◆◆ Drama & Discussion

••• Drama & Discussion

Edited by
STANLEY A. CLAYES
Loyola University

APPLETON-CENTURY-CROFTS / NEW YORK

Division of Meredith Corporation

ACKNOWLEDGMENTS

"Electra," from *Three Tragedies* by Sophocles, translated by H. D. F. Kitto. © Oxford University Press 1962. Reprinted by permission.

"Trial by Time: Electra," reprinted by permission of the publishers from Cedric H. Whitman, *Sophocles: A Study of Heroic Humanism*, Cambridge, Mass.: Harvard University Press, Copyright, 1951, by the President and Fellows of Harvard College.

"Hamlet and Orestes," reprinted by permission of the publishers from Gilbert Murray, *The Classical Tradition in Poetry*, Cambridge, Mass.: Harvard University Press, Copyright, 1927, by the President and Fellows of Harvard College, and Copyright, 1955, renewed by Gilbert Murray.

The Trojan Women and "A Pacifist in Periclean Athens," Reprinted from THREE GREEK PLAYS, *Prometheus Bound, Agamemnon, The Trojan Women*, Translated with Introductions by Edith Hamilton. By permission of W. W. Norton & Company, Inc. Copyright 1937 by W. W. Norton & Company, Inc.; Copyright Renewed 1965 by Doris Fielding Reid.

Robert Ornstein, "Historical Criticism and the Interpretation of Shakespeare," *Shakespeare Quarterly*, X (1959), pp. 3–9. Reprinted by permission.

Tiger at the Gates by Jean Giraudoux, translated by Christopher Fry. Copyright © 1955 by Christopher Fry. Reprinted by permission of Oxford University Press, Inc.

Jean Giraudoux, "Dissertation on the Theater," translated by M. S. Stanford, from *Littérature*. Reprinted by permission of Ninon Tallon Karlweis and Charles Scribner's Sons, Publishers.

Kenneth Tynan, "Notes on a Dead Language" and "[Review of] *Tiger at the Gates*," from *Curtains*, © 1961 by Kenneth Tynan. Reprinted by permission of Atheneum Publishers, and Longmans Green & Co., Ltd.

Federico García Lorca, "Blood Wedding," in *Three Tragedies*, translated by James Graham-Luján and Richard L. O'Connell. Copyright 1947, 1955 by New Directions. Reprinted by permission of the publisher, New Directions Publishing Corporation. All rights reserved. Permission to reprint or perform must be obtained from New Directions, 333 Sixth Avenue, New York, N. Y. 10014.

Bertolt Brecht, "From the *Mother Courage* Model," "Short Description of a New Technique of Acting Which Produces an Alienation Effect," and "Theatre for Pleasure or Theatre for Instruction," from *Brecht on Theatre*, edited and translated by John Willett. Copyright © 1957, 1963, and 1964 by Suhrkamp Verlag, Frankfurt am Main. Translation and notes © 1964 by John Willett. Reprinted by permission of Hill and Wang, Inc., and Methuen & Co., Ltd., Publishers.

Bertolt Brecht, *Mother Courage and Her Children: A Chronicle of the Thirty Years' War*, English version by Eric Bentley. Reprinted by permission of Grove Press, Inc. Copyright © 1955, 1959, 1961, 1962, 1963, 1966 by Eric Bentley.

Ronald Gaskell, "Theme and Form: Lorca's Blood Wedding," *Modern Drama*, V (February, 1963). Reprinted by permission.

George Bernard Shaw, *Saint Joan*. Copyright 1924, 1930, George Bernard Shaw. Copyright 1951, 1957, the Public Trustee as Executor of the Estate of George Bernard Shaw. Used by permission of The Public Trustee and Dodd, Mead and Company, Inc., and The Society of Authors.

The Lark by Jean Anouilh, translated by Christopher Fry. Copyright © 1956 by Christopher Fry. Reprinted by permission of Oxford University Press, Inc.

Jacques Guicharnaud, "Theatre as Proposition: Jean Giraudoux," *Modern French Theatre: from Giraudoux to Beckett*. Reprinted by permission of Yale University Press.

Preface

This selection of plays represents a variety of dramatic types and of historical periods, from a variety of cultures. Unlike other anthologies, whose scopes may be as wide and contents even more diverse, *Drama & Discussion* groups its plays—two, three or four—about discernible cores of subject and situation. While each play was chosen for its own dramatic appeal and value, a study of its similarities with others in its group should lead, by way of thought and discussion, to a full understanding of its essential differences in theme, technique, emphasis, attitude, meaning, and style.

Except in Part Five, each play is preceded by an introductory headnote of diverse length, focus, and authorship. In some cases, translators (Peter D. Arnott, H. D. F. Kitto, Edith Hamilton) provide pertinent mythological, linguistic, or cultural background. In others, editors (R. C. Bald, William E. Hart), critics (Jacques Guicharnaud, Francisco García-Lorca) and even dramatists themselves (Jean Anouilh, Bernard Shaw, Bertolt Brecht) furnish the initial comment. And here, as elsewhere, the differences are marked. For example, Shaw's "Preface to *Saint Joan*"—extensive, historical, and hortatory—contrasts sharply with Anouilh's program note to *The Lark*—brief, defensive, almost flippant. All of the commentary, whether it precedes or follows the play, was chosen to provide the student with information or an attitude that will lead him to something important in the play itself. In no case does analysis or explication bar the student from perceiving and pondering the drama on his own terms.

The substantial excerpts or complete essays in the discussion sections of Parts One through Five serve another function. They attempt to make explicit some—but by no means all or even most—of the differences in temper, creative and critical, at the basis of drama and its appreciation. Generalizations of a higher order, starting in Part Six with those of Aristotle, serve to raise more profound questions about the drama—its forms, audiences, and purposes.

An anthologist never produces, in fact, the drama collection he envisioned at the outset. Inevitably, regardless of his budget for permissions, some plays he values highly, both on their own merits and for their role in his proposed collection, prove to be unavailable—under any condition, or at any price. To list all the plays that might, for good reasons, have been included here would be pointless. For instructors who may wish to amplify their course in certain directions, however, let me suggest the following: *The Flies,* Jean-Paul Sartre's version of the Orestes story, and *Electra,* Jean Giraudoux's ironic treatment of the myth's central episode; *Waiting for Godot* by Samuel Beckett and *The American Dream* by Edward Albee, prime examples of the theme of alienation elaborated in terms of absurdist and anti-theater techniques. As for the Trojan story, Shakespeare's *Troilus and Cressida,* whose dramatic worth is now more keenly appreciated than it once was, complements well Euripides' *The Trojan Women* and Giraudoux's *Tiger at the Gates.*

My debt to others is too large and complex to acknowledge. An anthologist reads the work of playwrights and of critics, whose talents and perceptions vary widely; he also goes to the theater and tries to match his responses against those of friends. As he slowly elaborates his impressions into judgments (though never conclusively), he eventually loses sight of which reasoned acceptances and rejections are uniquely his own. If the present anthology has any major claim, it is on those whose understanding of drama is still young. What it attempts to offer is a useful common ground for encountering, at their very best, dramas as well as discussions they engender.

S.A.C.

Contents

Contents

Part Six

◆◆◆ Part One

AESCHYLUS

SOPHOCLES

SHAKESPEARE

◆ Introduction to *The Oresteia*

By PETER D. ARNOTT

AESCHYLUS AND GREEK TRAGEDY

Aeschylus lived through a crucial period in the history of Greece, and one which laid the foundations for many of that civilization's greatest achievements. In his city of Athens the rule of tyrants was superseded by an effective democracy which gave more people than ever before an active part in public affairs, and brought about a new surge of civic pride. While he was still of military age the Greek city-states, traditionally isolationist and fiercely jealous of each other, were forced to unite against the menace of Persian invasion. Persian armies twice entered Greece, and Aeschylus fought in the major battles of these campaigns. The sea-fight of Salamis, in which a small and predominantly Athenian force defeated the Persian armada, later served as background for his tragedy *The Persians,* the first Greek play that has come down to us complete. Greece emerged from the wars triumphant, though several cities had suffered great losses. This was particularly true of Athens, against which the Persians bore a special grudge. The city had to be abandoned and was twice sacked by the invading army. Athens' leadership in the resistance, however, had brought her greatly increased prestige. After the war a confederation was formed to provide against any future invasion. A number of states contributed to the maintenance of a joint fleet and treasury, with Athens eventually assuming charge of both. Little by little this confederacy was transformed into an Athenian empire, and the annual tribute of the subject states was used to rebuild the city on a more magnificent scale. Hand in hand with these territorial acquisitions went a new interest in the arts, the drama prominent among them.

Performances of tragedy had been given in Athens from about 535 B.C. as part of the great religious festivals. About the early writers and performances we know little. Tragedy appears originally to have consisted largely of choral song and pageantry. A chorus of fifty, which both sang and danced, carried the burden of the performance, assisted by a single actor who would take an occasional solo part. To Aeschylus is attributed the introduction of the second actor, which made more complex dramatic action possible and relieved the demands on the chorus. Sophocles, Aeschylus' younger contemporary and rival, introduced the third actor, an innovation which Aeschylus copied in the *Oresteia* and other later plays. Aeschylus' chorus probably still numbered fifty. It was later reduced to fifteen. Tradition associates this reduction with the performance of *The Eumenides,* whose horrific chorus of Furies threw the audience into a panic; there may well be a grain of truth in this story. In Aeschylus the chorus is still vital, and retains the dual function inherited from its origin in nondramatic performances. Its members can participate in the drama as characters—elders of Argos, slaves or Furies—or, when the playwright requires it, they can step outside the framework of the action to function as narrators or impersonal commentators, underlining a theme just stated in action or drawing a moral implication. The facility of direct address to the audience which this convention provides gave Greek tragedy, particularly in the hands of Aeschylus an enviable power and economy.

Apart from his technical innovations, Aeschylus seems to have been the first to enlarge the scope of tragedy to treat problems of significant importance. The Greeks expected drama, like all forms of art both literary and visual, to be functional, and provide some service to the state. Dramatists were regarded not merely as entertainers but as teachers, with the responsibility of filling the gap caused by the absence of any substantial body of ethical doctrine in the Greek

Peter D. Arnott, "Introduction to Oresteia," *Aeschylus: Agamemnon,* trans. and ed. by Peter D. Arnott

(New York: Appleton-Century-Crofts, 1964); pp. v-xiv. Copyright © 1964 by Meredith Publishing Company.

religion. Aeschylus employs tragedy to discuss moral, social, and religious problems. Even *The Persians,* a fiercely patriotic play based on events still fresh in the mind of his audience, transcends its subject matter to investigate the whole question of the balance between the human and the divine, and the misuse of human power. The *Oresteia,* while it is consistently exciting theater, at the same time poses vital questions about man's nature and destiny, his relationship to the gods and the nature of those gods, and the progress of civilization.

Aeschylus was revered by later generations as the father of Greek tragedy. His plays were the first to be officially preserved, and it is from the transcript made for the Athenian archives that they ultimately descend to us. He was credited with introducing many of the traditional features of the Greek theater—masks, costumes, settings—though some of these we know had been in use before his time. One signal posthumous honor was awarded him. Anyone wishing to revive a play of Aeschylus for a dramatic festival instead of entering an original play of his own would automatically be granted a chorus. This veneration, however, was not completely uncritical. There were not a few who found his language ponderous and stilted, his imagery incomprehensible. Aristophanes, the Greek comic writer of the later fifth century, satirizes Aeschylus freely in *The Frogs,* and makes a number of telling points. In the fourth century, when the plays of the great dramatists were frequently revived, Sophocles and Euripides were preferred to Aeschylus, not merely because their plays were simpler to stage but because of the difficulties of language and thought in Aeschylus already mentioned. These are valid criticisms, but small in comparison to the virtues of the Aeschylean method—the monumentality of his style, the constantly fresh implications of his cosmic themes, the grandeur of his thought and diction. Aeschylus has survived both on the stage and in the study, and still poses exciting challenges to scholar, to actor, and to director alike.

THE ORESTEIA

A tragic poet wishing to compete in the annual dramatic festivals at Athens was re-

quired to submit four plays, three tragedies and one satyr play. The latter was a short burlesque of popular mythology, played as an afterpiece to give the audience some light relief. Aeschylus was considered the best writer of satyr play of his time, and we must regret that none of his works in this genre has survived complete. The three tragedies could be completely independent of each other—a method favored by Sophocles and Euripides—or form a trilogy, in which each play, though complete in itself and capable of being performed independently, formed one act of a larger whole. This seems to have been the way in which Aeschylus preferred to work. *Seven Against Thebes* was the third play in such a sequence, *The Suppliant Women* the first; but the *Oresteia (Saga of Orestes),* comprising *Agamemnon, The Libation Bearers,* and *The Eumenides,* is the only trilogy that has survived complete.

The story on which Aeschylus bases these plays was a familiar one to Greek audiences, and furnished the plots of a number of tragedies. It was a long and complex story, beginning far earlier than the quarrel between Atreus and Thyestes which Aeschylus takes as his starting point. But a dramatist must use his material selectively, and Aeschylus restricts himself to the history of three generations. It is basically the brutal tale of a family feud, of which Greek legend contains many examples—the type of vendetta which still emerges from time to time in Greece and Sicily, and in other countries far from the Mediterranean. Atreus committed an atrocity against his brother Thyestes, for which a curse was laid upon him. Agamemnon, his son, is killed by his wife Clytemnestra and her lover Aegisthus, son of Thyestes; Clytemnestra in turn is killed by her son Orestes, honor bound to avenge his father; and Orestes himself is haunted by guilt and the fear of supernatural punishment until the curse is finally broken at the close of the trilogy. Since the tale was familiar to Aeschylus' audience, he takes us straight into the story of Agamemnon and we do not actually hear the curse recounted in full until almost the end of the first play. The primitive concept of justice embodied here was long a valid principle of Athenian law; it was not until comparatively late that the punishment of murder was taken out of the hands of the individual and entrusted to the state. It is a concept personified in the trilogy by the Erinyes, or Furies, demonic pursuers of the wrongdoer. Their presence is constantly felt, and becomes more tangible as the action proceeds. In *Agamemnon* they are unseen, though constantly referred or appealed to. In *The Libation Bearers* they appear as hallucinations, seen by Orestes after he has murdered his mother, but not by us. In *The Eumenides* they are seen by the audience too, terrible figures with snakey hair and blazing torches, and form the chorus, hunting down Orestes for his crime.

Agamemnon is a man cursed, and so naturally susceptible to trouble in whatever form it chooses to come. If we ask why Agamemnon dies, we find not one answer but several. He has angered his wife by the sacrifice of their child Iphigeneia, and further insulted her by bringing home a concubine, the prisoner of war Cassandra, to live in his palace. He has angered the gods by his arrogance and his unnecessary destruction of their temples in Troy. Aegisthus, living embodiment of the family curse, plots to kill him in revenge for the wrong done to his father. But behind all these particular causes we see a pattern working. The curse forces Agamemnon into situations where he is compelled to make a choice, and events are so arranged that any choice he makes will be disastrous. His brother Menelaus loses his wife, Helen, to Paris, Prince of Troy. Menelaus is bound in honor to attempt to reclaim his wife, and Agamemnon is bound by family ties to support him. But this can only be achieved at the cost of alienating his people. The chorus, speaking for the population of Argos, make it clear that they consider the Trojan War a useless and frivolous expedition, one that has brought suffering and hardship to many for the sake of a wanton woman. Another choice is forced upon him as soon as war is declared. The Greek fleet is delayed at Aulis by contrary winds, and the gods can be appeased only by the sacrifice of Iphigeneia. Thus the choice becomes one between public and private good. If he sacrifices his daughter he will alienate his family and deprive himself of a loved child. If he refuses, it will be tantamount to deserting the army. He chooses the public good, and thus brings retribution on his own head.

Aeschylus brilliantly weaves together two strains, one of triumph and one of impending fatality. On the one hand we hear of joy at the ending of the war and the fall of Troy, and the triumph of the king returning to his home victorious. But beneath this sounds a more somber note. Argos is empty of its men. There are only elders and boys, dominated by the scheming Clytemnestra. Agamemnon's supporters have been swept away in a storm. When he enters his city the triumph is hollow, and he is walking into a trap that his friends are powerless to prevent. Tempted by his wife, he enters his home over the purple carpet, symbolic of the arrogance of power and conquest, and is destroyed. So the city loses its benevolent ruler and falls under a tyranny; its only hope is the reappearance of Orestes.

The second play is much shorter than the first and different in mood. The joy of bloodshed has given place, in Aegisthus and Clytemnestra, to satiety and resignation. But the pattern of the curse reasserts itself. Orestes is faced with a choice similar to that which confounded his father. He is bound by filial duty to avenge his father's murder, but this can only be achieved by the hideous crime of murdering his mother. Once again, either choice is bound to be wrong. He wavers, but is finally urged to the deed; Clytemnestra and Aegisthus die, and Orestes is seen standing over their bodies as Clytemnestra stood in the first play. The chorus is misled into optimism. They hope that the curse is now worked out, and that the house may live happily. But Orestes in turn is pursued, not now by any mortal enemy but by the Furies. The dreary chain of crime and punishment is not yet at an end.

In the third play the issue transcends a mere family feud to assume cosmic significance. The whole meaning of justice is now involved, and the supernatural powers take up their various stands, using the trial of Orestes as a test case. On the one hand are the Furies. They stand for a concept of justice little removed from that of the jungle. If a man has died, another must die in punishment. For them, the fact of blood-guilt is in itself sufficient. They admit no degrees of wrong, no extenuating circumstances. They stand, too, for a primitive level of society in which the only valid tie is the blood-tie. Marriage, a social contract, has no place in their scheme. They argue that Orestes has killed a blood-relation, his mother, and so must be destroyed. Clytemnestra's deed was less reprehensible because the victim was merely her husband. Against them are ranged Apollo and Athena, personifications of law and wisdom for the Greeks. Their argument is the argument of civilization, that the bond of marriage is as valid as that of blood-relationship; Clytemnestra was no less guilty than Orestes. Eventually these gods, the newer deities of a more civilized and ordered society, triumph over the darker powers of an earlier age, and persuade them to change their natures. The Furies become beneficent spirits; the rule of law has conquered the spirit of revenge, the curse has been broken and Orestes may go free. Aeschylus deliberately appeals to the patriotic sentiments in his audience by setting this momentous decision in Athens and identifying the court as the Areopagus, the city's most venerable court of appeal. It is Athena, the city's, patron deity, who is ultimately responsible for this victory of light over darkness.

The *Oresteia*, then, is an allegory of civilization compressed into the story of a few generations. Aeschylus conceives of the gods, as well as men, as evolving from crude beginnings into something nobler and more elevated. The Furies change their natures; so does Apollo. In *Agamemnon* he appears as a malicious and vindictive god of the Homeric type, persecuting Cassandra because she has dared to oppose his desires. In *The Eumenides* he has become the embodiment of harmony and reason, the symbol of all that the Greeks of the classical age found most admirable in their own society. This motif of change and evolution is carried through the trilogy in more subtle ways also, in the shifting significance of recurrent images and me-

taphors. The net, a frequent symbol, at first implies scheming and destruction—the net that Zeus fastens around Troy, the meshes woven by the Furies for Agamemnon, the net of cunning fashioned by Clytemnestra for her husband, made visible as the mantle in which she traps his body as a fisherman catches a fish. Later it becomes a symbol of hope, the net to which Orestes and Electra cling. Persuasion, the force used by Clytemnestra for harm—to lie to the chorus and the herald, and to lure her husband to his doom—in Athena's mouth becomes a weapon for good, to turn the recalcitrant Furies from their dark courses.

The text of the *Oresteia* has suffered considerable damage over the centuries. Some passages have been lost completely. Orestes' opening speech in *The Libation Bearers* is the most serious instance of this. A number of verses have disappeared, and what we have—enough, fortunately, to give the sense—has largely been reconstructed from quotations in other authors. There are several other places where a line, or several lines, have clearly been lost. Sometimes there is no clue to the original content, and the most we can achieve is an intelligent guess. Aeschylus also suffered at the hands of the copyists. His fondness for a ponderous and exotic vocabulary troubled the scribes, who, on finding themselves confronted with unfamiliar words, assumed that they must be mistakes and replaced them with more conventional words of similar sound. Nor is it always clear to which character a particular speech should be attributed. There is thus considerable disagreement between different editors and translators, and the reader must expect a number of variations, some slight, some of considerable importance, in the various versions available.

◆◆ The Libation Bearers

By AESCHYLUS

Translated by Peter D. Arnott

Characters

ORESTES, son of the late king Agamemnon
 and Clytemnestra
ELECTRA, his sister
CLYTEMNESTRA, Queen of Argos
AEGISTHUS, Clytemnestra's lover, now King of
 Argos
CILISSA, Orestes' old nurse
PYLADES, friend of Orestes
PORTER
SERVANT, of Aegisthus
CHORUS, of slavewomen

Scene: at first, by the grave of Agamemnon;
 later, before the door of the royal palace.

[*The grave of* AGAMEMNON. ORESTES
kneels in prayer. His friend PYLADES
stands silent at a distance]

ORESTES. Hermes, spirit of the underworld
 And father's regent, lend to me
 Your strength, and stand my champion, I
  pray,
 For I have come home to my land again
 And on this mounded tomb invoke my
  father
 To listen and attend.

[*Laying a lock of hair upon the grave*]

A lock of hair to Inachus, for manhood;
Its fellow here, as token for the dead;
For I was not at hand to mourn your
  passing,
My father, or salute your burial.   10

[*The* CHORUS *of mourning women, with*
ELECTRA *among them, appear in the*
distance. They carry urns with libations
to pour over the grave]

But what is here now? What processional
Of women, in dignity of mourning black,
Is coming? What should I make this to
  mean?
A signal of new sorrow for the palace?
Or am I to suppose these women bring
Libations as late offerings to my father?
So it must be; for I think I see my sister
Electra among them, grief scored bold
Upon her face. Zeus, give me revenge
For my dead father; be my willing aid.   20
Pylades, let us give them room.
I must assure myself about this cry of
  women.

[ORESTES *and* PYLADES *conceal them-*
selves as the women approach the
grave]

Aeschylus, "The Libation Bearers," in *The Libation Bearers and the Eumenides*, trans. and ed. by Peter D. Arnott (New York: Appleton-Century-Crofts, 1964), pp. 1-45.

1 *Hermes* messenger-god, one of whose functions was to escort the spirits of the dead to the under-world. Thus he is frequently appealed to, both in this play and *The Eumenides* as the intermediary between the living and the dead. 7 *a lock of hair* common votive offering, particularly in acts of mourning. *Inachus* river-god of Argos

CHORUS. Forth from the palace gates, as I
    was bid,
  With urns I come, with drumming hands,
  Torn cheeks, the nails' fresh furrows
    A talisman of red,
  And in my heart old sorrow;
  With rending of my robes, with fingers
    tearing
  Wild at the linen on my breast
30 In grief of glad days gone.

  For in the dead watch Fright with stream-
    ing hair
  Shrilled from its cell, and to the dreaming
    house
  Told things to come, a gust of rancor
    stirring
  Fresh out of slumber,
  Beating ironfisted on the doors
  Of women. The seers swore by the gods
    their masters
  That anger was pulsing in the grave
  Against the murderers.

  So in hollow office of appeasement,
40 Earth, O Earth, in mock of holy law,
  She sends me forth. But there is fear
    At such a word.
  For who can ransom blood once spilled
  On the ground? O joyless hearth,
  O desolation of our house,
  Sun hid his face, the pestilence
  Of darkness fell thick on our palace
  At the killing of our kings.

  The splendor of our yesterdays, that stood
50 Triumphant, matchless and invincible
  To thrill men's hearts with story, is de-
    parted
  And terror comes.
  Success is god, and greater than god
  For mortal men. But Justice holds
  Her balance attentive, coming swift
  On some by day, for some waits ripening
  Till evenfall, and those remaining
  Are swallowed up in night.

Blood poured for mother earth to drink
Lies crusted, a living sore   60
To cry revenge. Destruction works
On the sinner, spiking him with plague
Till he is rotten through.

As once the chambers of virginity
Are forced, there is no remedy,
So all the waters of the world
Would seek to wash blood clean from guilty
Hands, and do their work in vain.

On me and on mine the gods imposed
The hard necessity of conquest   70
And from the dwellings of my fathers
Brought me here to be a slave.
So I can do no other but approve
My masters, right or wrong—my life
Is new come in their keeping,
And I must struggle to suppress
The heart's loathing.
But still there run behind the veil
Tears for the errant destiny of kings
And to the secret places of my heart   80
Comes the cold touch of horror.

  [ELECTRA *takes her place at the graveside*]

ELECTRA. You serving-maids, who set our
    house to rights,
  Since you have trod this path of prayer
    with me,
  Give me your counsel here. How should
    I speak
  As I pour these offerings on my father's
    grave?
  With what address, what sacramental
    words?
  That this is love's commission to her love,
  To husband from his wife—and this my
    mother?
  I would not dare. Then what accompani-
    ment
  Should herald these libations underground? 90
  I know not. Or could I say this—

That men believe that those who send
    such wreaths
As these, deserve to be repaid in kind
With presents worthy of their merits?
Or should I pour into the thirsty earth
Without a word, without a salutation,
In manner as he died, and fling the urn
    away
As one who would be rid of it forever,
And go my way without a backward
    glance?
100   This is the question, friends. Advise me.
We share a roof, a common hate.
So do not hide your counsels out of fear
Of . . . anyone. The free man and the
    slave,
Each has his destiny. So speak;
Perhaps you know a better.

CHORUS. If you will have it so, I'll speak my
    mind
Before your father's tomb, which is for me
A sacred shrine—
EL.   Then as you reverence
My father's grave, speak to me now.
110   CHORUS. Pour, and call blessings on men of
    goodwill—
EL. And where among my friends could I
    find any
To bear that name?
CHORUS. Yourself; then anyone who hates
    Aegisthus.
EL. You, then, and me. Is that to be my
    prayer?
CHORUS. You know what I mean. But you
    must say it.
EL. Whom else shall I number in this com-
    pany?
CHORUS. Remember Orestes, banished though
    he be.
EL. That was well spoken, my good instructor.
CHORUS. And for the ones who shed this
    blood, remember—
120   EL. What? I am strange to this, you must
    dictate to me.
CHORUS. To call someone against them, from
    this world
Or from the other—
EL. To judge, or to revenge? Explain yourself.

CHORUS. In plain words, to take life for life.
EL. May I so pray, without offence to heaven?
CHORUS. Why not? To pay your enemy in
    kind?
EL. God of darkness, Hermes, potent mes-
    senger
Of this world and the next, I summon you
To help me now, and call
The spirits of the underworld, that watch   130
My father's house, to hear me as I pray,
And summon Earth, that brings all things
    to life
And takes her rearing to her womb again.
As I pour out these vessels to the dead,
I call upon my father. Pity me,
And light Orestes' lamp within our house,
For we are homeless now, our mother's
    chattels
With which she purchased for herself a
    man,
Aegisthus, who was partner in your
    murder.
I am no better than a slave; Orestes   140
Is banished from his rich inheritance,
While they loll back in luxury, and reap
The harvest of your labor. Thus I pray,
My father, listen close. Let fortune bring
Orestes home, and let me show myself
More modest than my mother was, my
    hand
More virtuous.
These prayers for us. This for our enemies:
Father, I charge you show us your avenger.
Kill them who killed you. Render them   150
    this justice.
And let me set against their curse
My curse, to fall on them.
Bring us blessings from the underworld;
The gods be on our side, and Earth,
And justice triumphant.
Such is the litany to which I pour
These offerings.

    [*To the* CHORUS]

             And you, as the custom is,
Must crown the prayers with your lament,
    and sing
Your hymnal to the dead.

160 CHORUS. Let fall now for the fallen lord
     A watering of tears
     As pitchers are upturned
     On this holy mound, a bastion
     Against evil, and a curse that must be laid.
     Hear me, majesty; lord, as you lie dim,
     Give this your mind. What champion will
          rise
     To be our palace's deliverance?
     What warrior to wield the backbent
     Bow of Scythia, or come
170 Firmhilted to the handfight?
EL. The earth has drunk. My father has his
     due.

[*Seeing the lock of* ORESTES' *hair*]

     But here is something strange to tell,
     Something for all of us.
CHORUS. Tell me what you mean.
     Fear is stepping nimble in my heart.
EL. Look, on the tomb. A lock of hair.
CHORUS. Whose? Man's or woman's?
EL. Guess. Nobody could mistake it.
CHORUS. What is it? Your young years must
     teach my age.
180 EL. This curl could not have come from any
     head
     But mine.
CHORUS. His nearest hate him, they would
     never
     Cut hair in his mourning.
EL. But look at it—so very like—
CHORUS. Like whose hair? Tell me.
EL. My own. So like. Compare them.
CHORUS. Orestes? Has he come in secret
     To make this offering?
EL.   Yes, he has hair
     Like this.
CHORUS. He would not dare to come.
190 EL. He sent it, then; this shorn lock,
     A lovegift to his father.
CHORUS. Then I have no less cause to weep
     If he will never set foot in this land again.
EL. I too. The full tide of my anger now
     Has come, it is a knife to rend my heart.

169 *Bow of Scythia* the Scythians were famous
archers in antiquity

The dyke is down, the tears fall from my
     eyes
Unslaked, my grief is at the flood
To see this hair. Oh, how could I imagine
That this lock could have come from any
     other
In Argos? It was not the murderess   200
That cropped her hair, my mother—what a
     name
For her, that fiend who hates her children!
But how can I say straight and clear
This glory comes from him I love the best,
Orestes—oh, I am hope's fool!
If it had wit to speak, if it could tell me,
Then I should not be torn between two
     minds,
But know for sure if I should cast it out
For being fathered by a head I hate
Or if it is one blood with mine, my sor-   210
     row's partner
To grace this grave, and reverence my
     father.
But on the gods we call, who know
What tempests have beset our voyaging,
And if it is ordained we come safe home,
Great trunks from little seeds may grow.

[*Seeing footprints on the ground*]

A second witness! Marks upon the ground
Like those my feet have made, the very
     same . . .
No, there's a double set of footprints here,
One his, and one somebody's that was with
     him. . . .
The heel, the tracing of the toes; these
     measurements   220
Exactly fit with mine—I cannot bear it!
This is too much to think of!

[ORESTES *and* PYLADES *step from their
hiding place*]

OR. You may inform the gods your prayers
     are answered.
Now pray to be as lucky in the future.
EL. Why? What favor have I won from them?
OR. You are in sight of what you prayed to
     see so long.

EL. The man I prayed for—what is he to you?

OR. I know how you long to see Orestes.

EL. What makes you think my prayers are answered?

230 OR. Here I am. Look no further. You will never find
A closer friend.

EL. I do not know you. Are you playing tricks on me?

OR. If so, I play a trick upon myself.

EL. Have you come here to laugh at my misfortunes?

OR. If they are your misfortunes, they are mine.

EL. Let me pretend you are Orestes, then,
And bid you—

OR.   I am Orestes,
And you do not know me when you see me.
But when you saw this hair cut off in mourning,

240 When you looked on the earth my feet had trod,
Your mind flew on the instant to the thought
That what you saw was me.
Look, lay this lock of hair where it was cut;
It is your brother's—see, it matches yours.

[*Showing a child's garment*]

And look, the jerkin that you wove for me:
The texture, this embroidery of beasts—

[ELECTRA *is convinced, and weeps for joy*]

Control yourself, and do not let your joy
Outweigh discretion. I am well acquainted
With our dear friends, and how they hate us.

250 EL. Oh dearest treasure of our father's house,
Its hope, its future seed; how we have wept for you.
It shall be yours again. You have your father's strength
Behind you. Face that I have longed to see;
You have divided me, and made four loves from one.

One for my father—that is your name now;
One for my loving duty to my mother—
Her share is yours; to her I give my hate;
One for my sister's cruel sacrifice;
One for the brother true that I have found you,
The only one of all my family   260
To give me dignity.
So Might and Justice fight upon my side
And Zeus Almighty, greatest of them all,
To make a third.

OR. Zeus, O Zeus, look down at what has passed here.
Look at us both, the eagle's children,
Parentless, their father strangled
In the deadly embraces of a snake.
Their father's dead, and they must starve,
For they have not his art, to bring their   270
catch
Home to the lair, as he did. It is myself I mean
And this girl, Electra. We stand here in your sight
Two children, fatherless, and both alike
Cast from our homes. Our father
Was lavish in his tithes to honor you.
Destroy his young, you will look hard to find
Another hand so generous to feast you.
If you suffer the eagle's progeny to die
Who will believe you when you manifest yourself
Hereafter? If this ministering branch   280
Is left to wither, when the day comes round
To serve the altar, it will not be there
To wait on you with sacrifice. Take heed:
You may uplift this house and make it great
Although it seems to lie in ruins now.

CHORUS. Children, saviors of your father's house
Be silent, or some tattletale will warn
Our overlords. I hope I live to see them
Dead, and burning in the spitting fire!

OR. One thing will never fail, the potent   290
oracle

258 *my sister's cruel sacrifice* Iphigeneia, sacrificed by Agamemnon to win the gods' favor at the outset of the Trojan War

Of Apollo. It was he who bade me walk
This perilled way, and in the secret hours
Whispered to me a litany of horrors
To turn my blood to ice, should I neglect
To hound my father's murderers and kill
    them
As they killed him, round on them, gore
    them,
Strip them of all they have. If I should fail,
He said my own self would be forfeit; I
    should suffer
Miseries uncounted . . . he made it plain
And told how, when the dead are angry,   300
Their rancor rises as a pestilence
Up through the ground, to ride upon our
    bodies,
Creeping, feeding; cancer sets its teeth
In flesh once fair, and leaves its mark upon
Our faces, scabbed with silver scales.
He spoke of other visitations too,
Of Furies forming in the father's blood.
Dead things work by dark. Then mur-
    dered men
Come crying to their kin "Revenge!" and
    terror stalks
By night, to haunt him. Wild hallucina-   310
    tions
Come vivid on his eyes, although he screw
    them
Tight shut in the dark, and drive him forth
With barbs and scourges from the land
    that bred him.
For such an outcast there can be
No common bowl, no loving-cup,
No prayer at altars—there a sentry stands,
His father's ghost; no man will share a
    roof with him
Or take him in, till friendless and un-
    mourned
He shrivels up and dies in misery.
Such was the oracle. Could I then deny it?   320
Even if I could, the deed must still be
    done,
For there are many calls on me, unanimous
To urge me on—the gods' commandment,
Grief for my father—there is weight in
    this—

291 *Apollo* god of prophecy and Orestes' patron;
see note on v. 31

The press of poverty, and my desire
That the marvel of the earth, my country-
    men,
Whose glorious spirit subjugated Troy
Should not bow down before this pair of
    women—
For he is woman at heart; if I am one
He soon shall learn!   330

[ORESTES, ELECTRA *and the* CHORUS *join
in a lament over the tomb*]

CHORUS. O you presiding Destinies
By the will of god make ending
In the turnabout of justice.
Let hate cry quittance to hate once spoken.
So Justice proclaims herself aloud, exacting
Atonement; blood for blood
And stroke for stroke, do and be done by;
Thus the lesson three ages old.

OR. O terrible my father,
What word of mine, what act   340
Can blow fair to the far shore,
Where fast you lie, a light
The measure of your darkness?
And yet it has been called
A work of grace, to tell old glories
In mourning for the champions
Of the house of Atreus fallen.

CHORUS. Child, when a man dies flesh is
    frayed
And broken in the fire, but not his will.
He shows his wrath though late.   350
For the dead man there is mourning,
For the guilty man a finding,
And the deathsong for a parent and a father
Is a call to judgement, ranging through
The universe disquieted
To hunt and find.

EL. Hear me in turn, my father,
My weeping and long sorrow.
Here two children at your graveside
Raise our chant for the departed.   360
Your tomb is haven
For outcasts, and for those

347 *Atreus* Agamemnon's father.

Who pray for aid. What here is good,
What refuge from calamity?
Can we try a fall with fate?

CHORUS. Even from such as these the god
  At will can shape a gladder strain,
  And from the lamentation at the graveside
  A song of triumph may arise
370 Within the palace, to carry home
  The well-beloved, the dear unknown.

OR. If you had only died, my father,
  At Troy, upon the field of honor,
  And struck down by a foreign hand.
  Then had you left your house
  A legacy of glory, to your children
  As they walked abroad, undying
  Regard; then had you made
  A heavy tomb upon a foreign shore
380 But for your family light burden.

CHORUS. Welcome then would he have gone
  To those who loved him, to the nobled
    dead,
  And in the nether world
  Would have kept high state, in honor
  Held and majesty, first minister
  To the most mighty, to the kings of dark-
    ness.
  For he was monarch on earth, and ruled
  Those who command men's lives, who
    wield
  The sceptre of dominion.

390 EL. No, that was not a place
  For you to die, my father,
  Under the battlements of Troy,
  And by Scamander's ford to find
  A plot of ground among the herd,
  The reaping of the spear. Far better
  That those who killed him should have
    died as he did,
  And in far countries strangers to our sorrow
  Had heard tell of the manner of their
    passing.
CHORUS. Child, you talk of riches passing
  mortal,

393 *Scamander* river of Troy 401 *who live be-*
yond the wind the legendary Hyperboreans, who

Of miracles, felicity   400
  They only know who live beyond the wind.
  Dreams are free. But the double scourge
  Beats louder in the land; beneath
  The earth there is a mustering
  Of forces in our aid; our lords
  Have hands unclean, and the curse is on
    them;
  The children's day is coming.

OR. There now is a word
  To rivet the ear. O Zeus,
  Zeus, send up from below   410
  The laggard punisher
  For men of wrath and guilty hand
  And let the score be settled for the parents.

CHORUS. May it be given me to raise
  A cheer at the slaying of the man,
  The woman's dying. Why should I hide
  The thought that deep within flies free?
  For in the voyage of the heart
  There is a freight of hatred, and the wind
  Of wrath blows shrill.   420

EL. Zeus two-fisted come
  To smite them, yes, to smash
  Heads; let there be a place
  For faith again; where there is wrong
  I say let right be done; O hear me
  Earth, and dignities of darkness.

CHORUS. This is the law. Blood spilt upon
  the ground
  Cries out for more; the act
  Of desecration is a summons to the Fury
  Who for the dead once fallen heaps   430
  Havoc on havoc, new upon the old.

OR. O potentates of darkness, see,
  See, curses that come mighty from the
    dead,
  The house of Atreus, all that is left of us,
  Helpless, driven from our rightful homes.
  Where is there aid, O Zeus?

CHORUS. And my heart too has quivered

lived in the far north and were particular favorites
of Apollo

To hear your sorrow's utterance.
At such a word came despair,
440   A shadow on the heart. But when
I see you standing strong, there comes
Hope, and lightening of sorrow
At this fair sign.

EL. What shall our tale be then? What other
Than sorrows suffered for our parents' sake?
Fawn away, there can be no assuaging.
Anger ravens wolfish and implacable,
Child of the mother.

CHORUS. As in Aria the women beat their
   breasts
450   Then beat I mine, and in Cissian style
Made show of mourning. There was a sight
Of drumming fists, of blood-bruised flesh,
A dance of hands, plucking
Higher, lower, till my sorry head
Rang with their hammering.

EL. O ruthless, O relentless, O my mother,
Who in forced and meagre offices
Thought fit to bury him, a king
Far from his folk, without
460   The rites of mourning,
Without a tear, your husband.

OR. In such dishonor, say you?
But she shall pay for slighting him,
My father, by the help
Of the immortals, by the help
Of these my hands.
So let me kill her, and then die.

CHORUS. This too you must know. His limbs
   were lopped
And travestied, upon her word
470   Who ordered this his grave,
Intent to lay crushing grief
On your young life.
So was your father slighted.

EL. As you tell it, so he died. I was not by;
I had no rights there, I was nothing,
Only a cur that must be locked away

Inside, for fear she'd bite. I hid
The welling of my grief
Though tears came readier than smiles that
   day.
Hear this, and write it in your memory!   480

CHORUS. Yes, write, and let the tale bore deep
Into your heart. But bide your time
In patience still. So stands
The story now. You yearn
To know the end. Steadfast
Comes fittest to the fight.

OR. Pay heed, my father. Work beside your
   own.
EL. Your weeping daughter adds her voice
   to his.
CHORUS. And so cries all this company to-
   gether.
Obey, and come to light; make one   490
Against your enemies.

OR. Battle now match battle, right with right.
EL. O gods, bring justice and accomplishment.
CHORUS. Fear comes over me as I hear you
   pray.
Long destiny has waited; now
When summoned it may come.

O curse inborn, sour song
Of fate, the bloody chastisement.
O hard and heavy sorrows, grief
That has no easy end.   500

The cure is in the house, not brought
By other hands from distant places
But by its own, in agony and blood.
Thus we sing unto the dark ones.

But listen to our prayer, O blessed ones
Below, and send your willing aid
To these the children. Let them fight and
conquer.

OR. Father, who died out of the royal way,
I pray you make me master in your house.

449 *Aria, Cissian style* regions in Asia Minor. The
chorus liken their reaction to Agamemnon's death

to that of professional Asiatic mourners, with the
difference that their grief was sincere.

510 EL. I ask a like gift from your hands, my father:
Aegisthus' death, a husband for my own. . . .
OR. So when there is feasting here on earth
May you come welcome. If not, in the banquet days
When steaming meats are offered to the dead
No portion shall be yours.
EL.   Let me but come
Into my own, and on my bridal day
I'll bring gifts from the mansions of my fathers
To pour for you, and honor this tomb above all others.
OR. Earth, loose my father. Let him see my fight.
520 EL. Queen Persephone, give us grace and strength.
OR. Remember your laving and your death, my father—
EL. Remember the strange weaving that you wore—
OR. Hobbled in fetters forged by no man's hand, my father—
EL. And wrapped about in shroud of foul devising—
OR. Do these taunts sting you from your sleep, my father?
EL. And do you lift the head that we so love?
OR. Send forth your chastisement to fight with those
You love, or let us turn the hold on them
If you would change defeat to victory.
530 EL. And father, hear this cry, my last:
See these nestlings huddled on your tomb
And pity them, the girlchild and the boy together.
OR. And do not write an end to Pelops' line.
Through them you live, though you are in your grave.
EL. For when a man has died, his children keep
His fame alive; we are the corks upon the net

That hold the skein from sinking in the waters.
OR. For you these tears, so give them heed.
Reward our speech, and save yourself.
CHORUS. The tomb lacks nothing of its honor now. 540
Long have you spoken, and the debt of tears
Is paid. But if your mind is firm to act
Go on, and make experiment of fate!
OR. So be it. But there is a question still to ask
And to the point. Why did she send
These offerings? What persuaded her to make
These late amends for sorrow long past healing?
A miserable favor, lavished on
The dead, the mindless! What these gifts might mean
I could not start to guess. How small they weigh 550
Beside her sin! Spend blood, there needs no more,
And you may spend the world to pay for it
And lose your labor. Thus the proverb runs.
Speak, if you know. You'll find a ready ear.
CHORUS. I saw, and know, child. There was a dream,
A horror in the night; she woke in fear
And sent these offerings in mock of piety.
OR. What did she dream? If you know, tell all.
CHORUS. She gave birth to a snake—this was her story.
OR. And then? What was the sequel to this tale? 560
CHORUS. She wrapped it like a babe in cradle clothes.
OR. What did it ask for food, this beast new-born?
CHORUS. In the dream, she gave it her own breast to suck.
OR. How could she, and the nipple not be torn
By this foul thing?

520 *Persephone* wife of the god Hades and Queen of the Underworld   521 *your laving . . . strange weaving* Clytemnestra murdered Agamemnon in his bath, having entangled him in his own robe. It is this robe that Orestes displays to the chorus later in the play, vv. 1058ff.   533 *Pelops* remote ancestor of the house of Atreus

CHORUS   It sucked milk and clotted blood.

OR. No riddle here. This vision means a man—

CHORUS. Then she awoke, and screamed in terror,
And in the dark house at the mistress' cry
The shuttered lamps began to blink their eyes;
570 And thinking to find surgery for pain
She sent at once these offerings to the dead.

OR. I pray this earth, my father's sepulchre,
That this dream find accomplishment in me.
Thus I interpret; it is of a piece;
The serpent came from that same place
That brought forth me; she wrapped it in the robes
That cradled me; its mouth spread on the breast
That suckled me, and with lifegiving milk
Drew clotted blood, and at this dreadful thing
580 My mother screamed in fear; then surely she
Is doomed to die, and by no gentle hand
For bringing such a fearful prodigy
Into the world, and I am made the snake
To kill her, as this dream foretells.

CHORUS. Then you are the interpreter I trust
And cry amen. Expound the rest
To your friends now, who is to work, who wait—

OR. It can be quickly told. My sister must go home
And see that nothing of our plan leaks out,
590 So they who killed by treachery a man
Deserving of great honor, may be caught
By treachery, and in the selfsame net
May die; for thus Apollo prophesied,
The prophet-god who never yet has lied.
Accoutred like a traveller I'll come
Before the outer gates, with this man here
Whose name is Pylades, my friend, the bounden
Champion of men and mine. We'll both
Assume the accent of Parnassus, and talk

The way men do in Phocis. If nobody   600
Opens the gates for us and bids us welcome
Because the house is busy with its troubles,
We'll stay where we are, so anyone who passes
Will point and say "Is Aegisthus home?
Does he know they are here? Then why
Does he bar his doors to those who ask shelter?"
And if I gain admission at the gates
And find that man upon my father's throne
Or if he comes to look me up and down
And question me to my face, before he says   610
"Where is this stranger from?" I'll strike him dead,
And in the flashing of a sword he'll fall.
So the Fury, that has never yet been starved of slaughter,
Will drink pure blood, the third draught and the last.

[To ELECTRA]

Your part to manage everything within
The house, so all may hang together,

[To the CHORUS]

And yours, to keep a guard upon your tongue,
Speak when you should, be silent when you must.
And all the rest I summon this one here
To oversee, when I have made   620
All ready for the trial at arms.

[Exeunt ORESTES and PYLADES to disguise themselves, ELECTRA to the palace]

CHORUS. Great the progeny of nature, strange
And dreadful; in the cradle of the sea
Lurk monsters; in the hinterland
Of earth and heaven, fire
Has wings to fly; and birds
And creeping things can tell
The malice of the stormwinds.

600 Phocis district on the northern shore of the Gulf of Corinth, containing Mount Parnassus, traditional home of the Muses, and Delphi, the shrine of Apollo

But who could put to words the vaunting
630 Pride of man, the overmastering
Selfwill of woman, bedfellow
Of sorrows for mankind?
For when her passion turns
From wedlock and home, no beast
Or man can rage as she.

Let him who has a mind to plumb the
depths
Of things, learn how the sad Althaea once,
Armed with prescience of fire,
Devised death for her son, and burnt
640 The red brand that was of an age with him
Since he came forth crying from his
mother's womb,
Whose span was his, to the appointed day.

There is another written black in story,
Scylla, who dealt in death, and was se-
duced
By enemies to kill one of her nearest.
Tempted her bitch-heart was and won
By Minos' gift, the necklace wrought of
gold,
To cut from Nisus as he heedless slept
The lock of lasting life; and from this
world went he.

650 And now I have begun this bloody his-
tory
Should there not be a place
For the loveless wedlock that this house
Would fain see gone? You came
In guise of enemy upon
Your husband, working on him with
Your wiles, and sly as only woman may,
On your husband armored strong in might,
And over him you prized

A house whose hearth is barren of its fire,
The heart of the man-woman. 660

Of all the evils that the world can tell
Lemnos takes pride of place, a name
To fright the ear, a blasphemy,
And whatsoever dreadful thing
Shall pass, there will be one to christen it
"The crime of Lemnos." So angry were the
gods
That from earth the race has gone dis-
honored.
For what is evil in heaven's sight
Is so for men. Does any of these tales
Not fit our case? 670

Now stands the sword at the lifebreath
To thrust sharp home, and at the hilt
Is Justice aiding; for it is not fit
That those who trod the majesty of Zeus
Underfoot, should not be trampled
Down in their turn.

Now the anvil of Justice stands four-
square
And Fate the swordsmith has the edge
made keen.
For from the abyss of her mind the Fury,
Late come to honor, visits on the house 680
The child of blood shed in the former
time
To make atonement.

[*The palace.* ORESTES *and* PYLADES, *disguised as travellers, come to the door
and knock*]

OR. Boy, do you hear? There's someone
knocking!

---

619 **this one here** without the stage gesture which
would originally have accompanied these words, it
is impossible to say who is meant. It could be
Pylades, Agamemnon or Apollo. 637 the chorus
offer examples from mythology of women who
have been carried away by their passions. *Althaea*
was the mother of Meleager. When her son was
born the Fates told her that he would die when
a brand then burning in the fire was consumed.
She promptly extinguished the brand and locked
it away. When Meleager grew to manhood, he
quarrelled with his mother's brothers and killed

them. In her grief and anger Althaea rekindled the
brand and Meleager died. 644 *Scylla* daughter of
Nisus, king of Megara, often confused with the sea
monster of the same name. Her father's life depended on a lock of red hair growing on his head.
Minos, King of Crete, who was attacking Megara,
persuaded Scylla to sever it, thus killing Nisus and
causing the surrender of the city. 662 *Lemnos*
island off the coast of Asia Minor whose women,
according to tradition, had risen against their husbands and killed them

Is anyone there? Boy, I say! Who's at home?
For the third time, somebody come to the
  door,
If there is still shelter to be had here
Now that Aegisthus is in charge.
PORTER [*Within*]. All right, I hear you!
  Where are you from?
OR. Go tell the masters of this house.
690   They are the ones I seek. I bring strange
        news.
      And hurry; night's dark chariot comes
      Apace; this is the hour
      When merchants must drop anchor in a
        house
      That opens up its doors to travelling men.
      Send us someone in authority,
      The mistress, or her man, for preference.
      With women we must be polite, and talk
      Around the matter. Man to man speaks
        straight
      And to the point, without prevarication.

[*The door opens. Enter* CLYTEMNESTRA]

700   CLYTEMNESTRA. Travellers, you have only to
        state your needs.
      Such entertainment as this house can offer
      Is at your command—a warm bath, or a bed
      To magic weariness away, and honest
      Eyes to wait on you. But if
      You have more weighty business to discuss,
      That is the man's work, and we shall in-
        form him so.
      OR. Daulis is my home. I am a traveller from
        Phocis.
      I was on my way with merchandise to
        Argos
      On business of my own. When I turned off
        here,
710   A man I had met—we were strangers to
        each other—
      Asked my destination, and told me his.
      He was Strophius the Phocian—that came
        out
      In conversation—and he said to me
      "Since you must go to Argos anyway,
      Think to look out the parents of Orestes

712 *Strophius*   friend to Argos, to whose hands the
infant Orestes had been entrusted

And tell them he is dead. Do not forget.
Whatever his family decides to do,
Whether to bring him back, or have him
  buried
Out of his land, to lie forever among
  strangers,
Bring word accordingly, when you come   720
  back again,
For we have done but this—shed proper tears
Above his ashes, and unfolded them
In the belly of a brazen urn." That was
  all he told me.
But whether I talk to those who have
Authority and interest in this business
I do not know. I think his father should
  be told.
CLYT. Oh,
You tell of how the waters of our grief
Rise clear above our heads. O curse upon
  our house
That ever throws disaster in our way,
How little slips your eyes, with what sure   730
  aim
You send your shafts to strike down from
  afar
Even the things that carefully were set
Out of your path, to strip me desolate
Of those I love. So now it is Orestes,
He who was so well schooled to tread
  around
This slough of death. There was a hope
Of decency, of revel in our house;
By this we kept alive; now take that hope
And by its name write "Liar."
OR. I would have rather introduced myself   740
To entertainment so munificent
By telling of more pleasant things; for none
Could be more anxious to oblige than
  travellers
Their hosts. But I should have looked upon
  myself
As breaking a sacred trust, if I neglected
To carry this matter through. I gave my
  promise
To Strophius, and am under obligation
To you now, as your guest.
CLYT. This changes nothing. You will be re-
  ceived
According to your merits, and shall have   750

No less regard, while you are in our house.
If it had not been you who brought this
message
It would have been another. It is now
The hour when footsore travellers should
reap
The promise of their long day's march.

[*To her servants*]

Take him inside, to the guestrooms where
We lodge the menfolk, his attendants too
And fellow travellers. See that they receive
The comforts proper to a house like ours.
760 You have your orders. You are answerable
to me.
I shall go tell the master of the house
What I have heard, and with my friends
about me
Take the measure of this new disaster.

[CLYTEMNESTRA, ORESTES *and* PYLADES
go inside the palace]

CHORUS. Come friends and fellow servants all,
Is it not time for us to show
The power of our voices, and so aid
Orestes? O soverign Earth and sovereign
Mound of the tomb, who lie upon
The body of the sealord and our king,
770 Now hear us, grant us aid.
Now is the time ripe for Persuasion
To marshal all her wiles
And for the god of the dark journey,
Hermes,
And him that dwells in night, to stand
Sentinel as the sword comes to the match.

[*Enter* CILISSA]

The harm must be afoot, the traveller is
busy—
Here is Orestes' nurse in tears.
Where are you going from the gates, Cilissa,
With misery, the uninvited guest
780 Free ever of her company, to step beside
you?

774 *him that dwells in night* Agamemnon

CILISSA. Our mistress sent me hurrying to find
Aegisthus for the travellers, so he
Could talk to them man to man, and learn
The ins and outs of what they have to
tell him.
She had a wry face for her servants, but
behind
Her eyes she hid a smile that things had
worked
So well for her—but for this house
It's nothing short of tragedy—the tale
The travellers told, and that's plain
enough.
And it will be good news to that one   790
When he hears it. Oh, the pity of it!
All the troubles that we had, and never
Two alike, here in the house of Atreus,
More than a body could stand; oh, how
they vexed
This heart of mine! And yet I never
Had to endure anything like this.
The rest I got through when I set my mind
to it.
Orestes, bless him, plagued the life out of
me—
I had the rearing of him from his mother,
And all those times he got me up   800
By crying in the night—and what good
did it ever
Do me? Babes are little animals,
They can't think for themselves, you have
To guess what they want, what else can
you do?
The child in his cradle doesn't have the
words
To tell us if he's hungry, if he's thirsty,
Or wants to wet; no arguing
With young insides. I needed second sight,
And I was often wrong, believe me, and
had to be
His washerwoman too. Feed him, clean   810
up after him,
It was all the same job, and I
Doubled these offices, ever since I took
Orestes from his father's hands; and now
He's dead, they say; so much the worse
for me.
Well, I must go to find the man who
ruined

This house, and he'll be glad enough to
    hear it.
CHORUS. Did she say he was to come in state?
CIL. Say that again, so I may catch your
    meaning.
CHORUS. With his bodyguard, or by himself?
820 CIL. She told him to bring his servants
    armed—
CHORUS. Then as you hate your master, do
    not tell him this.
    Say he must come alone, so his informants
    May talk without constraint. Bid him hurry
    And be of good heart. It is the messenger
    Who takes the crooked word and makes it
    straight.
CIL. But are you happy over what I told you?
CHORUS. And if Zeus means to send a wind
    To blow away foul weather?
CIL.   How?
    Orestes is dead; the house has lost its hope.
830 CHORUS. Not yet. He would be a poor diviner
    Who traced things so.
CIL.   What do you mean?
    Do you know something we have not been
    told?
CHORUS. Go with your message, do as you are
    bid.
    The gods will take care of their own affairs.
CIL. I'll go, and do as you have told me;
    And heaven grant it turn out for the best!

    [*Exit*]

CHORUS. Grant this my prayer, O Zeus
    The godhead, father of Olympus,
    That those who long to see
840 This mansion set to rights may have their
    hope
    Accomplished; what I have said
    Is nothing if not just, O Zeus;
    Do you enforce it.

    O Zeus, rank him who now
    Is in the house above his enemies.
    For if you raise him to eminence
    Two and threefold will he repay you,
    Zeus, and cheerfully.

For be advised, this colt,
The orphan of a man much loved,   850
Is harnessed in the chariot
Of suffering; and you must set a measure
To the course, so we may never
See him break step, but extend himself
Full tilt across the ground.

O Zeus, rank him who now
Is in the house above his enemies.
For if you raise him to eminence
Two and threefold will he repay you,
Zeus, and cheerfully.   860

And you that haunt the inner sanctum
    of the house
In pride of wealth, O gods
That think as we do, hear us.
Come, rid us of this bloody stain
Of things done in olden time.
Make manifest your justice, let
Old murder breed in the house no more.

And you who live
At the mouthpiece of the world
Grant to those who fell in glory   870
This kindness, that they may look up again
To the house of a hero, and that eyes of
    love
May see it as a beacon shining, free
From enshrouding shadows.

And let the son of Maia give us fitting
    aid
For he is mightiest
To give a deed fair passage
If so he will, for many a time
He deigns to make dark word plain
Or wraps the eyes in shadows, speaking 880
Riddles that no clearer come by daylight.

And you who live
At the mouthpiece of the world
Grant to those who fell in glory
This kindness, that they may look up again
To the house of a hero, and that eyes of
    love

869 *the mouthpiece of the world* the meaning of
this whole passage is obscure; probably Apollo's

shrine at Delphi is meant   875 *the Son of Maia*
Hermes

May see it as a beacon shining, free
From enshrouding shadows.

Then at last will the house be rid
890 Of double evil; with united voice
We shall speed the work, as women may,
Break out the mourning song, and sing
"The ship sails fair."
Mine, mine to reap the argosy, and wreck
Is far from my beloved.

When the time comes for doing, be
Stoutedhearted; when she calls
"My child," shout her down
With cry of "Father," and act
900 The sin that is grace, her murder.

And with Orestes' mind combine
The heart of Perseus; for your friends
On earth and under it, perform
This favor, though it sting you sore.
Let death and blood
Run wild within, and bring upon the man
Who killed, a death in punishment.

[*Enter* AEGISTHUS]

AEGISTHUS. I do but as they bid me, and am
    come
In answer to the message. There are people
910 Lodging here, they say, who tell a tale
We never hoped to hear, the death
Of Orestes. This house has wounds still
    raw
From bloodshed long ago; now must it take
Another burden on itself, a thing
Of running blood? What can I make of
    this?
The living truth? The terrified imaginings

Of women make bubble-tales that burst
Upon the air. Can you say anything
Of this, to make me certain in my mind?
CHORUS. We heard the same. But go in to
    the travelers
920 And let them tell you. It is better always

902 *Perseus* mythical hero who killed the Gorgon,
she-monster with hair of snakes whose glance turned
men to stone

To go to the source than learn secondhand.
AEG. Yes, I should like to see this messenger
And ask if he was with him when he died
Or speaks the words of groping rumor only.
The mind must have an eye for trickery.

[*Exit*]

CHORUS. Zeus, Zeus, what shall I say? And
    where begin
My prayer for the gods' aid?
How, before the ending, find
Words worthy of my will?   930
For now the bloody cutting-edge
Comes close, to rend a man.
Now in the house of Agamemnon
Will he bring ruin upon all
Or light the fire of liberty again
And in the kingdom of his father
Live rich, the honored son.
To such a wrestle must Orestes come
The challenger, by the god's advisement
One against two; and may he throw them! 940

[*A cry within*]

Ah, what is that?
What has happened in the house?
Let us stand aside till the work is finished
So there may come no blame on us all
In this foul business, for the fight
Is at an end.

[*Enter* SERVANT *from the palace*]

SERVANT. Cry desolation, for our lord is dead,
And cry again, a triple cry of sorrow!
Aegisthus is gone. Come, no delay;
Open the portals of the women's chambers, 950
Slide back the bolts; we need young
    strength
To fight for us, a man, but not for him
Who is dead and gone; no purpose there.
Ahoy, ahoy!
I call on the deaf, on those who lie
In idle slumber and do nothing. Where
Is Clytemnestra, what does she do now?
Her head is on the block, and soon
Must fall, in measure as she did to others.

[*Enter* CLYTEMNESTRA]

960 CLYT. What is this? What means this shouting in the house?

SERVANT. Listen to me. The dead are killing the living.

CLYT. You speak in riddles, but I read you well.

By sleight we killed, by sleight we are to die.

Come, hurry, bring an axe to kill a man.

[*Exit* SERVANT]

Let us make certain, then. It must be he or I,

So far have I come now in this sad history.

[*Enter* ORESTES *with a drawn sword,* PYLADES *beside him*]

OR. You are the one I seek. His part is played.

CLYT. Are you dead, my love? Is brave Aegisthus gone?

OR. You love that man? Then in one tomb you shall

970 Be buried, and be faithful after death.

CLYT. Hold back, my son, have pity on this breast

My child, where often slumbering

You lay, and suckled milk to make you strong.

OR. Pylades, what shall I do? How may I kill my mother?

PYLADES. What of the oracles still unfulfilled

Apollo spoke at Delphi? Your sworn promise?

Better the world should hate you than the gods.

OR. Your word has won. You show the way that I must go.

[*To* CLYTEMNESTRA]

Come in, for I would kill you on his body.

980 In life you thought him better than my father;

Then sleep with him in death, if such you love

And give to him whom you should love your hate.

CLYT. You took my youth. May I not share your age?

OR. You killed my father. Would you share my house?

CLYT. The blame is Destiny's as well as mine.

OR. Then it is Destiny who kills you now.

CLYT. Have you no terror of a mother's curse?

OR. You bore me and then cast me out to sorrow.

CLYT. To live with friends. This was no casting out.

OR. I was born of a free father and you sold 990 me.

CLYT. Then where is the price that I received for you?

OR. I could not bring myself to tell your shame.

CLYT. Tell all, but tell your father's follies too.

OR. Blame not him. He toiled, you sat at home.

CLYT. Women suffer when the man is gone, my child.

OR. Man's labor feeds the women who sit idle.

CLYT. My child, I think you mean to kill your mother.

OR. I will not kill you. You will kill yourself.

CLYT. Take care. Your mother's curse will hound you down.

OR. My father's curse will find me if I fail. 1000

CLYT. This is the serpent that I bore and fed.

OR. Indeed the terror of your dreams spoke true.

You sinned in killing. Now be sinned against.

[ORESTES *and* PYLADES *drive* CLYTEMNESTRA *into the house*]

CHORUS. Even for these I can find tears, and for

Their coupled death. But since Orestes has been bold

To top this long and bloody history

We find it better that the light within

The house not be extinguished utterly.

In time there came to the sons of Priam
1010 Justice heavy in punishment
And on the house of Agamemnon came
The lions paired to battle two.
Then pressed he to the uttermost, the exile
To whom god had spoken, eager
Under heaven's admonition.

    Cry joy now for the mansions of our
      lords,
    The end of pain, the end of rich things
      wasted
    By two in infamy, the dark days gone.

    He came; and his part was to deceive,
1020 To scheme and conquer. In the fight
His hand was guided by the very child
Of Zeus—we mortals know her name
As Justice, and we have good cause—
She who in a blast of hate
Comes on her foes destroying.

    Cry joy now for the mansions of our
      lords,
    The end of pain, the end of rich things
      wasted
    By two in infamy, the dark days gone.

    As Apollo spoke from his deep-riven
1030 Cavern on Parnassus, so
Has it passed; the innocent deceit
Comes home to fight harm grown old.
Divinity has ways to keep
From going down to evil; it is fit
That we should laud the powers that reign
    in heaven.

    Now is there light to see, the bit
Is gone that held our house so hard.
So up, you halls, arise; for time
Too long have you lain fallen.

1040   Not long, and Time that brings all
To pass will enter in
Our gates, when the evil presence
Is cast from our hearth, and ceremonies
Have made all clean; then chance
Will come up ever fair for those
Who take their lodging here in aftertime.

    Now is there light to see, the bit
Is gone that held our house so hard.
So up, you halls, arise; for time
Too long have you lain fallen. 1050

    [*The doors open* ORESTES *is seen stand-
ing sword in hand over the bodies of*
CYTEMNESTRA *and* AEGISTHUS. *He holds
the robe in which* AGAMEMNON *was
killed*]

OR. See here the double lordship of this land
    Who killed my father and laid waste my
      house.
    A while they sat upon their thrones in
      state,
    And they are lovers still, as you may judge
    By what befell; their oath has kept its
      promise.
    Together they swore to kill my wretched
      father
    And die together; they are not forsworn.

    [*Displaying* AGAMEMNON's *robe*]

    See too, all you who look on this sad story,
    The trick they used to bind my wretched
      father,
    Chains for his hands, a halter for his feet. 1060
    Come, spread it out and make a circle
      round
    To show this net to catch a man.
    So may the father see—I mean not mine,
    But he who watches every living thing
    The Sun—my mother's filthy handiwork.
    So at the judgement day, whenever it shall
      come,
    He may appear to testify
    That I had just cause to pursue the death
    Of this my mother. On Aegisthus' death
    I waste no words. It is written, adulterers 1070
    Shall be punished—but she who worked so
      vile a thing
    Against her man, whose children she con-
      ceived
    And bore beneath her cincture, sweet load
      once,
    Now this you see, a curse, a thing of hate—

What do you think her now? A water-
snake, a viper
Who needs no fangs, whose very touch
Will rot a man, so venomous
Her mind, so quick to strike . . .
And this, what shall I call it? Has it any
name
1080   That one may say with decency? A snare
To catch an animal, a winding sheet,
A tenting for the bath? A net, a skein
We well could say, a robe to hobble feet—
The sort of thing a cozener might use
Who lived by catching travellers and rob-
bing them
Of money; such a trick as this
Would win him many victims, and would
keep
His heart warm inside him. . . .
May such a woman never come to share
1090   My home and bed; may heaven first de-
stroy me,
Before I have begotten me a child.

CHORUS. Sing sorrow for things done:
For you a hateful death, and for the
one
Who lives, the ripening of pain.

OR. Did she do this or not? This mantle
testifies
That it was dyed red by Aegisthus' sword.
Dip it and dip again, and still
The stain of blood and its accomplice,
Time,
Have spoilt the work. Now I can praise
him, now
1100   Make lamentation over him; and when
I speak to this, the robe that killed my
father,
I sorrow for the doing and the death,
For all our race, the tainted prize
Of this, my inconsiderable conquest.

CHORUS. No mortal man can live his life
Through to the end untouched by suf-
fering.
There is trouble here, and more to come.

OR. But hear me now; I cannot see the end;
My chariot has run me from the course,
1110   My rebel senses lead me where they will,
While fear draws breath to sing within
my heart

And it must dance to his angry tune.
While I
Have wits about me still, I call upon my
friends
To hear. I killed my mother, but I say
There was some right in this; my father's
blood
Had tainted her, she was a thing unclean
In heaven's sight.
And for the blandishments that made me
bold
To such a deed, I cite as culpable
Apollo, seer of Delphi, who proclaimed in   1120
oracles
That I could do this thing and still
Be innocent; but if I failed—
What then would come on me I will not
say.
Draw bow at hazard, you would never
Come within measure of my suffering.

[*He arrays himself as a suppliant*]

See me how I go forth, with wreath
Upon my head, with branch in hand,
To the centrestone of earth, Apollo's seat
And holy shrine, that famous place
Whose fire burns everlasting; I will go   1130
Out from my own, from blood that is my
own;
Apollo charged me that I should not turn
To any other sanctuary but his.
To all who live in Argos in the future time
I say remember how these evil things were
done
And speak for me when Menelaus comes.
And I shall go an outcast from my land
To walk among strangers, and leave be-
hind
In life, in death, this memory of me.

CHORUS. What you did was well. Do not let   1140
foul speech
Harness your mouth, or turn your tongue
to evil.
For you brought liberty to all who live
In Argos, when you came upon
This pair of snakes and cut their heads off
clean.

1126 *wreath, branch* customary emblems of the
suppliant 1136 *Menelaus* Agamemnon's brother

[ORESTES *points and cries out*]

OR. O servants of this house, they come
   In shapes of Gorgons, clad in robes of
     black,
   Their hair a nest of snakes; I cannot stay!
CHORUS. If any man has earned a father's
     love
   You are the one; so what imaginings
1150 Are these, that send you reeling? Stay,
   Be bold, you have good cause.
OR. I suffer, these are no imaginings
   But real; the hounding of my mother's hate.
CHORUS. It is the blood still wet on your
     hands
   That comes on you now to shake your
     senses.
OR. O Lord Apollo, are they coming yet?
   They weep, their eyes are running foul
     with blood.
CHORUS. There is one way to purify your-
     self. Apollo
   Will lay his hands on you, and make you
     free

Of this affliction.   1160
OR. You do not see them, but I see them.
   I must go forth, I can stay here no longer.

[*Exit*]

CHORUS. Good luck go with you, then, and
     may the god
   Look kindly on you, and preserve you safe
   In fortune.
   Now for the third time
   Has storm come from the race, to blow
   Upon the palace of our kings, and passed.
   One was the child-feast,
   The grief and desolation of Thyestes.   1170
   Two was the death of kings, when the lord
   Of the Achaean host was struck
   Down in the bath.
   Three was the coming of the savior
   Or death—which shall I call it?
   When will there be an ending, when
   Will wrath be spent, and fate lulled to   1177
     slumber?

1146 Gorgons Orestes sees the Furies advancing on him, still invisible to the chorus. They were traditionally represented as women with hair of snakes and carrying blazing torches—thus resembling the Gorgons, to whom Orestes compare them. See note on v. 902   *1169 the child-feast* Atreus, Agamemnon's father, had killed his brother *Thyestes'* children and served them up as a feast   *1172 Achaean* Greek

◆ Some Notes on the Myth of Electra

By H. D. F. KITTO

The story of the Pelopid dynasty, of the Curse in the House of Atreus, is too well known to need summarizing here. There are however three points in Sophocles' handling of it which may deserve brief comment: two of them illustrate the great freedom with which the Greek poets remodelled myth to suit their immediate purpose.

1. Aeschylus and Euripides both represent Orestes as being pursued by the Erinyes (Furies, Avengers) because of his killing of Clytemnestra; Sophocles' play not only contains no hint of such a pursuit; it actually makes the Erinyes, with Ares and Hermes, divine partners in the act of vengeance (vv. 1362-4). The reason is plain enough: Sophocles' theme is that a crime like that of Aegisthus and Clytemnestra will naturally, if not even inevitably, generate its own retribution; therefore he makes the divine powers —Zeus, Apollo, the Erinyes—favour those who are, in the nature of the case, seeking to avenge the crime and to reverse the lawless usurpation.

2. Sophocles' version of the sacrifice of Iphigeneia at Aulis is different from what Aeschylus had devised. Aeschylus made Artemis demand the sacrifice not because of something that Agamemnon had already done, but because of what he was proposing to do, namely to sacrifice lives in a 'war for a wanton woman': he may abandon his war and save his daughter, or he may kill his daughter, fight and win his war—and then return to face the retribution that awaits the man who has blood on his hands. Sophocles returns to what was in fact the traditional story, the incident of the stag; he also makes Artemis raise not adverse winds but no winds at all, so that the fleet could sail neither to Troy nor back home. Again the reason is clear: Sophocles wishes Agamemnon to be as guiltless as may be.

3. The earlier part of the myth, all that concerns Atresus and Thyestes, Sophocles naturally omits, as irrelevant to his theme; he does however, in his first ode, go back to an even earlier incident, 'the chariot-race of Pelops'—and one wonders why. The story, in brief, is as follows. Pelops ('Ruddy-face'), the founder of the dynasty, was a young hero from Asia Minor. He risked all in making a dangerous bid for the hand of Hippodameia, daughter of Oenomaus, king of Elis in the Peloponnesus, 'island of Pelops'; the terms were that any suitor had to run a chariot race with Oenomaus: if he won, the lady was his; if he lost, he was to be killed. Previous suitors had lost; Pelops won, either through his own skill and the aid of a god, or (in the version followed by Sophocles) by bribing Oenomaus' charioteer MYRTILUS to remove a linch-pin from Oenomaus' chariot so that the king was thrown out and killed. Myrtilus himself then offered insult to Hippodameia and was flung from a cliff into the sea by Pelops; but before he drowned he uttered a curse on Pelops. This was the beginning of the long chain of disaster in the Pelopid house. The reason why in this detail alone Sophocles harked back to the earliest part of the myth is presumably that in his play the vengeance taken by Orestes and Electra is going to square all accounts, with the restoration of the lawful heir; therefore he refers, thus briefly, to the beginning of all the trouble. Further, it is at least interesting to observe that the final triumph also involves a chariot race, though a fictitious one.

AMPHIARÄUS (or Amphiareus). There is a passing allusion to this hero in the Electra (vv. 830 ff.). He, a wise man and a prophet, was a brother-in-law to the king of Argos, Adrastus, who gave help to Polyneices in his attack on Thebes. Disapproving of the whole expedition, and knowing that it was doomed, Amphiaraus was reluctant to join it, but he was over-persuaded by his wife Eriphyle,

H. D. F. Kitto, "Some Notes on the Myth of Electra," *Sophocles: Three Tragedies*, trans. by H. D. F. Kitto (New York: Oxford University Press, 1964), pp. 156-157.

whom Polyneices had bribed with a golden necklace. When the defeated Argives were in flight from Thebes the earth opened and swallowed Amphiaraus alive, with his chariot.

It is for this reason that he is said, in the play, to be living and ruling in the underworld.

◆ On the Pronunciation of Greek Names

By H. D. F. KITTO

By tradition, we give Greek proper names a Latin spelling, and then pronounce them in the English way, with the stress accent natural to English, though observing for the most part the original distinction between long and short vowels. As a convention this is intelligible, but there is nothing sacrosanct about it. For example, the Greek name Kithairon is spelt Cithaeron and then pronounced something like Sitheerun, but if an actor or producer dislikes hissing, why should he not revert to something like the Greek form? The Greek Iokaste is traditionally spelt Jocasta and the first syllable is pronounced like Joe; it is because I find this a nasty sound that I have partially reverted to the Greek spelling, as also with the name Phokis. On the other hand, it would be silly to disguise the familiar Mycenae by saying Mykenae. In the following list, my circumflex accent denotes a long syllable; the acute accent marks the syllable which normally carries our English stress; it may be assumed that the vowel is short unless it has the circumflex accent. *Ch* should always be made hard, unless indeed an aspirated *k* (as in *loch*) is preferred. The dipththong *ae* is the Latinization of *ai*; pronunciation in English varies between a long *e* ('see') and *i* (as in *high*). Surely, so long as we are consistent, we are entitled to apply our ideas of euphony. *Oe* regularly becomes the long *e* (though not in America), and final *eus* rhymes with *deuce*.

Annotated List of Proper Names

Abae: an oracular shrine in Phokis.

Acheron: 'Lamentation': one of the rivers of the underworld.

Aetólia (Eetólia: Ayetolia would be pedantic)

Agênôr: an ancient king of Tyre, father of Cadmus. (g hard)

Ámphiareús (stress on the first and fourth syllables)

Amphîôn: a mythical musician whose music raised the walls of Thebes.

Amphitrîtê: a sea-goddess.

Aulis (Awlis traditional, Owlis pedantic)

Boeôtia (Bee-ó-shya): the region in which Thebes was the largest city.

Chrysóthemis (stress on the second syllable; the *y* represents a long vowel, but the fact is commonly ignored)

Dêmêtêr: a goddess of vegetation, especially of corn.

Dircê (Dirke): a river near Thebes.

Dionŷsus

Eteoclês (the first three syllables are all short; some stress the first, some the second)

Haemôn (Heemon, Haymon, Highmon, are all possible pronunciations)

Hêlios: the Sun-god.

Iphianassa (stress on the first and fourth syllables)

Ismênus: a river near Thebes, and a local god.

Ister: the Danube.

Lábdacus

Menoeceus (Menoikeus may be preferred to Meneekeus or Meneeseus)

Meropê

Pélops (not Peelops)

Phánoteus

Polydôrus

Pýlades (Pill-a-dês; though one often hears Pighl-a-des)

Pŷthô: the priestess at Delphi; also Delphi in general.

Erinys (plural: Erinyes): commonly rendered Furies or Avengers. These were the agents of Dike, which we translate as best we can: Justice, or Retribution, according to the context. Dike really means something like 'the way in which things regularly happen'; the Erinyes therefore punish or correct infringements of the established and proper order, whether in the moral or the physical universe. Thus in the *Iliad,* when Achilles' horse has spoken to him to warn him, it is the Erinyes which stop the horse's mouth.

H. D. F. Kitto "On the Pronunciation of Greek Names," *Ibid.* pp. 154-155.

◆◆ Electra

By SOPHOCLES

Translated by H. D. F. Kitto

Characters

ORESTES, only son of Agamemnon and Clytemnestra

PYLADES, his friend (He has no speaking part)

PAEDAGOGUS, an old slave, personal attendant of Orestes

ELECTRA, daughter of Agamemnon and Clytemnestra

CHRYSOTHEMIS, her sister

CLYTEMNESTRA

AEGISTHUS

CHORUS of women of Mycenae

Scene: Mycenae, in Argos, before the royal palace

The time of the action is some fifteen or twenty years after the return of Agamemnon from the Trojan War and his murder at the hands of Clytemnestra his wife, and Aegisthus his cousin and her paramour. The murderers have usurped Agamemnon's crown and estate. The date of the first production of the play is unknown: probably some time between 425 and 415 B.C. The events here enacted were dramatized, very differently, by Aeschylus in the *Choephori* or *Libation-bearers*, and by Euripides in his *Electra*. These two plays are extant; so too are the *Orestes* and *Iphigeneia in Tauris* of Euripides, in which he developed his version of the myth.

Sophocles, "Electra," in *Sophocles: Three Tragedies*, trans. by H. D. F. Kitto (New York: Oxford University Press, 1964), pp. 99–149.

Enter ORESTES, PYLADES *and the* PAEDAGOGUS, *with two attendants*

PAEDAGOGUS. Here is the land of Argos. From this place
Your father Agamemnon led the Greeks
To Troy. How many years have you been longing
To see what now your eyes can look upon:
The ancient city Argos, once the home
Of Io and her father Inachus.
Now look upon it: there, the market-place
That bears Apollo's name, and to the left
Is Hera's famous temple. The place where we
Are standing now—my son, this is Mycenae, 10
Golden Mycenae, and the blood-drenched palace
Of Pelops' dynasty is here, the place
From which your sister saved you, as a baby,
When they had murdered Agamemnon. I
Took you to safety, I have brought you up
To manhood. Now you must avenge your father.
So now, Orestes, you and Pylades
Your loyal friend, resolve with no delay
What you will do. For dawn has come; the stars
Have vanished from the darkness of the sky; 20
The birds are striking up their morning songs;
People will soon be stirring. Little time
Is left to you; the hour has come for action.

ORESTES. My friend, my loyal servant: every-
    thing
You say or do proclaims your true devo-
    tion.
Just as a horse, if he is thoroughbred,
Will keep his mettle even in old age,
Will never flinch, but in the face of danger
Prick up his ears, so you are ever first
30 To proffer help and to encourage me.
You then shall hear my plan, and as you
    listen
Give it your sharp attention, to amend
Whatever seems amiss.
I went to Delphi, and I asked Apollo
How best I might avenge my father's death
On those who murdered him. The god's
    reply
Was brief; it went like this: *Not with an
    army*
But with your own right hand, by strata-
    gem,
Give them what they have earned, and kill
    them both.
40 Therefore, since this is what the god has
    said,
Your part shall be to have yourself ad-
    mitted
Inside the palace when the moment fa-
    vours.
Find out what is afoot; return to me
And tell me what you can.—They will not
    know you;
You have grown old, so many years have
    passed;
Your silver hair will keep them from sus-
    pecting.
Your story shall be this, that you have
    come
From foreign parts, from Phanoteus of
    Phokis—
For he is one of their most trusted allies;
50 Tell them Orestes has been killed, and give
Your oath that it is true: he met his death
Competing in the Pythian Games at Del-
    phi,
Flung from his racing-chariot. Let this be
The tale. And for myself, the god com-
    manded
That I should first go to my father's tomb
And pay my tribute with a lock of hair

And wine-libation. This then will I do;
And I will find the urn which you have
    told me
Lies hidden in a thicket, and with that
I will come back. This urn of beaten   60
    bronze
Shall bring them joy—though not for long;
    for it
(So we will tell them) holds the ash and
    cinders
Of this my body that the fire consumed.—
Why should I fear an omen, if I say that I
Am dead, when by this story I fulfil
My life's true purpose, to secure my ven-
    geance?
No need to fear a tale that brings me gain.
For I have heard of those philosophers
Who were reported dead: when they re-
    turned,
Each to his city, they were honoured more.   70
And so, I trust, may I, through this pre-
    tence,
Look down triumphant like the sun in
    heaven
Upon my enemies.
Only do thou, my native soil; you, gods of
    Argos,
Receive and prosper me. House of my
    fathers,
Receive me with your blessing! The gods
    have sent me,
And I have come to purify and purge you.
Do not reject me, drive me not away,
But let me enter into my possessions;
Let me rebuild my father's fallen house.   80
    Such is my prayer. My friend, go to your
    task
And do it well. We go to ours; for Time
Calls only once, and that determines all.
ELECTRA [*within*]. Ah me! Ah me!
PAEDAGOGUS. Listen, my son: I thought I
    heard a cry
From near the gates, a cry of bitter grief.
ORESTES. Electra, my unhappy sister! Could
    It be her cry?—Let us wait and listen.
PAEDAGOGUS. No. The command that God has
    given us,
That must come first, to offer your libations   90
At Agamemnon's tomb. His aid will bring
Victory to us, and ruin to his foes.

[*Exeunt* ORESTES, PYLADES, *the* PAEDAG-OGUS, *and attendants. Enter* ELECTRA]

ELECTRA. Thou holy light,
(*anapaests: chanted*) Thou sky that art earth's
    canopy,
How many bitter cries of mine
Have you not heard, when shadowy night
Has given place to days of mourning!
And when the night has come again
My hateful bed alone can tell
100   The tears that I have shed within
This cruel palace. O my father!
No Trojan spear, no god of war,
Brought death to you on foreign soil.
My mother killed you, and her mate
Aegisthus! As a woodman fells
An oak, they took a murderous axe
    And cut you down.
And yet no other voice but mine
110   Cries out upon this bloody deed.
I only, father, mourn your death.
    Nor ever will
I cease from dirge and sad lament
So long as I behold the sun
By day and see the stars by night;
But like the sorrowing nightingale
Who mourns her young unceasingly,
Here at the very gates will I
Proclaim my grief for all to hear.

You powers of Death! you gods below!
120   Avenging Spirits, who behold
Each deed of blood, each faithless act
Dishonouring the marriage-vow,
Desert me not. Come to my aid!
Avenge my father's death!
And send my brother; bring to me
Orestes! For I can no more
Sustain this grief; it crushes me.

[*Enter the* CHORUS]

Strophe I

CHORUS. Electra, child of a most pitiless
    mother,

Why are you so wasting your life in un-
    ceasing
Grief and despair? Agamemnon   130
Died long ago. Treachery filled the heart,
Your mother's heart, that gave him,
Snared, entrapped, to a shameful sup-
    planter who killed him.
   If I may dare to say it, may
   Those who did such a thing
   Suffer the same themselves.
ELECTRA. O my noble, generous friends,
   You are here, I know, to comfort me in my
    sorrow.
   Welcome to me, most welcome, is your
    coming.
But ask me not to abandon my grief   140
   Or cease to mourn my father.
No, my friends; give, as always you give
   me, your love and devotion,
   But bear with my grief; I cannot betray
   my sorrow.

Antistrophe I

CHORUS. But he has gone to the land to which
    we all must
   Go. Neither by tears nor by mourning
    can
   He be restored from the land of the
    dead.
   Yours is a grief beyond the common
    measure,
    A grief that knows no ending,
   Consuming your own life, and all in
    vain.
    For how can mourning end wrong?   150
   Cannot you part yourself from your long
    Sorrow and suffering?
ELECTRA. Hard the heart, unfeeling the mind,
   Of one who should forget a father, cruelly
    slain.
   Her will my heart follow, the sad nightin-
    gale,
    Bird of grief, always lamenting
    Itys, Itys, her child.
And O, Niobe, Queen of Sorrow, to thee
   do I turn, as a goddess
Weeping for ever, in thy mountain-tomb.

Strophe II

160 CHORUS. Not upon you alone, my child,
Has come the heavy burden of grief
That chafes you more than those with
whom you live,
The two bound to you by kindred blood.
See how Chrysothemis lives, and Iphia-
nassa,
Your two sisters within.
He also lives, your brother,
Although in exile, suffering grief;
And glory awaits Orestes, for
He will come by the kindly guidance of
Zeus, and be
170 Received with honour and welcome, here
in Mycenae.
ELECTRA. But I, year after year, waiting for
him,
Tread my weary path, unwedded, childless,
Bathed in tears, burdened with endless
sorrow.
For the wrongs he has suffered, the crimes
of which I have told him,
He cares nothing. Messages come; all are
belied;
He longs to be here, but not enough to
come!

Antistrophe II

CHORUS. Comfort yourself, take comfort,
child;
Zeus is still King in the heavens.
He sees all; he overrules all things.
180 Leave this bitter grief and anger to him.
Do not go too far in hatred with those you
hate,
Nor be forgetful of him.
Time has power to heal all wounds.
Nor will he who lives in the rich
Plain of Crisa, near the sea,
Agamemnon's son, neglect his own father.
ELECTRA. But how much of my life has now
been spent,
Spent in despair! My strength will soon
be gone.
I am alone, without the comfort of chil-
dren; no

Husband to stand beside me, and share 190
the burden;
Spurned like a slave, dressed like a slave,
fed on the scraps,
I serve, disdained by all—in the house of
my fathers!

Strophe III

CHORUS. Pitiful the cry at his return,
Your father's cry in the banquet-hall,
When the straight, sharp blow of an axe
was launched at him.
Guile was the plotter, lust was the slayer,
Hideous begetters of a hideous crime,
Whether the hand that wrought the deed
Was a mortal hand, or a Spirit loosed from
Hell.
ELECTRA. That day of horrors beyond all 200
other horrors!
Hateful and bitter beyond all other days!
That accursed night of banqueting
Filled with fear and blood!
My father looked, and saw two murderers
aiming
A deadly, cowardly blow at him,
A blow that has betrayed my life
To slavery, to ruin.
O God that rulest Heaven and Earth,
Make retribution fall on them!
What they have done, that may they 210
suffer.
Leave them not to triumph!

Antistrophe III

CHORUS. Yet you should be wise, and say no
more.
It is yourself and what you do
That brings upon yourself this cruel out-
rage.
Your sullen, irreconcilable heart,
Breeding strife and enmity,
Adds to your own misery.
To fight with those that hold the power
is folly.
ELECTRA. I know, I know my bitter and hate-
ful temper;

220 But see what I have to suffer! That con-
      strains me.
    Because of that, I cannot help
    But give myself to frenzied hate
So long as life shall last. My gentle friends,
    What words of comfort or persuasion
    Can prevail, to reconcile
    My spirit with this evil?
    No; leave me, leave me; do not try.
    These are ills past remedy.
    Never shall I depart from sorrow
230 And tears and lamentation.

Epode

CHORUS. In love and friendship, like a
      mother,
  I beg you: do not make, my child,
  Trouble on top of trouble.
ELECTRA. In what I suffer, is there modera-
      tion?
  To be neglectful of the dead, can that be
      right?
  Where among men is that accounted
      honour?
  I'll not accept praise from them!
  Whatever happiness is mine,
I'll not enjoy dishonourable ease,
240   Forget my grief, or cease to pay
  Tribute of mourning to my father.
For if the dead shall lie there, nothing but
      dust and ashes,
And they who killed him do not suffer
      death in return,
  Then, for all mankind,
Fear of the gods, respect for men, have
      vanished.
CHORUS-LEADER. Your cause I make my own.
      So, if my words
  Displease you, I recall them and let yours
  Prevail; for I will always follow you.
ELECTRA. My friends, these lamentations are
      a sore
250 Vexation to you, and I am ashamed.
  But bear with me: I can do nothing else.
  What woman would not cry to Heaven,
      if she
  Had any trace of spirit, when she saw
  Her father suffering outrage such as I

Must look on every day—and every night?
And it does not decrease, but always grows
More insolent. There is my mother: she,
My mother! has become my bitterest en-
      emy.
And then, I have to share my house with
      those
Who murdered my own father; I am ruled   260
By them, and what I get, what I must do
Without, depends on them. What happy
      days,
Think you, mine are, when I must see
      Aegisthus
Sitting upon my father's throne, wearing
My father's robes, and pouring his libations
Beside the hearth-stone where they mur-
      dered him?
And I must look upon the crowning out-
      rage,
The murderer lying in my father's bed
With my abandoned mother—if I must
Call her a mother who dare sleep with him!   270
She is so brazen that she lives with that
Defiler; vengeance from the gods is not
A thought that frightens her! As if exulting
In what she did she noted carefully
The day on which she treacherously killed
My father, and each month, when that day
      comes,
She holds high festival and sacrifices
Sheep to the Gods her Saviours. I look on
In misery, and weep with breaking heart.
This cruel mockery, her Festival   280
Of Agamemnon, is to me a day
Of bitter grief—and I must grieve alone.
And then, I cannot even weep in peace:
This noble lady bids me stop, reviles
Me bitterly: 'You god-forsaken creature!
You hateful thing! Are you the only one
Who ever lost a father? Has none but you
Ever worn black? A curse upon you! May
The gods of Hades give you ample cause
To weep for evermore!'—So she reviles me.   290
But when she hears from someone that
      Orestes
May come, she flies into a frenzied rage,
Stands over me and screams: 'It's you I
      have
To thank for this, my girl! This is your
      work!

You stole Orestes from my hands, and sent
Him secretly away. But let me tell you,
I'll make you pay for this as you deserve.'
So, like a dog, she yelps, encouraged by
That glorious bridegroom who stands at her
    side,
300 That milksop coward, that abomination,
That warrior who shelters behind women.
    My cry is for Orestes and his coming
To put an end to this. O, I am sick
At heart from waiting; he is holding back,
And his delay has broken all my hopes.
Enduring this, my friends, how can I follow
Wisdom and piety? Among such evils
How can my conduct not be evil too?
CHORUS-LEADER. Come, tell me: is Aegisthus
    here, that you
310 Say this to us, or is he gone from home?
ELECTRA. If he were here, I'd not have
    dared to come
Outside the palace. No, he's in the country.
CHORUS-LEADER. If that is so, why then, I
    might perhaps
Myself be bold, and speak with you more
    freely.
ELECTRA. Say what you will; Aegisthus is not
    here.
CHORUS-LEADER. Then tell me of your
    brother: is there news
That he is coming, or is he still waiting?
ELECTRA. He promises—and that is all he does.
CHORUS-LEADER. So great an enterprise is not
    done quickly.
320 ELECTRA. Yet I was quick enough when I
    saved him!
CHORUS-LEADER. He'll not desert his friends.
    Have confidence.
ELECTRA. I have. If I had not I should have
    died.
CHORUS-LEADER. Hush, say no more! Chry-
    sothemis is coming,
Your sister, from the palace, carrying
Grave-offerings, that are given to the dead.
CHRYSOTHEMIS. Why have you come again
    outside the gate,
Spreading your talk? O, will you never
    learn?
Will nothing teach you? Why do you in-
    dulge
This vain resentment? I am sure of this:

Mine is as great as yours. If I could find   330
The power, they soon would learn how
    much I hate them.
But we are helpless; we should ride the
    storm
With shortened sail, not show our enmity
When we are impotent to do them harm.
Will you not do the same? The right may
    lie
On your side, not on mine, but since *they*
    rule,
I must submit, or lose all liberty.
ELECTRA. Shameful! that you, the child of
    such a father
Should have no thought for him, but only
    for
Your mother! All the wise advice you give   340
    me
You learn of her; none of it is your own.
But you must make your choice: to be a
    fool,
Like me, or to be prudent, and abandon
Those dearest to you. If you had the power,
You say, you'd show them how you hate
    them both—
And yet when I do all I can to avenge
Our father, do you help me? No; you try
To thwart me, adding cowardice on top
Of misery. Come, tell me—or let me
Tell you: if I give up my grief, what should   350
I gain? Do I not live? Barely, I know,
But well enough for me; and I give *them*
Continual vexation, and thereby
Honour the dead, if there is any feeling
Beyond the grave. You hate them, so you
    tell me:
Your tongue may hate them; what you do
    supports
Our father's enemies and murderers.
I will not yield to them, no, not for all
The toys and trinkets that give you such
    pleasure.
Enjoy your luxuries, your delicate food!   360
It is enough for me if I may eat
What does not turn my stomach. I have no
Desire to share in your high privileges.
And you would scorn them, if you knew
    your duty.
You might be known as Agamemnon's
    child,

But let them call you Clytemnestra's daugh-
ter,
And recognize your treason, who abandon
Your murdered father and your family.
CHORUS-LEADER. Do not give way to anger.
Each of you
370 Can with advantage listen to the other.
CHRYSOTHEMIS. I am well used to her tirades,
my friends;
I would not have provoked her, but that I
Know that the gravest danger threatens
her:
They are resolved to end her long com-
plaints.
ELECTRA. What is this awful thing? If it is
worse
Than *this* I will not say another word.
CHRYSOTHEMIS. I'll tell you everything I
know.—They have determined,
If you will not give up these protestations,
To imprison you in such a place that you
380 Will never see the sun again, but live
To sing your own laments in some dark
dungeon.
So think on this, or, when the blow has
fallen,
Do not blame me. Now is the time for pru-
dence.
ELECTRA. Will they do *that* to me?
CHRYSOTHEMIS.   They will; it is
Decreed, the moment that Aegisthus has
returned.
ELECTRA. Then let him come at once, for all
I care!
CHRYSOTHEMIS. How can you say it? Are
you mad?
ELECTRA.   At least,
I shall be out of sight of all of you.
CHRYSOTHEMIS. But to give up the life you
lead with us!
390 ELECTRA. A marvellous existence! One to
envy!
CHRYSOTHEMIS. It could be, if you would be-
have with sense.
ELECTRA. You'll not teach *me* to abandon
those I love.
CHRYSOTHEMIS. Not that, but to give in to
those who rule us.
ELECTRA. Let that be your excuse; I will not
make it!

CHRYSOTHEMIS. It is a duty, not to fall
through folly.
ELECTRA. I'll fall, if fall I must, avenging *him*.
CHRYSOTHEMIS. Our father will not blame me,
I am sure.
ELECTRA. Only a coward would rely on that!
CHRYSOTHEMIS. Will you not listen, and let
me persuade you?
ELECTRA. Never! I hope my judgements will 400
not fall
As low as that.
CHRYSOTHEMIS.   Then I will say no more.
I'll leave you now, and go upon my errand.
ELECTRA.Where are you going, with those
offerings?
CHRYSOTHEMIS. I am to lay them on our
father's tomb;
Our mother sent me.
ELECTRA.   She? Give offerings
To him who is her deadliest enemy?
CHRYSOTHEMIS. Say next: 'The husband slain
by her own hand'!
ELECTRA. Who thought of this? Or who per-
suaded her?
CHRYSOTHEMIS. She had a dream, I think,
that frightened her.
ELECTRA. Gods of our race! Be with us now, 410
at last!
CHRYSOTHEMIS. Do you find cause of hope in
this bad dream?
ELECTRA. Tell me the dream, and then per-
haps I'll know.
CHRYSOTHEMIS. I cannot tell you much.
ELECTRA.   But tell me *that*!
The safety or the ruin of a house
Will often turn upon a little thing.
CHRYSOTHEMIS. They say that in her dream
she saw our father
Returned to life and standing at her side;
He took the sceptre which he used to hold
Himself—the one that now Aegisthus car- 420
ries—
And planted it beside the hearth; from that
There grew, and spread, an over-arching
tree
That gave its shelter to the whole of Argos.
At sunrise, to allay her fear, she told
Her vision to the sun-god: one who stood
Nearby and heard reported it to me.
I cannot tell you more, except that I

Am sent because the dream has frightened
   her.
   So now, I beg you, in the name of all
430 The gods we worship, do as I advise:
Give up this folly which will be your ruin.
If you reject me now, you will return
To me when nothing I can do will help
   you.
ELECTRA. Dear sister, do not let these offerings
Come near his tomb; it is a thing that law
And piety forbid, to dedicate
To him gifts and libations that are sent
By her, his deadliest, bitterest enemy.
Bury them in the ground, or throw them to
440 The random winds, that none of them may
   reach him.
No; let them all be kept in store for her
In Hell, a treasure for her when she dies.
If she were not the most insensate woman
The world has ever seen, she'd not have
   dared
To try to crown the tomb of him she killed
With gifts inspired by enmity. Think:
   would they
Cause any gratitude in him? Did she not
   kill him?
And with such hatred, and with such dis-
   honour,
That she attacked even his lifeless body
450 And mangled it? You cannot think that
   gifts
Will gain her absolution from her crime?
Impossible! No, let them be, and make
A different offering at our father's grave:
Give him a lock of hair for token, one
Of yours, and one of mine—no lordly gifts,
But all I have; and give him too this girdle,
Poor, unadorned; and as you give them,
   kneel
Upon his grave; beseech him, from the world
Below, to look with favour on us, and
460 To give his aid against our enemies;
And that his son Orestes may be saved
To come in triumph and to trample on
His foes, that in the days to come we may
Grace him with gifts more splendid far
   than those
That we can offer now. For I believe,
I do believe, that in this dream, to her
So terrifying, the spirit of our father

Has played some part. However that may
   be,
My sister, do this service to yourself,
To me, and to the one we love beyond   470
All others, him who now is dead—our
   father.
CHORUS-LEADER. My child, if you are wise,
   you will do all
She bids you, for she speaks in piety.
CHRYSOTHEMIS. Do it I will; when duty's
   clear, there is
No cause to argue, but to do it quickly.
But, O my friends, I beg you, keep it secret,
This that I undertake. If it should come
To Clytemnestra's knowledge, then I fear
I should pay dearly for this enterprise.

[*Exit* CHRYSOTHEMIS]

Strophe I

CHORUS. If I have any foresight, any judge-   480
   ment to be trusted,
Retribution is at hand; her shadow falls
   before she comes.
She is coming, and she brings with her a
   power invincible.
   Confidence rises in my heart;
   The dream is good; it makes me glad.
The King, your father, is not sunk in dull
   forgetfulness,
Nor does the rusty two-edged axe forget
   the foul blow.

Antistrophe I

She will come swiftly and strongly, spring-
   ing on them from an ambush,
The Vengeance of the gods, coming in
   might. For they were swept
By a passion for a lawless and bloody mat-
   ing into crime.
   Therefore I feel glad confidence;   490
   The omen has not come in vain.
For evil doers must pay. Oracles and
   prophecies
Only deceive, if this dream is not now
   fulfilled.

Epode

That chariot-race of Pelops
Has become the cause of sorrow
And of suffering without end.
Since Myrtilus was thrown from
His golden car, and dashed to death into
500 The sea that roared beneath him,
Cruel violence and bloodshed
Have been quartered on this house.

[*Enter* CLYTEMNESTRA, *with a servant
carrying materials for a sacrifice*]

CLYTEMNESTRA. At large again, it seems—be-
cause Aegisthus
Is not at home to stop you. So you go
Roaming about, putting us all to shame!
But in *his* absence, you are not afraid
Of me! And yet you say to everyone
That I am cruel and tyrannical,
That I heap outrage both on you and yours.
510 I do no outrage; if my tongue reviles you,
It is because my tongue must answer yours.
Your father: that is always your excuse,
That he was killed by me.—By me! Of
course;
I know he was, and I do not deny it—
Because his own crime killed him, and
not I
Alone. And you, if you had known your
duty,
Ought to have helped, for I was helping
Justice.
This father of yours, whom you are always
mourning,
Had killed your sister, sacrificing her
520 To Artemis, the only Greek who could en-
dure
To do it—though his part, when he begot
her,
Was so much less than mine, who bore the
child.
So tell me why, in deference to whom,
He sacrificed her? For the Greeks, you say?
What right had they to kill a child of
mine?
But if you say he killed *my* child to serve
His brother Menelaus, should not he

Pay me for that? Did not this brother have
Two sons, and should they rather not have
died,
The sons of Helen who had caused the war   530
And Menelaus who had started it?
Or had the god of death some strange desire
To feast on mine, and not on Helen's chil-
dren?
Or did this most unnatural father love
His brother's children, not the one I bore
him?
Was not this father monstrous, criminal?
You will say No, but I declare he was,
And so would she who died—if she could
speak.
Therefore at what has happened I am not
Dismayed; and if you think me wrong,   540
correct
Your own mistakes before you censure
mine.
ELECTRA. This time at least you will not say
that I
Attacked you first, and then got such an
answer.
If you allow it, I'll declare the truth
On his behalf and on my sister's too.
CLYTEMNESTRA. I do allow it. Had you always
spoken
Like this, you would have given less
offence.
ELECTRA. Then listen. You admit you killed
my father:
Justly or not, could you say anything
More foul? But I can prove to you it was   550
No love of Justice that inspired the deed,
But the suggestions of that criminal
With whom you now are living. Go and ask
The Huntress Artemis why she becalmed
The fleet at windy Aulis.—No; *I* will tell
you;
We may not question gods.
My father once, they tell me, hunting in
A forest that was sacred to the goddess,
Started an antlered stag. He aimed, and
shot it,
Then made a foolish boast, of such a kind   560
As angered Artemis. Therefore she held up
The fleet, to make my father sacrifice
His daughter to her in requital for
The stag he'd killed. So came the sacrifice:

The Greeks were prisoners, they could neither sail
To Troy nor go back home; and so, in anguish,
And after long refusal, being compelled,
He sacrificed her. It was not to help
His brother. But even had it been for that,
570 As you pretend, what right had you to kill him?
Under what law? Be careful; if you set
This up for law, *Blood in return for blood,*
You may repent it; you would be the first
To die, if you were given your deserts.
But this is nothing but an empty pretext;
For tell me—if you will—why you are doing
What is of all things most abominable.
You take the murderer with whose help you killed
My father, sleep with him and bear him children;
580 Those born to you before, in lawful wedlock,
You have cast out. Is this to be applauded?
Will you declare this too is retribution?
You'll not say that; most shameful if you do—
Marrying enemies to avenge a daughter!
But there, one cannot even warn you, for
You shout aloud that I revile my mother.
You are no daughter's *mother,* but a slave's
Mistress to me! You and your paramour
Enforce on me a life of misery.
590 Your son Orestes, whom you nearly killed,
Is dragging out a weary life in exile.
You say I am sustaining him that he
May come as an avenger: would to God
I were! Go then, denounce me where you like—
Unfilial, disloyal, shameless, impudent.
I may be skilled in all these arts; if so,
I am at least a credit to my mother!

CHORUS-LEADER. She is so furious that she is beyond
All caring whether she be right or wrong.

600 CLYTEMNESTRA. Then why should I care what I say to her,
When she so brazenly insults her mother,
At her age too? She is so impudent
That there is nothing that she would not do.

ELECTRA. Then let me tell you, though you'll not believe it:
I *am* ashamed at what I do; I hate it.
But it is forced on me, despite myself,
By your malignity and wickedness.
Evil in one breeds evil in another.

CLYTEMNESTRA. You shameless creature! What I say, it seems,
And what I do give you too much to say. 610

ELECTRA. 'Tis you that say it, not I. You do the deeds,
And your ungodly deeds find me the words.

CLYTEMNESTRA. I swear by Artemis that when Aegisthus comes
Back home you'll suffer for this insolence.

ELECTRA. You see? You give me leave to speak my mind,
Then fly into a rage and will not listen.

CLYTEMNESTRA. Will you not even keep a decent silence
And let me offer sacrifice in peace
When I have let you rage without restraint?

ELECTRA. Begin your secrifice. I will not speak 620
Another word. You shall not say I stopped you.

CLYTEMNESTRA [*to the servant*]. Lift up the rich fruit-offering to Apollo
As I lift up my prayers to him, that he
Will give deliverance from the fears that now
Possess me.
Phoebus Apollo, god of our defence:
Hear my petition, though I keep it secret;
There is one present who has little love
For me. Should I speak openly, her sour
And clamorous tongue would spread malicious rumour 630
Throughout the city. Therefore, as I may
Not speak, give ear to my unspoken prayer.
Those visions of the doubtful dreams that came
When I was sleeping, if they bring good omen,
Then grant, O Lord Apollo, that they be
Fulfilled; if evil omen, then avert
That evil; let it fall upon my foes.
If there be any who, by trickery,
Would wrest from me the wealth I now enjoy,

640 Frustrate them. Let this royal power be mine,
This house of Atreus. So, until I die,
My peace untroubled, my prosperity
Unbroken, let me live with those with whom
I now am living, with my children round me—
Those who are not my bitter enemies.
    Such is my prayer; accept it graciously,
O Lord Apollo; give to all of us
Even as we ask. And there is something more.
I say not what it is; I must be silent;
650 But thou, being a god, wilt understand.
Nothing is hidden from the sons of Zeus.

[*A silence, while* CLYTEMNESTRA *makes her sacrifice. Enter the* PAEDAGOGUS]

PAEDAGOGUS [*to the chorus-leader*]. Might I inquire of you if I have come
To the royal palace of the lord Aegisthus?
CHORUS-LEADER. You have made no mistake, sir; this is it.
PAEDAGOGUS. The lady standing there perhaps might be
Aegisthus' wife? She well might be a queen!
CHORUS-LEADER. She is indeed the queen.
PAEDAGOGUS. My lady, greeting!
One whom you know—a friend—has sent me here
To you and to Aegisthus with good news.
660 CLYTEMNESTRA. Then you are very welcome. Tell me first,
Who is the friend who sent you?
PAEDAGOGUS.   Phanoteus
Of Phokis.—The news is of importance.
CLYTEMNESTRA. There sir, what is it? Tell me. Coming from
So good a friend, the news, I'm sure, is good.
PAEDAGOGUS. In short, it is Orestes. He is dead.
ELECTRA. Orestes, dead? O this is death to me!
CLYTEMNESTRA. What, dead?—Take no account of her.
PAEDAGOGUS. That is the news. Orestes has been killed.

ELECTRA. Orestes! Dead! Then what have I to live for?
CLYTEMNESTRA. That's your affair!—Now let 670 me hear the truth,
Stranger. What was the manner of his death?
PAEDAGOGUS. That was my errand, and I'll tell you all.
He came to Delphi for the Pythian Games,
That pride and glory of the land of Greece.
So, when he heard the herald's voice proclaim
The foot-race, which was first to be contested,
He stepped into the course, admired by all.
And soon he showed that he was swift and strong
No less than beautiful, for he returned
Crowned with the glory of a victory.   680
But though there's much to tell, I will be brief:
That man was never known who did the like.
Of every contest in the Festival
He won the prize, triumphantly. His name
Time and again was heard proclaimed: 'Victor:
Orestes, citizen of Argos, son
Of Agamemnon, who commanded all
The Greeks at Troy.' And so far, all was well.
But when the gods are adverse, human strength
Cannot prevail; and so it was with him.   690
For when upon another day, at dawn,
There was to be a contest of swift chariots,
He took his place—and he was one of many:
One from Achaea, one from Sparta, two
From Libya, charioteers of skill; Orestes
Was next—the fifth—driving Thessalian mares;
Then an Aetolian with a team of chestnuts;
The seventh was from Magnesia; the eighth
From Aenia—he was driving bays;
The ninth was from that ancient city   700
Athens;
The tenth and last was a Boeotian.
They drew their places. Then the umpire set them

Each at the station that had been allotted.
The brazen trumpet sounded; they were
    off.
They shouted to their horses, shook the
    reins;
You could hear nothing but the rattling din
Of chariots; clouds of dust arose; they all
Were bunched together; every driver
Goaded his horses, hoping so to pass
710 His rival's wheels and then his panting
    horses.
Foam from the horses' mouths was every-
    where—
On one man's wheels, upon another's back.
    So far no chariot had been overturned.
But now, the sixth lap finished and the
    seventh
Begun, the Aenian driver lost control:
His horses, hard of mouth, swerved sud-
    denly
And dashed against a Libyan team. From
    this
Single mishap there followed crash on
    crash;
The course was full of wreckage. Seeing
    this,
720 The Athenian—a clever charioteer—
Drew out and waited, till the struggling
    mass
Had passed him by. Orestes was behind,
Relying on the finish. When he saw
That only the Athenian was left
He gave his team a ringing cry, and they
Responded. Now the two of them raced
    level;
First one and then the other gained the
    lead,
But only by a head. And as he drove,
Each time he turned the pillar at the end,
730 Checking the inside horse he gave full rein
To the outer one, and so he almost grazed
The stone. Eleven circuits now he had
Safely accomplished; still he stood erect,
And still the chariot ran. But then, as he
Came to the turn, slackening the left-hand
    rein
Too soon, he struck the pillar. The axle-
    shaft
Was snapped in two, and he was flung
    headlong,

Entangled in the reins. The horses ran
Amok into mid-course and dragged
    Orestes
Along the ground. O, what a cry arose   740
From all the company when they saw him
    thrown!
That he, who had achieved so much,
    should meet
With such disaster, dashed to the ground,
    and now
Tossed high, until the other charioteers,
After a struggle with the horses, checked
    them
And loosed him, torn and bleeding, from
    the reins,
So mangled that his friends would not
    have known him.
    A funeral-pyre was made; they burned
    the body.
Two men of Phokis, chosen for the task,
Are bringing home his ashes in an urn—   750
A little urn, to hold so tall a man—
That in his native soil he may find burial.
Such is my tale, painful enough to hear;
For those of us who saw it, how much
    worse!
Far worse than anything I yet have seen.

CHORUS-LEADER. And so the ancient line of
    Argive kings
Has reached its end, in such calamity!

CLYTEMNESTRA. O Zeus! Am I to call this
    happy news,
Or sorrowful, but good? What bitterness,
If I must lose a son to save my life!   760

PAEDAGOGUS. My lady, why so sad?

CLYTEMNESTRA.   There is strange power
In motherhood: however terrible
Her wrongs, a mother never hates her
    child.

PAEDAGOGUS. So then it seems that I have
    come in vain.

CLYTEMNESTRA. No, not in vain! How can
    you say 'In vain,'
When you have brought to me the certain
    news
That he is dead who drew his life from
    mine
But then deserted me, who suckled him
And reared him, and in exile has become

770 A stranger to me? Since he left this
country
I have not seen him; but he charged me
with
His father's murder, and he threatened me
Such that by day or night I could not sleep
Except in terror; each single hour that came
Cast over me the shadow of my death.
　　But now . . . ! This day removes my
　　　fear of him—
And her! She was the worse affliction; she
Lived with me, draining me of life. But
now
Her threats are harmless; I can live in
peace.

780 ELECTRA. O my Orestes! Here is double
cause
For grief: you dead, and your unnatural
mother
Exulting in your death! O, is it just?

CLYTEMNESTRA. You are not! He is—being as
he is!

ELECTRA. Nemesis! Listen, and avenge Orestes.

CLYTEMNESTRA. She has heard already, and
has rightly judged.

ELECTRA. Do outrage to me now: your hour
has come.

CLYTEMNESTRA. But you will silence me, you
and Orestes!

ELECTRA. Not now, alas! It is we that have
been silenced.

CLYTEMNESTRA. My man, if you have stopped
her mouth, you do

790 Indeed deserve a very rich reward.

PAEDAGOGUS. Then I may go back home, if
all is well?

CLYTEMNESTRA. Back home? By no means!
That would not be worthy
Of me, or of the friend who sent you here.
No, come inside, and leave this woman
here
To shout her sorrows—and her brother's
too!

[*Exeunt* CLYTEMNESTRA *and the* PAEDA-
GOGUS, *into the palace*]

ELECTRA. What grief and pain she suffered!
Did you see it?—

How bitterly she wept, how wildly
mourned
Her son's destruction! Did you see it? No,
She left us laughing. O my brother! O
My dear Orestes! You are dead; your death　800
Has killed me too, for it has torn from
me
The only hope I had, that you would
come
At last in might, to be the avenger of
Your father, and my champion. But now
Where can I turn? For I am left alone,
Robbed of my father, and of you. Hence-
forth
I must go back again, for ever, into
bondage
To those whom most I hate, the murderers
Who killed my father. O, can this be
justice?
Never again will I consent to go　810
Under their roof; I'll lie down here, and
starve,
Outside their doors; and if *that* vexes them,
Let them come out and kill me. If they do,
I shall be glad; it will be misery
To go on living; I would rather die.

COMMOS

Strophe I

CHORUS. Zeus, where are thy thunderbolts?
(*mainly in slow three-time*) Where is the
bright eye of the Sun-God? if they look
down upon this
　　And see it not.
ELECTRA.　　(*An inarticulate cry of woe*)　820
CHORUS. My daughter, do not weep.
ELECTRA.　　(*Cry, as before*)
CHORUS. My child, say nothing impious.
ELECTRA. You break my heart.
CHORUS.　　　　　　But how?
ELECTRA. By holding out an empty hope.
Who now can avenge *him*?
His son Orestes is in his grave.
There is no comfort. O, let me be!
You do but make my grief the more.

Antistrophe I

830 CHORUS. But yet, there was a king of old,
Amphiareus: his wicked wife
Tempted by gold killed him, and yet
Though he is dead . . .
ELECTRA.   *(Cry, as before)*
CHORUS. He lives and reigns below.
ELECTRA.   *(Cry, as before)*
CHORUS. Alas indeed! The murderess . . .
ELECTRA. But she was killed!
CHORUS.   She was.
ELECTRA. I know! I know! Amphiareus
840 Had a champion to avenge him;
But I have none now left to me.
The one I had is in his grave.

Strophe II

CHORUS. Your fate is hard and cruel.
ELECTRA. How well I know it! Sorrow, pain,
Year upon year of bitter grief!
CHORUS. Yes, we have seen it all.
ELECTRA. O offer not, I beg you,
An empty consolation.
No longer can I look for help
850 From my noble and loyal brother.

Antistrophe II

CHORUS. Yet death must come to all men.
ELECTRA. But not like this! Dragged along,
Trampled on by horses' hooves!
CHORUS. No, do not think of it!
ELECTRA. O what an end! In exile,
Without a loving sister
To lay him in his grave, with none
To pay tribute of tears and mourning.

(Enter CHRYSOTHEMIS*)*

CHRYSOTHEMIS. Great happiness, dear sister,
is the cause
860 Of my unseemly haste; good news for you,
And joy. Release has come at last from all
The sufferings that you have so long endured.

ELECTRA. And where can you find any help
for my
Afflictions? They have grown past remedy.
CHRYSOTHEMIS. Orestes has come back to us!
I know it
As surely as I stand before you now.
ELECTRA. What, are you mad, poor girl? Do
you make fun
Of your calamity, and mine as well?
CHRYSOTHEMIS. I am not mocking you! I
swear it by
Our father's memory. He is here, among 870
us.
ELECTRA. You foolish girl! You have been
listening to
Some idle rumour. Who has told it you?
CHRYSOTHEMIS. No one has told me anything.
I know
From proof that I have seen with my own
eyes.
ELECTRA. What proof, unhappy girl? What
have you seen
To be inflamed with this disastrous hope?
CHRYSOTHEMIS. Do listen, I implore you; then
you'll know
If I am talking foolishly or not.
ELECTRA. Then tell me, if it gives you any
pleasure.
CHRYSOTHEMIS. I'll tell you everything I saw. 880
When I
Came near the tomb, I saw that offerings
Of milk had just been poured upon the
mound,
And it was wreathed with flowers. I looked,
and wondered;
I peered about, to see if anyone
Was standing near; then, as I seemed alone,
I crept a little nearer to the tomb,
And there, upon the edge, I saw a lock
Of hair; it had been newly cut.
Upon the moment, as I looked, there fell
Across my mind a picture, one that I 890
Have often dreamed of, and I knew that
these
Were offerings given by our beloved
brother.
I took them up with reverence; my eyes
Were filled with tears of joy; for I was
sure,
As I am now, that none but he has laid

This tribute on the grave. Who else should
   do it
But he, or you, or I? It was not I,
That is quite certain. You have not been
   there;
How could you? Even to worship at a
   shrine
900   They do not let you leave the house, un-
   punished.
As for our mother, she has little mind
To make such offerings—and we should
   have known it.
No, dear Electra, they are from Orestes.
Therefore take courage! There is no such
   thing
As joy unbroken, or unbroken sorrow.
We have known sorrow—nothing else;
   perhaps
Today great happiness begins for us.
ELECTRA. O you unhappy girl! You little
   know!
CHRYSOTHEMIS. Unhappy? Is this not the best
   of news?
910   ELECTRA. The truth is very difficult from your
   fancy.
CHRYSOTHEMIS. This is the truth. Mayn't I
   believe my eyes?
ELECTRA. Poor girl! He's dead! We cannot
   look to him
For our deliverance; our hopes are gone.
CHRYSOTHEMIS. Alas, alas! . . . Who told you
   this?
ELECTRA. One who was there; a man who
   saw him killed.
CHRYSOTHEMIS. Where is the man? This fills
   me with dismay!
ELECTRA. At home; and, to our mother, very
   welcome.
CHRYSOTHEMIS. Alas, alas! Who could it then
   have been
Who put those many offerings on the tomb?
920   ELECTRA. It will be someone who has laid
   them there
As a memorial of Orestes' death.
CHRYSOTHEMIS. O, this is ruin! I came hurry-
   ing back,
So happy, with my news, not knowing this
Calamity. But all the woes we had
Before are with us still, and worse are
   added!

ELECTRA. Yet even so, if you will work with
   me,
We can throw off the weight that wears us
   down.
CHRYSOTHEMIS. What, can I bring the dead
   to life again?
ELECTRA. That's not my meaning; I am not a
   fool.
CHRYSOTHEMIS. Then what assistance can I   930
   give to you?
ELECTRA. I need your courage in a certain
   venture.
CHRYSOTHEMIS. If it will help us, I will not
   refuse.
ELECTRA. Remember: nothing prospers with-
   out effort.
CHRYSOTHEMIS. You may command whatever
   strength I have.
ELECTRA. This then is what I have resolved
   to do.
You know, as I do, we have no support
Of friends; of what we had we have been
   stripped
By death. We two are left; we are alone.
For me, while I had news about our
   brother,
That he was well and strong, I lived in   940
   hope
That he would some time come and punish
   those
Who killed our father. Now that he is
   dead,
I turn to you, that you will join your hand
With mine, your sister's; help me, do not
   flinch:
Aegisthus, who has murdered our dear
   father—
We'll kill him! There's no reason now to
   keep
It back from you. You cannot wait, in-
   active,
Hoping for—nothing. What hope was left
   to you
That is not shattered? This is what you
   have:
Lasting resentment that you have been   950
   robbed
Of all the wealth that rightly should be
   yours;
Anger that they have let you live so long

Unmarried—and do not think that this will
    change:
Aegisthus is no fool; he can foresee,
If you or I had children, they would take
Revenge on him. Marriage is not for us.
Therefore be with me in my resolution.
This you will win: the praise of our dead
    father,
And of our brother, for your loyalty;
960 The freedom that is yours by right of birth;
A marriage worthy of your station, since
All look admiringly upon the brave.
Do you not see what glory you will win
Both for yourself and me by doing this?
For all will cry, Argive or foreigner,
When they behold us: 'See! there are the
    sisters
Who saved their father's house from desola-
    tion;
Who, when their enemies were firmly set
In power, avenged a murder, risking all.
970 Love and respect and honour are their due;
At festivals and public gatherings
Give them pre-eminence, for their bravery.'
So we shall be acclaimed by everyone;
As long as we shall live our glory will
Endure, and will not fade when we are
    dead.
    My sister, give consent! Stand by your
      father,
Work with your brother, put an end to my
Calamities and yours; for to the noble
A life of shameful suffering is disgraceful.
980 CHORUS-LEADER. In such a case, in speech or
    in reply,
Forethought and prudence are the best of
    helpers.
CHRYSOTHEMIS. Before she spoke at all, my
    friends, if she
Had any prudence she might have pre-
    served
Some caution, not have thrown it to the
    winds.
For what can you be thinking of, to arm
Yourself with utter recklessness, and call
On me to help you? Do you not reflect
You are a woman, not a man? how weak
You are, how strong your foes? that day by
    day
990 Their cause grows stronger, ours diminishes

And dwindles into nothing? Who can hope,
Plotting to overthrow so powerful
A man, not to be overwhelmed himself
In utter ruin? Our plight is desperate
Already; you will make it worse, far worse,
If you are heard saying such things as this.
It brings us nothing, if when we have won
That glorious repute, we die ignobly.
Mere death is not the worst; this is the
    worst,
To long for death and be compelled to live. 1000
No, I implore you, keep your rage in check
Before you bring destruction on us both
And devastation to our father's house.
What you have said shall be as if unsaid,
Of no effect; and you, before it is
Too late, must learn that since you have no
    strength
You have to yield to those that are in
    power.
CHORUS-LEADER. You must indeed. There is
    no better thing
For anyone than forethought and good
    sense.
ELECTRA. I had expected this; I thought that 1010
    you
Would spurn the offer that I made. And so
My hand alone must do it—for be sure,
It is a task that cannot be neglected.
CHRYSOTHEMIS. A pity you were not as bold
    as this
Before! You might have thwarted the as-
    sassins!
ELECTRA. I was too young to act. I had the
    will!
CHRYSOTHEMIS. Then try once more to be
    too young to act.
ELECTRA. It seems you are determined not to
    help me.
CHRYSOTHEMIS. Not in a venture that would
    be our ruin.
ELECTRA. How wise you are! And what a 1020
    coward too.
CHRYSOTHEMIS. Some day you'll praise my
    wisdom. I will bear it!
ELECTRA. I'll never trouble you so far as that!
CHRYSOTHEMIS. Who's wise, and who is fool-
    ish, time will show.
ELECTRA. Out of my sight! You are no use to
    me.

CHRYSOTHEMIS. I am, if you were wise
  enough to listen.

ELECTRA. Go to your mother; tell her everything!

CHRYSOTHEMIS. No; I refuse my help, but
  not from hatred.

ELECTRA. But in contempt! You make that
  very plain.

CHRYSOTHEMIS. Trying to save your life! Is
  that contempt?

1030 ELECTRA. Am I to do what you imagine
  right?

CHRYSOTHEMIS. Yes; and when you are right,
  I'll follow you.

ELECTRA. To be so plausible—and be so
  wrong!

CHRYSOTHEMIS. These are the very words I'd
  use of you.

ELECTRA. The right is on my side. Do you
  deny it?

CHRYSOTHEMIS. The right may lead a man to
  his destruction.

ELECTRA. That is no principle for me to follow.

CHRYSOTHEMIS. You'll think the same as I—
  when you have done it.

ELECTRA. Do it I will. You shall not frighten
  me.

CHRYSOTHEMIS. Give up this folly! Be advised
  by me!

1040 ELECTRA. No! There is nothing worse than
  bad advice.

CHRYSOTHEMIS. Can I say nothing that you
  will accept?

ELECTRA. I have considered, and I have determined.

CHRYSOTHEMIS. Then I will go, since you do
  not approve
  Of what I say, nor I of what you do.

ELECTRA. Go then, for your ways never can
  be mine
  However much you wish. It is mere folly
  To go in quest of the impossible.

CHRYSOTHEMIS. If this, to you, is wisdom,
  follow it;
  But when it leads you to disaster, then

1050 At last you'll learn mine was the better
  wisdom.

[*Exit* CHRYSOTHEMIS]

Strophe I

CHORUS. We see the birds of the air, with
  what
  Sure instinct they protect and nourish
Those who brought them to life and
  tended them.
  How can man disobey the laws of Na-
  ture?
  The anger of the gods, the law estab-
  lished,
  Enthroned in Heaven, will bring them
  retribution.
  There is a Voice the dead can hear:
Speak, O Voice, to the King, to Agamem-
  non,
A message of shame and sorrow and deep
  dishonour.

Antistrophe I

His house already was near to falling;   1060
Now a new cause of ruin threatens:
Discord comes to divide his champions
  Now no longer is daughter joined with
  daughter
  In loyalty and love, but strife divides
  them.
  Electra stands alone to face the tempest.
  Never has she ceased to mourn,
Faithful, careless of life, if she may purge
  this
Palace of those two Furies, a foul pol-
  lution.

Strophe II

He that is noble in spirit scorns
A life ignoble, darkened by shame,   1070
And chooses honour, my daughter,
As you chose to cleave to your father,
Accepting a life of sorrow.
Spurning dishonour, you have won a
  double fame:
  Courage is yours, and wisdom.

Antistrophe II

Still may I see you triumph, raised
Above your foes, restored to the power
And wealth of which they have robbed
you.
You have known nothing but sorrow;
1080　And yet by observing those great
Laws of the gods, in piety and reverence,
You crown your sorrow with glory.

[*Enter* ORESTES, PYLADES, *and attendants*]

ORESTES. Ladies, we wish to know if we have
been
Rightly directed to the place we look for.
CHORUS-LEADER. What is that you wish to
find?
ORESTES. Aegisthus,
If you could tell us where to find his
palace?
CHORUS-LEADER. But it is here. You have been
guided well.
ORESTES. Could one of you perhaps tell those
within
That we have come, whom they have long
awaited?
1090　CHORUS-LEADER [*indicating* ELECTRA]. She
best might do it; she is nearest to them.
ORESTES. Madam, we are from Phokis; tell
them, pray,
That we have certain business with Aegisthus.
ELECTRA. Alas, alas! You have not come with
something
To prove it true—the rumour that we
heard?
ORESTES. Of 'rumours' I know nothing. I am
sent
By Strophius, Orestes' friend, with news.
ELECTRA. O, tell me what it is! You frighten
me.
ORESTES. We bring him home; this little urn
contains
What now is left of him; for he is dead.
1100　ELECTRA. Ah, this is what I feared! I see your
burden;

Small weight for you, but heavy grief to
me.
ORESTES. It is—if that which moves your sor-
row is
Orestes' death: in *that* we bring his ashes.
ELECTRA. Then give it me, I beg you! If this
vessel
Now holds him, let me take it in my arms.
ORESTES. Men, give it her, whoever she may
be:
A friend; perhaps, one of his family.
This is no prayer of one who wished him
evil.

[ELECTRA *advances to the front of the
orchestra.* ORESTES *and* PYLADES *retire
near the palace gate*]

ELECTRA. Orestes! my Orestes! you have come
To this! The hopes with which I sent you　1110
forth
Are come to this! How radiant you were!
And now I hold you—so: a little dust!
O, would to God that I had died myself,
And had not snatched *you* from the edge of
death
To have you sent into a foreign land!
They would have killed you—but you
would have shared
Your father's death and burial; not been
killed
Far from your home, an exile, pitiably,
Alone, without your sister. Not for you,
The last sad tribute of a sister's hand!　1120
Some stranger washed your wounds, and
laid your body
On the devouring fire; the charity
Of strangers brings you home—so light a
burden,
And in so small a vessel!
　　　　　　　　O, my brother,
What love and tenderness I spent on you!
For you were my child rather than your
mother's;
I was your nurse—or you would not have
had
A nurse; *I* was the one you always called
Your *sister*—and it has come to nothing.
One single day has made it all in vain,　1130
And, like a blast of wind, has swept it all

To ruin. You are dead; my father too
Lies in his grave; your death is death to me,
Joy to our enemies: our mother—if
She *is* a mother!—dances in delight,
When you had sent me many a secret
   promise
That you would come and be revenged on
   her.
But no! A cruel fate has ruined you,
And ruined me, and brought it all to noth-
   ing:

1140 The brother that I loved is gone, and in
His place are ashes, and an empty shadow.
O pity! pity, grief and sorrow!
How cruel, cruel, is your home-coming,
My dearest brother! I can live no longer.
O take me with you! You are nothing; I
Am nothing, now. Let me henceforward be
A shade among the shades, with you. We
   lived
As one; so now in death, let us be one,
And share a common grave, as while you
   lived

1150 We shared a common life. O, let me die;
For death alone can put an end to grief.

CHORUS-LEADER. Your father died, Electra; he
   was mortal:
So has Orestes died; so shall we all.
Remember this, and do not grieve too
   much.

ORESTES. What answer can I make to this?
   What *can*
I say? I must, and yet I cannot, speak.

ELECTRA. Sir, what has troubled you? Why
   speak like this?

ORESTES. Are *you* the Princess? Can you be
   Electra?

ELECTRA. I *am* Electra, though I look so mean.

1160 ORESTES. To think that it has gone so far as
   this!

ELECTRA. But why such words of pity over *me*?

ORESTES.—Treated so harshly and with such
   dishonour!

ELECTRA. Ill words well spoken, stranger—of
   Electra.

ORESTES.—How cruel! Kept unmarried, and
   ill-used!

ELECTRA. Sir, why do you look at me so
   fixedly,
   And in such pity?

ORESTES.   Little did I know
My own unhapiness, how great it was.

ELECTRA. What words of mine have made you
   think of *that*?

ORESTES. No words; it is the sight of all you
   suffer.

ELECTRA. The sight of it? What you can see 1170
   is nothing!

ORESTES. How? What can be more terrible
   than this?

ELECTRA. To live, as I do, with the murderers.

ORESTES. What murderers? Who are these
   guilty men?

ELECTRA. My father's.—And they treat me as
   their slave!

ORESTES. But who has forced you to this servitude?

ELECTRA. She who has the name of mother—
   nothing else!

ORESTES. What does she do? Oppression? Violence?

ELECTRA. Violence, oppression, everything
   that's evil!

ORESTES. You have no champion? no one to
   oppose them?

ELECTRA. The one I had is dead: here are his 1180
   ashes.

ORESTES. A cruel life! How much I pity you.

ELECTRA. You are the only one who pities me!

ORESTES. I am the only one who shares your
   sorrow.

ELECTRA. Who are you? Can it be you are
   some kinsman?

ORESTES. Give back the urn, and I will tell
   you all.

ELECTRA. No, no, I beg you; do not be so
   cruel!

ORESTES. Do as I ask; you will do nothing
   wrong.

ELECTRA. It is all I have! You cannot take it
   from me!

ORESTES. You may not keep it.

ELECTRA.   O, my dear Orestes,
How cruel! I may not even bury you. 1190

ORESTES. Your talk of burial, your tears, are
   wrong.

ELECTRA. How is it wrong to mourn my
   brother's death?

ORESTES. You must not speak of him in words
   like these.

ELECTRA. Must I be robbed of *all* my rights
   in him?
ORESTES. You are robbed of nothing! *This* is
   not for you.
ELECTRA. Yes, if I hold Orestes in my arms!
ORESTES. This is Orestes only by a fiction.
ELECTRA. Then *where* is my unhappy
   brother's grave?
ORESTES. Nowhere. The living do not have a
   grave!
1200 ELECTRA. My friend! What do you mean?
ORESTES.   I mean—the truth.
ELECTRA. My brother is *alive?*
ORESTES.   If *I'm* alive!
ELECTRA. *You* are *Orestes?*
ORESTES.   Look upon this ring—
   Our father's ring.—Do you believe me now?
ELECTRA. O day of happiness!
ORESTES.   Great happiness!
ELECTRA. It is *your* voice?—And have you
   come?
ORESTES. My voice,
   And I am here!
ELECTRA.   I hold you in my arms?
ORESTES. You do—and may we nevermore be
   parted.
ELECTRA. O look, my friends! My friends of
   Argos, look!
1210 It is Orestes!—dead, by artifice,
   And by that artifice restored to us.
CHORUS-LEADER. To see him, and to see your
   happiness,
   My child, brings tears of joy into my eyes.

Strophe

[ELECTRA *sings,* ORESTES *speaks*]

ELECTRA. My brother is here! the son of my
   own dear father!
   You longed to see me, and now, at last,
   You have found me! O, you have come to
   me!
ORESTES. Yes, I have come: but wait; contain
   your joy
   In silence; they will hear us in the palace.
ELECTRA. O by the virgin-goddess, by Artemis,
1220   I despise them, those in the palace—

Women, useless and helpless!
   O, why should I fear them?
ORESTES. Remember: women may not be too
   weak
   To strike a blow. You have seen proof of it.
ELECTRA. Ah me! The foul crime, that no
   Darkness can ever hide, that no
   Oblivion can wash away, no
   Power on earth remove.
ORESTES. All this I know; but we will speak
   of it
   When we can speak of it without restraint.   1230

Antistrophe

ELECTRA. Each moment of time, now or to
   come, is time
   To proclaim aloud the abomination.
   At last, at last, I can speak with freedom.
ORESTES. You can; and yet, until the hour has
   come,
   By speaking freely we may lose our free-
   dom.
ELECTRA. How can I chain my tongue and
   repress my joy?
   Can I look upon you and be silent,
   Safe returned, my brother?
   It is more than I dared hope.
ORESTES. I waited long, but when the voice   1240
   of God
   Spoke, then I made no more delay.
ELECTRA. O, this is joy crowning joy, if
   Heaven has brought you home to me!
   I see the hand of God
   Working along with us.
ORESTES. To stem your flood of joy is hard,
   but yet
   There is some danger in this long rejoicing.

Epode

ELECTRA. So weary was the time of waiting!
   Now when you have come at last
   And all my sorrows have reached their   1250
   end,
   O, do not check my happiness.
ORESTES. Nor would I do it—but we must be
   prudent.

ELECTRA. My friends, I heard my brother's
   voice,
   And I had thought
   That I would never hear his voice again:
   How could I restrain my joy?
   Ah, now I have you; I can look upon
   The well-loved face that I could not forget
   Even in darkest sorrow.

1260 ORESTES. How much there is to hear!—our
   mother's sin
   And cruelty, that our ancestral wealth
   Is plundered, ravished, wantonly misused
   By that usurper. Yet our time is short
   And their misdeeds are more than can be
   told.
   But tell me what may help our present ven-
   ture:
   Where can I hide, or where can I confront
   Our foes, to turn their laughter into silence?

1270 And see to this: our mother must not read
   Our secret in your face. Conceal your joy
   When we go in; look sad, and mourn, as if
   The tale that you have heard were true.
   There will
   Be time enough to smile when we have
   conquered.

ELECTRA. My brother, what seems good to you
   shall be
   My law; your pleasure shall be mine, for
   mine
   Is nothing, except what you have brought
   to me,
   And to win all there is I would not cause
   A moment's pain to you, nor would that
   serve

1280 The favour of the gods, which now is with
   us.
      Now as to what you ask.—You surely
      know
   Aegisthus is abroad, not in the palace;
   But she is there, and you need have no fear
   That she will see a look of happiness
   Upon my face. The settled hatred which
   I have for her will banish any smile.
   I shall be weeping!—though my tears will
   be
   Of joy at your return. My tears today
   Flow in abundance; I have seen you dead,

1290 And now alive. So strange the day has been
   That if our father came and greeted us

I should not think it was a ghost; I should
Believe it. Therefore, being yourself a
   miracle
In your return, command me as you will;
For had you died, had I been left alone,
I should myself have ventured all, and
   found
Glorious deliverance, or a glorious death.

ORESTES. Hush! I can hear the steps of someone coming
   Out of the palace.

ELECTRA.   You are welcome, strangers.
   Enter; the burden that you bring is such   1300
   As no one could reject—and no one wel-
   come.

[*Enter the* PAEDAGOGUS, *from the
palace*]

PAEDAGOGUS. You reckless fools! What, have
   you got no sense?
   Do you not care whether you live or die?
   Are you demented? Don't you understand
   The peril you are in? Not one that
   threatens;
   No, it is here! Had I not stood on guard
   Inside the door they would have known
   your plot
   Before they saw you. As it is, I took
   Good care of that. So, make an end of talk
   And these interminable cries of joy.   1310
   Go in; delay is dangerous at such
   A moment. You must act, and make an end.

ORESTES. When I go in, how shall I find it
   there?

PAEDAGOGUS. All's well. Rely on this: they
   will not know you.

ORESTES. You have reported, then, that I am
   dead?

PAEDAGOGUS. I have; in their eyes you are
   dead and gone.

ORESTES. And are they glad? Or what have
   they been saying?

PAEDAGOGUS. We'll speak of that hereafter.
   All is well
   Within the palace—even what is shameful.

ELECTRA. In Heaven's name, who is this man,   1320
   Orestes?

ORESTES. Do you not know him?

ELECTRA.   I cannot even guess.

ORESTES. You know the man to whom you
gave me once?

ELECTRA. Which man? What are you saying?

ORESTES.   The man by whom
You had me secretly conveyed to Phokis.

ELECTRA. What, this is *he*?—the only one I
found
Remaining loyal at our father's murder?

ORESTES. That is the man; no need to ask
for proof.

ELECTRA. How glad I am! Dear friend, to you
alone
The house of Agamemnon owes deliverance.

1330   How come you here? Can you be really he
That saved us both from all that threatened
us?
Come, let me take your hands, those faith-
ful hands,
My friend! How could I not have known
you, when
You came to bring me joy—but joy con-
cealed
In words of deadly grief? I'll call you
father,
Give you a daughter's greeting—for to me
You are a father. How I hated you
A while ago; how much I love you now!

PAEDAGOGUS. It is enough. Though there is
much to tell,

1340   There will be many days and many nights
In which, Electra, you may tell it all.
One word with you, Orestes, Pylades:
This is your moment; now she is alone,
No men-at-arms are near. But if you wait,
Then you will have to face not only them,
But many more—men trained to use their
weapons.

ORESTES. Pylades, there is no longer time for
talk;
It seems the hour has come. So, let us go;
And as I go I give my reverence

1350   To all the gods that stand before the
house.

[ORESTES *enters the palace with* PY-
LADES, *praying before images on either
side of the gate.* ELECTRA *goes to the
altar where Clytemnestra's offerings are
still visible*]

ELECTRA. O Lord Apollo, listen to their
prayers,
Be gracious to them! Listen too to mine!
How often have I been thy suppliant
Bringing what gifts I had; and therefore
now,
Although my hands are empty, I beseech
thee,
I beg thee, I implore thee, Lord Apollo:
Give us thy favour, help our purposes,
And show mankind what chastisement the
gods
Inflict on those who practise wickedness.

[*Exit* ELECTRA, *into the palace*]

Strophe

CHORUS. Look where the god of death makes   1360
his way,
[*dochmiacs: swift tempo*] Fierce and implac-
able.
The Furies, champions of Justice,
Hounds of the gods, hot on the trail of
crime,
Have entered the palace.
Before me rises a vision:
Soon shall I see fulfilment.

Antistrophe

The minister of the gods, with stealthy foot,
Ushered within the palace,
The ancient home of his fathers,   1370
Holds in his hand a keen whetted sword,
With Hermes to guide him,
To shroud his designs in darkness
And lead him straight to vengeance.

[*Enter* ELECTRA]

ELECTRA. My friends, keep silent; wait. It will
not be
For long. Their hands are ready; soon
they'll strike.

CHORUS-LEADER. What are they doing now?

ELECTRA.   She has the urn,
Preparing it for burial; they are near her.

CHORUS-LEADER. And why have you come out?

ELECTRA. To stand on guard;
1380 To give the warning if Aegisthus comes.

CLYTEMNESTRA [*within*]. Ah . . . ! So many
Murderers, and not a single friend!

ELECTRA. Someone inside is screaming. Do
you hear it?

CHORUS-LEADER. I heard. . . . It makes me
shudder; it is fearful.

CLYTEMNESTRA. Aegisthus! O where are you?
They will kill me!

ELECTRA. There, yet another scream!

CLYTEMNESTRA. My son, my son!
Take pity on your mother!

ELECTRA. You had none
For him, nor for his father!

CHORUS [*sings*]. O my city! Ill-starred race of
our kings!
1390 So many years a doom has lain on you:
Now it is passing away.

CLYTEMNESTRA. Ah! . . . They have struck
me!

ELECTRA. Strike her again, if you have
strength enough!

CLYTEMNESTRA. Another blow!

ELECTRA. Pray God there'll be a third,
And that one for Aegisthus!

CHORUS. [*sings*]. The cry for vengeance is at
work; the dead are stirring.
Those who were killed of old now
Drink in return the blood of those who
killed them.

CHORUS-LEADER. See, they are coming, and
the blood-stained arm
1400 Drips sacrifice of death. It was deserved.

[*Enter* ORESTES *and* PYLADES]

ELECTRA. How is it with you both?

ORESTES. All's well, within
The palace, if Apollo's oracle was well.

ELECTRA. Then she is dead?

ORESTES. No longer need you fear
Your mother's insolence and cruelty.

CHORUS-LEADER. Be silent! I can see Aegisthus
coming.

ELECTRA. Stand back, Orestes.

ORESTES. Are you sure you see him?

ELECTRA. Yes, he is coming from the town.
He smiles;
We have him in our hands.

CHORUS [*sings*]. Back to the doorway quickly!
One
Task is accomplished; may the second 1410
prosper too!

ORESTES. It will. No fear of that.

ELECTRA. Then, to your station.

ORESTES. I go at once.

ELECTRA. And leave the rest to me.

CHORUS [*sings*]. Speak some gentle words to
him
That he may fall, unawares,
Into the retribution that awaits him.

[*Enter* AEGISTHUS]

AEGISTHUS. They tell me that some men have
come from Phokis
With news about Orestes; dead, they say,
Killed in a chariot-race. Where are these
men?
Will someone tell me? [*To* ELECTRA.] You!
Yes, you should know;
It will have special interest for you! 1420

ELECTRA. I know. Of course I know. I loved
my brother;
How then should I make little of his death?

AEGISTHUS. Then tell me where these men
are to be found.

ELECTRA. In there.
They've won their way to Clytemnestra's
heart.

AEGISTHUS. And is it true that they have
brought this message?

ELECTRA. More than the message: they
brought Orestes too.

AEGISTHUS. What, is the very body to be seen?

ELECTRA. It is; I do not envy you the sight.

AEGISTHUS. Our meetings have not always 1430
been so pleasant!

ELECTRA. If this proves to your liking, you are
welcome.

AEGISTHUS. I bid you all keep silence. Let the
doors
Be opened.

[*Enter, from the palace,* ORESTES *and*
PYLADES, *bearing the shouded body of*
CLYTEMNESTRA]

Citizens of Argos, look!
If there is any who had hopes in him,

That hope lies shattered. Look upon this
body
And learn that I am master—or the weight
Of my strong arm will make him learn the
lesson.

ELECTRA. I need no teaching; I have learned,
at last,
That I must live at peace with those that
rule.

1440 AEGISTHUS. Zeus! Here is one laid low, before
our eyes,
By the angry gods—and may no Nemesis
Attend my words, or I unsay them.—Now,
Turn back the shroud, and let me see the
face.
It was a kinsman, and I too must mourn.

ORESTES. This you should do; it is for you,
not me,
To look upon this face and take farewell.

AEGISTHUS. It is indeed for me, and I will
do it.—
Call Clyemnestra, if she is at hand.

ORESTES. She is not far away; look straight
before you.

[AEGISTHUS *takes the face-cloth from
the body*]

AEGISTHUS. God! What is this?

1450 ORESTES.   Some stranger, frightening you?

AEGISTHUS. Who are you, that have got me
in your clutches
For my destruction?

ORESTES.   Have you not seen already?
Someone you thought was dead is still
alive.

AEGISTHUS. Ah. . . . Now I understand.—You,
who speak,
You are Orestes!

ORESTES.   You could read the future
So well, yet were so blind.

AEGISTHUS.   Ah. . . . You have come
To kill me! Give me time, a little time,
To speak.

ELECTRA.   No, by the gods, Orestes! No
Long speech from him! No, not a single
word!

1460 He's face to face with death; there's nothing
gained

In gaining time. Kill him at once! And
when
You've killed him, throw the body out of
sight,
And let him have the funeral he deserves.
Animals shall eat him! Nothing less than
this
Will compensate for all that he has done.

ORESTES. Sir, come with me into the house;
this is
No time for talk. My business is your life.

AEGISTHUS. Why to the house? If you are
not ashamed
At what you do, then do it openly.

ORESTES. You shall not order me. Go in, and   1470
die
On the same spot on which you killed my
father.

AEGISTHUS. This house of Atreus must, it
seems, behold
Death upon death, those now and those to
come.

ORESTES. It will see yours; so much I can
foresee.

AEGISTHUS. You did not get this foresight
from your father!

ORESTES. You have too much to say; the time
is passing.
Go!

AEGISTHUS. Lead the way.

ORESTES.   You must go before me.

AEGISTHUS. That I may not escape you?

ORESTES.   That you may not
Be killed where *you* would choose. You
shall taste all
The bitterness of death.—If retribution   1480
Were swift and certain, and the lawless
man
Paid with his life, there would be fewer
villains.

[*Exeunt* ORESTES, PYLADES, ELECTRA,
AEGISTHUS]

CHORUS. Children of Atreus, now at last
Your sufferings are ended. You have won
Your own deliverance; now once more
Is the line of your fathers restored.

◆ Note on the Publication and Date of *Hamlet*

By R. C. BALD

Hamlet, in the form in which we know it, was first published at the end of 1604. A much shorter and debased version had been published in the previous year, and this First Quarto, as it is called, was certainly one of the "stolen and surreptitious" texts of which the editors of the collected edition of Shakespeare's plays in 1623 (the First Folio) complained in their preface. How the publishers of the First Quarto obtained the play has been much disputed; shorthand, memorization by someone in the theatre, a traitor actor who knew his own parts and remembered those of the others as best he could, have all been suggested. But, interesting as the First Quarto is, it represents Shakespeare's play very unsatisfactorily; the pirate was a poor hand at his job. When the Second Quarto was published in 1604, the title-page stated that it was "newly imprinted and enlarged to almost as much again as it was, according to the true and perfect copy."

Two other editions of *Hamlet* appeared before 1623, when the play was included in the First Folio. It has been convincingly argued that the Second Quarto was printed from Shakespeare's own manuscript, but the Folio version presents a slightly different text. *Hamlet* is the longest of Shakespeare's plays, and it is only natural that it should have been somewhat cut when it was acted. The Folio omits over 200 lines found in the Second Quarto, although it contains 85 others which the Quarto lacks. The Folio text seems to represent the acting version current in the theatre at the time Shakespeare's collected works were published.

Although the Second Quarto was not published until 1604, James Roberts, who printed it, acquired the right to publish the play as early as July 26, 1602, when he entered it in the Register of the Stationers' Company. *Hamlet* was clearly in existence before this

R. C. Bald, "Introduction" to William Shakespeare, *Hamlet,* R. C. Bald, ed. (New York: Appleton-Century-Crofts, 1946) pp. iii-vi.

date. On the other hand, it is not mentioned by Francis Meres in his *Palladis Tamia* in 1598. In that book Meres mentions Shakespeare several times and gives a list of twelve plays he had written. The omission of *Hamlet,* which seems to have been notably successful from the very beginning, suggests that the play had not yet appeared.

The earliest reference to Shakespeare's *Hamlet* is from the pen of Gabriel Harvey, a Cambridge scholar and a friend of the poet Spenser. At the end of a copy of Chaucer's poems, which he bought in 1598, Harvey wrote some notes about the poets of his own time, in which he states that Shakespeare's "Lucrece, & his tragedie of Hamlet, Prince of Denmarke, haue it in them, to please the wiser sort." An earlier statement in the same note to the effect that "the Earle of Essex much commends Albions England" suggests that the note was written while Essex was still alive, *i.e.* before his execution for treason on February 25, 1601.

Another clue to the date of the play has been found at II.ii.315 in the sentence "The humorous man shall end his part in peace." This has been interpreted as a reference to the original performance of Ben Jonson's play, *Every Man out of his Humour,* given in November 1599, when the audience so violently demonstrated its disapproval of the sudden conversion of Malicente ("the humorous man") at the end of the play that Jonson had to write a new ending for it.

Since *Hamlet* was referred to by Harvey at some date before February 1601 and itself appears to refer to an event which occurred late in 1599, it seems reasonable to assign the play to the year 1600. It was thus written when Shakespeare was approaching the height of his powers: after he had written nearly all his historical plays and most of his comedies, and while he was still fresh from the study of intellectual idealism and its consequences in the character of Brutus in the tragedy of *Julius Caesar.*

◆◆ Hamlet

By WILLIAM SHAKESPEARE

Characters

CLAUDIUS, King of Denmark
HAMLET, son to the former, and nephew to the present King
POLONIUS, lord chamberlain
HORATIO, friend to Hamlet
LAERTES, son to Polonius
VOLTIMAND,
CORNELIUS,
ROSENCRANTZ, } courtiers
GUILDENSTERN
OSRIC,
A Gentleman,
A Priest
MARCELLUS, } officers
BERNARDO,
FRANCISCO, a solider
REYNALDO, servant to Polonius
Players
Two Clowns, gravediggers
FORTINBRAS, prince of Norway
A Captain
English Ambassadors
GERTRUDE, Queen of Denmark, and mother to Hamlet
OPHELIA, daughter to Polonius
Lords, Ladies, Officers, Soldiers, Sailors, Messengers, and other Attendants
Ghost of Hamlet's Father

Scene: Denmark

William Shakespeare, *Hamlet*, R. C. Bald, ed. (New York: Appleton-Century-Crofts, 1946), pp. 1–112.

ACT I

Scene I

Enter BERNARDO *and* FRANCISCO, *two Sentinels.*

BERNARDO. Who's there?
FRANCISCO. Nay, answer me. Stand and unfold yourself.
BERNARDO. Long live the king!
FRANCISCO. Bernardo?
BERNARDO. He.
FRANCISCO. You come most carefully upon your hour.
BERNARDO. 'Tis now struck twelve; get thee to bed, Francisco.
FRANCISCO. For this relief much thanks: 'tis bitter cold,
And I am sick at heart.
BERNARDO. Have you had quiet guard?
FRANCISCO.   Not a mouse stirring. 10
BERNARDO. Well, good night:
If you do meet Horatio and Marcellus,
The rivals of my watch, bid them make haste.
FRANCISCO. I think I hear them. Stand, ho! Who is there?

Enter HORATIO *and* MARCELLUS.

HORATIO. Friends to this ground.
MARCELLUS.   And liegemen to the Dane.
FRANCISCO. Give you good night.
MARCELLUS.   O, farewell, honest soldier:
Who hath relieved you?

13 rivals partners

54

FRANCISCO.   Bernardo hath my place;
Give you good night.

Exit.

MARCELLUS.   Holla, Bernardo!
BERNARDO.   Say—
What, is Horatio there?
HORATIO.   A piece of him.
BERNARDO. Welcome, Horatio: welcome, good
Marcellus.
MARCELLUS. What, has this thing appeared
again tonight?
BERNARDO. I have seen nothing.
MARCELLUS. Horatio says 'tis but our fantasy,
And will not let belief take hold of him
Touching this dreaded sight twice seen of
us;
Therefore I have entreated him along
With us to watch the minutes of this night,
That, if again this apparition come,
He may approve our eyes and speak to it.
HORATIO. Tush, tush, 'twill not appear.
BERNARDO.   Sit down awhile,
And let us once again assail your ears,
That are so fortified against our story,
What we have two nights seen.
HORATIO.   Well, sit we down,
And let us hear Bernardo speak of this.
BERNARDO. Last night of all,
When yond same star that's westward from
the pole
Had made his course to illume that part of
heaven
Where now it burns, Marcellus and my-
self,
The bell then beating one—

Enter GHOST

MARCELLUS. Peace, break thee off, look where
it comes again!
BERNARDO. In the same figure like the king
that's dead.
MARCELLUS. Thou art a scholar, speak to it,
Horatio.
BERNARDO. Looks a' not like the king? mark
it, Horatio.

HORATIO. Most like; it harrows me with fear
and wonder.
BERNARDO. It would be spoke to.
MARCELLUS.   Question it, Horatio.
HORATIO. What art thou that usurp't this
time of night,
Together with that fair and warlike form
In which the majesty of buried Denmark
Did sometimes march? by heaven I charge
thee, speak!
MARCELLUS. It is offended.
BERNARDO.   See, it stalks away.
HORATIO. Stay! speak, speak, I charge thee,
speak!

Exit GHOST

MARCELLUS. 'Tis gone, and will not answer.
BERNARDO. How now, Horatio? you tremble
and look pale.
Is not this something more than fantasy?
What think you on't?
HORATIO. Before my God, I might not this be-
lieve
Without the sensible and true avouch
Of mine own eyes.
MARCELLUS.   Is it not like the king?
HORATIO. As thou art to thyself.
Such was the very armor he had on
When he the ambitious Norway combated;
So frowned he once, when in an angry
parle
He smote the sledded Polacks on the ice.
'Tis strange.
MARCELLUS. Thus twice before, and jump at
this dead hour,
With martial stalk hath he gone by our
watch.
HORATIO. In what particular thought to work
I know not,
But, in the gross and scope of my opinion,
This bodes some strange eruption to our
state.
MARCELLUS. Good now, sit down, and tell
me, he that knows,
Why this same strict and most observant
watch

---

29 *approve* corroborate   48 *Denmark* King of
Denmark   49 *sometimes* formerly   61 *Norway*
King of Norway   65 *jump* just   68 *gross and
scope* general range

So nightly toils the subject of the land,
And why such daily cast of brazen cannon
And foreign mart for implements of war,
Why such impress of shipwrights, whose
    sore task
Does not divide the Sunday from the week,
What might be toward that this sweaty
    haste
Doth make the night joint laborer with the
    day;
Who is't that can inform me?

HORATIO.   That can I;
80 At least the whisper goes so. Our last king,
Whose image even but now appeared to us,
Was as you know by Fortinbras of Norway,
Thereto pricked on by a most emulate
    pride,
Dared to the combat; in which our valiant
    Hamlet—
For so this side of our known world
    esteemed him—
Did slay this Fortinbras, who, by a sealed
    compact
Well ratified by law and heraldry,
Did forfeit, with his life, all those his lands
Which he stood seized of to the conqueror;
90 Against the which a moiety competent
Was gagéd by our king, which had re-
    turned
To the inheritance of Fortinbras,
Had he been vanquisher; as, by the same
    co-mart,
And carriage of the article designed,
His fell to Hamlet. Now sir, young Fortin-
    bras,
Of unimprovéd mettle hot and full,
Hath in the skirts of Norway here and
    there
Sharked up a list of lawless resolutes,
For food and diet, to some enterprise
100 That hath a stomach in't; which is no
    other—
As it doth well appear unto our state—
But to recover of us, by strong hand

And terms compulsatory, those foresaid
    lands
So by his father lost; and this, I take it,
Is the main motive of our preparations,
The source of this our watch, and the chief
    head
Of this posthaste and romage in the land.
BERNARDO. I think it be no other but e'en so;
Well may it sort that this portentous figure
Comes arméd through our watch so like   110
    the king
That was and is the question of these wars.
HORATIO. A mote it is to trouble the mind's
    eye.
In the most high and palmy state of Rome,
A little ere the mightiest Julius fell,
The graves stood tenantless and the sheeted
    dead
Did squeak and gibber in the Roman
    streets,
And even the like precurse of feared events,
As harbingers preceding still the fates
And prologue to the omen coming on,
Have heaven and earth together demon-   120
    strated
Unto our climatures and countrymen,
As stars with trains of fire, and dews of
    blood,
Disasters in the sun; and the moist star,
Upon whose influence Neptune's empire
    stands,
Was sick almost to doomsday with eclipse.
But soft, behold, lo where it comes again!

Enter GHOST

I'll cross it though it blast me. Stay, illusion;

He spreads his arms.

If thou hast any sound or use of voice,
Speak to me.
If there be any good thing to be done   130
That may to thee do ease and grace to me,

---

72 *toils* makes toil 74 *mart* trading 75 *impress* conscription 77 *toward* imminent 83 *emulate* ambitious 87 *heraldry* law of arms 89 *seized* possessed 90 *moiety competent* sufficient quantity 91 *gagéd* pledged 93 *co-mart* joint bargain 94 *carriage* effect 96 *unimprovéd* unused 97 *skirts* outlying parts 98 *list* company 100 *stomach* show of daring 106 *head* cause 107 *romage* activity 109 *sort* happen 117 *precurse* foretokening 118 *harbingers* forerunners 119 *omen* dire event 121 *climatures* regions of the earth 123 *the moist star* the moon

Speak to me.
If thou art privy to thy country's fate,
Which, happily, foreknowing may avoid,
O speak!
Or if thou hast uphoarded in thy life
Extorted treasure in the womb of earth,
For which they say you spirits oft walk in
death,

The cock crows.

Speak of it. Stay and speak! Stop it, Marcellus.
140 MARCELLUS. Shall I strike at it with my partisan?
HORATIO. Do if it will not stand.
BERNARDO.   'Tis here!
HORATIO.   'Tis here!

[*Exit* GHOST.]

MARCELLUS. 'Tis gone!
We do it wrong, being so majestical,
To offer it the show of violence,
For it is as the air invulnerable,
And our vain blows malicious mockery.
BERNARDO. It was about to speak when the
cock crew.
HORATIO. And then it started like a guilty
thing
Upon a fearful summons. I have heard,
150 The cock, that is the trumpet to the morn,
Doth with his lofty and shrill-sounding
throat
Awake the god of day and at his warning,
Whether in sea or fire, in earth or air,
The extravagant and erring spirit hies
To his confine; and of the truth herein
This present object made probation.
MARCELLUS. It faded on the crowing of the
cock.
Some say that ever 'gainst that season comes
Wherein our Savior's birth is celebrated
160 This bird of dawning singeth all night
long,
And then they say no spirit dare stir abroad;

The nights are wholesome; then on planets
strike,
No fairy takes, nor witch hath power to
charm,
So hallowed and so gracious is the time.
HORATIO. So have I heard, and do in part be-
lieve it.
But look, the morn, in russet mantle clad,
Walks o'er the dew of yon high eastern hill.
Break we our watch up, and by my advice
Let us impart what we have seen tonight
Unto young Hamlet, for upon my life   170
This spirit, dumb to us, will speak to him:
Do you consent we shall acquaint him
with it,
As needful in our loves, fitting our duty?
MARCELLUS. Let's do't, I pray; and I this
morning know
Where we shall find him most conven-
iently.

Exeunt.

Scene II

Flourish. Enter CLAUDIUS, *King of Denmark,* GERTRUDE *the Queen, Council-
lors,* POLONIUS *and his son* LAERTES,
HAMLET, *and others* [*including* VOLTI-
MAND *and* CORNELIUS].

KING. Though yet of Hamlet our dear
brother's death
The memory be green, and that it us be-
fitted
To bear our hearts in grief, and our whole
kingdom
To be contracted in one brow of woe;
Yet so far hath discretion fought with na-
ture,
That we with wisest sorrow think on him
Together with remembrance of ourselves:
Therefore our sometime sister, now our
queen,
The imperial jointress to this warlike state,

---

140 *partisan* spear 154 *extravagant* wandering
out of bounds 155 *confine* place of confinement
156 *probation* proof 162 *strike* exercise evil influence 163 *takes* enchants 9 *jointress* a
widow who holds a jointure, or life-interest, in an
estate

10 Have we, as 'twere with a defeated joy,
With an auspicious and a dropping eye,
With mirth in funeral and with dirge in
    marriage,
In equal scale weighing delight and dole,
Taken to wife: nor have we herein barred
Your better wisdoms, which have freely
    gone
With this affair along. For all, our thanks.
Now follows that you know, young Fortin-
    bras,
Holding a weak supposal of our worth,
Or thinking by our late dear brother's
    death
20 Our state to be disjoint and out of frame,
Colleaguéd with this dream of his advan-
    tage,
He hath not failed to pester us with mes-
    sage
Importing the surrender of those lands
Lost by his father, with all bonds of law,
To our most valiant brother. So much for
    him.
Now for ourself, and for this time of meet-
    ing.
Thus much the business is: we have here
    writ
To Norway, uncle of young Fortinbras—
Who, impotent and bedrid, scarcely hears
30 Of this his nephew's purpose—to suppress
His further gait herein, in that the levies,
The lists, and full proportions are all made
Out of his subject, and we here dispatch
You, good Cornelius, and you, Voltimand,
For bearers of this greeting to old Norway,
Giving to you no further personal power
To business with the king, more than the
    scope
Of these delated articles allow.
Farewell, and let your haste commend your
    duty.
40 CORNELIUS, VOLTIMAND. In that, and all
    things, will we show our duty.
KING. We doubt it nothing; heartily farewell.

Exeunt VOLTIMAND *and* CORNELIUS.

And now, Laertes, what's the news with
    you?
You told us of some suit, what is't, Laertes?
You cannot speak of reason to the Dane
And lose your voice; what wouldst thou
    beg, Laertes,
That shall not be my offer, not thy asking?
The head is not more native to the heart,
The hand more instrumental to the mouth,
Than is the throne of Denmark to thy
    father.
What wouldst thou have, Laertes?
LAERTES.   My dread lord, 50
Your leave and favor to return to France,
From whence though willingly I came to
    Denmark,
To show my duty in your coronation;
Yet now, I must confess, that duty done,
My thoughts and wishes bend again toward
    France
And bow them to your gracious leave and
    pardon.
KING. Have you your father's leave? What
    says Polonius?
POLONIUS. He hath, my lord, wrung from me
    my slow leave
By laborsome petition, and at last
Upon his will I sealed my hard consent;   60
I do beseech you give him leave to go.
KING. Take thy fair hour, Laertes; time be
    thine,
And thy best graces spend it at thy
    will!
But now, my cousin Hamlet, and my son—
HAMLET [*aside*]. A little more than kin, and
    less than kind.
KING. How is it that the clouds still hang on
    you?
HAMLET. Not so, my lord; I am too much in
    the sun.
QUEEN. Good Hamlet, cast thy nightéd color
    off
And let thine eye look like a friend on
    Denmark,
Do not for ever with thy vailéd lids   70
Seek for thy noble father in the dust;

---

14 *barred* ignored 20 *disjoint* disorganized 21
colleaguéd combined 31 *gait* progress 32 *proportions* estimates of forces and supplies 38 *delated* extended 44 *Dane* King of Denmark 45

lose your voice speak in vain 47 *native* linked
by nature to 48 *instrumental* serviceable 67 *sun:*
notice the pun with son 69 *Denmark* King of
Denmark 70 *vailéd* lowered

Thou know'st 'tis common; all that live
     must die,
Passing through nature to eternity.
HAMLET. Ay, madam, it is common.
QUEEN.   If it be,
Why seems it so particular with thee?
HAMLET. Seems, madam, nay it is; I know
     not "seems."
'Tis not alone my inky cloak, good mother,
Nor customary suits of solemn black,
Nor windy suspiration of forced breath,
80 No, nor the fruitful river in the eye,
Nor the dejected havior of the visage,
Together with all forms, moods, shapes of
     grief,
That can denote me truly; these indeed
     seem,
For they are actions that a man might play,
But I have that within which passes show;
These but the trappings and the suits of
     woe.
KING. 'Tis sweet and commendable in your
     nature, Hamlet,
To give these mourning duties to your
     father,
But you must know your father lost a
     father,
90 That father lost, lost his, and the survivor
     bound
In filial obligation for some term
To do obsequious sorrow; but to persever
In obstinate condolement is a course
Of impious stubbornness, 'tis unmanly
     grief;
It shows a will most incorrect to heaven,
A heart unfortified, a mind impatient,
An understanding simple and unschooled
For what we know must be, and is as com-
     mon
As any the most vulgar thing to sense;
100 Why should we in our peevish opposition
Take it to heart? Fie, 'tis a fault to heaven,
A fault against the dead, a fault to nature,
To reason most absurd, whose common
     theme

Is death of fathers, and who still hath
     cried,
From the first corse till he that died today,
"This must be so." We pray you throw to
     earth
This unprevailing woe, and think of us
As of a father, for let the world take note
You are the most immediate to our throne,
And with no less nobility of love   110
Than that which dearest father bears his
     son,
Do I impart toward you. For your intent
In going back to school in Wittenberg,
It is most retrograde to our desire,
And we beseech you bend you to remain
Here in the cheer and comfort of our eye,
Our chiefest courtier, cousin, and our son.
QUEEN. Let not thy mother lose her prayers,
     Hamlet;
I pray thee stay with us, go not to Witten-
     berg.
HAMLET. I shall in all my best obey you, 120
     madam.
KING. Why, 'tis a loving and a fair reply;
Be as ourself in Denmark. Madam, come;
This gentle and unforced accord of Ham-
     let
Sits smiling to my heart, in grace whereof,
No jocund health that Denmark drinks to-
     day
But the great cannon to the clouds shall tell,
And the king's rouse the heavens shall
     bruit again,
Re-speaking earthly thunder. Come away.

Flourish. Exeunt all except HAMLET.

HAMLET. O that this too too sullied flesh
     would melt,
Thaw and resolve itself into a dew,   130
Or that the Everlasting had not fixed
His canon 'gainst self slaughter! O God,
     God,
How weary, stale, flat, and unprofitable
Seem to me all the uses of this world!
Fie on't, ah fie, 'tis an unweeded garden
That grows to seed, things rank and gross
     in nature
Possess it merely. That it should come to
     this—

79 *suspiration* breathing 92 *obsequious* dutiful
114 *retrograde* opposed 127 *rouse* carousal
bruit again echo 132 *canon* ordinance

But two months dead, nay not so much,
    not two—
So excellent a king, that was to this
140 Hyperion to a satyr, so loving to my
    mother,
That he might not beteem the winds of
    heaven
Visit her face too roughly. Heaven and
    earth,
Must I remember? why, she would hang
    on him
As if increase of appetite had grown
By what it fed on, and yet within a
    month—
Let me not think on't, frailty, thy name is
    woman—
A little month, or ere those shoes were old
With which she followed my poor father's
    body,
Like Niobe all tears, why she, even she—
150 O God, a beast, that wants discourse of rea-
    son,
Would have mourned longer—married with
    my uncle,
My father's brother, but no more like my
    father
Than I to Hercules, within a month,
Ere yet the salt of most unrighteous tears
Had left the flushing in her gallèd eyes,
She married. O most wicked speed, to post
With such dexterity to incestuous sheets!
It is not, nor it cannot come to good;
But break, my heart, for I must hold my
    tongue.

        Enter HORATIO, MARCELLUS, *and* BER-
        NARDO.

HORATIO. Hail to your lordship!
160 HAMLET.   I am glad to see you well;
    Horatio—or I do forget myself.
HORATIO. The same, my lord, and your poor
    servant ever.
HAMLET. Sir, my good friend; I'll change that
    name with you;

And what make you from Wittenberg,
    Horatio?
Marcellus!
MARCELLUS. My good lord!
HAMLET. I am very glad to see you; good
    even, sir.
But what, in faith, make you from Witten-
    berg?
HORATIO. A truant disposition, good my lord.
HAMLET. I would not hear your enemy say so,
    Nor shall you do my ear that violence   170
To make it truster of your own report
Against yourself; I know you are no truant.
But what is your affair in Elsinore?
We'll teach you to drink deep ere you de-
    part.
HORATIO. My lord, I came to see your father's
    funeral.
HAMLET. I prithee do not mock me, fellow
    student;
I think it was to see my mother's wedding.
HORATIO. Indeed, my lord, it followed hard
    upon.
HAMLET. Thrift, thrift, Horatio, the funeral
    baked meats
Did coldly furnish forth the marriage tables.   180
Would I had met my dearest foe in heaven
Or ever I had seen that day, Horatio!
My father—methinks I see my father.
HORATIO. Where, my lord?
HAMLET.   In my mind's eye, Horatio.
HORATIO. I saw him once, a' was a goodly
    king.
HAMLET. A' was a man, take him for all in
    all,
I shall not look upon his like again.
HORATIO. My lord, I think I saw him yester-
    night.
HAMLET. Saw who?
HORATIO. My lord, the king your father.
HAMLET.   The king my father!   190
HORATIO. Season your admiration for a while
With an attent ear till I may deliver,
Upon the witness of these gentlemen,
This marvel to you.

---

140 *Hyperion* the sun-god 141 *beteem* permit
149 *Niobe* After the gods had killed all her children Niobe was turned into stone from which tears
gushed continually 150 *discourse* process 155

gallèd rubbed, inflamed 181 *dearest* bitterest
191 *season* moderate *admiration* astonishment
192 *attent* attentive

HAMLET. For God's love let me hear.

HORATIO. Two nights together had these gentlemen,
Marcellus and Bernardo, on their watch
In the dead waste and middle of the night
Been thus encountered: a figure like your father,
Arméd at point exactly, cap-a-pe,
Appears before them, and with solemn march
Goes slow and stately by them; thrice he walked
By their oppressed and fear-surprised eyes,
Within his truncheon's length, whilst they, distilled
Almost to jelly with the act of fear,
Stand dumb and speak not to him; this to me
In dreadful secrecy impart they did,
And I with them the third night kept the watch,
Where as they had delivered both in time,
Form of the thing, each word made true and good,
The apparition comes: I knew your father;
These hands are not more like.

HAMLET. But where was this?

MARCELLUS. My lord, upon the platform where we watched.

HAMLET. Did you not speak to it?

HORATIO. My lord, I did,
But answer made it none; yet once methought
It lifted up it head, and did address
Itself to motion like as it would speak:
But even then the morning cock crew loud,
And at the sound it shrunk in haste away
And vanished from our sight.

HAMLET. 'Tis very strange.

HORATIO. As I do live, my honored lord, 'tis true,
And we did think it writ down in our duty
To let you know of it.

HAMLET. Indeed, indeed, sirs, but this troubles me.
Hold you the watch tonight?

ALL. We do, my lord.

HAMLET. Armed, say you?

ALL. Armed, my Lord.

HAMLET. From top to toe?

ALL. My lord, from head to foot.

HAMLET. Then saw you not his face?

HORATIO. O yes, my lord, he wore his beaver up.

HAMLET. What, looked he frowningly? 230

HORATIO. A countenance more in sorrow than in anger.

HAMLET. Pale or red?

HORATIO. Nay, very pale.

HAMLET. And fixed his eyes upon you?

HORATIO. Most constantly.

HAMLET. I would I had been there.

HORATIO. It would have much amazed you.

HAMLET. Very like, very like. Stayed it long?

HORATIO. While one with moderate haste might tell a hundred.

BOTH. Longer, longer.

HORATIO. Not when I saw't.

HAMLET. His beard was grizzled, no?

HORATIO. It was as I have seen it in his life, 240
A sable silvered.

HAMLET. I will watch tonight,
Perchance 'twill walk again.

HORATIO. I warrant it will.

HAMLET. If it assume my noble father's person,
I'll speak to it though hell itself should gape
And bid me hold my peace; I pray you all,
If you have hitherto concealed this sight,
Let it be tenable in your silence still,
And whatsomever else shall hap tonight,
Give it an understanding but no tongue.
I will requite your loves; so fare you well: 250
Upon the platform 'twixt eleven and twelve
I'll visit you.

ALL. Our duty to your honor.

HAMLET. Your loves, as mine to you; farewell.

Exeunt.

My father's spirit in arms! all is not well;
I doubt some foul play; would the night were come!

---

199 *at point* completely *cap-a-pe* from head to foot 215 *it* its 229 *beaver* visor 237 *tell* count 241 *sable* black 247 *tenable* held back 255 *doubt* suspect

Till then sit still, my soul; foul deeds will
  rise,
Though all the earth o'erwhelm them, to
  men's eyes.

Exit.

Scene III

Enter LAERTES *and* OPHELIA, *his sister.*

LAERTES. My necessaries are embarked; fare-
  well.
And, sister, as the winds give benefit,
And convoy is assistant, do not sleep,
But let me hear from you.
OPHELIA.   Do you doubt that?
LAERTES. For Hamlet and the trifling of his
  favor,
Hold it a fashion and a toy in blood,
A violet in the youth of primy nature,
Forward, not permanent, sweet, not lasting,
The perfume and suppliance of a minute,
No more.
OPHELIA. No more but so?
10 LAERTES.   Think it no more.
For nature crescent does not grow alone
In thews and bulk, but as this temple
  waxes
The inward service of the mind and soul
Grows wide withal. Perhaps he loves you
  now,
And now no soil nor cautel doth besmirch
The virtue of his will; but you must fear,
His greatness weighed, his will is not his
  own,
For he himself is subject to his birth.
He may not, as unvalued persons do,
20 Carve for himself, for on his choice de-
  pends
The safety and health of this whole state,
And therefore must his choice be circum-
  scribed
Unto the voice and yielding of that body
Whereof he is the head. Then if he says
  he loves you,

It fits your wisdom so far to believe it
As he in his particular act and place
May give his saying deed, which is no
  further
Than the main voice of Denmark goes
  withal.
Then weigh what loss your honor may sus-
  tain
If with too credent ear you list his songs,   30
Or lose your heart, or your chaste treasure
  open
To his unmastered importunity.
Fear it, Ophelia, fear it, my dear sister,
And keep you in the rear of your affection,
Out of the shot and danger of desire.
The chariest maid is prodigal enough
If she unmask her beauty to the moon;
Virtue itself scapes not calumnious strokes;
The canker galls the infants of the spring
Too oft before their buttons be disclosed;   40
And in the morn and liquid dew of youth
Contagious blastments are most imminent.
Be wary, then best safety lies in fear;
Youth to itself rebels, though none else
  near.
OPHELIA. I shall the effect of this good lesson
  keep
As watchman to my heart. But, good my
  brother,
Do not, as some ungracious pastors do,
Show me the steep and thorny way to
  heaven,
Whiles like a puffed and reckless libertine
Himself the primrose path of dalliance   50
  treads,
And recks not his own rede.
LAERTES.   O fear me not.
I stay too long; but here my father comes.

Enter POLONIUS.

A double blessing is a double grace;
Occasion smiles upon a second leave.
POLONIUS. Yet here, Laertes! aboard, aboard,
  for shame!

3 *convoy* means of conveyance 7 *primy* early
11 *crescent* growing 12 *this temple* the body
15 *soil* blemish *cautel* deceit 23 *yielding*
consent 30 *credent* trustful 34-35 *keep . . . desire* do not go as far forward as affection will lead
you, but avoid danger by staying out of range 36
chariest most sparing 39 *canker* grub, caterpillar
galls injures *infants of the spring* young flowers
40 *buttons* buds 42 *blastments* blights 51
recks heeds *rede* advice

The wind sits in the shoulder of your sail,
And you are stayed for. There, my blessing
  with thee!
And these few precepts in thy memory
Look thou character. Give thy thoughts no
  tongue,
60 Nor any unproportioned though this act.
Be thou familiar, but by no means vulgar.
The friends thou hast, and their adoption
  tried,
Grapple them unto thy soul with hoops of
  steel,
But do not dull thy palm with entertainment
Of each new-hatched, unfledged comrade.
  Beware
Of entrance to a quarrel, but being in,
Bear't that th' opposéd may beware of thee.
Give every man thy ear, but few thy voice;
Take each man's censure, but reserve thy
  judgment.
70 Costly thy habit as thy purse can buy,
But not expressed in fancy; rich, not gaudy;
For the apparel oft proclaims the man,
And they in France of the best rank and
  station
Are often most select and generous, chief
  in that.
Neither a borrower nor a lender be,
For loan oft loses both itself and friend,
And borrowing dulls the edge of hus-
  bandry.
This above all, to thine ownself be true,
And it must follow, as the night the day,
80 Thou canst not then be false to any man.
Farewell; my blessing season this in thee!

LAERTES. Most humbly do I take my leave,
  my lord.
POLONIUS. The time invites you; go, your
  servants tend.
LAERTES. Farewell, Ophelia, and remember
  well
What I have said to you.
OPHELIA.   'Tis in my memory locked
And you yourself shall keep the key of it.
LAERTES. Farewell.

  Exit LAERTES.

POLONIUS. What is't, Ophelia, he hath said to
  you?
OPHELIA. So please you, something touching
  the Lord Hamlet.
POLONIUS. Marry, well bethought.   90
'Tis told me he hath very oft of late
Given private time to you, and you your-
  self
Have of your audience been most free and
  bounteous;
If it be so—as so 'tis put on me,
And that in way of caution—I must tell
  you
You do not understand yourself so clearly
As it behoves my daughter and your honor.
What is between you? give me up the truth.
OPHELIA. He hath, my lord, of late made
  many tenders
Of his affection to me.   100
POLONIUS. Affection, pooh! you speak like a
  green girl
Unsifted in such perilous circumstance.
Do you believe his tenders, as you call
  them?
OPHELIA. I do not know, my lord, what I
  should think.
POLONIUS. Marry, I will teach you: think
  yourself a baby
That you have ta'en these tenders for true
  pay,
Which are not sterling. Tender yourself
  more dearly,
Or (not to crack the wind of the poor
  phrase,
Running it thus) you'll tender me a fool.
OPHELIA. My lord, he hath importuned me   110
  with love
In honorable fashion.
POLONIUS. Ay, fashion you may call it; go to,
  go to.
OPHELIA. And hath given countenance to his
  speech, my lord,
With almost all the holy vows of heaven.
POLONIUS. Ay, springes to catch woodcocks.
  I do know,
When the blood burns, how prodigal the
  soul

59 *character* engrave 60 *unproportioned* unbal-
anced 69 *censure* opinion 77 *husbandry* economy 83 *tend* attend 99 *tenders* offers 102
unsifted untried 113 *countenance* confirmation
115 *springes* snares

Lends the tongue vows; these blazes, daughter,

Giving more light than heat, extinct in both,

Even in their promise, as it is a-making,

120 You must not take for fire. From this time

Be something scanter of your maiden presence;

Set your entreatments at a higher rate

Than a command to parley. For Lord Hamlet,

Believe so much in him that he is young,

And with a larger tether may he walk

Than may be given you: in few, Ophelia,

Do not believe his vows, for they are brokers,

Not of that dye which their investments show,

But mere implorators of unholy suits,

130 Breathing like sanctified and pious bawds,

The better to beguile. This is for all:

I would not, in plain terms, from this time forth

Have you so slander any moment leisure

As to give words or talk with the Lord Hamlet.

Look to't, I charge you; come your ways.

OPHELIA. I shall obey, my lord.

Exeunt.

Scene IV

Enter HAMLET, HORATIO, *and* MARCELLUS.

HAMLET. The air bites shrewdly, it is very cold.

HORATIO. It is a nipping and an eager air.

HAMLET. What hour now?

HORATIO.   I think it lacks of twelve.

MARCELLUS. No, it is struck.

HORATIO. Indeed? I heard it not; it then draws near the season

Wherein the spirit held his wont to walk.

A flourish of trumpets, and two pieces go off.

What does this mean, my lord?

HAMLET. The king doth wake tonight and takes his rouse,

Keeps wassail, and the swaggering upspring reels;

And as he drains his draughts of Rhenish down   10

The kettledrum and trumpet thus bray out

The triumph of his pledge.

HORATIO.   Is it a custom?

HAMLET. Ay, marry, is't;

But to my mind, though I am native here

And to the manner born, it is a custom

More honored in the breach than the observance.

This heavy-headed revel east and west

Makes us traduced and taxed of other nations;

They clepe us drunkards, and with swinish phrase

Soil our addition, and indeed it takes   20

From our achievements, though performed at height,

The pith and marrow of our attribute.

So, oft it chances in particular men

That for some vicious mole of nature in them,

As in their birth, wherein they are not guilty,

(Since nature cannot choose his origin)

By the o'ergrowth of some complexion,

Oft breaking down the pales and forts of reason,

Or by some habit that too much o'erleavens

The form of plausive manners—that these   30
men,

---

122 *entreatments* interviews 123 *parley* conference under a truce 127 *brokers* go-betweens 128 *investments* vestments, clothes 129 *implorators* solicitors 133 *slander* misuse *moment* momentary 2 *eager* sharp 9 *up-spring* a dance 10 *Rhenish* Rhine wine 18 *taxed of* upbraided

by 19 *clepe* call 20 *addition* title, honor 21 *at height* at the highest pitch of excellence 24 *mole of nature* natural defect 26 *his* its 27 *complexion* disposition 28 *pales* fences 29 *o'erleavens* modifies 30 *plausive* plausible

Carrying, I say, the stamp of one defect,
Being nature's livery, or fortune's star,
His virtues else—be they as pure as grace,
As infinite as man may undergo—
Shall in the general censure take corruption
From that particular fault: the dram of evil
Doth all the noble substance often dout
To his own scandal.

HORATIO.   Look, my lord, it comes!

Enter GHOST.

HAMLET. Angels and ministers of grace defend us!
40 Be thou a spirit of health or goblin damned,
Bring with thee airs from heaven or blasts from hell,
Be thy intents wicked or charitable,
Thou com'st in such a questionable shape,
That I will speak to thee; I'll call thee Hamlet,
King, father, royal Dane; O, answer me!
Let me not burst in ignorance, but tell
Why thy canonized bones hearséd in death
Have burst their cerements; why the sepulchre,
Wherein we saw thee quietly inurned,
50 Hath oped his ponderous and marble jaws
To cast thee up again! What may this mean
That thou, dead corse, again in complete steel
Revisits thus the glimpses of the moon,
Making night hideous, and we fools of nature
So horridly to shake our disposition
With thoughts beyond the reaches of our souls?
Say, why is this? wherefore? what should we do?

GHOST *beckons* HAMLET.

HORATIO. It beckons you to go away with it

As if it some impartment did desire
To you alone.

MARCELLUS. Look with what courteous action 60
It waves you to a more removéd ground;
But do not go with it.

HORATIO.   No, by no means.

HAMLET. It will not speak; then I will follow it.

HORATIO. Do not, my lord.

HAMLET.   Why, what should be the fear?
I do not set my life at a pin's fee,
And for my soul, what can it do to that,
Being a thing immortal as itself?
It waves me forth again, I'll follow it.

HORATIO. What if it tempt you toward the flood, my lord,
Or to the dreadful summit of the cliff 70
That beetles o'er his base into the sea,
And there assume some other horrible form,
Which might deprive your sovereignty of reason,
And draw you into madness? think of it:
The very place puts toys of desperation,
Without more motive, into every brain
That looks so many fathoms to the sea
And hears it roar beneath.

HAMLET.   It waves me still;
Go on, I'll follow thee.

MARCELLUS. You shall not go, my lord.

HAMLET.   Hold off your hands. 80

HORATIO. Be ruled, you shall not go.

HAMLET.   My fate cries out,
And makes each petty artere in this body
As hardy as the Nemean lion's nerve;
Still am I call'd; unhand me, gentlemen;
By heaven, I'll make a ghost of him that lets me;
I say, away! go on, I'll follow thee.

Exeunt GHOST *and* HAMLET.

HORATIO. He waxes desperate with imagination.

MARCELLUS. Let's follow; 'tis not fit thus to obey him.

32 *livery* badge *fortune's star* accidental mark
35 *censure* opinion 36 *dram* particle 37 *dout*
extinguish 38 *his* its *scandal* harm 48 *cerements* grave-cloths 55 *disposition* normal habit
of thought 65 *fee* value 71 *beetles* projects

73 *sovereignty of reason* supreme control exercised
by reason 75 *toys* trifles, fancies 82 *artere*
artery 83 *Nemean lion* the lion slain by Hercules
nerve sinew 85 *lets* hinders

HORATIO. Have after. To what issue will this come?

90 MARCELLUS. Something is rotten in the state of Denmark.

HORATIO. Heaven will direct it.

MARCELLUS.   Nay, let's follow him.

Exeunt.

Scene V

Enter GHOST *and* HAMLET.

HAMLET. Whither wilt thou lead me? speak, I'll go no further.

GHOST. Mark me.

HAMLET.   I will.

GHOST.   My hour is almost come,
   When I to sulphurous and tormenting flames
   Must render up myself.

HAMLET.   Alas, poor ghost!

GHOST. Pity me not, but lend thy serious hearing
   To what I shall unfold.

HAMLET.   Speak, I am bound to hear.

GHOST. So art thou to revenge, when thou shalt hear.

HAMLET. What?

GHOST. I am thy father's spirit,

10   Doomed for a certain term to walk the night,
   And for the day confined to fast in fires,
   Till the foul crimes done in my days of nature
   Are burnt and purged away: but that I am forbid
   To tell the secrets of my prison house,
   I could a tale unfold whose lightest word
   Would harrow up thy soul, freeze thy young blood,
   Make thy two eyes like stars start from their spheres,
   Thy knotted and combinéd locks to part,
   And each particular hair to stand an end,

20   Like quills upon the fretful porpentine.

19 *an end* on end 20 *porpentine* porcupine
21 *eternal blazon* proclamation of the secrets of
eternity 33 *Lethe* the river of oblivion

But this eternal blazon must not be
To ears of flesh and blood. List, list, O list!
If thou didst ever thy dear father love—

HAMLET. O God!

GHOST. Revenge his foul and most unnatural murder.

HAMLET. Murder!

GHOST. Murder most foul, as in the best it is,
   But this most foul, strange and unnatural.

HAMLET. Haste me to know't, that I with wings as swift
   As meditation or the thoughts of love   30
   May sweep to my revenge.

GHOST.   I find thee apt,
   And duller shouldst thou be than the fat weed
   That roots itself in ease on Lethe wharf,
   Wouldst thou not stir in this. Now, Hamlet, hear:
   'Tis given out that, sleeping in my orchard,
   A serpent stung me; so the whole ear of Denmark
   Is by a forgéd process of my death
   Rankly abused: but know, thou noble youth,
   The serpent that did sting thy father's life
   Now wears his crown.

HAMLET.   O my prophetic soul!   40
   My uncle?

GHOST. Ay, that incestuous, that adulterate beast,
   With witchcraft of his wit, with traitorous gifts—
   O wicked wit and gifts, that have the power
   So to seduce!—won to his shameful lust
   The will of my most seeming-virtuous queen;
   O Hamlet, what a falling-off was there!
   From me, whose love was of that dignity
   That it went hand in hand even with the vow
   I made to her in marriage, and to decline   50
   Upon a wretch whose natural gifts were poor
   To those of mine;
   But virtue, as it never will be moved,
   Though lewdness court it in a shape of heaven,
   So lust, though to a radiant angel linked,

Will sate itself in a celestial bed
And prey on garbage.
But soft, methinks I scent the morning air;
Brief let me be. Sleeping within my or-
chard,
60 My custom always of the afternoon,
Upon my secure hour thy uncle stole
With juice of curséd hebenon in a vial,
And in the porches of mine ears did pour
The leperous distilment, whose effect
Holds such an enmity with blood of man,
That swift as quicksilver it courses through
The natural gates and alleys of the body,
And with a sudden vigor it doth posset
And curd, like eager droppings into milk,
70 The thin and wholesome blood; so did it
mine,
And a most instant tetter barked about,
Most lazar-like, with vile and loathsome
crust
All my smooth body.
Thus was I sleeping by a brother's hand
Of life, of crown, of queen at once dis-
patched,
Cut off even in the blossoms of my sin,
Unhouseled, disappointed, unaneled,
No reckoning made, but sent to my account
With all my imperfections on my head;
80 O horrible, O horrible, most horrible!
If thou hast nature in thee, bear it not;
Let not the royal bed of Denmark be
A couch for luxury and damnéd incest.
But howsomever thou pursues this act,
Taint not thy mind, nor let thy soul con-
trive
Against thy mother aught; leave her to
heaven,
And to those thorns that in her bosom
lodge
To prick and sting her. Fare thee well at
once;
The glowworm shows the matin to be near,
90 And gins to pale his uneffectual fire.
Adieu, adieu, adieu: remember me.

Exit.

68 *posset* curdle 69 *eager* bitter 71 *tetter*
eruption of the skin *barked* crusted 72 *lazar-like*
like a leper 77 *unhouseled* without sacrament
unaneled without extreme unction 98 *table*

HAMLET. O all you host of heaven! O earth!
what else?
And shall I couple hell? O fie! Hold, hold
my heart,
And you, my sinews, grow not instant old,
But bear me stiffly up. Remember thee?
Ay, thou poor ghost, whiles memory holds
a seat
In this distracted globe. Remember thee?
Yea, from the table of my memory
I'll wipe away all trivial fond records,
All saws of books, all forms, all pressures 100
past,
That youth and observation copied there;
And thy commandment all alone shall live
Within the book and volume of my brain
Unmixed with baser matter; yes by heaven!
O most pernicious woman!
O villain, villain, smiling, damnéd villain!
My tables—meet it is I set it down
That one may smile, and smile, and be a
villain;
At least I'm sure it may be so in Denmark.
[*Writing.*]
So uncle, there you are. Now to my word; 110
It is "Adieu, adieu, remember me:"
I have sworn't.

MARCELLUS. }
HORATIO. } [*within*] My lord, my lord!

Enter HORATIO *and* MARCELLUS.

MARCELLUS. Lord Hamlet!
HORATIO. Heavens secure him!
HAMLET. So be it!
HORATIO. Illo, ho, ho, my lord!
HAMLET. Hillo, ho, ho, boy! come, bird, come.
MARCELLUS. How is't, my noble lord?
HORATIO. What news, my lord?
HAMLET. O, wonderful.
HORATIO. Good my lord, tell it.
HAMLET. No, you will reveal it.
HORATIO. Not I, my lord, by heaven.
MARCELLUS. Nor I, my lord. 120
HAMLET. How say you then, would heart of
man once think it?
But you'll be secret?

writing tablet 100 *saws* maxims *forms* sketches
pressures impressions 115 *Illo, ho, ho* the fal-
coner's call to his hawk

BOTH. Ay, by heaven, my lord.

HAMLET. There's never a villain dwelling in all Denmark
But he's an arrant knave.

HORATIO. There needs no ghost, my lord, come from the grave
To tell us this.

HAMLET.   Why right, you are in the right;
And so, without more circumstance at all,
I hold it fit that we shake hands and part;
You, as your business and desire shall point you,
130   For every man hath business and desire,
Such as it is, and for my own poor part,
Look you, I will go pray.

HORATIO. These are but wild and whirling words, my lord.

HAMLET. I'm sorry they offend you, heartily;
Yes, faith, heartily.

HORATIO.   There's no offence, my lord.

HAMLET. Yes, by Saint Patrick, but there is, Horatio,
And much offence too. Touching this vision here,
It is an honest ghost, that let me tell you;
For your desire to know what is between us
140   O'ermaster't as you may; and now, good friends,
As you are friends, scholars and soldiers,
Give me one poor request.

HORATIO. What is't, my lord? we will.

HAMLET. Never make known what you have seen tonight.

BOTH. My lord, we will not.

HAMLET.   Nay, but swear't.

HORATIO.   In faith,
My lord, not I.

MARCELLUS. Nor I, my lord, in faith.

HAMLET. Upon my sword.

MARCELLUS. We have sworn, my lord, already.

HAMLET. Indeed, upon my sword, indeed.

GHOST *cries under the stage.*

GHOST. Swear.

HAMLET. Ha, ha, boy, say'st thou so? art thou
150   there, truepenny?

Come on, you hear this fellow in the cellarage,
Consent to swear.

HORATIO.   Propose the oath, my lord.

HAMLET. Never to speak of this that you have seen,
Swear by my sword.

GHOST. Swear.

HAMLET. *Hic et ubique?* then we'll shift our ground.
Come hither, gentlemen,
And lay your hands again upon my sword.
Swear by my sword
Never to speak of this that you have heard.   160

GHOST. Swear by his sword.

HAMLET. Well said, old mole, canst work i'
the earth so fast?
A worthy pioner! Once more remove, good friends.

HORATIO. O day and night, but this is wondrous strange!

HAMLET. And therefore as a stranger give it welcome.
There are more things in heaven and earth, Horatio,
Than are dreamt of in your philosophy.
But come:
Here as before, never, so help you mercy,
How strange or odd some'er I bear myself—   170
As I perchance hereafter shall think meet
To put an antic disposition on—
That you, at such times seeing me, never shall
With arms encumbered thus, or this headshake,
Or by pronouncing of some doubtful phrase,
As "Well, well, we know," or "We could, an if we would,"
Or "If we list to speak," or "There be, an if they might,"
Or such ambiguous giving out, to note
That you know aught of me: this do swear,
So grace and mercy at your most need help   180
you.

GHOST. Swear.

HAMLET. Rest, rest, perturbéd spirit: [*They swear.*] so, gentlemen,
With all my love I do commend me to you,
And what so poor a man as Hamlet is

127 *circumstance* formality 156 *hic et ubique*
here and everywhere 163 *pioner* miner 172
antic odd, strange 174 *encumbered* folded

May do to express his love and friending
to you,
God willing, shall not lack. Let us go in
together,
And still your fingers on your lips, I pray.
The time is out of joint; O cursed spite
That ever I was born to set it right!
190 Nay come, let's go together.

Exeunt.

ACT II

Scene I

Enter old POLONIUS, *with his man*
REYNALDO.

POLONIUS. Give him this money and these
notes, Reynaldo.
REYNALDO. I will, my lord.
POLONIUS. You shall do marvellous wisely,
good Reynaldo,
Before you visit him, to make inquire
Of his behavior.
REYNALDO.   My lord, I did intend it.
POLONIUS. Marry, well said, very well said.
Look you, sir,
Inquire me first what Danskers are in
Paris,
And how, and who, what means, and
where they keep,
What company, at what expense, and
finding,
10 By this encompassment and drift of ques-
tion,
That they do know my son, come you more
nearer
Than your particular demands will touch
it;
Take you as 'twere some distant knowledge
of him,
As thus, "I know his father and his friends,

And in part him;" do you mark this,
Reynaldo?
REYNALDO. Ay, very well, my lord.
POLONIUS. "An in part him, but," you may
say, "not well;
But if't be he I mean he's very wild,
Addicted so and so," and there put on him
What forgeries you please; marry, none so 20
rank
As may dishonor him, take heed of that,
But, sir, such wanton, wild and usual slips
As are companions noted and most known
To youth and liberty.
REYNALDO.   As gaming, my lord.
POLONIUS. Ay, or drinking, fencing, swearing,
quarreling,
Drabbing—you may go so far.
REYNALDO. My lord, that would dishonor him.
POLONIUS. Faith, no, as you may season it
in the charge.
You must not put another scandal on him,
That he is open to incontinency—   30
That's not my meaning; but breathe his
faults so quaintly
That they may seem the taints of liberty,
The flash and outbreak of a fiery mind,
A savageness in unreclaiméd blood,
Of general assault.
REYNALDO.   But, my good lord—
POLONIUS. Wherefore should you do this?
REYNALDO.   Ay, my lord,
I would know that.
POLONIUS.   Marry, sir, here's my drift,
And I believe it is a fetch of warrant:
You laying these slight sullies on my son,
As 'twere a thing a little soiled i' the   40
working,
Mark you,
Your party in converse, him you would
sound,
Having ever seen in the prenominate
crimes
The youth you breathe of guilty, be assured
He closes with you in this consequence,
"Good sir," or so, or "friend," or "gentle-
man,"

---

7 *Danskers* Danes 8 *keep* resort 10 *encompassment* circuitous route 28 *season* modify
charge accusation 31 *quaintly* skilfully 32
taints faults 34 *unreclaiméd* unrestrained 35
of general assault which attack everyone 38 *fetch*
device *of warrant* justifiable 43 *prenominate*
aforementioned 45 *in this consequence* to this
effect 47 *addition* title

According to the phrase or the addition
Of man and country.

REYNALDO.   Very good, my lord.

POLONIUS. And then, sir, does a' this—a' does—
50   What was I about to say? By the mass,
      I was
About to say something; where did I leave?

REYNALDO. At "closes in the consequence,"
At "friend or so, and gentleman."

POLONIUS. At "closes in the consequence," ay,
      marry;
He closes with you thus: "I know the
      gentleman,
I saw him yesterday, or th'other day,
Or then, or then, with such, or such, and,
      as you say,
There was a' gaming, there o'ertook in's
      rouse,
There falling out at tennis," or perchance
60   "I saw him enter such a house of sale,"
Videlicet, a brothel, or so forth. See you
      now,
Your bait of falsehood takes this carp of
      truth,
And thus do we of wisdom and of reach,
With windlasses and with assays of bias,
By indirections find directions out;
So by my former lecture and advice
Shall you my son. You have me, have
      you not?

REYNALDO. My lord, I have.

POLONIUS.   God be wi' ye, fare ye well.

REYNALDO. Good my lord!

70 POLONIUS. Observe his inclination in yourself.

REYNALDO. I shall, my lord.

POLONIUS. And let him ply his music.

REYNALDO.   Well, my lord.

POLONIUS. Farewell!

Exit REYNALDO.

Enter OPHELIA.

                    How now, Ophelia,
                    what's the matter?

OPHELIA. O my lord, my lord, I have been
      so affrighted!

POLONIUS. With what, i' the name of God?

OPHELIA. My lord, as I was sewing in my
      closet,
Lord Hamlet with his doublet all unbraced,
No hat upon his head, his stockings fouled,
Ungartered and down-gyvéd to his ankle,
Pale as his shirt, his knees knocking each
      other,
And with a look so piteous in purport   80
As if he had been looséd out of hell
To speak of horrors—he comes before me.

POLONIUS. Mad for thy love?

OPHELIA.   My lord, I do not know,
But truly I do fear it.

POLONIUS.   What said he?

OPHELIA. He took me by the wrist and held
      me hard,
Then goes he to the length of all his arm,
And with his other hand thus o'er his brow
He falls to such perusal of my face
As a' would draw it. Long stayed he so;
At last, a little shaking of mine arm   90
And thrice his head thus waving up and
      down,
He raised a sigh so piteous and profound
As it did seem to shatter all his bulk
And end his being; that done, he lets
      me go:
And with his head over his shoulder turned
He seemed to find his way without his eyes,
For out o' doors he went without their
      helps,
And to the last bended their light on me.

POLONIUS. Come, go with me; I will go seek
      the king.   100
This is the very ecstasy of love,
Whose violent property fordoes itself,
And leads the will to desperate under-
      takings,
As oft as any passion under heaven
That does afflict our natures. I am sorry.
What, have you given him any hard words
      of late?

OPHELIA. No, my good lord, but as you did
      command

---

58 *o'ertook* overcome *rouse* carousal, cups 63
reach capacity 64 *windlasses* crafty devices
assays of bias roundabout attempts 65 *indirections*
indirect means 77 *doublet* jacket 79 *downgyvéd*
hanging down like gyves or fetters 101 *ecstasy* madness 102 *property* propensity *fordoes* ruins

I did repel his letters, and denied
His access to me.

POLONIUS.   That hath made him mad.

110 I am sorry that with better heed and judg-
ment
I had not quoted him; I feared he did but
trifle
And meant to wreck thee; but, beshrew my
jealousy,
By heaven it is as proper to our age
To cast beyond ourselves in our opinions,
As it is common for the younger sort
To lack discretion. Come, go we to the
king,
This must be known; which, being kept
close, might move
More grief to hide than hate to utter love.
Come.

Exeunt.

Scene II

Flourish. Enter KING *and* QUEEN,
ROSENCRANTZ *and* GUILDENSTERN,
with others.

KING. Welcome, dear Rosencrantz and Guild-
enstern.
Moreover that we much did long to see
you,
The need we have to use you did provoke
Our hasty sending. Something have you
heard
Of Hamlet's transformation—so I call it,
Sith nor the exterior nor the inward man
Resembles that it was. What it should be,
More than his father's death, that thus hath
put him
So much from the understanding of him-
self
10 I cannot dream of: I entreat you both
That, being of so young days brought up
with him
And sith so neighbored to his youth and
havior,

That you vouchsafe your rest here in our
court
Some little time; so by your companies
To draw him on to pleasures, and to gather
So much as from occasion you may glean,
Whether aught to us unknown afflicts him
thus,
That opened lies within our remedy.

QUEEN. Good gentlemen, he hath much
talked of you,
And sure I am two men there are not living 20
To whom he more adheres. If it will please
you
To show us so much gentry and good will
As to expend you time with us awhile,
For the supply and profit of our hope,
Your visitation shall receive such thanks
As fits a king's remembrance.

ROSENCRANTZ.   Both your majesties
Might, by the sovereign power you have
of us,
Put your dread pleasures more into com-
mand
Than to entreaty.

GUILDENSTERN.   But we both obey,
And here give up ourselves in the full 30
bent
To lay our service freely at your feet,
To be commanded.

KING. Thanks, Rosencrantz and gentle Guildenstern.

QUEEN. Thanks, Guildenstern and gentle Rosencrantz,
And I beseech you instantly to visit
My too much changéd son. Go, some of
you,
And bring these gentlemen where Hamlet
is.

GUILDENSTERN. Heavens make our presence
and our practices
Pleasant and helpful to him!

QUEEN.   Ay, amen!

Exeunt ROSENCRANTZ, GUILDENSTERN
[*and some Attendants.*]

Enter POLONIUS.

---

111 quoted observed   114 cast beyond ourselves
go too far   117 move cause   118 to hide if
hidden   to utter love if love is told   12 havior

way of life   18 opened made known   21 adheres
is attached   22 gentry courtesy   30 in the full
bent to the full

40 POLONIUS. The ambassadors from Norway, my good lord,
  Are joyfully returned.
KING. Thou still hast been the father of good news.
POLONIUS. Have I, my lord? Assure you, my good liege,
  I hold my duty, as I hold my soul,
  Both to my God and to my gracious king;
  And I do think, or else this brain of mine
  Hunts not the trail of policy so sure
  As it hath used to do, that I have found
  The very cause of Hamlet's lunacy.
50 KING. O speak of that, that do I long to hear.
POLONIUS. Give first admittance to the ambassadors;
  My news shall be the fruit to that great feast.
KING. Thyself do grace to them, and bring them in.

  [*Exit* POLONIUS.]

  He tells me, my dear Gertrude, he hath found
  The head and source of all your son's distemper.
QUEEN. I doubt it is no other but the main,
  His father's death and our o'erhasty marriage.
KING. Well, we shall sift him.

  Enter POLONIUS, VOLTIMAND *and* CORNELIUS.

                 Welcome, my good friends.
  Say, Voltimand, what from our brother Norway?
60 VOLTIMAND. Most fair return of greetings and desires.
  Upon our first, he sent out to suppress
  His nephew's levies, which to him appeared
  To be a preparation 'gainst the Polack,
  But better looked into, he truly found
  It was against your highness; whereat grieved
  That so his sickness, age, and impotence

Was falsely borne in hand, sends out arrests
  On Fortinbras; which he in brief obeys,
  Receives rebuke from Norway, and in fine
  Makes vow before his uncle never more   70
  To give the assay of arms against your majesty:
  Whereon old Norway, overcome with joy,
  Gives him threescore thousand crowns in annual fee,
  And his commission to employ those soldiers,
  So levied as before, against the Polack,
  With an entreaty, herein further shown,

  [*Gives a paper.*]

  That it might please you to give quiet pass
  Through your dominions for this enterprise
  On such regards of safety and allowance
  As therein are set down.
KING.   It likes us well;   80
  And at our more considered time we'll read,
  Answer, and think upon this business.
  Meantime we thank you for your well-took labor.
  Go to your rest; at night we'll feast together;
  Most welcome home!

  Exeunt AMBASSADORS.

POLONIUS.   This business is well ended.
  My liege and madam, to expostulate
  What majesty should be, what duty is,
  Why day is day, night night, and time is time,
  Were nothing but to waste night, day and time.
  Therefore, since brevity is the soul of wit,   90
  And tediousness the limbs and outward flourishes,
  I will be brief. Your noble son is mad;
  Mad call I it, for, to define true madness,
  What is't but to be nothing else but mad?
  But let that go.
QUEEN.   More matter with less art.

47 *policy* conduct of public affairs 53 *grace* honor 61 *upon our first* on our first raising the issue 67 *falsely borne in hand* deceived *arrests* staying orders 69 *in fine* in conclusion 79 *regards* conditions 86 *expostulate* explain

POLONIUS. Madam, I swear I use no art at all.
That he is mad 'tis true; 'tis true 'tis pity,
And pity 'tis 'tis true; a foolish figure,
But farewell it, for I will use no art.
100 Mad let us grant him then, and now remains
That we find out the cause of this effect,
Or rather say, the cause of this defect,
For this effect defective comes by cause:
Thus it remains, and the remainder thus.
Perpend:
I have a daughter—have while she is mine—
Who in her duty and obedience, mark,
Hath given me this; now gather, and surmise.

[*Reads*] *the letter.*

110 "To the celestial and my soul's idol, the
most beautified Ophelia,"—
That's an ill phrase, a vile phrase, "beautified" is a vile phrase; but you shall hear.
Thus:

[*Reads.*]

"In her excellent white bosom, these," &c.—
QUEEN. Came this from Hamlet to her?
POLONIUS. Good madam, stay awhile; I will
be faithful.

[*Reads.*]

"Doubt thou the stars are fire,
Doubt that the sun doth move,
Doubt truth to be a liar,
But never doubt I love.
"O dear Ophelia, I am ill at these numbers,
120 I have not art to reckon my groans; but
that I love thee best, O most best, believe
it. Adieu.
"Thine evermore, most dear lady,
whilst this machine is to him, HAMLET."
This in obedience hath my daughter
shown me,

And more above, hath his solicitings,
As they fell out by time, by means and
place,
All given to mine ear.
KING.   But how hath she
Received his love?
POLONIUS.   What do you think of me?
KING. As of a man faithful and honorable.
POLONIUS. I would fain prove so. But what   130
might you think,
When I had seen this hot love on the
wing—
As I perceived it, I must tell you that,
Before my daughter told me—what might
you,
Or my dear majesty your queen here, think,
If I had played the desk or table-book,
Or given my heart a winking, mute and
dumb,
Or looked upon this love with idle sight—
What might you think? No, I went round
to work,
And my young mistress thus I did bespeak:
"Lord Hamlet is a prince, out of thy star;   140
This must not be:" and then I prescripts
gave her
That she should lock herself from his resort,
Admit no messengers, receive no tokens.
Which done, she took the fruits of my
advice;
And he repelled (a short tale to make)—
Fell into a sadness, then into a fast,
Thence to a watch, thence into a weakness,
Thence to a lightness, and by this declension
Into the madness wherein now he raves,   150
And all we mourn for.
KING.   Do you think 'tis this?
QUEEN. It may be, very like.
POLONIUS. Hath there been such a time, I
would fain know that,
That I have positively said "'Tis so,"
When it proved otherwise?
KING.   Not that I know.
POLONIUS. [*pointing to his head and shoulder*]. Take this from this, if this be
otherwise;

98 *figure* trope, figure of speech 120 *numbers* verses 137 *given my heart a winking* shut the eyes of my heart 139 *round* directly 141 *star* sphere 142 *prescripts* orders 148 *watch* sleeplessness 149 *lightness* lightheadedness *declension* decline

If circumstances lead me, I will find
Where truth is hid, though it were hid
indeed
Within the centre.
KING.   How may we try it further?
POLONIUS. You know sometimes he walks four
160   hours together
Here in the lobby.
QUEEN.   So he does, indeed.
POLONIUS. At such a time I'll loose my daugh-
ter to him;
Be you and I behind an arras then;
Mark the encounter; if he love her not,
And be not from his reason fallen thereon,
Let me be no assistant for a state
But keep a farm and carters.
KING.   We will try it.

Enter HAMLET *reading on a book.*

QUEEN. But look where sadly the poor wretch
comes reading.
POLONIUS. Away, I do beseech you both,
away;
I'll board him presently.

Exeunt KING *and* QUEEN.

170   O give me leave,
How does my good Lord Hamlet?
HAMLET. Well, God-a-mercy.
POLONIUS. Do you know me, my lord?
HAMLET. Excellent well, you are a fishmonger.
POLONIUS. Not I, my lord.
HAMLET. Then I would you were so honest
a man.
POLONIUS. Honest, my lord!
HAMLET. Ay sir, to be honest, as this world
goes, is to be one man picked out of ten
thousand.
180 POLONIUS. That's very true, my lord.
HAMLET. For if the sun breed maggots in a
dead dog, being a good kissing carrion—
Have you a daughter?
POLONIUS. I have, my lord.
HAMLET. Let her not walk i' the sun; concep-
tion is a blessing, but as your daughter may
conceive—friend, look to't.

POLONIUS. [*aside*]. How say you by that? Still
harping on my daughter. Yet he knew me
not at first; a' said I was a fishmonger: A'
is far gone, far gone, and truly in my youth
I suffered much extremity for love, very
near this. I'll speak to him again.—What do
you read, my lord?
HAMLET. Words, words, words.   190
POLONIUS. What is the matter, my lord?
HAMLET. Between who?
POLONIUS. I mean the matter that you read,
my lord.
HAMLET. Slanders, sir; for the satirical rogue
says here, that old men have gray beards,
that their faces are wrinkled, their eyes
purging thick amber and plum-tree gum,
and that they have a plentiful lack of wit,
together with most weak hams; all which,
sir, though I most powerfully and potently
believe, yet I hold it not honesty to have it
thus set down; for yourself, sir, shall grow   200
old as I am, if, like a crab, you could go
backward.
POLONIUS. [*aside*]. Though this be madness,
yet there is method in't.—Will you walk
out of the air, my lord?
HAMLET. Into my grave?
POLONIUS. Indeed, that's out of the air.—
[*Aside*] How pregnant sometimes his replies are! a happiness that often madness
hits on, which reason and sanity could not
so prosperously be delivered of. I will leave
him, and suddenly contrive the means of
meeting between him and my daughter.—
My honorable lord, I will most humbly   210
take my leave of you.
HAMLET. You cannot, sir, take from me any
thing that I will more willing part withal:
except my life, except my life, except my
life.
POLONIUS. Fare you well, my lord.
HAMLET. These tedious old fools!

Enter ROSENCRANTZ *and* GUILDENSTERN.

POLONIUS. You go to seek the Lord Hamlet;
there he is.

---

159 *centre* centre of the earth   165 *thereon* for
this reason   170 *board* accost   *presently* at once
172   *God-a-mercy* thank-you   174 *fishmonger*
could have meant "procurer"   182 *good kissing*
carion flesh good for kissing   191 *matter* (1) subject matter (2) subject of a quarrel   196 *purging*
oozing   206 *pregnant* apt   213 *withal* with

ROSENCRANTZ. [*to* POLONIUS]. God save you, sir!

[*Exit* POLONIUS.]

GUILDENSTERN. My most honored lord!

220 ROSENCRANTZ. My dear lord!

HAMLET. My excellent good friends! How dost thou, Guildenstern? Ah, Rosencrantz! Good lads, how do you both?

ROSENCRANTZ. As the indifferent children of the earth.

GUILDENSTERN. Happy, in that we are not overhappy; On Fortune's cap we are not the very button.

HAMLET. Nor the soles of her shoe?

ROSENCRANTZ. Neither, my lord.

HAMLET. Then you live about her waist, or in
230 the middle of her favors.

GUILDENSTERN. Faith, her privates we.

HAMLET. In the secret parts of Fortune? O most true, she is a strumpet. What news?

ROSENCRANTZ. None, my lord, but that the world's grown honest.

HAMLET. Then is doomsday near; but your news is not true. Let me question more in particular: what have you, my good friends, deserved at the hands of Fortune, that she sends you to prison hither?

GUILDENSTERN. Prison, my lord?

240 HAMLET. Denmark's a prison.

ROSENCRANTZ. Then is the world one.

HAMLET. A goodly one, in which there are many confines, wards and dungeons, Denmark being one o' the worst.

ROSENCRANTZ. We think not so, my lord.

HAMLET. Why then 'tis none to you; for there is nothing either good or bad, but thinking makes it so: to me it is a prison.

ROSENCRANTZ. Why then your ambition makes it one; 'tis too narrow for your mind.

250 HAMLET. O God, I could be bounded in a nutshell, and count myself a king of infinite space, were it not that I have bad dreams.

GUILDENSTERN. Which dreams indeed are ambition; for the very substance of the ambitious is merely the shadow of a dream.

HAMLET. A dream itself is but a shadow.

ROSENCRANTZ. Truly, and I hold ambition of so airy and light a quality, that it is but a shadow's shadow.

HAMLET. Then are our beggars bodies, and our monarchs and outstretched heroes the beggars' shadows. Shall we to the court? 260 for, by my fay, I cannot reason.

BOTH. We'll wait upon you.

HAMLET. No such matter; I will not sort you with the rest of my servants, for, to speak to you like an honest man, I am most dreadfully attended. But in the beaten way of friendship, what make you at Elsinore?

ROSENCRANTZ. To visit you, my lord, no other occasion.

HAMLET. Beggar that I am, I am even poor in thanks, but I thank you; and sure, dear friends, my thanks are too dear a halfpenny. Were you not sent for? Is it your own inclining? Is it a free visitation? Come, 270 come, deal justly with me, come, come; nay, speak.

GUILDENSTERN. What should we say, my lord?

HAMLET. Why, any thing but to the purpose. You were sent for, and there is a kind of confession in your looks, which your modesties have not craft enough to color; I know the good king and queen have sent for you.

ROSENCRANTZ. To what end, my lord?

HAMLET. That you must teach me. But let me conjure you, by the rights of our fellowship, by the consonancy of our youth, by 280 the obligation of our ever-preserved love, and by what more dear a better proposer can charge you withal, be even and direct with me whether you were sent for or no.

ROSENCRANTZ. [*aside to* GUILDENSTERN]. What say you?

HAMLET. [*aside*]. Nay then, I have an eye of you.—If you love me, hold not off.

224 *indifferent* ordinary 226 *button* top 242 *confines* cells 243 *wards* sections of a prison 258 *beggars: i.e.* the men without ambition *monarchs and . . . heroes: i.e.* ambitious men 259 *outstretched* enlarged, *i.e.* larger than ordinary men

269 *too dear a halfpenny* of little worth 270 *free* unforced 279 *consonancy* accord 281 *proposer* questioner 282 *even* fair 289 *prevent* come before *discovery* disclosure

GUILDENSTERN. My lord, we were sent for.

HAMLET. I will tell you why; so shall my anticipation prevent your discovery, and your secrecy to the king and queen molt no feather. I have of late—but wherefore I know not—lost all my mirth, foregone all custom of exercises; and indeed it goes so heavily with my disposition, that this goodly frame the earth seems to me a sterile promontory; this most excellent canopy the air, look you, this brave o'erhanging firmament, this majestical roof fretted with golden fire, why, it appeareth no thing to me but a foul and pestilent congregation of vapors. What a piece of work is man, how noble in reason, how infinite in faculties, in form and moving, how express and admirable in action, how like an angel in apprehension, how like a god! the beauty of the world, the paragon of animals! And yet to me what is this quintessence of dust? man delights not me, no, nor woman neither, though by your smiling you seem to say so.

ROSENCRANTZ My lord, there was no such stuff in my thoughts.

HAMLET. Why did you laugh then, when I said "man delights not me"?

ROSENCRANTZ. To think, my lord, if you delight not in man, what lenten entertainment the players shall receive from you; we coted them on the way, and hither are they coming, to offer you service.

HAMLET. He that plays the king shall be welcome, his majesty shall have tribute of me; the adventurous knight shall use his foil and target, the lover shall not sigh gratis, the humorous man shall end his part in peace, the clown shall make those laugh whose lungs are tickle o' the sere, and the lady shall say her mind freely, or the blank verse shall halt for't. What players are they?

ROSENCRANTZ. Even those you were wont to take such delight in, the tragedians of the city.

HAMLET. How chances it they travel? their residence, both in reputation and profit, was better both ways.

ROSENCRANTZ. I think their inhibition comes by the means of the late innovation.

HAMLET. Do they hold the same estimation they did when I was in the city? are they so followed?

ROSENCRANTZ. No indeed, are they not.

HAMLET. How comes it? do they grow rusty?

ROSENCRANTZ. Nay, their endeavor keeps in the wonted pace; but there is, sir, an eyrie of children, little eyases, that cry out on the top of question, and are most tyrannically clapped for't: these are now the fashion, and so berattle the common stages (so they call them) that many wearing rapiers are afraid of goosequills, and dare scarce come thither.

HAMLET. What, are they children? who maintains 'em? how are they escoted? Will they pursue the quality no longer than they can sing? will they not say afterwards, if they should grow themselves to common players (as it is most like, if their means are no better) their writers do them wrong, to make them exclaim against their own succession?

ROSENCRANTZ. Faith, there has been much to do on both sides, and the nation holds it no sin to tarre them to controversy; there was for a while no money bid for argument, unless the poet and the player went to cuffs in the question.

HAMLET. Is't possible?

GUILDENSTERN. O, there has been much throwing about of brains.

HAMLET. Do the boys carry it away?

ROSENCRANTZ. Ay, that they do, my lord—Hercules and his load too.

HAMLET. It is not very strange, for my uncle is king of Denmark, and those that would

---

290 *molt no feather* suffer no loss 291 *forgone* given up 296 *fretted* adorned 299 *express* well-devised 301 *paragon* model of excellence 309 *lenten* meagre 310 *coted* overtook 314 *target* shield 315 *humorous* eccentric 316 *tickle o' the sere* ready to go off at any moment

323 *inhibition* prohibition 330 *eyrie* nest, brood *eyases* young hawks 333 *berattle* berate 334 *goosequills* pens 337 *escoted* supported *quality* profession 342 *succession* future 344 *tarre* incite 345 *argument* plot of a play 350 *Hercules and his load* the sign outside the Globe Theater

make mows at him while my father lived,
give twenty, forty, fifty, and hundred ducats
apiece for his picture in little. 'Sblood, there
is something in this more than natural, if
philosophy could find it out.

Flourish for the players.

GUILDENSTERN. There are the players.

HAMLET. Gentlemen, you are welcome to Elsinore. Your hands, come then. The appurtenance of welcome is fashion and cere-
360 mony; let me comply with you in this garb,
lest my extent to the players which, I tell
you, must show fairly outwards, should
more appear like entertainment than yours.
You are welcome: but my uncle-father and
aunt-mother are deceived.

GUILDENSTERN. In what, my dear lord?

HAMLET. I am but mad north-north-west;
when the wind is southerly I know a hawk
from a handsaw.

Enter POLONIUS.

POLONIUS. Well be with you, gentlemen.

HAMLET. Hark you, Guildenstern, and you
too, at each ear a hearer; that great baby
370 you see there is not yet out of his swad-
dling-clouts.

ROSENCRANTZ. Happily he is the second time
come to them, for they say an old man is
twice a child.

HAMLET. I will prophesy he comes to tell me
of the players; mark it. You say right, sir; o'
Monday morning, 'twas then indeed.

POLONIUS. My lord, I have news to tell you.

HAMLET. My lord, I have news to tell you.
When Roscius was an actor in Rome—

POLONIUS. The actors are come hither, my
lord.

380 HAMLET. Buz, buz!

POLONIUS. Upon my honor—

HAMLET. Then came each actor on his ass—

POLONIUS. The best actors in the world, either
for tragedy, comedy, history, pastoral, pastoral-comical, historical-pastoral, tragical-
historical, tragical-comical-historical-pastoral,
scene individable, or poem unlimited; Seneca cannot be too heavy, nor Plautus too
light for the law of writ and the liberty.
These are the only men.

HAMLET. O Jephthah, judge of Israel, what a
treasure hadst thou!   390

POLONIUS. What a treasure had he, my lord?

HAMLET. Why,
"One fair daughter and no more,
  The which he lovéd passing well."

POLONIUS. [*aside*]. Still on my daughter.

HAMLET. Am I not i' the right, old Jephthah?

POLONIUS. If you call me Jephthah, my lord,
I have a daughter that I love passing well.

HAMLET. Nay, that follows not.

POLONIUS. What follows then, my lord?   400

HAMLET. Why,
"As by lot, God wot,"
and then, you know,
"It came to pass, as most like it was";
the first row of the pious chanson will
show you more, for look where my abridg-
ment comes.

Enter four or five PLAYERS.

You are welcome, masters, welcome all; I
am glad to see thee well. Welcome, good
friends. O my old friend, thy face is
valanced since I saw thee last; comest thou
to beard me in Denmark? What, my young   410
lady and mistress! by'r lady, your ladyship
is nearer to heaven than when I saw you
last by the altitude of a chopine. Pray God
your voice, like a piece of uncurrent gold,
be not cracked within the ring. Masters,
you are all welcome. We'll e'en to't like
French falconers, fly at any thing we see;

352 *mows* faces, grimaces   358 *appurtenance* ac-
companiment 359 *comply* observe the formalities
361 *outwards* on the outside   *entertainment* welcome 366 *hawk* (1) falcon (2) plasterer's mor-
tarboard *handsaw* (1) heron (2) carpenter's tool
370 *clouts* clothes 386 *individable* unchanged
unlimited: i.e., ignoring the unities 388 *writ*
writing *liberty* the area outside city jurisdiction,

i.e., those who do not heed the rules   405 *chanson*
song 406 *my abridgement* that which cuts me
short 409 *valanced* fringed   410 *young lady and
mistress* the boy who played the leading female
parts 412 *chopine* high-heeled shoe   413 *uncurrent* not legal tender   414 *ring* (1) tone (2)
outer ring round the design of a coin

we'll have a speech straight; come, give us
a taste of your quality, come, a passionate
speech.

FIRST PLAYER. What speech, my good lord?

HAMLET. I heard thee speak me a speech once,
420　but it was never acted, or if it was, not
above once, for the play, I remember,
pleased not the million; 'twas caviary to
the general, but it was—as I received it,
and others whose judgments in such matters cried in the top of mine—an excellent
play, well digested in the scenes, set down
with as much modesty as cunning. I remember one said there were no sallets in
the lines to make the matter savory, nor no
matter in the phrase that might indict the
author of affection, but called it an honest
method, as wholesome as sweet, and by
very much more handsome than fine. One
430　speech in't I chiefly loved; 'twas Aeneas'
tale to Dido, and thereabout of it especially
where he speaks of Priam's slaughter. If it
live in your memory, begin at this line—let
me see, let me see:
　"The rugged Pyrrhus, like the Hyrcanian
　　beast,"
—'tis not so; it begins with Pyrrhus:
　"The rugged Pyrrhus, he whose sable
　　arms,
　Black as his purpose, did the night re-
　　semble
　When he lay couchéd in the ominous
　　horse,
　Hath now this dread and black com-
　　plexion smeared
440　With heraldry more dismal; head to foot
　Now is he total gules, horridly tricked
　With blood of fathers, mothers, daugh-
　　ters, sons,
　Baked and impasted with the parching
　　streets
　That lend a tyrannous and damnéd
　　light

To their lord's murder; roasted in wrath
　and fire
And thus o'er-sizéd with coagulate gore,
With eyes like carbuncles, the hellish
　Pyrrhus
Old grandsire Priam seeks."—
So proceed you.

POLONIUS. 'Fore God, my lord, well spoken,　450
with good accent and good discretion.

FIRST PLAYER.　　　　　　"Anon he finds him
　Striking too short at Greeks; his antique
　　sword,
　Rebellious to his arms, lies where it falls,
　Repugnant　to　command；　unequal
　　matched,
　Pyrrhus at Priam drives, in rage strikes
　　wide,
　But with the whiff and wind of his fell
　　sword
　The unnervéd father falls. Then sense-
　　less Ilium,
　Seeming to feel this blow, with flaming
　　top
　Stoops to his base, and with a hideous　460
　　crash
　Takes prisoner Pyrrhus' ear, for lo! his
　　sword,
　Which was declining on the milky head
　Of reverend Priam, seemed i' the air to
　　stick;
　So, as a painted tyrant, Pyrrhus stood
　And, like a neutral to his will and matter,
　　Did nothing.
　But as we often see against some storm
　A silence in the heavens, the rack stand
　　still,
　The bold winds speechless, and the orb
　　below
　As hush as death, anon the dreadful　470
　　thunder
　Doth rend the region; so, after Pyrrhus'
　　pause,
　A rouséd vengeance sets him new a-work,

422 *general* public　423 *cried in the top of*
spoke with more authority than　424 *digested* arranged　425 *modesty* moderation　426 *sallets*
salads　428 *affection* affectation　429 *handsome*
stately　431 *Aeneas' tale to Dido* In the *Aeneid*
Aeneas relates to Dido the story of the fall of Troy
434 *Hyrcanian beast* tiger　436 *sable* black
440 *heraldry* heraldic device　441 *gules* the

heraldic word for 'red' *tricked* colored (another
heraldic term)　446 *o'ersizéd* glued over *coagulate* clotted　447 *carbuncles* red semi-precious
stones　457 *fell* fierce　458 *unnervéd* feeble in
sinew *Illium* the citadel of Troy　460 *stoops to
his base* collapses to the ground　467 *against* in
expectation of　468 *rack* clouds

And never did the Cyclops' hammers fall
On Mars's armour, forged for proof
   eterne,
With less remorse than Pyrrhus' bleeding
   sword
Now falls on Priam.
Out, out, thou strumpet Fortune! All you
   gods
In general synod take away her power,
Break all the spokes and fellies from her
   wheel,
480 And bowl the round nave down the hill
   of heaven,
As low as to the fiends!"

POLONIUS. This is too long.

HAMLET. It shall to the barber's with your beard; prithee, say on, he's for a jig or a tale of bawdry, or he sleeps; say on, come to Hecuba.

FIRST PLAYER. "But who, ah woe! had seen the mobled queen—"

HAMLET. "The mobled queen"?

POLONIUS. That's good, "mobled queen" is good.

FIRST PLAYER. "Run barefoot up and down, threatening the flames
490 With bisson rheum, a clout upon that head
Where late the diadem stood, and for a robe
About her lank and all o'er-teeméd loins,
A blanket in the alarm of fear caught up;
Who this had seen, with tongue in venom steeped,
'Gainst Fortune's state would treason have pronounced;
But if the gods themselves did see her then,
When she saw Pyrrhus make malicious sport
In mincing with his sword her husband's limbs,
The instant burst of clamor that she made—
500 Unless things mortal move them not at all—

Would have made milch the burning
   eyes of heaven,
And passion in the gods."

POLONIUS. Look whether he has not turned his color, and has tears in's eyes. Prithee no more.

HAMLET. 'Tis well; I'll have thee speak out the rest soon. Good my lord, will you see the players well bestowed? Do you hear, let them be well used, for they are the abstract and brief chronicles of the time; after your death you were better have a 510 bad epitaph than their ill report while you live.

POLONIUS. My lord, I will use them according to their desert.

HAMLET. God's bodkin, man, much better; use every man after his desert, and who shall scape whipping? Use them after your own honor and dignity; the less they deserve, the more merit is in your bounty. Take them in.

POLONIUS. Come, sirs.

HAMLET. Follow him, friends; we'll hear a play tomorrow.

Exit POLONIUS [*with all the* PLAYERS *except the First.*]

Dost thou hear me, old friend; can you 520 play the Murder of Gonzago?

FIRST PLAYER. Ay, my lord.

HAMLET. We'll ha't tomorrow night. You could for a need study a speech of some dozen or sixteen lines, which I would set down and insert in't, could you not?

FIRST PLAYER. Ay, my lord.

HAMLET. Very well. Follow that lord, and look you mock him not.

[*Exit* FIRST PLAYER.]

My good friends, I'll leave you till night; you are welcome to Elsinore.

ROSENCRANTZ. Good my lord! 530

Exeunt.

---

473 *Cyclops* the workmen of Vulcan 474 *proof* invulnerability 479 *fellies* rim 480 *nave* hub 484 *jig* comic dialogue in song 486 *mobled* muffled 490 *bisson* blinding *rheum* moisture, tears *clout* cloth 492 *o'erteemed* (because, it was said, Hecuba had had fifty children) 501 *milch* tearful *burning eyes of heaven* the stars 506 *bestowed* lodged

HAMLET. Ay, so, God bye to you.
      Now I am alone.
O what a rogue and peasant slave am I!
Is it not monstrous that this player here
But in a fiction, in a dream of passion,
Could force his soul so to his own conceit
That from her working all his visage
    wanned,
Tears in his eyes, distraction in his aspect,
A broken voice, and his whole function
    suiting
540 With forms to his conceit? and all for
    nothing,
For Hecuba.
What's Hecuba to him, or he to Hecuba,
That he should weep for her? What would
    he do
Had he the motive and the cue for passion
That I have? He would drown the stage
    with tears,
And cleave the general ear with horrid
    speech,
Make mad the guilty and appal the free,
Confound the ignorant, and amaze indeed
The very faculties of eyes and ears;
550 Yet I,
A dull and muddy-mettled rascal, peak
Like John-a-dreams, unpregnant of my
    cause,
And can say nothing; no, not for a king,
Upon whose property and most dear life
A damned defeat was made. Am I a
    coward?
Who calls me villain, breaks my pate across,
Plucks off my beard and blows it in my
    face,
Tweaks me by the nose, gives me the lie i'
    the throat
As deep as to the lungs? who does me this,
    ha?
560 'Swounds, I should take it: for it cannot be
But I am pigeon-livered, and lack gall
To make oppression bitter, or ere this
I should ha' fatted all the region kites
With this slave's offal. Bloody, bawdy vil-
    lain!

Remorseless, treacherous, lecherous, kind-
    less villain!
O vengeance!
Why, what an ass am I! This is most brave,
That I, the son of a dear father murdered,
Prompted to my revenge by heaven and
    hell,
Must like a whore, unpack my heart with 570
    words,
And fall a-cursing, like a very drab,
A stallion!
Fie upon't, foh! About, my brains; hum, I
    have heard
That guilty creatures sitting at a play
Have by the very cunning of the scene
Been struck so to the soul, that presently
They have proclaimed their malefactions;
For murder, though it have no tongue, will
    speak
With most miraculous organ. I'll have these
    players
Play something like the murder of my 580
    father
Before mine uncle; I'll observe his looks,
I'll tent him to the quick; if a' do blench
I know my course. The spirit that I have
    seen
May be a devil, and the devil hath power
To assume a pleasing shape; yea, and per-
    haps
Out of my weakness and my melancholy,
As he is very potent with such spirits,
Abuses me to damn me; I'll have grounds
More relative than this; the play's the thing
Wherein I'll catch the conscience of the 590
    king.

    Exit.

ACT III

Scene I

Enter KING, QUEEN, POLONIUS, OPHELIA,
ROSENCRANTZ, GUILDENSTERN, LORDS.

---

536 *conceit* feeling, imagination 539 *function*
behavior 551 *muddy-mettled* poor-spirited *peak*
mope 552 *John-a-dreams* a dreamy fellow *un-*
pregnant unproductive 555 *defeat* destruction
565 *kindless* unnatural 576 *presently* at once
582 *tent* probe 589 *relative* relevant

KING. And can you by no drift of circumstance

Get from him why he puts on this confusion,

Grating so harshly all his days of quiet

With turbulent and dangerous lunacy?

ROSENCRANTZ. He does confess he feels himself distracted,

But from what cause a' will by no means speak.

GUILDENSTERN. Nor do we find him forward to be sounded,

But with a crafty madness keeps aloof

When we would bring him on to some confession

Of his true state.

10 QUEEN. Did he receive you well?

ROSENCRANTZ. Most like a gentleman.

GUILDENSTERN. But with much forcing of his disposition.

ROSENCRANTZ. Niggard of question, but of our demands

Most free in his reply.

QUEEN. Did you assay him

To any pastime?

ROSENCRANTZ. Madam, it so fell out, that certain players

We o'er-raught on the way; of these we told him,

And there did seem in him a kind of joy

To hear of it: they are here about the court

20 And, as I think, they have already order

This night to play before him.

POLONIUS. 'Tis most true,

And he beseeched me to entreat your majesties

To hear and see the matter.

KING. With all my heart; and it doth much content me

To hear him so inclined.

Good gentlemen, give him a further edge,

And drive his purpose into these delights.

ROSENCRANTZ. We shall, my lord.

Exeunt ROSENCRANTZ *and* GUILDENSTERN.

KING. Sweet Gertrude, leave us too,

For we have closely sent for Hamlet hither,

That he, as 'twere by accident, may here 30

Affront Ophelia;

Her father and myself, lawful espials,

Will so bestow ourselves that, seeing unseen,

We may of their encounter frankly judge,

And gather by him, as he is behaved,

If't be the affliction of his love or no

That thus he suffers for.

QUEEN. I shall obey you;

And for your part, Ophelia, I do wish

That your good beauties be the happy cause

Of Hamlet's wildness; so shall I hope your 40
virtues

Will bring him to his wonted way again,

To both your honors.

OPHELIA. Madam, I wish it may.

[*Exit* QUEEN.]

POLONIUS. Ophelia, walk you here. Gracious, so please you.

We will bestow ourselves. [*To* OPHELIA]
Read on this book,

That show of such an exercise may color

Your loneliness. We are oft to blame in this—

'Tis too much proved—that with devotion's visage

And pious action we do sugar o'er

The devil himself.

KING. [*aside*]. O 'tis too true;

How smart a lash that speech doth give 50
my conscience!

The harlot's cheek, beautied with plastering art,

Is not more ugly to the thing that helps it

Than is my deed to my most painted word:

O heavy burden!

POLONIUS. I hear him coming; let's withdraw, my lord.

Exeunt.

Enter HAMLET.

17 o'er-raught overtook *31 affront* confront *32 espials* spies *45 color* excuse

HAMLET. To be or not to be, that is the question,

Whether 'tis nobler in the mind to suffer
The slings and arrows of outrageous for-
   tune,
Or to take arms against a sea of troubles,
60 And by opposing end them? To die, to
   sleep—
No more; and by a sleep to say we end
The heartache and the thousand natural
   shocks
That flesh is heir to, 'tis a consummation
Devoutly to be wished. To die, to sleep;
To sleep, perchance to dream; ay, there's
   the rub,
For in that sleep of death what dreams
   may come
When we have shuffled off this mortal coil
Must give us pause; there's the respect
That makes calamity of so long life;
70 For who would bear the whips and scorns
   of time,
The oppressor's wrong, the proud man's
   contumely,
The pangs of despised love, the law's delay,
The insolence of office and the spurns
That patient merit of the unworthy takes,
When he himself might his quietus make
With a bare bodkin? who would fardels
   bear,
To grunt and sweat under a weary life,
But that the dread of something after
   death,
The undiscovered country, from whose
   bourn
80 No traveler returns, puzzles the will,
And makes us rather bear those ills we
   have
Than fly to others that we know not of?
Thus conscience does make cowards of us
   all,
And thus the native hue of resolution
Is sicklied o'er with the pale cast of thought,
And enterprises of great pitch and moment
With this regard their currents turn awry,
And lose the name of action. Soft you now,
The fair Ophelia! Nymph, in thy orisons
Be all my sins remembered.

OPHELIA.   Good my lord, 90
How does your honor for this many a day?
HAMLET. I humbly thank you, well, well, well.
OPHELIA. My lord, I have remembrances of
   yours
That I have longéd long to re-deliver;
I pray you now receive them.
HAMLET.   No, not I,
I never gave you aught.
OPHELIA. My honored lord, you know right
   well you did,
And with them words of so sweet breath
   composed
As made these things more rich; their
   perfume lost,
Take these again, for to the noble mind 100
Rich gifts wax poor when givers prove un-
   kind.
There, my lord.
HAMLET. Ha, ha, are you honest?
OPHELIA. My lord?
HAMLET. Are you fair?
OPHELIA. What means your lordship?
HAMLET. That if you be honest and fair, your
   honesty should admit no discourse to your
   beauty.
OPHELIA. Could beauty, my lord, have better 110
   commerce than with honesty?
HAMLET. Ay, truly, for the power of beauty
   will sooner transform honesty from what it
   is to a bawd than the force of honesty can
   translate beauty into his likeness; this was
   sometime a paradox, but now the time gives
   it proof. I did love you once.
OPHELIA. Indeed, my lord, you made me believe so.
HAMLET. You should not have believed me,
   for virtue cannot so inoculate our old stock,
   but we shall relish of it; I loved you not.
OPHELIA. I was the more deceived. 120
HAMLET. Get thee to a nunnery; why wouldst
   thou be a breeder of sinners? I am myself
   indifferent honest, but yet I could accuse
   me of such things, that it were better my
   mother had not borne me: I am very proud,
   revengeful, ambitious, with more offences
   at my beck than I have thoughts to put

---

65 *rub* obstruction 71 *contumely* scorn 75
quietus settlement 76 *bodkin* dagger *fardels*
burdens 79 *bourn* boundary 86 *pitch* height

87 *awry* aside 89 *orisons* prayers 109 *commerce* association 118 *inoculate* engraft *relish
of* smack of, have a trace of

them in, imagination to give them shape, or time to act them in. What should such fellows as I do crawling between earth and heaven? We are arrant knaves, all; believe none of us; go thy ways to a nunnery.
130 Where's your father?

OPHELIA. At home, my lord.

HAMLET. Let the doors be shut upon him, that he may play the fool no where but in's own house. Farewell.

OPHELIA. O help him, you sweet heavens!

HAMLET. If thou dost marry, I'll give thee this plague for thy dowry: be thou as chaste as ice, as pure as snow, thou shalt not escape calumny. Get thee to a nunnery, go: farewell. Or if thou wilt needs marry, marry a fool, for wise men know well enough what monsters you make of them. To a nunnery
140 go, and quickly too. Farewell.

OPHELIA. O heavenly powers restore him!

HAMLET. I have heard of your paintings too, well enough; God hath given you one face, and you make yourselves another; you jig, you amble, and you lisp; you nickname God's creatures, and make your wantonness your ignorance. Go to, I'll not more on't; it hath made me mad. I say we will have no more marriage; those that are married already, all but one, shall live; the rest shall keep as they are. To a nunnery, go.

Exit.

150 OPHELIA. O what a noble mind is here o'erthrown!
The courtier's, soldier's, scholar's eye, tongue, sword,
The expectancy and rose of the fair state,
The glass of fashion and the mould of form,
The observed of all observers, quite, quite down,
And I of ladies most deject and wretched,
That sucked the honey of his music vows,
Now see that noble and most sovereign reason
Like sweet bells jangled, out of tune and harsh,

That unmatched form and feature of blown youth
Blasted with ecstasy; O woe is me   160
To have seen what I have seen, see what I see!

Re-enter KING *and* POLONIUS.

KING. Love! his affections do not that way tend,
Nor what he spake, though it lacked form a little,
Was not like madness. There's something in his soul
O'er which his melancholy sits on brood,
And I do doubt the hatch and the disclose
Will be some danger; which for to prevent
I have in quick determination
Thus set it down: he shall with speed to England,
For the demand of our neglected tribute.   170
Haply the seas, and countries different,
With variable objects, shall expel
This something-settled matter in his heart,
Whereon his brains still beating puts him thus
From fashion of himself. What think you on't?

POLONIUS. It shall do well; but yet do I believe
The origin and commencement of his grief
Sprung from neglected love. How now, Ophelia?
You need not tell us what Lord Hamlet said;
We heard it all. My lord, do as you please,   180
But, if you hold it fit, after the play
Let his queen mother all alone entreat him
To show his grief; let her be round with him,
And I'll be placed, so please you, in the ear
Of all their conference. If she find him not,
To England send him, or confine him where
Your wisdom best shall think.

KING.   It shall be so;
Madness in great ones must not unwatch'd go.

Exeunt.

153 *glass* mirror *mould* model *form* behavior
160 *ecstasy* madness 173 *something-settled*
somewhat settled 183 *round* direct

Scene II

Enter HAMLET *and three of the* PLAYERS.

HAMLET. Speak the speech, I pray you, as I pronounced it to you, trippingly on the tongue; but if you mouth it, as many of our players do, I had as lief the town crier spoke my lines. Nor do not saw the air too much with your hand, thus, but use all gently, for in the very torrent, tempest, and as I may say whirlwind of your passion, you must acquire and beget a temperance that may give it smoothness. O, it offends me to the soul to hear a robustious periwig-pated fellow tear a passion to tatters, to
10 very rags, to split the ears of the groundlings, who for the most part are capable of nothing but inexplicable dumb shows and noise: I would have such a fellow whipped for o'erdoing Termagant; it out-herods Herod: pray you avoid it.

FIRST PLAYER. I warrant your honor.

HAMLET. Be not too tame neither, but let your own discretion be your tutor; suit the action to the word, the word to the action, with this special observance, that you o'erstep not the modesty of nature: for
20 any thing so o'erdone is from the purpose of playing, whose end, both at the first and now, was and is, to hold as 'twere the mirror up to nature, to show virtue her own feature, scorn her own image, and the very age and body of the time his form and pressure. Now this overdone or come tardy off, though it make the unskilful laugh, cannot but make the judicious grieve; the censure of the which one must in your allowance o'erweigh a whole theatre of others. O there be players that I have seen play—and heard others praise, and that highly—not to speak it profanely, that neither having the accent of Christians
30 nor the gait of Christian, pagan, nor man, have so strutted and bellowed, that I have thought some of nature's journeymen had made men, and not made them well, they imitated humanity so abominably.

FIRST PLAYER. I hope we have reformed that indifferently with us, sir.

HAMLET. O reform it altogether, and let those that play your clowns speak no more than is set down for them, for there be of them that will themselves laugh, to set on some 40 quantity of barren spectators to laugh too, though in the mean time some necessary question of the play be then to be considered; that's villanous, and shows a most pitiful ambition in the fool that uses it. Go, make you ready.

Exeunt PLAYERS.

Enter POLONIUS, ROSENCRANTZ, *and* GUILDENSTERN.

How now, my lord? will the king hear this piece of work?

POLONIUS. And the queen too, and that presently.

HAMLET. Bid the players make haste.

Exit POLONIUS.

Will you two help to hasten them?

ROSENCRANTZ, GUILDENSTERN. We will, my lord.

Exeunt they two.

HAMLET. What, ho, Horatio!   50

Enter HORATIO.

HORATIO. Here, sweet lord, at your service.

HAMLET. Horatio, thou art e'en as just a man As e'er my conversation coped withal.

HORATIO. O my dear lord—

HAMLET.   Nay, do not think I flatter, For what advancement may I hope from thee

That no revenue hast but thy good spirits
To feed and clothe thee? Why should the
  poor be flattered?
No, let the candied tongue lick absurd
  pomp,
And crook the pregnant hinges of the knee
60 Where thrift may follow fawning. Dost
  thou hear?
Since my dear soul was mistress of her
  choice,
And could of men distinguish her election,
She hath sealed thee for herself, for thou
  hast been
As one in suffering all that suffers nothing,
A man that fortune's buffets and rewards
Hast ta'en with equal thanks; and blessed
  are those
Whose blood and judgment are so well
  co-medled,
That they are not a pipe for fortune's finger
To sound what stop she please. Give me
  that man
70 That is not passion's slave, and I will wear
  him
In my heart's core, ay, in my heart of heart,
As I do thee. Something too much of this.
There is a play tonight before the king;
One scene of it comes near the circum-
  stance
Which I have told thee of my father's
  death;
I prithee, when thou seest that act a-foot,
Even with the very comment of thy soul
Observe my uncle. If his occulted guilt
Do not itself unkennel in one speech,
80 It is a damnéd ghost that we have seen,
And my imaginations are as foul
As Vulcan's stithy. Give him heedful note,
For I mine eyes will rivet to his face,
And after we will both our judgments
  join
In censure of his seeming.
HORATIO.   Well, my lord;
  If he steal aught the whilst this play is
  playing,
  And scape detecting, I will pay the theft.

HAMLET. They are coming to the play, I must
  be idle;
Get you a place.

Enter Trumpets and Kettledrums, KING,
QUEEN, POLONIUS, OPHELIA, ROSEN-
CRANTZ, GUILDENSTERN, *and other Lords
attendant with his Guard carrying
torches. Danish march. Sound a flourish.*

KING. How fares our cousin Hamlet?   90
HAMLET. Excellent, i' faith, of the chame-
  leon's dish; I eat the air, promise-crammed:
  you cannot feed capons so.
KING. I have nothing with this answer, Ham-
  let; these words are not mine.
HAMLET. No, nor mine now. [*To* POLONIUS]
  My lord, you played once i' the university,
  you say?
POLONIUS. That did I, my lord, and was
  accounted a good actor.
HAMLET. What did you enact?
POLONIUS. I did enact Julius Cæsar; I was 100
  killed i' the Capitol; Brutus killed me.
HAMLET. It was a brute part of him to kill so
  capital a calf there. Be the players ready?
ROSENCRANTZ. Ay, my lord, they stay upon
  your patience.
QUEEN. Come hither, my dear Hamlet, sit
  by me.
HAMLET. No, good mother, here's metal more
  attractive.

[*Lying down at* OPHELIA's *feet.*]

POLONIUS [*to the* KING]. O ho, do you mark
  that?
HAMLET. Lady, shall I lie in your lap?
OPHELIA. No, my lord.   110
HAMLET. I mean, my head upon your lap?
OPHELIA. Ay, my lord.
HAMLET. Do you think I meant country
  matters?
OPHELIA. I think nothing, my lord.

59 *pregnant* supple   60 *thrift* profit   62 *election*
choice   67 *blood* passion   *co-medled* blended
78 *occulted* hidden   82 *stithy* smithy   85 *censure* judging   *seeming* behavior   88 *idle* insane   91 *the chameleon's dish* air, on which the
chameleon was supposed to live   94 *are not mine*
are not an answer to my question   104 *stay upon
your patience* await your leisure

HAMLET. That's a fair thought to lie between maid's legs.

OPHELIA. What is, my lord?

HAMLET. Nothing.

OPHELIA. You are merry, my lord.

HAMLET. Who, I?

120 OPHELIA. Ay, my lord.

HAMLET. O God, your only jig-maker. What should a man do but be merry? for, look you, how cheerfully my mother looks, and my father died within's two hours.

OPHELIA. Nay, 'tis twice two months, my lord.

HAMLET. So long? Nay then, let the devil wear black, for I'll have a suit of sables. O heavens, die two months ago, and not forgotten yet? Then there's hope a great man's memory may outlive his life half a 130 year, but by'r lady a' must build churches then, or else shall a' suffer not thinking on, with the hobbyhorse, whose epitaph is, "For O, for O, the hobbyhorse is forgot."

Hautboys play. The dumb-show enters.

Enter a King and a Queen very lovingly; the Queen embracing him, and he her. She kneels, and makes show of protestation unto him. He takes her up, and declines his head upon her neck: he lays him down upon a bank of flowers: she, seeing him asleep, leaves him. Anon comes in another man, takes off his crown, kisses it, pours poison in the sleeper's ears, and leaves him. The Queen returns; finds the King dead, and makes passionate action. The Poisoner with some three or four comes in again, seems to condole with her. The dead body is carried away. The Poisoner woos the Queen with gifts: she seems harsh awhile, but in the end accepts his love.

Exeunt.

OPHELIA. What means this, my lord?

HAMLET. Marry, this is miching mallecho, it means mischief.

OPHELIA. Belike this show imports the argument of the play.

Enter PROLOGUE.

HAMLET. We shall know by this fellow; the players cannot keep counsel, they'll tell all.

OPHELIA. Will a' tell us what this show 140 meant?

HAMLET. Ay, or any show that you'll show him; be not you ashamed to show, he'll not shame to tell you what it means.

OPHELIA. You are naught, you are naught; I'll mark the play.

PROLOGUE. For us and for our tragedy,
          Here stooping to your clemency,
          We beg your hearing patiently.

          [*Exit.*]

HAMLET. Is this a prologue, or the posy of a ring?

OPHELIA. 'Tis brief, my lord.   150

HAMLET. As woman's love.

          Enter [*two* PLAYERS *as*] King *and* Queen.

PLAYER KING. Full thirty times hath Phœbus' cart gone round
     Neptune's salt wash and Tellus' orbéd ground,
     And thirty dozen moons with borrowed sheen
     About the world have times twelve thirties been
     Since love our hearts, and Hymen did our hands
     Unite commutual in most sacred bands.

PLAYER QUEEN. So many journeys may the sun and moon
     Make us again count o'er ere love be done!
     But woe is me, you are so sick of late, 160
     So far from cheer and from your former state,
     That I distrust you. Yet, though I distrust,
     Discomfort you my lord, it nothing must,
     For women fear too much, even as they love,

127 sables furs *134 miching mallecho* skulking mischief *144 naught* indecent *149 posy* in-scription *152 Phoebus' cart* the sun *157 commutual* mutually *162 distrust* fear for

And women's fear and love hold
    quantity:
In neither aught, or in extremity.
Now what my love is proof hath made
    you know,
And as my love is sized, my fear is so;
Where love is great, the littlest doubts
    are fear;
170 Where little fears grow great, great love
    grows there.
PLAYER KING. Faith, I must leave thee, love,
    and shortly too;
My operant powers their functions leave
    to do;
And thou shalt live in this fair world
    behind,
Honored, beloved, and haply one as kind
For husband shalt thou—
PLAYER QUEEN.   O confound the rest!
Such love must needs be treason in my
    breast.
In second husband let me be accurst,
None wed the second but who killed the
    first.
HAMLET. [*aside*]. Wormwood, wormwood.
180 PLAYER QUEEN. The instances that second
    marriage move
Are base respects of thrift, but none of
    love;
A second time I kill my husband dead
When second husband kisses me in bed.
PLAYER KING. I do believe you think what
    now you speak,
But what we do determine oft we break.
Purpose is but the slave to memory,
Of violent birth but poor validity,
Which now like fruit unripe sticks on
    the tree,
But fall unshaken when they mellow be.
190 Most necessary 'tis that we forget
To pay ourselves what to ourselves is
    debt;
What to ourselves in passion we propose,
The passion ending, doth the purpose lose.
The violence of either grief or joy
Their own enactures with themselves
    destroy;

Where joy most revels, grief doth most
    lament;
Grief joys, joy grieves, on slender
    accident.
This world is not for aye, nor 'tis not
    strange
That even our loves should with our
    fortunes change;
For 'tis a question left us yet to prove,   200
Whether love lead fortune, or else
    fortune love.
The great man down, you mark his
    favorite flies;
The poor advanced makes friends of
    enemies.
And hitherto doth love on fortune tend,
For who not needs shall never lack a
    friend,
And who in want a hollow friend doth
    try,
Directly seasons him his enemy.
But, orderly to end where I begun,
Our wills and fates do so contrary run,
That our devices still are overthrown;   210
Our thoughts are ours, their ends none
    of our own;
So think thou wilt no second husband
    wed,
But die thy thoughts when thy first lord
    is dead.
PLAYER QUEEN. Nor earth to me give food,
    nor heaven light,
Sport and repose lock from me day and
    night,
To desperation turn my trust and hope,
An anchor's cheer in prison be my scope,
Each opposite that blanks the face of joy,
Meet what I would have well, and it
    destroy,
Both here and hence pursue me lasting   220
    strife,
If once a widow ever I be wife!
HAMLET. If she should break it now!
PLAYER KING. 'Tis deeply sworn. Sweet, leave
    me here a while;
My spirits grow dull, and fain I would
    beguile
The tedious day with sleep.

Sleeps.

---

172 *operant* active 195 *enactures* fulfilment,
performances 207 *seasons* ripens 217 *anchor's*
hermit's 218 *blanks* turns pale

PLAYER QUEEN.　　　　　Sleep rock thy brain,
And never come mischance between us
　　twain!

Exit.

HAMLET. Madam, how like you this play?

QUEEN. The lady doth protest too much,
　methinks.

HAMLET. O, but she'll keep her word.

230　KING. Have you heard the argument? Is there
　no offence in't?

HAMLET. No, no, they do but jest, poison in
　jest; no offence i' the world.

KING. What do you call the play?

HAMLET. The Mousetrap. Marry, how? Tro-
　pically. This play is the image of a murder
　done in Vienna; Gonzago is the duke's
　name, his wife Baptista; you shall see anon
　'tis a knavish piece of work, but what o'
　that? your majesty and we that have free

240　souls, it touches us not; let the galled jade
　wince, our withers are unwrung.

Enter LUCIANUS.

This is one Lucianus, nephew to the king.

OPHELIA. You are as good as a chorus, my
　lord.

HAMLET. I could interpret between you and
　your love, if I could see the puppets dally-
　ing.

OPHELIA. You are keen, my lord, you are keen.

HAMLET. It would cost you a groaning to take
　off mine edge.

OPHELIA. Still better and worse.

250　HAMLET. So you must take your husbands.
　Begin murderer, leave thy damnable faces,
　and begin. Come: "the croaking raven doth
　bellow for revenge."

LUCIANUS. Thoughts black, hands apt, drugs
　fit, and time agreeing,
　Confederate season, else no creature
　　seeing,
　Thou mixture rank, of midnight weeds
　　collected,

With Hecate's ban thrice blasted, thrice
　infected,
Thy natural magic and dire property
On wholesome life usurps immediately.

Pours the poison in his ears.

HAMLET. A' poisons him i' the garden for his
　estate. His name's Gonzago; the story is
　extant, and written in very choice Italian;　260
　you shall see anon how the murderer gets
　the love of Gonzago's wife.

OPHELIA. The king rises.

HAMLET. What, frightened with false fire?

QUEEN. How fares my lord?

POLONIUS. Give o'er the play.

KING. Give me some light; away!

POLONIUS. Lights, lights, lights!

Exeunt all but HAMLET *and* HORATIO.

HAMLET. Why, let the stricken deer go weep,
　The hart ungallèd play,
For some must watch while some must　270
　　sleep;
　Thus runs the world away.
Would not this, sir, and a forest of feathers
　—if the rest of my fortunes turn Turk with
　me—with two Provincial roses on my razed
　shoes, get me a fellowship in a cry of
　players, sir?

HORATIO. Half a share.

HAMLET. A whole one, I.
For thou dost know, O Damon dear,
　This realm dismantled was
Of Jove himself, and now reigns here　280
　A very, very—pajock.

HORATIO. You might have rhymed.

HAMLET. O good Horatio, I'll take the ghost's
　word for a thousand pound. Didst perceive?

HORATIO. Very well, my lord.

HAMLET. Upon the talk of the poisoning?

HORATIO. I did very well note him.

HAMLET. Ah, ha! Come, some music! come,
　the recorders!
　For if the king like not the comedy,　290

---

230 *argument* outline of the plot　235 *tropically*
figuratively　240 *galled* chafed　*jade* horse
withers shoulders of horse　*unwrung* not irritated
255 *Hecate* goddess of witchcraft　272 *forest of*
feathers bunch of feathers sometimes part of an
actor's costume　273 *Provincial roses* large rosettes
worn by actors　274 *razed* slashed　*cry* pack
281 *pajock* peacock　289 *recorders* flageolets

Why then belike—he likes it not, perdy. Come, some music!

Enter ROSENCRANTZ *and* GUILDENSTERN.

GUILDENSTERN. Good my lord, vouchsafe me a word with you.

HAMLET. Sir, a whole history.

GUILDENSTERN. The king, sir—

HAMLET. Ay, sir, what of him?

GUILDENSTERN. Is in his retirement marvellous distempered.

HAMLET. With drink, sir?

GUILDENSTERN. No, my lord, with choler.

300 HAMLET. Your wisdom should show itself more richer to signify this to the doctor, for for me to put him to his purgation would perhaps plunge him into more choler.

GUILDENSTERN. Good my lord, put your discourse into some frame, and start not so wildly from my affair.

HAMLET. I am tame, sir; pronounce.

GUILDENSTERN. The queen your mother, in most great affliction of spirit, hath sent me to you.

HAMLET. You are welcome.

GUILDENSTERN. Nay, good my lord, this cour310 tesy is not of the right breed. If it shall please you to make me a wholesome answer, I will do your mother's commandment; if not, your pardon and my return shall be the end of my business.

HAMLET. Sir, I cannot.

GUILDENSTERN. What, my lord?

HAMLET. Make you a wholesome answer—my wit's diseased; but, sir, such answer as I can make, you shall command, or rather, as you say, my mother; therefore no more, but to the matter: my mother, you say,—

320 ROSENCRANTZ. Then thus she says: your behavior hath struck her into amazement and admiration.

HAMLET. O wonderful son, that can so stonish a mother! But is there no sequel at the heels of this mother's admiration? impart.

ROSENCRANTZ. She desires to speak with you in her closet ere you go to bed.

HAMLET. We shall obey, were she ten times our mother. Have you any further trade with us?

ROSENCRANTZ. My lord, you once did love me.

HAMLET. And do still, by these pickers and 330 stealers.

ROSENCRANTZ. Good my lord, what is your cause of distemper? you do surely bar the door upon your own liberty, if you deny your griefs to your friend.

HAMLET. Sir, I lack advancement.

ROSENCRANTZ. How can that be, when you have the voice of the king himself for your succession in Denmark?

HAMLET. Ay, sir, but "while the grass grows" —the proverb is something musty.

Enter the PLAYERS *with recorders.*

O, the recorders; let me see one. To withdraw with you—why do you go about to recover the wind of me, as if you would 340 drive me into a toil?

GUILDENSTERN. O, my lord, if my duty be too bold, my love is too unmannerly.

HAMLET. I do not well understand that. Will you play upon this pipe?

GUILDENSTERN. My lord, I cannot.

HAMLET. I pray you.

GUILDENSTERN. Believe me, I cannot.

HAMLET. I do beseech you.

GUILDENSTERN. I know no touch of it, my 350 lord.

HAMLET. 'Tis as easy as lying; govern these ventages with your fingers and thumb, give it breath with your mouth, and it will discourse most eloquent music. Look you, these are the stops.

GUILDENSTERN. But these cannot I command to any utterance of harmony; I have not the skill.

HAMLET. Why, look you now, how unworthy a thing you make of me! You would play upon me, you would seem to know my

---

297 *distempered* out of sorts 304 *frame* coherent form 311 *wholesome* reasonable 325 *closet* private room 330 *pickers and stealers* hands 337 *'while the grass grows':* the proverb continues 'oft starves the silly steed' 340 *recover the wind* get to windward 341 *toil* trap 343 *unmannerly* extreme 351 *ventages* wind-holes, stops

stops, you would pluck out the heart of my mystery, you would sound me from my
360 lowest note to the top of my compass; and there is much music, excellent voice, in this little organ, yet cannot you make it speak. 'Sblood, do you think I am easier to be played on than a pipe? Call me what instrument you will, though you can fret me, yet you cannot play upon me.

Enter POLONIUS.

God bless you, sir!
POLONIUS. My lord, the queen would speak with you, and presently.
370 HAMLET. Do you see yonder cloud that's almost in shape of a camel?
POLONIUS. By the mass and 'tis, like a camel indeed.
HAMLET. Methinks it is like a weasel.
POLONIUS. It is backed like a weasel.
HAMLET. Or like a whale?
POLONIUS. Very like a whale.
HAMLET. Then I will come to my mother by and by. They fool me to the top of my bent. I will come by and by.
POLONIUS. I will say so.

Exit.

380 HAMLET. By and by is easily said.
Leave me, friends.

[*Exeunt all but* HAMLET.]

'Tis now the very witching time of night,
When churchyards yawn, and hell itself breathes out
Contagion to this world: now could I drink hot blood,
And do such bitter business as the day
Would quake to look on. Soft, now to my mother.
O heart, lose not thy nature, let not ever
The soul of Nero enter this firm bosom;
Let me be cruel, not unnatural.

I will speak daggers to her, but use none;   390
My tongue and soul in this be hypocrites;
How in my words somever she be shent,
To give them seals never, my soul, consent!

Exit.

Scene III

Enter KING, ROSENCRANTZ *and* GUILDEN-STERN.

KING. I like him not, nor stands it safe with us
To let his madness range. Therefore prepare you;
I your commission will forthwith dispatch,
And he to England shall along with you:
The terms of our estate may not endure
Hazard so near us as doth hourly grow
Out of his brawls.
GUILDENSTERN. We will ourselves provide.
Most holy and religious fear it is
To keep those many many bodies safe
That live and feed upon your majesty.   10
ROSENCRANTZ. The single and peculiar life is bound,
With all the strength and armor of the mind,
To keep itself from noyance, but much more
That spirit upon whose weal depends and rests
The lives of many. The cess of majesty
Dies not alone, but like a gulf doth draw
What's near it with it; or it is a massy wheel
Fixed on the summit of the highest mount,
To whose huge spokes ten thousand lesser things
Are mortised and adjoined; which, when   20
it falls,
Each small annexment, petty consequence,
Attends the boisterous ruin. Never alone
Did the king sigh, but with a general groan.

---

362 *organ* instrument 388 *Nero* (who had his mother Agrippina put to death) 392 *shent* reproved 393 *give them seals* ratify by means of actions 5 *terms* conditions *estate* rank 7 *pro-*vide prepare 11 *peculiar* individual 13 *noyance* harm 15 *cess* cessation 16 *gulf* whirlpool 20 *mortised* fitted 21 *annexment* attachment 22 *ruin* crash

KING. Arm you, I pray you, to this speedy
  voyage,
For we will fetters put upon this fear
Which now goes too free-footed.
ROSENCRANTZ.   We will haste us.

  Exeunt ROSENCRANTZ *and* GUILDEN-
  STERN.

  Enter POLONIUS.

POLONIUS. My lord, he's going to his mother's
  closet.
Behind the arras I'll convey myself
To hear the process; I'll warrant she'll tax
  him home,
30 And as you said, and wisely was it said,
'Tis meet that some more audience than a
  mother,
Since nature makes them partial, should
  o'erhear
The speech, of vantage. Fare you well, my
  liege;
I'll call upon you ere you go to bed
And tell you what I know.
KING.   Thanks, dear my lord.

  Exit [POLONIUS.]

O, my offence is rank, it smells to heaven;
It hath the primal eldest curse upon't,
A brother's murder! Pray can I not,
Though inclination be as sharp as will;
40 My stronger guilt defeats my strong intent,
And, like a man to double business bound,
I stand in pause where I shall first begin,
And both neglect. What if this curséd hand
Were thicker than itself with brother's
  blood,
Is there not rain enough in the sweet
  heavens
To wash it white as snow? Whereto serves
  mercy
But to confront the visage of offence?
And what's in prayer but this twofold force,
To be forestalléd ere we come to fall,

Or pardoned being down? Then I'll look 50
  up;
My fault is past. But O, what form of
  prayer
Can serve my turn? "Forgive me my foul
  murder"?
That cannot be, since I am still possess'd
Of those effects for which I did the murder,
My crown, mine own ambition, and my
  queen.
May one be pardoned, and retain the
  offence?
In the corrupted currents of this world
Offence's gilded hand may shove by justice,
And oft 'tis seen the wicked prize itself
Buys out the law, but 'tis not so above; 60
There is no shuffling, there the action lies
In his true nature, and we ourselves com-
  pelled,
Even to the teeth and forehead of our
  faults,
To give in evidence. What then? what rests?
Try what repentance can; what can it not?
Yet what can it when one can not repent?
O wretched state! O bosom black as death!
O liméd soul, that, struggling to be free,
Art more engaged! Help, angels! make assay;
Bow, stubborn knees, and, heart with 70
  strings of steel,
Be soft as sinews of the new-born babe!
All may be well.

  [*Retires and kneels.*]

  Enter HAMLET.

HAMLET. Now might I do it pat, now a' is
  a-praying,
And now I'll do't, and so a' goes to heaven,
And so am I revenged. That would be
  scann'd:
A villain kills my father, and for that
I, his sole son, do this same villain send
To heaven.
Why, this is hire and salary, not revenge.
A' took my father grossly, full of bread, 80

29 *process* proceedings *tax* take to task 33 *of
vantage* from a vantage point 37 *primal eldest
curse* the curse of Cain 47 *offence* guilt 56
offence results of guilt 58 *gilded* furnished with

bribes 61 *shuffling* trickery 68 *liméd* entrapped 69 *engaged* entangled 73 *pat* readily
80 *full of bread* in full enjoyment of pleasure

With all his crimes broad blown, as flush
    as May,
And how his audit stands who knows save
    heaven?
But in our circumstance and course of
    thought
'Tis heavy with him: and am I then re-
    venged
To take him in the purging of his soul,
When he is fit and seasoned for his pas-
    sage?
No.
Up, sword, and know thou a more horrid
    hent:
When he is drunk, asleep, or in his rage,
90 Or in the incestuous pleasure of his bed,
At game a-swearing, or about some act
That has no relish of salvation in't;
Then trip him, that his heels may kick at
    heaven,
And that his soul may be as damned and
    black
As hell, whereto it goes. My mother stays;
This physic but prolongs thy sickly days.

    Exit.

KING. My words fly up, my thoughts remain
    below;
Words without thoughts never to heaven
    go.

    Exit.

Scene IV

Enter QUEEN *and* POLONIUS.

POLONIUS. A' will come straight. Look you
    lay home to him;
Tell him his pranks have been too broad
    to bear with,
And that your grace hath screened and
    stood between

Much heat and him. I'll silence me even
    here.
Pray you, be round with him.
HAMLET. [*within*]. Mother, mother, mother!
QUEEN.   I'll warrant you;
Fear me not: withdraw, I hear him coming.

    [POLONIUS *goes behind the arras.*]

    Enter HAMLET.

HAMLET. Now, mother, what's the matter?
QUEEN. Hamlet, thou hast thy father much
    offended.
HAMLET. Mother, you have my father much   10
    offended.
QUEEN. Come, come, you answer with an idle
    tongue.
HAMLET. Go, go, you question with a wicked
    tongue.
QUEEN. Why, how now, Hamlet?
HAMLET.   What's the matter now?
QUEEN. Have you forgot me?
HAMLET.   No, by the rood, not so!
    You are the queen, your husband's brother's
        wife,
    And—would it were not so!—you are my
        mother.
QUEEN. Nay, then I'll set those to you that
    can speak.
HAMLET. Come, come, and sit you down; you
    shall not budge;
    You go not till I set you up a glass
    Where you may see the inmost part of you.   20
QUEEN. What wilt thou do? thou wilt not
    murder me?
    Help, help, ho!
POLONIUS. [*behind*]. What, ho! help, help,
    help!
HAMLET. [*drawing*]. How now? a rat? Dead
    for a ducat, dead!

    [*Makes a pass through the arras and
    kills* POLONIUS.]

POLONIUS. [*behind*]. O, I am slain!
QUEEN. O me, what hast thou done?

---

81 *broad blown* in full bloom *flush* vigorous
82 *audit* account 86 *seasoned* prepared 88
hent opportunity 1 *lay home* speak severely 2

broad unrestrained 5 *round* downright 14 *rood*
cross

HAMLET.   Nay, I know not;
  Is it the king?
QUEEN. O, what a rash and bloody deed is this!
HAMLET. A bloody deed! almost as bad, good
    mother,
  As kill a king, and marry with his brother.
QUEEN. As kill a king!
30 HAMLET.   Ay, lady, it was my word.

    [*Lifts up the arras, and sees* POLONIUS.]

  Thou wretched, rash, intruding fool, fare-
    well!
  I took thee for thy better; take thy fortune;
  Thou find'st to be too busy is some danger.
  Leave wringing of your hands; peace sit
    you down
  And let me wring your heart, for so I shall,
  If it be made a penetrable stuff,
  If damnéd custom have not brassed it so
  That it be proof and bulwark against sense.
QUEEN. What have I done, that thou darest
    wag thy tongue
  In noise so rude against me?
40 HAMLET.   Such an act
  That blurs the grace and blush of modesty,
  Calls virtue hypocrite, takes off the rose
  From the fair forehead of an innocent love,
  And sets a blister there, makes marriage-
    vows
  As false as dicers' oaths; O, such a deed
  As from the body of contraction plucks
  The very soul, and sweet religion makes
  A rhapsody of words. Heaven's face does
    glow,
  And this solidity and compound mass,
50 With heated visage as against the doom,
  Is thought-sick at the act.
QUEEN.   Ay me, what act,
  That roars so loud and thunders in the
    index?
HAMLET. Look here upon this picture, and
    on this,
  The counterfeit presentment of two brothers.

  See what a grace was seated on this brow:
  Hyperion's curls, the front of Jove himself,
  An eye like Mars, to threaten and com-
    mand,
  A station like the herald Mercury
  New-lighted on a heaven-kissing hill,
  A combination and a form indeed,   60
  Where every god did seem to set his seal,
  To give the world assurance of a man;
  This was your husband. Look you now
    what follows;
  Here is your husband, like a mildewed ear
  Blasting his wholesome brother. Have you
    eyes?
  Could you on this fair mountain leave to
    feed,
  And batten on this moor? Ha! have you
    eyes?
  You cannot call it love, for at your age
  The heyday in the blood is tame, it's hum-
    ble,
  And waits upon the judgment; and what   70
    judgment
  Would step from this to this? Sense sure
    you have,
  Else could you not have motion, but sure
    that sense
  Is apoplexed, for madness would not err,
  Nor sense to ecstasy was ne'er so thralled
  But it reserved some quantity of choice
  To serve in such a difference. What devil
    was't
  That thus hath cozened you at hoodman-
    blind?
  Eyes without feeling, feeling without sight,
  Ears without hands or eyes, smelling sans all,
  Or but a sickly part of one true sense   80
  Could not so mope.
  O shame, where is thy blush? Rebellious
    hell,
  If thou canst mutine in a matron's bones,
  To flaming youth let virtue we as wax
  And melt in her own fire; proclaim no
    shame

33 *busy* prying, meddlesome 37 *custom* habit
38 *proof* armor *sense* feeling 46 *contraction*
contract, obligation 48 *glow* redden, blush for
shame 50 *against* at the approach of 52 *index*
preliminaries, table of contents 54 *presentment*
representation 56 *Hyperion* the sun god *front*
forehead 58 *station* attitude 64 *ear* (of wheat)

67 *batten* gorge, pasture 69 *heyday* youth 70
waits upon defers to 73 *apoplexed* subject to
aberrations or fits 74 *ecstasy* madness *thralled*
in bondage 76 *serve* employ *difference* power
of distinguishing 77 *cozened* deceived *hood-
man-blind* blind-man's-buff 81 *so mope* be so
uncertain 83 *mutine* mutiny, rebel

When the compulsive ardor gives the
    charge,
Since frost itself as actively doth burn,
And reason panders will.
QUEEN.   O Hamlet, speak no more;
    Thou turn'st my eyes into my very soul,
90 And there I see such black and grainéd
        spots
    As will not leave their tinct.
HAMLET.   Nay, but to live
    In the rank sweat of an enseaméd bed,
    Stewed in corruption, honeying and mak-
        ing love
    Over the nasty sty—
QUEEN.   O speak to me no more;
    These words like daggers enter in mine
        ears;
    No more, sweet Hamlet.
HAMLET.   A murderer and a villain,
    A slave that is not twentieth part the tithe
    Of your precedent lord, a vice of kings,
    A cutpurse of the empire and the rule,
100 That from a shelf the precious diadem stole
    And put it in his pocket—
QUEEN   No more.
HAMLET. A king of shreds and patches—

    Enter GHOST.

    Save me, and hover o'er me with your
        wings,
    You heavenly guards! What would your
        gracious figure?
QUEEN. Alas, he's mad.
HAMLET. Do you not come your tardy son to
        chide,
    That, lapsed in time and passion, lets go by
    The important acting of your dread com-
        mand?
    O, say!
110 GHOST. Do not forget; this visitation
    Is but to whet thy almost blunted purpose.
    But look, amazement on thy mother sits.
    O step between her and her fighting soul;
    Conceit in weakest bodies strongest works.

Speak to her, Hamlet.
HAMLET.   How is it with you, lady?
QUEEN. Alas, how is't with you,
    That you do bend your eye on vacancy,
    And with the incorporal air do hold dis-
        course?
    Forth at your eyes your spirits wildly peep,
    And, as the sleeping soldiers in the alarm,   120
    Your bedded hairs like life in excrements,
    Start up and stand an end. O gentle son,
    Upon the heat and flame of thy distemper
    Sprinkle cool patience. Whereon do you
        look?
HAMLET. On him, on him! Look you, how
        pale he glares!
    His form and cause conjoined, preaching to
        stones,
    Would make them capable. Do not look
        upon me,
    Lest with this piteous action you convert
    My stern effects; then what I have to do
    Will want true color—tears perchance for   130
        blood.
QUEEN. To whom do you speak this?
HAMLET.   Do you see nothing there?
QUEEN. Nothing at all; yet all that is I see.
HAMLET. Nor did you nothing hear?
QUEEN.   No, nothing but ourselves.
HAMLET. Why, look you there! look, how it
        steals away!
    My father, in his habit as he lived!
    Look, where he goes, even now, out at the
        portal!

    Exit GHOST.

QUEEN. This is the very coinage of your brain;
    This bodiless creation ecstasy
    Is very cunning in.
HAMLET.   Ecstasy!
    My pulse as yours doth temperately keep   140
        time
    And makes as healthful music; it is not
        madness
    That I have uttered. Bring me to the test,

86 *compulsive* compelling *gives the charge* orders the attack 88 *panders* is subservient to
90 *grainéd* ingrained 91 *tinct* color, dye 92
enseaméd greasy 97 *tithe* tenth part 98 *precedent* previous *vice* clown 99 *cutpurse* pickpocket 113 *fighting* struggling 114 *conceit*
imagination 121 *excrements* outgrowths 122 *an*
on 127 *capable* able to feel 129 *effects* deeds
130 *color* appearance *for* instead of

And I the matter will reword, which mad-
ness
Would gambol from. Mother, for love of
grace
Lay not that flattering unction to your soul,
That not your trespass but my madness
speaks;
It will but skin and film the ulcerous place
Whiles rank corruption, mining all within,
Infects unseen. Confess yourself to heaven,
150 Repent what's past, avoid what is to come,
And do not spread the compost on the
weeds
To make them ranker. Forgive me this my
virtue,
For in the fatness of these pursy times
Virtue itself of vice must pardon beg,
Yea, curb and woo for leave to do him good.
QUEEN. O Hamlet, thou hast cleft my heart
in twain.
HAMLET. O, throw away the worser part of it,
And live the purer with the other half.
Good night, but go not to my uncle's bed;
160 Assume a virtue, if you have it not.
That monster custom, who all sense doth eat
Of habits evil, is angel yet in this,
That to the use of actions fair and good
He likewise gives a frock or livery
That aptly is put on. Refrain tonight,
And that shall lend a kind of easiness
To the next abstinence; the next more easy,
For use almost can change the stamp of
nature,
And either curb the devil, or throw him out
170 With wondrous potency. Once more, good
night,
And when you are desirous to be blessed,
I'll blessing beg of you.—For this same lord,

[*Pointing to* POLONIUS.]

I do repent; but heaven hath pleased it so,
To punish me with this, and this with me,

That I must be their scourge and minister.
I will bestow him and will answer well
The death I gave him. So again, good
night.
I must be cruel only to be kind;
Thus bad begins, and worse remains be-
hind.
One word more, good lady.
QUEEN.   What shall I do?   180
HAMLET. Not this, by no means, that I bid
you do;
Let the bloat king tempt you again to bed,
Pinch wanton on your cheek, call you his
mouse,
And let him for a pair of reechy kisses,
Or paddling in your neck with his damned
fingers,
Make you to ravel all this matter out
That I essentially am not in madness,
But mad in craft. 'Twere good you let him
know,
For who, that's but a queen, fair, sober,
wise,
Would from a paddock, from a bat, a gib,   190
Such dear concernings hide? who would
do so?
No, in despite of sense and secrecy,
Unpeg the basket on the house's top,
Let the birds fly, and like the famous ape,
To try conclusions, in the basket creep
And break your own neck down.
QUEEN. Be thou assured, if words be made of
breath
And breath of life, I have no life to breathe
What thou hast said to me.
HAMLET. I must to England; you know that?
QUEEN.   Alack,   200
I had forgot; 'tis so concluded on.
HAMLET. There's letters sealed, and my two
schoolfellows,
Whom I will trust as I will adders fanged,
They bear the mandate; they must sweep
my way

---

145 *unction* ointment 148 *mining* undermining
152 *virtue* apparent self-righteousness 153 *fatness*
grossness *pursy* corpulent 155 *curb* bow 161
sense feeling, sensitiveness 162 *of* from 164
livery uniform 165 *aptly* easily 168 *use* habit
stamp form, impression 175 *scourge* instrument
of punishment *minister* agent 176 *bestow* hide

182 *bloat* bloated 183 *wanton* wantonly 184
reechy reeking, dirty 186 *ravel . . . out* unravel 188 *in craft:* i.e., pretendedly 190 *paddock* toad *gib* cat 191 *dear concernings* matters of personal importance 204 *mandate* orders
sweep prepare

And marshal me to knavery. Let it work,
For 'tis the sport to have the enginer
Hoist with his own petar, and't shall go
    hard
But I will delve one yard below their mines,
And blow them at the moon: O 'tis most
    sweet
210 When in one line two crafts directly meet.
This man shall set me packing;
I'll lug the guts into the neighbor room.
Mother, good night indeed. This counsellor
Is now most still, most secret, and most
    grave,
Who was in life a foolish prating knave.
Come, sir, to draw toward an end with you.
Good night, mother.

Exit HAMLET *tugging in* POLONIUS.

ACT IV

Scene I

Enter KING, *and* QUEEN, *with* ROSEN-
CRANTZ *and* GUILDENSTERN.

KING. There's matter in these sighs, these pro-
    found heaves,
You must translate; 'tis fit we understand
    them.
Where is your son?
QUEEN. Bestow this place on us a little while.

[*Exeunt* ROSENCRANTZ *and* GUILDEN-
STERN.]

Ah, mine own lord, what have I seen to-
    night!
KING. What, Gertrude, how does Hamlet?
QUEEN. Mad as the sea and wind when both
    contend
Which is the mightier; in his lawless fit,
Behind the arras hearing something stir,
10 Whips out his rapier, cries "a rat, a rat!"
And in this brainish apprehension kills
The unseen good old man.

KING.   O heavy deed!
It had been so with us had we been there.
His liberty is full of threats to all—
To you yourself, to us, to every one.
Alas, how shall this bloody deed be an-
    swered?
It will be laid to us, whose providence
Should have kept short, restrained, and out
    of haunt
This mad young man; but so much was our
    love,
We would not understand what was most   20
    fit;
But like the owner of a foul disease,
To keep it from divulging, let it feed
Even on the pith of life. Where is he gone?
QUEEN. To draw apart the body he hath
    killed,
O'er whom his very madness, like some ore
Among a mineral of metals base,
Shows itself pure; a' weeps for what is done.
KING. O Gertrude, come away!
The sun no sooner shall the mountains
    touch,
But we will ship him hence, and this vile   30
    deed
We must, with all our majesty and skill,
Both countenance and excuse. Ho, Guild-
    enstern!

Enter ROSENCRANTZ *and* GUILDENSTERN.

Friends both, go join you with some further
    aid;
Hamlet in madness hath Polonious slain,
And from his mother's closet hath he
    dragged him.
Go seek him out; speak fair, and bring the
    body
Into the chapel. I pray you haste in this.

Exeunt ROSENCRANTZ *and* GUILDEN-
STERN.

Come, Gertrude, we'll call up our wisest
    friends,
And let them know both what we mean to
    do

205 *marshal* lead 206 *enginer* engineer 207
hoist blown up *petar* mine, bomb 208 *delve*
dig, tunnel *11 brainish apprehension* imaginary

fear *18 out of haunt* out of the way *25 ore*
precious metal *26 mineral* vein *32 countenance*
acknowledge

40 And what's untimely done; [so haply slander—]
Whose whisper o'er the world's diameter,
As level as the cannon to his blank,
Transports his poisoned shot—may miss our name,
And hit the woundless air. O, come away!
My soul is full of discord and dismay.

Exeunt.

Scene II

Enter HAMLET.

HAMLET. Safely stowed
GENTLEMEN [*within*]. Hamlet, Lord Hamlet!
HAMLET. What noise? who calls on Hamlet?
O, here they come.

Enter ROSENCRANTZ *and* GUILDENSTERN.

ROSENCRANTZ. What have you done, my lord, with the dead body?
HAMLET. Compounded it with dust, whereto 'tis kin.
ROSENCRANTZ. Tell us where 'tis that we may take it thence,
And bear it to the chapel.
HAMLET. Do not believe it.
10 ROSENCRANTZ. Believe what?
HAMLET. That I can keep your counsel and not mine own. Besides, to be demanded of a sponge! what replication should be made by the son of a king?
ROSENCRANTZ. Take you me for a sponge, my lord?
HAMLET. Ay, sir, that soaks up the king's countenance, his rewards, his authorities. But such officers do the king best service in the end: he keeps them, like an ape, in the corner of his jaw—first mouthed, to be last swallowed; when he needs what you have gleaned, it is but squeezing you, and
20 sponge, you shall be dry again.
ROSENCRANTZ. I understand you not, my lord.

HAMLET. I am glad of it; a knavish speech sleeps in a foolish ear.
ROSENCRANTZ. My lord, you must tell us where the body is, and go with us to the king.
HAMLET. The body is with the king, but the king is not with the body. The king is a thing—
GUILDENSTERN. A thing, my lord!
HAMLET. Of nothing; bring me to him. Hide fox, and all after. 30

Exeunt.

Scene III

Enter KING, *and two or three.*

KING. I have sent to seek him, and to find the body.
How dangerous is it that this man goes loose;
Yet must not we put the strong law on him;
He's loved of the distracted multitude,
Who like not in their judgment, but their eyes,
And where 'tis so, the offender's scourge is weighted,
But never the offence. To bear all smooth and even,
This sudden sending him away must seem
Deliberate pause; diseases desperate grown
By desperate appliance are relieved, 10
Or not at all.

Enter ROSENCRANTZ.

How now, what hath befallen?
ROSENCRANTZ. Where the dead body is bestowed, my lord,
We cannot get from him.
KING. But where is he?
ROSENCRANTZ. Without, my lord; guarded, to know your pleasure.
KING. Bring him before us.

---

42 *blank* target 6 *compounded* mixed 15 *countenance* favor 22 *sleeps* is not understood

4 *distracted* unstable 6 *scourge* punishment 10 *appliance* medical treatment

ROSENCRANTZ. Ho, Guildenstern! bring in my
lord.

Enter HAMLET. *and* GUILDENSTERN.

KING. Now, Hamlet, where's Polonius?
HAMLET. At supper.
KING. At supper! where?
20 HAMLET. Not where he eats, but where a' is
eaten; a certain convocation of politic
worms are e'en at him. Your worm is your
only emperor for diet; we fat all creatures
else to fat us, and we fat ourselves for
maggots; your fat king and your lean beggar is but variable service—two dishes, but
to one table; that's the end.
KING. Alas, alas!
HAMLET. A man may fish with the worm that
hath eat of a king, and eat of the fish that
hath fed of that worm.
KING. What dost thou mean by this?
30 HAMLET. Nothing but to show you how a
king may go a progress through the guts of
a beggar.
KING. Where is Polonius?
HAMLET. In heaven. Send thither to see; if
your messenger find him not there, seek
him i' the other place yourself. But if indeed you find him not within this month,
you shall nose him as you go up the stairs
into the lobby.
KING. Go seek him there.

[To some Attendants.]

HAMLET. A' will stay till you come.

[Exeunt Attendants.]

KING. Hamlet, this deed, for thine especial
safety—
40   Which we do tender, as we dearly grieve
For that which thou hast done—must send
thee hence

With fiery quickness; therefore prepare
thyself;
The bark is ready, and the wind at help,
The associates tend, and every thing is bent
For England.
HAMLET.   For England!
KING.   Ay, Hamlet.
HAMLET.   Good.
KING. So is it, if thou knew'st our purposes.
HAMLET. I see a cherub that sees them. But
come; for England! Farewell, dear mother.
KING. Thy loving father, Hamlet.
HAMLET. My mother; father and mother is   50
man and wife, man and wife is one flesh,
and so my mother. Come, for England!

[Exit.]

KING. Follow him at foot; tempt him with
speed aboard.
Delay it not; I'll have him hence tonight.
Away! for every thing is sealed and done
That else leans on the affair; pray you,
make haste.

[Exeunt ROSENCRANTZ *and* GUILDEN-
STERN.]*

And, England, if my love thou hold'st at
aught—
As my great power thereof may give thee
sense,
Since yet thy cicatrice looks raw and red
After the Danish sword, and thy free awe   60
Pays homage to us—thou mayst not coldly
set
Our sovereign process, which imports at full
By letters congruing to that effect
The present death of Hamlet. Do it, Eng-
land;
For like the hectic in my blood he rages,
And thou must cure me; till I know 'tis
done,

21 *convocation of politic worms . . . emperor for
diet* (a punning allusion to the Diets of the Holy
Roman Empire held at Worms) 24 *variable service*
different courses 31 *progress* state journey made
by a king 40 *tender* care for *dearly* deeply
44 *tend* wait 56 *leans on* concerns 57 *England* King of England *hold'st at aught* valuest
at all 58 *give thee sense* make thee perceive 59
cicatrice scar 61 *coldly set* disregard 62 *process* command 63 *congruing* amounting 64
present immediate 65 *hectic* fever

Howe'er my haps, my joys were ne'er begun.

Exit.

Scene IV

Enter FORTINBRAS, *with his Army over the stage.*

FORTINBRAS. Go, captain, from me greet the
  Danish king;
Tell him that by his license Fortinbras
Claims the conveyance of a promised march
Over his kingdom. You know the rendez-
  vous.
If that his majesty would aught with us,
We shall express our duty in his eye;
And let him know so.
CAPTAIN.   I will do't, my lord.
FORTINBRAS. Go softly on.

  [*Exeunt* FORTINBRAS *and his Forces.*]

  Enter HAMLET, ROSENCRANTZ, [GUILDEN-
  STERN *and others.*]

HAMLET. Good sir, whose powers are these?
10 CAPTAIN. They are of Norway, sir.
HAMLET. How purposed, sir, I pray you?
CAPTAIN. Against some part of Poland.
HAMLET. Who commands them, sir?
CAPTAIN. The nephew to old Norway, Fortin-
  bras.
HAMLET. Goes it against the main of Poland,
  sir,
Or for some frontier?
CAPTAIN. Truly to speak, and with no addi-
  tion,
We go to gain a little patch of ground
That hath in it no profit but the name.
20 To pay five ducats, five, I would not farm
  it,
Nor will it yield to Norway or the Pole
A ranker rate, should it be sold in fee.

HAMLET. Why then, the Polack never will
  defend it.
CAPTAIN. Yes, it is already garrisoned.
HAMLET. Two thousand souls and twenty
  thousand ducats
Will not debate the question of this straw;
This is the imposthume of much wealth
  and peace,
That inward breaks, and shows no cause
  without
Why the man dies. I humbly thank you,
  sir.
CAPTAIN. God be wi' you, sir.

  [*Exit.*]

ROSENCRANTZ. Will't please you go, my lord? 30
HAMLET. I'll be with you straight. Go a little
  before.

  [*Exeunt all except* HAMLET.]

How all occasions do inform against me,
And spur my dull revenge! What is a man
If his chief good and market of his time
Be but to sleep and feed? a beast, no more.
Sure, he that made us with such large dis-
  course
Looking before and after, gave us not
That capability and godlike reason
To fust in us unused. Now, whether it be
Bestial oblivion, or some craven scruple 40
Of thinking too precisely on the event—
A thought which, quartered, hath but one
  part wisdom,
And ever three parts coward—I do not
  know
Why yet I live to say "This thing's to do,"
Sith I have cause, and will, and strength,
  and means
To do't. Examples gross as earth exhort me:
Witness this army of such mass and charge,
Led by a delicate and tender prince,
Whose spirit, with divine ambition puffed,
Makes mouths at the invisible event, 50
Exposing what is mortal and unsure

---

67 *haps* fortunes 3 *conveyance* convoy 9
powers forces 15 *main* principal part 17 *addition* exaggeration 22 *ranker* higher *in fee*
outright 27 *imposthume* ulcer 32 *inform against*
denounce 34 *market* profit 36 *discourse* power
of reasoning 39 *fust* grow mouldy 40 *oblivion*
forgetfulness 41 *event* outcome 47 *charge* expense 50 *makes mouths at* makes faces at, defies

To all that fortune, death and danger dare,
Even for an eggshell. Rightly to be great
Is not to stir without great argument,
But greatly to find quarrel in a straw
When honor's at the stake. How stand I
    then
That have a father killed, a mother stained,
Excitements of my reason and my blood,
And let all sleep? while to my shame I see
60 The imminent death of twenty thousand
    men,
That for a fantasy and trick of fame
Go to their graves like beds, fight for a plot
Whereon the numbers cannot try the cause,
Which is not tomb enough and continent
To hide the slain? O, from this time forth
My thoughts be bloody, or be nothing
    worth!

    Exit.

Scene V

Enter QUEEN, HORATIO, *and a* GENTLE-
MAN.

QUEEN. I will not speak with her.
GENTLEMAN. She is importunate, indeed dis-
    tract;
    Her mood will needs be pitied.
QUEEN.   What would she have?
GENTLEMAN. She speaks much of her father,
    says she hears
    There's tricks i' the world, and hems, and
    beats her heart,
    Spurns enviously at straws, speaks things
    in doubt
    That carry but half sense; her speech is
    nothing,
    Yet the unshapéd use of it doth move
    The hearers to collection; they aim at it,
10 And botch the words up fit to their own
    thoughts,

Which, as her winks and nods and gestures
    yield them,
Indeed would make one think there might
    be thought,
Though nothing sure, yet much unhappily.
HORATIO. 'Twere good she were spoken with,
    for she may strew
Dangerous   conjectures   in   ill-breeding
    minds;
Let her come in.

    [*Exit* GENTLEMAN.]

QUEEN. To my sick soul, as sin's true nature
    is,
Each top seems prologue to some great
    amiss;
So full of artless jealousy is guilt,
It spills itself in fearing to be spilt.   20

    Enter OPHELIA *distracted.*

OPHELIA. Where is the beauteous majesty of
    Denmark?
QUEEN. How now, Ophelia?
OPHELIA [*sings*]. How should I your true love
    know
            From another one?
        By his cockle hat and staff,
            And his sandal shoon.
QUEEN. Alas, sweet lady, what imports this
    song?
OPHELIA. Say you? Nay, pray you, mark.
[*Sings.*] He is dead and gone, lady,
            He is dead and gone;
        At his head a grass-green turf,   30
            At his heels a stone
            O, ho!
QUEEN. Nay, but Ophelia—
OPHELIA. Pray you, mark.
[*Sings.*] White his shroud as the mountain
    snow—

    Enter KING.

---

58 *blood* passion, anger 61 *trick* whim 64 *continent* receptacle 2 *distract* distracted, unbal-
anced 5 *tricks* deceits 6 *spurns enviously at
straws* takes offence at trifles 7 *nothing* nonsense 8 *unshapéd* incoherent 9 *collection* attempt to collect some meaning from it 10 *botch*

patch 15 *ill-breeding* liable to misinterpret 18
toy trifle *amiss* misfortune 19 *artless* uncon-
trolled *jealousy* suspicion 25 *cockle hat and staff*
insignia of a pilgrim 26 *shoon* shoes 27 *imports*
means

QUEEN. Alas, look here, my lord.

OPHELIA. [*sings*]. Larded all with sweet
  flowers,
  Which bewept to the grave did not go
  With true-love showers.

40 KING. How do you, pretty lady?

OPHELIA. Well, God 'ild you! They say the
  owl was a baker's daughter. Lord, we know
  what we are, but know not what we may
  be. God be at your table!

KING. Conceit upon her father.

OPHELIA. Pray you, let's have no words of this;
  but when they ask you what it means, say
  you this:
  [*Sings.*] To-morrow is Saint Valentine's day,
    All in the morning bedtime,
    And I a maid at your window,
50   To be your Valentine.
    Then up he rose, and donned his
    clo'es,
    And dupped the chamber door.
    Let in the maid, that out a maid
    Never departed more.

KING. Pretty Ophelia!

OPHELIA. Indeed, la, without an oath I'll make
  an end on't:
  [*Sings.*] By Gis and by Saint Charity,
    Alack and fie for shame!
60   Young men will do't if they come
    to't,
    By Cock, they are to blame.

    Quoth she, "Before you tumbled me,
    You promised me to wed."
  He answers
    So would I ha' done by yonder sun,
    And thou hadst not come to my
    bed.

KING. How long hath she been thus?

OPHELIA. I hope all will be well. We must be
  patient, but I cannot choose but weep to
  think they would lay him i' the cold
  ground. My brother shall know of it; and
70 so I thank you for your good counsel.
  Come, my coach! Good night, ladies; good
night, sweet ladies; good night, good night.

  Exit.

KING. Follow her close; give her good watch,
  I pray you.

  [*Exit* HORATIO.]

O, this is the poison of deep grief; it springs
All from her father's death—and now be-
hold!
O Gertrude, Gertrude,
When sorrows come, they come not single
  spies,
But in batallions: first, her father slain;
Next, your son gone, and he most violent
  author
Of his own just remove; the people mud-   80
  died,
Thick and unwholesome in their thoughts
  and whispers
For good Polonius' death; and we have
  done but greenly
In hugger-mugger to inter him; poor Op-
  helia
Divided from herself and her fair judg-
  ment,
Without the which we are pictures, or
  mere beasts;
Last, and as much containing as all these,
Her brother is in secret come from France,
Feeds on his wonder, keeps himself in
  clouds,
And wants not buzzers to infect his ear
With pestilent speeches of his father's   90
  death,
Wherein necessity, of matter beggared,
Will nothing stick our person to arraign
In ear and ear. O my dear Gertrude, this,
Like to a murdering-piece, in many places
Gives me superfluous death.

  A noise within.

---

37 *larded* decked 41 *'ild* yield, *i.e.,* reward 44
conceit thought 48 *betime* early 52 *dupped*
opened 58 *Gis* Jesus 80 *muddied* confused
82 *greenly* unskilfully 83 *hugger-mugger* surreptitious haste 88 *wonder* uncertainty *in clouds*
secluded 89 *buzzers* those who repeat rumors
92 *nothing stick* hesitate not at all *arraign* accuse 94 *murdering-piece* piece of artillery loaded
so as to scatter its shot.

QUEEN.   Alack, what noise is this?
KING. Where are my Switzers? Let them
    guard the door.

Enter a MESSENGER.

What is the matter?
GENTLEMAN.   Save yourself, my lord;
    The ocean, overpeering of his list,
    Eats not the flats with more impiteous haste
100 Then young Laertes, in a riotous head,
    O'erbears your officers. The rabble call him
        lord,
    And, as the world were now but to begin,
    Antiquity forgot, custom not known,
    The ratifiers and props of every word,
    They cry, "Choose we; Laertes shall be
        king!"
    Caps, hands, and tongues applaud it to the
        clouds,
    "Laertes shall be king, Laertes king!"

A noise within.

QUEEN. How cheerfully on the false trail they
        cry!
    O this is counter, you false Danish dogs!
110 KING. The doors are broke.

Enter LAERTES *with others.*

LAERTES. Where is this king? Sirs, stand you
        all without.
DANES. No, let's come in.
LAERTES.   I pray you, give me leave.
DANES. We will, we will.

[*They retire without the door.*]

LAERTES. I thank you; keep the door. O thou
        vile king,
    Give me my father.
QUEEN.   Calmly, good Laertes.
LAERTES. That drop of blood that's calm pro-
        claims me bastard,

Cries cuckold to my father, brands the
        harlot
Even here between the chaste unsmirchéd
        brow
Of my true mother.
KING.   What is the cause, Laertes,
    That thy rebellion looks so giant-like?   120
Let him go, Gertrude, do not fear our per-
        son;
There's such divinity doth hedge a king,
That treason can but peep to what it would,
Acts little of his will. Tell me, Laertes,
Why thou art thus incensed. Let him go,
        Gertrude.
Speak, man.
LAERTES. Where is my father?
KING.   Dead.
QUEEN.   But not by him.
KING. Let him demand his fill.
LAERTES. How came he dead? I'll not be
        juggled with.
    To hell allegiance, vows to the blackest   130
        devil,
    Conscience and grace to the profoundest
        pit!
    I dare damnation. To this point I stand,
    That both the worlds I give to negligence,
    Let come what comes, only I'll be revenged
    Most throughly for my father.
KING.   Who shall stay you?
LAERTES. My will, not all the world's:
    And for my means, I'll husband them so
        well,
    They shall go far with little.
KING.   Good Laertes,
    If you desire to know the certainty
    Of your dear father's death, is't writ in   140
        your revenge
    That swoopstake you will draw both friend
        and foe,
    Winner and loser?
LAERTES. None but his enemies.
KING.   Will you know them then?
LAERTES. To his good friends thus wide I'll
        ope my arms,

---

96 *Switzers* Swiss guards 98 *overpeering* pressing across *list* boundary 99 *impiteous* pitiless
100 *head* armed band 104 *word* pledge 109
counter following the scent backwards 121 *fear*
fear for 123 *peep* have a glimpse of *would* desires 132 *to this point I stand* I stand firm on
this one thing 133 *both the worlds:* i.e., this and
the next *give to negligence* am indifferent to
135 *throughly* thoroughly 141 *swoopstake* at
random

And, like the kind life-rendering pelican,
Repast them with my blood.
KING.   Why, now you speak
Like a good child and a true gentleman.
That I am guiltless of your father's death,
And am most sensibly in grief for it,
150 It shall as level to your judgment 'pear
As day does to your eye.

[*A noise within*]

                              Let her come in.
LAERTES. How now, what noise is that?

Enter OPHELIA.

O heat, dry up my brains; tears seven-times
salt,
Burn out the sense and virtue of mine eyes!
By heaven, thy madness shall be paid with
weight,
Till our scale turn the beam. O rose of
May,
Dear maid, kind sister, sweet Ophelia!
O heavens, is't possible a young maid's wits
Should be as mortal as an old man's life?
160 Nature is fine in love, and where 'tis fine,
It sends some precious instance of itself
After the thing it loves.
OPHELIA [*sings*]. They bore him barefaced
on the bier,
            (Hey non nonny, nonny,
            hey nonny)
            And in his grave rained
            many a tear—
Fare you well, my dove!
LAERTES. Hadst thou thy wits, and didst per-
suade revenge,
It could not move thus.
OPHELIA. You must sing "A-down a-down,
an you call him a-down-a."
170 O, how the wheel becomes it! It is the false
steward, that stole his master's daughter.
LAERTES. This nothing's more than matter.
OPHELIA. There's rosemary, that's for remem-

brance—pray you, love, remember; and
there is pansies, that's for thoughts.
LAERTES. A document in madness, thoughts
and remembrance fitted.
OPHELIA. There's fennel for you, and colum-
bines; there's rue for you, and here's some
for me—we may call it herb of grace o'
Sundays. O, you must wear your rue with 180
a difference. There's a daisy; I would give
you some violets, but they withered all
when my father died. They say a' made
a good end—
[*Sings.*] For bonny sweet Robin is all my
joy.
LAERTES. Thought and afflictions, passion,
hell itself,
She turns to favor and to prettiness.
OPHELIA [*sings*].
      And will a' not come again?
      And will a' not come again?
        No, no, he is dead;
        Go to thy death-bed;   190
      He never will come again.
      His beard was as white as snow,
      All flaxen was his poll;
        He is gone, he is gone,
        And we cast away moan;
      God ha' mercy on his soul!
And of all Christian souls, I pray God.
God be wi' you.

Exit.

LAERTES. Do you see this, O God?
KING. Laertes, I must commune with your grief,
Or you deny me right. Go but apart,   200
Make choice of whom your wisest friends
you will,
And they shall hear and judge 'twixt you
and me.
If by direct or by collateral hand
They find us touched, we will our kingdom
give,
Our crown, our life, and all that we call
ours,

---

145 *life-rendering:* i.e., because it was supposed to feed its young on its own blood 146 *repast* feed 149 *sensibly* feelingly 156 *beam* ballance 160 *fine* sensitive 161 *instance* token 172 *nothing* nonsense *matter* sense 176 *document* piece of instruction 186 *favor* beauty 193 *poll* head 199 *commune with* share 203 *collateral hand* indirect means 204 *touched* involved

To you in satisfaction; but if not,
Be you content to lend your patience to us,
And we shall jointly labor with your soul
To give it due content.

LAERTES.   Let this be so.
210 His means of death, his obscure funeral,
No trophy, sword, nor hatchment o'er his
   bones,
No noble rite nor formal ostentation,
Cry to be heard, as 'twere from heaven to
   earth,
That I must call't in question.
KING.   So you shall,
And where the offence is let the great axe
   fall.
I pray you, go with me.

Exeunt.

Scene VI

Enter HORATIO *with an* ATTENDANT.

HORATIO. What are they that would speak
   with me?
SERVANT. Seafaring men, sir; they say they
   have letters for you.
HORATIO. Let them come in.

[*Exit* ATTENDANT.]

I do not know from what part of the world
I should be greeted, if not from Lord Hamlet.

Enter SAILORS.

SAILOR. God bless you, sir.
HORATIO. Let him bless thee too.
SAILOR. A' shall, sir, an't please him. There's
10   a letter for you, sir; it came from the ambassador that was bound for England; if
   your name be Horatio, as I am let to know
   it is.
HORATIO [*reads*]. "Horatio, when thou shalt

have overlooked this, give these fellows
some means to the king; they have letters
for him. Ere we were two days old at sea,
a pirate of very warlike appointment gave
us chase. Finding ourselves too slow of sail,
we put on a compelled valor, and in the
grapple I boarded them; on the instant they
got clear of our ship, so I alone became
their prisoner. They have dealt with me
like thieves of mercy, but they knew what   20
they did; I am to do a good turn for them.
Let the king have the letters I have sent,
and repair thou to me with as much speed
as thou wouldest fly death. I have words
to speak in thine ear will make thee dumb,
yet are they much too light for the bore
of the matter. These good fellows will
bring thee where I am. Rosencrantz and
Guildenstern hold their course for England; of them I have much to tell thee.
Farewell.

   He that thou knowest thine, HAMLET."
Come, I will make you way for these your   30
   letters,
And do't the speedier, that you may direct
   me
To him from whom you brought them.

Exeunt.

Scene VII

Enter KING *and* LAERTES.

KING. Now must your conscience my acquit-
   tance seal,
And you must put me in your heart for
   friend,
Sith you have heard, and with a knowing
   ear,
That he which hath your noble father slain
Pursued my life.
LAERTES.   It well appears; but tell me
Why you proceeded not against these feats,
So crimeful and so capital in nature,

---

211 *hatchment* coat of arms 212 *ostentation*
ceremony 213 *cry to be heard* demand explanation 215 *axe: i.e.,* of vengeance 20 *thieves of*
mercy merciful robbers 25 *bore* caliber, *i.e.,* importance 1 *acquittance* acquittal *seal* confirm
6 *feats* deeds

As by your safety, greatness, wisdom, all things else,
You mainly were stirred up.

KING.   O, for two special reasons,
Which may to you perhaps seem much unsinewed,
But yet to me they are strong. The queen his mother
Lives almost by his looks; and for myself—
My virtue or my plague, be't either which—
She is so conjunctive to my life and soul
That, as the star moves not but in his sphere,
I could not but by her. The other motive,
Why to a public count I might not go,
Is the great love the general gender bear him,
Who, dipping all his faults in their affection,
Would, like the spring that turneth wood to stone,
Convert his gyves to graces, so that my arrows,
Too slightly timbered for so loud a wind,
Would have reverted to my bow again,
And not where I had aimed them.

LAERTES. And so have I a noble father lost,
A sister driven into desperate terms,
Whose worth, if praises may go back again,
Stood challenger on mount of all the age
For her perfections; but my revenge will come.

KING. Break not your sleeps for that; you must not think
That we are made of stuff so flat and dull
That we can let our beard be shook with danger
And think it pastime. You shortly shall hear more;
I loved your father, and we love ourself,
And that, I hope, will teach you to imagine—

Enter a MESSENGER *with letters.*

How now! what news?

MESSENGER. Letters, my lord, from Hamlet;
This to your majesty, this to the queen.

KING. From Hamlet? who brought them?

MESSENGER. Sailors, my lord, they say; I saw them not.
They were given me by Claudio; he received them
Of him that brought them.

KING.   Laertes, you shall hear them.
Leave us.

Exit MESSENGER.

[*Reads.*] "High and mighty, You shall know I am set naked on your kingdom. Tomorrow shall I beg leave to see your kingly eyes, when I shall, first asking your pardon thereunto, recount the occasion of my sudden and more strange return.

                    HAMLET."

What should this mean? Are all the rest come back?
Or is it some abuse, and no such thing?

LAERTES. Know you the hand?

KING. 'Tis Hamlet's character. "Naked"—
And in a postscript here, he says "alone."
Can you devise me?

LAERTES. I am lost in it, my lord; but let him come.
It warms the very sickness in my heart
That I shall live and tell him to his teeth,
"Thus diddest thou."

KING.   If it be so, Laertes—
As how should it be so? how otherwise?—
Will you be ruled by me?

LAERTES.   Ay, my lord;
So you will not o'errule me to a peace.

KING. To thine own peace. If he be now returned,
As checking at his voyage, and that he means
No more to undertake it, I will work him
To an exploit, now ripe in my device,
Under the which he shall not choose but fall:
And for his death no wind of blame shall breathe,

---

9 *mainly* powerfully 10 *much unsinewed* very weak 14 *conjunctive* united 17 *count* trial 18 *general gender* common people 21 *gyves* fetters 26 *terms* straits 27 *go back again: i.e.,* to what she once was 28 *on mount* on high 29 *for* to defend 50 *abuse* deceit 51 *character* handwriting 62 *checking at* fighting shy of

But even his mother shall uncharge the
   practice,
And call it accident.

LAERTES.   My lord, I will be ruled;
The rather if you could devise it so
That I might be the organ.

70 KING.   It falls right.
You have been talked of since your travel
   much,
And that in Hamlet's hearing, for a quality
Wherein they say you shine; your sum of
   parts
Did not together pluck such envy from
   him
As did that one, and that, in my regard,
Of the unworthiest siege.

LAERTES.   What part is that, my lord?

KING. A very riband in the cap of youth,
Yet needful too, for youth no less becomes
The light and careless livery that it wears
80 Than settled age his sables and his weeds,
Importing health and graveness. Two
   months since,
Here was a gentleman of Normandy.
I have seen myself, and served against, the
   French,
And they can well on horseback, but this
   gallant
Had witchcraft in't; he grew unto his seat,
And to such wondrous doing brought his
   horse
As he had been incorpsed and demi-na-
   tured
With the brave beast, so far he topped my
   thought
That I, in forgery of shapes and tricks,
Come short of what he did.

90 LAERTES.   A Norman was't?

KING. A Norman.

LAERTES. Upon my life, Lamord.

KING.   The very same.

LAERTES. I know him well; he is the brooch
   indeed

And gem of all the nation.

KING. He made confession of you,
And gave you such a masterly report
For art and exercise in your defence,
And for your rapier most especial,
That he cried out 'twould be a sight indeed
If one could match you; the scrimers of   100
   their nation
He swore had neither motion, guard, nor
   eye,
If you opposed them. Sir, this report of his
Did Hamlet so envenom with his envy,
That he could nothing do but wish and
   beg
Your sudden coming o'er to play with him.
Now, out of this—

LAERTES.   What out of this, my lord?

KING. Laertes, was your father dear to you?
Or are you like the painting of a sorrow,
A face without a heart?

LAERTES.   Why ask you this?

KING. Not that I think you did not love your   110
   father,
But that I know love is begun by time,
And that I see, in passages of proof,
Time qualifies the spark and fire of it.
There lives within the very flame of love
A kind of wick or snuff that will abate it
And nothing is at a like goodness still,
For goodness, growing to a plurisy,
Dies in his own too-much; that we would
   do
We should do when we would, for this
   "would" changes
And hath abatements and delays as many   120
As there are tongues, are hands, are acci-
   dents,
And then this "should" is like a spendthrift
   sigh,
That hurts by easing. But, to the quick
   of the ulcer—
Hamlet comes back; what would you un-
   dertake

---

67 *uncharge* fail to suspect *practice* plot 70
organ instrument 73 *parts* talents 76 *siege*
rank 77 *riband* ornament 78 *becomes* is appropriately clad in 79 *livery* costume 80 *sables*
blacks (or furs) *weeds* garments 87 *incorpsed
and demi-natured* united and made half 88
topped exceeded 89 *forgery* invention, imagination 93 *brooch* ornament 96 *masterly report*

report of mastery or skill 97 *art* skill *exercise*
agility 100 *scrimers* fencers 112 *passages of
proof* incidents which test 113 *qualifies* weak-
ens 115 *snuff* burnt part of the wick 116 *still*
always 117 *plurisy* excess 118 *that* what
123 *hurts by easing* damages while it gives relief
(because sighs were supposed to draw blood from
the heart) *quick* sensitive part

To show yourself in deed your father's son
More than in words?

LAERTES.   To cut his throat i' the church.

KING. No place, indeed, should murder sanc-
tuarize;
Revenge should have no bounds. But, good
Laertes,
Will you do this, keep close within your
chamber.
130 Hamlet returned shall know you are come
home;
We'll put on those shall praise your excel-
lence,
And set a double varnish on the fame
The Frenchman gave you, bring you in
fine together
And wager on your heads. He, being re-
miss,
Most generous, and free from all contriving,
Will not peruse the foils, so that with ease,
Or with a little shuffling, you may choose
A sword unbated, and in a pass of practice
Requite him for your father.

LAERTES.   I will do't,
140 And for that purpose I'll anoint my sword.
I bought an unction of a mountebank,
So mortal, that but dip a knife in it,
Where it draws blood no cataplasm so rare,
Collected from all simples that have virtue,
Under the moon, can save the thing from
death
That is but scratched withal. I'll touch my
point
With this contagion, that, if I gall him
slightly,
It may be death.

KING.   Let's further think of this,
Weigh what convenience both of time and
means
150 May fit us to our shape. If this should fail,
And that our drift look through our bad
performance,
'Twere better not assayed; therefore this
project

Should have a back or second that might
hold
If this should blast in proof. Soft, let me
see;
We'll make a solemn wager on your cun-
nings.
I ha't;
When in your motion you are hot and
dry—
As make your bouts more violent to that
end—
And that he calls for drink, I'll have pre-
ferred him
A chalice for the nonce, whereon but sip- 160
ping,
If he by chance escape your venomed stuck,
Our purpose may hold there.

Enter QUEEN.

                            But stay, what noise?

QUEEN. One woe doth tread upon another's
heel,
So fast they follow; your sister's drowned,
Laertes.

LAERTES. Drowned! O where?

QUEEN. There is a willow grows askant the
brook
That shows his hoary leaves in the glassy
stream;
Therewith fantastic garlands did she make
Of cornflowers, nettles, daisies, and long
purples
That liberal shepherds give a grosser name, 170
But our cold maids do dead men's fingers
call them.
There, on the pendant boughs her crownet
weeds
Clambering to hang, an envious sliver
broke,
When down her weedy trophies and herself
Fell in the weeping brook. Her clothes
spread wide,
And mermaid-like awhile they bore her up,

---

133 *in fine* eventually 135 *contriving* plotting
136 *peruse* scan carefully 138 *unbated* not
blunted 141 *unction* ointment mountebank
pedlar of patent medicines 142 *mortal* deadly
143 *cataplasm* poultice 144 *simples* herbs 146
withal with 147 *gall* scratch 150 *shape* plan
151 *drift* purpose *look* become visible 153

back supporter 154 *blast* come to ruin *in
proof* when put to the test 155 *cunnings* skills
157 *motion* activity 159 *preferred* offered 160
chalice cup *nonce* occasion 161 *stuck* thrust
166 *askant* alongside 172 *pendent* hanging
173 *crownet* coronet *sliver* bough

Which time she chanted snatches of old
lauds,
As one incapable of her own distress,
Or like a creature native and indued
180 Unto that element; but long it could not
be
Till that her garments, heavy with their
drink,
Pulled the poor wretch from her melodious
lay
To muddy death.

LAERTES.   Alas, then, she is drowned?

QUEEN. Drowned, drowned.

LAERTES. Too much of water hast thou, poor
Ophelia,
And therefore I forbid my tears; but yet
It is our trick; nature her custom holds,
Let shame say what it will; when these are
gone,
The woman will be out. Adieu, my lord;
190 I have a speech of fire, that fain would
blaze,
But that this folly douts it.

Exit.

KING.   Let's follow, Gertrude.
How much I had to do to calm his rage!
Now fear I this will give it start again;
Therefore let's follow.

Exeunt.

ACT V

Scene I

Enter two CLOWNS, [*with spades, etc.*]

FIRST CLOWN. Is she to be buried in Christian
burial when she wilfully seeks her own
salvation?

SECOND CLOWN. I tell thee she is; therefore

make her grave straight. The crowner hath
sat on her, and finds it Christian burial.

FIRST CLOWN. How can that be, unless she
drowned herself in her own defence?

SECOND CLOWN. Why, 'tis found so.

FIRST CLOWN. It must be *se offendendo*; it
cannot be else. For here lies the point: if 10
I drown myself wittingly, it argues an act,
and an act hath three branches; it is, to
act, to do, to perform: argal, she drowned
herself wittingly.

SECOND CLOWN. Nay, but hear you, goodman,
delver—

FIRST CLOWN. Give me leave. Here lies the
water—good; here stands the man—good;
if the man go to this water and drown himself, it is, will he nill he, he goes—mark you
that; but if the water come to him and
drown him, he drowns not himself; argal,
he that is not guilty of his own death
shortens not his own life.

SECOND CLOWN. But is this law?   20

FIRST CLOWN. Ay marry, is't—crowner's quest
law.

SECOND CLOWN. Will you ha' the truth on't?
If this had not been a gentlewoman, she
should have been buried out o' Christian
burial.

FIRST CLOWN. Why, there thou say'st; and the
more pity that great folk should have countenance in this world to drown or hang
themselves, more than their even Christian.
Come, my spade; there is no ancient gentlemen but gardeners, ditchers, and grave-
makers—they hold up Adam's profession.   30

SECOND CLOWN. Was he a gentleman?

FIRST CLOWN. A' was the first that ever bore
arms.

SECOND CLOWN. Why, he had none.

FIRST CLOWN. What, art a heathen? How
dost thou understand the Scripture? The
Scripture says Adam digged; could he dig
without arms? I'll put another question to
thee; if thou answerest me not to the purpose, confess thyself—

---

177 *lauds* hymns 178 *incapable* unconscious
179 *indued* accustomed 180 *that element:* i.e.,
water 191 *douts* puts out 4 *straight* immediately *crowner* coroner 9 *se offendendo* a blun-
der for 'se defendendo,' in self-defence 12 *argal*
ergo, therefore 13 *delver* digger 16 *will he nill
he* willy-nilly 21 *quest* inquest 25 *there thou
say'st* there you're saying something 26 *countenance* permission 27 *even* fellow 32 *bore arms*
(a pun) had a coat of arms, the sign of gentle birth

SECOND CLOWN. Go to.

40 FIRST CLOWN. What is he that builds stronger than either the mason, the shipwright, or the carpenter?

SECOND CLOWN. The gallowsmaker, for that frame outlives a thousand tenants.

FIRST CLOWN. I like thy wit well, in good faith; the gallows does well, but how does it well? it does well to those that do ill; now, thou dost ill to say the gallows is built stronger than the church; argal, the gallows may do well to thee. To't again, come.

SECOND CLOWN. "Who builds stronger than a
50 mason, a shipwright, or a carpenter?"

FIRST CLOWN. Ay, tell me that and unyoke.

SECOND CLOWN. Marry, now I can tell.

FIRST CLOWN. To't.

SECOND CLOWN. Mass, I cannot tell.

Enter HAMLET *and* HORATIO *afar off.*

FIRST CLOWN. Cudgel thy brains no more about it, for your dull ass will not mend his pace with beating, and when you are asked this question next, say "a grave-maker;" the houses he makes lasts till doomsday. Go, get thee to Yaughan, and fetch me a stoup of liquor.

[Exit SECOND CLOWN.
He digs, and] sings.

60 In youth when I did love, did love,
  Methought it was very sweet
To contract—O—the time for—a—my behove,
  O—methought there—a—was nothing—a—
  meet.

HAMLET. Has this fellow no feeling of his business, that a' sings in gravemaking?

HORATIO. Custom hath made it in him a property of easiness.

HAMLET. 'Tis e'en so; the hand of little employment hath the daintier sense.

70 FIRST CLOWN. *Sings.* But age with his stealing steps

Hath clawed me in his clutch,
And hath shipped me intil the land,
  As if I had never been such.

[Throws up a skull.]

HAMLET. That skull had a tongue in it, and could sing once; how the knave jowls it to the ground, as if it were Cain's jawbone, that did the first murder! This might be the pate of a politician, which this ass now o'er-reaches; one that would circumvent God, might it not?

HORATIO. It might, my lord.

HAMLET. Or of a courtier, which could say 80 "Good morrow, sweet lord! How dost thou, good lord?" This might be my lord such-a-one, that praised my lord such-a-one's horse, when a' meant to beg it—might it not?

HORATIO. Ay, my lord.

HAMLET. Why, e'en so—and now my Lady Worm's, chapless, and knocked about the mazzard with a sexton's spade; here's fine revolution, and we had the trick to see't. Did these bones cost no more the breeding, but to play at loggats with 'em? mine ache to think on't.

FIRST CLOWN. *Sings.* A pickaxe and a spade, 90
  a spade,
  For and a shrouding-sheet;
O, a pit of clay for to be made
  For such a guest is meet.

[Throws up another skull.]

HAMLET. There's another; why may not that be the skull of a lawyer? Where be his quiddities now, his quillets, his cases, his tenures, and his tricks? why does he suffer this mad knave now to knock him about the sconce with a dirty shovel, and will not tell him of his action of battery? Hum! This fellow might be in's time a great

51 *unyoke* make an end to it 59 *stoup* mug
62 *behove* benefit 63 *meet* fitting 66 *custom* habit *property* characteristic 68 *easiness* indifference 69 *daintier sense* finer feeling 72 *intil* into 75 *jowls* flings 77 *o'er-reaches* gets the better of 86 *chapless* without a jawbone *mazzard* pate 89 *loggats* a game like bowls 95 *quiddities* definitions *quillets* quibbles 96 *tenures* terms of holding land 97 *sconce* skull 99 *battery* assault

100 buyer of land, with his statues, his recognizances, his fines, his double vouchers, his recoveries; is this the fine of his fines, and the recovery of his recoveries, to have his fine pate full of fine dirt? will his vouchers vouch him no more of his purchases, and double ones too, than the length and breadth of a pair of indentures? The very conveyances of his lands will scarcely lie in this box, and must the inheritor himself have no more, ha?

HORATIO. Not a jot more, my lord.

HAMLET. Is not parchment made of sheepskins?

110 HORATIO. Ay, my lord, and of calfskins too.

HAMLET. They are sheep and calves which seek out assurance in that. I will speak to this fellow. Whose grave's this, sirrah?

FIRST CLOWN. Mine, sir.

[*Sings.*] O, a pit of clay for to be made
    For such a guest is meet.

HAMLET. I think it be thine indeed, for thou liest in't.

FIRST CLOWN. You lie out on't, sir, and therefore 'tis not yours; for my part, I do not lie in't, yet it is mine.

120 HAMLET. Thou dost lie in't, to be in't and say it is thine; 'tis for the dead, not for the quick; therefore thou liest.

FIRST CLOWN. 'Tis a quick lie, sir; 'twill away again from me to you.

HAMLET. What man dost thou dig it for?

FIRST CLOWN. For no man, sir.

HAMLET. What woman, then?

FIRST CLOWN. For none, neither.

HAMLET. Who is to be buried in't?

FIRST CLOWN. One that was a woman, sir;
130 but, rest her soul, she's dead.

HAMLET. How absolute the knave is! we must speak by the card, or equivocation will undo us. By the Lord, Horatio, this three years I have took note of it, the age is grown so picked that the toe of the peasant comes so near the heel of the courtier he

galls his kibe. How long hast thou been gravemaker?

FIRST CLOWN. Of all the days i' the year, I came to't that day that our last king Hamlet overcame Fortinbras.

HAMLET. How long is that since?

FIRST CLOWN. Cannot you tell that? every 140 fool can tell that; it was the very day that young Hamlet was born—he that is mad and sent into England.

HAMLET. Ay, marry, why was he sent into England?

FIRST CLOWN. Why, because a' was mad: a' shall recover his wits there or, if a' do not, 'tis no great matter there.

HAMLET. Why?

FIRST CLOWN. 'Twill not be seen in him there; there the men are as mad as he.

HAMLET. How came he mad? 150

FIRST CLOWN. Very strangely, they say.

HAMLET. How strangely?

FIRST CLOWN. Faith, e'en with losing his wits.

HAMLET. Upon what ground?

FIRST CLOWN. Why, here in Denmark: I have been sexton here, man and boy, thirty years.

HAMLET. How long will a man lie i' the earth ere he rot?

FIRST CLOWN. Faith, if a' be not rotten before a' die—as we have many pocky corses now- 160 adays that will scarce hold the laying in— he will last you some eight year or nine year. A tanner will last you nine year.

HAMLET. Why he more than another?

FIRST CLOWN. Why sir, his hide is so tanned with his trade that a' will keep out water a great while; and your water is a sore decayer of your whoreson dead body. Here's a skull now; this skull hath lien yon i' the earth three-and-twenty years.

HAMLET. Whose was it?

FIRST CLOWN. A whoreson mad fellow's it 170 was; whose do you think it was?

HAMLET. Nay, I know not.

100 *statutes and recognizances* two different kinds of bonds 101 *fines . . . double vouchers* various types of procedure for transferring land *fine* end 105 *indentures* legal documents on parchment 106 *conveyances* deeds 111 *seek out assurance* put their trust 118 *out on't* outside it 121 *quick*

living 131 *absolute* positive 132 *by the card* by the compass, precisely *equivocation* double meanings 134 *picked* fastidious 135 *galls his kibe* scrapes the chilblains on his heels 154 *upon what ground* for what cause 160 *pocky* diseased 161 *hold the laying in* last till burial

FIRST CLOWN. A pestilence on him for a mad rogue! a' poured a flagon of Rhenish on my head once. This same skull, sir, was Yorick's skull, the king's jester.

HAMLET. This?

FIRST CLOWN. E'en that.

HAMLET. Let me see. [*Takes the skull.*] Alas, poor Yorick! I knew him, Horatio: a fellow
180 of infinite jest, of most excellent fancy; he hath borne me on his back a thousand times, and now how abhorred in my imagination it is! my gorge rises at it. Here hung those lips that I have kissed I know not how oft. Where be your gibes now? your gambols, your songs, your flashes of merriment that were wont to set the table on a roar? Not one now to mock your own grinning? quite chapfallen? Now get you to my lady's chamber, and tell her, let her paint an inch thick, to this favor she must come; make her laugh at that. Prithee, Horatio, tell me one thing.

190 HORATIO. What's that, my lord?

HAMLET. Dost thou think Alexander looked o' this fashion i' the earth?

HORATIO. E'en so.

HAMLET. And smelt so? pah!

[*Puts down the skull.*]

HORATIO. E'en so, my lord.

HAMLET. To what base uses we may return, Horatio! Why may not imagination trace the noble dust of Alexander till a' find it stopping a bunghole?

HORATIO. 'Twere to consider too curiously to consider so.

200 HAMLET. No, faith, not a jot; but to follow him thither with modesty enough, and likelihood to lead it, as thus: Alexander died, Alexander was buried, Alexander returneth to dust; the dust is earth, of earth we make loam, and why of that loam whereto he was converted might they not stop a beer barrel?

Imperious Cæsar, dead and turned to clay,
Might stop a hole to keep the wind away.
O, that that earth which kept the world in awe
Should patch a wall to expel the winter's flaw!
But soft, but soft awhile; here comes the king, 210

Enter KING, QUEEN, LAERTES, *and a Coffin, with Lords Attendant,* [*a* DOCTOR OF DIVINITY *following.*]

The queen, the courtiers. Who is this they follow?
And with such maiméd rites? This doth betoken
The corse they follow did with desperate hand
Fordo it own life; 'twas of some estate.
Couch we awhile, and mark.

[*Retiring with* HORATIO.]

LAERTES. What ceremony else?

HAMLET.   That is Laertes,
A very noble youth; mark.

LAERTES. What ceremony else?

DOCTOR. Her obsequies have been as far enlarged
As we have warranty. Her death was 220 doubtful
And, but that great command o'ersways the order,
She should in ground unsanctified have lodged
Till the last trumpet; for charitable prayers,
Shards, flints and pebbles should be thrown on her:
Yet here she is allowed her virgin crants,
Her maiden strewments, and the bringing home
Of bell and burial.

LAERTES. Must there no more be done?

DOCTOR.   No more be done.

---

174 Rhenish Rhine wine *186 chapfallen* (1) jawless (2) dejected *188 favor* appearance *201 modesty* moderation *212 maiméd rites* incomplete ceremonial *214 fordo* destroy *estate* rank *215 couch* hide *220 have warranty* are permitted *doubtful* uncertain *221 great command:* i.e., that of the King *o'ersways* overrules *223 for* instead of *224 shards* broken pottery *225 crants* garland *226 strewments* strewing of flowers on the grave *bringing home* laying to rest

230 We should profane the service of the dead
To sing a requiem and such rest to her
As to peace-parted souls.
LAERTES.   Lay her i' the earth,
And from her fair and unpolluted flesh
May violets spring! I tell thee, churlish
    priest,
A ministering angel shall my sister be,
When thou liest howling.
HAMLET.   What, the fair Ophelia!
QUEEN. Sweets to the sweet; farewell!

        [*Scattering flowers*]

I hoped thou shouldst have been my Ham-
    let's wife;
I thought thy bride-bed to have decked,
    sweet maid,
And not have strewed thy grave.
LAERTES.   O, treble woe
240 Fall ten times treble on that curséd head
Whose wicked deed thy most ingenious
    sense
Deprived thee of! Hold off the earth awhile,
Till I have caught her once more in mine
    arms;

        Leaps in the grave.

Now pile your dust upon the quick and
    dead,
Till of this flat a mountain you have made
To o'ertop old Pelion or the skyish head
Of blue Olympus.
HAMLET [*advancing*]. What is he whose grief
Bears such an emphasis, whose phrase of
    sorrow
Conjures the wandering stars and makes
    them stand
250 Like wonder-wounded hearers? This is I,
Hamlet the Dane.

        Leaps in after LAERTES.

LAERTES.   The devil take thy soul!

[*Grappling with him.*]

HAMLET. Thou pray'st not well.
I prithee take thy fingers from my throat,
For, though I am not splenitive and rash,
Yet have I in me something dangerous,
Which let thy wisdom fear. Hold off thy
    hand!
KING. Pluck them asunder.
QUEEN.   Hamlet, Hamlet!
ALL. Gentlemen—
HORATIO.   Good my lord, be quiet.

        [*The Attendants part them, and they
        come out of the grave.*]

HAMLET. Why, I will fight with him upon
    this theme
Until my eyelids will no longer wag.   260
QUEEN. O my son, what theme?
HAMLET. I loved Ophelia; forty thousand
    brothers
Could not with all their quantity of love
Make up my sum. What wilt thou do for
    her?
KING. O, he is mad, Laertes.
QUEEN. For love of God, forbear him.
HAMLET. 'Swounds, show me what thou'lt do:
Woo't weep? woo't fight? woo't fast? woo't
    tear thyself?
Woo't drink up eisel? eat a crocodile?
I'll do't. Dost thou come here to whine,   270
To outface me with leaping in her grave?
Be buried quick with her, and so will I:
And if thou prate of mountains, let them
    throw
Millions of acres on us, till our ground,
Singeing his pate against the burning zone,
Make Ossa like a wart! Nay, an thou'lt
    mouth,
I'll rant as well as thou.
QUEEN.   This is mere madness:
And thus awhile the fit will work on him;
Anon, as patient as the female dove
When that her golden couplets are dis-   280
    closed,

---

241 *sense* senses 244 *quick* living 246 *Pelion
. . . Olympus* (according to the Greek legend,
the Titans piled Mt. Pelion on Mt. Ossa in their
attempt to storm Mt. Olympus) 254 *splenitive*
excitable 266 *forbear him* leave him alone 269
eisel vinegar 271 *outface* outdo 280 *couplets*
twins *disclosed* hatched

His silence will sit drooping.
HAMLET.   Hear you, sir;
What is the reason that you use me thus?
I loved you ever: but it is no matter;
Let Hercules himself do what he may,
The cat will mew, and the dog will have
    his day.

Exit.

KING. I pray you, good Horatio, wait upon
    him.

Exit HORATIO.

[*To* LAERTES] Strengthen your patience in
    our last night's speech;
We'll put the matter to the present push.
Good Gertrude, set some watch over your
    son.
290 This grave shall have a living monument:
An hour of quiet shortly shall we see;
Till then, in patience our proceeding be.

Exeunt.

Scene II

Enter HAMLET *and* HORATIO.

HAMLET. So much for this, sir; now shall you
    see the other.
You do remember all the circumstance?
HORATIO. Remember it, my lord!
HAMLET. Sir, in my heart there was a kind
    of fighting
That would not let me sleep; methought
    I lay
Worse than the mutines in the bilboes.
    Rashly,
And praised be rashness for it—let us know
Our indiscretion sometimes serves us well
When our deep plots do pall, and that
    should learn us

There's a divinity that shapes our ends,   10
Rough-hew them how we will—
HORATIO.   That is most certain.
HAMLET. Up from my cabin,
My sea-gown scarfed about me, in the dark
Groped I to find out them, had my desire,
Fingered their packet, and in fine withdrew
To mine own room again, making so bold,
My fears forgetting manners, to unseal
Their grand commission; where I found,
    Horatio—
O royal knavery!—an exact command,
Larded with many several sorts of reasons,   20
Importing Denmark's health and England's
    too,
With, ho! such bugs and goblins in my life,
That on the supervise, no leisure bated,
No, not to stay the grinding of the axe,
My head should be struck off.
HORATIO.   Is't possible?
HAMLET. Here's the commission; read it at
    more leisure.
But wilt thou hear now how I did proceed?
HORATIO. I beseech you.
HAMLET. Being thus benetted round with val-
    lanies—
Or I could make a prologue to my brains,   30
They had begun the play—I sat me down,
Devised a new commission, wrote it fair;
I once did hold it, as our statists do,
A baseness to write fair, and labored much
How to forget that learning, but, sir, now
It did me yeoman's service; wilt thou know
The effect of what I wrote?
HORATIO.   Ay, good my lord.
HAMLET. An earnest conjuration from the king,
As England was his faithful tributary
As love between them like the palm might   40
    flourish,
As peace should still her wheaten garland
    wear
And stand a comma 'tween their amities,
And many such-like "as'es" of great charge,
That, on the view and knowing of these
    contents,

---

288 *present push* immediate test 6 *mutines*
mutineers *bilboes* irons 9 *pall* fail 15 *fine*
conclusion 20 *larded* adorned 21 *importing*
concerning 22 *bugs* bugbears 23 *supervise*
perusal *bated* subtracted 30 *or* ere, before 33

statists statesmen 36 *yeoman's service* sturdy
service 38 *conjuration* exhortation 39 *tributary*
vassal 42 *comma* connecting link 43 *charge*
force

Without debatement further, more or less,
He should the bearers put to sudden death,
Not shriving-time allowed.

HORATIO.   How was this sealed?

HAMLET. Why, even in that was heaven or-
    dinant.
  I had my father's signet in my purse,
50 Which was the model of that Danish seal;
  Folded the writ up in the form of the other,
  Subscribed it, gave't the impression, placed
    it safely,
  The changeling never known. Now, the
    next day
  Was our seafight, and what to this was
    sequent
  Thou know'st already.

HORATIO. So Guildenstern and Rosencrantz
    go to't.

HAMLET. Why, man, they did make love to
    this employment;
  They are not near my conscience; their
    defeat
  Does by their own insinuation grow;
60 'Tis dangerous when the baser nature comes
  Between the pass and fell incensèd points
  Of mighty opposites.

HORATIO.   Why, what a king is this!

HAMLET. Does it not, think thee, stand me
    now upon—
  He that hath killed my king, and whored
    my mother,
  Popped in between the election and my
    hopes,
  Thrown out his angle for my proper life,
  And with such cozenage—is't not perfect
    conscience
  To quit him with this arm? and is't not to
    be damned
  To let this canker of our nature come
70 In further evil?

HORATIO. It must be shortly known to him
    from England
  What is the issue of the business there.

HAMLET. It will be short; the interim is mine,

And a man's life's no more than to say
  "one."
But I am very sorry, good Horatio,
That to Laertes I forgot myself;
For, by the image of my cause, I see
The portraiture of his; I'll court his favors;
But sure the bravery of his grief did put me
Into a towering passion.

HORATIO.   Peace, who comes here?   80

Enter young OSRIC, *a courtier.*

OSRIC. Your lordship is right welcome back to
  Denmark.

HAMLET. I humbly thank you, sir. [*Aside to*
  HORATIO.] Dost know this water-fly?

HORATIO. [*aside to* HAMLET]. No, my good lord.

HAMLET [*aside to* HORATIO]. Thy state is the
  more gracious, for 'tis a vice to know him.
  He hath much land, and fertile: let a beast
  be lord of beasts, and his crib shall stand
  at the king's mess; 'tis a chough, but, as I
  say, spacious in the possession of dirt.

OSRIC. Sweet lord, if your lordship were at   90
  leisure, I should impart a thing to you
  from his majesty.

HAMLET. I will receive it, sir, with all dili-
  gence of spirit. Put your bonnet to his
  right use; 'tis for the head.

OSRIC. I thank your lordship, it is very hot.

HAMLET. No, believe me, 'tis very cold; the
  wind is northerly.

OSRIC. It is indifferent cold, my lord, indeed.

HAMLET. But yet methinks it is very sultry
  and hot, or my complexion—

OSRIC. Exceedingly, my lord; it is very sultry—
  as 'twere—I cannot tell how. But, my lord,   100
  his majesty bade me signify to you, that a'
  has laid a great wager on your head; sir,
  this is the matter—

HAMLET. I beseech you, remember—

[HAMLET *motions him to put on his
  hat.*]

---

47 *shriving-time* time for confession 48 *ordinant*
propitious 52 *subscribed* signed *impression* (of
the seal) 54 *sequent* subsequent 58 *defeat*
destruction 59 *insinuation* intrusion 60 *baser*
of lower rank 61 *pass* thrust *fell* fierce 63
does it not . . . stand me now upon am I not now

obliged 66 *angle* fishing-line *proper* own 67
cozenage deceit *conscience* justice 68 *quit*
repay 69 *canker* cancer 73 *interim* time between 78 *portraiture* picture, portrayal 79 *bravery* display, ostentation 88 *mess* table *chough*
jackdaw 96 *indifferent* moderately

OSRIC. Nay, good my lord; for my ease, in good faith. Sir, here is newly come to court Laertes; believe me, an absolute gentleman, full of most excellent differences, of very soft society and great showing: indeed, to speak feelingly of him, he is the card or calendar of gentry, for you shall find in him the continent of what parts a gentleman would see.

HAMLET. Sir, his definement suffers no perdition in you, though I know to divide him inventorially would dizzy the arithmetic of memory, and yet but yaw neither, in respect of his quick sail. But, in the verity of extolment, I take him to be a soul of great article, and his infusion of such dearth and rareness as, to make true diction of him, his semblance is his mirror, and who else would trace him, his umbage, nothing more.

OSRIC. Your lordship speaks most infallibly of him.

HAMLET. The concernancy, sir? why do we wrap the gentleman in our more rawer breath?

OSRIC. Sir?

HORATIO. Is't not possible to understand in another tongue? You will to't, sir, really.

HAMLET. What imports the nomination of this gentleman?

OSRIC. Of Laertes?

HORATIO. His purse is empty already; all's golden words are spent.

HAMLET. Of him, sir.

OSRIC. I know you are not ignorant—

HAMLET. I would you did, sir; yet, in faith, if you did, it would not much approve me; well, sir.

OSRIC. You are not ignorant of what excellence Laertes is—

HAMLET. I dare not confess that, lest I should compare with him in excellence; but to know a man well were to know himself.

OSRIC. I mean, sir, for his weapon; but in the imputation laid on him by them, in his meed he's unfellowed.

HAMLET. What's his weapon?

OSRIC. Rapier and dagger.

HAMLET. That's two of his weapons; but, well.

OSRIC. The king, sir, hath wagered with him six Barbary horses, against the which he has impawned, as I take it, six French rapiers and poniards, with their assigns, as girdle, hangers, and so. Three of the carriages, in faith, are very dear to fancy, very responsive to the hilts, most delicate carriages, and of very liberal conceit.

HAMLET. What call you the carriages?

HORATIO. I knew you must be edified by the margent ere you had done.

OSRIC. The carriages, sir, are the hangers.

HAMLET. The phrase would be more germane to the matter, if we could carry a cannon by our sides; I would it might be hangers till then. But, on: six Barbary horses against six French swords, their assigns, and three liberal-conceited carriages; that's the French bet against the Danish. Why is this "impawned," as you call it?

OSRIC. The king, sir, hath laid, sir, that in a dozen passes between yourself and him, he shall not exceed you three hits; he hath laid on twelve for nine, and it would come to immediate trial, if your lordship would vouch-safe the answer.

HAMLET. How if I answer no?

OSRIC. I mean, my lord, the opposition of your person in trial.

HAMLET. Sir, I will walk here in the hall. If

106 *differences* accomplishments 107 *of very soft society* pleasant company *great showing* fine appearance 108 *card or calendar* pattern *gentry* gentlemanliness 109 *continent* sum total *parts* good qualities 111 *definement* description *perdition* loss 112 *divide him inventorially* make a list of his qualities 113 *arithmetic* reckoning power *but* only *yaw* fail to hold its course, *i.e.,* come short of the mark 114 *in the verity of extolment* to praise him accurately 115 *article* scope *infusion* character 116 *dearth* scarcity *make true diction* speak truly 117 *semblable* resemblance, equal 118 *trace* copy *umbrage*

shadow 120 *concernancy* purport 121 *rawer* cruder 125 *nomination* mention 132 *approve me* be to my advantage 134 *compare with* rival 137 *imputation* reputation 138 *meed* desert *unfellowed* unequalled 143 *impawned* staked 144 *assigns* appurtenances 145 *carriages* hangers 146 *dear* pleasing *fancy* taste *responsive* well-matched 147 *liberal conceit* elegant design 149 *edified* instructed *margent* marginal note 152 *germane* suitable 153 *cannon* (Hamlet is referring to 'gun-carriages') 160 *laid* stipulated *for* instead of 167 *breathing* exercise

110

120

130

140

150

160

it please his majesty, it is the breathing
time of day with me. Let the foils be
brought, the gentleman willing, and the
king hold his purpose, I will win for him
170   an I can; if not, I will gain nothing but my
shame and the odd hits.

OSRIC. Shall I redeliver you e'en so?

HAMLET. To this effect, sir; after what flourish your nature will.

OSRIC. I commend my duty to your lordship.

HAMLET. Yours, yours. [*Exit* OSRIC.] He does
well to commend it himself; there are no
tongues else for's turn.

HORATIO. This lapwing runs away with the
shell on his head.

180   HAMLET. A' did comply with his dug before
a' sucked it. Thus has he—and many more
of the same bevy that I know the drossy age
dotes on—only got the tune of the time and,
out of an habit of encounter, a kind of
yesty collection, which carries them
through and through the most fanned and
winnowed opinions, and do but blow them
to their trial, the bubbles are out.

    Enter a LORD.

LORD. My lord, his majesty commended him
to you by young Osric, who brings back
to him that you attend him in the hall; he
sends to know if your pleasure hold to play
with Laertes, or that you will take longer
time.

190   HAMLET. I am constant to my purposes; they
follow the king's pleasure; if his fitness
speaks, mine is ready, now or whensoever,
provided I be so able as now.

LORD. The king and queen and all are coming down.

HAMLET. In happy time.

LORD. The queen desires you to use some
gentle entertainment to Laertes before you
fall to play.

HAMLET. She well instructs me.

    [*Exit* LORD.]

HORATIO. You will lose this wager, my lord.

HAMLET. I do not think so; since he went
into France, I have been in continual prac-   200
tice; I shall win at the odds. But thou
wouldst not think how ill all's here about
my heart—but it is no matter.

HORATIO. Nay, good my lord—

HAMLET. It is but foolery, but it is such a kind
of gain-giving as would perhaps trouble a
woman.

HORATIO. If your mind dislike anything, obey
it; I will forestall their repair hither, and
say you are not fit.

HAMLET. Not a whit, we defy augury. There
is special providence in the fall of a sparrow. If it be now, 'tis not to come; if it be
not to come, it will be now; if it be not   210
now, yet it will come—the readiness is all.
Since no man has aught of what he leaves,
what is't to leave betimes? Let be.

    *A table prepared with flagons of wine
    on it. Trumpets and drums. [Enter]
    officers with cushions. Then enter* KING,
    QUEEN, [OSRIC] *and all the state. Foils
    and daggers [brought in]. [Then enter]*
    LAERTES.

KING. Come, Hamlet, come and take this hand
from me.

    [*The* KING *puts* LAERTES' *hand into*
    HAMLET's.]

HAMLET. Give me your pardon, sir. I have
done you wrong,
But pardon't, as you are a gentleman.
This presence knows,
And you must needs have heard, how I am
punished
With sore distraction. What I have done
That might your nature, honor and ex-   220
ception
Roughly awake, I here proclaim was mad-
ness.

171 *redeliver you* take back your reply   177 *lapwing* a bird said to be able to run as soon as
it was hatched   179 *comply* compliment   181
drossy degenerate   182 *encounter* formal greeting   *yesty* frothy   183 *carries them through*
makes them impress   184 *fanned and winnowed*
experienced   195 *entertainment* greeting, welcome   204 *gain-giving* misgiving   207 *repair*
coming   213 *betimes* early   217 *this presence*
those present   220 *exception* objection

Was't Hamlet wronged Laertes? never
   Hamlet.
If Hamlet from himself be ta'en away,
And when he's not himself does wrong
   Laertes,
Then Hamlet does it not, Hamlet denies it.
Who does it then? his madness. If't be so,
Hamlet is of the faction that is wronged;
His madness is poor Hamlet's enemy.
Sir, in this audience,
230 Let my disclaiming from a purposed evil
Free me so far in your most generous
   thoughts,
That I have shot my arrow o'er the house,
And hurt my brother.
LAERTES.   I am satisfied in nature,
Whose motive, in this case, should stir me
   most
To my revenge; but in my terms of honor
I stand aloof, and will no reconcilement
Till by some elder masters of known honor
I have a voice and precedent of peace
To keep my name ungored. But till that
   time
240 I do receive your offered love like love,
And will not wrong it.
HAMLET.   I embrace it freely,
And will this brother's wager frankly play.
Give us the foils. Come on.
LAERTES.   Come, one for me.
HAMLET. I'll be your foil, Laertes; in mine ig-
   norance
Your skill shall, like a star i' the darkest
   night,
Stick fiery off indeed.
LAERTES.   You mock me, sir.
HAMLET. No, by this hand.
KING. Give them the foils, young Osric. Cou-
   sin Hamlet,
You know the wager?
HAMLET.   Very well, my lord;
250 Your grace has laid the odds o' the weaker
   side.
KING. I do not fear it; I have seen you both;
But since he's bettered, we have therefore
   odds.

LAERTES. This is too heavy; let me see another.
HAMLET. This likes me well. These foils have
   all a length?

   Prepare to play.

OSRIC. Ay, my good lord.
KING. Set me the stoups of wine upon that
   table.
If Hamlet give the first or second hit,
Or quit in answer of the third exchange,
Let all the battlements their ordnance fire;
The king shall drink to Hamlet's better 260
   breath,
And in the cup an union shall he throw
Richer than that which four successive
   kings
In Denmark's crown have worn. Give me
   the cups,
And let the kettle to the trumpet speak,
The trumpet to the cannoneer without,
The cannons to the heavens, the heaven to
   earth,
"Now the king drinks to Hamlet." Come,
   begin;
And you, the judges, bear a wary eye.

   Trumpets the while.

HAMLET. Come on, sir.
LAERTES.   Come, my lord.

   They play.

HAMLET.   One.
LAERTES.   No.
HAMLET.   Judgment.
OSRIC. A hit, a very palpable hit.

   *Drums; flourish of trumpets; a piece
   goes off.*

LAERTES.   Well; again. 270
KING. Stay, give me drink. Hamlet, this pearl
   is thine;

---

227 *of the faction* on the side   233 *in nature: i.e.,*
as a son 239 *ungored* uninjured 244 *foil*
something that sets off another by contrast 246

stick fiery off stand out brilliantly 256 *stoups*
goblets 258 *quit in answer of* score a hit in
261 *union* pearl 264 *kettle* kettledrum

Here's to thy health. Give him the cup.

HAMLET. I'll play this bout first; set it by awhile.

Come. [*They play.*] Another hit; what say you?

LAERTES. A touch, a touch, I do confess't.

KING. Our son shall win.

QUEEN.   He's fat, and scant of breath.
Here, Hamlet, take my napkin, rub thy brows;
The queen carouses to thy fortune, Hamlet.

HAMLET. Good madam!

KING.   Gertrude, do not drink.

280 QUEEN. I will, my lord; I pray you, pardon me.

   [*Drinks.*]

KING [*aside*]. It is the poisoned cup; it is too late.

HAMLET. I dare not drink yet, madam; by and by.

QUEEN. Come, let me wipe thy face.

LAERTES. My lord, I'll hit him now.

KING.   I do not think't.

LAERTES [*aside*]. And yet it is almost against my conscience.

HAMLET. Come, for the third, Laertes, you but dally;
I pray you, pass with your best violence;
I am afeared you make a wanton of me.

LAERTES. Say you so? come on.

   Play.

290 OSRIC. Nothing, neither way.

LAERTES. Have at you now!

[*Laertes wounds* HAMLET; *then*] *in scuffling, they change rapiers,* [*and* HAMLET *wounds* LAERTES.]

KING.   Part them; they are incensed.

HAMLET. Nay, come, again.

   The QUEEN *falls.*

OSRIC.   Look to the queen there, ho!

HORATIO. They bleed on both sides. How is it, my lord?

OSRIC. How is't, Laertes?

LAERTES. Why, as a woodcock to mine own springe,
Osric; I am justly killed with mine own treachery.

HAMLET. How does the queen?

KING.   She swoons to see them bleed.

QUEEN. No, no, the drink, the drink—O my dear Hamlet—
The drink, the drink!—I am poisoned.

   [*Dies.*]

HAMLET. O villany! Ho! let the door be 300 locked;
Treachery! seek it out.

LAERTES. It is here, Hamlet; Hamlet, thou art slain;
No medicine in the world can do thee good,
In thee there is not half an hour of life;
The treacherous instrument is in thy hand,
Unbated and envenomed. The foul practice
Hath turned itself on me; lo, here I lie,
Never to rise again. Thy mother's poisoned.
I can no more; the king, the king's to blame.

HAMLET. The point envenomed too! 310
Then, venom, to thy work.

   Hurts the KING.

ALL. Treason! treason!

KING. O yet defend me, friends; I am but hurt.

HAMLET. Here, thou incestuous, murderous, damnéd Dane,
Drink off this potion; is thy union here?
Follow my mother.

   KING *dies.*

LAERTES.   He is justly served;
It is a poison tempered by himself.

276 *fat* sweaty *scant* short 288 *wanton* spoilt child 295 *woodcock* the silliest of all birds *springe* snare 306 *unbated* unblunted *practice* plot

Exchange forgiveness with me, noble Hamlet;

Mine and my father's death come not upon thee,

320 Nor thine on me!

Dies.

HAMLET. Heaven make thee free of it! I follow thee.

I am dead, Horatio. Wretched queen, adieu!

You that look pale and tremble at this chance,

That are but mutes or audience to this act,

Had I but time—as this fell sergeant, death,

Is strict in his arrest—O, I could tell you—

But let it be.—Horatio, I am dead,

Thou livest; report me and my cause aright

To the unsatisfied.

HORATIO.   Never believe it;

330 I am more an antique Roman than a Dane.

Here's yet some liquor left.

HAMLET.   As thou'rt a man,

Give me the cup. Let go; by heaven, I'll have't.

O good Horatio, what a wounded name,

Things standing thus unknown, shall live behind me!

If thou didst ever hold me in thy heart,

Absent thee from felicity awhile,

And in this harsh world draw thy breath in pain

To tell my story.

March afar off, and shout within.

What warlike noise is this?

OSRIC. Young Fortinbras, with conquest come from Poland,

340 To the ambassadors of England gives

This warlike volley.

HAMLET.   O, I die, Horatio;

The potent poison quite o'er-crows my spirit;

I cannot live to hear the news from England,

But I do prophesy the election lights

On Fortinbras; he has my dying voice;

So tell him, with the occurrents, more and less,

Which have solicited—the rest is silence.

Dies.

HORATIO. Now cracks a noble heart; good night, sweet prince,

And flights of angels sing thee to thy rest!

Why does the drum come hither?   350

Enter FORTINBRAS, *the* ENGLISH AMBASSADORS *with drum, colors, and Attendants.*

FORTINBRAS. Where is this sight?

HORATIO.   What is it you would see?

If aught of woe or wonder, cease your search.

FORTINBRAS. This quarry cries on havoc. O proud Death,

What feast is toward in thin eternal cell,

That thou so many princes at a shot

So bloodily hast struck?

FIRST AMBASSADOR.   The sight is dismal,

And our affairs from England come too late;

The ears are senseless that should give us hearing,

To tell him his commandment is fulfilled,

That Rosencrantz and Guildenstern are   360
dead;

Where should we have our thanks?

HORATIO.   Not from his mouth,

Had it the ability of life to thank you;

He never gave commandment for their death.

But since, so jump upon this bloody question,

You from the Polack wars, and you from England,

Are here arrived, give order that these bodies

---

325 *sergeant* a sheriff's officer 342 *o'er-crows* overcomes 345 *voice* vote 346 *occurrents* occurrences 347 *solicited* prompted (this) 353 *quarry* heap of dead *cries* proclaims *havoc* slaughter 364 *jump* exactly *question* affair 367 *stage* platform

High on a stage be placéd to the view,
And let me speak to the yet unknowing
   world
How these things came about; so shall you
   hear
370   Of carnal, bloody and unnatural acts,
Of accidental judgments, casual slaughters,
Of deaths put on by cunning and forced
   cause,
And, in this upshot, purposes mistook
Fall'n on the inventors' heads: all this
   can I
Truly deliver.
FORTINBRAS. Let us haste to hear it,
And call the noblest to the audience.
For me, with sorrow I embrace my fortune;
I have some rights of memory in this king-
   dom,
Which now to claim my vantage doth in-
   vite me.
380   HORATIO. Of that I shall have also cause to
   speak,
And from his mouth whose voice will draw
   on more;
But let this same be presently performed,
Even while men's minds are wild; lest more
   mischance
On plots and errors happen.
FORTINBRAS.   Let four captains
Bear Hamlet like a soldier to the stage,
For he was likely, had he been put on,
To have proved most royally; and for his
   passage
The soldiers' music and the rites of war
Speak loudly for him.
Take up the bodies; such a sight as this   390
Becomes the field, but here shows much
   amiss.
Go bid the soldiers shoot.

*Exeunt marching; after the which, a
peal of ordnance are shot off.*

371 *casual* chance 372 *put on* brought about
378 *of memory* not forgotten 379 *vantage* opportunity 382 *presently* immediately 383 *wild*
disturbed 384 *on* over and above

◆ *from* Trial by Time: *Electra*

By CEDRIC H. WHITMAN

Sophocles' drama of *Electra* has always been the great enigma. Critics like Jebb, and others who accredit Sophocles with various forms of religious orthodoxy, have been seriously embarrassed in their attempts to explain the moral attitude of this amazing piece. The story of how Electra and Orestes avenged the murder of their father by slaying their mother was followed, as everyone knew, by the story of Orestes' consequent madness and pursuit by the Furies, until he was finally purified of his guilt in the court of the Areopagus at Athens. What did Sophocles mean by allowing his Orestes to do the dreadful deed scot-free, as if it were something admirable? The characters are drawn in such a way that the hero, or at least the heroine, could be treated as guilty of all manner of breaches of sophrosyne; * all the usual "faults" appear. But even the closest adherents of the hamartia theory † are peculiarly lacking in suggestions about a play whose heroine, however stubborn or extreme she may be, gets everything she wants, murders her mother, and goes off in triumph. There is not the sign or hint of a Fury; Orestes is a stainless hero, and the play has been scornfully called a "mixture of matricide and good spirits."

Nothing could be further from the truth. The classic assumptions about Sophocles nowhere reveal their fallacy and sterility so completely as they do in the case of the *Electra*. Some have tried to read the Furies into the play, or claim that Sophocles thought any crime was justified if it was commanded by a god. Others, in a reckless confusion as to what Sophocles was pious about, maintain that he was too religious to change a sacred myth. Anthropologists speculate on the relative importance of mothers and fathers in early Greece, and arrive at different answers. Some call the play art for art's sake and drop the moral issue. Finally, there are those who, feeling the need for sin and punishment in a tragedy, deflect the tragic essence from Electra to Clytaemnestra, as Creon in the *Antigone* is sometimes regarded as the tragic hero, because it is he who has been wrong and comes to final grief. But whereas Creon can perhaps claim a little sympathy at the end, the characters of Clytaemnestra and Aegisthus are of such manifest and unrelieved blackness that one must recall the truism of Aristotle, that there is nothing tragic in seeing a thorough villain get his just deserts. Indeed, Aristotle's observation is especially *à propos*. For if the *Electra* is rightly to be called a tragedy —and no other name suits its strained and weary atmosphere so aptly—its tragic core must not be sought in the matricide, which for Sophocles was not the climax but merely the denouement.

When this play was produced, Aeschylus had been dead perhaps forty years, and his *Oresteia* was already a classic monument in the religious and cultural history of Athens. For in that trilogy, Athens had, perhaps for the first time, stepped in her own person, as it were, upon the tragic stage, and in her favorite role of defender and dispenser of justice. Whoever should write again the story of Orestes would have to remember that the intense scenes of the *Choephori*‡ were unforgettably imbedded in the minds of his audience. No one could have known better than Sophocles did that Aeschylus, though a little stiff at times, a little archaic and ritualistic in his approach to the drama, was possessed of an incomparable dramatic genius; the archaic style was not merely a prelude to the achievement of the Periclean times, but complete in itself, an early efflorescence, but as Aeschylus left it, perfect. So far as the tragedy of Orestes went, the *Choephori* could hardly be im-

Cedric H. Whitman, "Trial by Time: Electra," *Sophocles: A Study in Heroic Humanism*, (Cambridge, Mass.: Harvard University Press, 1951), pp. 153–163.

* *sophrosyne* integration and harmony of character.

† *hamartia theory* the theory of the tragic flaw, either a moral weakness or an error of judgment or both, a distinction on which Aristotle is vague.

‡ *Choephori* the second play of the *Oresteia* trilogy by Aeschylus.

proved. There was the prologue, with the sorrowful prayer of Orestes at the neglected tomb of Agamemnon, the meeting between Electra and Orestes, and the great moment when mother and son face each other, when Orestes wavers a moment and Pylades, recalling the god's injunction, pronounces his one utterance and decides the issue. Finally, there is the last speech of Orestes, when the Furies are coming and the web of bloodshed and misery seems to stretch interminably into the future. It is all complete; the rest is lyric and invocation of the thirsty spirit of the murdered king, where the roots of the poetry go deeply into the ancient chthonian * substratum of Greek religion, seeking the moral impetus by which Clytaemnestra and her paramour shall die.

Sophocles never intended to supplant this masterpiece, or "correct" it with a more civilized version, such as Euripides wrote. Why, then, did he write a play about Orestes at all, when the perfect one was already written? The answer is, he did not; he wrote a play about Electra, who does little more than appear in Aeschylus. He begins indeed with Orestes, but in what a different spirit! Instead of the lonely exile, returning with his only friend to the tomb of his slain father, the Orestes of Sophocles enters before the palace in a bright, clear atmosphere, accompanied not only by Pylades, but also by his old Pedagogue who introduces him to the landmarks of his homeland, whence he had been sent in infancy by Electra, to escape the hands of Aegisthus and Clytaemnestra. It is early morning, the birds are singing, and Orestes is full of confidence and hope, anxious to do the deed of deliverance; only after planning his vengeance in detail does he mention the tomb of Agamemnon. Orestes has come not to suffer, but to triumph. He is singularly free of any emotional involvement with the situation and views it like a stranger or a god. The Pedagogue too is significant, for he is a visible symbol of the young hero's *paideia*, his training for greatness. In a few lines Orestes is depicted, chivalrous and noble, with no problem and no special dramatic interest; he retires shortly and remains away until he is needed. He is so unlike the rest of the play in tone and character that it

seems almost as if Sophocles conceived him as a sort of frame for Electra, who is the real tragic picture; the frame is formal and chaste and does not partake of the colors of the picture, but only emphasizes them, as a frame should do. Orestes hears Electra's voice briefly in the beginning, and in the end he meets and consoles her. But he is scatheless and outside all the evil, and obviously more a symbol than a character.

The contrast of Electra's entrance is a carefully designed shock. After the calm air of Orestes and his friends, there suddenly appears the tortured and lonely figure, who chants a long monody in restless meter, and calls the "holy light" to witness her agony. Electra and Orestes are ill-matched by the standards set by Aeschylus, who unites sister and brother in grief and vengeance. Sophocles' Electra is alone, and when she is finally allowed to meet her brother, Sophocles devises the scene with characteristic subtlety, so that it resembles less the meeting of two people with a common cause than the meeting of a person with an image of an unexpected inner self. In any case, what here in the prologue is intense contrast becomes later in the recognition scene a mysterious revelation. Orestes does not join Electra in her suffering, but she rather is able to join him in his strength and victory.

The lyric dirge, which, consistently with the plastic style of the later drama, supplants the more formal parodos † of the chorus, allows us to gain direct insight into the soul of Electra before her scene with her sister, Chrysothemis, in which she appears in a harsher and less sympathetic light. In these lyric portions we see her from within, as she seems to herself, pouring out her faithfulness to her father's memory, her hatred of Aegisthus and Clytaemenestra, her passionate adherence to her own anguish—while the chorus gently dissuades her, in well-worn terms, from increasing her own misery by a stubborn resistance to those in power. But Electra defends her position. The sight of Aegisthus in power compels her not to yield, but to resist the more. "In the midst of evils," she says, "there is every need to make evil one's daily bread." [1] She cannot be gentle and polite. She does not say exactly why that which compels

---

* *chthonian*   refers to spirits of the underworld.
† *parodos*   first song of the whole chorus. See *The Poetics*, Chapter 12.

[1] *El.* 308 f. [307 f.] [Line numbers in brackets indicate appropriate quotations as given in translations in this anthology. SAC]

others to obedience compels her to rebellion, but the reason becomes clear through the action of the play.

The scene with Chrysothemis, on the other hand, shows us how Electra looks to others—stubborn, sullen, insanely rebellious, even masochistic. Chrysothemis has done the sensible thing, accepted the fact that Agamemnon is dead and Aegisthus is her master. Therefore, she lives in the palace, dressed finely and well fed, while Electra starves in rags. Out of friendliness, Chrysothemis has come to warn her sister that Aegisthus is planning to thrust her into the dungeon to be rid of her.[2] Chrysothemis would gladly do anything she could against Aegisthus, but what could she do? Let Electra be wise and yield, and cease to oppose those stronger than herself. It is wonderful indeed how completely the weak and shallow Chrysothemis has won generations of readers to her side. Electra, they feel, is self-willed and wearisome, and indeed she should learn the lesson of sophrosyne. For some reason, Sophoclean scholars have, almost to a man, concluded that Chrysothemis, though weak, is fundamentally right, and that Sophocles spoke personally through this, almost the least attractive of his characters. Heroism is always ill-timed; but a plea for common sense, whenever it is made, invariably finds sympathizers.

Electra, however, scorns the advice and with her bitter replies drives Chrysothemis back into the palace. As in the case of other Sophoclean protagonists, her violent impatience with advice-givers who understand nothing has been conceived as brutality, blindness, or irreligion. But it is none of these; it rises from an imperative moral conviction, upon which Sophocles must have set the seal of his approval; for Electra is victorious in the end, and there is no trace of her harshness' being punished.

The exit of Chrysothemis brings the first third of the play to a close, and as yet there has been no real action or major conflict. Sophocles seems to have been anxious to let Electra's position be well defined and rounded off before plunging her into the actual events of the play. There is none of the quick deftness of the *Antigone*, where a similar picture of two sisters with equally sharp contrasts is drawn in ninety-nine lines. Instead there is a detailed molding, with infinite chiaroscuro and echoes of varying speech-tone in the verse, so that, as with a living person, one feels one knows Electra, but not what she signifies. It is easier to see Antigone's significance than to understand how she could be flesh and blood.

The portrait complete, Sophocles begins the principal action with a verbal duel between Electra and Clytaemnestra—her "mother no-mother." Of the three dramatists, Sophocles makes the most definite use of the political implications of the murder of Agamemnon. To Aeschylus, Aegisthus is a usurper and Clytaemnestra a murderess, but they are woven into a gigantic nexus of crime already generations old; Agamemnon himself was not guiltless, though his murderers are worse; the problem is one of crime. Euripides, on the other hand, made less of the criminality of the royal pair and showed Clytaemnestra as a mild, weary woman, mellowing with time and full of human sympathies, while his Aegisthus is by no means unappealing. But Sophocles drew them as tyrants who, having slain the good, lawful king, now ruled by terror alone, fearful themselves of the return of Orestes, and fearful even of the helpless Electra who daily reminds them of their crime. The debate between mother and daughter about Clytaemnestra's justification for killing Agamemnon has been taken too much at face value. Herein the critics have tried to find the answer to the moral problem of the play, but their search is made difficult by the fact that Electra seems to condemn the law of blood for blood while her actions confirm it.

Clytaemnestra urges that her destruction of Agamemnon was justified because he had sacrificed Iphigenia in order to obtain a wind to Troy and thus "gratify his brother."[3] Electra answers:

But if he did so—for I'll even grant
Your tale, that he did that to please his brother,
Should he have died at your hands? By what
    law?
Beware of making this a law for men,
Lest it bring grief and penitence to you.
For if we are to slay each other, you
Should die first, if you get what you deserve.
Take care, then, lest you urge a hollow plea.[4]

2 *El.* 379 f. [377 f.]
3 *El.* 528–546. [526–541]

4 *El.* 577–584. [569–575]

Such are Electra's words, but the point of that debate lies not in the arguments—all of them old and stale as both characters know—but in the fact that Clytaemnestra is forced constantly to take refuge in these rationalizations, failing which she has only force left; while Electra, who is honest and does not fear force, is free to say what she will, to mock, taunt, and even to threaten. Once more we see the bewildering irony of Sophocles: Clytaemnestra protests her innocence with labored consistency and reveals her corruption in every line. Electra makes no attempt to formulate a real answer; she replies almost flippantly in her supreme scorn, but with the voice of the free and heroic individual. Essentially, it is the freedom of the enslaved Electra in contrast to the suppressed terror of the queen, trapped in her own bestiality, which makes this strange scene true. Clytaemnestra's fear is paramount. She originally entered because a terrifying dream had driven her to make a propitiatory sacrifice to the shade of Agamemnon;[5] now, as the scene with her daughter reaches an impasse, she turns to the altar of Apollo where, like Macbeth, she cannot say "amen," but utters dark prayers hinting the death of both her children.

The remaining scenes of the play rise steadily in tension almost to the end. The long *rhesis*, or set speech, of the Pedagogue, relating the fictitious death of Orestes, is followed by a second scene with Chrysothemis where once more the famous Sophoclean irony is used to its fullest effect. Chrysothemis has found a lock of hair on Agamemnon's grave and has guessed it to be Orestes'. She is right, of course, but Electra, who has heard the Pedagogue's tale, convinces her that her brother is dead. Such passion and authority are in her words that she almost makes the audience feel that Chrysothemis was a fool to have thought Orestes had returned, as well as utterly gauche and irresponsible to have come bringing optimistic news at such a time. Even in her right moments Chrysothemis is made to bear out her morally unrealistic character. To the audience, as to Electra, Orestes is dead; Sophocles has so far prevailed that Chrysothemis seems the deluded one. That is because a new and greater truth is arising in Electra: now that there is no further hope of salvation

from without, she is ready to seek the means to salvation within; she will kill Aegisthus herself. Chrysothemis is shocked and retires from any participation in the deed, but Electra persists, and prepares herself.

Then follows the recognition scene, where Orestes in disguise presents the supposed urn of his own ashes to his sister, and finally is so moved by her convulsive lament that he reveals himself. The marvels of this episode are well known. With the coming of Orestes, the play is virtually complete and the frame has met all around. Orestes, without even a shudder, slays first Clytaemnestra and then Aegisthus, and the play ends with a triumphant cry of deliverance from the chorus.

Euripides objected violently to this play and wrote his own *Electra* in answer to it. Presumably Sophocles, in this work at least, was not fully comprehended even by his contemporaries. Euripides, no less than modern scholars, was blinded by the tremendous authority of Aeschylus, who seemed to have fixed the myth's outlines permanently; and morally his own play differs from that of Aeschylus only in that he can find in the matricide no justice at all. For him as for Aeschylus, the murder of Clytaemnestra constitutes the major problem, and the belief that it did so for Sophocles is what has led scholars astray. They feel that Electra and Orestes must be wrong, and either conclude that the play is a failure because Sophocles apparently does not agree, or else hunt diligently through the text for minute relics of the Aeschylean moral, and failing to find them, make them up.

Some indeed have recognized that the vengeance of Orestes is treated by Sophocles as a perfectly justifiable deed, but are still so far influenced by Aeschylus as to feel that this vengeance is the main point of the drama, and that Sophocles' purpose was to justify either the "sacred story," or else a kind of hard world-order, in which occasional matricide may be a means to a moral society, sanctified by an unmerciful Divine Justice. But Greek myths were not holy writ. They were the values and thoughts of the early Greeks in dramatic form, and they were always subject to reinterpretation, and even, in the course of time, revision. Thus Euripides' attack on the story of Electra was a confession of his inability to understand it as it stood;

---

[5] *El.* 417 ff. [417 ff.] Cf. 780 ff. [733 ff.]

for Sophocles, however, it had a meaning, which he extracted. He did not defend it, as a fundamentalist defends the Bible. Neither did he defend any merciless divine world order, for when the world seemed too cruel to him, he said so, as he did in the *Trachiniae* and the *Oedipus Rex*. Sophocles championed neither myth nor matricide; his eyes were fixed elsewhere.

That this is true is proven by the focus of the tragic conflict. In the *Choephori,* there is conflict between Orestes' conscience and the command of Apollo. But in Sophocles' play, there is nothing of the sort. It is, in fact, just this lack of conflict which has occasioned all the embarrassment. Vengeance runs a straight course; its justice is never questioned, but assumed for a purpose. The case is similar to that of the *Oedipus Rex,* which must not be approached as if the main problem were the guilt or innocence of Oedipus; his innocence is assumed as the first premise of the play. So here, Sophocles wrote a play in which matricide was incidentally treated as just, in order to make clear a different and more interesting point. That point lies where the moral conflict lies.

Oddly enough, the belief that Sophocles was a poet who wrote only for art's sake and cared little for the moral problems of his plays pointed to the discovery of the real moral conflict in the *Electra.* Tycho von Wilamowitz, whose limited approach permitted him to pass by the religious question, recognized that the *raison d'etre* of the play must lie in its most intense moment—the great scene of recognition—and that the murder was merely an unavoidable part of the story. To Wilamowitz, everything said in the play about the murder, including the long debate on blood vengeance, seemed irrelevant and inconclusive, while the recognition scene, the climax of the portrait of Electra, showed Sophocles' real purpose. This scene, he concluded, was the chief "work of art" for which the larger one, the play, existed. The *Electra* is indeed a work of art, and, as is not generally the case with Sophocles, the art shows. For this reason, presumably, it remains a favorite virtuoso piece for eminent actresses to the present day. But it is more than a cadenza: it was not written merely as a setting for a superb recognition scene. And yet the fact that this scene is the most highly

developed one in the work is important, not for Wilamowitz' reasons, but because it brings to pass the long-desired coming of Orestes. The dramatic conflict which culminates in this scene is the problem of Electra's salvation, and herein lies the secret of the drama. How was Electra, powerless before tyrants, to activate the moral integrity for which she stood? The recognition scene tells how Electra was saved, and how Orestes came back to her; the moral has to do with Electra's endurance, not with Orestes' vengeance.

If such an emphasis seems new and surprising after the *Choephori,* it should be noted that up until the time of Aeschylus, probably, Orestes was a stainless hero, whose act was looked upon as the deliverance of his country. Homer, though he seems to veil the murder of Clytaemnestra, presents Orestes without Furies, and with the gods' approval. So also does Pindar. The one reference to him in the Epic Cycle and the few fragments of Stesichorus show nothing very definite, though the latter probably treated the story as Homer had done. It would seem therefore that Sophocles, though he differed from Aeschylus, stood in the main stream of tradition when he omitted the Furies and treated the murders as simple justice.

The *Choephori,* however, existed; if Sophocles was to write a play about Electra's suffering and triumph, he had to make the matricide seem sufficiently justified so that the play could free itself from the prejudices created by Aeschylus. Electra, it is true, was never punished in any case, even in Aeschylus, but Orestes himself must appear purely as a deliverer and the play must end on a note of victory and peace. Such a task seems to have been almost beyond even Sophocles' surpassing powers. The *Oresteia* of Aeschylus remained an unforgettable landmark, and even today the mind inevitably drifts back to the scene of Clytaemnestra's ghost. And yet, taken by itself, the *Electra* lacks nothing to make it a sympathetic play. Every artistic device is deployed with almost indescribable skill and tact; if the play fails, it is only because Sophocles chose to illustrate tragic endurance by a myth which had already been used by an equally great artist to illustrate something else. The fact that the matricide actually was justified in the end of the *Oresteia* does not make it any easier to accept its immediate justification here. Sophocles must have foreseen fully the prejudice which the superb Clytaemnestra of Aeschylus would create in the minds of his audience.

One means of obviating this prejudice was to avoid any scene in which Clytaemnestra faces her son. There is no such terrible dialogue as occurs in the *Choephori*, with Pylades the silent suddenly speaking like the Delphic Oracle itself; there is no such sickening enticement scene as Euripides used to his purpose. Orestes goes calmly into the palace, we here some brief commotion, a cry for mercy, and then the two grim echoes of the dying words of Aeschylus' Agamemnon, which, of course, bring the queen's original crime strongly to mind.[6] Electra calls to her brother to strike again; then, as he comes out, the chorus murmurs approval. Electra asks if the deed is done, and Orestes answers, "Fear no more that your mother's arrogance will dishonor you."[7]

The subject then changes to Aegisthus, who is approaching, and the brief remainder of the play is devoted to a somewhat more developed treatment of his destruction. In contrast to the brief scene of Clytaemnestra's death, the children here play triumphantly with their victim, who appears in an odious enough light as he gloats over what he supposes to be Electra's grief[8] and happily announces to all the Mycenaeans that their last hope is gone, and they must now submit to his "bridle."[9] He is presently allowed to discover his mistake, while Orestes, with a dreadful leisureliness, looks on. Strangely enough, it is impossible to feel any sympathy with Aegisthus. In sixty-odd lines Sophocles has created an astonishingly repulsive figure, a veritable model of pettiness, effeminacy, and tyranny. The quiet scorn of Orestes and Electra's weary disgust are limned suddenly in the light of a universal judgment. Instead of warped outcasts, they emerge as a human norm asserting itself over something indescribably contemptible. "Slay him quickly," says Electra, "and throw him out of our sight."[10] Orestes does so, but very calmly. His commands are spoken ironically, in a

strangely low, almost courteous tone, in marked contrast to the martinet manner of Aegisthus: "You might go inside quickly," he says, using the mildest form of the Greek imperative. As he edges his victim slowly inside the doors, though it is clear what is about to happen, there is no savagery, no violence, but only a calm invincible determination, capped with a claim of justice and order.

Thus, the death of Clytaemnestra is only an introduction to the death of Aegisthus; and Sophocles, so far as we know, is alone in placing the murders in this order. He could have done this for no other purpose than to let Orestes emerge as the hero which he is in the *Odyssey*, instead of as the half-guilty fate-driven sufferer of Aeschylus. Homer similarly endeavored to veil the horror of matricide, by saying merely that Orestes killed Aegisthus and then made a tomb for him and also for his "hateful mother." Within the framework of the tribal custom of vendetta, the Homeric Orestes is held up as an example of heroic behavior, while Clytaemnestra, of course, can be mentioned only with reserve, and at that, branded with the epithet of "hateful."[38] The Homeric account seems therefore to be the true background for Sophocles, which should not be surprising, since Sophocles was frequently far more directly dependent upon Homer for his ideas of heroism and arete* than on his older contemporary, Aeschylus.

But it was not enough simply to pass quickly over the matricide. It had to be made to seem just. In order to present Electra as an example of heroic fortitude, Sophocles set out to recreate the situation in the light of the old epic, in which Clytaemnestra deserved her fate. He took his cue from Homer therefore, and made her completely loathsome.[39] The fact that she is more credible perhaps in either Aeschylus or Euripides only proves that here she is made for an occasion. Sophocles would hardly have taken all this trouble merely to show his contemporaries that Clytaemnestra really was an evil woman, and his artistic integrity would have prevented him from stacking the cards so heavily against the queen, if he really were treating the problem of her

---

[6] *El.* 1415 f. [1392 f.]
[7] *El.* 1426 f. [1404 f.] The reference is designedly made to Clytaemnestra's criminal treatment of her daughter, in order to prevent sympathy from rising for her.

[8] *El.* 1445 ff. [1419 ff.]
[9] *El.* 1458–1463. [1433–1437.]
[10] *El.* 1487 ff. [1461 ff.]
* *arete* the manly virtues, chiefly courage.

deserts. In short, he is too honest to say, "Clytaemnestra must have been wicked, for a god commanded her death"; instead he says, "Clytaemnestra was admittedly a murderess; supposing she and Aegisthus were, as Homer says, a pair of weak and heartless tyrants, what a soul Electra must have had! . . ."

◆ *Hamlet* and *Orestes*

By GILBERT MURRAY

In the first of these studies we considered the conscious study and imitation of classical literature revealed in Milton's poetry. In the second we considered the origin of that classical literature itself—not indeed the models which it consciously imitated, but the quarry out of which its marbles were hewn, or the spring whose waters ran in its great rivers. In the last chapter we saw how this original raw material of poetry, the primitive religious Molpê, for the most part was not wrought to its highest forms except by passing through fire and torment, and that for this reason poetry still, in a sense, finds its models in the Heroic Age. But the unconscious tradition in poetry is not only greater in extent, it also reaches much further back into the past, than any deliberate human imitation.

I propose now to consider the influence of this unconscious tradition in a region where its presence has not been suspected.*

My subject is the study of two great tragic characters, Hamlet and Orestes, regarded as traditional types. I do not compare play with play, but simply character with character, though in the course of the comparison I shall naturally consider the situations in which my heroes are placed and the other persons with whom they are associated.

Orestes in Greek is very clearly a traditional character. He occurs in poem after poem, in tragedy after tragedy, varying slightly in each one but always true to type. He is, I think, the most central and typical tragic hero on the Greek stage; and he occurs in no less than seven of our extant tragedies—eight if we count the *Iphigenia in Aulis,* where he is an infant—whereas Oedipus, for instance, only comes in three and Agamemnon in four. I

shall use all these seven plays as material: namely, Aeschylus, *Choephoroe* and *Eumenides;* Sophocles, *Electra;* and Euripides, *Electra, Orestes, Iphigenia in Tauris* and *Andromache.* And we must realize that before any of these plays was written Orestes was a well-established character both in religious worship and in epic and lyric tradition.

As for *Hamlet,* I note, in passing, the well-known fragments of evidence which indicate the existence of a Hamlet tragedy before the publication of Shakespeare's Second Quarto in 1604. These are:

1602. A phrase in Dekker's *Satiromastix,* "My name's Hamlet: Revenge!"

1598. Gabriel Harvey's remarks about Shakespeare's *Hamlet.* The true date of this entry is disputed.

1596. Lodge, *Wit's Miserie and the World's Madness:* "He looks as pale as the ghost which cried so miserally at the theator like an oysterwife, Hamlet, revenge."

1594. Henslowe's Diary records a play called *Hamlet* as acted at Newington Butts Theatre on June 9.

The earliest reference seems to be in Nash's *Epistle* prefixed to Greene's *Menaphon:* it is dated 1589, but was perhaps printed in 1587. "Yet English Seneca read by candle light yeeldes many good sentences, as Bloud is a beggar, and so foorth: and if you intreate him faire in a frosty morning, he will affoord you whole Hamlets, I should say handfulls of tragicall speeches."

The play of *Hamlet* is extant in three main forms:

The First Quarto, dated 1603, but perhaps printed in 1602. It is entitled "The Tragicall Historie of Hamlet *Prince of Denmark* by

Gilbert Murray, *"Hamlet and Orestes," The Classical Tradition in Poetry* (Cambridge, Mass.: Harvard University Press, 1927), pp. 205–240.

* Gilbert Murray means by "unconscious tradition" the mainstream of ideas and art, of which the Graeco-Roman is the most important element, which has come down to us and influences us even when we are not conscious of it. "It is a stream from which commonness has been strained away. It has formed the higher intelligence of Europe. At the same time it is ubiquitous and unescapable." (*The Classical Tradition in Poetry,* p. 7.) [Throughout this essay footnotes to *Electra* refer to Euripides' *Electra* unless they specify Sophocles'. Line numbers in brackets indicate appropriate quotations as given in translations in this anthology. SAC]

William Shake-speare, As it hath been at divers times acted by his Highnesse servants in the Cittie of London: as also in the two Vniversities of Cambridge and Oxford and else-where." It is much shorter than the *Hamlet* which we commonly read, having only 2,143 lines, many of them incomplete, as against the 3,891 of the Globe edition. It differs from our version also in the order of the scenes and to some extent in plot. For instance, the Queen's innocence of her husband's murder is made quite explicit: when she hears how it was wrought she exclaims:

But, as I have a soule, I sweare by Heaven
I never knew of this most horride murder;

and thereafter she acts confidentially with Hamlet and Horatio. Also some of the names are different: for Polonius we have Corambis, and for Reynaldo, Montano.

The Second Quarto, dated 1604, describes itself as "enlarged to almoste as much againe as it was, according to the true and perfecte coppie."

Thirdly, there is the Folio of 1623. This omits a good deal that was in the Second Quarto, and contains some passages which are not in that edition but have their parallels in the First Quarto.

Thus *Hamlet,* like most of the great Elizabethan plays, presents itself to us as a whole that has been gradually built up, not as a single definitive creation made by one man in one effort. There was an old play called *Hamlet* extant about 1587, perhaps written by Kyd. It was worked over and improved by Shakespeare; improved doubtless again and again in the course of its different productions. We can trace additions; we can even trace changes of mind or repentances, as when the Folio of 1623 goes back to a discarded passage in the First Quarto. It is a live and growing play, apt no doubt to be slightly different at each performance, and growing steadily more profound, more rich, and more varied in its appeal.

And before it was an English play, it was a Scandinavian story: a very ancient Northern tale, not invented by any person, but just living, and doubtless from time to time growing and decaying, in oral tradition. It is recorded at length, of course with some remodelling, both conscious and unconscious,

by Saxo Grammaticus in his great *History of the Danes* (*Gesta Danorum*), Books III and IV. Saxo wrote about the year 1185; he calls his hero Amlethus, or Amloði, Prince of Jutland, and has worked in material that seems to come from the classical story of Brutus—Brutus the Fool, who cast out the Tarquins—and the deeds of Anlaf Curan, King of Ireland. But the story of Hamlet existed long before Saxo; for the prose *Edda* happens to quote a song by the poet Snaebjørn, composed about 980, with a passing reference to "Amloði." And it must mean our Amloði; for our Amloði in his pretended madness was a great riddle-maker, and the song refers to one of his best riddles. He speaks in Saxo of the sand as meal ground by the sea; and Snaebjørn's song calls the sea "Amloði's meal-bin."

Besides Saxo we have a later form of the same legend in the Icelandic *Ambales Saga.* The earliest extant manuscripts of this belong to the seventeenth century.

Thus our sources for *Hamlet* will be (1) the various versions of the play known to us, (2) the story of Saxo Grammaticus and the *Ambales Saga,* and (3) some occasional variants of these sagas.[1]

II

Now to our comparison.

1. The general situation. In all the versions, both Northern and Greek, the hero is the son of a king who has been murdered and succeeded on the throne by a younger kinsman—a cousin, Aegisthus, in the Greek; a younger brother, Feng or Claudius, in the Northern. The dead king's wife has married his murderer. The hero, driven by supernatural commands, undertakes and carries through the duty of vengeance.

In Shakespeare the hero dies as his vengeance is accomplished; but this seems to be an innovation. In Saxo, *Ambales,* and the Greek he duly succeeds to the kingdom. In Saxo there is no mention of a ghost; the duty of vengeance is perhaps accepted as natural. In *Ambales,* however, there are angels; in the English, a ghost; in the Greek, dreams and visions of the dead father, and an oracle.

[1] There are, of course, numerous variants and offshoots of the Hamlet story. See *Corpus Hamleticum* by Professor Josef Schick of Munich.

2. In all versions of the story there is some shyness about the mother-murder. In Saxo the mother is not slain; in Shakespeare she is slain by accident, not deliberately murdered; in *Ambales* she is warned and leaves the burning hall just in time. In one of the variants the mother refuses to leave the hall and is burnt with her husband.[2] In the Greek versions she is deliberately slain, but the horror of the deed unseats the hero's reason. We shall consider this mother more at length later on.

3. In all the versions the hero is in some way under the shadow of madness. This is immensely important, indeed essential, in his whole dramatic character. It is present in all the versions, but is somewhat different in each.

In *Hamlet* the madness is assumed, but I trust I am safe in saying that there is something in the hero's character which at least makes one wonder if it is entirely assumed. I think the same may be said of Amloði and Ambales.

In the Greek the complete madness comes only as a result of the mother-murder; yet here too there is that in the hero's character which makes it easy for him to go mad. In the *Choephoroe*, where we see him before the deed, he is not normal. His language is strange and broken amid its amazing eloquence; he is a haunted man. In other plays, after the deed, he is seldom actually raving. But, like Hamlet in his mother's chamber, he sees visions which others cannot:

You cannot see them: only I can see.[3]

He indulges freely in soliloquies;[4] especially, like Hamlet, he is subject to paralyzing doubts and hesitations, alternating with hot fits. For instance, once in the *Iphigenia* he suddenly wishes to fly and give up his whole enterprise, and has to be checked by Pylades:

O God, where hast thou brought me? what new snare
Is this?—I slew my mother, I avenged

My father at thy bidding. I have ranged
A homeless world, hunted by shapes of pain. . . .
. . . We still have time to fly for home,
Back to the galley quick, ere worse things come.

PYLADES
To fly we dare not, brother: 't is a thing
Not of our custom.[5]

Again, in the *Electra* he suspects that the god who commands him to take vengeance may be an evil spirit in disguise:

How if some fiend of Hell
Hid in God's likeness spake that oracle?

One is reminded of Hamlet's words:

The spirit that I have seen
May be the devil.[6]

At the moment before the actual crisis he is seized with horror and tries to hold back. In the *Choephoroe* this is given in a line or two:

Pylades,
What can I? Dare I let my mother live?[7]

or with a different punctuation: "Let me spare my mother!" In the *Electra* it is a whole scene, where he actually for the moment forgets what it is that he has to do; he only remembers that it has something to do with his mother. Again he vows, too late, after the mother-murder, that, if his dead father had known all, he would never have urged him to such a deed; he would rather

have knelt down
And hung his wreath of prayers about my beard,
To leave him unavenged.[8]

In Shakespeare this belief is made a fact: the Ghost specially charges Hamlet not to kill Gertrude:

Taint not thy mind, nor let thy soul contrive
Against thy Mother aught.[9]

[2] Halfdan is killed by his brother Frodi, who also takes his wife. Halfdan's sons, Helgi and Hroar, eventually burn Frodi at a feast. See Professor Elton's appendix to his translation of Saxo, edited by York Powell.
[3] *Choephoroe*, 1061 [1161]; cf. *Orestes*, 255–279.
[4] *Iphigenia in Tauris*, 77–94, *Electra* 367–390; cf.

Iphigenia in Tauris, 940–978; *Choephoroe*, 268–305 [290–330], and last scene.
[5] *Iphigenia in Tauris*, 93–103.
[6] *Electra*, 979; *Hamlet*, II, 2.
[7] *Choephoroe*, 899 [975].
[8] *Orestes*, 288–293.
[9] *Hamlet*, I, 5; cf. also the tone in III, 4.

Is it too much to say that, in all these strangely characteristic speeches of Orestes, every line might have been spoken by Hamlet, and hardly a line by any other tragic character except those directly influenced by Orestes or Hamlet?

Now what do we find in the sagas? Both in Saxo and in *Ambales* the madness is assumed, entirely or mainly, but in its quality also it is utterly different from that of Shakespeare's hero. The saga Hamlet is not a highly wrought and sensitive man with his mind shaken by a terrible experience, he is a Fool, a gross Jester, covered with dirt and ashes, grinning and mowing and eating like a hog, spared by the murderer simply because he is considered too witless to be dangerous. The name "Amloði" itself means a fool. This side is emphasised most in *Ambales*, but it is clear enough in Saxo also and explains why he has combined his hero with the Fool, Brutus. Hamlet is a Fool, though his folly is partly assumed and hides unsuspected cunning.

4. The Fool.—It is very remarkable that Shakespeare, who did such wonders in his idealized and half-mystic treatment of the real Fool, should also have made his greatest tragic hero out of a Fool transfigured. Let us spend a few moments on noticing the remnants of the old Fool that subsist in the transfigured hero of the tragedies. For one thing, as has often been remarked, Hamlet's actual language is at times exactly that of the regular Shakespearean Fool: for example, with Polonius in Act II, scene 2; just before the play in Act III, scene 2, and after. But apart from that, there are other significant elements.

(*a*) The Fool's disguise.—Amloði and Brutus and Shakespeare's Hamlet feign madness; Orestes does not. Yet the element of disguise is very strong in Orestes. He is always disguising his feelings: he does so in the *Choephoroe*, Sophocles' *Electra*, Euripides' *Electra* and *Iphigenia in Tauris*. In two passages further, he narrates how, in other circumstances, he had to disguise them:

> I suffered in silence and made pretence not
>   to see.[1]
> I suffered, Oh, I suffered; but as things
>   drove me I endured.[2]

This is like Shakespeare's Hamlet. It is also very like the saga Hamlet, who deliberately laughs in pretended idiocy to see his brother hanged.

Again, it is a marked feature of Orestes to be present in disguise, especially when he is supposed to be dead, and then at some crisis to reveal himself with startling effect. He is apt to be greeted by such words as "Undreamed-of phantom!" or "Who is this risen from the dead?" [3] He is present disguised and unknown in the *Choephoroe*, Sophocles' *Electra*, Euripides' *Electra* and *Iphigenia in Tauris*; he is in nearly every case supposed to be dead. In the *Choephoroe* and Sophocles' *Electra* he brings the funeral urn that is supposed to contain his own ashes; in the *Iphigenia* he interrupts his own funeral rites.

No other character in Greek tragedy behaves in this extraordinary way. But Saxo's Amloði does. When Amloði goes to England, he is supposed to be dead, and his funeral feast is in progress, when he walks in, "striking all men utterly aghast." [4]

In *Hamlet* there is surely a remnant of this motive, considerably softened. In Act V, 2, the Gravedigger scene, Hamlet has been present in disguise while the Gravedigger and the public thought he was in England, and the King and his confidants must have believed him dead, as they do in Saxo. Then comes the funeral—not his own, but Ophelia's; he stays hidden for a time, and then springs out, revealing himself: "This is I, Hamlet the Dane!" The words seem like an echo of that cry that is so typical in the Greek tragedies: "'Tis I, Orestes, Agamemnon's son!" [5] One is reminded, too, of the quotation from the pre-Shakespearean *Hamlet* in Dekker's *Satiromastix* of 1602: "My name's Hamlet! Revenge!" It may well be that these melodramatic appearances were more prominent in the tradition before Shakespeare.

(*b*) The disorder of the Fool.—This disguise motive has led us away from the Fool, though it is closely connected with him. Another curious element of the Fool that lingers on is his dirtiness and disorder in dress. Saxo says that Amloði "remained always in his mother's house, utterly listless and unclean,

---

[1] *Iphigenia in Tauris*, 956
[2] *Andromache*, 980.
[3] *Orestes*, 385, 879, 478 f.; *Iphigenia*, 1361 (cf. 1321).

[4] *Gesta Danorum*, IV, 95.
[5] *Andromache*, 884; *Iphigenia*, 1361; cf. his sudden apparitions in *Choephoroe*, 212 ff., *Electra* 220, also the recognition scenes.

flinging himself on the ground and bespattering his person with foul dirt." [6] Ambales was worse; enough to say that he slept in his mother's room and "ashes and filth reeked off him." [7] We remember Ophelia's description of Hamlet's coming to her chamber:

> *his doublet all unbraced;*
> *No hat upon his head; his stockings fouled,*
> *Ungartered and down gyvèd to the ankle,*
> *Pale as his shirt . . .*[8]

Similarly, Orestes, at the beginning of the play that bears his name, is found with his sister, ghastly pale, with foam on his mouth, gouts of rheum in his eyes, his long hair matted with dirt and "made wild with long unwashenness." "Poor curls, poor filthy face," his sister says to him.[9] In the *Electra*, too, he is taken for a brigand,[1] which suggests some lack of neatness in dress; in the *Iphigenia* we hear of his foaming at the mouth and rolling on the ground.[2] In both plays, it is true, Orestes carries with him an air of princely birth, but so, no doubt, did Hamlet, whatever state his stockings were in.

(c) *The Fool's rudeness of speech.*—Besides being dirty and talking in riddles, the Fool was abusive and gross in his language. This is the case to some degree in Saxo, though no doubt the monk has softened Amloði's words. It is much emphasized in Ambales. That hero's language is habitually outrageous, especially to women. This outrageousness of speech has clearly descended to Hamlet, in whom it seems to be definitely intended as a morbid trait. He is obsessed by revolting images. He does

> *like a whore unpack his heart in words*
> *And fall a-cursing like a very drab,*

and he rages at himself because of it.

(d) *The Fool on women.*—Now the general style of Greek tragedy will not admit any gross language. So Orestes has lost this trait. But a trace of it perhaps remains. Both Orestes and Hamlet are given to expressing violently cynical opinions about women.[3] The *Orestes* bristles with parallels to the ravings of Hamlet's "Get-thee-to-a-nunnery" scene.[4] The hero is haunted by his "most pernicious woman." All women want to murder their husbands; it is only a question of time. Then they will fly in tears to their children, show their breasts, and cry for sympathy. We may, perhaps, couple with these passages the famous speech where he denies any blood relationship with his mother,[5] and the horrible mad line where he says he could never weary of killing evil women.[6]

Both heroes also tend—if I may use such an expression—to bully any woman they are left alone with. Amloði in Saxo mishandles his foster-sister—though the passage is obscure—and utters violent reproaches to the Queen. (The scene is taken over by Shakespeare.) Ambales is habitually misbehaving in this way. Hamlet bullies Ophelia cruelly and "speaks daggers" to the Queen. He never meets any other woman. Orestes is very surly to Iphigenia;[7] draws his sword on Electra in one play, and takes her for a devil in another;[8] holds his dagger at the throat of Hermione till she faints;[9] denounces, threatens, and kills Clytemnestra, and tries to kill Helen. There are not many tragic heroes with such an extreme anti-feminist record.

The above, I think, are, all of them, elements that go deep into the character of the hero as a stage figure. I will now add some slighter and more external points of resemblance.

1. In both traditions the hero has been away from home when the main drama begins, Orestes in Phocis, Hamlet in Wittenberg. This point, as we shall see later, has some significance.

2. The hero in both traditions—and in both rather strangely—goes on a ship, is captured by enemies who want to kill him, but escapes. And as Hamlet has a sort of double escape, first from the King's treacherous letter, and next from the pirates, so Orestes, in the *Iphigenia*, escapes once from the Taurians who catch him on the shore, and again from the pursuers in the ship. Ambales has similar

---

[6] *Saxo*, 88.
[7] *Hamlet*, II, i.
[8] *Electra*, 219.
[9] *Ambales*, pp. 73–75, 77.
[1] *Orestes*, 219–226; cf. 880 ff.
[2] *Iphigenia in Tauris*, 307 f.
[3] *Orestes*, 246–251, 566–572, 935–942.

[4] *Hamlet*, III, 1.
[5] *Orestes*, 552 ff., based on the quibble in Aeschylus' *Eumenides*, 657–661.
[6] *Orestes*, 1590.
[7] *Iphigenia*, 482 ff.
[8] *Electra*, 220 ff.; *Orestes*, 264.
[9] *Orestes*, 1575 ff.

adventures at sea; and the original Amloði seems to have had nautical connexions, since the sea was his meal-bin, and the ship's rudder his knife.[1]

3. Much more curious, and indeed extraordinary, is the following point, which occurs in Saxo, *Ambales,* and the Greek, but not in Shakespeare. We have seen that the hero is always a good deal connected with the dead, with graves and ghosts and funerals. In the sagas on one occasion he wins a great battle after a preliminary defeat, by a somewhat ghastly strategem. He picks up his dead—or his dead and wounded—and ties them upright to stakes and rocks, so that, when his pursuers renew their attack, they find themselves affronted by an army of dead men standing upright, and fly in dismay. Now in the *Electra,* Orestes prays to his father:

Girt with thine own dead armies wake,
Oh wake,[2]

or, quite literally, "Come bringing every dead man as a fellow-fighter." One would almost think here that there was some direct influence—of course with a misunderstanding. But the parallel may be a mere chance.

4. I would not lay much stress on the coincidence about the serpent. Clytemnestra dreams that she gives birth to a serpent, which bites her breast. Orestes, hearing of it, accepts the omen: he will be the serpent. And at the last moment, Clytemnestra so recognizes him:

Oh God;
This is the serpent that I bore and suckled.

We are reminded of the Ghost's words:

The serpent that did sting thy father's life
Now wears his crown.[3]

However, Shakespeare abounds in serpents, and I have found no trace of this serpent motive in the sagas.

5. Nor yet would I make anything of the

point that both Hamlet and Orestes on one occasion have the enemy in their power and put off killing him in order to provide a worse death afterwards. This is important in *Hamlet*—

Now might I do it pat, now he is praying,[4]

but only occurs as a slight incident in Sophocles' *Electra,*[5] and may be due merely to the Greek rule of having no violent deaths on the stage. Nor is there much significance in the fact that in both traditions the hero has a scene in which he hears the details of his father's death and bursts into uncontrollable grief.[6] Such a scene is in both cases almost unavoidable.

Let us now follow this father for a little while. He was, perhaps naturally, a great warrior. He "slew Troy's thousands"; he "smote the sledded Polacks on the ice." It is a particular reproach that the son of such a man should be so slow-tempered, "peaking like John-a-dreams," and so chary of shedding blood.[7] The father was also generally idealized and made magnificent. He has some manly faults yet "He was a man, taking him all in all." He was "a king of kings."[8] A special contrast is drawn between him and his successor:

It was so easy to be true. A King
Was thine, not feebler, not in any thing
Below Aegisthus; one whom Hellas chose
Above all kings.[9]

One might continue: "Look on this picture and on this."

We may also notice that the successor, besides the vices which are necessary, or at least desirable, in his position, is in both cases accused of drunkenness,[1] which seems irrelevant and unusual.

Lastly, and more important, one of the greatest horrors about the father's death in both traditions is that he died without the due religious observances. In the Greek tragedies, this lack of religious burial is almost the central horror of the whole story. Wher-

---

[1] See also a pamphlet, *Grotta Söngr and the Orkney and Shetland Quern,* by A. W. Johnston, 1912.
[2] *Electra,* 680.
[3] *Choephoroe,* 527–550, 928 [575–584, 1001]; *Orestes,* 479; *Hamlet,* I, 5.
[4] *Hamlet,* III, 3.
[5] Sophocles, *Electra,* 1491 ff. [1478 ff.]

[6] *Choephoroe,* 430 ff. [456 ff.]; Euripides, *Electra,* 290; *Hamlet,* I, 5, "Oh, all you host of heaven," etc.
[7] *Electra,* 275 ff., 336 ff.; cf. 130, 245.
[8] *Ibid.,* 1066 ff.
[9] *Ibid.,* 320 ff., 917, 1080.
[1] *Hamlet,* I, 4; *Electra,* 326.

ever it is mentioned it comes as something
intolerable, maddening; it breaks Orestes
down. A good instance is the scene in the
Choephoroe, where Orestes and Electra are
kneeling at their father's grave, awakening the
dead and working their own passion to the
murder point.

ELECTRA

Ah, pitiless one, my mother, mine enemy!
With an enemy's burial didst thou bury him:
thy King without his people, without dying
rites; thine husband without a tear!

ORESTES

All, all, in dishonour thou tellest it, woe is
me! And for that dishonouring she shall pay
her punishment: by the will of the Gods, by
the will of my hands: Oh, let me but slay, and
then perish!

He is now ripe for the hearing of the last
horror:

LEADER OF THE CHORUS

His body was mangled to lay his ghost! There,
learn it all . . .

and the scene becomes hysterical.[2]

The atmosphere is quite different in the
English. But the lack of dying rites remains,
and retains a strange dreadfulness:

> *Cut off even in the blossom of my sin,*
> *Unhousel'd, disappointed, unanel'd.*

To turn to the other characters: in both
the dramatic traditions the hero has a faithful
friend and confidant, who also arrives from
Phocis-Wittenberg, and advises him about his
revenge. This friend, when the hero is threatened with death, wishes to die too, but is
prevented by the hero and told to "absent him
from felicity awhile." [3] This motive is worked
out more at length in the Greek than in the
English.

Also the friendship between Orestes and
Pylades is more intense than—between Hamlet and Horatio; naturally, since devoted
friendship always plays a greater part in
antiquity. But Hamlet's words are strong:

> *Give me that man*
> *That is not passion's slave, and I will wear*
> *him*

> *In my heart's core, ay, in my heart of heart,*
> *As I do thee.*[4]

I find no Pylades-Horatio in the sagas;
though there is a brother to Hamlet, sometimes older and sometimes a twin. In some of
the variants also, such as the stories of Helgi
and Hroar, there are pairs of avengers, one
of whom is mad, or behaves like a madman.

Next comes a curious point. At first sight
it seems as if all the Electra motive were
lacking in the modern play, all the Ophelia—
Polonius motive in the ancient. Yet I am not
sure.

In all the ancient plays Orestes is closely
connected with a strange couple—a young
woman and a very old man. They are his
sister Electra and her only true friend, an old
and trusted servant of the dead King, who
saved Orestes' life in childhood. In Euripides
this old man habitually addresses Electra as
"my daughter"—not merely as "child" ($\pi\alpha\hat{\iota}\varsigma$),
but really "daughter" ($\theta\upsilon\gamma\acute{\alpha}\tau\eta\rho$),[5] while she
in return carefully avoids calling him
"Father," because that is to her a sacred name
and she will never use it lightly. But in
Sophocles she says emphatically:

> *"Hail, Father. For it is as if in thee*
> *I saw my father!"* [6]

In the Elizabethan play this couple—if we
may so beg the question—has been transformed. The sister is now the mistress,
Ophelia; the old servant of the King—for so
we must surely describe Polonius or Corambis—remains, but has become Ophelia's real
father. And the relations of both to the hero
are quite different.

The change is made more intelligible when
we look at the sagas. There the young woman
is not a sister but a foster-sister; like Electra
she helps Amloði, like Ophelia she is his beloved. The old servant of the King is not her
father—so far like the Greek; but there the
likeness stops. He spies on Amloði in his
mother's chamber and is killed for his pains,
as in the English.

We may notice, further, that in all the
Electra plays alike a peculiar effect is got
from Orestes' first sight of his sister, either

---

[2] *Choephoroe*, 435 ff. [456 ff.] cf. Sophocles, *Electra*,
443 ff.; Euripides, *Electra*, 289, 323 ff.
[3] *Orestes*, 1069 ff.; *Iphigenia*, 675 ff.; *Hamlet*, V, 2.

[4] *Hamlet*, III, 2.
[5] Euripides, *Electra*, 493, 563.
[6] Sophocles, *Electra*, 1361 [1335].

walking in a funeral procession or alone in mourning garb.[7] He takes her for a slave, and cries, "Can that be the unhappy Electra?" A similar but stronger effect is reached in *Hamlet*,[8] when Hamlet, seeing an unknown funeral procession approach, gradually discovers whose it is and cries in horror: "What, the fair Ophelia?"

Lastly, there is something peculiar, at any rate in the Northern tradition,—I will take the Greek later,—about the hero's mother. Essentially it is this: she has married the murderer of her first husband and is in part implicated in the murder, and yet the tradition instinctively keeps her sympathetic. In our *Hamlet* she is startled to hear that her first husband was murdered, yet one does not feel clear that she is perfectly honest with herself. She did not know Claudius had poisoned him, but probably that was because she obstinately refused to put together things which she did know and which pointed towards that conclusion. At any rate, though she does not betray Hamlet, she sticks to Claudius and shares his doom. In the First Quarto she is more definitely innocent of the murder; when she learns of it she changes sides, protects Hamlet, and acts in confidence with Horatio. In Saxo her attitude is as ambiguous as in the later *Hamlet;* she is friendly to Amloði and does not betray him, yet does not turn against Feng either.

A wife who loves her husband and bears him children, and then is wedded to his slayer and equally loves him, and does it all in a natural and unemotional manner: it seems somewhat unusual.

And one's surprise is a little increased to find that in Saxo Amloði's wife, Hermutrude, behaves in the same way as his mother has done. On Amloði's death she marries his slayer, Wiglek. Again, there is an Irish king, historical to a great degree, who has got deeply entangled with the Hamlet story. His name is Anlaf Curan. Now his wife, Gormflaith, carried this practice so far that the chronicler comments on it. After Anlaf's defeat at Tara she married his conqueror Malachy, and on Malachy's defeat she married Malachy's conqueror Brian. We will consider later the Greek parallels to this enigmatic lady. For

the present we must admit that she is very unlike the Clytemnestra of Greek tragedy, whose motives are studied in every detail, who boldly hates her husband and murders him. But there are traces in Homer of a far less passionate Clytemnestra.

III

Now I hope I have not tried artificially to make a case or to press my facts too hard. I think it will be conceded that the points of similarity, some fundamental and some perhaps superficial, between these two tragic heroes are rather extraordinary, and are made the more striking by the fact that Hamlet and Orestes are respectively the very greatest or most famous heroes of the world's two great ages of tragedy.

The points of similarity, we must notice, fall into two parts. There are, first, the broad similarities of situation between what we may call the original sagas on both sides; that is, the general story of Orestes and of Hamlet respectively. But, secondly, there is something much more remarkable: when these sagas were worked up into tragedies, quite independently and on very different lines, by the great dramatists of Greece and England, not only do most of the old similarities remain, but a number of new similarities are developed. That is, Aeschylus, Euripides, and Shakespeare are strikingly similar in certain points which do not occur at all in Saxo or *Ambales* or the Greek epic. For instance, the hero's madness is the same in Shakespeare and Euripides, but is totally different from the madness in Saxo or *Ambales*.

What is the connexion? All critics seem to be agreed that Shakespeare did not study these Greek tragedians directly. And, if any one should suggest that he did, there are many considerations which would, I think, make that hypothesis unserviceable. Of course, it is likely enough that some of Shakespeare's university friends, who knew Greek, may have told him in conversation of various stories or scenes or effects in Greek plays. Miss Spens suggests the name of Marston. She shows that he consciously imitated the Greek—for instance, in getting a special effect out of the absence of funeral rites—and probably had considerable influence on Shakespeare. This is a highly important line of

[7] *Choephoroe*, 16 [221]; Sophocles, *Electra*, 80 [87]; Euripides, *Electra*, 107 ff.
[8] Act V, scene 1.

inquiry, but such an explanation would not carry us very far with Shakespeare, and would be no help with Saxo.

Neither can it be indirect imitation through Seneca. Orestes only appears once in the whole of Seneca, and then he is a baby unable to speak.[9] And in any case Saxo does not seem to have studied Seneca.

Will Scandinavian mercenaries at the Court of Byzantium help us? Or, simpler perhaps, will the Roman conquest of Britain? Both these channels were doubtless important in opening up a connexion between the North and the Mediterranean, and revealing to the Northmen the rich world of classical story. But neither explanation is at all adequate. It might possibly provide a bridge between the traditional Orestes and Saxo's Amloði; but they are not in any pressing need of a bridge. It does not provide any bridge where it is chiefly wanted, between the Orestes of tragedy and Shakespeare's Hamlet.

There seems to have been, so far as our recorded history goes, no chance of imitation, either direct or indirect. Are we thrown back, then, on a much broader and simpler though rather terrifying hypothesis, that the field of tragedy is by nature so limited that these similarities are inevitable? Certain situations and stories and characters—certain subjects, we may say, for shortness—are naturally tragic; these subjects are quite few in number, and, consequently, two poets or sets of poets trying to find or invent tragic subjects are pretty sure to fall into the same paths. I think there is some truth in this suggestion; and I shall make use of something like it later. But I do not think that in itself it is enough, or nearly enough, to explain such close similarities, both detailed and fundamental, as those we are considering. I feel as I look at these two traditions that there must be a connexion somewhere.

There is none within the limits of our historical record; but can there be any outside? There is none between the dramas, nor even directly between the sagas, but can there be some original connexion between the myths, or the primitive religious rituals, on which the dramas are ultimately based? And can it be that in the last analysis the similarities be-

tween Euripides and Shakespeare are simply due to the natural working out, by playwrights of special genius, of the dramatic possibilities latent in that original seed? If this is so, it will lead us to some interesting conclusions.

To begin with, then, can we discover the original myth out of which the Greek Orestes-saga has grown? (I do not deny the possible presence of an historical element also; but if history is there, there is certainly myth mixed up with it.) The saga contains two parts:

(1) Agamemnon, "king of men," is dethroned and slain by a younger kinsman, the banished Aegisthus, who is helped by the Queen. (2) His successor, in turn, dreads and tries to destroy the next heir to the throne, Orestes, who, however, comes home secretly and, helped by a Young Queen, Electra, slays him and the Queen with him.

The story falls into its place in a clearly marked group of Greek or pre-Greek legends. Let us recall the primeval kings of the world in Hesiod.

First there was Ouranos and his wife Gaia. Ouranos lived in dread of his children, and "hid them away" till his son Kronos rose and cast him out, helped by the Queen-Mother Gaia.

Then came King Kronos with his wife Rhea. He, too, feared his children and "swallowed them," till his son Zeus rose and cast him out, helped by the Queen-Mother Rhea.

Then, thirdly—but the story cannot continue. For Zeus is still ruling and cannot have been cast out. But he was saved by a narrow margin. He was about to marry the sea-maiden Thetis, when Prometheus warned him that, if he did so, the son of Thetis would be greater than he and cast him out from heaven. And, great as is my love for Thetis, I have little doubt that she would have been found helping her son in his criminal behaviour.

In the above cases the new usurper is represented as the son of the old King and Queen. Consequently the Queen-Mother, though she helps him, does not marry him, as she does when he is merely a younger kinsman. But there is one great saga in which the marriage of mother and son has remained, quite unsoftened and unexpurgated.

---

[9] Seneca, *Agamemnon*, 910–943.

In Thebes King Laïus and his wife Jocasta knew that their son would slay and dethrone his father. Laïus orders the son's death, but he is saved by the Queen-Mother, and, after slaying and dethroning his father, marries her. She is afterwards slain or dethroned with him, as Clytemnestra is with Aegisthus, and Gertrude with Claudius.

There is clearly a common element in all these stories, and the reader will doubtless have recognised it. It is the world-wide ritual story of what we may call the Golden-Bough Kings. That ritual story is, as I have tried to show elsewhere, the fundamental conception that forms the basis of Greek tragedy, and not Greek tragedy only. It forms the basis of the traditional Mummers' Play, which, though deeply degraded and vulgarized, is not quite dead yet in the countries of Northern Europe and lies at the root of so large a part of all the religions of mankind.

It is unnecessary, I hope, to make any long explanation of the Vegetation-kings or Year-daemons. But there are perhaps two points that we should remember, to save us from confusion later on. First, there are two early modes of reckoning: you can reckon by seasons or half-years, by summers and winters; or you can reckon with the whole year as your unit. On the first system a Summer-king or Vegetation-spirit is slain by Winter and rises from the dead in the spring. On the second each Year-king comes first as a wintry slayer, weds the queen, grows proud and royal, and then is slain by the Avenger of his predecessor. These two conceptions cause some confusion in the myths, as they do in most forms of the Mummers' Play.

The second point to remember is that this death and vengeance was really enacted among our remote ancestors in terms of human bloodshed. The sacred king really had "slain the slayer" and was doomed himself to be slain. The queen might either be taken on by her husband's slayer, or else slain with her husband. It is no pale myth or allegory that has so deeply dyed the first pages of human history. It is man's passionate desire for the food that will save him from starvation, his passionate memory of the streams of blood, willing and unwilling, that have been shed to keep him alive. But for all this subject I must refer the reader to the classic expositions of the *Golden Bough*, and their bril-liant development in Dr. Jane Harrison's *Themis*.

Thus Orestes, the madman and king-slayer, takes his place beside Brutus the Fool, who expelled the Tarquins, and Amloði the Fool, who burnt King Feng at his winter feast. The great Greek scholar, Hermann Usener, some years since, on quite other grounds, identified Orestes as a Winter-god, a slayer of the Summer.[1] He is the man of the cold mountains who slays annually the Red Neoptolemus at Delphi; he is the ally of death and the dead; he comes suddenly in the dark; he is mad and raging, like the Winter-god Maimaktes and the November storms. In Athenian ritual, it seems, a cloak was actually woven for him in late autumn, lest he should be too cold.[2] Thus he is quite unlike the various bright heros who slay dragons of darkness; he finds his comrade in the Bitter Fool—may we say the bitter Amloði?—of many Mummers' Plays, who is the Slayer of the Joyous King.

This is all very well for Orestes; but can we talk thus of Hamlet-Amloði? Is it possible to bring him into the region of myth, and myth of the same kind that we find in Greece? Here I am quite off my accustomed beat, and must speak with diffidence and under correction from my betters. But it seems beyond doubt, even to my most imperfect scrutiny of the material, that the same forms of myth and the same range of primitive religious conceptions are to be found in Scandinavia as in other Aryan countries.

There are several wives in the Ynglinga saga who seem to belong to the Gaia–Rhea–Clytemnestra–Jocasta type. For instance, King Vanlandi was married to Drifa of Finland, and was killed by her in conjunction with their son Visburr, who succeeded to the kingdom. (The slaying was done by witchcraft; but no jury could, I think, exculpate Visburr.)

Visburr in turn married the daughter of Aude the Wealthy. Like Agamemnon, he was unfaithful to his wife, so she left him and sent her two sons to talk to him, and duly, in the proper ritual manner, to burn him in his house—just as the Hamlet of saga burned King Feng, just as the actual Northern villagers at their festival burned the Old Year.

---

[1] *Heilige Handlung*, in the *Archiv für Religionswissenschaft*, 1904.
[2] Aristophanes, *Birds*, 712.

Again, there are clear traces of kings who are sacrificed and are succeeded by their slayers. Most of the Yngling kings die in sacrificial ways. One is confessedly sacrificed to avert famine, one killed by a sacrificial bull, one falls off his horse in a temple and dies, one burns himself on a pyre at a festival. Another—like Ouranos and Kronos and the other child-swallowers—sacrifices one of his sons periodically in order to prolong his own life. I cite these cases merely to show that such ideas were apparently current in primitive Norse society as well as elsewhere. But the matter is really clinched by Saxo himself. He not only gives us the tale of Ole, King of the Beggars, who came in disguise, with one servant dressed as a woman, to King Thore's house, got himself hailed as king in mockery, and then slew Thore and took the crown. He definitely tells us, in a story about the Sclavs, that "by public law of the ancients the succession to the throne belonged to him who should slay the king." [3]

So that when we find that the Hamlet of saga resembles Orestes so closely; when we find that he is the Bitter Fool and king-slayer; when especially we find that this strange part of wedding—if not helping—their husband's slayer and successor is played alike by Hamlet's mother, whatever her name, Gerutha, Gertrude, or Amba; and by Amloði's mother and by Ambales' mother, and by the mother of divers variants of Hamlet, like Helgi and Hroar; and by Hamlet's wife, and by the wife of Anlaf Curan, who is partly identified with Hamlet, we can hardly hesitate to draw the same sort of conclusion as would naturally follow in a Greek story. Hamlet is more deeply involved in this Clytemnestra-like atmosphere than any person I know of outside Hesiod. And one cannot fail to be reminded of Oedipus and Jocasta by the fact, which is itself of no value in the story but is preserved both in Saxo and the *Ambales Saga*, that Amloði slept in his mother's chamber. [4]

There is something strangely characteristic in the saga treatment of this ancient Queen-Mother, a woman under the shadow of adultery, the shadow of incest, the shadow of murder, who is yet left in most of the stories a motherly and sympathetic character. Clytem-nestra is an exception, and perhaps Gorm-flaith. But Gaia, Rhea, and even Jocasta, are all motherly and sympathetic. So is Gerutha, the wife of Ørvandil and the mother of Amleth, and Amba the mother of Ambales. [5] So is Groa, the usual wife of Ørvandil, who is probably the same person as Gerutha. "Groa," says Professor Rydberg, "was a tender person devoted to the members of her family." The trait remains even in Shakespeare. "Gertrude," says Professor Bradley, "had a soft animal nature. . . . She loved to be happy like a sheep in the sun, and to do her justice she loved to see others happy, like more sheep in the sun." Just the right character for our Mother Earth! For, of course, that is who she is. The Greek stories speak her name openly: Gaia and Rhea are confessed Earth-Mothers, Jocasta only a few stages less so. One cannot apply moral disapproval to the annual re-marriages of Mother Earth with the new Spring-god; nor yet possibly to the impersonal and compulsory marriages of the human queen in certain very primitive stages of society. But later on, when life has become more self-conscious and sensitive, if once a poet or dramatist gets to thinking of the story, and tries to realise the position and feelings of this eternally traitorous wife, this eternally fostering and protecting mother, he cannot but feel in her that element of inward conflict which is the seed of great drama. She is torn between husband, lover, and son; and the avenging son, the mother-murderer, how is he torn?

English tragedy has followed the son. Yet Gerutha, Amba, Gertrude, Hermutrude, Gormflaith, Gaia, Rhea, Jocasta—there is tragedy in all of them, and it is in the main the same tragedy. Why does the most tragic of all of them, Clytemnestra, stand out of the picture?

We can only surmise. For one thing, Clytemnestra, like Gertrude in some stories, has both the normal experiences of the primitive king's wife. She both marries her husband's slayer and is slain by his avenger; and both parts of her story are equally emphasised, which is not the case with the other heroines. Their deaths are generally softened or ignored. But, apart from this, I am inclined

---

[3] *Gesta Danorum*, 254, 277.
[4] Saxo, 88; *Ambales*, p. 119, *et ante*, ed. Gollancz.
[5] In the extant form of the *Ambales Saga* Amba's

personal chastity is preserved by a miracle; such an exception approves the rule.

to lay most stress on the deliberate tragic art of Aeschylus. He received perhaps from the tradition a Clytemnestra not much more articulate than Gerutha; but it needed only a turn of the wrist to change her from a silent and passive figure to a woman seething with tragic passions. If Saxo had been a man like Aeschylus, or if Shakespeare had made Gertrude his central figure instead of Hamlet, Clytemnestra would perhaps not have stood so much alone.

And what of Hamlet himself as a mythical character? I find, almost to my surprise, exactly the evidence I should have liked to find. Hamlet in Saxo is the son of Horvendillus or Ørvandil, an ancient Teutonic god connected with dawn and the spring. His great toe, for instance, is now the morning star. (It was frozen off; that is why it shines like ice.) His wife was Groa, who is said to be the Green Earth; he slew his enemy Collerus—Kollr the Hooded, or perhaps the Cold —in what Saxo calls "a sweet and spring-green spot" in a budding wood. He was slain by his brother and avenged by his son. The sort of conclusion towards which I, on my different lines, was groping had already been drawn by several of the recognized Scandinavian authorities: notably by Professor Gollancz (who especially calls attention to the part played by the hero's mother), by Adolf Zinzow, and by Victor Rydberg. Professor Elton is more guarded, but his conclusions point, on the whole, in the same direction. And the whole of the evidence has been greatly strengthened since these words were first published, by the appearance of Miss Phillpotts's remarkable book, *The Elder Edda.*[6]

Thus, if these arguments are trustworthy, we finally run the Hamlet-saga to earth in the same ground as the Orestes-saga: in that prehistoric and world-wide ritual battle of Summer and Winter, of Life and Death, which has played so vast a part in the mental development of the human race and especially, as Mr. E. K. Chambers has shown us, in the history of mediaeval drama. Both

heroes have the notes of the winter about them rather than summer, though both are on the side of right against wrong. Hamlet is no joyous and triumphant slayer. He is clad in black, he rages, he is the Bitter Fool who must slay the King.[7]

IV

It seems a strange thing, this gradual shaping and reshaping of a primitive folk-tale, in itself rather empty and devoid of character, until it issues in a great tragedy which shakes the world. Yet in Greek literature, I am sure, the process is a common, almost a normal, one. Myth is defined by a Greek writer as τὰ λεγόμενα ἐπὶ τοῖς δρωμένοις, "the things said over a ritual act." For a certain agricultural rite, let us suppose, you tore a cornsheaf in pieces and scattered the grain; and to explain why you did so, you told a myth. "There was once a young and beautiful prince who was torn in pieces. . . ." Was he torn by hounds or wild beasts in requital for some strange sin? Or was he utterly innocent, torn by mad Thracian women or devilish Titans, or the working of an unjust curse? As the group in the village talks together, and begins to muse and wonder and make unconscious poetry, the story gets better and stronger and ends by being the tragedy of Pentheus or Hippolytus or Actaeon or Dionysus himself. Of course, an element of history must be present also. Life was not eventless in primitive times any more than it is now. Things happened, and people were moved by them at the time and talked about them afterwards. But to observe exactly, and to remember and report exactly, is one of the very latest and rarest of human accomplishments. By the help of much written record and much mental training we can now manage it pretty well. But early man was at the time too excited to observe, and afterwards too indifferent to record, and always too much beset by fixed forms of thought ever to take in concrete facts exactly.

[6] Gollancz, *Hamlet in Iceland,* Introduction; Zinzow, *Die Hamlet Saga an und mit verwandten Sagen erläutert,* 1877; Rydberg, *Teutonic Mythology,* English tr. by Anderson, 1889; Elton, Appendix II to his translation of Saxo, edited by York Powell; Bertha S. Phillpotts, *The Elder Edda* (Cambridge, 1920). Rydberg goes so far as to identify Hamlet with Ørvandil's famous son Swipdag. "Two Disser-

tations on the Hamlet of Saxo and of Shakespeare" by R. G. Latham contain linguistic and mythological suggestions. I have not come across the works of Gubernatis mentioned in Ward, *English Dramatic Literature,* ii, 165.

[7] I believe this figure of the Fool to be capable of further analysis, but will not pursue the question here.

(As a matter of fact, he did not even wish to do so; he was aiming at something quite different.) In any case, the facts, as they happened, were thrown swiftly into the same crucible as the myths. Men did not research. They did not keep names and dates distinct. They talked together and wondered and followed their musings, till an historical king of Ireland grew very like the old mythical Amloði, an historical king of Mycenae took on part of the story of a primitive Ouranos or Sky-King wedded to an Earth-Mother. And in later times it was the myth that lived and grew rather than the history. The things that thrill and amaze us in *Hamlet* or the *Agamemnon* are not any historical particulars about mediaeval Elsinore or pre-historic Mycenae, but things belonging to the old stories and the old magic rites, which stirred and thrilled our forefathers five and six thousand years ago; set them dancing all night on the hills, tearing beasts and men in pieces, and giving up their own bodies to a ghastly death, in hope thereby to keep the green world from dying and to be the saviours of their own people.

I am not trying to utter a paradox, or even to formulate a theory. I am not for a moment questioning or belittling the existence, or the overwhelming artistic value, of individual genius. I trust no one will suspect me of so doing. I am simply trying to understand a phenomen on which seems, before the days of the printed book and the widespread reading public, to have occurred quite normally and constantly in works of imaginative literature, and doubtless in some degree is occurring still.

What does our hypothesis imply? It seems to imply, first, a great unconscious solidarity and continuity, lasting from age to age, among all the children of the poets, both the makers and the callers-forth, both the artists and the audiences. In artistic creation, as in all the rest of life, the traditional element is far larger, the purely inventive element far smaller, than the unsophisticated man supposes.

Further, it implies that in the process of *traditio*—that is, of being handed on from generation to generation, constantly modified and expurgated, re-felt and re-thought—a subject sometimes shows a curious power of almost eternal durability. It can be vastly altered; it may seem utterly transformed. Yet some inherent quality still remains, and significant details are repeated quite unconsciously by generation after generation of poets. Nay, more. It seems to show that often there is latent in some primitive myth a wealth of detailed drama, waiting only for the dramatist of genius to discover it and draw it forth. Of course, we must not exaggerate this point. We must not say that *Hamlet* or the *Electra* is latent in the original ritual as a flower is latent in the seed. The seed, if it just gets its food, is bound to develop along a certain fixed line; the myth or ritual is not. It depends for its development on too many live people and too many changing and complex conditions. We can only say that some natural line of growth is there, and in the case before us it seems to have asserted itself both in large features and in fine details, in a rather extraordinary way. The two societies in which the Hamlet and Orestes tragedies arose were very dissimilar; the poets were quite different in character, and quite independent; even the particular plays themselves differed greatly in plot and setting and technique and most other qualities; the only point of contact lies at their common origin many thousand years ago, and yet the fundamental identity still shows itself, almost unmistakable.

This conception may seem strange; but after all, in the history of religion it is already a proved and accepted fact, this "almost eternal durability" of primitive conceptions and even primitive rites. Our hypothesis will imply that what is already known to happen in religion may also occur in imaginative drama.

If this is so, it seems only natural that those subjects, or some of those subjects, which particularly stirred the interest of primitive men, should still have an appeal to certain very deep-rooted human instincts. I do not say that they will always move us now; but, when they do, they will tend to do so in ways which we recognize as particularly profound and poetical. This comes in part from their original quality; in part, I suspect, it depends on mere repetition. We all know the emotional charm possessed by famous and familiar words and names, even to hearers who do not understand the words and know little of the bearers of the names. I suspect that a charm of that sort lies in these stories and situations, which are—I cannot quite keep clear of metaphor—deeply implanted in the memory of the race, stamped, as it were, upon our physical organism. We have forgotten their faces and their voices; we say that they are strange to us. Yet there is that within us which leaps at the sight of them, a cry of the blood which tells us we have known them always.

Of course, it is an essential part of the whole process of Tradition that the mythical material is constantly castigated and rekindled by comparison with real life. That is where realism comes in, and literary skill and imagination. An element drawn from real life was there, no doubt, even at the beginning. The earliest myth-maker never invented in a vacuum. He really tried—in Aristotle's famous phrase—to tell "the sort of thing that would happen"; only his conception of "what would happen" was, by our standards, a little wild. Then, as man's experience of life grew larger and calmer and more objective, his conception of "the sort of thing that would happen" grew more competent. It grew ever nearer to

the truth of Nature, to its variety, to its reasonableness, to its infinite subtlety. And in the greatest ages of literature there seems to be, among other things, a power of preserving due proportion between these opposite elements—the expression of boundless primitive emotion and the subtle and delicate representation of life. In plays like *Hamlet* or the *Agamemnon* or the *Electra* we have certainly fine and flexible character-study, a varied and well-wrought story, a full command of the technical instruments of the poet and the dramatist; but we have also, I suspect, strange, unanalyzed vibration below the surface, an undercurrent of desires and fears and passions, long slumbering yet eternally familiar, which have for thousands of years lain near the root of our most intimate emotions and been wrought into the fabric of our most magical dreams. How far into past ages this stream may reach back, I dare not even surmise; but it seems as if the power of stirring it or moving with it were one of the last secrets of genius.

◆ Historical Criticism and the Interpretation of Shakespeare

By ROBERT ORNSTEIN

There is no doubt that Shakespeare scholarship has advanced far beyond the Romantic criticism which confused literature and life. Yet it is possible that future generations will in their turn smile at the naïveté of some of our Shakespeare studies, particularly those concerned with the ethics of the plays. In recent decades the definition of Shakespeare's moral attitudes has been viewed as a problem in the history of ideas that can be solved by the accumulation of objective factual evidence. At best such an approach over-simplifies a complex aesthetic problem; at worst it ignores the essential realities of dramatic art. Professor E. E. Stoll suggested some years ago that we cannot intelligently discuss Shakespeare's characters unless we understand how the impression of character is created in poetic drama. I would suggest, in addition, that we cannot accurately interpret Shakespeare's moral intention unless we understand how moral judgments are translated into the artifice of poetic drama and apprehended by an audience.

It has been too frequently assumed that the moral interpretation of Shakespeare is the province of the scholarly researcher, who relates the thought and action of a play to the commonplace political, moral, and religious beliefs of the Elizabethan age. But the same assumptions about a dramatist and his cultural milieu which lead scholars to interpret Shakespeare by means of La Primaudaye, Charron, and Coeffeteau should lead us to interpret *A Streetcar Named Desire* by reference to Norman Vincent Peale, a latter-day ethical psychologist no less influential than his Renaissance counterparts. To be sure, Dr. Peale sheds some light on the tragedy of Blanche Du Bois: she has no mustard seeds, no "Attitude of Gratitude"; she might possibly have been saved had she been more of a positive thinker. We would not be surprised, moreover, to find striking similarities between

Robert Ornstein, "Historical Criticism and the Interpretation of Shakespeare," *Shakespeare Quarterly*, X (Winter, 1959), pp. 3–9.

Mitch's views on marriage and motherhood and those of Dr. Peale. Still we must insist that Tennessee Williams' view of life is not Dr. Peale's. We must distinguish between popular and intellectual levels of thought when discussing the cultural milieu of any dramatist. And we must recognize the difference between a moral intuition expressed in art and the traditional platitudes of systematized ethics.

That scholarly research enriches our understanding of Shakespeare is undeniable; that it affords a unique revelation of the meaning of the plays is debatable. The very nature of Elizabethan dramaturgy—the immediate plunge into dramatic action—demands that the moral apprehension of character be immediate. Motivation may be complex, subterranean, even inscrutable. The psychological depths of a character like Iago may be dark indeed; but we penetrate to that darkness in a very few moments. In their moral natures the characters of Shakespearian tragedy are infinitely more transparent than the men and women we live among.

The art that creates this moral transparency is not easily analyzed, but it is an art—a mastery of language and of living speech, not a mastery of philosophy or theology. We apprehend a philosopher's moral vision intellectually, a dramatist's aesthetically. In the most prurient love scenes of Fletcher's plays, for example, there is no rational confusion of moral values. We do not accuse Fletcher of tampering with moral categories but of failing to translate a rhetorical morality into the presentation of character. We are *told* that adultery is evil but it appears attractive; we listen to moral sentiments even while our erotic impulses are aroused. Fletcher illustrates (negatively, of course) the fact that the moral apprehension of drama is an aesthetic experience which depends upon the immediately created impression of character, thought, and action. In other words, the moral judgment in art must be translated into qualitative, affective terms; it must communicate an almost sensuous awareness of the beauty of virtue and the sordidness of vice. Biblical and theological allusions may deepen this immediate "sensuous" impression of character in action, but they cannot substitute for it if the drama is to live upon the stage.

The difference between Shakespeare and Fletcher is not that between an objective and an objectional dramatist but between one who appeals to and refines our deepest moral intuitions and one who places theatrical effect above moral perception. Although Shakespeare does not use his art to propagandize, although he does not pattern experience according to rigid formulae, he nevertheless imposes immediately on his audience's sensibility a particular moral criticism of life. In the great tragedies almost every line is calculated to elicit a specific emotional response—to shape a particular moral judgment. But the art that elicits and shapes that judgment is so sophisticated that it hides itself. We *seem* to know the moral nature of Goneril or Iago intuitively. Moreover Shakespeare's moral vision is so humane that it accords always with the empirical truths of human experience; through his eyes we see life clearly and whole.

If we turn to the Closet scene in *Hamlet,* we can see the extent to which Shakespeare's poetic and dramatic art shapes our moral responses. Consider the evidence objectively and rationally: An overwrought, passionate youth, bent upon revenge, strikes out in a blind fury at someone hidden behind the arras. He *hopes* that it will be the King, but he has no assurance that it will be, especially since he left Claudius at prayer in the preceding scene. Hamlet does not intend to kill Polonius, but at the moment he does not seem too much concerned about whom he may kill, and the preceding dialogue would lead us to believe that without Polonius' intervention he might possibly have killed his own mother. When he sees his error he is not stricken with remorse; instead he quips sardonically about Polonius' "policy," lectures to his mother on *her* guilt, and finally with a brutal callousness lugs the guts off the stage. Why do we not think of Hamlet then and thereafter as a murderer who, giving rein to his passions, dyed his hand indelibly in an innocent (or relatively innocent) man's blood? The answer is that the murder of Polonius does not dis-

turb us because it does not disturb Hamlet; it is not near our conscience because it is not near his.

Here is a paradox that illuminates the difference between literature and life. In the ordinary world a criminal's remorse softens a spectator's condemnation while callousness and indifference to a criminal act seem chilling signs of unregeneracy. But in drama a guilty conscience may have an almost opposite effect on the spectator because conscience damns: it is the internalized moral chorus through which the dramatist and his audience contemplate the moral significance of a criminal act. It was convenient for Shakespeare that Elizabethans believed that most criminals suffer pangs of remorse, but that conventional belief does not explain the artistic function of conscience in Shakespearian tragedy. For example, the coldblooded treachery by which Richard III murders his brother should arouse a deeper moral revulsion than Macbeth's tormented and anguished decision to kill Duncan. However, just the reverse is true. The very loathing with which Macbeth contemplates his crime burns his guilt into our consciousness, while Richard's high-spirited lack of conscience temporarily suspends moral judgment and allows a moral holiday in which we can momentarily enjoy his outwitting of those who would play the same deadly, amoral game. When a pattern of retribution begins to impose itself on Richard's successes, then the signs of gnawing conscience in Richard and his henchmen dissipate the mood of melodramatic farce and engage a deeper moral response to Richard's villainy.

To return to the Closet scene, I would suggest that were Hamlet more sensitive about Polonius' death we would think the worse of him. The very accusation of his conscience would brand him a murderer in our eyes. But as the scene stands, instead of contemplating his guilt in killing Polonius, Hamlet shifts his mother's attention (and our own) away from his act to Gertrude's guilt in marrying Claudius. Because the moral significance of Hamlet's act is not contemplated, we feel no bizarre incongruity when he lectures to Gertrude on ethics while Polonius' body lies at his feet. Nor do we smile sardonically when in the midst of his moral exhortation Hamlet begs forgiveness for his virtue.

I do not mean that in this crucial scene Shakespeare juggles our moral responses or that he preserves our sympathy with Hamlet by avoiding condemnation of what should be condemned. I mean rather that our moral response to this scene is a complex aesthetic experience that is influenced by the total artifice of the play. What is not near Hamlet's conscience is not near our own because he is our moral interpreter. He is the voice of ethical sensibility in a sophisticated, courtly milieu; his bitter asides, which penetrate Claudius' façade of kingly virtue and propriety, initiate, so to speak, the moral action of the play. And throughout the play our identification with Hamlet's moral vision is such that we hate what he hates, admire what he admires. As centuries of Shakespeare criticism reveal, we accuse Hamlet primarily of what he accuses himself: namely, his slowness to revenge. And we accept the morality of blood revenge instantaneously and unquestioningly because Hamlet the idealist does. Indeed, nothing that we can learn about Renaissance attitudes towards revenge can alter that acceptance.

Our moral impression of Hamlet's character derives primarily from what he says rather than what he does. It is an almost intuitive awareness of the beauty, depth, and refinement of his moral nature, upon which is thrust a savage burden of revenge and of disillusion. If Shakespeare's characters are illusions created by dramatic artifice, then what we love in Hamlet is an illusion within an illusion: i.e., the suggestion of Hamlet's former self, the Hamlet whom Ophelia remembers and who poignantly reappears in the conversations with Horatio, particularly those just before the catastrophe. Through his consummate artistry Shakespeare creates within us a sympathy with Hamlet which becomes almost an act of faith—a confidence in the untouched and untouchable core of his spiritual nature. This act of faith, renewed by the great speeches throughout the play, allows us to accept Hamlet's brutality towards Ophelia, his reaction to Polonius' death, his savage refusal to kill Claudius at prayer, and his Machiavellian delight in disposing of Rosencrantz and Guildenstern. Without the memory of the great soliloquies which preceded it, our impression of the Closet scene would be vastly different. And, in fact, to attempt to define Hamlet's character by weighing his motives and actions against any system of Renaissance thought is to stage *Hamlet* morally without the Prince of Denmark: i.e., without the felt impression of Hamlet's moral nature which is created by poetic nuance.

Equally important in shaping our reaction to the Closet scene is our response to Polonius. So far as a rational moral judgment of Hamlet's "crime" is concerned, it does not matter who besides Claudius was behind the arras. Yet the audience's reaction would be vastly different if, let us say, Ophelia were the eavesdropper. Believing the worst of her, Hamlet might as callously dismiss her death, but from that moment the audience would part moral company with him. Polonius is, of course, more expendable. While we may not share Hamlet's cynical contempt, we cannot escape feeling that the foolish, doting, prying old man received the just wages of a dupe and spy; he did find it dangerous to be too busy.

Even the moralistic critic derives satisfaction in seeing Polonius hoist with his own petard; and yet nothing which the ancient Councilor does warrants death—indeed, if eavesdropping be a mortal offense, God help the wicked! Although he snoops, pries, and carries out Claudius' plans, it is without evil purpose; there is absolutely no suggestion that he acts except for the general (and his personal) good in discovering the cause of Hamlet's melancholy. He is as ignorant of Claudius' crimes as are the bystanders who are bewildered by the final slaughter. Our "satisfaction" with Polonius' death, then, must lie outside the realm of moral philosophy; and strictly speaking it is not moral at all. By legal obligation the good citizen must inform on his neighbors' misdemeanors, but who does not despise the informer whether he is outside or within the law? To society and even to the law, the devious means are repugnant, however moral the intention. A deeply engrained "folk" morality (built up, I imagine, through centuries of police oppression) cherishes openness, candor, and directness; we realize that no man is safe and no life secure in an atmosphere of mutual suspicion and distrust.

Thus the audience feels quite rightly that Polonius does not belong behind the arras. But one could quote a dozen Renaissance moral and political authorities who insist that a high Minister of State, entrusted with the security and well-being of a nation, has the right (nay, the duty) to go about the law, to spy and use suspect means to achieve a worthwhile end. Consider the long controversy over the Duke in *Measure for Measure*. The many essays on the play reveal that some very respectable critics see the Duke as a snooper, a meddler in other men's lives, a well-intentioned official who resorts to repugnant stratagems to achieve a moral goal. Scholars insist that this impression is mistaken and unhistorical; they quote Renaissance political, moral, and religious treatises to demonstrate that the Duke has a perfect justification for his deeds and that a Renaissance audience would not have been disturbed by what seems devious or sordid to a modern reader. Perhaps so, but let us be consistent in our criticism. If our moral judgment of the Duke is to be based, not on the immediate impression of his character but on the weight of Renaissance commonplace opinion, then the same should be true of our judgment of Polonius. Or, conversely, if a mass of carefully selected Renaissance opinions cannot obliterate our distaste for Polonius' policy, then it cannot obliterate a similar response to the Duke's policy.

I do not mean to identify Polonius and the Duke. Our response to Vincentio is far more complex because he plays a more significant and many-sided role. And if it is true, as critics argue, that the action of *Measure for Measure* proceeds on an allegorical as well as realistic level, then our apprehension of the Duke's dramatic role must be different from that of Polonius. But we cannot escape from the immediate impression of the Duke's character by defining his role analogically. The symbolic vision which allegory embodies in art cannot dictate our response to the immediate realities of life or to the image of life presented on a stage; it can only build upon that response, illuminating the shared qualities of "thing" and idea—the analogical relationships between character and concept—

which allow the mind to move freely between the realistic and symbolic levels of action. When the mind of the audience cannot move freely in this way because the analogical relationships are obscurely, ingeniously, or casuistically contrived, then the allegory is decadent. When the symbolic vision seeks to identify the devious and the Divine, then the allegory is immoral.

Consider another instructive parallel, this time between Hamlet and Othello. We are told that Othello is damned to everlasting torments because he murdered innocence and did not, according to strict theology, repent. If so, what shall we say of Hamlet? He does not strangle Ophelia, but he shocks and torments her, humiliates her before the Court, suggests that she is and treats her like a whore, murders her father and thus drives her insane. Othello's crimes against Desdemona have at least the extenuating circumstance of Iago's diabolical malice. Hamlet's brutality toward Ophelia is the product of his own hypersensitive imagination and the sexual nausea produced by the shock of his mother's infidelity. At her funeral he shouts melodramatically that he loved her but offers no apology for his treatment of her and recognizes no guilt. How shall Othello be damned and flights of angels sing Hamlet to his rest?[1]

Needless to say, we feel that the endings of *Hamlet* and *Othello* are inevitable and "right". This is so, not because we can by scholarly documentation "prove" that Hamlet was inspired always by moral or religious motives and that Othello fell beyond repentance, but because Shakespeare emphasizes the unsullied core of Hamlet's goodness (the exquisite moral sensibility temporarily o'erthrown) while he emphasizes the degradation of Othello's noble spirit. He shapes different judgments of character by creating different artistic perspectives. Like Polonius, Ophelia is a minor character; Hamlet's "crimes" against her are placed in proportion and overshadowed by the larger moral action of the play. Desdemona is the heroine;

---

[1] I do not argue that Horatio's exquisite farewell to his Prince proves the blessed state of Hamlet's immortal soul. On the contrary, unless a character were literally God's spy he would scarcely have authoritative knowledge of the Divine Judgment. We cannot dogmatize about the function of imagery drawn from popular religious beliefs in Shakespeare's plays, but we can demand consistency in critical methods. If the imagery of hell in Othello's last speeches indicates his damnation, then the apocalyptic references at the end of *Lear* ("Is this the promised end?/Or image of that *horror?*" [my italics]) must indicate a failure of belief in Providential Order, a sense of cosmic dissolution and disillusion.

Othello's crime against her *is* the moral action of the play.

To put it differently, in *Hamlet* and *Othello* as in *Lear* Shakespeare presents heroes who are sinned against as well as sinning, who may be pitied as victims and condemned as wrongdoers. He is interested in dramatic situations which although unambiguous admit diametrically opposite moral emphases. In *Othello* his emphasis is upon the brutality of the destructive impulse. As we watch the unsuspecting Desdemona prepare for bed, our hearts steel against sympathy for the "abused" Othello. After this knowledge of Desdemona's purity, innocence, and love, what forgiveness for Othello? But without altering either his characterizations or the incidents of his fable, Shakespeare might have created a very different judgment of Othello's deed. Were the scene mentioned above eliminated, were the focus in the last scenes shifted to Iago's sin (to the crime against Othello's innocence) we might accept as inevitable and "right" a very different final impression; we might look upon the tormented Othello as one who deserves more pity than blame. A theological gloss of Othello's last speeches cannot tell us how to judge Othello nor can we discover by this means the particular moral emphasis which Shakespeare creates through the total design of his play. One doubts, moreover, that the mystery of Hamlet's "innocence" can be solved either by Renaissance theology or moral philosophy. The codes which govern society cannot easily admit what an audience knows during a performance of *Hamlet*: namely, that a man's spirit may be superior not only to his fate but even to his own acts.

Thus while scholarship can make the interpretation of Shakespeare more scientific, it cannot make of interpretation a science based upon factual information. The dichotomy of scholarly fact and aesthetic impression is finally misleading because the refined, disciplined aesthetic impression *is* the fact upon which the interpretation of Shakespeare must ultimately rest; that is to say, all scholarly evidence outside the text of a play is related to it by inferences which must themselves be supported by aesthetic impressions.[2] The attempt of historical criticism to recapture (in so far as it is possible) Shakespeare's own artistic intention is, or should be, the goal of all responsible criticism. But we must insist that that intention is fully realized in the play and can be grasped only from the play. A study of Renaissance thought may guide us to what is central in Shakespeare's drama; it may tell us why Shakespeare's vision of life is what it is. But we can apprehend his vision only as aesthetic experience. When the long history of Shakespeare studies indicates that certain characterizations are ambiguous, scholarly information cannot erase those ambiguities, for they arise either from detached, ironic, or ambivalent conceptions of character or from failures to translate univocal judgments into effective artifice. To announce that Ulysses' speech on order and degree is a great statement of Elizabethan commonplaces is merely to accent the irony of its dramatic context and to define more sharply the problem which the critical faculty alone can solve.

There will always be a welcome variety in the interpretation of Shakespeare. And there will always be eccentric interpretations, but they will not long withstand the assault of common sense, the sensitive and scrupulous examination of the text, and the insistence that Shakespeare's art is dramatic in intention —created for theatrical performance. Historical

[2] How shall we decide which of the Elizabethan views of melancholy are relevant to Shakespeare's portrait of Hamlet? Certainly not every obscure and contradictory Elizabethan opinion is part of the background of the play. If we are not to stress coincidental parallels or make erroneous assumptions about Shakespeare's beliefs, the selection of scholarly evidence must be an act of critical judgment. A scholar must begin with a conception of Hamlet's character if he is to find the contemporary thought which underlay Shakespeare's dramatic portrait. Thus while scholarly documentation validates a critical impression, that documentation will be apposite and illuminating only if based upon a sensitive and perceptive reading of the text.

Moreover, unless we are to assume that Shakespeare was incapable of original insights into human nature, we cannot say that an interpretation of character is mistaken because we cannot find sanction for it in Elizabethan treatises on moral philosophy or psychology. The Romantic notion that Hamlet loses his will to action in thought may be mistaken (I think it is mistaken), but it is not mistaken simply because Elizabethan courtiers were (or were supposed to be) men of action as well as thought. Beaumont and Fletcher's Amintor and Philaster are proof that the Romantic conception of Hamlet was plausible to the Elizabethan artistic mind, if not to the compiler of courtesy books.

criticism has, of course, eliminated eccentric interpretations, but it has also, in some respects, fostered them by substituting completely unliterary standards for the traditional standards of critical perceptivity. We need now to redefine what is eccentric in interpretation by first redefining the legitimate criteria of critical judgment and the proper relationship between scholarship and criticism in Shakespeare studies. Only through the cooperation of scholarship and criticism will we arrive at an understanding of Shakespeare's art that precludes the dogmatism of the learned and the uninformed.

◆ from *Hamlet* and Greek Drama

By H. D. F. KITTO

'There is an old saying that high prosperity, when it reaches its peak, dies not childless, but has offspring; out of good fortune is born misery without end. But my thought takes a lonely path of its own. It is wickedness that begets a numerous offspring, resembling its parents; but in the house that pursues Justice, prosperity breeds fair fortune. Among the wicked, old sin breeds new sin, and a wicked spirit of recklessness, with black ruin for the family.'[1] *Hamlet* might serve as an illustration of this Aeschylean text. Claudius, the 'limed soul', in struggling to be free, is still more engaged, and in his struggle he smears others with the same deadly concoction in which he himself is held fast.

To begin with, there are the consequences, to Claudius, of the death of Polonius. No fewer than three times does he speak of the danger in which this involves him:

> *O heavy deed!*
> *It had been so with us, had we been*
> * there . . .*
> *Alas, how shall this bloody deed be an-*
> *swered?*
> *It will be laid to us, whose providence*
> *Should have kept short, restrain'd, and out*
> * of haunt*
> *This mad young man.*

Again:

> *So, haply, slander—*
> *Whose whisper o'er the world's diameter*
> *As level as the cannon to its blank*
> *Transports his poisoned shot—may miss*
> * our name*
> *And hit the woundless air.*

Again:

> *How dangerous is it that this man goes*
> * loose!*

H. D. F. Kitto, "*Hamlet* and Greek Drama," *Form and Meaning in Drama* (London: Methuen, 1960), pp. 317–337.

[1] *Agamemnon* 751-771, paraphrased.

> *Yet must not we put the strong law on him:*
> *He's loved of the distracted multitude . . .*

Therefore, as we now learn, the King will add another treacherous crime to his tally: Hamlet is to be murdered in England:

> *Till I know 'tis done,*
> *Howe'er my haps, my joys were ne'er*
> *begun.*

This evil intention is frustrated, and the failure of the King's plot is presented by Shakespeare in a way that must be carefully observed. Unlike the Greek dramatists, Shakespeare did not work in a convention that permitted him to use the gods in his theatre; nevertheless, references to Providence now become very frequent, and perhaps we should not dismiss them too lightly. For instance, if we remain with our feet firmly planted on the most prosaic level we can find, secure in the knowledge that at least we can fall no lower, we shall have to say, when the pirate-ship turns up, that the magnificent Shakespeare is condescending to a stale contrivance that would discredit a second-rate melodrama; and having said this we shall for very shame begin to cast about for excuses or explanations, like the prosaic critics who do not understand why Aeschylus freezes the Strymon.

We will go back to the point where Hamlet is being sent to England. He has his suspicions, and the way in which they are conveyed to us is worth noting:

HAMLET: *For England!*
KING: *Aye, Hamlet.*
HAMLET: *Good.*
KING: *So 'tis, if thou knew'st our purposes.*
HAMLET: *I see a cherub that sees them.*

One of the older editors explains: Hamlet means that he divines them, or has an inkling of them. That is indeed what he means, but what he says is: 'I see a cherub that sees them', and the phrase is not idly chosen.

But before he puts Hamlet on board ship, Shakespeare contrives, in a rough and ready way, that he shall meet the Norwegian Captain, and in an even rougher and readier way, he clears the stage for a final soliloquy. At first sight this soliloquy is not easy to understand. But the meaning of the whole passage becomes plain when we see that it is a parallel to the Pyrrhus-Hecuba passage. Superficially, each of them is superfluous—proof enough that Shakespeare thought them necessary. Each ends with a soliloquy, and each soliloquy with an important declaration. Naturally, to these formal resemblances an inner one corresponds, as is clear from the fact that each soliloquy asks the same torturing question: Why cannot I act? But how far, or how deep, does the resemblance go?

In each case Hamlet is contrasted with someone who *can* act. The earlier passage showed us that Hamlet, by no means deficient in passion, cannot give rein to it, like the Player. Now he is set over against Fortinbras, and the theme is Honour.

> *How all occasions do inform against me*
> *And spur my dull revenge! What is a man*
> *If his chief good and market of his time*
> *Be but to sleep and feed? A beast, no more.*
> *Sure, He that made us with such large dis-*
>   *course,*
> *Looking before and after, gave us not*
> *That capability and godlike reason*
> *To fust in us unused . . .*

If any man has 'that capability and godlike reason' it is Hamlet himself; no one could be more of a man, less of a beast that only sleeps and feeds. So that when, a moment later, he again asks himself the baffling question

> *Why yet I live to say* This thing's to do,

we know that the answer is not 'bestial oblivion.' Nor is it cowardice. The answer is hidden from Hamlet, but it would indeed be a strange play if it were also hidden from us. First he was held back by a sense of evil that paralysed him—an evil that he came to think barely credible. The paralysis disappeared; he convinced his reason, and was ready to do it—not out of passion but as a necessary act of justice. Yet it was precisely his reasoning that betrayed him: if only he

had known what Claudius knew so well at that moment, Claudius would have been dead. To follow Reason is godlike, but can be perilous to such as are not gods.

Now he is confronted with something which seems to him to deny all reason:

> *Why then, the Polack never will defend it.*

He has before him men who are following a different guide to conduct—twenty thousand men going to their graves like beds, all for so miserable plot of ground,

> *Led by a delicate and tender prince*
> *Whose spirit with divine ambition puffed*
> *Makes mouths at the invisible event*
> *Exposing what is mortal and unsure*
> *To all that fortune, death and danger dare*
> *Even for an eggshell.*

True greatness, he reflects, is to demand indeed great argument before acting, but to find that argument even in a straw, 'when honour's at the stake.' 'How stand I then?'

Inspired by this example, Hamlet decides: he must follow where Honour beckons. But we must observe how the speech ends, for the end illuminates much:

> *O from this time forth*
> *My thoughts be bloody, or be nothing*
>   *worth.*

To Fortinbras, following Honour is—we must not say easy, but at least simple; to Hamlet, placed as he is, it is not. We must not sentimentalise him. He was ready to 'make a ghost of him that lets me,' and he has little compunction in sending Rosencrantz and Guildenstern to their death; nevertheless, he has already told us, twice, what he thinks of this business. Shakespeare makes it quite plain what is happening to him—that he feels himself being inexorably dragged down, as on a 'massy wheel,' to actions which, being free, he would condemn. 'Hell itself breathes out contagion to this world,' and he is affected by it. The same thought he repeats to Gertrude:

> *They must sweep my way*
> *And marshal me to knavery.*

The path of honour, to Fortinbras, is straightforward; in Denmark, Hamlet's fineness must necessarily suffer corruption.

It has been the burden of all Hamlet's self-questionings hitherto, that he is losing his honour.

> Who calls me villain? breaks my pate across,
> Plucks off my beard, and blows it in my
> face?

Now, having surmounted his paralysis, having convinced his reason, having reconciled himself to 'knavery,' he becomes resolute. But by now it is dangerously late; Claudius is fully warned and deeply committed. Indeed, the question is whether the villain Claudius will not destroy Hamlet, and triumph. In the event, villainy does triumph, to the extent that it destroys Hamlet; but we can hardly fail to notice how often, in what remains of the play, Shakespeare reminds us that there is an overruling Providence which, though it will not intervene to save Hamlet, does intervene to defeat Claudius, and does guide events to a consummation in which evil frustrates itself, even though it destroys the innocent by the way.

We may not follow Hamlet's fortunes yet without distorting the structure; for Shakespeare now engages our interest in other events, and these are not merely contemporaneous with those but are also complementary to them, cohering with them in the wide design of the play. As in the first six scenes, we must be prepared for significant juxtaposition.

What we are to be concerned with is the madness and then the death of Ophelia, the return of Laertes, the willingness of 'the false Danish dogs' to rebel against Claudius, the failure of his present plot against Hamlet, and the hatching of the new double plot by Claudius and Laertes together. If we try to take, as the essence of the play, the duel between Hamlet and Claudius, or the indecision of Hamlet, or any other theme which is only a part, not the whole, of the play, then much of this act is only peripheral; but everything coheres closely and organically when we see that the central theme is the disastrous growth of evil.

How, for instance, does Shakespeare introduce the madness of Ophelia? In a very arresting way indeed:

> I will not speak with her.

These few words reveal much. We last saw Gertrude utterly contrite at the sins which Hamlet had revealed to her. She has received a straight hint that she is living with her husband's murderer; she has seen Polonius killed, and his daughter crazed—all this the direct or indirect consequence of the villainy in which she has been a partner. No wonder that she would avoid being confronted with this latest disaster: 'I will not speak with her.'

But Horatio tells her that she must, lest worse happen:

> 'Twere good she were spoken with, for she
> may strew
> Dangerous   conjectures   in   ill-breeding
> minds.

She gives way, hoping to make the best of it:

> Let her come in.—
> To my sick soul, as sin's true nature is,
> Each toy seems prelude to some great amiss.
> So full of artless jealousy is guilt,
> It spills itself in fearing to be spilt.

She is frightened by her knowledge of her own guilt, but against this she sets the thought that too great consciousness of guilt, and too great circumspection in hiding it, may of themselves reveal that guilt to the world. It is one of the themes that run through the play, that sin breaks through every attempt to keep it secret: 'Foul deeds will rise.' The oath of the cellarage-scene was sworn in vain.

After this it is the King's turn to show what offspring his own sins are breeding for him, and what he says does but repeat, more urgently, what he has said before.[2]

> When sorrows come, they come not single
> spies,
> But in battalias.

Polonius is dead, Hamlet gone, the people mudded—

>   and we have done but greenly
> In hugger-mugger to inter him—

and Laertes has come secretly from France, to

[2] In Act III, Scene 5.

hear 'pestilent speeches of his father's death.'

> O my dear Gertrude, this,
> Like to a murdering-piece, in many places
> Gives me superfluous death.

Immediately upon this comes Laertes, at the head of an incipient rebellion. The Court may be subservient and complaisant, but among the people Claudius commands little respect:

> Thick and unwholesome in their thoughts
>   and whispers
> For good Polonius' death,

and bearing 'great love' for the exiled Prince. Claudius has given a handle to any enemy he may have, and the people are willing to take from him the crown which he has done so much to win. But he is equal to the occasion; Hamlet has gone to his death, and Laertes can be talked over.

With Laertes he has little trouble:

LAERTES: *And so have I a noble father lost;*
A sister driven into desperate terms,
Whose worth, if praises may go
    back again,
Stood challenger on mount of all
    the age.
KING: *Break not your sleeps for that: you*
    must not think
That we are made of stuff so flat
    and dull,
That we can let our beard be shook
    with danger,
And think it pastime. You shortly
    shall hear more:
I loved your father, and we love
    ourself;
And that, I hope, will teach you
    to imagine—
        Enter a Messenger.

Sophocles too used Messengers in this way. Claudius is confronted with news which we have briefly learned already. His plot has failed; Hamlet is back in Denmark. To Claudius it is incredible:

> How should it be? how otherwise?

The full story of his escape we are still to learn, but we may suspect that there was indeed a cherub that saw the King's purposes. But for the plot that has failed he substitutes another, since he 'loves himself.' Laertes consents—like two other men, now dead—to serve Claudius:

KING: *Will you be ruled by me?*
LAERTES: *I will, my lord,*
So you will not o'errule me to a
    peace.
KING: *To thine own peace.*

But hardly so, since it involves Laertes first in treachery, then in death.

Again a Messenger interrupts the King:

KING: *. . . wherein but sipping,*
If he by chance escape your ven-
    omed stuck,
Our purpose may hold there.—
        Enter the Queen.
            How now, sweet Queen?
QUEEN: *One woe doth tread upon another's*
    heel,
So fast they follow.—Your sister's
    drowned, Laertes.

Death has struck again. It is the fitting climax to this part of the play. Since it began, with the Queen's vain declaration: 'I will not speak with her,' our thoughts have not been encouraged to stray very far from the idea of evil breeding evil, and leading to ruin. Each *toy is* prelude to some great amiss. The present one reaches its consummation in the scene that follows; and the horrible spectacle of Hamlet and Laertes struggling with each other beside the grave [3] points the way to the end. Sophocles, in the *Electra*, has a vivid image of the irresistible advance of Vengeance on the criminals:

> See how Ares (Violence) advances, breath-
>   ing implacable slaughter

except that the word which I have translated 'advances' really means 'grazes its way forward,' as a flock will slowly and deliberately eat its way across a pasture, in a way which nothing but satiety will stop. The same feeling of inevitability prevails here.

At the end of the Churchyard-scene we

---

[3] Not *in* the grave. To what Granville Barker has to say about this (*Introduction to Hamlet*, 162 f.) add that Ophelia's body is not coffined—or how could Laertes say: 'Hold off the earth awhile, Till I have caught her once more in mine arms'?

are told what happened on the North Sea.
We last saw Hamlet being sent away, under
guard, for 'instant death.' It looked as if
Claudius might triumph. But Hamlet is home
again. All we know of the manner of his
escape is what we have learned from his
letter to Horatio; everything turned on the
veriest accident—seconded by Hamlet's own
impetuous valour. Shakespeare now chooses
to amplify the story; and the colour he gives
it is surely a definite and significant one,
and entirely harmonious with the colours of
the whole play.

> *Sir, in my heart there was a kind of fighting*
> *That would not let me sleep.*

This time, as when he killed Polonius, and as
always henceforth, Hamlet yields to the
prompting of the occasion:

> HAMLET: *Rashly—*
> *And praised be rashness for it: let*
> *us know*
> *Our indiscretion sometimes serves*
> *us well*
> *When our deep plots do pall; and*
> *that should teach us*
> *There's a divinity that shapes our*
> *ends*
> *Rough-hew them how we will,—*
> HORATIO: *That is most certain.*
> HAMLET: *Up from my cabin . . .*

This is a very different Hamlet from the one
who sought confirmation—or disproof—of
what the Ghost had told him, and who
sought more than mere death for Claudius.
It is the Hamlet who did the 'rash and bloody
deed' on Polonius, where also 'rashness' serves
the ends of Providence.

As for what Hamlet did to Rosencrantz and
Guildenstern, we must be on our guard
against seeing the obvious and missing what
is significant. There is no irrelevant reproof
in Horatio's brief comment:

> *So Rosencrantz and Guildenstern go to 't.*

Hamlet continues:

> *Why, man, they did make love to this em-*
> *ployment.*
> *They are not on my conscience; their defeat*
> *Doth by their own insinuation grow.*
> *'Tis dangerous when the baser nature*
> *comes*

> *Between the pass and fell incensèd points*
> *Of mighty opposites.*

This is not Hamlet trying to exculpate himself. Shakespeare is not interested in that
kind of thing here. He is saying: 'This is
what happens in life, when foolish men allow
themselves to be used by such as Claudius,
and to get themselves involved in desperate
affairs like these.' To prove that this is what
he meant, we may once more reflect what
Horatio might have said, and then listen to
what he does say:

> *Why, what a King is this!*

How could Shakespeare more decisively draw
our attention away from a nice and private
appraisal of Hamlet's character, as expressed
in this affair, and direct it to the philosophic
or 'religious' framework in which it is set?
Horatio says just what Laertes says later: 'The
King! the King's to blame.'

It was a lucky chance, though not an unlikely one, that Hamlet had his father's signet
in his purse; but this is how Hamlet puts it:

> *Why, even in this was Heaven ordinant.*

It was also a lucky chance that the pirate ship
caught up with them at this time; and our
natural response is: Here too Heaven was
ordinant. But it was no lucky chance that
Hamlet (with his well-known indecision)
was the first and only man to board the pirate.

Once more, the English tragic poet recalls
the Greek. In the *Agamemnon* 'some god'
took the helm of the King's ship, saved it from
the storm, and brought it to land, that Agamemnon might suffer what Justice demanded.
Hamlet is a hero very different from Agamemnon, but he too is brought safely back
from the sea by Providence; it is no part of
the universal design that villainy should triumph. And further: it is through the actions
of men that the designs of Providence are
fulfilled—through the reckless courage of
Hamlet, through the valour and intelligence
of the Greeks, in the *Persae*, through the
resolution of Electra and Orestes in Sophocles' play. The gods and men are 'partners,'
μεταίτιοι. This is not to say that the religion
or philosophy of Shakespeare was the same
as that of Aeschylus and Sophocles, nor that
his drama was influenced by theirs, either

directly or indirectly; only that they were all tragic poets, grappling with the same fundamental realities, and expressing themselves in what is recognisably the same dramatic language.

Once more Hamlet and Claudius confront each other, and Claudius, we know, has another deadly plot ready. Horatio warns Hamlet that the time is short; but Hamlet replies 'The interim is mine.'

But there is no interim at all; the tide has run out, and Hamlet seems to feel it: 'If his fitness speaks, mine is ready.' That Claudius is fit for death is plain enough; but what of Hamlet? 'I will forstall their repair hither,' says Horatio, 'and say you are not fit.' Every word in this dialogue makes us feel that the tragic action is at last poised, ready for the catastrophe. Hamlet has his 'gaingiving,' but he defies augury: 'Mine is ready.' Even more forcibly we are made to feel that Providence is working in the events; an eternal Law is being exemplified: 'There is a special providence in the fall of a sparrow.' But if Providence is working, what is the catastrophe intended to reveal?

The significant design of the catastrophe is unmistakeable. The action of the play began with poison, and it ends with a double poison, that of Claudius and that of Laertes. Gertrude, left to Heaven as the Ghost had commanded, drinks Claudius's poison literally as she had once done metaphorically. Claudius is killed by both, for Hamlet first runs him through with Laertes' poisoned sword, and then makes him drink his own poisoned cup. Laertes himself confesses: 'I am most justly slain by my own treachery'; and in his dying reconciliation with Hamlet he accepts, in effect, what Hamlet had said to him earlier in his own defence:

> *Hamlet does it not, Hamlet denies it.*
> *Who does it then? His madness. If 't be so,*
> *Hamlet is of the faction that is wronged.*

For Hamlet's 'madness' was but the reflection of the evil with which he found himself surrounded, of which Claudius was the most prolific source. So Laertes declares: 'The King! The King's to blame.' Hamlet's death shall not come on Laertes, nor the death of Polonius on Hamlet, but both on Claudius. Horatio, on the other hand, is forcibly prevented from sharing in this common death.

He has stood outside the action; he has not been tainted. What is taking place is something like the working-out of Dikê, and in this there is no place for heroic suicide. Hamlet is destroyed not because evil works mechanically, but because his nature was such that he could not confront it until too late.

> *Fie, 'tis an unweeded garden,*
> *That grows to seed; things rank and gross*
> *in nature*
> *Possess it merely.*

Weeds can choke flowers. These weeds have choked Ophelia, and at last they choke Hamlet, because he could not do the coarse work of eradicating them. First, his comprehensive awareness of evil, reversing every habit of his mind, left him prostrate in anguish and apathy; then, the desire for vengeance being aroused, he missed everything by trying to encompass too much; finally, pursuing Honour when it was nearly too late, he found it, but only in his own death. So finely poised, so brittle a nature as Hamlet's, is especially vulnerable to the destructive power of evil.

In the first act, the sinister Claudius drank to Hamlet's health, and guns proclaimed to Heaven and Earth the 'heavy-headed revel.' Now in the last scene the guns roar again: Claudius is drinking to Hamlet's death. The action has completed its circle. The guns remind us of what Hamlet said when first they spoke: some vicious mole of nature, like their birth, wherein they are not guilty; the overgrowth of some complexion that breaks down the pales and forts of reason; some habit that o'erleavens, or works too strongly for, plausive manners—all these bring corruption to a man whose virtues else may be 'pure as grace, as infinite as man may undergo.' All this we see fulfilled in Hamlet. Gertrude's sin, his 'birth,' has worked in his mind to spoil it; his philosophic 'complexion,' too absolute, was overthrown and turned to 'madness'; his habit of 'godlike reason' betrayed him at the great crisis.

But does Hamlet 'in the general censure take corruption'? This is a question which Shakespeare answers by letting off guns for a third time.

> *Let four captains*
> *Bear Hamlet, like a soldier, to the stage;*
> *For he was likely, had he been put on,*

T' have proved most royally: and for his
   passage
The soldiers' music and the rites of war
Speak loudly for him.

This time the guns proclaim neither swinish coarseness nor black treachery, but Honour.

This examination of *Hamlet* has been based on the same assumptions as our examination of certain Greek plays: that the dramatist said exactly what he meant, through the medium of his art, and means therefore exactly what he has said. We have tried therefore to observe what in fact he has said, considering every scene and every considerable passage (as one would in analysing a picture, for example, or a piece of music), not passing over this or that because it did not happen to interest us, or illustrate our point; nor being too ready to disregard a passage on the grounds that it was put there for some extraneous reason; remembering too that a dramatist can 'say' things by means other than words. I do not so flatter myself as to suppose that anything new has been brought to light. Nevertheless, if this general account of the play is acceptable, if its structure has been made to appear purposeful, in details big and small, such that the interpretation (blunders excepted) carries some measure of authority, then the critical method and the assumptions on which it is based may be held to be sound. It seems to me that this may be true.

As we said at the outset, the first thing that strikes us, or should strike us, when we contemplate the play is that it ends in the complete destruction of the two houses that are concerned. The character of Hamlet and the inner experience that he undergoes are indeed drawn at length and with great subtlety, and we must not overlook the fact; nevertheless, the architectonic pattern just indicated is so vast as to suggest at once that what we are dealing with is no individual tragedy of character, however profound, but something more like religious drama; and this means that unless we are ready, at every step, to relate the dramatic situation to its religious or philosophical background—in other words, to look at the play from a point of view to which more recent drama has not accustomed us—then we may not see either the structure

or the meaning of the play as Shakespeare thought them.

Why do Rosencrantz and Guildenstern die, and Ophelia, and Laertes? Are these disasters casual by-products of 'the tragedy of a man who could not make up his mind'? Or are they necessary parts of a firm structure? Each of these disasters we can refer to something that Hamlet has done or failed to do, and we can say that each reveals something more of Hamlet's character; but if we see no more than this we are short-sighted, and are neglecting Shakespeare's plain directions in favour of our own. We are told much more than this when we hear Horatio, and then Laertes, cry 'Why, what a King is this!', 'The King, the King's to blame'; also when Guildenstern says, with a deep and unconscious irony 'We here give up ourselves . . . ,' and when Laertes talks of 'contagious blastments.' Shakespeare puts before us a group of young people, friends or lovers, none of them wicked, one of them at least entirely virtuous, all surrounded by the poisonous air of Denmark (which also Shakespeare brings frequently and vividly before our minds), all of them brought to death because of its evil influences. Time after time, either in some significant patterning or with some phrase pregnant with irony, he makes us see that these people are partners in disaster, all of them borne down on the 'massy wheel' to 'boisterous ruin.'

In this, the natural working-out of sin, there is nothing mechanical. That is the philosophic reason why character and situation must be drawn vividly. Neither here nor in Greek drama have we anything to do with characters who are puppets in the hands of Fate. In both, we see something of the power of the gods, or the designs of Providence; but these no more override or reduce to unimportance the natural working of individual character than the existence, in the physical world, of universal laws overrides the natural behaviour of natural bodies. It is indeed precisely in the natural behaviour of men, and its natural results, in given circumstances, that the operation of the divine laws can be discerned. In *Hamlet,* Shakespeare draws a complete character, not for the comparatively barren purpose of 'creating' a Hamlet for our admiration, but in order to show how he, like the others, is inevitably engulfed by the evil that has been set in motion, and how he himself becomes the cause of further ruin. The conception which unites these eight persons in one coherent catastrophe may be said to be this: evil, once started on its course, will so work as to attack and overthrow impartially the good and the bad; and if the dramatist makes us feel, as he does, that a Providence is ordinant in all this, that, as with the Greeks, is his way of universalising the particular event.

Claudius, the arch-villain, driven by crime into further crime, meets at last what is manifestly divine justice. 'If his fitness speaks . . .' says Hamlet; the 'fitness' of Claudius has been speaking for a long time. At the opposite pole stands Ophelia, exposed to corruption through uncorrupted, but pitifully destroyed as the chain of evil uncoils itself. Then Gertrude, one of Shakespeare's most tragic characters: she is the first, as Laertes is the last, to be tainted by Claudius; but while he dies in forgivenes and reconciliation, no such gentle influence alleviates her end. In the bedchamber scene Hamlet had pointed out to her the hard road to amendment; has she tried to follow it? On this, Shakespeare is silent; but her last grim experience of life is to find that 'O my dear Hamlet, the drink, the drink! I am poisoned'—poisoned, as she must realise, by the cup that her new husband had prepared for the son whom she loved so tenderly. After her own sin, and as a direct consequence of it, everything that she holds dear is blasted. Her part in this tragedy is indeed a frightening one. She is no Claudius, recklessly given to crime, devoid of any pure or disinterested motive. Her love for her son shines through every line she speaks; this, and her affection for Ophelia, show us the Gertrude that might have been, if a mad passion had not swept her into the arms of Claudius. By this one sin she condemned herself to endure, and, still worse, to understand, all its devastating consequences: her son driven 'mad,' killing Polonius, denouncing herself and her crime in cruel terms that she cannot rebut, Ophelia driven out of her senses and into her grave—nearly a criminal's grave; all her hopes irretrievably ruined. One tragic little detail, just before the end, shows how deeply Shakespeare must have pondered on his Gertrude. We know that she has seen the wild struggle in the graveyard between Laertes and Hamlet. When the Lord enters, to invite Hamlet to the fencing-match, he says: 'The Queen desires you to use some gentle entertainment to Laertes before you fall to play.' 'She well instructs me,' says Hamlet. What can this mean, except that she has vague fears of Laertes' anger, and a pathetic hope that Hamlet might appease it, by talk more courteous than he had used in the graveyard? It recalls her equally pathetic wish that Ophelia's beauty and virtue might 'bring him to his wonted ways again.' The mischief is always much greater than her worst fears. We soon see how Hamlet's gentle entertainment is received by Laertes; and she, in the blinding flash in which she dies, learns how great a treachery had been prepared against her Hamlet.

We cannot think of Gertrude's death, and the manner of it, without recalling what the Ghost had said: Leave her to Heaven. But if we are to see the hand of Providence—whatever that may signify—in her death, can we do other with the death of Polonius? A 'casual slaughter'? A 'rash and bloody deed'? Certainly; and let us by all means blame Hamlet for it, as also for the callousness with which he sends Rosencrantz and Guildenstern to their doom; but if we suppose that Shakespeare contrived these things only to show us what Hamlet was like, we shall be treating as secular drama what Shakespeare designed as something bigger. In fact, Hamlet was *not* like this, any more than he was, by nature, hesitant or dilatory; any more than Ophelia was habitually mad. This is what he has become. The dramatist does indeed direct us to regard the killing of Polonius in two aspects at once: it is a sudden, unpremeditated attack made by Hamlet, 'mad,' on one who he hopes will prove to be Claudius; and at the same time it is the will of Heaven:

> For this same lord
> I do repent; but Heaven hath pleased it so
> To punish me with this and this with me,
> That I must be their scourge and minister.

Surely this is exactly the same dramaturgy that we meet in Sophocles' *Electra*. When Orestes comes out from killing his mother, Electra asks him how things are. 'In the *palace*,' [4] he says, 'all is well—if Apollo's oracle

[4] I italicise this word in order to represent Sophocles' untranslateable μέν, which suggests a coming antithesis that in fact is not expressed.

was well.' Perhaps it was a 'rash and bloody deed'; it seems to bring Orestes little joy. We may think of it what we like; Sophocles does not invite us to approve, and if we suppose that he does, we have not understood his play, or his gods. Apollo approves, and Orestes, though he acts for his own reasons, is the gods' 'scourge and minister.' Polonius, no unworthy Counsellor of this King, a mean and crafty man whose soul is mirrored in his language no less than in his acts, meets a violent death while spying; and that such a man should so be killed is, in a large sense, right. Hamlet may 'repent'; Orestes may feel remorse at a dreadful act, but in each case Heaven was ordinant.

The death of Laertes too is a coherent part of this same pattern. To this friend of Hamlet's we can attribute one fault; nor are we taken by surprise when we meet it, for Shakespeare has made his preparations. Laertes is a noble and generous youth, but his sense of honour has no very secure foundations—and Polonius' farewell speech to him makes the fact easy to understand. His natural and unguarded virtue, assailed at once by his anger, his incomplete understanding of the facts, and the evil suggestions of Claudius, gives way; he falls into treachery, and through it, as he comes to see, he is 'most justly killed.'

Of Rosencrantz and Guildenstern, two agreeable though undistinguished young men, flattered and suborned and cruelly destroyed, there is no more to be said; but there remains Hamlet, last and greatest of the eight. Why must he be destroyed? It would be true to say that he is destroyed simply because he has failed to destroy Claudius first; but this is 'truth' as it is understood between police-inspectors, on duty. The dramatic truth must be something which, taking this in its stride, goes much deeper; and we are justified in saying 'must be' since this catastrophe too is presented as being directed by Providence, and therefore inevitable and 'right.' If 'there is a special providence in the fall of a sparrow,' there surely is in the fall of a Hamlet.

Of the eight victims, we have placed Claudius at one pole and Ophelia at the other; Hamlet, plainly, stands near Ophelia. In both Hamlet and Ophelia we can no doubt detect faults: she ought to have been able to see through Polonius, and he should not have hesitated. But to think like this is to behave like a judge, one who must stand outside the drama and sum up from a neutral point of view; the critic who tries to do this would be better employed in a police-court than in criticism. We must remain within the play, not try to peer at the characters through a window of our own constructing. If we do remain within the play, we observe that what Shakespeare puts before us, all the time, is not faults that we can attribute to Ophelia and Hamlet, but their virtues; and when he does make Hamlet do things deserving of blame, he also makes it evident on whom the blame should be laid. The impression with which he leaves us is not the tragedy that one so fine as Hamlet should be ruined by one fault; it is the tragedy that one so fine should be drawn down into the gulf; and, beyond this, that the poison let loose in Denmark should destroy indiscriminately the good, the bad and the indifferent. Good and bad, Hamlet and Claudius, are coupled in the one sentence 'If his fitness speaks, mine is ready.' That Claudius is 'fit and seasoned for his passage' is plain enough is it not just as plain that Hamlet is equally 'ready'? What has he been telling us, throughout the play, but that life can henceforth have no meaning or value to him? Confronted by what he sees in Denmark, he, the man of action, has been reduced to impotence; the man of reason has gone 'mad'; the man of religion has been dragged down to 'knavery,' and has felt the contagions of Hell. There is room, though not very much, for subtle and judicious appraisal of his character and conduct; the core of his tragedy is not here, but in the fact that such surpassing excellence is, like the beauty and virtue of Ophelia, brought to nothing by evil. Through all the members of these two doomed houses the evil goes on working, in a concatenation

> Of carnal, bloody and unnatural acts,
> Of accidental judgments, casual slaughters,
> Of deaths put on by cunning and forced cause,

until none are left, and the slate is wiped clean.

The structure of *Hamlet*, then, suggests that we should treat it as religious drama, and when we do, it certainly does not lose either in significance or in artistic integrity. As we have seen more than once, it has fundamental things in common with Greek religious drama —yet in other respects it is very different, being so complex in form and texture. It may be worth while to enquire, briefly, why this should be so.

One naturally compares it with the two Greek revenge-tragedies, the *Choephori* and Sophocles' *Electra*, but whether we do this, or extend the comparison to other Greek religious tragedies like the *Agamemnon* or *Oedipus Tyrannus* or *Antigone*, we find one difference which is obviously pertinent to our enquiry: in the Greek plays the sin, crime or error which is the mainspring of the action is specific, while in Hamlet it is something more general, a quality rather than a single act. Thus, although there are crimes enough in the *Oresteia*, what we are really concerned with, throughout the trilogy, is the problem of avenging or punishing crime. The *Agamemnon* is full of hybris, blind folly, blood-lust, adultery, treachery; but what humanity is suffering from, in the play, is not these sins in themselves, but a primitive conception of Justice, one which uses, and can be made to justify, these crimes, and leads to chaos; and the trilogy ends not in any form of reconciliation or forgiveness among those who have injured each other, nor in any purging of sin, or acceptance of punishment, but in the resolution of the dilemma.

Hamlet resembles the *Choephori* in this, that the murder of a King, and adultery, or something like it, are the crimes which have to be avenged; also that these can be avenged only through another crime, though perhaps a sinless one; but the differences are deep and far-reaching. They are not merely that Orestes kills, and Hamlet shrinks from killing. We may say that both in the Greek trilogy and in Shakespeare's play the Tragic Hero, ultimately, is humanity itself; and what humanity is suffering from, in *Hamlet* is not a specific evil, but Evil itself. The murder is only the chief of many manifestations of it, the particular case which is the mainspring of the tragic action.

This seems to be typical. In the *Antigone* a whole house is brought down in ruin, and, again, the cause is quite a specific one. It is nothing like the comprehensive wickedness of Iago, or the devouring ambition of Macbeth, or the consuming and all-excluding love of Antony and Cleopatra. It is, quite precisely, that Creon makes, and repeats, a certain error of judgment, ἁμαρτία; and I use the phrase 'error of judgment' meaning not that it is venial, nor that it is purely intellectual, but that it is specific. It is not a trivial nor a purely intellectual mistake if a man, in certain circumstances, rejects the promptings of humanity, and thinks that the gods will approve; but this is what Creon does, and the tragedy springs from this and from nothing else. He is not a wicked man—not lecherous or envious or ambitious or vindictive. All this is irrelevant. He is simply the man to make and maintain this one specific and disastrous error.

This contrast between the specific and the general obviously has a close connexion with the contrast between the singleness of the normal Greek tragic structure and the complexity of *Hamlet*. In the first place, since Shakespeare's real theme is not the moral or theological or social problem of crime and vengeance, still less its effect on a single mind and soul, but the corroding power of sin, he will present it not as a single 'error of judgment' but as a hydra with many heads. We have shown, let us hope, how this explains, or helps to explain, such features of the play as, so to speak, the simultaneous presentation of three Creons: Claudius, Gertrude and Polonius, each of them, in his own degree, an embodiment of the general evil. Hence too the richer character-drawing. Claudius is a drunkard, and the fact makes its own contribution to the complete structure; if Sophocles had made Creon a drunkard, it would have been an excrescence on the play. Hence too the frequent changes of scene in the first part of the play; also the style of speech invented for Polonius and Osric. The general enemy is the rottenness that pervades Denmark; therefore it is shown in many persons and many guises.

Then, not only are the sources of the corruption diverse, but so are its ramifications too. We are to see how it spreads, whether from Claudius or from Gertrude or from Polonius, and how it involves one after another, destroying as it goes. To be sure, Greek tragedy shows us something similar—but it is not the same. For example, the condemnation of Antigone leads to the death of Haemon, and that to the death of Eurydice; in the *Oresteia* too there is a long succession of crime. In fact, we remarked above that Claudius recalls the *Agamemnon* and its πρώταρχος ἄτη, the crime that sets crime in motion. So he does; but there is a big difference. Both in *Hamlet* and in the Greek plays crime leads to crime, or disaster to disaster, in this linear fashion, but in *Hamlet* it spreads in another way too, one which is not Greek: it spreads from soul to soul, as a contagion, as when Laertes is tempted by Claudius, or, most notably, when, by his mother's example and Polonius' basely inspired interference, Hamlet's love is corrupted into lewdness, or when he turns against his two compromised friends and pitilessly sends them to death.

Extension of evil in this fashion is, I think, foreign to Greek tragedy. Clearly, it involves a dramatic form which is complexive, not linear and single, like the Greek. Of his successive victims, Sophocles does not even mention Haemon until the middle of the play, and Eurydice not until the end; and the effect is most dramatic. In *Hamlet* there are eight victims, all of whom we have to watch, from time to time, as they become more and more deeply involved.

Further, not only are more people involved at the same time in this more generalised Tragic Flaw, but they are involved more intimately, which again makes for a richer dramatic texture. We may compare Hamlet with Orestes. Externally, they are in a similar position. But when Aeschylus has shown us that Orestes is an avenger pure in heart, and that his dilemma is from every point of view an intolerable one, it is not far wrong to say that his interest in Orestes, as a character, is exhausted; anything more would be unnecessary. Hamlet exists in a different kind of tragedy, one which requires that we should see how the contagion gradually spreads over his whole spirit and all his conduct.

The same contrast exists between Hamlet and Sophocles' Orestes and Electra. She, one might say, is drawn much more intimately than the Orestes of Aeschylus. True; but still she is drawn, so to speak, all at once: There is the situation, here is Electra, and this is the way in which it makes her act. It is not Sophocles' conception to show how her mother's continuing crime gradually warps her mind, by a stealthy growth of evil. If she is warped, it has all happened already. His dramatic interest in the characters of the avengers is focussed on this, that they, being what they are, and being affected by Clytemnestra's crime in this way, will naturally act as they do.

It is, in short, a general statement which I think will bear examination, that Greek tragedy presents sudden and complete disaster, or one disaster linked to another in linear fashion, while Shakespearean tragedy presents the complexive, menacing spread of ruin; and that at least one explanation of this is that the Greek poets thought of the tragic error as the breaking of a divine law (or sometimes, in Aeschylus, as the breaking down of a temporary divine law), while Shakespeare saw it as an evil quality which, once it has broken loose, will feed on itself and on anything else that it can find until it reaches its natural end. So, for example in *Macbeth*: in 'noble Macbeth,' ambition is stimulated, and is not controlled by reason or religion; it meets with a stronger response from Lady Macbeth, and grows insanely into a monstrous passion that threatens a whole kingdom. It is a tragic conception which is essentially dynamic, and demands the very unhellenic fluidity and expansiveness of expression which the Elizabethan theatre afforded. Whether this is a reflection of some profound difference between Greek and Christian thought is a question which I am not competent to discuss.

◆◆◆ Part Two

EURIPIDES
GIRAUDOUX

◆ A Pacifist in Periclean Athens

By EDITH HAMILTON

The greatest piece of anti-war literature there is in the world was written 2,350 years ago. This is a statement worth a thought or two. Nothing since, no description or denunciation of war's terrors and futilities, ranks with *The Trojan Women*, which was put upon the Athenian stage by Euripides in the year 416 B.C. In that faraway age a man saw with perfect clarity what war was, and wrote what he saw in a play of surpassing power, and then—nothing happened. No one was won over to his side—no band of eager disciples took up his idea and went preaching it to a war-ridden world. That superlatively efficient war-machine, Rome, described by one of her own historians as having fought continuously for eight hundred years, went on to greater and greater efficiency, with never a glimmer from Euripides to disturb her complacency. In the long annals of literature no writer is recorded who took over his point of view. A few objectors to war are known to us. They crop out sporadically through the ages, but rarely and never with Euripides' deliberate intention of showing war up for what it is. And except for Christ, to whom non-resistance was fundamental, we do not know of anyone else who disbelieved in violence as a means of doing good. None of Christ's followers seem to have followed Him there until comparatively modern times. Not one medieval saint stands out to oppose the thousands of saintly believers in the holiness of this war or that. One soldier there was in the early days of Christianity, a simple, uneducated man, who refused to fight when he was converted, because, as he explained, Christ did not approve of men killing each other. But he was easily silenced—and the Church never denounced his executioners. He never came near to being made a saint. His very name, Marcellus, is known only to the curious. That was doctrine too dangerous for the

Edith Hamilton, "A Pacifist in Periclean Athens," in *Three Greek Plays*, trans. by Edith Hamilton (New York: Norton, 1937), pp. 19–29.

Fathers of the Church. Christians refuse to fight? Rather, set up a cross as the banner of a triumphant army, conquering under that standard, killing in His name.

The men of religion, along with the men of letters, passed by, unseeing, the road Euripides had opened, and each usually vied with the other in glorifying and magnifying noble, heroic and holy war.

Consider the greatest of all, Shakespeare. He never bothered to think war through. Of course, that was not his way with anything. He had another method. Did he believe in "Contumelious, beastly, mad-brain'd war"? Or in "Pride, pomp and circumstance of glorious war"? He says as much on the one side as on the other.

"We few, we happy few, we band of brothers," King Henry cries before Agincourt:

This day is called the feast of Crispian;
And gentlemen of England now abed
Shall think themselves accursed they were
    not here,
And hold their manhoods cheap whiles any
    speaks
That fought with us upon Saint Crispin's
    day.

And then a few pages on:

                    If impious war
Array'd in flames like to the Prince of
    fiends,
Do, with his smirched complexion, all fell
    feats
Enlink'd to waste and desolation—

It is not possible to know what Shakespeare really thought about war, if he really thought about it at all. Always that disconcerting power of imagination blocks the way to our knowledge of him. He saw eye to eye with Henry on one page and with the citizens of Harfleur on the next, and what he saw when he looked only for himself, he did not care to record.

In our Western world Euripides stands

alone. He understood what the world has only begun today to understand.

"The burden of the valley of vision," wrote Isaiah, when he alone knew what could save his world from ruin. To perceive an overwhelmingly important truth of which no one else sees a glimmer, is loneliness such as few even in the long history of the world can have had to suffer. But Euripides suffered it for the greater part of his long life. The valley of vision was his abiding place.

He was the youngest of the three Greek tragic poets, but only a few years younger than Sophocles, who, indeed, survived him. The difference between the two men was great. Each had the keen discernment and the profound spiritual perception of the supreme artist. Each lived and suffered through the long-drawn-out war, which ended in the crushing defeat of Athens, and together they watched the human deterioration brought about during those years. But what they saw was not the same. Sophocles never dreamed of a world in which such things could not be. To him the way to be enabled to endure what was happening, the only way for a man to put life through no matter what happened, was to face facts unwaveringly and accept them, to perceive clearly and bear steadfastly the burden of the human lot, which is as it is and never will be different. To look at the world thus, with profundity, but in tranquillity of spirit, without bitterness, has been given to few, and to no other writer so completely as to Sophocles.

But Euripides saw clearest of all not what is, but what might be. So rebels are made. Great rebels all know the valley of vision. They see possibilities: this evil and that ended; human life transformed; people good and happy. "And there shall be neither sorrow nor crying, nor any more pain: for the former things are passed away." The clarity with which they see brings them anguish; they have a passion of longing to make their vision a reality. They feel, like a personal experience, the giant agony of the world. Not many among the greatest stand higher than Euripides in this aristocracy of humanity.

Sophocles said, "Nothing is wrong which gods command." Euripides said, "If gods do evil, then they are not gods." Two different worlds are outlined in those two ideas. Submission is the rule of the first. Not ours to pass judgment upon the divine. "There are thoughts too great for mortal men," was ever Sophocles' idea, or, in the words of another great Greek writer, "To long for the impossible is a disease of the soul." Keep then within the rational limit; "Sail not beyond the pillars of Heracles." But in the second world, Euripides' world, there can be no submission, because what reigns there is a passion for justice and a passion of pity for suffering. People who feel in that way do not submit to the inevitable, or even really perceive it. But they perceive intolerably what is wrong and under that tremendous impetus they are ready to throw all security aside, to call everything into question, to tear off the veils that hide ugly things, and often, certainly in Euripides' case, to give up forever peace of mind.

Two years before the end of the war Euripides died, not in Athens, but away up north in savage Thrace, lonelier in his death even than in his life. The reason he left his city is not recorded, but it was a compelling one. Men did not give up their home in Greek and Roman days unless they must. All we are told is a single sentence in the ancient *Life of Euripides* that he had to go away because of "the malicious exultation" aroused against him in the city. It is not hard to discover why.

Athens was fighting a life-and-death war. She did not want to think about anything. Soldiers must not think. If they begin to reason why, it is very bad for the army. Above all, they must not think about the rights and wrongs of the war. Athens called that being unpatriotic, not to say traitorous, just as emphatically as the most Aryan Nazi today could. And Euripides kept making her think. He put play after play on the stage which showed the hideousness of cruelty and the pitifulness of human weakness and human pain. The Athenians took their theater very seriously, and they were as keen and as sensitive an audience as has ever been in the world. It was unheard of in Athens to forbid a play because it was not in accordance with the ruling policy, but many a politician must have felt very uneasy as he listened to what Euripides had to say.

The war lasted twenty-seven years. Thucydides, the great historian of the time, remarks that "War, teaching men by violence, fits their characters to their condition," and two of his austere black-laid-on-white pictures illustrate with startling clarity how quickly the Athenians went downhill under that teaching.

They had been fighting for three years only when an important island in the Aegean revolted. Athens sent a big fleet against her and captured her, and in furious anger voted to put all the men to death and make slaves of the women and children. They dispatched a ship to carry the order to the general in command, and then, true to the spirit of the city that was still so great, they realized the shocking thing they had done, and they sent another boat to try to overtake the first and bring it back, or, if that was impossible, to get to the island in time to prevent the massacre. We are told how the rowers rowed as none ever before, and how they did arrive in time. And Athens felt that weight of guilt lifted, and rejoiced.

But as the war went on men did not feel guilty when terrible deeds were done. They grew used to them. Twelve years later, when the war had lasted fifteen years, another island offended Athens, not by revolting, only by trying to keep neutral. It was a tiny island, in itself of no importance, but by that time Athens was incapable of weighing pros and cons. She took the island, she killed all the men and enslaved all the women and children, and we hear of no one who protested. But a few months later one man showed what he thought, not only of this terrible deed but of the whole horrible business of war. Euripides brought out *The Trojan Women*.

There is no plot in *The Trojan Women* and almost no action. After a ten-year war a town has been taken by storm and the men in it killed. Except for two subordinate parts the characters are all women. Their husbands are dead, their children taken from them, and they are waiting to be shipped off to slavery. They talk about what has happened and how they feel, and this talk makes up the substance of the play. They are very unlike each other, so that we see the situation from different points of view. There is the wife of the king, an old woman, whose husband was cut down before her eyes, in their home as he clung to the altar; her sons, too, are dead, and she, a queen, is to be a slave to the conquerors. There is her daughter, a holy virgin, dedicated to the service of the god of truth, now to be the concubine of the victorious

commander-in-chief. Her daughter-in-law too, wife of her dearest and most heroic son, she is to belong to the son of the man who killed him and misused him after death. Helen, the beautiful, is there as well, maneuvering to regain her power over the husband she betrayed, but, in the play, unsuccessful and led away to die. And there are a number of other women, not great or impressive at all except through their sufferings, pitiful creatures weeping for the loss of home, husband, children, and everything sweet and pleasant gone forever.

That is the whole of it. Not one gleam of light anywhere. Euripides had asked himself what war is like when one looks straight at it, and this is his answer. He knew his Homer. It was the Greek Bible. And that theme of glorious poetry about the dauntless deeds of valiant men, heroically fighting for the most beautiful woman in the world, turns in his hands into a little group of broken-hearted women.

A soldier from the victorious army, who comes to bring them orders, is surprised and irritated to find himself moved to pity them; but he shrugs his shoulders and says, "Well—that's war."

The pomp and pride and glorious circumstance are all gone. When the play opens it is just before dawn, and the only light in the darkness comes fitfully from the burning city. Against that background two gods talk to each other and at once Euripides makes clear what he thinks about war as a method of improving life in any way for anyone.

In the old stories about what happened after Troy fell, told for hundreds of years before Euripides, curiously the conquering Greeks did not come off well. They had an exceedingly bad voyage back, and even those who escaped storm and shipwreck found terrible things waiting for them at home. In those faraway times, long before history began, it would seem that some men had learned what our world hardly yet perceives, that inevitably victors and vanquished must in the end suffer together. It was one of those strange prophetic insights which occasionally disturb the sluggish flow of the human spirit, but seem to accomplish nothing for centuries of time. Euripides, however, had discovered the meaning behind the stories.

He makes his two gods decide that the fall

of Troy shall turn out no better for the Greeks than for the Trojans. "Give the Greek ships a bitter homecoming," Athena, once the ally of the Greeks, says fiercely to the god of the sea. He agrees that when they set sail for Greece he will "make the wild Aegean roar until shores and reefs and cliffs will hold dead men, bodies of many dead," and when she leaves him he meditates for a moment on human folly: "The fools, who lay a city waste, so soon to die themselves."

"Mother," the Trojan queen's daughter says, "I will show you,

"This town, now, yes, Mother,
is happier than the Greeks—
They came here to the banks of that
  Scamander,
and tens of thousands died. For what?
No man had moved their land-marks
or laid siege to their high-walled towns.
But those whom war took never saw their
  children.
No wife with gentle hand shrouded them
  for their grave.
They lie in a strange land. And in their
  homes
are sorrows too, the very same.
Lonely women who died. Old men who
  waited
for sons that never came.
This is the glorious victory they won.
But we—we Trojans died to save our people.
Oh, fly from war if you are wise. But if
  war comes,
to die well is to win the victor's crown."

But many whom war kills cannot win that crown. The women talk little about the heroes, much about the helpless. They think of the children who are

Crying, crying,
calling to us with tears,
Mother, I am all alone—

They see the capture of the city through their eyes; the terrible moment of the Greeks' entry as childish ears heard it:

A shout rang out in the town,
a cry of blood through the houses,
and a frightened child caught his mother's
  skirt
and hid himself in her cloak,
while War came forth from his hiding
  place.

A child's death is the chief action in this play about war. A little boy, hardly grown beyond babyhood, is taken from his mother by the Greeks to be killed. She holds him in her arms and talks to him. She bids him:

Go die, my best-beloved, my own, my
  treasure,
in cruel hands.
Weeping, my little one? There, there,
you cannot know. You little thing
curled in my arms, how sweet the fragrance of you—
Kiss me. Never again. Come closer, closer—
Your mother who bore you—put your arms
  around her neck.
Now kiss me, lips to lips—

When the little dead body is brought back, the mother is gone, hurried away to a Greek ship. Only the grandmother is there to receive it. She holds his hands,

Dear hands, the same dear shape your
  father's had,
how loosely now you fall. And dear proud
  lips
forever closed.

She remembers the small boy climbing on to her bed in the morning and telling her what he would do when he was grown up.

Not you, but I, old, homeless, childless,
must lay you in your grave, so young,
so miserably dead.

"The poet of the world's grief," Euripides was called: in this play about war he sounded the deepest depths of that grief. How not, he would have said, since no other suffering approaches that which war inflicts.

◆◆ The Trojan Women

By EURIPIDES
Translated by Edith Hamilton

Characters

POSEIDON

PALLAS ATHENA

HECUBA, Queen of Troy, wife of Priam, mother of Hector, Paris, and Cassandra

CASSANDRA

ANDROMACHE, wife of Hector

HELEN

TALTHYBIUS, herald of the Greeks

CHORUS OF CAPTIVE TROJAN WOMEN

GREEK SOLDIERS

(*The scene is a space of waste ground except for a few huts to right and left, where the women selected for the Greek leaders are housed. Far in the background Troy, the wall in ruins, is slowly burning, as yet more smoke than flame. In front a woman with white hair lies on the ground. It is just before dawn. A tall dim figure is seen, back of the woman.*)

POSEIDON. I am the sea god. I have come
up from the salt sea depths of the Aegean,
from where the sea nymphs' footsteps fall,
weaving the lovely measures of the dance.
For since that day I built the towers of stone
around this town of Troy, Apollo with me,
—and straight we raised them, true by line
and plummet—
good will for them has never left my heart,
my Trojans and their city.

Euripides, "The Trojan Women," in *Three Greek Plays*, trans. by Edith Hamilton (New York: Norton, 1937), pp. 30–90.

City? Smoke only—all is gone,
perished beneath Greek spears.
A horse was fashioned, big with arms.
Parnassus was the workman's home,
in Phocia, and his name Epeius.
The skill he had Athena gave him.
He sent it through the walls—it carried death.
The wooden horse, so men will call it always,
which held and hid those spears.
A desert now where groves were. Blood drips down
from the gods' shrines. Beside his hearth
Priam lies dead upon the altar steps
of Zeus, the hearth's protector.
While to the Greek ships pass the Trojan treasure,
gold, gold in masses, armor, clothing,
stripped from the dead.
The Greeks who long since brought war to the town,
—ten times the seed was sown before Troy fell—
wait now for a fair wind for home,
the joyful sight of wife and child again.
Myself defeated by the Argive goddess
Hera and by Athena, both in league together—
I too must take my leave of glorious Troy,
forsake my altars. When a town is turned
into a desert, things divine fall sick.
Not one to do them honor.
Scamander's stream is loud with lamentation,
so many captive women weeping.
Their masters drew lots for them. Some will go

to Arcady and some to Thessaly.
Some to the lords of Athens, Theseus' sons.
Huts here hold others spared the lot, but chosen
for the great captains.
With them, like them a captive of the spear,
the Spartan woman, Helen.
But if a man would look on misery,
it is here to see—Hecuba lies there
before the gates. She weeps.
Many tears for many griefs.
And one still hidden from her.
But now upon Achilles' grave her daughter
was killed—Polyxena. So patiently she died.
Gone is her husband, gone her sons, all dead.
One daughter whom the Lord Apollo loved,
yet spared her wild virginity, Cassandra,
Agamemnon, in the dark, will force upon his bed.
No thought for what was holy and was God's.
O city happy once, farewell.
O shining towers, crumbling now
beneath Athena's hand, the child of God,
or you would still stand firm on deep foundations.

(As he turns to go the goddess PALLAS ATHENA enters.)

ATHENA. Am I allowed to speak to one who is my father's nearest kinsman,
a god among gods honored, powerful?
If I put enmity aside, will he?
POSEIDON. He will, most high Athena. We are kin,
old comrades too, and these have magic power.
ATHENA. Thanks for your gentleness. What I would say
touches us both, great king.
POSEIDON. A message from the gods? A word from Zeus?
Some spirit, surely?
ATHENA. No, but for Troy's sake, where we stand, I seek
your power to join my own with it.
POSEIDON. What! Now—at last? Has that long hatred left you?

Pity—when all is ashes—burned to ashes?
ATHENA. The point first, please. Will you make common cause
with me? What I wish done will you wish, too?
POSEIDON. Gladly. But what you wish I first must know.
You come to me for Troy's sake or for Greece?
ATHENA. I wish to make my Trojan foes rejoice,
and give the Greeks a bitter home-coming.
POSEIDON. The way you change! Here—there —then back again.
Now hate, now love—no limit ever.
ATHENA. You know how I was outraged and my temple.
POSEIDON. Oh that—when Ajax dragged Cassandra out?
ATHENA. And not one Greek to punish him— not one to blame him.
POSEIDON. Even though your power ruined Troy for them.
ATHENA. Therefore with you I mean to hurt them.
POSEIDON. Ready for all you wish. But—hurt them? How?
ATHENA. Give them affliction for their coming home.
POSEIDON. Held here, you mean? Or out on the salt sea?
ATHENA. Whenever the ships sail.
Zeus shall send rain, unending rain, and sleet,
and darkness blown from heaven.
He will give me—he has promised—his thunderbolt,
to strike the ships with fire. They shall burn.
Your part, to make your sea-roads roar—
wild waves and whirlwinds,
while dead men choke the winding bay.
So Greeks shall learn to reverence my house
and dread all gods.
POSEIDON. These things shall be. No need of many words
to grant a favor. I will stir the sea,
the wide Aegean. Shores and reefs and cliffs

will hold dead men, bodies of many dead.
Off to Olympus with you now, and get
those fiery arrows from the hand of Zeus.
Then when a fair wind sends the Greeks
  to sea,
watch the ships sail.

(*Exit* ATHENA.)

Oh, fools, the men who lay a city waste,
giving to desolation temples, tombs,
the sanctuaries of the dead—so soon
to die themselves.

(*Exit* POSEIDON.)

(*The two gods have been talking before daylight, but now the day begins
to dawn and the woman lying on the
ground in front moves. She is* HECUBA,
the aged queen of Troy.)

HECUBA. Up from the ground—O weary head,
  O breaking neck.
This is no longer Troy. And we are not
the lords of Troy.
Endure. The ways of fate are the ways of
  the wind.
Drift with the stream—drift with fate.
No use to turn the prow to breast the
  waves.
Let the boat go as it chances.
Sorrow, my sorrow.
What sorrow is there that is not mine,
grief to weep for.
Country lost and children and husband.
Glory of all my house brought low.
All was nothing—nothing, always.
Keep silent? Speak?
Weep then? Why? For what?

(*She begins to get up.*)

Oh, this aching body—this bed—
it is very hard. My back pressed to it—
Oh, my side, my brow, my temples.
Up! Quick, quick. I must move.
Oh, I'll rock myself this way, that way,

to the sound of weeping, the song of tears,
dropping down forever.
The song no feet will dance to ever,
for the wretched, the ruined.

O ships, O prows, swift oars,
out from the fair Greek bays and harbors,
over the dark shining sea,
you found your way to our holy city,
and the fearful music of war was heard,
the war song sung to flute and pipe,
as you cast on the shore your cables,
ropes the Nile dwellers twisted and coiled,
and you swung, oh, my grief, in Troy's
  waters.

What did you come for? A woman?
A thing of loathing, of shame,
to husband, to brother, to home.
She slew Priam, the king,
father of fifty sons,
she wrecked me upon
the reef of destruction.
Who am I that I wait *
here at a Greek king's door?
A slave that men drive on,
an old gray woman that has no home.
Shaven head brought low in dishonor.
O wives of the bronze-armored men who
  fought,
and maidens, sorrowing maidens,
plighted to shame,
see—only smoke left where was Troy.
Let us weep for her.
As a mother bird cries to her feathered
  brood,
so will I cry.
Once another song I sang
when I leaned on Priam's scepter,
and the beat of dancing feet
marked the music's measure.
Up to the gods
the song of Troy rose at my signal.

(*The door of one of the huts opens
and a woman steals out, then another,
and another.*)

---

* This is the way Professor Murray translates the
line and the one following. The translation is so
simple and beautiful, I cannot bear to give it up
for a poorer one of my own.

FIRST WOMAN. Your cry, O Hecuba—oh, such a cry—
What does it mean? There in the tent
we heard you call so piteously,
and through our hearts flashed fear.
In the tent we were weeping, too,
for we are slaves.

HECUBA. Look, child, there where the Greek ships lie—

ANOTHER WOMAN. They are moving. The men hold oars.

ANOTHER. O God, what will they do? Carry me off
over the sea in a ship far from home?

HECUBA. You ask and I know nothing,
but I think ruin is here.

ANOTHER WOMAN. Oh, we are wretched. We shall hear the summons.
Women of Troy, go forth from your home,
for the Greeks set sail.

HECUBA. But not Cassandra, oh, not her.
She is mad—she has been driven mad.
Leave her within.
Not shamed before the Greeks—not that grief too.
I have enough.
O Troy, unhappy Troy, you are gone
and we, the unhappy, leave you,
we who are living and we who are dead.

(*More women now come out from a second hut.*)

A WOMAN. Out of the Greek king's tent
trembling I come, O Queen,
to hear my fate from you.
Not death—They would not think of death
for a poor woman.

ANOTHER. The sailors—they are standing on the prow.
Already they are running out the oars.

ANOTHER. (*she comes out of a third hut and several follow her.*)
It is so early—but a terror woke me.
My heart beats so.

ANOTHER. Has a herald come from the Greek camp?
Whose slave shall I be? I—bear that?

HECUBA. Wait for the lot drawing. It is near.

ANOTHER. Argos shall it be, or Phthia?

or an island of the sea?
A Greek soldier lead me there,
far, far from Troy?

HECUBA. And I a slave—to whom—where—how?
You old gray woman, patient to endure,
you bee without a sting,
only an image of what was alive.
or the ghost of one dead.
I watch a master's door?
I nurse his children?
Once I was queen in Troy.

ONE WOMAN TO ANOTHER. Poor thing. What are your tears
to the shame before you?

THE OTHER. The shuttle will still pass through my hands,
but the loom will not be in Troy.

ANOTHER. My dead sons. I would look at them once more.
Never again.

ANOTHER. Worse to come.
A Greek's bed—and I—

ANOTHER. A night like that? Oh, never—
oh, no—not that for me.

ANOTHER. I see myself a water carrier,
dipping my pitcher in the great Pierian spring.

ANOTHER. The land of Theseus, Athens, it is known
to be a happy place. I wish I could go there.

ANOTHER. But not to the Eurotas, hateful river,
where Helen lived. Not there, to be a slave
to Menelaus who sacked Troy.

ANOTHER. Oh, look. A man from the Greek army—
a herald. Something strange has happened,
he comes so fast. To tell us—what?
What will he say? Only Greek slaves are here,
waiting for orders.

(*Enter* TALTHYBIUS *with soldiers.*)

TALTHYBIUS. You know me, Hecuba. I have often come
with messages to Troy from the Greek camp.

Talthybius—these many years you've known
me.

I bring you news.

HECUBA. It has come, women of Troy. Once
we only feared it.

TALTHYBIUS. The lots are drawn, if that is
what you feared.

HECUBA. Who—where? Thessaly? Phthia?
Thebes?

TALTHYBIUS. A different man takes each.
You're not to go together.

HECUBA. Then which takes which? Has any
one good fortune?

TALTHYBIUS. I know, but ask about each one,
not all at once.

HECUBA. My daughter, who—who drew her?
Tell me—
Cassandra. She has had so much to bear.

TALTHYBIUS. King Agamemnon chose her out
from all.

HECUBA. Oh! but—of course—to serve his
Spartan wife?

TALTHYBIUS. No, no—but for the king's own
bed at night.

HECUBA. Oh, never. She is God's, a virgin,
always.
That was God's gift to her for all her life.

TALTHYBIUS. He loved her for that same
strange purity.*

HECUBA. Throw away, daughter, the keys of
the temple.
Take off the wreath and the sacred stole.

TALTHYBIUS. Well, now—a king's bed is not
so bad.

HECUBA. My other child you took from me
just now?

TALTHYBIUS. (*speaking with constraint.*)
Polyxena, you mean? Or someone else?

HECUBA. Her. Who drew her?

TALTHYBIUS. They took her off to watch
Achilles' tomb.

HECUBA. To watch a tomb? My daughter?
That a Greek custom?
What strange ritual is that, my friend?

TALTHYBIUS. (*speaking fast and trying to put
her off.*)
Just think of her as happy—all well with
her.

HECUBA. Those words—Why do you speak
like that?
She is alive?

TALTHYBIUS. (*determined not to tell her.*)
What happened was—well, she is free from
trouble.

HECUBA. (*wearily giving the riddle up.*)
Then Hector's wife—my Hector, wise in
war—
Where does she go, poor thing—Andromache?

TALTHYBIUS. Achilles' son took her. He chose
her out.

HECUBA. And I, old gray head, whose slave
am I,
creeping along with my crutch?

TALTHYBIUS. Slave of the king of Ithaca,
Odysseus.

HECUBA. Beat, beat my shorn head! Tear,
tear my cheek!
His slave—vile lying man. I have come to
this—
There is nothing good he does not hurt—a
lawless beast.
He twists and turns, this way and that,
and back again.
A double tongue, as false in hate as false
in love.
Pity me, women of Troy,
I have gone. I am lost—oh, wretched.
An evil fate fell on me,
a lot the hardest of all.

A WOMAN. You know what lies before you,
Queen, but I—
What man among the Greeks owns me?

TALTHYBIUS. (*to the soldiers.*)
Off with you. Bring Cassandra here. Be
quick,
you fellows. We must give her to the
chief,
into his very hand. And then these here
to all the other generals. But what's that—
that flash of light inside there?

(*Light shines through the crevices of
one of the huts.*)

Set fire to the huts—is that their plan,
these Trojan women? Burn themselves to
death

* This line, too, is Professor Murray's, and retained
here for the reason given above.

rather than sail to Greece. Choosing to die
   instead.
How savagely these days the yoke bears
   down
on necks so lately free.
Open there, open the door. (*Aside.*) As
   well for them perhaps,
but for the Greeks—they'd put the blame
   on me.
HECUBA. No, no, there is nothing burning. It
   is my daughter,
Cassandra. She is mad.

(CASSANDRA *enters from the hut dressed
like a priestess, a wreath in her hair, a
torch in her hand. She does not seem
to see anyone.*)

CASSANDRA. Lift it high—in my hand—light
   to bring.
I praise him. I bear a flame.
With my torch I touch to fire
this holy place.
Hymen, O Hymen.
Blessed the bridegroom,
   blessed am I
to lie with a king in a king's bed in Argos.
   Hymen, O Hymen.
Mother, you weep
tears for my father dead,
mourning for the beloved
   country lost.
I for my bridal here
lift up the fire's flame
to the dawn, to the splendor,
to you, O Hymen.
Queen of night,
give your starlight
to a virgin bed,
as of old you did.
Fly, dancing feet.
Up with the dance.
   Oh, joy, oh, joy!
Dance for my father dead,
   most blest to die.
Oh, holy dance!
Apollo—you?
Lead on then.
There in the laurel grove
I served your altar.

Dance, Mother, come.
Keep step with me.
Dear feet with my feet
   tracing the measure
   this way and that.
Sing to the Marriage god,
oh, joyful song.
Sing for the bride, too,
joyously all.
Maidens of Troy,
dressed in your best,
honor my marriage.
Honor too him
whose bed fate drives me to share.
A WOMAN. Hold her fast, Queen, poor frenzied girl.
She might rush straight to the Greek camp.
HECUBA. O fire, fire, when men make marriages
you light the torch, but this flame flashing
   here
is for grief only. Child, such great hopes
   once I had.
I never thought that to your bridal bed
Greek spears would drive you.
Give me your torch. You do not hold it
   straight,
you move so wildly. Your sufferings, my
   child,
have never taught you wisdom.
You never change. Here! someone take the
   torch
into the hut. This marriage needs no songs,
but only tears.
CASSANDRA. O Mother, crown my triumph
   with a wreath.
Be glad, for I am married to a king.
Send me to him, and if I shrink away,
drive me with violence. If Apollo lives,
my marriage shall be bloodier than Helen's.
Agamemnon, the great, the glorious lord
   of Greece—
I shall kill him, Mother, lay his house as
   low
as he laid ours, make him pay for all
he made my father suffer, brothers, and—
But no. I must not speak of that—that axe
which on my neck—on others' too—
nor of that murder of a mother.
All, all because he married me and so

pulled his own house down.
But I will show you. This town now, yes,
    Mother,
is happier than the Greeks. I know that I
    am mad,
but Mother, dearest, now, for this one time
I do not rave.
One woman they came hunting, and one
    love,
Helen, and men by tens of thousands died.
Their king, so wise, to get what most he
    hated
destroyed what most he loved,
his joy at home, his daughter, killing her
for a brother's sake, to get him back a
    woman
who had fled because she wished—not
    forced to go.
And when they came to the banks of the
    Scamander
those thousands died. And why?
No man had moved their landmarks
or laid siege to their high-walled towns.
But those whom war took never saw their
    children.
No wife with gentle hands shrouded them
    for their grave.
They lie in a strange land. And in their
    homes
are sorrows, too, the very same.
Lonely women who died, old men who
    waited
for sons that never came—no son left to
    them
to make the offering at their graves.
That was the glorious victory they won.
But we—we Trojans died to save our peo-
    ple,
no glory greater. All those the spear slew,
friends bore them home and wrapped them
    in their shroud
with dutiful hands. The earth of their own
    land
covered them. The rest, through the long
    days they fought,
had wife and child at hand, not like the
    Greeks,
whose joys were far away.
And Hector's pain—your Hector. Mother,
    hear me.

This is the truth: he died, the best, a hero.
Because the Greeks came, he died thus.
Had they stayed home, we never would
    have known him.
This truth stands firm: the wise will fly
    from war.
But if war comes, to die well is to win
the victor's crown.
The only shame is not to die like that.
So, Mother, do not pity Troy,
or me upon my bridal bed.

TALTHYBIUS. (*has been held awestruck
through all this, but can bear no more.*)
Now if Apollo had not made you mad
I would have paid you for those evil words,
bad omens, and my general sailing soon.

(*Grumbles to himself.*)

The great, who seem so wise, have no more
    sense
than those who rank as nothing.
Our king, the first in Greece, bows down
before this mad girl, loves her, chooses her
out of them all. Well, I am a poor man,
but I'd not go to bed with her.

(*Turns to* CASSANDRA.)

Now, you—you know your mind is not
    quite right.
So all you said against Greece and for Troy,
I never heard—the wind blew it away.
Come with me to the ship now.

(*Aside.*)

A grand match for our general, she is.

(*To* HECUBA, *gently.*)

And you, do follow quietly when Odysseus'
    men come.
His wife's a good, wise woman, so they say.
CASSANDRA. (*seeming to see* TALTHYBIUS *for
the first time and looking him over haughtily.*)
A strange sort of slave, surely.
Heralds such men are called,
hated by all, for they are tyrants' tools.

You say my mother goes to serve Odysseus?

(She turns away and speaks to herself.)

But where then is Apollo's word, made
    clear
to me, that death will find her here?
And—no, that shame I will not speak of.
Odysseus! wretched—but he does not know.
    Soon all these sorrows, mine and Troy's,
    will seem
compared to his like golden hours.
Ten years behind him here, ten years
    before him.
Then only, all alone, will he come home,
and there find untold trouble has come first.
But his cares—why let fly one word at him?
Come, let us hasten to my marriage.
We two shall rest, the bridegroom and the
    bride,
within the house of death.
O Greek king, with your dreams of gran-
    deur yet to come,
vile as you are, so shall your end be,
in darkness—all light gone.
And me—a cleft in the hills,
washed by winter rains,
his tomb near by.
There—dead—cast out—naked—
and wild beasts seeking food—
It is I there—I myself—Apollo's servant.
O flowers of the God I love, mysterious
    wreaths,
away. I have forgotten temple festival,
I have forgotten joy.
Off. I tear them from my neck.
Swift winds will carry them
up to you, O God of truth.
My flesh still clean, I give them back to
    you.
Where is the ship? How do I go on board?
Spread the sail—the wind comes swift.
Those who bring vengeance—three are they,
And one of them goes with you on the sea.
Mother, my Mother, do not weep. Farewell,
dear City. Brothers, in Troy's earth laid, my
    father,
a little time and I am with you.
You dead, I shall come to you a victor.
Those ruined by my hand who ruined us.

(She goes out with TALTHYBIUS *and the
soldiers.* HECUBA, *motionless for a moment, falls.)*

A WOMAN. The Queen! See—see—she is fall-
    ing.
Oh, help! She cannot speak.
Miserable slaves, will you leave her on the
    ground,
old as she is. Up—lift her up.
HECUBA. Let me be. Kindness not wanted is
    unkindness.
I cannot stand. Too much is on me.
Anguish here and long since and to come—
O God—Do I call to you? You did not help.
But there is something that cries out for
    God
when trouble comes.
Oh, I will think of good days gone,
days to make a song of,
crowning my sorrow by remembering.
We were kings and a king I married.
Sons I bore him, many sons.
That means little—but fine, brave lads.
They were the best in all Troy.
No woman, Trojan, Greek, or stranger,
had sons like mine to be proud of.
I saw them fall beneath Greek spears.
My hair I shore at the grave of the dead.
Their father—I did not learn from others
that I must weep for him—these eyes be-
    held him.
I, my own self, saw him fall murdered
upon the altar, when his town was lost.
My daughters, maidens reared to marry
    kings,
are torn from me. For the Greeks I reared
    them.
All gone—no hope that I shall look upon
their faces any more, or they on mine.
And now the end—no more can lie be-
    yond—
The tasks they know for my age hardest,
    mine.
The door to shut and open, bowing low
—I who bore Hector—meal to grind; upon
the ground lay this old body down that
    once
slept in a royal bed; torn rags around me,
torn flesh beneath.

And all this misery and all to come
because a man desired a woman.
Daughter, who knew God's mystery and
　joy,
what strange chance lost you your vir-
　ginity?
And you, Polyxena—where are you gone?
No son, no daughter, left to help my need,
and I had many, many—
Why lift me up? What hope is there to
　hold to?
　This slave that once went delicately in
　　Troy,
take her and cast her on her bed of clay,
rocks for her pillow, there to fall and die,
wasted with tears. Count no one happy,
however fortunate, before he dies.
CHORUS. Sing me, O Muse, a song for Troy,
　a strange song sung to tears,
　a music for the grave.
　O lips, sound forth a melody
　　for Troy.

A four-wheeled cart brought the horse to
　the gates,
brought ruin to me,
　captured, enslaved me.
Gold was the rein and the bridle,
deadly the arms within,
and they clashed loud to heaven as the
　threshold was passed.

High on Troy's rock the people cried,
"Rest at last, trouble ended.
Bring the carven image in.
Bear it to Athena,
fit gift for the child of God."

Who of the young but hurried forth?
Who of the old would stay at home?
With song and rejoicing they brought
　death in,
treachery and destruction.

All that were in Troy,
hastening to the gate,
drew that smooth-planed horse of wood
carven from a mountain pine,
where the Greeks were hiding,
where was Troy's destruction,

gave it to the goddess,
gift for her, the virgin,
driver of the steeds that never die.

With ropes of twisted flax,
as a ship's dark hull is drawn to land,
they brought it to her temple of stone,
to her floor that soon would run with blood,
　to Pallas Athena.

　On their toil and their joy
the dark of evening fell,
but the lutes of Egypt still rang out
　to the songs of Troy.

And girls with feet light as air
dancing, sang happy songs.
The houses blazed with light
through the dark splendor,
　and sleep was not.
A GIRL. I was among the dancers.
I was singing to the maiden of Zeus,
the goddess of the hills.
A shout rang out in the town,
a cry of blood through the houses,
and a frightened child caught his mother's
　skirt
and hid himself in her cloak.
Then War came forth from his hiding
　place—
Athena, the virgin, devised it.
Around the altars they slaughtered us.
Within on their beds lay headless men,
young men cut down in their prime.
This was the triumph-crown of Greece.
We shall bear children for her to rear,
grief and shame to our country.

　(*A chariot approaches, loaded with
　spoils. In it sits a woman and a child.*)

A WOMAN. Look, Hecuba, it is Andromache.
See, in the Greek car yonder.
Her breast heaves with her sobs and yet
the baby sleeps there, dear Astyanax,
　the son of Hector.
ANOTHER. Most sorrowful of women, where
　do you go?
Beside you the bronze armor that was
　Hector's,

the spoil of the Greek spear, stripped from
  the dead.
Will Achilles' son use it to deck his
  temples?

ANDROMACHE. I go where my Greek masters
  take me.

HECUBA. Oh, our sorrow—our sorrow.

ANDROMACHE. Why should you weep? This
  sorrow is mine.

HECUBA. O God—

ANDROMACHE. What has come to me is mine.

HECUBA. My children—

ANDROMACHE. Once we lived, not now.

HECUBA. Gone—gone—happiness—Troy—

ANDROMACHE. And you bear it.

HECUBA. Sons, noble sons, all lost.

ANDROMACHE. Oh, sorrow is here.

HECUBA. For me—for me.

ANDROMACHE. For the city, in its shroud of
  smoke.
  Come to me, O my husband.

HECUBA. What you cry to lies in the grave.
  My son, wretched woman, mine.

ANDROMACHE. Defend me—me, your wife.

HECUBA. My son, my eldest son,
  whom I bore to Priam,
  whom the Greeks used shamefully,
  come to me, lead me to death.

ANDROMACHE. Death—oh, how deep a desire.

HECUBA. Such is our pain—

ANDROMACHE. For a city that has fallen,
  fallen.

HECUBA. For anguish heaped upon anguish.

ANDROMACHE. For the anger of God against
  Paris,
  your son, who fled from death,
  who laid Troy's towers low
  to win an evil love.
  Dead men—bodies—blood—
  vultures hovering—
  Oh, Athena the goddess is there, be sure,
  and the slave's yoke is laid upon Troy.

HECUBA. O country, desolate, empty.

ANDROMACHE. My tears fall for you.

HECUBA. Look and see the end—

ANDROMACHE. Of the house where I bore my
  children.

HECUBA. O children, your mother has lost her
  city,
  and you—you have left her alone.

Only grief is mine and mourning.
Tears and more tears, falling, falling.
The dead—they have forgotten their pain.
They weep no more.

A WOMAN. (*aside to another.*) Tears are sweet
  in bitter grief,
  and sorrow's song is lamentation.

ANDROMACHE. Mother of him whose spear
  of old brought death
  to Greeks unnumbered, you see what is
  here.

HECUBA. I see God's hand that casts the
  mighty down
  and sets on high the lowly.

ANDROMACHE. Driven like cattle captured in
  a raid,
  my child and I—the free changed to a slave.
  Oh, changed indeed.

HECUBA. It is fearful to be helpless. Men
  just now
  have taken Cassandra—forced her from me.

ANDROMACHE. And still more for you—more
  than that—

HECUBA. Number my sorrows, will you?
  Measure them?
  One comes—the next one rivals it.

ANDROMACHE. Polyxena lies dead upon Achilles tomb,
  a gift to a corpse, to a lifeless thing.

HECUBA. My sorrow! That is what Talthybius meant—
  I could not read his riddle. Oh, too plain.

ANDROMACHE. I saw her there and left the
  chariot
  and covered her dead body with my cloak,
  and beat my breast.

HECUBA. Murdered—my child. Oh, wickedly!
  Again I cry to you. Oh, cruelly slain!

ANDROMACHE. She has died her death, and
  happier by far
  dying than I alive.

HECUBA. Life cannot be what death is, child.
  Death is empty—life has hope.

ANDROMACHE. Mother, O Mother, hear a
  truer word.
  Now let me bring joy to your heart.
  I say to die is only not to be,
  and rather death than life with bitter grief.
  They have no pain, they do not feel their
  wrongs.

But the happy who has come to wretchedness,
his soul is a lost wanderer,
the old joys that were once, left far behind.
She is dead, your daughter—to her the same
as if she never had been born.
She does not know the wickedness that
killed her.
While I—I aimed my shaft at good repute.
I gained full measure—then missed happiness.
For all that is called virtuous in a woman
I strove for and I won in Hector's house.
Always, because we women, whether right
or wrong,
are spoken ill of
unless we stay within our homes, my longing
I set aside and kept the house.
Light talk, glib women's words,
could never gain an entrance there.
My own thoughts were enough for me,
best of all teachers to me in my home.
Silence, a tranquil eye, I brought my husband,
knew well in what I should rule him,
and when give him obedience.
And this report of me came to the Greeks
for my destruction. When they captured
me
Achilles' son would have me.
I shall be a slave to those who murdered—
O Hector, my beloved—shall I thrust him
aside,
open my heart to the man that comes to me,
and be a traitor to the dead?
And yet to shrink in loathing from him
and make my masters hate me—
One night, men say, one night in a man's
bed
will make a woman tame—
Oh, shame! A woman throw her husband
off
and in a new bed love another—
Why, a young colt will not run in the yoke
with any but her mate—not a dumb beast
that has no reason, of a lower nature.
O Hector, my beloved, you were all to me,
wise, noble, mighty, in wealth, in manhood, both.

No man had touched me when you took
me,
took me from out my father's home
and yoked a girl fast to you.
And you are dead, and I, with other plunder,
am sent by sea to Greece. A slave's yoke
there.
Your dead Polyxena you weep for,
what does she know of pain like mine?
The living must have hope. Not I, not any
more.
I will not lie to my own heart. No good
will ever come.
But oh, to think it would be sweet.

A WOMAN. We stand at the same point of
pain. You mourn your ruin,
and in your words I hear my own calamity.

HECUBA. Those ships— I never have set foot
on one,
but I have heard of them, seen pictures of
them.
I know that when a storm comes which
they think
they can ride out, the sailors do their best,
one by the sail, another at the helm,
and others bailing.
But if great ocean's raging overwhelms
them,
they yield to fate.
They give themselves up to the racing
waves.
So in my many sorrows I am dumb.
I yield, I cannot speak.
The great wave from God has conquered
me.
But, O dear child, let Hector be,
and let be what has come to him.
Your tears will never call him back.
Give honor now to him who is your master.
Your sweet ways—use them to allure him.
So doing you will give cheer to your
friends.
Perhaps this child, my own child's son,
you may rear to manhood and great aid for
Troy,
and if ever you should have more children,
they might build her again. Troy once more
be a city!
Oh—one thought leads another on.

But why again that servant of the Greeks?
I see him coming. Some new plan is here.

(Enter TALTHYBIUS *with soldiers. He is troubled and advances hesitatingly.)*

TALTHYBIUS. Wife of the noblest man that was in Troy,
O wife of Hector, do not hate me.
Against my will I come to tell you.
The people and the kings have all resolved—
ANDROMACHE. What is it? Evil follows words like those.
TALTHYBIUS. This child they order—Oh, how can I say it—
ANDROMACHE. Not that he does not go with me to the same master—
TALTHYBIUS. No man in Greece shall ever be his master.
ANDROMACHE. But—leave him here—all that is left of Troy?
TALTHYBIUS. I don't know how to tell you. What is bad,
words can't make better—
ANDROMACHE. I feel you kind. But you have not good news.
TALTHYBIUS. Your child must die. There, now you know
the whole, bad as it is.
ANDROMACHE. Oh, I have heard an evil worse than a slave in her master's bed.
TALTHYBIUS. It was Odysseus had his way. He spoke
to all the Greeks.
ANDROMACHE. O God. There is no measure to my pain.
TALTHYBIUS. He said a hero's son must not grow up—
ANDROMACHE. God, on his own sons may that counsel fall.
TALTHYBIUS.—but from the towering wall of Troy be thrown.
Now, now—let it be done—that's wiser.
Don't cling so to him. Bear your pain
the way a brave woman suffers.
You have no strength—don't look to any help.
There's no help for you anywhere. Think—think.

The city gone—your husband too. And you
a captive and alone, one woman—how
can you do battle with us? For your own good
I would not have you try, and draw
hatred down on you and be shamed.
Oh, hush—never a curse upon the Greeks.
If you say words that make the army angry
the child will have no burial, and without pity—
Silence now. Bear your fate as best you can.
So then you need not leave him dead without a grave,
and you will find the Greeks more kind.
ANDROMACHE. Go die, my best beloved, my own, my treasure,
in cruel hands, leaving your mother comfortless.
Your father was too noble. That is why they kill you. He could save others,
he could not save you for his nobleness.
My bed, my bridal—all for misery—
when long ago I came to Hector's halls
to bear my son—oh, not for Greeks to slay,
but for a ruler over teeming Asia.
Weeping, my little one? There, there.
You cannot know what waits for you.
Why hold me with your hands so fast, cling so fast to me?
You little bird, flying to hide beneath my wings.
And Hector will not come—he will not come,
up from the tomb, great spear in hand, to save you.
Not one of all his kin, of all the Trojan might.
How will it be? Falling down—down—oh, horrible.
And his neck—his breath—all broken.
And none to pity. You little thing,
curled in my arms, you dearest to your mother,
how sweet the fragrance of you.
All nothing then—this breast from where
your baby mouth drew milk, my travail too,
my cares, when I grew wasted watching you.

Kiss me—Never again. Come, closer, closer.
Your mother who bore you—put your arms
    around my neck.
Now kiss me, lips to lips.
O Greeks, you have found out ways to
    torture
that are not Greek.
A little child, all innocent of wrong—
you wish to kill him.
O Helen, evil growth, that was sown by
    Tyndareus,
you are no child of Zeus, as people say.
Many the fathers you were born of,
Madness, Hatred, Red Death, whatever
    poison
the earth brings forth—no child of Zeus,
but Greece's curse and all the world's.
God curse you, with those beautiful eyes
that brought to shame and ruin
Troy's far-famed plains.
Quick! take him—seize him—cast him
    down—
if so you will. Feast on his flesh.
God has destroyed me, and I cannot—
I cannot save my child from death.
Oh hide my head for shame and fling me
into the ship.

(She falls, then struggles to her knees.)

My fair bridal—I am coming—
Oh, I have lost my child, my own.
A WOMAN. O wretched Troy, tens of thou-
    sands lost
for a woman's sake, a hateful marriage bed.
TALTHYBIUS. *(drawing the child away.)*
    Come, boy, let go. Unclasp those loving
        hands,
    poor mother.
    Come now, up, up, to the very height,
    where the towers of your fathers crown the
        wall,
    and where it is decreed that you must die.

(To the soldiers.)

Take him away.

A herald who must bring such orders
should be a man who feels no pity,
and no shame either—not like me.
HECUBA. Child, son of my poor son, whose
    toil was all in vain,
we are robbed, your mother and I, oh,
    cruelly—
robbed of your life. How bear it?
What can I do for you, poor piteous child?
Beat my head, my breast—all I can give
    you.
Troy lost, now you—all lost.
The cup is full. Why wait? For what?
Hasten on—swiftly on to death.

*(The soldiers, who have waited while
HECUBA speaks, go out with the child
and TALTHYBIUS. One of them takes
ANDROMACHE to the chariot and drives
off with her.)*

CHORUS. The waves make a ring around
    Salamis.
The bees are loud in the island.
King Telamon built him a dwelling.
It fronted the holy hills,
where first the gray gleaming olive
Athena showed to men,
the glory of shining Athens,
her crown from the sky.
He joined himself to the bowman,
the son of Alcmena, for valorous deeds.
Troy, Troy he laid waste, my city,
long ago when he went forth from Greece.
When he led forth from Greece the bravest
in his wrath for the steeds* withheld,
and by fair-flowing Simois stayed his oar
that had brought him over the sea.
Cables there made the ship fast.
In his hand was the bow that never missed.
It brought the king to his death.
Walls of stone that Phoebus had built
he wrecked with the red breath of fire.
He wasted the plain of Troy.
Twice her walls have fallen. Twice
a blood-stained spear struck her down,
    laid her in ruin.

* When Troy was destroyed the first time, the reason was that the Trojan king had promised two
immortal horses to Hercules ("the son of Alcmena")
but did not give them to him. Hercules in revenge
ruined the city. The son of this king was Ganymede,
cup-bearer to Zeus.

In vain, O you who move
with delicate feet where the wine-cups are
    gold,
son of that old dead king,
who fill with wine the cup Zeus holds,
service most fair—
she who gave you birth is afire.
The shores of the sea are wailing for her.
As a bird cries over her young,
women weep for husbands, for children,
for the old, too, who gave them birth.
Your dewy baths are gone,
and the race-course where you ran.
Yet your young face keeps the beauty of
    peace
in joy, by the throne of Zeus.
While Priam's land
lies ruined by Greek spearsmen.

Love, O Love,
once you came to the halls of Troy,
and your song rose up to the dwellers in
    heaven.
How did you then exalt Troy high,
binding her fast to the gods, by a union—
No—I will not speak blame of Zeus.
But the light of white-winged Dawn, dear
    to men,
is deadly over the land this day,
shining on fallen towers.
And yet Dawn keeps in her bridal bower
her children's father, a son of Troy.
Her chariot bore him away to the sky.
It was gold, and four stars drew it.
Hope was high then for our town.
But the magic that brought her the love of
    the gods
has gone from Troy.

> (*As the song ends* MENELAUS *enters
> with a bodyguard of soldiers.*)

MENELAUS. How bright the sunlight is to-
    day—
this day, when I shall get into my power
Helen, my wife. For I am Menelaus,
the man of many wrongs.
I came to Troy and brought with me my
    army,
not for that woman's sake, as people say,

but for the man who from my house,
and he a guest there, stole away my wife.
Ah, well, with God's help he has paid the
    price,
he and his country, fallen beneath Greek
    spears.
I am come to get her—wretch—I cannot
    speak her name
who was my wife once.
In a hut here, where they house the cap-
    tives,
she is numbered with the other Trojan
    women.
The men who fought and toiled to win her
    back,
have given her to me—to kill, or else,
if it pleases me, to take her back to Argos.
And it has seemed to me her death in Troy
is not the way. I will take her overseas,
with swift oars speeding on the ship,
and there in Greece give her to those to kill
whose dearest died because of her.

> (*To his men.*)

Attention! Forward to the huts.
Seize her and drag her out by that long
    blood-drenched hair—

> (*Stops suddenly and controls himself.*)

And when fair winds come, home with her
to Greece.

> (*Soldiers begin to force the door of one
> of the huts.*)

HECUBA. (*comes slowly forward.*)
O thou who dost uphold the world,
whose throne is high above the world,
thou, past our seeking hard to find, who art
    thou?
God, or Necessity of what must be,
or Reason of our reason?
Whate'er thou art, I pray to thee,
seeing the silent road by which
all mortal things are led by thee to justice.
MENELAUS. What have we here? A queer
    prayer that.
HECUBA. (*she comes still nearer to him and he
recognizes her.*)

Kill her, Menelaus? You will? Oh, blessings on you!

But—shun her, do not look at her.

Desire for her will seize you, conquer you.

For through men's eyes she gets them in her power.

She ruins them and ruins cities too.

Fire comes from her to burn homes,

magic for death. I know her—so do you,

and all these who have suffered.

(HELEN *enters from the hut. The soldiers do not touch her. She is very gentle and undisturbed.*)

HELEN. (*with sweet, injured dignity. Not angry at all.*)

Menelaus, these things might well make a woman fear.

Your men with violence have driven me from my room,

have laid their hands upon me.

Of course I know—almost I know—you hate me,

but yet I ask you, what is your decision,

yours and the Greeks? Am I to live or not?

MENELAUS. Nothing more clear. Unanimous, in fact.

Not one who did not vote you should be given me,

whom you have wronged, to kill you.

HELEN. Am I allowed to speak against the charge?

To show you If I die that I shall die

most wronged and innocent?

MENELAUS. I have come to kill you, not to argue with you.

HECUBA. Oh, hear her. She must never die unheard.

Then, Menelaus, let me answer her.

The evil that she did in Troy, you do not know.

But I will tell the story. She will die.

She never can escape.

MENELAUS. That means delay. Still—if she wants to speak,

she can. I grant her this because of what you say,

not for her sake. She can be sure of that.

HELEN. And perhaps, no matter if you think I speak

the truth or not, you will not talk to me,

since you believe I am your enemy.

Still, I will try to answer what I think

you would say if you spoke your mind,

and my wrongs shall be heard as well as yours.

First: who began these evils? She, the day

when she gave birth to Paris. Who next was guilty?

The old king who decreed the child should live,

and ruined Troy and me—Paris, the hateful,

the firebrand.

What happened then? Listen and learn.

This Paris—he was made the judge for three,

all yoked together in a quarrel—goddesses.

Athena promised he should lead the Trojans

to victory and lay all Greece in ruins.

And Hera said if he thought her the fairest

she would make him lord of Europe and of Asia.

But Aphrodite—well, she praised my beauty—

astonishing, she said—and promised him

that she would give me to him if he judged

that she was loveliest. Then, see what happened.

She won, and so my bridal brought all Greece

great good. No strangers rule you,

no foreign spears, no tyrant.

Oh, it was well for Greece, but not for me,

sold for my beauty and reproached besides

when I deserved a crown.

But—to the point. Is that what you are thinking?

Why did I go—steal from your house in secret?

That man, Paris, or any name you like to call him,

his mother's curse—oh, when he came to me

a mighty goddess walked beside him.

And you, poor fool, you spread your sails for Crete,

left Sparta—left him in your house.
Ah well—Not you, but my own self I ask,
what was there in my heart that I went
    with him,
a strange man, and forgot my home and
    country?
Not I, but Aphrodite. Punish her,
be mightier than Zeus who rules
the other gods, but is her slave.
She is my absolution—
One thing with seeming justice you might
    say.
When Paris died and went down to the
    grave,
and when no god cared who was in my
    bed,
I should have left his house—gone to the
    Greeks.
Just what I tried to do—oh, many times.
I have witnesses—the men who kept the
    gates,
the watchmen on the walls. Not once, but
    often
they found me swinging from a parapet,
a rope around this body, stealthily
feeling my way down.
The Trojans then no longer wanted me,
but the man who next took me—and by
    force—
would never let me go.
My husband, must I die, and at your
    hands?
You think that right? Is that your justice?
I was forced—by violence. I lived a life
that had no joy, no triumph. In bitterness
I lived a slave.
Do you wish to set yourself above the gods?
Oh, stupid, senseless wish!
A WOMAN. O Queen, defend your children
    and your country.
Her soft persuasive words are deadly.
She speaks so fair and is so vile.
A fearful thing.
HECUBA. Her goddesses will fight on my side
    while
I show her for the liar that she is.
Not Hera, not virgin Athena, do I think
would ever stoop to folly great enough
to sell their cities. Hera sell her Argos,
Athena Athens, to be the Trojan's slave!

playing like silly children there on Ida,
and each one in her insolence demanding
the prize for beauty. Beauty—why was
    Hera
so hot for it? That she might get herself
a better mate than Zeus?
Athena—who so fled from marriage that she
    begged
one gift from Zeus, virginity.
But she would have the prize, you say. And
    why?
To help her hunt some god to marry her?
Never make gods out fools to whitewash
    your own evil.
No one with sense will listen to you.
And Aphrodite, did you say—who would
    not laugh?
—must take my son to Menelaus' house?
Why? Could she not stay quietly in heaven
and send you on—and all your town—to
    Troy?
My son was beautiful exceedingly.
You saw him—your own desire was enough.
No need of any goddess.
Men's follies—they are Aphrodite.
She rose up from the sea-foam; where the
    froth
and foam of life are, there she is.
It was my son. You saw him in his Eastern
    dress
all bright with gold, and you were mad
    with love.
Such little things had filled your mind in
    Argos,
busied with this and that.
Once free of Sparta and in Troy where
    gold,
you thought, flowed like a river, you would
    spend
and spend, until your spendthrift hand
had drowned the town.
Your luxuries, your insolent excesses,
Menelaus' halls had grown too small for
    them.
Enough of that. By force you say he took
    you?
You cried out? Where? No one in Sparta
    heard you.
Young Castor was there and his brother
    too,

not yet among the stars.
And when you came to Troy and on your
track the Greeks,
and death and agony in battle,
if they would tell you, "Greece has won
today,"
you would praise this man here, Menelaus,
to vex my son, who feared him as a rival.
Then Troy had victories, and Menelaus
was nothing to you.
Looking to the successful side—oh yes,
you always followed there.
There was no right or wrong side in your
eyes.
And now you talk of ropes—letting your
body down
in secret from the wall, longing to go.
Who found you so?
Was there a noose around your neck?
A sharp knife in your hand? Such ways
as any honest woman would have found,
who loved the husband she had lost?
Often and often I would tell you, Go,
my daughter. My sons will find them other
wives.
I will help you. I will send you past the
lines
to the Greek ships. Oh, end this war
between our foes and us. But this was
bitter to you.
In Paris' house you had your insolent way.
You liked to see the Eastern men fall at
your feet.
These were great things to you.
Look at the dress you wear, your ornaments.
Is that the way to meet your husband?
You should not dare to breathe the same air
with him.
Oh, men should spit upon you.
Humbly, in rags, trembling and shivering,
with shaven head—so you should come,
with shame at last, instead of shameless-
ness,
for all the wickedness you did.
King, one word more and I am done.
Give Greece a crown, be worthy of your-
self.
Kill her. So shall the law stand for all
women,

that she who plays false to her husband's
bed,
shall die.
A WOMAN. O son of an ancient house, O
King, now show
that you are worthy of your fathers.
The Greeks called you a woman, shamed
you
with that reproach. Be strong. Be noble.
Punish her.
MENELAUS. (*impatiently.*) I see it all as you
do. We agree.
She left my house because she wanted to—
went to a stranger's bed. Her talk of Aphro-
dite—
big words, no more. (*Turns to* HELEN.) Go.
Death is near.
Men there are waiting for you. In their
hands are stones.
Die—a small price for the Greeks' long
suffering.
You shall not any more dishonor me.
HELEN. (*kneeling and clinging to him.*)
No! No! Upon my knees—see, I am praying
to you.
It was the gods, not me. Oh, do not kill
me.
Forgive.
HECUBA. The men she murdered. Think of
those
who fought beside you—of their children
too.
Never betray them. Hear that prayer.
MENELAUS. (*roughly.*) Enough, old woman.
She is nothing to me.
Men, take her to the ships and keep her
safe
until she sails.
HECUBA. But not with you! She must not set
foot on your ship.
MENELAUS. (*bitterly.*) And why? Her weight
too heavy for it?
HECUBA. A lover once, a lover always.
MENELAUS. (*pauses a moment to think.*)
Not so when what he loved has gone.
But it shall be as you would have it.
Not on the same ship with me. The advice
is good.
And when she gets to Argos she shall die
a death hard as her heart.

So in the end she will become a teacher,
teach women chastity—no easy thing,
but yet her utter ruin will strike terror
into their silly hearts,
even women worse than she.

CHORUS. And so your temple in Ilium,
your altar of frankincense,
are given to the Greek,
the flame from the honey, the corn and the
    oil,
the smoke from the myrrh floating upward,
the holy citadel.
And Ida, the mountain where the ivy
    grows,
and rivers from the snows rush through the
    glens,
and the boundary wall of the world
where the first sunlight falls,
the blessed home of the dawn.

The sacrifice is gone, and the glad call
of dancers, and the prayers at evening to
    the gods
that last the whole night long.
Gone too the golden images,
and the twelve Moons, to Trojans holy.
Do you care, do you care, do you heed
    these things,
O God, from your throne in high heaven?
My city is perishing.
ending in fire and onrushing flame.

A WOMAN. O dear one, O my husband,
you are dead, and you wander
unburied, uncared for, while over-seas
the ships shall carry me,
swift-winged ships darting onward,
on to the land the riders love,
Argos, where the towers of stone
built by giants reach the sky.

ANOTHER. Children, our children.
At the gate they are crying, crying,
calling to us with tears,
Mother, I am all alone.
They are driving me away
to a black ship, and I cannot see you.

ANOTHER. Where, oh where? To holy Sala-
    mis,
with swift oars dipping?
Or to the crest of Corinth,
the city of two seas,

where the gates King Pelops built
for his dwelling stand?

ANOTHER. Oh, if only, far out to sea,
the crashing thunder of God
would fall down, down on Menelaus' ship,
crashing down upon her oars,
the Aegean's wild-fire light.
He it was drove me from Troy.
He is driving me in tears
over to Greece to slavery.

ANOTHER. And Helen, too, with her mirrors
    of gold,
looking and wondering at herself,
as pleased as a girl.
May she never come to the land of her
    fathers,
never see the hearth of her home,
her city, the temple with brazen doors
of goddess Athena.
Oh, evil marriage that brought
shame to Greece, the great,
And to the waters of Simois
sorrow and suffering.

(TALTHYBIUS *approaches with a few soldiers. He is carrying the dead child.*)

ANOTHER WOMAN. Before new sufferings are
    grown old
come other new.
Look, unhappy wives of Troy,
the dead Astyanax.
They threw him from the tower as one
    might pitch a ball.
Oh, bitter killing.
And now they have him there.

TALTHYBIUS. (*he gives the body into* HECUBA'S
arms.)

One ship is waiting, Hecuba, to take
    aboard
the last of all the spoil Achilles' son was
    given,
and bear it with the measured beat of oars
to Thessaly's high headlands.
The chief himself has sailed because of
    news
he heard, his father's father
driven from his land by his own son.
So, more for haste even than before,
he went and with him went Andromache.

She drew tears from me there upon the ship
mourning her country, speaking to Hector's grave,
begging a burial for her child, your Hector's son,
who thrown down from the tower lost his life.
And this bronze-fronted shield, the dread of many a Greek,
which Hector used in battle,
that it should never, so she prayed,
hang in strange halls, her grief before her eyes,
nor in that bridal chamber where she must be a wife,
Andromache, this dead boy's mother.
She begged that he might lie upon it in his grave,
instead of cedar wood or vault of stone.
And in your arms she told me I must lay him,
for you to cover the body, if you still
have anything, a cloak left—
And to put flowers on him if you could,
since she has gone. Her master's haste
kept her from burying her child.
So now, whenever you have laid him out,
we'll heap the earth above him, then
up with the sails!
Do all as quickly as you can. One trouble
I saved you. When we passed Scamander's stream
I let the water run on him and washed his wounds.
I am off to dig his grave now, break up the hard earth.
Working together, you and I,
will hurry to the goal, oars swift for home.

HECUBA. Set the shield down—the great round shield of Hector.
I wish I need not look at it.

(TALTHYBIUS *goes out with the soldiers.*)

You Greeks, your spears are sharp but not your wits.
You feared a child. You murdered him.
Strange murder. You were frightened, then? You thought

he might build up our ruined Troy? And yet
when Hector fought and thousands at his side,
we fell beneath you. Now, when all is lost,
the city captured and the Trojans dead,
a little child like this made you afraid.
The fear that comes when reason goes away—
Myself, I do not wish to share it.

(*She dismisses the Greeks and their ways.*)

Beloved, what a death has come to you.
If you had fallen fighting for the city,
if you had known strong youth and love
and godlike power, if we could think
you had known happiness—if there is
happiness anywhere—
But now—you saw and knew, but with your soul
you did not know, and what was in your house
you could not use.
Poor little one. How savagely our ancient walls,
Apollo's towers, have torn away the curls
your mother's fingers wound and where she pressed
her kisses—here where the broken bone grins white—
Oh no—I cannot—
Dear hands, the same dear shape your father's had,
how loosely now you fall. And dear proud lips
forever closed. False words you spoke to me
when you would jump into my bed, call me sweet names
and tell me, Grandmother, when you are dead,
I'll cut off a great lock of hair and lead my soldiers all
to ride out past your tomb.
Not you, but I, old, homeless, childless,
must lay you in your grave, so young,
so miserably dead.

Dear God. How you would run to greet
me.
And I would nurse you in my arms, and
oh,
so sweet to watch you sleep. All gone.
What could a poet carve upon your tomb?
"A child lies here whom the Greeks feared
and slew."
Ah, Greece should boast of that.
Child, they have taken all that was your
father's,
but one thing, for your burying, you shall
have,
the bronze-barred shield.
It kept safe Hector's mighty arm, but now
it has lost its master.
The grip of his own hand has marked it
—dear to me then—
His sweat has stained the rim. Often and
often
in battle it rolled down from brows and
beard
while Hector held the shield close.
Come, bring such covering for the pitiful
dead body
as we still have. God has not left us much
to make a show with. Everything I have
I give you, child.
    O men, secure when once good fortune
comes—
fools, fools. Fortune's ways—
here now, there now. She springs
away—back—and away, an idiot's dance.
No one is ever always fortunate.

(*The women have come in with cover-
ings and garlands.*)

A WOMAN. Here, for your hands, they bring
you clothing for the dead,
got from the spoils of Troy.
HECUBA. (*shrouding the body and putting
garlands beside it.*)
Oh, not because you conquered when the
horses raced,
or with the bow outdid your comrades,
your father's mother lays these wreaths beside you,
and of all that was yours, gives you this
covering.

A woman whom God hates has robbed you,
taken your life, when she had taken your
treasure
and ruined all your house.
A WOMAN. Oh, my heart! As if you touched
it—touched it.
Oh, this was once our prince, great in the
city.
HECUBA. So on your wedding day I would
have dressed you,
the highest princess of the East your bride.
Now on your body I must lay the raiment,
all that is left of the splendor that was
Troy's.
And the dear shield of Hector, glorious in
battle,
mother of ten thousand triumphs won,
it too shall have its wreath of honor,
undying it will lie beside the dead.
More honorable by far than all the armor
Odysseus won, the wicked and the wise.
A WOMAN. You, O child, our bitter sorrow,
earth will now receive.
Mourn, O Mother.
HECUBA. Mourn, indeed.
A WOMAN. Weeping for all the dead.
HECUBA. Bitter tears.
A WOMAN. Your sorrows that can never be
forgotten.

(*The funeral rite is now begun,* HEBUCA
symbolically healing the wounds.)

HECUBA. I heal your wounds; with linen I
bind them.
Ah, in words only, not in truth—
a poor physician.
But soon among the dead your father
will care for you.
A WOMAN. Beat, beat your head.
Lift your hands and let them fall,
moving in measure.
HECUBA. O Women. Dearest—
A WOMAN. Oh, speak to us. Your cry—what
does it mean?
HECUBA. Only this the gods would have,
pain for me and pain for Troy,
those they hated bitterly.
Vain, vain, the bulls we slew.
And yet—had God not bowed us down,

not laid us low in dust,
none would have sung of us or told our
     wrongs
in stories men will listen to forever.
Go: lay our dead in his poor grave,
with these last gifts of death given to him.
I think those that are gone care little
how they are buried. It is we, the living,
our vanity.

(*Women lift the shield with the body
on it and carry it out.*)

A WOMAN. Poor mother—her high hopes were
     stayed on you
and they are broken.
They called you happy at your birth,
a good man's son.
Your death was miserable exceedingly.
ANOTHER. Oh, see, see—
On the crested height of Troy
fiery hands. They are flinging torches.
Can it be
some new evil?
Something still unknown?
TALTHYBIUS. (*stops as he enters and speaks
     off stage.*)
Captains, attention. You have been given
     charge
to burn this city. Do not let your torches
     sleep.
Hurry the fire on.
When once the town is level with the
     ground
then off for home and glad goodbye to
     Troy.
And you, you Women—I will arrange for
     you
as well, one speech for everything—
whenever a loud trumpet-call is sounded,
go to the Greek ships, to embark.
Old woman, I am sorriest for you,
follow. Odysseus' men are here to get you.
He drew you—you must leave here as his
     slave.
HECUBA. The end then. Well—the height of
     sorrow, I stand there.
Troy is burning—I am going.
But—hurry, old feet, if you can,
a little nearer—here, where I can see

my poor town, say goodbye to her.
You were so proud a city, in all the East
the proudest. Soon your name the whole
     world knew,
will be taken from you. They are burning
     you
and leading us away, their slaves.
O God—What makes me say that word?
The gods—I prayed, they never listened.
Quick, into the fire—Troy, I will die with
     you.
Death then—oh, beautiful.
TALTHYBIUS. Out of your head, poor thing,
     with all you've suffered.
Lead her away—Hold her, don't be too
     gentle.
She must be taken to Odysseus.
Give her into his hands. She is his—

(*Shakes his head.*)

his prize.

(*It grows darker.*)

A WOMAN. Ancient of days, our country's
     Lord,
Father, who made us,
You see your children's sufferings.
Have we deserved them?
ANOTHER. He sees—but Troy has perished,
     the great city.
No city now, never again.
ANOTHER. Oh, terrible!
The fire lights the whole town up.
The inside rooms are burning.
The citadel—it is all flame now.
ANOTHER. Troy is vanishing.
War first ruined her.
And what was left is rushing up in smoke,
the glorious houses fallen.
First the spear and then the fire.
HECUBA. (*she stands up and seems to be call-
     ing to someone far away.*)
Children, hear, your mother is calling.
A WOMAN. (*gently.*) They are dead, those
     you are speaking to.
HECUBA. My knees are stiff, but I must kneel.
Now, strike the ground with both my
     hands—

A WOMAN. I too, I kneel upon the ground.
I call to mine down there.
Husband, poor husband.

HECUBA. They are driving us like cattle—
taking us away.

A WOMAN. Pain, all pain.

ANOTHER. To a slave's house, from my country.

HECUBA. Priam, Priam, you are dead,
and not a friend to bury you.
The evil that has found me—
do you know?

A WOMAN. No. Death has darkened his eyes.
He was good and the wicked killed him.

HECUBA. O dwellings of the gods and O dear
city,
the spear came first and now
only the red flame lives there.

A WOMAN. Fall and be forgotten. Earth is
kind.

ANOTHER. The dust is rising, spreading out
like a great wing of smoke.
I cannot see my house.

ANOTHER. The name has vanished from the
land,
and we are gone, one here, one there.
And Troy is gone forever.

(*A great crash is heard.*)

HECUBA. Did you hear? Did you know—

A WOMAN. The fall of Troy—

ANOTHER. Earthquake and flood and the city's
end—

HECUBA. Trembling body—old weak limbs,
you must carry me on to the new day of
slavery.

(*A trumpet sounds.*)

A WOMAN. Farewell, dear city.
Farewell, my country, where once my children lived.
On to the ships—
There below, the Greek ships wait.

(*The trumpet sounds again and the
women pass out.*)

◆ *from* Theatre as Proposition: Jean Giraudoux

By JACQUES GUICHARNAUD

. . . At a time when theatre demands no more than immobility from a spectator so that it can painlessly graze him, Giraudoux demands cooperation, the presence of heart and imagination. Hence the "difficulty" of his theatre. His importance in the history of modern French theatre is both to have demanded a very active collaboration on the part of the spectator and to have given back the theatre its function of elucidating the world in fundamental terms. Certain types of theatre may force the spectator to use his mind so as to understand a particularly rare and complex problem. Others may pick up the notions of destiny, death, or love, and feed them to the passive spectator. Giraudoux's theatre is made neither for those in search of intellectual rarities, nor for the passive; it is made for a "normal" audience—the norm being defined as the audience of Greek tragedy, of the Spanish theatre of the *Siglo de Oro,* of Shakespeare, of French Classicism.

Those who want to understand in the theatre do not understand theatre . . . The theatre is not a theorem, but a spectacle, not a lesson, but a philter. It should enter your imagination and your senses more than your mind . . .

say the actors in *l'Impromptu de Paris.* Moreover in *Visitations,* Giraudoux wrote that theatre must reveal to the spectator

. . . these surprising truths: that the living must live, that the living must die, that autumn follows after summer, spring after winter, that there are the four elements, and happiness, and billions of catastrophes, that life is a reality, that it is a dream, that man lives by peace, that man lives by blood, in brief, what they will never know. . . .[1]

Such affirmations may seem in contradiction with the judgment of many critics for whom Giraudoux's theatre consists in works of the mind, their revelations far indeed from the commonplaces of the last quotation. Actually the misunderstanding about Giraudoux that reigned during the thirties can be reduced to the following: his method is complicated and baffling; therefore the idea expressed must itself be difficult to understand. And in fact Giraudoux's theatre offers quite the contrary. It is presented as an initiation to simplicity, in other words a reevaluation of simplicity through the detours that must be made in order to rediscover it. The objective is to exasperate the mind by an accumulation of intellectual subtleties, to the point that an emotional adhesion beyond all comprehension will spring from the network of multiple lines that the intelligence has been following.

Knowledge of a certain order can be acquired only through the delirium of an inferior order. In certain religions the individual must subject his body to the most extreme violations in order to reach mysticism. Giraudoux's postulate seems to be that a manifest truth can be reached and experienced beyond intellection through a paroxysm of the intelligence. Preciosity, burlesque, humanist rationalism, and Aristotelian rationalism are actually so many means of making the mind so dizzy that it bows to the unchallengeable and striking fact of life. The spectator of good faith is expected to relive the adventure of Creation—the very Creation that the writer relived at the time of composition, that also of the director, from the blocking on paper to the performance—from ideas, form, or essences to the synthetic emotion of the human adventure.

In *la Guerre de Troie n'aura pas lieu**[*] peace, represented both mythically and negatively by the title and the first line of the play (immediately challenged by the second, whence the drama):

Jacques Guicharnaud, "Theatre as Proposition: Jean Giraudoux," *Modern French Theatre: from Giraudoux to Beckett* (New Haven, Conn.: Yale University Press, 1961), pp. 38–41.

[1] Giraudoux, *Visitations,* Ides et Calendes, Neuchâtel

and Paris, 1947. Translation by Bert M-P. Leefmans, *The Kenyon Review,* 1954.
[*] [Literally, "The Trojan War will not take place"; adapted for the English version of the play as *Tiger at the Gates.* SAC]

Andromache: There will be no Trojan War,
            Cassandra.
Cassandra: I'll take that bet, Andromache.

is specified in the very first scene, then becomes "happiness," then "beauty"—all abstract notions—then the "sun" of that day, then evocative expressions like a "fisherman's house," the "murmur of seashells," and is finally, through a double ambiguity, embodied in a character, Hector. We thus go from what is most abstract in peace (its negative definition: the absence of war) to one man who will take its defense.

The concrete images remain vague enough for each spectator to give peace the face of his choice. The "fisherman's house," the "murmur of seashells," the sun that spreads its "mother of pearl" over the unspecified landscape all indicate a Mediterranean universe without particularizing it, suggesting its essence, from which the spectator can imagine his own fisherman's house, murmur, sun. Owl, station, train, birch tree, cat, silk, fur, hand, armor—Giraudoux's glossary always directs the spectator toward a certain concrete category, concrete feeling, concrete landscape. He never individualizes it; he is satisfied to emphasize its dominant feature. It is up to the spectator to bring about the final individualization. . . .

◆◆ Tiger at the Gates

By JEAN GIRAUDOUX

Translated by Christopher Fry

Characters

HECTOR
ANDROMACHE, wife to Hector
CASSANDRA, sister to Hector
LAUNDRESS
PARIS, brother to Hector
FIRST OLD MAN
SECOND OLD MAN
PRIAM, King of Troy,
    father to Hector
DEMOKOS, a Poet,
    Leader of the Senate
HECUBA, mother to Hector
MATHEMATICIAN
LADY IN WAITING
POLYXENE, young sister to Hector
HELEN
MESSENGER
TROILUS, young brother to Hector
ABNEOS, a Senator
BUSIRIS, a Lawyer
AJAX, a Greek Captain
ULYSSES
A TOPMAN, Officer on Paris' Ship
OLPIDES, Sailor on Paris' Ship
SENATOR
SAILOR

ACT I

ANDROMACHE. There's not going to be a Trojan War, Cassandra!

Jean Giraudoux, *Tiger at the Gates*, trans. by Christopher Fry (New York: Oxford University Press, 1955), pp. 1–74.

CASSANDRA. I shall take that bet, Andromache.

ANDROMACHE. The Greeks are quite right to protest. We are going to receive their ambassador very civilly. We shall wrap up his little Helen and give her back to him.

CASSANDRA. We shall receive him atrociously. We shall refuse to give Helen back. And there *will* be a Trojan War.

ANDROMACHE. Yes, if Hector were not here. But he is here, Cassandra, he is home again. You can hear the trumpets. At this moment he is marching into the city, victorious. And Hector is certainly going to have something to say. When he left, three months ago, he promised me this war would be the last.

CASSANDRA. It is the last. The next is still ahead of him.

ANDROMACHE. Doesn't it ever tire you to see and prophesy only disasters?

CASSANDRA. I see nothing. I prophesy nothing. All I ever do is to take account of two great stupidities: the stupidity of men, and the wild stupidity of the elements.

ANDROMACHE. Why should there be a war? Paris and Helen don't care for each other any longer.

CASSANDRA. Do you think it will matter if Paris and Helen don't care for each other any longer? Has destiny ever been interested in whether things were still true or not?

ANDROMACHE. I don't know what destiny is.

CASSANDRA. I'll tell you. It is simply the relentless logic of each day we live.

ANDROMACHE. I don't understand abstractions.

CASSANDRA. Never mind. We can try a metaphor. Imagine a tiger. You can understand that? It's a nice, easy metaphor. A sleeping tiger.

ANDROMACHE. Let it sleep.

CASSANDRA. There's nothing I should like better. But certain cocksure statements have been prodding him out of his sleep. For some considerable time Troy has been full of them.

ANDROMACHE. Full of what?

CASSANDRA. Of cocksure statements, a confident belief that the world, and the supervision of the world, is the province of mankind in general, and Trojan men and women in particular.

ANDROMACHE. I don't follow you.

CASSANDRA. Hector at this very moment is marching into Troy?

ANDROMACHE. Yes. Hector at this very moment has come home to his wife.

CASSANDRA. And Hector's wife is going to have a child?

ANDROMACHE. Yes; I am going to have a child.

CASSANDRA. Don't you call these statements a little overconfident?

ANDROMACHE. Don't frighten me, Cassandra.

(A YOUNG LAUNDRESS *goes past with an armful of linen*)

LAUNDRESS. What a beautiful day, miss!

CASSANDRA. Does it seem so, indeed?

LAUNDRESS. It's the most beautiful Spring day Troy has seen this year.

(*Exit*)

CASSANDRA. Even the laundrymaid is confident!

ANDROMACHE. And so she should be, Cassandra. How can you talk of a war on a day like this? Happiness is falling on us out of the sky.

CASSANDRA. Like a blanket of snow.

ANDROMACHE. And beauty, as well. Look at the sunshine. It is finding more mother-of-pearl on the rooftops of Troy than was ever dragged up from the bed of the sea. And do you hear the sound coming up from the fishermen's houses, and the movement of the trees, like the murmuring of

sea shells? If ever there were a chance to see men finding a way to live in peace, it is today. To live in peace, in humility. And to be immortal.

CASSANDRA. Yes, I am sure those cripples who have been carried out to lie in their doorways feel how immortal they are.

ANDROMACHE. And to be good. Do you see that horseman, in the advance-guard, leaning from his saddle to stroke a cat on the battlements? Perhaps this is also going to be the first day of true fellowship between men and the animals.

CASSANDRA. You talk too much. Destiny, the tiger, is getting restive, Andromache!

ANDROMACHE. Restive, maybe, in young girls looking for husbands; but not otherwise.

CASSANDRA. You are wrong. Hector has come home in triumph to the wife he adores. The tiger begins to rouse, and opens one eye. The incurables lie out on their benches in the sun and feel immortal. The tiger stretches himself. Today is the chance for peace to enthrone herself over all the world. The tiger licks his lips. And Andromache is going to have a son! And the horsemen have started leaning from their saddles to stroke tom-cats on the battlements! The tiger starts to prowl.

ANDROMACHE. Be quiet!

CASSANDRA. He climbs noiselessly up the palace steps. He pushes open the doors with his snout. And here he is, here he is!

(HECTOR's *voice*: Andromache!)

ANDROMACHE. You are lying! It is Hector!

CASSANDRA. Whoever said it was not?

(*Enter* HECTOR)

ANDROMACHE. Hector!

HECTOR. Andromache!

(THEY *embrace*)

And good morning to you, too, Cassandra. Ask Paris to come to me, if you will. As soon as he can.

(CASSANDRA *lingers*)

Have you something to tell me?

ANDROMACHE. Don't listen to her! Some catastrophe or other!

HECTOR. Tell me.

CASSANDRA. Your wife is going to have a child.

(*Exit* CASSANDRA)

(HECTOR *takes* ANDROMACHE *in his arms, leads her to a stone bench, and sits beside her. A short pause*)

HECTOR. Will it be a son or a daughter?

ANDROMACHE. Which did you want to create when you called it into life?

HECTOR. A thousand boys. A thousand girls.

ANDROMACHE. Why? Because it would give you a thousand women to hold in your arms? You are going to be disappointed. It will be a son, one single son.

HECTOR. That may very well be. Usually more boys are born than girls at the end of a war.

ANDROMACHE. And before a war? Which, before a war?

HECTOR. Forget wars, Andromache, even this war. It's over. It lost you a father and a brother, but it gave you back a husband.

ANDROMACHE. It has been too kind. It may think better of it presently.

HECTOR. Don't worry. We won't give it the chance. Directly I leave you I shall go into the square, and formally close the Gates of War. They will never open again.

ANDROMACHE. Close them, then. But they will open again.

HECTOR. You can even tell me the day, perhaps?

ANDROMACHE. I can even tell you the day: the day when the cornfields are heavy and golden, when the vines are stooping, ready for harvest, and every house is sheltering a contented couple.

HECTOR. And peace, no doubt, at its very height?

ANDROMACHE. Yes. And my son is strong and glowing with life.

(HECTOR *embraces her*)

HECTOR. Perhaps your son will be a coward.

That's one possible safeguard.

ANDROMACHE. He won't be a coward. But perhaps I shall have cut off the index finger of his right hand.

HECTOR. If every mother cut off her son's right-hand index finger, the armies of the world would fight without index fingers. And if they cut off their son's right legs, the armies would be one-legged. And if they put out their eyes, the armies would be blind, but there would still be armies: blind armies groping to find the fatal place in the enemy's groin, or to get at his throat.

ANDROMACHE. I would rather kill him.

HECTOR. There's a truly maternal solution to war!

ANDROMACHE. Don't laugh. I can still kill him before he is born.

HECTOR. Don't you want to see him at all, not even for a moment? After that, you would think again. Do you mean never to see your son?

ANDROMACHE. It is your son that interests me. Hector, it's because he is yours, because he is you, that I'm so afraid. You don't know how like you he is. Even in this no-man's-land where he is waiting, he already has everything, all those qualities you brought to this life we live together. He has your tenderness, your silences. If you love war, he will love it. Do you love war?

HECTOR. Why ask such a question?

ANDROMACHE. Admit, sometimes you love it.

HECTOR. If a man can love what takes away hope, and happiness, and all those nearest to his heart.

ANDROMACHE. And you know it can be so. Men do love it.

HECTOR. If they let themselves be fooled by that little burst of divinity the gods give them at the moment of attack.

ANDROMACHE. Ah, there, you see! At the moment of attack you feel like a god.

HECTOR. More often not as much as a man. But sometimes, on certain mornings, you get up from the ground feeling lighter, astonished, altered. Your whole body, and the armour on your back, have a different weight, they seem to be made of a different metal. You are invulnerable. A tenderness comes over you, submerging you, a kind of tenderness of battle: you are tender because you are pitiless; what, in fact, the tenderness of the gods must be. You advance towards the enemy slowly, almost absentmindedly, but lovingly. And you try not to crush a beetle crossing your path. You brush off the mosquito without hurting it. You never at any time had more respect for the life you meet on your way.

ANDROMACHE. And then the enemy comes?

HECTOR. Then the enemy comes, frothing at the mouth. You pity him; you can see him there, behind the swollen veins and the whites of his eyes, the helpless, willing little man of business, the well-meaning husband and son-in-law who likes to grow his own vegetables. You feel a sort of love for him. You love the wart on his cheek and the cast in his eye. You love him. But he comes on; he is insistent. Then you kill him.

ANDROMACHE. And you bend over the wretched corpse as though you are a god; but you are not a god; you can't give back his life again.

HECTOR. You don't wait to bend over him. There are too many more waiting for you, frothing at the mouth and howling hate. Too many more unassuming, law-abiding family men.

ANDROMACHE. Then you kill them.

HECTOR. You kill them. Such is war.

ANDROMACHE. All of them: you kill them all?

HECTOR. This time we killed them all. Quite deliberately. They belonged to an incorrigibly warlike race, the reason why wars go on and multiply in Asia. Only one of them escaped.

ANDROMACHE. In a thousand years time, there the warlike race will be again, descended from that one man. His escape made all that slaughter futile after all. My son is going to love war, just as you do.

HECTOR. I think, now that I've lost my love for it, I hate it.

ANDROMACHE. How do you come to hate what you once worshipped?

HECTOR. You know what it's like when you find out a friend is a liar? Whatever he says, after that, sounds false, however true it may be. And strangely enough, war used to promise me many kinds of virtue: goodness, generosity, and a contempt for anything base and mean. I felt I owed it all my strength and zest for life, even my private happiness, you, Andromache. And until this last campaign there was no enemy I haven't loved.

ANDROMACHE. Very soon you will say you only kill what you love.

HECTOR. It's hard to explain how all the sounds of war combined to make me think it was something noble. The galloping of horse in the night, the clatter of bowls and dishes where the cooks were moving in and out of the firelight, the brush of silk and metal against your tent as the nightpatrol went past, and the cry of the falcon wheeling high above the sleeping army and their unsleeping captain: it all seemed then so right, marvellously right.

ANDROMACHE. But not this time: this time war had no music for you?

HECTOR. Why was that? Because I am older? Or was it just the kind of weariness with your job which, for instance, a carpenter will be suddenly seized by, with a table half finished, as I was seized one morning, standing over an adversary of my own age, about to put an end to him? Up to that time, a man I was going to kill had always seemed my direct opposite. This time I was kneeling on a mirror, the death I was going to give was a kind of suicide. I don't know what the carpenter does at such a time, whether he throws away his hammer and plane, or goes on with it. I went on with it. But after that nothing remained of the perfect trumpet note of war. The spear as it slid against my shield rang suddenly false; so did the shock of the killed against the ground, and, some hours later, the palace crumbling into ruin. And, moreover, war knew that I understood, and gave up any pretence of shame. The cries of the dying sounded false. I had come to that.

ANDROMACHE. But it all still sounded right for the rest of them.

HECTOR. The rest of them heard it as I did.

The army I brought back hates war.

ANDROMACHE. An army with poor hearing.

HECTOR. No. When we first came in sight of Troy, an hour ago, you can't imagine how everything in that moment sounded true for them. There wasn't a regiment which didn't halt, racked to the heart by this sense of returning music. So much so, we were afraid to march boldly in through the gates: we broke up into groups outside the walls. It feels like the only job worthy of a good army, laying peaceful siege to the open cities of your own country.

ANDROMACHE. You haven't understood, this is where things are falser than anywhere. War is here, in Troy, Hector. That is what welcomed you at the gates.

HECTOR. What do you mean?

ANDROMACHE. You haven't heard that Paris has carried off Helen?

HECTOR. They told me so. What else?

ANDROMACHE. Did you know that the Greeks are demanding her back? And their ambassador arrives today? And if we don't give her up, it means war.

HECTOR. Why shouldn't we give her up? I shall give her back to them myself.

ANDROMACHE. Paris will never agree to it.

HECTOR. Paris will agree, and very soon. Cassandra is bringing him to me.

ANDROMACHE. But Paris can't agree. His honour, as you all call it, won't let him. Nor his love either, he may tell you.

HECTOR. Well, we shall see. Run and ask Priam if he will let me speak to him at once. And set your heart at rest. All the Trojans who have been fighting, or who can fight, are against a war.

ANDROMACHE. There are still the others, remember.

(*As* ANDROMACHE *goes . . .*
CASSANDRA *enters with* PARIS)

CASSANDRA. Here is Paris.

HECTOR. Congratulations, Paris, I hear you have been very well occupied while we were away.

PARIS. Not badly. Thank you.

HECTOR. What is this story they tell me about Helen?

PARIS. Helen is a very charming person. Isn't she, Cassandra?

CASSANDRA. Fairly charming.

PARIS. Why these reservations today? It was only yesterday you said you thought she was extremely pretty.

CASSANDRA. She is extremely pretty, and fairly charming.

PARIS. Hasn't she the ways of a young, gentle gazelle?

CASSANDRA. No.

PARIS. But you were the one who first said she was like a gazelle.

CASSANDRA. I made a mistake. Since then I have seen a gazelle again.

HECTOR. To hell with gazelles! Doesn't she look any more like a woman than that?

PARIS. She isn't the type of woman we know here, obviously.

CASSANDRA. What is the type of woman we know here?

PARIS. Your type, my dear sister. The fearfully unremote sort of woman.

CASSANDRA. When your Greek makes love she is a long way off, I suppose?

PARIS. You know perfectly well what I'm trying to say. I have had enough of Asiatic women. They hold you in their arms as though they were glued there, their kisses are like battering-rams, their words chew right into you. The more they undress the more elaborate they seem, until when they're naked they are more overdressed than ever. And they paint their faces to look as though they mean to imprint themselves on you. And they do imprint themselves on you. In short, you are definitely *with* them. But Helen is far away from me, even held in my arms.

HECTOR. Very interesting! But, one wonders, is it really worth a war, to allow Paris to make love at a distance?

CASSANDRA. With distance. He loves women to be distant but right under his nose.

PARIS. To have Helen with you not with you is worth anything in the world.

HECTOR. How did you fetch her away? Willingly, or did you compel her?

PARIS. Listen, Hector! You know women as well as I do. They are only willing when you compel them, but after that they're as enthusiastic as you are.

HECTOR. On horseback, in the usual style of seducers, leaving a heap of horse manure under the windows.

PARIS. Is this a court of enquiry?

HECTOR. Yes, it is. Try for once to answer precisely and accurately. Have you insulted her husband's house, or the Greek earth?

PARIS. The Greek water, a little. She was bathing.

CASSANDRA. She is born of the foam, is she? This cold one is born of the foam, like Venus.

HECTOR. You haven't disfigured the walls of the palace with offensive drawings, as you usually do? You didn't shout to the echoes any word which they would at once repeat to the betrayed husband?

PARIS. No. Menelaus was naked on the river bank, busy removing a crab from his big toe. He watched my boat sail past as if the wind were carrying his clothes away.

HECTOR. Looking furious?

PARIS. The face of a king being nipped by a crab isn't likely to look beatific.

HECTOR. No onlookers?

PARIS. My crew.

HECTOR. Perfect!

PARIS. Why perfect? What are you getting at?

HECTOR. I say perfect, because you have done nothing irrevocable. In other words: she was undressed, so neither her clothes nor her belongings have been insulted. Nothing except her body, which is negligible. I've enough acquaintance with the Greeks to know they will concoct a divine adventure out of it, to their own glory, the story of this little Greek queen who goes down into the sea, and quietly comes up again a few months later, with a look on her face of perfect innocence.

CASSANDRA. We can be quite sure of the look on her face.

PARIS. You think that I'm going to take Helen back to Menelaus?

HECTOR. We don't ask so much of you, or of her. The Greek ambassador will take care

of it. He will put her back in the sea himself, like a gardener planting water-lilies, at a particular chosen spot. You will give her into his hands this evening.

PARIS. I don't know whether you are allowing yourself to notice how monstrous you are being, to suppose that a man who has the prospect of a night with Helen will agree to giving it up.

CASSANDRA. You still have an afternoon with Helen. Surely that's more Greek?

HECTOR. Don't be obstinate. We know you of old. This isn't the first separation you've accepted.

PARIS. My dear Hector, that's true enough. Up to now I have always accepted separations fairly cheerfully. Parting from a woman, however well you love her, induces a most pleasant state of mind, which I know how to value as well as anybody. You come out of her arms and take your first lonely walk through the town, and, the first little dressmaker you meet, you notice with a shock of surprise how fresh and unconcerned she looks, after that last sight you have had of the dear face you parted from, her nose red with weeping. Because you have come away from such broken, despairing farewells, the laundrygirls and the fruitsellers laughing their heads off, more than make up for whatever you've lost in the parting. By losing one person your life has become entirely re-peopled. All the women in the world have been created for you afresh; they are all your own, in the liberty, honour, and peace of your conscience. Yes, you're quite right: when a love-affair is broken off it reaches its highest point of exaltation. Which is why I shall never be parted from Helen, because with Helen I feel as though I had broken with every other woman in the world, and that gives me the sensation of being free a thousand times over instead of once.

HECTOR. Because she doesn't love you. Everything you say proves it.

PARIS. If you like. But, if I had to choose one out of all the possible ways of passion, I would choose the way Helen doesn't love me.

HECTOR. I'm extremely sorry. But you will give her up.

PARIS. You are not the master here.

HECTOR. I am your elder brother, and the future master.

PARIS. Then order me about in the future. For the present, I obey my father.

HECTOR. That's all I want! You're willing that we should put this to Priam and accept his judgment?

PARIS. Perfectly willing.

HECTOR. On your soleman word? We both swear to accept that?

CASSANDRA. Mind what you're doing, Hector! Priam is mad for Helen. He would rather give up his daughters.

HECTOR. What nonsense is this?

PARIS. For once she is telling the truth about the present instead of the future.

CASSANDRA. And all our brothers, and all our uncles, and all our great-great uncles! Helen has a guard-of-honour which includes every old man in the city. Look there. It is time for her walk. Do you see, there's a fringe of white beards draped all along the battlements?

HECTOR. A beautiful sight. The beards are white, and the faces red.

CASSANDRA. Yes; it's the blood pressure. They should be waiting at the Scamander Gate, to welcome the victorious troops. But no; they are all at the Sceean Gate, waiting for Helen.

HECTOR. Look at them, all leaning forward as one man, like storks when they see a rat going by.

CASSANDRA. The rat is Helen.

PARIS. Is it?

CASSANDRA. There she is: on the second terrace, standing to adjust her sandal, and giving careful thought to the crossing of her legs.

HECTOR. Incredible. All the old men of Troy are there looking down at her.

CASSANDRA. Not all. There are certain crafty ones looking up at her.

(*Cries offstage:* Long live Beauty!)

HECTOR. What are they shouting?

PARIS. They're shouting 'Long live Beauty!'

CASSANDRA. I quite agree with them, if they mean that they themselves should die as quickly as possible.

(*Cries offstage:* Long live Venus!)

HECTOR. And what now?

CASSANDRA. 'Long live Venus.' They are shouting only words without R's in them because of their lack of teeth. Long live Beauty, long live Venus, long live Helen. At least they imagine they're shouting, though, as you can hear, all they are doing is simply increasing a mumble to its highest power.

HECTOR. What has Venus to do with it?

CASSANDRA. They imagine it was Venus who gave us Helen. To show her gratitude to Paris for awarding her the apple on first sight.

HECTOR. That was another brilliant stroke of yours.

PARIS. Stop playing the elder brother!

(*Enter* TWO OLD MEN)

1st OLD MAN. Down there we see her better.

2nd OLD MAN. We had a very good view.

1st OLD MAN. But she can hear us better from up here. Come on. One, two, three!

BOTH. Long live Helen!

2nd OLD MAN. It's a little tiring, at our age, to have to climb up and down these impossible steps all the time, according to whether we want to look at her or to cheer her.

1st OLD MAN. Would you like us to alternate? One day we will cheer her? Another day we will look at her?

2nd OLD MAN. You are mad! One day without looking at Helen, indeed! Goodness me, think what we've seen of her today! One, two, three!

BOTH. Long live Helen!

1st OLD MAN. And now down we go again!

(THEY *run off*)

CASSANDRA. You see what they're like, Hector.

I don't know how their poor lungs are going to stand it.

HECTOR. But our father can't be like this.

PARIS. Hector, before we have this out in front of my father, I suppose you wouldn't like to take just one look at Helen.

HECTOR. I don't care a fig about Helen. Ah: greetings to you, father!

(PRIAM *enters, with* HECUBA, ANDRO-MACHE, *the poet* DEMOKOS *and another old man.* HECUBA *leads by the hand little* POLYXENE)

PRIAM. What was it you said?

HECTOR. I said that we should make haste to shut the Gates of War, father, see them bolted and padlocked, so that not even a gnat can get between them.

PRIAM. I thought what you said was somewhat shorter.

DEMOKOS. He said he didn't care a fig about Helen.

PRIAM. Look over here.

(HECTOR *obeys*)

Do you see her?

HECUBA. Indeed he sees her. Who, I ask myself, doesn't see her, or hasn't seen her? She takes the road which goes the whole way round the city.

DEMOKOS. It is Beauty's perfect circle.

PRIAM. Do you see her?

HECTOR. Yes, I see her. What of it?

DEMOKOS. Priam is asking you what you see.

HECTOR. I see a young woman adjusting her sandal.

CASSANDRA. She takes some time to adjust her sandal.

PARIS. I carried her off naked; she left her clothes in Greece. Those are your sandals, Cassandra. They're a bit big for her.

CASSANDRA. Anything's too big for these little women.

HECTOR. I see two charming buttocks.

HECUBA. He sees what all of you see.

PRIAM. I'm sorry for you!

HECTOR. Why?

PRIAM. I had no idea that the young men of Troy had come to this.

HECTOR. What have they come to?

PRIAM. To being impervious to beauty.

DEMOKOS. And, consequently, ignorant of love. And, consequently, unrealistic. To us who are poets reality is love or nothing.

HECTOR. But the old men, you think, can appreciate love and beauty?

HECUBA. But of course. If you make love, or if you are beautiful, you don't need to understand these things.

HECTOR. You come across beauty, father, at every street corner. I'm not alluding to Helen, though at the moment she condescends to walk our streets.

PRIAM. You are being unfair, Hector. Surely there have been occasions in your life when a woman has seemed to be more than merely herself, as though a radiance of thoughts and feelings glowed from her flesh, taking a special brilliance from it.

DEMOKOS. As a ruby represents blood.

HECTOR. Not to those who have seen blood. I have just come back from a close acquaintance with it.

DEMOKOS. A symbol, you understand. Soldier though you are, you have surely heard of symbolism! Surely you have come across women who as soon as you saw them seemed to you to personify intelligence, harmony, gentleness, whatever it might be?

HECTOR. It has happened.

DEMOKOS. And what did you do?

HECTOR. I went closer, and that was the end of it. And what does this we see here personify?

DEMOKOS. We have told you before: Beauty.

HECUBA. Then send her quickly back to the Greeks if you want her to personify that for long. Blonde beauty doesn't usually last for ever.

DEMOKOS. It's impossible to talk to these women!

HECUBA. Then don't talk *about* women. You're not showing much gallantry, I might say; nor patriotism either. All other races choose one of their own women as their symbol, even if they have flat noses and lips like two fishes on a plate. It's only you who have to go outside your own country to find it.

HECTOR. Listen, father: we are just back from a war, and we have come home exhausted. We have made quite certain of peace on our continent for ever. From now on we mean to live in happiness, and we mean our wives to be able to love us without anxiety, and to bear our children.

DEMOKOS. Wise principles, but war has never prevented wives from having children.

HECTOR. So explain to me wny we have come back to find the city transformed, all because of Helen? Explain to me what you think she has given to us, worth a quarrel with the Greeks?

MATHEMATICIAN. Anybody will tell you! I can tell you myself!

HECUBA. Listen to the mathematician!

MATHEMATICIAN. Yes, listen to the mathematician! And don't think that mathematicians have no concern with women! We're the land-surveyors of your personal landscape. I can't tell you how we mathematicians suffer to see any slight disproportion of the flesh, on the chin or the thigh, any infringement of your geometrical desirability. Well now, until this day mathematicians have never been satisfied with the countryside surrounding Troy. The line linking the plain with the hills seemed to us too slack: the line from the hills to the mountains too taut. Now, since Helen came, the country has taken on meaning and vigour. And, what is particularly evident to true mathematicians, space and volume have now found in Helen a common denominator. We can abolish all the instruments we have invented to reduce the universe to a manageable equation. There are no more feet and inches, ounces, pounds, milligrams or leagues. There is only the weight of Helen's footfall, the length of Helen's arm, the range of Helen's look or voice; and the movement of the air as she goes past is the measure of the winds. That is what the mathematicians will tell you.

HECUBA. The old fool is crying.

PRIAM. My dear son, you have only to look at this crowd, and you will understand what Helen is. She is a kind of absolution. To each one of these old men, whom you can see now like a frieze of grotesque heads all round the city walls: to the old swindler, the old thief, the old pandar, to all the old failures, she has shown they always had a secret longing to rediscover the beauty they had lost. If throughout their lives beauty had always been as close at hand as Helen is today, they would never have tricked their friends, or sold their daughters, or drunk away their inheritance. Helen is like a pardon to them: a new beginning for them, their whole future.

HECTOR. These old men's ancient futures are no concern of mine.

DEMOKOS. Hector, as a poet I approach things by the way of poetry. Imagine if beauty, never, at any time, touched our language. Imagine there being no such word as 'delight.'

HECTOR. We should get on well enough without it. I get on without it already. 'Delight' is a word I use only when I'm absolutely driven to it.

DEMOKOS. Well, then the word 'desirable': you could get on without that as well, I suppose?

HECTOR. If it could be bought only at the cost of war, yes, I could get on without the word 'desirable.'

DEMOKOS. One of the most beautiful words there are was found only at the cost of war: the word 'courage.'

HECTOR. It has been well paid for.

HECUBA. And the word 'cowardice' was inevitably found at the same time.

PRIAM. My son, why do you so deliberately not understand us?

HECTOR. I understand you very well. With the help of a quibble, by pretending to persuade us to fight for beauty you want to get us to fight for a woman.

PRIAM. Would you never go to war for any woman?

HECTOR. Certainly not!

HECUBA. And he would be unchivalrously right.

CASSANDRA. If there were only one woman, then perhaps he would go to war for her. But we have exceeded that number, quite extravagantly.

DEMOKOS. Wouldn't you go to war to rescue Andromache?

HECTOR. Andromache and I have already made our secret plans for escaping from any prison in the world, and finding our way back to each other again.

DEMOKOS. Even if there's no hope of it on earth?

HECTOR. Even then.

HECUBA. You have done well to unmask them, Hector. They want you to make war for the sake of a woman; it's the kind of love-making men believe in who are past making love in any other way.

DEMOKOS. And doesn't that make you all the more valuable?

HECUBA. Ah yes! You may say so!

DEMOKOS. Excuse me, but I can't agree with you. The sex which gave me my mother will always have my respect, even its least worthy representatives.

HECUBA. We know that. You have, as we know, shown your respect for instance to——

(*The* SERVANTS *who have stood by to hear the argument burst out laughing*)

PRIAM. Hecuba! Daughters! What can this mean? Why on earth are you all so up in arms? The Council are considering giving the city a public holiday in honour of one of your sex.

ANDROMACHE. I know of only one humiliation for a woman: injustice.

DEMOKOS. It's painful to say so, but there's no one knows less what a woman is than a woman.

(*The* YOUNG SERVANT, *passing:* Oh, dear! dear!*)

HECUBA. We know perfectly well. I will tell you myself what a woman is.

DEMOKOS. Don't let them talk, Priam. You never know what they might say.

HECUBA. They might tell the truth.

PRIAM. I have only to think of one of you, my dears, to know what a woman is.

DEMOKOS. In the first place, she is the source

of our energy. You know that, Hector. The soldiers who haven't a portrait of a woman in their kit aren't worth anything.

CASSANDRA. The source of your pride, yes, I agree.

HECUBA. Of your vices.

ANDROMACHE. She is a poor bundle of uncertainty, a poor mass of fears, who detests whatever is difficult, and adores whatever is vulgar and easy.

HECTOR. Dear Andromache!

HECUBA. It's very simple. I have been a woman for fifty years, and I've never yet been able to discover precisely what it is I am.

DEMOKOS. Secondly, whether she likes it or not, she's the only reward for courage. Ask any soldier. To kill a man is to merit a woman.

ANDROMACHE. She loves cowards and libertines. If Hector were a coward or a libertine I shouldn't love him less; I might even love him more.

PRIAM. Don't go too far, Andromache. You will prove the very opposite of what you want to prove.

POLYXENE. She is greedy. She tells lies.

DEMOKOS. So we're to say nothing of her fidelity, her purity: we are not to mention them?

THE SERVANT. Oh, dear! dear!

DEMOKOS. What did you say?

THE SERVANT. I said 'Oh, dear! dear!' I say what I think.

POLYXENE. She breaks her toys. She puts them headfirst into boiling water.

HECUBA. The older we women grow, the more clearly we see what men really are: hypocrites, boasters, he-goats. The older men grow, the more they doll us up with every perfection. There isn't a slut you've hugged behind a wall who isn't transformed in your memories into a loved and lovely creature.

PRIAM. Have you ever deceived me, Hecuba?

HECUBA. Only with yourself; scores of time with yourself.

DEMOKOS. Has Andromache ever deceived Hector?

HECUBA. You can leave Andromache out of

this. There is nothing she could recognize in the sad histories of erring women.

ANDROMACHE. But I know if Hector were not my husband, if he were a club-footed, bandy-legged fisherman I should run after him and find him in his hovel, and lie down on the pile of oyster-shells and sea-weed, and give him a son in adultery.

POLYXENE. She pretends to go to sleep at night, but she's really playing games in her head with her eyes shut.

HECUBA (*to* POLYXENE). You may well say so! It's dreadful! You know how I scold you for it!

THE SERVANT. The only thing worse than a woman is a man; there are no words to describe him.

DEMOKOS. Then more's the pity if a woman deceives us! More's the pity if she scorns her own value and dignity! If she can't be true to a pattern of perfection which would save her from the ravages of conscience, we have to do it for her.

THE SERVANT. Oh, the kind guardian angel!

PARIS. One thing they've forgotten to say of themselves: they are never jealous.

PRIAM. My dear daughters, the fact that you're so furious is a proof in itself that we are right. I can't conceive of any greater unselfishness than the way you now fight for peace, when peace will give you idle, feeble, chicken-hearted husbands, and war would turn them into men.

DEMOKOS. Into heroes.

HECUBA. Yes, we know the jargon. In war-time a man is called a hero. It doesn't make him any braver, and he runs for his life. But at least it's a hero who is running away.

ANDROMACHE. Father, I must beg you to listen. If you have such a fondness for women, listen to what they have to say to you, for I can promise I speak for all the women in the world. Let us keep our husbands as they are. The gods took care to see they were surrounded with enough obstacles and dangers to keep them brave and vigorous. Quite enough if they had nothing to cope with except floods and storms! Or only wild animals! The small

game, foxes and hares and pheasants, which a woman can scarcely distinguish from the heather they hide in, prove a man's quickness of eye far better than this target you propose: the enemy's heart hiding in flesh and metal. Whenever I have seen a man kill a stag or an eagle, I have offered up thanks to them. I know they died for Hector. Why should you want me to owe Hector to the deaths of other men?

PRIAM. I don't want it, my dear child. But why do you think you are here now, all looking so beautiful, and valiantly demanding peace? Why: because your husbands and your fathers, and their fathers, and theirs, were fighting men. If they had been too lazy and self-indulgent to spring to arms, if they hadn't known how this dull and stupid business we call life suddenly leaps into flame and justifies itself through the scorn men have for it, you would find *you* were the cowards now, and you would be clamouring for war. A man has only one way of being immortal on this earth: he has to forget he is mortal.

ANDROMACHE. Why, exactly so, father: you're only too right. The brave men die in war. It takes great luck or judgment not to be killed. Once at least the head has to bow and the knee has to bend to danger. The soldiers who march back under the triumphal arches are death's deserters. How can a country increase in strength and honour by sending them both to their graves?

PRIAM. Daughter, the first sign of cowardice in a people is their first moment of decay.

ANDROMACHE. But which is the worse cowardice? To appear cowardly to others, and make sure of peace? Or to be cowardly in your own eyes, and let loose a war?

DEMOKOS. Cowardice is not to prefer death on every hand rather than the death of one's native land.

HECUBA. I was expecting poetry at this point. It never lets us down.

ANDROMACHE. Everyone always dies for his country. If you have lived in it, well and wisely and actively, you die for it too.

HECUBA. It would be better if only the old

men fought the wars. Every country is the country of youth. When its youth dies it dies with them.

DEMOKOS. All this nonsense about youth! In thirty years time youth is nothing but these old men you talk about.

CASSANDRA. Wrong.

HECUBA. Wrong! When a grown man reaches forty we change him for an old one. He has completely disappeared. There's only the most superficial resemblance between the two of them. Nothing is handed on from one to the other.

DEMOKOS. I still take a serious concern in my fame as a poet.

HECUBA. Yes, that's quite true. And your rheumatism.

(*Another outburst of laughter from the* SERVANTS)

HECTOR. And you can listen to all this without saying a word, Paris? Can you still not decide to give up an adventure to save us from years of unhappiness and massacre?

PARIS. What do you want me to say? My case is an international problem.

HECTOR. Are you really in love with Helen, Paris?

CASSANDRA. They've become now a kind of symbol of love's devotion. They don't still have to love each other.

PARIS. I worship Helen.

CASSANDRA (*at the rampart*). Here she is.

HECTOR. If I persuade her to set sail, will you agree?

PARIS. Yes, I'll agree.

HECTOR. Father, if Helen is willing to go back to Greece, will you hold her here by force?

PRIAM. Why discuss the impossible?

HECTOR. Do you call it impossible? If women are a tenth of what you say they are, Helen will go of her own free will.

PARIS. Father, now *I'm* going to ask you to let him do what he wants. You have seen what it's like. As soon as the question of Helen cropped up, this whole tribe royal turned itself into a family conclave of all the poor girl's sisters-in-law, mother- and

father-in-law, brother-in-law, worthy of the best middle-class tradition. I doubt if there's anything more humiliating than to be cast for the part of the seducer son in a large family. I've had quite enough of their insinuations. I accept Hector's challenge.

DEMOKOS. Helen's not only yours, Paris. She belongs to the city. She belongs to our country.

MATHEMATICIAN. She belongs to the landscape.

HECUBA. You be quiet, mathematician.

CASSANDRA. Here's Helen; here she is.

HECTOR. Father, I must ask you to let me handle this. Listen; they are calling us to go to the ceremony, to close the Gates of War. Leave this to me. I'll join you soon.

PRIAM. Do you really agree to this, Paris?

PARIS. I'm eager for it.

PRIAM. Very well, then; let it be so. Come along, the rest of you; we will see that the Gates of War are made ready.

CASSANDRA. Those poor gates. They need more oil to shut them than to open them.

(PARIS *and the rest withdraw.* DEMOKOS *stays*)

HECTOR. What are you waiting for?

DEMOKOS. The visitation of my genius.

HECTOR. Say that again?

DEMOKOS. Every time Helen walks my way I am thrown into a transport of inspiration. I shake all over, break into sweat, and improvise. Good heavens, here it is! (*He declaims:*)

Beautiful Helen, Helen of Sparta,
　Singular as the evening star,
　The gods forbid that we should part a
　Pair as fair as you and Paris are.

HECTOR. Your line-endings give me a headache.

DEMOKOS. It's an invention of mine. I can obtain effects even more surprising. Listen: (*declaims*)

Face the great Hector with no qualm,
　Troy's glory though he be, and the
　　　world's terror:
He is the storm, and you the after-calm,
　Yours is the right, and his the
　　　boist'rous error.

HECTOR. Get out!

DEMOKOS. What are you glaring at? You look as though you have as little liking for poetry as you have for war.

HECTOR. They make a pretty couple! Now vanish.

(*Exit* DEMOKOS)

(*Enter* CASSANDRA)

CASSANDRA. Helen!

(*Enter* HELEN *and* PARIS)

PARIS. Here he is, Helen darling; this is Hector. He has a proposition to make to you, a perfectly simple proposition. He wants to hand you over to the Greeks, and prove to you that you don't love me. Tell me you do love me, before I leave you with him. Tell me in your own words.

HELEN. I adore you, my sweet.

PARIS. Tell me how beautiful the wave was which swept you away from Greece.

HELEN. Magnificent! A magnificent wave! Where did you see a wave? The sea was so calm.

PARIS. Tell me you hate Menelaus.

HELEN. Menelaus? I hate him.

PARIS. You haven't finished yet. I shall never again return to Greece. Say that.

HELEN. You will never again return to Greece.

PARIS. No, no, this is about you, my darling.

HELEN. Oh, of course! How silly I am! I shall never again return to Greece.

PARIS. I didn't make her say it.—Now it's up to you.

(*He goes off*)

HECTOR. Is Greece a beautiful country?

HELEN. Paris found it ravishing.

HECTOR. I meant is Greece itself beautiful, apart from Helen?

HELEN. How very charming of you.

HECTOR. I was simply wondering what it is really like.

HELEN. Well, there are quite a great many

kings, and a great many goats, dotted about on marble.

HECTOR. If the kings are in gold, and the goats angora, that would look pretty well when the sun was rising.

HELEN. I don't get up very early.

HECTOR. And a great many gods as well, I believe? Paris tells me the sky is crawling with them; he tells me you can see the legs of goddesses hanging down from the clouds.

HELEN. Paris always goes about with his nose in the air. He may have seen them.

HECTOR. But you haven't?

HELEN. I am not gifted that way. I will look out for them when I go back there again.

HECTOR. You were telling Paris you would never be going back there.

HELEN. He asked me to tell him so. I adore doing what Paris wants me to do.

HECTOR. I see. Is that also true of what you said about Menelaus? Do you not, after all, hate him?

HELEN. Why should I hate him?

HECTOR. For the one reason which might certainly make for hate. You have seen too much of him.

HELEN. Menelaus? Oh, no! I have never seen Menelaus. On the contrary.

HECTOR. You have never seen your husband?

HELEN. There are some things, and certain people, that stand out in bright colours for me. They are the ones I can see. I believe in them. I have never been able to see Menelaus.

HECTOR. Though I suppose he must have come very close to you sometimes.

HELEN. I have been able to touch him. But I can't honestly tell you I saw him.

HECTOR. They say he never left your side.

HELEN. Apparently. I must have walked across him a great many times without knowing it.

HECTOR. Whereas you have seen Paris.

HELEN. Vividly; in the clearest outline against the sky and the sun.

HECTOR. Does he still stand out as vividly as he did? Look down there: leaning against the rampart.

HELEN. Are you sure that's Paris, down there?

HECTOR. He is waiting for you.

HELEN. Good gracious! He's not nearly as clear as usual!

HECTOR. And yet the wall is freshly white-washed. Look again: there he is in profile.

HELEN. It's odd how people waiting for you stand out far less clearly than people you are waiting for.

HECTOR. Are you sure that Paris loves you?

HELEN. I don't like knowing about other people's feelings. There is nothing more embarrassing. Just as when you play cards and you see your opponent's hand. You are sure to lose.

HECTOR. What about yourself? Do you love him?

HELEN. I don't much like knowing my own feelings either.

HECTOR. But, listen: when you make love with Paris, when he sleeps in your arms, when you are circled round with Paris, overwhelmed with Paris, haven't you any thoughts about it?

HELEN. My part is over. I leave any thinking to the universe. It does it much better than I do.

HECTOR. Have there been many others, before Paris?

HELEN. Some.

HECTOR. And there will be others after him, wouldn't you say, as long as they stand out in clear relief against the sky, or the wall, or the white sheets on the bed? It is just as I thought it was. You don't love Paris particularly, Helen; you love men.

HELEN. I don't dislike them. They're as pleasant as soap and a sponge and warm water; you feel cleansed and refreshed by them.

HECTOR. Cassandra! Cassandra!

CASSANDRA (*entering*). What do you want?

HECTOR. Cassandra, Helen is going back this evening with the Greek ambassador.

HELEN. I? What makes you think so?

HECTOR. Weren't you telling me that you didn't love Paris particularly?

HELEN. That was your interpretation. Still, if you like.

HECTOR. I quote my authority. You have the same liking for men as you have for a cake of soap.

HELEN. Yes; or pumice stone perhaps is better. What about it?

HECTOR. Well, then, you're not going to hesitate in your choice between going back to Greece, which you don't mind, and a catastrophe as terrible as war?

HELEN. You don't understand me at all, Hector. Of course I'm not hesitating. It would be very easy to say 'I will do this or that, so that this can happen or that can happen.' You've discovered my weakness and you are overjoyed. The man who discovers a woman's weakness is like the huntsman in the heat of the day who finds a cool spring. He wallows in it. But you mustn't think, because you have convinced me, you've convinced the future, too. Merely by making children behave as you want them to, you don't alter the course of destiny.

HECTOR. I don't follow your Greek shades and subtleties.

HELEN. It's not a question of shades and subtleties. It's no less than a question of monsters and pyramids.

HECTOR. Do you choose to leave here, yes or no?

HELEN. Don't bully me. I choose what happens in the way I choose men, or anything else. I choose whatever is not indefinite and vague. I choose what I see.

HECTOR. I know, you said that: what you see in the brightest colours. And you don't see yourself returning to Menelaus in a few days' time?

HELEN. No. It's very difficult.

HECTOR. We could no doubt persuade your husband to dress with great brilliance for your return.

HELEN. All the purple dye from all the murex shells in the sea wouldn't make him visible to me.

HECTOR. Here you have a rival, Cassandra. Helen can read the future, too.

HELEN. No, I can't read the future. But when I imagine the future some of the pictures I see are coloured, and some are dull and drab. And up to now it has always been the coloured scenes which have happened in the end.

HECTOR. We are going to give you back to the Greeks at high noon, on the blinding sand, between the violet sea and the ochre-coloured wall. We shall all be in golden armour with red skirts; and my sisters, dressed in green and standing between my white stallion and Priam's black mare, will return you to the Greek ambassador, over whose silver helmet I can imagine tall purple plumes. You see that, I think?

HELEN. No, none of it. It is all quite sombre.

HECTOR. You are mocking me, aren't you?

HELEN. Why should I mock you? Very well, then. Let us go, if you like! Let us go and get ready to return me to the Greeks. We shall see what happens.

HECTOR. Do you realize how you insult humanity, or is it unconscious?

HELEN. I don't know what you mean.

HECTOR. You realize that your coloured picture-book is holding the world up to ridicule? While we are all battling and making sacrifices to bring about a time we can call our own, there are you, looking at your pictures which nothing in all eternity can alter. What's wrong? Which one has made you stop and stare at it with those blind eyes? I don't doubt it's the one where you are standing here on the ramparts, watching the battle going on below. Is it the battle you see?

HELEN. Yes.

HECTOR. And the city is in ruins or burning, isn't that so?

HELEN. Yes. It's a vivid red.

HECTOR. And what about Paris? You are seeing his body dragged behind a chariot?

HELEN. Oh, do you think that is Paris? I see what looks like a flash of sunlight rolling in the dust. A diamond sparkling on his hand. Yes, it is! Often I don't recognize faces, but I always recognize the jewellery. It's his ring, I'm quite certain.

HECTOR. Exactly. Do I dare to ask you about Andromache, and myself, the scene of Andromache and Hector? You are looking at us. Don't deny it. How do you see us? Happy, grown old, bathed in light?

HELEN. I am not trying to see it.

HECTOR. The scene of Andromache weeping over the body of Hector, does that shine clearer?

HELEN. You seem to know. But sometimes I see things shining, brilliantly shining, and they never happen. No one is infallible.

HECTOR. You needn't go on. I understand. There is a son between the weeping mother and the father stretched on the ground?

HELEN. Yes. He is playing with his father's tangled hair. He is a sweet boy.

HECTOR. And these scenes are there in your eyes, down in the depths of them. Could I see them there?

HELEN. I don't know. Look.

HECTOR. Nothing. Nothing except the ashes of all those fires, the gold and the emerald in dust. How innocent it is, this crystal where the future is waiting. But there should be tears bathing it, and where are they? Would you cry, Helen, if you were going to be killed?

HELEN. I don't know. But I should scream. And I feel I shall scream if you go on at me like this, Hector. I am going to scream.

HECTOR. You will leave for Greece this evening, Helen, otherwise I shall kill you.

HELEN. But I want to leave! I'm prepared to leave. All that I'm trying to tell is that I simply can't manage to distinguish the ship that is going to carry me there. Nothing is shining in the least, neither the metal on the mast, nor the ring in the captain's nose, nor the cabin-boy's eyes, nor anything.

HECTOR. You will go back on a grey sea under a grey sun. But we must have peace.

HELEN. I cannot see peace.

HECTOR. Ask Cassandra to make her appear for you. Cassandra is a sorceress. She can summon up shapes and spirits.

A MESSENGER (*entering*). Hector, Priam is asking for you. The priests are opposed to our shutting the Gates of War. They say the gods will consider it an insult.

HECTOR. It is curious how the gods can never speak for themselves in these difficult matters.

MESSENGER. They have spoken for themselves. A thunderbolt has fallen on the temple, several men have been killed, the entrails of the victims have been consulted, and they are unanimously against Helen's return to Greece.

HECTOR. I would give a good deal to be able to consult the entrails of the priests . . . I'll follow you.

(*The* MESSENGER *goes*)

Well, now, Helen, do we agree about this?

HELEN. Yes.

HECTOR. From now on you will say what I tell you to say? You will do what I tell you to do?

HELEN. Yes.

HECTOR. When we come in front of Ulysses you won't contradict me, you will bear out everything I say?

HELEN. Yes.

HECTOR. Do you hear this, Cassandra? Listen to this solid wall of negation which says Yes! They have all given in to me. Paris has given in to me, Priam has given in to me, Helen has given in to me. And yet I can't help feeling that in each of these apparent victories I have been defeated. You set out, thinking you are going to have to wrestle with giants; you brace yourself to conquer them, and you find yourself wrestling with something inflexible reflected in a woman's eye. You have said yes beautifully, Helen, and you're brimful of a stubborn determination to defy me!

HELEN. That's possible. But how can I help it? It isn't my own determination.

HECTOR. By what peculiar vagary did the world choose to place its mirror in this obtuse head?

HELEN. It's most regrettable, obviously. But can you see any way of defeating the obstinacy of a mirror?

HECTOR. Yes. I've been considering that for the past several minutes.

ANOTHER MESSENGER (*entering*). Hector, make haste. They are in a turmoil of revolt down on the beach. The Greek ships have been sighted, and they have hoisted their flag not masthead but hatchway. The honour of our navy is at stake. Priam is

afraid the ambassador may be murdered as soon as he lands.

HECTOR. I leave you in charge of Helen, Cassandra. I must go and give my orders.

HELEN. If you break the mirror, will what is reflected in it cease to exist?

HECTOR. That is the whole question.

(*Exit* HECTOR)

CASSANDRA. I never see anything at all, you know, either coloured or not. But I can feel the weight on me of every person who comes towards me. I know what is in store for them by the sensation of suffering which flows into my veins.

HELEN. Is it true that you are a sorceress? Could you really make Peace take shape and appear for us?

CASSANDRA. Peace? Very easily. She is always standing in her beggarly way on every threshold. Wait . . . you will see her now.

(PEACE *appears*)

HELEN. Oh, how pretty she is!

PEACE. Come to my rescue, Helen: help me!

HELEN. But how pale and wan she is.

PEACE. Pale and wan? What do you mean? Don't you see the gold shining in my hair?

HELEN. Gold? Well, perhaps a golden grey. It's very original.

PEACE. Golden grey? Is my gold now grey?

(*She disappears*)

CASSANDRA. I think she means to make herself clearer.

(PEACE *re-appears, outrageously painted*)

PEACE. Is that better now?

HELEN. I don't see her as well as I did before.

PEACE. Is that better?

CASSANDRA. Helen doesn't see you as well as she did.

PEACE. But you can see me: you are speaking to me.

CASSANDRA. It's my speciality to speak to the invisible.

PEACE. What is going on, then? Why are all the men in the city and along the beach making such a pandemonium?

CASSANDRA. Apparently their gods are insulted, and their honour is at stake.

PEACE. Their gods! Their honour!

CASSANDRA. Yes . . . You are ill!

The curtain falls.

ACT II

(A palace enclosure. At each corner a view of the sea. In the middle a monument, the Gates of War. They are wide open.)

(HELEN. *The young* TROILUS)

HELEN. You, you, hey! You down there! Yes, it's you I'm calling. Come here.

TROILUS. No.

HELEN. What is your name?

TROILUS. Troilus.

HELEN. Come here.

TROILUS. No.

HELEN. Come here, Troilus!

(TROILUS *draws near*)

That's the way. You obey when you're called by your name: you are still very like a puppy. It's rather beguiling. Do you know you have made me call out to a man for the first time in my life. They keep so close to my side I have only usually to move my lips. I have called out to sea-gulls, to dogs, to the echoes, but never before to a man. You will pay for that. What's the matter? Are you trembling?

TROILUS. No, I'm not.

HELEN. You tremble, Troilus.

TROILUS. Yes, I do.

HELEN. Why are you always just behind me? If I walk with my back to the sun and suddenly stop, the head of your shadow stubs itself against my feet. That doesn't matter, as long as it doesn't overshoot them. Tell me what you want.

TROILUS. I don't want anything.

HELEN. Tell me what you want, Troilus!

TROILUS. Everything! I want everything!

HELEN. You want everything. The moon?

TROILUS. Everything! Everything and more!

HELEN. You're beginning to talk like a real man already; you want to kiss me!

TROILUS. No!

HELEN. You want to kiss me, isn't that it, Troilus?

TROILUS. I would kill myself directly afterwards!

HELEN. Come nearer. How old are you?

TROILUS. Fifteen. Alas!

HELEN. Bravo that alas. Have you kissed girls of your own age?

TROILUS. I hate them.

HELEN. But you have kissed them?

TROILUS. Well, yes, you're bound to kiss them, you kiss them all. I would give my life not to have kissed any of them.

HELEN. You seem prepared to get rid of quite a number of lives. Why haven't you said to me frankly: Helen, I want to kiss you! I don't see anything wrong in your kissing me. Kiss me.

TROILUS. Never.

HELEN. And then, when the day came to an end, you would have come quietly to where I was sitting on the battlements watching the sun go down over the islands, and you would have turned my head towards you with your hands—from golden it would have become dark, only shadow now, you would hardly have been able to see me— and you would have kissed me, and I should have been very happy. Why this is Troilus, I should have said to myself: young Troilus is kissing me! Kiss me.

TROILUS. Never.

HELEN. I see. You think, once you have kissed me, you would hate me?

TROILUS. Oh! Older men have all the luck, knowing how to say what they want to!

HELEN. You say it well enough.

(*Enter* PARIS)

PARIS. Take care, Helen, Troilus is a dangerous fellow.

HELEN. On the contrary. He wants to kiss me.

PARIS. Troilus, you know that if you kiss Helen, I shall kill you?

HELEN. Dying means nothing to him; no matter how often.

PARIS. What's the matter with him? Is he crouching to spring? Is he going to take a leap at you? He's too nice a boy. Kiss Helen, Troilus. I'll let you.

HELEN. If you can make up his mind to it you're cleverer than I am.

(TROILUS *who was about to hurl himself on* HELEN *immediately draws back*)

PARIS. Listen, Troilus! Here's a committee of our revered elders coming to shut the Gates of War. Kiss Helen in front of them; it will make you famous. You want to be famous, don't you, later on in life?

TROILUS. No. I want nobody to have heard of me.

PARIS. You don't want to be famous? You don't want to be rich and powerful?

TROILUS. No. Poor. Ugly.

PARIS. Let me finish! So that you can have all the women you want.

TROILUS. I don't want any, none at all, none.

PARIS. Here come the senators! Now you can chooose: either you kiss Helen in front of them, or I shall kiss her in front of you. Would you rather I did it? All right! Look! . . . Why this was a new version of kiss you gave me, Helen. What was it?

HELEN. The kiss I had ready for Troilus.

PARIS. You don't know what you're missing, my boy! Are you leaving us? Goodbye, then.

HELEN. We shall kiss one another, Troilus. I'll answer for that.

(TROILUS *goes*)

Troilus!

PARIS (*slightly unnerved*). You called very loudly, Helen.

(*Enter* DEMOKOS)

DEMOKOS. Helen, one moment! Look me full in the face. I've got here in my hand a magnificent bird which I'm going to set free. Are you looking? Here it is. Smooth back your hair, and smile a beautiful smile.

PARIS. I don't see how the bird will fly any better if Helen smooths her hair and gives a beautiful smile.

HELEN. It can't do me any harm, anyway.

DEMOKOS. Don't move. One! Two! Three! There! It's all over, you can go now.

HELEN. Where was the bird?

DEMOKOS. It's a bird who knows how to make himself invisible.

HELEN. Ask him next time to tell you how he does it.

(*She goes*)

PARIS. What is this nonsense?

DEMOKOS. I am writing a song on the subject of Helen's face. I needed to look at it closely, to engrave it, smiling, on my memory.

(*Enter* HECUBA, POLYXENE, ABNEOS, *the* MATHEMATICIAN, *and some* OLD MEN)

HECUBA. Well, are you going to shut these Gates for us?

DEMOKOS. Certainly not. We might well have to open them again this very evening.

HECUBA. It is Hector's wish. And Hector will persuade Priam.

DEMOKOS. That is as we shall see. And what's more I have a surprise in store for Hector.

POLYXENE. Where do the Gates lead to, mama?

ABNEOS. To war, my child. When they are open it means there is war.

DEMOKOS. My friends . . .

HECUBA. War or not, it's an absurd symbolism, your Gateway, and those two great doors always left open look very unsightly. All the dogs stop there.

MATHEMATICIAN. This is no domestic matter. It concerns war and the Gods.

HECUBA. Which is just as I said: the Gods never remember to shut their doors.

POLYXENE. I remember to shut them very well, don't I, mama?

PARIS. And you even include your fingers in them, don't you, my pretty one?

DEMOKOS. May I ask for a moment of silence, Paris? Abneos, and you, Mathematician, and you, my friends: I asked you to meet here earlier than the time fixed for the ceremony so that we could hold our first council. And it promises well that this first council of war should be, not a council of generals, but a council of intellectuals. For it isn't enough in war-time to have our soldiers drilled, well-armed, and spectacular. It is absolutely necessary to bring their enthusiasm up to fever pitch. The physical intoxication which their officers will get from them by a generous allowance of cheap wine supplied at the right moment, will still be ineffective against the Greeks, unless it is reinforced by the spiritual and moral intoxication which the poets can pour into them. If we are too old to fight we can at least make sure that the fighting is savage. I see you have something to say on the subject, Abneos.

ABNEOS. Yes. We must make a war-song.

DEMOKOS. Very proper. A war requires a war-song.

PARIS. We have done without one up to now.

HECUBA. War itself sings quite loud enough.

ABNEOS. We have done without one because up to now we were fighting only barbarians. It was nothing more than a hunt, and the hunting horn was all we needed. But now with the Greeks we're entering a different region of war altogether.

DEMOKOS. Exactly so, Abneos. The Greeks don't fight with everybody.

PARIS. We already have a national anthem.

ABNEOS. Yes. But it's a song of peace.

PARIS. If you sing a song of peace with enough gestures and grimaces it becomes a war-song. What are the words we have already?

ABNEOS. You know them perfectly well. There's no spirit in them:

'We cut and bind the harvest,
We tread the vineyard's blood.'

DEMOKOS. At the very most it's a war-song against farm produce. You won't frighten the Spartans by threatening a wheatfield.

PARIS. Sing it with a spear in your hand, and a dead body at your feet, you will be surprised.

HECUBA. It includes the word 'blood,' there's always that.

PARIS. The word 'harvest' as well. War rather approves of the word 'harvest.'

ABNEOS. Why discuss it, when Demokos can invent an entirely new one in a couple of hours.

DEMOKOS. A couple of hours is rather short.

HECUBA. Don't be afraid; it's more than you need for it. And after the song will come the hymn, and after the hymn the cantata. As soon as war is declared it will be impossible to hold the poets back. Rhyme is still the most effective drum.

DEMOKOS. And the most useful, Hecuba: you don't know how wisely you speak. I know war. As long as war isn't with us, and the Gates are shut, each of us is free to insult it and execrate it as we will. But once war comes, its pride and autocracy is huge. You can gain its goodwill only by flattery and adoration. So the mission of those who understand how to speak and write is to compliment and praise war ceaselessly and indiscriminately, otherwise we shut ourselves out from his favour.

PARIS. Have you got an idea for your song already?

DEMOKOS. A marvellous idea, which no one will understand better than you. War must be tired of the mask we always give it, of Medusa's venomous hair and a Gorgon's lips. I have had the notion to compare War's face with Helen's. It will be enchanted by the comparison.

POLYXENE. What does War look like, mama?

HECUBA. Like your Aunt Helen.

POLYXENE. She is very pretty.

DEMOKOS. Then the discussion is closed. You can expect the war-song. Why are you looking worried, Mathematician?

MATHEMATICIAN. Because there are other things far more urgent than this war-song, far more urgent!

DEMOKOS. You think we should discuss the question of medals, false information, atrocity stories, and so on?

MATHEMATICIAN. I think we should discuss the insulting epithets.

HECUBA. The insulting epithets?

MATHEMATICIAN. Before they hurl their spears the Greek fighting-men hurl insults. You third cousin of a toad, they yell! You son of a sow!—They insult each other, like that! And they have a good reason for it. They know that the body is more vulnerable when self-respect has fled. Soldiers famous for their composure lose it immediately when they're treated as warts or maggots. We Trojans suffer from a grave shortage of insults.

DEMOKOS. The Mathematician is quite right. We are the only race in the world which doesn't insult its enemies before it kills them.

PARIS. You don't think it's enough that the civilians insult the enemy civilians?

MATHEMATICIAN. The armies have to show the same hatred the civilians do. You know what dissemblers armies can be in this way. Leave them to themselves and they spend their time admiring each other. Their front lines very soon become the only ranks of real brotherhood in the world. So naturally, when the theatre of war is so full of mutual consideration, hatred is driven back on to the schools, the salons, the trades-people. If our soldiers aren't at least equal to the Greeks in the fury of their epithets, they will lose all taste for insults and calumny, and as a natural consequence all taste for war.

DEMOKOS. Suggestion adopted! We will organize a cursing parade this evening.

PARIS. I should have thought they're big enough to find their own curses.

DEMOKOS. What a mistake! Could you, adroit as you are, find your own effective curses?

PARIS. I believe so.

DEMOKOS. You fool yourself. Come and stand face to face with Abneos and begin.

PARIS. Why Abneos?

DEMOKOS. Because he lends himself to this sort of thing, with his corpulence and one thing and another.

ABNEOS. Come on, then, speak up, you piece of pie-crust!

PARIS. No. Abneos doesn't inspire me. I'll start with you, if you don't mind.

DEMOKOS. With me? Certainly. You can let fly at ten paces. There we are. Begin.

HECUBA. Take a good look at him. You will be inspired.

PARIS. You old parasite! You filthy-footed iambic pentameter!

DEMOKOS. Just one second. To avoid any mistake you had better say who it is you're addressing.

PARIS. You're quite right! Demokos! Bloodshot bullock's eye! You fungus-ridden plum-tree!

DEMOKOS. Grammatically reasonable, but very naive. What is there in a fungus-ridden plum-tree to make me rise up foaming at the lips?

HECUBA. He also called you a bloodshot bullock's eye.

DEMOKOS. Bloodshot bullock's eye is better. But you see how you flounder, Paris? Search for something that can strike home to me. What are my faults, in your opinion?

PARIS. You are cowardly: your breath smells, and you have no talent.

DEMOKOS. You're asking for trouble!

PARIS. I was trying to please you.

POLYXENE. Why are we scolding Uncle Demokos, mama?

HECUBA. Because he is a cuckoo, dearest!

DEMOKOS. What did you say, Hecuba?

HECUBA. I was saying that you're a cuckoo, Demokos. If cuckoos had the absurdity, the affectation, the ugliness and the stench of vultures, you would be a cuckoo.

DEMOKOS. Wait a bit, Paris! Your mother is better at this than you are. Model yourselves on her. One hour's exercise each day for each soldier, and Hecuba has given us the superiority in insults which we badly need. As for the war-song, I'm not sure it wouldn't be wiser to entrust that to her as well.

HECUBA. If you like. But if so, I shouldn't say that war looks like Helen.

DEMOKOS. What would you say it looks like, in your opinion?

HECUBA. I will tell you when the Gates have been shut.

(Enter PRIAM, HECTOR, ANDROMACHE, *and presently* HELEN. *During the closing of the Gates,* ANDROMACHE *takes little* POLYXENE *aside and whispers a secret or an errand to her)*

HECTOR. As they nearly are.

DEMOKOS. One moment, Hector!

HECTOR. Aren't we ready to begin the ceremony?

HECUBA. Surely? The hinges are swimming in oil.

HECTOR. Well, then.

PRIAM. What our friends want you to understand, Hector, is that war is ready, too. Consider carefully. They're not mistaken. If you shut these Gates, in a minute we may have to open them again.

HECUBA. Even one minute of peace is worth taking.

HECTOR. Father, you should know what peace means to men who have been fighting for months. It's like solid ground to someone who was drowning or sinking in the quicksands. Do let us get our feet on to a few inches of peace, touch it, if only with the tips of our toes.

PRIAM. Hector: consider: inflicting the word peace on to the city today is as ruthless as though you gave it poison. You will take her off her guard, undermine her iron determination, debase, with the word peace, the accepted values of memory, affection, and hope. The soldiers will rush to buy the bread of peace, to drink the wine of peace, to hold in their arms the woman of peace, and in an hour you will put them back to face a war.

HECTOR. The war will never take place!

(The sound of clamour near the Gates)

DEMOKOS. No? Listen!

HECTOR. Shut the Gates. This is where we shall meet the Greeks. Conversation will be bitter enough as it is. We must receive them in peace.

PRIAM. My son, are we even sure we should let the Greeks disembark?

HECTOR. Disembark they shall. This meeting with Ulysses is our last chance of peace.

DEMOKOS. Disembark they shall not. Our honour is at stake. We shall be the laughing-stock of the whole world.

HECTOR. And you're taking it upon yourself to recommend to the Senate an action which would certainly mean war?

DEMOKOS. Upon myself? No, not at all. Will you come forward now, Busiris. This is where your mission begins.

HECTOR. Who is this stranger?

DEMOKOS. He is the greatest living expert on the rights of nations. It's a lucky chance he should be passing through Troy today. You can't say that he's a biased witness. He is neutral. Our Senate is willing to abide by his decision, a decision which all other nations will agree with tomorrow.

HECTOR. And what is your opinion?

BUSIRIS. My opinion, Princes, based on my own observation and further enquiry, is that the Greeks, in relation to Troy, are guilty of three breaches of international law. If you give them permission to disembark you will have sacrificed your position as the aggrieved party, and so lost the universal sympathy which would certainly have been yours in the conflict to follow.

HECTOR. Explain yourself.

BUSIRIS. Firstly, they have hoisted their flag hatchway and not masthead. A ship of war, my dear Princes and colleagues, hoists its flag hatchway only when replying to a salute from a boat carrying cattle. Clearly, then, so to salute a city and a city's population is an insult. As it happens, we have a precedent. Last year the Greeks hoisted their flag hatchway when they were entering the port of Orphea. The reply was incisive. Orphea declared war.

HECTOR. And what happened?

BUSIRIS. Orphea was beaten. Orphea no longer exists, nor the Orpheans either.

HECUBA. Perfect.

BUSIRIS. But the annihilation of a people doesn't alter in the least their superior moral position.

HECTOR. Go on.

BUSIRIS. Secondly, on entering your territorial

waters the Greeks adopted the formation known as frontal. At the last congress there was some talk of including this formation in the paragraph of measures called defensive-aggressive. I was very happy to be able to get it restored under its proper heading of aggressive-defensive: so without doubt it is now one of the subtle forms of naval manœuvre which is a disguised form of blockade: that is to say, it constitutes a fault of the first degree! We have a precedent for this, as well. Five years ago the Greek navy adopted the frontal formation when they anchored outside Magnesia. Magnesia at once declared war.

HECTOR. Did they win it?

BUSIRIS. They lost it. There's not one stone of Magnesia still standing on another. But my redraft of the paragraph is still standing.

HECUBA. I congratulate you. We were beginning to be anxious.

HECTOR. Go on.

BUSIRIS. The third fault is not so serious. One of the Greek triremes has crept close in to shore without permission. Its captain, Ajax, the most unruly and impossible man among the Greeks, is climbing up towards the city, shouting scandal and provocation, and swearing he would like to kill Paris. But this is a very minor matter, from the international point of view; because it isn't, in any way, a formal breach of the law.

DEMOKOS. You have your information. The situation can only be resolved in one of two ways. To swallow an outrage, or return it. Choose.

HECTOR. Oneah, go and find Ajax. Head him off in this direction.

PARIS. I'm waiting here for him.

HECTOR. You will be good enough to stay in the Palace until I call for you. As for you, Busiris, you must understand that our city has no intention of being insulted by the Greeks.

BUSIRIS. I am not surprised. Troy's incorruptible pride is a legend all the world over.

HECTOR. You are going to provide me, here and now, with an argument which will allow our Senate to say that there has been no fault whatever on the part of our visitors, and with our pride untouched we welcome them here as our guests.

DEMOKOS. What nonsense is this?

BUSIRIS. It isn't in keeping with the facts, Hector.

HECTOR. My dear Busiris, all of us here know there's no better way of exercising the imagination than the study of law. No poet ever interpreted nature as freely as a lawyer interprets truth.

BUSIRIS. The Senate asked me for an opinion: I gave it.

HECTOR. And I ask you for an interpretation. An even subtler point of law.

BUSIRIS. It goes against my conscience.

HECTOR. Your conscience has seen Orphea destroyed, Magnesia destroyed: is it now contemplating, just as light-heartedly, the destruction of Troy?

HECUBA. Yes. He comes from Syracuse.

HECTOR. I do beg of you, Busiris. The lives of two countries depend on this. Help us.

BUSIRIS. Truth is the only help I can give you.

HECTOR. Precisely. Discover a truth which saves us. What is the use of justice if it doesn't hammer out a shield for innocent people? Forge us a truth. If you can't, there is one thing I can tell you, quite simply: we shall hold you here for as long as the war goes on.

BUSIRIS. What are you saying?

DEMOKOS. You're abusing your position, Hector!

HECUBA. During war we imprison the rights of man. There seems no reason why we shouldn't imprison a lawyer.

HECTOR. I mean what I say, Busiris. I've never failed yet to keep my promises, or my threats. And now either these guards are going to take you off to prison for a year or two, or else you leave here, this evening, heaped with gold. With this in mind, you can dispassionately examine the evidence once again.

BUSIRIS. Actually there are certain mitigating arguments.

HECTOR. I was sure there were.

BUSIRIS. In the case of the first fault, for instance, when the cattle-boat salute is given in certain seas where the shores are fertile, it could be interpreted as a salute from the sailors to the farmers.

HECTOR. That would be, in fact, the logical interpretation. The salute of the sea to the earth.

BUSIRIS. Not to mention that the cargo of cattle might easily be a cargo of bulls. In that case the homage would verge on flattery.

HECTOR. There you are. You've understood what I meant. We've arrived at our point of view.

BUSIRIS. And as to the frontal formation, that could as easily mean a promise as a provocation. Women wanting children give themselves not from the side but face to face.

HECTOR. Decisive argument.

BUSIRIS. Then, again, the Greek ships have huge carved nymphs for figureheads. A woman who comes towards you naked and open-armed is not a threat but an offer. An offer to talk, at any rate.

HECTOR. So there we have our honour safe and sound, Demokos. The next step is to make this consultation with Busiris public. Meanwhile, Minos, tell the port authorities to let Ulysses disembark without any loss of time.

DEMOKOS. It's no use even trying to discuss honour with these fighting men. They trade on the fact that you can't treat them as cowards.

MATHEMATICIAN. At any rate, Hector, deliver the Oration for the Dead. That will make you think again.

HECTOR. There's not going to be an Oration for the Dead.

PRIAM. But it's a part of the ceremony. The victorious general must always speak in honour of the dead when the Gates are closed.

HECTOR. An Oration for the Dead of a war is a hypocritical speech in defence of the living, a plea for acquittal. I am not so sure of my innocence.

DEMOKOS. The High Command is not responsible.

HECTOR. Alas, no one is: nor the Gods either. Besides, I have given my oration for the dead already. I gave it to them in their last minute of life, when they were lying on the battlefield, on a little slope of olive-trees, while they could still attend me with what was left of their sight and hearing. I can tell you what I said to them. There was one, disembowelled, already turning up the whites of his eyes, and I said to him: 'It's not so bad, you know, it's not so bad; you will do all right, old man.' And one with his skull split in two; I said: 'You look pretty comical with that broken nose.' And my little equerry, with his left arm hanging useless and his last blood flowing out of him; and I said, 'It's a good thing for you it's the left arm you've splintered.' I am happy I gave them one final swig of life; it was all they asked for; they died drinking it. And there's nothing else to be said. Shut the Gates.

POLYXENE. Did the little equerry die, as well?

HECTOR. Yes, puss-cat. He died. He stretched out his right arm. Someone I couldn't see took him by his perfect hand. And then he died.

DEMOKOS. Our general seems to confuse remarks made to the dying with the Oration for the Dead.

PRIAM. Why must you be so stubborn, Hector?

HECTOR. Very well: you shall have the Oration. (*He takes a position below the gates*) —You who cannot hear us, who cannot see us, listen to these words, look at those who come to honour you. We have won the war. I know that's of no moment to you. You are the victors, too. But we are victorious, and still live. That's where the difference is between us and why I'm ashamed. I don't know whether, among the crowd of the dead, any privilege is given to men who died victorious. But the living, whether victorious or not, have privilege enough. We have our eyes. We see the sun. We do what all men do under the sun. We eat. We drink. By the moon, we sleep with our wives. And with yours, now you have gone.

DEMOKOS. You insult the dead!

HECTOR. Do you think so?

DEMOKOS. Either the dead or the living.

HECTOR. There is a distinction.

PRIAM. Come to the peroration, Hector. The Greeks are coming ashore.

HECTOR. I will come to it now . . . Breathe in this incense, touch these offerings, you who can neither smell nor touch. And understand, since I speak to you sincerely, I haven't an equal tenderness and respect for all of you. Though all of you are the dead, with you as with us who survive there are men of courage and men of fear, and you can't make me confuse, for the sake of a ceremony, the dead I admire with those I can't admire. But what I have to say to you today is that war seems to me the most sordid, hypocritical way of making all men equal: and I accept death neither as a punishment or expiation for the coward, nor as a reward to the living. So, whatever you may be, absent, forgotten, purposeless, unresting, without existence, one thing is certain when we close these Gates: we must ask you to forgive us, we, the deserters who survive you, who feel we have stolen two great privileges, I hope the sound of their names will never reach you: the warmth of the living body, and the sky.

POLYXENE. The gates are shutting, mama!

HECUBA. Yes, darling.

POLYXENE. The dead men are pushing them shut.

HECUBA. They help, a little.

POLYXENE. They're helping quite a lot, especially over on the right.

HECTOR. Is it done? Are they shut?

GUARD. Tight as a clam.

HECTOR. We're at peace, father, we're at peace.

HECUBA. We're at peace!

POLYXENE. It feels much better, doesn't it, mama?

HECTOR. Indeed it does.

POLYXENE. I feel much better, anyway.

(*The sound of the* GREEKS' *music*)

A MESSENGER. The Greeks have landed, Priam!

DEMOKOS. What music! What frightful music! It's the most anti-Trojan music there could possibly be! Let's go and give them a welcome to match it.

HECTOR. Receive them royally, bring them here safely. You are responsible.

MATHEMATICIAN. At any rate we ought to counter with some Trojan music. Hector, if we can't be indignant any other way, you can authorize a battle of music.

CROWD. The Greeks! The Greeks!

MESSENGER. Ulysses is on the landing-stage, Priam. Where are we to take him?

PRIAM. Conduct him here. Send word to us in the palace when he comes. Keep with us, Paris. We don't want you too much in evidence just yet.

HECTOR. Let's go and prepare what we shall say to the Greeks, father.

DEMOKOS. You'd better prepare it somewhat better than your speech for the dead; you're likely to meet more contradiction.

(*Exeunt* PRIAM *and his* SONS)

If you are going with them, tell us before you go, Hecuba, what it is you think war looks like.

HECUBA. You insist on knowing?

DEMOKOS. If you've seen what it looks like, tell us.

HECUBA. Like the bottom of a baboon. When the baboon is up in a tree, with its hind end facing us, there is the face of war exactly: scarlet, scaley, glazed, framed in a clotted, filthy wig.

DEMOKOS. So he has two faces: this you describe, and Helen's.

(*Exit*)

ANDROMACHE. Here is Helen now. Polyxene, you remember what you have to say to her?

POLYXENE. Yes.

ANDROMACHE. Go to her, then.

(*Enter* HELEN)

HELEN. Do you want to talk to me, darling?

POLYXENE. Yes, Aunt Helen.

HELEN. It must be important, you're so very tense.

POLYXENE. Yes, Aunt Helen.

HELEN. Is it something you can't tell me without standing so stiffly?

POLYXENE. No, Aunt Helen.

HELEN. Do tell me, then; you make me feel terrible when you stand there like a little stick.

POLYXENE. Aunt Helen, if you love anyone, please go away.

HELEN. Why should I go away, darling?

POLYXENE. Because of the war.

HELEN. Do you know about war already, then?

POLYXENE. I don't exactly know about it. I think it means we have to die.

HELEN. And do you know what dying is?

POLYXENE. I don't exactly. I think it means we don't feel anything any more.

HELEN. What exactly was it that Andromache told you to ask me?

POLYXENE. If you love us at all, please to go away.

HELEN. That doesn't seem to me very logical. If you loved someone you wouldn't leave them?

POLYXENE. Oh, no! Never!

HELEN. Which would you rather do: go right away from Hebuca, or never feel anything any more?

POLYXENE. Oh, never feel anything! I would rather stay, and never feel anything any more.

HELEN. You see how badly you put things to me. If I'm to leave you, I mustn't love you. Would you rather I didn't love you?

POLYXENE. Oh, no! I want you to love me.

HELEN. In other words, you didn't know what you were saying, did you?

POLYXENE. No.

HECUBA. (*offstage*). Polyxene!

(*Enter* HECUBA)

Are you deaf, Polyxene? Why did you shut your eyes when you saw me? Are you playing at being a statue? Come with me.

HELEN. She is teaching herself not to feel anything. But she has no gift for it.

HECUBA. Can you hear me, Polyxene? And see me?

POLYXENE. Yes, I can hear you. I can see you, too.

HECUBA. Why are you crying? Don't you like to see and hear me?

POLYXENE. If I do, you will go away.

HECUBA. I think it would be better, Helen, if you left Polyxene alone. She is too sensitive to touch the insensitive, even through your beautiful dress and your beautiful voice.

HELEN. I quite agree with you. I advise Andromache to carry her own messages. Kiss me, Polyxene. I shall go away this evening, since that is what you would like.

POLYXENE. Don't go! Don't go!

HELEN. Bravo! You are quite loosened up again!

HECUBA. Are you coming with us, Andromache?

ANDROMACHE. No: I shall wait here.

(*Exeunt* HECUBA *and* POLYXENE)

HELEN. You want an explanation?

ANDROMACHE. I believe it's necessary.

HELEN. Listen to the way they're shouting and arguing down below. Isn't that enough? Do you and I have to have explanations, too? And what explanations, since I'm leaving here anyway?

ANDROMACHE. Whether you go or stay isn't any longer the problem.

HELEN. Tell Hector that. You will make his day easier.

ANDROMACHE. Yes, Hector is obsessed by the thought of getting you away. All men are the same. They take no notice of the stag in the thicket because they're already chasing the hare. Perhaps men can hunt like that. But not the gods.

HELEN. If you have discovered what the gods are after in this affair, I congratulate you.

ANDROMACHE. I don't know that the gods are after anything. But there is something the universe is after. Ever since this morning, it seems to me, everything has begged and cried out for it, men, animals, even the leaves on the trees and my own child, not yet born.

HELEN. Cried out for what?

ANDROMACHE. That you should love Paris.

HELEN. If they know so certainly that I don't love Paris, they are better informed than I am.

ANDROMACHE. But you don't love him! You could love him, perhaps. But, at present, you are both living in a misunderstanding.

HELEN. I live with him happily, amicably, in complete agreement. We understand each other so well, I don't really see how this can be called a misunderstanding.

ANDROMACHE. Agreement is never reached in love. The life of a wife and husband who love each other is never at rest. Whether the marriage is true or false, the marriage portion is the same: elemental discord. Hector is my absolute opposite. He shares none of my tastes. We pass our days either getting the better of one another, or sacrificing ourselves. There is no tranquillity for lovers.

HELEN. And if I went pale whenever I saw Paris: and my eyes filled with tears, and the palms of my hands were moist, you think Menelaus would be delighted, and the Greeks pleased and quite satisfied?

ANDROMACHE. It wouldn't much matter then what the Greeks thought.

HELEN. And the war would never happen?

ANDROMACHE. Perhaps, indeed, it would never happen. Perhaps if you loved him, love would call to the rescue one of its own equals: generosity or intelligence. No one, not even destiny itself, attacks devotion lightheartedly. And even if the war did happen, why, I think even then——

HELEN. Then it wouldn't be the same war, I suppose.

ANDROMACHE. Oh, no, Helen! You know what this struggle is going to be. Fate would never take so many precautions for an ordinary quarrel. It means to build the future on this war, the future of our countries and our peoples, and our ways of thinking. It won't be so bad if our thoughts and our future are built on the story of a man

and a woman who truly love each other. But fate hasn't noticed yet that you are lovers only on paper, officially. To think that we're going to suffer and die only for a pair of theoretical lovers: and the splendour and calamity of the age to come will be founded on a trivial adventure between two people who don't love each other—that's what is so horrible.

HELEN. If everybody thinks that we love each other, it comes to the same thing.

ANDROMACHE. They don't think so. But no one will admit that he doesn't. Everyone, when there's war in the air, learns to live in a new element: falsehood. Everybody lies. Our old men don't worship beauty: they worship themselves, they worship ugliness. And this indignation the Greeks are showing us is a lie. God knows, they're amused enough at what you can do with Paris! Their boats, in the bay, with their patriotic anthems and their streamers flying, are a falsehood of the sea. And Hector's life and my son's life, too, are going to be played out in hypocrisy and pretence.

HELEN. So?

ANDROMACHE. I beg of you, Helen. You see how I'm pressed against you as though I were begging you to love me. Love Paris! Or tell me that I'm mistaken! Tell me that you would kill yourself if Paris were to die! Tell me that you would even let yourself be disfigured if it would keep him alive. Then the war will only be a scourge, not an injustice.

HELEN. You are being very difficult. I don't think my way of loving is as bad as all that. Certainly I don't get upset and ill when Paris leaves me to play bowls or go fishing for eels. But I do feel commanded by him, magnetically attracted. Magnetism is a kind of love, as much as devotion. And it's an old and fruitful passion in its own way, as desperate devotion and passionate weeping are in theirs. I'm as content in this love as a star in a constellation. It's my own centre of gravity; I shine there; it's the way I breathe, and the way I take life in my arms. And it's easy to see what sons this love can produce: tall, clear-cut boys, of great distinction, with fine fingers and short noses. What will it all become if I fill it with jealousy, with emotion, and anxiety? The world is nervous enough already: look at yourself!

ANDROMACHE. Fill it with pity, Helen. That's the only help the world needs.

HELEN. There we are; I knew it would come; the word has been said.

ANDROMACHE. What word?

HELEN. The word 'pity.' You must talk to someone else. I'm afraid I'm not very good at pity.

ANDROMACHE. Because you don't know unhappiness.

HELEN. Maybe. It could also be that I think of unhappy people as my equals, I accept them, and I don't think of my health and my position and beauty as any better than their misery. It's a sense of brotherhood I have.

ANDROMACHE. You're blaspheming, Helen.

HELEN. I am sure people pity others to the same extent that they would pity themselves. Unhappiness and ugliness are mirrors they can't bear to look into. I haven't any pity for myself. You will see, if war breaks out. I'll put up with hunger and pain better than you will. And insults, too. Do you think I don't hear what the Trojan women say when I'm going past them? They treat me like a slut. They say that the morning light shows me up for what they think me. It may be true, or it may not be. It doesn't matter to me, one way or the other.

ANDROMACHE. Stop, Helen!

HELEN. And of course I can see, in what your husband called the coloured picture-book in my head, pictures of Helen grown old, flabby, toothless, sitting hunched-up in the kitchen, sucking sweets. I can see the white enamel I've plastered over my wrinkles, and the bright colours the sweets are, very clearly. But it leaves me completely indifferent.

ANDROMACHE. I am lost.

HELEN. Why? If you're content with one perfect couple to make the war acceptable, there is always you and Hector, Andromache.

(*Enter* AJAX, *then* HECTOR)

AJAX. Where is he? Where's he hiding himself? A coward! A typical Trojan!

HECTOR. Who are you looking for?

AJAX. I'm looking for Paris.

HECTOR. I am his brother.

AJAX. Beautiful family! I am Ajax! What's your name?

HECTOR. My name's Hector.

AJAX. It ought to be pimp!

HECTOR. I see that Greece has sent over her diplomats. What do you want?

AJAX. War.

HECTOR. Not a hope. Why do you want it?

AJAX. Your brother carried off Helen.

HECTOR. I am told she was willing.

AJAX. A Greek woman can do what she likes. She doesn't have to ask permission from you. He carried her off. It's a reason for war.

HECTOR. We can offer our apologies.

AJAX. What's a Trojan apology? We're not leaving here without your declaration of war.

HECTOR. Declare it yourselves.

AJAX. All right, we will. As from this evening.

HECTOR. That's a lie. You won't declare war. There isn't an island in the archipelago that will back you if we aren't in any way responsible. And we don't intend to be.

AJAX. Will you declare it yourself, personally, if I call you a coward?

HECTOR. That is a name I accept.

AJAX. I've never known such unmilitary reaction! Suppose I tell you what the people of Greece thinks of Troy, that Troy is a cess-pit of vice and stupidity?

HECTOR. Troy is obstinate. You won't get your war.

AJAX. Suppose I spit on her?

HECTOR. Spit.

AJAX. Suppose I strike you, you, one of her princes?

HECTOR. Try it.

AJAX. Suppose I slap your face, you disgusting

example of Troy's conceit and her spurious
honour?

HECTOR. Strike.

AJAX (*striking him*). There. If this lady's
your wife she must be proud of you.

HECTOR. I know her. She is proud.

(*Enter* DEMOKOS)

DEMOKOS. What's all the noise about? What
does this drunkard want, Hector?

HECTOR. He has got what he wants.

DEMOKOS. What is going on, Andromache?

ANDROMACHE. Nothing.

AJAX. Two times nothing. A Greek hits Hector, and Hector puts up with it.

DEMOKOS. Is this true, Hector?

HECTOR. Completely false, isn't it, Helen?

HELEN. The Greeks are great liars. Greek
men, I mean.

AJAX. Is it natural for him to have one cheek
redder than the other?

HECTOR. Yes. I am healthier on that side.

DEMOKOS. Tell the truth, Hector. Has he
dared to raise his hand against you?

HECTOR. That is my concern.

DEMOKOS. It's the concern of war. You are the
figurehead of Troy.

HECTOR. Exactly. No one is going to slap a
figurehead.

DEMOKOS. Who are you, you brute? I am Demokos, second son of Achichaos!

AJAX. The second son of Achichaos? How do
you do? Tell me: is it as serious to slap a
second son of Archichaos as to strike Hector?

DEMOKOS. Quite as serious, you drunk. I am
the head of the senate. If you want war,
war to the death, you have only to try.

AJAX. All right. I'll try. (*He slaps* DEMOKOS)

DEMOKOS. Trojans! Soldiers! To the rescue!

HECTOR. Be quiet, Demokos!

DEMOKOS. To arms! Troy's been insulted!
Vengeance!

HECTOR. Be quiet, I tell you.

DEMOKOS. I *will* shout! I'll rouse the city!

HECTOR. Be quiet! If you won't, I shall hit
you, too!

DEMOKOS. Priam! Anchises! Come and see the
shame of Troy burning on Hector's face!

(HECTOR *strikes* DEMOKOS. AJAX *laughs.
During the scene,* PRIAM *and his lords
group themselves ready to receive*
ULYSSES)

PRIAM. What are you shouting for, Demokos?

DEMOKOS. I have been struck.

AJAX. Go and complain to Achichaos!

PRIAM. Who struck you?

DEMOKOS. Hector! Ajax! Ajax! Hector!

PARIS. What is he talking about? He's mad!

HECTOR. Nobody struck him, did they, Helen?

HELEN. I was watching most carefully, and I
didn't notice anything.

AJAX. Both his cheeks are the same colour.

PARIS. Poets often get upset for no reason. It's
what they call their inspiration. We shall
get a new national anthem out of it.

DEMOKOS. You will pay for this, Hector.

VOICES. Ulysses! Here is Ulysses!

(AJAX *goes amicably to* HECTOR)

AJAX. Well done. Plenty of pluck. Noble
adversary. A beautiful hit.

HECTOR. I did my best.

AJAX. Excellent method, too. Straight elbow.
The wrist on an angle. Safe position for
the carpus and metacarpus. Your slap must
be stronger than mine is.

HECTOR. I doubt it.

AJAX. You must be able to throw a javelin
magnificently with this iron forearm and
this shoulder-bone for a pivot.

HECTOR. Eighty yards.

AJAX. My deepest respect! My dear Hector,
forgive me. I withdraw my threats, I take
back my slap. We have enemies in common, in the sons of Achichaos. I won't fight
with anybody who shares with me an enmity for the sons of Achichaos. Not another
mention of war. I don't know what Ulysses
has got in mind, but count on me to arrange the whole thing.

(*He goes towards* ULYSSES *and comes
back with him*)

ANDROMACHE. I love you, Hector.

HECTOR (*showing his cheek*). Yes; but don't kiss me just yet.

ANDROMACHE. You have won this round, as well. Be confident.

HECTOR. I win every round. But still with each victory the prize escapes me.

ULYSSES. Priam and Hector?

PRIAM. Yes. And behind us, Troy, and the suburbs of Troy, and the land of Troy, and the Hellespont.

ULYSSES. I am Ulysses.

PRIAM. This is Anchises.

ULYSSES. There are many people here for a diplomatic conversation.

PRIAM. And here is Helen.

ULYSSES. Good morning, my queen.

HELEN. I've grown younger here, Ulysses. I've become a princess again.

PRIAM. We are ready to listen to you.

AJAX. Ulysses, you speak to Priam. I will speak to Hector.

ULYSSES. Priam, we have come to take Helen home again.

AJAX. You do understand, don't you, Hector? We can't have things happening like this.

ULYSSES. Greece and Menelaus cry out for vengeance.

AJAX. If deceived husbands can't cry out for vengeance, what can they do?

ULYSSES. Deliver Helen over to us within an hour. Otherwise it means war.

HECTOR. But if we give Helen back to you give us your assurance there will be peace.

AJAX. Utter tranquillity.

HECTOR. If she goes on board within an hour, the matter is closed.

AJAX. And all is forgotten.

HECTOR. I think there's no doubt we can come to an understanding, can we not, Helen?

HELEN. Yes, no doubt.

ULYSSES. You don't mean to say that Helen is being given back to us?

HECTOR. Exactly that. She is ready.

AJAX. What about her baggage? She is sure to have more to take back than when she came.

HECTOR. We return her to you, bag and baggage, and you guarantee peace. No reprisals, no vengeance!

AJAX. A woman is lost, a woman is found, and we're back where we were. Perfect! Isn't it, Ulysses?

ULYSSES. Just wait a moment. I guarantee nothing. Before we say there are going to be no reprisals we have to be sure there has been no cause for reprisals. We have to make sure that Menelaus will find Helen exactly as she was when she was taken from him.

HECTOR. How is he going to discover any difference?

ULYSSES. A husband is very perceptive when a world-wide scandal has put him on his guard. Paris will have had to have respected Helen. And if that isn't so . . .

CROWD. Oh, no! It isn't so!

ONE VOICE. Not exactly!

HECTOR. And if it is so?

ULYSSES. Where is this leading us, Hector?

HECTOR. Paris has not touched Helen. They have both taken me into their confidence.

ULYSSES. What is this absurd story?

HECTOR. The true story, isn't it, Helen?

HELEN. Why does it seem to you so extraordinary?

A VOICE. It's terrible! It puts us to shame!

HECTOR. Why do you have to smile, Ulysses? Do you see the slightest indication in Helen that she has failed in her duty?

ULYSSES. I'm not looking for one. Water leaves more mark on a duck's back than dishonour does on a woman.

PARIS. You're speaking to a queen.

ULYSSES. Present queens excepted, naturally. So, Paris, you have carried off this queen, carried her off naked; and I imagine that you didn't go into the water wearing all your armour; and yet you weren't seized by any taste or desire for her?

PARIS. A naked queen is dressed in her dignity.

HELEN. She has only to remember to keep it on.

ULYSSES. How long did the voyage last? I took three days with my ships, which are faster than yours.

VOICES. What are these intolerable insults to the Trojan navy?

A VOICE. Your winds are faster! Not your ships!

ULYSSES. Let us say three days, if you like. Where was the queen during those three days?

PARIS. Lying down on the deck.

ULYSSES. And Paris was where? In the crow's nest?

HELEN. Lying beside me.

ULYSSES. Was he reading as he lay beside you? Or fishing for goldfish?

HELEN. Sometimes he fanned me.

ULYSSES. Without ever touching you?

HELEN. One day, the second day, I think it was, he kissed my hand.

ULYSSES. Your hand! I see. An outbreak of the animal in him.

HELEN. I thought it was more dignified to take no notice.

ULYSSES. The rolling of the ship didn't throw you towards each other? I don't think it's an insult to the Trojan navy to suggest that its ships roll?

A VOICE. They roll much less than the Greek ships pitch!

AJAX. Pitch? Our Greek ships? If they seem to be pitching it's because of their high prows and their scooped-out sterns!

A VOICE. Oh, yes! The arrogant face and the flat behind, that's Greek all right.

ULYSSES. And what about the three nights you were sailing? The stars appeared and vanished again three times over the pair of you. Do you remember nothing of those three nights?

HELEN. I don't know. Oh, yes! I'd forgotten. I learnt a lot more about the stars.

ULYSSES. While you were asleep, perhaps, he might have taken you . . .

HELEN. A mosquito can wake me.

HECTOR. They will both swear to you, if you like, by our goddess Aphrodite.

ULYSSES. We can do without that. I know what Aphrodite is. Her favourite oath is a perjury.—It's a curious story you're telling me: and it will certainly destroy the idea that the rest of the Archipelago has always had of the Trojans.

PARIS. Why, what do they think of us in the Archipelago?

ULYSSES. You're thought of as less accomplished at trading than we are, but handsome and irresistible. Go on with your story, Paris. It's an interesting contribution to the study of human behaviour. What good reason could you have possibly had for respecting Helen when you had her at your mercy?

PARIS. I . . . I loved her.

HELEN. If you don't know what love is, Ulysses, I shouldn't venture on the subject.

ULYSSES. You must admit, Helen, you would never have followed him if you had known the Trojans were impotent.

VOICES. Shame! Muzzle him! Bring your women here, and you'll soon see! And your grandmother!

ULYSSES. I expressed myself badly. I meant that Paris, the handsome Paris, is impotent.

A VOICE. Why don't you say something, Paris? Are you going to make us the laughing-stock of the world?

PARIS. Hector, you can see, this is a most unpleasant situation for me!

HECTOR. You have to put up with it only a few minutes longer. Goodbye, Helen. And I hope your virtue will become as proverbial as your frailty might have done.

HELEN. That doesn't worry me. The centuries always give us the recognition we deserve.

ULYSSES. Paris the impotent, that's a very good surname! If you care to, Helen, you can kiss him for once.

PARIS. Hector!

FIRST TOPMAN. Are you going to tolerate this farce, commander?

HECTOR. Be quiet! I am in charge here!

TOPMAN. And a rotten job you make of it! We've stood quite enough. We'll tell you, we, Paris's own seamen, we'll tell you what he did with your queen!

VOICES. Bravo! Tell him!

TOPMAN. He's sacrificing himself on his brother's orders. I was an officer on board his ship. I saw everything.

HECTOR. You were quite wrong.

TOPMAN. Do you think a Trojan sailor doesn't know what he sees? I can tell the sex of a seagull thirty yards off. Come over here, Olpides. Olpides was up in the crow's nest. He saw everything from on top. I was standing on the stairs in the hatchway.

My head was exactly on a level with them, like a cat on the end of a bed. Shall I tell him, Trojans?

HECTOR. Silence!

VOICES. Tell him! Go on and tell him!

TOPMAN. And they hadn't been on board more than two minutes, wasn't that true, Olpides?

OLPIDES. Only time enough for the queen to dry herself, being just come up out of the water, and to comb the parting into her hair again. I could see her parting, from her forehead over to the nape of her neck, from where I was.

TOPMAN. And he sent us all down into the hold, except the two of us who he couldn't see.

OLPIDES. And without a pilot, the ship drifted due north. There was no wind, and yet the sails were bellied out full.

TOPMAN. And when I looked out from where I was hiding, what I should have seen was the outline of one body, but what I did see was in the shape of two, like a wheaten loaf and rye bread, baking in the oven together.

OLPIDES. But from up where I was, I more often saw one body than two, but sometimes it was white, and sometimes it was golden brown.

TOPMAN. So much for impotence! And as for respectful, inexpressive love, and unspoken affection, you tell him, Olpides, what you heard from your ledge up there! Women's voices carry upwards, men's voice stay on the ground. I shall tell you what Paris said.

OLPIDES. She called him her ladybird, her little ewe-lamb.

TOPMAN. And he called her his lion, his panther. They reversed the sexes. Because they were being so affectionate. It's not unusual.

OLPIDES. And then she said: 'You are my darling oak-tree, I put my arms round you as if you were an oak-tree.' When you're at sea you think about trees, I suppose.

TOPMAN. And he called her his birch-tree: 'My trembling silver birch-tree!' I remember the word birch-tree very well. It's a Russian tree.

OLPIDES. And I had to say up in the crow's nest all night. You don't half get thirsty up there, and hungry, and everything else.

TOPMAN. And when at last they got up from the deck to go to bed they swayed on their feet. And that's how your wife Penelope would have got on with Trojan impotence.

VOICES. Bravo! Bravo!

A WOMAN'S VOICE. All praise to Paris.

A JOVIAL MAN. Render to Paris what belongs to Paris!

HECTOR. This is a pack of lies, isn't it, Helen?

ULYSSES. Helen is listening enraptured.

HELEN. I forgot they were talking about me. They sound so wonderfully convincing.

ULYSSES. Do you dare to say they are lying, Paris?

PARIS. In some of the particulars, yes, I think they are.

TOPMAN. We're not lying, either in the general or the particular. Are we, Olpides? Do you deny the expressions of love you used? Do you deny the word panther?

PARIS. Not especially the word panther.

TOPMAN. Well, birch-tree, then? I see. It's the phrase 'trembling silver birch-tree' that embarrasses you. Well, like it or not, you used it. I swear you used it, and anyway what is there to blush about in the word 'birch-tree'? I have seen these silver birch-trees trembling against the snow in winter-time, by the shores of the Caspian, with their rings of black bark apparently separated by rings of space, so that you wondered what was carrying the branches. And I've seen them at the height of summer, beside the canal at Astrakhan, with their white rings like fresh mushrooms. And the leaves talked and made signs to me. To see them quivering, gold above and silver underneath, it makes your heart melt! I could have wept like a woman, isn't that true, Olpides? That's how I feel about the birch-tree.

CROWD. Bravo! Bravo!

ANOTHER SAILOR. And it wasn't only the topman and Olpides who saw them, Priam. The entire crew came wriggling up through the hatches and peering under the handrails. The whole ship was one great spy-glass.

THIRD SAILOR. Spying out love.

ULYSSES. There you have it, Hector!

HECTOR. Be quiet, the lot of you.

TOPMAN. Well, keep this quiet, if you can!

(IRIS *appears in the sky*)

PEOPLE. Iris! Iris!

PARIS. Has Aphrodite sent you?

IRIS. Yes, Aphrodite sent me, and told me that I should say to you that love is the world's chief law. Whatever strengthens love becomes in itself sacred, even falsehood, avarice, or luxury. She takes all lovers under her protection, from the king to the goatherd. And she forbids both of you, Hector and Ulysses, to separate Paris from Helen. Or else there will be war.

PARIS AND THE OLD MEN. Thank you, Iris.

HECTOR. Is there any message from Pallas Athene?

IRIS. Yes; Pallas Athene told me that I should say to you that reason is the chief law of the world. All who are lovers, she wishes me to say, are out of their minds. She would like you to tell her quite frankly what is more ridiculous than the mating of cocks with hens or flies with flies. And she orders both of you, Hector, and Ulysses to separate Helen from this Paris of the curly hair. Or else there will be war.

HECTOR AND THE WOMEN. Thank you, Iris!

PRIAM. Oh, my son, it isn't Aphrodite nor Pallas Athene who rules the world. What is it Zeus commands us to do in this time of uncertainty?

IRIS. Zeus, the master of the Gods, told me that I should say to you that those who see in the world nothing but love are as foolish as those who cannot see it at all. It is wise, Zeus, master of the Gods informs you, it is wise sometimes to make love, and at other times not to make love. The decision he gives to Hector and Ulysses, is to separate Helen and Paris without separating them. He orders all the rest of you to go away and leave the negotiators to face each other. And let them so arrange matters that there will be no war. Or else—he swears to you: he swears there will be war.

(*Exit* IRIS)

HECTOR. At your service, Ulysses!

ULYSSES. At your service.

(ALL *withdraw*)

(*A great rainbow is seen in the sky*)

HELEN. How very like Iris to leave her scarf behind.

HECTOR. Now we come to the real tussle, Ulysses.

ULYSSES. Yes: out of which either war or peace is going to come.

HECTOR. Will war come of it?

ULYSSES. We shall know in five minutes time.

HECTOR. If it's to be a battle of words, my chances are small.

ULYSSES. I believe it will be more a battle of weight. It's as though we were one on each side of a pair of scales. How we weigh in the balance will be what counts in the end.

HECTOR. How we weigh in the balance? And what is my weight, Ulysses? My weight is a young man, a young woman, an unborn child. Joy of life, belief in life, a response to whatever's natural and good.

ULYSSES. And my weight is the mature man, the wife thirty-five years old, the son whose height I measure each month with notches against the doorpost of the palace. My weight is the pleasures of living, and a mistrust of life.

HECTOR. Hunting, courage, loyalty, love.

ULYSSES. Circumspection in the presence of the gods, of men, and everything else.

HECTOR. The Phrygian oak-tree, all the leafy, thick-set oak-trees that grow on our hills with our curly-coated oxen.

ULYSSES. The power and wisdom of the olive-tree.

HECTOR. I weigh the hawk, I look straight into the sun.

ULYSSES. I weigh the owl.

HECTOR. I weigh the whole race of humble peasants, hardworking craftsmen, thousands of ploughs and looms, forges and anvils . . . Why is it, when I put all these in the scale in front of you, all at once they seem to me to weigh so light?

ULYSSES. I am the weight of this incorruptible, unpitying air of these coasts and islands.

HECTOR. Why go on? The scales have tipped.

ULYSSES. To my side? Yes, I think so.

HECTOR. And you want war?

ULYSSES. I don't want it. But I'm less sure whether war may not want us.

HECTOR. Our peoples have brought us together to prevent it. Our meeting itself shows that there is still some hope.

ULYSSES. You are young, Hector! It's usual on the eve of every war, for the two leaders of the peoples concerned to meet privately at some innocent village, on a terrace in a garden overlooking a lake. And they decide together that war is the world's worst scourge, and as they watch the rippling reflections in the water, with magnolia petals dropping on to their shoulders, they are both of them peace-loving, modest and friendly. They study one another. They look into each other's eyes. And, warmed by the sun and mellowed by the claret, they can't find anything in the other man's face to justify hatred, nothing, indeed, which doesn't inspire human affection, nothing incompatible in their languages any more, or in their particular way of scratching the nose or drinking wine. They really are exuding peace, and the world's desire for peace. And when their meeting is over, they shake hands in a most sincere brotherly fashion, and turn to smile and wave as they drive away. And the next day war breaks out. And so it is with us both at this moment. Our peoples, who have drawn aside, saying nothing while we have this interview, are not expecting us to win a victory over the inevitable. They have merely given us full powers, isolated here together, to stand above the catastrophe and taste the essential brotherhood of enemies. Taste it. It's a rare dish. Savour it. But that is all. One of the privileges of the great is to witness catastrophes from a terrace.

HECTOR. Do you think this is a conversation between enemies we are having?

ULYSSES. I should say a duet before the full orchestra. Because we have been created sensible and courteous, we can talk to each other, an hour or so before the war, in the way we shall talk to each other long after it's over, like old antagonists. We are merely having our reconciliation before the struggle instead of after it. That may be unwise. If one day one of us should have to kill the other, it might be as well if it wasn't a friend's face we recognized as the body dropped to the ground. But, as the universe well knows, we are going to fight each other.

HECTOR. The universe might be mistaken. One way to recognize error is the fact that it's universal.

ULYSSES. Let's hope so. But when destiny has brought up two nations, as for years it has brought up yours and mine, to a future of similar invention and authority, and given to each a different scale of values (as you and I saw just now, when we weighed pleasure against pleasure, conscience against conscience, even nature itself against nature): when the nation's architects and poets and painters have created for them opposing kingdoms of sound, and form, and subtlety, when we have a Trojan tile roof, a Theban arch, Phrygian red, Greek blue: the universe knows that destiny wasn't preparing alternative ways for civilization to flower. It was contriving the dance of death, letting loose the brutality and human folly which is all that the gods are really contented by. It's a mean way to contrive things, I agree. But we are Heads of State, you and I; we can say this between ourselves: it is Destiny's way of contriving things, inevitably.

HECTOR. And this time it has chosen to match Greece with Troy?

ULYSSES. This morning I was still in doubt. As soon as I stepped on to your landing stage I was certain of it.

HECTOR. You mean you felt yourself on enemy soil?

ULYSSES. Why will you always harp on the word enemy? Born enemies don't fight. Nations you would say were designed to go to war against each other—by their skins, their language, their smell: always jealous of each other, always hating each other—they're not the ones who fight. You will find the real antagonists in nations fate has groomed and made ready for the same war.

HECTOR. And you think we have been made ready for the Greek war?

ULYSSES. To an astonishing extent. Just as nature, when she foresees a struggle between two kinds of insects, equips them with weaknesses and weapons which correspond, so we, living well apart, unknown to ourselves, not even suspecting it, have both been gradually raised up to the level where war begins. All our weapons and habits correspond with each other and balance against each other like the beams of a gable. No other women in the world excite less brutality in us, or less desire, than your wives and daughters do; they give us a joy and an anguish of heart which is a sure sign of impending war between us. Doom has transfigured everything here with the colour of storm: your grave buildings shaking with shadow and fire, the neighing horses, figures disappearing into the dark of a colonnade: the future has never impressed me before with such startling clarity. There is nothing to be done. You're already living in the light of the Greek war.

HECTOR. And do the rest of the Greeks think this?

ULYSSES. What they think is no more reassuring. The rest of the Greeks think Troy is wealthy, her warehouses bulging, her soil prolific. They think that they, on the other hand, are living cramped on a rock. And your golden temples and golden wheatfields flashed from your promontories a signal our ships will never forget. It isn't very wise to have such golden gods and vegetables.

HECTOR. This is more like the truth, at last. Greece has chosen Troy for her prey. Then why a declaration of war? It would have been simpler to have taken Troy by surprise when I was away with the army. You would have had her without striking a blow.

ULYSSES. There's a kind of permission for war which can be given only by the world's mood and atmosphere, the feel of its pulse. It would have been madness to undertake a war without that permission. We didn't have it.

HECTOR. But you have it now.

ULYSSES. I think we do.

HECTOR. But why against us? Troy is famous for her arts, her justice, her humanity.

ULYSSES. A nation doesn't put itself at odds with its destiny by its crimes, but by its faults. Its army may be strong, its treasury well filled, its poets at the height of inspiration. But one day, why it is no one knows, because of some simple event, such as the citizens wantonly cutting down the trees, or their prince wickedly making off with a woman, or the children getting out of hand, the nation is suddenly lost. Nations, like men, die by imperceptible disorders. We recognize a doomed people by the way they sneeze or pare their nails. There's no doubt you carried off Helen badly.

HECTOR. What fairness of proportion can you see between the rape of one woman, and the possible destruction of a whole people, yours or mine, in war?

ULYSSES. We are speaking of Helen. You and Paris have made a great mistake about Helen. I've known her fifteen years, and watched her carefully. There's no doubt about it: she is one of the rare creatures destiny puts on the earth for its own personal use. They're apparently quite unimportant. It might be not even a person, but a small town, or a village: a little queen, or a child; but if you lay hands on them, watch out! It's very hard to know how to recognize one of these hostages of fate among all the other people and places. You haven't recognized it. You could have laid hands with impunity on our great admirals or one of our kings. Paris could have let himself go with perfect safety in a Spartan bed, or a Theban bed, with generous returns twenty times over; but he chose the shallowest brain, the hardest heart, the narrowest understanding of sex. And so you are lost.

HECTOR. We are giving Helen back to you.

ULYSSES. The insult to destiny can't be taken back.

HECTOR. What are we discussing, then? I'm beginning to see what is really behind your words. Admit it. You want our wealth! You had Helen carried off to give you an honourable pretext for war! I blush for Greece. She will be responsible and ashamed for the rest of time.

ULYSSES. Responsible and ashamed? Do you think so? The two words hardly agree. Even if we believed we were responsible for the war, all our generation would have to do would be to deny it, and lie, to appease the conscience of future generations. And we shall lie. We'll make that sacrifice.

HECTOR. Ah, well, the die is cast, Ulysses. On with the war! The more I hate it, the more I find growing in me an irresistible need to kill. If you won't help me, it were better you should leave here.

ULYSSES. Understand me, Hector; you have my help. Don't ask me to interpret fate. All I have tried to do is to read the world's hand, in the great lines of desert caravans, the wake of ships, and the track of migrant birds and wandering peoples. Give me your hand. There are lines there, too. We won't search to see if their lesson tells the same story. We'll suppose that these three little lines at the base of Hector's hand contradict the waves, the wings, and the furrows. I am inquisitive by nature, and not easily frightened. I'm quite willing to join issue with fate. I accept your offer of Helen. I will take her back to Menelaus. I've more than enough eloquence to convince a husband of his wife's virtue. I will even persuade Helen to believe it herself. And I'll leave at once, to avoid any chance of disturbance. Once back on my ship perhaps we can take the risk of running war on to the rocks.

HECTOR. Is this part of Ulysses' cunning, or his greatness?

ULYSSES. In this particular instance, I'm using my cunning against destiny, not against you. It's my first attempt, so I deserve some credit for it. I am sincere, Hector. If I wanted war, I should have asked for a ransom more precious to you than Helen. I am going now. But I can't shake off the feeling that the road from here to my ship is a long way.

HECTOR. My guard will escort you.

ULYSSES. As long as the road of a visiting king, when he knows there has been a threat against his life. Where are the assassins hiding? We're lucky if it's not in the heavens themselves. And the distance from here to the corner of the palace is a long way. A long way, taking this first step. Where is it going to carry me among all these perils? Am I going to slip and kill myself? Will part of the cornice fall down on me? It's all new stonework here; at any moment a stone may be dislodged. But courage. Let us go. (*He takes a first step*)

HECTOR. Thank you, Ulysses.

ULYSSES. The first step is safely over. How many more?

HECTOR. Four hundred and sixty.

ULYSSES. Now the second! You know what made me decide to go, Hector?

HECTOR. Yes. Your noble nature.

ULYSSES. Not precisely. Andromache's eyelashes dance as my wife Penelope's do.

(*Enter* ANDROMACHE *and* CASSANDRA)

HECTOR. Were you there all the time, Andromache?

ANDROMACHE. Let me take your arm. I've no more strength.

HECTOR. Did you hear what we said?

ANDROMACHE. Yes. I am broken.

HECTOR. You see, we needn't despair.

ANDROMACHE. We needn't despair for ourselves, perhaps. But for the world, yes. That man is terrible. All the unhappiness of the world is in me.

HECTOR. A moment or two more, and Ulysses will be on board. You see how fast he is travelling. You can follow his progress from here. There he is, on a level with the fountains. What are you doing?

ANDROMACHE. I haven't the strength any longer to hear any more. I am covering up my ears. I won't take my hands away until we know what our fate is to be.

HECTOR. Find Helen, Cassandra!

(AJAX *enters, more drunk than ever. He sees* ANDROMACHE. *Her back is towards him*)

CASSANDRA. Ulysses is waiting for you down at the harbour, Ajax. Helen will be brought to you there.

AJAX. Helen! To hell with Helen! This is the one I want to get my arms around.

CASSANDRA. Go away, Ajax. That is Hector's wife.

AJAX. Hector's wife! Bravo! I've always liked my friends' wives, my best friends' wives!

CASSANDRA. Ulysses is already half-way there. Hurry.

AJAX. Don't worry, my dear. She's got her hands over her ears. I can say what I like, she can't hear me. If I touched her, now, if I kissed her, certainly! But words she can't hear, what's the matter with that?

CASSANDRA. Everything is the matter with that. Go away, Ajax!

(AJAX, *while* CASSANDRA *tries to force him away from* ANDROMACHE *and* HECTOR, *slowly raises his javelin*)

AJAX. Do you think so? Then I might as well touch her. Might as well kiss her. But chastely, always chastely, with your best friends' wives! What's the most chaste part of your wife, Hector, her neck? So much for her neck. Her ear has a pretty little look of chastity to me. So much for her ear. I'll tell you what I've always found the chastest thing about a woman . . . Let me alone, now; let me alone! She can't even hear when I kiss her . . . You're so cursed strong! All right, I'm going, I said I was going. Goodbye.

(He goes)

(HECTOR *imperceptibly lowers his javelin. At this moment* DEMOKOS *bursts in*)

DEMOKOS. What's this cowardice? You're giving Helen back? Trojans, to arms! They've betrayed us. Fall in! And your war-song is ready! Listen to your war-song!

HECTOR (*striking him*). Have that for your war-song!

DEMOKOS (*falling*). He has killed me!

HECTOR. The war isn't going to happen, Andromache!

(He tries to take ANDROMACHE's *hands from her ears: she resists, her eyes fixed on* DEMOKOS. *The curtain which had begun to fall is lifted little by little*)

ABNEOS. They have killed Demokos! Who killed Demokos?

DEMOKOS. Who killed me? Ajax! Ajax! Kill him!

ABNEOS. Kill Ajax!

HECTOR. He's lying. I am the man who struck him.

DEMOKOS. No. It was Ajax.

ABNEOS. Ajax has killed Demokos. Catch him! Punish him!

HECTOR. I struck you, Demokos, admit it! Admit it, or I'll put an end to you!

DEMOKOS. No, my dear Hector, my good dear Hector. It was Ajax. Kill Ajax!

CASSANDRA. He is dying, just as he lived, croaking like a frog.

ABNEOS. There. They have taken Ajax. There. They have killed him!

HECTOR (*drawing* ANDROMACHE's *hands away from her ears*). The war will happen.

(The Gates of War slowly open, to show HELEN kissing TROILUS)

CASSANDRA. The Trojan poet is dead. And now the Grecian poet will have his word.

The curtain finally falls

◆ *from* Dissertation on the Theater

By JEAN GIRAUDOUX

The problem of the theater and of spectacles, which has played a leading and sometimes decisive role in the history of nations, has lost none of its importance in an age when the eight or seven-hour day has multiplied the time available to every citizen for leisure and amusement. The sole form of a nation's moral or artistic education is theater. It provides, in the evening, the only worthwhile course in adult education; it is the only way by which the most humble and least educated part of the public can have personal contact with the loftiest conflicts and can create for itself a secular religion—rites and saints, sentiments and passions. Some nations dream, but for those who do not there is theater. The intellectual clarity of the French people does not in any way imply rejection of great spiritual presences. The cult of the dead, this domineering cult of heroes, really proves that the French love to see exalted figures, close to them yet inaccessible, enact, in a higher, unlimited region of nobleness, their own humble and limited lives. . . .

The theater, the novel, and even literary criticism, instead of being incidental to a superficial and tranquilly bourgeois life, have again become, in our own age as in every full and anguished age, greatly needed implements. That quartering of literature into so many fragments, performed for the benefit of salons and gala gatherings in a blissful century when novelists, journalists, dramatists and philosophers were encouraged to form so many independent and hostile brotherhoods, now no longer has any reason to continue. The man of letters feels at home in the theater, newspaper office and advertising agency: he invades them. The heart of literature, the magnet that will again pull so many scattered bits into one group, has again been found; it is the writer, it is writing. Every great upheaval in thought and manners diminishes the importance of literary genres as

such, but it heightens a hundredfold the function of the writer by returning his universality to him. Our age does not ask the man of letters to produce more works—streets and alleys are filled with these unwanted effects—it craves from him above all a language. What it no longer expects is to have the writer, either as clown or happy monarch, enunciate his truths in tame, well-made plays and novels, in criticisms as contemptible as flattery. What the public of our age does expect of a writer is that he reveal truth as he sees it, that he disclose, so the public might organize its thought and feeling, the secret of which he alone is trustee—style. Our age also craves the same thing of theater. The protests of persons who do not wish to distinguish between dramatic works that have as their goal the formation of the public and those that aim only to fawn or to please are now no longer of any consequence; for the theater-going public does not experience, in hearing a dramatic work, what the semiliterate call boredom. A seat in the theater has for the public the extraterritoriality of an embassy in the kingdom of antiquity or of heroic ages, in the realm of the illogical and of the fantastic. And the public, while at the theater, intends to uphold the solemn character of this realm. The affection the public nourishes for verse drama lies in this very veneration of style and vocabulary. It likes the craftsmanship of well-turned verses, the care and scruple that this presupposes on the part of the poet. But when a writer reveals that prose is not slipshod, not coarse, not obscene, not indifferent, the public asks nothing more than to believe it. It is stirred to see actors and actresses suddenly exchanging, in place of that paper money that is the usual theatrical style, sentences which reveal that what a people possesses of greatest value, its language, is also a fund of gold.

Jean Giraudoux, "Dissertation on the Theatre," trans. by M. S. Stanford, *Littérature* (Paris: Editions Bernard Grasset, 1941), pp. 198–199, 203–204.

◆ Notes on a Dead Language *and* Review of *Tiger at the Gates*

By KENNETH TYNAN

Notes on a Dead Language

When the London theatre takes to its bed, the habit of criticism is to scourge the invalid; the sick-room resounds with bullying cries of "Who are the new English playwrights?" A more acute inquiry might be: "Who were the old ones?" For the brute fact is that no Englishman since the third decade of the seventeenth century has written an acknowledged dramatic masterpiece. Note that I say "acknowledged"; I might make claims for Otway or Dryden, you for Pinero or Maugham, but in the general censure we should be outvoted. The truth would out: that the legend of English drama springs partly from Shakespeare, our luminous accident, and mostly from an Irish conspiracy to make us ashamed of our weakness. English drama is a procession of glittering Irishmen: Farquhar, Goldsmith, Sheridan, Shaw, Wilde, Synge, and O'Casey are there; and even Congreve slips in on a quibble, since his Irish upbringing served to correct the fault of his English birth. We should not mourn that there are no great English playwrights; we should marvel that there are any English playwrights at all.

Come closer; observe how few fine plays have been written *about* the English in the last three hundred years. High drama presupposes high colloquial speech, which, since Cromwell, has been a rarity on English lips. We will accept eloquence from a Tartar emperor, a Dublin pickpocket or a New York taxi-driver, but we would rightly baulk at verbal beauty in a Yarmouth policeman. When Shakespeare was born, our language was being pelted with imports, from France, from Italy, from classical translations; "thought," as Virginia Woolf said, "plunged into a sea of words and came up dripping." A stock-pot was bubbling which everyone tasted and tried out in speech; and drama evolved out of an epidemic of logorrhoea.

Kenneth Tynan, "Notes on a Dead Language" and "[Review of] *Tiger at the Gates*," *Curtains* (New York, Atheneum, 1961), pp. 95–98.

For half a century we have watched a similar process in America, where a clash of immigrant tongues has produced the same experimental play of language. In England the riot is over. Lexicography has battened on the invaders, and our dictionaries swell with the slain; a memorable phrase flies sometimes from a typewriter into print, but seldom from a larynx into a listening ear. Christopher Fry has performed prodigies of artificial respiration; the words are there, and richly he deploys them; but do they not resemble the bright, life-stimulating dyes which American morticians apply to the faces of the dead? To gain admission to drama, words must be used; they must put on flesh, throng the streets, and bellow through the buses. Dylan Thomas' *Under Milk Wood* was one of the last outposts of the living vernacular, a memory of a time when a phrase was as concrete a thing as a brick; and Thomas, remember, was not English, but a Welshman writing about Welshmen.

The sudden onslaught of a million immigrants of mixed nationalities might help. Until then, I propose an agonising reappraisal of our theatrical status, which is now that of a showroom for foreign goods. A swarm of Continental plays crowds our stage-door; our part, as hosts, is to provide for them translators of genius. Mr. Fry, who is now adapting Anouilh's *L'Alouette* and Giraudoux' *La Guerre de Troie n'aura pas lieu*, has set a noble, instructive, and realistic example.

Review of *Tiger at the Gates*

In spite of a few bad performances and a setting uniquely hideous, I do not believe that anyone could emerge from *Tiger at the Gates* unaware that what had just hit him was a masterpiece. For this is Giraudoux' *La Guerre de Troie n'aura pas lieu*, brought to us at last, after twenty years of impatience, in a methodical translation by Christopher Fry. It remains the final comment on the superfluity of war, and the highest peak in the mountain-range of modern French theatre. At the lowest estimate, it is a great occasional play, in the sense that its impact might be doubled if war seemed imminent; but to call it dated because nowadays we are at peace is to ignore its truest warning, which is that nothing more surely rouses the sleeping tiger of war than the prospect of universal tranquillity.

What is to engage us is the process whereby the Trojan war nearly failed to happen. Returning disillusioned from one campaign, Hector finds another impending; to send Helen back to the Greeks he will undergo any humiliation, even the dishonour of his wife. Paris, his brother, gives in to him easily, but Helen is harder to persuade. The fates, in choosing her for their instrument, have endowed her with an icy indifference to Hector's enormous compassion. "I'm sure," she says, "that people pity each other to the same extent that they pity themselves." Yet she, too, puts herself in his hands.

Breaking all precedents, Hector refuses to make the traditional speech of homage to his fallen soldiers; instead, we have the majestic tirade in which he rejoices with those who survived, the cowards who live to make love to the wives of the dead. His last stumbling-block is Ulysses, wily and circumspect, who reminds him, as they amicably chat, that a convivial "meeting at the summit" is always the preamble to war; but even he agrees to gamble against destiny and take Helen home in peace. In the play's closing moments, war is declared. To reveal how would be an insult to those who know the text and a terrible deprivation to those who do not. Enough to say that history passes into the keeping of (Max Beerbohm's phrase) "those incomparable poets, Homer."

I cannot but marvel at the virtuosity of Giraudoux' prose. It embraces grandeur and littleness in one gigantic clasp; having carved a heroic group in granite, it can turn to the working of tiny heads on cherry-stones. No playwright of our time can change gear so subtly, from majestic gloom to crystalline wit. Sometimes, in the mass debates, the verbal glitter is overpowering, but in duologues Giraudoux has no rival. Hector's scenes with Helen in the first act and with Ulysses in the second ring in the mind like doubloons flung down on marble. Is it objected that English actors jib at long stretches of ornate prose? Or that they are unused to playing tragic scenes for laughs and comic scenes for tears? If so, they had better relearn their craft. The player who thinks Giraudoux unactable is in the wrong profession. Harold Clurman, the director, has tried hard to teach old dogs new tricks, but the right note of vocal aristocracy is only intermittently struck. Listening to Giraudoux should be like watching a series of lightning water-colours, dashed off by a master; some of the present company make do with ponderous cartoons, licking the lead and plunging it deep into the paper. This is the case with Walter Fitzgerald's Ulysses, a dour and laboured performance; and Diane Cilento, though fetchingly got up in what I can best describe as a Freudian slip, gives us paste jewellery instead of the baleful diamond Giraudoux had in mind for Helen. It is Michael Redgrave, as Hector, who bears the evening's brunt. He is clearly much happier in the emotional bits than in the flicks of wit which spark and speckle them; but, even so, this is a monumental piece of acting, immensely moving, intelligent in action, and in repose never less than a demi-god. In the presence of such an actor and such a play, I will forgive much. Especially do I feel for anyone unlucky enough to have to stumble and clamber over the obstacle-course of Loudon Sainthill's set. It is enough to make a chamois nervy.

◆◆◆ Part Three

SYNGE

LORCA

BRECHT

◆ *from* Introduction to *Riders to the Sea*

By WILLIAM E. HART

Between the silent cliffs of Clare and the Connemara coast are the Aran Islands, scene of *Riders to the Sea*. The play takes its title from a dramatic feature of life on the two small islands of Inishmaan and Inisheer. Because of the tides and shallows, coastal steamers and sometimes even smaller transports awaiting passengers and livestock must anchor far offshore. Consequently, islanders intent on shipping horses and cattle to the mainland must ride them into the sea and with the help of the agile island rowboats, the curaghs, tow the animals through the treacherous currents out to the steamer. In a sea that is seldom calm it is a hazardous business for man and beast. At the back of the curagh sits an island man who tethers the swimming animal until it is at the point of exhaustion. Then with a quick movement he pulls the beast's head over the gunnel and struggles to keep it alive and floating until it is hoisted aboard the steamer. This is one of the unique aspects of island life so powerfully captured in Robert Flaherty's splendid documentary film *Man of Aran* (1934).

Life on Aran has changed little from what it was when, at Yeats' uninspired recommendation, J. M. Synge went to the islands in 1898. There, in what he later called "The Last Fortress of the Celt," Synge found the raw material for most of his plays—the strange rhythms and rich imaginative language of his poetic speech, his artist's spirit and the soul of Ireland. He came upon a life that affected his simple, passionate heart—a life that was described in his prose work *The Aran Islands*. Later, Synge recollected his Aran experience in the peace of Wicklow and dramatized one tragic episode. First published in 1903, *Riders to the Sea* has been translated into at least eight languages and in 1937 was made into an opera by Vaughan Williams.

William E. Hart, "Introduction to *Riders to the Sea*," in John Millington Synge, *Playboy of the Western World* and *Riders to the Sea*, William E. Hart, ed. (New York: Appleton-Century-Crofts, 1966), pp. 79–80. Copyright © 1966 by Meredith Publishing Company.

◆◆ Riders to the Sea

By JOHN MILLINGTON SYNGE

Characters

MAURYA, an old woman
BARTLEY, her son
CATHLEEN, her daughter
NORA, a younger daughter
MEN and WOMEN

Scene: An Island off the West of Ireland.

(*Cottage kitchen, with nets, oilskins, spinning wheel, some new boards standing by the wall, etc.* CATHLEEN, *a girl of about twenty, finishes kneading cake, and puts it down in the pot-oven by the fire; then wipes her hands, and begins to spin at the wheel.* NORA, *a young girl, puts her head in at the door.*)

NORA (*in a low voice*). Where is she?

CATHLEEN. She's lying down, God help her, and maybe sleeping, if she's able.

(NORA *comes in softly, and takes a bundle from under her shawl.*)

CATHLEEN (*spinning the wheel rapidly*). What is it you have?

NORA. The young priest is after bringing[1] them. It's a shirt and a plain stocking were got off a drowned man in Donegal.[2]

(CATHLEEN *stops her wheel with a sudden movement, and leans out to listen.*)

NORA. We're to find out if it's Michael's they are, some time herself[3] will be down looking by the sea.

CATHLEEN. How would they be Michael's, Nora? How would he go the length of that way to the far north?

NORA. The young priest says he's known the like of it. "If it's Michael's they are," says he, "you can tell herself he's got a clean burial[4] by the grace of God, and if they're not his, let no one say a word about them, for she'll be getting her death."[5] says he, "with crying and lamenting."

(*The door which* NORA *half closed is blown open by a gust of wind.*)

CATHLEEN (*looking out anxiously*). Did you ask him would he stop Bartley going[6] this day with the horses to the Galway fair?[7]

NORA. "I won't stop him," says he, "but let you not be afraid. Herself does be saying prayers half through the night, and the Almighty God won't leave her destitute," says he, "with no son living."

CATHLEEN. Is the sea bad by the white rocks, Nora?

NORA. Middling bad, God help us. There's a great roaring in the west, and it's worse it'll be getting when the tide's turned to[8] the

John Millington Synge, "Riders to the Sea," in *Playboy of the Western World* and *Riders to the Sea*, William E. Hart, ed. (New York: Appleton-Century-Crofts, 1966), pp. 83–99. Copyright © 1966 by Meredith Publishing Company.

1 *after bringing* has just brought 2 *Donegal* bay, seaport, and county more than a hundred miles north of Aran 3 *herself* their mother Maurya, the woman of the house 4 *clean burial* ritual burial 5 *getting her death* Anglo-Irish idiom for *to die of* 6 *going* from going 7 *Galway fair* the natural mainland trade center for the islanders. Originally the phrase read "going this day to Connemara" 8 *turned to* turned against to form a fierce sea

wind. (*She goes over to the table with the bundle.*) Shall I open it now?

CATHLEEN. Maybe she'd wake up on us, and come in before we'd done. (*Coming to the table*) It's a long time we'll be, and the two of us crying.

NORA (*goes to the inner door and listens*). She's moving about on the bed. She'll be coming in a minute.

CATHLEEN. Give me the ladder, and I'll put them up in the turf-loft, the way[9] she won't know of them at all, and maybe when the tide turns she'll be going down to see would he be floating from the east.

(*They put the ladder against the gable of the chimney;* CATHLEEN *goes up a few steps and hides the bundle in the turf-loft.* MAURYA *comes from the inner room.*)

MAURYA (*looking up at* CATHLEEN *and speaking querulously*). Isn't it turf enough[10] you have for this day and evening?

CATHLEEN. There's a cake baking at the fire for a short space (*throwing down the turf*), and Bartley will want it when the tide turns if he goes to Connemara.[11]

(NORA *picks up the turf and puts it round the pot-oven.*)

MAURYA (*sitting down on a stool at the fire*). He won't go this day with the wind rising from the south and west. He won't go this day, for the young priest will stop him surely.

NORA. He'll not stop him, mother, and I heard Eamon Simon and Stephen Pheety and Colum Shawn saying he would go.

MAURYA. Where is he itself?

NORA. He went down to see would there be another boat sailing in the week, and I'm thinking it won't be long till he's here now, for the tide's turning at the green head, and the hooker's[12] tacking from the east.

CATHLEEN. I hear some one passing the big stones.

NORA (*looking out*). He's coming now, and he in a hurry.

BARTLEY (*comes in and looks round the room. Speaking sadly and quietly*). Where is the bit of new rope,[13] Cathleen, was bought in Connemara?

CATHLEEN (*coming down*). Give it to him, Nora; it's on a nail by the white boards. I hung it up this morning, for the pig with the black feet was eating it.

NORA (*giving him a rope*). Is that it, Bartley?

MAURYA. You'd do right to leave that rope, Bartley, hanging by the boards. (*Bartley takes the rope.*) It will be wanting[14] in this place, I'm telling you, if Michael is washed up to-morrow morning, or the next morning, or any morning in the week, for it's a deep grave we'll make him by the grace of God.

BARTLEY (*beginning to work with the rope*). I've no halter the way I can ride down on the mare, and I must go now quickly. This is the one boat going for two weeks or beyond it,[15] and the fair will be a good fair for horses I heard them saying below.

MAURYA. It's a hard thing[16] they'll be saying below if the body is washed up and there's no man in it[17] to make the coffin, and I after giving a big price for the finest white boards you'd find in Connemara.

(*She looks round at the boards.*)

BARTLEY. How would it be washed up, and we[18] after looking each day for nine days, and a strong wind blowing a while back from the west and south?

[9] *the way* so that   [10] *turf enough* there is no peat on the islands so each family at great expense must buy turf brought over in boatloads from Connemara   [11] *Connemara* the mountainous district of the Galway coast due north of Aran. In Synge's time all the horses from the island were taken by boat to Connemara to graze in the hills from June to September   [12] *hooker* a stout, one-masted fishing-smack used also to transport horses and cattle between the islands and the mainland   [13] *new rope* to make a halter so he can ride the horses down into the sea to meet the Galway boat   [14] *wanting* needed to lower coffin into grave   [15] *beyond it* or more   [16] *hard thing* bitter remarks   [17] *in it* here in the house   [18] *and we* when we're

MAURYA. If it isn't found itself,[19] that wind is raising the sea, and there was a star up against the moon,[20] and it rising in the night. If it was a hundred horses, or a thousand horses you had itself, what is the price of a thousand horses against a son where there is one son only?

BARTLEY (*working at the halter, to* CATHLEEN). Let you go down each day, and see the sheep aren't jumping in on the rye, and if the jobber[21] comes you can sell the pig with the black feet if there is a good price going.

MAURYA. How would the like of her get a good price for a pig?

BARTLEY (*to* CATHLEEN). If the west wind holds with the last bit of the moon let you and Nora get up weed enough for another cock for the kelp.[22] It's hard set[23] we'll be from this day with no one in it[24] but one man to work.

MAURYA. It's hard set we'll be surely the day you're drownd'd with the rest. What way[25] will I live and the girls with me, and I an old woman looking for the grave?

(BARTLEY *lays down the halter, takes off his old coat, and puts on a newer one of the same flannel.*)

BARTLEY (*to* NORA). Is she coming to the pier?

NORA (*looking out*). She's passing the green head and letting fall her sails.

BARTLEY (*getting his purse and tobacco*). I'll have half an hour to go down, and you'll see me coming again in two days, or in three days, or maybe in four days if the wind is bad.

MAURYA (*turning round to the fire, and putting her shawl over her head*). Isn't it a hard and cruel man won't hear a word from an old woman, and she holding him from the sea?

CATHLEEN. It's the life of a young man to be going on the sea, and who would listen to an old woman with one thing and she saying it over?

BARTLEY (*taking the halter*). I must go now quickly. I'll ride down on the red mare, and the gray pony'll run behind me. . . . The blessing of God on you.

(*He goes out.*)

MAURYA (*crying out as he is in the door*). He's gone now, God spare us, and we'll not see him again. He's gone now, and when the black night is falling I'll have no son left me in the world.

CATHLEEN. Why wouldn't you give him your blessing[26] and he looking round in the door? Isn't it sorrow enough is on every one in this house without your sending him out with an unlucky word behind him, and a hard word in his ear?

(MAURYA *takes up the tongs and begins raking the fire aimlessly without looking round.*)

NORA (*turning towards her*). You're taking away the turf from the cake.

CATHLEEN (*crying out*). The Son of God forgive us, Nora, we're after forgetting his bit of bread.

(*She comes over to the fire.*)

NORA. And it's destroyed[27] he'll be going till dark night, and he after eating nothing since the sun went up.

CATHLEEN (*turning the cake out of the oven*). It's destroyed he'll be, surely. There's no sense left on any person in a house where an old woman will be talking for ever.

(MAURYA *sways herself on her stool.*)

CATHLEEN (*cutting off some of the bread and rolling it in a cloth; to* MAURYA). Let you

---

19 *If . . . itself* even if 20 *star . . . moon* an omen in local folklore 21 *jobber* a livestock dealer 22 *weed . . . cock . . . kelp* seaweed heaped in a conical shaped mound, a rick, left to dry and then burned. The residue is left to harden and then sold for its iodine content 23 *hard set* bad off 24 *in it* here 25 *What way* How 26 *blessing* commonly considered bad luck not to return the blessing to one going off on a journey 27 *destroyed* Anglo-Irish intensive for fatigued, exhausted

go down now to the spring well and give him this and he passing.[28] You'll see him then and the dark word will be broken, and you can say "God speed you," the way he'll be easy[29] in his mind.

MAURYA (*taking the bread*). Will I be in it[30] as soon as himself?

CATHLEEN. If you go now quickly.

MAURYA (*standing up unsteadily*). It's hard set I am to walk.

CATHLEEN (*looking at her anxiously*). Give her the stick, Nora, or maybe she'll slip on the big stones.

NORA. What stick?

CATHLEEN. The stick Michael brought from Connemara.

MAURYA (*taking a stick* NORA *gives her*). In the big world the old people do be leaving things after them for their sons and children, but in this place it is the young men do be leaving things behind for them that do be old.

(*She goes out slowly.* NORA *goes over to the ladder.*)

CATHLEEN. Wait, Nora, maybe she'd turn back quickly. She's that sorry, God help her, you wouldn't know the thing she'd do.

NORA. Is she gone round by the bush?[31]

CATHLEEN (*looking out*). She's gone now. Throw it down quickly, for the Lord knows when she'll be out of it[32] again.

NORA (*getting the bundle from the loft*). The young priest said he'd be passing to-morrow, and we might go down and speak to him below if it's Michael's they are surely.

CATHLEEN (*taking the bundle*). Did he say what way they were found?

NORA (*coming down*). "There were two men," says he, "and they rowing round with poteen[33] before the cocks crowed, and the oar of one of them caught the body, and they passing the black cliffs[34] of the north."

CATHLEEN (*trying to open the bundle*). Give

me a knife, Nora, the string's perished[35] with the salt water, and there's a black knot[36] on it you wouldn't loosen in a week.

NORA (*giving her a knife*). I've heard tell it was a long way to Donegal.

CATHLEEN (*cutting the string*). It is surely. There was a man here a while ago—the man sold us that knife—and he said if you set off walking from the rocks beyond, it would be in seven days you'd be in Donegal.

NORA. And what time would a man take, and he floating?

(CATHLEEN *opens the bundle and takes out a bit of a stocking. They look at them eagerly.*)

CATHLEEN (*in a low voice*). The Lord spare us, Nora! isn't it a queer hard thing to say if it's his they are surely?

NORA. I'll get his shirt off the hook the way[37] we can put the one flannel on the other. (*She looks through some clothes hanging in the corner.*) It's not with them, Cathleen, and where will it be?

CATHLEEN. I'm thinking Bartley put it on him in the morning, for his own shirt was heavy with the salt in it (*pointing to the corner*). There's a bit of a sleeve was of the same stuff. Give me that and it will do.

(NORA *brings it to her and they compare the flannel.*)

CATHLEEN. It's the same stuff, Nora; but if it is itself[38] aren't there great rolls of it in the shops of Galway, and isn't it many another man may have a shirt of it as well as Michael himself?

NORA (*who has taken up the stocking and counted the stitches, crying out*). It's Michael, Cathleen, it's Michael; God spare his soul, and what will herself[39] say when she hears this story, and Bartley on the sea?

---

[28] *and he passing* when he's passing [29] *easy* calm, tranquil [30] *in it* there [31] *bush* an easy landmark on those treeless limestone wastes [32] *out of it* out of the house [33] *poteen* illicit whiskey [34] *black cliffs* perhaps the stupendous cliffs of

Slieve League rising nearly 2,000 feet out of the Atlantic on the north shore of Donegal Bay [35] *perished* contracted and hardened [36] *black knot* exceedingly hard to undo [37] *the way* so that [38] *if it is itself* even if it is [39] *herself* Maurya

CATHLEEN (*taking the stocking*). It's a plain stocking.

NORA. It's the second one of the third pair I knitted, and I put up three score stitches, and I dropped four of them.

CATHLEEN (*counts the stitches*). It's that number is in it (*crying out*). Ah, Nora, isn't it a bitter thing to think of him floating that way to the far north, and no one to keen[40] him but the black hags[41] that do be flying on the sea?

NORA (*swinging herself half round, and throwing out her arms on the clothes*). And isn't it a pitiful thing when there is nothing left of a man who was a great rower and fisher, but a bit of an old shirt and a plain stocking?

CATHLEEN (*after an instant*). Tell me is herself coming, Nora? I hear a little sound on the path.

NORA (*looking out*). She is, Cathleen. She's coming up to the door.

CATHLEEN. Put these things away before she'll come in. Maybe it's easier she'll be after giving her blessing to Bartley, and we won't let on[42] we've heard anything the time he's on the sea.

NORA (*helping* CATHLEEN *to close the bundle*). We'll put them here in the corner.

(*They put them into a hole in the chimney corner.* CATHLEEN *goes back to the spinning-wheel.*)

NORA. Will she see it was crying I was?

CATHLEEN. Keep your back to the door the way the light'll not be on you.

(NORA *sits down at the chimney corner, with her back to the door.* MAURYA *comes in very slowly, without looking at the girls, and goes over to her stool at the other side of the fire. The cloth with the bread is still in her hand. The girls look at each other, and* NORA *points to the bundle of bread.*)

CATHLEEN (*after spinning for a moment*). You didn't give him his bit of bread?

(MAURYA *begins to keen softly, without turning round.*)

CATHLEEN. Did you see him riding down?

(MAURYA *goes on keening.*)

CATHLEEN (*a little impatiently*). God forgive you; isn't it a better thing to raise your voice and tell what you seen, than to be making lamentation for a thing that's done? Did you see Bartley, I'm saying to you.

MAURYA (*with a weak voice*). My heart's broken from this day.

CATHLEEN (*as before*). Did you see Bartley?

MAURYA. I seen the fearfulest thing.

CATHLEEN (*leaves her wheel and looks out*). God forgive you; he's riding the mare now over the green head, and the gray pony behind him.

MAURYA (*starts, so that her shawl falls back from her head and shows her white tossed hair. With a frightened voice*). The gray pony behind him. . . .

CATHLEEN (*coming to the fire*). What is it ails you, at all?

MAURYA (*speaking very slowly*). I've seen the fearfulest thing any person has seen, since the day Bride Dara seen the dead man with the child in his arms.

CATHLEEN AND NORA. Uah.

(*They crouch down in front of the old woman at the fire.*)

NORA. Tell us what it is you seen.

MAURYA. I went down to the spring well, and I stood there saying a prayer to myself. Then Bartley came along, and he riding on the red mare with the gray pony[43] behind him. (*She puts up her hands, as if to hide something from her eyes.*) The Son of God spare us, Nora!

---

[40] *keen* the ritual "Irish cry" of lamentation for the dead. Though improvised to a degree, it has several traditional phrases for it, each with many repetitions of the words "Och, ochone" (Woe, woe!). The words are more spoken than sung. [41] *black hags* cormorants [42] *won't let on* pretend we haven't heard [43] *red mare . . . gray pony* other than being the traditional ballad colors for life and death, red and gray are also the predominant colors of the island clothing

CATHLEEN. What is it you seen?

MAURYA. I seen Michael himself.

CATHLEEN (*speaking softly*). You did not, mother. It wasn't Michael you seen, for his body is after being found in the far north, and he's got a clean burial by the grace of God.

MAURYA (*a little defiantly*). I'm after seeing him this day, and he riding and galloping. Bartley came first on the red mare; and I tried to say "God speed you," but something choked the words in my throat. He went by quickly; and "the blessing of God on you," says he, and I could say nothing. I looked up then, and I crying, at the gray pony, and there was Michael upon it—with fine clothes on him, and new shoes on his feet.

CATHLEEN (*begins to keen*). It's destroyed we are from this day. It's destroyed, surely.

NORA. Didn't the young priest say the Almighty God won't leave her destitute with no son living?

MAURYA (*in a low voice, but clearly*). It's little the like of him[44] knows of the sea. . . . Bartley will be lost now, and let you call in Eamon and make me a good coffin out of the white boards, for I won't live after them. I've had a husband, and a husband's father, and six sons in this house—six fine men, though it was a hard birth I had with every one of them and they coming to the world—and some of them were found and some of them were not found, but they're gone now the lot of them. . . . There were Stephen, and Shawn, were lost in the great wind, and found after in the Bay of Gregory[45] of the Golden Mouth, and carried up the two of them on one plank, and in by that door.

(*She pauses for a moment, the girls start as if they heard something through the door that is half open behind them.*)

NORA (*in a whisper*). Did you hear that, Cathleen? Did you hear a noise in the north-east?

CATHLEEN (*in a whisper*). There's some one after crying out by the seashore.

MAURYA (*continues without hearing anything*). There was Sheamus and his father, and his own father again, were lost in a dark night, and not a stick or sign was seen of them when the sun went up. There was Patch after was drowned out of a curagh[46] that turned over. I was sitting here with Bartley, and he a baby, lying on my two knees, and I seen two women, and three women, and four women coming in, and they crossing themselves, and not saying a word. I looked out then, and there were men coming after them, and they holding a thing in the half of a red sail, and water dripping out of it—it was a dry day, Nora—and leaving a track to the door.

(*She pauses again with her hand stretched out towards the door. It opens softly and old women begin to come in, crossing themselves on the threshold, and kneeling down in front of the stage with their backs to the people, and the white waist-bands of the red petticoats they wear over their heads just seen from behind.*)

MAURYA (*half in a dream, to* CATHLEEN). Is it Patch, or Michael, or what is it at all?

CATHLEEN. Michael is after being found in the far north, and when he is found there how could he be here in this place?

MAURYA. There does be a power[47] of young men floating round in the sea, and what way would they know if it was Michael they had, or another man like him, for when a man is nine days in the sea, and the wind blowing, it's hard set his own mother would be to say what man was in it.[48]

CATHLEEN. It's Michael, God spare him, for they're after sending us a bit of his clothes from the far north.

---

44 *like of him* men who live by the sea and not by the Chapel alone know it's little the sea cares for God or man 45 *Bay of Gregory* Gregory Sound separates the island of Inishmore from Inish-maan 46 *curagh* a very light, open boat made of a frame-work of lath covered with tarred canvas 47 *a power* a large number 48 *was in it* was there, who it was

(*She reaches out and hands* MAURYA *the clothes that belonged to Michael.* MAURYA *stands up slowly, and takes them in her hands.* NORA *looks out.*)

NORA. They're carrying a thing among them and there's water dripping out of it and leaving a track by the big stones.

CATHLEEN (*in a whisper to the women who have come in*). Is it Bartley it is?

ONE OF THE WOMEN. It is surely, God rest his soul.

(*Two younger women come in and pull out the table. Then men carry in the body of* BARTLEY, *laid on a plank, with a bit of a sail over it, and lay it on the table.*)

CATHLEEN (*to the women, as they are doing so*). What way was he drowned?

ONE OF THE WOMEN. The gray pony knocked him over into the sea, and he was washed out where there is a great surf on the white rocks.

(MAURYA *has gone over and knelt down at the head of the table. The women are keening softly and swaying themselves with a slow movement.* CATHLEEN *and* NORA *kneel at the other end of the table. The men kneel near the door.*)

MAURYA (*raising her head and speaking as if she did not see the people around her*). They're all gone now, and there isn't anything more the sea can do to me. . . . I'll have no call[49] now to be up crying and praying when the wind breaks from the south, and you can hear the surf is in the east, and the surf is in the west, making a great stir with the two noises, and they hitting one on the other. I'll have no call now to be going down and getting Holy Water[50] in the dark nights after Samhain,[51] and I won't care what way the sea is when the other women will be keening. (*To*

NORA) Give me the Holy Water, Nora, there's a small cup still on the dresser.

(NORA *gives it to her.*)

MAURYA (*drops Michael's clothes across* BARTLEY'S *feet, and sprinkles the Holy Water over him*). It isn't that I haven't prayed for you, Bartley, to the Almighty God. It isn't that I haven't said prayers in the dark night till you wouldn't know what I'd be saying; but it's a great rest I'll have now, and it's time surely. It's a great rest I'll have now, and great sleeping in the long nights after Samhain, if it's only a bit of wet flour we do have to eat, and maybe a fish that would be stinking.

(*She kneels down again, crossing herself, and saying prayers under her breath.*)

CATHLEEN (*to an old man*). Maybe yourself and Eamon would make a coffin when the sun rises. We have fine white boards herself bought, God help her, thinking Michael would be found, and I have a new cake you can eat while you'll be working.

THE OLD MAN (*looking at the boards*). Are there nails with them?

CATHLEEN. There are not, Colum; we didn't think of the nails.

ANOTHER MAN. It's a great wonder she wouldn't think of the nails, and all the coffins she's seen made already.

CATHLEEN. It's getting old she is, and broken.

(MAURYA *stands up again very slowly and spreads out the pieces of Michael's clothes beside the body, sprinkling them with the last of the Holy Water.*)

NORA (*in a whisper to* CATHLEEN). She's quiet now and easy; but the day Michael was drowned you could hear her crying out from this to the spring well. It's fonder she was of Michael, and would any one have thought that?

---

49 *no call* no need   50 *Holy Water* water blessed for ritual use and commonly kept in Catholic homes for benediction and to ward off danger   51 *Samhain*

(pron. Sòw-in) All Souls Day, 1 November, the feast of the Dead and the old name for the beginning of winter

CATHLEEN (*slowly and clearly*). An old woman will be soon tired with anything she will do, and isn't it nine days herself is after crying and keening, and making great sorrow in the house?

MAURYA (*puts the empty cup mouth downwards on the table, and lays her hands together on* BARTLEY'*s feet*). They're all together this time, and the end is come. May the Almighty God have mercy on Bartley's soul, and on Michael's soul, and on the souls of Sheamus and Patch, and Stephen and Shawn (*bending her head*); and may He have mercy on my soul, Nora, and on the soul of every one is left living in the world.

(*She pauses, and the keen rises a little more loudly from the women, then sinks away.*)

MAURYA (*continuing*). Michael has a clean burial in the far north, by the grace of the Almighty God. Bartley will have a fine coffin out of the white boards, and a deep grave surely. What more can we want than that? No man at all can be living for ever, and we must be satisfied.

(*She kneels down again and the curtain falls slowly.*)

◆ *from* Prologue to *Three Tragedies*

By FRANCISCO GARCÍA-LORCA

. . . *Blood Wedding* was inspired by a newspaper account of an incident almost identical with the plot of the play, which took place in Almería. However, many years passed before he decided to write the play; it had a gestation period almost as long as *Doña Rosita* did.

After grasping reality, it was as though he needed to draw away from it, to dream on it anew, then to incorporate the live persons into his own poetic mythology. It is perfectly apparent that the characters in *Blood Wedding* went through this evolutionary process.

I do not know how many times he told me about the play. Then he would forget it; later it would reappear, but transformed (he never wrote down a play's outline) until, fully conceived at last in his fantasy, he wrote it. If I remember correctly, *Blood Wedding* only took a week to write; but in maturing it took years.

Most times he did not himself know what was going to happen in a play—yet it would later surprise me how he would have foreseen, in a first act, what would have its justification in a third. The part he turned over to a process of unconscious cerebration was enormous. . . .

His procedure in writing for the theatre did not vary greatly from the one he adopted for poetry. What was perhaps a play's essential part he entrusted to instinct. If he had not been a born playwright he could never have brought a dramatic work to realization.

In *Blood Wedding* there is a palpable (and I do not know if I should add, but involuntary) intention of taking the play's atmosphere away from any nature of a newspaper story. From the field of the very human passions of concrete beings he removes to an unreal world, one in which the appearances of mysterious and fantastic players (as in the personification of the Moon and Death) are possible. Then he makes the flesh-and-blood characters rise to a plane less real, one which converts them into forces whose incentives are outside themselves. At the play's climax, one of the characters says this:

"For the fault is not mine;
the fault is the earth's."

And a lesser one:

"Blood that sees the light
is drunk up by the earth."

In this fusion with nature—for more than nature it is Earth herself they tread on—the characters have lost individuality. They have moved away from the newspaper account from which they came but they have gained in human and poetic significance. They have been converted into anonymous beings who possess a country's generic character, who are opposed by a tragic personage, their fate, and who are led by this fate among songs and premonitions toward death. As the great poet, Pedro Salinas, says, "*Blood Wedding* gives body, dramatic realization, and the category of great art to a concept of human life borne along time's length in a people's innermost being and traditionally remembered and kept alive in it: the concept of human fatality."

Thus there is a greater abundance of poetic themes in this work; the turning to verse in climatic situations is frequent. Even more: the moments of the play's greatest dramatic intensity are in verse. But Federico never turns to this technical device without a careful preparation. The final episode of the next to last scene, an episode unequaled in dramatic sensuality, is preceded by a series of fantastic appearances which makes the use of verse and of the characters' poetic expressions seem natural. This to such a degree that the episode is imbued with a tone that surpasses in realism the scenes of greater realistic intention.

To some critics this is the play which best achieves an integration of poetry and drama. It is the most spontaneous and simple because the poet does not struggle against his poetic instinct; he gives himself over to it, but without forgetfulness of his previous experiences.

Francisco García-Lorca, "Prologue," to Federico García Lorca, *Three Tragedies*, trans. by James Graham-Luján and Richard L. O'Connell (New York: New Directions, 1947), pp. 19–21.

◆◆ Blood Wedding

By FEDERICO GARCÍA LORCA
Translated by James Graham-Luján and Richard O'Connell

Characters

THE MOTHER
THE BRIDE
THE MOTHER-IN-LAW
LEONARDO'S WIFE
THE SERVANT WOMAN
THE NEIGHBOR WOMAN
YOUNG GIRLS
LEONARDO
THE BRIDEGROOM
THE BRIDE'S FATHER
THE MOON
DEATH (as a Beggar Woman)
WOODCUTTERS
YOUNG MEN

ACT I

Scene 1

A room painted yellow.

BRIDEGROOM, *entering.* Mother.
MOTHER. What?
BRIDEGROOM. I'm going.
MOTHER. Where?
BRIDEGROOM. To the vineyard.

He starts to go.

MOTHER. Wait.
BRIDEGROOM. You want something?

MOTHER. Your breakfast, son.
BRIDEGROOM. Forget it. I'll eat grapes. Give me the knife.
MOTHER. What for?
BRIDEGROOM, *laughing.* To cut the grapes with.
MOTHER, *muttering as she looks for the knife.* Knives, knives. Cursed be all knives, and the scoundrel who invented them.
BRIDEGROOM. Let's talk about something else.
MOTHER. And guns and pistols and the smallest little knife—and even hoes and pitchforks.
BRIDEGROOM. All right.
MOTHER. Everything that can slice a man's body. A handsome man, full of young life, who goes out to the vineyards or to his own olive groves—his own because he's inherited them . . .
BRIDEGROOM, *lowering his head.* Be quiet.
MOTHER. . . . and then that man doesn't come back. Or if he does come back it's only for someone to cover him over with a palm leaf or a plate of rock salt so he won't bloat. I don't know how you dare carry a knife on your body—or how I let this serpent

She takes a knife from a kitchen chest.

stay in the chest.
BRIDEGROOM. Have you had your say?
MOTHER. If I lived to be a hundred I'd talk of nothing else. First your father; to me he smelled like a carnation and I had him for barely three years. Then your brother.

Federico García Lorca, "Blood Wedding," in *Three Tragedies,* trans. by James Graham-Luján and Richard L. O'Connell (New York: New Directions, 1947), pp. 31–99.

Oh, is it right—how can it be—that a small thing like a knife or a pistol can finish off a man—a bull of a man? No, I'll never be quiet. The months pass and the hopelessness of it stings in my eyes and even to the roots of my hair.

BRIDEGROOM, *forcefully.* Let's quit this talk!

MOTHER. No. No. Let's not quit this talk. Can anyone bring me your father back? Or your brother? Then there's the jail. What do they mean, jail? They eat there, smoke there, play music there! My dead men choking with weeds, silent, turning to dust. Two men like two beautiful flowers. The killers in jail, carefree, looking at the mountains.

BRIDEGROOM. Do you want me to go kill them?

MOTHER. No . . . If I talk about it it's because . . . Oh, how can I help talking about it, seeing you go out that door? It's . . . I don't like you to carry a knife. It's just that . . . that I wish you wouldn't go out to the fields.

BRIDEGROOM, *laughing.* Oh, come now!

MOTHER. I'd like it if you were a woman. Then you wouldn't be going out to the arroyo now and we'd both of us embroider flounces and little woolly dogs.

BRIDEGROOM, *he puts his arm around his mother and laughs.* Mother, what if I should take you with me to the vineyards?

MOTHER. What would an old lady do in the vineyards? Were you going to put me down under the young vines?

BRIDEGROOM, *lifting her in his arms.* Old lady, old lady—you little old, little old lady!

MOTHER. Your father, he used to take me. That's the way with men of good stock; good blood. Your grandfather left a son on every corner. That's what I like. Men, men; wheat, wheat.

BRIDEGROOM. And I, Mother?

MOTHER. You, what?

BRIDEGROOM. Do I need to tell you again?

MOTHER, *seriously.* Oh!

BRIDEGROOM. Do you think it's bad?

MOTHER. No.

BRIDEGROOM. Well, then?

MOTHER. I don't really know. Like this, sud-denly, it always surprises me. I know the girl is good. Isn't she? Well behaved. Hard working. Kneads her bread, sews her skirts, but even so when I say her name I feel as though someone had hit me on the forehead with a rock.

BRIDEGROOM. Foolishness.

MOTHER. More than foolishness. I'll be left alone. Now only you are left me—I hate to see you go.

BRIDEGROOM. But you'll come with us.

MOTHER. No. I can't leave your father and brother here alone. I have to go to them every morning and if I go away it's possible one of the Félix family, one of the killers, might die—and they'd bury him next to ours. And that'll never happen! Oh, no! That'll never happen! Because I'd dig them out with my nails and, all by myself, crush them against the wall.

BRIDEGROOM, *sternly.* There you go again.

MOTHER. Forgive me.

Pause.

How long have you known her?

BRIDEGROOM. Three years. I've been able to buy the vineyard.

MOTHER. Three years. She used to have another sweetheart, didn't she?

BRIDEGROOM. I don't know. I don't think so. Girls have to look at what they'll marry.

MOTHER. Yes. I looked at nobody. I looked at your father, and when they killed him I looked at the wall in front of me. One woman with one man, and that's all.

BRIDEGROOM. You know my girl's good.

MOTHER. I don't doubt it. All the same, I'm sorry not to have known what her mother was like.

BRIDEGROOM. What difference does it make now?

MOTHER, *looking at him.* Son.

BRIDEGROOM. What is it?

MOTHER. That's true! You're right! When do you want me to ask for her?

BRIDEGROOM, *happily.* Does Sunday seem all right to you?

MOTHER, *seriously.* I'll take her the bronze

earrings, they're very old—and you buy
her . . .

BRIDEGROOM. You know more about that . . .

MOTHER. . . . you buy her some open-work
stockings—and for you, two suits—three! I
have no one but you now!

BRIDEGROOM. I'm going. Tomorrow I'll go see
her.

MOTHER. Yes, yes—and see if you can make
me happy with six grandchildren—or as
many as you want, since your father didn't
live to give them to me.

BRIDEGROOM. The first-born for you!

MOTHER. Yes, but have some girls. I want
to embroider and make lace, and be at
peace.

BRIDEGROOM. I'm sure you'll love my wife.

MOTHER. I'll love her.

*She starts to kiss him but changes her
mind.*

Go on. You're too big now for kisses. Give
them to your wife.

Pause. To herself.

When she is your wife.

BRIDEGROOM. I'm going.

MOTHER. And that land around the little mill
—work it over. You've not taken good care
of it.

BRIDEGROOM. You're right. I will.

MOTHER. God keep you.

*The Son goes out. The Mother remains
seated—her back to the door. A Neighbor Woman with a 'kerchief on her
head appears in the door.*

Come in.

NEIGHBOR. How are you?

MOTHER. Just as you see me.

NEIGHBOR. I came down to the store and
stopped in to see you. We live so far away!

MOTHER. It's twenty years since I've been up
to the top of the street.

NEIGHBOR. You're looking well.

MOTHER. You think so?

NEIGHBOR. Things happen. Two days ago

they brought in my neighbor's son with
both arms sliced off by the machine.

She sits down.

MOTHER. Rafael?

NEIGHBOR. Yes. And there you have him.
Many times I've thought your son and
mine are better off where they are—sleeping, resting—not running the risk of being
left helpless.

MOTHER. Hush. That's all just something
thought up—but no consolation.

NEIGHBOR, *sighing.* Ay!

MOTHER, *sighing.* Ay!

Pause.

NEIGHBOR, *sadly.* Where's your son?

MOTHER. He went out.

NEIGHBOR. He finally bought the vineyard?

MOTHER. He was lucky.

NEIGHBOR. Now he'll get married.

MOTHER, *as though reminded of something,
she draws her chair near The Neighbor.*
Listen.

NEIGHBOR, *in a confidential manner.* Yes.
What is it?

MOTHER. You know my son's sweetheart?

NEIGHBOR. A good girl!

MOTHER. Yes, but . . .

NEIGHBOR. But who knows her really well?
There's nobody. She lives out there alone
with her father—so far away—fifteen miles
from the nearest house. But she's a good
girl. Used to being alone.

MOTHER. And her mother?

NEIGHBOR. Her mother I *did* know. Beautiful.
Her face glowed like a saint's—but *I* never
liked her. She didn't love her husband.

MOTHER, *sternly.* Well, what a lot of things
certain people know!

NEIGHBOR. I'm sorry. I didn't mean to offend
—but it's true. Now, whether she was decent or not nobody said. That wasn't discussed. She was haughty.

MOTHER. There you go again!

NEIGHBOR. You asked me.

MOTHER. I wish no one knew anything about
them—either the live one or the dead

one—that they were like two thistles no one
even names but cuts off at the right moment.

NEIGHBOR. You're right. Your son is worth a
lot.

MOTHER. Yes—a lot. That's why I look after
him. They told me the girl had a sweetheart some time ago.

NEIGHBOR. She was about fifteen. He's been
married two years now—to a cousin of hers,
as a matter of fact. But nobody remembers
about their engagement.

MOTHER. How do you remember it?

NEIGHBOR. Oh, what questions you ask!

MOTHER. We like to know all about the
things that hurt us. Who was the boy?

NEIGHBOR. Leonardo.

MOTHER. What Leonardo?

NEIGHBOR. Leonardo Félix.

MOTHER. Félix!

NEIGHBOR. Yes, but—how is Leonardo to
blame for anything? He was eight years
old when those things happened.

MOTHER. That's true. But I hear that name—
Félix—and it's all the same.

Muttering.

Félix, a slimy mouthful.

She spits.

It makes me spit—spit so I won't kill!

NEIGHBOR. Control yourself. What good will
it do?

MOTHER. No good. But you see how it is.

NEIGHBOR. Don't get in the way of your son's
happiness. Don't say anything to him.
You're old. So am I. It's time for you and
me to keep quiet.

MOTHER. I'll say nothing to him.

NEIGHBOR, *kissing her.* Nothing.

MOTHER, *calmly.* Such things . . . !

NEIGHBOR. I'm going. My men will soon be
coming in from the fields.

MOTHER. Have you ever known such a hot
sun?

NEIGHBOR. The children carrying water out
to the reapers are black with it. Goodbye,
woman.

MOTHER. Goodbye.

*The Mother starts toward the door at
the left. Halfway there she stops and
crosses herself.*

Curtain

Scene 2

*A room painted rose with copperware
and wreaths of common flowers. In the
center of the room is a table with a
tablecloth. It is morning.*

*Leonardo's Mother-in-law sits in one
corner holding a child in her arms and
rocking it. His Wife is in the other
corner mending stockings.*

MOTHER-IN-LAW.
    Lullaby, my baby
    once there was a big horse
    who didn't like water.
    The water was black there
    under the branches.
    When it reached the bridge
    it stopped and it sang.
    Who can say, my baby,
    what the stream holds
    with its long tail
    in its green parlor?

WIFE, *softly.*
    Carnation, sleep and dream,
    the horse won't drink from the stream.

MOTHER-IN-LAW.
    My rose, asleep now lie,
    the horse is starting to cry.
    His poor hooves were bleeding,
    his long mane was frozen,
    and deep in his eyes
    stuck a silvery dagger.
    Down he went to the river,
    Oh, down he went down!
    And his blood was running,
    Oh, more than the water.

WIFE.
    Carnation, sleep and dream,
    the horse won't drink from the stream.

MOTHER-IN-LAW.

> My rose, asleep now lie,
> the horse is starting to cry.

WIFE.

> He never did touch
> the dank river shore
> though his muzzle was warm
> and with silvery flies.
> So, to the hard mountains
> he could only whinny
> just when the dead stream
> covered his throat.
> Ay-y-y, for the big horse
> who didn't like water!
> Ay-y-y, for the snow-wound
> big horse of the dawn!

MOTHER-IN-LAW.

> Don't come in! Stop him
> and close up the window
> with branches of dreams
> and a dream of branches.

WIFE.

> My baby is sleeping.

MOTHER-IN-LAW.

> My baby is quiet.

WIFE.

> Look, horse, my baby
> has him a pillow.

MOTHER-IN-LAW.

> His cradle is metal.

WIFE.

> His quilt a fine fabric.

MOTHER-IN-LAW.

> Lullaby, my baby.

WIFE.

> Ay-y-y, for the big horse
> who didn't like water!

MOTHER-IN-LAW.

> Don't come near, don't come in!
> Go away to the mountains
> and through the grey valleys,
> that's where your mare is.

WIFE, *looking at the baby.*

> My baby is sleeping.

MOTHER-IN-LAW.

> My baby is resting.

WIFE, *softly.*

> Carnation, sleep and dream,
> The horse won't drink from the stream.

MOTHER-IN-LAW, *getting up, very softly.*

> My rose, asleep now lie
> for the horse is starting to cry.

She carries the child out. Leonardo enters.

LEONARDO. Where's the baby?

WIFE. He's sleeping.

LEONARDO. Yesterday he wasn't well. He cried during the night.

WIFE. Today he's like a dahlia. And you? Were you at the blacksmith's?

LEONARDO. I've just come from there. Would you believe it? For more than two months he's been putting new shoes on the horse and they're always coming off. As far as I can see he pulls them off on the stones.

WIFE. Couldn't it just be that you use him so much?

LEONARDO. No. I almost never use him.

WIFE. Yesterday the neighbors told me they'd seen you on the far side of the plains.

LEONARDO. Who said that?

WIFE. The women who gather capers. It certainly surprised me. Was it you?

LEONARDO. No. What would I be doing there, in that wasteland?

WIFE. That's what I said. But the horse was streaming sweat.

LEONARDO. Did you see him?

WIFE. No. Mother did.

LEONARDO. Is she with the baby?

WIFE. Yes. Do you want some lemonade?

LEONARDO. With good cold water.

WIFE. And then you didn't come to eat!

LEONARDO. I was with the wheat weighers. They always hold me up.

WIFE, *very tenderly, while she makes the lemonade.* Did they pay you a good price?

LEONARDO. Fair.

WIFE. I need a new dress and the baby a bonnet with ribbons.

LEONARDO, *getting up.* I'm going to take a look at him.

WIFE. Be careful. He's asleep.

MOTHER-IN-LAW, *coming in.* Well! Who's been racing the horse that way? He's down there, worn out, his eyes popping from their sockets as though he'd come from the ends of the earth.

LEONARDO, *acidly*. I have.

MOTHER-IN-LAW. Oh, excuse me! He's your horse.

WIFE, *timidly*. He was at the wheat buyers.

MOTHER-IN-LAW. He can burst for all of me!

She sits down. Pause.

WIFE. Your drink. Is it cold?

LEONARDO. Yes.

WIFE. Did you hear they're going to ask for my cousin?

LEONARDO. When?

WIFE. Tomorrow. The wedding will be within a month. I hope they're going to invite us.

LEONARDO, *gravely*. I don't know.

MOTHER-IN-LAW. His mother, I think, wasn't very happy about the match.

LEONARDO. Well, she may be right. She's a girl to be careful with.

WIFE. I don't like to have you thinking bad things about a good girl.

MOTHER-IN-LAW, *meaningfully*. If he does, it's because he knows her. Didn't you know he courted her for three years?

LEONARDO. But I left her.

To his Wife.

Are you going to cry now? Quit that!

He brusquely pulls her hands away from her face.

Let's go see the baby.

They go in with their arms around each other. A Girl appears. She is happy. She enters running.

GIRL. Señora.

MOTHER-IN-LAW. What is it?

GIRL. The groom came to the store and he's bought the best of everything they had.

MOTHER-IN-LAW. Was he alone?

GIRL. No. With his mother. Stern, tall.

She imitates her.

And such extravagance!

MOTHER-IN-LAW. They have money.

GIRL. And they bought some open-work stockings! Oh, such stockings! A woman's dream of stockings! Look: a swallow here,

She points to her ankle.

a ship here,

She points to her calf.

and here,

She points to her thigh.

a rose!

MOTHER-IN-LAW. Child!

GIRL. A rose with the seeds and the stem! Oh! All in silk.

MOTHER-IN-LAW. Two rich families are being brought together.

Leonardo and his Wife appear.

GIRL. I came to tell you what they're buying.

LEONARDO, *loudly*. We don't care.

WIFE. Leave her alone.

MOTHER-IN-LAW. Leonardo, it's not that important.

GIRL. Please excuse me.

She leaves, weeping.

MOTHER-IN-LAW. Why do you always have to make trouble with people?

LEONARDO. I didn't ask for your opinion.

He sits down.

MOTHER-IN-LAW. Very well.

Pause.

WIFE, *to Leonardo*. What's the matter with you? What idea've you got boiling there inside your head? Don't leave me like this, not knowing anything.

LEONARDO. Stop that.

WIFE. No. I want you to look at me and tell me.

LEONARDO. Let me alone.

He rises.

WIFE. Where are you going, love?
LEONARDO, *sharply.* Can't you shut up?
MOTHER-IN-LAW, *energetically, to her daughter.* Be quiet!

Leonardo goes out.

The baby!

She goes into the bedroom and comes out again with the baby in her arms. The Wife has remained standing, unmoving.

MOTHER-IN-LAW.
　　His poor hooves were bleeding,
　　his long mane was frozen,
　　and deep in his eyes
　　stuck a silvery dagger.
　　Down he went to the river,
　　Oh, down he went down!
　　And his blood was running,
　　Oh, more than the water.
WIFE, *turning slowly, as though dreaming.*
　　Carnation, sleep and dream,
　　the horse is drinking from the stream.
MOTHER-IN-LAW.
　　My rose, asleep now lie
　　the horse is starting to cry.
WIFE.
　　Lullaby, my baby.
MOTHER-IN-LAW.
　　Ay-y-y, for the big horse
　　who didn't like water!
WIFE, *dramatically.*
　　Don't come near, don't come in!
　　Go away to the mountains!
　　Ay-y-y, for the snow-wound,
　　big horse of the dawn!
MOTHER-IN-LAW, *weeping.*
　　My baby is sleeping . . .
WIFE, *weeping, as she slowly moves closer.*
　　My baby is resting . . .
MOTHER-IN-LAW.
　　Carnation, sleep and dream,
　　the horse won't drink from the stream.

WIFE, *weeping, and leaning on the table.*
　　My rose, asleep now lie,
　　the horse is starting to cry.

Curtain

Scene 3

Interior of the cave where The Bride lives. At the back is a cross of large rose colored flowers. The round doors have lace curtains with rose colored ties. Around the walls, which are of a white and hard material, are round fans, blue jars, and little mirrors.

SERVANT. Come right in . . .

She is very affable, full of humble hypocrisy. The Bridegroom and his Mother enter. The Mother is dressed in black satin and wears a lace mantilla; The Bridegroom in black corduroy with a great golden chain.

Won't you sit down? They'll be right here.

She leaves. The Mother and Son are left sitting motionless as statues. Long pause.

MOTHER. Did you wear the watch?
BRIDEGROOM. Yes.

He takes it out and looks at it.

MOTHER. We have to be back on time. How far away these people live!
BRIDEGROOM. But this is good land.
MOTHER. Good; but much too lonesome. A four hour trip and not one house, not one tree.
BRIDEGROOM. This is the wasteland.
MOTHER. Your father would have covered it with trees.
BRIDEGROOM. Without water?
MOTHER. He would have found some. In the three years we were married he planted ten cherry trees,

Remembering.

those three walnut trees by the mill, a whole vineyard and a plant called Jupiter which had scarlet flowers—but it dried up.

Pause.

BRIDEGROOM, *referring to The Bride.* She must be dressing.

> *The Bride's Father enters. He is very old, with shining white hair. His head is bowed. The Mother and The Bridegroom rise. They shake hands in silence.*

FATHER. Was it a long trip?
MOTHER. Four hours.

> *They sit down.*

FATHER. You must have come the longest way.
MOTHER. I'm too old to come along the cliffs by the river.
BRIDEGROOM. She gets dizzy.

Pause.

FATHER. A good hemp harvest.
BRIDEGROOM. A really good one.
FATHER. When I was young this land didn't even grow hemp. We've had to punish it, even weep over it, to make it give us anything useful.
MOTHER. But now it does. Don't complain. I'm not here to ask you for anything.
FATHER, *smiling.* You're richer than I. Your vineyards are worth a fortune. Each young vine a silver coin. But—do you know?—what bothers me is that our lands are separated. I like to have everything together. One thorn I have in my heart, and that's the little orchard there, stuck in between my fields—and they won't sell it to me for all the gold in the world.
BRIDEGROOM. That's the way it always is.
FATHER. If we could just take twenty teams of oxen and move your vineyards over here,

and put them down on that hillside, how happy I'd be!
MOTHER. But why?
FATHER. What's mine is hers and what's yours is his. That's why. Just to see it all together. How beautiful it is to bring things together!
BRIDEGROOM. And it would be less work.
MOTHER. When I die, you could sell ours and buy here, right alongside.
FATHER. Sell, sell? Bah! Buy, my friend, buy everything. If I had had sons I would have bought all this mountainside right up to the part with the stream. It's not good land, but strong arms can make it good, and since no people pass by, they don't steal your fruit and you can sleep in peace.

Pause.

MOTHER. You know what I'm here for.
FATHER. Yes.
MOTHER. And?
FATHER. It seems all right to me. They have talked it over.
MOTHER. My son has money and knows how to manage it.
FATHER. My daughter too.
MOTHER. My son is handsome. He's never known a woman. His good name cleaner than a sheet spread out in the sun.
FATHER. No need to tell you about my daughter. At three, when the morning star shines, she prepares the bread. She never talks: soft as wool, she embroiders all kinds of fancy work and she can cut a strong cord with her teeth.
MOTHER. God bless her house.
FATHER. May God bless it.

> *The Servant appears with two trays. One with drinks and the other with sweets.*

MOTHER, *to The Son.* When would you like the wedding?
BRIDEGROOM. Next Thursday.
FATHER. The day on which she'll be exactly twenty-two years old.
MOTHER. Twenty-two! My oldest son would

be that age if he were alive. Warm and manly as he was, he'd be living now if men hadn't invented knives.

FATHER. One mustn't think about that.

MOTHER. Every minute. Always a hand on your breast.

FATHER. Thursday, then? Is that right?

BRIDEGROOM. That's right.

FATHER. You and I and the bridal couple will go in a carriage to the church which is very far from here; the wedding party on the carts and horses they'll bring with them.

MOTHER. Agreed.

The Servant passes through.

FATHER. Tell her she may come in now.

To The Mother.

I shall be much pleased if you like her.

The Bride appears. Her hands fall in a modest pose and her head is bowed.

MOTHER. Come here. Are you happy?

BRIDE. Yes, señora.

FATHER. You shouldn't be so solemn. After all, she's going to be your mother.

BRIDE. I'm happy. I've said "yes" because I wanted to.

MOTHER. Naturally.

She takes her by the chin.

Look at me.

FATHER. She resembles my wife in every way.

MOTHER. Yes? What a beautiful glance! Do you know what it is to be married, child?

BRIDE, *seriously.* I do.

MOTHER. A man, some children and a wall two yards thick for everything else.

BRIDEGROOM. Is anything else needed?

MOTHER. No. Just that you all live—that's it! Live long!

BRIDE. I'll know how to keep my word.

MOTHER. Here are some gifts for you.

BRIDE. Thank you.

FATHER. Shall we have something?

MOTHER. Nothing for me.

To The Son.

But you?

BRIDEGROOM. Yes, thank you.

He takes one sweet, The Bride another.

FATHER, *to The Bridegroom.* Wine?

MOTHER. He doesn't touch it.

FATHER. All the better.

Pause. All are standing.

BRIDEGROOM, *to The Bride.* I'll come tomorrow.

BRIDE. What time?

BRIDEGROOM. Five.

BRIDE. I'll be waiting for you.

BRIDEGROOM. When I leave your side I feel a great emptiness, and something like a knot in my throat.

BRIDE. When you are my husband you won't have it any more.

BRIDEGROOM. That's what I tell myself.

MOTHER. Come. The sun doesn't wait.

To The Father.

Are we agreed on everything?

FATHER. Agreed.

MOTHER, *to The Servant.* Goodbye, woman.

SERVANT. God go with you!

The Mother kisses The Bride and they begin to leave in silence.

MOTHER, *at the door.* Goodbye, daughter.

The Bride answers with her hand.

FATHER. I'll go out with you.

They leave.

SERVANT. I'm bursting to see the presents.

BRIDE, *sharply.* Stop that!

SERVANT. Oh, child, show them to me.

BRIDE. I don't want to.

SERVANT. At least the stockings. They say they're all open work. Please!

BRIDE. I said no.

SERVANT. Well, my Lord. All right then. It looks as if you didn't want to get married.

BRIDE, _biting her hand in anger_. Ay-y-y!

SERVANT. Child, child! What's the matter with you? Are you sorry to give up your queen's life? Don't think of bitter things. Have you any reason to? None. Let's look at the presents.

She takes the box.

BRIDE, _holding her by the wrists_. Let go.

SERVANT. Ay-y-y, girl!

BRIDE. Let go, I said.

SERVANT. You're stronger than a man.

BRIDE. Haven't I done a man's work? I wish I were.

SERVANT. Don't talk like that.

BRIDE. Quiet, I said. Let's talk about something else.

The light is fading from the stage. Long pause.

SERVANT. Did you hear a horse last night?

BRIDE. What time?

SERVANT. Three.

BRIDE. It might have been a stray horse—from the herd.

SERVANT. No. It carried a rider.

BRIDE. How do you know?

SERVANT. Because I saw him. He was standing by your window. It shocked me greatly.

BRIDE. Maybe it was my fiancé. Sometimes he comes by at that time.

SERVANT. No.

BRIDE. You saw him?

SERVANT. Yes.

BRIDE. Who was it?

SERVANT. It was Leonardo.

BRIDE, _strongly_. Liar! You liar! Why should he come here?

SERVANT. He came.

BRIDE. Shut up! Shut your cursed mouth.

The sound of a horse is heard.

SERVANT, _at the window_. Look. Lean out. Was it Leonardo?

BRIDE. It was!

Quick Curtain

ACT II

Scene 1

The entrance hall of The Bride's house. A large door in the back. It is night. The Bride enters wearing ruffled white petticoats full of laces and embroidered bands, and a sleeveless white bodice. The Servant is dressed the same way.

SERVANT. I'll finish combing your hair out here.

BRIDE. It's too warm to stay in there.

SERVANT. In this country it doesn't even cool off at dawn.

The Bride sits on a low chair and looks into a little hand mirror. The Servant combs her hair.

BRIDE. My mother came from a place with lots of trees—from a fertile country.

SERVANT. And she was so happy!

BRIDE. But she wasted away here.

SERVANT. Fate.

BRIDE. As we're all wasting away here. The very walls give off heat. Ay-y-y! Don't pull so hard.

SERVANT. I'm only trying to fix this wave better. I want it to fall over your forehead.

The Bride looks at herself in the mirror.

How beautiful you are! Ay-y-y!

She kisses her passionately.

BRIDE, _seriously_. Keep right on combing.

SERVANT, _combing_. Oh, lucky you—going to put your arms around a man; and kiss him; and feel his weight.

BRIDE. Hush.

SERVANT. And the best part will be when

you'll wake up and you'll feel him at your side and when he caresses your shoulders with his breath, like a little nightingale's feather.

BRIDE, *sternly.* Will you be quiet.

SERVANT. But, child! What *is* a wedding? A wedding is just that and nothing more. Is it the sweets—or the bouquets of flowers? No. It's a shining bed and a man and a woman.

BRIDE. But you shouldn't talk about it.

SERVANT. Oh, that's something else again. But fun enough too.

BRIDE. Or bitter enough.

SERVANT. I'm going to put the orange blossoms on from here to here, so the wreath will shine out on top of your hair.

She tries on the sprigs of orange blossom.

BRIDE, *looking at herself in the mirror.* Give it to me.

She takes the wreath, looks at it and lets her head fall in discouragement.

SERVANT. Now what's the matter?

BRIDE. Leave me alone.

SERVANT. This is no time for you to start feeling sad.

Encouragingly.

Give me the wreath.

The Bride takes the wreath and hurls it away.

Child! You're just asking God to punish you, throwing the wreath on the floor like that. Raise your head! Don't you want to get married? Say it. You can still withdraw.

The Bride rises.

BRIDE. Storm clouds. A chill wind that cuts through my heart. Who hasn't felt it?

SERVANT. You love your sweetheart, don't you?

BRIDE. I love him.

SERVANT. Yes, yes. I'm sure you do.

BRIDE. But this is a very serious step.

SERVANT. You've got to take it.

BRIDE. I've already given my word.

SERVANT. I'll put on the wreath.

BRIDE, *she sits down.* Hurry. They should be arriving by now.

SERVANT. They've already been at least two hours on the way.

BRIDE. How far is it from here to the church?

SERVANT. Five leagues by the stream, but twice that by the road.

The Bride rises and The Servant grows excited as she looks at her.

SERVANT.
> Awake, O Bride, awaken,
> On your wedding morning waken!
> The world's rivers may all
> Bear along your bridal Crown!

BRIDE, *smiling.* Come now.

SERVANT, *enthusiastically kissing her and dancing around her.*
> Awake,
> with the fresh bouquet
> of flowering laurel.
> Awake,
> by the trunk and branch
> of the laurels!

The banging of the front door latch is heard.

BRIDE. Open the door! That must be the first guests.

She leaves. The Servant opens the door.

SERVANT, *in astonishment.* You!

LEONARDO. Yes, me. Good morning.

SERVANT. The first one!

LEONARDO. Wasn't I invited?

SERVANT. Yes.

LEONARDO. That's why I'm here.

SERVANT. Where's your wife?

LEONARDO. I came on my horse. She's coming by the road.

SERVANT. Didn't you meet anyone?

LEONARDO. I *passed* them on my horse.

SERVANT. You're going to kill that horse with so much racing.

LEONARDO. When he dies, he's dead!

Pause.

SERVANT. Sit down. Nobody's up yet.

LEONARDO. Where's the bride?

SERVANT. I'm just on my way to dress her.

LEONARDO. The bride! She ought to be happy!

SERVANT, *changing the subject.* How's the baby?

LEONARDO. What baby?

SERVANT. Your son.

LEONARDO, *remembering, as though in a dream.* Ah!

SERVANT. Are they bringing him?

LEONARDO. No.

Pause. Voices sing distantly.

VOICES.

    Awake, O Bride, awaken,
    On your wedding morning waken!

LEONARDO.

    Awake, O Bride, awaken,
    On your wedding morning waken!

SERVANT. It's the guests. They're still quite a way off.

LEONARDO. The bride's going to wear a big wreath, isn't she? But it ought not to be so large. One a little smaller would look better on her. Has the groom already brought her the orange blossom that must be worn on the breast?

BRIDE, *appearing, still in petticoats and wearing the wreath.* He brought it.

SERVANT, *sternly.* Don't come out like that.

BRIDE. What does it matter?

Seriously.

Why do you ask if they brought the orange blossom? Do you have something in mind?

LEONARDO. Nothing. What would I have in mind?

Drawing near her.

You, you know me; you know I don't. Tell me so. What have I ever meant to you? Open your memory, refresh it. But two oxen and an ugly little hut are almost nothing. That's the thorn.

BRIDE. What have you come here to do?

LEONARDO. To see your wedding.

BRIDE. Just as I saw yours!

LEONARDO. Tied up by you, done with your two hands. Oh, they can kill me but they can't spit on me. But even money, which shines so much, spits sometimes.

BRIDE. Liar!

LEONARDO. I don't want to talk. I'm hot-blooded and I don't want to shout so all these hills will hear me.

BRIDE. My shouts would be louder.

SERVANT. You'll have to stop talking like this.

To The Bride.

You don't have to talk about what's past.

The Servant looks around uneasily at the doors.

BRIDE. She's right. I shouldn't even talk to you. But it offends me to the soul that you come here to watch me, and spy on my wedding, and ask about the orange blossom with something on your mind. Go and wait for your wife at the door.

LEONARDO. But, can't you and I even talk?

SERVANT, *with rage.* No! No, you can't talk.

LEONARDO. Ever since I got married I've been thinking night and day about whose fault it was, and every time I think about it, out comes a new fault to eat up the old one; but always there's a fault left!

BRIDE. A man with a horse knows a lot of things and can do a lot to ride roughshod over a girl stuck out in the desert. But I have my pride. And that's why I'm getting married. I'll lock myself in with my husband and then I'll have to love him above everyone else.

LEONARDO. Pride won't help you a bit.

He draws near to her.

BRIDE. Don't come near me!

LEONARDO. To burn with desire and keep quiet about it is the greatest punishment we can bring on ourselves. What good was pride to me—and not seeing you, and letting you lie awake night after night? No good! It only served to bring the fire down on me! You think that time heals and walls hide things, but it isn't true, it isn't true! When things get that deep inside you there isn't anybody can change them.

BRIDE, *trembling*. I can't listen to you. I can't listen to your voice. It's as though I'd drunk a bottle of anise and fallen asleep wrapped in a quilt of roses. It pulls me along, and I know I'm drowning—but I go on down.

SERVANT, *seizing Leonardo by the lapels*. You've got to go right now!

LEONARDO. This is the last time I'll ever talk to her. Don't you be afraid of anything.

BRIDE. And I know I'm crazy and I know my breast rots with longing; but here I am—calmed by hearing him, by just seeing him move his arms.

LEONARDO. I'd never be at peace if I didn't tell you these things. I got married. Now you get married.

SERVANT. But she *is* getting married!

Voices are heard singing, nearer.

VOICES.
Awake, O Bride, awaken,
On your wedding morning waken!

BRIDE.
Awake, O Bride, awaken.

She goes out, running toward her room.

SERVANT. The people are here now.

To Leonardo.

Don't you come near her again.

LEONARDO. Don't worry.

He goes out to the left. Day begins to break.

FIRST GIRL, *entering.*

Awake, O Bride, awaken,
the morning you're to marry;
sing round and dance round;
balconies a wreath must carry.

VOICES.
Bride, awaken!

SERVANT, *creating enthusiasm.*
Awake,
with the green bouquet
of love in flower.
Awake,
by the trunk and the branch
of the laurels!

SECOND GIRL, *entering.*
Awake,
with her long hair,
snowy sleeping gown,
patent leather boots with silver—
her forehead jasmines crown.

SERVANT.
Oh, shepherdess,
the moon begins to shine!

FIRST GIRL.
Oh, gallant,
leave your hat beneath the vine!

FIRST YOUNG MAN, *entering, holding his hat on high.*
Bride, awaken,
for over the fields
the wedding draws nigh
with trays heaped with dahlias
and cakes piled high.

VOICES.
Bride, awaken!

SECOND GIRL.
The bride
has set her white wreath in place
and the groom
ties it on with a golden lace.

SERVANT.
By the orange tree,
sleepless the bride will be.

THIRD GIRL, *entering.*
By the citron vine,
gifts from the groom will shine.

Three Guests come in.

FIRST YOUTH.
Dove, awaken!

In the dawn
shadowy bells are shaken.

GUEST.
The bride, the white bride
today a maiden,
tomorrow a wife.

FIRST GIRL.
Dark one, come down
trailing the train of your silken gown.

GUEST.
Little dark one, come down,
cold morning wears a dewy crown.

FIRST GUEST.
Awaken, wife, awake,
orange blossoms the breezes shake.

SERVANT.
A tree I would embroider her
with garnet sashes wound,
And on each sash a cupid,
with "Long Live" all around.

VOICES.
Bride, awaken.

FIRST YOUTH.
The morning you're to marry!

GUEST.
The morning you're to marry
how elegant you'll seem;
worthy, mountain flower,
of a captain's dream.

FATHER, *entering.*
A captain's wife
the groom will marry.
He comes with his oxen the treasure to
carry!

THIRD GIRL.
The groom
is like a flower of gold.
When he walks,
blossoms at his feet unfold.

SERVANT.
Oh, my lucky girl!

SECOND YOUTH.
Bride, awaken.

SERVANT.
Oh, my elegant girl!

FIRST GIRL.
Through the windows
hear the wedding shout.

SECOND GIRL.
Let the bride come out.

FIRST GIRL.
Come out, come out!

SERVANT.
Let the bells
ring and ring out clear!

FIRST YOUTH.
For here she comes!
For now she's near!

SERVANT.
Like a bull, the wedding
is arising here!

*The Bride appears. She wears a black
dress in the style of 1900, with a bustle
and large train covered with pleated
gauzes and heavy laces. Upon her hair,
brushed in a wave over her forehead,
she wears an orange blossom wreath.
Guitars sound. The Girls kiss The
Bride.*

THIRD GIRL. What scent did you put on your
hair?

BRIDE, *laughing.* None at all.

SECOND GIRL, *looking at her dress.* This cloth
is what you can't get.

FIRST YOUTH. Here's the groom!

BRIDEGROOM. Salud!

FIRST GIRL, *putting a flower behind his ear.*
The groom
is like a flower of gold.

SECOND GIRL.
Quiet breezes
from his eyes unfold.

The Groom goes to The Bride.

BRIDE. Why did you put on those shoes?

BRIDEGROOM. They're gayer than the black
ones.

LEONARDO'S WIFE, *entering and kissing The
Bride.* Salud!

They all speak excitedly.

LEONARDO, *entering as one who performs a
duty.*
The morning you're to marry
We give you a wreath to wear.

LEONARDO'S WIFE.
> So the fields may be made happy
> with the dew dropped from your hair!

MOTHER, *to The Father.* Are those people here, too?

FATHER. They're part of the family. Today is a day of forgiveness!

MOTHER. I'll put up with it, but I don't forgive.

BRIDEGROOM. With your wreath, it's a joy to look at you!

BRIDE. Let's go to the church quickly.

BRIDEGROOM. Are you in a hurry?

BRIDE. Yes. I want to be your wife right now so that I can be with you alone, not hearing any voice but yours.

BRIDEGROOM. That's what I want!

BRIDE. And not seeing any eyes but yours. And for you to hug me so hard, that even though my dead mother should call me, I wouldn't be able to draw away from you.

BRIDEGROOM. My arms are strong. I'll hug you for forty years without stopping.

BRIDE, *taking his arm, dramatically.* Forever!

FATHER. Quick now! Round up the teams and carts! The sun's already out.

MOTHER. And go along carefully! Let's hope nothing goes wrong.

The great door in the background opens.

SERVANT, *weeping.*
> As you set out from your house,
> oh, maiden white,
> remember you leave shining
> with a star's light.

FIRST GIRL.
> Clean of body, clean of clothes
> from her home to church she goes.

They start leaving.

SECOND GIRL.
> Now you leave your home
> for the church!

SERVANT.
> The wind sets flowers
> on the sands.

THIRD GIRL.
> Ah, the white maid!

SERVANT.
> Dark winds are the lace
> of her mantilla.

They leave. Guitars, castanets and tambourines are heard.

Leonardo and his Wife are left alone.

WIFE. Let's go.

LEONARDO. Where?

WIFE. To the church. But not on your horse. You're coming with me.

LEONARDO. In the cart?

WIFE. Is there anything else?

LEONARDO. I'm not the kind of man to ride in a cart.

WIFE. Nor I the wife to go to a wedding without her husband. I can't stand any more of this!

LEONARDO. Neither can I!

WIFE. And why do you look at me that way? With a thorn in each eye.

LEONARDO. Let's go!

WIFE. I don't know what's happening. But I think, and I don't want to think. One thing I do know. I'm already cast off by you. But I have a son. And another coming. And so it goes. My mother's fate was the same. Well, I'm not moving from here.

Voices outside.

VOICES.
> As you set out from your home
> and to the church go
> remember you leave shining
> with a star's glow.

WIFE, *weeping.*
> Remember you leave shining
> with a star's glow!
> I left my house like that too. They could have stuffed the whole countryside in my mouth. I was that trusting.

LEONARDO, *rising.* Let's go!

WIFE. But you with me!

LEONARDO. Yes.

Pause.

Start moving!

They leave.

VOICES.

As you set out from your home
and to the church go,
remember you leave shining
with a star's glow.

Slow Curtain

Scene 2

The exterior of The Bride's Cave Home,
in white gray and cold blue tones. Large
cactus trees. Shadowy and silver tones.
Panoramas of light tan tablelands, every-
thing hard like a landscape in popular
ceramics.

SERVANT, *arranging glasses and trays on a*
table.

A-turning,
the wheel was a-turning
and the water was flowing,
for the wedding night comes.
May the branches part
and the moon be arrayed
at her white balcony rail.

In a loud voice.

Set out the tablecloths!

In a pathetic voice.

A-singing,
bride and groom were singing
and the water was flowing
for their wedding night comes.
Oh, rime-frost, flash!—
and almonds bitter
fill with honey!

In a loud voice.

Get the wine ready!

In a poetic tone.

Elegant girl,
most elegant in the world,
see the way the water is flowing,
for your wedding night comes.
Hold your skirts close in
under the bridegroom's wing
and never leave your house,
for the Bridegroom is a dove
with his breast a firebrand
and the fields wait for the whisper
of spurting blood.
A-turning
the wheel was a-turning
and the water was flowing
and your wedding night comes.
Oh, water, sparkle!

MOTHER, *entering.* At last!

FATHER. Are we the first ones?

SERVANT. No. Leonardo and his wife arrived
a while ago. They drove like demons. His
wife got here dead with fright. They made
the trip as though they'd come on horseback.

FATHER. That one's looking for trouble. He's
not of good blood.

MOTHER. What blood would you expect him
to have? His whole family's blood. It comes
down from his great grandfather, who
started in killing, and it goes on down
through the whole evil breed of knife
wielding and false smiling men.

FATHER. Let's leave it at that!

SERVANT. But how can she leave it at that?

MOTHER. It hurts me to the tips of my veins.
On the forehead of all of them I see only
the hand with which they killed what was
mine. Can you really see me? Don't I seem
mad to you? Well, it's the madness of not
having shrieked out all my breast needs to.
Always in my breast there's a shriek standing tiptoe that I have to beat down and
hold in under my shawls. But the dead are
carried off and one has to keep still. And
then, people find fault.

She removes her shawl.

FATHER. Today's not the day for you to be
remembering these things.

MOTHER. When the talk turns on it, I have to

speak. And more so today. Because today I'm left alone in my house.

FATHER. But with the expectation of having someone with you.

MOTHER. That's my hope: grandchildren.

They sit down.

FATHER. I want them to have a lot of them. This land needs hands that aren't hired. There's a battle to be waged against weeds, the thistles, the big rocks that come from one doesn't know where. And those hands have to be the owner's, who chastises and dominates, who makes the seeds grow. Lots of sons are needed.

MOTHER. And some daughters! Men are like the wind! They're forced to handle weapons. Girls never go out into the street.

FATHER, *happily.* I think they'll have both.

MOTHER. My son will cover her well. He's of good seed. His father could have had many sons with me.

FATHER. What I'd like is to have all this happen in a day. So that right away they'd have two or three boys.

MOTHER. But it's not like that. It takes a long time. That's why it's so terrible to see one's own blood spilled out on the ground. A fountain that spurts for a minute, but costs us years. When I got to my son, he lay fallen in the middle of the street. I wet my hands with his blood and licked them with my tongue—because it was my blood. You don't know what that's like. In a glass and topaz shrine I'd put the earth moistened by his blood.

FATHER. Now you must hope. My daughter is wide-hipped and your son is strong.

MOTHER. That's why I'm hoping.

They rise.

FATHER. Get the wheat trays ready!

SERVANT. They're all ready.

LEONARDO'S WIFE, *entering.* May it be for the best!

MOTHER. Thank you.

LEONARDO. Is there going to be a celebration?

FATHER. A small one. People can't stay long.

SERVANT. Here they are!

Guests begin entering in gay groups. The Bride and Groom come in arm-in-arm. Leonardo leaves.

BRIDEGROOM. There's never been a wedding with so many people!

BRIDE, *sullen.* Never.

FATHER. It was brilliant.

MOTHER. Whole branches of families came.

BRIDEGROOM. People who never went out of the house.

MOTHER. Your father sowed well, and now you're reaping it.

BRIDEGROOM. There were cousins of mine whom I no longer knew.

MOTHER. All the people from the seacoast.

BRIDEGROOM, *happily.* They were frightened of the horses.

They talk.

MOTHER, *to The Bride.* What are you thinking about?

BRIDE. I'm not thinking about anything.

MOTHER. Your blessings weigh heavily.

Guitars are heard.

BRIDE. Like lead.

MOTHER, *stern.* But they shouldn't weigh so. Happy as a dove you ought to be.

BRIDE. Are you staying here tonight?

MOTHER. No. My house is empty.

BRIDE. You ought to stay!

FATHER, *to The Mother.* Look at the dance they're forming. Dances of the far away seashore.

Leonardo enters and sits down. His wife stands rigidly behind him.

MOTHER. They're my husband's cousins. Stiff as stones at dancing.

FATHER. It makes me happy to watch them. What a change for this house!

He leaves.

BRIDEGROOM, *to The Bride.* Did you like the orange blossom?

BRIDE, *looking at him fixedly.* Yes.

BRIDEGROOM. It's all of wax. It will last forever. I'd like you to have had them all over your dress.

BRIDE. No need of that.

Leonardo goes off to the right.

FIRST GIRL. Let's go and take out your pins.

BRIDE, *to The Groom.* I'll be right back.

LEONARDO'S WIFE. I hope you'll be happy with my cousin!

BRIDEGROOM. I'm sure I will.

LEONARDO'S WIFE. The two of you here; never going out; building a home. I wish I could live far away like this, too!

BRIDEGROOM. Why don't you buy land? The mountain-side is cheap and children grow up better.

LEONARDO'S WIFE. We don't have any money. And at the rate we're going . . . !

BRIDEGROOM. Your husband is a good worker.

LEONARDO'S WIFE. Yes, but he likes to fly around too much; from one thing to another. He's not a patient man.

SERVANT. Aren't you having anything? I'm going to wrap up some wine cakes for your mother. She likes them so much.

BRIDEGROOM. Put up three dozen for her.

LEONARDO'S WIFE. No, no. A half-dozen's enough for her!

BRIDEGROOM. But today's a day!

LEONARDO'S WIFE, *to The Servant.* Where's Leonardo?

BRIDEGROOM. He must be with the guests.

LEONARDO'S WIFE. I'm going to go see.

She leaves.

SERVANT, *looking off at the dance.* That's beautiful there.

BRIDEGROOM. Aren't you dancing?

SERVANT. No one will ask me.

Two Girls pass across the back of the stage; during this whole scene the background should be an animated crossing of figures.

BRIDEGROOM, *happily.* They just don't know anything. Lively old girls like you dance better than the young ones.

SERVANT. Well! Are you tossing me a compliment, boy? What a family yours is! Men among men! As a little girl I saw your grandfather's wedding. What a figure! It seemed as if a mountain were getting married.

BRIDEGROOM. I'm not as tall.

SERVANT. But there's the same twinkle in your eye. Where's the girl?

BRIDEGROOM. Taking off her wreath.

SERVANT. Ah! Look. For midnight, since you won't be sleeping, I have prepared ham for you, and some large glasses of old wine. On the lower shelf of the cupboard. In case you need it.

BRIDEGROOM, *smiling.* I won't be eating at midnight.

SERVANT, *slyly.* If not you, maybe the bride.

She leaves.

FIRST YOUTH, *entering.* You've got to come have a drink with us!

BRIDEGROOM. I'm waiting for the bride.

SECOND YOUTH. You'll have her at dawn!

FIRST YOUTH. That's when it's best!

SECOND YOUTH. Just for a minute.

BRIDEGROOM. Let's go.

They leave. Great excitement is heard. The Bride enters. From the opposite side Two Girls come running to meet her.

FIRST GIRL. To whom did you give the first pin; me or this one?

BRIDE. I don't remember.

FIRST GIRL. To me, you gave it to me here.

SECOND GIRL. To me, in front of the altar.

BRIDE, *uneasily, with a great inner struggle.* I don't know anything about it.

FIRST GIRL. It's just that I wish you'd . . .

BRIDE, *interrupting.* Nor do I care. I have a lot to think about.

SECOND GIRL. Your pardon.

Leonardo crosses at the rear of the stage.

BRIDE, *she sees Leonardo.* And this is an up-
setting time.

FIRST GIRL. We wouldn't know anything
about that!

BRIDE. You'll know about it when your time
comes. This step is a very hard one to take.

FIRST GIRL. Has she offended you?

BRIDE. No. You must pardon me.

SECOND GIRL. What for? But *both* the pins
are good for getting married, aren't they?

BRIDE. Both of them.

FIRST GIRL. Maybe now one will get married
before the other.

BRIDE. Are you so eager?

SECOND GIRL, *shyly.* Yes.

BRIDE. Why?

FIRST GIRL. Well . . .

*She embraces The Second Girl. Both go
running off. The Groom comes in very
slowly and embraces The Bride from
behind.*

BRIDE, *in sudden fright.* Let go of me!

BRIDEGROOM. Are you frightened of me?

BRIDE. Ay-y-y! It's you?

BRIDEGROOM. Who else would it be?

Pause.

Your father or me.

BRIDE. That's true!

BRIDEGROOM. Of course, your father would
have hugged you more gently.

BRIDE, *darkly.* Of course!

BRIDEGROOM, *embracing her strongly and a
little bit brusquely.* Because he's old.

BRIDE, *curtly.* Let me go!

BRIDEGROOM. Why?

He lets her go.

BRIDE. Well . . . the people. They can see us.

*The Servant crosses at the back of the
stage again without looking at The
Bride and Bridegroom.*

BRIDEGROOM. What of it? It's consecrated
now.

BRIDE. Yes, but let me be . . . Later.

BRIDEGROOM. What's the matter with you?
You look frightened!

BRIDE. I'm all right. Don't go.

Leonardo's Wife enters.

LEONARDO'S WIFE. I don't mean to intrude . . .

BRIDEGROOM. What is it?

LEONARDO'S WIFE. Did my husband come
through here?

BRIDEGROOM. No.

LEONARDO'S WIFE. Because I can't find him,
and his horse isn't in the stable either.

BRIDEGROOM, *happily.* He must be out racing
it.

*The Wife leaves, troubled. The Servant
enters.*

SERVANT. Aren't you two proud and happy
with so many good wishes?

BRIDEGROOM. I wish it were over with. The
bride is a little tired.

SERVANT. That's no way to act, child.

BRIDE. It's as though I'd been struck on the
head.

SERVANT. A bride from these mountains must
be strong.

To The Groom.

You're the only one who can cure her, because she's yours.

She goes running off.

BRIDEGROOM, *embracing The Bride.* Let's go
dance a little.

He kisses her.

BRIDE, *worried.* No. I'd like to stretch out on
my bed a little.

BRIDEGROOM. I'll keep you company.

BRIDE. Never! With all these people here?
What would they say? Let me be quiet for
a moment.

BRIDEGROOM. Whatever you say! But don't be
like that tonight!

BRIDE, *at the door.* I'll be better tonight.

BRIDEGROOM. That's what I want.

The Mother appears.

MOTHER. Son.

BRIDEGROOM. Where've you been?

MOTHER. Out there—in all that noise. Are you happy?

BRIDEGROOM. Yes.

MOTHER. Where's your wife?

BRIDEGROOM. Resting a little. It's a bad day for brides!

MOTHER. A bad day? The only good one. To me it was like coming into my own.

The Servant enters and goes toward The Bride's room.

Like the breaking of new ground; the planting of new trees.

BRIDEGROOM. Are you going to leave?

MOTHER. Yes. I ought to be at home.

BRIDEGROOM. Alone.

MOTHER. Not alone. For my head is full of things: of men, and fights.

BRIDEGROOM. But now the fights are no longer fights.

The Servant enters quickly; she disappears at the rear of the stage, running.

MOTHER. While you live, you have to fight.

BRIDEGROOM. I'll always obey you!

MOTHER. Try to be loving with your wife, and if you see she's acting foolish or touchy, caress her in a way that will hurt her a little: a strong hug, a bite and then a soft kiss. Not so she'll be angry, but just so she'll feel you're the man, the boss, the one who gives orders. I learned that from your father. And since you don't have him, I have to be the one to tell you about these strong defenses.

BRIDEGROOM. I'll always do as you say.

FATHER, *entering.* Where's my daughter?

BRIDEGROOM. She's inside.

The Father goes to look for her.

FIRST GIRL. Get the bride and groom! We're going to dance a round!

FIRST YOUTH, *to The Bridegroom.* You're going to lead it.

FATHER, *entering.* She's not there.

BRIDEGROOM. No?

FATHER. She must have gone up to the railing.

BRIDEGROOM. I'll go see!

He leaves. A hubbub of excitement and guitars is heard.

FIRST GIRL. They've started it already!

She leaves.

BRIDEGROOM, *entering.* She isn't there.

MOTHER, *uneasily.* Isn't she?

FATHER. But where could she have gone?

SERVANT, *entering.* But where's the girl, where is she?

MOTHER, *seriously.* That we don't know.

The Bridegroom leaves. Three guests enter.

FATHER, *dramatically.* But, isn't she in the dance?

SERVANT. She's not in the dance.

FATHER, *with a start.* There are a lot of people. Go look!

SERVANT. I've already looked.

FATHER, *tragically.* Then where is she?

BRIDEGROOM, *entering.* Nowhere. Not anywhere.

MOTHER, *to The Father.* What does this mean? Where is your daughter?

Leonardo's Wife enters.

LEONARDO'S WIFE. They've run away! They've run away! She and Leonardo. On the horse. With their arms around each other, they rode off like a shooting star!

FATHER. That's not true! Not my daughter!

MOTHER. Yes, your daughter! Spawn of a wicked mother, and he, he too. But now she's my son's wife!

BRIDEGROOM, *entering.* Let's go after them! Who has a horse?

MOTHER. Who has a horse? Right away! Who has a horse? I'll give him all I have—my eyes, my tongue even. . . .

VOICE. Here's one.

MOTHER, *to The Son.* Go! After them!

He leaves with two young men.

No. Don't go. Those people kill quickly and well . . . but yes, run, and I'll follow!

FATHER. It couldn't be my daughter. Perhaps she's thrown herself in the well.

MOTHER. Decent women throw themselves in water; not that one! But now she's my son's wife. Two groups. There are two groups here.

They all enter.

My family and yours. Everyone set out from here. Shake the dust from your heels! We'll go help my son.

The people separate into two groups.

For he has his family: his cousins from the sea, and all who came from inland. Out of here! On all roads. The hour of blood has come again. Two groups! You with yours and I with mine. After them! After them!

Curtain

ACT III

Scene 1

A forest. It is nighttime. Great moist tree trunks. A dark atmosphere. Two violins are heard. Three Woodcutters enter.

FIRST WOODCUTTER. And have they found them?

SECOND WOODCUTTER. No. But they're looking for them everywhere.

THIRD WOODCUTTER. They'll find them.

SECOND WOODCUTTER. Sh-h-h!

THIRD WOODCUTTER. What?

SECOND WOODCUTTER. They seem to be coming closer on all the roads at once.

FIRST WOODCUTTER. When the moon comes out they'll see them.

SECOND WOODCUTTER. They ought to let them go.

FIRST WOODCUTTER. The world is wide. Everybody can live in it.

THIRD WOODCUTTER. But they'll kill them.

SECOND WOODCUTTER. You have to follow your passion. They did right to run away.

FIRST WOODCUTTER. They were deceiving themselves but at the last blood was stronger.

THIRD WOODCUTTER. Blood!

FIRST WOODCUTTER. You have to follow the path of your blood.

SECOND WOODCUTTER. But blood that sees the light of day is drunk up by the earth.

FIRST WOODCUTTER. What of it? Better dead with the blood drained away than alive with it rotting.

THIRD WOODCUTTER. Hush!

FIRST WOODCUTTER. What? Do you hear something?

THIRD WOODCUTTER. I hear the crickets, the frogs, the night's ambush.

FIRST WOODCUTTER. But not the horse.

THIRD WOODCUTTER. No.

FIRST WOODCUTTER. By now he must be loving her.

SECOND WOODCUTTER. Her body for him; his body for her.

THIRD WOODCUTTER. They'll find them and they'll kill them.

FIRST WOODCUTTER. But by then they'll have mingled their bloods. They'll be like two empty jars, like two dry arroyos.

SECOND WOODCUTTER. There are many clouds and it would be easy for the moon not to come out.

THIRD WOODCUTTER. The bridegroom will find them with or without the moon. I saw him set out. Like a raging star. His face the color of ashes. He looked the fate of all his clan.

FIRST WOODCUTTER. His clan of dead men lying in the middle of the street.

SECOND WOODCUTTER. There you have it!

THIRD WOODCUTTER. You think they'll be able to break through the circle?

SECOND WOODCUTTER. It's hard to. There are knives and guns for ten leagues 'round.

THIRD WOODCUTTER. He's riding a good horse.

SECOND WOODCUTTER. But he's carrying a woman.

FIRST WOODCUTTER. We're close by now.

SECOND WOODCUTTER. A tree with forty branches. We'll soon cut it down.

THIRD WOODCUTTER. The moon's coming out now. Let's hurry.

From the left shines a brightness.

FIRST WOODCUTTER.
 O rising moon!
 Moon among the great leaves.

SECOND WOODCUTTER.
 Cover the blood with jasmines!

FIRST WOODCUTTER.
 O lonely moon!
 Moon among the great leaves.

SECOND WOODCUTTER.
 Silver on the bride's face.

THIRD WOODCUTTER.
 O evil moon!
 Leave for their love a branch in shadow.

FIRST WOODCUTTER.
 O sorrowing moon!
 Leave for their love a branch in shadow.

They go out. The Moon appears through the shining brightness at the left. The Moon is a young woodcutter with a white face. The stage takes on an intense blue radiance.

MOON.
 Round swan in the river
 and a cathedral's eye,
 false dawn on the leaves,
 they'll not escape; these things am I!
 Who is hiding? And who sobs
 in the thornbrakes of the valley?
 The moon sets a knife
 abandoned in the air

which being a leaden threat
yearns to be blood's pain.
Let me in! I come freezing
down to walls and windows!
Open roofs, open breasts
where I may warm myself!
I'm cold! My ashes
of somnolent metals
seek the fire's crest
on mountains and streets.
But the snow carries me
upon its mottled back
and pools soak me
in their water, hard and cold.
But this night there will be
red blood for my cheeks,
and for the reeds that cluster
at the wide feet of the wind.
Let there be neither shadow nor bower,
and then they can't get away!
O let me enter a breast
where I may get warm!
A heart for me!
Warm! That will spurt
over the mountains of my chest;
let me come in, oh let me!

To the branches.

I want no shadows. My rays
must get in everywhere,
even among the dark trunks I want
the whisper of gleaming lights,
so that this night there will be
sweet blood for my cheeks,
and for the reeds that cluster
at the wide feet of the wind.
Who is hiding? Out, I say!
No! They will not get away!
I will light up the horse
with a fever bright as diamonds.

He disappears among the trunks, and the stage goes back to its dark lighting. An Old Woman comes out completely covered by thin green cloth. She is barefooted. Her face can barely be seen among the folds. This character does not appear in the cast.

BEGGAR WOMAN.

> That moon's going away, just when
>   they're near.
> They won't get past here. The river's
>   whisper
> and the whispering tree trunks will
>   muffle
> the torn flight of their shrieks.
> It has to be here, and soon. I'm worn
>   out.
> The coffins are ready, and white sheets
> wait on the floor of the bedroom
> for heavy bodies with torn throats.
> Let not one bird awake, let the breeze,
> gathering their moans in her skirt,
> fly with them over black tree tops
> or bury them in soft mud.

Impatiently.

Oh, that moon! That moon!

*The Moon appears. The intense blue
light returns.*

MOON. They're coming. One band through
the ravine and the other along the river.
I'm going to light up the boulders. What
do you need?

BEGGAR WOMAN. Nothing.

MOON. The wind blows hard now, with a
double edge.

BEGGAR WOMAN. Light up the waistcoat and
open the buttons; the knives will know the
path after that.

MOON.

> But let them be a long time a-dying.
>   So the blood
> will slide its delicate hissing between
>   my fingers.
> Look how my ashen valleys already
>   are waking
> in longing for this fountain of shud-
>   dering gushes!

BEGGAR WOMAN. Let's not let them get past
the arroyo. Silence!

MOON. There they come!

He goes. The stage is left dark.

BEGGAR WOMAN. Quick! Lots of light! Do you
hear me? They can't get away!

*The Bridegroom and The First Youth
enter. The Beggar Woman sits down
and covers herself with her cloak.*

BRIDEGROOM. This way.

FIRST YOUTH. You won't find them.

BRIDEGROOM, *angrily.* Yes, I'll find them.

FIRST YOUTH. I think they've taken another
path.

BRIDEGROOM. No. Just a moment ago I felt the
galloping.

FIRST YOUTH. It could have been another
horse.

BRIDEGROOM, *intensely.* Listen to me. There's
only one horse in the whole world, and this
one's it. Can't you understand that? If
you're going to follow me, follow me
without talking.

FIRST YOUTH. It's only that I want to . . .

BRIDEGROOM. Be quiet. I'm sure of meeting
them there. Do you see this arm? Well, it's
not my arm. It's my brother's arm, and my
father's, and that of all the dead ones in
my family. And it has so much strength
that it can pull this tree up by the roots,
if it wants to. And let's move on, because
here I feel the clenched teeth of all my
people in me so that I can't breathe easily.

BEGGAR WOMAN, *whining.* Ay-y-y!

FIRST YOUTH. Did you hear that?

BRIDEGROOM. You go that way and then circle
back.

FIRST YOUTH. This is a hunt.

BRIDEGROOM. A hunt. The greatest hunt there
is.

*The Youth goes off. The Bridegroom
goes rapidly to the left and stumbles
over The Beggar Woman, Death.*

BEGGAR WOMAN. Ay-y-y!

BRIDEGROOM. What do you want?

BEGGAR WOMAN. I'm cold.

BRIDEGROOM. Which way are you going?

BEGGAR WOMAN, *always whining like a beggar.*
Over there, far away . . .

BRIDEGROOM. Where are you from?

BEGGAR WOMAN. Over there . . . very far away.

BRIDEGROOM. Have you seen a man and a woman running away on a horse?

BEGGAR WOMAN, *awakening.* Wait a minute . . .

She looks at him.

Handsome young man.

She rises.

But you'd be much handsomer sleeping.

BRIDEGROOM. Tell me; answer me. Did you see them?

BEGGAR WOMAN. Wait a minute . . . What broad shoulders! How would you like to be laid out on them and not have to walk on the soles of your feet which are so small?

BRIDEGROOM, *shaking her.* I asked you if you saw them! Have they passed through here?

BEGGAR WOMAN, *energetically.* No. They haven't passed; but they're coming from the hill. Don't you hear them?

BRIDEGROOM. No.

BEGGAR WOMAN. Do you know the road?

BRIDEGROOM. I'll go, whatever it's like!

BEGGAR WOMAN. I'll go along with you. I know this country.

BRIDEGROOM, *impatiently.* Well, let's go! Which way?

BEGGAR WOMAN, *dramatically.* This way!

They go rapidly out. Two violins, which represent the forest, are heard distantly. The Woodcutters return. They have their axes on their shoulders. They move slowly among the tree trunks.

FIRST WOODCUTTER.
　　O rising death!
　　Death among the great leaves.

SECOND WOODCUTTER.
　　Don't open the gush of blood!

FIRST WOODCUTTER.
　　O lonely death!
　　Death among the dried leaves.

THIRD WOODCUTTER.
　　Don't lay flowers over the wedding!

SECOND WOODCUTTER.
　　O sad death!
　　Leave for their love a green branch.

FIRST WOODCUTTER.
　　O evil death!
　　Leave for their love a branch of green!

They go out while they are talking. Leonardo and The Bride appear.

LEONARDO.
　　Hush!

BRIDE.
　　From here I'll go on alone.
　　You go now! I want you to turn back.

LEONARDO.
　　Hush, I said!

BRIDE.
　　With your teeth, with your hands,
　　　anyway you can,
　　take from my clean throat
　　the metal of this chain,
　　and let me live forgotten
　　back there in my house in the ground.
　　And if you don't want to kill me
　　as you would kill a tiny snake,
　　set in my hands, a bride's hands,
　　the barrel of your shotgun.
　　Oh, what lamenting, what fire,
　　sweeps upward through my head!
　　What glass splinters are stuck in my
　　　tongue!

LEONARDO.
　　We've taken the step now; hush!
　　because they're close behind us,
　　and I must take you with me.

BRIDE.
　　Then it must be by force!

LEONARDO.
　　By force? Who was it first
　　went down the stairway?

BRIDE.
　　I went down it.

LEONARDO.
　　And who was it put
　　a new bridle on the horse?

BRIDE.
　　I myself did it. It's true.

LEONARDO.

> And whose were the hands
> strapped spurs to my boots?

BRIDE.

> The same hands, these that are yours,
> but which when they see you would
>   like
> to break the blue branches
> and sunder the purl of your veins.
> I love you! I love you! But leave me!
> For if I were able to kill you
> I'd wrap you 'round in a shroud
> with the edges bordered in violets.
> Oh, what lamenting, with fire,
> sweeps upward through my head!

LEONARDO.

> What glass splinters are stuck in my
>   tongue!
> Because I tried to forget you
> and put a wall of stone
> between your house and mine.
> It's true. You remember?
> And when I saw you in the distance
> I threw sand in my eyes.
> But I was riding a horse
> and the horse went straight to your
>   door.
> And the silver pins of your wedding
> turned my red blood black.
> And in me our dream was choking
> my flesh with its poisoned weeds.
> Oh, it isn't my fault—
> the fault is the earth's—
> and this fragrance that you exhale
> from your breasts and your braids.

BRIDE.

> Oh, how untrue! I want
> from you neither bed nor food,
> yet there's not a minute each day
> that I don't want to be with you,
> because you drag me, and I come,
> then you tell me to go back
> and I follow you,
> like chaff blown on the breeze.
> I have left a good, honest man,
> and all his people,
> with the wedding feast half over
> and wearing my bridal wreath.
> But you are the one will be punished
> and that I don't want to happen.

> Leave me alone now! You run away!
> There is no one who will defend you.

LEONARDO.

> The birds of early morning
> are calling among the trees.
> The night is dying
> on the stone's ridge.
> Let's go to a hidden corner
> where I may love you forever,
> for to me the people don't matter,
> nor the venom they throw on us.

He embraces her strongly.

BRIDE.

> And I'll sleep at your feet,
> to watch over your dreams.
> Naked, looking over the fields,
> as though I were a bitch.
> Because that's what I am! Oh, I look
>   at you
> and your beauty sears me.

LEONARDO.

> Fire is stirred by fire.
> The same tiny flame
> will kill two wheat heads together.
> Let's go!

BRIDE.

> Where are you taking me?

LEONARDO.

> Where they cannot come,
> these men who surround us.
> Where I can look at you!

BRIDE, *sarcastically.*

> Carry me with you from fair to fair,
> a shame to clean women,
> so that people will see me
> with my wedding sheets
> on the breeze like banners.

LEONARDO.

> I, too, would want to leave you
> if I thought as men should.
> But wherever you go, I go.
> You're the same. Take a step. Try.
> Nails of moonlight have fused
> my waist and your thighs.

*This whole scene is violent, full of great
sensuality.*

BRIDE.

    Listen!

LEONARDO.

    They're coming.

BRIDE.

                      Run!
It's fitting that I should die here,
with water over my feet,
with thorns upon my head.
And fitting the leaves should mourn
   me,
a woman lost and virgin.

LEONARDO.

    Be quiet. Now they're appearing.

BRIDE.

                    Go now!

LEONARDO.

    Quiet. Don't let them hear us.

The Bride hesitates.

BRIDE.

    Both of us!

LEONARDO, *embracing her.*

             Any way you want!
If they separate us, it will be
because I am dead.

BRIDE.

          And I dead too.

They go out in each other's arms.

*The Moon appears very slowly. The
stage takes on a strong blue light. The
two violins are heard. Suddenly two
long, ear-splitting shrieks are heard, and
the music of the two violins is cut short.
At the second shriek The Beggar
Woman appears and stands with her
back to the audience. She opens her
cape and stands in the center of the
stage like a great bird with immense
wings. The Moon halts. The curtain
comes down in absolute silence.*

Curtain

Scene 2

The Final Scene

*A white dwelling with arches and thick
walls. To the right and left are white
stairs. At the back, a great arch and a
wall of the same color. The floor also
should be shining white. This simple
dwelling should have the monumental
feeling of a church. There should not
be a single gray nor any shadow, not
even what is necessary for perspective.*

*Two Girls dressed in dark blue are
winding a red skein.*

FIRST GIRL.

    Wool, red wool,
what would you make?

SECOND GIRL.

    Oh, jasmine for dresses,
fine wool like glass.
At four o'clock born,
at ten o'clock dead.
A thread from this wool yarn,
a chain 'round your feet
a knot that will tighten
the bitter white wreath.

LITTLE GIRL, *singing.*

    Were you at the wedding?

FIRST GIRL.

    No.

LITTLE GIRL.

    Well, neither was I!
What could have happened
'midst the shoots of the vineyards?
What could have happened
'neath the branch of the olive?
What really happened
that no one came back?
Were you at the wedding?

SECOND GIRL.

    We told you once, no.

LITTLE GIRL, *leaving.*

    Well, neither was I!

SECOND GIRL.

    Wool, red wool,
what would you sing?

FIRST GIRL.
> Their wounds turning waxen
> balm-myrtle for pain.
> Asleep in the morning,
> and watching at night.

LITTLE GIRL, *in the doorway.*
> And then, the thread stumbled
> on the flinty stones,
> but mountains, blue mountains,
> are letting it pass.
> Running, running, running,
> and finally to come
> to stick in a knife blade,
> to take back the bread.

She goes out.

SECOND GIRL.
> Wool, red wool,
> what would you tell?

FIRST GIRL.
> The lover is silent,
> crimson the groom,
> at the still shoreline
> I saw them laid out.

She stops and looks at the skein.

LITTLE GIRL, *appearing in the doorway.*
> Running, running, running,
> the thread runs to here.
> All covered with clay
> I feel them draw near.
> Bodies stretched stiffly
> in ivory sheets!

*The Wife and Mother-in-law of Leo-
nardo appear. They are anguished.*

FIRST GIRL. Are they coming yet?

MOTHER-IN-LAW, *harshly.* We don't know.

SECOND GIRL. What can you tell us about
the wedding?

FIRST GIRL. Yes, tell me.

MOTHER-IN-LAW, *curtly.* Nothing.

LEONARDO'S WIFE. I want to go back and
find out all about it.

MOTHER-IN-LAW, *sternly.*
> You, back to your house.
> Brave and alone in your house.

> To grow old and to weep.
> But behind closed doors.
> Never again. Neither dead nor alive.
> We'll nail up our windows
> and let rains and nights
> fall on the bitter weeds.

LEONARDO'S WIFE. What could have happened?

MOTHER-IN-LAW.
> It doesn't matter what.
> Put a veil over your face.
> Your children are yours,
> that's all. On the bed
> put a cross of ashes
> where his pillow was.

They go out.

BEGGAR WOMAN, *at the door.* A crust of bread,
little girls.

LITTLE GIRL. Go away!

The Girls huddle close together.

BEGGAR WOMAN. Why?

LITTLE GIRL. Because you whine; go away!

FIRST GIRL. Child!

BEGGAR WOMAN.
> I might have asked for your eyes! A
>   cloud
> of birds is following me. Will you
>   have one?

LITTLE GIRL. I want to get away from here!

SECOND GIRL, *to The Beggar Woman.* Don't
mind her!

FIRST GIRL. Did you come by the road
through the arroyo?

BEGGAR WOMAN. I came that way!

FIRST GIRL, *timidly.* Can I ask you something?

BEGGAR WOMAN.
> I saw them: they'll be here soon; two
>   torrents
> still at last, among the great boulders,
> two men at the horse's feet.
> Two dead men in the night's splendor.

With pleasure.

> Dead, yes, dead.

FIRST GIRL. Hush, old woman, hush!

BEGGAR WOMAN.

 Crushed flowers for eyes, and their
  teeth
 two fistfuls of hard-frozen snow.
 Both of them fell, and the Bride
  returns
 with bloodstains on her skirt and hair.
 And they come covered with two
  sheets
 carried on the shoulders of two tall
  boys.
 That's how it was; nothing more.
  What was fitting.
 Over the golden flower, dirty sand.

*She goes. The Girls bow their heads
and start going out rhythmically.*

FIRST GIRL.

 Dirty sand.

SECOND GIRL.

 Over the golden flower.

LITTLE GIRL.

 Over the golden flower
 they're bringing the dead from the
  arroyo.
 Dark the one,
 dark the other.
 What shadowy nightingale flies and
  weeps
 over the golden flower!

*She goes. The stage is left empty. The
Mother and a Neighbor Woman appear. The Neighbor is weeping.*

MOTHER. Hush.
NEIGHBOR. I can't.
MOTHER. Hush, I said.

At the door.

Is there nobody here?

She puts her hands to her forehead.

My son ought to answer me. But now my
son is an armful of shrivelled flowers. My
son is a fading voice beyond the mountains
now.

With rage, to The Neighbor.

Will you shut up? I want no wailing in
this house. Your tears are only tears from
your eyes, but when I'm alone mine will
come—from the soles of my feet, from my
roots—burning more than blood.

NEIGHBOR. You come to my house; don't you
stay here.

MOTHER. I want to be here. Here. In peace.
They're all dead now: and at midnight I'll
sleep, sleep without terror of guns or
knives. Other mothers will go to their windows, lashed by rain, to watch for their
sons' faces. But not I. And of my dreams
I'll make a cold ivory dove that will carry
camellias of white frost to the graveyard.
But no; not graveyard, not graveyard: the
couch of earth, the bed that shelters them
and rocks them in the sky.

*A woman dressed in black enters, goes
toward the right, and there kneels. To
The Neighbor.*

Take your hands from your face. We have
terrible days ahead. I want to see no one.
The earth and I. My grief and I. And these
four walls. Ay-y-y! Ay-y-y!

She sits down, overcome.

NEIGHBOR. Take pity on yourself!
MOTHER, *pushing back her hair.* I must be
calm.

She sits down.

Because the neighbor women will come and
I don't want them to see me so poor. So
poor! A woman without even one son to
hold to her lips.

*The Bride appears. She is without her
wreath and wears a black shawl.*

NEIGHBOR, *with rage, seeing The Bride.*
Where are you going?

BRIDE. I'm coming here.

MOTHER, *to The Neighbor.* Who is it?

NEIGHBOR. Don't you recognize her?

MOTHER. That's why I asked who it was. Because I don't want to recognize her, so I won't sink my teeth in her throat. You snake!

She moves wrathfully on The Bride, then stops. To The Neighbor.

Look at her! There she is, and she's crying, while I stand here calmly and don't tear her eyes out. I don't understand myself. Can it be I didn't love my son? But, where's his good name? Where is it now? Where is it?

She beats The Bride who drops to the floor.

NEIGHBOR. For God's sake!

She tries to separate them.

BRIDE, *to The Neighbor*. Let her; I came here so she'd kill me and they'd take me away with them.

To The Mother.

But not with her hands; with grappling hooks, with a sickle—and with force—until they break on my bones. Let her! I want her to know I'm clean, that I may be crazy, but that they can bury me without a single man ever having seen himself in the whiteness of my breasts.

MOTHER. Shut up, shut up; what do I care about that?

BRIDE. Because I ran away with the other one; I ran away!

With anguish.

You would have gone, too. I was a woman burning with desire, full of sores inside and out, and your son was a little bit of water from which I hoped for children, land, health; but the other one was a dark river, choked with brush, that brought near me the undertone of its rushes and its whispered song. And I went along with your son who was like a little boy of cold water—and the other sent against me hundreds of birds who got in my way and left white frost on my wounds, my wounds of a poor withered woman, of a girl caressed by fire. I didn't want to; remember that! I didn't want to. Your son was my destiny and I have not betrayed him, but the other one's arm dragged me along like the pull of the sea, like the head toss of a mule, and he would have dragged me always, always—even if I were an old woman and all your son's sons held me by the hair!

A Neighbor enters.

MOTHER. She is not to blame; nor am I!

Sarcastically.

Who is, then? It's a delicate, lazy, sleepless woman who throws away an orange blossom wreath and goes looking for a piece of bed warmed by another woman!

BRIDE. Be still! Be still! Take your revenge on me; here I am! See how soft my throat is; it would be less work for you than cutting a dahlia in your garden. But never that! Clean, clean as a new-born little girl. And strong enough to prove it to you. Light the fire. Let's stick our hands in; you, for your son, I, for my body. *You'll* draw yours out first.

Another Neighbor enters.

MOTHER. But what does your good name matter to me? What does your death matter to me? What does anything about anything matter to me? Blesséd be the wheat stalks, because my sons are under them; blesséd be the rain, because it wets the face of the dead. Blesséd be God, who stretches us out together to rest.

Another Neighbor enters.

BRIDE. Let me weep with you.

MOTHER. Weep. But at the door.

The Girl enters. The Bride stays at the door. The Mother is at the center of the stage.

LEONARDO'S WIFE, *entering and going to the left.*

He was a beautiful horseman,
now he's a heap of snow.
He rode to fairs and mountains
and women's arms.
Now, the night's dark moss
crowns his forehead.

MOTHER.

A sunflower to your mother,
a mirror of the earth.
Let them put on your breast
the cross of bitter rosebay;
and over you a sheet
of shining silk;
between your quiet hands
let water form its lament.

WIFE.

Ay-y-y, four gallant boys
come with tired shoulders!

BRIDE.

Ay-y-y, four gallant boys
carry death on high!

MOTHER.

Neighbors.

LITTLE GIRL, *at the door.*

They're bringing them now.

MOTHER.

It's the same thing.
Always the cross, the cross.

WOMEN.

Sweet nails,
cross adored,
sweet name
of Christ our Lord.

BRIDE. May the cross protect both the quick and the dead.

MOTHER.

Neighbors: with a knife,
with a little knife,
on their appointed day, between two
and three,
these two men killed each other for
love.
With a knife,
with a tiny knife
that barely fits the hand,
but that slides in clean
through the astonished flesh
and stops at the place
where trembles, enmeshed,
the dark root of a scream.

BRIDE.

And this is a knife,
a tiny knife
that barely fits the hand;
fish without scales, without river,
so that on their appointed day, between two and three,
with his knife,
two men are left stiff,
with their lips turning yellow.

MOTHER.

And it barely fits the hand
but it slides in clean
through the astonished flesh
and stops there, at the place
where trembles enmeshed
the dark root of a scream.

The Neighbors, kneeling on the floor, sob.

Curtain

◆ From the *Mother Courage* Model

By BERTOLT BRECHT

MODELS

After the great war life still goes on in our ruined cities, but it is a different life, the life of different or differently composed circles, guided or handicapped by a new environment whose newness consists in its degree of destruction. Where the great piles of rubble lie, the costly foundations lie too, the drainage system and the gas and electricity network. Even the large building that has remained intact will have been sympathetically affected by the damage and confusion around it, and may sometimes act as a barrier to planning. Temporary structures have to be built, and the danger is that they will remain. All this is reflected in art, for our way of thinking is part of our way of living. Where the theatre is concerned we put forward models to fill the gap. They at once run into strong resistance from all supporters of the old ways, of the routine that masquerades as experience and the conventionality that calls itself creative freedom. And they are not helped by those who take them up without having learnt how to use them. Meant to simplify matters, they are not simple to handle. They are intended not to render thought unnecessary but to provoke it: not as a substitute for artistic creation but as its stimulus.

To start with one has to imagine that the printed text's conclusions about certain events —in this case, Mother Courage's adventures and setbacks—have been to some extent filled in; it has now been established that when the woman's dead son was brought to her she was sitting beside her dumb daughter, and so forth: the sort of conclusion which an artist painting some historic incident can arrive at by cross-examining eye-witnesses. He can make use of them to change particular details as for one reason or another he may think advisable. Until a high standard has been achieved in the lively and intelligent copying

of models (and in setting them up) it would be wrong to copy too much. Such things as the Cook's makeup or Courage's costume should not be imitated. The model must not be pressed too far.

Pictures and descriptions of a performance are not enough. One does not learn much by reading that a character moves in a particular direction after a given sentence, even if the tone of speech, the way of walking and a convincing reason can all be supplied (which is very difficult). The persons available for the imitation are quite different from those in the pattern; with them it would never have come about. Anyone who deserves the name of artist is unique; he represents generalities in a special way. He can neither be perfectly imitated nor give a perfect imitation. Nor is it anyway so important for artists to imitate art as to imitate life. The use of models is a particular kind of art, and just so much can be learnt from it. The aim must be neither to copy the patterns exactly nor to break away from it at once.

In studying what follows—a number of explanations and discoveries emerging from the rehearsal of a play—what matters is that seeing how certain problems are solved should lead one to see the problems themselves.

[A paragraph then discusses the relation of photographs to the actual performance, from the point of view of light and shade, etc.]

MUSIC

Paul Dessau's music for *Mother Courage* is not meant to be particularly easy; like the stage set, it left something to be supplied by the audience; it was up to them to link voice and melody aurally. Art is no Land of Cockaigne. In order to make the transition to the musical part, to let music get its word in, we lowered a musical emblem from the flies whenever a song came which did not arise directly out of the action, or arose from it but none the less remained clearly apart. This

Bertolt Brecht, "From the *Mother Courage* Model," in *Brecht on Theatre,* trans. by John Willett (New York: Hill and Wang, 1964), pp. 215–220.

consisted of a trumpet, a drum, a flag and electric globes that lit up: a slight and delicate thing, pleasant to look at, even if scene nine found it shot to pieces. Some people thought it a pure frivolity, an unrealistic element. But one ought not to disapprove too much of frivolity in the theatre so long as it is kept within bounds. Nor on the other hand was it purely unrealistic, in that it lifted the music above the reality of the action; it served us as a visible sign of the shift to another artistic level—that of music—and gave the right impression of musical insertions instead of leading people to think quite wrongly that the songs sprang from the action. Those who take exception to this are quite simply against anything intermittent, inorganic, pieced-together, and this is primarily because they are against any breaking of the illusion. What they ought to have objected to was not the tangible symbol of music but the manner of fitting the musical items into the play: i.e., as insertions.

The musicians were placed so that they could be seen, in one of the stage boxes, and thanks to this their performances became little concerts, independent contributions made at suitable points in the play. The box communicated with the stage, so a musician or two could occasionally go backstage for trumpet calls or when music occurred as part of the action.

We began with the overture. It was slightly thin, as it was performed by four players only; all the same it was a reasonably ceremonious preparation for the confusions of war.

STAGE DESIGN

For the production which we are describing, at the Deutsches Theater in Berlin, we used the famous scheme devised by Teo Otto for the Zurich Schauspielhaus during the war. There was a permanent framework of huge screens, making use of such materials as were available in the military encampments of the seventeenth century: tenting, wooden posts lashed together with ropes, etc. Structures like the parsonage and the peasants' cottage were introduced three-dimensionally, using realistic building methods and materials, but in the form of an artistic indication, giv-

ing only as much of the structure as served the acting. Coloured projections were thrown on the cyclorama, and the revolving stage was used to convey travel. We varied the size and position of the screens, and used them only for the camp scenes, so as to distinguish these from the scenes on the road. The Berlin stage designer made his own versions of the structures (in scenes 2, 4, 5, 9, 10, 11), but on the same general lines. We dispensed with the background projections used in Zurich, and suspended the various countries' names above the stage in large black letters. Our lighting was white and even and as brilliant as our equipment allowed. This enabled us to get rid of any remnants of 'atmosphere' such as would have given the incidents a slightly romantic flavour. Nearly all the rest we kept, often down to the smallest details (chopping block, fireplace, etc.), particularly the admirable positionings of the waggon, which meant a lot since these determined from the outset much of the grouping and of the sequence of events.

Extraordinarily little is lost by sacrificing complete freedom of 'artistic creation.' One has to make a start somewhere, with something, and it may as well be with something that has been properly thought out. Freedom comes with the principle of contradiction, which is continually active and vocal in us all.

REALISTIC THEATRE AND ILLUSION

Goethe, writing in 1826, spoke of the 'inadequacy of the English wooden stage' of Shakespeare's day. He says: 'There is no trace here of these aids to naturalness which we have become accustomed to thanks to the improvement in machinery, in the art of perspective and in the wardrobe.' 'Who,' he asks, 'would tolerate such a scheme today? Under those conditions Shakespeare's plays would become highly interesting fairy-tales narrated by a number of players who had tried to create an impression by making up as the characters, coming and going and carrying out the movements required by the story, but left it to the audience to imagine as many paradises and palaces as they liked on the empty stage.'

Since he wrote these words there has been a hundred years' improvement in the mechanical equipment of our theatres; 'aids to naturalness' have led to such emphasis being put on illusion that we newcomers would sooner think of Shakespeare on an empty stage than a Shakespeare who had ceased to stimulate or provoke any use of the imagination.

In Goethe's day this improvement in the mechanics of illusion was hardly thinkable, for the machinery was so imperfect, so much 'in the childhood of its beginnings' that theatre itself was still a reality, and imagination and inventiveness alike could be used to turn nature into art. The various scenes of the action were still theatrical displays in which the stage designer gave an artistic and poetic interpretation of the places concerned.

The bourgeois classical theatre was happily situated half-way along the road to naturalistic illusionism, at a point where the stage machinery provided enough elements of illusion to improve the representation of some aspects of reality, but not so much as to make the audience feel that it was no longer in a theatre—i.e. stopping short of the point where art comes to mean obliterating all the clues that show art to be involved. There was no electricity, so lighting effects were still primitive; if lack of taste decreed that there should be a sunset, lack of proper mechanical resources prevented the worst horrors. The Meiningers' authenticity of costume came later; it was usually handsome if not always beautiful, and it was after all compensated by an inauthentic mode of speech. In short, wherever it failed in the business of deception the theatre still proved to be theatre. Restoring the theatre's reality as theatre is now a precondition for any possibility of arriving at realistic images of human social life. Too much heightening of the illusion in the setting, together with a 'magnetic' way of acting that gives the spectator the illusion of being present at a fleeting, accidental, 'real' event, create such an impression of naturalness that one can no longer interpose one's judgment, imagination or reactions, and must simply conform by sharing in the experience and becoming one of 'nature's' objects. The illusion created by the theatre must be a partial one, in order that it may always be recognized

as an illusion. Reality, however complete, has to be altered by being turned into art, so that it can be seen to be alterable and be treated as such.

And this is why we too are inquiring into naturalness: we want to alter the nature of our social life.

ELEMENTS OF ILLUSION?

No doubt the sight of the cyclorama behind a completely empty stage (in the Prologue and in the seventh and last scenes) creates the illusion of a flat landscape with a huge sky. There is no objection to this, for there must be some stirring of poetry in the spectator's soul for such an illusion to come about. Thanks to the ease with which it is created the actors can suggest at the start that here is a wide horizon lying open to the business enterprise of the small family with their canteen, then at the end that the exhausted seeker after happiness is faced by a measureless devastation. And we can always hope that this impression of substance will combine with a formal one: that the spectator will be able to share in the initial void from which everything arises, by seeing the bare empty stage, soon to be inhabited. This, he realizes, is the *tabula rasa* on which the actors have been working for weeks, testing first one detail then another, learning the incidents of the chronicle by portraying them, and portraying them by judging them. And now we are starting, and Courage's waggon comes rolling on to the stage.

If in big matters there is such a thing as a beautiful approximation, in small there is not. What counts in a realistic portrayal is carefully worked out details of costumes and props, for here the audience's imagination can add nothing. Any implements connected with working and eating must have been most lovingly made. Nor can the costumes be as for a folklore festival; they have to show signs of individuality and social class. They are worn longer or shorter, of cheaper or more expensive material, more or less carefully looked after, etc.

The costumes for this production of *Mother Courage* were by Palm.

WHAT IS A PERFORMANCE OF MOTHER COURAGE AND HER CHILDREN PRIMARILY MEANT TO SHOW?

That in wartime big business is not conducted by small people. That war is a continuation of business by other means, making the human virtues fatal even to those who exercise them. That no sacrifice is too great for the struggle against war.

[*Couragemodell 1949*, East Berlin, 1958]

◆◆ Mother Courage and Her Children

By BERTOLT BRECHT

English Version by Eric Bentley

Characters

MOTHER COURAGE
KATTRIN, her dumb daughter
EILIF, her elder son
SWISS CHEESE, her younger son
RECRUITING OFFICER
SERGEANT
COOK
SWEDISH COMMANDER
CHAPLAIN
ORDNANCE OFFICER
YVETTE POTTIER
MAN WITH THE BANDAGE
ANOTHER SERGEANT
OLD COLONEL
CLERK
YOUNG SOLDIER
OLDER SOLDIER
PEASANT
PEASANT WOMAN
YOUNG MAN
OLD WOMAN
ANOTHER PEASANT
ANOTHER PEASANT WOMAN
YOUNG PEASANT
LIEUTENANT
VOICE

1

Spring, 1624. In Dalarna, the Swedish Commander Oxenstierna is recruiting for the campaign in Poland. The canteen woman Anna Fierling, commonly known as Mother Courage, loses a son.

Highway outside a town. A SERGEANT *and a* RECRUITING OFFICER *stand shivering.*

RECRUITING OFFICER. How the hell can you line up a squadron in a place like this? You know what I keep thinking about, Sergeant? Suicide. I'm supposed to knock four platoons together by the twelfth—four platoons the Chief's asking for! And they're so friendly around here, I'm scared to go to sleep at night. Suppose I do get my hands on some character and squint at him so I don't notice he's pigeon-chested and has varicose veins. I get him drunk and relaxed, he signs on the dotted line. I pay for the drinks, he steps outside for a minute, I have a hunch I should follow him to the door, and am I right? Off he's shot like a louse from a scratch. You can't take a man's word any more, Sergeant. There's no loyalty left in the world, no trust, no faith, no sense of honor. I'm losing my confidence in mankind, Sergeant.

SERGEANT. What they could use around here is a good war. What else can you expect with peace running wild all over the place? You know what the trouble with peace is? No organization. And when do you get organization? In a war. Peace is one big waste of equipment. Anything goes, no one gives a damn. See the way they eat? Cheese on pumpernickel, bacon on the

Bertolt Brecht, *Mother Courage and Her Children,* English version by Eric Bentley (New York: Grove Press, Black Cat Edition, 1966), pp. 19–111.

cheese? Disgusting! How many horses have they got in this town? How many young men? Nobody knows! They haven't bothered to count 'em! That's peace for you! I've been in places where they haven't had a war for seventy years and you know what? The people haven't even been given names! They don't know who they are! It takes a war to fix that. In a war, everyone registers, everyone's name's on a list. Their shoes are stacked, their corn's in the bag, you count it all up—cattle, men, *et cetera*—and you take it away! That's the story: no organization, no war!

RECRUITING OFFICER. It's the God's truth.

SERGEANT. Of course, a war's like any good deal: hard to get going. But when it does get moving, it's a pisser, and they're all scared of peace, like a dice player who can't stop—'cause when peace comes they have to pay up. Of course, *until* it gets going, they're just as scared of war, it's such a novelty!

RECRUITING OFFICER. Hey, look, here's a canteen wagon. Two women and a couple of fellows. Stop the old lady, Sergeant. And if there's nothing doing this time, you won't catch me freezing my ass in the April wind any longer.

A harmonica is heard. A canteen wagon rolls on, drawn by two young fellows. MOTHER COURAGE is sitting on it with her dumb daughter, KATTRIN.

MOTHER COURAGE. A good day to you, Sergeant!

SERGEANT (*barring the way*). Good day to *you!* Who d'you think *you* are?

MOTHER COURAGE. Tradespeople.

She sings.

Stop all the troops: here's Mother Courage!
Hey, Captain, let them come and buy!
For they can get from Mother Courage
Boots they will march in till they die!
Your marching men do not adore you

(Packs on their backs, lice in their hair)
But it's to death they're marching for you
And so they need good boots to wear!
   Christians, awake! Winter is gone!
   The snows depart! Dead men sleep on!
   Let all of you who still survive
   Get out of bed and look alive!

Your men will walk till they are dead, sir,
But cannot fight unless they eat.
The blood they spill for you is red, sir,
What fires that blood is my red meat.
Cannon is rough on empty bellies:
First with my meat they should be crammed.
Then let them go and find where hell is
And give my greetings to the damned!
   Christians, awake! Winter is gone!
   The snows depart! Dead men sleep on!
   Let all of you who still survive
   Get out of bed and look alive!

SERGEANT. Halt! Where are you from, riffraff?

EILIF. Second Finnish Regiment!

SERGEANT. Where are your papers?

MOTHER COURAGE. Papers?

SWISS CHEESE. But this is Mother Courage!

SERGEANT. Never heard of her. Where'd she get a name like that?

MOTHER COURAGE. They call me Mother Courage 'cause I was afraid I'd be ruined, so I drove through the bombardment of Riga like a madwoman, with fifty loaves of bread in my cart. They were going moldy, what else could I do?

SERGEANT. No funny business! Where are your papers?

MOTHER COURAGE (*rummaging among papers in a tin box and clambering down from her wagon*). Here, Sergeant! Here's a missal—I got it in Altötting to wrap my cucumbers in. Here's a map of Moravia—God knows if I'll ever get there—the birds can have it if I don't. And here's a document saying my horse hasn't got hoof and mouth disease—pity he died on us, he cost fifteen guilders, thank God I didn't pay it. Is that enough paper?

SERGEANT. Are you pulling my leg? Well,

you've got another guess coming. You need a license and you know it.

MOTHER COURAGE. Show a little respect for a lady and don't go telling these grown children of mine I'm pulling anything of yours. What would I want with you? My license in the Second Protestant Regiment is an honest face. If *you* wouldn't know how to read it, that's not my fault, I want no rubber stamp on it anyhow.

RECRUITING OFFICER. Sergeant, we have a case of insubordination on our hands. Do you know what we need in the army? Discipline!

MOTHER COURAGE. I was going to say sausages.

SERGEANT. Name?

MOTHER COURAGE. Anna Fierling.

SERGEANT. So you're all Fierlings.

MOTHER COURAGE. I was talking about me.

SERGEANT. And I was talking about your children.

MOTHER COURAGE. Must they all have the same name? (*Pointing to the elder son.*) This fellow, for instance, I call him Eilif Noyocki. Why? He got the name from his father who told me he was called Koyocki. Or was it Moyocki? Anyhow, the lad remembers him to this day. Only the man he remembers is someone else, a Frenchman with a pointed beard. But he certainly has his father's brains—that man could whip the breeches off a farmer's backside before he could turn around. So we all have our own names.

SERGEANT. You're all called something different?

MOTHER COURAGE. Are you pretending you don't understand?

SERGEANT (*pointing at the younger son*). He's Chinese, I suppose.

MOTHER COURAGE. Wrong again. Swiss.

SERGEANT. After the Frenchman?

MOTHER COURAGE. Frenchman? What Frenchman? Don't confuse the issue, Sergeant, or we'll be here all day. He's Swiss, but he happens to be called Feyos, a name that has nothing to do with his father, who was called something else—a military engineer, if you please, and a drunkard.

SWISS CHEESE *nods, beaming; even* KATTRIN *smiles.*

SERGEANT. Then how come his name's Feyos?

MOTHER COURAGE. Oh, Sergeant, you have no imagination. *Of course* he's called Feyos: when he came, I was with a Hungarian. He didn't mind. He had a floating kidney, though he never touched a drop. He was a very *honest* man. The boy takes after him.

SERGEANT. But that wasn't his father!

MOTHER COURAGE. I said: he took after him. I call him Swiss Cheese. Why? Because he's good at pulling wagons. (*Pointing to her daughter.*) And that is Kattrin Haupt, she's half German.

SERGEANT. A nice family, I must say!

MOTHER COURAGE. And we've seen the whole wide world together—this wagonload and me.

SERGEANT. We'll need all that in writing. (*He writes.*) You're from Bamberg in Bavaria. What are you doing *here*?

MOTHER COURAGE. I can't wait till the war is good enough to come to Bamberg.

RECRUITING OFFICER. And you two oxen pull the cart. Jacob Ox and Esau Ox! D'you ever get out of harness?

EILIF. Mother! May I smack him in the puss? I'd like to.

MOTHER COURAGE. I'd like *you* to stay where you are. And now, gentlemen, what about a brace of pistols? Or a belt? Sergeant? Yours is worn clean through.

SERGEANT. It's something else *I'm* looking for. These lads of yours are straight as birch trees, strong limbs, massive chests. . . . What are such fine specimens doing out of the army?

MOTHER COURAGE (*quickly*). A soldier's life is not for sons of mine!

RECRUITING OFFICER. Why not? It means money. It means fame. Peddling shoes is woman's work. (*To* EILIF.) Step this way and let's see if that's muscle or chicken fat.

MOTHER COURAGE. It's chicken fat. Give him a good hard look, and he'll fall right over.

RECRUITING OFFICER. Yes, and kill a calf in the falling! (*He tries to hustle* EILIF *away.*)

MOTHER COURAGE. Let him alone! He's not for you!

RECRUITING OFFICER. He called my face a puss. That is an insult. The two of us will now go and settle the affair on the field of honor.

EILIF. Don't worry, Mother, I can handle him.

MOTHER COURAGE. Stay here. You're never happy till you're in a fight. He has a knife in his boot and he knows how to use it.

RECRUITING OFFICER. I'll draw it out of him like a milk tooth. Come on, young fellow!

MOTHER COURAGE. Officer, I'll report you to the Colonel, and he'll throw you in jail. His lieutenant is courting my daughter.

SERGEANT. Go easy. (*To* MOTHER COURAGE.) What have you got against the service, wasn't his own father a soldier? Didn't you say he died a soldier's death?

MOTHER COURAGE. This one's just a baby. You'll lead him like a lamb to the slaughter. I know you, you'll get five guilders for him.

RECRUITING OFFICER (*to* EILIF). First thing you know, you'll have a lovely cap and high boots, how about it?

EILIF. Not from you.

MOTHER COURAGE. "Let's you and me go fishing," said the angler to the worm. (*To* SWISS CHEESE.) Run and tell everybody they're trying to steal your brother! (*She draws a knife.*) Yes, just you try, and I'll cut you down like dogs! We sell cloth, we sell ham, we are peaceful people!

SERGEANT. You're peaceful all right: your knife proves that. Why, you should be ashamed of yourself. Give me that knife, you hag! You admit you live off the war, what else *could* you live off? Now tell me, how can we have a war without soldiers?

MOTHER COURAGE. Do they have to be mine?

SERGEANT. So that's the trouble. The war should swallow the peach stone and spit out the peach, hm? Your brood should get fat off the war, but the poor war must ask nothing in return, it can look after itself, can it? Call yourself Mother Courage and then get scared of the war, your bread-winner? Your sons aren't scared, I know that much.

EILIF. Takes more than a war to scare me.

SERGEANT. Correct! Take me. The soldier's life hasn't done *me* any harm, has it? I enlisted at seventeen.

MOTHER COURAGE. You haven't reached seventy.

SERGEANT. I will, though.

MOTHER COURAGE. Above ground?

SERGEANT. Are you trying to rile me, telling me I'll die?

MOTHER COURAGE. Suppose it's the truth? Suppose I see it's your fate? Suppose I *know* you're just a corpse on furlough?

SWISS CHEESE. She can look into the future. Everyone says so.

RECRUITING OFFICER. Then by all means look into the sergeant's future. It might amuse him.

SERGEANT. I don't believe in that stuff.

MOTHER COURAGE. Helmet!

The SERGEANT *gives her his helmet.*

SERGEANT. It means less than a crap in the grass. Anything for a laugh.

MOTHER COURAGE (*taking a sheet of parchment and tearing it in two*). Eilif, Swiss Cheese, Kattrin! So shall we all be torn in two if we let ourselves get too deep into this war! (*To the* SERGEANT.) I'll give you the bargain rate, and do it free. Watch! Death is black, so I draw a black cross.

SWISS CHEESE. And the other she leaves blank, see?

MOTHER COURAGE. I fold them, put them in the helmet, and mix 'em up together, the way we're all mixed up together from our mother's womb on. Now draw!

The SERGEANT *hesitates.*

RECRUITING OFFICER (*to* EILIF). I don't take just anybody. I'm choosy. And you've got guts, I like that.

SERGEANT (*fishing around in the helmet*). It's silly. Means as much as blowing your nose.

SWISS CHEESE. The black cross! Oh, his number's up!

RECRUITING OFFICER. Don't let them get under your skin. There aren't enough bullets to go around.

SERGEANT (*hoarsely*). You cheated me!

MOTHER COURAGE. You cheated yourself the day you enlisted. And now we must drive on. There isn't a war every day in the week, we must get to work.

SERGEANT. Hell, you're not getting away with this! We're taking that bastard of yours with *us*!

EILIF. I'd like that, Mother.

MOTHER COURAGE. Quiet—you Finnish devil, you!

EILIF. And Swiss Cheese wants to be a soldier, too.

MOTHER COURAGE. That's news to me. I see I'll have to draw lots for all three of you. (*She goes to the back to draw the crosses on bits of paper.*)

RECRUITING OFFICER (*to* EILIF). People've been saying the Swedish soldier is religious. That kind of loose talk has hurt us a lot. One verse of a hymn every Sunday—and then only if you have a voice . . .

MOTHER COURAGE (*returning with the slips and putting them in the* SERGEANT's *helmet*). So they'd desert their old mother, would they, the scoundrels? They take to war like a cat to cream. But I'll consult these slips, and they'll see the world's no promised land, with a "Join up, son, you're officer material!" Sergeant, I'm afraid for them, very afraid they won't get through this war. They have terrible qualities, all three. (*She holds the helmet out to* EILIF.) There. Draw your lot. (EILIF *fishes in the helmet, unfolds a slip. She snatches it from him.*) There you have it: a cross. Unhappy mother that I am, rich only in a mother's sorrows! He dies. In the springtime of his life, he must go. If he's a soldier, he must bite the dust, that's clear. He's too brave, like his father. And if he doesn't use his head, he'll go the way of all flesh, the slip proves it. (*Hectoring him.*) Will you use your head?

EILIF. Why not?

MOTHER COURAGE. It's using your head to stay with your mother. And when they make fun of you and call you a chicken, just laugh.

RECRUITING OFFICER. If you're going to wet your pants, I'll try your brother.

MOTHER COURAGE. I told you to laugh. Laugh! Now it's your turn, Swiss Cheese. You should be a better bet, you're honest. (*He fishes in the helmet.*) Why are you giving that slip such a funny look? You've drawn a blank for sure. It can't be there's a cross on it. It can't be I'm going to lose *you*. (*She takes the slip.*) A cross? Him too! Could it be 'cause he's so simple? Oh, Swiss Cheese, you'll be a goner too, if you aren't honest, honest, honest the whole time, the way I always brought you up to be, the way you always bring me all the change when you buy me a loaf. It's the only way you can save yourself. Look, Sergeant, if it isn't a black cross!

SERGEANT. It's a cross! I don't understand how *I* got one. I always stay well in the rear. (*To the* OFFICER.) But it can't be a trick: it gets *her* children too.

SWISS CHEESE. It gets me too. But I don't accept it!

MOTHER COURAGE (*to* KATTRIN). And now all I have left for certain is you, you're a cross in yourself, you have a good heart. (*She holds the helmet up high toward the wagon but takes the slip out herself.*) Oh, I could give up in despair! There must be some mistake, I didn't mix them right. Don't be too kind, Kattrin, just don't, there's a cross in your path too. Always be very quiet, it can't be hard, you can't speak. Well, so now you know, all of you: be careful, you'll need to be. Now let's climb on the wagon and move on. (*She returns the helmet to the* SERGEANT *and climbs on the wagon.*)

RECRUITING OFFICER (*to the* SERGEANT). Do something!

SERGEANT. I don't feel very well.

RECRUITING OFFICER. Maybe you caught a chill when you handed over your helmet in this wind. Get her involved in a business transaction! (*Aloud.*) That belt, Sergeant, you could at least take a look at it. These good people live by trade, don't they? Hey, all of you, the sergeant wants to buy the belt!

MOTHER COURAGE. Half a guilder. A belt like

that is worth two guilders. (*She clambers
down again from the wagon.*)

SERGEANT. It isn't new. But there's too much
wind here. I'll go and look at it behind the
wagon. (*He does so.*)

MOTHER COURAGE. I don't find it windy.

SERGEANT. Maybe it's worth half a guilder at
that. There's silver on it.

MOTHER COURAGE (*following him behind the
wagon*). A solid six ounces worth!

RECRUITING OFFICER (*to* EILIF). And we can
have a drink, just us men. I'll advance you
some money to cover it. Let's go.

EILIF *stands undecided.*

MOTHER COURAGE. Half a guilder, then.

SERGEANT. I don't understand it. I always stay
in the rear. There's no safer spot for a sergeant to be. You can send the others on
ahead in quest of fame. My appetite is
ruined. I can tell you right now: I won't be
able to get anything down.

MOTHER COURAGE. You shouldn't take on so,
just because you can't eat. Just stay in the
rear. Here, take a slug of brandy, man.
(*She gives him brandy.*)

RECRUITING OFFICER (*taking* EILIF *by the arm
and making off toward the back*). Ten
guilders in advance and you're a soldier of
the king and a stout fellow and the women
will be mad about you. And you can give
me a smack in the puss for insulting you.

Both leave.

Dumb KATTRIN *jumps down from the
wagon and lets out harsh cries.*

MOTHER COURAGE. Coming, Kattrin, coming!
The sergeant's just paying up. (*She bites
the half guilder.*) I'm suspicious of all
money, I've been badly burned, Sergeant.
But this money's good. And now we'll be
going. Where's Eilif?

SWISS CHEESE. Gone with the recruiting officer.

MOTHER COURAGE (*standing quite still, then*).
Oh, you simpleton! (*To* KATTRIN.) You
can't speak, I know. You are innocent.

SERGEANT. That's life. Take a slug yourself,
Mother. Being a soldier isn't the worst that
could happen. You want to live off war and
keep you and yours out of it, do you?

MOTHER COURAGE. You must help your
brother now, Kattrin.

*Brother and sister get into harness to-
gether and pull the wagon.* MOTHER
COURAGE *walks at their side. The wagon
gets under way.*

SERGEANT (*looking after them*).
When a war gives you all you earn
One day it may claim something in re-
turn!

2

*In the years 1625 and 1626 Mother
Courage journeys through Poland in the
baggage train of the Swedish army. She
meets her son again before the fortified
town of Wallhof.—Of the successful
sale of a capon and great days for the
brave son.*

Tent of the SWEDISH COMMANDER.
*Kitchen next to it. Thunder of cannon.
The* COOK *is quarreling with* MOTHER
COURAGE, *who is trying to sell him a
capon.*

COOK. Sixty hellers for that miserable bird?

MOTHER COURAGE. Miserable bird? This fat
fowl? Your Commander is a glutton. Woe
betide you if you've nothing for him to eat.
This capon is worth sixty hellers to you.

COOK. They're ten hellers a dozen on every
corner.

MOTHER COURAGE. A capon like this on every
corner! With a siege going on and people
all skin and bones? Maybe you can get a
field rat! I said maybe. Because we're all
out of *them* too. Don't you see the soldiers
running five deep after one hungry little
field rat! All right then, in a siege, my
price for a giant capon is fifty hellers.

COOK. But we're not "in a siege," we're doing the besieging, it's the other side that's "in a siege," when will you get this into your head?

MOTHER COURAGE. A fat lot of difference that makes, *we* haven't got a thing to eat either. They took everything into the town with them before all this started, and now they've nothing to do but eat and drink, I hear. It's us I'm worried about. Look at the farmers around here, they haven't a thing.

COOK. Certainly they have. They hide it.

MOTHER COURAGE (*triumphant*). They have not! They're ruined, that's what. They're so hungry I've seen 'em digging up roots to eat. I could boil your leather belt and make their mouths water with it. That's how things are around here. And I'm expected to let a capon go for forty hellers!

COOK. Thirty. Not forty. I said thirty hellers.

MOTHER COURAGE. I say this is no ordinary capon. It was a talented animal, so I hear. It would only feed to music—one march in particular was its favorite. It was so intelligent it could count. Forty hellers is too much for all this? I know *your* problem: if you don't find something to eat and quick, the Chief will—cut—your—fat—head—off!

COOK. All right, just watch. (*He takes a piece of beef and lays his knife on it.*) Here's a piece of beef, I'm going to roast it. I give you one more chance.

MOTHER COURAGE. Roast it, go ahead, it's only one year old.

COOK. One *day* old! Yesterday it was a cow. I saw it running around.

MOTHER COURAGE. In that case it must have started stinking before it died.

COOK. I don't care if I have to cook it for five hours. We'll see if it's still hard after that. (*He cuts into it.*)

MOTHER COURAGE. Put plenty of pepper in, so the Commander won't smell the smell.

The SWEDISH COMMANDER, *a* CHAPLAIN, *and* EILIF *enter the tent.*

COMMANDER (*clapping* EILIF *on the shoulder*). In the Commander's tent with you, my son! Sit at my right hand, you happy warrior! You've played a hero's part, you've served the Lord in his own Holy War, *that's* the thing! And you'll get a gold bracelet out of it when we take the town if *I* have any say in the matter! We come to save their souls and what do they do, the filthy, shameless peasant pigs? Drive their cattle away from *us,* while they stuff their priests with beef at both ends! But you showed 'em. So here's a can of red wine for you, we'll drink together! (*They do so.*) The chaplain gets the dregs, he's pious. Now what would you like for dinner, my hearty?

EILIF. How about a slice of meat?

COOK. Nothing to eat, so he brings company to eat it!

MOTHER COURAGE *makes him stop talking; she wants to listen.*

EILIF. Tires you out, skinning peasants. Gives you an appetite.

MOTHER COURAGE. Dear God, it's my Eilif!

COOK. Who?

MOTHER COURAGE. My eldest. It's two years since I saw him, he was stolen from me in the street. He must be in high favor if the Commander's invited him to dinner. And what do you have to eat? Nothing. You hear what the Commander's guest wants? Meat! Better take my advice, buy the capon. The price is one guilder.

The COMMANDER *has sat down with* EILIF *and the* CHAPLAIN.

COMMANDER (*roaring*). Cook! Dinner, you pig, or I'll have your head!

COOK. This is blackmail. Give me the damn thing!

MOTHER COURAGE. A miserable bird like this?

COOK. You were right. Give it here. It's highway robbery, fifty hellers.

MOTHER COURAGE. I said one guilder. Nothing's too high for my eldest, the Commander's guest of honor.

COOK (*giving her the money*). Well, you might at least pluck it till I have a fire going.

MOTHER COURAGE (*sitting down to pluck the capon*). I can't wait to see his face when he sees me. This is my brave and clever son. I have a stupid one as well but he's honest. The daughter is nothing. At least, she doesn't talk: we must be thankful for small mercies.

COMMANDER. Have another can, my son, it's my favorite Falernian. There's only one cask left—two at the most—but it's worth it to meet a soldier that still believes in God! The shepherd of our flock here just looks on, he only preaches, he hasn't a clue how anything gets done. So now, Eilif, my son, give us the details: tell us how you fixed the peasants and grabbed the twenty bullocks. And let's hope they'll soon be here.

EILIF. In one day's time. Two at the most.

MOTHER COURAGE. Now that's considerate of Eilif—to bring the oxen tomorrow—otherwise my capon wouldn't have been so welcome today.

EILIF. Well, it was like this. I found out that the peasants had hidden their oxen and—on the sly and chiefly at night—had driven them into a certain wood. The people from the town were to pick them up there. I let them get their oxen in peace—they ought to know better than me where they are, I said to myself. Meanwhile I made my men crazy for meat. Their rations were short and I made sure they got shorter. Their mouths'd water at the sound of any word beginning with MEA . . . , like measles.

COMMANDER. Smart fella.

EILIF. Not bad. The rest was a snap. Only the peasants had clubs and outnumbered us three to one and made a murderous attack on us. Four of them drove me into a clump of trees, knocked my good sword from my hand, and yelled, "Surrender!" What now, I said to myself, they'll make mincemeat of me.

COMMANDER. What did you do?

EILIF. I laughed.

COMMANDER. You what?

EILIF. I laughed. And so we got to talking. I came right down to business and said:

"Twenty guilders an ox is too much, I bid fifteen." Like I wanted to buy. That foxed 'em. So while they were scratching their heads, I reached for my good sword and cut 'em to pieces. Necessity knows no law, huh?

COMMANDER. What do *you* say, shepherd of the flock?

CHAPLAIN. Strictly speaking, that saying is not in the Bible. Our Lord made five hundred loaves out of five so that no such necessity would arise. When he told men to love their neighbors, their bellies were full. Things have changed since his day.

COMMANDER (*laughing*). Things have changed! A swallow of wine for those wise words, you pharisee! (*To* EILIF.) You cut 'em to pieces in a good cause, our fellows were hungry and you gave 'em to eat. Doesn't it say in the Bible "Whatsoever thou doest for the least of these my children, thou doest for me?" And what *did* you do for 'em? You got 'em the best steak dinner they ever tasted. Moldy bread is not what they're used to. They always ate white bread, and drank wine in their helmets, before going out to fight for God.

EILIF. I reached for my good sword and cut 'em to pieces.

COMMANDER. You have the makings of a Julius Caesar, why, you should be presented to the King!

EILIF. I've seen him—from a distance of course. He seemed to shed a light all around. I must try to be like him!

COMMANDER. I think you're succeeding, my boy! Oh, Eilif, you don't know how I value a brave soldier like you! I treat such a chap as my very own son. (*He takes him to the map.*) Take a look at our position, Eilif, it isn't all it might be, is it?

MOTHER COURAGE *has been listening and is now plucking angrily at her capon.*

MOTHER COURAGE. He must be a very bad Commander.

COOK. Just a gluttonous one. Why bad?

MOTHER COURAGE. Because he needs *brave*

soldiers, that's why. If his plan of campaign was any good, why would he need *brave* soldiers, wouldn't plain, ordinary soldiers do? Whenever there are great virtues, it's a sure sign something's wrong.

COOK. You mean, it's a sure sign something's right.

MOTHER COURAGE. I mean what I say. Why? When a general or a king is stupid and leads his soldiers into a trap, they need this virtue of courage. When he's tightfisted and hasn't enough soldiers, the few he does have need the heroism of Hercules—another virtue. And if he's slovenly and doesn't give a damn about anything, they have to be as wise as serpents or they're finished. Loyalty's another virtue and you need plenty of it if the king's always asking too much of you. All virtues which a well-regulated country with a good king or a good general wouldn't need. In a good country virtues wouldn't be necessary. Everybody could be quite ordinary, middling, and, for all I care, cowards.

COMMANDER. I bet your father was a soldier.

EILIF. I've heard he was a great soldier. My mother warned me. I know a song about that.

COMMANDER. Sing it to us. (*Roaring.*) Bring that meat!

EILIF. It's called The Song of the Wise Woman and the Soldier.

He sings and at the same time does a war dance with his saber:

A shotgun will shoot and a jackknife will knife,
If you wade in the water, it will drown you,
Keep away from the ice, if you want my advice,
Said the wise woman to the soldier.

But that young soldier, he loaded his gun,
And he reached for his knife, and he started to run:
For marching never could hurt him!
From the north to the south he will march through the land

With his knife at his side and his gun in his hand:
That's what the soldiers told the wise woman.

Woe to him who defies the advice of the wise!
If you wade in the water, it will drown you!
Don't ignore what I say or you'll rue it one day,
Said the wise woman to the soldier.

But that young soldier, his knife at his side
And his gun in his hand, he steps into the tide:
For water never could hurt him!
When the new moon is shining on yonder church tower
We are all coming back: go and pray for that hour:
That's what the soldiers told the wise woman.

MOTHER COURAGE (*continues the song from her kitchen, beating on a pan with a spoon*).
Then the wise woman spoke: you will vanish like smoke
Leaving nothing but cold air behind you!
Just watch the smoke fly! Oh God, don't let him die!
Said the wise woman to the soldier.

EILIF. What's that?

MOTHER COURAGE (*singing on*).

And the lad who defied the wise woman's advice,
When the new moon shone, floated down with the ice:
He waded in the water and it drowned him.
The wise woman spoke, and they vanished like smoke,
And their glorious deeds did not warm us.
Your glorious deeds do not warm us!

COMMANDER. What a kitchen I've got! There's no end to the liberties they take!

EILIF *has entered the kitchen and embraced his mother.*

EILIF. To see you again! Where are the others?

MOTHER COURAGE (*in his arms*). Happy as ducks in a pond. Swiss Cheese is paymaster with the Second Regiment, so at least he isn't in the fighting. I couldn't keep him out altogether.

EILIF. Are your feet holding up?

MOTHER COURAGE. I've a bit of trouble getting my shoes on in the morning.

The COMMANDER *has come over.*

COMMANDER. So you're his mother! I hope you have more sons for me like this fellow.

EILIF. If I'm not the lucky one: to be feasted by the Commander while you sit listening in the kitchen!

MOTHER COURAGE. Yes. I heard all right. (*She gives him a box on the ear.*)

EILIF (*his hand on his cheek*). Because I took the oxen?

MOTHER COURAGE. No. Because you didn't surrender when the four peasants let fly at you and tried to make mincemeat of you! Didn't I teach you to take care of yourself? You Finnish devil, you!

The COMMANDER *and the* CHAPLAIN *stand laughing in the doorway.*

3

Three years pass and Mother Courage, with parts of a Finnish regiment, is taken prisoner. Her daughter is saved, her wagon likewise, but her honest son dies.

A camp. The regimental flag is flying from a pole. Afternoon. All sorts of wares hanging on the wagon. MOTHER COURAGE'S *clothesline is tied to the* wagon *at one end, to a cannon at the other. She and* KATTRIN *are folding the washing on the cannon. At the same time she is bargaining with an* ORDNANCE OFFICER *over a bag of bullets.* SWISS CHEESE, *in paymaster's uniform now, looks on.* YVETTE POTTIER, *a very good-looking young person, is sewing at a colored hat, a glass of brandy before her. She is in stocking feet. Her red boots are near by.*

OFFICER. I'm letting you have the bullets for two guilders. Dirt cheap. 'Cause I need the money. The Colonel's been drinking with the officers for three days and we're out of liquor.

MOTHER COURAGE. They're army property. If they find 'em on me, I'll be courtmartialed. You sell your bullets, you bastards, and send your men out to fight with nothing to shoot with.

OFFICER. Oh, come on, you scratch my back, and I'll scratch yours.

MOTHER COURAGE. I won't take army stuff. Not at *that* price.

OFFICER. You can resell 'em for five guilders, maybe eight, to the Ordnance Officer of the Fourth Regiment. All you have to do is give him a receipt for twelve. He hasn't a bullet left.

MOTHER COURAGE. Why don't you do it yourself?

OFFICER. I don't trust him. We're friends.

MOTHER COURAGE (*taking the bag*). Give it here. (*To* KATTRIN.) Take it around to the back and pay him a guilder and a half. (*As the* OFFICER *protests.*) I said a guilder and a half! (KATTRIN *drags the bag away. The* OFFICER *follows.* MOTHER COURAGE *speaks to* SWISS CHEESE.) Here's your underwear back, take care of it; it's October now, autumn may come at any time; I purposely don't say it must come, I've learned from experience there's nothing that must come, not even the seasons. But your books *must* balance now you're the regimental paymaster. *Do* they balance?

SWISS CHEESE. Yes, Mother.

MOTHER COURAGE. Don't forget they made

you paymaster because you're honest and so simple you'd never think of running off with the cash. Don't lose that underwear.

SWISS CHEESE. No, mother. I'll put it under the mattress. (*He starts to go.*)

OFFICER. I'll go with you, paymaster.

MOTHER COURAGE. Don't teach him any monkey business.

Without a good-by the OFFICER *leaves with* SWISS CHEESE.

YVETTE (*waving to him*). You might at least say good-by!

MOTHER COURAGE (*to* YVETTE). I don't like that. *He's* no sort of company for my Swiss Cheese. But the war's not making a bad start. Before all the different countries get into it, four or five years'll have gone by like nothing. If I look ahead and make no mistakes, business will be good. Don't you know you shouldn't drink in the morning with your illness?

YVETTE. Who says I'm ill? That's libel!

MOTHER COURAGE. They all say so.

YVETTE. They're all liars. I'm desperate, Mother Courage. They all avoid me like a stinking fish. Because of those lies. So what am I arranging my hat for? (*She throws it down.*) That's why I drink in the morning. I never used to, it gives you crow's feet. But what's the difference? Every man in the regiment knows me. I should have stayed at home when my first was unfaithful. But pride isn't for the likes of us, you eat dirt or down you go.

MOTHER COURAGE. Now don't you start again with your friend Peter and how it all happened—in front of my innocent daughter.

YVETTE. She's the one that should hear it. So she'll get hardened against love.

MOTHER COURAGE. That's something no one ever gets hardened against.

YVETTE. I'll tell you about it, and get it off my chest. I grew up in Flanders' fields, that's where it starts, or I'd never even have caught sight of him and I wouldn't be here in Poland today. He was an army cook, blond, a Dutchman, but thin. Kattrin, beware of thin men! I didn't. I didn't even

know he'd had another girl before me and she called him Peter Piper because he never took his pipe out of his mouth the whole time, it meant so little to him.

She sings "The Fraternization Song."

When I was almost seventeen
The foe came to our land
And laying aside his saber
He took me gently by the hand.

First came the May Day Rite
Then came the May Day night.
The pipes played and the drums did beat.
The foe paraded down the street.
And then with us they took their ease
And fraternized behind the trees.

Our foes they came in plenty.
A cook was my own foe.
I hated him by daylight
But in the dark I loved him so.

First comes the May Day Rite
Then comes the May Day night.
The pipes play and the drums do beat.
The foe parades down every street.
And then with us they take their ease
And fraternize behind the trees.

The heavens seemed to open
Such passion did I feel.
But my people never understood
The love I felt was real.

One day the sun rose slow
On all my pain and woe.
My loved one, with the other men,
Presented arms and stood at ease
Then marched away past all those trees
And never did come back again.

I made the mistake of running after him, I never found him. It's five years ago now. (*With swaying gait she goes behind the wagon.*)

MOTHER COURAGE. You've left your hat.

YVETTE. For the birds.

MOTHER COURAGE. Let this be a lesson to you, Kattrin, never start anything with a soldier. The heavens do seem to open, so watch

out! Even with men who're not in the army
life's no honeypot. He tells you he'd like to
kiss the ground under your feet—did you
wash 'em yesterday, while we're on the
subject?—and then if you don't look out,
your number's up, you're his slave for life.
Be glad you're dumb, Kattrin: you'll never
contradict yourself, you'll never want to
bite your tongue off because you spoke out
of turn. Dumbness is a gift from God. Here
comes the Commander's cook, what's bothering *him?*

Enter the COOK *and the* CHAPLAIN.

CHAPLAIN. I bring a message from your son
Eilif. The cook came with me. You've
made, ahem, an impression on him.
COOK. I thought I'd get a little whiff of the
balmy breeze.
MOTHER COURAGE. You're welcome to that if
you behave yourself, and even if you don't
I think I can handle you. But what does
Eilif want? I don't have any money.
CHAPLAIN. Actually, I have something to tell
his brother, the paymaster.
MOTHER COURAGE. He isn't here. And he isn't
anywhere else either. He's not his brother's
paymaster, and I won't have him led into
temptation. Let Eilif try it on with someone else! (*She takes money from the purse
at her belt.*) Give him this. It's a sin. He's
speculating in mother love, he ought to be
ashamed of himself.
COOK. Not for long. He has to go with his
regiment now—to his death maybe. Send
some more money, or you'll be sorry. You
women are hard—and sorry afterward. A
glass of brandy wouldn't cost very much,
but you refuse to provide it, and six feet
under goes your man and you can't dig
him up again.
CHAPLAIN. All very touching, my dear cook,
but to fall in this war is not a misfortune,
it's a blessing. This is a war of religion. Not
just any old war but a special one, a religious one, and therefore pleasing unto God.
COOK. Correct. In one sense it's a war because
there's fleecing, bribing, plundering, not to
mention a little raping, but it's different

from all other wars because it's a war of
religion. That's clear. All the same, it makes
you thirsty.
CHAPLAIN (*to* MOTHER COURAGE, *pointing at
the* COOK). I tried to hold him off but he
said you'd bewitched him. He dreams about
you.
COOK (*lighting a clay pipe*). Brandy from the
fair hand of a lady, that's for me. And
don't embarrass me any more: the stories
the chaplain was telling me on the way
over still have me blushing.
MOTHER COURAGE. A man of his cloth! I must
get you both something to drink or you'll
be making improper advances out of sheer
boredom.
CHAPLAIN. That is indeed a temptation, said
the court chaplain, and gave way to it.
(*Turning toward* KATTRIN *as he walks.*)
And who is this captivating young person?
MOTHER COURAGE. She's not a captivating
young person, she's a respectable young person.

The CHAPLAIN *and the* COOK *go with*
MOTHER COURAGE *behind the cart, and
one hears them talk politics.*

MOTHER COURAGE. The trouble here in Poland is that the Poles *would* keep meddling.
It's true our King moved in on them with
man, beast, and wagon, but instead of
keeping the peace the Poles attacked the
Swedish King when he was in the act of
peacefully withdrawing. So they were
guilty of a breach of the peace and their
blood is on their own heads.
CHAPLAIN. Anyway, our King was thinking of
nothing but freedom. The Kaiser enslaved
them all, Poles and Germans alike, so our
King *had* to liberate them.
COOK. Just what *I* think. Your health! Your
brandy is first-rate, I'm never mistaken in
a face.

KATTRIN *looks after them, leaves the
washing, goes to the hat, picks it up, sits
down, and takes up the red boots.*

And the war is a war of religion. (*Singing*

while KATTRIN *puts the boots on.*) "A mighty fortress is our God . . ." (*He sings a verse or so of Luther's hymn.*) And talking of King Gustavus, this freedom he tried to bring to Germany cost him a pretty penny. Back in Sweden he had to levy a salt tax, the poorer folks didn't like it a bit. Then, too, he had to lock up the Germans and even cut their heads off, they clung so to slavery and their Kaiser. Of course, if no one had *wanted* to be free, the King would have got quite mad. First it was just Poland he tried to protect from bad men, especially the Kaiser, then his appetite grew with eating, and he ended up protecting Germany too. Now Germany put up a pretty decent fight. So the good King had nothing but worries in return for his outlay and his goodness, and of course he had to get his money back with taxes, which made bad blood, but he didn't shrink even from that. For he had one thing in his favor anyway, God's Holy Word, which was all to the good, because otherwise they could have said he did it for profit. That's how he kept his conscience clear. He always put conscience first.

MOTHER COURAGE. It's plain you're no Swede, or you'd speak differently of the Hero King.

CHAPLAIN. What's more, you eat his bread.

COOK. I don't eat his bread. I bake his bread.

MOTHER COURAGE. He's unbeatable. Why? His men believe in him. (*Earnestly.*) To hear the big fellows talk, they wage war from fear of God and for all things bright and beautiful, but just look into it, and you'll see they're not so silly: they want a good profit out of it, or else the little fellows like you and me wouldn't back 'em up.

COOK. That's right.

CHAPLAIN. And as a Dutchman you'd do well to see which flag's flying here before you express an opinion!

MOTHER COURAGE. All good Protestants forever!

COOK. A health!

KATTRIN *has begun to strut about with* YVETTE's *hat on, copying* YVETTE's *sexy walk. Suddenly cannon and shots.*

Drums. MOTHER COURAGE, *the* COOK, *and the* CHAPLAIN *rush around to the front of the cart, the last two with glasses in their hands. The* ORDNANCE OFFICER *and a* SOLDIER *come running to the cannon and try to push it along.*

MOTHER COURAGE. What's the matter? Let me get my washing off that gun, you slobs! (*She tries to do so.*)

OFFICER. The Catholics! Surprise attack! We don't know if we can get away! (*To the* SOLDIER.) Get that gun! (*He runs off.*)

COOK. For heaven's sake! I must go to the Commander. Mother Courage, I'll be back in a day or two—for a short conversation. (*He rushes off.*)

MOTHER COURAGE. Hey, you've left your pipe!

COOK (*off*). Keep it for me, I'll need it!

MOTHER COURAGE. This *would* happen just when we were making money.

CHAPLAIN. Well, I must be going too. Yes, if the enemy's so close, it can be dangerous. "Blessed are the peacemakers," a good slogan in war time! If only I had a cloak.

MOTHER COURAGE. I'm lending no cloaks. Not even to save a life, I'm not. I've had experience in that line.

CHAPLAIN. But I'm in special danger. Because of my religion.

MOTHER COURAGE (*bringing him a cloak*). It's against my better judgment. Now run!

CHAPLAIN. I thank you, you're very generous, but maybe I'd better stay and sit here. If I run, I might attract the enemy's attention, I might arouse suspicion.

MOTHER COURAGE (*to the* SOLDIER). Let it alone, you dolt, who's going to pay you for this? It'll cost you your life, let me hold it for you.

SOLDIER (*running away*). You're my witness: I tried!

MOTHER COURAGE. I'll swear to it! (*Seeing* KATTRIN *with the hat.*) What on earth are you up to—with a whore's hat! Take if off this minute! Are you mad? With the enemy coming? (*She tears the hat off her head.*) Do you want them to find you and make a whore of you? And she has the boots on too, straight from Babylon. I'll soon fix that.

(*She tries to get them off.*) Oh, God, Chaplain, help me with these boots, I'll be right back. (*She runs to the wagon.*)

YVETTE (*entering and powdering her face*). What's that you say: the Catholics are coming? Where's my hat? Who's been trampling on it? I can't run around in that, what will they think of me? And I don't even have a mirror. (*To the* CHAPLAIN.) How do I look—too much powder?

CHAPLAIN. Just, er, right.

YVETTE. And where are my red boots? (*She can't find them because* KATTRIN *is hiding her feet under her skirt.*) I left them here! Now I've got to go barefoot to my tent, it's a scandal! (*Exit.*)

SWISS CHEESE *comes running in carrying a cash box.* MOTHER COURAGE *enters with her hands covered with ashes.*

MOTHER COURAGE (*to* KATTRIN). Ashes! (*To* SWISS CHEESE.) What have you got there?

SWISS CHEESE. The regimental cash box.

MOTHER COURAGE. Throw it away! Your paymastering days are over!

SWISS CHEESE. It's a trust! (*He goes to the back.*)

MOTHER COURAGE (*to the* CHAPLAIN). Off with your pastor's cloak, Chaplain, or they'll recognize you, cloak or no cloak. (*She is rubbing ashes into* KATTRIN'S *face.*) Keep still. A little dirt, and you're safe. A calamity! The sentries were drunk. Well, one must hide one's light under a bushel, as they say. When a soldier sees a clean face, there's one more whore in the world. Especially a Catholic soldier. For weeks on end, no grub. Then, when the plundering starts and they steal some, the jump on top of the women-folk. That should do. Let me look at you. Not bad. Looks like you've been rolling in muck. Don't tremble. Nothing can happen to you now. (*To* SWISS CHEESE.) Where've you left the cash box?

SWISS CHEESE. I thought I'd just put it in the wagon.

MOTHER COURAGE (*horrified*). What! In my wagon? God punish you for a prize idiot! If I just look away for a moment! They'll hang all three of us!

SWISS CHEESE. Then I'll put it somewhere else. Or escape with it.

MOTHER COURAGE. You'll stay where you are. It's too late.

CHAPLAIN (*still changing his clothes*). For heaven's sake: the flag!

MOTHER COURAGE (*taking down the flag*). God in heaven! I don't notice it any more. I've had it twenty-five years.

The thunder of cannon grows.

Three days later. Morning. The cannon is gone. MOTHER COURAGE, KATTRIN, *the* CHAPLAIN, *and* SWISS CHEESE *sit anxiously eating.*

SWISS CHEESE. This is the third day I've been sitting here doing nothing, and the Sergeant, who's always been patient with me, may be slowly beginning to ask, "Where on earth is Swiss Cheese with that cash box?"

MOTHER COURAGE. Be glad they're not on the trail.

CHAPLAIN. What about me? I can't hold a service here or I'll be in hot water. It is written, "Out of the abundance of the heart, the tongue speaketh." But woe is me if *my* tongue speaketh!

MOTHER COURAGE. That's how it is. Here you sit—one with his religion, the other with his cash box, I don't know which is more dangerous.

CHAPLAIN. We're in God's hands now!

MOTHER COURAGE. I hope we're not *that* desperate, but it *is* hard to sleep nights. 'Course it'd be easier if *you* weren't here, Swiss Cheese, all the same I've not done badly. I told them I was against the Antichrist, who's a Swede with horns on his head. I told them I noticed his left horn's a bit threadbare. When they cross-examined me, I always asked where I could buy holy candles a bit cheaper. I know these things because Swiss Cheese's father was a Catholic and made jokes about it. They didn't quite believe me but they needed a canteen, so they turned a blind eye. Maybe it's all for the best. We're prisoners. But so are lice in fur.

CHAPLAIN. The milk is good. As far as quantity goes, we may have to reduce our Swedish appetites somewhat. We are defeated.

MOTHER COURAGE. Who's defeated? The defeats and victories of the fellows at the top aren't always defeats and victories for the fellows at the bottom. Not at all. There've been cases where a defeat is a victory for the fellows at the bottom, it's only their honor that's lost, nothing serious. In Livonia once, our Chief took such a knock from the enemy, in the confusion I got a fine gray mare out of the baggage train, it pulled my wagon seven months—till we won and there was an inventory. But in general both defeat and victory are a costly business for us that haven't got much. The best thing is for politics to get stuck in the mud. (*To* SWISS CHEESE.) Eat!

SWISS CHEESE. I don't like it. How will the sergeant pay his men?

MOTHER COURAGE. Soldiers in flight don't get paid.

SWISS CHEESE. Well, they could claim to be. No pay, no flight. They can refuse to budge.

MOTHER COURAGE. Swiss Cheese, your sense of duty worries me. I've brought you up to be honest because you're not very bright. But don't overdo it. And now I'm going with the chaplain to buy a Catholic flag and some meat. There's no one can hunt out meat like him, sure as a sleepwalker. He can tell a good piece of meat from the way his mouth waters. A good thing they let me stay in the business. In business you ask what price, not what religion. And Protestant trousers keep you just as warm.

CHAPLAIN. As the mendicant monk said when there was talk of the Lutherans turning the whole world upside down: Beggars will *always* be needed. (MOTHER COURAGE *disappears into the wagon.*) She's worried about the cash box. Up to now they've ignored us—as if we were part of the wagon —but can it last?

SWISS CHEESE. I can get rid of it.

CHAPLAIN. That's almost *more* dangerous.

Suppose you're seen. They have spies. Yesterday morning one jumped out of the very hole I was relieving myself in. I was so scared I almost broke out in prayer—*that* would have given me away all right! I believe their favorite way of finding a Protestant is smelling his excrement. The spy was a little brute with a bandage over one eye.

MOTHER COURAGE (*clambering out of the wagon with a basket*). I've found you out, you shameless hussy! (*She holds up* YVETTE's *red boots in triumph.*) Yvette's red boots! She just swiped them—because you went and told her she was a captivating person. (*She lays them in the basket.*) Stealing Yvette's boots! But *she* disgraces herself for money, *you* do it for nothing—for pleasure! I told you, you must wait for the peace. No soldiers! Save your proud peacock ways for peacetime!

CHAPLAIN. I don't find her proud.

MOTHER COURAGE. Prouder than she can afford to be. I like her when people say "I never noticed the poor thing." I like her when she's a stone in Dalarna, where there's nothing but stones. (*To* SWISS CHEESE.) Leave the cash box where it is, do you hear? And pay attention to your sister, she needs it. Between the two of you, you'll be the death of me yet. I'd rather take care of a bag of fleas.

She leaves with the CHAPLAIN. KATTRIN *clears the dishes away.*

SWISS CHEESE. Not many days more when you can sit in the sun in your shirtsleeves. (KATTRIN *points to a tree.*) Yes, the leaves are yellow already. (*With gestures,* KATTRIN *asks if he wants a drink.*) I'm not drinking, I'm thinking. (*Pause.*) She says she can't sleep. So I *should* take the cash box away. I've found a place for it. I'll keep it in the mole hole by the river till the time comes. I might get it tonight before sunrise and take it to the regiment. How far can they have fled in three days? The Sergeant's eyes'll pop out of his head. "I give you the cash box to take care of, and what do you do," he'll say, "but hand it right back to me: you've disappointed me most pleasantly, Swiss Cheese." Yes, Kattrin, I *will* have a glass now!

When KATTRIN *reappears behind the wagon two men confront her. One of them is a* SERGEANT. *The other doffs his hat and flourishes it in a showy greeting. He has a bandage over one eye.*

MAN WITH THE BANDAGE. Good morning, young lady. Have you seen a man from the Second Protestant Regiment?

Terrified, KATTRIN *runs away, spilling her brandy. The two men look at each other and then withdraw after seeing* SWISS CHEESE.

SWISS CHEESE (*starting up from his reflection*). You're spilling it! What's the matter with you, have you hurt your eye? I don't understand. Yes, and I must be going, too. I've decided it's the thing to do. (*He stands up. She does all she can to make him aware of the danger he is in. He only pushes her away.*) I'd like to know what you mean. I know you mean well, poor thing, you just can't get it out. And don't trouble yourself about the brandy, I'll live to drink so much of it, what's one glass? (*He takes the cash box out of the wagon and puts it under his coat.*) I'll be back right away. But don't hold me up or I'll have to scold you. Yes, I know you mean well. If you could only speak!

When she tries to hold him back he kisses her and pulls himself free. Exit. She is desperate and runs up and down, emitting little sounds. MOTHER COURAGE *and the* CHAPLAIN *return.* KATTRIN *rushes at her mother.*

MOTHER COURAGE. What *is* it, what *is* it, Kattrin? Control yourself! Has someone done something to you? Where is Swiss Cheese? (*To the* CHAPLAIN.) Don't stand around,

get that Catholic flag up! (*She takes a Catholic flag out of her basket and the* CHAPLAIN *runs it up the pole.*)

CHAPLAIN (*bitterly*). All good Catholics forever!

MOTHER COURAGE. Now, Kattrin, calm down and tell all about it, your mother understands you. What, that little bastard of mine's taken the cash box away? I'll box his ears for him, the rascal! Now take your time and don't try to talk, use your hands. I don't like it when you howl like a dog, what'll the chaplain think of you? You're giving him the creeps. A man with one eye was here?

CHAPLAIN. That fellow with one eye is an informer! Have they caught Swiss Cheese? (KATTRIN *shakes her head, shrugs her shoulders.*) This is the end.

Voices off. The two men bring in SWISS CHEESE.

SWISS CHEESE. Let me go. I've nothing on me. You're breaking my shoulder! I am innocent.

SERGEANT. This is where he comes from. These are his friends.

MOTHER COURAGE. Us? Since when?

SWISS CHEESE. I don't even know 'em. I was just getting my lunch here. Ten hellers it cost me. Maybe you saw me sitting on that bench. It was too salty.

SERGEANT. Who *are* you people, anyway?

MOTHER COURAGE. Law-abiding citizens! It's true what he says. He bought his lunch here. And it was too salty.

SERGEANT. Are you pretending you don't know him?

MOTHER COURAGE. I can't know all of them, can I? *I* don't ask, "What's your name and are you a heathen?" If they pay up, they're not heathens to me. Are you a heathen?

SWISS CHEESE. Oh, no!

CHAPLAIN. He sat there like a law-abiding fellow and never once opened his mouth. Except to eat. Which is necessary.

SERGEANT. Who do you think *you* are?

MOTHER COURAGE. Oh, he's my barman. And

you're thirsty, I'll bring you a glass of brandy. You must be footsore and weary!

SERGEANT. No brandy on duty. (*To* SWISS CHEESE.) You were carrying something. You must have hidden it by the river. We saw the bulge in your shirt.

MOTHER COURAGE. Sure it was him?

SWISS CHEESE. I think you mean another fellow. There *was* a fellow with something under his shirt, I saw him. I'm the wrong man.

MOTHER COURAGE. I think so too. It's a misunderstanding. Could happen to anyone. Oh, I know what people are like, I'm Mother Courage, you've heard of me, everyone knows about me, and I can tell you this: he looks honest.

SERGEANT. We're after the regimental cash box. And we know what the man looks like who's been keeping it. We've been looking for him two days. It's you.

SWISS CHEESE. No, it's not!

SERGEANT. And if you don't shell out, you're dead, see? Where is it?

MOTHER COURAGE (*urgently*). 'Course he'd give it to you to save his life. He'd up and say, *I've* got it, here it is, you're stronger than me. He's not *that* stupid. Speak, little stupid, the sergeant's giving you a chance!

SWISS CHEESE. What if I haven't got it?

SERGEANT. Come with us. We'll get it out of you. (*They take him off.*)

MOTHER COURAGE (*shouting after them*). He'd tell you! He's not *that* stupid! And don't you break his shoulder! (*She runs after them.*)

The same evening. The CHAPLAIN *and* KATTRIN *are rinsing glasses and polishing knives.*

CHAPLAIN. Cases of people getting caught like this are by no means unknown in the history of religion. I am reminded of the Passion of Our Lord and Savior. There's an old song about it.

He sings "The Song of the Hours."

In the first hour of the day

Simple Jesus Christ was
Presented as a murderer
To the heathen Pilate.

Pilate found no fault in him
No cause to condemn him
So he sent the Lord away.
Let King Herod see him!

Hour the third: the Son of God
Was with scourges beaten
And they set a crown of thorns
On the head of Jesus.

And they dressed him as a king
Joked and jested at him
And the cross to die upon
He himself must carry.

Six: they stripped Lord Jesus bare.
To the cross they nailed him.
When the blood came gushing, he
Prayed and loud lamented.

Each upon his cross, two thieves
Mocked him like the others.
And the bright sun crept away
Not to see such doings.

Nine: Lord Jesus cried aloud
That he was forsaken!
In a sponge upon a pole
Vinegar was fed him.

Then the Lord gave up the ghost
And the earth did tremble.
Temple curtains split in twain.
Cliffs fell in the ocean.

Evening: they broke the bones
Of the malefactors.
Then they took a spear and pierced
The side of gentle Jesus.

And the blood and water ran
And they laughed at Jesus.
Of this simple son of man
Such and more they tell us.

MOTHER COURAGE (*entering, excited*). It's life and death. But the Sergeant will still listen to us. The only thing is, he musn't know it's our Swiss Cheese, or they'll say we helped him. It's only a matter of money, but where can *we* get money? Isn't Yvette here yet? I talked to her on the way over. She's picked up a Colonel who may be willing to buy her a canteen business.

CHAPLAIN. You'd sell the wagon, everything?

MOTHER COURAGE. Where else would I get the money for the Sergeant?

CHAPLAIN. What are you to live off?

MOTHER COURAGE. That's just it.

Enter YVETTE *with a hoary old* COLONEL.

YVETTE (*embracing* MOTHER COURAGE). *Dear* Mistress Courage, we meet again. (*Whispering.*) He didn't say no. (*Aloud.*) This is my friend, my, um, business adviser. I happened to hear you might sell your wagon. Due to special circumstances, I'd like to think about it.

MOTHER COURAGE. I want to pawn it, not sell it. And nothing hasty. In war time you don't find another wagon like that so easy.

YVETTE (*disappointed*). Only pawn it? I thought you wanted to sell. I don't know if I'm interested. (*To the* COLONEL.) What do *you* think, my dear?

COLONEL. I quite agree with you, bunny.

MOTHER COURAGE. It's only for pawn.

YVETTE. I thought you *had* to have the money.

MOTHER COURAGE (*firmly*). I do have to have it. But I'd reather wear my feet off looking for an offer than just sell. Why? We live off the wagon. It's an opportunity for you, Yvette. Who knows when you'll have another such? Who knows when you'll find another business adviser?

COLONEL. Take it, take it!

YVETTE. My friend thinks I should go ahead, but I'm not sure, if it's only for pawn. You think we should buy it outright, don't you?

COLONEL. I do, bunny, I do!

MOTHER COURAGE. Then you must go and find something that's for sale. Maybe you'll find it—if you have the time, and your friend goes with you, let's say in about a week, or two weeks, you may find the right thing.

YVETTE. Yes, we can certainly look around for something. I love going around looking, I love going around with you, Poldy . . .

COLONEL. Really? Do you?

YVETTE. Oh, it's lovely! I could take two weeks of it!

COLONEL. Really, could you?

YVETTE. If you get the money, when are you thinking of paying it back?

MOTHER COURAGE. In two weeks. Maybe one.

YVETTE. I can't make up my mind. Poldy, advise me, *chéri*! (*She takes the* COLONEL *to one side.*) She'll *have* to sell, don't worry. That Lieutenant—the blond one, you know the one I mean—he'll lend me the money. He's *mad* about me, he says I remind him of someone. What do you advise?

COLONEL. Oh, I have to warn you against *him*. He's no good. He'll exploit the situation. I told you, bunny, I told you *I'd* buy you something, didn't I tell you that?

YVETTE. I simply can't let you!

COLONEL. Oh, please, please!

YVETTE. Well, if you think the Lieutenant might exploit the situation I *will* let you!

COLONEL. I do think so.

YVETTE. So you advise me to?

COLONEL. I do, bunny, I do!

YVETTE (*returning to* MOTHER COURAGE). My friend says all right. Write me out a receipt saying the wagon's mine when the two weeks are up—with everything in it. I'll just run through it all now, the two hundred guilders can wait. (*To the* COLONEL.) You go ahead to the camp, I'll follow, I must go over all this so nothing'll be missing later from *my* wagon!

COLONEL. Wait, I'll help you up! (*He does so.*) Come soon, honey bun! (*Exit.*)

MOTHER COURAGE. Yvette, Yvette!

YVETTE. There aren't many boots left!

MOTHER COURAGE. Yvette, this is no time to go through the wagon, yours or not yours. You promised you'd talk to the Sergeant about Swiss Cheese. There isn't a minute to lose. He's up before the court-martial one hour from now.

YVETTE. I just want to count these shirts again.

MOTHER COURAGE (*dragging her down the steps by the skirt*). You hyena, Swiss Cheese's life's at stake! And don't say who the money comes from. Pretend he's your sweetheart, for heaven's sake, or we'll all get it for helping him.

YVETTE. I've arranged to meet One Eye in the bushes. He must be there by now.

CHAPLAIN. And don't hand over all two hundred, a hundred and fifty's sure to be enough.

MOTHER COURAGE. Is it your money? I'll thank you to keep your nose out of this, I'm not doing *you* out of your porridge. Now run, and no haggling, remember his life's at stake. (*She pushes* YVETTE *off.*)

CHAPLAIN. I didn't want to talk you into anything, but what are we going to live on? You have an unemployable daughter around your neck.

MOTHER COURAGE. I'm counting on that cash box, smart aleck. They'll pay his expenses out of it.

CHAPLAIN. You think she can work it?

MOTHER COURAGE. It's in her own interest: I pay the two hundred and she gets the wagon. She knows what she's doing, she won't have her Colonel on the string forever. Kattrin, go and clean the knives, use pumice stone. And don't *you* stand around like Jesus in Gethsemane. Get a move on, wash those glasses. There'll be over fifty cavalrymen here tonight, and you'll be saying you're not used to being on your feet. "Oh my poor feet, in church I never had to run around like this!" I think they'll let us have him. Thanks be to God they're corruptible. They're not wolves, they're human and after money. God is merciful, and men are bribable, that's how His will is done on earth as it is in Heaven. Corruption is our only hope. As long as there's corruption, there'll be merciful judges and even the innocent may get off.

YVETTE *comes in panting.*

YVETTE. They'll do it for two hundred if you make it snappy—these things change from one minute to the next. I'd better take One Eye to my Colonel at once. He confessed he had the cash box, they put the thumbscrews on him. But he threw it in the river when he noticed them coming up behind him. So it's gone. Shall I run and get the money from my Colonel?

MOTHER COURAGE. The cash box gone? How'll I ever get my two hundred back?

YVETTE. So you thought you could get it from the cash box? I *would* have been sunk. Not a hope, Mother Courage. If you want your Swiss Cheese, you'll have to pay. Or should I let the whole thing drop, so you can keep your wagon?

MOTHER COURAGE. I wasn't figuring on this. But you needn't hound me, you'll get the wagon, it's yours already, and it's been mine seventeen years. I need a minute to think it over, it's all so sudden. What can I do? I *can't* pay two hundred. You *should* have haggled with them. I must hold on to something, or any passer-by can kick me in the ditch. Go and say I'll pay a hundred and twenty or the deal's off. Even then I lose the wagon.

YVETTE. They won't do it. And anyway, One Eye's in a hurry. He keeps looking over his shoulder all the time, he's so worked up. Hadn't I better give them the whole two hundred?

MOTHER COURAGE (*desperate*). I can't pay it! I've been working thirty years. She's twenty-five and still no husband. I have her to think of. So leave me alone. I know what I'm doing. A hundred and twenty or no deal.

YVETTE. You know best. (*She runs off.*)

MOTHER COURAGE *turns away and slowly walks a few paces to the rear. Then she turns around, looks neither at the* CHAPLAIN *nor her daughter, and sits down to help* KATTRIN *polish the knives.*

MOTHER COURAGE. Don't break the glasses, they're not ours. Watch what you're doing, you're cutting yourself. Swiss Cheese will be back, I'll give two hundred, if I have to. You'll get your brother back. With eighty guilders we could pack a hamper with goods and begin again. It wouldn't be the end of the world.

CHAPLAIN. The Bible says: the Lord will provide.

MOTHER COURAGE. Rub them dry, I said.

They clean the knives in silence.

They say the war will stop soon. How would it? I ask. And no one can answer me. (*Slowly.*) The King and the Pope are mortal enemies, their Faith is different. They must go for each other till one of them drops dead, neither of them can relax till then. Even so they can't get on with it. Why not? The Emperor is in the way, and they both have something against him. They're not going to fight each other to the death with the Emperor lurking about till they're half dead so he can fall on both of 'em! No, they're banding together against the Emperor so he'll drop dead first and they can go for each other.

Suddenly KATTRIN *runs sobbing behind the wagon.*

Someone once offered me five hundred guilders for the wagon. I didn't take it. My Eilif, wherever he may be, thought I'd taken it and cried all night.

YVETTE *comes running in.*

YVETTE. They won't do it. I warned you. One Eye was going to drop it then and there. There's no point, he said. He said the drums would roll any second now and that's the sign a verdict has been reached. I offered a hundred and fifty, he didn't even shrug. I could hardly get him to stay there while I came here.

MOTHER COURAGE. Tell him I'll pay two hundred. Run!

YVETTE *runs.* MOTHER COURAGE *sits, silent. The* CHAPLAIN *has stopped doing the glasses.*

I believe—I've haggled too long.

In the distance, a roll of drums. The CHAPLAIN *stands up and walks toward the rear.* MOTHER COURAGE *remains seated. It grows dark. It gets light again.* MOTHER COURAGE *has not moved.* YVETTE *appears, pale.*

YVETTE. Now you've done it—with your haggling. You can keep the wagon now. He got eleven bullets in him. I don't know why I still bother about you, you don't deserve it, but I just happened to learn they don't think the cash box is really in the river. They suspect it's here, they think you're connected with him. I think they're going to bring him here to see if you'll give yourself away when you see him. You'd better not know him or we're in for it. And I'd better tell you straight, they're just behind me. Shall I keep Kattrin away? (MOTHER COURAGE *shakes her head.*) Does she know? Maybe she never heard the drums or didn't understand.

MOTHER COURAGE. She knows. Bring her.

YVETTE *brings* KATTRIN, *who walks over to her mother and stands by her.* MOTHER COURAGE *takes her hand. Two men come on with a stretcher; there is a sheet on it and something underneath. Beside them, the* SERGEANT. *They put the stretcher down.*

SERGEANT. Here's a man we can't identify. But he has to be registered to keep the records straight. He bought a meal from you. Look at him, see if you know him. (*He pulls back the sheet.*) Do you know him? (MOTHER COURAGE *shakes her head.*) What? You never saw him before he took that meal? (MOTHER COURAGE *shakes her head.*) Lift him up. Throw him in the carrion pit. He has no one that knows him.

They carry him off.

4

Mother Courage sings "The Song of the Great Capitulation."

Outside an officer's tent. MOTHER COURAGE *waits. A* CLERK *looks out of the tent.*

CLERK. I know you. You had a Protestant paymaster with you, he was hiding out with you. Better make no complaint.

MOTHER COURAGE. But I'm innocent and if I give up it'll look as if I have a bad conscience. They cut everything in my wagon to ribbons with their sabers and then claimed a fine of five thalers for nothing and less than nothing.

CLERK. For your own good, keep your trap shut. We haven't many canteens, so we let you stay in business, especially if you've a bad conscience and have to pay a fine now and then.

MOTHER COURAGE. I'm going to file a complaint.

CLERK. As you wish. Wait here till the Captain has time. (*He withdraws into the tent.*)

A YOUNG SOLDIER *comes storming in.*

YOUNG SOLDIER. Screw the Captain! Where *is* the son of a bitch? Swiping my reward, spending it on brandy for his whores, I'll rip his belly open!

AN OLDER SOLDIER (*coming after him*). Shut your hole, you'll wind up in the stocks.

YOUNG SOLDIER. Come out, you thief, I'll make lamb chops out of you! I was the only one in the squad who swam the river and *he* grabs my money, I can't even buy myself a beer. Come on out! And let me slice you up!

OLDER SOLDIER. Holy Christ, he'll destroy himself!

YOUNG SOLDIER. Let me go or I'll run *you* down too. This has got to be settled!

OLDER SOLDIER. Saved the Colonel's horse and didn't get the reward. He's young, he hasn't been at it long.

MOTHER COURAGE. Let him go. He doesn't have to be chained, he's not a dog. Very reasonable to want a reward. Why else should he want to shine?

YOUNG SOLDIER. He's in there pouring it down! You're all nice. I've done something special, I want the reward!

MOTHER COURAGE. Young man, don't scream at *me,* I have my own troubles. And go easy with your voice, you may need it when the Captain comes. The Captain'll come and you'll be hoarse and can't make a sound, so he'll have to deny himself the pleasure of sticking you in the stocks till you pass out. The screamers don't scream long, only half an hour, after which they have to be sung to sleep, they're all in.

YOUNG SOLDIER. I'm not all in, and sleep's out of the question. I'm hungry. They're making their bread out of acorns and hempseed, and not even much of that. He's whoring on my money, and I'm hungry. I'll murder him!

MOTHER COURAGE. I understand: you're hungry. Last year your Commander ordered you people out of the streets and into the fields. So the crops got trampled down. I could have got ten guilders for boots, if anyone'd had ten guilders, and if I'd had any boots. He didn't expect to be around this year, but he is, and there's famine. I understand: you're angry.

YOUNG SOLDIER. It's no use your talking. I won't stand for injustice!

MOTHER COURAGE. You're quite right. But how long? How long won't you stand for injustice? One hour? Or two? You haven't asked yourself that, have you? And yet it's the main thing. It's pure misery to sit in the stocks. Especially if you leave it till then to decide you do stand for injustice.

YOUNG SOLDIER. I don't know why I listen to you. Screw that Captain! Where is he?

MOTHER COURAGE. You listen because you know I'm right. Your rage has calmed down already. It was a short one and you'd need a long one. But where would you find it?

YOUNG SOLDIER. Are you trying to say it's not right to ask for the money?

MOTHER COURAGE. Just the opposite. I only say, your rage won't last. You'll get nowhere with it, it's a pity. If your rage was a long one, I'd urge you on. Slice him up, I'd advise you. But what's the use if you *don't* slice him up because you can feel

your tail between your legs? You stand
there and the Captain lets you have it.
OLDER SOLDIER. You're quite right, he's crazy.
YOUNG SOLDIER. All right, we'll see whether I
slice him up or not. (*He draws his sword.*)
When he comes out, I slice him up!
CLERK (*looking out*). The Captain will be out
in a minute. (*In the tone of military command.*) Be seated!

The YOUNG SOLDIER *sits.*

MOTHER COURAGE. And he *is* seated. What
did I tell you? You are seated. They know
us through and through. They know how
they must work it. Be seated! And we sit.
And in sitting there's no revolt. Better not
stand up again—not the way you did before
—don't stand up again. And don't be em-
barassed in front of me, I'm no better, not
a scrap. They've drawn our teeth, haven't
they? If we say boo, it's bad for business.
Let me tell you about the great capitulation.

She sings "The Song of the Great Capitulation."

Long ago when I was a green beginner
I believed I was a special case.

(None of your ordinary run of the mill
girls, with my looks and my talent, and my
love of the higher things in life!)

And if I picked a hair out of my dinner
I would put the cook right in his place.

(All or nothing. Anyhow, never the second
best, I am the master of my Fate. I'll take
no orders from no one.)

Then a little bird whispered in my ear:
"That's all very well, but wait a year
And you will join the big brass band
And with your trumpet in your hand
You'll march in lockstep with the rest.
Then one day, look! The battalions
wheel!
The whole thing swings from east to
west!

And falling on your knees, you'll squeal:
The Lord God, He knows best!
(But don't give *me* that!)"

And a month or two before that year was
over
I had learned to drink their cup of tea.

(Two children round your neck, and the
price of bread and what all!)

And the day soon came when I was to
discover
They had me just where they wanted
me.

(You must get in good with people. If you
scratch my back, I'll scratch yours. Don't
stick your neck out.)

And that little bird whispered in my ear:
"You didn't even take a year!
And you have joined the big brass band
And with your trumpet in your hand
You marched in lockstep with the rest.
But one day, look! The battalions
wheeled!
The whole thing swung from east to
west!
And falling on your knees, you squealed:
The Lord God, He knows best!
(But don't give *me* that!)"

Yes, our hopes are high, our plans
colossal!
And we hitch our wagon to a star!

(Where there's a will there's a way. One
can't hold a good man down.)

We can move mountains, says St. Paul
the great Apostle
And yet: how heavy one cigar!

(We must cut our coat according to our
cloth.)

For that little bird whispers in your ear:
"That's all very well but wait a year
And we will join the big brass band
And with our trumpet in our hand

We march in lockstep with the rest.
But one day, look! The battalions wheel!
The whole thing swings from east to
west!
And falling on our knees, we squeal:
The Lord God, He knows best!
(But don't give *me* that!)"

And so I think you should stay here with
your sword drawn if you're set on it and
your anger is big enough. You have good
cause, I admit. But if your anger is a short
one, you'd better go.

YOUNG SOLDIER. Kiss my ass. (*He stumbles
off, the other* SOLDIER *following him.*)

CLERK (*sticking his head out*). The Captain
is ready now. You can file your complaint.

MOTHER COURAGE. I've thought better of it.
I'm not complaining. (*Exit.*)

The CLERK *looks after her, shaking his
head.*

5

*Two years have passed. The war covers
wider and wider territory. Forever on
the move, the little wagon crosses Poland, Moravia, Bavaria, Italy, and again
Bavaria. 1631. Tilly's victory at Magde-
burg costs Mother Courage four officers'
shirts.*

*The wagon stands in a war-ravaged vil-
lage. Faint military music from the distance. Two* SOLDIERS *are being served at
a counter by* KATTRIN *and* MOTHER
COURAGE. *One of them has a woman's
fur coat about his shoulders.*

MOTHER COURAGE. What, you can't pay? No
money, no brandy! They can play victory
marches, they should pay their men.

FIRST SOLDIER. I want my brandy! I arrived
too late for plunder. The Chief allowed one
hour to plunder the town, it's a swindle.

He's not inhuman, he says. So I suppose
they bought him off.

CHAPLAIN (*staggering in*). There are more in
the farmhouse. A family of peasants. Help
me someone. I need linen!

The second SOLDIER *goes with him.*
KATTRIN *is getting very excited. She
tries to get her mother to bring linen
out.*

MOTHER COURAGE. I have none. I sold all my
bandages to the regiment. I'm not tearing
up my officers' shirts for these people.

CHAPLAIN (*calling over his shoulder*). I said
I need linen!

MOTHER COURAGE (*stopping* KATTRIN *from
entering the wagon*). Not a thing! They
can't pay, and why? They have nothing
and they pay nothing!

CHAPLAIN (*to a* WOMAN *he is carrying in*).
Why did you stay out there in the line of
fire?

WOMAN. Our farm—

MOTHER COURAGE. Think they'd ever let go
of *anything*? And now I'm supposed to pay.
Well, I won't!

FIRST SOLDIER. They're Protestants, why
should they be Protestants?

MOTHER COURAGE. Protestant, Catholic, what
do *they* care? Their farm's gone, that's
what.

SECOND SOLDIER. They're not Protestants anyway, they're Catholics.

FIRST SOLDIER. In a bombardment we can't
pick and choose.

A PEASANT (*brought on by the* CHAPLAIN).
My arm's gone.

CHAPLAIN. Where's that linen?

All look at MOTHER COURAGE, *who does
not budge.*

MOTHER COURAGE. I can't give you any. With
all I have to pay out—taxes, duties, bribes.
. . . (KATTRIN *takes up a board and threatens her mother with it, emitting gurgling
sounds.*) Are you out of your mind? Put
that board down or I'll let you have one,
you lunatic! I'm giving nothing, I don't

dare, I have myself to think of. (*The* CHAPLAIN *lifts her bodily off the steps of the wagon and sets her down on the ground. He takes out shirts from the wagon and tears them in strips.*) My shirts, my officers' shirts!

From the house comes the cry of a child in pain.

PEASANT. The child's still in there.

KATTRIN *runs in.*

CHAPLAIN (*to the* WOMAN). Stay where you are. She's getting it for you.

MOTHER COURAGE. Hold her back, the roof may fall in!

CHAPLAIN. I'm not going back in there!

MOTHER COURAGE (*pulled in both directions*). Go easy on my expensive linen.

The SECOND SOLDIER *holds her back.* KATTRIN *brings a baby out of the ruins.*

MOTHER COURAGE. Another baby to drag around, you must be pleased with yourself. Give it to its mother this minute! Or do I have to fight you again for hours till I get it from you? Are you deaf? (*To the* SECOND SOLDIER.) Don't stand about gawking, go back there and tell 'em to stop that music, I can see their victory without it. I have nothing but losses from your victory!

CHAPLAIN (*bandaging*). The blood's coming through.

KATTRIN *is rocking the child and half humming a lullaby.*

MOTHER COURAGE. There she sits, happy as a lark in all this misery. Give the baby back, the mother is coming to! (*She sees the* FIRST SOLDIER. *He had been handling the drinks, and is now trying to make off with the bottle.*) God's truth! You beast! You want another victory, do you? Then pay for it!

FIRST SOLDIER. I have nothing.

MOTHER COURAGE (*snatching the fur coat back*). Then leave this coat, it's stolen goods anyhow.

CHAPLAIN. There's still someone in there.

6

Before the city of Ingolstadt in Bavaria Mother Courage is present at the funeral of the fallen commander, Tilly. Conversations take place about war heroes and the duration of the war. The Chaplain complains that his talents are lying fallow and Kattrin gets the red boots. The year is 1632.

The inside of a canteen tent. The inner side of a counter at the rear. Rain. In the distance, drums and funeral music. The CHAPLAIN *and the regimental* CLERK *are playing draughts.* MOTHER COURAGE *and her daughter are taking an inventory.*

CHAPLAIN. The funeral procession is just starting out.

MOTHER COURAGE. Pity about the Chief— twenty-two pairs of socks—getting killed that way. They say it was an accident. There was a fog over the fields that morning, and the fog was to blame. The Chief called up another regiment, told 'em to fight to the death, rode back again, missed his way in the fog, went forward instead of back, and ran smack into a bullet in the thick of battle—only four lanterns left. (*A whistle from the rear. She goes to the counter. To a* SOLDIER.) It's a disgrace the way you're all skipping your Commander's funeral! (*She pours a drink.*)

CLERK. They shouldn't have handed the money out before the funeral. Now the men are all getting drunk instead of going to it.

CHAPLAIN (*to the* CLERK). Don't you have to be there?

CLERK. I stayed away because of the rain.

MOTHER COURAGE. It's different for you, the

rain might spoil your uniform. I hear they wanted to ring the bells for his funeral, which is natural, but it came out that the churches had been shot up by his orders, so the poor Commander won't be hearing any bells when they lower him in his grave. Instead, they'll fire off three shots so the occasion won't be *too* sober—sixteen leather belts.

A VOICE FROM THE COUNTER. Service! One brandy!

MOTHER COURAGE. Your money first. No, you *can't* come inside the tent, not with those boots on. You can drink outside, rain or no rain. I only let officers in here. (*To the* CLERK.) The Chief had his troubles lately, I hear. There was unrest in the Second Regiment because he didn't pay 'em. He said it was a war of religion and they must fight it free of charge.

Funeral march. All look toward the rear.

CHAPLAIN. Now they're filing past the body.

MOTHER COURAGE. I feel sorry for a Commander or an Emperor like that—when he might have had something special in mind, something they'd talk about in times to come, something they'd raise a statue to him for. The conquest of the world now, *that's* a goal for a Commander, he wouldn't know any better. . . . Lord, worms have got into the biscuits. . . . In short, he works his hands to the bone and then it's all spoiled by the common riffraff that only wants a jug of beer or a bit of company, not the higher things in life. The finest plans have always been spoiled by the littleness of them that should carry them out. Even Emperors can't do it all by themselves. They count on support from their soldiers and the people round about. Am I right?

CHAPLAIN (*laughing*). You're right, Mother Courage, till you come to the soldiers. They do what they can. Those fellows outside, for example, drinking their brandy in the rain, I'd trust 'em to fight a hundred years, one war after another, two at a time if necessary. And I wasn't trained as a commander.

MOTHER COURAGE. . . . Seventeen leather belts. . . . Then you don't think the war might end?

CHAPLAIN. Because a commander's dead? Don't be childish, they grow on trees. There are always heroes.

MOTHER COURAGE. Well, I wasn't asking for the sake of argument. I was wondering if I should buy up a lot of supplies. They happen to be cheap just now. But if the war ended, I might just as well throw them away.

CHAPLAIN. I realize you are serious, Mother Courage. Well, there've always been people going around saying some day the war will end. I say, you can't be sure the war will *ever* end. Of course it may have to pause occasionally—for breath, as it were—it can even meet with an accident—nothing on this earth is perfect—a war of which we could say it left nothing to be desired will probably never exist. A war can come to a sudden halt—from unforeseen causes—you can't think of everything—a little oversight, and the war's in the hole, and someone's got to pull it out again! The someone is the Emperor or the King or the Pope. They're such friends in need, the war has really nothing to worry about, it can look forward to a prosperous future.

A SOLDIER (*singing at the counter*).

One schnapps, mine host, make haste!
We have no time to waste:
We must be shooting, shooting, shooting
Our Emperor's foes uprooting!

Make it a double. This is a holiday.

MOTHER COURAGE. If I was sure you're right . . .

CHAPLAIN. Think it out for yourself: how *could* the war end?

SOLDIER (*off-stage*).

Two breasts, mine host, make haste!
We have no time to waste:
We must be hating, hating, hating
We cannot keep our Emperor waiting!

CLERK (*suddenly*). What about peace? Yes,

peace. I'm from Bohemia. I'd like to get home once in a while.

CHAPLAIN. Oh, you would, would you? Dear old peace! What happens to the hole when the cheese is gone?

SOLDIER (*off-stage*).

> Your blessing, priest, make haste!
> For we have no time to waste:
> We must be dying, dying, dying
> Our Emperor's greatness glorifying!

CLERK. In the long run you can't live without peace!

CHAPLAIN. Well, I'd say there's peace even in war, war has its islands of peace. For war satisfies *all* needs, even those of peace, yes, they're provided for, or the war couldn't keep going. In war—as in the very thick of peace—you can take a crap, and between one battle and the next there's always a beer, and even on the march you can snatch a nap—on your elbow maybe, in a gutter—something can always be managed. Of course you can't play cards during an attack, but neither can you while ploughing the fields in peace time: it's when the victory's won that there are possibilities. You have your leg shot off, and at first you raise quite an outcry as if it *was* something, but soon you calm down or take a swig of brandy, and you end up hopping about, and the war is none the worse for your little misadventure. And can't you be fruitful and multiply in the thick of slaughter—behind a barn or somewhere? Nothing can keep you from it very long in any event. And so the war has your offspring and can carry on. War is like love, it always finds a way. Why *should* it end?

KATTRIN *has stopped working. She stares at the* CHAPLAIN.

MOTHER COURAGE. Then I *will* buy those supplies, I'll rely on you. (KATTRIN *suddenly bangs a basket of glasses down on the ground and runs out.* MOTHER COURAGE *laughs.*) Kattrin! Lord, Kattrin's still going to wait for peace. I promised her she'll get a husband—when it's peace. (*She runs after her.*)

CLERK (*standing up*). I win. You were talking. You pay.

MOTHER COURAGE (*returning with* KATTRIN). Be sensible, the war'll go on a bit longer, and we'll make a bit more money, then peace'll be all the nicer. Now you go into the town, it's not ten minutes walk, and bring the things from the Golden Lion, just the more expensive ones, we can get the rest later in the wagon. It's all arranged, the clerk will go with you, most of the soldiers are at the Commander's funeral, nothing can happen to you. Do a good job, don't lose anything, Kattrin, think of your trousseau!

KATTRIN *ties a cloth around her head and leaves with the* CLERK.

CHAPLAIN. You don't mind her going with the clerk?

MOTHER COURAGE. She's not so pretty anyone would want to ruin her.

CHAPLAIN. The way you run your business and always come through is highly commendable, Mother Courage—I see how you got your name.

MOTHER COURAGE. The poor need courage. Why? They're lost. That they even get up in the morning is something—in *their* plight. Or that they plough a field—in war time. Even their bringing children into the world shows they have courage, for they have no prospects. They have to hang each other one by one and slaughter each other in the lump, so if they want to look each other in the face once in a while, well, it takes courage. That they put up with an Emperor and a Pope, that takes an unnatural amount of courage, for *they* cost you your life. (*She sits, takes a small pipe from her pocket and smokes it.*) You might chop me a bit of firewood.

CHAPLAIN (*reluctantly taking his coat off and preparing to chop wood*). Properly speaking, I'm a pastor of souls, not a woodcutter.

MOTHER COURAGE. But I don't have a soul. And I do need wood.

CHAPLAIN. What's that little pipe you've got there?

MOTHER COURAGE. Just a pipe.

CHAPLAIN. I think it's a very particular pipe.

MOTHER COURAGE. Oh?

CHAPLAIN. The cook's pipe in fact. The cook from the Oxenstierna Regiment.

MOTHER COURAGE. If you know, why beat about the bush?

CHAPLAIN. Because I don't know if you've been *aware* that's what you've been smoking. It was possible you just rummaged among your belongings and your fingers just lit on a pipe and you just took it. In pure absent-mindedness.

MOTHER COURAGE. How do you know that's not it?

CHAPLAIN. It isn't. You *are* aware of it. (*He brings the ax down on the block with a crash.*)

MOTHER COURAGE. What if I was?

CHAPLAIN. I must give you a warning, Mother Courage, it's my duty. You are unlikely to see the gentleman again but that's no pity, you're in luck. Mother Courage, he did not impress me as trustworthy. On the contrary.

MOTHER COURAGE. Really? He was such a nice man.

CHAPLAIN. Well! So that's what you call a nice man. I do not. (*The ax falls again.*) Far be it from me to wish him ill, but I cannot—cannot—describe him as nice. No, no, he's a Don Juan, a cunning Don Juan. Just look at that pipe if you don't believe me. You must admit it tells all.

MOTHER COURAGE. I see nothing special in it. It's been used, of course.

CHAPLAIN. It's bitten halfway through! He's a man of great violence! It is the pipe of a man of great violence, you can see *that* if you've any judgment left! (*He deals the block a tremendous blow.*)

MOTHER COURAGE. Don't bite my chopping block halfway through!

CHAPLAIN. I told you I had no training as a woodcutter. The care of souls was my field. Around here my gifts and capabilities are grossly misused. In physical labor my God-given talents find no—um—adequate expression—which is a sin. You

haven't heard me preach. Why, I can put such spirit into a regiment with a single sermon that the enemy's a mere flock of sheep to them and their own lives no more than smelly old shoes to be thrown away at the thought of final victory! God has given me the gift of tongues. I can preach you out of your senses!

MOTHER COURAGE. I need my senses. What would I do without them?

CHAPLAIN. Mother Courage, I have often thought that—under a veil of plain speech—you conceal a heart. You are human, you need warmth.

MOTHER COURAGE. The best way of warming this tent is to chop plenty of firewood.

CHAPLAIN. You're changing the subject. Seriously, my dear Courage, I sometimes ask myself how it would be if our relationship should be somewhat more firmly cemented. I mean, now the wild wind of war has whirled us so strangely together.

MOTHER COURAGE. The cement's pretty firm already. I cook your meals. And you lend a hand—at chopping firewood, for instance.

CHAPLAIN (*going over to her, gesturing with the ax*). You know what I mean by a close relationship. It has nothing to do with eating and woodcutting and such base necessities. Let your heart speak!

MOTHER COURAGE. Don't come at me like that with your ax, that'd be *too* close a relationship!

CHAPLAIN. This is no laughing matter, I am in earnest. I've thought it all over.

MOTHER COURAGE. Dear Chaplain, be a sensible fellow. I like you, and I don't want to heap coals of fire on your head. All I want is to bring me and my children through in that wagon. It isn't just mine, the wagon, and anyway I've no mind to start any adventures. At the moment I'm taking quite a risk buying these things when the Commander's fallen and there's all this talk of peace. Where would you go, if I was ruined? See? You don't even know. Now chop some firewood and it'll be warm of an evening, which is quite a lot in times like these. What was that? (*She stands up.* KATTRIN *enters, breathless, with a wound across the eye and forehead. She is dragging all sorts of articles, parcels, leather goods, a drum, etc.*) What is it, were you attacked? On the way back? She was attacked on the way back! I'll bet it was that soldier who got drunk on my liquor. I should never have let you go. Dump all that stuff! It's not bad, the wound is only a flesh wound. I'll bandage it for you, it'll all be healed up in a week. They're worse than animals. (*She bandages the wound.*)

CHAPLAIN. I reproach them with nothing. At home they never did these shameful things. The men who start the wars are responsible, they bring out the worst in people.

MOTHER COURAGE. Didn't the clerk walk you back home? That's because you're a respectable girl, he thought they'd leave you alone. The wound's not at all deep, it will never show. There: all bandaged up. Now, I've got something for you, rest easy. I've been keeping them secret. (*She digs* YVETTE's *red boots out of a bag.*) Well, what do you see? You always wanted them. Now you have them. (*She helps her to put the boots on.*) Put them on quick, before I change my mind. It will never show, though it wouldn't bother *me* if it did. The ones they like fare worst. They drag them around till they're finished. Those they don't care for they leave alone. I've seen so many girls, pretty as they come in the beginning, then all of a sudden they're so ugly they'd scare a wolf. They can't even go behind a tree on the street without having something to fear from it. They lead a frightful life. Like with trees: the tall, straight ones are cut down for roof timber, and the crooked ones can enjoy life. So this wound here is really a piece of luck. The boots have kept well. I gave them a good cleaning before I put them away.

> KATTRIN *leaves the boots and creeps into the wagon.*

CHAPLAIN (*when she's gone*). I hope she won't be disfigured?

MOTHER COURAGE. There'll be a scar. She needn't wait for peace now.

CHAPLAIN. She didn't let them get any of the stuff.

MOTHER COURAGE. Maybe I shouldn't have made such a point of it. If only I ever knew what went on inside her head. Once she stayed out all night, once in all the years. Afterward she seemed much the same, except that she worked harder. I could never get out of her what happened. I worried about it for quite a while. (*She picks up the things* KATTRIN *spilled and sorts them angrily.*) This is a war. A nice source of income, I must say!

Cannon shots.

CHAPLAIN. Now they're lowering the Commander into his grave! A historic moment.

MOTHER COURAGE. It's a historic moment to me when they hit my daughter over the eye. She's all but finished now, she'll never get a husband, and she's so mad about children! Even her dumbness comes from the war. A soldier stuck something in her mouth when she was little. I'll never see Swiss Cheese again, and where my Eilif is the Good Lord knows. Curse the war!

7

Mother Courage at the height of her business career.

A highway. The CHAPLAIN, MOTHER COURAGE, *and her daughter* KATTRIN *pull the wagon, and new wares are hanging from it.* MOTHER COURAGE *wears a necklace of silver coins.*

MOTHER COURAGE. I won't let you spoil my war for me. Destroys the weak, does it? Well, what does peace do for 'em huh? War feeds its people better.

She sings.

If war don't suit your disposition
When victory comes, you will be dead.
War is a business proposition:
But not with cheese, with steel instead!
 Christians, awake! Winter is gone!
 The snows depart! Dead men sleep on!
 Let all of you who still survive
 Get out of bed and look alive!

And staying in one place won't help either.
Those who stay at home are the first to go.

She sings.

 Too many seek a bed to sleep in:
 Each ditch is taken, and each cave
 And he who digs a hole to creep in
 Finds he has dug an early grave.
 And many a man spends many a
  minute
 In hurrying toward some resting place.
 You wonder, when at last he's in it
 Just why the fellow forced the pace.

The wagon proceeds.

8

1632. *In this same year Gustavus Adolphus fell in the battle of Lützen. The peace threatens Mother Courage with ruin. Her brave son performs one heroic deed too many and comes to a shameful end.*

A camp. A summer morning. In front of the wagon, an OLD WOMAN *and her son. The son is dragging a large bag of bedding.*

MOTHER COURAGE (*from inside the wagon*). Must you come at the crack of dawn?
YOUNG MAN. We've been walking all night, twenty miles it was, we have to be back today.
MOTHER COURAGE (*still inside*). What do I want with bed feathers? People don't even have houses.
YOUNG MAN. At least wait till you see 'em.
OLD WOMAN. Nothing doing here either, let's go.
YOUNG MAN. And let 'em sign away the roof over our heads for taxes? Maybe she'll pay three guilders if you throw in that bracelet. (*Bells start ringing.*) You hear, mother?
VOICES (*from the rear*). It's peace! The King of Sweden's been killed!

MOTHER COURAGE *sticks her head out of the wagon. She hasn't done her hair yet.*

MOTHER COURAGE. Bells! What are the bells for, middle of the week?
CHAPLAIN (*crawling out from under the wagon*). What's that they're shouting?
YOUNG MAN. It's peace.
CHAPLAIN. Peace!
MOTHER COURAGE. Don't tell me peace has broken out—when I've just gone and bought all these supplies!
CHAPLAIN (*calling, toward the rear*). Is it peace?
VOICE (*from a distance*). They say the war stopped three weeks ago. I've only just heard.
CHAPLAIN (*to* MOTHER COURAGE). Or why would they ring the bells?
VOICE. A great crowd of Lutherans have just arrived with wagons—they brought the news.
YOUNG MAN. It's peace, mother. (*The* OLD WOMAN *collapses.*) What's the matter?
MOTHER COURAGE (*back in the wagon*). Kattrin, it's peace! Put on your black dress, we're going to church, we owe it to Swiss Cheese! Can it be true?
YOUNG MAN. The people here say so too, the war's over. Can you stand up? (*The* OLD WOMAN *stands up, dazed.*) I'll get the harness shop going again now, I promise you. Everything'll be all right, father will get his bed back. . . . Can you walk? (*To the* CHAPLAIN.) She felt ill, it was the news. She didn't believe there'd ever be peace again. Father always said there would. We're going home. (*They leave.*)

MOTHER COURAGE (*off*). Give her some brandy.

CHAPLAIN. They've left already.

MOTHER COURAGE (*still off*). What's going on in the camp over there?

CHAPLAIN. They're all getting together. I think I'll go over. Shall I put my pastor's coat on again?

MOTHER COURAGE. Better get the exact news first, and not risk being taken for the Antichrist. I'm glad about the peace even though I'm ruined. At least I've got two of my children through the war. Now I'll see my Eilif again.

CHAPLAIN. And who may this be coming down from the camp? Well, if it isn't our Swedish Commander's cook!

COOK (*somewhat bedraggled, carrying a bundle*). Who's here? The chaplain!

CHAPLAIN. Mother Courage, a visitor!

MOTHER COURAGE *clambers out.*

COOK. Well, I promised I'd come over for a brief conversation as soon as I had time. I didn't forget your brandy, Mrs. Fierling.

MOTHER COURAGE. Jesus, the Commander's cook! After all these years! Where is Eilif, my eldest?

COOK. Isn't he here yet? He went on ahead yesterday, he was on his way over.

CHAPLAIN. I *will* put my pastor's coat on. I'll be back. (*He goes behind the wagon.*)

MOTHER COURAGE. He may be here any minute then. (*She calls toward the wagon.*) Kattrin, Eilif's coming! Bring a glass of brandy for the cook, Kattrin! (KATTRIN *doesn't come.*) Just pull your hair over it. Mr. Lamb is no stranger. (*She gets the brandy herself.*) She won't come out. Peace is nothing to her, it was too long coming. They hit her right over the eye. You can hardly see it now. But she thinks people stare at her.

COOK. Ah yes, war! (*He and* MOTHER COURAGE *sit.*)

MOTHER COURAGE. Cook, you come at a bad time: I'm ruined.

COOK. What? That's terrible!

MOTHER COURAGE. The peace has broken my neck. On the chaplain's advice I've gone and bought a lot of supplies. Now everybody's leaving and I'm holding the baby.

COOK. How could you listen to the chaplain? If I'd had time—but the Catholics were too quick for me—I'd have warned you against him. He's a windbag. Well, so now he's the big man round here!

MOTHER COURAGE. He's been doing the dishes for me and helping with the wagon.

COOK. With the wagon—him! And I'll bet he's told you a few of his jokes. He has a most unhealthy attitude to women. I tried to influence him but it was no good. He isn't sound.

MOTHER COURAGE. Are you sound?

COOK. If I'm nothing else, I'm sound. Your health!

MOTHER COURAGE. Sound! Only one person around here was ever sound, and I never had to slave as I did then. He sold the blankets off the children's beds in the spring, and he called my harmonica unchristian. You aren't recommending yourself if you *admit* you're sound.

COOK. You fight tooth and nail, don't you? I like that.

MOTHER COURAGE. Don't tell me you've been dreaming of my teeth and nails.

COOK. Well, here we sit, while the bells of peace do ring, and you pouring your famous brandy as only you know how!

MOTHER COURAGE. I don't think much of the bells of peace at the moment. I don't see how they can hand out all this pay that's in arrears. And then where shall I be with my famous brandy? Have you all been paid?

COOK (*hesitating*). Not exactly. That's why we disbanded. In the circumstances, I thought, why stay? For the time being, I'll look up a couple of friends. So here I sit—with you.

MOTHER COURAGE. In other words, you're broke.

COOK (*annoyed by the bells*). It's about time they stopped that racket! I'd like to set myself up in some business. I'm fed up with being their cook. I'm supposed to make do with tree roots and shoe leather, and then they throw my hot soup in my face! Being a cook nowadays is a dog's life. I'd sooner be a soldier, but of course, it's peace now. (*As the* CHAPLAIN *turns up, wearing his old coat.*) We'll talk it over later.

CHAPLAIN. The coat's pretty good. Just a few moth holes.

COOK. I don't know why you take the trouble. You won't find another pulpit. Who could you incite now to earn an honest living or risk his life for a cause? Besides, I have a bone to pick with you.

CHAPLAIN. Have you?

COOK. I have. You advised a lady to buy superfluous goods on the pretext that the war would never end.

CHAPLAIN (*hotly*). I'd like to know what business it is of yours?

COOK. It's unprincipled behavior! How can you give unwanted advice? And interfere with the conduct of other people's business?

CHAPLAIN. Who's interfering now, I'd like to know? (*To* MOTHER COURAGE.) I had no idea you were such a close friend of this gentleman and had to account to *him* for everything.

MOTHER COURAGE. Now don't get excited. The cook's giving his personal opinion. You can't deny your war was a flop.

CHAPLAIN. You have no respect for peace, Courage. You're a hyena of the battlefield!

MOTHER COURAGE. A what?

COOK. Who insults my girl friend insults me!

CHAPLAIN. I am *not* speaking to you, your intentions are only too transparent! (*To* MOTHER COURAGE.) But when I see *you* take peace between finger and thumb like a snotty old hanky, my humanity rebels! It shows that you want war, not peace, for what you get out of it. But don't forget the proverb: he who sups with the devil must use a long spoon!

MOTHER COURAGE. Remember what one fox said to another that was caught in a trap? "If you stay there, you're just asking for trouble!" There isn't much love lost between me and the war. And when it comes to calling me a hyena, you and I part company.

CHAPLAIN. Then why all this grumbling about the peace just as everyone's heaving a sigh of relief? Is it for the junk in your wagon?

MOTHER COURAGE. My goods are not junk. I live off them. *You've* been living off them.

CHAPLAIN. You live off war. Exactly.

COOK (*to the* CHAPLAIN). As a grown man, you should know better than to go around advising people. (*To* MOTHER COURAGE.) Now, in your situation you'd be smart to get rid of certain goods at once—before the prices sink to nothing. Get ready and get going, there isn't a moment to lose!

MOTHER COURAGE. That's sensible advice, I think I'll take it.

CHAPLAIN. Because the cook says so.

MOTHER COURAGE. Why didn't *you* say so? He's right, I must get to the market. (*She climbs into the wagon.*)

COOK. One up for me, Chaplain. You have no presence of mind. You should have said, "I gave you advice? Why, I was just talking politics!" And you shouldn't take me on as a rival. Cockfights are not becoming to your cloth.

CHAPLAIN. If you don't shut your trap, I'll murder you, cloth or no cloth!

COOK (*taking his boots off and unwinding the wrappings on his feet*). If you hadn't degenerated into a godless tramp, you could easily get yourself a parsonage, now its peace. Cooks won't be needed, there's nothing to cook, but there's still plenty to believe, and people will go right on believing it.

CHAPLAIN. Mr. Lamb, please don't drive me out! Since I became a tramp, I'm a somewhat better man. I couldn't preach to 'em any more.

YVETTE POTTIER *enters, decked out in black, with a stick. She is much older, fatter, and heavily powdered. Behind her, a* SERVANT.

YVETTE. Hullo, everybody! Is this Mother Courage's establishment?

CHAPLAIN. Quite right. And with whom have we the pleasure?

YVETTE. I am Madame Colonel Starhemberg, good people. Where's Mother Courage?

CHAPLAIN (*calling to the wagon*). Madame Colonel Starhemberg wants to speak to you!

MOTHER COURAGE (*from inside*). Coming!

YVETTE (*calling*). It's Yvette!

MOTHER COURAGE (*inside*). Yvette!

YVETTE. Just to see how you're getting on! (*As the* COOK *turns around in horror.*) Peter!

COOK. Yvette!

YVETTE. Of all things! How did *you* get here?

COOK. On a cart.

CHAPLAIN. Well! You know each other? Intimately?

YVETTE. I'll say. (*Scrutinizing the* COOK.) You're fat.

COOK. For that matter, *you're* no beanpole.

YVETTE. Anyway, it's lucky we've met, tramp. Now I can tell you what I think of you.

CHAPLAIN. Do so, tell him all, but wait till Mother Courage comes out.

COOK. Now don't make a scene . . .

MOTHER COURAGE (*coming out, laden with goods*). Yvette! (*They embrace.*) But why are you in mourning?

YVETTE. Doesn't it suit me? My husband, the colonel, died several years ago.

MOTHER COURAGE. The old fellow that nearly bought my wagon?

YVETTE. His elder brother.

MOTHER COURAGE. So you're not doing badly. Good to see one person who got somewhere in the war.

YVETTE. I've had my ups and downs.

MOTHER COURAGE. Don't let's speak ill of colonels. They make money like hay.

CHAPLAIN (*to the* COOK). If I were you, I'd put my shoes on again. (*To* YVETTE.) You promised to give us your opinion of this gentleman.

COOK. Now, Yvette, don't make a stink!

MOTHER COURAGE. He's a friend of mine, Yvette.

YVETTE. He's—Peter Piper, that's who.

MOTHER COURAGE. What!

COOK. Cut the nicknames. My name's Lamb.

MOTHER COURAGE (*laughing*). Peter Piper? Who turned the women's heads? And I've been keeping your pipe for you.

CHAPLAIN. And smoking it.

YVETTE. Lucky I can warn you against him.

He's a bad lot. You won't find worse on the whole coast of Flanders. He got more girls in trouble than . . .

COOK. That's a long time ago, it isn't true any more.

YVETTE. Stand up when you talk to a lady! Oh, how I loved that man; and all the time he was having a little bowlegged brunette. He got *her* into trouble too, of course.

COOK. I seem to have brought *you* luck!

YVETTE. Shut your trap, you hoary ruin! And you take care, Mother Courage, this type is still dangerous even in decay.

MOTHER COURAGE (*to* YVETTE). Come with me, I must get rid of this stuff before the prices fall.

YVETTE (*concentrating on the* COOK). Miserable cur!

MOTHER COURAGE. Maybe you can help me at army headquarters, you have contacts.

YVETTE. Seducer!

MOTHER COURAGE (*shouting into the wagon*). Kattrin, church is all off, I'm going to market!

YVETTE. Whore hunter!

MOTHER COURAGE (*still to* KATTRIN). When Eilif comes, give him something to drink!

YVETTE. That a man like him should have been able to turn me from the straight and narrow! I have my own star to thank that I rose none the less to the heights! But I've put an end to your tricks, Peter Piper, and one day—in a better life than this—the Lord God will reward me! Come, Mother Courage! (*She leaves with* MOTHER COURAGE.)

CHAPLAIN. As our text this morning let us take the saying: the mills of God grind slowly. And you complain of my jokes!

COOK. I never have any luck. I'll be frank, I was hoping for a good hot dinner, I'm starving. And now they'll be talking about me, and she'll get a completely wrong picture. I think I should go before she comes back.

CHAPLAIN. I think so too.

COOK. Chaplain, peace makes me sick. Mankind must perish by fire and sword, we're born and bred in sin! Oh, how I wish I was roasting a great fat capon for the Commander—God knows where *he's* got to—with mustard sauce and those little yellow carrots . . .

CHAPLAIN. Red cabbage—with capon, red cabbage.

COOK. You're right. But he always wanted yellow carrots.

CHAPLAIN. He never understood a thing.

COOK. You always put plenty away.

CHAPLAIN. Under protest.

COOK. Anyway, you must admit, those were the days.

CHAPLAIN. Yes, that I might admit.

COOK. Now you've called her a hyena, there's not much future for you here either. What are you staring at?

CHAPLAIN. It's Eilif!

Followed by two soldiers with halberds, EILIF *enters. His hands are fettered. He is white as chalk.*

CHAPLAIN. What's happened to you?

EILIF. Where's mother?

CHAPLAIN. Gone to town.

EILIF. They said she was here. I was allowed a last visit.

COOK (*to the* SOLDIERS). Where are you taking him?

A SOLDIER. For a ride.

The other SOLDIER *makes the gesture of throat cutting.*

CHAPLAIN. What has he done?

SOLDIER. He broke in on a peasant. The wife is dead.

CHAPLAIN. Eilif, how could you?

EILIF. It's no different. It's what I did before.

COOK. That was in war time.

EILIF. Shut your hole. Can I sit down till she comes?

SOLDIER. No.

CHAPLAIN. It's true. In war time they honored him for it. He sat at the Commander's right hand. It was bravery. Couldn't we speak with the military police?

SOLDIER. What's the use? Stealing cattle from a peasant, what's brave about that?

COOK. It was just stupid.

EILIF. If I'd been stupid, I'd have starved, smarty.

COOK. So you were bright and paid for it.

CHAPLAIN. At least we must bring Kattrin out.

EILIF. Let her alone. Just give me some brandy.

SOLDIER. No.

CHAPLAIN. What shall we tell your mother?

EILIF. Tell her it was no different. Tell her it was the same. Oh, tell her nothing.

The SOLDIERS *take him away.*

CHAPLAIN. I'll come with you, I'll . . .

EILIF. I don't need a priest!

CHAPLAIN. You don't know—yet. (*He follows him.*)

COOK (*calling after him*). I'll have to tell her, she'll want to see him!

CHAPLAIN. Better tell her nothing. Or maybe just that he was here, and he'll return, maybe tomorrow. Meantime I'll be back and can break the news. (*He leaves quickly.*)

The COOK *looks after him, shakes his head, then walks about uneasily. Finally, he approaches the wagon.*

COOK. Hello! Won't you come out? You want to sneak away from the peace, don't you? Well, so do I! I'm the Swedish Commander's cook, remember me? I was wondering if you've got anything to eat in there —while we're waiting for your mother. I wouldn't mind a bit of bacon—or even bread—just to pass the time. (*He looks in.*) She's got a blanket over her head.

The thunder of cannon.

MOTHER COURAGE *runs in, out of breath, still carrying the goods.*

MOTHER COURAGE. Cook, the peace is over, the war's on again, has been for three days! I didn't get rid of this stuff after all, thank God! There's a shooting match in the town already—with the Lutherans. We must get

away with the wagon. Pack, Kattrin!
What's on *your* mind? Something the matter?

COOK. Nothing.

MOTHER COURAGE. But there is. I see it in
your face.

COOK. Because the war's on again, most likely.
May it last till tomorrow evening, so I can
get something in my belly!

MOTHER COURAGE. You're not telling me.

COOK. Eilif was here. Only he had to go away
again.

MOTHER COURAGE. He was here? Then we'll
see him on the march. I'll be with our side
this time. How'd he look?

COOK. The same.

MOTHER COURAGE. He'll *never* change. And
the war couldn't get *him*, he's bright. Help
me with the packing. (*She starts it.*) Did
he tell you anything? Is he well in with
the Provost? Did he tell you about his
heroic deeds?

COOK (*darkly*). He's done one of them again.

MOTHER COURAGE. Tell me about it later.
(KATTRIN *appears.*) Kattrin, the peace is
over, we're on the move again. (*To the*
COOK.) What *is* the matter with you?

COOK. I'll enlist.

MOTHER COURAGE. A good idea. Where's the
Chaplain?

COOK. In the town. With Eilif.

MOTHER COURAGE. Stay with us a while,
Lamb, I need a bit of help.

COOK. This matter of Yvette . . .

MOTHER COURAGE. Hasn't done you any harm
at all in my eyes. Just the opposite. Where
there's smoke, there's fire, they say. You'll
come?

COOK. I may as well.

MOTHER COURAGE. The Twelfth Regiment's
under way. Into harness with you! Maybe
I'll see Eilif before the day is out, just
think! That's what I like best. Well, it
wasn't such a long peace, we can't grumble.
Let's go!

The COOK *and* KATTRIN *are in harness.*

MOTHER COURAGE *sings.*

From Ulm to Metz, past dome and
steeple
My wagon always moves ahead.
The war can care for all its people
So long as there is steel and lead.
Though steel and lead are stout sup-
porters
A war needs human beings too.
Report today to your headquarters!
If it's to last, this war needs you!

9

*The great war of religion has lasted six-
teen years and Germany has lost half its
inhabitants. Those who are spared in
battle die by plague. Over once blooming countryside hunger rages. Towns are
burned down. Wolves prowl the empty
streets. In the autumn of 1634 we find
Mother Courage in the Fichtelgebirge
not far from the road the Swedish army
is taking. Winter has come early and is
hard. Business is bad. Only begging remains. The cook receives a letter from
Utrecht and is sent packing.*

*In front of a half-ruined parsonage.
Early winter. A gray morning. Gusts of
wind.* MOTHER COURAGE *and the* COOK
at the wagon in shabby clothes.

COOK. There are no lights on. No one's up.

MOTHER COURAGE. But it's a parsonage. The
parson'll have to leave his feather bed and
ring the bells. Then he'll have some hot
soup.

COOK. Where'll he get it from? The whole
village is starving.

MOTHER COURAGE. The house is lived in.
There was a dog barking.

COOK. If the parson has anything, he'll hang
on to it.

MOTHER COURAGE. Maybe if we sang him
something . . .

COOK. I've had enough. (*Suddenly.*) I didn't
tell you, a letter came from Utrecht. My

mother's died of cholera, the inn is mine. There's the letter, if you don't believe me. I'll show it to you, though my aunt's railing about me and my ups and downs is none of your business.

MOTHER COURAGE (*reading*). Lamb, I'm tired of wandering, too. I feel like a butcher's dog taking meat to my customers and getting none myself. I've nothing more to sell and people have nothing to pay with. In Saxony someone tried to force a chestful of books on me in return for two eggs. And in Württemberg they would have let me have their plough for a bag of salt. Nothing grows any more, only thorn bushes. In Pomerania I hear the villagers have been eating their younger children. Nuns have been caught committing robbery.

COOK. The world's dying out.

MOTHER COURAGE. Sometimes I see myself driving through hell with this wagon and selling brimstone. And sometimes I'm driving through heaven handing our provisions to wandering souls! If only we could find a place where there's no shooting, me and my children—what's left of 'em—we might rest a while.

COOK. We could open this inn together. Think about it, Courage. *My* mind's made up. With or without you, I'm leaving for Utrecht. And today too.

MOTHER COURAGE. I must talk to Kattrin, it's a bit sudden, and I don't like to make my decisions in the cold on an empty stomach. (KATTRIN *emerges from the wagon.*) Kattrin, I've something to tell you. The cook and I want to go to Utrecht, he's been left an inn. You'd be able to stay put and get to know some people. Many a man'd be prepared to take on a girl with a position. Looks aren't everything. I like the idea. I get on well with the cook. I'll say this for him: he has a head for business. We'd be sure of our dinner, that would be all right, wouldn't it? You'd have your own bed, what do you think of *that*? In the long run, this is no life, on the road. You might be killed any time. You're eaten up with lice as it is. And we must decide now, because

otherwise we go north with the Swedes. They must be over there somewhere. (*She points left.*) I think we'll decide to go, Kattrin.

COOK. Anna, I must have a word with you alone.

MOTHER COURAGE. Go back inside, Kattrin.

KATTRIN *does so.*

COOK. I'm interrupting because there's a misunderstanding, Anna. I thought I wouldn't have to say it right out, but I see I must. If you're bringing *her,* it's all off. Do we understand each other?

KATTRIN *has her head out of the back of the wagon and is listening.*

MOTHER COURAGE. You mean I leave Kattrin behind?

COOK. What do you think? There's no room in the inn, it isn't one of those places with three counters. If the two of us look lively we can earn a living, but three's too many. Let Kattrin keep your wagon.

MOTHER COURAGE. I was thinking we might find her a husband in Utrecht.

COOK. Don't make me laugh. With that scar? And old as she is? And dumb?

MOTHER COURAGE. Not so loud!

COOK. Loud or soft, what is, is. That's another reason I can't have her in the inn. Customers don't like having something like that always before their eyes. You can't blame them.

MOTHER COURAGE. Shut up. I told you not to talk so loud.

COOK. There's a light in the parsonage, we can sing now!

MOTHER COURAGE. Cook, how could she pull the wagon by herself? The war frightens her. She can't bear it. She has terrible dreams. I hear her groan at night, especially after battles. What she sees in her dreams I don't know. She suffers from sheer pity. The other day I found her with a hedgehog that we'd run over.

COOK. The inn's too small. (*Calling.*) Worthy Sir, menials, and all within! We now pre-

sent the song of Solomon, Julius Caesar,
and other great souls who came to no good,
so you can see we're law-abiding folk too,
and have a hard time getting by, especially in winter.

*He sings "The Song of the Great Souls
of this Earth."*

King Solomon was very wise,
So what's his history?
He came to view this life with scorn,
Yes, he came to regret he ever had been
   born
Declaring: all is vanity.
King Solomon was very wise,
But long before the day was out
The consequence was clear, alas:
His wisdom 'twas that brought him to
   this pass.
A man is better off without.

For the virtues are dangerous in this world,
as our fine song tells. You're better off
without, you have a nice life, breakfast
included—some good hot soup maybe . . .
I'm an example of a man who's not had
any, and I'd like some. I'm a soldier, but
what good did my bravery do me in all
those battles? None at all. I might just as
well have wet my pants like a poltroon and
stayed at home. For why?

Old Julius Caesar, he was brave.
His fame shall never cease.
He sat like a god on an altar piece.
Yet they tore brave old Julius limb from
   valiant limb
And Brutus helped to slaughter him.
Old Julius was very brave
But long before the day was out
The consequence was clear, alas:
His bravery 'twas that brought him to
   this pass.
A man is better off without.

(*Under his breath.*) They don't even look
out. (*Aloud.*) Worthy Sir, menials, and
all within! You could say, no, courage isn't
the thing to fill a man's belly, try honesty,

that should be worth a dinner, at any rate
it must have *some* effect. Let's see.

You all know honest Socrates
Who always spoke the truth.
They owed him thanks for that, you'd
   think,
But what happened? Why, they put
   hemlock in his drink
And swore that he misled the youth.
How honest was this Socrates!
Yet long before the day was out
The consequence was clear, alas:
His honesty had brought him to this
   pass.
A man is better off without.

Yes, we're told to be unselfish and share
what we have, but what if we have nothing? And those who do share it don't have
an easy time either, for what's left when
you're through sharing? Unselfishness is a
very rare virtue—it doesn't pay.

Unselfish Martin could not bear
His fellow creatures' woes.
He met a poor man in the snows
And he gave this poor fellow half his
   cloak to wear:
So both of them fell down and froze.
His brothers' woes he could not bear,
So long before the day was out
The consequence was clear, alas:
Unselfishness had brought him to this
   pass.
A man is better off without.

That's how it is with us. We're law-abiding
folk, we keep to ourselves, don't steal,
don't kill, don't burn the place down. And
in this way we sink lower and lower and
the song proves true and there's no soup
going. And if we were different, if we were
thieves and killers, maybe we could eat our
fill! For virtues bring no reward, only
vices. Such is the world, need it be so?

God's ten commandments we have kept
And acted as we should.
It has not done us any good.

All you people who sit beside a roaring
  fire
O help us in our need so dire!
The ten commandments we have kept
And long before the day was out
The consequence was clear, alas:
Our godliness has brought us to this
  pass.
A man is better off without.

VOICE (*from above*). You there! Come up!
  There's some soup here for you!

MOTHER COURAGE. Lamb, I couldn't swallow
a thing. I don't say what you said is unreasonable, but was it your last word?
We've always understood each other.

COOK. Yes, Anna. Think it over.

MOTHER COURAGE. There's nothing to think
over. I'm not leaving her here.

COOK. You're going to be silly, but what can
I do? I'm not inhuman, it's just that the
inn's a small one. And now we must go
up, or there'll be nothing doing here too,
and we've been singing in the cold for
nothing.

MOTHER COURAGE. I'll fetch Kattrin.

COOK. Better stick something in your pocket
for her. If there are three of us, they'll
get a shock.

Exeunt.

KATTRIN *clambers out of the wagon with
a bundle. She makes sure they are both
gone. Then, on a wagon wheel, she lays
out a skirt of her mother's and a pair of
the cook's trousers side by side and easy
to see. She has just finished, and has
picked up her bundle, when* MOTHER
COURAGE *returns.*

MOTHER COURAGE (*with a plate of soup*).
Kattrin! Stay where you are, Kattrin!
Where do you think you're going with
that bundle? (*She examines the bundle.*)
She's packed her things. Were you listening? I told him there was nothing doing,
he can *have* Utrecht and his lousy inn,
what would we want with a lousy inn?
(*She sees the skirt and trousers.*) Oh,

you're a stupid girl, Kattrin, what if I'd
seen that and you gone? (*She takes hold
of* KATTRIN *who is trying to leave.*) And
don't think I've sent him packing on your
account. It was the wagon. You can't part
us, I'm too used to it, it was the wagon.
Now we're leaving and we'll put the cook's
things here where he'll find 'em, the
stupid man. (*She clambers up and throws
a couple of things down to go with the
trousers.*) There! He's fired. The last man
I'll take into *this* business! Now let's be
going, you and me. This winter'll pass, like
all the others. Get into harness, it looks like
snow.

*They harness themselves to the wagon,
turn it around, and start out. A gust
of wind. Enter the* COOK, *still chewing.
He sees his things.*

10

*During the whole of 1635 Mother
Courage and Kattrin pull the wagon
along the roads of central Germany in
the wake of the ever more tattered
armies.*

On the highway. MOTHER COURAGE *and*
KATTRIN *are pulling the wagon. They
come to a prosperous farmhouse. Someone inside is singing.*

VOICE.

In March a bush we planted
To make the garden gay.
In June we were enchanted:
A lovely rose was blooming
The balmy air perfuming!
Blest are they
Who have gardens gay!
In June we were enchanted.

When snow falls helter-skelter
And loudly blows the storm

Our farmhouse gives us shelter.
The winter's in a hurry
But we've no cause to worry.
We are warm
In the midst of the storm!
Our farmhouse gives us shelter.

MOTHER COURAGE *and* KATTRIN *have stopped to listen. Then they start out again.*

11

January, 1636. Catholic troops threaten the Protestant town of Halle. The stone begins to speak. Mother Courage loses her daughter and journeys onward alone. The war is not yet near its end.

The wagon, very far gone now, stands near a farmhouse with a straw roof. It is night. Out of the woods come a LIEUTENANT *and three* SOLDIERS *in full armor.*

LIEUTENANT. And there mustn't be a sound. If anyone yells, cut him down.

FIRST SOLDIER. But we'll have to knock—if we want a guide.

LIEUTENANT. Knocking's a natural noise, it's all right, could be a cow hitting the wall of the cowshed.

The SOLDIERS *knock at the farmhouse door. An* OLD PEASANT WOMAN *opens. A hand is clapped over her mouth. Two* SOLDIERS *enter.*

A MAN'S VOICE. What is it?

The SOLDIERS *bring out an* OLD PEASANT *and his son.*

LIEUTENANT (*pointing to the wagon on which* KATTRIN *has appeared*). There's one. (*A* SOLDIER *pulls her out.*) Is this everybody that lives here?

PEASANTS (*alternating*). That's our son. And that's a girl that can't talk. Her mother's in town buying up stocks because the shopkeepers are running away and selling cheap. They're canteen people.

LIEUTENANT. I'm warning you. Keep quiet. One sound and we'll crack you over the head with a pike. And I need someone to show us the path to the town. (*He points to the* YOUNG PEASANT.) You! Come here!

YOUNG PEASANT. I don't know any path!

SECOND SOLDIER (*grinning*). He don't know any path!

YOUNG PEASANT. I don't help Catholics.

LIEUTENANT (*to the* SECOND SOLDIER). Let him feel your pike in his side.

YOUNG PEASANT (*forced to his knees, the pike at his throat*). I'd rather die!

SECOND SOLDIER (*again mimicking*). He'd rather die!

FIRST SOLDIER. I know how to change his mind. (*He walks over to the cowshed.*) Two cows and a bull. Listen, you. If you aren't going to be reasonable, I'll saber your cattle.

YOUNG PEASANT. Not the cattle!

PEASANT WOMAN (*weeping*). Spare the cattle, Captain, or we'll starve!

LIEUTENANT. If he must be pigheaded!

FIRST SOLDIER. I think I'll start with the bull.

YOUNG PEASANT (*to the old one*). Do I have to? (*The older one nods.*) I'll do it.

PEASANT WOMAN. Thank you, thank you, Captain, for sparing us, for ever and ever, Amen.

The OLD MAN *stops her going on thanking him.*

FIRST SOLDIER. I knew the bull came first all right!

Led by the YOUNG PEASANT, *the* LIEUTENANT *and the* SOLDIERS *go on their way.*

OLD PEASANT. I wish we knew what it was. Nothing good, I suppose.

PEASANT WOMAN. Maybe they're just scouts. What are you doing?

OLD PEASANT (*setting a ladder against the roof and climbing up*). I'm seeing if they're alone. (*On the roof.*) Things are moving—all over. I can see armor. And cannon. There must be more than a regiment. God have mercy on the town and all within!

PEASANT WOMAN. Are there lights in the town?

OLD PEASANT. No, they're all asleep. (*He climbs down.*) There'll be an attack, and they'll all be slaughtered in their beds.

PEASANT WOMAN. The watchman'll give warning.

OLD PEASANT. They must have killed the watchman in the tower on the hill or he'd have sounded his horn before this.

PEASANT WOMAN. If there were more of us . . .

OLD PEASANT. But being that we're alone with that cripple . . .

PEASANT WOMAN. There's nothing we can do, is there?

OLD PEASANT. Nothing.

PEASANT WOMAN. We can't get down there. In the dark.

OLD PEASANT. The whole hillside's swarming with 'em.

PEASANT WOMAN. We could give a sign?

OLD PEASANT. And be cut down for it?

PEASANT WOMAN. No, there's nothing we can do. (*To* KATTRIN.) Pray, poor thing, pray! There's nothing we can do to stop this bloodshed, so even if you can't talk, at least pray! He hears, if no one else does. I'll help you. (*All kneel,* KATTRIN *behind.*) Our Father, which art in Heaven, hear our prayer, let not the town perish with all that lie therein asleep and fearing nothing.Wake them, that they rise and go to the walls and see the foe that comes with fire and sword in the night down the hill and across the fields. (*Back to* KATTRIN.) God protect our mother and make the watchman not sleep but wake ere it's too late. And save our son-in-law, too, O God, he's there with his four children, let them not perish, they're innocent, they know nothing—(*To* KATTRIN, *who groans.*)—one of them's not two years old, the eldest is seven. (KATTRIN *rises, troubled.*) Heavenly Father, hear us, only Thou canst help us or we die, for we are weak and have no sword nor nothing; we cannot trust our own strength but only Thine, O Lord; we are in Thy hands, our cattle, our farm, and the town too, we're all in Thy hands, and the foe is nigh unto the walls with all his power.

KATTRIN, *unperceived, has crept off to the wagon, has taken something out of it, put it under her apron, and has climbed up the ladder to the roof.*

Be mindful of the children in danger, especially the little ones, be mindful of the old folk who cannot move, and of all Christian souls, O Lord.

OLD PEASANT. And forgive us our trespasses as we forgive them that trespass against us. Amen.

Sitting on the roof, KATTRIN *takes a drum from under her apron and starts to beat it.*

PEASANT WOMAN. Heavens, what's she doing?

OLD PEASANT. She's out of her mind!

PEASANT WOMAN. Get her down, quick.

The OLD PEASANT *runs to the ladder but* KATTRIN *pulls it up on the roof.*

She'll get us in trouble.

OLD PEASANT. Stop it this minute, you silly cripple!

PEASANT WOMAN. The soldiers'll come!

OLD PEASANT (*looking for stones*). I'll stone you!

PEASANT WOMAN. Have you no pity, have you no heart? We have relations there too, four grandchildren, but there's nothing we can do. If they find us now, it's the end, they'll stab us to death!

KATTRIN *is staring into the far distance, toward the town. She goes on drumming.*

PEASANT WOMAN (*to the* PEASANT). I told you not to let that riffraff on your farm. What do *they* care if we lose our cattle?

LIEUTENANT (*running back with* SOLDIERS *and the* YOUNG PEASANT). I'll cut you all to bits!

PEASANT WOMAN. We're innocent, sir, there's nothing we can do. She did it, a stranger!

LIEUTENANT. Where's the ladder?

OLD PEASANT. On the roof.

LIEUTENANT (*calling*). Throw down the drum. I order you! (KATTRIN *goes on drumming.*) You're all in this, but you won't live to tell the tale.

OLD PEASANT. They've been cutting down fir trees around here. If we bring a tall enough trunk we can knock her off the roof . . .

FIRST SOLDIER (*to the* LIEUTENANT). I beg leave to make a suggestion. (*He whispers something to the* LIEUTENANT, *who nods.*) Listen, you! We have an idea—for your own good. Come down and go with us to the town. Show us your mother and we'll spare her.

KATTRIN *goes on drumming.*

LIEUTENANT (*pushing him away*). She doesn't trust you, no wonder with your face. (*He calls up to* KATTRIN:) Hey, you! Suppose I give you my word? I'm an officer, my word's my bond!

KATTRIN *drums harder.*

Nothing is sacred to her.

YOUNG PEASANT. Sir, it's not just because of her mother!

FIRST SOLDIER. This can't go on, they'll hear it in the town as sure as hell.

LIEUTENANT. We must make another noise with something. Louder than that drum. What can we make a noise with?

FIRST SOLDIER. But we musn't make a noise!

LIEUTENANT. A harmless noise, fool, a peace-time noise!

OLD PEASANT. I could start chopping wood.

LIEUTENANT. That's it! (*The* PEASANT *brings his ax and chops away.*) Chop! Chop harder! Chop for your life!

KATTRIN *has been listening, beating the drum less hard. Very upset, and peering around, she now goes on drumming.*

It's not enough. (*To the* FIRST SOLDIER.) You chop too!

OLD PEASANT. I've only one ax. (*He stops chopping.*)

LIEUTENANT. We must set fire to the farm. Smoke her out.

OLD PEASANT. That's no good, Captain. When they see fire from the town, they'll know everything.

During the drumming KATTRIN *has been listening again. Now she laughs.*

LIEUTENANT. She's laughing at us, that's too much, I'll have her guts if it's the last thing I do. Bring a musket!

Two SOLDIERS *off.* KATTRIN *goes on drumming.*

PEASANT WOMAN. I have it, Captain. That's their wagon over there, Captain. If we smash that, she'll stop. It's all they have, Captain.

LIEUTENANT (*to the* YOUNG PEASANT). Smash it! (*Calling.*) If you don't stop that noise, we'll smash your wagon!

The YOUNG PEASANT *deals the wagon a couple of feeble blows with a board.*

PEASANT WOMAN (*to* KATTRIN). Stop, you little beast!

KATTRIN *stares at the wagon and pauses. Noises of distress come out of her. But she goes on drumming.*

LIEUTENANT. Where are those sons of bitches with that gun?

FIRST SOLDIER. They can't have heard anything in the town or we'd hear their cannon.

LIEUTENANT (*calling*). They don't hear you. And now we're going to shoot you. I'll give you one more chance: throw down that drum!

YOUNG PEASANT (*dropping the board, screaming to* KATTRIN). Don't stop now! Or they're all done for. Go on, go on, go on . . .

The SOLDIER *knocks him down and beats him with his pike.* KATTRIN *starts crying but goes on drumming.*

PEASANT WOMAN. Not in the back, you're killing him!

The SOLDIERS *arrive with the musket.*

SECOND SOLDIER. The Colonel's foaming at the mouth. We'll be court-martialed.

LIEUTENANT. Set it up! Set it up! (*Calling while the musket is set up on forks.*) Once and for all: stop that drumming!

Still crying, KATTRIN *is drumming as hard as she can.*

Fire!

The SOLDIERS *fire.* KATTRIN *is hit. She gives the drum another feeble beat or two, then slowly collapses.*

LIEUTENANT. That's an end to the noise.

But the last beats of the drum are lost in the din of cannon from the town. Mingled with the thunder of cannon, alarm bells are heard in the distance.

FIRST SOLDIER. She made it.

12

Toward morning. The drums and pipes of troops on the march, receding. In front of the wagon MOTHER COURAGE *sits by* KATTRIN's *body. The* PEASANTS *of the last scene are standing near.*

PEASANTS. You must leave, woman. There's only one regiment to go. You can never get away by yourself.

MOTHER COURAGE. Maybe she's fallen asleep.

She sings.

Lullaby, baby, what's that in the hay?
The neighbor's kids cry but mine are gay.
The neighbor's kids are dressed in dirt:
Your silks are cut from an angel's skirt.
They are all starving: you have a pie.
If it's too stale, you need only cry.
Lullaby, baby, what's rustling there?
One lad fell in Poland. The other is—
where?

You shouldn't have told her about the children.

PEASANTS. If you hadn't gone off to the town to get your cut, maybe it wouldn't have happened.

MOTHER COURAGE. She's asleep now.

PEASANTS. She's not asleep, it's time you realized. She's gone. You must get away. There are wolves in these parts. And the bandits are worse.

MOTHER COURAGE. That's right. (*She goes and fetches a cloth from the wagon to cover up the body.*)

PEASANT WOMAN. Have you no one now? Someone you can go to?

MOTHER COURAGE. There's one. My Eilif.

PEASANT (*while* MOTHER COURAGE *covers the body*). Find him then. Leave *her* to us. We'll give her a proper burial. You needn't worry.

MOTHER COURAGE. Here's money for the expenses.

She pays the PEASANT. *The* PEASANT *and his son shake her hand and carry* KATTRIN *away.*

PEASANT WOMAN (*also taking her hand, and bowing, as she goes away*). Hurry!

MOTHER COURAGE (*harnessing herself to the wagon*). I hope I can pull the wagon by myself. Yes, I'll manage, there's not much in it now. I must get back into business.

Another regiment passes at the rear with pipe and drum.

MOTHER COURAGE *starts pulling the wagon.*

MOTHER COURAGE. Hey! Take me with you!

Soldiers are heard singing.

Dangers, surprises, devastations!
The war moves on, but will not quit.
And though it last three generations,
We shall get nothing out of it.
Starvation, filth, and cold enslave us.
The army robs us of our pay.

But God may yet come down and save
us:
His holy war won't end today.
    Christians, awake! Winter is gone!
    The snows depart! Dead men sleep on!
    Let all of you who still survive
    Get out of bed and look alive!

◆ *from* Theme and Form: Lorca's *Blood Wedding*

By RONALD GASKELL

The alertness of Lorca's dramatic imagination and the decisiveness of his rejection of the theatre of middle-class manners are apparent at least as early as 1930 in the brilliant little *Love of Don Perlimplin*. His finest work, however, is in the three rural tragedies, and of these *Blood Wedding*, if less deeply unified than *Yerma*, less compact than *The House of Bernarda Alba*, is at once the most original and the most impressive.

In summary the play could sound as banal as the newspaper account on which it was based. A girl elopes on her wedding day with a former lover; the husband pursues them, and the two men kill each other. The story has the picturesque sensationalism of a ballad, of the *Romancero Gitano*. But the strength of *Blood Wedding* springs less from the treatment of this story in terms of character and plot than from forces which the characters unconsciously embody. Lorca's achievement is to have invented a form, a pattern of speech and action, which reveals these forces.

In part the form is found in the restrictive code of Spanish village life. In the first scene of the play the suspicion that the Bride had a lover some years before is felt as ominous, and the intensity of the passion of the lovers in the forest springs from the Bride's recognition that she is in the grip of a force more savage than her own chastity. In the scene with the Mother at the end, again, it is this virgin pride that gives the speeches of the girl their vehemence. In keeping with this fierce insistence on virginity, and indeed an important reason for it, is the conception of marriage as an alliance between two families. This point is established firmly in the first act: implicitly by the subordination of the Bridegroom to his Mother and of the Bride to her Father—the economy of characters is typical of Lorca—explicitly by the formality of the scene in which the marriage is arranged. Such a mar-

riage, it is taken for granted, can never be broken, since infidelity would outrage not only honour but the institution of property which society has succeeded in consecrating. The strength of this convention of sexual ethics, and hence the strength of the passions needed to disrupt it, is brought sharply into focus before the wedding by the girl's retort to Leonardo:

> I have my pride. And that's why I'm getting married. I'll lock myself in with my husband and then I'll have to love him above everyone else.

Leonardo, significantly, is the one character named in the play: the interloper, the apparently free individual whose abduction of the Bride challenges the law by which society has striven to tame the sexual energy that threatens its stability.

In *Yerma* and *The House of Bernarda Alba* this energy beats against a rigid obstacle: the indifference of Yerma's husband (buttressed by the moral code that binds her to him), the social conventions embodied in Bernarda's tyranny over her daughters. Honour and destiny, the two concepts basic to Spanish drama, are in conflict. So also in *Blood Wedding*; but here the convention of honour goes into action through the vendetta between the Bridegroom's family and Leonardo's which the elopement instantly reopens. The essential theme of the play, in short, is the opposition between death and life. For it is more than personal desire that flings the Bride and Leonardo together. There is no affection; and Leonardo's freedom to leave the wife and child who check, and so intensify, his passion is only apparent. In reality he, no less than the Bride, is carried by a force beyond his control: the force that rides in the blood of the stallion smashing at the wall of Bernarda's house, the force that drives the mountain spring where the washerwomen of *Yerma* sing of generation. In its impersonal strength no less than in its forward thrust, the thrust that gives the plays their momentum, sexual

Ronald Gaskell, "Theme and Form: Lorca's *Blood Wedding*," *Modern Drama*, V (February, 1963), pp. 431–437.

energy is the dramatic core of the three tragedies. And the purpose of this energy is made clear in *Blood Wedding* through the Mother's hunger for grandchildren as well as, more subtly, through the iterated imagery of earth and water. . . .

The substance of the dialogue in *Blood Wedding,* as in all the plays after *Mariana Pineda,* is prose; verse is reserved for passages of exceptional emotional intensity. Lorca therefore makes no attempt to work out an all-purpose rhythm, such as Eliot has sought, in which the most ordinary conversation can be carried on. On the contrary, the verse, when he uses verse, is formal—taut, usually eight-syllable lines, often linked by repetition, and tightened by the assonances closing every second line:

> Que yo no tengo la culpa,
> que la culpa es de la tierra
> y de ese olor que te sale
> de los pechos y las trenzas.

Since the purpose of these strongly marked rhythms is to express and control emotion, the verse of *Blood Wedding* is largely concentrated in the third act. (In the first two acts verse is used only for the lullaby, the epithalamion, and the recitative of the Servant before the wedding feast.) The limpid prose of the Woodcutters moves unobtrusively into verse to prepare for the soliloquies of the Moon and the Beggarwoman; these are broken by the staccato prose of the Bridegroom and his companion hunting for the lovers; then the litany of the Woodcutters, moved into a related key, leads to the passionate duet of Leonardo and the Bride. In the final scene the disordered emotions of the Bride and the Mother are vented in prose to deepen the clarity of the ending which follows.

By mingling prose with verse in this way Lorca sacrifices the unity that a single mode of speech could provide. But the gain in dramatic contrasts is considerable, and the transitions between prose and verse are skilfully managed. For one thing, Lorca's prose is terse, so that the tightening of syntax and rhythm becomes apparent only gradually.[1]

[1] Early in the third act, for example, where the Woodcutters move into verse at the rising of the moon.

(Eliot, having chosen urban speech as the staple of his later plays, has been driven to weaken his metric disastrously to compass similar transitions.) Lorca's prose, moreover, shares with his verse an unforced energy of metaphor. The normal concerns of his characters are with things immediately present to their senses—vines, olives, corn, sheep—so that images come to their lips naturally. Lorca's strength as a poet, in his plays as in his lyrics, is the freshness and precision of his images. If the verse of *Blood Wedding* is more highly charged than prose, so that it convinces less by its resemblance to speech than by its sustained intensity, the difference is only one of degree. The prose is curt, the verse more vivid and more concise.

It is this conciseness of metaphor that gives the style its cutting edge. So the Moon, searching the forest for the lovers:

> Who is hiding? Out I say!
> No! They will not get away!
> I will light up the horse
> With a fever of diamonds.

Writing of this order gives dramatic force to the passion of the lovers and to the bitterness of the Mother at the close of the play. Frequently also, and notably in *Blood Wedding,* Lorca goes on to use images as an expression of his theme. *Doña Rosita* is organised round a single image, the rose whose growth and fading parallels the life of the forsaken girl. The theme of *Yerma* (the name means "barren") is developed through an imagery of earth and water. In *Blood Wedding* the knife which is to be the instrument of death is wanted in the first scene, and references to it are scattered through the second and third acts. The blood that the Moon thirsts for, the blood of life, of warmth, is also the blood of violent death; the two currents of meaning flow together with the killing of the Bridegroom, the Mother's hope of further life. The horse, symbolic as in *The House of Bernarda Alba* of male sexuality, is related repeatedly to Leonardo. And the earth/water image appears persistently. The home of the Bride has to be reached through a wasteland. "Your father would have covered it with trees," the Mother tells her son. "Without water?" "He would have found some." The Servant, arranging glasses for the guests in the second act, hums to herself:

Turning,
The wheel was turning,
And the water was flowing,
For the wedding night comes.

The Mother recalls her own wedding day:

To me it was like coming into my own. Like the breaking of new ground; the planting of new trees.

The full strength of the image is released in the anguish of the Bride confronting the Mother in the final scene:

You would have gone too. I was a woman burning with desire, full of sores inside and out, and your son was a little drop of water from which I hoped for children, land, health; but the other was a dark river, choked with brushwood, that brought me the undertone of its rushes and its whispered song. And I went along with your son who was like a little boy of cold water, and the other sent against me hundreds of birds who got in my way. . . . I didn't want to, remember that! I didn't want to. Your son was my destiny and I have not betrayed him, but the arm of the other dragged me along like the pull of the sea.

The image, in a country as dry as Spain, is doubtless obvious enough. What gives it such dramatic force is its intimate relation, here as in *Yerma,* to the theme of the play. In *Yerma* the image is at least as important as any of the characters. For to say that Lorca uses water and earth to define Yerma's passion for children would be inexact. Yerma is herself the image through which he articulates most clearly that urge towards life that is compressed in the verbal metaphors. In this, as in so much else, Lorca differs radically from Synge, with whom he has been compared. For Synge, nature is the world as it impinges on the senses of men and women: the cry of a curlew, the smell of gorse, the tide turning in the wind. For Lorca, in the

rural tragedies at least, nature is fecundity, balked by social conventions but too powerful ever to be mastered. Women, and perhaps men also, are driven by a power that they perceive only rarely, as Leonardo perceives it in the forest with the Bride in his arms:

Oh, it isn't my fault—
The fault is the earth's.

This is not to say that Lorca's characters are faintly defined, on the contrary. But they are defined less through motives and habits than by their relation to the central theme of the play, and they are significant not as persons but as part of the pattern through which the theme is clarified.

This dramatisation, not of the conflicts of men and women, but of the rhythm of the earth . . . takes the plays to the verge of ritual. As in ritual, emotion of permanent and profound significance is restrained, ordered, and so expressed in its fullest strength, through a pattern of speech and action. . . .

Blood Wedding, probably the earliest of the three tragedies, is from this point of view the least satisfying. For the elements of ritual —the epithalamion, the litany of the Woodcutters, the choric ending—though dramatically justified and impressive, are not completely fused with the stringent naturalism of the first act. (The Woodcutters, in particular, are rather awkward in production.) *Yerma* and *The House of Bernarda Alba* suggest the two kinds of structure between which the play seems to hesitate. Yet the greater power of *Blood Wedding* is not to be ascribed to the violence of the action. Essentially, the strength of the play is in the exploration of its theme through imagery and rhythm, and so in the deepening of the action by a dramatic realisation of the forces that drive the characters to their appointed end.

◆ Short Description of a New Technique of Acting Which Produces an Alienation Effect

By BERTOLT BRECHT

What follows represents an attempt to describe a technique of acting which was applied in certain theatres (1) with a view to taking the incidents portrayed and alienating them from the spectator. The aim of this technique, known as the alienation effect, was to make the spectator adopt an attitude of inquiry and criticism in his approach to the incident. The means were artistic.

The first condition for the A-effect's application to this end is that stage and auditorium must be purged of everything 'magical' and that no 'hypnotic tensions' should be set up. This ruled out any attempt to make the stage convey the flavour of a particular place (a room at evening, a road in the autumn), or to create atmosphere by relaxing the tempo of the conversation. The audience was not 'worked up' by a display of temperament or 'swept away' by acting with tautened muscles; in short, no attempt was made to put it in a trance and give it the illusion of watching an ordinary unrehearsed event. As will be seen presently, the audience's tendency to plunge into such illusions has to be checked by specific artistic means (3).

The first condition for the achievement of the A-effect is that the actor must invest what he has to show with a definite gest of showing. It is of course necessary to drop the assumption that there is a fourth wall cutting the audience off from the stage and the consequent illusion that the stage action is taking place in reality and without an audience. That being so, it is possible for the actor in principle to address the audience direct.

It is well known that contact between audience and stage is normally made on the basis of empathy. Conventional actors devote their efforts so exclusively to bringing about this psychological operation that they may be said to see it as the principal aim of their art (5). Our introductory remarks will already have made it clear that the technique which produces an A-effect is the exact opposite of that which aims at empathy. The actor applying it is bound not to try to bring about the empathy operation.

Yet in his efforts to reproduce particular characters and show their behaviour he need not renounce the means of empathy entirely. He uses these means just as any normal person with no particular acting talent would use them if he wanted to portray someone else, i.e. show how he behaves. This showing of other people's behaviour happens time and again in ordinary life (witnesses of an accident demonstrating to newcomers how the victim behaved, a facetious person imitating a friend's walk, etc.), without those involved making the least effort to subject their spectators to an illusion. At the same time they do feel their way into their characters' skins with a view to acquiring their characteristics.

As has already been said, the actor too will make use of this psychological operation. But whereas the usual practice in acting is to execute it during the actual performance, in the hope of stimulating the spectator into a similar operation, he will achieve it only at an earlier stage, at some time during rehearsals.

To safeguard against an unduly 'impulsive,' frictionless and uncritical creation of characters and incidents, more reading rehearsals can be held than usual. The actor should refrain from living himself into the part prematurely in any way, and should go on functioning as long as possible as a reader (which does not mean a reader-aloud). An important step is memorizing one's first impressions.

When reading his part the actor's attitude should be one of a man who is astounded and

Bertolt Brecht, "A Short Description of a New Technique of Acting Which Produces an Alienation Effect," in *Brecht on Theatre*, trans. by John Willett (New York: Hill and Wang, 1964), pp. 136–147.

contradicts. Not only the occurrence of the incidents, as he reads about them, but the conduct of the man he is playing, as he experiences it, must be weighed up by him and their peculiarities understood; none can be taken as given, as something that 'was bound to turn out that way,' that was 'only to be expected from a character like that.' Before memorizing the words he must memorize what he felt astounded at and where he felt impelled to contradict. For these are dynamic forces that he must preserve in creating his performance.

When he appears on the stage, besides what he actually is doing he will at all essential points discover, specify, imply what he is not doing; that is to say he will act in such a way that the alternative emerges as clearly as possible, that his acting allows the other possibilities to be inferred and only represents one out of the possible variants. He will say for instance 'You'll pay for that,' and not say 'I forgive you.' He detests his children; it is not the case that he loves them. He moves down stage left and not up stage right. Whatever he doesn't do must be contained and conserved in what he does. In this way every sentence and every gesture signifies a decision; the character remains under observation and is tested. The technical term for this procedure is 'fixing the "not . . . but".'

The actor does not allow himself to become completely transformed on the stage into the character he is portraying. He is not Lear, Harpagon, Schweik; he shows them. He reproduces their remarks as authentically as he can; he puts forward their way of behaving to the best of his abilities and knowledge of men; but he never tries to persuade himself (and thereby others) that this amounts to a complete transformation. Actors will know what it means if I say that a typical kind of acting without this complete transformation takes place when a producer or colleague shows one how to play a particular passage. It is not his own part, so he is not completely transformed; he underlines the technical aspect and retains the attitude of someone just making suggestions.

Once the idea of total transformation is abandoned the actor speaks his part not as if he were improvising it himself but like a quotation (7). At the same time he obviously has

to render all the quotation's overtones, the remark's full human and concrete shape; similarly the gesture he makes must have the full substance of a human gesture even though it now represents a copy.

Given this absence of total transformation in the acting there are three aids which may help to alienate the actions and remarks of the characters being portrayed:

1. Transposition into the third person.
2. Transposition into the past.
3. Speaking the stage directions out loud.

Using the third person and the past tense allows the actor to adopt the right attitude of detachment. In addition he will look for stage directions and remarks that comment on his lines, and speak them aloud at rehearsal ('He stood up and exclaimed angrily, not having eaten: . . . ,' or 'He had never been told so before, and didn't know if it was true or not,' or 'He smiled, and said with forced nonchalance: . . .'). Speaking the stage directions out loud in the third person results in a clash between two tones of voice, alienating the second of them, the text proper. This style of acting is further alienated by taking place on the stage after having already been outlined and announced in words. Transposing it into the past gives the speaker a standpoint from which he can look back at his sentence. The sentence too is thereby alienated without the speaker adopting an unreal point of view; unlike the spectator, he has read the play right through and is better placed to judge the sentence in accordance with the ending, with its consequences, than the former, who knows less and is more of a stranger to the sentence.

This composite process leads to an alienation of the text in the rehearsals which generally persists in the performance too (9). The directness of the relationship with the audience allows and indeed forces the actual speech delivery to be varied in accordance with the greater or smaller significance attaching to the sentences. Take the case of witnesses addressing a court. The underlinings, the characters' insistence on their remarks, must be developed as a piece of effective virtuosity. If the actor turns to the audience it must be a whole-hearted turn rather than the asides and soliloquizing technique of the old-fashioned theatre. To get the full A-effect from the poetic medium the actor should start at rehearsal by paraphrasing the verse's content in vulgar prose, possibly accompanying this by the gestures designed for the verse. A daring and beautiful handling of verbal media will alienate the text. (Prose can be alienated by translation into the actor's native dialect.)

Gesture will be dealt with below, but it can at once be said that everything to do with the emotions has to be externalized; that is to say, it must be developed into a gesture. The actor has to find a sensibly perceptible outward expression for his character's emotions, preferably some action that gives away what is going on inside him. The emotion in question must be brought out, must lose all its restrictions so that it can be treated on a big scale. Special elegance, power and grace of gesture bring about the A-effect.

A masterly use of gesture can be seen in Chinese acting. The Chinese actor achieves the A-effect by being seen to observe his own movements.

Whatever the actor offers in the way of gesture, verse structure, etc., must be finished and bear the hallmarks of something rehearsed and rounded-off. The impression to be given is one of ease, which is at the same time one of difficulties overcome. The actor must make it possible for the audience to take his own art, his mastery of technique, lightly too. He puts an incident before the spectator with perfection and as he thinks it really happened or might have happened. He does not conceal the fact that he has rehearsed it, any more than an acrobat conceals his training, and he emphasizes that it is his own (actor's) account, view, version of the incident.

Because he doesn't identify himself with him he can pick a definite attitude to adopt towards the character whom he portrays, can show what he thinks of him and invite the spectator, who is likewise not asked to identify himself, to criticize the character portrayed.

The attitude which he adopts is a socially critical one. In his exposition of the incidents and in his characterization of the person he tries to bring out those features which come within society's sphere. In this way his performance becomes a discussion (about social conditions) with the audience he is addressing. He prompts the spectator to justify or abolish these conditions according to what class he belongs to (13).

The object of the A-effect is to alienate the social gest underlying every incident. By social gest is meant the mimetic and gestural expression of the social relationships prevailing between people of a given period (14).

It helps to formulate the incident for society, and to put it across in such a way that society is given the key, if titles are thought up for the scenes. These titles must have a historical quality.

This brings us to a crucial technical device: historicization.

The actor must play the incidents as historical ones. Historical incidents are unique, transitory incidents associated with particular periods. The conduct of the persons involved in them is not fixed and 'universally human'; it includes elements that have been or may be overtaken by the course of history, and is subject to criticism from the immediately following period's point of view. The conduct of those born before us is alienated[1] from us by an incessant evolution.

It is up to the actor to treat present-day events and modes of behaviour with the same detachment as the historian adopts with regard to those of the past. He must alienate these characters and incidents from us.

Characters and incidents from ordinary life, from our immediate surroundings, being familiar, strike us as more or less natural. Alienating them helps to make them seem remarkable to us. Science has carefully developed a technique of getting irritated with the everyday, 'self-evident,' universally accepted occurrence, and there is no reason why this infinitely useful attitude should not be taken over by art (17). It is an attitude which arose in science as a result of the growth in human productive powers. In art the same motive applies.

As for the emotions, the experimental use of the A-effect in the epic theatre's German productions indicated that this way of acting too can stimulate them, though possibly a different class of emotion is involved from those of the orthodox theatre (18). A critical attitude on the audience's part is a thoroughly artistic one (19). Nor does the actual practice of the A-effect seem anything like so unnatural as its description. Of course it is a way of acting that has nothing to do with

[1] *Entfremdet.*

stylization as commonly practised. The main advantage of the epic theatre with its A-effect, intended purely to show the world in such a way that it becomes manageable, is precisely its quality of being natural and earthly, its humour and its renunciation of all the mystical elements that have stuck to the orthodox theatre from the old days.

Appendix

(selected notes)

3. E. g. such mechanical means as very brilliant illumination of the stage (since a half-lit stage plus a completely darkened auditorium makes the spectator less level-headed by preventing him from observing his neighbour and in turn hiding him from his neighbour's eyes) and also *making visible the sources of light.*

MAKING VISIBLE THE SOURCES OF LIGHT

There is a point in showing the lighting apparatus openly, as it is one of the means of preventing an unwanted element of illusion; it scarcely disturbs the necessary concentration. If we light the actors and their performance in such a way that the lights themselves are within the spectator's field of vision we destroy part of his illusion of being present at a spontaneous, transitory, authentic, unrehearsed event. He sees that arrangements have been made to show something; something is being repeated here under special conditions, for instance in a very brilliant light. Displaying the actual lights is meant to be a counter to the old-fashioned theatre's efforts to hide them. No one would expect the lighting to be hidden at a sporting event, a boxing match for instance. Whatever the points of difference between the modern theatre's presentations and those of a sporting promoter, they do not include the same concealment of the sources of light as the old theatre found necessary.

(Brecht: 'Der Bühnenbau des epischen Theaters')

5. Cf. these remarks by Poul Reumert, the best-known Danish actor:

. . . If I feel I am *dying*, and if I *really* feel it, then so does everybody else; if I act as though

I had a dagger in my hand, and am entirely filled by the one idea of killing the child, then everybody shudders. . . . The whole business is a matter of mental activity being communicated by emotions, or the other way round if you prefer it: a feeling so strong as to be an obsession, which is translated into thoughts. If it comes off it is the most infectious thing in the world; anything external is then a matter of complete indifference. . . .

And Rapaport, 'The Work of the Actor,' *Theater Workshop,* October 1936:

. . . On the stage the actor is surrounded entirely by fictions. . . . The actor must be able to regard all this as though it were true, as though he were convinced that all that surrounds him on the stage is a living reality and, along with himself, he must convince the audience as well. This is the central feature of our method of work on the part. . . . Take any object, a cap for example; lay it on the table or on the floor and try to regard it as though it were a rat; make believe that it is a rat, and not a cap. . . . Picture what sort of rat it is; what size, colour? . . . We thus commit ourselves to believe quite naïvely that the object before us is something other than it is and, at the same time, learn to compel the audience to believe. . . .

This might be thought to be a course of instruction for conjurers, but in fact it is a course of acting, supposedly according to Stanislavsky's method. One wonders if a technique that equips an actor to make the audience see rats where there aren't any can really be all that suitable for disseminating the truth. Given enough alcohol it doesn't take acting to persuade almost anybody that he is seeing rats: pink ones.

7. QUOTATION

Standing in a free and direct relationship to it, the actor allows his character to speak and move; he presents a report. He does not have to make us forget that the text isn't spontaneous, but has been memorized, is a fixed quantity; the fact doesn't matter, as we anyway assume that the report is not about himself but about others. His attitude would be the same if he were simply speaking from his own memory. [. . .]

8. The epic actor has to accumulate far more material than has been the case till now. What he has to represent is no longer himself as king, himself as scholar, himself as gravedigger, etc., but just kings, scholars, gravediggers, which means that he has to look around him in the world of reality. Again, he has to learn how to imitate: something that is discouraged in modern acting on the ground that it destroys his individuality.

9. The theatre can create the corresponding A-effect in the performance in a number of ways. The Munich production of *Edward II* for the first time had titles preceding the scenes, announcing the contents. The Berlin production of *The Threepenny Opera* had the titles of the songs projected while they were sung. The Berlin production of *Mann ist Mann* had the actors' figures projected on big screens during the action.

13. Another thing that makes for freedom in the actor's relationship with his audience is that he does not treat it as an undifferentiated mass. He doesn't boil it down to a shapeless dumpling in the stockpot of the emotions. He does not address himself to everybody alike; he allows the existing divisions within the audience to continue, in fact he widens them. He has friends and enemies in the audience; he is friendly to the one group and hostile to the other. He takes sides, not necessarily with his character but if not with it then against it. (At least, that is his basic attitude, though it too must be variable and change according to what the character may say at different stages. There may, however, also be points at which everything is in the balance and the actor must withhold judgment, though this again must be expressly shown in his acting.)

14. If *King Lear* (in Act I, scene I) tears up a map when he divides his kingdom between his daughters, then the act of division is alienated. Not only does it draw our attention to his kingdom, but by treating the kingdom so plainly as his own private property he throws some light on the basis of the feudal idea of the family. In *Julius Caesar* the tyrant's murder by Brutus is

alienated if during one of his monologues accusing Caesar of tyrannical motives he himself maltreats a slave waiting on him. Weigel as *Maria Stuart* suddenly took the crucifix hanging round her neck and used it coquettishly as a fan, to give herself air. (See too Brecht: 'Übungsstücke für Schauspieler' in *Versuche II,* p. 107.)

17. THE A-EFFECT AS A PROCEDURE IN EVERYDAY LIFE

The achievement of the A-effect constitutes something utterly ordinary, recurrent; it is just a widely-practised way of drawing one's own or someone else's attention to a thing, and it can be seen in education as also in business conferences of one sort or another. The A-effect consists in turning the object of which one is to be made aware, to which one's attention is to be drawn, from something ordinary, familiar, immediately accessible, into something peculiar, striking and unexpected. What is obvious is in a certain sense made incomprehensible, but this is only in order that it may then be made all the easier to comprehend. Before familiarity can turn into awareness the familiar must be stripped of its inconspicuousness; we must give up assuming that the object in question needs no explanation. However frequently recurrent, modest, vulgar it may be it will now be labelled as something unusual.

A common use of the A-effect is when someone says: 'Have you ever really looked carefully at your watch?' The questioner knows that I've looked at it often enough, and now his question deprives me of the sight which I've grown used to and which accordingly has nothing more to say to me. I used to look at it to see the time, and now when he asks me in this importunate way I realize that I have given up seeing the watch itself with an astonished eye; and it is in many ways an astonishing piece of machinery. Similarly it is an alienation effect of the simplest sort if a business discussion starts off with the sentence: 'Have you ever thought what happens to the waste from your factory which is pumped into the river twenty-four hours a day?' This waste wasn't just swept down the river unobserved; it was carefully channelled into the river; men and machines have worked on it; the river has changed colour, the waste has flowed away most conspicuously, but just as waste. It was superfluous to the process of manufacture, and now it is to become material for manufacture; our eye turns to it with interest. The asking of the question has alienated it, and intentionally so. The very simplest sentences that apply in the A-effect are those with 'Not . . . But': (He didn't say 'come in' but 'keep moving.' He was not pleased but amazed). They include an expectation which is justified by experience but, in the event, disappointed. One might have thought that . . . but one oughtn't to have thought it. There was not just one possibility but two; both are introduced, then the second one is alienated, then the first as well. To see one's mother as a man's wife one needs an A-effect; this is provided, for instance, when one acquires a stepfather. If one sees one's teacher hounded by the bailiffs an A-effect occurs: one is jerked out of a relationship in which the teacher seems big into one where he seems small. An alienation of the motor-car takes place if after driving a modern car for a long while we drive an old Model T Ford. Suddenly we hear explosions once more; the motor works on the principle of explosion. We start feeling amazed that such a vehicle, indeed any vehicle not drawn by animal-power, can move; in short, we understand cars, by looking at them as something strange, new, as a triumph of engineering and to that extent something unnatural. Nature, which certainly embraces the motor-car, is suddenly imbued with an element of unnaturalness, and from now on this is an indelible part of the concept of nature.

The expression 'in fact' can likewise certify or alienate. (He wasn't in fact at home; he said he would be, but we didn't believe him and had a look; or again, we didn't think it possible for him not to be at home, but it was a fact.) The term 'actually' is just as conducive to alienation. ('I don't actually agree.') Similarly the Eskimo definition 'A car is a wingless aircraft that crawls along the ground' is a way of alienating the car.

In a sense the alienation effect itself has been alienated by the above explanation; we have taken a common, recurrent, universally-practiced operation and tried to draw attention to it by illuminating its peculiarity. But we have achieved the effect only with those people who have truly ('in fact') grasped that it does 'not' result from every representation 'but' from certain ones: only 'actually' is it familiar.

18. ABOUT RATIONAL AND EMOTIONAL POINTS OF VIEW

The rejection of empathy is not the result of a rejection of the emotions, nor does it lead to such. The crude aesthetic thesis that emotions can only be stimulated by means of empathy is wrong. None the less a non-aristotelian dramaturgy has to apply a cautious criticism to the emotions which it aims at and incorporates. Certain artistic tendencies like the provocative behaviour of Futurists and Dadaists and the icing-up of music point to a crisis of the emotions. Already in the closing years of the Weimar Republic the post-war German drama took a decisively rationalistic turn. Fascism's grotesque emphasizing of the emotions, together perhaps with the no less important threat to the rational element in Marxist aesthetics, led us to lay particular stress on the rational. Nevertheless there are many contemporary works of art where one can speak of a decline in emotional effectiveness due to their isolation from reason, or its revival thanks to a stronger rationalist message. This will surprise no one who has not got a completely conventional idea of the emotions.

The emotions always have a quite definite class basis; the form they take at any time is historical, restricted and limited in specific ways. The emotions are in no sense universally human and timeless.

The linking of particular emotions with particular interests is not unduly difficult so long as one simply looks for the interests corresponding to the emotional effects of works of art. Anyone can see the colonial adventures of the Second Empire looming behind Delacroix's paintings and Rimbaud's 'Bateau Ivre.'

If one compares the 'Bateau Ivre,' say, with Kipling's 'Ballad of East and West,' one can see the difference between French mid-nineteenth-century colonialism and British colonialism at the beginning of the twentieth. It is less easy to explain the effect that such poems have on ourselves, as Marx already noticed.

Apparently emotions accompanying social progress will long survive in the human mind as emotions linked with interests, and in the case of works of art will do so more strongly than might have been expected, given that in the meantime contrary interests will have made themselves felt. Every step forward means the end of the previous step forward, because that is where it starts and goes on from. At the same time it makes use of this previous step, which in a sense survives in men's consciousness as a step forward, just as it survives in its effects in real life. This involves a most interesting type of generalization, a continual process of abstraction. Whenever the works of art handed down to us allow us to share the emotions of other men, of men of a bygone period, different social classes, etc., we have to conclude that we are partaking in interests which really were universally human. These men now dead represented the interests of classes that gave a lead to progress. It is a very different matter when Fascism today conjures up on the grandest scale emotions which for most of the people who succumb to them are not determined by interest.

19. IS THE CRITICAL ATTITUDE AN INARTISTIC ONE?

An old tradition leads people to treat a critical attitude as a predominantly negative one. Many see the difference between the scientific and artistic attitudes as lying precisely in their attitude to criticism. People cannot conceive of contradiction and detachment as being part of artistic appreciation. Of course such appreciation normally includes a higher level, which appreciates critically, but the criticism here only applies to matters of technique; it is quite a different matter from being required to observe not a representation of the world but the world itself in a critical, contradictory, detached manner.

To introduce this critical attitude into art, the negative element which it doubtless includes must be shown from its positive side: this criticism of the world is active, practical, positive. Criticizing the course of a river means improving it, correcting it. Criticism of society is ultimately revolution; there you have criticism taken to its logical conclusion and playing an active part. A critical attitude of this type is an operative factor of productivity; it is deeply enjoyable as such, and if we commonly use the term 'arts' for enterprises that improve people's lives why should art proper remain aloof from arts of this sort?

['Kurze Beschreibung einer neuen Technik der Schauspielkunst, die einen Verfremdungseffekt hervorbringt,' from *Versuche II*, 1951, less notes 2, 4, 6, 10, 11, 15, 16 and part of 7.]

◆ *Riders to the Sea, Blood Wedding* and *Mother Courage*

By JAMES GRAHAM-LUJÁN

The differences between sentimentality and compassion are so great that what these three unsentimental and profoundly compassionate plays tell us is moving indeed, but most of all unexpected. *Riders to the Sea, Blood Wedding,* and *Mother Courage* share the single theme of the sacrifices of women for their sons. What the plays tell us about mothers is this: that they are capable of withstanding any terrible blow in the protection of their sons, but that, finally, when the sons die, the mothers will resign themselves to outlasting them.

These three plays, as representative of one theme, set off the minds and talents of three important playwrights in an interplay of ideas, correspondences and theatrical methods. If we look at the plays from one angle, we come upon the surprising knowledge that *Riders to the Sea* and *Blood Wedding* are the same play, written in the same language, even, but that *Mother Courage* is audaciously different, since it seems to forswear the plot development, fascinating in its tragic inevitability, that animates the first two.

But from the point of view of the knowing use and exploitation of theatrical device, it is *Riders to the Sea* which emerges as an austere ritual. The other two plays are not only frank in their theatricality but seem a celebration of the theatre's empathetic resources.

When we begin to examine the play of correspondences, we come upon the matter of the similarities between *Riders to the Sea* and *Blood Wedding.* In each play there is a mother who, having lost a husband and a son, tries to keep a last remaining son safe at home. But the son will go; and surely no son worthy of the family's honor can be confined. So, at the moment when he does go, there is a strangely destructive reaction in the mother. In *Riders to the Sea,* Maurya lets Bartley go, fatefully, without giving him her blessing. The mother in *Blood Wedding* knows that her son goes to meet those who

"kill quickly and well," yet she calls for a horse, and the horse carries her son to the deadly, appointed meeting. Thus do these mothers seem to invite destruction.

At these moments there is a further correspondence beyond that of going to meet death, and it appears in the coincidence of the horses. In *Riders to the Sea,* Bartley rides his mare and leads his gray pony; and the gray pony, ridden by the ghost of drowned Michael, knocks Bartley into the sea. In neither play have we seen the horses, but the playwrights make us believe that we have. The writers, then, have created a truth—not an actual truth, but a theatrical one.

We do not enumerate other correspondences, for the sake of leaving to the reader the delight of their discovery. The correspondences are present, different ones for different readers, since great plays share this quality with the sea shell: the ability to make a private music for the private ear.

We need only say that between the two plays seeming differences may only be differences of proportion in the ratio of a one-act play to a play in three acts. Synge needs only to mention the supernatural. Cathleen, speaking of the reappearance of Michael's body after death by drowning, says, ". . . Ah, Nora, isn't it a bitter thing to think of him floating that way to the far north, and no one to keen him but the black hags that do be flying on the sea?" But Lorca makes a whole scene, in Act III, of the intervention of supernatural forces. Moreover, Lorca accompanies the scene with a baroque music whose development toward the resolution of its theme helps convince us of the inevitability of the death of the bridegroom.

The splendor of the baroque music is part of Lorca's celebration of theatrical resource. Brecht shares this joy with Lorca, but seems to commit a paradox. Lorca enriches his stage with several stories. He breaks our hearts in the resolution of these stories; and he finally heals us in the courage of his personages. Brecht develops no story or suspense line at all. His play wanders with the wanderings of Mother Courage, and correctly so, since her interest is concentrated upon survival. Yet, in refusing to engage our attention with the device of suspense, Brecht coolly exacts our empathy with his mastery of theatrical effect. Scenes are ornamented with songs and with lettered banners. The banners encapsulate narrative material and indicate locale. Mother Courage spills her energy upon the frozen ground while remaining before our shocked gaze through the mechanical device of a turntable.

Probably the most heartbreaking use of mechanical resource is to be found in Brecht's treatment of the character of Mother Courage's daughter, Kattrin. The playwright presents her to us as daringly as any artist whose medium is language can do: wordlessly, because she is dumb. Yet, dumb, in the scene of her death, she grinds upon our nerves intolerably, by beating on a drum until a soldier's bullet kills her. Brecht has committed an irony upon us. We grieve over her death even as we are glad the drum is still.

Being human, we become fond of one play or another, and then we begin to insist upon its excellence beyond the others: *Riders to the Sea,* for the perfection of its form and for the eloquent idiom the playwright invented for it; *Blood Wedding,* for its overwhelming passions sung in a rhetoric only the great are able to wield; and *Mother Courage,* for a succession of definitive images burnt into our cognizance like caustic.

Synge and Lorca share a victory only great poets may attain: the invention of an idiom which sounds true to the speech of peasants but which is also noble. Synge, taking his direction from the accent of the Aran Islands, arrives at eloquence itself. Lorca probably knew Synge's play as *Jinetes hacia el mar,* in a translation by Juan Ramón Jiménez, a great translator who undertook translation from English to Spanish for the best of reasons: for love of the original. In Lorca, however, the dialogues encompass a wider range of emotions.

In Brecht, the achievement is a different one. We do not know where he stands, or what judgment he himself makes upon the alarming lives of his beings. We are free to make our own interpretations, and in so doing we interpret ourselves.

◆◆◆Part Four

SHAW

ANOUILH

◆ Preface to *Saint Joan*

By BERNARD SHAW

JOAN THE ORIGINAL AND PRESUMPTUOUS

Joan of Arc, a village girl from the Vosges, was born about 1412; burnt for heresy, witchcraft, and sorcery in 1431; rehabilitated after a fashion in 1456; designated Venerable in 1904; declared Blessed in 1908; and finally canonized in 1920. She is the most notable Warrior Saint in the Christian calendar, and the queerest fish among the eccentric worthies of the Middle Ages. Though a professed and most pious Catholic, and the projector of a Crusade against the Husites, she was in fact one of the first Protestant martyrs. She was also one of the first apostles of Nationalism, and the first French practitioner of Napoleonic realism in warfare as distinguished from the sporting ransom-gambling chivalry of her time. She was the pioneer of rational dressing for women, and, like Queen Christina of Sweden two centuries later, to say nothing of Catalina de Erauso and innumerable obscure heroines who have disguised themselves as men to serve as soldiers and sailors, she refused to accept the specific woman's lot, and dressed and fought and lived as men did.

As she contrived to assert herself in all these ways with such force that she was famous throughout western Europe before she was out of her teens (indeed she never got out of them), it is hardly surprising that she was judicially burnt, ostensibly for a number of capital crimes which we no longer punish as such, but essentially for what we call unwomanly and insufferable presumption. At eighteen Joan's pretensions were beyond those of the proudest Pope or the haughtiest emperor. She claimed to be the ambassador and plenipotentiary of God, and to be, in effect, a member of the Church Triumphant whilst still in the flesh on earth. She patronized her own king, and summoned the English king to repentance and obedience to her commands. She lectured, talked down, and overruled statesmen and prelates. She poohed the plans of generals, leading their troops to victory on plans of her own. She had an unbounded and quite unconcealed contempt for official opinion, judgment, and authority, and for War Office tactics and strategy. Had she been a sage and monarch in whom the most venerable hierarchy and the most illustrious dynasty converged, her pretensions and proceedings would have been as trying to the official mind as the pretensions of Caesar were to Cassius. As her actual condition was pure upstart, there were only two opinions about her. One was that she was miraculous: the other that she was unbearable.

JOAN AND SOCRATES

If Joan had been malicious, selfish, cowardly, or stupid, she would have been one of the most odious persons known to history instead of one of the most attractive. If she had been old enough to know the effect she was producing on the men whom she humiliated by being right when they were wrong, and had learned to flatter and manage them, she might have lived as long as Queen Elizabeth. But she was too young and rustical and inexperienced to have any such arts. When she was thwarted by men whom she thought fools, she made no secret of her opinion of them or her impatience with their folly; and she was naïve enough to expect them to be obliged to her for setting them right and keeping them out of mischief. Now it is always hard for superior wits to understand the fury roused by their exposures of the stupidities of comparative dullards. Even Socrates, for all his age and experience, did not defend himself at his trial like a man who understood the long accumulated fury that had burst on him, and was clamoring for his death. His accuser, if born 2300 years later, might have been picked out of any first class carriage on a suburban railway during the evening or morning rush from or to the City; for he had

Bernard Shaw, "Preface," *Saint Joan* (Baltimore: Penguin, 1951), pp. 7–48.

really nothing to say except that he and his like could not endure being shewn up as idiots every time Socrates opened his mouth. Socrates, unconscious of this, was paralyzed by his sense that somehow he was missing the point of the attack. He petered out after he had established the fact that he was an old soldier and a man of honorable life, and that his accuser was a silly snob. He had no suspicion of the extent to which his mental superiority had roused fear and hatred against him in the hearts of men towards whom he was conscious of nothing but good will and good service.

CONTRAST WITH NAPOLEON

If Socrates was as innocent as this at the age of seventy, it may be imagined how innocent Joan was at the age of seventeen. Now Socrates was a man of argument, operating slowly and peacefully on men's minds, whereas Joan was a woman of action, operating with impetuous violence on their bodies. That, no doubt, is why the contemporaries of Socrates endured him so long, and why Joan was destroyed before she was fully grown. But both of them combined terrifying ability with a frankness, personal modesty, and benevolence which made the furious dislike to which they fell victims absolutely unreasonable, and therefore inapprehensible by themselves. Napoleon, also possessed of terrifying ability, but neither frank nor disinterested, had no illusions as to the nature of his popularity. When he was asked how the world would take his death, he said it would give a gasp of relief. But it is not so easy for mental giants who neither hate nor intend to injure their fellows to realize that nevertheless their fellows hate mental giants and would like to destroy them, not only enviously because the juxtaposition of a superior wounds their vanity, but quite humbly and honestly because it frightens them. Fear will drive men to any extreme; and the fear inspired by a superior being is a mystery which cannot be reasoned away. Being immeasurable it is unbearable when there is no presumption or guarantee of its benevolence and moral responsibility: in other words, when it has no official status. The legal and conven-

tional superiority of Herod and Pilate, and of Annas and Caiaphas, inspires fear; but the fear, being a reasonable fear of measurable and avoidable consequences which seem salutary and protective, is bearable; whilst the strange superiority of Christ and the fear it inspires elicit a shriek of Crucify Him from all who cannot divine its benevolence. Socrates has to drink the hemlock, Christ to hang on the cross, and Joan to burn at the stake, whilst Napoleon, though he ends in St Helena, at least dies in his bed there; and many terrifying but quite comprehensible official scoundrels die natural deaths in all the glory of the kingdoms of this world, proving that it is far more dangerous to be a saint than to be a conqueror. Those who have been both, like Mahomet and Joan, have found that it is the conqueror who must save the saint, and that defeat and capture mean martyrdom. Joan was burnt without a hand lifted on her own side to save her. The comrades she had led to victory and the enemies she had disgraced and defeated, the French king she had crowned and the English king whose crown she had kicked into the Loire, were equally glad to be rid of her.

WAS JOAN INNOCENT OR GUILTY?

As this result could have been produced by a crapulous inferiority as well as by a sublime superiority, the question which of the two was operative in Joan's case has to be faced. It was decided against her by her contemporaries after a very careful and conscientious trial; and the reversal of the verdict twenty-five years later, in form a rehabilitation of Joan, was really only a confirmation of the validity of the coronation of Charles VII. It is the more impressive reversal by a unanimous Posterity, culminating in her canonization, that has quashed the original proceedings, and put her judges on their trial, which, so far, has been much more unfair than their trial of her. Nevertheless the rehabilitation of 1456, corrupt job as it was, really did produce evidence enough to satisfy all reasonable critics that Joan was not a common termagant, not a harlot, not a witch, not a blasphemer, no more an idolator than the Pope himself, and not ill conducted in any sense apart from her soldiering, her wearing of men's clothes, and her audacity, but on the contrary good-humored, an intact virgin, very pious, very temperate (we should call her meal of bread soaked in the common wine which is the drinking water of France ascetic), very kindly, and, though a brave and hardy soldier, unable to endure loose language or licentious conduct. She went to the stake without a stain on her character except the overweening presumption, the superbity as they called it, that led her thither. It would therefore be waste of time now to prove that the Joan of the first part of the Elizabethan chronicle play of Henry VI (supposed to have been tinkered by Shakespear) grossly libels her in its concluding scenes in deference to Jingo patriotism. The mud that was thrown at her has dropped off by this time so completely that there is no need for any modern writer to wash up after it. What is far more difficult to get rid of is the mud that is being thrown at her judges, and the whitewash which disfigures her beyond recognition. When Jingo scurrility had done its worst to her, sectarian scurrility (in this case Protestant scurrility) used her stake to beat the Roman Catholic Church and the Inquisition. The easiest way to make these institutions the villains of a melodrama was to make The Maid its heroine. That melodrama may be dismissed as rubbish. Joan got a far fairer trial from the Church and the Inquisition than any prisoner of her type and in her situation gets nowadays in any official secular court; and the decision was strictly according to law. And she was not a melodramatic heroine: that is, a physically beautiful lovelorn parasite on an equally beautiful hero, but a genius and a saint, about as completely the opposite of a melodramatic heroine as it is possible for a human being to be.

Let us be clear about the meaning of the terms. A genius is a person who, seeing farther and probing deeper than other people, has a different set of ethical valuations from theirs, and has energy enough to give effect to this extra vision and its valuations in whatever manner best suits his or her specific talents. A saint is one who having practised heroic virtues, and enjoyed revelations or powers of the order which The Church classes technically as supernatural, is eligible for canonization. If a historian is an Anti-Feminist, and does not believe women to be capable of genius in the traditional masculine departments, he will never make anything of Joan, whose genius was turned to practical account mainly in soldiering and politics. If he is Rationalist enough to deny that saints exist, and to hold that new ideas cannot come otherwise than by conscious ratiocination, he will never catch Joan's likeness. Her ideal biographer must be free from nineteenth century prejudices and biases; must understand the Middle Ages, the Roman Catholic Church, and the Holy Roman Empire much more intimately than our Whig historians have ever understood them; and must be capable of throwing off sex partialities and their romance, and regarding woman as the female of the human species, and not as a different kind of animal with specific charms and specific imbecilities.

JOAN'S GOOD LOOKS

To put the last point roughly, any book about Joan which begins by describing her as a beauty may be at once classed as a romance. Not one of Joan's comrades, in village, court, or camp, even when they were straining themselves to please the king by praising her, ever claimed that she was pretty. All the men who alluded to the matter declared most emphatically that she was unattractive sexually to a degree that seemed to them miraculous, considering that she was in the bloom of youth, and neither ugly, awkward, deformed, nor unpleasant in her person. The evident truth is that like most women of her hardy managing type she seemed neutral in the conflict of sex because men were too much afraid of her to fall in love with her. She herself was not sexless: in spite of the virginity she had vowed up to a point, and preserved to her death, she never excluded the possibility of marriage for herself. But marriage, with its preliminary of the attraction, pursuit, and capture of a husband, was not her business: she had something else to do. Byron's formula, 'Man's love is of man's life a thing apart: 'tis woman's whole existence,' did not apply to her any more than to George Washington or any other masculine worker on the heroic scale. Had she lived in our time, picture postcards might have been sold of her as a general: they would not have been sold of her as a sultana. Nevertheless there is one reason for crediting her with a very remarkable face. A sculptor of her time in Orleans made a statue of a helmeted young woman with a face that is unique in art in point of being evidently not an ideal face but a portrait, and yet so uncommon as to be unlike any real woman one has ever seen. It is surmised that Joan served unconsciously as the sculptor's model. There is no proof of this; but those extraordinarily spaced eyes raise so powerfully the question 'If this woman be not Joan, who is she?' that I dispense with further evidence, and challenge those who disagree with me to prove a negative. It is a wonderful face, but quite neutral from the point of view of the operatic beauty fancier.

Such a fancier may perhaps be finally chilled by the prosaic fact that Joan was the defendant in a suit for breach of promise of marriage, and that she conducted her own case and won it.

JOAN'S SOCIAL POSITION

By class Joan was the daughter of a working farmer who was one of the headmen of his village, and transacted its feudal business for it with the neighboring squires and their lawyers. When the castle in which the villagers were entitled to take refuge from raids became derelict, he organized a combination of half a dozen farmers to obtain possession of it so as to occupy it when there was any danger of invasion. As a child, Joan could please herself at times with being the young lady of this castle. Her mother and brothers were able to follow and share her fortune at court without making themselves notably ridiculous. These facts leave us no excuse for the popular romance that turns every heroine into either a princess or a beggarmaid. In the somewhat similar case of Shakespear a whole inverted pyramid of wasted research has been based on the assumption that he was an illiterate laborer, in the face of the plainest evidence that his father was a man of business, and at one time a very prosperous one,

married to a woman of some social pretensions. There is the same tendency to drive Joan into the position of a hired shepherd girl, though a hired shepherd girl in Domrémy would have deferred to her as the young lady of the farm.

The difference between Joan's case and Shakespear's is that Shakespear was not illiterate. He had been to school, and knew as much Latin and Greek as most university passmen retain: that is, for practical purposes, none at all. Joan was absolutely illiterate. 'I do not know A from B' she said. But many princesses at that time and for long after might have said the same. Marie Antoinette, for instance, at Joan's age could not spell her own name correctly. But this does not mean that Joan was an ignorant person, or that she suffered from the diffidence and sense of social disadvantage now felt by people who cannot read or write. If she could not write letters, she could and did dictate them and attach full and indeed excessive importance to them. When she was called a shepherd lass to her face she very warmly resented it, and challenged any woman to compete with her in the household arts of the mistresses of well furnished houses. She understood the political and military situation in France much better than most of our newspaper fed university women-graduates understand the corresponding situation of their own country today. Her first convert was the neighboring commandant at Vaucouleurs; and she converted him by telling him about the defeat of the Dauphin's troops at the Battle of Herrings so long before he had official news of it that he concluded she must have had a divine revelation. This knowledge of and interest in public affairs was nothing extraordinary among farmers in a war-swept countryside. Politicians came to the door too often sword in hand to be disregarded: Joan's people could not afford to be ignorant of what was going on in the feudal world. They were not rich; and Joan worked on the farm as her father did, driving the sheep to pasture and so forth; but there is no evidence or suggestion of sordid poverty, and no reason to believe that Joan had to work as a hired servant works, or indeed to work at all when she preferred to go to confession, or dawdle about waiting for visions and listening to the church bells to hear voices in them. In short, much more of a young lady, and even of an intellectual, than most of the daughters of our petty bourgeoisie.

JOAN'S VOICES AND VISIONS

Joan's voices and visions have played many tricks with her reputation. They have been held to prove that she was mad, that she was a liar and impostor, that she was a sorceress (she was burned for this), and finally that she was a saint. They do not prove any of these things; but the variety of the conclusions reached shew how little our matter-of-fact historians know about other people's minds, or even about their own. There are people in the world whose imagination is so vivid that when they have an idea it comes to them as an audible voice, sometimes uttered by a visible figure. Criminal lunatic asylums are occupied largely by murderers who have obeyed voices. Thus a woman may hear voices telling her that she must cut her husband's throat and strangle her child as they lie asleep; and she may feel obliged to do what she is told. By a medico-legal superstition it is held in our courts that criminals whose temptations present themselves under these illusions are not responsible for their actions, and must be treated as insane. But the seers of visions and the hearers of revelations are not always criminals. The inspirations and intuitions and unconsciously reasoned conclusions of genius sometimes assume similar illusions. Socrates, Luther, Swedenborg, Blake saw visions and heard voices just as Saint Francis and Saint Joan did. If Newton's imagination had been of the same vividly dramatic kind he might have seen the ghost of Pythagoras walk into the orchard and explain why the apples were falling. Such an illusion would have invalidated neither the theory of gravitation nor Newton's general sanity. What is more, the visionary method of making the discovery would not be a whit more miraculous than the normal method. The test of sanity is not the normality of the method but the reasonableness of the discovery. If Newton had been informed by Pythagoras that the moon was made of green cheese, then Newton would have been locked up. Gravitation, being a reasoned hypothesis which fitted remarkably well into the Copernican version of the observed physical facts of the universe, established Newton's reputation for extraordinary intelligence, and would have done so no matter how fantastically he had arrived at it. Yet his theory of gravitation is not so impressive a mental feat as his astounding chronology, which establishes him as the king of mental conjurors, but a Bedlamite king whose authority no one now accepts. On the subject of the eleventh horn of the beast seen by the prophet Daniel he was more fantastic than Joan, because his imagination was not dramatic but mathematical and therefore extraordinarily susceptible to numbers: indeed if all his works were lost except his chronology we should say that he was as mad as a hatter. As it is, who dares diagnose Newton as a madman?

In the same way Joan must be judged a sane woman in spite of her voices because they never gave her any advice that might not have come to her from her mother wit exactly as gravitation came to Newton. We can all see now, especially since the late war threw so many of our women into military life, that Joan's campaigning could not have been carried on in petticoats. This was not only because she did a man's work, but because it was morally necessary that sex should be left out of the question as between her and her comrades-in-arms. She gave this reason herself when she was pressed on the subject; and the fact that this entirely reasonable necessity came to her imagination first as an order from God delivered through the mouth of Saint Catherine does not prove that she was mad. The soundness of the order proves that she was unusually sane; but its form proves that her dramatic imagination played tricks with her senses. Her policy was also quite sound: nobody disputes that the relief of Orleans, followed up by the coronation at Rheims of the Dauphin as a counterblow to the suspicions then current of his legitimacy and consequently of his title, were military and political masterstrokes that saved France. They might have been planned by Napoleon or any other illusionproof genius. They came to Joan as an instruction from her Counsel, as she called her visionary saints;

but she was none the less an able leader of men for imagining her ideas in this way.

THE EVOLUTIONARY APPETITE

What then is the modern view of Joan's voices and visions and messages from God? The nineteenth century said that they were delusions, but that as she was a pretty girl, and had been abominably ill-treated and finally done to death by a superstitious rabble of medieval priests hounded on by a corrupt political bishop, it must be assumed that she was the innocent dupe of these delusions. The twentieth century finds this explanation too vapidly commonplace, and demands something more mystic. I think the twentieth century is right, because an explanation which amounts to Joan being mentally defective instead of, as she obviously was, mentally excessive, will not wash. I cannot believe, nor, if I could, could I expect all my readers to believe, as Joan did, that three ocularly visible well dressed persons, named respectively Saint Catherine, Saint Margaret, and Saint Michael, came down from heaven and gave her certain instructions with which they were charged by God for her. Not that such a belief would be more improbable or fantastic than some modern beliefs which we all swallow; but there are fashions and family habits in belief, and it happens that, my fashion being Victorian and my family habit Protestant, I find myself unable to attach any such objective validity to the form of Joan's visions.

But that there are forces at work which use individuals for purposes far transcending the purpose of keeping these individuals alive and prosperous and respectable and safe and happy in the middle station in life, which is all any good bourgeois can reasonably require, is established by the fact that men will, in the pursuit of knowledge and of social readjustments for which they will not be a penny the better, and are indeed often many pence the worse, face poverty, infamy, exile, imprisonment, dreadful hardship, and death. Even the selfish pursuit of personal power does not nerve men to the efforts and sacrifices which are eagerly made in pursuit of extensions of our power over nature, though these extensions may not touch the personal life of the seeker at any point. There is no more mystery about this appetite for knowledge and power than about the appetite for food: both are known as facts and as facts only, the difference between them being that the appetite for food is necessary to the life of the hungry man and is therefore a personal appetite, whereas the other is an appetite for evolution, and therefore a superpersonal need.

The diverse manners in which our imaginations dramatize the approach of the superpersonal forces is a problem for the psychologist, not for the historian. Only, the historian must understand that visionaries are neither impostors nor lunatics. It is one thing to say that the figure Joan recognized as St Catherine was not really St Catherine, but the dramatization by Joan's imagination of that pressure upon her of the driving force that is behind evolution which I have just called the evolutionary appetite. It is quite another to class her visions with the vision of two moons seen by a drunken person, or with Brocken spectres, echoes and the like. Saint Catherine's instructions were far too cogent for that; and the simplest French peasant who believes in apparitions of celestial personages to favored mortals is nearer to the scientific truth about Joan than the Rationalist and Materialist historians and essayists who feel obliged to set down a girl who saw saints and heard them talking to her as either crazy or mendacious. If Joan was mad, all Christendom was mad too; for people who believe devoutly in the existence of celestial personages are every whit as mad in that sense as the people who think they see them. Luther, when he threw his inkhorn at the devil, was no more mad than any other Augustinian monk: he had a more vivid imagination, and had perhaps eaten and slept less: that was all.

THE MERE ICONOGRAPHY DOES NOT MATTER

All the popular religions in the world are made apprehensible by an array of legendary personages, with an Almighty Father, and sometimes a mother and divine child, as the central figures. These are presented to the mind's eye in childhood; and the result is a hallucination which persists strongly throughout life when it has been well impressed.

Thus all the thinking of the hallucinated adult about the fountain of inspiration which is continually flowing in the universe, or about the promptings of virtue and the revulsions of shame: in short, about aspiration and conscience, both of which forces are matters of fact more obvious than electro-magnetism, is thinking in terms of the celestial vision. And when in the case of exceptionally imaginative persons, especially those practising certain appropriate austerities, the hallucination extends from the mind's eye to the body's, the visionary sees Krishna or the Buddha or the Blessed Virgin or St Catherine as the case may be.

THE MODERN EDUCATION WHICH JOAN ESCAPED

It is important to everyone nowadays to understand this, because modern science is making short work of the hallucinations without regard to the vital importance of the things they symbolize. If Joan were reborn today she would be sent, first to a convent school in which she would be mildly taught to connect inspiration and conscience with St Catherine and St Michael exactly as she was in the fifteenth century, and then finished up with a very energetic training in the gospel of Saints Louis Pasteur and Paul Bert, who would tell her (possibly in visions but more probably in pamphlets) not to be a superstitious little fool, and to empty out St Catherine and the rest of the Catholic hagiology as an obsolete iconography of exploded myths. It would be rubbed into her that Galileo was a martyr, and his persecutors incorrigible ignoramuses, and that St Teresa's hormones had gone astray and left her incurably hyperpituitary or hyperadrenal or hysteroid or epileptoid or anything but asteroid. She would have been convinced by precept and experiment that baptism and receiving the body of her Lord were contemptible superstitions, and that vaccination and vivisection were enlightened practices. Behind her new Saints Louis and Paul there would be not only Science purifying Religion and being purified by it, but hypochondria, melancholia, cowardice, stupidity, cruelty, muckraking curiosity, knowledge without wisdom, and

everything that the eternal soul in Nature loathes, instead of the virtues of which St Catherine was the figure head. As to the new rites, which would be the saner Joan? the one who carried little children to be baptized of water and the spirit, or the one who sent the police to force their parents to have the most villainous racial poison we know thrust into their veins? the one who told them the story of the angel and Mary, or the one who questioned them as to their experiences of the Edipus complex? the one to whom the consecrated wafer was the very body of the virtue that was her salvation, or the one who looked forward to a precise and convenient regulation of her health and her desires by a nicely calculated diet of thyroid extract, adrenalin, thymin, pituitrin, and insulin, with pick-me-ups of hormone stimulants, the blood being first carefully fortified with antibodies against all possible infections by inoculations of infected bacteria and serum from infected animals, and against old age by surgical extirpation of the reproductive ducts or weekly doses of monkey gland?

It is true that behind all these quackeries there is a certain body of genuine scientific physiology. But was there any the less a certain body of genuine psychology behind St Catherine and the Holy Ghost? And which is the healthier mind? the saintly mind or the monkey gland mind? Does not the present cry of Back to the Middle Ages, which has been incubating ever since the pre-Raphaelite movement began, mean that it is no longer our Academy pictures that are intolerable, but our credulities that have not the excuse of being superstitious, our cruelties that have not the excuse of barbarism, our persecutions that have not the excuse of religious faith, our shameless substitution of successful swindlers and scoundrels and quacks for saints as objects of worship, and our deafness and blindness to the calls and visions of the inexorable power that made us, and will destroy us if we disregard it? To Joan and her contemporaries we should appear as a drove of Gadarene swine, possessed by all the unclean spirits cast out by the faith and civilization of the Middle Ages, running violently down a steep place into a hell of high explosives. For us to set up our condition as a standard of sanity, and declare Joan mad because she never condescended to it, is to prove that we are not only lost but irredeemable. Let us then once for all drop all nonsense about Joan being cracked, and accept her as at least as sane as Florence Nightingale, who also combined a very simple iconography of religious belief with a mind so exceptionally powerful that it kept her in continual trouble with the medical and military panjandrums of her time.

FAILURES OF THE VOICES

That the voices and visions were illusory, and their wisdom all Joan's own, is shewn by the occasions on which they failed her, notably during her trial, when they assured her that she would be rescued. Here her hopes flattered her; but they were not unreasonable: her military colleague La Hire was in command of a considerable force not so very far off; and if the Armagnacs, as her party was called, had really wanted to rescue her, and had put anything like her own vigor into the enterprise, they could have attempted it with very fair chances of success. She did not understand that they were glad to be rid of her, nor that the rescue of a prisoner from the hands of the Church was a much more serious business for a medieval captain, or even a medieval king, than its mere physical difficulty as a military exploit suggested. According to her lights her expectation of a rescue was reasonable; therefore she heard Madame Saint Catherine assuring her it would happen, that being her way of finding out and making up her own mind. When it became evident that she had miscalculated: when she was led to the stake, and La Hire was not thundering at the gates of Rouen nor charging Warwick's men at arms, she threw over Saint Catherine at once, and recanted. Nothing could be more sane or practical. It was not until she discovered that she had gained nothing by her recantation but close imprisonment for life that she withdrew it, and deliberately and explicitly chose burning instead: a decision which shewed not only the extraordinary decision of her character, but also a Rationalism carried to its ultimate human test of suicide. Yet even in this the illusion persisted; and she announced her relapse as dictated to her by her voices.

JOAN A GALTONIC VISUALIZER

The most sceptical scientific reader may therefore accept as a flat fact, carrying no implication of unsoundness of mind, that Joan was what Francis Galton and other modern investigators of human faculty call a visualizer. She saw imaginary saints just as some other people see imaginary diagrams and landscapes with numbers dotted about them, and are thereby able to perform feats of memory and arithmetic impossible to non-visualizers. Visualizers will understand this at once. Non-visualizers who have never read Galton will be puzzled and incredulous. But a very little inquiry among their acquaintances will reveal to them that the mind's eye is more or less a magic lantern, and that the street is full of normally sane people who have hallucinations of all sorts which they believe to be part of the normal permanent equipment of all human beings.

JOAN'S MANLINESS AND MILITARISM

Joan's other abnormality, too common among uncommon things to be properly called a peculiarity, was her craze for soldiering and the masculine life. Her father tried to frighten her out of it by threatening to drown her if she ran away with the soldiers, and ordering her brothers to drown her if he were not on the spot. This extravagance was clearly not serious: it must have been addressed to a child young enough to imagine that he was in earnest. Joan must therefore as a child have wanted to run away and be a soldier. The awful prospect of being thrown into the Meuse and drowned by a terrible father and her big brothers kept her quiet until the father had lost his terrors and the brothers yielded to her natural leadership; and by that time she had sense enough to know that the masculine and military life was not a mere matter of running away from home. But the taste for it never left her, and was fundamental in determining her career.

If anyone doubts this, let him ask himself why a maid charged with a special mission from heaven to the Dauphin (this was how Joan saw her very able plan for retrieving the desperate situation of the uncrowned king) should not have simply gone to the court as a

maid, in woman's dress, and urged her counsel upon him in a woman's way, as other
women with similar missions had come to his
mad father and his wise grandfather. Why
did she insist on having a soldier's dress and
arms and sword and horse and equipment,
and on treating her escort of soldiers as comrades, sleeping side by side with them on the
floor at night as if there were no difference of
sex between them? It may be answered that
this was the safest way of traveling through
a country infested with hostile troops and
bands of marauding deserters from both sides.
Such an answer has no weight because it applies to all the women who travelled in
France at that time, and who never dreamt
of travelling otherwise than as women. But
even if we accept it, how does it account for
the fact that when the danger was over, and
she could present herself in court in feminine
attire with perfect safety and obviously with
greater propriety, she presented herself in her
man's dress, and instead of urging Charles,
like Queen Victoria urging the War Office to
send Roberts to the Transvaal, to send
D'Alençon, De Rais, La Hire and the rest to
the relief of Dunois at Orleans, insisted that
she must go herself and lead the assault in
person? Why did she give exhibitions of her
dexterity in handling a lance, and of her seat
as a rider? Why did she accept presents of armor and chargers and masculine surcoats,
and in every action repudiate the conventional character of a woman? The simple
answer to all these questions is that she was
the sort of woman that wants to lead a man's
life. They are to be found wherever there are
armies on foot or navies on the seas, serving
in male disguise, eluding detection for astonishingly long periods, and sometimes, no
doubt, escaping it entirely. When they are
in a position to defy public opinion they
throw off all concealment. You have your
Rosa Bonheur painting in male blouse and
trousers, and George Sand living a man's life
and almost compelling her Chopins and De
Mussets to live women's lives to amuse her.
Had Joan not been one of those 'unwomanly
women,' she might have been canonized
much sooner.

But it is not necessary to wear trousers and
smoke big cigars to live a man's life any more
than it is necessary to wear petticoats to live
a woman's. There are plenty of gowned and
bodiced women in ordinary civil life who
manage their own affairs and other people's,
including those of their menfolk, and are entirely masculine in their tastes and pursuits.
There always were such women, even in the
Victorian days when women had fewer legal
rights than men, and our modern women
magistrates, mayors, and members of Parliament were unknown. In reactionary Russia
in our own century a woman soldier organized an effective regiment of amazons,
which disappeared only because it was Alders-
hottian enough to be against the Revolution.
The exemption of women from military service is founded, not on any natural inaptitude
that men do not share, but on the fact that
communities cannot reproduce themselves
without plenty of women. Men are more
largely dispensable, and are sacrificed accordingly.

WAS JOAN SUICIDAL?

These two abnormalities were the only
ones that were irresistably prepotent in Joan;
and they brought her to the stake. Neither
of them was peculiar to her. There was nothing peculiar about her except the vigor and
scope of her mind and character, and the
intensity of her vital energy. She was accused
of a suicidal tendency; and it is a fact that
when she attempted to escape from Beaurevoir Castle by jumping from a tower said to
be sixty feet high, she took a risk beyond
reason, though she recovered from the crash
after a few days fasting. Her death was deliberately chosen as an alternative to life
without liberty. In battle she challenged death
as Wellington did at Waterloo, and as Nelson
habitually did when he walked his quarter
deck during his battles with all his decorations
in full blaze. As neither Nelson nor Wellington nor any of those who have performed
desperate feats, and preferred death to cap-
tivity, has been accused of suicidal mania,
Joan need not be suspected of it. In the
Beaurevoir affair there was more at stake
than her freedom. She was distracted by the
news that Compiègne was about to fall; and
she was convinced that she could save it if
only she could get free. Still, the leap was so
perilous that her conscience was not quite
easy about it; and she expressed this, as

usual, by saying that Saint Catherine had forbidden her to do it, but forgave her afterwards for her disobedience.

JOAN SUMMED UP

We may accept and admire Joan, then, as a sane and shrewd country girl of extraordinary strength of mind and hardihood of body. Everything she did was thoroughly calculated; and though the process was so rapid that she was hardly conscious of it, and ascribed it all to her voices, she was a woman of policy and not of blind impulse. In war she was as much a realist as Napoleon: she had his eye for artillery and his knowledge of what it could do. She did not expect besieged cities to fall Jerichowise at the sound of her trumpet, but, like Wellington, adapted her methods of attack to the peculiarities of the defence; and she anticipated the Napoleonic calculation that if you could only hold on long enough the other fellow will give in: for example, her final triumph at Orleans was achieved after her commander Dunois had sounded the retreat at the end of a day's fighting without a decision. She was never for a moment what so many romances and playwrights have pretended: a romantic young lady. She was a thorough daughter of the soil in her peasantlike matter-of-factness and doggedness, and her acceptance of great lords and kings and prelates as such without idolatry or snobbery, seeing at a glance how much they were individually good for. She had the respectable countrywoman's sense of the value of public decency, and would not tolerate foul language and neglect of religious observances, nor allow disreputable women to hang about her soldiers. She had one pious ejaculation 'En nom Dé!' and one meaningless oath 'Par mon martin'; and this much swearing she allowed to the incorrigibly blasphemous La Hire equally with herself. The value of this prudery was so great in restoring the self-respect of the badly demoralized army that, like most of her policy, it justified itself as soundly calculated. She talked to and dealt with people of all classes, from laborers to kings, without embarrassment or affection, and got them to do what she wanted when they were not afraid or corrupt. She could coax and she could hustle, her tongue having

a soft side and a sharp edge. She was very capable: a born boss.

JOAN'S IMMATURITY AND IGNORANCE

All this, however, must be taken with one heavy qualification. She was only a girl in her teens. If we could think of her as a managing woman of fifty we should seize her type at once; for we have plenty of managing women among us of that age who illustrate perfectly the sort of person she would have become had she lived. But she, being only a lass when all is said, lacked their knowledge of men's vanities and of the weight and proportion of social forces. She knew nothing of iron hands in velvet gloves: she just used her fists. She thought political changes much easier than they are, and, like Mahomet in his innocence of any world but the tribal world, wrote letters to kings calling on them to make millennial rearrangements. Consequently it was only in the enterprises that were really simple and compassable by swift physical force, like the coronation and the Orleans campaign, that she was successful.

Her want of academic education disabled her when she had to deal with such elaborately artificial structures as the great ecclesiastical and social institutions of the Middle Ages. She had a horror of heretics without suspecting that she was herself a heresiarch, one of the precursors of a schism that rent Europe in two, and cost centuries of bloodshed that is not yet staunched. She objected to foreigners on the sensible ground that they were not in their proper place in France; but she had no notion of how this brought her into conflict with Catholicism and Feudalism, both essentially international. She worked by commonsense; and where scholarship was the only clue to institutions she was in the dark, and broke her shins against them, all the more rudely because of her enormous self-confidence, which made her the least cautious of human beings in civil affairs.

This combination of inept youth and academic ignorance with great natural capacity, push, courage, devotion, originality and oddity, fully accounts for all the facts in Joan's career, and makes her a credible historical and human phenomenon; but it clashes most discordantly both with the idolatrous romance that has grown up round her, and the be-littling scepticism that reacts against that romance.

THE MAID IN LITERATURE

English readers would probably like to know how these idolizations and reactions have affected the books they are most familiar with about Joan. There is the first part of the Shakespearean, or pseudo-Shakespearean trilogy of Henry VI, in which Joan is one of the leading characters. This portrait of Joan is not more authentic than the descriptions in the London papers of George Washington in 1780, of Napoleon in 1803, the German Crown Prince in 1915, or of Lenin in 1917. It ends in mere scurrility. The impression left by it is that the playwright, having begun by an attempt to make Joan a beautiful and romantic figure, was told by his scandalized company that English patriotism would never stand a sympathetic representation of a French conqueror of English troops, and that unless he at once introduced all the old charges against Joan of being a sorceress and harlot, and assumed her to be guilty of all of them, his play could not be produced. As likely as not, this is what actually happened: indeed there is only one other apparent way of accounting for the sympathetic representa-tion of Joan as a heroine culminating in her eloquent appeal to the Duke of Burgundy, followed by the blackguardly scurrility of the concluding scenes. That other way is to as-sume that the original play was wholly scuri-lous, and that Shakespeare touched up the earlier scenes. As the work belongs to a period at which he was only beginning his practice as a tinker of old works, before his own style was fully formed and hardened, it is impossible to verify this guess. His finger is not unmistakably evident in the play, which is poor and base in its moral tone; but he may have tried to redeem it from downright infamy by shedding a momentary glamor on the figure of The Maid.

When we jump over two centuries to Schiller, we find Die Jungfrau von Orleans drowned in a witch's caldron of raging ro-mance. Schiller's Joan has not a single point of contact with the real Joan, nor indeed with any mortal woman that ever walked this earth. There is really nothing to be said of his play but that it is not about Joan at all, and can hardly be said to pretend to be; for he makes her die on the battlefield, find-ing her burning unbearable. Before Schiller came Voltaire, who burlesqued Homer in a mock epic called La Pucelle. It is the fashion to dismiss this with virtuous indignation as an obscene libel; and I certainly cannot de-fend it against the charge of extravagant inde-corum. But its purpose was not to depict Joan, but to kill with ridicule everything that Vol-taire righteously hated in the institutions and fashions of his own day. He made Joan ridiculous, but not contemptible nor (com-paratively) unchaste; and as he also made Homer and St Peter and St Denis and the brave Dunois ridiculous, and the other hero-ines of the poem very unchaste indeed, he may be said to have let Joan off very easily. But indeed the personal adventures of the characters are so outrageous, and so Homeric-ally free from any pretence at or even possi-bility of historical veracity, that those who affect to take them seriously only make them-selves Pecksniffian. Samuel Butler believed The Iliad to be a burlesque of Greek Jingoism and Greek religion, written by a hostage or a slave; and La Pucelle makes Butler's theory almost convincing. Voltaire represents Agnes Sorel, the Dauphin's mistress, whom Joan never met, as a woman with a consuming passion for the chastest concubinal fidelity, whose fate it was to be continually falling into the hands of licentious foes and suffering the worst extremities of rapine. The combats in which Joan rides a flying donkey, or in which, taken unaware with no clothes on, she defends Agnes with her sword, and in-flicts appropriate mutilations on her assail-ants, can be laughed at as they are intended to be without scruple; for no sane person could mistake them for sober history; and it may be that their ribald irreverence is more wholesome than the beglamored sentimen-tality of Schiller. Certainly Voltaire should not have asserted that Joan's father was a priest; but when he was out to *écraser l'in-fâme* (the French Church) he stuck at noth-ing.

So far, the literary representations of The Maid were legendary. But the publication by Quicherat in 1841 of the reports of her trial and rehabilitation placed the subject on a new footing. These entirely realistic documents created a living interest in Joan which Voltaire's mock Homerics and Schiller's romantic nonsense missed. Typical products of that interest in America and England are the histories of Joan by Mark Twain and Andrew Lang. Mark Twain was converted to downright worship of Joan directly by Quicherat. Later on, another man of genius, Anatole France, reacted against the Quicheratic wave of enthusiasm, and wrote a Life of Joan in which he attributed Joan's ideas to clerical prompting and her military success to an adroit use of her by Dunois as a *mascotte*: in short, he denied that she had any serious military or political ability. At this Andrew saw red, and went for Anatole's scalp in a rival Life of her which should be read as a corrective to the other. Lang had no difficulty in shewing that Joan's ability was not an unnatural fiction to be explained away as an illusion manufactured by priests and soldiers, but a straightforward fact.

It has been lightly pleaded in explanation that Anatole France is a Parisian of the art world, into whose scheme of things the able, hardheaded, hardhanded female, though she dominates provincial France and business Paris, does not enter; whereas Lang was a Scot, and every Scot knows that the grey mare is as likely as not to be the better horse. But this explanation does not convince me. I cannot believe that Anatole France does not know what everybody knows. I wish everybody knew all that he knows. One feels antipathies at work in his book. He is not anti-Joan; but he is anti-clerical, anti-mystic, and fundamentally unable to believe that there ever was any such person as the real Joan.

Mark Twain's Joan, skirted to the ground, and with as many petticoats as Noah's wife in a toy ark, is an attempt to combine Bayard with Esther Summerson from Bleak House into an unimpeachable American school teacher in armor. Like Esther Summerson she makes her creator ridiculous, and yet, being the work of a man of genius, remains a credible human goodygoody in spite of her creator's infatuation. It is the description rather than the valuation that is wrong. Andrew Lang and Mark Twain are equally determined to make Joan a beautiful and most ladylike Victorian; but both of them recognize and insist on her capacity for leadership, though the Scots scholar is less romantic about it than the Mississippi pilot. But then Lang was, by lifelong professional habit, a critic of biographies rather than a biographer, whereas Mark Twain writes his biography frankly in the form of a romance.

PROTESTANT MISUNDERSTANDINGS OF THE MIDDLE AGES

They had, however, one disability in common. To understand Joan's history it is not enough to understand her character: you must understand her environment as well. Joan in a nineteenth-twentieth century environment is as incongruous a figure as she would appear were she to walk down Piccadilly today in her fifteenth-century armor. To see her in her proper perspective you must understand Christendom and the Catholic Church, the Holy Roman Empire and the Feudal System, as they existed and were understood in the Middle Ages. If you confuse the Middle Ages with the Dark Ages, and are in the habit of ridiculing your aunt for wearing 'medieval clothes,' meaning those in vogue in the eighteen-nineties, and are quite convinced that the world has progressed enormously, both morally and mechanically, since Joan's time, then you will never understand why Joan was burnt, much less feel that you might have voted for burning her yourself if you had been a member of the court that tried her; and until you feel that you know nothing essential about her.

That the Mississippi pilot should have broken down on this misunderstanding is natural enough. Mark Twain, the Innocent Abroad, who saw the lovely churches of the Middle Ages without a throb of emotion, author of A Yankee at the Court of King Arthur, in which the heroes and heroines of medieval chivalry are guys seen through the eyes of a street arab, was clearly out of court from the beginning. Andrew Lang was better read; but, like Walter Scott, he enjoyed medieval history as a string of Border romances rather than as the record of a high European civilization based on a catholic faith. Both of them were baptized as Protestants, and impressed by all their schooling and most of their reading with the belief that Catholic bishops who burnt heretics were persecutors capable of any villainy; that all heretics were Albigensians or Husites or Jews or Protestants of the highest character; and that the Inquisition was a Chamber of Horrors invented expressly and exclusively for such burnings. Accordingly we find them representing Peter Cauchon, Bishop of Beauvais, the judge who sent Joan to the stake, as an unconscionable scoundrel, and all the questions put to her as 'traps' to ensnare and destroy her. And they assume unhesitatingly that the two or three score of canons and doctors of law and divinity who sat with Cauchon as assessors, were exact reproductions of him on slightly less elevated chairs and with a different head-dress.

COMPARATIVE FAIRNESS OF JOAN'S TRIAL

The truth is that Cauchon was threatened and insulted by the English for being too considerate to Joan. A recent French writer denies that Joan was burnt, and holds that Cauchon spirited her away and burnt somebody or something else in her place, and that the pretender who subsequently personated her at Orleans and elsewhere was not a pretender but the real authentic Joan. He is able to cite Cauchon's pro-Joan partiality in support of his view. As to the assessors, the objection to them is not that they were a row of uniform rascals, but that they were political partisans of Joan's enemies. This is a valid objection to all such trials; but in the absence of neutral tribunals they are unavoidable. A trial by Joan's French partisans would have been as unfair as the trial by her French opponents; and an equally mixed tribunal would have produced a deadlock. Such recent trials as those of Edith Cavell by a German tribunal and Roger Casement by an English one were open to the same objection; but they went forward to the death nevertheless, because neutral tribunals were not available. Edith, like Joan, was an arch heretic: in the middle of the war she declared before the world that 'Patriotism is not enough.' She nursed enemies back to health, and assisted their prisoners to escape, making it abundantly clear that she would help any fugitive or distressed person without asking whose side he was

on, and acknowledging no distinction before Christ between Tommy and Jerry and Pitou the *poilu*. Well might Edith have wished that she could bring the Middle Ages back, and have fifty civilians, learned in the law or vowed to the service of God, to support two skilled judges in trying her case according to the Catholic law of Christendom, and to argue it out with her at sitting after sitting for many weeks. The modern military Inquisition was not so squeamish. It shot her out of hand; and her countrymen, seeing in this a good opportunity for lecturing the enemy on his intolerance, put up a statue to her, but took particular care not to inscribe on the pedestal 'Patriotism is not enough,' for which omission, and the lie it implies, they will need Edith's intercession when they are themselves brought to judgment, if any heavenly power thinks such moral cowards capable of pleading to an intelligible indictment.

The point need be no further labored. Joan was persecuted essentially as she would be persecuted today. The change from burning to hanging or shooting may strike us as a change for the better. The change from careful trial under ordinary law to recklessly summary military terrorism may strike us as a change for the worse. But as far as toleration is concerned the trial and execution in Rouen in 1431 might have been an event of today; and we may charge our consciences accordingly. If Joan had to be dealt with by us in London she would be treated with no more toleration than Miss Sylvia Pankhurst, or the Peculiar People, or the parents who keep their children from the elementary school, or any of the others who cross the line we have to draw, rightly or wrongly, between the tolerable and the intolerable.

JOAN NOT TRIED AS A POLITICAL OFFENDER

Besides, Joan's trial was not, like Casement's, a national political trial. Ecclesiastical courts and the courts of the Inquisition (Joan was tried by a combination of the two) were Courts Christian: that is, international courts; and she was tried, not as a traitress, but as a heretic, blasphemer, sorceress and idolater. Her alleged offences were not political offences against England, nor against the Bur-

gundian faction in France, but against God
and against the common morality of Christendom. And although the idea we call Nationalism was so foreign to the medieval conception
of Christian society that it might almost have
been directly charged against Joan as an
additional heresy, yet it was not so charged;
and it is unreasonable to suppose that the
political bias of a body of Frenchmen like the
assessors would on this point have run
strongly in favor of the English foreigners
(even if they had been making themselves
particularly agreeable in France instead of
just the contrary) against a Frenchwoman
who had vanquished them.

The tragic part of the trial was that Joan,
like most prisoners tried for anything but the
simplest breaches of the ten commandments,
did not understand what they were accusing
her of. She was much more like Mark Twain
than like Peter Cauchon. Her attachment to
the Church was very different from the
Bishop's, and does not, in fact, bear close
examination from his point of view. She
delighted in the solaces the Church offers to
sensitive souls: to her, confession and communion were luxuries beside which the vulgar pleasures of the senses were trash. Her
prayers were wonderful conversations with
her three saints. Her piety seemed super-
human to the formally dutiful people whose
religion was only a task to them. But when
the Church was not offering her her favorite
luxuries, but calling on her to accept its
interpretation of God's will, and to sacrifice
her own, she flatly refused, and made it clear
that her notion of a Catholic Church was
one in which the Pope was Pope Joan. How
could the Church tolerate that, when it had
just destroyed Hus, and had watched the
career of Wycliffe with a growing anger that
would have brought him, too, to the stake,
had he not died a natural death before the
wrath fell on him in his grave? Neither Hus
nor Wycliffe was as bluntly defiant as Joan:
both were reformers of the Church like
Luther; whilst Joan, like Mrs. Eddy, was
quite prepared to supersede St Peter as the
rock on which the Church was built, and,
like Mahomet, was always ready with a private revelation from God to settle every question and fit every occasion.

The enormity of Joan's pretension was
proved by her own unconsciousness of it,
which we call her innocence, and her friends
called her simplicity. Her solutions of the
problems presented to her seemed, and indeed mostly were, the plainest commonsense,
and their revelation to her by her Voices was
to her a simple matter of fact. How could
plain commonsense and simple fact seem to
her to be that hideous thing, heresy? When
rival prophetesses came into the field, she
was down on them at once for liars and hum-
bugs; but she never thought of them as heretics. She was in a state of invincible ignorance
as to the Church's view; and the Church
could not tolerate her pretensions without
either waiving its authority or giving her a
place beside the Trinity during her lifetime
and in her teens, which was unthinkable.
Thus an irresistible force met an immovable
obstacle, and developed the heat that consumed poor Joan.

Mark and Andrew would have shared her
innocence and her fate had they been dealt
with by the Inquisition: that is why their
accounts of the trial are as absurd as hers
might have been could she have written one.
All that can be said for their assumption that
Cauchon was a vulgar villain, and that the
questions put to Joan were traps, is that it has
the support of the inquiry which rehabilitated
her twenty-five years later. But this rehabilitation was as corrupt as the contrary proceeding
applied to Cromwell by our Restoration re-
actionaries. Cauchon had been dug up, and
his body thrown into the common sewer.
Nothing was easier than to accuse him of
cozenage, and declare the whole trial void
on that account. That was what everybody
wanted, from Charles the Victorious, whose
credit was bound up with The Maid's, to the
patriotic Nationalist populace, who idolized
Joan's memory. The English were gone; and
a verdict in their favor would have been an
outrage on the throne and on the patriotism
which Joan had set on foot.

We have none of these overwhelming motives of political convenience and popularity
to bias us. For us the first trial stands valid;
and the rehabilitation would be negligible
but for the mass of sincere testimony it produced as to Joan's engaging personal character. The question then arises: how did The
Church get over the verdict at the first trial
when it canonized Joan five hundred years
later?

THE CHURCH UNCOMPROMISED BY ITS AMENDS

Easily enough. In the Catholic Church, far more than in law, there is no wrong without a remedy. It does not defer to Joanesque private judgment as such, the supremacy of private judgment for the individual being the quintessence of Protestantism; nevertheless it finds a place for private judgment *in excelsis* by admitting that the highest wisdom may come as a divine revelation to an individual. On sufficient evidence it will declare that individual a saint. Thus, as revelation may come by way of an enlightenment of the private judgment no less than by the words of a celestial personage appearing in a vision, a saint may be defined as a person of heroic virtue whose private judgment is privileged. Many innovating saints, notably Francis and Clare, have been in conflict with the Church during their lives, and have thus raised the question whether they were heretics or saints. Francis might have gone to the stake had he lived longer. It is therefore by no means impossible for a person to be excommunicated as a heretic, and on further consideration canonized as a saint. Excommunication by a provincial ecclesiastical court is not one of the acts for which the Church claims infallibility. Perhaps I had better inform my Protestant readers that the famous Dogma of Papal Infallibility is by far the most modest pretension of the kind in existence. Compared with our infallible democracies, our infallible medical councils, our infallible astronomers, our infallible parliaments, the Pope is on his knees in the dust confessing his ignorance before the throne of God, asking only that as to certain historical matters on which he has clearly more sources of information open to him than anyone else his decision shall be taken as final. The Church may, and perhaps some day will, canonize Galileo without compromising such infallibility as it claims for the Pope, if not without compromising the infallibility claimed for the Book of Joshua by simple souls whose rational faith in more important things has become bound up with a quite irrational faith in the chronicle of Joshua's campaigns as a treatise on physics. Therefore the Church will probably not canonize Galileo yet awhile, though it might do worse. But it has been able to canonize Joan without any compromise at all. She never doubted that the sun went round the earth: she had seen it so too often.

Still, there was a great wrong done to Joan and to the conscience of the world by her burning. *Tout comprendre, c'est tout pardonner,* which is the Devil's sentimentality, cannot excuse it. When we have admitted that the tribunal was not only honest and legal, but exceptionally merciful in respect of sparing Joan the torture which was customary when she was obdurate as to taking the oath, and that Cauchon was far more self-disciplined and conscientious both as priest and lawyer than any English judge ever dreams of being in a political case in which his party and class prejudices are involved, the human fact remains that the burning of Joan of Arc was a horror, and that a historian who would defend it would defend anything. The final criticism of its physical side is implied in the refusal of the Marquesas islanders to be persuaded that the English did not eat Joan. Why, they ask, should anyone take the trouble to roast a human being except with that object? They cannot conceive its being a pleasure. As we have no answer for them that is not shameful to us, let us blush for our more complicated and pretentious savagery before we proceed to unravel the business further, and see what other lessons it contains for us.

CRUELTY, MODERN AND MEDIEVAL

First, let us get rid of the notion that the mere physical cruelty of the burning has any special significance. Joan was burnt just as dozens of less interesting heretics were burnt in her time. Christ, in being crucified, only shared the fate of thousands of forgotten malefactors. They have no pre-eminence in mere physical pain: much more horrible executions than theirs are on record, to say nothing of the agonies of so-called natural death at its worst.

Joan was burnt more than five hundred years ago. More than three hundred years later: that is, only about a hundred years before I was born, a woman was burnt on Stephen's Green in my native city of Dublin for coining, which was held to be treason. In my preface to the recent volume on English Prisons under Local Government, by Sidney and Beatrice Webb, I have mentioned that when I was already a grown man I saw Richard Wagner conduct two concerts, and that when Richard Wagner was a young man he saw and avoided a crowd of people hastening to see a soldier broken on the wheel by the more cruel of the two ways of carrying out that hideous method of execution. Also that the penalty of hanging, drawing, and quartering, unmentionable in its details, was abolished so recently that there are men living who have been sentenced to it. We are still flogging criminals, and clamoring for more flogging. Not even the most sensationally frightful of these atrocities inflicted on its victim the misery, degradation, and conscious waste and loss of life suffered in our modern prisons, especially the model ones, without, as far as I can see, rousing any more compunction than the burning of heretics did in the Middle Ages. We have not even the excuse of getting some fun out of our prisons as the Middle Ages did out of their stakes and wheels and gibbets. Joan herself judged this matter when she had to choose between imprisonment and the stake, and chose the stake. And thereby she deprived The Church of the plea that it was guiltless of her death, which was the work of the secular arm. The Church should have confined itself to excommunicating her. There it was within its rights: she had refused to accept its authority or comply with its conditions; and it could say with truth 'You are not one of us: go forth and find the religion that suits you, or found one for yourself.' It had no right to say 'You may return to us now that you have recanted; but you shall stay in a dungeon all the rest of your life.' Unfortunately, The Church did not believe that there was any genuine soul saving religion outside itself; and it was deeply corrupted, as all the Churches were and still are, by primitive Calibanism (in Browning's sense), or the propitiation of a dreaded deity by suffering and sacrifice. Its method was not cruelty for cruelty's sake, but cruelty for the salvation of Joan's soul. Joan, however, believed that the saving of her soul was her own business, and not that of *les gens d'église*. By using that term as she did, mistrustfully and contemptuously, she announced herself as, in germ, an anti-Clerical as thoroughgoing as Voltaire or Anatole France. Had

she said in so many words 'To the dustbin with the Church Militant and its blackcoated officials: I recognize only the Church Triumphant in heaven,' she would hardly have put her view more plainly.

CATHOLIC ANTI-CLERICALISM

I must not leave it to be inferred here that one cannot be an anti-Clerical and a good Catholic too. All the reforming Popes have been vehement anti-Clericals, veritable scourges of the clergy. All the great Orders arose from dissatisfaction with the priests: that of the Franciscans with priestly snobbery, that of the Dominicans with priestly laziness and Laodiceanism, that of the Jesuits with priestly apathy and ignorance and indiscipline. The most bigoted Ulster Orangeman or Leicester Low Church bourgeois (as described by Mr Henry Nevinson) is a mere Gallio compared to Machiavelli, who, though no Protestant, was a fierce anti-Clerical. Any Catholic may, and many Catholics do, denounce any priest or body of priests, as lazy, drunken, idle, dissolute, and unworthy of their great Church and their function as the pastors of their flocks of human souls. But to say that the souls of the people are no business of the Churchmen is to go a step further, a step across the Rubicon. Joan virtually took that step.

CATHOLICISM NOT YET CATHOLIC ENOUGH

And so, if we admit, as we must, that the burning of Joan was a mistake, we must broaden Catholicism sufficiently to include her in its charter. Our Churches must admit that no official organization of mortal men whose vocation does not carry with it extraordinary mental powers (and this is all that any Church Militant can in the face of fact and history pretend to be), can keep pace with the private judgment of persons of genius except when, by a very rare accident, the genius happens to be Pope, and not even then unless he is an exceedingly overbearing Pope. The Churches must learn humility as well as teach it. The Apostolic Succession cannot be secured or confined by the laying on of hands: the tongues of fire have descended on heathens and outcasts too often for that, leaving anointed Churchmen to scandalize History as worldly rascals. When the Church Militant behaves as if it were already the Church Triumphant, it makes these appalling blunders about Joan and Bruno and Galileo and the rest which make it so difficult for a Freethinker to join it; and a Church which has no place for Freethinkers: nay, which does not inculcate and encourage freethinking with a complete belief that thought, when really free, must by its own law take the path that leads to The Church's bosom, not only has no future in modern culture, but obviously has no faith in the valid science of its own tenets, and is guilty of the heresy that theology and science are two different and opposite impulses, rivals for human allegiance.

I have before me the letter of a Catholic priest. 'In your play,' he writes, 'I see the dramatic presentation of the conflict of the Regal, sacerdotal, and Prophetical powers, in which Joan was crushed. To me it is not the victory of any one of them over the others that will bring peace and the Reign of the Saints in the Kingdom of God, but their fruitful interaction in a costly but noble state of tension.' The Pope himself could not put it better; nor can I. We must accept the tension, and maintain it nobly without letting ourselves be tempted to relieve it by burning the thread. This is Joan's lesson to The Church; and its formulation by the hand of a priest emboldens me to claim that her canonization was a magnificently Catholic gesture as the canonization of a Protestant saint by the Church of Rome. But its special value and virtue cannot be apparent until it is known and understood as such. If any simple priest for whom this is too hard a saying tells me that it was not so intended, I shall remind him that the Church is in the hands of God, and not, as simple priests imagine, God in the hands of the Church; so if he answers too confidently for God's intentions he may be asked 'Hast thou entered into the springs of the sea? or hast thou walked in the recesses of the deep?' And Joan's own answer is also the answer of old: 'Though He slay me, yet will I trust in Him; *but I will maintain my own ways before Him.*'

THE LAW OF CHANGE IS THE LAW OF GOD

When Joan maintained her own ways she claimed, like Job, that there was not only God and the Church to be considered, but the Word made Flesh: that is, the unaveraged individual, representing life possibly at its highest actual human evolution and possibly at its lowest, but never at its merely mathematical average. Now there is no deification of the democratic average in the theory of the Church: it is an avowed hierarchy in which the members are sifted until at the end of the process an individual stands supreme as the Vicar of Christ. But when the process is examined it appears that its successive steps of selection and election are of the superior by the inferior (the cardinal vice of democracy), with the result that great popes are as rare and accidental as great kings, and that it has sometimes been safer for an aspirant to the Chair and the Keys to pass as a moribund dotard than as an energetic saint. At best very few popes have been canonized, or could be without letting down the standard of sanctity set by the self-elected saints.

No other result could have been reasonably expected; for it is not possible that an official organization of the spiritual needs of millions of men and women, mostly poor and ignorant, should compete successfully in the selection of its principals with the direct choice of the Holy Ghost as it flashes with unerring aim upon the individual. Nor can any College of Cardinals pray effectively that its choice may be inspired. The conscious prayer of the inferior may be that his choice may light on a greater than himself; but the sub-conscious intention of his self-preserving individuality must be to find a trustworthy servant for his own purposes. The saints and prophets, though they may be accidentally in this or that official position or rank, are always really self-selected, like Joan. And since neither Church nor State, by the secular necessities of its constitution, can guarantee even the recognition of such self-chosen missions, there is nothing for us but to make it a point of honor to privilege heresy to the last bearable degree on the simple ground that all evolution in thought and conduct must at first appear as heresy and misconduct. In short, though all society is founded on intolerance, all improvement is founded on tolerance, or the recognition of the fact that the law of evolution is Ibsen's law of change. And as the law of God in any sense of the word which can now command a faith proof against science is a law of evolution, it follows that the law of God is a law of change, and that when the Churches set themselves against change as such, they are setting themselves against the law of God.

CREDULITY, MODERN AND MEDIEVAL

When Abernethy, the famous doctor, was asked why he indulged himself with all habits he warned his patients against as unhealthy, he replied that his business was that of a direction post, which points out the way to a place, but does not go thither itself. He might have added that neither does it compel the traveller to go thither, nor prevent him from seeking some other way. Unfortunately our clerical direction posts always do coerce the traveller when they have the political power to do so. When the Church was a temporal as well as a spiritual power, and for long after to the full extent to which it could control or influence the temporal power, it enforced conformity by persecutions that were all the more ruthless because their intention was so excellent. Today, when the doctor has succeeded to the priest, and can do practically what he likes with parliament and the press through the blind faith in him which has succeeded to the far more critical faith in the parson, legal compulsion to take the doctor's prescription, however poisonous, is carried to an extent that would have horrified the Inquisition and staggered Archbishop Laud. Our credulity is grosser than that of the Middle Ages, because the priest had no such direct pecuniary interest in our sins as the doctor has in our diseases: he did not starve when all was well with his flock, nor prosper when they were perishing, as our private commercial doctors must. Also the medieval cleric believed that something extremely unpleasant would happen to him after death if he was unscrupulous, a belief now practically extinct among persons receiving a dogmatically materialist education.

Our professional corporations are Trade Unions without souls to be damned; and they will soon drive us to remind them that they have bodies to be kicked. The Vatican was never soulless: at worst it was a political conspiracy to make the Church supreme temporally as well as spiritually. Therefore the question raised by Joan's burning is a burning question still, though the penalties involved are not so sensational. That is why I am probing it. If it were only an historical curiosity I would not waste my readers' time and my own on it for five minutes.

TOLERATION, MODERN AND MEDIEVAL

The more closely we grapple with it the more difficult it becomes. At first sight we are disposed to repeat that Joan should have been excommunicated and then left to go her way, though she would have protested vehemently against so cruel a deprivation of her spiritual food; for confession, absolution, and the body of her Lord were first necessaries of life to her. Such a spirit as Joan's might have got over that difficulty as the Church of England got over the Bulls of Pope Leo, by making a Church of her own, and affirming it to be the temple of the true and original faith from which her persecutors had strayed. But as such a proceeding was, in the eyes of both Church and State at that time, a spreading of damnation and anarchy, its toleration involved a greater strain on faith in freedom than political and ecclesiastical human nature could bear. It is easy to say that the Church should have waited for the alleged evil results instead of assuming that they would occur, and what they would be. That sounds simple enough; but if a modern Public Health Authority were to leave people entirely to their own devices in the matter of sanitation, saying, 'We have nothing to do with drainage or your views about drainage; but if you catch smallpox or typhus we will prosecute you and have you punished very severely like the authorities in Butler's Erewhon,' it would either be removed to the County Asylum or reminded that A's neglect of sanitation may kill the child of B two miles off, or start an epidemic in which the most conscientious sanitarians may perish.

We must face the fact that society is

founded on intolerance. There are glaring cases of the abuse of intolerance; but they are quite as characteristic of our own age as of the Middle Ages. The typical modern example and contrast is compulsory inoculation replacing what was virtually compulsory baptism. But compulsion to inoculate is objected to as a crudely unscientific and mischievous anti-sanitary quackery, not in the least because we think it wrong to compel people to protect their children from disease. Its opponents would make it a crime, and will probably succeed in doing so; and that will be just as intolerant as making it compulsory. Neither the Pasteurians nor their opponents the Sanitarians would leave parents free to bring up their children naked, though that course also has some plausible advocates. We may prate of toleration as we will; but society must always draw a line somewhere between allowable conduct and insanity or crime, in spite of the risk of mistaking sages for lunatics and saviors for blasphemers. We must persecute, even to the death; and all we can do to mitigate the danger of persecution is, first, to be very careful what we persecute, and second, to bear in mind that unless there is a large liberty to shock conventional people, and a well informed sense of the value of originality, individuality, and eccentricity, the result will be apparent stagnation covering a repression of evolutionary forces which will eventually explode with extravagant and probably destructive violence.

VARIABILITY OF TOLERATION

The degree of tolerance attainable at any moment depends on the strain under which society is maintaining its cohesion. In war, for instance, we suppress the gospels and put Quakers in prison, muzzle the newspapers, and make it a serious offence to shew a light at night. Under the strain of invasion the French Government in 1792 struck off 4000 heads, mostly on grounds that would not in time of settled peace have provoked any Government to chloroform a dog; and in 1920 the British Government slaughtered and burnt in Ireland to persecute the advocates of a constitutional change which it had presently to effect itself. Later on the Fascisti in Italy did everything that the Black and Tans did in Ireland, with some grotesquely ferocious variations, under the strain of an unskilled attempt at industrial revolution by Socialists who understood Socialism even less than Capitalists understand Capitalism. In the United States an incredibly savage persecution of Russians took place during the scare spread by the Russian Bolshevik revolution after 1917. These instances could easily be multiplied; but they are enough to shew that between a maximum of indulgent toleration and a ruthlessly intolerant Terrorism there is a scale through which toleration is continually rising or falling, and that there was not the smallest ground for the self-complacent conviction of the nineteenth century that it was more tolerant than the fifteenth, or that such an event as the execution of Joan could not possibly occur in what we call our own more enlightened times. Thousands of women, each of them a thousand times less dangerous and terrifying to our Governments than Joan was to the Government of her day, have within the last ten years been slaughtered, starved to death, burnt out of house and home, and what not that Persecution and Terror could do to them, in the course of Crusades far more tyrannically pretentious than the medieval Crusades which proposed nothing more hyperbolical than the rescue of the Holy Sepulchre from the Saracens. The Inquisition, with its English equivalent the Star Chamber, are gone in the sense that their names are now disused; but can any of the modern substitutes for the Inquisition, the Special Tribunals and Commissions, the punitive expeditions, the suspensions of the Habeas Corpus Act, the proclamations of martial law and of minor states of siege, and the rest of them, claim that their victims have as fair a trial, as well considered a body of law to govern their cases, or as conscientious a judge to insist on strict legality of procedure as Joan had from the Inquisition and from the spirit of the Middle Ages even when her country was under the heaviest strain of civil and foreign war? From us she would have had no trial and no law except a Defence of The Realm Act suspending all law; and for judge she would have had, at best, a bothered major, and at worst a promoted advocate in ermine and scarlet to whom the scruples of a trained ecclesiastic like Cauchon would seem ridiculous and ungentlemanly.

THE CONFLICT BETWEEN GENIUS AND
DISCIPLINE

Having thus brought the matter home to ourselves, we may now consider the special feature of Joan's mental constitution which made her so unmanageable. What is to be done on the one hand with rulers who will not give any reason for their orders, and on the other with people who cannot understand the reasons when they are given? The government of the world, political, industrial, and domestic, has to be carried on mostly by the giving and obeying of orders under just these conditions. 'Don't argue: do as you are told' has to be said not only to children and soldiers, but practically to everybody. Fortunately most people do not want to argue: they are only too glad to be saved the trouble of thinking for themselves. And the ablest and most independent thinkers are content to understand their own special department. In other departments they will unhesitatingly ask for and accept the instructions of a policeman or the advice of a tailor without demanding or desiring explanations.

Nevertheless, there must be some ground for attaching authority to an order. A child will obey its parents, a soldier his officer, a philosopher a railway porter, and a workman a foreman, all without question, because it is generally accepted that those who give the orders understand what they are about, and are duly authorized and even obliged to give them, and because, in the practical emergencies of daily life, there is no time for lessons and explanations, or for arguments as to their validity. Such obediences are as necessary to the continuous operation of our social system as the revolutions of the earth are to the succession of night and day. But they are not so spontaneous as they seem: they have to be very carefully arranged and maintained. A bishop will defer to and obey a king; but let a curate venture to give him an order, however necessary and sensible, and the bishop will forget his cloth and damn the curate's impudence. The more obedient a man is to accredited authority the more jealous he is of allowing any unauthorized person to order him about.

With all this in mind, consider the career of Joan. She was a village girl, in authority over sheep and pigs, dogs and chickens, and to some extent over her father's hired laborers when he hired any, but over no one else on earth. Outside the farm she had no authority, no prestige, no claim to the smallest deference. Yet she ordered everybody about, from her uncle to the king, the archbishop, and the military General Staff. Her uncle obeyed her like a sheep, and took her to the castle of the local commander, who, on being ordered about, tried to assert himself, but soon collapsed and obeyed. And so on up to the king, as we have seen. This would have been unbearably irritating even if her orders had been offered as rational solutions of the desperate difficulties in which her social superiors found themselves just then. But they were not so offered. Nor were they offered as the expression of Joan's arbitrary will. It was never 'I say so,' but always 'God says so.'

JOAN AS THEOCRAT

Leaders who take that line have no trouble with some people, and no end of trouble with others. They need never fear a lukewarm reception. Either they are messengers of God, or they are blasphemous impostors. In the Middle Ages the general belief in witchcraft greatly intensified this contrast, because when an apparent miracle happened (as in the case of the wind changing at Orleans) it proved the divine mission to the credulous, and proved a contract with the devil to the sceptical. All through, Joan had to depend on those who accepted her as an incarnate angel against those who added to an intense resentment of her presumption a bigoted abhorrence of her as a witch. To this abhorrence we must add the extreme irritation of those who did not believe in the voices, and regarded her as a liar and impostor. It is hard to conceive anything more infuriating to a statesman or a military commander, or to a court favorite, than to be overruled at every turn, or to be robbed of the ear of the reigning sovereign, by an impudent young upstart practising on the credulity of the populace and the vanity and silliness of an immature prince by exploiting a few of those lucky coincidences which pass as miracles with uncritical people. Not only were the envy, snobbery, and competitive ambition of the baser natures exacerbated by Joan's success, but among the friendly ones that were clever enough to be critical a quite reasonable scepticism and mistrust of her ability, founded on a fair observation of her obvious ignorance and temerity, were at work against her. And as she met all remonstrances and all criticisms, not with arguments or persuasion, but with a flat appeal to the authority of God and a claim to be in God's special confidence, she must have seemed, to all who were not infatuated by her, so insufferable that nothing but an unbroken chain of overwhelming successes in the military and political field could have saved her from the wrath that finally destroyed her.

UNBROKEN SUCCESS ESSENTIAL IN THEOCRACY

To forge such a chain she needed to be the King, the Archbishop of Rheims, the Bastard of Orleans, and herself into the bargain; and that was impossible. From the moment when she failed to stimulate Charles to follow up his coronation with a swoop on Paris she was lost. The fact that she insisted on this whilst the king and the rest timidly and foolishly thought they could square the Duke of Burgundy, and effect a combination with him against the English, made her a terrifying nuisance to them; and from that time onward she could do nothing but prowl about the battlefields waiting for some lucky chance to sweep the captains into a big move. But it was to the enemy that the chance came: she was taken prisoner by the Burgundians fighting before Compiègne, and at once discovered that she had not a friend in the political world. Had she escaped she would probably have fought on until the English were gone, and then had to shake the dust of the court off her feet, and retire to Domrémy as Garibaldi had to retire to Caprera.

MODERN DISTORTIONS OF JOAN'S HISTORY

This, I think, is all that we can now pretend to say about the prose of Joan's career. The romance of her rise, the tragedy of her execution, and the comedy of the attempts of posterity to make amends for that execution, belong to my play and not to my preface, which must be confined to a sober essay on the facts. That such an essay is badly needed can be ascertained by examining any of our standard works of reference. They give accurately enough the facts about the visit to Vaucouleurs, the annunciation to Charles at Chinon, the raising of the siege of Orleans and the subsequent battles, the coronation at Rheims, the capture at Compiègne, and the trial and execution at Rouen, with their dates and the names of the people concerned; but they all break down on the melodramatic legend of the wicked bishop and the entrapped maiden and the rest of it. It would be far less misleading if they were wrong as to the facts, and right in their view of the facts. As it is, they illustrate the too little considered truth that the fashion in which we think changes like the fashion of our clothes, and that it is difficult, if not impossible, for most people to think otherwise than in the fashion of their own period.

HISTORY ALWAYS OUT OF DATE

This, by the way, is why children are never taught contemporary history. Their history books deal with periods of which the thinking has passed out of fashion, and the circumstances no longer apply to active life. For example, they are taught history about Washington, and told lies about Lenin. In Washington's time they were told lies (the same lies) about Washington, and taught history about Cromwell. In the fifteenth and sixteenth centuries they were told lies about Joan, and by this time might very well be told the truth about her. Unfortunately the lies did not cease when the political circumstances became obsolete. The Reformation, which Joan had unconsciously anticipated, kept the questions which arose in her case burning up to our own day (you can see plenty of the burnt houses still in Ireland), with the result that Joan has remained the subject of anti-Clerical lies, of specifically Protestant lies, and of Roman Catholic evasions of her unconscious Protestantism. The truth sticks in our throats with all the sauces it is served with: it will never go down until we take it without any sauce at all.

THE REAL JOAN NOT MARVELLOUS ENOUGH FOR US

But even in its simplicity, the faith demanded by Joan is one which the anti-metaphysical temper of nineteenth-century civilization, which remains powerful in England and America, and is tyrannical in France, contemptuously refuses her. We do not, like her contemporaries, rush to the opposite extreme in a recoil from her as from a witch self-sold to the devil, because we do not believe in the devil nor in the possibility of commercial contracts with him. Our credulity, though enormous, is not boundless; and our stock of it is quite used up by our mediums, clairvoyants, hand readers, slate writers, Christian Scientists, psycho-analysts, electronic vibration diviners, therapeutists of all schools registered and unregistered, astrologers, astronomers who tell us that the sun is nearly a hundred million miles away and that Betelgeuse is ten times as big as the whole universe, physicists who balance Betelgeuse by describing the incredible smallness of the atom, and a host of other marvel mongers whose credulity would have dissolved the Middle Ages in a roar of sceptical merriment. In the Middle Ages people believed that the earth was flat, for which they had at least the evidence of their senses: we believe it to be round, not because as many as one per cent of us could give the physical reasons for so quaint a belief, but because modern science has convinced us that nothing that is obvious is true, and that everything that is magical, improbable, extraordinary, gigantic, microscopic, heartless, or outrageous is scientific.

I must not, by the way, be taken as implying that the earth is flat, or that all or any of our amazing credulities are delusions or impostures. I am only defending my own age against the charge of being less imaginative than the Middle Ages. I affirm that the nineteenth century, and still more the twentieth, can knock the fifteenth into a cocked hat in point of susceptibility to marvels and saints and prophets and magicians and monsters and fairy tales of all kinds. The proportion of marvel to immediately credible statement in the latest edition of the Encyclopædia Britannica is enormously greater than in the Bible.

The medieval doctors of divinity who did not pretend to settle how many angels could dance on the point of a needle cut a very poor figure as far as romantic credulity is concerned beside the modern physicists who have settled to the billionth of a millimetre every movement and position in the dance of the electrons. Not for words would I question the precise accuracy of these calculations or the existence of electrons (whatever they may be). The fate of Joan is a warning to me against such heresy. But why the men who believe in electrons should regard themselves as less credulous than the men who believed in angels is not apparent to me. If they refuse to believe, with the Rouen assessors of 1431, that Joan was a witch, it is not because that explanation is too marvellous, but because it is not marvellous enough.

THE STAGE LIMITS OF HISTORICAL REPRESENTATION

For the story of Joan I refer the reader to the play which follows. It contains all that need be known about her; but as it is for stage use I have had to condense into three and a half hours a series of events which in their historical happening were spread over four times as many months; for the theatre imposes unities of time and place from which Nature in her boundless wastefulness is free. Therefore the reader must not suppose that Joan really put Robert de Baudricourt in her pocket in fifteen minutes, nor that her excommunication, recantation, relapse, and death at the stake were a matter of half an hour or so. Neither do I claim more for my dramatizations of Joan's contemporaries than that some of them are probably slightly more like the originals than those imaginary portraits of all the Popes from Saint Peter onward through the Dark Ages which are still gravely exhibited in the Uffizi in Florence (or were when I was there last). My Dunois would do equally well for the Duc d'Alençon. Both left descriptions of Joan so similar that, as a man always describes himself unconsciously whenever he describes anyone else, I have inferred that these goodnatured young men were very like one another in mind; so I have lumped the twain into a single figure, thereby saving the theatre manager a salary and a suit of armor. Dunois' face, still on record at Châteaudun, is a suggestive help. But I really know no more about these men and their circle than Shakespear knew about Falconbridge and the Duke of Austria, or about Macbeth and Macduff. In view of things they did in history, and have to do again in the play, I can only invent appropriate characters for them in Shakespear's manner.

A VOID IN THE ELIZABETHAN DRAMA

I have, however, one advantage over the Elizabethans. I write in full view of the Middle Ages, which may be said to have been rediscovered in the middle of the nineteenth century after an eclipse of about four hundred and fifty years. The Renascence of antique literature and art in the sixteenth century, and the lusty growth of Capitalism, between them buried the Middle Ages; and their resurrection is a second Renascence. Now there is not a breath of medieval atmosphere in Shakespear's histories. His John of Gaunt is like a study of the old age of Drake. Although he was a Catholic by family tradition, his figures are all intensely Protestant, individualist, sceptical, self-centred in everything but their love affairs, and completely personal and selfish even in them. His kings are not statesmen: his cardinals have no religion: a novice can read his plays from one end to the other without learning that the world is finally governed by forces expressing themselves in religions and laws which make epochs rather than by vulgarly ambitious individuals who make rows. The divinity which shapes our ends, rough hew them how we will, is mentioned fatalistically only to be forgotten immediately like a passing vague apprehension. To Shakespear as to Mark Twain, Cauchon would have been a tyrant and a bully instead of a Catholic, and the inquisitor Lemaître would have been a Sadist instead of a lawyer. Warwick would have had no more feudal quality than his successor the King Maker has in the play of Henry VI. We should have seen them all completely satisfied that if they would only to their own selves be true they could not then be false to any man (a precept which represents the reaction against medievalism at its intensest) as if they were beings in the air, without public responsibilities of any kind. All Shakespear's characters are so: that is why they seem natural to our middle classes, who are comfortable and irresponsible at other people's expense, and are neither ashamed of that condition nor even conscious of it. Nature abhors this vacuum in Shakespear; and I have taken care to let the medieval atmosphere blow through my play freely. Those who see it performed will not mistake the startling event it records for a mere personal accident. They will have before them not only the visible and human puppets, but the Church, the Inquisition, the Feudal System, with divine inspiration always beating against their too inelastic limits: all more terrible in their dramatic force than any of the little mortal figures clanking about in plate armor or moving silently in the frocks and hoods of the order of St Dominic.

TRAGEDY, NOT MELODRAMA

There are no villains in the piece. Crime, like disease, is not interesting: it is something to be done away with by general consent, and that is all about it. It is what men do at their best, with good intentions, and what normal men and women find that they must and will do in spite of their intentions, that really concern us. The rascally bishop and the cruel inquisitor of Mark Twain and Andrew Lang are as dull as pickpockets; and they reduce Joan to the level of the even less interesting person whose pocket is picked. I have represented both of them as capable and eloquent exponents of The Church Militant and The Church Litigant, because only by doing so can I maintain my drama on the level of high tragedy and save it from becoming a mere police court sensation. A villain in a play can never be anything more than a *diabolus ex machina,* possibly a more exciting expedient than a *deus ex machina,* but both equally mechanical, and therefore interesting only as mechanism. It is, I repeat, what normally innocent people do that concerns us; and if Joan had not been burnt by normally innocent people in the energy of their righteousness her death at their hands would have no more significance than the Tokyo earthquake, which burnt a great many maidens. The tragedy of such murders is that they are not committed by murderers. They are judicial murders, pious murders; and this contradiction at once brings an element of comedy into the tragedy: the angels may weep at the murder, but the gods laugh at the murderers.

THE INEVITABLE FLATTERIES OF TRAGEDY

Here then we have a reason why my drama of Saint Joan's career, though it may give the essential truth of it, gives an inexact picture of some accidental facts. It goes almost without saying that the old Jeanne d'Arc melodramas, reducing everything to a conflict of villain and hero, or in Joan's case villain and heroine, not only miss the point entirely, but falsify the characters, making Cauchon a scoundrel, Joan a prima donna, and Dunois a lover. But the writer of high tragedy and comedy, aiming at the innermost attainable truth, must needs flatter Cauchon nearly as much as the melodramatist vilifies him. Although there is, as far as I have been able to discover, nothing against Cauchon that convicts him of bad faith or exceptional severity in his judicial relations with Joan, or of as much anti-prisoner, pro-police, class and sectarian bias as we now take for granted in our own courts, yet there is hardly more warrant for classing him as a great Catholic churchman, completely proof against the passions roused by the temporal situation. Neither does the inquisitor Lemaître, in such scanty accounts of him as are now recoverable, appear quite so able a master of his duties and of the case before him as I have given him credit for being. But it is the business of the stage to make its figures more intelligible to themselves than they would be in real life; for by no other means can they be made intelligible to the audience. And in this case Cauchon and Lemaître have to make intelligible not only themselves but the Church and the Inquisition, just as Warwick has to make the feudal system intelligible, the three between them having thus to make a twentieth-century audience conscious of an epoch fundamentally different from its own. Obviously the real Cauchon, Lemaître, and Warwick could not have done this: they were part of the Middle Ages themselves, and therefore as unconscious of its peculiarities as of the atomic formula of the air they breathed. But the play would be unintelligible if I had not endowed them with enough of this consciousness to enable them to explain their attitude to the twentieth century. All I claim is that by this inevitable sacrifice of verisimilitude I have secured in the only possible way sufficient veracity to justify me in claiming that as far as I can gather from the available documentation, and from such powers of divination as I possess, the things I represent these three exponents of the drama as saying are the things they actually would have said if they had known what they were really doing. And beyond this neither drama nor history can go in my hands.

SOME WELL-MEANT PROPOSALS FOR THE IMPROVEMENT OF THE PLAY

I have to thank several critics on both sides of the Atlantic, including some whose admiration for my play is most generously enthusiastic, for their heartfelt instructions as to how it can be improved. They point out that by the excision of the epilogue and all the references to such undramatic and tedious matters as the Church, the feudal system, the Inquisition, the theory of heresy and so forth, all of which, they point out, would be ruthlessly blue pencilled by any experienced manager, the play could be considerably shortened. I think they are mistaken. The experienced knights of the blue pencil, having saved an hour and a half by disemboweling the play, would at once proceed to waste two hours in building elaborate scenery, having real water in the river Loire and a real bridge across it, and staging an obviously sham fight for possession of it, with the victorious French led by Joan on a real horse. The coronation would eclipse all previous theatrical displays, shewing, first, the procession through the streets of Rheims, and then the service in the cathedral, with special music written for both. Joan would be burnt on the stage, as Mr Matheson Lang always is in The Wandering Jew, on the principle that it does not matter in the least why a woman is burnt provided she is burnt, and people can pay to see it done. The intervals between the acts whilst these splendors were being built up and then demolished by the stage carpenters would seem eternal, to the great profit of the refreshment bars. And the weary and demoralized audience would lose their last trains and curse me for writing such inordinately long and intolerably dreary and meaningless plays. But the applause of the press would be unanimous. Nobody who knows the stage history of Shakespear will doubt that this is what would happen if I knew my business so little as to listen to these well intentioned but disastrous counsellors: indeed it probably will happen when I am no longer in control of the performing rights. So perhaps it will be as well for the public to see the play while I am still alive.

THE EPILOGUE

As to the epilogue, I could hardly be expected to stultify myself by implying that Joan's history in the world ended unhappily with her execution, instead of beginning there. It was necessary by hook or crook to shew the canonized Joan as well as the incinerated one; for many a woman has got herself burnt by carelessly whisking a muslin skirt into the drawing-room fireplace, but getting canonized is a different matter, and a more important one. So I am afraid the epilogue must stand.

TO THE CRITICS,
LEST THEY SHOULD FEEL IGNORED

To a professional critic (I have been one myself) theatre-going is the curse of Adam. The play is the evil he is paid to endure in the sweat of his brow; and the sooner it is over, the better. This would seem to place him in irreconcilable opposition to the paying playgoer, from whose point of view the longer the play, the more entertainment he gets for his money. It does in fact so place him, especially in the provinces, where the playgoer goes to the theatre for the sake of the play solely, and insists so effectively on a certain number of hours' entertainment that touring managers are sometimes seriously embarrassed by the brevity of the London plays they have to deal in.

For in London the critics are reinforced by a considerable body of persons who go to the theatre as many others go to church, to display their best clothes and compare them with other people's; to be in the fashion, and have something to talk about at dinner parties; to adore a pet performer; to pass the evening anywhere rather than at home: in short, for any or every reason except interest in dramatic art as such. In fashionable centres the number of irreligious people who go to church, of unmusical people who go to concerts and operas, and of undramatic people who go to the theatre, is so prodigious that sermons have been cut down to ten minutes and plays to two hours; and, even at that, congregations sit longing for the benediction and audiences for the final curtain, so that they may get away to the lunch or supper they really crave for, after arriving as late as (or later than) the hour of beginning can possibly be made for them.

Thus from the stalls and in the Press an atmosphere of hypocrisy spreads. Nobody says straight out that genuine drama is a tedious nuisance, and that to ask people to endure more than two hours of it (with two long intervals of relief) is an intolerable imposition. Nobody says 'I hate classical tragedy and comedy as I hate sermons and symphonies; but I like police news and divorce news and any kind of dancing or decoration that has an aphrodisiac effect on me or on my wife or husband. And whatever superior people may pretend, I cannot associate pleasure with any sort of intellectual activity; and I dont believe anyone else can either.' Such things are not said; yet nine-tenths of what is offered as criticism of the drama in the metropolitan Press of Europe and America is nothing but a muddled paraphrase of it. If it does not mean that, it means nothing.

I do not complain of this, though it complains very unreasonably of me. But I can take no more notice of it than Einstein of the people who are incapable of mathematics. I write in the classical manner for those who pay for admission to a theatre because they like classical comedy or tragedy for its own sake, and like it so much when it is good of its kind and well done that they tear themselves away from it with reluctance to catch the very latest train or omnibus that will take them home. Far from arriving late from an eight or half-past eight o'clock dinner so as to escape at least the first half-hour of the performance, they stand in queues outside the theatre doors for hours beforehand in bitingly cold weather to secure a seat. In countries where a play lasts a week, they bring baskets of provisions and sit it out. These are the patrons on whom I depend for my bread. I do not give them performances twelve hours long, because circumstances do not at present make such entertainments feasible; though a performance beginning after breakfast and ending at sunset is as possible physically and artistically in Surrey or Middlesex as in Ober-Ammergau; and an all-night sitting in a theatre would be at least as enjoyable as an all-night sitting in the House of Commons, and much more useful. But in St Joan I have done my best by going to the well-established classical limit of three and a half hours' practically continuous playing, barring the one interval imposed by considerations which have nothing to do with art. I know that this is hard on the pseudo-critics and on the fashionable people whose playgoing is a hypocrisy. I cannot help feeling some compassion for them when they assure me that my play, though a great play, must fail hopelessly, because it does not begin at a quarter to nine and end at eleven. The facts are overwhelmingly against them. They forget that all men are not as they are. Still, I am sorry for them; and though I cannot for their sakes undo my work and help the people who hate the theatre to drive out the people who love it, yet I may point out to them that they have several remedies in their own hands. They can escape the first part of the play by their usual practice of arriving late. They can escape the epilogue by not waiting for it. And if the irreducible minimum thus attained is still too painful, they can stay away altogether. But I deprecate this extreme course, because it is good neither for my pocket nor for their own souls. Already a few of them, noticing that what matters is not the absolute length of time occupied by a play, but the speed with which that time passes, are discovering that the theatre, though purgatorial in its Aristotelian moments, is not necessarily always the dull place they have so often found it. What do its discomforts matter when the play makes us forget them?

Ayot St Lawrence
May 1924

◆◆ Saint Joan

By BERNARD SHAW

Characters

BERTRAND DE POULENGEY
STEWARD
JOAN
ROBERT DE BAUDRICOURT
THE ARCHBISHOP OF RHEIMS
MGR DE LA TRÉMOUILLE
COURT PAGE
GILLES DE RAIS
CAPTAIN LA HIRE
THE DAUPHIN (later CHARLES VII)
DUCHESS DE LA TRÉMOUILLE
DUNOIS, Bastard of Orleans
DUNOIS' PAGE
RICHARD DE BEAUCHAMP, Earl of Warwick
CHAPLAIN DE STOGUMBER
PETER CAUCHON, Bishop of Beauvais
WARWICK'S PAGE
THE INQUISITOR
D'ESTIVET
DE COURCELLES
BROTHER MARTIN LADVENU
THE EXECUTIONER
AN ENGLISH SOLDIER
A GENTLEMAN OF 1920

Scene I

A fine spring morning on the river Meuse, between Lorraine and Champagne, in the year 1429 A.D., in the castle of Vaucouleurs.

Bernard Shaw, *Saint Joan* (Baltimore: Penguin, 1951). pp. 49–159.

Captain Robert de Baudricourt, a military squire, handsome and physically energetic, but with no will of his own, is disguising that defect in his usual fashion by storming terribly at his steward, a trodden worm, scanty of flesh, scanty of hair, who might be any age from 18 to 55, being the sort of man whom age cannot wither because he has never bloomed.

The two are in a sunny stone chamber on the first floor of the castle. At a plain strong oak table, seated in chair to match, the captain presents his left profile. The steward stands facing him at the other side of the table, if so deprecatory a stance as his can be called standing. The mullioned thirteenth-century window is open behind him. Near it in the corner is a turret with a narrow arched doorway leading to a winding stair which descends to the courtyard. There is a stout fourlegged stool under the table, and a wooden chest under the window.

ROBERT. No eggs! No eggs!! Thousand thunders, man, what do you mean by no eggs?
STEWARD. Sir: it is not my fault. It is the act of God.
ROBERT. Blasphemy. You tell me there are no eggs; and you blame your Maker for it.
STEWARD. Sir: what can I do? I cannot lay eggs.
ROBERT [*sarcastic*] Ha! You jest about it.
STEWARD. No, sir, God knows. We all have to go without eggs just as you have, sir. The hens will not lay.
ROBERT. Indeed! [*Rising*] Now listen to me, you.

STEWARD [*humbly*] Yes, sir.

ROBERT. What am I?

STEWARD. What are you, sir?

ROBERT [*coming at him*] Yes: what am I? Am I Robert, squire of Baudricourt and captain of this castle of Vaucouleurs; or am I a cowboy?

STEWARD. Oh, sir, you know you are a greater man here than the king himself.

ROBERT. Precisely. And now, do you know what you are?

STEWARD. I am nobody, sir, except that I have the honor to be your steward.

ROBERT [*driving him to the wall, adjective by adjective*] You have not only the honor of being my steward, but the privilege of being the worst, most incompetent, drivelling snivelling jibbering jabbering idiot of a steward in France. [*He strides back to the table*].

STEWARD [*cowering on the chest*] Yes, sir: to a great man like you I must seem like that.

ROBERT [*turning*] My fault, I suppose. Eh?

STEWARD [*coming to him deprecatingly*] Oh, sir: you always give my most innocent words such a turn!

ROBERT. I will give your neck a turn if you dare tell me when I ask you how many eggs there are that you cannot lay any.

STEWARD [*protesting*] Oh sir, oh sir—

ROBERT. No: not oh sir, oh sir, but no sir, no sir. My three Barbary hens and the black are the best layers in Champagne. And you come and tell me that there are no eggs! Who stole them? Tell me that, before I kick you out through the castle gate for a liar and a seller of my goods to thieves. The milk was short yesterday, too: do not forget that.

STEWARD [*desperate*] I know, sir. I know only too well. There is no milk: there are no eggs: tomorrow there will be nothing.

ROBERT. Nothing! You will steal the lot: eh?

STEWARD. No, sir: nobody will steal anything. But there is a spell on us: we are bewitched.

ROBERT. That story is not good enough for me. Robert de Baudricourt burns witches and hangs thieves. Go. Bring me four dozen eggs and two gallons of milk here in this room before noon, or Heaven have mercy on your bones! I will teach you to make a fool of me. [*He resumes his seat with an air of finality*].

STEWARD. Sir: I tell you there are no eggs. There will be none—not if you were to kill me for it—as long as The Maid is at the door.

ROBERT. The Maid! What maid? What are you talking about?

STEWARD. The girl from Lorraine, sir. From Domrémy.

ROBERT [*rising in fearful wrath*] Thirty thousand thunders! Fifty thousand devils! Do you mean to say that that girl, who had the impudence to ask to see me two days ago, and whom I told you to send back to her father with my orders that he was to give her a good hiding, is here still?

STEWARD. I have told her to go, sir. She wont.

ROBERT. I did not tell you to tell her to go: I told you to throw her out. You have fifty men-at-arms and a dozen lumps of able-bodied servants to carry out my orders. Are they afraid of her?

STEWARD. She is so positive, sir.

ROBERT [*seizing him by the scruff of the neck*] Positive! Now see here. I am going to throw you downstairs.

STEWARD. No, sir. Please.

ROBERT. Well, stop me by being positive. It's quite easy: any slut of a girl can do it.

STEWARD [*hanging limp in his hands*] Sir, sir: you cannot get rid of her by throwing me out [*Robert has to let him drop. He squats on his knees on the floor, contemplating his master resignedly*]. You see, sir, you are much more positive than I am. But so is she.

ROBERT. I am stronger than you are, you fool.

STEWARD. No, sir: it isnt that: it's your strong character, sir. She is weaker than we are: she is only a slip of a girl; but we cannot make her go.

ROBERT. You parcel of curs: you are afraid of her.

STEWARD [*rising cautiously*] No sir: we are afraid of you; but she puts courage into us. She really doesn't seem to be afraid of anything. Perhaps you could frighten her, sir.

ROBERT [*grimly*] Perhaps. Where is she now?

STEWARD. Down in the courtyard, sir, talking to the soldiers as usual. She is always talking to the soldiers except when she is praying.

ROBERT. Praying! Ha! You believe she prays, you idiot. I know the sort of girl that is always talking to soldiers. She shall talk to me a bit. [*He goes to the window and shouts fiercely through it*] Hallo, you there!

A GIRL'S VOICE [*bright, strong and rough*] Is it me, sir?

ROBERT. Yes, you.

THE VOICE. Be you captain?

ROBERT. Yes, damn your impudence, I be captain. Come up here. [*To the soldiers in the yard*] Shew her the way, you. And shove her along quick. [*He leaves the window, and returns to his place at the table, where he sits magisterially*].

STEWARD [*whispering*] She wants to go and be a soldier herself. She wants you to give her soldier's clothes. Armor, sir! And a sword! Actually! [*He steals behind Robert*].

Joan appears in the turret doorway. She is an ablebodied country girl of 17 or 18, respectably dressed in red, with an uncommon face; eyes very wide apart and bulging as they often do in very imaginative people, a long well-shaped nose with wide nostrils, a short upper lip, resolute but full-lipped mouth, and handsome fighting chin. She comes eagerly to the table, delighted at having penetrated to Baudricourt's presence at last, and full of hope as to the results. His scowl does not check or frighten her in the least. Her voice is normally a hearty coaxing voice, very confident, very appealing, very hard to resist.

JOAN [*bobbing a curtsey*] Good morning, captain squire. Captain: you are to give me a horse and armor and some soldiers, and send me to the Dauphin. Those are your orders from my Lord.

ROBERT [*outraged*] Orders from your lord! And who the devil may your lord be? Go back to him, and tell him that I am neither duke nor peer at his orders: I am squire of Baudricourt; and I take no orders except from the king.

JOAN [*reassuringly*] Yes, squire: that is all right. My Lord is the King of Heaven.

ROBERT. Why, the girl's mad. [*To the steward*] Why didnt you tell me so, you blockhead?

STEWARD. Sir: do not anger her: give her what she wants.

JOAN [*impatient, but friendly*] They all say I am mad until I talk to them, squire. But you see that it is the will of God that you are to do what He has put into my mind.

ROBERT. It is the will of God that I shall send you back to your father with orders to put you under lock and key and thrash the madness out of you. What have you to say to that?

JOAN. You think you will, squire; but you will find it all coming quite different. You said you would not see me; but here I am.

STEWARD [*appealing*] Yes, sir. You see, sir.

ROBERT. Hold your tongue, you.

STEWARD [*abjectly*] Yes, sir.

ROBERT [*to Joan, with a sour loss of confidence*] So you are presuming on my seeing you, are you?

JOAN [*sweetly*] Yes, squire.

ROBERT [*feeling that he has lost ground, brings down his two fists squarely on the table, and inflates his chest imposingly to cure the unwelcome and only too familiar sensation*] Now listen to me. I am going to assert myself.

JOAN [*busily*] Please do, squire. The horse will cost sixteen francs. It is a good deal of money: but I can save it on the armor. I can find a soldier's armor that will fit me well enough: I am very hardy; and I do not need beautiful armor made to my measure like you wear. I shall not want many soldiers: the Dauphin will give me all I need to raise the siege of Orleans.

ROBERT [*flabbergasted*] To raise the siege of Orleans!

JOAN [*simply*] Yes, squire: that is what God is sending me to do. Three men will be enough for you to send with me if they are good men and gentle to me. They have promised to come with me. Polly and Jack and—

ROBERT. Polly!! You impudent baggage, do you dare call squire Bertrand de Poulengey Polly to my face?

JOAN. His friends call him so, squire: I did not know he had any other name. Jack—

ROBERT. That is Monsieur John of Metz, I suppose?

JOAN. Yes, squire. Jack will come willingly: he is a very kind gentleman, and gives me money to give to the poor. I think John Godsave will come, and Dick the Archer, and their servants John of Honecourt and Julian. There will be no trouble for you, squire: I have arranged it all: you have only to give the order.

ROBERT [*contemplating her in a stupor of amazement*] Well, I am damned!

JOAN [*with unruffled sweetness*] No, squire: God is very merciful; and the blessed saints Catherine and Margaret, who speak to me every day [*he gapes*], will intercede for you. You will go to paradise; and your name will be remembered for ever as my first helper.

ROBERT [*to the steward, still much bothered but changing his tone as he pursues a new clue*] Is this true about Monsieur de Poulengey?

STEWARD [*eagerly*] Yes, sir, and about Monsieur de Metz too. They both want to go with her.

ROBERT [*thoughtful*] Mf! [*He goes to the window, and shouts into the courtyard*] Hallo! You there: send Monsieur de Poulengey to me, will you? [*He turns to Joan*] Get out; and wait in the yard.

JOAN [*smiling brightly at him*] Right, squire. [*She goes out*].

ROBERT [*to the steward*] Go with her, you, you dithering imbecile. Stay within call; and keep your eye on her. I shall have her up here again.

STEWARD. Do so in God's name, sir. Think of those hens, the best layers in Champagne; and—

ROBERT. Think of my boot; and take your backside out of reach of it.

The steward retreats hastily and finds himself confronted in the doorway by Bertrand de Poulengey, a lymphatic French gentleman-at-arms, aged 36 or thereabout, employed in the department of the provost-marshal, dreamily absentminded, seldom speaking unless spoken to, and then slow and obstinate in reply; altogether in contrast to the self-assertive, loud-mouthed, superficially energetic, fundamentally will-less Robert. The steward makes way for him, and vanishes.*

Poulengey salutes, and stands awaiting orders.

ROBERT [*genially*] It isnt service, Polly. A friendly talk. Sit down [*He hooks the stool from under the table with his instep*].

Poulengey, relaxing, comes into the room: places the stool between the table and the window: and sits down ruminatively. Robert, half sitting on the end of the table, begins the friendly talk.

ROBERT. Now listen to me, Polly. I must talk to you like a father.

Poulengey looks up at him gravely for a moment, but says nothing.

ROBERT. It's about this girl you are interested in. Now, I have seen her. I have talked to her. First, she's mad. That doesnt matter. Second, she's not a farm wench. She's a bourgeoise. That matters a good deal. I know her class exactly. Her father came here last year to represent his village in a lawsuit: he is one of their notables. A farmer. Not a gentleman farmer: he makes money by it, and lives by it. Still, not a laborer. Not a mechanic. He might have a cousin a lawyer, or in the Church. People of this sort may be of no account socially; but they can give a lot of bother to the authorities. That is to say, to me. Now no doubt it seems to you a very simple thing to take this girl away, humbugging her into the belief that you are taking her to the Dauphin. But if you get her into trouble, you may get me into no end of a mess, as I am her father's lord, and responsible for her protection. So friends or no friends, Polly, hands off her.

POULENGEY [*with deliberate impressiveness*] I should as soon think of the Blessed Virgin herself in that way, as of this girl.

ROBERT [*coming off the table*] But she says you and Jack and Dick have offered to go with her. What for? You are not going to tell me that you take her crazy notion of going to the Dauphin seriously, are you?

POULENGEY [*slowly*] There is something about her. They are pretty foulmouthed and foulminded down there in the guardroom, some of them. But there hasnt been a word that has anything to do with her being a woman. They have stopped swearing before her. There is something. Something. It may be worth trying.

ROBERT. Oh, come, Polly! pull yourself together. Commonsense was never your strong point; but this is a little too much. [*He retreats disgustedly*].

POULENGEY [*unmoved*] What is the good of commonsense? If we had any commonsense we should join the Duke of Burgundy and the English king. They hold half the country, right down to the Loire. They have Paris. They have this castle: you know very well that we had to surrender it to the Duke of Bedford, and that you are only holding it on parole. The Dauphin is in Chinon, like a rat in a corner, except that he wont fight. We dont even know that he is the Dauphin: his mother says he isnt; and she ought to know. Think of that! the queen denying the legitimacy of her own son!

ROBERT. Well, she married her daughter to the English king. Can you blame the woman?

POULENGEY. I blame nobody. But thanks to her, the Dauphin is down and out; and we may as well face it. The English will take Orleans: the Bastard will not be able to stop them.

ROBERT. He beat the English the year before last at Montargis. I was with him.

POULENGEY. No matter: his men are cowed now; and he cant work miracles. And I tell you that nothing can save our side now but a miracle.

ROBERT. Miracles are all right, Polly. The only difficulty about them is that they dont happen nowadays.

POULENGEY. I used to think so. I am not so sure now. [*Rising, and moving ruminatively towards the window*] At all events this is not a time to leave any stone unturned. There is something about the girl.

ROBERT. Oh! You think the girl can work miracles, do you?

POULENGEY. I think the girl herself is a bit of a miracle. Anyhow, she is the last card left in our hands. Better play her than throw up the game. [*He wanders to the turret*].

ROBERT [*wavering*] You really think that?

POULENGEY. [*turning*] Is there anything else left for us to think?

ROBERT [*going to him*] Look here, Polly. If you were in my place would you let a girl like that do you out of sixteen francs for a horse?

POULENGEY. I will pay for the horse.

ROBERT. You will!

POULENGEY. Yes: I will back my opinion.

ROBERT. You will really gamble on a forlorn hope to the tune of sixteen francs?

POULENGEY. It is not a gamble.

ROBERT. What else is it?

POULENGEY. It is a certainty. Her words and her ardent faith in God have put fire into me.

ROBERT [*giving him up*] Whew! You are as mad as she is.

POULENGEY [*obstinately*] We want a few mad people now. See where the sane ones have landed us!

ROBERT [*his irresoluteness now openly swamping his affected decisiveness*] I shall feel like a precious fool. Still, if you feel sure—?

POULENGEY. I feel sure enough to take her to Chinon—unless you stop me.

ROBERT. This is not fair. You are putting the responsibility on me.

POULENGEY. It is on you whichever way you decide.

ROBERT. Yes: thats just it. Which way am I to

decide? You dont see how awkward this is for me. [*Snatching at a dilatory step with an unconscious hope that Joan will make up his mind for him*] Do you think I ought to have another talk to her?

POULENGEY [*rising*] Yes. [*He goes to the window and calls*] Joan!

JOAN's VOICE. Will he let us go, Polly?

POULENGEY. Come up. Come in. [*Turning to Robert*] Shall I leave you with her?

ROBERT. No: stay here; and back me up.

Poulengey sits down on the chest. Robert goes back to his magisterial chair, but remains standing to inflate himself more imposingly. Joan comes in, full of good news.

JOAN. Jack will go halves for the horse.

ROBERT. Well!! [*He sits, deflated*].

POULENGEY [*gravely*] Sit down, Joan.

JOAN [*checked a little, and looking to Robert*] May I?

ROBERT. Do what you are told.

Joan curtsies and sits down on the stool between them. Robert outfaces his perplexity with his most peremptory air.

ROBERT. What is your name?

JOAN [*chattily*] They always call me Jenny in Lorraine. Here in France I am Joan. The soldiers call me The Maid.

ROBERT. What is your surname?

JOAN. Surname? What is that? My father sometimes calls himself d'Arc; but I know nothing about it. You met my father. He—

ROBERT. Yes, yes; I remember. You come from Domrémy in Lorraine, I think.

JOAN. Yes; but what does it matter? we all speak French.

ROBERT. Dont ask questions: answer them. How old are you?

JOAN. Seventeen: so they tell me. It might be nineteen. I dont remember.

ROBERT. What did you mean when you said that St Catherine and St Margaret talked to you every day?

JOAN. They do.

ROBERT. What are they like?

JOAN [*suddenly obstinate*] I will tell you nothing about that: they have not given me leave.

ROBERT. But you actually see them; and they talk to you just as I am talking to you?

JOAN. No: it is quite different. I cannot tell you: you must not talk to me about my voices.

ROBERT. How do you mean? voices?

JOAN. I hear voices telling me what to do. They come from God.

ROBERT. They come from your imagination.

JOAN. Of course. That is how the messages of God come to us.

POULENGEY. Checkmate.

ROBERT. No fear! [*To Joan*] So God says you are to raise the siege of Orleans?

JOAN. And to crown the Dauphin in Rheims Cathedral.

ROBERT [*gasping*] Crown the D—! Gosh!

JOAN. And to make the English leave France.

ROBERT [*sarcastic*] Anything else?

JOAN [*charming*] Not just at present, thank you, squire.

ROBERT. I suppose you think raising a siege is as easy as chasing a cow out of a meadow. You think soldiering is anybody's job?

JOAN. I do not think it can be very difficult if God is on your side, and you are willing to put your life in His hand. But many soldiers are very simple.

ROBERT [*grimly*] Simple! Did you ever see English soldiers fighting?

JOAN. They are only men. God made them just like us; but He gave them their own country and their own language; and it is not His will that they should come into our country and try to speak our language.

ROBERT. Who has been putting such nonsense into your head? Don't you know that soldiers are subject to their feudal lord, and that it is nothing to them or to you whether he is the duke of Burgundy or the king of England or the king of France? What has their language to do with it?

JOAN. I do not understand that a bit. We are all subject to the King of Heaven; and He gave us our countries and our languages, and meant us to keep to them. If it were not so it would be murder to kill an Englishman in battle; and you, squire, would be in great danger of hell fire. You must not think about your duty to your feudal lord, but about your duty to God.

POULENGEY. It's no use, Robert: she can choke you like that every time.

ROBERT. Can she, by Saint Dennis! We shall see. [*To Joan*] We are not talking about God: we are talking about practical affairs. I ask you again, girl, have you ever seen English soldiers fighting? Have you ever seen them plundering, burning, turning the countryside into a desert? Have you heard no tales of their Black Prince who was blacker than the devil himself, or of the English king's father?

JOAN. You must not be afraid, Robert—

ROBERT. Damn you, I am not afraid. And who gave you leave to call me Robert?

JOAN. You were called so in church in the name of our Lord. All the other names are your father's or your brother's or anybody's.

ROBERT. Tcha!

JOAN. Listen to me, squire. At Domrémy we had to fly to the next village to escape from the English soldiers. Three of them were left behind, wounded. I came to know these three poor goddams quite well. They had not half my strength.

ROBERT. Do you know why they are called goddams?

JOAN. No. Everyone calls them goddams.

ROBERT. It is because they are always calling on their God to condemn their souls to perdition. That is what goddam means in their language. How do you like it?

JOAN. God will be merciful to them; and they will act like His good children when they go back to the country He made for them, and made them for. I have heard the tales of the Black Prince. The moment he touched the soil of our country the devil entered into him, and made him a black fiend. But at home, in the place made for him by God, he was good. It is always so. If I went into England against the will of God to conquer England, and tried to live there and speak its language, the devil would ener tnito me; and when I was old

I should shudder to remember the wickedness I did.

ROBERT. Perhaps. But the more devil you were the better you might fight. That is why the goddams will take Orleans. And you cannot stop them, nor ten thousand like you.

JOAN. One thousand like me can stop them. Ten like me can stop them with God on our side. [*She rises impetuously, and goes at him, unable to sit quiet any longer*]. You do not understand, squire. Our soldiers are always beaten because they are fighting only to save their skins; and the shortest way to save your skin is to run away. Our knights are thinking only of the money they will make in ransoms: it is not kill or be killed with them, but pay or be paid. But I will teach them all to fight that the will of God may be done in France; and then they will drive the poor goddams before them like sheep. You and Polly will live to see the day when there will not be an English soldier on the soil of France; and there will be but one king there: not the feudal English king, but God's French one.

ROBERT [*to Poulengey*] This may be all rot, Polly; but the troops might swallow it, though nothing that we can say seems able to put any fight into them. Even the Dauphin might swallow it. And if she can put fight into him, she can put it into anybody.

POULENGEY. I can see no harm in trying. Can you? And there is something about the girl—

ROBERT [*turning to Joan*] Now listen you to me; and [*desperately*] dont cut in before I have time to think.

JOAN [*plumping down on the stool again, like an obedient schoolgirl*] Yes, squire.

ROBERT. Your orders are that you are to go to Chinon under the escort of this gentleman and three of his friends.

JOAN [*radiant, clasping her hands*] Oh, squire! Your head is all circled with light, like a saint's.

POULENGEY. How is she to get into the royal presence?

ROBERT [*who has looked up for his halo*

rather apprehensively] I dont know: how did she get into my presence? If the Dauphin can keep her out he is a better man than I take him for. [*Rising*] I will send her to Chinon; and she can say I sent her. Then let come what may: I can do no more.

JOAN. And the dress? I may have a soldier's dress, maynt I, squire?

ROBERT. Have what you please. I wash my hands of it.

JOAN [*wildly excited by her success*] Come, Polly. [*She dashes out*].

ROBERT [*shaking Poulengey's hand*] Goodbye, old man, I am taking a big chance. Few other men would have done it. But as you say, there is something about her.

POULENGEY. Yes: there is something about her. Goodbye. [*He goes out*].

Robert, still very doubtful whether he has not been made a fool of by a crazy female, and a social inferior to boot, scratches his head and slowly comes back from the door.

The steward runs in with a basket.

STEWARD. Sir, sir—

ROBERT. What now?

STEWARD. The hens are laying like mad, sir. Five dozen eggs!

ROBERT [*stiffens convulsively: crosses himself: and forms with his pale lips the words*] Christ in heaven! [*Aloud but breathless*] She did come from God.

Scene II

Chinon, in Touraine. An end of the throne room in the castle, curtained off to make an antechamber. The Archbishop of Rheims, close on 50, a full-fed prelate with nothing of the ecclesiastic about him except his imposing bearing, and the Lord Chamberlain, Monseigneur de la Trémouille, a monstrous ar-rogant wineskin of a man, are waiting for the Dauphin. There is a door in the wall to the right of the two men. It is late in the afternoon on the 8th of March, 1429. The Archbishop stands with dignity whilst the Chamberlain, on his left, fumes about in the worst of tempers.

LA TRÉMOUILLE. What the devil does the Dauphin mean by keeping us waiting like this? I don't know how you have the patience to stand there like a stone idol.

THE ARCHBISHOP. You see, I am an archbishop; and an archbishop is a sort of idol. At any rate he has to learn to keep still and suffer fools patiently. Besides, my dear Lord Chamberlain, it is the Dauphin's royal privilege to keep you waiting, is it not?

LA TRÉMOUILLE. Dauphin be damned! saving your reverence. Do you know how much money he owes me?

THE ARCHBISHOP. Much more than he owes me, I have no doubt, because you are a much richer man. But I take it he owes you all you could afford to lend him. That is what he owes me.

LA TRÉMOUILLE. Twenty-seven thousand: that was his last haul. A cool twenty-seven thousand!

THE ARCHBISHOP. What becomes of it all? He never has a suit of clothes that I would throw to a curate.

LA TRÉMOUILLE. He dines on a chicken or a scrap of mutton. He borrows my last penny; and there is nothing to shew for it. [*A page appears in the doorway*]. At last!

THE PAGE. No, my lord: it is not His Majesty. Monsieur de Rais is approaching.

LA TRÉMOUILLE. Young Bluebeard! Why announce him?

THE PAGE. Captain La Hire is with him. Something has happened, I think.

Gilles de Rais, a young man of 25, very smart and self-possessed, and sporting the extravagance of a little curled beard dyed blue at a clean-shaven court, comes in. He is determined to make himself agreeable, but lacks natural joyousness, and is not really pleasant. In fact when he defies the Church some eleven years later he is accused of trying to extract pleasure from horrible cruelties, and hanged. So far, however, there is no shadow of the gallows on him. He advances gaily to the Archbishop. The page withdraws.

BLUEBEARD. Your faithful lamb, Archbishop. Good day, my lord. Do you know what has happened to La Hire?

LA TRÉMOUILLE. He has sworn himself into a fit, perhaps.

BLUEBEARD. No: just the opposite. Foul Mouthed Frank, the only man in Touraine who could beat him at swearing, was told by a soldier that he shouldnt use such language when he was at the point of death.

THE ARCHBISHOP. Nor at any other point. But was Foul Mouthed Frank on the point of death?

BLUEBEARD. Yes: he has just fallen into a well and been drowned. La Hire is frightened out of his wits.

Captain La Hire comes in: a war dog with no court manners and pronounced camp ones.

BLUEBEARD. I have just been telling the Chamberlain and the Archbishop. The Archbishop says you are a lost man.

LA HIRE [*striding past Bluebeard, and planting himself between the Archbishop and La Trémouille*] This is nothing to joke about. It is worse than we thought. It was not a soldier, but an angel dressed as a soldier.

THE ARCHBISHOP ⎫
THE CHAMBERLAIN ⎬ [*exclaiming all together*] An angel!
BLUEBEARD ⎭

LA HIRE. Yes, an angel. She has made her way from Champagne with half a dozen men through the thick of everything: Burgundians, goddams, deserters, robbers, and Lord knows who; and they never met a

soul except the country folk. I know one of them: de Poulengey. He says she's an angel. If ever I utter an oath again may my soul be blasted to eternal damnation!

THE ARCHBISHOP. A very pious beginning, Captain.

Bluebeard and La Trémouille laugh at him. The page returns.

THE PAGE. His Majesty.

They stand perfunctorily at court attention. The Dauphin, aged 26, really King Charles the Seventh since the death of his father, but as yet uncrowned, comes in through the curtains with a paper in his hands. He is a poor creature physically; and the current fashion of shaving closely, and hiding every scrap of hair under the headcovering or headdress, both by women and men, makes the worst of his appearance. He has little narrow eyes, near together, a long pendulous nose that droops over his thick short upper lip, and the expression of a young dog accustomed to be kicked, yet incorrigible and irrepressible. But he is neither vulgar nor stupid; and he has a cheeky humor which enables him to hold his own in conversation. Just at present he is excited, like a child with a new toy. He comes to the Archbishop's left hand. Bluebeard and La Hire retire towards the curtains.

CHARLES. Oh, Archbishop, do you know what Robert de Baudricourt is sending me from Vaucouleurs?

THE ARCHBISHOP [*contemptuously*] I am not interested in the newest toys.

CHARLES [*indignantly*] It isn't a toy. [*Sulkily*] However, I can get on very well without your interest.

THE ARCHBISHOP. Your Highness is taking offence very unnecessarily.

CHARLES. Thank you. You are always ready with a lecture, arnt you?

LA TRÉMOUILLE [*roughly*] Enough grumbling. What have you got there?

CHARLES. What is that to you?

LA TRÉMOUILLE. It is my business to know what is passing between you and the garrison at Vaucouleurs. [*He snatches the paper from the Dauphin's hand, and begins reading it with some difficulty, following the words with his finger and spelling them out syllable by syllable.*]

CHARLES [*mortified*] You all think you can treat me as you please because I owe you money, and because I am no good at fighting. But I have the blood royal in my veins.

THE ARCHBISHOP. Even that has been questioned, your Highness. One hardly recognizes in you the grandson of Charles the Wise.

CHARLES. I want to hear no more of my grandfather. He was so wise that he used up the whole family stock of wisdom for five generations, and left me the poor fool I am, bullied and insulted by all of you.

THE ARCHBISHOP. Control yourself, sir. These outbursts of petulance are not seemly.

CHARLES. Another lecture! Thank you. What a pity it is that though you are an archbishop saints and angels dont come to see you!

THE ARCHBISHOP. What do you mean?

CHARLES. Aha! Ask that bully there [*pointing to La Trémouille*].

LA TRÉMOUILLE [*furious*] Hold your tongue. Do you hear?

CHARLES. Oh, I hear. You neednt shout. The whole castle can hear. Why dont you go and shout at the English, and beat them for me?

LA TRÉMOUILLE [*raising his fist*] You young—

CHARLES [*running behind the Archbishop*] Dont you raise your hand to me. It's high treason.

LA HIRE. Steady, Duke! Steady!

THE ARCHBISHOP [*resolutely*] Come, come! this will not do. My Lord Chamberlain: please! please! we must keep some sort of order. [*To the Dauphin*] And you, sir: if you cannot rule your kingdom, at least try to rule yourself.

CHARLES. Another lecture! Thank you.

LA TRÉMOUILLE [*handing over the paper to the Archbishop*] Here: read the accursed thing for me. He has sent the blood boiling into my head: I cant distinguish the letters.

CHARLES [*coming back and peering round La Trémouille's left shoulder*] I will read it for you if you like. I can read, you know.

LA TRÉMOUILLE [*with intense contempt, not at all stung by the taunt*] Yes: reading is all you are fit for. Can you make it out, Archbishop?

THE ARCHBISHOP. I should have expected more commonsense from de Baudricourt. He is sending some cracked country lass here—

CHARLES [*interrupting*] No: he is sending a saint: an angel. And she is coming to me: to me, the king, and not to you, Archbishop, holy as you are. She knows the blood royal if you dont. [*He struts up to the curtains between Bluebeard and La Hire*].

THE ARCHBISHOP. You cannot be allowed to see this crazy wench.

CHARLES [*turning*] But I am the king; and I will.

LA TRÉMOUILLE [*brutally*] Then she cannot be allowed to see you. Now!

CHARLES. I tell you I will. I am going to put my foot down—

BLUEBEARD [*laughing at him*] Naughty! What would your wise grandfather say?

CHARLES. That just shews your ignorance, Bluebeard. My grandfather had a saint who used to float in the air when she was praying, and told him everything he wanted to know. My poor father had two saints, Marie de Maillé and the Gasque of Avignon. It is in our family; and I dont care what you say: I will have my saint too.

THE ARCHBISHOP. This creature is not a saint. She is not even a respectable woman. She does not wear women's clothes. She is dressed like a soldier, and rides round the country with soldiers. Do you suppose such a person can be admitted to your Highness's court?

LA HIRE. Stop. [*Going to the Archbishop*] Did you say a girl in armor, like a soldier?

THE ARCHBISHOP. So de Baudricourt describes her.

LA HIRE. But by all the devils in hell—Oh, God forgive me, what am I saying?—by Our Lady and all the saints, this must be the angel that struck Foul Mouthed Frank dead for swearing.

CHARLES [*triumphant*] You see! A miracle!

LA HIRE. She may strike the lot of us dead if we cross her. For Heaven's sake, Archbishop, be careful what you are doing.

THE ARCHBISHOP [*severely*] Rubbish! Nobody has been struck dead. A drunken blackguard who has been rebuked a hundred times for swearing has fallen into a well, and been drowned. A mere coincidence.

LA HIRE. I do not know what a coincidence is. I do know that the man is dead, and that she told him he was going to die.

THE ARCHBISHOP. We are all going to die, Captain.

LA HIRE [*crossing himself*] I hope not. [*He backs out of the conversation*].

BLUEBEARD. We can easily find out whether she is an angel or not. Let us arrange when she comes that I shall be the Dauphin, and see whether she will find me out.

CHARLES. Yes: I agree to that. If she cannot find the blood royal I will have nothing to do with her.

THE ARCHBISHOP. It is for the Church to make saints: let de Baudricourt mind his own business, and not dare usurp the function of his priest. I say this girl shall not be admitted.

BLUEBEARD. But, Archbishop—

THE ARCHBISHOP [*sternly*] I speak in the Church's name. [*To the Dauphin*] Do you dare say she shall?

CHARLES [*intimidated but sulky*] Oh, if you make it an excommunication matter, I have nothing more to say, of course. But you havnt read the end of the letter. De Baudricourt says she will raise the siege of Orleans, and beat the English for us.

LA TRÉMOUILLE. Rot!

CHARLES. Well, will you save Orleans for us, with all your bullying?

LA TRÉMOUILLE [*savagely*] Do not throw that in my face again: do you hear? I have done more fighting than you ever did or ever will. But I cannot be everywhere.

THE DAUPHIN. Well, thats something.

BLUEBEARD [*coming between the Archbishop and Charles*] You have Jack Dunois at the head of your troops in Orleans: the brave Dunois, the handsome Dunois, the wonderful invincible Dunois, the darling of all the ladies, the beautiful bastard. Is it likely that the country lass can do what he cannot do?

CHARLES. Why doesnt he raise the siege, then?

LA HIRE. The wind is against him.

BLUEBEARD. How can the wind hurt him at Orleans? It is not on the Channel.

LA HIRE. It is on the river Loire; and the English hold the bridgehead. He must ship his men across the river and upstream, if he is to take them in the rear. Well, he cannot, because there is a devil of a wind blowing the other way. He is tired of paying the priests to pray for a west wind. What he needs is a miracle. You tell me that what the girl did to Foul Mouthed Frank was no miracle. No matter: it finished Frank. If she changes the wind for Dunois, that may not be a miracle either; but it may finish the English. What harm is there in trying?

THE ARCHBISHOP [*who has read the end of the letter and become more thoughtful*] It is true that de Baudricourt seems extraordinarily impressed.

LA HIRE. De Baudricourt is a blazing ass; but he is a soldier; and if he thinks she can beat the English, all the rest of the army will think so too.

LA TRÉMOUILLE [*to the Archbishop, who is hesitating*] Oh, let them have their way. Dunois' men will give up the town in spite of him if somebody does not put some fresh spunk into them.

THE ARCHBISHOP. The Church must examine the girl before anything decisive is done about her. However, since his Highness desires it, let her attend the Court.

LA HIRE. I will find her and tell her. [*He goes out*].

CHARLES. Come with me, Bluebeard; and

let us arrange so that she will not know who I am. You will pretend to be me. [*He goes out through the curtains*].

BLUEBEARD. Pretend to be that thing! Holy Michael! [*He follows the Dauphin*].

LA TRÉMOUILLE. I wonder will she pick him out!

THE ARCHBISHOP. Of course she will.

LA TRÉMOUILLE. Why? How is she to know?

THE ARCHBISHOP. She will know what everyone in Chinon knows: that the Dauphin is the meanest-looking and worst-dressed figure in the Court, and that the man with the blue beard is Gilles de Rais.

LA TRÉMOUILLE. I never thought of that.

THE ARCHBISHOP. You are not so accustomed to miracles as I am. It is part of my profession.

LA TRÉMOUILLE [*puzzled and a little scandalized*] But that would not be a miracle at all.

THE ARCHBISHOP [*calmly*] Why not?

LA TRÉMOUILLE. Well, come! what is a miracle?

THE ARCHBISHOP. A miracle, my friend, is an event which creates faith. That is the purpose and nature of miracles. They may seem very wonderful to the people who witness them, and very simple to those who perform them. That does not matter: if they confirm or create faith they are true miracles.

LA TRÉMOUILLE. Even when they are frauds, do you mean?

THE ARCHBISHOP. Frauds deceive. An event which creates faith does not deceive: therefore it is not a fraud, but a miracle.

LA TRÉMOUILLE [*scratching his neck in his perplexity*] Well, I suppose as you are an archbishop you must be right. It seems a bit fishy to me. But I am no churchman, and dont understand these matters.

THE ARCHBISHOP. You are not a churchman; but you are a diplomatist and a soldier. Could you make our citizens pay war taxes, or our soldiers sacrifice their lives, if they knew what is really happening instead of what seems to them to be happening?

LA TRÉMOUILLE. No, by Saint Dennis: the fat would be in the fire before sundown.

THE ARCHBISHOP. Would it not be quite easy to tell them the truth?

LA TRÉMOUILLE. Man alive, they wouldn't believe it.

THE ARCHBISHOP. Just so. Well, the Church has to rule men for the good of their souls as you have to rule them for the good of their bodies. To do that, the Church must do as you do: nourish their faith by poetry.

LA TRÉMOUILLE. Poetry! I should call it humbug.

THE ARCHBISHOP. You would be wrong, my friend. Parables are not lies because they describe events that have never happened. Miracles are not frauds because they are often—I do not say always—very simple and innocent contrivances by which the priest fortifies the faith of his flock. When this girl picks out the Dauphin among his courtiers, it will not be a miracle for me, because I shall know how it has been done, and my faith will not be increased. But as for the others, if they feel the thrill of the supernatural, and forget their sinful clay in a sudden sense of the glory of God, it will be a miracle and a blessed one. And you will find that the girl herself will be more affected than anyone else. She will forget how she really picked him out. So, perhaps, will you.

LA TRÉMOUILLE. Well, I wish I were clever enough to know how much of you is God's archbishop and how much the most artful fox in Touraine. Come on, or we shall be late for the fun; and I want to see it, miracle or no miracle.

THE ARCHBISHOP [*detaining him a moment*] Do not think that I am a lover of crooked ways. There is a new spirit rising in men: we are at the dawning of a wider epoch. If I were a simple monk, and had not to rule men, I should seek peace for my spirit with Aristotle and Pythagoras rather than with the saints and their miracles.

LA TRÉMOUILLE. And who the deuce was Pythagoras?

THE ARCHBISHOP. A sage who held that the earth is round, and that it moves round the sun.

LA TRÉMOUILLE. What an utter fool! Couldnt he use his eyes?

They go out together through the curtains, which are presently withdrawn, revealing the full depth of the throne room with the Court assembled. On the right are two Chairs of State on a dais. Bluebeard is standing theatrically on the dais, playing the king, and, like the courtiers, enjoying the joke rather obviously. There is a curtained arch in the wall behind the dais; but the main door, guarded by men-at-arms, is at the other side of the room; and a clear path across is kept and lined by the courtiers. Charles is in this path in the middle of the room. La Hire is on his right. The Archbishop, on his left, has taken his place by the dais: La Trémouille at the other side of it. The Duchess de la Trémouille, pretending to be the Queen, sits in the Consort's chair, with a group of ladies in waiting close by, behind the Archbishop.

The chatter of the courtiers makes such a noise that nobody notices the appearance of the page at the door.

THE PAGE. The Duke of—[*Nobody listens*]. The Duke of—[*The chatter continues. Indignant at his failure to command a hearing, he snatches the halberd of the nearest man-at-arms, and thumps the floor with it. The chatter ceases; and everybody looks at him in silence*]. Attention! [*He restores the halberd to the man-at-arms*]. The Duke of Vendôme presents Joan the Maid to his Majesty.

CHARLES [*putting his finger on his lip*] Ssh! [*He hides behind the nearest courtier, peering out to see what happens*].

BLUEBEARD [*majestically*] Let her approach the throne.

Joan, dressed as a soldier, with her hair bobbed and hanging thickly round her face, is led by a bashful and speechless nobleman, from whom she detaches her-self to stop and look round eagerly for the Dauphin.

THE DUCHESS [*to the nearest lady in waiting*] My dear! Her hair!

All the ladies explode in uncontrollable laughter.

BLUEBEARD [*trying not to laugh, and waving his hand in deprecation of their merriment*] Ssh—ssh! Ladies! Ladies!!

JOAN [*not at all embarrassed*] I wear it like this because I am a soldier. Where be Dauphin?

A titter runs through the Court as she walks to the dais.

BLUEBEARD [*condescendingly*] You are in the presence of the Dauphin.

Joan looks at him sceptically for a moment, scanning him hard up and down to make sure. Dead silence, all watching her. Fun dawns in her face.

JOAN. Coom, Bluebeard! Thou canst not fool me. Where be Dauphin?

A roar of laughter breaks out as Gilles, with a gesture of surrender, joins in the laugh, and jumps down from the dais beside La Trémouille. Joan, also on the broad grin, turns back, searching along the row of courtiers, and presently makes a dive, and drags out Charles by the arm.

JOAN [*releasing him and bobbing him a little curtsey*] Gentle little Dauphin, I am sent to you to drive the English away from Orleans and from France, and to crown you king in the cathedral at Rheims, where all true kings of France are crowned.

CHARLES [*triumphant, to the Court*] You see, all of you: she knew the blood royal. Who dare say now that I am not my father's son? [*To Joan*] But if you want me to be crowned at Rheims you must talk to the Archbishop, not to me. There he is [*he is standing behind her*]!

JOAN [*turning quickly, overwhelmed with emotion*] Oh, my lord! [*She falls on both knees before him, with bowed head, not daring to look up*] My lord: I am only a poor country girl; and you are filled with the blessedness and glory of God Himself; but you will touch me with your hands, and give me your blessing, wont you?

BLUEBEARD [*whispering to La Trémouille*] The old fox blushes.

LA TRÉMOUILLE. Another miracle!

THE ARCHBISHOP [*touched, putting his hand on her head*] Child: you are in love with religion.

JOAN [*startled: looking up at him*] Am I? I never thought of that. Is there any harm in it?

THE ARCHBISHOP. There is no harm in it, my child. But there is danger.

JOAN [*rising, with a sunflush of reckless happiness irradiating her face*] There is always danger, except in heaven. Oh, my lord, you have given me such strength, such courage. It must be a most wonderful thing to be Archbishop.

The Court smiles broadly: even titters a little.

THE ARCHBISHOP. [*drawing himself up sensitively*] Gentlemen: your levity is rebuked by this maid's faith. I am, God help me, all unworthy; but your mirth is a deadly sin.

Their faces fall. Dead silence.

BLUEBEARD. My lord: we were laughing at her, not at you.

THE ARCHBISHOP. What? Not at my unworthiness but at her faith! Gilles de Rais: this maid prophesied that the blasphemer should be drowned in his sin—

JOAN [*distressed*] No!

THE ARCHBISHOP [*silencing her by a gesture*] I prophesy now that you will be hanged in yours if you do not learn when to laugh and when to pray.

BLUEBEARD. My lord: I stand rebuked. I am sorry: I can say no more. But if you prophesy that I shall be hanged, I shall never be able to resist temptation, because I shall always be telling myself that I may as well be hanged for a sheep as a lamb.

The courtiers take heart at this. There is more tittering.

JOAN [*scandalized*] You are an idle fellow, Bluebeard; and you have great impudence to answer the Archbishop.

LA HIRE [*with a huge chuckle*] Well said, lass! Well said!

JOAN [*impatiently to the Archbishop*] Oh, my lord, will you send all these silly folks away so that I may speak to the Dauphin alone?

LA HIRE [*goodhumoredly*] I can take a hint. [*He salutes; turns on his heel; and goes out*].

THE ARCHBISHOP. Come, gentlemen. The Maid comes with God's blessing, and must be obeyed.

The courtiers withdraw, some through the arch, others at the opposite side. The Archbishop marches across to the door, followed by the Duchess and La Trémouille. As the Archbishop passes Joan, she falls on her knees, and kisses the hem of his robe fervently. He shakes his head in instinctive remonstrance; gathers the robe from her; and goes out. She is left kneeling directly in the Duchess's way.

THE DUCHESS [*coldly*] Will you allow me to pass, please?

JOAN [*hastily rising, and standing back*] Beg pardon, maam, I am sure.

The Duchess passes on. Joan stares after her; then whispers to the Dauphin.

JOAN. Be that Queen?

CHARLES. No. She thinks she is.

JOAN [*again staring after the Duchess*] Oo-oo-

ooh! [*Her awestruck amazement at the figure cut by the magnificently dressed lady is not wholly complimentary*].

LA TRÉMOUILLE [*very surly*] I'll trouble your Highness not to gibe at my wife. [*He goes out. The others have already gone*].

JOAN [*to the Dauphin*] Who be old Gruff-and-Grum?

CHARLES. He is the Duke de la Trémouille.

JOAN. What be his job?

CHARLES. He pretends to command the army. And whenever I find a friend I can care for, he kills him.

JOAN. Why dost let him?

CHARLES [*petulantly moving to the throne side of the room to escape from her magnetic field*] How can I prevent him? He bullies me. They all bully me.

JOAN. Art afraid?

CHARLES. Yes: I am afraid. It's no use preaching to me about it. It's all very well for these big men with their armor that is too heavy for me, and their swords that I can hardly lift, and their muscle and their shouting and their bad tempers. They like fighting: most of them are making fools of themselves all the time they are not fighting; but I am quiet and sensible; and I dont want to kill people: I only want to be left alone to enjoy myself in my own way. I never asked to be a king: it was pushed on me. So if you are going to say 'Son of St Louis: gird on the sword of your ancestors, and lead us to victory' you may spare your breath to cool your porridge; for I cannot do it. I am not built that way; and there is an end of it.

JOAN [*trenchant and masterful*] Blethers! We are all like that to begin with. I shall put courage into thee.

CHARLES. But I dont want to have courage put into me. I want to sleep in a comfortable bed, and not live in continual terror of being killed or wounded. Put courage into the others, and let them have their bellyful of fighting; but let me alone.

JOAN. It's no use, Charlie: thou must face what God puts on thee. If thou fail to make thyself king, thoult be a beggar: what else art fit for? Come! Let me see thee sitting on the throne. I have looked forward to that.

CHARLES. What is the good of sitting on the throne when the other fellows give all the orders? However! [*he sits enthroned, a piteous figure*] here is the king for you! Look your fill at the poor devil.

JOAN. Thourt not king yet, lad: thourt but Dauphin. Be not led away by them around thee. Dressing up dont fill empty noddle. I know the people: the real people that make thy bread for thee; and I tell thee they count no man king of France until the holy oil has been poured on his hair, and himself consecrated and crowned in Rheims Cathedral. And thou needs new clothes, Charlie. Why does not Queen look after thee properly?

CHARLES. We're too poor. She wants all the money we can spare to put on her own back. Besides, I like to see her beautifully dressed; and I dont care what I wear myself: I should look ugly anyhow.

JOAN. There is some good in thee, Charlie; but it is not yet a king's good.

CHARLES. We shall see. I am not such a fool as I look. I have my eyes open; and I can tell you that one good treaty is worth ten good fights. These fighting fellows lose all on the treaties that they gain on the fights. If we can only have a treaty, the English are sure to have the worst of it, because they are better at fighting than at thinking.

JOAN. If the English win, it is they that will make the treaty: and then God help poor France! Thou must fight, Charlie, whether thou will or no. I will go first to hearten thee. We must take our courage in both hands: aye, and pray for it with both hands too.

CHARLES [*descending from his throne and again crossing the room to escape from her dominating urgency*] Oh do stop talking about God and praying. I cant bear people who are always praying. Isnt it bad enough to have to do it at the proper times?

JOAN [*pitying him*] Thou poor child, thou hast never prayed in thy life. I must teach thee from the beginning.

CHARLES. I am not a child: I am a grown

man and a father; and I will not be taught any more.

JOAN. Aye, you have a little son. He that will be Louis the Eleventh when you die. Would you not fight for him?

CHARLES. No: a horrid boy. He hates me. He hates everybody, selfish little beast! I dont want to be bothered with children. I dont want to be a father; and I dont want to be a son: especially a son of St Louis. I dont want to be any of these fine things you all have your heads full of: I want to be just what I am. Why cant you mind your own business, and let me mind mine?

JOAN [*again contemptuous*] Minding your own business is like minding your own body: it's the shortest way to make yourself sick. What is my business? Helping mother at home. What is thine? Petting lapdogs and sucking sugarsticks. I call that muck. I tell thee it is God's business we are here to do: not our own. I have a message to thee from God; and thou must listen to it, though thy heart break with the terror of it.

CHARLES. I dont want a message; but can you tell me any secrets? Can you do any cures? Can you turn lead into gold, or anything of that sort?

JOAN. I can turn thee into a king, in Rheims Cathedral; and that is a miracle that will take some doing, it seems.

CHARLES. If we go to Rheims, and have a coronation, Anne will want new dresses. We cant afford them. I am all right as I am.

JOAN. As you are! And what is that? Less than my father's poorest shepherd. Thourt not lawful owner of thy own land of France till thou be consecrated.

CHARLES. But I shall not be lawful owner of my own land anyhow. Will the consecration pay off my mortgages? I have pledged my last acre to the Archbishop and that fat bully. I owe money even to Bluebeard.

JOAN [*earnestly*] Charlie: I come from the land, and have gotten my strength working on the land; and I tell thee that the land is thine to rule righteously and keep God's peace in, and not to pledge at the pawn-shop as a drunken woman pledges her children's clothes. And I come from God to tell thee to kneel in the cathedral and solemnly give thy kingdom to Him for ever and ever, and become the greatest king in the world as His steward and His bailiff, His soldier and His servant. The very clay of France will become holy: her soldiers will be the soldiers of God: the rebel dukes will be rebels against God: the English will fall on their knees and beg thee let them return to their lawful homes in peace. Wilt be a poor little Judas, and betray me and Him that sent me?

CHARLES [*tempted at last*] Oh, if I only dare!

JOAN. I shall dare, dare, and dare again, in God's name! Art for or against me?

CHARLES [*excited*] I'll risk it, I warn you I shant be able to keep it up; but I'll risk it. You shall see. [*Running to the main door and shouting*] Hallo! Come back, everybody. [*To Joan, as he runs back to the arch opposite*] Mind you stand by and dont let me be bullied. [*Through the arch*] Come along, will you: the whole Court. [*He sits down in the royal chair as they all hurry in to their former places, chattering and wondering*]. Now I'm in for it; but no matter: here goes! [*To the page*] Call for silence, you little beast, will you?

THE PAGE [*snatching a halberd as before and thumping it repeatedly*] Silence for His Majesty the King. The King speaks. [*Peremptorily*] Will you be silent there? [*Silence*].

CHARLES [*rising*] I have given the command of the army to The Maid. The Maid is to do as she likes with it. [*He descends from the dais*].

General amazement. La Hire, delighted, slaps his steel thighpiece with his gauntlet.

LA TRÉMOUILLE [*turning threateningly towards Charles*] What is this? I command the army.

Joan quickly puts her hand on Charles's shoulder as he instinctively recoils.

Charles, with a grotesque effort culminating in an extravagant gesture, snaps his fingers in the Chamberlain's face.

JOAN. Thourt answered, old Gruff-and-Grum. [*Suddenly flashing out her sword as she divines that her moment has come*] Who is for God and His Maid? Who is for Orleans with me?

LA HIRE [*carried away, drawing also*] For God and His Maid! To Orleans!

ALL THE KNIGHTS [*following his lead with enthusiasm*] To Orleans!

Joan, radiant, falls on her knees in thanksgiving to God. They all kneel, except the Archbishop, who gives his benediction with a sigh, and La Trémouille, who collapses, cursing.

Scene III

Orleans, April 29th, 1429. Dunois, aged 26, is pacing up and down a patch of ground on the south bank of the silver Loire, commanding a long view of the river in both directions. He has had his lance stuck up with a pennon, which streams in a strong east wind. His shield with its bend sinister lies beside it. He has his commander's baton in his hand. He is well built, carrying his armor easily. His broad brow and pointed chin give him an equilaterally triangular face, already marked by active service and responsibility, with the expression of a good-natured and capable man who has no affections and no foolish illusions. His page is sitting on the ground, elbows on knees, cheeks on fists, idly watching the water. It is evening; and both man and boy are affected by the loveliness of the Loire.

DUNOIS [*halting for a moment to glance up at the streaming pennon and shake his head wearily before he resumes his pacing*] West wind, west wind, west wind. Strumpet: steadfast when you should be wanton, wanton when you should be steadfast. West wind on the silver Loire: what rhymes to Loire? [*He looks again at the pennon, and shakes his fist at it*] Change, curse you, change, English harlot of a wind, change. West, west, I tell you. [*With a growl he resumes his march in silence, but soon begins again*] West wind, wanton wind, wilful wind, womanish wind, false wind from over the water, will you never blow again?

THE PAGE [*bounding to his feet*] See! There! There she goes!

DUNOIS [*startled from his reverie: eagerly*] Where? Who? The Maid?

THE PAGE. No: the kingfisher. Like blue lightning. She went into that bush.

DUNOIS [*furiously disappointed*] Is that all? You infernal young idiot: I have a mind to pitch you into the river.

THE PAGE [*not afraid, knowing his man*] It looked frightfully jolly, that flash of blue. Look! There goes the other!

DUNOIS [*running eagerly to the river brim*] Where? Where?

THE PAGE [*pointing*] Passing the reeds.

DUNOIS [*delighted*] I see.

They follow the flight till the bird takes cover.

THE PAGE. You blew me up because you were not in time to see them yesterday.

DUNOIS. You knew I was expecting The Maid when you set up your yelping. I will give you something to yelp for next time.

THE PAGE. Arnt they lovely? I wish I could catch them.

DUNOIS. Let me catch you trying to trap them, and I will put you in the iron cage for a month to teach you what a cage feels like. You are an abominable boy.

THE PAGE [*laughs, and squats down as before*]!

DUNOIS [*pacing*] Blue bird, blue bird, since I am friend to thee, change thou the wind for me. No: it does not rhyme. He who has

sinned for thee: thats better. No sense in
it, though. [*He finds himself close to the
page*] You abominable boy! [*He turns away
from him*] Mary in the blue snood, kingfisher color: will you grudge me a west
wind?

A SENTRY'S VOICE WESTWARD. Halt! Who goes
there?

JOAN'S VOICE. The Maid.

DUNOIS. Let her pass. Hither, Maid! To me!

*Joan, in splendid armor, rushes in in a
blazing rage. The wind drops; and the
pennon flaps idly down the lance; but
Dunois is too much occupied with Joan
to notice it.*

JOAN [*bluntly*] Be you Bastard of Orleans?

DUNOIS [*cool and stern, pointing to his
shield*] You see the bend sinister. Are you
Joan the Maid?

JOAN. Sure.

DUNOIS. Where are your troops?

JOAN. Miles behind. They have cheated me.
They have brought me to the wrong side
of the river.

DUNOIS. I told them to.

JOAN. Why did you? The English are on the
other side!

DUNOIS. The English are on both sides.

JOAN. But Orleans is on the other side. We
must fight the English there. How can we
cross the river?

DUNOIS [*grimly*] There is a bridge.

JOAN. In God's name, then, let us cross the
bridge, and fall on them.

DUNOIS. It seems simple; but it cannot be
done.

JOAN. Who says so?

DUNOIS. I say so; and older and wiser heads
than mine are of the same opinion.

JOAN [*roundly*] Then your older and wiser
heads are fatheads: they have made a fool
of you; and now they want to make a fool
of me too, bringing me to the wrong side of
the river. Do you not know that I bring
you better help than ever came to any
general or any town?

DUNOIS [*smiling patiently*] Your own?

JOAN. No: the help and counsel of the King
of Heaven. Which is the way to the bridge?

DUNOIS. You are impatient, Maid.

JOAN. Is this a time for patience? Our enemy
is at our gates; and here we stand doing
nothing. Oh, why are you not fighting?
Listen to me: I will deliver you from fear.
I—

DUNOIS [*laughing heartily, and waving her
off*] No, no, my girl: if you delivered me
from fear I should be a good knight for a
story book, but a very bad commander of
the army. Come! let me begin to make a
soldier of you. [*He takes her to the water's
edge*]. Do you see those two forts at this
end of the bridge? the big ones?

JOAN. Yes. Are they ours or the goddams'?

DUNOIS. Be quiet, and listen to me. If I were
in either of those forts with only ten men
I could hold it against an army. The English have more than ten times ten goddams
in those forts to hold them against us.

JOAN. They cannot hold them against God.
God did not give them the land under
those forts: they stole it from Him. He gave
it to us. I will take those forts.

DUNOIS. Single-handed?

JOAN. Our men will take them. I will lead
them.

DUNOIS. Not a man will follow you.

JOAN. I will not look back to see whether anyone is following me.

DUNOIS [*recognizing her mettle, and clapping
her heartily on the shoulder*] Good. You
have the makings of a soldier in you. You
are in love with war.

JOAN [*startled*] Oh! And the Archbishop said
I was in love with religion.

DUNOIS. I, God forgive me, am a little in love
with war myself, the ugly devil! I am like
a man with two wives. Do you want to be
like a woman with two husbands?

JOAN [*matter-of-fact*] I will never take a husband. A man in Toul took an action against
me for breach of promise; but I never promised him. I am a soldier: I do not want to
be thought of as a woman. I will not dress
as a woman. I do not care for the things
women care for. They dream of lovers, and
of money. I dream of leading a charge, and

of placing the big guns. You soldiers do not know how to use the big guns: you think you can win battles with a great noise and smoke.

DUNOIS [*with a shrug*] True. Half the time the artillery is more trouble than it is worth.

JOAN. Aye, lad; but you cannot fight stone walls with horses: you must have guns, and much bigger guns too.

DUNOIS [*grinning at her familiarity, and echoing it*] Aye, lass; but a good heart and a stout ladder will get over the stoniest wall.

JOAN. I will be first up the ladder when we reach the fort, Bastard. I dare you to follow me.

DUNOIS. You must not dare a staff officer, Joan: only company officers are allowed to indulge in displays of personal courage. Besides, you must know that I welcome you as a saint, not as a soldier. I have daredevils enough at my call, if they could help me.

JOAN. I am not a daredevil: I am a servant of God. My sword is sacred: I found it behind the altar in the church of St Catherine, where God hid it for me; and I may not strike a blow with it. My heart is full of courage, not of anger. I will lead; and your men will follow: that is all I can do. But I must do it: you shall not stop me.

DUNOIS. All in good time. Our men cannot take those forts by a sally across the bridge. They must come by water, and take the English in the rear on this side.

JOAN [*her military sense asserting itself*] Then make rafts and put big guns on them; and let your men cross to us.

DUNOIS. The rafts are ready; and the men are embarked. But they must wait for God.

JOAN. What do you mean? God is waiting for them.

DUNOIS. Let Him send us a wind then. My boats are downstream: they cannot come up against both wind and current. We must wait until God changes the wind. Come: let me take you to the church.

JOAN. No. I love church; but the English will not yield to prayers: they understand nothing but hard knocks and slashes. I will not go to church until we have beaten them.

DUNOIS. You must: I have business for you there.

JOAN. What business?

DUNOIS. To pray for a west wind. I have prayed; and I have given two silver candlesticks; but my prayers are not answered. Yours may be: you are young and innocent.

JOAN. Oh yes: you are right. I will pray: I will tell St Catherine: she will make God give me a west wind. Quick: shew me the way to the church.

THE PAGE [*sneezes violently*] At-cha!!!

JOAN. God bless you, child! Coom, Bastard.

They go out. The page rises to follow. He picks up the shield, and is taking the spear as well when he notices the pennon, which is now streaming eastward.

THE PAGE [*dropping the shield and calling excitedly after them*] Seigneur! Seigneur! Mademoiselle!

DUNOIS [*running back*] What is it? The kingfisher? [*He looks eagerly for it up the river*].

JOAN [*joining them*] Oh, a kingfisher! Where?

THE PAGE. No: the wind, the wind, the wind [*pointing to the pennon*]: that is what made me sneeze.

DUNOIS [*looking at the pennon*] The wind has changed. [*He crosses himself*] God has spoken. [*Kneeling and handing his baton to Joan*] You command the king's army. I am your soldier.

THE PAGE [*looking down the river*] The boats have put off. They are ripping upstream like anything.

DUNOIS [*rising*] Now for the forts. You dared me to follow. Dare you lead?

JOAN [*bursting into tears and flinging her arms round Dunois, kissing him on both cheeks*] Dunois, dear comrade in arms, help me. My eyes are blinded with tears. Set my foot on the ladder, and say 'Up, Joan.'

DUNOIS [*dragging her out*] Never mind the tears: make for the flash of the guns.

JOAN [*in a blaze of courage*] Ah!

DUNOIS [*dragging her along with him*] For God and Saint Dennis!

THE PAGE [*shrilly*] The Maid! The Maid! God and The Maid! Hurray-ay-ay! [*He snatches up the shield and lance, and capers out after them, mad with excitement*].

Scene IV

A tent in the English camp. A bull-necked English chaplain of 50 is sitting on a stool at a table, hard at work writing. At the other side of the table an imposing nobleman, aged 46, is seated in a handsome chair turning over the leaves of an illuminated Book of Hours. The nobleman is enjoying himself: the chaplain is struggling with suppressed wrath. There is an unoccupied leather stool on the nobleman's left. The table is on his right.

THE NOBLEMAN. Now this is what I call workmanship. There is nothing on earth more exquisite than a bonny book, with well-placed columns of rich black writing in beautiful borders, and illuminated pictures cunningly inset. But nowadays, instead of looking at books, people read them. A book might as well be one of those orders for bacon and bran that you are scribbling.

THE CHAPLAIN. I must say, my lord, you take our situation very coolly. Very coolly indeed.

THE NOBLEMAN [*supercilious*] What is the matter?

THE CHAPLAIN. The matter, my lord, is that we English have been defeated.

THE NOBLEMAN. That happens, you know. It is only in history books and ballads that the enemy is always defeated.

THE CHAPLAIN. But we are being defeated over and over again. First, Orleans—

THE NOBLEMAN [*poohpoohing*] Oh, Orleans!

THE CHAPLAIN. I know what you are going to say, my lord: that was a clear case of witchcraft and sorcery. But we are still being defeated. Jargeau, Meung, Beaugency, just like Orleans. And now we have been butchered at Patay, and Sir John Talbot taken prisoner. [*He throws down his pen, almost in tears*] I feel it, my lord: I feel it very deeply. I cannot bear to see my countrymen defeated by a parcel of foreigners.

THE NOBLEMAN. Oh! you are an Englishman, are you?

THE CHAPLAIN. Certainly not, my lord: I am a gentleman. Still, like your lordship, I was born in England; and it makes a difference.

THE NOBLEMAN. You are attached to the soil, eh?

THE CHAPLAIN. It pleases your lordship to be satirical at my expense: your greatness privileges you to be so with impunity. But your lordship knows very well that I am not attached to the soil in a vulgar manner, like a serf. Still, I have a feeling about it; [*with growing agitation*] and I am not ashamed of it; and [*rising wildly*] by God, if this goes on any longer I will fling my cassock to the devil, and take arms myself, and strangle the accursed witch with my own hands.

THE NOBLEMAN [*laughing at him goodnaturedly*] So you shall, chaplain: so you shall, if we can do nothing better. But not yet, not quite yet.

The Chaplain resumes his seat very sulkily.

THE NOBLEMAN [*airily*] I should not care very much about the witch—you see, I have made my pilgrimage to the Holy Land; and the Heavenly Powers, for their own credit, can hardly allow me to be worsted by a village sorceress—but the Bastard of Orleans is a harder nut to crack; and as he has been to the Holy Land too, honors are easy between us as far as that goes.

THE CHAPLAIN. He is only a Frenchman, my lord.

THE NOBLEMAN. A Frenchman! Where did you pick up that expression? Are these

Burgundians and Bretons and Picards and Gascons beginning to call themselves Frenchmen, just as our fellows are beginning to call themselves Englishmen? They actually talk of France and England as their countries. Theirs, if you please! What is to become of me and you if that way of thinking comes into fashion?

THE CHAPLAIN. Why, my lord? Can it hurt us?

THE NOBLEMAN. Men cannot serve two masters. If this cant of serving their country once takes hold of them, goodbye to the authority of their feudal lords, and goodbye to the authority of the Church. That is, goodbye to you and me.

THE CHAPLAIN. I hope I am a faithful servant of the Church; and there are only six cousins between me and the barony of Stogumber, which was created by the Conqueror. But is that any reason why I should stand by and see Englishmen beaten by a French bastard and a witch from Lousy Champagne?

THE NOBLEMAN. Easy, man, easy: we shall burn the witch and beat the bastard all in good time. Indeed I am waiting at present for the Bishop of Beauvais, to arrange the burning with him. He has been turned out of his diocese by her faction.

THE CHAPLAIN. You have first to catch her, my lord.

THE NOBLEMAN. Or buy her. I will offer a king's ransom.

THE CHAPLAIN. A king's ransom! For that slut!

THE NOBLEMAN. One has to leave a margin. Some of Charles's people will sell her to the Burgundians; the Burgundians will sell her to us; and there will probably be three or four middlemen who will expect their little commissions.

THE CHAPLAIN. Monstrous. It is all those scoundrels of Jews: they get in every time money changes hands. I would not leave a Jew alive in Christendom if I had my way.

THE NOBLEMAN. Why not? The Jews generally give value. They make you pay; but they deliver the goods. In my experience the men who want something for nothing are invariably Christians.

A page appears.

THE PAGE. The Right Reverend the Bishop of Beauvais: Monseigneur Cauchon.

Cauchon, aged about 60, comes in. The page withdraws. The two Englishmen rise.

THE NOBLEMAN [*with effusive courtesy*] My dear Bishop, how good of you to come! Allow me to introduce myself: Richard de Beauchamp, Earl of Warwick, at your service.

CAUCHON. Your lordship's fame is well known to me.

WARWICK. This reverend cleric is Master John de Stogumber.

THE CHAPLAIN [*glibly*] John Bowyer Spenser Neville de Stogumber, at your service, my lord: Bachelor of Theology, and Keeper of the Private Seal to His Eminence the Cardinal of Winchester.

WARWICK [*to Cauchon*] You call him the Cardinal of England, I believe. Our king's uncle.

CAUCHON. Messire John de Stogumber: I am always the very good friend of His Eminence. [*He extends his hand to the chaplain, who kisses his ring*].

WARWICK. Do me the honor to be seated. [*He gives Cauchon his chair, placing it at the head of the table*].

Cauchon accepts the place of honor with a grave inclination. Warwick fetches the leather stool carelessly, and sits in his former place. The chaplain goes back to his chair.

Though Warwick has taken second place in calculated deference to the Bishop, he assumes the lead in opening the proceedings as a matter of course. He is still cordial and expansive; but there is a new note in his voice which means that he is coming to business.

WARWICK. Well, my Lord Bishop, you find us in one of our unlucky moments. Charles is to be crowned at Rheims, practically by the young woman from Lorraine; and—I must not deceive you, nor flatter your hopes—we cannot prevent it. I suppose it will make a great difference to Charles's position.

CAUCHON. Undoubtedly. It is a masterstroke of The Maid's.

THE CHAPLAIN [*again agitated*] We were not fairly beaten, my lord. No Englishman is ever fairly beaten.

Cauchon raises his eyebrow slightly, then quickly composes his face.

WARWICK. Our friend here takes the view that the young woman is a sorceress. It would, I presume, be the duty of your reverend lordship to denounce her to the Inquisition, and have her burnt for that offence.

CAUCHON. If she were captured in my diocese: yes.

WARWICK [*feeling that they are getting on capitally*] Just so. Now I suppose there can be no reasonable doubt that she is a sorceress.

THE CHAPLAIN. Not the least. An arrant witch.

WARWICK [*gently reproving the interruption*] We are asking for the Bishop's opinion, Messire John.

CAUCHON. We shall have to consider not merely our own opinions here, but the opinions—the prejudices, if you like—of a French court.

WARWICK [*correcting*] A Catholic court, my lord.

CAUCHON. Catholic courts are composed of mortal men, like other courts, however sacred their function and inspiration may be. And if the men are Frenchmen, as the modern fashion calls them, I am afraid the bare fact that an English army has been defeated by a French one will not convince them that there is any sorcery in the matter.

THE CHAPLAIN. What! Not when the famous Sir Talbot himself has been defeated and actually taken prisoner by a drab from the ditches of Lorraine!

CAUCHON. Sir John Talbot, we all know, is a fierce and formidable soldier, Messire; but I have yet to learn that he is an able general. And though it pleases you to say that he has been defeated by this girl, some of us may be disposed to give a little of the credit to Dunois.

THE CHAPLAIN [*contemptuously*] The Bastard of Orleans!

CAUCHON. Let me remind—

WARWICK [*interposing*] I know what you are going to say, my lord. Dunois defeated me at Montargis.

CAUCHON [*bowing*] I take that as evidence that the Seigneur Dunois is a very able commander indeed.

WARWICK. Your lordship is the flower of courtesy. I admit, on our side, that Talbot is a mere fighting animal, and that it probably served him right to be taken at Patay.

THE CHAPLAIN [*chafing*] My lord: at Orleans this woman had her throat pierced by an English arrow, and was seen to cry like a child from the pain of it. It was a death wound; yet she fought all day; and when our men had repulsed all her attacks like true Englishmen, she walked alone to the wall of our fort with a white banner in her hand; and our men were paralyzed, and could neither shoot nor strike whilst the French fell on them and drove them on to the bridge, which immediately burst into flames and crumbled under them, letting them down into the river, where they were drowned in heaps. Was this your bastard's generalship? or were those flames of hell, conjured up by witchcraft?

WARWICK. You will forgive Messire John's vehemence, my lord; but he has put our case. Dunois is a great captain, we admit; but why could he do nothing until the witch came?

CAUCHON. I do not say that there were no supernatural powers on her side. But the names on that white banner were not the names of Satan and Beelzebub, but the blessed names of our Lord and His holy mother. And your commander who was drowned—Clahz-da I think you call him—

WARWICK. Glasdale. Sir William Glasdale.

CAUCHON. Glass-dell, thank you. He was no

saint; and many of our people think that he was drowned for his blasphemies against The Maid.

WARWICK [*beginning to look very dubious*] Well, what are we to infer from all this, my lord? Has The Maid converted you?

CAUCHON. If she had, my lord, I should have known better than to have trusted myself here within your grasp.

WARWICK [*blandly deprecating*] Oh! oh! My lord!

CAUCHON. If the devil is making use of this girl—and I believe he is—

WARWICK [*reassured*] Ah! You hear, Messire John? I knew your lordship would not fail us. Pardon my interruption. Proceed.

CAUCHON. If it be so, the devil has longer views than you give him credit for.

WARWICK. Indeed? In what way? Listen to this, Messire John.

CAUCHON. If the devil wanted to damn a country girl, do you think so easy a task would cost him the winning of half a dozen battles? No, my lord: any trumpery imp could do that much if the girl could be damned at all. The Prince of Darkness does not condescend to such cheap drudgery. When he strikes, he strikes at the Catholic Church, whose realm is the whole spiritual world. When he damns, he damns the souls of the entire human race. Against that dreadful design The Church stands ever on guard. And it is as one of the instruments of that design that I see this girl. She is inspired, but diabolically inspired.

THE CHAPLAIN. I told you she was a witch.

CAUCHON [*fiercely*] She is not a witch. She is a heretic.

THE CHAPLAIN. What difference does that make?

CAUCHON. You, a priest, ask me that! You English are strangely blunt in the mind. All these things that you call witchcraft are capable of a natural explanation. The woman's miracles would not impose on a rabbit: she does not claim them as miracles herself. What do her victories prove but that she has a better head on her shoulders than your swearing Glass-dells and mad bull Talbots, and that the courage of faith, even though it be a false faith, will always outstay the courage of wrath?

THE CHAPLAIN [*hardly able to believe his ears*] Does your lordship compare Sir John Talbot, three times Governor of Ireland, to a mad bull? !!!

WARWICK. It would not be seemly for you to do so, Messire John, as you are still six removes from a barony. But as I am an earl, and Talbot is only a knight, I may make bold to accept the comparison. [*To the Bishop*] My lord: I wipe the slate as far as the witchcraft goes. None the less, we must burn the woman.

CAUCHON. I cannot burn her. The Church cannot take life. And my first duty is to seek this girl's salvation.

WARWICK. No doubt. But you do burn people occasionally.

CAUCHON. No. When The Church cuts off an obstinate heretic as a dead branch from the tree of life, the heretic is handed over to the secular arm. The Church has no part in what the secular arm may see fit to do.

WARWICK. Precisely. And I shall be the secular arm in this case. Well, my lord, hand over your dead branch; and I will see that the fire is ready for it. If you will answer for The Church's part, I will answer for the secular part.

CAUCHON [*with smouldering anger*] I can answer for nothing. You great lords are too prone to treat The Church as a mere political convenience.

WARWICK [*smiling and propitiatory*] Not in England, I assure you.

CAUCHON. In England more than anywhere else. No, my lord: the soul of this village girl is of equal value with yours or your king's before the throne of God; and my first duty is to save it. I will not suffer your lordship to smile at me as if I were repeating a meaningless form of words, and it were well understood between us that I should betray the girl to you. I am no mere political bishop: my faith is to me what your honor is to you; and if there be a loophole through which this baptized child of God can creep to her salvation, I shall guide her to it.

THE CHAPLAIN [*rising in a fury*] You are a traitor.

CAUCHON [*springing up*] You lie, priest. [*Trembling with rage*] If you dare do what this woman has done—set your country above the holy Catholic Church—you shall go to the fire with her.

THE CHAPLAIN. My lord: I—I went too far. I— [*he sits down with a submissive gesture*].

WARWICK [*who has risen apprehensively*] My lord: I apologize to you for the word used by Messire John de Stogumber. It does not mean in England what it does in France. In your language traitor means betrayer: one who is perfidious, treacherous, unfaithful, disloyal. In our country it means simply one who is not wholly devoted to our English interests.

CAUCHON. I am sorry: I did not understand. [*He subsides into his chair with dignity*].

WARWICK [*resuming his seat, much relieved*] I must apologize on my own account if I have seemed to take the burning of this poor girl too lightly. When one has seen whole countrysides burnt over and over again as mere items in military routine, one has to grow a very thick skin. Otherwise one might go mad: at all events, I should. May I venture to assume that your lordship also, having to see so many heretics burned from time to time, is compelled to take— shall I say a professional view of what would otherwise be a very horrible incident?

CAUCHON. Yes: it is a painful duty: even, as you say, a horrible one. But in comparison with the horror of heresy it is less than nothing. I am not thinking of this girl's body, which will suffer for a few moments only, and which must in any event die in some more or less painful manner, but of her soul, which may suffer to all eternity.

WARWICK. Just so; and God grant that her soul may be saved! But the practical problem would seem to be how to save her soul without saving her body. For we must face it, my lord: if this cult of The Maid goes on, our cause is lost.

THE CHAPLAIN [*his voice broken like that of a man who has been crying*] May I speak, my lord?

WARWICK. Really, Messire John, I had rather you did not, unless you can keep your temper.

THE CHAPLAIN. It is only this. I speak under correction; but The Maid is full of deceit: she pretends to be devout. Her prayers and confessions are endless. How can she be accused of heresy when she neglects no observance of a faithful daughter of The Church?

CAUCHON [*flaming up*] A faithful daughter of The Church! The Pope himself at his proudest dare not presume as this woman presumes. She acts as if she herself were The Church. She brings the message of God to Charles; and The Church must stand aside. She will crown him in the cathedral of Rheims: she, not The Church! She sends letters to the king of England giving him God's command through her to return to his island on pain of God's vengeance, which she will execute. Let me tell you that the writing of such letters was the practice of the accursed Mahomet, the anti-Christ. Has she ever in all her utterances said one word of The Church? Never. It is always God and herself.

WARWICK. What can you expect? A beggar on horseback! Her head is turned.

CAUCHON. Who has turned it? The devil. And for a mighty purpose. He is spreading this heresy everywhere. The man Hus, burnt only thirteen years ago at Constance, infected all Bohemia with it. A man named WcLeef, himself an anointed priest, spread the pestilence in England; and to your shame you let him die in his bed. We have such people here in France too: I know the breed. It is cancerous: if it be not cut out, stamped out, burnt out, it will not stop until it has brought the whole body of human society into sin and corruption, into waste and ruin. By it an Arab camel driver drove Christ and His Church out of Jerusalem, and ravaged his way west like a wild beast until at last there stood only the Pyrenees and God's mercy between France and damnation. Yet what did the camel driver do at the beginning more than this shepherd girl is doing? He had his voices from the angel Gabriel: she has her voices from St Catherine and St Margaret and the Blessed Michael. He declared himself the messenger of God, and wrote in God's name to the kings of the earth. Her letters to them are going forth daily. It is not the Mother of God now to who we must look for intercession, but to Joan the Maid. What will the world be like when The Church's accumulated wisdom and knowledge and experience, its councils of learned, venerable pious men, are thrust into the kennel by every ignorant laborer or dairymaid whom the devil can puff up with the monstrous self-conceit of being directly inspired from heaven? It will be a world of blood, of fury, of devastation, of each man striving for his own hand: in the end a world wrecked back into barbarism. For now you have only Mahomet and his dupes, and the Maid and her dupes; but what will it be when every girl thinks herself a Joan and every man a Mahomet? I shudder to the very marrow of my bones when I think of it. I have fought it all my life; and I will fight it to the end. Let all this woman's sins be forgiven her except only this sin; for it is the sin against the Holy Ghost; and if she does not recant in the dust before the world, and submit herself to the last inch of her soul to her Church, to the fire she shall go if she once falls into my hand.

WARWICK [*unimpressed*] You feel strongly about it, naturally.

CAUCHON. Do not you?

WARWICK. I am a soldier, not a churchman. As a pilgrim I saw something of the Mahometans. They were not so ill-bred as I had been led to believe. In some respects their conduct compared favorably with ours.

CAUCHON [*displeased*] I have noticed this before. Men go to the East to convert the infidels. And the infidels pervert them. The Crusader comes back more than half a Saracen. Not to mention that all Englishmen are born heretics.

THE CHAPLAIN. Englishmen heretics!!! [*Appealing to Warwick*] My lord: must we endure this? His lordship is beside himself. How can what an Englishman believes be heresy? It is a contradiction in terms.

CAUCHON. I absolve you, Messire de Stogumber, on the ground of invincible ignorance. The thick air of your country does not breed theologians.

WARWICK. You would not say so if you heard us quarrelling about religion, my lord! I am sorry you think I must be either a heretic or a blockhead because, as a travelled man, I know that the followers of Mahomet profess great respect for our Lord, and are more ready to forgive St Peter for being a fisherman than your lordship is to forgive Mahomet for being a camel driver. But at least we can proceed in this matter without bigotry.

CAUCHON. When men call the zeal of the Christian Church bigotry I know what to think.

WARWICK. They are only east and west views of the same thing.

CAUCHON [*bitterly ironical*] Only east and west! Only!!

WARWICK. Oh, my Lord Bishop, I am not gainsaying you. You will carry The Church with you; but you have to carry the nobles also. To my mind there is a stronger case against The Maid than the one you have so forcibly put. Frankly, I am not afraid of this girl becoming another Mahomet, and superseding The Church by a great heresy. I think you exaggerate that risk. But have you noticed that in these letters of hers, she proposes to all the kings of Europe, as she has already pressed on Charles, a transaction which would wreck the whole social structure of Christendom?

CAUCHON. Wreck The Church. I tell you so.

WARWICK [*whose patience is wearing out*] My lord: pray get The Church out of your head for a moment; and remember that there are temporal institutions in the world as well as spiritual ones. I and my peers represent the feudal aristocracy as you represent The Church. We are the temporal power. Well, do you not see how this girl's idea strikes at us?

CAUCHON. How does her idea strike at you, except as it strikes at all of us, through The Church?

WARWICK. Her idea is that the kings should give their realms to God, and then reign as God's bailiffs.

CAUCHON [*not interested*] Quite sound theologically, my lord. But the king will hardly care, provided he reign. It is an abstract idea: a mere form of words.

WARWICK. By no means. It is a cunning device to supersede the aristocracy, and make the king sole and absolute autocrat. Instead of the king being merely the first among his peers, he becomes their master. That we cannot suffer: we call no man master. Nominally we hold our lands and dignities from the king, because there must be a keystone to the arch of human society; but we hold our lands in our own hands, and defend them with our own swords and those of our own tenants. Now by The Maid's doctrine the king will take our lands—our lands!—and make them a present to God; and God will then vest them wholly in the king.

CAUCHON. Need you fear that? You are the makers of kings after all. York or Lancaster in England, Lancaster or Valois in France: they reign according to your pleasure.

WARWICK. Yes; but only as long as the people follow their feudal lords, and know the king only as a travelling show, owning nothing but the highway that belongs to everybody. If the people's thoughts and hearts were turned to the king, and their lords became only the king's servants in their eyes, the king could break us across his knee one by one; and then what should we be but liveried courtiers in his halls?

CAUCHON. Still you need not fear, my lord. Some men are born kings: and some are born statesmen. The two are seldom the same. Where would the king find counsellors to plan and carry out such a policy for him?

WARWICK [*with a not too friendly smile*] Perhaps in the Church, my lord.

Cauchon, with an equally sour smile, shrugs his shoulders, and does not contradict him.

WARWICK. Strike down the barons; and the cardinals will have it all their own way.

CAUCHON [*conciliatory, dropping his polemical tone*] My lord: we shall not defeat The Maid if we strive against one another. I know well that there is a Will to Power in the world. I know that while it lasts there will be a struggle between the Emperor and the Pope, between the dukes and the political cardinals, between the barons and the kings. The devil divides us and governs. I see you are no friend to The Church: you are an earl first and last, as I am a churchman first and last. But can we not sink our differences in the face of a common enemy? I see now that what is in your mind is not that this girl has never once mentioned The Church, and thinks only of God and herself, but that she has never once mentioned the peerage, and thinks only of the king and herself.

WARWICK. Quite so. These two ideas of hers are the same idea at bottom. It goes deep, my lord. It is the protest of the individual soul against the interference of priest or peer between the private man and his God. I should call it Protestantism if I had to find a name for it.

CAUCHON [*looking hard at him*] You understand it wonderfully well, my lord. Scratch an Englishman, and find a Protestant.

WARWICK [*playing the pink of courtesy*] I think you are not entirely void of sympathy with The Maid's secular heresy, my lord. I leave you to find a name for it.

CAUCHON. You mistake me, my lord. I have no sympathy with her political presumptions. But as a priest I have gained a knowledge of the minds of the common people; and there you will find yet another most dangerous idea. I can express it only by such phrases as France for the French, England for the English, Italy for the Italians, Spain for the Spanish, and so forth. It is sometimes so narrow and bitter in country folk that it surprises me that this country girl can rise above the idea of her village for its villagers. But she can. She does. When she threatens to drive the English from the soil of France she is undoubtedly thinking of the whole extent of country in which French is spoken. To her the French-speaking people are what the Holy Scriptures describe as a nation. Call this side of her heresy Nationalism if you will: I can find you no better name for it. I can only tell you that it is essentially anti-Catholic and anti-Christian; for the Catholic Church knows only one realm, and that is the realm of Christ's kingdom. Divide that kingdom into nations, and you dethrone Christ. Dethrone Christ, and who will stand between our throats and the sword? The world will perish in a welter of war.

WARWICK. Well, if you will burn the Protestant, I will burn the Nationalist, though perhaps I shall not carry Messire John with me there. England for the English will appeal to him.

THE CHAPLAIN. Certainly England for the English goes without saying: it is the simple law of nature. But this woman denies to England her legitimate conquests, given her by God because of her peculiar fitness to rule over less civilized races for their own good. I do not understand what your lordships mean by Protestant and Nationalist: you are too learned and subtle for a poor clerk like myself. But I know as a matter of plain commonsense that the woman is a rebel; and that is enough for me. She rebels against Nature by wearing man's clothes, and fighting. She rebels against The Church by usurping the divine authority of the Pope. She rebels against God by her damnable league with Satan and his evil spirits against our army. And all these rebellions are only excuses for her great rebellion against England. That is not to be endured. Let her perish. Let her burn. Let her not infect the whole flock. It is expedient that one woman die for the people.

WARWICK [*rising*] My lord: we seem to be agreed.

CAUCHON [*rising also, but in protest*] I will not imperil my soul. I will uphold the justice of the Church. I will strive to the utmost for this woman's salvation.

WARWICK. I am sorry for the poor girl. I hate these severities. I will spare her if I can.

THE CHAPLAIN [*implacably*] I would burn her with my own hands.

CAUCHON [*blessing him*] Sancta simplicitas!

Scene V

The ambulatory in the cathedral of Rheims, near the door of the vestry. A pillar bears one of the stations of the cross. The organ is playing the people out of the nave after the coronation. Joan is kneeling in prayer before the station. She is beautifully dressed, but still in male attire. The organ ceases as Dunois, also splendidly arrayed, comes into the ambulatory from the vestry.

DUNOIS. Come, Joan! you have had enough praying. After that fit of crying you will catch a chill if you stay here any longer. It is all over: the cathedral is empty; and the streets are full. They are calling for The Maid. We have told them you are staying here alone to pray; but they want to see you again.

JOAN. No: let the king have all the glory.

DUNOIS. He only spoils the show, poor devil. No, Joan: you have crowned him; and you must go through with it.

JOAN [*shakes her head reluctantly*].

DUNOIS [*raising her*] Come come! it will be over in a couple of hours. It's better than the bridge at Orleans: eh?

JOAN. Oh, dear Dunois, how I wish it were the bridge at Orleans again! We lived at that bridge.

DUNOIS. Yes, faith, and died too: some of us.

JOAN. Isnt it strange, Jack? I am such a coward: I am frightened beyond words before a battle; but it is so dull afterwards

when there is no danger: oh, so dull! dull!
dull!

DUNOIS. You must learn to be abstemious in
war, just as you are in your food and drink,
my little saint.

JOAN. Dear Jack: I think you like me as a
soldier likes his comrade.

DUNOIS. You need it, poor innocent child of
God. You have not many friends at court.

JOAN. Why do all these courtiers and knights
and churchmen hate me? What have I
done to them? I have asked nothing for
myself except that my village shall not be
taxed; for we cannot afford war taxes. I
have brought them luck and victory: I have
set them right when they were doing all
sorts of stupid things: I have crowned
Charles and made him a real king; and all
the honors he is handing out have gone
to them. Then why do they not love
me?

DUNOIS [*rallying her*] Sim-ple-ton! Do you
expect stupid people to love you for shewing them up? Do blundering old military
dug-outs love the successful young captains
who supersede them? Do ambitious politicians love the climbers who take the front
seats from them? Do archbishops enjoy
being played off their own altars, even by
saints? Why, I should be jealous of you
myself if I were ambitious enough.

JOAN. You are the pick of the basket here,
Jack: the only friend I have among all
these nobles. I'll wager your mother was
from the country. I will go back to the
farm when I have taken Paris.

DUNOIS. I am not so sure that they will let
you take Paris.

JOAN [*startled*] What!

DUNOIS. I should have taken it myself before
this if they had all been sound about it.
Some of them would rather Paris took you,
I think. So take care.

JOAN. Jack: the world is too wicked for me.
If the goddams and the Burgundians do
not make an end of me, the French will.
Only for my voices I should lose all heart.
That is why I had to steal away to pray
here alone after the coronation. I'll tell you
something, Jack. It is in the bells I hear

my voices. Not to-day, when they all rang:
that was nothing but jangling. But here in
this corner, where the bells come down
from heaven, and the echoes linger, or in
the fields, where they come from a distance through the quiet of the countryside,
my voices are in them. [*The cathedral clock
chimes the quarter*] Hark! [*She becomes
rapt*] Do you hear? 'Dear-child-of-God':
just what you said. At the half-hour they
will say 'Be-brave-go-on.' At the three-
quarters they will say 'I-am-thy-Help.' But
it is at the hour, when the great bell goes
after 'God-will-save-France': it is then that
St Margaret and St Catherine and sometimes even the blessed Michael will say
things that I cannot tell beforehand. Then,
oh then—

DUNOIS [*interrupting her kindly but not sympathetically*] Then, Joan, we shall hear
whatever we fancy in the booming of the
bell. You make me uneasy when you talk
about your voices: I should think you were
a bit cracked if I hadnt noticed that you
give me very sensible reasons for what
you do, though I hear you telling others
you are only obeying Madame Saint
Catherine.

JOAN [*crossly*] Well, I have to find reasons
for you, because you do not believe in my
voices. But the voices come first; and I
find the reasons after: whatever you may
choose to believe.

DUNOIS. Are you angry, Joan?

JOAN. Yes. [*Smiling*] No: not with you. I
wish you were one of the village babies.

DUNOIS. Why?

JOAN. I could nurse you for awhile.

DUNOIS. You are a bit of a woman after all.

JOAN. No: not a bit: I am a soldier and nothing else. Soldiers always nurse children
when they get a chance.

DUNOIS. That is true. [*He laughs*].

*King Charles, with Bluebeard on his
left and La Hire on his right, comes
from the vestry, where he has been dis-
robing. Joan shrinks away behind the
pillar. Dunois is left between Charles
and La Hire.*

DUNOIS. Well, your Majesty is an anointed king at last. How do you like it?

CHARLES. I would not go through it again to be emperor of the sun and moon. The weight of those robes! I thought I should have dropped when they loaded that crown on to me. And the famous holy oil they talked so much about was rancid: phew! The Archbishop must be nearly dead: his robes must have weighed a ton: they are stripping him still in the vestry.

DUNOIS [*drily*] Your Majesty should wear armor oftener. That would accustom you to heavy dressing.

CHARLES. Yes: the old jibe! Well, I am not going to wear armor: fighting is not my job. Where is The Maid?

JOAN [*coming forward between Charles and Bluebeard, and falling on her knee*] Sire: I have made you king: my work is done. I am going back to my father's farm.

CHARLES [*surprised, but relieved*] Oh, are you? Well, that will be very nice.

Joan rises, deeply discouraged.

CHARLES [*continuing heedlessly*] A healthy life, you know.

DUNOIS. But a dull one.

BLUEBEARD. You will find the petticoats tripping you up after leaving them off for so long.

LA HIRE. You will miss the fighting. It's a bad habit, but a grand one, and the hardest of all to break yourself of.

CHARLES [*anxiously*] Still, we dont want you to stay if you would really rather go home.

JOAN [*bitterly*] I know well that none of you will be sorry to see me go. [*She turns her shoulder to Charles and walks past him to the more congenial neighborhood of Dunois and La Hire*].

LA HIRE. Well, I shall be able to swear when I want to. But I shall miss you at times.

JOAN. La Hire: in spite of all your sins and swears we shall meet in heaven; for I love you as I love Pitou, my old sheep dog. Pitou could kill a wolf. You will kill the English wolves until they go back to their country and become good dogs of God, will you not?

LA HIRE. You and I together: yes.

JOAN. No: I shall last only a year from the beginning.

ALL THE OTHERS. What!

JOAN. I know it somehow.

DUNOIS. Nonsense!

JOAN. Jack: do you think you will be able to drive them out?

DUNOIS [*with quiet conviction*] Yes: I shall drive them out. They beat us because we thought battles were tournaments and ransom markets. We played the fool while the goddams took war seriously. But I have learnt my lesson, and taken their measure. They have no roots here. I have beaten them before; and I shall beat them again.

JOAN. You will not be cruel to them, Jack?

DUNOIS. The goddams will not yield to tender handling. We did not begin it.

JOAN [*suddenly*] Jack: before I go home, let us take Paris.

CHARLES [*terrified*] Oh no no. We shall lose everything we have gained. Oh dont let us have any more fighting. We can make a very good treaty with the Duke of Burgundy.

JOAN. Treaty! [*She stamps with impatience*].

CHARLES. Well, why not, now that I am crowned and anointed? Oh, that oil!

The Archbishop comes from the vestry, and joins the group between Charles and Bluebeard.

CHARLES. Archbishop: The Maid wants to start fighting again.

THE ARCHBISHOP. Have we ceased fighting, then? Are we at peace?

CHARLES. No: I suppose not; but let us be content with what we have done. Let us make a treaty. Our luck is too good to last; and now is our chance to stop before it turns.

JOAN. Luck! God has fought for us; and you call it luck! And you would stop while there are still Englishmen on this holy earth of dear France!

THE ARCHBISHOP [*sternly*] Maid: the king addressed himself to me, not to you. You forget yourself. You very often forget yourself.

JOAN [*unabashed, and rather roughly*] Then speak, you; and tell him that it is not God's will that he should take his hand from the plough.

THE ARCHBISHOP. If I am not so glib with the name of God as you are, it is because I interpret His will with the authority of the Church and of my sacred office. When you first came you respected it, and would not have dared to speak as you are now speaking. You came clothed with the virtue of humility; and because God blessed your enterprises accordingly, you have stained yourself with the sin of pride. The old Greek tragedy is rising among us. It is the chastisement of hubris.

CHARLES. Yes: she thinks she knows better than everyone else.

JOAN [*distressed, but naïvely incapable of seeing the effect she is producing*] But I do know better than any of you seem to. And I am not proud: I never speak unless I know I am right.

BLUEBEARD ⎫ [*exclaiming* ⎰ Ha ha!
CHARLES   ⎬   *together*] ⎱ Just so.

THE ARCHBISHOP. How do you know you are right?

JOAN. I always know. My voices—

CHARLES. Oh, your voices, your voices. Why dont the voices come to me? I am king, not you.

JOAN. They do come to you; but you do not hear them. You have not sat in the field in the evening listening for them. When the angelus rings you cross yourself and have done with it; but if you prayed from your heart, and listened to the thrilling of the bells in the air after they stop ringing, you would hear the voices as well as I do. [*Turning brusquely from him*] But what voices do you need to tell you what the blacksmith can tell you: that you must strike while the iron is hot? I tell you we must make a dash at Compiègne and relieve it as we relieved Orleans. Then Paris will open its gates; or if not, we will break through them. What is your crown worth without your capital?

LA HIRE. That is what I say too. We shall go through them like a red hot shot through a pound of butter. What do you say, Bastard?

DUNOIS. If our cannon balls were all as hot as your head, and we had enough of them, we could conquer the earth, no doubt. Pluck and impetuosity are good servants in war, but bad masters: they have delivered us into the hands of the English every time we have trusted to them. We never know when we are beaten: that is our great fault.

JOAN. You never know when you are victorious: that is a worse fault. I shall have to make you carry looking-glasses in battle to convince you that the English have not cut off all your noses. You would have been besieged in Orleans still, you and your councils of war, if I had not made you attack. You should always attack; and if you only hold on long enough the enemy will stop first. You dont know how to begin a battle; and you dont know how to use your cannons. And I do.

She squats down on the flags with crossed ankles, pouting.

DUNOIS. I know what you think of us, General Joan.

JOAN. Never mind that, Jack. Tell them what you think of me.

DUNOIS. I think that God was on your side; for I have not forgotten how the wind changed, and how our hearts changed when you came; and by my faith I shall never deny that it was in your sign that we conquered. But I tell you as a soldier that God is no man's daily drudge, and no maid's either. If you are worthy of it He will sometimes snatch you out of the jaws of death and set you on your feet again; but that is all: once on your feet you must fight with all your might and all your craft. For He has to be fair to your enemy too: dont forget that. Well, He set us on our feet through you at Orleans; and the glory of it has carried us through a few good battles here to the coronation. But if we presume on it further, and trust to God to do the work we should do ourselves, we shall be defeated; and serve us right!

JOAN. But—

DUNOIS. Sh! I have not finished. Do not think, any of you, that these victories of ours were won without generalship. King Charles: you have said no word in your proclamation of my part in this campaign; and I make no complaint of that; for the people will run after The Maid and her miracles and not after the Bastard's hard work finding troops for her and feeding them. But I know exactly how much God did for us through The Maid, and how much He left me to do by my own wits; and I tell you that your little hour of miracles is over, and that from this time on he who plays the war game best will win—if the luck is on his side.

JOAN. Ah! if, if, if, if! If ifs and ans were pots and pans there'd be no need of tinkers. [*Rising impetuously*] I tell you, Bastard, your art of war is no use, because your knights are no good for real fighting. War is only a game to them, like tennis and all their other games: they make rules as to what is fair and what is not fair, and heap armor on themselves and on their poor horses to keep out the arrows; and when they fall they cant get up, and have to wait for their squires to come and lift them to arrange about the ransom with the man that has poked them off their horse. Cant you see that all the like of that is gone by and done with? What use is armor against gunpowder? And if it was, do you think men that are fighting for France and for God will stop to bargain about ransoms, as half your knights live by doing? No: they will fight to win, and they will give up their lives out of their own hand into the hand of God when they go into battle, as I do. Common folks understand this. They cannot afford armor and cannot pay ransoms; but they followed me half naked into the moat and up the ladder and over the wall. With them it is my life or thine, and God defend the right! You may shake your

head, Jack; and Bluebeard may twirl his billygoat's beard and cock his nose at me; but remember the day your knights and captains refused to follow me to attack the English at Orleans! You locked the gates to keep me in; and it was the townsfolk and the common people that followed me, and forced the gate, and shewed you the way to fight in earnest.

BLUEBEARD [*offended*] Not content with being Pope Joan, you must be Caesar and Alexander as well.

THE ARCHBISHOP. Pride will have a fall, Joan.

JOAN. Oh, never mind whether it is pride or not: is it true? is it commonsense?

LA HIRE. It is true. Half of us are afraid of having our handsome noses broken; and the other half are out for paying off their mortgages. Let her have her way, Dunois: she does not know everything; but she has got hold of the right end of the stick. Fighting is not what it was; and those who know least about it often make the best job of it.

DUNOIS. I know all that. I do not fight in the old way: I have learnt the lesson of Agincourt, of Poitiers and Crecy. I know how many lives any move of mine will cost; and if the move is worth the cost I make it and pay the cost. But Joan never counts the cost at all: she goes ahead and trusts to God: she thinks she has God in her pocket. Up to now she has had the numbers on her side; and she has won. But I know Joan; and I see that some day she will go ahead when she has only ten men to do the work of a hundred. And then she will find that God is on the side of the big battalions. She will be taken by the enemy. And the lucky man that makes the capture will receive sixteen thousand pounds from the Earl of Ouareek.

JOAN [*flattered*] Sixteen thousand pounds! Eh, laddie, have they offered that for me? There cannot be so much money in the world.

DUNOIS. There is, in England. And now tell me, all of you, which of you will lift a finger to save Joan once the English have got her? I speak first, for the army. The day after she has been dragged from her horse by a goddam or a Burgundian, and he is not struck dead: the day after she is locked in a dungeon, and the bars and bolts do not fly open at the touch of St Peter's angel: the day when the enemy finds out that she is as vulnerable as I am and not a bit more invincible, she will not be worth the life of a single soldier to us; and I will not risk that life, much as I cherish her as a companion-in-arms.

JOAN. I dont blame you, Jack: you are right. I am not worth one soldier's life if God lets me be beaten; but France may think me worth my ransom after what God has done for her through me.

CHARLES. I tell you I have no money; and this coronation, which is all your fault, has cost me the last farthing I can borrow.

JOAN. The Church is richer than you. I put my trust in the Church.

THE ARCHBISHOP. Woman: they will drag you through the streets, and burn you as a witch.

JOAN [*running to him*] Oh, my lord, do not say that. It is impossible. I a witch!

THE ARCHBISHOP. Peter Cauchon knows his business. The University of Paris has burnt a woman for saying that what you have done was well done, and according to God.

JOAN [*bewildered*] But why? What sense is there in it? What I have done is according to God. They could not burn a woman for speaking the truth.

THE ARCHBISHOP. They did.

JOAN. But you know that she was speaking the truth. You would not let them burn me.

THE ARCHBISHOP. How could I prevent them?

JOAN. You would speak in the name of the Church. You are a great prince of the Church. I would go anywhere with your blessing to protect me.

THE ARCHBISHOP. I have no blessing for you while you are proud and disobedient.

JOAN. Oh, why will you go on saying things like that? I am not proud and disobedient. I am a poor girl, and so ignorant that I do not know A from B. How could I be proud? And how can you say that I am disobedient when I always obey my voices, because they come from God.

THE ARCHBISHOP. The voice of God on earth is the voice of the Church Militant; and all the voices that come to you are the echoes of your own wilfulness.

JOAN. It is not true.

THE ARCHBISHOP [*flushing angrily*] You tell the Archbishop in his cathedral that he lies; and yet you say you are not proud and disobedient.

JOAN. I never said you lied. It was you that as good as said my voices lied. When have they ever lied? If you will not believe in them: even if they are only the echoes of my own commonsense, are they not always right? and are not your earthly counsels always wrong?

THE ARCHBISHOP [*indignantly*] It is waste of time admonishing you.

CHARLES. It always comes back to the same thing. She is right; and everyone else is wrong.

THE ARCHBISHOP. Take this as your last warning. If you perish through setting your private judgment above the instructions of your spiritual directors, the Church disowns you, and leaves you to whatever fate your presumption may bring upon you. The Bastard has told you that if you persist in setting up your military conceit above the counsels of your commanders—

DUNOIS [*interposing*] To put it quite exactly, if you attempt to relieve the garrison in Compiègne, without the same superiority in numbers you had at Orleans—

THE ARCHBISHOP. The army will disown you, and will not rescue you. And His Majesty the King has told you that the throne has not the means of ransoming you.

CHARLES. Not a penny.

THE ARCHBISHOP. You stand alone: absolutely alone, trusting to your own conceit, your own ignorance, your own headstrong presumption, your own impiety in hiding all these sins under the cloak of a trust in God. When you pass through these doors into the sunlight, the crowd will cheer you. They will bring you their little children and their invalids to heal: they will kiss your hands and feet, and do what they can, poor simple souls, to turn your head, and madden you with the self-confidence that is leading you to your destruction. But you will be none the less alone: they cannot save you. We and we only can stand between you and the stake at which our enemies have burnt that wretched woman in Paris.

JOAN [*her eyes skyward*] I have better friends and better counsel than yours.

THE ARCHBISHOP. I see that I am speaking in vain to a hardened heart. You reject our protection, and are determined to turn us all against you. In future, then fend for yourself; and if you fail, God have mercy on your soul.

DUNOIS. That is the truth, Joan. Heed it.

JOAN. Where would you all have been now if I had heeded that sort of truth? There is no help, no counsel, in any of you. Yes: I am alone on earth: I have always been alone. My father told my brothers to drown me if I would not stay to mind his sheep while France was bleeding to death: France might perish if only our lambs were safe. I thought France would have friends at the court of the king of France; and I find only wolves fighting for pieces of her poor torn body. I thought God would have friends everywhere, because He is the friend of everyone; and in my innocence I believed that you who now cast me out would be like strong towers to keep harm from me. But I am wiser now; and nobody is any the worse for being wiser. Do not think you can frighten me by telling me that I am alone. France is alone; and God is alone; and what is my loneliness before the loneliness of my country and my God? I see now that the loneliness of God is His strength: what would He be if He listened to your jealous little counsels? Well, my loneliness shall be my strength too; it is better to be alone with God; His friendship will not fail me, nor His counsel, nor His love. In His strength I will dare, and dare, and dare, until I die. I will go out now to the common people, and let the love in their eyes comfort me for the hate in yours.

You will all be glad to see me burnt; but if I go through the fire I shall go through it to their hearts for ever and ever. And so, God be with me!

She goes from them. They stare after her in glum silence for a moment. Then Gilles de Rais twirls his beard.

BLUEBEARD. You know, the woman is quite impossible. I dont dislike her, really; but what are you to do with such a character?

DUNOIS. As God is my judge, if she fell into the Loire I would jump in in full armor to fish her out. But if she plays the fool at Compiègne, and gets caught, I must leave her to her doom.

LA HIRE. Then you had better chain me up; for I could follow her to hell when the spirit rises in her like that.

THE ARCHBISHOP. She disturbs my judgment too: there is a dangerous power in her outbursts. But the pit is open at her feet; and for good or evil we cannot turn her from it.

CHARLES. If only she would keep quiet, or go home!

They follow her dispiritedly.

Scene VI

Rouen, 30th May 1431. A great stone hall in the castle, arranged for a trial-at-law, but not a trial-by-jury, the court being the Bishop's court with the Inquisition participating: hence there are two raised chairs side by side for the Bishop and the Inquisitor as judges. Rows of chairs radiating from them at an obtuse angle are for the canons, the doctors of law and theology, and the Dominican monks, who act as assessors. In the angle is a table for the scribes, with stools. There is also a heavy rough wooden stool for the prisoner. All these are at the inner end of the hall. The further end is open to the courtyard through a row of arches. The court is shielded from the weather by screens and curtains.

Looking down the great hall from the middle of the inner end, the judicial chairs and scribes' table are to the right. The prisoner's stool is to the left. There are arched doors right and left. It is a fine sunshiny May morning.

Warwick comes in through the arched doorway on the judges' side, followed by his page.

THE PAGE [*pertly*] I suppose your lordship is aware that we have no business here. This is an ecclesiastical court; and we are only the secular arm.

WARWICK. I am aware of that fact. Will it please your impudence to find the Bishop of Beauvais for me, and give him a hint that he can have a word with me here before the trial, if he wishes?

THE PAGE [*going*] Yes, my lord.

WARWICK. And mind you behave yourself. Do not address him as Pious Peter.

THE PAGE. No, my lord. I shall be kind to him, because, when The Maid is brought in, Pious Peter will have to pick a peck of pickled pepper.

Cauchon enters through the same door with a Dominican monk and a canon, the latter carrying a brief.

THE PAGE. The Right Reverend his lordship the Bishop of Beauvais. And two other reverend gentlemen.

WARWICK. Get out; and see that we are not interrupted.

THE PAGE. Right, my lord [*he vanishes airily*].

CAUCHON. I wish your lordship good-morrow.

WARWICK. Good-morrow to your lordship. Have I had the pleasure of meeting your friends before? I think not?

CAUCHON [*introducing the monk, who is on his right*] This, my lord, is Brother John Lemaître, of the order of St Dominic. He is acting as deputy for the Chief Inquisitor into the evil of heresy in France. Brother John: the Earl of Warwick.

WARWICK. Your Reverence is most welcome. We have no Inquisitor in England, unfortunately; though we miss him greatly, especially on occasions like the present.

The Inquisitor smiles patiently, and bows. He is a mild elderly gentleman, but has evident reserves of authority and firmness.

CAUCHON [*introducing the Canon, who is on his left*] This gentleman is Canon John D'Estivet, of the Chapter of Bayeux. He is acting as Promoter.

WARWICK. Promoter?

CAUCHON. Prosecutor, you would call him in civil law.

WARWICK. Ah! prosecutor. Quite, quite. I am very glad to make your acquaintance, Canon D'Estivet.

D'Estivet bows [He is on the young side of middle age, well mannered, but vulpine beneath his veneer].

WARWICK. May I ask what stage the proceedings have reached? It is now more than nine months since The Maid was captured at Compiègne by the Burgundians. It is fully four months since I bought her from the Burgundians for a very handsome sum, solely that she might be brought to justice. It is nearly three months since I delivered her up to you, my Lord Bishop, as a person suspected of heresy. May I suggest that you are taking a rather unconscionable time to make up your minds about a very plain case? Is this trial never going to end?

THE INQUISITOR [*smiling*] It has not yet begun, my lord.

WARWICK. Not yet begun! Why, you have been at it eleven weeks!

CAUCHON. We have not been idle, my lord. We have held fifteen examinations of The Maid: six public and nine private.

THE INQUISITOR [*always patiently smiling*]

You see, my lord, I have been present at only two of these examinations. They were proceedings of the Bishop's court solely, and not of the Holy Office. I have only just decided to associate myself—that is, to associate the Holy Inquisition—with the Bishop's court. I did not at first think that this was a case of heresy at all. I regarded it as a political case, and The Maid as a prisoner of war. But having now been present at two of the examinations, I must admit that this seems to be one of the gravest cases of heresy within my experience. Therefore everything is now in order, and we proceed to trial this morning. [*He moves towards the judicial chairs*].

CAUCHON. This moment, if your lordship's convenience allows.

WARWICK [*graciously*] Well, that is good news, gentlemen. I will not attempt to conceal from you that our patience was becoming strained.

CAUCHON. So I gathered from the threats of your soldiers to drown those of our people who favor The Maid.

WARWICK. Dear me! At all events their intentions were friendly to you, my lord.

CAUCHON [*sternly*] I hope not. I am determined that the woman shall have a fair hearing. The justice of the Church is not a mockery, my lord.

THE INQUISITOR [*returning*] Never has there been a fairer examination within my experience, my lord. The Maid needs no lawyers to take her part: she will be tried by her most faithful friends, all ardently desirous to save her soul from perdition.

D'ESTIVET. Sir: I am the Promoter; and it has been my painful duty to present the case against the girl; but believe me, I would throw up my case today and hasten to her defence if I did not know that men far my superiors in learning and piety, in eloquence and persuasiveness, have been sent to reason with her, to explain to her the danger she is running, and the ease with which she may avoid it. [*Suddenly bursting into forensic eloquence, to the disgust of Cauchon and the Inquisitor, who have listened to him so far with patronizing ap-*

proval] Men have dared to say that we are acting from hate; but God is our witness that they lie. Have we tortured her? No. Have we ceased to exhort her; to implore her to have pity on herself; to come to the bosom of her Church as an erring but beloved child? Have we—

CAUCHON [*interrupting drily*] Take care, Canon. All that you say is true; but if you make his lordship believe it I will not answer for your life, and hardly for my own.

WARWICK [*deprecating, but by no means denying*] Oh, my lord, you are very hard on us poor English. But we certainly do not share your pious desire to save The Maid: in fact I tell you now plainly that her death is a political necessity which I regret but cannot help. If the Church lets her go—

CAUCHON [*with fierce and menacing pride*] If the Church lets her go, woe to the man, were he the Emperor himself, who dares lay a finger on her! The Church is not subject to political necessity, my lord.

THE INQUISITOR [*interposing smoothly*] You need have no anxiety about the result, my lord. You have an invincible ally in the matter: one who is far more determined than you that she shall burn.

WARWICK. And who is this very convenient partisan, may I ask?

THE INQUISITOR. The Maid herself. Unless you put a gag in her mouth you cannot prevent her from convicting herself ten times over every time she opens it.

D'ESTIVET. That is perfectly true, my lord. My hair bristles on my head when I hear so young a creature utter such blasphemies.

WARWICK. Well, by all means do your best for her if you are quite sure it will be of no avail. [*Looking hard at Cauchon*] I should be sorry to have to act without the blessing of the Church.

CAUCHON [*with a mixture of cynical admiration and contempt*] And yet they say Englishmen are hypocrites! You play for your side, my lord, even at the peril of your soul. I cannot but admire such devotion; but I dare not go so far myself. I fear damnation.

WARWICK. If we feared anything we could never govern England, my lord. Shall I send your people in to you?

CAUCHON. Yes: it will be very good of your lordship to withdraw and allow the court to assemble.

Warwick turns on his heel, and goes out through the courtyard. Cauchon takes one of the judicial seats; and D'Estivet sits at the scribes' table, studying his brief.

CAUCHON [*casually, as he makes himself comfortable*] What scoundrels these English nobles are!

THE INQUISITOR [*taking the other judicial chair on Cauchon's left*] All secular power makes men scoundrels. They are not trained for the work; and they have not the Apostolic Succession. Our own nobles are just as bad.

The Bishop's assessors hurry into the hall, headed by Chaplain de Stogumber and Canon de Courcelles, a young priest of 30. The scribes sit at the table, leaving a chair vacant opposite D'Estivet. Some of the assessors take their seats: others stand chatting, waiting for the proceedings to begin formally. De Stogumber, aggrieved and obstinate, will not take his seat: neither will the Canon, who stands on his right.

CAUCHON. Good morning, Master de Stogumber. [*To the Inquisitor*] Chaplain to the Cardinal of England.

THE CHAPLAIN [*correcting him*] Of Winchester, my lord. I have to make a protest, my lord.

CAUCHON. You make a great many.

THE CHAPLAIN. I am not without support, my lord. Here is Master de Courcelles, Canon of Paris, who associates himself with me in my protest.

CAUCHON. Well, what is the matter?

THE CHAPLAIN [*sulkily*] Speak you, Master de Courcelles, since I do not seem to enjoy his lordship's confidence. [*He sits down in dudgeon next to Cauchon, on his right*].

COURCELLES. My lord: we have been at great pains to draw up an indictment of The Maid on sixty-four counts. We are now told that they have been reduced, without consulting us.

THE INQUISITOR. Master de Courcelles: I am the culprit. I am overwhelmed with admiration for the zeal displayed in your sixty-four counts; but in accusing a heretic, as in other things, enough is enough. Also you must remember that all the members of the court are not so subtle and profound as you, and that some of your very great learning might appear to them to be very great nonsense. Therefore I have thought it well to have your sixty-four articles cut down to twelve—

COURCELLES [*thunderstruck*] Twelve!!!

THE INQUISITOR. Twelve will, believe me, be quite enough for your purpose.

THE CHAPLAIN. But some of the most important points have been reduced almost to nothing. For instance, The Maid has actually declared that the blessed saints Margaret and Catherine, and the holy Archangel Michael, spoke to her in French. That is a vital point.

THE INQUISITOR. You think, doubtless, that they should have spoken in Latin?

CAUCHON. No: he thinks they should have spoken in English.

THE CHAPLAIN. Naturally, my lord.

THE INQUISITOR. Well, as we are all here agreed, I think, that these voices of The Maid are the voices of evil spirits tempting her to her damnation, it would not be very courteous to you, Master de Stogumber, or to the King of England, to assume that English is the devil's native language. So let it pass. The matter is not wholly omitted from the twelve articles. Pray take your places, gentlemen; and let us proceed to business.

All who have not taken their seats, do so.

THE CHAPLAIN. Well, I protest. That is all.

COURCELLES. I think it hard that all our work

should go for nothing. It is only another example of the diabolical influence which this woman exercises over the court. [*He takes his chair, which is on the Chaplain's right*].

CAUCHON. Do you suggest that I am under diabolical influence?

COURCELLES. I suggest nothing, my lord. But it seems to me that there is a conspiracy here to hush up the fact that The Maid stole the Bishop of Senlis's horse.

CAUCHON [*keeping his temper with difficulty*] This is not a police court. Are we to waste our time on such rubbish?

COURCELLES [*rising, shocked*] My lord: do you call the Bishop's horse rubbish?

THE INQUISITOR [*blandly*] Master de Courcelles: The Maid alleges that she paid handsomely for the Bishop's horse, and that if he did not get the money the fault was not hers. As that may be true, the point is one on which The Maid may well be acquitted.

COURCELLES. Yes, if it were an ordinary horse. But the Bishop's horse! how can she be acquitted for that? [*He sits down again, bewildered and discouraged*].

THE INQUISITOR. I submit to you, with great respect, that if we persist in trying The Maid on trumpery issues on which we may have to declare her innocent, she may escape us on the great main issue of heresy, on which she seems so far to insist on her own guilt. I will ask you, therefore, to say nothing, when The Maid is brought before us, of these stealings of horses, and dancings round fairy trees with the village children, and prayings at haunted wells, and a dozen other things which you were diligently inquiring into until my arrival. There is not a village girl in France against whom you could not prove such things: they all dance round haunted trees, and pray at magic wells. Some of them would steal the Pope's horse if they got the chance. Heresy, gentlemen, heresy is the charge we have to try. The detection and suppression of heresy is my peculiar business: I am here as an inquisitor, not as an ordinary magistrate. Stick to the heresy, gentlemen; and leave the other matters alone.

CAUCHON. I may say that we have sent to the girl's village to make inquiries about her, and there is practically nothing serious against her.

THE CHAPLAIN [*rising and clamoring together*] Nothing serious, my lord—

COURCELLES What! The fairy tree not—

CAUCHON [*out of patience*] Be silent, gentlemen; or speak one at a time.

Courcelles collapses into his chair, intimidated.

THE CHAPLAIN [*sulkily resuming his seat*] That is what The Maid said to us last Friday.

CAUCHON. I wish you had followed her counsel, sir. When I say nothing serious, I mean nothing that men of sufficiently large mind to conduct an inquiry like this would consider serious. I agree with my colleague the Inquisitor that it is on the count of heresy that we must proceed.

LADVENU [*a young but ascetically fine-drawn Dominican who is sitting next Courcelles, on his right*] But is there any great harm in the girl's heresy? Is it not merely her simplicity? Many saints have said as much as Joan.

THE INQUISITOR. [*dropping his blandness and speaking very gravely*] Brother Martin: if you had seen what I have seen of heresy, you would not think it a light thing even in its most apparently harmless and even lovable and pious origins. Heresy begins with people who are to all appearance better than their neighbors. A gentle and pious girl, or a young man who has obeyed the command of our Lord by giving all his riches to the poor, and putting on the garb of poverty, the life of austerity, and the rule of humility and charity, may be the founder of a heresy that will wreck both Church and Empire if not ruthlessly stamped out in time. The records of the Holy Inquisition are full of histories we dare not give to the world, because they are beyond the belief of honest men and innocent women; yet they all began with saintly simpletons. I have seen this again and again. Mark what I say: the woman who quarrels with her clothes, and puts on the dress of a man, is like the man who throws off his fur gown and dresses like John the Baptist: they are followed, as surely as the night follows the day, by bands of wild women and men who refuse to wear any clothes at all. When maids will neither marry nor take regular vows, and men reject marriage and exalt their lusts into divine inspirations, then, as surely as the summer follows the spring, they begin with polygamy, and end by incest. Heresy at first seems innocent and even laudable; but it ends in such a monstrous horror of un-natural wickedness that the most tender-hearted among you, if you saw it at work as I have seen it, would clamor against the mercy of the Church in dealing with it. For two hundred years the Holy Office has striven with these diabolical madnesses; and it knows that they begin always by vain and ignorant persons setting up their own judgment against the Church, and taking it upon themselves to be the interpreters of God's will. You must not fall into the common error of mistaking these simple-tons for liars and hypocrites. They believe honestly and sincerely that their diabolical inspiration is divine. Therefore you must be on your guard against your natural compassion. You are all, I hope, merciful men: how else could you have devoted your lives to the service of our gentle Savior? You are going to see before you a young girl, pious and chaste; for I must tell you, gentlemen, that the things said of her by our English friends are supported by no evidence, whilst there is abundant testi-mony that her excesses have been excesses of religion and charity and not of worldli-ness and wantonness. This girl is not one of those whose hard features are the sign of hard hearts, and whose brazen looks and lewd demeanor condemn them before they are accused. The devilish pride that has led her into her present peril has left no mark on her countenance. Strange as it may seem to you, it has even left no mark on her character outside those special matters

in which she is proud; so that you will see a diabolical pride and a natural humility seated side by side in the selfsame soul. Therefore be on your guard. God forbid that I should tell you to harden your hearts; for her punishment if we condemn her will be so cruel that we should forfeit our own hope of divine mercy were there one grain of malice against her in our hearts. But if you hate cruelty—and if any man here does not hate it I command him on his soul's salvation to quit this holy court—I say, if you hate cruelty, remember that nothing is so cruel in its consequences as the toleration of heresy. Remember also that no court of law can be so cruel as the common people are to those whom they suspect of heresy. The heretic in the hands of the Holy Office is safe from violence, is assured of a fair trial, and cannot suffer death, even when guilty, if repentance fol-lows sin. Innumerable lives of heretics have been saved because the Holy Office has taken them out of the hands of the people, and because the people have yielded them up, knowing that the Holy Office would deal with them. Before the Holy Inquisi-tion existed, and even now when its officers are not within reach, the unfortunate wretch suspected of heresy, perhaps quite ignorantly and unjustly, is stoned, torn in pieces, drowned, burned in his house with all his innocent children, without a trial, unshriven, unburied save as a dog is buried: all of them deeds hateful to God and most cruel to man. Gentlemen: I am compas-sionate by nature as well as by my pro-fession; and though the work I have to do may seem cruel to those who do not know how much more cruel it would be to leave it undone, I would go to the stake myself sooner than do it if I did not know its righteousness, its necessity, its essential mercy. I ask you to address yourself to this trial in that conviction. Anger is a bad counsellor: cast out anger. Pity is some-times worse: cast out pity. But do not cast out mercy. Remember only that justice comes first. Have you anything to say, my lord, before we proceed to trial?

CAUCHON. You have spoken for me, and spoken better than I could. I do not see how any sane man could disagree with a word that has fallen from you. But this I will add. The crude heresies of which you have told us are horrible; but their horror is like that of the black death: they rage for a while and then die out, because sound and sensible men will not under any incitement be reconciled to nakedness and incest and polygamy and the like. But we are confronted today throughout Europe with a heresy that is spreading among men not weak in mind nor diseased in brain: nay, the stronger the mind, the more obstinate the heretic. It is neither discredited by fantastic extremes nor corrupted by the common lusts of the flesh; but it, too, sets up the private judgment of the single erring mortal against the considered wisdom and experience of the Church. The mighty structure of Catholic Christendom will never be shaken by naked madmen or by the sins of Moab and Ammon. But it may be betrayed from within, and brought to barbarous ruin and desolation, by this arch heresy which the English Commander calls Protestantism.

THE ASSESSORS [*whispering*] Protestantism! What was that? What does the Bishop mean? Is it a new heresy? The English Commander, he said. Did you ever hear of Protestantism? etc., etc.

CAUCHON [*continuing*] And that reminds me. What provision has the Earl of Warwick made for the defence of the secular arm should The Maid prove obdurate, and the people be moved to pity her?

THE CHAPLAIN. Have no fear on that score, my lord. The noble earl has eight hundred men-at-arms at the gates. She will not slip through our English fingers even if the whole city be on her side.

CAUCHON [*revolted*] Will you not add, God grant that she repent and purge her sin?

THE CHAPLAIN. That does not seem to me to be consistent; but of course I agree with your lordship.

CAUCHON [*giving him up with a shrug of contempt*] The court sits.

THE INQUISITOR. Let the accused be brought in.

LADVENU [*calling*] The accused. Let her be brought in.

> *Joan, chained by the ankles, is brought in through the arched door behind the prisoner's stool by a guard of English soldiers. With them is the Executioner and his assistants. They lead her to the prisoner's stool, and place themselves behind it after taking off her chain. She wears a page's black suit. Her long imprisonment and the strain of the examinations which have preceded the trial have left their mark on her; but her vitality still holds; she confronts the court unabashed, without a trace of the awe which their formal solemnity seems to require for the complete success of its impressiveness.*

THE INQUISITOR [*kindly*] Sit down, Joan. [*She sits on the prisoner's stool*]. You look very pale today. Are you not well?

JOAN. Thank you kindly: I am well enough. But the Bishop sent me some carp; and it made me ill.

CAUCHON. I am sorry. I told them to see that it was fresh.

JOAN. You meant to be good to me, I know; but it is a fish that does not agree with me. The English thought you were trying to poison me—

CAUCHON } [*together*] { What!
THE CHAPLAIN } { No, my lord.

JOAN [*continuing*] They are determined that I shall be burnt as a witch; and they sent their doctor to cure me; but he was forbidden to bleed me because the silly people believe that a witch's witchery leaves her if she is bled; so he only called me filthy names. Why do you leave me in the hands of the English? I should be in the hands of the Church. And why must I be chained by the feet to a log of wood? Are you afraid I will fly away?

D'ESTIVET [*harshly*] Woman: it is not for you to question the court: it is for us to question you.

COURCELLES. When you were left unchained, did you not try to escape by jumping from a tower sixty feet high? If you cannot fly like a witch, how is it that you are still alive?

JOAN. I suppose because the tower was not so high then. It has grown higher every day since you began asking me questions about it.

D'ESTIVET. Why did you jump from the tower?

JOAN. How do you know that I jumped?

D'ESTIVET. You were found lying in the moat. Why did you leave the tower?

JOAN. Why would anybody leave a prison if they could get out?

D'ESTIVET. You tried to escape?

JOAN. Of course I did; and not for the first time either. If you leave the door of the cage open the bird will fly out.

D'ESTIVET [*rising*] That is a confession of heresy. I call the attention of the court to it.

JOAN. Heresy, he calls it! Am I a heretic because I try to escape from prison?

D'ETIVET. Assuredly, if you are in the hands of the Church, and you wilfully take yourself out of its hands, you are deserting the Church; and that is heresy.

JOAN. It is great nonsense. Nobody could be such a fool as to think that.

D'ETIVET. You hear, my lord, how I am reviled in the execution of my duty by this woman. [*He sits down indignantly*].

CAUCHON. I have warned you before, Joan, that you are doing yourself no good by these pert answers.

JOAN. But you will not talk sense to me. I am reasonable if you will be reasonable.

THE INQUISITOR [*interposing*] This is not yet in order. You forget, Master Promoter, that the proceedings have not been formally opened. The time for questions is after she has sworn on the Gospels to tell us the whole truth.

JOAN. You say this to me every time. I have said again and again that I will tell you all that concerns this trial. But I cannot tell you the whole truth: God does not allow the whole truth to be told. You do not understand it when I tell it. It is an old

saying that he who tells too much truth is sure to be hanged. I am weary of this argument: we have been over it nine times already. I have sworn as much as I will swear; and I will swear no more.

COURCELLES. My lord: she should be put to the torture.

THE INQUISITOR. You hear, Joan? That is what happens to the obdurate. Think before you answer. Has she been shewn the instruments?

THE EXECUTIONER. They are ready, my lord. She has seen them.

JOAN. If you tear me limb from limb until you separate my soul from my body you will get nothing out of me beyond what I have told you. What more is there to tell that you could understand? Besides, I cannot bear to be hurt; and if you hurt me I will say anything you like to stop the pain. But I will take it all back afterwards; so what is the use of it?

LADVENU. There is much in that. We should proceed mercifully.

COURCELLES. But the torture is customary.

THE INQUISITOR. It must not be applied wantonly. If the accused will confess voluntarily, then its use cannot be justified.

COURCELLES. But this is unusual and irregular. She refuses to take the oath.

LADVENU [*disgusted*] Do you want to torture the girl for the mere pleasure of it?

COURCELLES [*bewildered*] But it is not a pleasure. It is the law. It is customary. It is always done.

THE INQUISITOR. That is not so, Master, except when the inquiries are carried on by people who do not know their legal business.

COURCELLES. But the woman is a heretic. I assure you it is always done.

CAUCHON [*decisively*] It will not be done today if it is not necessary. Let there be an end of this. I will not have it said that we proceeded on forced confessions. We have sent our best preachers and doctors to this woman to exhort and implore her to save her soul and body from the fire: we shall not now send the executioner to thrust her into it.

COURCELLES. Your lordship is merciful, of course. But it is a great responsibility to depart from the usual practice.

JOAN. Thou art a rare noodle, Master. Do what was done last time is thy rule, eh?

COURCELLES [*rising*] Thou wanton: dost thou dare to call me noodle?

THE INQUISITOR. Patience, Master, patience: I fear you will soon be only too terribly avenged.

COURCELLES [*mutters*] Noodle indeed! [He *sits down, much discontented*].

THE INQUISITOR. Meanwhile, let us not be moved by the rough side of a shepherd lass's tongue.

JOAN. Nay: I am no shepherd lass, though I have helped with the sheep like anyone else. I will do a lady's work in the house—spin or weave—against any woman in Rouen.

THE INQUISITOR. This is not a time for vanity, Joan. You stand in great peril.

JOAN. I know it: have I not been punished for my vanity? If I had not worn my cloth of gold surcoat in battle like a fool, that Burgundian soldier would never have pulled me backwards off my horse; and I should not have been here.

THE CHAPLAIN. If you are so clever at woman's work why do you not stay at home and do it?

JOAN. There are plenty of other women to do it; but there is nobody to do my work.

CAUCHON. Come! we are wasting time on trifles. Joan: I am going to put a most solemn question to you. Take care how you answer; for your life and salvation are at stake on it. Will you for all you have said and done, be it good or bad, accept the judgment of God's Church on earth? More especially as to the acts and words that are imputed to you in this trial by the Promoter here, will you submit your case to the inspired interpretation of the Church Militant?

JOAN. I am a faithful child of the Church. I will obey the Church—

CAUCHON [*hopefully leaning forward*] You will?

JOAN.—provided it does not command anything impossible.

Cauchon sinks back in his chair with a heavy sigh. The Inquisitor purses his lips and frowns. Ladvenu shakes his head pitifully.

D'ESTIVET. She imputes to the Church the error and folly of commanding the impossible.

JOAN. If you command me to declare that all that I have done and said, and all the visions and revelations I have had, were not from God, then that is impossible: I will not declare it for anything in the world. What God made me do I will never go back on; and what He has commanded or shall command I will not fail to do in spite of any man alive. That is what I mean by impossible. And in case the Church should bid me do anything contrary to the command I have from God, I will not consent to it, no matter what it may be.

THE ASSESSORS [*shocked and indignant*] Oh! The Church contrary to God! What do you say now? Flat heresy. This is beyond everything, etc., etc.

D'ESTIVET [*throwing down his brief*] My lord: do you need anything more than this?

CAUCHON. Woman: you have said enough to burn ten heretics. Will you not be warned? Will you not understand?

THE INQUISITOR. If the Church Militant tells you that your revelations and visions are sent by the devil to tempt you to your damnation, will you not believe that the Church is wiser than you?

JOAN. I believe that God is wiser than I; and it is His commands that I will do. All the things that you call my crimes have come to me by the command of God. I say that I have done them by the order of God: it is impossible for me to say anything else. If any Churchman says the contrary I shall not mind him: I shall mind God alone, whose command I always follow.

LADVENU [*pleading with her urgently*] You do not know what you are saying, child. Do you want to kill yourself? Listen. Do you not believe that you are subject to the Church of God on earth?

JOAN. Yes. When have I ever denied it?

LADVENU. Good. That means, does it not, that you are subject to our Lord the Pope, to the cardinals, the archbishops, and the bishops for whom his lordship stands here today?

JOAN. God must be served first.

D'ESTIVET. Then your voices command you not to submit yourself to the Church Militant?

JOAN. My voices do not tell me to disobey the Church; but God must be served first.

CAUCHON. And you, and not the Church, are to be the judge?

JOAN. What other judgment can I judge by but my own?

THE ASSESSORS [*scandalized*] Oh! [*They cannot find words*].

CAUCHON. Out of your own mouth you have condemned yourself. We have striven for your salvation to the verge of sinning ourselves: we have opened the door to you again and again; and you have shut it in our faces and in the face of God. Dare you pretend, after what you have said, that you are in a state of grace?

JOAN. If I am not, may God bring me to it: if I am, may God keep me in it!

LADVENU. That is a very good reply, my lord.

COURCELLES. Were you in a state of grace when you stole the Bishop's horse?

CAUCHON [*rising in a fury*] Oh, devil take the Bishop's horse and you too! We are here to try a case of heresy; and no sooner do we come to the root of the matter than we are thrown back by idiots who understand nothing but horses. [*Trembling with rage, he forces himself to sit down*].

THE INQUISITOR. Gentlemen, gentlemen: in clinging to these small issues you are The Maid's best advocates. I am not surprised that his lordship has lost patience with you. What does the Promoter say? Does he press these trumpery matters?

D'ESTIVET. I am bound by my office to press everything; but when the woman confesses a heresy that must bring upon her the doom of excommunication, of what consequence is it that she has been guilty also of offences which expose her to minor penances? I share the impatience of his lordship as to these minor charges. Only, with great respect, I must emphasize the gravity of two very horrible and blasphemous crimes which she does not deny. First, she has intercourse with evil spirits, and is therefore a sorceress. Second, she wears men's clothes, which is indecent, unnatural, and abominable; and in spite of our most earnest remonstrances and entreaties, she will not change them even to receive the sacrament.

JOAN. Is the blessed St Catherine an evil spirit? Is St Margaret? Is Michael the Archangel?

COURCELLES. How do you know that the spirit which appears to you is an archangel? Does he not appear to you as a naked man?

JOAN. Do you think God cannot afford clothes for him?

The assessors cannot help smiling, especially as the joke is against Courcelles.

LADVENU. Well answered, Joan.

THE INQUISITOR. It is, in effect, well answered. But no evil spirit would be so simple as to appear to a young girl in a guise that would scandalize her when he meant her to take him for a messenger from the Most High. Joan: the Church instructs you that these apparitions are demons seeking your soul's perdition. Do you accept the instruction of the Church?

JOAN. I accept the messenger of God. How could any faithful believer in the Church refuse him?

CAUCHON. Wretched woman: again I ask you, do you know what you are saying?

THE INQUISITOR. You wrestle in vain with the devil for her soul, my lord: she will not be saved. Now as to this matter of the man's dress. For the last time, will you put off that impudent attire, and dress as becomes your sex?

JOAN. I will not.

D'ESTIVET [*pouncing*] The sin of disobedience, my lord.

JOAN [*distressed*] But my voices tell me I must dress as a soldier.

LADVENU. Joan, Joan: does not that prove to you that the voices are the voices of evil spirits? Can you suggest to us one good reason why an angel of God should give you such shameless advice?

JOAN. Why, yes: what can be plainer commonsense? I was a soldier living among soldiers. I am a prisoner guarded by soldiers. If I were to dress as a woman they would think of me as a woman; and then what would become of me? If I dress as a soldier they think of me as a soldier, and I can live with them as I do at home with my brothers. That is why St Catherine tells me I must not dress as a woman until she gives me leave.

COURCELLES. When will she give you leave?

JOAN. When you take me out of the hands of the English soldiers. I have told you that I should be in the hands of the Church, and not left night and day with four soldiers of the Earl of Warwick. Do you want me to live with them in petticoats?

LADVENU. My lord: what she says is, God knows, very wrong and shocking; but there is a grain of worldly sense in it such as might impose on a simple village maiden.

JOAN. If we were as simple in the village as you are in your courts and palaces, there would soon be no wheat to make bread for you.

CAUCHON. That is the thanks you get for trying to save her, Brother Martin.

LADVENU. Joan: we are all trying to save you. His lordship is trying to save you. The Inquisitor could not be more just to you if you were his own daughter. But you are blinded by a terrible pride and self-sufficiency.

JOAN. Why do you say that? I have said nothing wrong. I cannot understand.

THE INQUISITOR. The blessed St Athanasius has laid it down in his creed that those who cannot understand are damned. It is not enough to be simple. It is not enough even to be what simple people call good. The simplicity of a darkened mind is no better than the simplicity of a beast.

JOAN. There is great wisdom in the simplicity of a beast, let me tell you; and sometimes great foolishness in the wisdom of scholars.

LADVENU. We know that, Joan: we are not so foolish as you think us. Try to resist the temptation to make pert replies to us. Do you see that man who stands behind you [*he indicates the Executioner*]?

JOAN [*turning and looking at the man*] Your torturer? But the Bishop said I was not to be tortured.

LADVENU. You are not to be tortured because you have confessed everything that is necessary to your condemnation. That man is not only the torturer: he is also the Executioner. Executioner: let The Maid hear your answers to my questions. Are you prepared for the burning of a heretic this day?

THE EXECUTIONER. Yes, Master.

LADVENU. Is the stake ready?

THE EXECUTIONER. It is. In the market-place. The English have built it too high for me to get near her and make the death easier. It will be a cruel death.

JOAN [*horrified*] But you are not going to burn me now?

THE INQUISITOR. You realize it at last.

LADVENU. There are eight hundred English soldiers waiting to take you to the market-place the moment the sentence of excommunication has passed the lips of your judges. You are within a few short moments of that doom.

JOAN [*looking round desperately for rescue*] Oh God!

LADVENU. Do not despair, Joan. The Church is merciful. You can save yourself.

JOAN [*hopefully*] Yes: my voices promised me I should not be burnt. St Catherine bade me be bold.

CAUCHON. Woman: are you quite mad? Do you not yet see that your voices have deceived you?

JOAN. Oh no: that is impossible.

CAUCHON. Impossible! They have led you straight to your excommunication, and to the stake which is there waiting for you.

LADVENU [*pressing the point hard*] Have they kept a single promise to you since you were taken at Compiègne? The devil has betrayed you. The Church holds out its arms to you.

JOAN [*despairing*] Oh, it is true: it is true: my voices have deceived me. I have been mocked by devils: my faith is broken. I have dared and dared; but only a fool will walk into a fire: God, who gave me my commonsense, cannot will me to do that.

LADVENU. Now God be praised that He has saved you at the eleventh hour! [*He hurries to the vacant seat at the scribes' table, and snatches a sheet of paper, on which he sets to work writing eagerly*].

CAUCHON. Amen!

JOAN. What must I do?

CAUCHON. You must sign a solemn recantation of your heresy.

JOAN. Sign? That means to write my name. I cannot write.

CAUCHON. You have signed many letters before.

JOAN. Yes; but someone held my hand and guided the pen. I can make my mark.

THE CHAPLAIN [*who has been listening with growing alarm and indignation*] My lord: do you mean that you are going to allow this woman to escape us?

THE INQUISITOR. The law must take its course, Master de Stogumber. And you know the law.

THE CHAPLAIN [*rising, purple with fury*] I know that there is no faith in a Frenchman. [*Tumult, which he shouts down*]. I know what my lord the Cardinal of Winchester will say when he hears of this. I know what the Earl of Warwick will do when he learns that you intend to betray him. There are eight hundred men at the gate who will see that this abominable witch is burnt in spite of your teeth.

THE ASSESSORS [*meanwhile*] What is this? What did he say? He accuses us of treachery! This is past bearing. No faith in a Frenchman! Did you hear that? This is an intolerable fellow. Who is he? Is this what English Churchmen are like? He must be mad or drunk, etc., etc.

THE INQUISITOR [*rising*] Silence, pray! Gentlemen: pray silence! Master Chaplain: bethink you a moment of your holy office: of what you are, and where you are. I direct you to sit down.

THE CHAPLAIN [*folding his arms doggedly, his face working convulsively*] I will NOT sit down.

CAUCHON. Master Inquisitor: this man has called me a traitor to my face before now.

THE CHAPLAIN. So you are a traitor. You are all traitors. You have been doing nothing but begging this damnable witch on your knees to recant all through this trial.

THE INQUISITOR [*placidly resuming his seat*] If you will not sit, you must stand: that is all.

THE CHAPLAIN. I will NOT stand [*he flings himself back into his chair*].

LADVENU [*rising with the paper in his hand*] My lord: here is the form of recantation for The Maid to sign.

CAUCHON. Read it to her.

JOAN. Do not trouble. I will sign it.

THE INQUISITOR. Woman: you must know what you are putting your hand to. Read it to her, Brother Martin. And let all be silent.

LADVENU [*reading quietly*] 'I, Joan, commonly called The Maid, a miserable sinner, do confess that I have most grievously sinned in the following articles. I have pretended to have revelations from God and the angels and the blessed saints, and perversely rejected the Church's warnings that these were temptations by demons. I have blasphemed abominably by wearing an immodest dress, contrary to the Holy Scripture and the canons of the Church. Also I have clipped my hair in the style of a man, and, against all the duties which have made my sex specially acceptable in heaven, have taken up the sword, even to the shedding of human blood, inciting men to slay each other, invoking evil spirits to delude them, and stubbornly and most blasphemously imputing these sins to Almighty God. I confess to the sin of sedition, to the sin of idolatry, to the sin of disobedience, to the sin of pride, and to the sin of heresy. All of which sins I now renounce and abjure and depart from, humbly thanking you Doctors and Masters who have brought me back to the truth and into the grace of our Lord. And I will never return to my errors, but will remain in communion with our Holy Church and in obedience to our Holy Father the Pope of Rome. All this I swear by God Almighty and the Holy Gospels, in witness whereto I sign my name to this recantation.'

THE INQUISITOR. You understand this, Joan?

JOAN [*listless*] It is plain enough, sir.

THE INQUISITOR. And it is true?

JOAN. It may be true. If it were not true, the fire would not be ready for me in the market-place.

LADVENU [*taking up his pen and a book, and going to her quickly lest she should compromise herself again*] Come, child: let me guide your hand. Take the pen. [*She does so; and they begin to write, using the book as a desk*] J.E.H.A.N.E. So. Now make your mark by yourself.

JOAN [*makes her mark, and gives him back the pen, tormented by the rebellion of her soul against her mind and body*] There!

LADVENU [*replacing the pen on the table, and handing the recantation to Cauchon with a reverence*] Praise be to God, my brothers, the lamb has returned to the flock; and the shepherd rejoices in her more than in ninety and nine just persons. [*He returns to his seat*].

THE INQUISITOR [*taking the paper from Cauchon*] We declare thee by this act set free from the danger of excommunication in which thou stoodest. [*He throws the paper down to the table*].

JOAN. I thank you.

THE INQUISITOR. But because thou has sinned most presumptuously against God and the Holy Church, and that thou mayst repent thy errors in solitary contemplation, and be shielded from all temptation to return to them, we, for the good of thy soul, and for a penance that may wipe out thy sins and bring thee finally unspotted to the throne of grace, do condemn thee to eat the bread of sorrow and drink the water of affliction to the end of thy earthly days in perpetual imprisonment.

JOAN [*rising in consternation and terrible anger*] Perpetual imprisonment! Am I not then to be set free?

LADVENU [*mildly shocked*] Set free, child, after such wickedness as yours! What are you dreaming of?

JOAN. Give me that writing. [*She rushes to the table; snatches up the paper; and tears it into fragments*] Light your fire: do you think I dread it as much as the life of a rat in a hole? My voices were right.

LADVENU. Joan! Joan!

JOAN. Yes: they told me you were fools [*the word gives great offence*], and that I was not to listen to your fine words nor trust to your charity. You promised me my life; but you lied [*indignant exclamations*]. You think that life is nothing but not being stone dead. It is not the bread and water I fear: I can live on bread: when have I asked for more? It is no hardship to drink water if the water be clean. Bread has no sorrow for me, and water no affliction. But to shut me from the light of the sky and the sight of the fields and flowers; to chain my feet so that I can never again ride with the soldiers nor climb the hills; to make me breathe foul damp darkness, and keep from me everything that brings me back to the love of God when your wickedness and foolishness tempt me to hate Him: all this is worse than the furnace in the Bible that was heated seven times. I could do without my warhorse; I could drag about in a skirt; I could let the banners and the trumpets and the knights and soldiers pass me and leave me behind as they leave the other women, if only I could still hear the wind in the trees, the larks in the sunshine, the young lambs crying through the healthy frost, and the blessed blessed church bells that send my angel voices floating to me on the wind. But without these things I cannot live; and by your wanting to take them away from me, or from any human creature, I know that your counsel is of the devil, and that mine is of God.

THE ASSESSORS [*in great commotion*] Blasphemy! blasphemy! She is possessed. She said our counsel was of the devil. And hers of God. Monstrous! The devil is in our midst, etc., etc.

D'ESTIVET [*shouting above the din*] She is a

relapsed heretic, obstinate, incorrigible, and altogether unworthy of the mercy we have shewn her. I call for her excommunication.

THE CHAPLAIN [*to the Executioner*] Light your fire, man. To the stake with her.

The Executioner and his assistants hurry out through the courtyard.

LADVENU. You wicked girl: if your counsel were of God would He not deliver you?

JOAN. His ways are not your ways. He wills that I go through the fire to His bosom; for I am His child, and you are not fit that I should live among you. That is my last word to you.

The soldiers seize her.

CAUCHON [*rising*] Not yet.

They wait. There is a dead silence. Cauchon turns to the Inquisitor with an inquiring look. The Inquisitor nods affirmatively. They rise solemnly, and intone the sentence antiphonally.

CAUCHON. We decree that thou art a relapsed heretic.

THE INQUISITOR. Cast out from the unity of the Church.

CAUCHON. Sundered from her body.

THE INQUISITOR. Infected with the leprosy of heresy.

CAUCHON. A member of Satan.

THE INQUISITOR. We declare that thou must be excommunicate.

CAUCHON. And now we do cast thee out, segregate thee, and abandon thee to the secular power.

THE INQUISITOR. Admonishing the same secular power that it moderate its judgment of thee in respect of death and division of the limbs. [*He resumes his seat*].

CAUCHON. And if any true sign of penitence appear in thee, to permit our Brother Martin to administer to thee the sacrament of penance.

THE CHAPLAIN. Into the fire with the witch

[*he rushes at her, and helps the soldiers to push her out*].

Joan is taken away through the court-yard. The assessors rise in disorder, and follow the soldiers, except Ladvenu, who has hidden his face in his hands.

CAUCHON [*rising again in the act of sitting down*] No, no: this is irregular. The representative of the secular arm should be here to receive her from us.

THE INQUISITOR [*also on his feet again*] That man is an incorrigible fool.

CAUCHON. Brother Martin: see that everything is done in order.

LADVENU. My place is at her side, my Lord. You must exercise your own authority. [*He hurries out*].

CAUCHON. These English are impossible: they will thrust her straight into the fire. Look!

He points to the courtyard, in which the glow and flicker of fire can now be seen reddening the May daylight. Only the Bishop and the Inquisitor are left in the court.

CAUCHON [*turning to go*] We must stop that.

THE INQUISITOR [*calmly*] Yes; but not too fast, my lord.

CAUCHON [*halting*] But there is not a moment to lose.

THE INQUISITOR. We have proceeded in perfect order. If the English choose to put themselves in the wrong, it is not our business to put them in the right. A flaw in the procedure may be useful later on: one never knows. And the sooner it is over, the better for that poor girl.

CAUCHON [*relaxing*] That is true. But I suppose we must see this dreadful thing through.

THE INQUISITOR. One gets used to it. Habit is everything. I am accustomed to the fire: it is soon over. But it is a terrible thing to see a young and innocent creature crushed between these mighty forces, the Church and the law.

CAUCHON. You call her innocent!

THE INQUISITOR. Oh, quite innocent. What

does she know of the Church and the Law? She did not understand a word we were saying. It is the ignorant who suffer. Come, or we shall be late for the end.

CAUCHON [*going with him*] I shall not be sorry if we are: I am not so accustomed as you.

They are going out when Warwick comes in, meeting them.

WARWICK. Oh, I am intruding. I thought it was all over. [*He makes a feint of retiring*].

CAUCHON. Do not go, my lord. It is all over.

THE INQUISITOR. The execution is not in our hands, my lord; but it is desirable that we should witness the end. So by your leave— [*He bows, and goes out through the courtyard*].

CAUCHON. There is some doubt whether your people have observed the forms of law, my lord.

WARWICK. I am told that there is some doubt whether your authority runs in this city, my lord. It is not in your diocese. However, if you will answer for that I will answer for the rest.

CAUCHON. It is to God that we both must answer. Good morning, my lord.

WARWICK. My lord: good morning.

They look at one another for a moment with unconcealed hostility. Then Cauchon follows the Inquisitor out. Warwick looks round. Finding himself alone, he calls for attendance.

WARWICK. Hallo: some attendance here! [*Silence*]. Hallo, there! [*Silence*]. Hallo! Brian, you young blackguard, where are you? [*Silence*]. Guard! [*Silence*]. They have all gone to see the burning: even that child.

The silence is broken by someone frantically howling and sobbing.

WARWICK. What in the devil's name—?

The Chaplain staggers in from the courtyard like a demented creature, his face streaming with tears, making the piteous sounds that Warwick has heard. He stumbles to the prisoner's stool, and throws himself upon it with heartrending sobs.

WARWICK [*going to him and patting him on the shoulder*] What is it, Master John? What is the matter?

THE CHAPLAIN [*clutching at his hand*] My lord, my lord: for Christ's sake pray for for my wretched guilty soul.

WARWICK [*soothing him*] Yes, yes: of course I will. Calmly, gently—

THE CHAPLAIN [*blubbering miserably*] I am not a bad man, my lord.

WARWICK. No, no: not at all.

THE CHAPLAIN. I meant no harm. I did not know what it would be like.

WARWICK [*hardening*] Oh! You saw it, then?

THE CHAPLAIN. I did not know what I was doing. I am a hotheaded fool; and I shall be damned to all eternity for it.

WARWICK. Nonsense! Very distressing, no doubt; but it was not your doing.

THE CHAPLAIN [*lamentably*] I let them do it. If I had known, I would have torn her from their hands. You don't know: you havnt seen: it is so easy to talk when you dont know. You madden yourself with words: you damn yourself because it feels grand to throw oil on the flaming hell of your own temper. But when it is brought home to you; when you see the thing you have done; when it is blinding your eyes, stifling your nostrils, tearing your heart, then—then—[*Falling on his knees*] O God, take away this sight from me! O Christ, deliver me from this fire that is consuming me! She cried to Thee in the midst of it: Jesus! Jesus! She is in Thy bosom; and I am in hell for evermore.

WARWICK [*summarily hauling him to his feet*] Come come, man! you must pull yourself together. We shall have the whole town talking of this. [*He throws him not too gently into a chair at the table*] If you have not the nerve to see these things, why do you not as I do, and stay away?

THE CHAPLAIN [*bewildered and submissive*] She asked for a cross. A soldier gave her

two sticks tied together. Thank God he
was an Englishman! I might have done it:
but I did not: I am a coward, a mad dog,
a fool. But he was an Englishman too.

WARWICK. The fool! they will burn him too
if the priests get hold of him.

THE CHAPLAIN [*shaken with a convulsion*]
Some of the people laughed at her. They
would have laughed at Christ. They were
French people, my lord: I know they were
French.

WARWICK. Hush! someone is coming. Control
yourself.

*Ladvenu comes back through the court-
yard to Warwick's right hand, carrying
a bishop's cross which he has taken from
a church. He is very grave and composed.*

WARWICK. I am informed that it is all over,
Brother Martin.

LADVENU [*enigmatically*] We do not know,
my lord. It may have only just begun.

WARWICK. What does that mean, exactly?

LADVENU. I took this cross from the church
for her that she might see it to the last:
she had only two sticks that she put into
her bosom. When the fire crept round us,
and she saw that if I held the cross before
her I should be burnt myself, she warned
me to get down and save myself. My lord:
a girl who could think of another's danger
in such a moment was not inspired by the
devil. When I had to snatch the cross from
her sight, she looked up to heaven. And I
do not believe that the heavens were empty.
I firmly believe that her Savior appeared to
her then in His tenderest glory. She called
to Him and died. This is not the end for
her, but the beginning.

WARWICK. I am afraid it will have a bad
effect on the people.

LADVENU. It had, my lord, on some of them.
I heard laughter. Forgive me for saying that
I hope and believe it was English laughter.

THE CHAPLAIN [*rising frantically*] No: it was
not. There was only one Englishman there
that disgraced his country; and that was
the mad dog, de Stogumber. [*He rushes
wildly out, shrieking*] Let them torture
him. Let them burn him. I will go pray
among her ashes. I am no better than Judas:
I will hang myself.

WARWICK. Quick, Brother Martin: follow
him: he will do himself some mischief.
After him, quick.

*Ladvenu hurries out, Warwick urging
him. The Executioner comes in by the
door behind the judges' chairs; and
Warwick, returning, finds himself face
to face with him.*

WARWICK. Well, fellow: who are you?

THE EXECUTIONER [*with dignity*] I am not
addressed as fellow, my lord. I am the
Master Executioner of Rouen: it is a highly
skilled mystery. I am come to tell your
lordship that your orders have been obeyed.

WARWICK. I crave your pardon, Master Executioner; and I will see that you lose nothing by having no relics to sell. I have your
word, have I, that nothing remains, not a
bone, not a nail, not a hair?

THE EXECUTIONER. Her heart would not burn,
my lord; but everything that was left is at
the bottom of the river. You have heard
the last of her.

WARWICK [*with a wry smile, thinking of what
Ladvenu said*] The last of her? Hm! I
wonder!

Epilogue

*A restless fitfully windy night in June
1456, full of summer lightning after
many days of heat. King Charles the
Seventh of France, formerly Joan's
Dauphin, now Charles the Victorious
aged 51, is in bed in one of his royal
chateaux. The bed, raised on a dais of
two steps, is towards the side of the
room so as to avoid blocking a tall lancet window in the middle. Its canopy
bears the royal arms in embroidery. Except for the canopy and the huge down*

pillows there is nothing to distinguish it from a broad settee with bed-clothes and a valance. Thus its occupant is in full view from the foot.

Charles is not asleep: he is reading in bed, or rather looking at the pictures in Fouquet's Boccaccio with his knees doubled up to make a reading-desk. Beside the bed on his left is a little table with a picture of the Virgin, lighted by candles of painted wax. The walls are hung from ceiling to floor with painted curtains which stir at times in the draughts. At first glance the prevailing yellow and red in these hanging pictures is somewhat flamelike when the folds breathe in the wind.

The door is on Charles's left, but in front of him close to the corner farthest from him. A large watchman's rattle, handsomely designed and gaily painted, is in the bed under his hand.

Charles turns a leaf. A distant clock strikes the half-hour softly. Charles shuts the book with a clap; throws it aside; snatches up the rattle; and whirls it energetically, making a deafening clatter. Ladvenu enters, 25 years older, strange and stark in bearing, and still carrying the cross from Rouen. Charles evidently does not expect him; for he springs out of bed on the farther side from the door.

CHARLES. Who are you? Where is my gentleman of the bedchamber? What do you want?

LADVENU [*solemnly*] I bring you glad tidings of great joy. Rejoice, O king; for the taint is removed from your blood, and the stain from your crown. Justice, long delayed, is at last triumphant.

CHARLES. What are you talking about? Who are you?

LADVENU. I am Brother Martin.

CHARLES. And who, saving your reverence, may Brother Martin be?

LADVENU. I held this cross when The Maid perished in the fire. Twenty-five years have passed since then: nearly ten thousand days. And on every one of those days I have prayed to God to justify His daughter on earth as she is justified in heaven.

CHARLES [*reassured, sitting down on the foot of the bed*] Oh, I remember now. I have heard of you. You have a bee in your bonnet about The Maid. Have you been at the inquiry?

LADVENU. I have given my testimony.

CHARLES. Is it over?

LADVENU. It is over.

CHARLES. Satisfactorily?

LADVENU. The ways of God are very strange.

CHARLES. How so?

LADVENU. At the trial which sent a saint to the stake as a heretic and a sorceress, the truth was told; the law was upheld; mercy was shewn beyond all custom; no wrong was done but the final and dreadful wrong of the lying sentence and the pitiless fire. At this inquiry from which I have just come, there was shameless perjury, courtly corruption, calumny of the dead who did their duty according to their lights, cowardly evasion of the issue, testimony made of idle tales that could not impose on a ploughboy. Yet out of this insult to justice, this defamation of the Church, this orgy of lying and foolishness, the truth is set in the noonday sun on the hilltop; the white robe of innocence is cleansed from the smirch of the burning faggots; the holy life is sanctified; the true heart that lived through the flame is consecrated; a great lie is silenced for ever; and a great wrong is set right before all men.

CHARLES. My friend: provided they can no longer say that I was crowned by a witch and a heretic, I shall not fuss about how the trick has been done. Joan would not have fussed about it if it came all right in the end: she was not that sort: I knew her. Is her rehabilitation complete? I made it pretty clear that there was to be no nonsense about it.

LADVENU. It is solemnly declared that her judges were full of corruption, cozenage, fraud, and malice. Four falsehoods.

CHARLES. Never mind the falsehoods: her judges are dead.

LADVENU. The sentence on her is broken, annulled, annihilated, set aside as non-existent, without value or effect.

CHARLES. Good. Nobody can challenge my consecration now, can they?

LADVENU. Not Charlemagne nor King David himself was more sacredly crowned.

CHARLES [*rising*] Excellent. Think of what that means to me!

LADVENU. I think of what it means to her!

CHARLES. You cannot. None of us ever knew what anything meant to her. She was like nobody else; and she must take care of herself wherever she is; for *I* cannot take care of her; and neither can you, whatever you may think: you are not big enough. But I will tell you this about her. If you could bring her back to life, they would burn her again within six months, for all their present adoration of her. And you would hold up the cross, too, just the same. So [*crossing himself*] let her rest; and let you and I mind our own business, and not meddle with hers.

LADVENU. God forbid that I should have no share in her, nor she in me! [*He turns and strides out as he came, saying*] Henceforth my path will not lie through palaces, nor my conversation be with kings.

CHARLES [*following him towards the door, and shouting after him*] Much good may it do you, holy man! [*He returns to the middle of the chamber, where he halts, and says quizzically to himself*] That was a funny chap. How did he get in? Where are my people? [*He goes impatiently to the bed, and swings the rattle. A rush of wind through the open door sets the walls swaying agitatedly. The candles go out. He calls in the darkness*] Hallo! Someone come and shut the windows: everything is being blown all over the place. [*A flash of summer lightning shews up the lancet windows. A figure is seen in silhouette against it*] Who is there? Who is that? Help? Murder! [*Thunder. He jumps into bed, and hides under the clothes*].

JOAN'S VOICE. Easy, Charlie, easy. What art making all that noise for? No one can hear thee. Thourt asleep. [*She is dimly seen in a pallid greenish light by the bedside*].

CHARLES [*peeping out*] Joan! Are you a ghost, Joan?

JOAN. Hardly even that, lad. Can a poor burnt-up lass have a ghost? I am but a dream that thourt dreaming. [*The light increases: they become plainly visible as he sits up*] Thou looks older, lad.

CHARLES. I am older. Am I really asleep?

JOAN. Fallen asleep over thy silly book.

CHARLES. That's funny.

JOAN. Not so funny as that I am dead, is it?

CHARLES. Are you really dead?

JOAN. As dead as anybody ever is, laddie. I am out of the body.

CHARLES. Just fancy! Did it hurt much?

JOAN. Did what hurt much?

CHARLES. Being burnt.

JOAN. Oh, that! I cannot remember very well. I think it did at first; but then it all got mixed up; and I was not in my right mind until I was free of the body. But do not thou go handling fire and thinking it will not hurt thee. How hast been ever since?

CHARLES. Oh, not so bad. Do you know, I actually lead my army out and win battles? Down into the moat up to my waist in mud and blood. Up the ladders with the stones and hot pitch raining down. Like you.

JOAN. No! Did I make a man of thee after all, Charlie?

CHARLES. I am Charles the Victorious now. I had to be brave because you were. Agnes put a little pluck into me too.

JOAN. Agnes! Who was Agnes?

CHARLES. Agnes Sorel. A woman I fell in love with. I dream of her often. I never dreamed of you before.

JOAN. Is she dead, like me?

CHARLES. Yes. But she was not like you. She was very beautiful.

JOAN [*laughing heartily*] Ha ha! I was no beauty: I was always a rough one: a regular soldier. I might almost as well have been a man. Pity I wasnt: I should not have bothered you all so much then. But my head was in the skies; and the glory of God was upon me; and, man or woman, I should have bothered you as long as your noses were in the mud. Now tell me what has happened since you wise men knew no better than to make a heap of cinders of me?

CHARLES. Your mother and brothers have sued the courts to have your case tried over again. And the courts have declared that your judges were full of corruption and cozenage, fraud and malice.

JOAN. Not they. They were as honest a lot of poor fools as ever burned their betters.

CHARLES. The sentence on you is broken, annihilated, annulled: null, non-existent, without value or effect.

JOAN. I was burned, all the same. Can they unburn me?

CHARLES. If they could, they would think twice before they did it. But they have decreed that a beautiful cross be placed where the stake stood, for your perpetual memory and for your salvation.

JOAN. It is the memory and the salvation that sanctify the cross, not the cross that sanctifies the memory and the salvation. [*She turns away, forgetting him*] I shall outlast that cross. I shall be remembered when men will have forgotten where Rouen stood.

CHARLES. There you go with your self-conceit, the same as ever! I think you might say a word of thanks to me for having had justice done at last.

CAUCHON [*appearing at the window between them*] Liar!

CHARLES. Thank you.

JOAN. Why, if it isnt Peter Cauchon! How are you, Peter? What luck have you had since you burned me?

CAUCHON. None. I arraign the justice of Man. It is not the justice of God.

JOAN. Still dreaming of justice, Peter? See what justice came to with me! But what has happened to thee? Art dead or alive?

CAUCHON. Dead. Dishonored. They pursued me beyond the grave. They excommunicated my dead body: they dug it up and flung it into the common sewer.

JOAN. Your dead body did not feel the spade and the sewer as my live body felt the fire.

CAUCHON. But this thing that they have done against me hurts justice; destroys faith; saps the foundation of the Church. The solid earth sways like the treacherous sea beneath the feet of men and spirits alike when the innocent are slain in the name of law, and their wrongs are undone by slandering the pure of heart.

JOAN. Well, well, Peter, I hope men will be the better for remembering me; and they would not remember me so well if you had not burned me.

CAUCHON. They will be the worse for remembering me: they will see in me evil triumphing over good, falsehood over truth, cruelty over mercy, hell over heaven. Their courage will rise as they think of you, only to faint as they think of me. Yet God is my witness I was just: I was merciful: I was faithful to my light: I could do no other than I did.

CHARLES [*scrambling out of the sheets and enthroning himself on the side of the bed*] Yes: it is always you good men that do the big mischiefs. Look at me! I am not Charles the Good, nor Charles the Wise, nor Charles the Bold. Joan's worshippers may even call me Charles the Coward because I did not pull her out of the fire. But I have done less harm than any of you. You people with your heads in the sky spend all your time trying to turn the world upside down; but I take the world as it is, and say that top-side-up is right-side-up; and I keep my nose pretty close to the ground. And I ask you, what king of France has done better, or been a better fellow in his little way?

JOAN. Art really king of France, Charlie? Be the English gone?

DUNOIS [*coming through the tapestry on Joan's left, the candles relighting themselves at the same moment, and illuminating his armor and surcoat cheerfully*] I have kept my word: the English are gone.

JOAN. Praised be God! now is fair France a province in heaven. Tell me all about the fighting, Jack. Was it thou that led them? Wert thou God's captain to thy death?

DUNOIS. I am not dead. My body is very comfortably asleep in my bed at Chateaudun; but my spirit is called here by yours.

JOAN. And you fought them my way, Jack: eh? Not the old way, chaffering for ransoms; but The Maid's way: staking life against death, with the heart high and humble and void of malice, and nothing counting under God but France free and French. Was it my way, Jack?

DUNOIS. Faith, it was any way that would win. But the way that won was always your way. I give you best, lassie. I wrote a fine letter to set you right at the new trial. Perhaps I should never have let the priests burn you; but I was busy fighting; and it was the Church's business, not mine. There was no use in both of us being burned, was there?

CAUCHON. Ay! put the blame on the priests. But I, who am beyond praise and blame, tell you that the world is saved neither by its priests nor its soldiers, but by God and His Saints. The Church Militant sent this woman to the fire; but even as she burned, the flames whitened into the radiance of the Church Triumphant.

The clock strikes the third quarter. A rough male voice is heard trolling an improvised tune.

Rum tum trumpledum,
Bacon fat and rumpledum,
Old Saint mumpledum,
Pull his tail and stumpledum
O my Ma—ry Ann!

A ruffianly English soldier comes

through the curtains and marches between Dunois and Joan.

DUNOIS. What villainous troubadour taught you that doggrel?

THE SOLDIER. No troubadour. We made it up ourselves as we marched. We were not gentlefolks and troubadours. Music straight out of the heart of the people, as you might say. Rum tum trumpledum, Bacon fat and rumpledum, Old Saint mumpledum, Pull his tail and stumpledum: that dont mean anything you know; but it keeps you marching. Your servant, ladies and gentlemen. Who asked for a saint?

JOAN. Be you a saint?

THE SOLDIER. Yes, lady, straight from hell.

DUNOIS. A saint, and from hell!

THE SOLDIER. Yes, noble captain: I have a day off. Every year, you know. Thats my allowance for my one good action.

CAUCHON. Wretch! In all the years of your life did you do only one good action?

THE SOLDIER. I never thought about it: it came natural like. But they scored it up for me.

CHARLES. What was it?

THE SOLDIER. Why, the silliest thing you ever heard of. I—

JOAN [*interrupting him by strolling across to the bed, where she sits beside Charles*] He tied two sticks together, and gave them to a poor lass that was going to be burned.

THE SOLDIER. Right. Who told you that?

JOAN. Never mind. Would you know her if you saw her again?

THE SOLDIER. Not I. There are so many girls! and they all expect you to remember them as if there was only one in the world. This one must have been a prime sort; for I have a day off every year for her; and so, until twelve o'clock punctually, I am a saint, at your service, noble lords and lovely ladies.

CHARLES. And after twelve?

THE SOLDIER. After twelve, back to the only place fit for the likes of me.

JOAN [*rising*] Back there! You! that gave the lass the cross!

THE SOLDIER [*excusing his unsoldierly con-*

duct] Well, she asked for it; and they were going to burn her. She had as good a right to a cross as they had; and they had dozens of them. It was her funeral, not theirs. Where was the harm in it?

JOAN. Man: I am not reproaching you. But I cannot bear to think of you in torment.

THE SOLDIER [*cheerfully*] No great torment, lady. You see I was used to worse.

CHARLES. What! worse than hell?

THE SOLDIER. Fifteen years' service in the French wars. Hell was a treat after that.

Joan throws up her arms, and takes refuge from despair of humanity before the picture of the Virgin.

THE SOLDIER [*continuing*]—Suits me somehow. The day off was dull at first, like a wet Sunday. I dont mind it so much now. They tell me I can have as many as I like as soon as I want them.

CHARLES. What is hell like?

THE SOLDIER. You wont find it so bad, sir. Jolly. Like as if you were always drunk without the trouble and expense of drinking. Tip top company too: emperors and popes and kings and all sorts. They chip me about giving that young judy the cross; but I dont care: I stand up to them proper, and tell them that if she hadnt a better right to it than they, she'd be where they are. That dumbfounds them, that does. All they can do is gnash their teeth, hell fashion; and I just laugh, and go off singing the old chanty: Rum tum trumple—Hullo! Who's that knocking at the door?

They listen. A long gentle knocking is heard.

CHARLES. Come in.

The door opens; and an old priest, white-haired, bent, with a silly but benevolent smile, comes in and trots over to Joan.

THE NEWCOMER. Excuse me, gentle lords and ladies. Do not let me disturb you. Only a poor old harmless English rector. Formerly chaplain to the cardinal: to my lord of Winchester, John de Stogumber, at your service. [*He looks at them inquiringly*] Did you say anything? I am a little deaf, unfortunately. Also a little—well, not always in my right mind, perhaps; but still, it is a small village with a few simple people. I suffice: I suffice: they love me there; and I am able to do a little good. I am well connected, you see; and they indulge me.

JOAN. Poor old John! What brought thee to this state?

DE STOGUMBER. I tell my folks they must be very careful. I say to them, 'If you only saw what you think about you would think quite differently about it. It would give you a great shock. Oh, a great shock.' And they all say 'Yes, parson: we all know you are a kind man, and would not harm a fly.' That is a great comfort to me. For I am not cruel by nature, you know.

THE SOLDIER. Who said you were?

DE STOGUMBER. Well, you see, I did a very cruel thing once because I did not know what cruelty was like. I had not seen it, you know. That is the great thing: you must see it. And then you are redeemed and saved.

CAUCHON. Were not the sufferings of our Lord Christ enough for you?

DE STOGUMBER. No. Oh no: not at all. I had seen them in pictures, and read of them in books, and been greatly moved by them, as I thought. But it was no use: it was not our Lord that redeemed me, but a young woman whom I saw actually burned to death. It was dreadful: oh, most dreadful. But it saved me. I have been a different man ever since, though a little astray in my wits sometimes.

CAUCHON. Must then a Christ perish in torment in every age to save those that have no imagination?

JOAN. Well, if I saved all those he would have been cruel to if he had not been cruel to me, I was not burnt for nothing, was I?

DE STOGUMBER. Oh no; it was not you. My

sight is bad: I cannot distinguish your features: but you are not she: oh no: she was burned to a cinder: dead and gone, dead and gone.

THE EXECUTIONER [*stepping from behind the bed curtains on Charles's right, the bed being between them*] She is more alive than you, old man. Her heart would not burn; and it would not drown. I was a master at my craft: better than the master of Paris, better than the master of Toulouse; but I could not kill The Maid. She is up and alive everywhere.

THE EARL OF WARWICK [*sallying from the bed curtains on the other side, and coming to Joan's left hand*] Madam: my congratulations on your rehabilitation. I feel that I owe you an apology.

JOAN. Oh, please dont mention it.

WARWICK [*pleasantly*] The burning was purely political. There was no personal feeling against you, I assure you.

JOAN. I bear no malice, my lord.

WARWICK. Just so. Very kind of you to meet me in that way: a touch of true breeding. But I must insist on apologizing very amply. The truth is, these political necessities sometimes turn out to be political mistakes; and this one was a veritable howler; for your spirit conquered us, madam, in spite of our faggots. History will remember me for your sake, though the incidents of the connection were perhaps a little unfortunate.

JOAN. Ay, perhaps just a little, you funny man.

WARWICK. Still, when they make you a saint, you will owe your halo to me, just as this lucky monarch owes his crown to you.

JOAN [*turning from him*] I shall owe nothing to any man: I owe everything to the spirit of God that was within me. But fancy me a saint! What would St Catherine and St Margaret say if the farm girl was cocked up beside them!

A clerical-looking gentleman in black frockcoat and trousers, and tall hat, in the fashion of the year 1920, suddenly appears before them in the corner on

their right. They all stare at him. Then they burst into uncontrollable laughter.

THE GENTLEMAN. Why this mirth, gentlemen?

WARWICK. I congratulate you on having invented a most extraordinarily comic dress.

THE GENTLEMAN. I do not understand. You are all in fancy dress: I am properly dressed.

DUNOIS. All dress is fancy dress, is it not, except our natural skins?

THE GENTLEMAN. Pardon me: I am here on serious business, and cannot engage in frivolous discussions. [*He takes out a paper, and assumes a dry official manner*]. I am sent to announce to you that Joan of Arc, formerly known as The Maid, having been the subject of an inquiry instituted by the Bishop of Orleans—

JOAN [*interrupting*] Ah! They remember me still in Orleans.

THE GENTLEMAN [*emphatically, to mark his indignation at the interruption*]—by the Bishop of Orleans into the claim of the said Joan of Arc to be canonized as a saint—

JOAN [*again interrupting*] But I never made any such claim.

THE GENTLEMAN [*as before*]—the Church has examined the claim exhaustively in the usual course, and, having admitted the said Joan successively to the ranks of Venerable and Blessed,—

JOAN [*chuckling*] Me venerable!

THE GENTLEMAN.—has finally declared her to have been endowed with heroic virtues and favored with private revelations, and calls the said Venerable and Blessed Joan to the communion of the Church Triumphant as Saint Joan.

JOAN [*rapt*] Saint Joan!

THE GENTLEMAN. On every thirtieth day of May, being the anniversary of the death of the said most blessed daughter of God, there shall in every Catholic church to the end of time be celebrated a special office in commemoration of her; and it shall be lawful to dedicate a special chapel to her, and to place her image on its altar in every such church. And it shall be lawful and laudable for the faithful to kneel and address their prayers through her to the Mercy Seat.

JOAN. Oh no. It is for the saint to kneel. [*She falls on her knees, still rapt*].

THE GENTLEMAN [*putting up his paper, and retiring beside the Executioner*] In Basilica Vaticana, the sixteenth day of May, nineteen hundred and twenty.

DUNOIS [*raising Joan*] Half an hour to burn you, dear Saint, and four centuries to find out the truth about you!

DE STOGUMBER. Sir: I was chaplain to the Cardinal of Winchester once. They always would call him the Cardinal of England. It would be a great comfort to me and to my master to see a fair statue to The Maid in Winchester Cathedral. Will they put one there, do you think?

THE GENTLEMAN. As the building is temporarily in the hands of the Anglican heresy, I cannot answer for that.

A vision of the statue in Winchester Cathedral is seen through the window.

DE STOGUMBER. Oh look! look! that is Winchester.

JOAN. Is that meant to be me? I was stiffer on my feet.

The vision fades.

THE GENTLEMAN. I have been requested by the temporal authorities of France to mention that the multiplication of public statues to The Maid threatens to become an obstruction to traffic. I do so as a matter of courtesy to the said authorities, but must point out on behalf of the Church that The Maid's horse is no greater obstruction to traffic than any other horse.

JOAN. Eh! I am glad they have not forgotten my horse.

A vision of the statue before Rheims Cathedral appears.

JOAN. Is that funny little thing me too?

CHARLES. That is Rheims Cathedral where you had me crowned. It must be you.

JOAN. Who has broken my sword? My sword was never broken. It is the sword of France.

DUNOIS. Never mind. Swords can be mended. Your soul is unbroken; and you are the soul of France.

The vision fades. The Archbishop and the Inquisitor are now seen on the right and left of Cauchon.

JOAN. My sword shall conquer yet: the sword that never struck a blow. Though men destroyed my body, yet in my soul I have seen God.

CAUCHON [*kneeling to her*] The girls in the field praise thee; for thou hast raised their eyes; and they see that there is nothing between them and heaven.

DUNOIS [*kneeling to her*] The dying soldiers praise thee, because thou art a shield of glory between them and the judgment.

THE ARCHBISHOP [*kneeling to her*] The princes of the Church praise thee, because thou hast redeemed the faith their worldlinesses have dragged through the mire.

WARWICK [*kneeling to her*] The cunning counsellors praise thee, because thou hast cut the knots in which they have tied their own souls.

DE STOGUMBER [*kneeling to her*] The foolish old men on their deathbeds praise thee, because their sins against thee are turned into blessings.

THE INQUISITOR [*kneeling to her*] The judges in the blindness and bondage of the law praise thee, because thou hast vindicated the vision and the freedom of the living soul.

THE SOLDIER [*kneeling to her*] The wicked out of hell praise thee, because thou hast shewn them that the fire that is not quenched is a holy fire.

THE EXECUTIONER [*kneeling to her*] The tormentors and executioners praise thee, because thou hast shewn that their hands are guiltless of the death of the soul.

CHARLES [*kneeling to her*] The unpretending praise thee, because thou hast taken upon thyself the heroic burdens that are too heavy for them.

JOAN. Woe unto me when all men praise me! I bid you remember that I am a saint, and that saints can work miracles. And now tell me: shall I rise from the dead, and come back to you a living woman?

A sudden darkness blots out the walls of the room as they all spring to their feet in consternation. Only the figures and the bed remain visible.

JOAN. What! Must I burn again? Are none of you ready to receive me?

CAUCHON. The heretic is always better dead. And mortal eyes cannot distinguish the saint from the heretic. Spare them. [*He goes out as he came*].

DUNOIS. Forgive us, Joan: we are not yet good enough for you. I shall go back to my bed. [*He also goes*].

WARWICK. We sincerely regret our little mistake; but political necessities, though occasionally erroneous, are still imperative; so if you will be good enough to excuse me— [*He steals discreetly away*].

THE ARCHBISHOP. Your return would not make me the man you once thought me. The utmost I can say is that though I dare not bless you, I hope I may one day enter into your blessedness. Meanwhile, however —[*He goes*].

THE INQUISITOR. I who am of the dead, testified that day that you were innocent. But I do not see how The Inquisition could possibly be dispensed with under existing circumstances. Therefore— [*He goes*].

DE STOGUMBER. Oh, do not come back: you must not come back. I must die in peace. Give us peace in our time, O Lord! [*He goes*].

THE GENTLEMAN. The possibility of your resurrection was not contemplated in the recent proceedings for your canonization. I must return to Rome for fresh instructions. [*He bows formally, and withdraws*].

THE EXECUTIONER. As a master in my profession I have to consider its interests. And, after all, my first duty is to my wife and children. I must have time to think over this. [*He goes*].

CHARLES. Poor old Joan! They have all run away from you except this blackguard who has to go back to hell at twelve o'clock. And what can I do but follow Jack Dunois' example, and go back to bed too? [*He does so*].

JOAN [*sadly*] Goodnight, Charlie.

CHARLES [*mumbling in his pillows*] Goo ni. [*He sleeps. The darkness envelops the bed*].

JOAN [*to the soldier*] And you, my one faithful? What comfort have you for Saint Joan?

THE SOLDIER. Well, what do they all amount to, these kings and captains and bishops and lawyers and such like? They just leave you in the ditch to bleed to death; and the next thing is, you meet them down there, for all the airs they give themselves. What I say is, you have as good a right to your notions as they have to theirs, and perhaps better. [*Settling himself for a lecture on the subject*] You see, it's like this. If—[*the first stroke of midnight is heard softly from a distant bell*]. Excuse me: a pressing appointment—[*He goes on tiptoe*].

The last remaining rays of light gather into a white radiance descending on Joan. The hour continues to strike.

JOAN. O God that madest this beautiful earth, when will it be ready to receive Thy saints? How long, O Lord, how long?

◆ Note on *The Lark*

By JEAN ANOUILH

The play that follows makes no attempt to explain the mystery of Joan.

The persistent effort of so-called modern minds to explain mysteries is, in any case, one of the most naive and foolish activities indulged in by the puny human brain since it became overstocked with shallow political and scientific notions, and can yield nothing, in the long run, but the nostalgic satisfaction of the small boy who discovers at last that his mechanical duck was made up of two wheels, three springs and a screw. The little boy holds in his hands three springs, two wheels and a screw, objects which are doubtless reassuring, but he has lost his mechanical duck, and he has usually not found an explanation.

For my own part I always refuse to tell children how things work, even when I know; and in the case of Joan I must confess that I did not know.

Some nights, when I am feeling depressed, I try to be rational and I say: the situation—social, political and military—was ripe for the phenomenon of Joan; a little shepherdess, one of the countless little shepherdesses who had seen the Virgin or heard voices, and who happened to be called Joan, came to fill a gap in the works, and then everything began turning. If it hadn't been this one, another would have been found—there were candidates before and after her. When she was burnt, her place was taken by a little shepherd from the Landes, who led his countrymen to a few incomplete victories and was in his turn taken prisoner and burnt, without anyone thinking of making him into a hero or a saint. (As regards the hypothesis familiar to Catholics, at least in France, that God had begun to worry about France and sent Joan to save her, I must point out as a matter of general interest and without drawing any conclusion therefrom that Joan was officially recognized as a saint and not as a martyr. She was canonized for 'the excellence of her theological virtues' and not because she died for her faith—her faith being identical with the cause of France, which, even in 1920, was hardly acceptable from the Vatican's point of view. Joan was thus a saint who died as a result of a political intrigue, and God did not necessarily take sides against Henry VI of Lancaster. It's a pity, but it's true.)

Be that as it may, all this is typical of that reassuring sort of explanation which explains nothing, but which allows Monsieur Homais to go to sleep in peace after his cup of camomile tea.

And, supported by accurate texts and irrefutable evidence, it affords the same peaceful slumbers to Professor Homais, an academic bigwig. For a couple of generations, matter-of-fact people sleep thus, reassured, and then one day, by chance, in Michelet or in an illustrated paper, somebody reads one of Joan's answers at the trial, an authentic answer, a single, simple little answer, and the whole of Professor Homais' work collapses, as did the dialectic of the seventy judges in their stiff robes who spent long months harassing that weary, undernourished little girl, haggard and thin (yes, I know she was a big healthy girl, but I couldn't care less), and so strangely stubborn.

You cannot explain Joan, any more than you can explain the tiniest flower growing by the wayside. There's just a little living flower that has always known, ever since it was a microscopic seed, how many petals it would have and how big they would grow, exactly how blue its blue would be and how its delicate scent would be compounded. There's just the phenomenon of Joan, as there is the phenomenon of a daisy or of the sky or of a bird. What pretentious creatures men are, if that's not enough for them.

Children, even when they are growing older, are allowed to make a bunch of daisies or play at imitating bird-song, even if they know nothing about botany or ornithology. That is just about what I have done.

Jean Anouilh, "Note on *The Lark*," in *The Lark*, trans. by Christopher Fry (New York: Oxford University Press, 1956).

◆◆ The Lark

By JEAN ANOUILH

Translated by Christopher Fry

Characters

BEAUCHAMP, Earl of Warwick
CAUCHON, Bishop of Beauvais
JOAN
HER FATHER
HER MOTHER
HER BROTHER
THE PROMOTER
THE INQUISITOR
BROTHER LADVENU
ROBERT DE BEAUDRICOURT, Squire of Vaucouleurs
BOUDOUSSE, a guard
AGNES SOREL
THE YOUNG QUEEN
CHARLES, the Dauphin
QUEEN YOLANDE
ARCHBISHOP OF RHEIMS
M. DE LA TRÉMOUILLE
PAGE TO THE DAUPHIN
CAPTAIN LA HIRE
THE HANGMAN
AN ENGLISH SOLDIER

PART ONE

A simple, neutral setting. The stage is empty at first; then the characters enter by twos and threes. The costumes are plain. JOAN *wears man's clothes through-*

Jean Anouilh, *The Lark*, trans. by Christopher Fry (New York: Oxford University Press, 1956), pp. 1–103.

out the play. WARWICK *is the last to enter.*

WARWICK. Well now; is everyone here? If so, let's have the trial and be done with it. The sooner she is found guilty and burned the better for all concerned.

CAUCHON. But my lord, before we do that we have the whole story to play: Domrémy, the Voices, Vaucouleurs, Chinon, the Coronation.

WARWICK. Theatrical poppycock! You can tell that story to the children: the beautiful white armour, the fluttering standard, the gentle and implacable warrior maid. The statues of her can tell that story, later on, when policies have changed. We might even put up a statue ourselves in London, though I know at the moment that sounds wildly improbable: but you never know, in a few hundred years it might suit His Majesty's Government for some reason or other. But, as for now, I am Beauchamp, Earl of Warwick; and I've got my grubby little witch lying on the straw in the dungeon at Rouen, and a fine packet of trouble she has been, and a pretty sum she has cost us; but the money's been paid, and the next thing is to put her on trial and burn her.

CAUCHON. Not immediately. Before we come to that, there's the whole of her life to go through. It won't take very long, my lord.

WARWICK (*going to a corner resignedly*). Well, if you insist. An Englishman knows how to wait. (*Anxiously.*) I hope you're not expecting me to stand by while you go through that monstrous farce of a coronation again. And all the battles as well—Orleans, Patay, Beaugency?—I may as well tell you now, I should find that in very poor taste.

CAUCHON (*smiling*). Put your mind at rest, my lord. There are too few of us here to stage the battles.

WARWICK. Good.

CAUCHON. Joan.

She looks up.

You may begin.

JOAN. May I begin wherever I like?

CAUCHON. Yes.

JOAN. I like remembering the beginning: at home, in the fields, when I was still a little girl looking after the sheep, the first time I heard the Voices, that is what I like to remember. . . . It is after the evening Angelus. I am very small and my hair is still in pigtails. I am sitting in the field, thinking of nothing at all. God is good and keeps me safe and happy, close to my mother and my father and my brother, in the quiet countryside of Domrémy, while the English soldiers are looting and burning villages up and down the land. My big sheep-dog is lying with his head in my lap; and suddenly I feel his body ripple and tremble, and a hand seems to have touched my shoulder, though I know no one has touched me, and the voice says—

SOMEONE IN THE CROWD. Who is going to be the voice?

JOAN. I am, of course. I turned to look. A great light was filling the shadows behind me. The voice was gentle and grave. I had never heard it before, and all it said to me was: "Be a good and sensible child, and go often to church." But I *was* good, and I *did* go to church often, and I showed I was sensible by running away to safety. That was all that happened the first time. And I didn't say anything about it when I got home; but after supper I went back. The moon was rising; it shone on the white sheep; and that was all the light there was. And then came the second time; the bells were ringing for the noonday Angelus. The

light came again, in bright sunlight, but brighter than the sun, and that time I saw him.

CAUCHON. You saw whom?

JOAN. A man in a white robe, with two white wings reaching from the sky to the ground. He didn't tell me his name that day, but later on I found out that he was the blessed St. Michael.

WARWICK. Is it absolutely necessary to have her telling these absurdities all over again?

CAUCHON. Absolutely necessary, my lord.

WARWICK *goes back to his corner in silence, and smells the rose he has in his hand.*

JOAN (*in the deep voice of the Archangel*).—Joan, go to the help of the King of France, and give him back his kingdom. (*She replies in her own voice.*) Oh sir, you haven't looked at me; I am only a young peasant girl, not a great captain who can lead an army.—You will go and search out Robert de Beaudricourt, the Governor of Vaucouleurs. He will give you a suit of clothes to dress you like a man, and he will take you to the Dauphin. St. Catherine and St. Margaret will protect you. (*She suddenly drops to the floor sobbing with fear.*)—Please, please pity me, holy sir! I'm a little girl; I'm happy here alone in the fields. I've never had to be responsible for anything, except my sheep. The Kingdom of France is far beyond anything I can do. If you will only look at me you will see I am small, and ignorant. The realm of France is too heavy, sir. But the King of France has famous Captains, as strong as you could need and they're used to doing these things. If they lose a battle they sleep as soundly as ever. They simply say the snow or the wind was against them; and they just cross all the dead men off their roll. But I should always remember I had killed them. Please have pity on me! . . . No such thing. No pity. He had gone already, and there I was, with France on my shoulders. Not to mention the work on the farm, and my father, who wasn't easy.

Her FATHER, *who has been wandering around her* MOTHER, *suddenly speaks.*

FATHER. Where has that girl got to?

MOTHER (*going on with her knitting*). She is out in the fields.

FATHER. Well, I was out in the fields, and I'm back home again. It's six o'clock. She's no business to be out in the fields.

BROTHER. She's sitting under the Fairy Tree, staring at nothing. I saw her when I went to fetch in the bull.

PROMOTER (*from among the crowd*). The Fairy Tree! Note that, gentlemen, if you will. Note the superstition. The beginning of witchcraft already. The Fairy Tree! I ask you to note that!

CAUCHON. There are Fairy Trees all over France, my Lord Promoter. It's in our own interest not to refuse the fairies to these little girls.

PROMOTER (*primly*). We have our saints. That should be sufficient.

CAUCHON (*conciliating him*). Later on, certainly. But I mean while they are still very young; as Joan was; not yet fifteen.

PROMOTER. By fifteen they know everything: they're as old as Eve.

CAUCHON. Not Joan: Joan at that time was very simple and innocent. It will be another matter when we come to the trial; I shan't spare her Voices then. But a little girl shall keep her fairies. (*Firmly.*) And these discussions are under my charge.

The PROMOTER *bows, and retires, unmollified.*

FATHER (*bursting out afresh, to the* BROTHER). So that's where you say she is? And what does she think she's doing there, sitting under the tree?

BROTHER. Try and find out! She's just staring in front of her as if she was expecting something. And it isn't the first time either.

FATHER. Well, why didn't you tell me when you saw her before, then? Aren't you old enough to know what trouble there is with girls of her age, you little fool? What do you think she was expecting, eh? Somebody, not something, idiot! She's got a lover, and you know it! Give me my stick!

MOTHER (*gently, still knitting*). You know quite well, Joan's as innocent as a baby.

FATHER. Maybe she is. And girls as innocent as babies can come to you one evening and hold up their faces to be kissed, and the next morning, though you've kept them locked in their room all night, what has happened? You can't see into their eyes at all: they're avoiding you, and lying to you. They're the devil, all at once.

PROMOTER (*raising a finger*). The word has been said, my lords, and by her father!

MOTHER. How do you know that? The day I married you I was as innocent as Joan, and I daresay you could look into my eyes just as well next morning.

FATHER (*muttering*). That's nothing to do with it.

MOTHER. Who are these other girls you've known, then, that you've never told me about?

FATHER (*thundering to cover his embarrassment*). I tell you it's got nothing to do with it! We're not talking about other girls, we're talking about Joan! Hand me that stick. I'm going to look for her, and if she's been meeting somebody on the quiet I'll skin them alive!

JOAN (*smiling gently*). I was meeting someone on the quiet, and his solemn voice was saying: "Joan! Joan! What are you waiting for? There's a great sorrow in the realm of France."—"Holy Sir of Heaven, I'm so afraid; I'm only a young village girl; surely you've made a mistake?"— "Does God make mistakes, Joan?" (*She turns to her Judges.*) How could I have answered Yes?

PROMOTER (*shrugging*). You should have made the sign of the cross.

JOAN. I did, and the Archangel made it, too, all the time keeping his eyes carefully on mine, and the church clock sounded.

PROMOTER. You should have cried: *Vade retro Satanus!*

JOAN. I don't know Latin, my Lord.

PROMOTER. Don't be an idiot! The devil understands French. You should have cried: Get thee behind me, foul Satan, and don't tempt me again.

JOAN. But, my Lord, it was St. Michael.

PROMOTER (*sneering*). So he told you. And you were fool enough to believe him.

JOAN. Yes, I believed him. He couldn't have been the devil. He shone with light; he was beautiful.

PROMOTER (*losing his temper*). So is the devil, so is the devil, I tell you!

JOAN (*scandalised*). Oh, my Lord!

CAUCHON (*calming the PROMOTER with a gesture*). These subtle theological points, my lord Promoter, are proper for debating between ourselves, but they're beyond the understanding of this poor girl. No good is served by shocking her.

JOAN (*to the PROMOTER*). You're telling a lie, Canon! I haven't any of your learning, but I know the devil is ugly, and all that's beautiful is the work of God.

PROMOTER (*sneering*). Very charming, simple and stupid! Do you think the devil is stupid? He's a thousand times more intelligent than you and I put together. Do you think when he comes to snare a soul he would come like a horror of the flesh, with black ploughed skin and a snouting tusk like a rhinoceros? If he did, souls would fly to virtue at the sight of him. I tell you he chooses a moonlit summer night, and comes with coaxing hands, with eyes that receive you into them like water that drowns you, with naked women's flesh, transparent, white . . . beautiful——

CAUCHON (*stopping him sternly*). Canon! You are losing your way! This is very far from Joan's devil, if she has seen one. I beg you not to confuse your devil with hers.

PROMOTER (*flushed and confused in front of the smiling crowd*). I beg your pardon, my lord; there is only one devil.

CAUCHON. Go on, Joan.

JOAN (*still troubled*). If the devil is beautiful, how can we know him?

PROMOTER. By asking your parish priest.

JOAN. Can we never know by ourselves?

PROMOTER. No. That is why there is no salvation outside the church.

JOAN. Only rich people have a parish priest always at hand. It's hard for the poor.

PROMOTER. It is hard for everyone to escape damnation.

CAUCHON. My lord Promoter, let her talk with her Voices in peace and quiet. It is the beginning of the story. We mustn't reproach her with them yet.

JOAN (*continuing*). Another time it was St. Catherine and St. Margaret who came to me. (*She turns to the PROMOTER with a slightly mischievous defiance.*) They were beautiful, too.

PROMOTER (*blushing, but unable to prevent himself*). Did they appear to you naked?

JOAN (*smiling*). Oh, my lord! Do you imagine that God can't afford clothes for the saints in heaven?

The CROWD chuckles at this answer, and the PROMOTER sits down confused.

CAUCHON. You see, you make us all smile with your questions, my lord Promoter. Be wise enough to keep your interruptions until we come to the serious heart of this business. And when we do so, particularly when we come to judge her, remember that the soul in this little arrogant body is in our care. Aren't you risking very much confusion in her mind, to suggest to her that good and evil are no more than a question of clothes? It is true, certainly, that our saints are traditionally represented as clothed; yet, on the other hand——

JOAN (*to the PROMOTER*). Our Lord is naked on the cross.

CAUCHON (*turning to her*). I was going to say so, Joan, if you had not prevented me. It isn't for you to correct the reverend Canon. You forget who you are; you forget that we are your priests, your masters and your judges. Beware of your pride, Joan. If the devil one day wins you for his own, that is the way he will come to you.

JOAN. I know I am proud. But if God didn't mean me to be proud, why did He send an Archangel to see me, and saints with the light of heaven on them to speak to me? Why did He promise I should persuade all the people I have persuaded—men as learned and as wise as you—and say I should ride in white armour, with a bright sword given me by the King, to lead France into battle: and it has been so. He had only to leave me looking after the sheep, and I don't think pride would ever have entered my head.

CAUCHON. Weigh your words, Joan; weigh your thoughts. It is your Saviour you are accusing now.

JOAN (*crossing herself*). God guide me. His will be done, if His will is to make me proud and damned. That is His right, as well.

PROMOTER (*unable to contain himself*). Terrible! What she says is terrible! God's will to damn a soul? And you all listen to this without a murmur, my lords? I see here the seed of a fearful heresy which will one day tear the Church apart.

The INQUISITOR *has risen. He is an intelligent-looking man, spare and hard, speaking with great quietness.*

INQUISITOR. Listen carefully to what I am going to ask you, Joan. Do you think you are in a state of grace at this moment?

JOAN (*firmly*). At what moment, my lord? Is it the beginning, when I hear my Voices, or the end, when my King and all my friends have deserted me, when I doubt and recant and the Church receives me again?

INQUISITOR. Don't evade my question. Do you think you are in a state of grace?

All the PRIESTS *are watching her in silence; it seems a dangerous question.*

LADVENU (*rising*). My lord Inquisitor, it is a formidable question for a simple girl who believes in all sincerity that God has called her. I ask that her reply shall not be held against her: she is risking quite unwittingly——

INQUISITOR. Quiet, Brother Ladvenu! I ask

what I consider good to ask. Let her answer my question. Do you think you are in a state of grace, Joan?

JOAN. If I am not, may God in His goodness set me there. If I am, may God in His goodness keep me so.

The PRIESTS *murmur. The* INQUISITOR *sits again, inscrutable.*

LADVENU (*quietly*). Well answered, Joan.

PROMOTER (*muttering, annoyed by* JOAN's *success*). What of it? The devil has cunning, or he wouldn't be the devil. It isn't the first time he has been asked that question. We know what he is; he has his answers all ready.

WARWICK (*bored, to* CAUCHON). No doubt this is all very interesting, my lord, but if you go on at this rate we shall never get to the trial, never have her burnt, never get anywhere. I said she could take us over the old ground again, if you thought it so necessary, but let her get on with it. And let us come to the essentials. His Majesty's Government have to discredit this wretched little Charles Valois, at once; it's imperative that we should let Christendom know that the Coronation was all a humbug, the performance of a witch, a heretic, an army's whore.

CAUCHON. My lord, we're trying her only for heresy.

WARWICK. I know that; but I have to make more of it for the sake of the troops. The findings of your trial, I'm afraid, will be too rarefied for my soldiers. Propaganda, my lord Archbishop, is black or white. The main thing is to say something pretty staggering, and repeat it often enough until you turn it into a truth. It's a new idea, but, believe me, it will make its way. The essential thing, so far as I am concerned, is that the girl should be a nonentity, whatever she is in fact. And what she is in fact is of no particular importance to His Majesty's Government. Personally, I must admit, I find the girl attractive. The way she takes the wind out of your sails gives me a lot of pleasure; her seat on a horse is very good: that's rare in a woman. If the circumstances had been different, and she had belonged to my own set, I should have enjoyed a day's hunting with her. But unfortunately there's been this damned Coronation, and that was nobody's notion but hers in the first place. Really, my lords, what impudence! To have himself crowned King of France right under our noses: a Valois, King of France! and to do it at Rheims, our territory! To dare to pick France out of our pockets, and pilfer the English heritage! Luckily, God is on the side of England, as he satisfactorily proved at Agincourt. God and our right. Two ideas completely synonymous. And moreover, inscribed on our coat-of-arms. So rattle her through the rest of it, and have her burned, and not so much talk. Earlier on I was joking. I give it ten years, and this whole incident will have been forgotten.

CAUCHON (*sighing*). God grant so, my lord.

WARWICK. Where had we got to?

FATHER (*coming forward with his stick*). To where I was going out to find her, sitting under her tree, waiting to get herself into trouble, the little bitch. And I can tell you she'll be sorry she ever began it! (*He drags* JOAN *up by the wrists.*) What are you doing here, eh? Tell me what you're waiting about here for, when you know you ought to be indoors, eating your supper!

JOAN (*stammering, shy at being surprised, raising her arm to protect her face*). I didn't know it was so late. I had lost count of the time.

FATHER. That's it, you lost count of the time! And what else have you lost that you daren't tell me? (*He shakes her abominably.*) Who made you forget it was so late? I heard you as I came along, calling out goodbye to somebody. Well, who was it?

JOAN. St. Michael, father.

FATHER (*giving her a resounding slap on the face*). You make fun at your father, you'll be sorry! I won't have any girl of mine sitting out in the fields waiting for any man who wants to find her. You'll marry the decent fellow we choose for you, or I'll break every bone in your body!

JOAN. I've done nothing wrong, father: truthfully it was the blessed St. Michael who spoke to me.

FATHER. And when you can't hide your sinning any longer, and every day it grows bigger in you for all to see, and you've killed your mother with grief, and your brothers have to join the army to get away from the scandal in the village, it will be the Holy Ghost who brought it on us, I suppose? I'll tell the priest: not content with whoring, you have to blaspheme: and you'll be shut up in a convent on bread and water, my girl.

JOAN (*kneeling before him*). Father, stop shouting, you can't hear what I say. I promise you, by our Saviour, I'm telling you the truth. They've been coming for a long time now to ask things of me. It is always at the mid-day Angelus or the evening Angelus; always when I'm praying, when I am least sinful and nearest to God. Above all doubt, surely it must be true. St. Michael has appeared to me, and St. Margaret, and St. Catherine. They speak to me, and they answer when I question them, and each one says the same as the others.

FATHER (*pulling her about*). Why should St. Michael speak to you, you little idiot? Does he speak to me? Natural enough, if he had something to say to us, he'd say it to me, the head of the family. Does he speak to our priest?

JOAN. Father, as well as shaking me and shouting at me, try to understand what I'm saying. I'm so alone, and they want me to do so much. For three years I've been trying not to believe them, but all that time they've been saying the same thing. These Voices I hear: I can't go on fighting them all by myself. I've got to do what they say.

FATHER. The voices you hear? Do you want to drive me mad?

JOAN. They say it can't wait any longer; the time has come when I have to say "Yes."

FATHER. What can't wait any longer, idiot? What are they telling you to do, what you call these Voices? Voices! Well, it's better than being deaf!

JOAN. They tell me to go and save the realm of France which is in grave danger of being destroyed. Is it true?

FATHER. Heavens above! Of course the realm of France is in danger of being destroyed. It isn't the first time, and it won't be the last: and she always gets out of it. Leave it in God's hands; there's nothing you can do about it, you poor girl. Even a man can't do anything about it, unless he's a soldier.

JOAN. But I can. My Voices have said so.

FATHER (*laughing*). Oh, you can, can you? Dear me! You're sharper than all our great captains, of course, who can't do anything these days except be beaten every time they fight?

JOAN. Yes, father.

FATHER. Yes, father! Perhaps you're not a bad girl, but worse. You're a mad, idiot girl. What do you think you can do then, poor idiot?

JOAN. What my Voices tell me. I can ask the Squire of Beaudricourt for an armed escort. And when I've got my escort, I can go straight to the Dauphin at Chinon, to tell him that he's the rightful King; and I can lead him out at the head of the soldiers to save Orleans; and then I can persuade him to be consecrated with holy oil by the Archbishop, and then we can hurl the English into the sea.

FATHER (*suddenly understanding*). Now you're explaining yourself, at last, you filthy little slut! You want to go off with the soldiers, like the lowest of the low?

JOAN (*smiling mysteriously*). No, father, like the highest under God, riding first into the battle, and not looking back until I have saved France. (*Suddenly sad.*) And after that is done, what happens is God's will.

FATHER. I've heard enough shameless lying! I won't stand any more of it! I'll teach you what happens to girls who go chasing after soldiers, pretending to save France!

He savagely and unmercifully beats and kicks her.

JOAN (*crying*). Stop, father, stop! stop!

The FATHER *has taken off his belt, and starts to leather her, gasping with effort.*

LADVENU (*rising, very pale*). This must be stopped! He means to injure her.

CAUCHON (*gently*). We can do nothing, Brother Ladvenu. At this part of the story we have never met Joan; we don't get to know her until the trial. We can only act our parts, each his own, good or bad, as they are written, and in his turn. And later on, you know, we shall do worse things than this to her. (*He turns to* WARWICK.) This domestic scene is not very pleasant to witness, my lord?

WARWICK (*with a gesture*). Why not? We're firm believers in corporal punishment in England; it forms the character. I myself have been flogged many times as a boy; and I took it extremely well.

The FATHER, *at last too exhausted to go on, wipes the sweat off his forehead, and shouts at* JOAN, *lying crumpled at his feet.*

FATHER. There! you carrion! Do you still want to save France? (*He turns to the others, rather ashamed of himself.*) Well, sirs, what would you have done in my place if your daughter had said that to you?

MOTHER (*coming forward*). Have you killed her?

FATHER. Not this time. But if she talks any more about going off with the soldiers, I'll drown that girl of yours in the river with my own hands, do you hear me? And if I'm nowhere about, I give her brother full permission to do it for me. (*He strides off.*)

The MOTHER *bends over* JOAN *and dries her face.*

MOTHER. Joan, my little Joan, my little Joan. Did he hurt you?

JOAN (*giving a pathetic smile when she recognises her* MOTHER). Yes. He meant me to feel it.

MOTHER. He's your father, Joan; you must bear it patiently.

JOAN (*in a small voice*). I do bear it, mother. I prayed while he beat me: prayed that our heavenly Father would forgive him.

MOTHER (*shocked*). Our heavenly Father doesn't have to forgive fathers for beating their daughters. It's their right.

JOAN. And I prayed for him to understand.

MOTHER (*fondling her*). Understand what, my silly one? Why did you have to tell him all this nonsense?

JOAN (*in agony*). Someone has to understand; otherwise I'm by myself, and I have to face them alone!

MOTHER (*rocking her in her arms*). Now, now, now, you don't have to upset yourself. You remember when you were little, we would rock away your nightmares together. But now you're nearly a woman: nearly too big to hold in my arms any more, and I can tell you it's no good breaking your heart to make men understand anything. All you can do is say "yes" to whatever they think, and wait till they've gone out to the fields. Then you can be mistress in your own house again. Your father's a good man; but if I didn't trick him sometimes for his own good I don't know where we should be. Who is it, Joan? You can tell your mother. Don't you even know his name, perhaps? And yet I don't know but it must be someone in the village. Why, your father might even agree to him; he's not against a good marriage for you. We might even be able to persuade him he chose the boy himself, the poor old stupid. You know what men are: roar a lot, and lay down the law, and bang you about: but, the same as with a bull, you can lead them by the nose.

JOAN. It isn't marriage that I have to think of, mother. The blessed St. Michael has told me I should leave the village, put on a man's clothes, and go and find his highness the Dauphin, to save the realm of France.

MOTHER (*severely*). Joan, I speak nicely and gently to you, but I won't have you talking wickedness. And I won't have you put on a man's clothes, not if you beg at my grave. Have my daughter a man! You let me catch you, my goodness!

JOAN. But, mother, I should have to, if I'm to ride horseback with the soldiers. It's the blessed St. Michael who says so.

MOTHER. I don't care what the blessed St. Michael says, you shall never go off on a horse. Joan of Arc on a horse! It would be the talk of the village.

JOAN. But the lady of Vaucouleurs rides a horse to hawking.

MOTHER. You will not ride a horse, never! It isn't the station of life you were born to. Such grand ideas, indeed!

JOAN. But if I don't ride a horse, how can I lead the soldiers?

MOTHER. And you won't go with the soldiers, either, you wicked girl! I'd rather see you cold and dead. You see, how you make me talk the same as your father. There are some things we feel the same about. A daughter spins, and scrubs, and stays at home. Your grandmother never left this village, and neither have I, and neither will you, and when you have a daughter of your own, neither will she. (*She suddenly bursts into tears.*) Going off with the soldiers! Do you want to kill me?

JOAN (*throwing herself into her mother's arms, crying too*). No, mother!

MOTHER. You do: I can see you do. And you'll destroy yourself in the end if you don't get these thoughts out of your head. (*Exit.*)

JOAN *straightens herself up, still in tears, while her* MOTHER *goes back to the* CROWD.

JOAN. You see, holy St. Michael, it isn't possible; they won't ever understand. No one will. It is better that I should give up at once. Our Lord has said that we have to obey our father and mother. (*She speaks with the voice of the Archangel*).

—But first, Joan, you have to obey God.

—But if God commands the impossible?

—Then you have to attempt the impossible, calmly and quietly. It is a cause for pride, Joan, that God gives you something of His burden to carry.

After a pause.

—My Lord, do you think our Saviour can want a daughter to make her parents weep, and leave them alone to break their hearts, perhaps to die? That's hard to understand.

—He has said, I come to bring not peace, but a sword. I am come to set the brother against the sister and the son against the father. God came to bring struggle, Joan; not to make the way easy, but to make the way harder. He doesn't ask the impossible of everybody, but He does ask it of you. That is all. (JOAN *looks up, and says simply.*)—Well, I will go.

A VOICE (*from somewhere out of the shadows behind*). Proud and arrogant!

JOAN (*disturbed*). Who is calling me proud and arrogant? (*After a pause, in the voice of the Archangel.*)

—It was you, Joan. And when you begin to do what God is asking, it will be what the world calls you. But if you give yourself humbly into the hands of God, you can bear this blame of pride.

—It is heavy to bear, my Lord!

—Yes, it is heavy. But God knows that you are strong.

A silence. She looks straight in front of her, and suddenly becomes a little girl again, happy and decided.

All right, then. It's all decided. I shall go and find my Uncle Durand. With him I always get my own way. He's as easy to manage as a tame sparrow. I shall kiss him on both cheeks, and on the top of his head, and sit on his lap, and he will say "Oh Lord, Oh Lord," and take me to Vaucouleurs!

BROTHER. You're a silly donkey! Why did you have to go and tell the old people all that stuff? Next time, if you give me a ha'penny, I won't say a word about where I saw you.

JOAN (*leaping cheerfully at him*). Oh, so it was you who told them, you beastly little pig? Sneak, sneak, I'll give you a tweak! Tell tales out of school, duck him in a muddy pool! There's your halfpenny, lardy-head. Tell-tale-tit, your tongue shall be split, and all the children in the town shall have a little bit!

They fight like urchins. She chases straight across the stage towards BEAU-DRICOURT *who has come forward to take the centre of the stage.*

BEAUDRICOURT. Well, what is it? What does she want? What is it you want, you infernal nuisance? What's this nonsensical story I hear—

JOAN *collides head first with* BEAUDRICOURT's *great paunch. He is half winded, gives a yell of pain, grabs her by the arm and lifts her level with his nose, apoplectic with rage.*

What the devil do you want, you horrible mosquito? What the devil do you mean, playing the fool outside my gates for three days on end? What the devil are these tales you've been telling the guards until their eyes pop out as far as their noses?

JOAN (*breathless with her running and poised on tip-toe in the arms of the giant*). I want a horse, my lord, a man's clothes, and an escort, to go to Chinon to see his highness the Dauphin.

BEAUDRICOURT. And my boot, you want that, too, of course?

JOAN. If you like, my lord, and a good clout, as long as I get the horse as well.

BEAUDRICOURT (*still holding her*). You know about me and you know what I want; the village girls have told you all about it, haven't they? They come along to see me, usually to beg for the life of a brother, or their old father who's been caught poaching on my lands. If the girl is pretty,

I always hook him down off the gallows, being amiable at heart. If she's ugly, I hang the old chap, to make an example of him. But it's always the pretty ones who come; they manage to dig up one in the family somehow; with the admirable result that I have a fine reputation for benevolence in the neighbourhood. So now you know the rate of exchange, and we can come to terms.

JOAN (*simply*). I don't know what you're trying to say, my lord. The blessed St. Michael sent me to you.

BEAUDRICOURT (*crossing himself anxiously with his free hand*). You don't have to bring the saints into this. That was all right for the guards, to get you in to see me. But now you're here, and you can leave the saints in their proper places. And I wouldn't be surprised if you get your horse. An old jade for a young maid; it's a reasonable bargain. Are you a virgin?

JOAN. Yes, my lord.

BEAUDRICOURT (*looking at her all the time*). I agree to the horse.

JOAN. That isn't all I want, my lord.

BEAUDRICOURT. A greedy child, I see! Well, go on; you're amusing me. If I pay well for my pleasures it helps me to believe I really want them. You understand where this conversation is leading?

JOAN (*frankly*). No, my lord.

BEAUDRICOURT. Splendid. The bed's no place for brains. What else do you want besides the horse? The taxes are coming in very well this autumn; I don't mind being generous.

JOAN. An escort of men-at-arms, my lord, to accompany me to Chinon.

BEAUDRICOURT (*freeing her, changing his tone*). Now listen to me, if we're to get on together: I may be easygoing, but I won't stand any impudence. I'm the master here and you're using up my patience fast. I can just as well have you whipped for forcing your way in her, and send you home with nothing except the marks on your backside. So behave yourself. Why do you want to go to Chinon?

JOAN. To find his highness the Dauphin.

BEAUDRICOURT. Well, well, you mean to get on! Why not the Duke of Burgundy while you're about it? In theory, you might have a sporting chance with him: the Duke's as hot as a buck rabbit. Whereas, as you probably know, the Dauphin when it comes to war and women . . . I don't know what you expect to get from him.

JOAN. An army, my lord, which I can lead to Orleans.

BEAUDRICOURT. Ah: if you're mad it's another thing altogether. I'm not getting involved in any scandal. (*He turns to the crowd upstage.*) Hey, there, Boudousse!

A GUARD *comes forward.*

Take her away and give her a ducking, and then lock her up. You can send her back to her father tomorrow evening. But no beating, I don't want any trouble; the girl's mad.

JOAN (*calmly, held by the* GUARD). You can lock me up, my lord: I don't mind that; but when they let me out tomorrow evening I shall come back again. So it would be simpler if you let me talk to you now.

BEAUDRICOURT. Ten million thunders! Don't I frighten you?

JOAN. No, my lord. Not at all.

BEAUDRICOURT (*to the* GUARD). Get back to your post! you don't need to stand about, listening to this.

The GUARD *goes, and when he has gone* BEAUDRICOURT *asks uneasily*

And why don't I frighten you? I frighten everybody.

JOAN (*quietly*). You are very good, my lord.

BEAUDRICOURT. Good? Good? I've told you, that depends on the price.

JOAN. And what's more, very intelligent. There are many people I will have to convince before I can do everything my Voices want; so its lucky the first person I have to deal with, the one everything really depends on, should turn out to be the most intelligent.

BEAUDRICOURT (*slightly puzzled, asks in a*

casual voice while he pours himself some wine). You're an odd girl, in your way. How did you come to notice that I'm intelligent?

JOAN. Because you're very handsome, my lord.

BEAUDRICOURT (*with a furtive glance into the metal mirror beside him*). Oh, tush! I suppose, twenty years ago, I might say that I pleased the ladies; and I've taken care of myself, not let myself get too old too soon; that's all it is.—It's quite peculiar and unsettling to have a conversation like this with a farm girl I've never heard of, who happens to drop in like a stray kitten. (*He sighs.*) On the whole I vegetate here. My lieutenants are a poor bunch: hardly a brain between them. And while we're on the subject, what's this connection you find between intellect and beauty? I've usually heard quite the opposite: handsome people are always stupid; that's the general opinion.

JOAN. That's the opinion of the plain people, who like to believe God can't manage both things at once.

BEAUDRICOURT (*flattered*). Ah, well, you've made a point there. But then, take myself for example. I know, as you so kindly say, I'm not one of the plain people; but I wonder sometimes, am I, after all, very intelligent? No, no, don't protest. It's a question I have to ask now and again. I can tell you this, between ourselves, as you're not anyone in particular. Obviously I'm more intelligent than my lieutenants, that's only natural, being officer in command. If that wasn't an established fact there wouldn't be an army at all. But even so, I sometimes meet with problems which I find very troublesome. They ask me to decide something, some tactical or administrative point, and quite suddenly, I don't know why, my mind is a blank. There it is, nothing but a sort of fog. Mark you, nobody knows that. I get out of it, without my face showing any change of expression; I make a decision all right. And that's the essential thing when you're in command, of course: make a decision, whatever it is.

Until you've had some experience you're apt to get flustered: but you realise after a bit, it all amounts to the same thing, whatever you decide. Still, I should like to see myself doing better. Vaucouleurs, as you see, is of no great size. I'm looking forward to the day when I make a really important decision: one of those momentous decisions, of great consequence to the nation: not a question of somebody who hasn't paid his taxes, or half a dozen prisoners to be hanged: but something a bit exceptional, which would get me noticed and talked about higher up. (*He stops dreaming, and looks at her.*) I don't know what in the world I'm doing telling you all this. You can't do anything about it, and God help you, you're half crazy into the bargain.

JOAN (*smiling gently*). I know why. I knew it would happen, because they told me so. Listen, Robert——

BEAUDRICOURT (*startled*). What are you doing calling me by my Christian name?

JOAN. It's God's name for you, Robert. Now listen, Robert, and don't bluster again, because it isn't any use. What is the important decision, which will get you noticed and talked about higher up? I can tell you, Robert. It's me.

BEAUDRICOURT. What are you talking about?

JOAN (*coming to him*). I'll tell you, if you'll listen. First of all, you have to stop thinking of me as a girl, that's what is getting you confused. And I don't mean much to you anyway, do I?

He hesitates, afraid of being cheated; she flares up.

Robert, if you want to help yourself, you have to help me, too! When I tell you the truth, acknowledge it and say Yes: otherwise we shall never get anywhere.

BEAUDRICOURT (*muttering, rather shamefaced*). Well, no . . .

JOAN (*severely*). What do you mean, no?

BEAUDRICOURT. I mean, yes, it's true. I'm not particular about you. (*Adding politely.*) Though, mind you, you're a pretty enough little thing . . .

JOAN. All right, you don't have to think you've upset me. I'm very happy the point is cleared up. And now you can imagine you have already given me the suit of clothes I asked for, and we can discuss things together, sensibly and calmly, as man to man.

BEAUDRICOURT (*still suspicious*). Discuss what?

JOAN (*sitting on the edge of the table, finishing the dregs in the wine glass*). Your own important decision, my splendid Robert. Your great achievement which will make everyone take notice of you. Think of all of them, there at Bourges. They don't know whether they're praying or cursing, or which saint to turn to next. The English are everywhere. And you know the French army. Good boys, who have still got fight in them, but they're discouraged. They've got it into their heads that the English will always be the strongest, and there's nothing to be done. Dunois the Bastard; he's a good captain; intelligent, which is rare in the army, but no one listens to him any more, and he's getting tired of it. So he spends his days having a high old time with the women in the camp (and that's something else I shall have to deal with): and he's far too cock-a-hoop, like all bastards. "The affairs of France aren't his concern: let that milksop Charles get his country out of the tangle for himself." Then there's La Hire, and there's Xantrailles: prize angry bulls: they always want to charge in head first, slashing and thrusting like old heroes in the chronicles. They belong among the champions of single combat, who don't understand how to use their cannons, and always get killed to no purpose whatever, the way they did at Agincourt. They're wonderful at getting killed, but it isn't any help. That's true, isn't it, Robert. You can't treat war like a tournament. You have to win. You have to be cunning. (*She touches her forehead.*) You have to wage it here. With all your intelligence, Robert, you know that better than I do.

BEAUDRICOURT. I've always said so. Nowadays we don't think enough. Take my lieutenants: always spoiling for a fight, and that's all they can think of. And the men who know how to think get overlooked; nobody dreams of using them.

JOAN. Nobody. So they have to think for themselves. It's a lucky thing you have had such a tremendous idea. It's certain to alter everything.

BEAUDRICOURT (*uneasily*). I have an idea?

JOAN. Don't question it, Robert; be very proud of it. Your brain is working at great speed, clearly and concisely. It's a sad thing to think that, in the whole of France at this moment, no one sees things clearly, except you.

BEAUDRICOURT. You believe so?

JOAN. I tell you so.

BEAUDRICOURT. And what is it I see?

JOAN. You see simply that the people of France have to be given a spirit and a faith. And it so happens that you have with you at this moment a young country girl. St. Michael has appeared to her, and St. Catherine and St. Margaret, or at least she says they have. You are not so sure about it, but for the time being it's not important. And this is where you show yourself to be so remarkable. You say to yourself: Here's a little peasant girl, of no consequence at all; all right. If by any chance she really has been sent by God, then nothing could stop her, and it can't be proved one way or the other whether God sent her or not. She certainly got in to see me, without my permission, and I've been listening to her for half an hour; nobody could deny that. And then, like a sword of lightning, the idea strikes home to you. You say to yourself: If she has the power to convince me, why shouldn't she convince the Dauphin and Dunois and the Archbishop? They're men, just as I'm a man; as a matter of fact, between ourselves, rather less intelligent. Moreover, why shouldn't she convince our soldiers that the English in the main are exactly like themselves, half courage and half a wish to save their skins; pummel them hard enough at the right moment, and you send them staggering out of Orleans. It's magnificent how you marshal the whole situation in your mind. What our fellows need, you are saying to yourself: what they need is someone to rouse their spirit and prove to them that God is still with them. This is where you show yourself a born leader, Robert.

BEAUDRICOURT (*pitifully*). You think that?

JOAN. I know it. And very soon so will everyone else. Like all great politicians, you're a realist, Robert. You say to yourself: I, Beaudricourt, have my doubts about her coming from God, but I'll send her off to them, and if they think she is, it will have the same effect whether it's true or false. By a stroke of good luck my courier is leaving for Bourges tomorrow morning—

BEAUDRICOURT. Who told you that? It's a secret.

JOAN. I found it out. (*She continues.*) I pick half a dozen strong men for an escort, give her a horse and send her off with the courier. At Chinon, as far as I can see, she will work things out for herself. (*She looks at him admiringly.*) My word, my word, Robert!

BEAUDRICOURT. What?

JOAN. You have a marvellous intelligence to think of all that.

BEAUDRICOURT (*wiping his forehead, worn out*). Yes.

JOAN. Only, please give me a quiet horse, because I don't know how to ride one yet.

BEAUDRICOURT (*delighted*). You're going to break your neck, my girl!

JOAN. I don't think so. St. Michael will hold me on. I tell you what, Robert: I'll have a wager with you. I'll bet you a suit of clothes—the man's clothes which you still haven't said you'll give me—against a punch on the nose. Bring two horses into the courtyard and we'll gallop them together. If I fall off, you can lose faith in me. Is that fair? (*She offers him her hand.*) Agreed? And whoever doesn't pay up is a man of mud!

BEAUDRICOURT (*getting up*). Agreed! I need to move about a bit. I wouldn't have believed how tiring it is to think so much. (*He calls.*) Boudousse!

Enter the GUARD.

GUARD. Do I take her away and give her a ducking, sir?

BEAUDRICOURT. No, you idiot! You fetch her some breeches, and bring us a couple of horses. We're taking a gallop together.

GUARD. What about the Council, sir? It's four o'clock.

BEAUDRICOURT. It can wait till tomorrow. Today I've used my brains quite enough.

He goes. JOAN *passes the astonished* GUARD *and sticks out her tongue. They lose themselves in the crowd up stage.*

WARWICK (*to* CAUCHON). I can see this girl had quality. Very entertaining, to watch her playing the old fish, didn't you think so?

CAUCHON. Rather too crude for my taste, my lord. Something subtler than that will be needed when she comes to deal with Charles.

WARWICK. My lord Bishop, the tricks that you and I use in our way of business aren't so remarkably different from hers. Whether we're ruling the world with a mace or a crozier, in the long run, we do it by persuading fools that what we make them think is their own opinion. No need for any intervention of God in that. Which is why I found it so entertaining. (*He bows politely towards the* BISHOP.) Entertaining, at least, if one isn't professionally concerned, of course, as you are. Have you faith yourself, my lord Bishop? Forgive my bluntness; but between ourselves. I'm interested to know.

CAUCHON (*simply*). A child's faith, my lord. And that is why I shall make problems for you during the trial, and why we shall go as far as ever we can to save Joan, even though we have been sincere collaborators with the English rule, which seemed to us then the only reasonable solution to chaos. It was very easy for those who were at Bourges to call us traitors, when they had the protection of the French army. We were in occupied Rouen.

WARWICK. I don't like the word "occupied":

You forget the Treaty of Troyes. You were quite simply on His Majesty's territory.

CAUCHON. In the midst of His Majesty's army, and the execution of His Majesty's hostages; submitting to the curfew, and the condescension of His Majesty's food-supplies. We were men, with the frailty of men, who wanted to go on living, and yet at the same time to save Joan if we could. It was not in any way a happy part that we were called upon to fill.

WARWICK (*smiling*). There was nothing to stop you becoming martyrs, my dear fellow, if that would have made it more inspiring for you. My eight hundred soldiers were quite ready.

CAUCHON. We knew it. They took great pleasure in shouting their insults at us, hammering on the door with the butts of their halberds, to remind us they were there. We temporised for nine months before we would deliver Joan up to you; this little girl, forsaken by everyone; nine months to make her say Yes. Future times will be pleased to say we were barbarous. But I fancy, for all their fine principles, they will take to expediency faster than we did; in every camp.

WARWICK. Nine months, that's quite true. What a difficult confinement this trial has been. Our Holy Mother Church takes her time, when she's asked to give birth to a small matter of policy. But the nightmare is over. The mother and child are both doing well.

CAUCHON. I have pondered deeply over these things, my lord. The health of the mother, as you put it, is our one concern. And that is why, when we saw there could be no alternative, we sacrificed the child in good faith. Ever since that day of Joan's arrest, God has been dead to us. Neither she, whatever she may imagine, nor we, certainly, have heard Him any more. We have gone on, following our daily custom; our pre-eminent duty, to defend the old house, this great and wise human building which is all that remains to us in the absence of God. From the time we were fifteen years old, we were taught how to defend it. Joan had no such help, and yet, though her faith fell on dreadful days, when she was left alone by men and by God, she also has gone on, recovering at once after the single moment when she weakened, bearing herself with her curious mixture of humility and insolence, of grandeur and good sense, even up to execution and death. We weren't able to understand it then; we had our eyes buried in our mother's skirts, like children grown old. And yet, precisely in this loneliness, in the desert of a vanished God, in the privation and misery of the animal, the man is indeed great who continues to lift his head. Greatly alone.

WARWICK. Yes, well, no doubt. But if our business is politics we can't afford to brood about such men. We seem fated, as a rule, to meet them among the people we condemn to execution.

CAUCHON (*quietly, after a pause*). It is a consolation to me sometimes to think of those old priests who, though they were deeply offended by her insolent answers, nevertheless, even with English swords at their back, tried for nine months not to commit the irreparable.

WARWICK. Enough of fine phrases, Bishop. Nothing is irreparable in politics. I tell you we shall raise a handsome statue to her in London one day, when the right time comes.

He turns towards the people of Chinon, who have been putting up a small palace set during this conversation.

But now let's come to Chinon, my lord. I've got a profound disrespect for that lounging little idler, Charles, but he's a character who never fails to amuse me.

CHARLES *is with the two Queens and* AGNES SOREL.

AGNES. But Charles, it's impossible! You can't let me appear at the ball looking such a frump. Your mistress in one of last year's steeple-hats.

QUEEN. And your Queen, Charles! The Queen of France! What would they say?

CHARLES (*playing cup-and-ball, dropping into his throne*). They would say the King of France isn't worth a farthing. Which is quite right.

QUEEN. And think how the English court would laugh! The Duchess of Bedford, and Gloucester's wife, to say nothing of the Cardinal of Winchester's mistress! Now there's someone who knows how to dress.

AGNES. Imagine, Charles, if they're wearing our newest fashions over there before we are!

CHARLES. At least they pay for them. Fashion is practically the only thing we can sell them: our fashions and our cooking. They are the only things which still give us some prestige with the foreigners.

YOLANDE. We have to defend this prestige. The girls aren't altogether wrong, Charles. It's most important there should be no question at this ball that ladies of the court of France are the best dressed women in the world. No one has ever been able to decide, remember, exactly where triviality begins. A steeple-hat the English have never seen before might be as good as a great victory.

CHARLES (*with a dry laugh*). A victory which isn't going to stop them making off with Orleans, mother-in-law! According to the latest reports, Orleans is lost. And you think we should counter-attack with a new fashion.

AGNES. Certainly. You've no idea what a dangerous blow it will be to their confidence. If you want a victory, Charles, here is one you can have for nothing.

CHARLES. For nothing? You make me laugh! How much did you say these steeple-hats would come to?

AGNES. Six thousand francs, my darling. That's next to nothing, when you remember they're completely embroidered with pearls. And the pearls are a good investment. When the steeple-hat isn't fashionable any more you can always sell the pearls at a profit and put it towards the army's back pay.

CHARLES. Six thousand francs! But where do you think I can find six thousand francs, you poor little fool?

QUEEN (*softly*). Twelve thousand francs, Charles, because there are two of us, remember. You wouldn't want your mistress to be better dressed than your wife.

CHARLES (*raising his hands to heaven*). Twelve thousand francs! They've gone out of their minds!

AGNES. Of course there's a simpler model, but I wouldn't advise it. You would forfeit the moral effect we should have on the stupid English. And that, after all, is the effect we're after.

CHARLES. Twelve thousand francs! Enough to pay three-quarters of Dunois's army. I don't understand how you can encourage them, mother-in-law, a woman of your good judgment.

YOLANDE. It's because I'm a woman of good judgment that I support them, Charles. Have you ever found me opposing anything that might be for your good or the dignity of the throne? I am the mother of your Queen, and yet it was I who introduced you to Agnes when I saw clearly how it might help you.

QUEEN. Please, mother, don't brag about it!

YOLANDE. Daughter, Agnes is a very charming girl who perfectly knows her place. It was quite as important to you as to me, that Charles should decide to become a man. And the kingdom had even more need of it than we had. A little more pride, dear girl; at the moment you have thoughts like a tradesman's wife! Before Charles could become a man he had to be given a woman.

QUEEN (*acidly*). I was a woman, it seems to me, and his wife, what is more.

YOLANDE. I don't want to wound you, my dearest girl: but only slightly a woman. I can say this to you, because I was very much the same. Good sense, intelligence—more than you have—but that was all. Which is why I was always willing that the King, your father, should have his mistresses. Be his Queen, run his house, give him a son and heir, and leave the rest to other people. We can't do everything. And anyway, love is scarcely an honest woman's concern. We don't do well at it. Besides, you will thank me later on: one sleeps so much better alone. And Charles is far more manly since he knew Agnes. You are more manly, aren't you, Charles?

CHARLES. Yesterday I said "No" to the Archbishop. He tried to scare me, he sent La Trémouille in first to roar at me, and then he threatened to excommunicate me. All the old tricks. But I held firm.

AGNES. And thanks to whom?

CHARLES. Thanks to Agnes! We had rehearsed the whole scene in bed.

YOLANDE. What did the Archbishop want? You didn't tell me.

CHARLES (*caressing* AGNES *absent-mindedly*). I can't remember. To give up Paris to the Duke of Burgundy, or something of the sort, in return for a year's truce. I might say it wouldn't really have meant anything at all. The Duke's in Paris already. But it was a matter of principle: Paris is France, and France is mine. At least I encourage myself to believe it is. So I said "No." The Archbishop made such a great fuss about it, the Duke must have promised him a pretty good sum.

AGNES. And what would have happened, Charles dear, if you had said "yes" in spite of me?

CHARLES. You would have had a headache for a week, and although, I suppose, if I had to, I could do without Paris, I couldn't do without you.

AGNES. Well, then, my darling, if I have helped you to save Paris, you can surely buy me the new steeple-hat, and one for your little Queen, too, because you have said some very hurtful things to her, without noticing it, as usual, you bad boy. You don't want me to be ill for a whole week, do you? You wouldn't know what to do with yourself.

CHARLES. All right, then, order your steeple-hats. I always have to say "yes" to somebody, if it isn't the Archbishop, it's you. But I may as well tell you, I haven't the least idea how I'm going to pay for them.

AGNES. You're going to sign a draft on the Treasury, Charles, and we will see what happens later. Come along, little Majesty, we will try them on together. Would you rather have this rose-coloured one, or the sky-blue? I think myself the rose is the one which will suit you best.

CHARLES. What do you mean? Have you got them already?

AGNES. You're very slow at understanding, my dearest! Surely you can see, if we were to have them in time for the ball we had to order them a month ago? But we were so sure you would say "Yes," weren't we, Your Majesty? You shall see what a sensation this causes in London! It's a great victory for France, you know, Charles!

They take to their heels.

CHARLES (*sitting back on his throne again*). There's nothing you can do but laugh, the way they harp on victories. La Trémouille, Dunois, they're all the same! There is always going to be a great victory. But everything has to be paid for, including great victories, these days. And suppose I can't afford a great victory? Suppose France is above my means? (*He takes his writing desk, muttering.*) Ah well, we shall see! I can always sign a draft on the Treasury. Let's hope it will please the tradesmen. The Treasury is empty, but there's nothing on this paper to say so. (*He turns towards the* QUEEN YOLANDE.) You wouldn't like a steeple-hat too, while I'm doing it? You needn't mind saying so. My signature isn't worth the ink it's written in.

YOLANDE (*coming to him*). I'm past the age for steeple-hats, Charles. I want something else.

CHARLES (*wearily*). To make me a great King, I know! It gets very boring in the end, everybody wants to make me a great King. Even Agnes. Even in bed. Imagine how jolly that is. I wish you would all try and get it into your heads, I'm an unimportant, insignificant Valois, and to make a King of me would need a miracle. I know my grandfather Charles was a great king; but he lived before the war when everything was much cheaper. Besides, he was rich. But my father and mother spent it all, so whether you like it or not, I can't afford to be a great king; I haven't got the money, and I haven't got the courage; you all know I haven't. Courage is far too dangerous in a world full of bullying brutes. That fat pig La Trémouille was in a raging temper the other day, and drew his sword on me. We were alone together: nobody there to defend me. He was quite prepared to give me a jab with it, the beastly hooligan! I only just had time to dodge behind the throne. So you see what we've come to. Drawing his sword on the King! I should have sent for the constable to arrest him, except that unfortunately he is the constable, and I'm not sure that I am the King. That's why they treat me like this; they know that I may be only a bastard.

YOLANDE. It's nobody but yourself, Charles, who is always saying so.

CHARLES. When I look at the legitimate faces all round me I hope I am a bastard. It's a charming day and age to live in, when a man isn't considered anybody unless he can brandish an eight-pound sword, and stroll about in a suit of armour which would sink a galleon. When they put it on me, I'm welded into the ground; a great help to my dignity. And I don't like fighting. I don't like hitting, and I don't like being hit. And what's more, if you want to know, I'm frightened of it. (*He turns towards her crossly.*) What other impossibilities do you want me to do?

YOLANDE. I want you to receive this girl from Vaucouleurs. She says God sent her; and furthermore she says she has come to deliver Orleans. The people can think and talk of nothing else, and they're only waiting now to hear that you agree to receive her.

CHARLES. Then they're going to find I'm not as ridiculous as they think I am. Give audience to an eccentric peasant girl? Really, mother-in-law, for a woman of good sense you disappoint me.

YOLANDE. I've given you Agnes, because I thought it was for your good, Charles, though against my interest as a mother. Now I tell you to accept this girl from Domrémy. She seems to possess some exceptional power, or so everybody says, which is a point to be considered.

CHARLES (*bored*). I don't like virgins. I know, you're going to tell me again that I'm not virile enough. But they frighten me. And, anyway, I have Agnes, who still pleases me quite well enough. Don't think I'm reproaching you, but for someone who is a queen and my mother-in-law, you have a very remarkable vocation.

YOLANDE (*smiles*). You don't understand me, Charles, or else you're pretending not to. I'm asking you to take this peasant girl into your counsel, not into your bed.

CHARLES. In that case, in spite of all the respect I owe you, I have to tell you you're absolutely mad. Into my council, with the Archbishop, and La Trémouille, who believes that he sprang from Jupiter's thigh? Do you want them to knock my head off?

YOLANDE (*gently*). I think a peasant in your counsels is exactly what you all need. The nobility governs the kingdom, which is as it should be; God has entrusted it into their hands. But, without presuming to criticise the wisdom of providence, I wonder sometimes that he hasn't given them what he gives so generously to humbler men, a better measure of simplicity and common sense.

CHARLES (*ironically*). And courage!

YOLANDE (*gently*). And courage, Charles.

CHARLES. As far as I can understand you, you recommend turning the government over to the people? To the good people who have all the virtues. You've read the history of tyrants, I suppose?

YOLANDE. No, Charles. In my day, knowledge was not encouraged in young women.

CHARLES. But I've read it: the endless procession of horrors and scandals; and I amuse myself sometimes by imagining how the procession will go on in the future. They will certainly try what you recommend. They'll try everything. Men of the people will become masters of the kingdoms, maybe for centuries, the time it takes for a meteor to cross the sky; and that will be the time for massacres and the most monstrous errors. And what will they find, at the great account, when all is done? They'll find that not even the most vile, capricious, and cruel of the princes have cost the world as much as one of these virtuous men. Give France a powerful man of action, born of the people, whose ambition is to make the people happy, whatever it may entail, and see how they'll come to wish to God they had their poor lazy Charles back again, with his everlasting game of cup-and-ball. At least I've no theories about organizing the happy life. A negative virtue, perhaps, but more valuable than they realise yet.

YOLANDE. You should give up this cup-and-ball game, Charles, and this habit of sitting upside down on your throne. It's no behaviour for a king.

CHARLES. You would be sensible to let me be as I am. When the ball misses the cup, it drops on to my nose and nobody else's. But sit me on the throne the right way up, with the orb in one hand and the sceptre in the other, then whenever I make a mistake the ball will drop on everybody's nose.

Enter the ARCHBISHOP *and* LA TRÉMOUILLE. *He sits like a king on his throne.*

CHARLES. Archbishop, Constable, you've come at the perfect moment. I am starting to govern. You see I have here the orb and the sceptre.

ARCHBISHOP (*taking his eye-glass*). It's a cup-and-ball!

CHARLES. Unimportant, Archbishop: symbolism, after all. That isn't something I have to teach a prince of the Church. Your announced visit to me, my lord, must mean you wish for an audience.

ARCHBISHOP. I haven't come to be playful, Sire. I know very well the minority opinion, which cares to intrigue and agitate on

every possible occasion, is trying to persuade you to see this notorious peasant girl you have heard of. The Constable and I are here, Sire, to say it is not our intention to admit her.

CHARLES (*to* QUEEN YOLANDE). What did I tell you?—I have taken note of what you recommend, my lord, and I shall consider what course to follow. Now you may go; the audience is over.

ARCHBISHOP. I will remind you, Sire, we are not here for your amusement.

CHARLES. Whenever I talk like a king for a moment, they always think I'm amusing myself. (*He lies back on his throne with the cup and ball.*) Very well, then; leave me to amuse myself in peace.

ARCHBISHOP. This girl's miraculous reputation is spreading across the country ahead of her; it was here before she arrived; it's already causing excitement in beseiged Orleans. God has taken her by the hand and leads her: this is the story. God has decided that she shall save France and drive the English back across the sea; and other such nonsense. God will expect you to receive her into the royal presence, and nothing is going to prevent her. I don't know why they're so anxious that God should concern Himself in their affairs. And naturally she has performed miracles; it would have surprised me more if she hadn't. A soldier called her I don't know what when she arrived at Chinon. She told him that he was wrong to swear, because soon he would be standing before his Redeemer. And an hour later this boorish fellow missed his footing, and fell into the well in the servants' yard, and drowned himself. That blundering step of a drunkard has done more for the girl's reputation than a great victory ever did for Dunois. Apparently the opinion is unanimous, from the lowest kennel-boy to the highest lady in your court: only this wretched girl can save us. A preposterous infatuation!—I speak to you, sir, of the gravest matters of the realm, and you play at cup-and-ball.

CHARLES. My lord, let us be clear about this. Do you want me to play at cup-and-ball, or do you want me to govern? (*He sits up.*) Do you want me to govern?

ARCHBISHOP (*disturbed*). Sir, we don't ask you to go as far as that. We wish you to notice and appreciate the efforts we are making . . .

CHARLES. I assure you, I notice them; I appreciate them; and I find them quite useless, my lord. Everyone expects me to see this girl, isn't it so?

ARCHBISHOP. I haven't said that!

CHARLES. Well, I'm not at all curious to see her. I'm not fond of new faces; we have to know too many people as it is. And messengers from God aren't usually very enlivening. But I want to be a good king, and content my people people. I shall see this peasant girl, if only to take the wind out of her sails. Have you spoken to her yourself, Archbishop?

ARCHBISHOP. I have other things to do, sir, when you consider that I carry the whole burden of the kingdom's affairs.

CHARLES. Quite so. And I have nothing else to do except play at cup-and-ball. So I shall see her to save you the trouble: and I shall tell you frankly what I think of her. You can trust me to do that, my lord. I know you don't easily credit me with any qualities worth having, but at least you will agree that I'm a frivolous man: a quite useful condition for this interview. I'm very soon bored by anyone who takes himself seriously. I am going to receive this girl, and if she can make me want to listen to her talking about the welfare of the kingdom, which no one has ever done yet without making me yawn, then there's no doubt about her performing miracles.

ARCHBISHOP (*muttering*). A peasant girl in the presence of the king!

CHARLES (*simply*). You will remember, I think, that some of all kinds have been admitted to my presence. I don't mean M. de la Trémouille, who springs, of course, direct from Jupiter's thigh. But, for instance, yourself, my lord:—I think I remember being told you were the grandson of a wine merchant. There is no reproach in that. What could be more natural? You have carried the wine from your cellars to the altar. And as for myself, as you frequently have told me, it's a moot point whether I'm the son of a king. So we'd better not play the ancestry game, my lord, or we shall be making ourselves altogether ridiculous. (*To* QUEEN YOLANDE.) Come with me, and help me get ready for her. I've thought of a very amusing joke. We can disguise one of the pages in a royal doublet, if we can find one that isn't too shabby; sit him on the throne, which I am sure he will manage better than I can, and I shall hide myself in the crowd. Then we can listen to a solemn harangue from the messenger of God to a page-boy! It ought to be irresistible, don't you think so?

They go out.

ARCHBISHOP (*to* LA TRÉMOUILLE). Do we let him do it? It's a game to him, like everything else. It shouldn't be dangerous. And once he has seen her, the people may very well calm down again. In a fortnight they will have found some other messenger of God to infatuate them, and the girl will be forgotten.

LA TRÉMOUILLE. I command the army, Archbishop, and I can only tell you, the official doctor of the nation has nothing more to say. We're now entirely in the hands of the bone-setters, the faith-healers, the quacks. In other words, what you call messengers from God. What do we risk?

ARCHBISHOP (*anxiously*). Constable, wherever God concerns himself everything is a risk. If the unlikely should be true, and He really has sent this girl to us: if, in fact, He means to take our part, then our troubles are only beginning. We shall be shaken out of all custom and orthodoxy, contrive to win four or five battles, and then will come the problems, the complications. Long experience as a man, both in the church and in government, teaches me that never, never must we draw God's attention to us. It is better to remain very small, Constable, very small and unnoticed.

The COURTIERS *take their places with the* QUEENS; *a* PAGE *sits on the throne;* CHARLES *slips into the crowd. The* ARCHBISHOP *concludes in an undertone.*

Everybody is grouped round the throne where the little PAGE *sits;* CHARLES *is in the crowd.* JOAN *enters alone, looking very small and simple among the armour and the court fashions. They make a way for her to pass to the throne. She is about to kneel, hesitates, blushes, looking at the* PAGE.

YOLANDE (*whispering in her ear*). You must kneel, child, before the king.

JOAN *turns towards her, puzzled; then suddenly she looks at all the silent people who are watching her, and advances silently in the crowd, who make way for her. She goes towards* CHARLES, *who tries to hide from her. When he sees that she is about to reach him, he almost runs to hide behind the others, but she follows him, almost running, too. She finds him in a corner and falls on her knees.*

CHARLES (*embarrassed in the silence*). What do you want with me?

JOAN. Gentle Dauphin, I am called Joan the Maid. God has brought me to you, to tell you that you will be anointed and crowned in the city of Rheims. You will be viceroy of the King of Heaven, who is King of France.

CHARLES (*awkwardly*). Well, that is very nice. But Rheims belongs to the English, I understand. How would I get there?

JOAN (*still on her knees*). By your own strength, gentle Dauphin; by beating them. We will start with Orleans, and then we can go to Rheims.

LA TRÉMOUILLE (*coming up*). Little lunatic! Isn't that what all the army commanders have been trying to do for months? I am the head of them; I know something about it. And they haven't got there.

JOAN (*getting up*). I will get there.

LA TRÉMOUILLE. Will you indeed? And how will you get there?

JOAN. With the help of God Who sends me.

LA TRÉMOUILLE. I see. So God has arranged for us to retake Orleans?

JOAN. Yes, my lord; and to hunt the English out of France.

LA TRÉMOUILLE (*jeering*). A very beautiful thought! But God can't convey His own messages Himself? He has to have you to do it for Him?

JOAN. Yes, my lord.

ARCHBISHOP (*approaching her*). Young woman . . .

JOAN *sees him, kneels and kisses the hem of his robe. He gives her his ring to kiss, and motions her to rise.*

You say that God wishes to deliver the kingdom of France. If such is indeed His will, He has no need of armies, or you to lead them.

JOAN. Oh, my lord, does God care for those who have no care? First the soldiers must fight, and then He will give the victory.

CHARLES. How did you recognise me without my crown?

JOAN. Gentle Dauphin, it was a good joke to put your crown on this boy, it doesn't take much to see that he's really a little nobody.

CHARLES. You're mistaken. The boy is the son of a great lord.

JOAN. Great lords are not the king.

CHARLES (*troubled*). Who told you I was the king? I didn't look like a king.

JOAN. God told me, gentle Dauphin: Who appointed you from the beginning of time, through your father and your grandfather and all the line of kings, to be viceroy of His kingdom.

The ARCHBISHOP *and* LA TRÉMOUILLE *exchange a look of annoyance.*

ARCHBISHOP. Sire. The girl's answers are interesting: they show a remarkable good sense. But in a matter as delicate as this you cannot surround yourself with precautions too strict or thorough. A commission of learned theologians must question and examine her very closely. We will then discuss their report in Council, and decide if it is timely for you to give this girl a longer hearing. There's no need for her to importune you any further today. First of all I shall interrogate her myself. Come here, my daughter.

CHARLES. Not at all. (*He stops* JOAN.) Stay where you are. (*He turns to the* ARCHBISHOP, *taking* JOAN's *hand to give himself courage.*) I was the one she recognised. I was the one she spoke to. I wish you to leave me alone with her: all of you.

ARCHBISHOP. This blunt dismissal, sir: it is quite extraordinary, it is improper! Apart from all else, you should at least think of your own security . . .

CHARLES (*fearful for a moment, but he looks at* JOAN *and pulls himself together*). I am the only judge of that. (*He recites:*) Through my father, my grandfather, and all the line of kings . . . (*He winks at* JOAN.) Isn't that right? (*He turns to the others, imperturbable.*) Leave us, my lords, when the king commands it.

They ALL *bow, and go.*

CHARLES *keeps his regal pose for a moment, and then explodes with laughter.*

They've gone, they've gone! Did I do that, or did you? It's the first time in my life I have ever made myself obeyed. (*He looks at her, suddenly anxious.*) I hope there is nothing in what the Archbishop was trying to suggest. You haven't come here to kill me? There isn't a knife hidden about you somewhere?

He looks at her, and she smiles gravely.

No. You reassure me. I had forgotten, among all these pirates in my court, how reassuring a smile could be. Are there many of you in my kingdom with such honest faces?

JOAN (*still smiling gravely*). Yes, sir, very many.

CHARLES. But I never see you. Only ruffians, hypocrites, and whores: my entourage. Though of course there's my little queen, who has a certain amount of charm but not many brains. (*He goes back to his throne, his feet on the rail, and sighs*). Well, there you are. I suppose now you have to start boring me. You're going to tell me to become a great king.

JOAN (*gently*). Yes, Charles.

CHARLES. Don't let's bother. We shall have to stay shut up here together for an hour at least, to impress them. If you talk to me about God and the kingdom of France for an hour, I shall never last out. I propose instead we talk about something quite different. Do you play cards?

JOAN (*opening her eyes wide*). I don't know what it is.

CHARLES. It's an amusing game they invented for Papa, to distract him during his illness. You'll see, I shall teach you. I've played so often now I've got tired of it, but I think you may like it if you've never played before. (*He goes to rummage about in a chest.*) I hope they haven't stolen them from me. They steal everything here. And a pack of cards, you know, costs a lot of money. Only the royal princes have them. Mine were left to me by my father. I shall never have enough money to buy myself another pack. If those devils have stolen them . . . No, here they are. (*He returns with the cards.*) You knew Papa was mad, did you? Sometimes I hope I'm really his son, so that I can be sure I'm the true king; and then, at other times I hope I'm a bastard, so that I don't have to dread going mad before I'm thirty.

JOAN (*gently*). And which of the two would you prefer, Charles?

CHARLES (*turning in surprise*). Good heavens, are you calling me Charles? This is turning out to be a most surprising day. I believe I'm not going to be bored, for once; it's marvellous.

JOAN. Not now, Charles, or ever again.

CHARLES. Extraordinary.—Which of the two would I prefer? Well, I suppose on the days when I have some courage I would rather take the risk of going mad, and be the true king; and on the days when I haven't I would rather let everything go, and retire on my twopence-ha'penny to somewhere abroad, and live in peace. Have you met Agnes?

JOAN. No.

CHARLES (*shuffling the cards*). No, of course you haven't. Retiring wouldn't do for her. And I couldn't afford her then. She is always wanting me to buy her things.

JOAN (*suddenly grave*). And today: are you feeling brave today, Charles?

CHARLES. Today? (*He ponders a moment*). Yes, it seems to me I feel fairly brave. Not very, but fairly. Well, you saw how I packed off the Archbishop.

JOAN. How would you like to be brave all the time, from today onwards?

CHARLES (*leaning forward, interested*). Do you mean you know the secret?

JOAN. Yes.

CHARLES. Are you some sort of a witch? You needn't be afraid to tell me; it isn't something I object to. I promise you I won't repeat it. Those executions horrify me. I was taken once to see them burn a heretic. I was sick all night.

JOAN (*smiling*). No, I'm not a witch, Charles. But I know the secret.

CHARLES. Would you sell it to me, without letting the others know about it? I'm not very well off, but I could make you a draft on the Treasury.

JOAN. I will give it to you, Charles.

CHARLES (*suspiciously*). For nothing?

JOAN. Yes.

CHARLES. Then I'm not interested. A secret is either no good, or far beyond my means. Disinterested people are too rare, at any price (*He shuffles the cards*). I've taken to behaving like a fool, so that I shall be left in peace, but I know more than you think I know. I'm not so easily gulled.

JOAN. You know too much.

CHARLES. Too much? You can never know too much.

JOAN. Sometimes; it is possible.

CHARLES. I have to defend myself. You would soon see, if you were here in my position! If you were alone, among a lot of brutes whose one idea is to stab you when you are least expecting it, and if you've been born a weak sort of fellow, as I was, you would soon realise the only way to steer safely through it is by being more clever than they are. And I am; much more clever. Which is why I more or less hang on to my throne.

JOAN (*puts her hand on his arm*). I shall be with you now, defending you.

CHARLES. Do you think you will?

JOAN. And I'm strong. I'm not afraid of anything.

CHARLES (*sighing*). You're very lucky! (*He deals the cards*). Sit down on the cushion; I'm going to teach you to play cards.

JOAN (*smiling, sitting close to the throne*). All right. And then I'll teach you something.

CHARLES. What?

JOAN. Not to be afraid. And not to know too much.

CHARLES. Now pay attention. You see the cards, and these pictures on them? There's something of everything here: knaves, queens, kings: the same as in the world: and here are the commoners: spades, hearts, clubs, diamonds. Those are the troops. There are plenty of them, you can lose as many as you like. You deal the cards without looking at them, and fate either gives you a good hand, or a bad hand, and then the battle begins. The higher cards can capture the lower cards. Which do you think is the strongest?

JOAN. The king is.

CHARLES. Well, he is almost the strongest, but there's one stronger still. This card here, for instance, the single heart. Do you know what it's called?

JOAN. God, of course: because He's the only one who commands kings.

CHARLES (*annoyed*). No, it isn't at all. For goodness sake let God alone for five minutes. For the time being we're playing cards. It's called the ace.

JOAN. Then the game of cards is ridiculous. What can be stronger than a king, except God?

CHARLES. The ace, in fact. The ace, or God if you like; but there's one in each camp. You see: ace of hearts, ace of spades, ace of clubs, ace of diamonds. One for each of them. You're not so intelligent as I thought you were. Do you think the English don't say their prayers, as well as us? And, what's more, to a God who protects them, and gives them victories over us. And my cousin, the Duke of Burgundy, he has a God for Burgundy, in just the same way: a smallish one, maybe, but a bold one, a cunning one, who gets my cousin out of difficulties very well. God is with everybody, my girl. He marks the points, and keeps the score. But, in the long run, He plumps for the people who have the most money and the biggest armies. So why do you imagine He should be with France, now that France has got nothing at all?

JOAN. Perhaps for that reason: because she has nothing at all, Charles.

CHARLES (*shrugging his shoulders*). You don't know Him!

JOAN. I do. God isn't with the strongest; He is with the bravest. There's the difference. God hasn't any love for cowards.

CHARLES. Then He doesn't love me. And if He doesn't love me, why do you expect me to love Him? All He had to do was to give me some courage. I don't ask for anything better.

JOAN (*severely*). Do you think He's your nurse, with no one else to think about but you? Why can't you make the best of what you have got; I know He has made you weak in the legs. . .

CHARLES. You've noticed that? He ought to have managed better than that. Particularly with the present fashions. It's because of my legs that Agnes can't bring herself to love me. If He had only an eye for proportion, and hadn't given me my big knees as well. . .

JOAN. Well, I grant you that. He didn't go to much trouble over your knees. But there was something else that more concerned Him; His eye was on your head and your heart, Charles, where you most resemble Him. And there it is He makes you free,

to be whatever you will. You can use them to play cards, or to outmanœuvre the Archbishop for a time, though in the end you have to pay for it; or else you can use them to make the house of Valois glorious again, and remake the kingdom. Your little queen gave you a son, Charles. What are you going to leave the boy when you die? This wretched scrap of France, nibbled by the English? If so, when he grows up, the boy will be able to say, as you did just now, that God hasn't any interest in him. You are God, Charles, to your little son; and you have to take care of him.

CHARLES (*groans*). But I keep telling you, everything frightens me.

JOAN (*coming nearer to him*). You shall have the secret now, Charles. But don't give me away when I tell you first that everything frightens me, too. Do you know why M. de la Trémouille isn't afraid of anything?

CHARLES. Because he is strong.

JOAN. No. Because he is stupid. He never imagines anything. Wild boars, and bulls, and barrel-headed oxen are never afraid of anything, either. And I tell you this: it has been even more complicated for me to get to you than it will be for you to get to Orleans and refashion your kingdom. I had to explain to my father, and that was a bad enough beginning. He wouldn't believe I wanted anything, except to go dragging off after the soldiers; and so he beat me, and, my goodness, the English don't hit any harder than he does. And then I had to make my mother cry; there was nothing worse than that; and then to convince Beaudricourt, who didn't want to think of anything except adding one more to his list of sins. Don't think I haven't been afraid. I was afraid all the time, from the very beginning.

CHARLES. Then how have you done it?

JOAN. Just as I should have done without the fear. That's all the difficulty there is, Charles. Try it once, and see. You say: one thing is obvious, I'm frightened, which is nobody's business but mine, and now on I go. And on you go. And if you see something ahead which nothing can overcome . . .

CHARLES. Like Trémouille enjoying one of his rages—

JOAN. Yes, if you like. Or the unshakeable English facing Orleans in their fortress built like rocks. You say: Here it is—they outnumber us, their walls are as thick as the length of a giant's arm, their cannons out-thunder thunder, their arrows out-rain the rain. So be it. I'm frightened. Now I've realised how frightening it is, on we go.—And the English are so astonished, they begin to be frightened themselves, and you get through! You get through because you think deeper, imagine more, and get your fear over first. That's the secret of it.

CHARLES. But is it always so successful?

JOAN. Always. As long as you turn and face what frightens you. But the first step has to be yours; He waits for that.

CHARLES (*after a pause*). You think we could try your secret?

JOAN. We have to try it.

CHARLES (*suddenly frightened by his temerity*). Tomorrow, perhaps. By tomorrow I shall have had time to prepare for it.

JOAN. No, Charles; now; you're ready now.

CHARLES. Do you mean that I'm ready to call the Archbishop and La Trémouille? That I'm ready to tell them that I've given you command of the army, and then sit calmly back and watch their faces?

JOAN. Absolutely ready.

CHARLES. I'm scared out of my life.

JOAN. Then the worst is over. One thing is essential: you mustn't be still frightened after you've called them. Are you sure you are as frightened as you possibly can be?

CHARLES (*his hand on his belly*). Oh yes, I agree with you.

JOAN. Wonderful! That's an enormous advantage. When they start to be frightened, you will have got over it already. The whole scheme is to be afraid first, before the battle begins. You'll soon see. I'll call them. (*She calls offstage*). My Lord Archbishop, M. de la Trémouille! M. le Dauphin wishes to speak to you.

CHARLES (*taken by panic*). Oh dear, I'm so frightened! Goodness, goodness, I'm so frightened.

JOAN. That's it, that's right Charles; more frightened still!

CHARLES (*his teeth chattering*). I can't be more frightened: it's impossible!

JOAN. Then we have the victory! God has joined you; He says "Charles is afraid, but still he calls them." In eight hours we shall hold Orleans!

Enter the ARCHBISHOP *and* LA TRÉMOUILLE, *surprised.*

ARCHBISHOP. You called us, your Highness?

CHARLES (*suddenly, after a last look at* JOAN). Yes: I've come to a decision, my lord, and it also concerns you, M. de la Trémouille. I am giving the command of my royal army to this Maid here. (*He suddenly shouts*). If you don't agree, M. de la Trémouille, I must ask you to surrender your sword to me. You are under arrest!

LA TRÉMOUILLE *and the* ARCHBISHOP *stand petrified.*

JOAN (*clapping her hands*). Well done! Now you know how simple it is! Do you see their faces, Charles? Look at them: do look at them! Who is frightened now, Charles?

She bursts out laughing; CHARLES *begins to laugh as well: they rock with laughter, unable to stop; and the* ARCHBISHOP *and* LA TRÉMOUILLE *seem turned to stone.*

(JOAN *drops suddenly on to her knees, crying*) Thank you, God!

CHARLES (*also kneeling*). On your knees, M. de la Trémouille, on to your knees! And give us your blessing, Archbishop: no hesitating: give us your blessing! Now that we've all been thoroughly frightened, we must make straight for Orleans!

LA TRÉMOUILLE *is on his knees, stupified by the blow. The* ARCHBISHOP, *be-*

wildered, mechanically gives his bless-
ing.

PART TWO

WARWICK (*laughing and coming forward with* CAUCHON). In point of fact, that wasn't exactly how it happened. They called a meeting of the Council, and discussed the matter for hours. In the end they agreed to use Joan as a sort of flagpole to nail their colours to: an attractive little mascot, well qualified to charm the general public into letting themselves be killed. The best we could do to restore the balance was to treble the men's drink ration before they went into action, though it had nothing like as good an effect. We started being beaten from that time on, against all the laws of strategy. I know some people have said there was nothing miraculous about that. They maintain that our system of isolated forts around Orleans was ludicrous, and all the enemy had to do was attack: which is what Joan made them agree to try. But that's not true. Sir John Talbot was no fool. He knew his job thoroughly well; as he has proved again and again, both before this regrettable business, and since. His system of fortification was theoretically impregnable. No: we must have the grace to admit there was more in it than that: a strong element of the imponderable—or God, as you might say, my Lord Bishop—which the rules of strategy don't provide for. Without question, it was Joan: singing like a lark in the sky over the heads of your French armies on the march. I am very fond of France, my Lord: which is why I should be most unhappy if we lost her. This lark singing in the sky, while we all take aim to shoot her down: that seems very like France to me. Or at least like the best of her. In her time she has had plenty of fools, rogues and blunderers; but every now

and then a lark sings in her sky, and the fools and the rogues can be forgotten. I am very fond of France.

CAUCHON (*gently*). But still you take aim and shoot her down.

WARWICK. A man is a mass of contradictions, my lord Bishop. It isn't unusual in him to kill what he loves. I love animals, but I hunt them, too.

He suddenly gets up, looking stern. He raps with his stick on his boot, and makes a sign to TWO SOLDIERS *who come forward.*

Come along now: the lark has been caught. The cage of Compiègne has shut her in. The singing is over; and Charles and his court are leaving her there, without a second glance. They're going back to their old political methods, now that their little mascot isn't bringing them luck any more.

Indeed, CHARLES, LA TRÉMOUILLE, *and the* ARCHBISHOP *have slyly got up and edged away from* JOAN, *who is on her knees, praying. She starts up astonished to be alone, and sees* CHARLES *deserting her. The* GUARDS *begin to drag her away.*

CAUCHON. Your king has left you, Joan! There's no reason now to go on defending him. Yesterday we read you the letter he has sent to every town, telling them to say he repudiates you.

JOAN (*after a pause, quietly*). He is my king.

CHARLES (*in a low voice to the* ARCHBISHOP). That letter is going to be thrown in our teeth for a long time yet.

ARCHBISHOP (*also aside*). It had to be, sir: it was absolutely necessary. At this juncture, the cause of France cannot be linked in any way with Joan's.

CAUCHON. Joan: listen carefully, and try to understand what I'm saying. Your king is not our king. A treaty in rightful and due form has made Henry the Sixth of Lancaster King of France and England. Your trial is not a political trial. We are simply trying with all our power and with all our faith to lead a lost sheep back into the fold of our Holy Mother Church. But as men, Joan, we consider ourselves to be faithful subjects of His Majesty King Henry. We have as great and sincere a love of France as you: and because of that we recognise him as our sovereign: so that France can rise up again out of her ruins, dress her wounds, and be free of this appalling, interminable war which has drained all her strength. The useless resistance of the man you call your king, and his absurd pretentions to a throne which isn't his, appear to us to be acts of rebellion and terrorism against a peace which was almost assured. The puppet whom you served is not our master, be certain of that.

JOAN. Say what you like, you can't alter the truth. This is the king God gave you. Thin as he is, with his long legs and his big, bony knees.

CHARLES (*to the* ARCHBISHOP). This is really most disagreeable.

ARCHBISHOP. For a little while we have to have patience; but they mean to hurry through the trial and burn her, and after that we shall not be disturbed. You must surely admit, sir, the English have done us a good turn, making themselves responsible for her arrest and execution. If they hadn't done it, we ourselves should have had to, some day or other. She was becoming impossible!

They withdraw, unnoticed.

CAUCHON. We know by many of your answers, insolent though they were, that you're not slow of understanding, Joan. Put yourself for a moment in our place. How can you suppose that we, men with most earnest human convictions, can agree that God has sent you to oppose the cause you defend? How can you think, only because you say Voices have spoken to you, that we should believe God to be against us?

JOAN. You will know when we have beaten you.

CAUCHON (*shrugging*). You are answering like a self-willed, obstinate child. Considering the question now as priests and defenders of our Holy Mother Church, have we any better reason to put faith in what you tell us? Do you think you are the first who has heard Voices?

JOAN. No, of course not.

CAUCHON. Neither the first, nor the last, Joan. Now, do you believe that each time a little girl goes to her village priest and says: I have seen some saint, or the Blessed Virgin, I have heard Voices which have told me to do one thing or another—that her priest should believe and encourage her: and how long then would the Church still remain?

JOAN. I don't know.

CAUCHON. You don't know; but you are full of good sense, and that is why I am trying to lead you to reason with me. Have you not been in command in battle, Joan?

JOAN. Yes, I was in command of hundreds of good soldiers who followed me, and believed me.

CAUCHON. You were in command. And if on the morning of some attack one of your soldiers had heard Voices persuading him to attack by another gate than the one you had chosen, or not to attack at all, what would you have done?

JOAN (*speechless for a moment, before she suddenly bursts out laughing*). My lord Bishop, it's easy to see you're a priest! It's clear you don't know much about our men. They can drink and swear and fight, but they're not ones for hearing Voices!

CAUCHON. A joke is no answer, Joan. But you gave your answer before you spoke, in the second of hesitation when you were held and disarmed by what I said to you. And you see it is true: that the Church Militant is an army in a world still overrun by infidels and the powers of evil. The Church owes obedience to our Holy Father the Pope and his bishops, as your soldiers owed obedience to you and your lieutenants. If a soldier says on the morning of attack that Voices have told him not to advance, in yours or any army in the world

he would be silenced. And far more brutally than this effort of ours to reason
with you.

JOAN (*gathering herself together, on the defensive*). You have a right to hit at me
with all your power. And my right is to
say No, and go on believing.

CAUCHON. Don't make yourself a prisoner of
your own pride, Joan. You can surely see
that we have no possible reason, either as
men or as priests, to believe that your mission is divinely inspired. You alone have a
reason to believe so; encouraged by the
fiend who means to damn you, and also,
as long as you were useful to them, by
those whom you served. You served them;
and yet the way they behaved before your
capture, and their explicit repudiation
since, certainly proves that the most intelligent of them never believed you. No one
believes you, Joan, any longer, except the
common people, who believe everything,
and tomorrow they will believe half a
dozen others. You are quite alone.

> JOAN *makes no reply, sitting small and
> quiet among them all.*

I beg you not to imagine that your strong
will and your stubborn resistance to us is
a sign that God is upholding you. The
devil has also got intelligence and a tough
hide. His mind had the flash of a star
among the angels before he rebelled.

JOAN (*after a pause*). I am not intelligent,
my lord. I am a peasant girl, the same as
any other in my village. But when something is black I cannot say it is white, that
is all.

> *Another pause.*

PROMOTER (*suddenly rising up behind her*).
What was the sign you gave to the man
you are calling your king, to make him
trust you with his army?

JOAN. I don't know what you mean: what
sign I gave.

PROMOTER. Did you make him sip mandra-
gora, to be a protection against harm?

JOAN. I don't know what you mean by man-
dragora.

PROMOTER. Your secret has a name, whether
it's a potion or a formula, and we mean to
know it. What did you give him at Chinon
to make him so heroic all of a sudden? A
Hebrew name? The devil speaks all languages, but he delights in Hebrew.

JOAN (*smiling*). No, my lord: it has a French
name. I gave him courage.

CAUCHON. And so you think that God, or at
least the power you believe to be God, took
no part in this.

JOAN. He always takes part, my lord Bishop.
When a girl speaks two words of good
sense and someone listens, there He is.
But He is thrifty; when those two words
of good sense will do, He isn't likely to
throw away a miracle.

LADVENU (*quietly*). The answer's a good one,
in all humility, my lord: it can't be held
against her.

PROMOTER (*with venom, to* JOAN). I see, I
see! So you don't believe in such miracles
as we are shown in the gospels? You deny
what was done by Our Lord Jesus at the
marriage of Cana? You deny that He raised
Lazarus from the dead?

JOAN. No, my lord. What is written in Holy
Scripture was surely done. He changed
the water into wine just as easily as He
created them. And it was more extraordinary for Him, the Master of life and death,
to make Lazarus live again, than for me to
thread a needle.

PROMOTER (*yelping*). Listen to that! Listen to
that! She says there is no such thing as a
miracle!

JOAN. No, my lord. I say that a true miracle
is not done with a magic wand or incanta-
tion. The gypsies on our village green
can do miracles of that sort. The true
miracle is done by men themselves, with
the mind and the courage which God has
given to them.

CAUCHON. Are you measuring the gravity of
your words, Joan? You seem to be telling us
quite calmly that God's true miracle on
earth is man, who is nothing but sin and
error, blindness and futility. . . .

JOAN. And strength, too, and courage, and light sometimes when he is deepest in sin. I have seen men during the battles. . . .

LADVENU. My lord, Joan is talking to us in her rough and ready language about things which come instinctively from her heart, which may be wrong but are surely simple and genuine. Her thoughts are not so schooled that she can shape them to our way of argument. Perhaps by pressing her with questions we run the risk of making her say more than she meant, or something different from her belief.

CAUCHON. Brother Ladvenu, we shall try and estimate as fairly as we can what part lack of skill plays in her answers. But our duty is to question her to the last point of doubt. We are not perfectly sure, remember, that our concern now is *only* the question of Joan. So then, Joan, you excuse man all his faults, and think him one of God's greatest miracles, even the only one?

JOAN. Yes, my lord.

PROMOTER (*yelping, beside himself*). It's blasphemy! Man is filth, lust, a nightmare of obscenity!

JOAN. Yes, my lord. He sins; he is evil enough. And then something happens: it may be he is coming out of a brothel, roaring out his bawdy songs in praise of a good time, and suddenly he has thrown himself at the reins of a runaway horse to save some child he has never seen before; his bones broken, he dies at peace.

PROMOTER. But he dies like an animal, without a priest, in the full damnation of sin.

JOAN. No, my lord; he dies in the light which was lighted within him when the world began. He behaved as a man, both in doing evil and doing good, and God created him in that contradiction to make his difficult way.

A storm of indignation from the PRIESTS *when they hear this said. The* INQUISITOR *quietens them, and suddenly rises.*

INQUISITOR (*calmly*). Joan. I have let you speak throughout this trial, with scarcely a question to you. I wanted you to find your way clearly to your position. It has taken some time. The Promoter could see only the Devil, the Bishop only the pride of a young girl intoxicated with success; I waited for something else to show itself. Now it has happened—I represent the Holy Inquisition. My Lord the Bishop told you just now, with great humanity, how his human feelings linked him with the English cause, which he considers just; and how they were confounded by his sentiments as priest and bishop, charged with the defence of our Mother Church. But I have come from the heart of Spain. This is the first time I have been sent to France. I know nothing of either the Armagnac faction, or of the English. It is indifferent to me who shall rule France, whether your prince or Henry of Lancaster. As for that strict discipline of our Mother Church which will not tolerate those who play a lone hand, however well-intentioned, but directs them back into the fold: I'll not say that is indifferent to me; but it is perhaps a secondary task, which the Inquisition leaves to the Bishops and the parish priests. The Holy Inquisition has something higher and more secret to defend than the temporal integrity of the Church. She wrestles on an invisible ground, inwardly, with an enemy only she knows how to detect, of whom only she can estimate the danger. It has been her care sometimes to take up arms against an Emperor; at other times the same solemnity, the same vigilance, the same fixity of purpose have been deployed against some old apparently inoffensive scholar, or a herdsman buried away in a mountain village, or a young girl. The princes of the earth laugh very heartily to see the Inquisition give itself such endless care, when for them a piece of rope or a sergeant's signature on a death warrant would be enough. The Inquisition lets them laugh. It knows how to recognise the enemy; it knows better than to underestimate him wherever he may be found. And its enemy is not the devil, not the devil with the cloven hooves, the chastener of troublesome children, whom my lord

Promoter sees on every side. His enemy, you yourself spoke his name, when at last you came into the open: his only enemy, is man. Stand up. Joan, and answer me. I am your interrogator now.

JOAN rises and turns towards him. He asks in an expressionless voice.

Are you a Christian?

JOAN. Yes, my lord.

INQUISITOR. You were baptized, and in your earliest years you lived in the shadow of the church whose walls touched the walls of your home. The church bells ruled over your day, your playtime, your work, and your prayers. The emissaries we sent to your village have all come back with the same story: you were a little girl full of piety. Sometimes, instead of playing and running about with other children, though you were not a solemn child, you delighted to play, yet you would slip away into the church, and for a long time you would be there alone, kneeling, not even praying, but gazing at the coloured glass of the window.

JOAN. Yes. I was happy.

INQUISITOR. You had a friend you loved very dearly, a little girl called Haumette.

JOAN. Yes, my lord.

INQUISITOR. And when you made up your mind to leave for Vaucouleurs, already believing that you would never go back, you said goodbye to all your other friends, but you passed her house by.

JOAN. Yes. I was afraid to be too unhappy.

INQUISITOR. But you cared for more than only those you loved most. You cared for old people in sickness, children in poverty. And later on, when you fought in your first battle, you stood among the wounded and cried very bitterly.

JOAN. French blood was being shed; it was hard to bear.

INQUISITOR. Not only because it was French blood. A bully who had captured two English soldiers in a skirmish outside Orleans, knocked one of them down because he didn't move fast enough for him. You

jumped off your horse, took the man's head on your knee, wiped the blood from his mouth, and helped him in his dying, calling him your little son, and promising him Heaven.

JOAN. How is it you can know that, my lord?

INQUISITOR. The Holy Inquisition knows everything, Joan. It weighed your human tenderness in the scales before it sent me to judge you.

LADVENU (*rising*). My Lord Inquisitor, I am happy to hear you recalling all these details which until now have been passed over in silence. Yes, indeed, everything we know of Joan since her earliest years has been gentleness, humility, and Christian charity.

INQUISITOR (*turning upon him, suddenly stern*). Silence, Brother Ladvenu! I ask you to remember that I stand here for the Holy Inquisition, alone qualified to make the distinction between Charity, the theological virtue, and the uncommendable, graceless, cloudy drink of the milk of human kindness. (*He passes his eye over them all.*) Ah, my Masters! How quickly your hearts can be melted. The accused has only to be a little girl, looking at you with a pair of wide-open eyes, and with a ha'porth of simple kindness, and you're all ready to fall over yourselves to absolve her. Very good guardians of the faith we have here! I see that the Holy Inquisition has enough to occupy it still: and still so much has to be cut away, cut, cut, always the dead wood to be cut away: and after us, others will go on, still pruning, hacking away without mercy, clearing the ranks of unruliness, so that the forest will be sound from root to branch.

A pause, and then LADVENU replies.

LADVENU. Our Saviour also loved with this loving-kindness, my lord. He said: Suffer the little children to come unto me. He put His hand on the shoulder of the woman taken in adultery, and said to her: Go in peace.

INQUISITOR. I tell you to be silent, Brother Ladvenu! Otherwise I shall have to investigate your case as well as Joan's. Lessons from the Gospels are read to the congregations, and we ask the parish priests to explain them. But we have not translated them into the vulgar tongue, or put them into every hand to make of them what they will. How mischievous that would be, to leave untutored souls to let their imaginations play with the texts which only we should interpret. (*He quietens down.*) You are young, Brother Ladvenu, and you have a young man's generosity. But you must not suppose that youth and generosity find grace in the eyes of the faith's defenders. Those are transitory ills which experience will cure. I see that we should have considered your age, and not your learning which I believe is remarkable, before we invited you to join us here. Experience will soon make plain to you that youth, generosity, human tenderness are names of the enemy. At least, I trust it may. Surely you can see, if we were so unwise as to put these words you have spoken into the hands of simple people, they would draw from them a love of Man. And love of Man excludes the love of God.

LADVENU (*quietly*). And yet He chose to become a man . . .

INQUISITOR (*turning suddenly to* CAUCHON, *curtly*). My lord Bishop, in virtue of your discretionary power as president of these debates, I ask you to dispense for today with the collaboration of your young assessor. I shall inform you, when the session is over, what conclusions will be entered against him, if needs be. (*He suddenly thunders.*) Against him or against whomsoever! For no one is of too great importance to be put out of our care: understand so! I would denounce myself, if God should allow me to be misled. (*He gravely crosses himself and ends.*) May He mercifully watch over me!

A breath of fear whispers through the tribunal. CAUCHON *says simply, with a gesture of distress to* BROTHER LADVENU.

CAUCHON. Leave us, Brother Ladvenu.

LADVENU (*before he moves off*). My lord Inquisitor, I owe you obedience, as I do my Reverend Lord Bishop. I will go, saying no more: except that my prayers must be to our Lord Jesus that He shall lead you to remember the fragility of your small enemy who faces you now.

INQUISITOR (*not answering until he has gone, and then speaking quietly*). Small, fragile, tender, pure: and therefore formidable. (*He turns to* JOAN *and says in his neutral tone.*) The first time you heard your Voices you were not yet fifteen. On that occasion they simply said to you: "Be a good and sensible child, and go often to church." In fact you were a happy and contented little girl. And the unhappiness of France was only old men's talk. And yet one day you felt you should leave the village.

JOAN. My Voices told me that I must.

INQUISITOR. One day you felt that you must take upon yourself the unhappiness of others around you. And you knew even then everything that would come of it: how glorious your ride would be, how soon it would come to an end, and once your King had been anointed, how you would find yourself where you are now, surrounded and alone, the faggots heaped up in the market place, waiting to be set alight. You know this is—

JOAN. My Voices told me that I should be captured, and then delivered.

INQUISITOR. Delivered! They very well might use that word: and you guessed in what way it might be taken, how ambiguously as a word from heaven. Death is a deliverance, certainly. And you set off all the same, in spite of your father and mother, and in spite of all the grave difficulties ahead of you.

JOAN. Yes, my lord; it had to be. If I had been the daughter of a hundred mothers and a hundred fathers: still it would have had to be.

INQUISITOR. So that you could help your fellow men to keep possession of the soil where they were born, which they fondly imagine belongs to them.

JOAN. Our Lord couldn't want the English to pillage, and kill and overrule us in our own country. When they have gone back across the sea, they can be God's children then in their own land. I shall pick no quarrel with them then.

PROMOTER. Presumption! Pride! Don't you think you would have done better to go on with your sewing and spinning beside your mother?

JOAN. I had something else to do, my lord. There have always been plenty of women to do women's work.

INQUISITOR. When you found yourself in such direct communication with heaven did it never occur to you to consecrate your life to prayer, supplicating that heaven itself should expel the English from France?

JOAN. God likes to see action first, my lord. Prayer is extra. It was simpler to explain to Charles that he ought to attack, and he believed me, and gentle Dunois believed me, too. And so did La Hire and Xantrailles, my fine couple of angry bulls! We had some joyful battles, all of us together. It was good to face every new day with friends, ready to turn on the English, ready to rescue France, ready to—

PROMOTER. Kill, Joan? Ready to kill? And does Our Lord tell us to kill for what we want, as though we had fangs and claws?

JOAN does not reply.

CAUCHON (*gently*). You loved the war, Joan . . .

JOAN (*simply*). Yes. It is one of the sins which I have most need of God's forgiveness for. Though in the evening I would look across the battlefield and cry to see that the joyous beginning to the morning had gone down in a heap of dead.

PROMOTER. And the next day, you began again?

JOAN. God wished it. While there remained one Englishman in France. It isn't difficult to understand. There was work to be done first, that was all. You are learned, and you think too much. You can't understand the simple things, but the dullest of my soldiers understands them. Isn't that true, La Hire?

LA HIRE strides forward, in huge armour, gay and alarming.

LA HIRE. You bet it's true.

Everybody finds himself pushed into the shade: this one figure is clear. A vague music of the fife is heard. JOAN goes quietly up to him, incredulous, and touches him with her finger.

JOAN. La Hire . . .

LA HIRE (*taking up again the comradeship of the battle mornings*). Well, Miss, we've had the bit of praying we agreed to have: what's the next thing? Do we take a bash at them this morning?

JOAN (*throwing herself into his arms*). It is La Hire, my dear, fat La Hire! You smell so good!

LA HIRE (*embarrassed*). A glass of wine and an onion. It's my usual morning meal. Excuse me, Miss: I know you don't like it, but I did my praying beforehand so that God shouldn't take against my breath. Don't come too near: I know I stink in a way.

JOAN (*pressed against him*). No: it's good.

LA HIRE. You don't want to make me feel awkward. Usually you tell me I stink and it's a shame for a Christian. Usually you say that if the wind carries in that direction I shall give us away to the goddams, I stink so much; and we shall ruin our ambush because of me. One quite small onion and two tots of red wine, no more. Of course, let's be honest, no water with it.

JOAN. Well, I was a fool if I said so. If an onion has a right to stink why shouldn't you?

LA HIRE. It's what war does for you. Be a clerk, or a priest, or a linen draper: no smell. But be a captain, you're bound to sweat. As for washing, up in the line: a man doesn't see the interest in it. There was no need to add the onion, I suppose:

I ought to do with a bit of garlic sausage like the other fellows: it's better behaved when you come to conversation. But, look here, you wouldn't call it a sin, would you, eating the onion?

JOAN (*smiling*). No, La Hire: not a sin.

LA HIRE. You never know with you, you know.

JOAN. Have I pestered you with sins, La Hire? I was silly to tease you so much: it's odd, but there you are, a great bear smelling of sweat and onions and red wine, and you kill, and swear, and think of nothing except the girls . . .

LA HIRE (*very astonished*). Who, me?

JOAN. You. Yes. Look astonished, you old rogue. And yet you shine in the hand of God as bright as a new penny.

LA HIRE. Is that a fact? I should have thought I'd bitched my chance of paradise years ago. But you think if I keep on praying as arranged, a bit every day, I might still get there?

JOAN. They're expecting you. I know that God's paradise must be full of ruffians like you.

LA HIRE. Is that a fact? It would make all the difference to feel that there were a few kindred spirits around. I wasn't much looking forward to being in a crowd of saints and bishops looking like Heaven's village idiot.

JOAN (*gaily thumping him*). Great jackass! Of course Heaven's full of dunces. Hasn't our Lord said so? It may even be they're the only ones who get in: the others have had so many brains to sin with, they never get past the door.

LA HIRE (*uneasily*). You don't think, between ourselves, we'll get bored to death, do you, always on our best behaviour? Any fighting at all, do you imagine?

JOAN. All the day long.

LA HIRE (*respectfully*). Wait, now. Only when God isn't looking at us.

JOAN. But He's looking at you all the time, crackpot! He sees everything. And what's more, He is going to enjoy watching you at it. "Go it, La Hire," He'll say: "Bash the stuffing out of old Xantrailles! Pitch into him, now! Show him what you're made of!"

LA HIRE. Is that a fact?

JOAN. Not in those words perhaps, but in His own way.

LA HIRE. By God Almighty. (*Enthusiastically.*)

JOAN (*suddenly stern*). La Hire!

LA HIRE (*hanging his head*). Sorry, Miss.

JOAN (*pitilessly*). If you swear He will throw you out.

LA HIRE (*stammering*). I was feeling pleased, you see: had to thank Him somehow.

JOAN. So He thought. But don't do it again! We've talked quite enough for one morning. Let's get up on horseback and take a look at the day.

LA HIRE. It's dead country this morning. Not a soul to see.

They ride imaginary horses side by side.

JOAN. Look, we've got France all to ourselves—shall we ever see the world to better advantage? Here on horseback side by side: this is how it will be, La Hire, when the English have gone. Smell the wet grass, La Hire, isn't this why men go fighting? To ride out together smelling the world when the light of day is just beginning to discover it.

LA HIRE. So anyone can who likes to take a walk in his garden.

JOAN. No. I think death has to be somewhere near before God will show us the world like this.

LA HIRE. Suppose we should meet some English, who might also be liking the good smells of the morning?

JOAN. We attack them, we smite them, and send them flying. That's what we're here for!

A little pause.

(*She suddenly cries.*) Stop!

They draw in their horses.

There are three English over there. They've

seen us. They're running away! No! Now
they've turned back again: they've seen
there are only two of us. They're attacking. You're not afraid, La Hire? No use
counting on me; I'm only a girl, and I've
got no sword. Will you fight them alone?

LA HIRE (*brandishing his sword with a delighted roar*). Hell, yes, by God I will!
(*Shouting to the sky as he charges.*) I
didn't say anything, God, I didn't say anything. Pay no attention . . .

*He charges into the middle of the Tri-
bunal: they scatter as he swings his
sword to left and right. He disappears
still fighting.*

JOAN. He didn't say anything, God. He didn't
say anything! He is as good as a French
loaf. So all my soldiers are, though they
kill, and loot, and swear: good as your
wolves are, God, whom you created innocent. I will answer for all of them!

*JOAN is deep in prayer. The Tribunal
has re-formed round her: the light has
come back. JOAN raises her head, sees
them, seems to shake herself free of a
dream.*

La Hire and Xantrailles! Oh, we're not at
the end of things yet. You can be sure they
will come and deliver me with two or
three or four hundred men . . .

CAUCHON (*quietly*). They came, Joan: right
up to the gates of Rouen to find out how
many of the English were in the town,
and then they went away again.

JOAN (*dashed*). Oh, they went away? Without fighting? (*A silence; she looks up.*)
Why, they have gone to find reinforce-
ments, of course. I myself taught them, it
is no good to attack willynilly, as they did
at Agincourt.

CAUCHON. They withdrew to the South of the
Loire; Charles is down there, disbanding
his armies. He is tired of the war, and if
he can he will make a treaty, to secure at
least his own small portion of France. They
will never come back again, Joan.

JOAN. That isn't true! La Hire will come
back, even if he hasn't a chance.

CAUCHON. La Hire is only the captain of an
army of mercenaries, who sold himself and
his men to another Prince as soon as he
found that yours was out to make peace.
He is marching at this moment towards
Germany, to find another country to plunder; simply that.

JOAN. It isn't true!

CAUCHON (*rising*). Have I ever lied to you,
Joan? It is true. Then why will you sacrifice yourself to defend those who have
deserted you? The only men on earth who
are trying to save you—paradoxical though
it may seem—are ourselves, your old enemies and now your judges. Recant, Joan:
your resistance helps no one now; your
friends are betraying you. Return to the
arms of your Mother Church. Humble
yourself, she will lift you up again. I am
convinced that deep in your heart you have
never ceased to be one of her daughters.

JOAN. Yes, I am a daughter of the Church!

CAUCHON. Then give yourself into the care
of your mother, Joan, without question.
She will weigh your burden of error, and
so release you from the anguish of judging
it for yourself. You needn't think of anything any more: you will do your penance,
whether it be heavy or light, and at last
you will be at peace. Surely you have a
great need of peace.

JOAN (*after a pause*). In what concerns the
Faith, I trust myself to the Church. But
what I have done I shall never wish to
undo.

*A stir among the priests. The INQUISI-
TOR breaks in.*

INQUISITOR. Do you hear, my Masters? Do you
see Man raising up his head, like a serpent ready to strike us dead? Do you understand now what it is you have to judge?
These heavenly Voices have deafened you
as well as the girl, on my word they have!
You have been labouring to discover what
devil has been behind her actions. Would
it were only a question of the devil. His

trial would soon be over. The devil speaks our language. In his time he was an angel, and we understand him. The sum of his blasphemies, his insults, even his hatred of God, is an act of faith. But man, calm and transparent as he seems, frightens me infinitely more. Look at him: in chains, disarmed, deserted, no longer sure even in himself (isn't that so, Joan?) that the Voices which have been silent for so long have ever truly spoken. Does he throw himself down, supplicating God to hold him again in His hand? Does he at least implore his Voices to come back and give light to his path? No. He turns away, suffers the torture, suffers humiliation and beating, suffers like a dumb animal, while his eyes fasten on the invincible image of himself; (*he thunders*) himself, his only true God! That is what I fear! And he replies—repeat it, Joan; you are longing to say it again; "But what I have done . . ."

JOAN (*quietly*) . . . I shall never wish to undo.

INQUISITOR (*repeats*). "But what I have done I shall never wish to undo!" You hear those words? And you will hear them said on the scaffold, at the stake, in the torture chamber, wherever they come to suffer for the errors they commit. And centuries hence they will be saying it; the hunting down of Man will go on endlessly. However powerful we become one day in one shape or another, however inexorably the Idea shall dominate the world, however rigorous, precise and subtle its organisation and its police, there will always be a man who has escaped, a man to hunt, who will presently be caught, presently be killed: a man who, even so, will humiliate the Idea at the highest point of its Power, simply because he will say "No" without lowering his eyes. (*He hisses through his teeth, looking at* JOAN *with hatred.*) An insolent breed! (*He turns again towards the Tribunal.*) Do you need to question her any more? Do you need to ask her why she threw herself from the height of the tower where she was imprisoned, whether to escape, or to destroy herself against the commandments of God? Why she has left her father and mother, put on the clothes of a man, and wears them still, against the commandments of the Church? She will give you the same reply, the reply of Man: What I have done, I have done. It is mine, and my doing. No one can take it from me; no one can make me disown it. All that you can do is kill me, to make me cry out no matter what under the torture, but make me say "Yes," you cannot do. (*He cries to them.*) Ah well: by some means or other he must be taught to say say "Yes," whatever it may cost the world. As long as one remains who will not be broken, the Idea, even if it dominates and pervades all the rest of mankind, will be in danger of perishing. That is why I require Joan's excommunication, her rejection from the bosom of the Church and that she should be given over to the secular arm for punishment. (*He adds neutrally, reciting a formula.*) Beseeching it nevertheless to limit its sentence on this side of death and the mutilation of the limbs. (*He turns to* JOAN.) This will be a paltry victory against you, Joan, but at least it will silence you. And, up to now, we have not thought of a better. (*He sits down again in silence.*)

CAUCHON (*gently*). My Lord Inquisitor is the first to ask for your excommunication, Joan. In a moment I am afraid my Lord Promoter will ask for the same thing. Each one of us will speak his mind and then I shall have to give my decision. Before lopping the dead branch, which you have become, and casting it far from her, your Holy Mother Church, to whom the one lost sheep is more dear than all the others, remember that, entreats you now for the last time.

CAUCHON *makes a sign, and a man comes forward.*

Do you know this man, Joan?

She turns to look and gives a little shudder of fear.

It is the master hangman of Rouen. In a

short while from now you will belong to him, unless you give your soul into our keeping so that we can save it. Is the stake ready, Master Hangman?

HANGMAN. Quite ready, my lord. Higher than the regulation stake, such was the orders: so that the girl can be got a good view of from all sides. The nuisance of it for her is that I shan't be able to help her at all, she will be too high up.

CAUCHON. What do you call helping her, Master Hangman?

HANGMAN. A trick of the trade, my lord: it's the custom, when there aren't any special instructions. You wait till the first flames get up, and then I climb up behind, under the cover of the smoke, and strangle the party. Then it's only the corpse that burns, and it isn't so bad. But with the instructions I've had, it's too high, and I won't be able to get up there. (*He adds simply*) So, naturally, it will take longer.

CAUCHON. Do you hear that, Joan?

JOAN (*softly*). Yes.

CAUCHON. I am going to offer you once more the hand of your Mother, the great hand which opens towards you to take you back and save you. But the delay can't be for long. You hear the noise outside, as though the sea had come up to the door? That is the sound of the crowd, who already have been waiting for you since daybreak. They came early to get good places: and there they are still, eating the food they brought with them, grumbling at their children, joking and singing, and asking the soldiers how long it will be before things begin to happen. They are not bad people. They are the same men and women who would have cheered you if you had captured Rouen. But things have turned out differently, that's all, and so instead they come to see you burned. As nothing very much ever happens to them, they make their adventures out of the triumphs or the deaths of the world's great ones. You will have to forgive them, Joan. All their lives long they pay dearly for being the common people; they deserve these little distractions.

JOAN (*quietly*). I do forgive them. And I forgive you, as well, my lord.

PROMOTER. Appalling, abominable pride! My lord the Bishop troubles to talk to you like a father, in the hope of saving your miserable soul, and you have the effrontery to say that you forgive him!

JOAN. My lord talks to me gently, but I don't know whether it is to save me or to overthrow me. And since in a little while he will have to burn me anyway, I forgive him.

CAUCHON. Joan: try to understand that there is something absurd in your refusal. You are not an unbeliever. The God you claim as your own is ours also. And we are, in fact, those whom God has ordained to guide you, through the apostle Peter upon whom His Church is built. God did not say to His creatures: You will understand My will from Me. He said "Thou art Peter, and upon this rock I will build My church. . . . and its priests will be your shepherds. . . ." Do you think us unworthy priests, Joan?

JOAN (*quietly*). No.

CAUCHON. Then why will you not do as God has said? Why will you not resign your fault to the Church, as you did when you were a small girl, at home in your village? Has your faith so changed?

JOAN (*crying out in anguish*). I want to submit to the Church. I want to receive the Holy Sacrament, but you won't let me!

CAUCHON. We will give it to you after your confession, and when your penance has begun; we only wait for you to say "Yes." You are brave, we know that indeed: but your flesh is still frail: you are surely afraid of dying?

JOAN (*quietly*). Yes. I'm afraid. But what else can I do?

CAUCHON. I think well enough of you, Joan, to know that fear in itself is not enough to make you draw back. But you should have another, greater fear: the fear of being deceived, and of laying yourself open to eternal damnation. Now, what risk do you run, even if your Voices are from God, if you perform the act of submission to the priests of His church? If we do not believe in your Voices, and if nevertheless God has really spoken to you, then it is we who have committed the monstrous sin of ignorance, presumption and pride, and we who will have to make expiation through all eternity. We will take this risk for you, Joan, and you risk nothing. Say to us: "I submit to you." say simply "Yes." and you will be at peace, blameless, and safe in your redemption.

JOAN (*suddenly exhausted*). Why will you torture me so gently, my lord? I would far rather you beat me.

CAUCHON (*smiling*). If I beat you, Joan, I should only add to your pride: your pride which wishes to see you persecuted and killed. I reason with you because God gifted you with reason and good sense. I beseech you, because I know you have gentle feeling. I am an old man, Joan; I have no more ambitions in this world, and, like each of us here, I have put many to death in defence of the Church, as you have put many to death in defence of your Voices. It is enough. I am tired. I wish to die without adding to those deaths the death of a little girl. Help me.

JOAN (*after a pause*). What do I have to say?

CAUCHON. First of all you must understand that by insisting that God sent you, you no longer help anything or anyone. It is only playing into the hands of the English and the Executioner. Your king himself has declared in his letters that he doesn't in any way wish to owe the possession of his crown to a divine intervention of which you were the instrument.

JOAN *turns towards* CHARLES *in distress.*

CHARLES. Put yourself in my place, Joan! If there had to be a miracle to crown me King of France, it means I wasn't naturally king at all. It means I wasn't the true son of my father, or else my coronation would have followed of its own accord. All the other kings in my family have been crowned without needing a miracle. Divine help is all very well in its way, but sus-

pect. And it's even more suspect when it stops. Since that unhappy Paris business, we've been beaten at every step; and then you let yourself be captured at Compiègne. They've got a little verdict up their sleeve for you, to denounce you as a witch, a heretic, the devil's intermediary, all in one. I prefer people to think you were never sent by anyone. God or devil. In that way, God has neither helped me, nor thrown me over. I won because I was the strongest at the time; I am being beaten now because I am the weakest, for the moment. That is healthy politics, if you understand?

JOAN (*softly*). Yes, I understand.

CAUCHON. I'm thankful to see you're wiser at last. We have put so many questions to you, you became confused. I am going to ask you three more, three essential ones. If you answer "Yes" three times, we shall all of us be saved, you who are going to die, and we who are putting you to death.

JOAN (*quietly, after a pause*). Ask them. I will see whether I can answer them.

CAUCHON. The first question is the really important one. If you answer "Yes," the other answers will take care of themselves. Listen carefully, weighing each word: "Do you humbly put yourself into the hands of the Holy Apostolic Church of Rome; of our Holy Father the Pope and his bishops, that they shall estimate your deeds and judge you? Do you surrender yourself entirely and undoubtedly, and do you ask to be received again into the bosom of the Church?" It is enough for you to answer "Yes."

JOAN, *after a pause, looks around her without moving. At last she speaks.*

JOAN. Yes, but . . .

INQUISITOR (*in a level voice*). With no "but."

JOAN. I do not wish to be made to deny what my Voices have said to me. I do not wish to be made to bear witness against my king, or to say anything which will dim the glory of his coronation which is his, irrevocably, now and for ever.

The INQUISITOR *shrugs his shoulders.*

INQUISITOR. Such is the voice of man. There is only one way of bringing him to silence.

CAUCHON (*becoming angry*). Joan, Joan, Joan, are you mad? Do you not see this man in red who is waiting for you? Realise, understand, this is my last effort to save you, after this there is nothing more I can do. The Church still wishes to believe that you are one of her daughters. She has weighed with care the form her question should take, to help you on the path, and you cavil and try to bargain. There is no bargaining with your Mother, you impudent girl! You should beg her on your knees to wrap you in her cloak of love and protect you. Our Lord suffered far more than you in the humiliation and injustice of His Passion. Did He bargain or cavil when He came to die for you? Your suffering bears no comparison with His: scourged, mocked, spat upon: crowned with thorns, and nailed in a long agony between two thieves; you can never hope to rival His suffering! And He asks, through us, only one thing of you, that you submit to the judgment of His Church, and you hesitate.

JOAN (*after a pause, tears in her eyes*). Forgive me, my lord. I hadn't thought that Our Saviour might wish it. It is true that He has surely suffered more than I. (*A short pause, again, and she says*) I submit.

CAUCHON. Do you humbly and without any restriction supplicate the Holy Catholic Church to receive you again into her bosom, and do you defer to her judgment?

JOAN. I humbly supplicate my Mother Church to receive me again into her bosom, and I surrender myself to her judgment.

CAUCHON (*with a sigh of relief*). Good, Joan; well done. The rest will be simple enough now. Do you promise never again to take up arms?

JOAN. There is still work to be done . . .

CAUCHON. The work, as you call it, will be done by others. Don't be foolish, Joan. You are in chains, a prisoner, and in great danger of being burned. So whether you say yes or no the work will not be done by you. Your part is played out. The English have you in their grasp, and they'll not let you fight again. You said to us just now that when a girl has two words of good sense God is there performing His miracle. If God is protecting you, this is the time for Him to bring you the two words of good sense. So you promise never again to take up arms?

JOAN (*groaning*). But if my King still needs me?

CHARLES (*hastily*). Oh, goodness me! If it's me you're thinking about you can say yes at once. I don't need you any more.

JOAN (*heavily*). Then, yes; yes.

CAUCHON. Do you promise never to wear again these man's clothes, which is contrary to all the rules of decency and Christian modesty?

JOAN (*tired of the question*). You have asked me that ten times. The clothes are nothing. My Voices told me to wear them.

PROMOTER. The devil told you! Who except the devil would incite a girl to overthrow decency?

JOAN (*quietly*). Common sense, my lord.

PROMOTER (*sneering*). Common sense? Common sense is your strong card! Are breeches on a girl common sense?

JOAN. Of course, my lord. I had to ride horseback with the soldiers; I had to wear what they wore so that they wouldn't think of me as a girl, but as a soldier like themselves.

PROMOTER. A worthless reply! A girl who isn't damned to begin with wouldn't wish to ride with the soldiers!

CAUCHON. Even though it may be that these clothes had their purpose during the war, why do you still refuse to dress as a woman? The fighting's over, you are in our hands; yet you still refuse.

JOAN. It is necessary.

CAUCHON. Why?

JOAN (*hesitating for a moment, blushing*). If I were in a Church prison, I wouldn't refuse then.

PROMOTER. You hear this nonsense, my lord? What hair splitting: what deliberate prevarication! Why should she agree to modesty in a Church prison, and not where she is? I don't understand it, and I don't wish to!

JOAN (*smiling sadly*). And yet it is very easy to understand, my lord. You don't have to be very wise to see it.

PROMOTER. It is very easy to understand, and I don't understand because I'm a fool, I suppose? Will you note that, my lord? She insults me, in the exercise of my public office. She treats her indecency as something to glory in, boasts of it, in fact, takes a gross delight in it, I've no doubt! If she submits to the Church, as she apparently wants to, I may have to give up my chief accusation of heresy; but as long as she refuses to put off this diabolical dress, I shall persist in my charge of witchcraft, even though pressure is put upon me by the conspiracy to shield her which I see presides over this debate. I shall appeal, if necessary, to the Council of Basle! The devil is in this, my lord, the devil is in it! I can feel his terrible presence! He it is who is making her refuse to give up these clothes of immodesty and vice, no doubt of that.

JOAN. Put me in a Church prison, and I shall give them up.

PROMOTER. You shall not make your bargains with the Church: my lord has already told you so. You will give up this dress altogether, or you will be condemned as a witch and burnt!

CAUCHON. If you accept the principle, Joan, why don't you wish to obey us now, in the prison where you are?

JOAN. I'm not alone there.

PROMOTER. Well? you're not alone there. Well? What of that?

JOAN. The English soldiers are on guard in the cell, all through the day, and through the night.

PROMOTER. Well? (*A pause*). Do you mean to go on? Your powers of invention have failed you already, is that it? I should have thought the devil was more ingenious! You feel that you've been caught out, my girl, and it makes you blush.

CAUCHON (*quietly*). You must answer him, Joan. I think I understand but it must be you who tells us so.

JOAN (*after a moment of hesitation*). The nights are long, my lord. I am in chains. I do my best to keep awake, but sleep sometimes is too strong for me. (*She stops*).

PROMOTER (*more and more obtuse*). Well, what then? The nights are long, you are in chains, you want to sleep. What then?

JOAN (*quietly*). I can defend myself better if I wear these clothes.

CAUCHON (*heavily*). Has this been so all the time of the trial?

JOAN. Ever since I was captured, my lord, each night; and when you send me back there in the evening, it begins again. I've got into the way of not sleeping now, which is why my answers are so sleepy and muddled when I'm brought before you in the mornings. But each night seems longer; and the soldiers are strong, and full of tricks. I should as soon wear a woman's dress on the battlefield.

CAUCHON. Why don't you call the officer, and he would defend you?

JOAN (*after a pause*). They told me they would be hanged if I called for help.

WARWICK (*to* CAUCHON). Incredible. I never heard of such a thing! Quite possible in the French army. But in the English army, no, quite ridiculous. I shall inquire into this.

CAUCHON. If you would return, Joan, back to your Mother the Church who is waiting for you: promise to change from these clothes to the dress of a girl: the Church from now on would see you had no such fears.

JOAN. Then I do promise.

CAUCHON (*giving a deep sigh*). Good. Thank you, Joan, you have helped me. I was afraid for a time we should have no power to save you. We shall read your promise to adjure your sins: the document is all ready, you have only to sign it.

JOAN. I don't know how to write.

CAUCHON. You will make a cross. My lord Inquisitor, allow me to recall Brother Ladvenu so that he may read this to the prisoner. It is Brother Ladvenu who is responsible, at my request, for drawing up this paper. And, moreover, we have all to be here now, to pronounce sentence, now that Joan has returned to us. (*He leans towards him.*) You should be gratified, my lord: Man has said "Yes."

INQUISITOR (*a pallid smile on his thin lips*). I am waiting until the conclusion; until the conclusion.

CAUCHON *calls to the* GUARD.

CAUCHON. Recall Brother Ladvenu!

PROMOTER (*whispering*). My lord Inquisitor, you won't allow them to do this?

INQUISITOR (*with a vague gesture*). If she has said "Yes" . . .

PROMOTER. My lord Bishop has conducted the enquiry with an indulgence towards the girl which I can't begin to understand! And yet I have reliable information that he feeds well from the English manger. Does he feed even more rapaciously from the French? That is what I ask myself.

INQUISITOR (*smiling*). It is not what I ask myself, my lord Promoter. It is not of eating, well or better, that I am thinking, but of something graver. (*He falls on to his knees, oblivious of all around him.*) O Lord! It has pleased You to grant that Man should humble himself at the eleventh hour in the person of this young girl. It has been Your will that this time he shall say "Yes." But why has it also pleased You to let an evident and earthly tenderness be born in the heart of this old man who was judging her? Will you never grant, O Lord, that this world should be unburdened of every trace of humanity, so that at last we may in peace consecrate it to Thy glory alone?

BROTHER LADVENU *has come forward.*

CAUCHON. She is saved, Brother Ladvenu, Joan is saved. She has agreed to return to us, and to Holy Mother Church. Read her the act of Abjuration, and she will sign it.

LADVENU. Thank you, Joan. I was praying for you, I prayed that this might be possible. (*He reads*) 'I, Joan, known as the Maid, confess to having sinned, by pride, obstinacy, and wrong-doing, in pretending to receive revelation from Our Lord God, Father of all Men, through the means of His angels and His blessed Saints. I confess to having blasphemed by wearing immodest clothing, contrary to the ruling of our Holy Mother Church; and to having, by persuasion, incited men to kill one another. I foreswear and abjure all these sins; I vow upon the Holy Gospels no more to wear these clothes or to bear arms. I promise to surrender myself in humility to our Holy Mother Church, and to our Holy Father the Pope of Rome, and to his Bishops, that they shall weigh and estimate my sins and wickedness. I beseech the Church to receive me again into her bosom; and I declare myself ready to suffer the sentence which it will please her to inflict upon me. In token of which I have signed my name to this Act of Abjuration which I profess I have understood.'

JOAN (*who seems now like a shy and awkward girl*). Do I make a circle or a cross? I can't write my name.

LADVENU. I will guide your hand. (*He helps her to sign.*)

CAUCHON. There; it is done, Joan; and the Church rejoices to see her daughter safely returned: and you know she rejoices more for the one lost sheep than for the ninety-and-nine safely enfolded. Your soul is saved, and your body will not be delivered up to the executioner. We condemn you only, through the mercy and the grace of God, to live the rest of your days a prisoner, in penitence of these errors, eating the bread of sorrow, drinking the water of anguish, so that in solitary contemplation you may repent; and by these means we shall admit you free of the danger of excommunication into which you were fallen. You may go in peace. (*He makes the sign of the cross over her.*) Take her away.

The SOLDIERS *lead* JOAN *away.*

The assembly breaks up into groups, conversing among themselves.

WARWICK (*coming up to* CAUCHON). Good enough, my lord; good enough. I was wondering for a moment or so what irresponsible whim was urging you to save the girl, and whether you hadn't a slight inclination to betray your king.

CAUCHON. Which king, my lord?

WARWICK (*with a touch of frigidity*). I said your king. I imagine you have only one? Yes; very uncertain for a time whether His Majesty was going to get his money's worth, owing to this fancy of yours. But then, when I thought about it, I could see this method would discredit young Charles equally well, without the disadvantages of martyrdom, which are unpredictable, when you think of the sort of sentimental reactions we get from the public. The resolute, unshakeable girl, tied to the stake and burning in the flames, would have seemed, even so, something of a triumph for the French cause. This admission of guilt, on the other hand, is properly disgraceful. Perfect.

The CHARACTERS *move away.*

The lighting changes.

JOAN *is brought on by a* GUARD. AGNES SOREL *and* QUEEN YOLANDE *slip in beside her.*

AGNES (*coming forward*). Joan, Joan, my dear; we're so very happy it has all turned out well for you. Congratulations!

YOLANDE. Dying is quite useless, my little Joan: and whatever we do in life should have a use of some kind. People may have different opinions about the way my life has been lived, but at least I've never done anything absolutely useless.

AGNES. It was all so very stupid. Usually I adore political trials, and I particularly begged Charles to get me a seat; to watch someone fighting for his life is desperately exciting, as a rule. But really I didn't feel in the least happy when I was there. All the time I kept saying to myself: This is so very stupid: this poor little tomboy: she is going to get herself killed, and all for nothing. (*She takes* CHARLES' *arm.*) Being alive is much better, you know, in every way.

CHARLES. Yes, of course it is; and when you practically ruined your chances, just because of me—well, I was very touched, naturally, but I didn't know how to make you understand that you were getting everything quite wrong. In the first place, as you might expect, I had taken the precaution to disown you, on the advice of that old fox of an Archbishop; but, more than that, I don't like people being devoted to me. I don't like being loved. It creates obligations, and obligations are detestable.

JOAN *does not look at them; she hears their prattle without seeming to hear it. Then suddenly she speaks quietly.*

JOAN. Take care of Charles. I hope he keeps his courage.

AGNES. Of course he will; why shouldn't he? My way with him is not so different from yours. I don't want him to be a poor little king who is always being beaten, any more than you do; and you shall see, I shall make our Charles a great King yet, and without getting myself burnt, either. (*She adds in a low voice.*) I suppose it may be rather disillusioning to say so, Joan, (though, of course, the two sexes are presumably what God wanted): but I do seem to get as much out of Charles by my little campaigns in the bedroom as ever you did with swords and angels.

JOAN (*murmuring*). Poor Charles . . .

AGNES. Why poor? He is perfectly happy, like all egoists: and one of these days he is going to be a great king into the bargain.

YOLANDE. We shall see that done, Joan: not your way, but ours, and effectively enough.

AGNES (*with a gesture to the little* QUEEN). Even her little Majesty will help. She has just given him a second son. It is all she can do, but she does it very well. So if the first son dies there is no feverish worry.

The succession is assured. You can be quite happy, Joan, that you're leaving everything in good order at the Court of France.

CHARLES (*after a sneeze*). Are you coming, my dear? This prison atmosphere is deadly, so damp it would really be healthier to sit in the river. Goodbye, Joan, for the moment; we'll come and visit you from time to time.

JOAN. Goodbye, Charles.

CHARLES. Goodbye, goodbye . . . I might say, if ever you come back to Court, you will have to call me Sire, like anybody else. I've seen to that, since my coronation. Even La Trémouille does it. It's a great victory.

They go off, rustling their robes.

JOAN (*murmuring*). Goodbye, Sire. I am glad I got you that privilege at least.

The light changes again, as the GUARD *leads her to a three-legged stool; she is alone now in her cell.*

Blessed St. Michael, blessed ladies Catherine and Margaret, are you never going to come again and speak to me? Why have you left me alone since the English captured me? You were there to see me safely to victory: but it's now, in the suffering time, that I need you most. I know it would be too simple, too easy, if God always held me by the hand: where would the merit be? I know He took my hand at the beginning because I was still too small to be alone, and later He thought I could make my own way. But I am not very big yet, God. It was very difficult to follow clearly everything the Bishop said to me. With the Canon it was easy: I could see where he was wrong, and where he was wicked, and I was ready to give him any answer which would make him furious. But the Bishop spoke so gently, and it often seemed to me he was right. Are you sure that you meant that, God? Did you mean me to feel so afraid of suffering, when the man said he would have no chance to strangle me before the flames could reach me? Are you sure that you want me to live? (*A pause. She seems to be waiting for an answer, her eyes on the sky.*) No word for me? I shall have to answer that question for myself, as well. (*A pause. She nods.*) Perhaps I am only proud and self-willed after all? Perhaps after all, I did imagine everything?

Another pause. She suddenly bursts into tears, her head on the stool. WARWICK *comes quickly on to the stage, preceded by a* GUARD *who leaves them at once.* WARWICK *stops, and looks at* JOAN, *surprised.*

WARWICK. Are you crying?

JOAN. Yes, my lord.

WARWICK. And I came here to congratulate you! That was a very happy solution to it all, I thought, the outcome of the trial, very. I told Cauchon, I was delighted you managed to avoid an execution. Quite apart from my own personal sympathy for you, the suffering is really frightful, you know, and quite useless, and most unpleasant to watch. I'm perfectly convinced you've done right to steer clear of martyrdom; better for us all. I congratulate you most sincerely. It was astonishing, considering the peasant stock you come from, that you should behave with such distinction. A gentleman is always ready, when he must, to die for his honour or his king, but it's only the riff-raff who get themselves killed for nothing. And then I was very entertained to see you queen the Inquisitor's pawn. A sinister character, that Inquisitor fellow! I detest intellectuals more than anybody. These fleshless people, what unpleasant fossils they are!—Are you really a virgin?

JOAN. Yes.

WARWICK. Well, yes, of course you are. No woman would have spoken quite in the way you did. My fiancée in England, who's a very innocent girl, reasons exactly like a boy herself, and, like you, there's no gainsaying her. There's an Indian proverb—I don't know whether you may have heard it —which says it takes a virgin to walk on water. (*He gives a little laugh.*) We shall see how long she manages that, once she becomes Lady Warwick! Being a virgin is a state of grace. We adore them, and revere them, and yet, the sad thing is, as soon as we meet one we're in the greatest possible hurry to make a woman of her: and we expect the miracle to go on as if nothing had happened. Madmen! Just as soon as ever this campaign is over—it won't be long now, I hope: your little Charles is tottering to a fall—but as soon as it is, back I go to England, to do that very same idiotic thing. Warwick Castle is a very beautiful place, a bit big, a bit severe, but very beautiful. I breed superb horses—and my fiancée rides rather well, not as well as you do, but rather well. So she ought to be very happy there. We shall go fox-hunting, of course, and entertain fairly lavishly from time to time. I'm only sorry the circumstances make it so difficult to invite you over. (*An awkward pause.*) Well, there it is, I thought I'd pay you this visit, rather like shaking hands after a match, if you know what I mean. I hope I haven't disturbed you. Are my men behaving themselves now?

JOAN. Yes.

WARWICK. I should think they will certainly transfer you to a Church prison. But in any case, until they do, if there's any sign of a lapse, don't hesitate to report it to me. I'll have the blackguard hung. It's not really possible to have a whole army of gentlemen, but we can try. (*He bows.*) Madam.

He starts to go. JOAN *calls him back.*

JOAN. My lord!

WARWICK (*returning*). Yes?

JOAN (*without looking at him*). It would have been better, wouldn't it, if I had been burned?

WARWICK. I told you, for His Majesty's Government, the admission of guilt was just as good.

JOAN. But for me?

WARWICK. Unprofitable suffering. An ugly business. No, really, it wouldn't have been better. It would have been, as I told you just now, slightly plebeian, and ill-bred, and more than slightly stupid, to insist on dying just to embarrass everybody and make a demonstration.

JOAN (*as though to herself*). But I am ill-bred, I am stupid. And then, remember, my lord, my life isn't prepared and perfected like yours, running so orderly and smoothly between war, hunting, and your beautiful bride waiting for you in England. What is left of me when I am not Joan any longer?

WARWICK. Life isn't going to be very gay for you, I agree, not at first, anyway. But things will adjust themselves in time, I don't think you need have any doubt of that.

JOAN. But I don't want things to adjust themselves. I don't want to live through however long this 'in time' of yours will be. (*She gets up like a sleepwalker, and stares blindly ahead.*) Do you see Joan after living through it, when things have adjusted themselves: Joan, set free, perhaps, and vegetating at the French Court on her small pension?

WARWICK (*impatient*). My dear girl, I can tell you, in six months there won't be a French Court!

JOAN (*almost laughing, though sadly*). Joan accepting everything, Joan fat and complacent, Joan doing nothing but eat. Can you see me painted and powdered, trying to look fashionable, getting entangled in her skirts, fussing over her little dog, or trailing a man at her heels: who knows, perhaps with a husband?

WARWICK. Why not? Everything has to come to an end sometime. I'm going to be married myself.

JOAN (*suddenly cries out in another voice*). But I don't want everything to come to an end! Or at least not an end like that, an end which is no end at all. Blessed St. Michael: St. Margaret: St. Catherine! You may be silent now, but I wasn't born until you first spoke to me, that day in the fields: my life truly began when I did what you told me to do, riding horseback with a sword in my hand. And that is Joan, and no other one. Certainly not one sitting placid in her convent, pasty-faced and going to pieces in comfort: continuing to live as a tolerable habit: set free, they would call it! You kept yourself silent, God, while all the priests were trying to speak at once, and everything became a confusion of words. But You told St. Michael to make it clear to me in the very beginning, that when You're silent You have then the most certain trust in us. It is the time when You let us take on everything alone. (*She draws herself up.*) Well, I take it on, O God: I take it upon myself! I give Joan back to You: true to what she is, now and forever! Call your soldiers, Warwick; call them, call them, quickly now: for I tell you I withdraw my admission of guilt: I take back my promises: they can pile their faggots, and set up their stake: they can have their holiday after all!

WARWICK (*bored*). Now for God's sake don't let's have any such nonsense, I do implore you. I told you, I'm very satisfied with things as they are. And besides, I loathe executions. I couldn't bear to watch you going through anything of the kind.

JOAN. You have to have courage, that's all; I shall have courage. (*She looks at his pale face and puts a hand on his shoulder.*) You're a good dear fellow, in spite of your gentlemanly poker-face; but there isn't anything you can do: we belong, as you say, to different ways of life. (*She unexpectedly gives him a little kiss on the cheeks, and runs off, calling.*) Soldiers, goddams! Hey there, goddams! Fetch me the clothes I wore to fight in, and when I'm back in my breeches tell all my judges Joan is herself again!

> WARWICK *remains alone, wiping his cheek.*

WARWICK. How out of place this all is. What bad form. It's impossible to get on well with these French for long.

A great clamour.

CROWD. Death to the witch! Burn the heretic! Kill her, kill her, kill her!

> All the actors return quickly, grasping faggots: the EXECUTIONER dragging JOAN with the help of TWO ENGLISH SOLDIERS. LADVENU follows, very pale. The movement is rapid and brutal. The EXECUTIONER, with someone's help, perhaps the PROMOTER'S, makes a stake with the benches from the trial scene. They make JOAN climb up, they tie her to the stake, and nail a defamatory inscription over her head. The CROWD yells.

CROWD. To the stake with the witch! To the stake! Shave her head, the soldier's bitch! To the stake! To the stake! Burn her!

WARWICK. Stupidity! Absurd stupidity! This is something we could have done without, perfectly well.

JOAN. A cross! Let me have a cross, a cross to hold: pity me!

PROMOTER. No, no! No cross for a witch!

JOAN. Give me a cross, a cross to hold, a crucifix!

CAUCHON. Ladvenu! To the parish church! Run, Ladvenu!

> LADVENU *runs off.*

PROMOTER (*to the* INQUISITOR). This is most irregular! Aren't you going to protest, my lord?

INQUISITOR (*staring at* JOAN). With or without a cross, she has to be silenced, and quickly! Look at her, defying us. Are we never going to be able to master this flaunting spirit of man?

JOAN. A cross!

> An ENGLISH SOLDIER has taken two sticks, ties them together and calls to JOAN.

SOLDIER. Hold on, wait a bit, my girl: here you are! What are they talking about, these two priests? They make me vomit. She's got a right to a cross, like anybody else.

PROMOTER (*rushing forward*). She is a heretic! I forbid you to give it to her!

SOLDIER (*jostling him off*). You choke yourself.

He offers the improvised cross to JOAN, who clasps it against her, and kisses it.

PROMOTER (*rushing to WARWICK*). My lord! This man ought to be arrested as a heretic. I insist that you arrest him immediately!

WARWICK. You make me tired, sir. I have eight hundred men like that, each one more heretical than the others. They are what I use to fight the wars with.

INQUISITOR (*to the EXECUTIONER*). Will you hurry and light the fire? Let the smoke cover her quickly, and hide her away out of our sight! (*To WARWICK.*) We must make haste! In five minutes everybody will have swung to her side, they will all be for her!

WARWICK. I'm very much afraid that has already happened.

LADVENU *runs in with a cross.*

PROMOTER (*yelling*). Don't dare to give her the cross, Brother Ladvenu!

CAUCHON. Let him alone, Canon: I order you to let him alone.

PROMOTER. I shall refer this matter to the court of Rome!

CAUCHON. You can refer it to the devil, if you like: for the present moment, the orders to be obeyed here are mine.

All this is rapid, hurly-burly, improvised, like a police operation.

INQUISITOR (*running from one to the other nervously*). We must be quick! We must be quick! We must be quick!

LADVENU (*who has climbed up to the stake*). Courage, Joan. We are all praying for you.

JOAN. Thank you, little brother. But get down: the flames will catch you: you will be burnt as well.

INQUISITOR (*who can't bear it any more, to the EXECUTIONER*). Well, man, have you done it yet, have you done it?

EXECUTIONER (*climbing down*). Yes, it's done, my lord, it's alight. In two minutes, you'll see, the flames will have reached her.

INQUISITOR (*with a sigh of relief*). At last!

CAUCHON. (*falling on his knees*). O God, forgive us!

They all kneel, and start the prayers for the dead. The PROMOTER, in a fury of hatred, remains standing.

Get down on your knees, Canon!

The PROMOTER looks like a cornered animal: he kneels.

INQUISITOR (*who dare not look, to LADVENU who is near him and holding the cross for JOAN*). Is she looking straight in front of her?

LADVENU. Yes, my lord.

INQUISITOR. Without flinching?

LADVENU. Yes, my lord.

INQUISITOR (*almost sorrowfully*). And there is almost a smile on her lips, is there not?

LADVENU. Yes, my lord.

INQUISITOR (*with bowed head, overwhelmed, heavily*). I shall never be able to master him.

LADVENU (*radiant with confidence and joy*). No, my lord!

JOAN (*murmuring, already twisted with pain*). Blessed Michael, Margaret, and Catherine, you were brighter than those flames: let your Voices burn me. O Lord Jesus, let them speak to me. Speak to me. In the fields, in the heat of the sun. Noon.

AGNES (*kneeling in a corner with CHARLES and the QUEEN*). Poor little Joan. It is monstrous and stupid. Do you think she is suffering already?

CHARLES (*wiping his forehead and looking away*). There is still the agony to come.

The murmur of the prayers for the dead drowns the voices. Suddenly BEAUDRICOURT bursts on to the stage, breathless from running.

BEAUDRICOURT. Stop! Stop! Stop!

Everyone is startled; a moment of uncertainty.

To CAUCHON.

This can't be the way it goes! Grant a stay of execution, and let me have time to think! For, as I said to her when she first came to me, I don't think clearly when suddenly put to it. But one thing I do see: we haven't done what we said we'd do. We haven't performed the coronation! We said that we were going to play everything! And we haven't at all. It isn't justice to her. And she has a right to see the coronation performed: it's a part of her story.

CACHON (*struck by this*). We did say so, indeed; you are right to remind us. You remember, gentlemen: the whole of her life to go through, was what we said. We were in too great a hurry to bring her to an end. We were committing an injustice!

CHARLES. You see! I knew they would forget my coronation. No one ever remembers my coronation. And look what it cost me.

WARWICK. Well, really! The coronation, now! And at this time of the day, as though their little victory came last. It would be most improper for me to attend any such ceremony; I shall go away. As far as I'm concerned it is all over, and Joan is burnt. His Majesty's Government has obtained its political objective.

He goes.

CAUCHON. Unchain her! Drag away the faggots! Give her the sword and the standard again!

He goes.

Everyone joyously drags down the stake and faggots.

CAUCHON. This man is quite right. The real end of Joan's story, the end which will never come to an end, which they will always tell, long after they have forgotten our names or confused them all together: it isn't the painful and miserable end of the cornered animal caught at Rouen: but the lark singing in the open sky. Joan at Rheims in all her glory. The true end of the story is a kind of joy. Joan of Arc: a story which ends happily.

They have quickly set up an altar where the stake was standing. Bells suddenly ring out proudly. A procession forms with CHARLES, JOAN *a little behind him, then the* QUEENS, LA TRÉMOUILLE, *etc. The procession moves towards the altar.* EVERYONE *kneels. Only* JOAN *remains standing, leaning on her standard, smiling upward, like a statue of her. The* ARCHBISHOP *puts the crown on* CHARLES' *head. Bells, a salute of cannon, a flight of doves, a play of light perhaps, which throws the reflection of the cathedral stained glass across the scene, transforming it. The Curtain falls slowly on this beautiful illustration from a school prize.*

◆ *from* Bernard Shaw's *Saint Joan*

By LUIGI PIRANDELLO

. . . As we look carefully and deeply at this work of Shaw, taken as a whole, we cannot help detecting in it that curious half-humorous melancholy which is peculiar to the disillusioned idealist. Shaw has always had too keen a sense of reality not to be aware of the conflict between it and his social and moral ideals. The various phases of reality, as they were yesterday, as they are today, as they will be tomorrow, come forward in the persons who represent them before the ideal phantom of Joan (now a Saint without her knowing it). Each of these persons justifies his own manner of being, and confesses the sin of which he was guilty, but in such a way as to show that he is unable really to mend his ways—so true is it that each is today as he was yesterday, and will be tomorrow as he is today. Joan listens to them all, but she is not angry. She has for them just tolerant pity. She can only pray that the world may some time be made beautiful enough to be a worthy abode for the saints!

This new tolerance and pity rise from the most secret depths of poetry that exist in Shaw. Whenever, instead of tolerating, instead of pitying, he loses his temper at the shock of reality against his ideals, and then, for fear of betraying his anger—which would be bad mannered—begins to harass himself and his hearers with the dazzling brilliancy of his paradoxes, Shaw, the artist properly speaking, suffers more or less seriously—he falls to the level of the *jeu d'esprit* which is amusing in itself, through it irremediably spoils the work of art. I may cite in point a passage in the second act of *Saint Joan* where the Archbishop expatiates on the differences between fraud and miracles. 'Frauds deceive,' says he. 'An event which creates faith does not deceive, therefore it is not a fraud but a miracle.' Such word play is for amusement only. A work that would do something more than amuse must always respect the deeper demands of art, and so respecting these, the witticism is no longer a witticism but true art.

Luigi Pirandello, "Bernard Shaw's *Saint Joan*," *The Shavian*, II (June, 1964), pp. 9–12; originally published by *The New York Times* (January, 1924).

In none of Shaw's work that I can think of have considerations of art been so thoroughly respected as in *Saint Joan*. The four acts of this drama begin, as they must begin, with Joan's request for soldiers of Robert de Beaudricourt to use in driving the English from 'the sweet land of France.' And they end, as they must end, with the trial and execution of Joan. Shaw calls this play a chronicle. In fact, the drama is built up episode by episode, moment by moment some of them rigorously particular and free from generality—truly in the style of the chroniclers—though usually they tend to be what I call deliberate 'constructiveness.' The hens have not been laying, when suddenly they begin to lay. The wind has long been blowing from the east, and suddenly it begins blowing from the west. Two miracles! Then there are other simple, naïve things, such as the recognition of the 'blood royal' in the third act, which likewise seems to be a miracle.

But these moments are interspersed with other moments of irony and satire, of which either the Church or the English are the victims. However, this attempt to present the chronicle inside what is really history does not seem to me quite as happy as it was in *Caesar and Cleopatra*. In *Saint Joan*, history, or rather character historically conceived, weighs a bit too heavily on the living fluid objectivity of the chronicle, and the events in the play somehow lose that sense of the unexpected, which is the breath of true life. We know in advance where we are going to come out. The characters, whether historical or typical, do not quite free themselves from the fixity that history has forced upon them and from the significant rôle they are to play in history.

Joan herself, who is presented to us as a fresh creature of the open fields, full of burning faith and self-confidence, remains that way from the beginning to the end of the play: and she makes a little too obvious her intention not to be reciting a historical rôle and to remain that dear, frank, innocent, inspired child that she is. Yes, Joan, as she really was in her own little individual history, must have been much as Shaw imagined her.

But he seems to look on her once and for all, so to speak, quite without regard for the various situations in which she will meet life in the course of the story.

And she is kept thus simple and unilinear by the author just to bring her airy, refreshing ingenuousness into contrast with the artificial, sophisticated—or, as I say, 'deliberate' or 'constructed'—complexity of her accusers. There is, in other words, something mechanical, fore-ordained, fixed, about her character. Much more free and unobstructed in his natural impulses, much more independent of any deliberate restraints, and accordingly much more 'living' (from my point of view) is the Chaplain, de Stogumber, the truly admirable creation in this drama, and a personage on which Shaw has surely expended a great deal of affectionate effort.

At a certain moment Joan's faith in her 'voices' is shaken. And this charming little creature, hitherto steadfastly confident in the divine inspiration which has many times saved her from death in battle, is suddenly filled with terror at the torment awaiting her. She says she is ready to sign the recantation of all that she has said and done. And she does sign it. But then, on learning from her judges that the sentence of death is only to be changed into a sentence of life imprisonment, she seizes the document in a sudden burst of emotion and tears it to pieces. 'Death is far better than this!' she cries. She could never live without the free air of the fields, the beauty of the green meadows, the warm light of the sun. And she falls fainting into the arms of the executioners, who drag her off to the stake.

At this moment Shaw carries his protagonists to a summit of noble poetry with which any other author would be content; and we may be sure that any other author would have lowered the curtain on this scene. But Shaw cannot resist the pressure and the inspiration of the life he well knows must be surging in such circumstances in his other character—the Chaplain. He rushes on toward a second climax of not less noble poetry, depicting with magnificent elan the mad remorse, the hopeless penitence of Stogumber, thus adding to our first crisis of exquisite anguish another not less potent and overwhelming.

Rarely has George Bernard Shaw attained higher altitudes of poetic emotion than here.

There is a truly great poet in Shaw; but this combative Anglo-Irishman is often willing to forget that he is a poet, so interested is he in being a citizen of his country, or a man of the twentieth-century society, with a number of respectable ideas to defend, a number of sermons to preach, a number of antagonists to rout from the intellectual battlefield. But here, in *Saint Joan*, the poet comes into his own again, with only a subordinate rôle left, as a demanded compensation, to irony and satire. To be sure *Saint Joan* has all the savor and all the attractiveness of Shaw's witty polemical dialogue. But for all of these keen and cutting thrusts to left and right in Shaw's usual style of propaganda, *Saint Joan* is a work of poetry from beginning to end.

This play represents in marvellous fashion what, among so many elements of negation, is the positive element, indeed the fundamental underpinning, in the character, thought and art of this great writer—an outspoken Puritanism, which brooks no go-betweens and no mediations between man and God; a vigorous and independent vital energy, that frees itself restlessly and with joyous scorn from all the stupid and burdensome shackles of habit, routine and tradition, to conquer for itself a natural law more consonant with the poet's own being, and therefore more rational and more sound. Joan, in fact, cries to her judges: 'If the Church orders me to declare that all that I have done and said, that all the visions and revelations I have had were not from God, then that is impossible. I will not declare it for anything in the world. What God made me do, I will never go back on; and what He has commanded, or shall command, I will not fail to do, in spite of any man alive. That is what I mean by impossible. And in case the Church should bid me do anything contrary to the command I have from God, I will not consent to it, no matter what it may be.'

Joan, at bottom, quite without knowing it, and still declaring herself a faithful daughter of the Church, is a Puritan, like Shaw himself—affirming her own life impulse, her unshakable, her even tyrannical will to live, by accepting death itself. Joan, like Shaw, cannot exist without a life that is free and fruitful. When she tears up her recantation in the face of her deaf and blind accusers, she exemplifies the basic germ of Shaw's art, which is the germ also of his spiritual life.

◆ *from* Theory *and* The Tragic Role

By JOHN HARVEY

Theory

The evolution of art forms across the ages has been attributed to just about everything from gigantic political and social upheavals to a lonely artist's yearning to be different. But whatever the origins, every innovation has sought to justify itself as a triumph of truth over convention. . . .

At a time when scholars are outpacing one another to "explain" theatre through its origins, whether of ancient rite or medieval ritual, at a time when even those supposedly frivolous men of the theatre are grimly expounding on the birth of drama, tracing it all the way back to primitive man's impersonation of beast to lure game—at this juncture Jean Anouilh contributes a delightfully impish theory of his own: the meaning of theatre lies in its nature as "play," that simple game of pretending which we all loved as children. Unfortunately, most of us have grown up to find ourselves more often spectators than participants at such games. We now require interpreters to maintain the make-believe before us and dramatists to supply the matter for our increasingly uninventive minds. And, for its own part, the game of theatre continues to press its demands upon us: we can never stop playing, never expect to behold reality incarnate and be passively amused. Rather must we remain willful accomplices to the game, accepting its rules and conventions, freely tasting of it with intellect and feeling.

Active complicity is essential to Anouilh's theatre. "I have always thought that we should make the audience and critics rehearse, too," says the Author in *La Grotte* (*LG*, p. 11). Once Anouilh went so far as to upbraid his critics for an unwillingness to

play *his* game of theatre instead of their own old-fashioned one. The metaphor was not fortuitous when he wrote of himself: "On the one hand, the playwright (who has all our sympathy) and, on the other, the majority of the critics, did not decide to play the same game. What can you do with your colored marbles when all the 'nice' little classmates decide to play house? The recess is a fizzle, naturally."[1]

In a word, then, theatre for Jean Anouilh is a *jeu*; it is a game of pretending, a game of the intellect involving creator, interpreter, and spectator alike. Appropriately, his favorite dramatists of the past have all possessed what he calls a "marvelous sense of play"—Racine, who played with passions; Molière, who played with human foibles; Marivaux, who played with amorists; and last, Giraudoux, whom he regards as the "prince of play." . . .

Pretending is probably as generic to Anouilh the man as to Anouilh the dramatist. Take the word *minimistafia* as it recurs throughout his work. In *Romèo et Jeannette* the heroine, reminiscing about her past, mentions a childhood charm, some red paper called minimistafia, which she used to eat to find courage. Fourteen years later, in *L'Hurluberlu,* Anouilh returned to the same charm but dramatized its powers. The General's son, Toto, admits he is afraid of another boy, and the General gives him some red blotting paper called minimistafia: "When you feel you're going to be afraid, you bite off a little bit." And not only does Toto immediately bite into some before a reproving curate, but later in the play it is the General himself, his noble world having crumbled about him, who asks Toto for a speck. Very solemnly, father and son chew the red paper, seeking in it the courage to continue playing that comedy called life. In a third encounter:

John Harvey, "Theory" and "The Tragic Role," *Anouilh* (New Haven: Yale University Press, 1964), pp. 1, 5–10, 90–96.

[1] *Le Figaro* (Jan. 23, 1952).

We were at Erquy . . . we were in the garden playing cowboys and Indians. He was General Butterfly and I was private Squint-Eye—he had come up with that one. "Private Squint-Eye," he said, "go to the end of the path and see if there are any Indians around." I started, nearly dead with fright, wondering, "How can I protect papa?" He said, "You mustn't be afraid. Here, wait a minute." Taking on a mysterious air, he produced a piece of a red blotter and explained: "It's a minimistafia. I have some more. Whenever you're afraid, you bite off a little bit and chew. See? It's a charm that destroys fear!"

With these words a young French actress has looked back upon her childhood with her father, Jean Anouilh.[2]

Accepting Anouilh's definition of theatre as a game of the intellect, one wonders what bearing it will have on the plays themselves. The author has explained what it meant to him when he first embraced the notion in 1936 during the composition of *Le Voyageur sans bagage.* He no longer felt compelled to "submit" to a subject—that is, to treat it in its simple or rigorous naturalness. He discovered that an artist could and should "toy" with his material, be it in comedy or tragedy. The discovery here was simply the value of distortion—a value never too hard to defend: "A drama that has this toying resembles a musical composition. The toying won't make the drama less true, it won't even reduce its verisimilitude. On the contrary, the drama seems to draw even closer to truth as the author toys more and better with it."[3] Thus spoke Anouilh in an interview in 1936. Fifteen years later, in *La Répétition,* he was still asserting that "theatre's truth is the least natural thing in the world," and defining the playwright's task "to create—by every artifice possible—something truer than truth" (*PB* p. 387). In illustration of these little paradoxes, he has on various occasions recounted the following anecdote: "A child, when he wants to persuade his mother not to send him to school, will pretend to be ill. Generally, he is a poor actor; his mother knows he's not really sick. But when this same child plays at being ill in front of other children, he reveals himself to be a

remarkable actor. This, essentially, is the truth of the theatre." [4]

Pausing before so much truth, we recall that Picasso once dispatched the same notion in his aphorism, "Art is a lie that shows us the truth." The stage, of course, is just a *bigger* lie—so big, say a few writers, that the only truth it can possibly show us is itself: "In the theatre *acting* is the essential truth, a truth more important than the psychological background of events," wrote Giraudoux in his first play.[5] Fortunately, Jean Anouilh escaped the pit of preciosity; he has employed the lie of the stage to convey important truths, truths about life and people.

For the moment we shall not dwell on the exact nature of these truths, but instead turn to the deformations that enclose them. Significantly, Anouilh has not set them in just any lies. Rather, he has framed his psychological and metaphysical truths in the most glaring, hackneyed, and threadbare conventions of the stage. Convinced that theatre is play, he has not shrunk from the consequence that the more obvious, the more accomplished the playing (and the French word for playing, *le jeu,* also means acting), the better the theatre. It follows that moments of supreme truth in these works occur amidst the greatest pertending: it is during a rehearsal (*La Répétition*) of a scene from Marivaux that an aging aristocrat encounters love for the first time in his life; for over an hour the petals of a daisy (*La Marguerite*) are stripped away, revealing love's many facets, but the horrid and naked truth of this passion does not emerge until the final curtain falls on two children playing house.

Theatre for Jean Anouilh means the opening of a big red curtain; and when the curtain has opened, the faces of theatricalism will be varied. Over the years they have included the use of a chorus (*Antigone*), spectacle (*Le Bal des voleurs*), distorted time sequences (*L'Alouette*), distorted history (anachronisms, the Saxon Becket), visible fantasy (the make-believe horseback riding in *L'Alouette*), wildly incredible stock situations (identical twins, long-lost sons), the play within the play (whereby the artificiality of

---

[2] Voldemar Lestienne, "La Grande Fille de Monsieur Anouilh" [Catherine Anouilh], *Elle* (Nov. 6, 1959), p. 58.

[3] *Les Nouvelles littéraires* (Jan. 10, 1946).
[4] *Ibid.* (March 27, 1937).
[5] *Siegfried,* III.2.

the secondary play is legitimized), or even arch reminders to the audience that they are witnessing a show. But these are only the trappings of Anouilh's theatricalism. There is far more behind them.

The Tragic Role

Anouilh's approach to tragedy is essentially a theatrical one. For him the stage is set for tragedy when an individual feels himself rooted to a role, irrevocably trapped in a part. What role? what part? The hero himself is not sure. All he knows is that it is *his* role, and as he plays out this still imperfectly illumined part, the tragedy unfolds. The climax is the epiphany; it is the moment of revelation when the hero finally discovers not his guilt or *hubris* but his very identity, the meaning of his role. And what is this meaning? Invariably, the role reduces itself to a lust for purity, to a thirst for perfection and principle—in a word, to idealism. Tragic circumstances have given the hero a choice: either he may compromise his ideals or else play out this demanding part to the end, to his death. In such a scheme destiny is no longer reflected in the flow and combination of external events; outside circumstances are in fact irrelevant, and all the impressive talk of well-oiled machines and rat traps to the contrary, the only fate weighing upon Anouilh's heroes is that of their own predestined idealism. This is why tragedy itself becomes for the playwright little more than a matter of *distribution,* of casting.

By building his tragedies around the disclosure of a hero's pre-established mission, Anouilh appears to have set himself apart from his contemporaries. True, Giraudoux once advocated in *Electre* the "declaring" of oneself, by which term he meant the acceptation and playing out of one's inner destiny. But there the notion was only incidental, and in later works Giraudoux abandoned it altogether. In fact, both in essays and subsequent drama (*La Guerre de Troie,* in particular) he went on to insist that an *external* destiny was vital to tragedy. He once even defined tragedy as man's perception of this superior force leading him about as by a leash.[1] As for existentialist drama, it would seem that Anouilh's tragedy lies at the furthermost pole from it; for what possibility do Anouilh's heroes have freely to decide what they are or to form themselves through their acts? Even Leonard Pronko, after noting several parallels between Anouilh's and existentialist theatre, admitted that in Anouilh the notion of roles was inherently deterministic. He could describe the freedom enjoyed by the playwright's tragic heroes only as illusory or, at best, confused.[2]

Anouilh's tragedies are often called metaphysical, because they treat man's unacceptable place in the universe. But could they not with equal logic be classified as tragedies of character? The emphasis is placed not on the idealism per se but on the gradual revelation of this idealism to the hero. Conflict anchors itself within each protagonist: having placed his values beyond himself, the hero is impelled at once toward life and toward the ideal; he seeks to reconcile the necessary with the impossible. It would seem that the success or failure of such tragedy should depend to a large extent on the impact of the hero on the spectators. Thus the playwright's principal task should be the fullest possible development of his tragic hero. Nevertheless, it is for this very character development that Anouilh has frequently been censured. Hubert Gignoux, Anouilh's most discerning critic during the Liberation, complained that the personalities of these heroes were more important to him than their tragic destinies: psychological drama stifles the tragedy, he said. . . .

Anouilh's concept of tragedy involves two dramaturgical problems. The first is how to make the fatality of a role so convincing that spectators will not reject it as arbitrary. The second is how, while operating within this closed universe, to make the revelation of a role exciting not only in its suddenness but in its context of grandeur and mortal struggle. Basically, the author's problem has been to reconcile predestination with dramatic disclosure: How can the hero be trapped in his part and not know what that part is? It is a tricky problem and one that Anouilh has attempted to resolve through a number of expedients.

Just which plays are the tragedies? None

---

[1] "Bellac et la tragédie," *Littérature* (Paris, 1941), p. 297.
[2] Pronko, *Anouilh,* pp. 60–75.

is so designated in the collected works, though *Antigone* was originally so labeled. Besides *Antigone*, we should include *Médée, L'Alouette, Becket,* and the fragment *Oreste.* Immediately obvious is a recourse to figures from myth and history, figures whose fates are readily acceptable as foredoomed.

Although it was not published until 1945, *Oreste* is generally held to be anterior to *Antigone.* The author has trapped the characters of his first tragedy in a Sartre-like hell: already cognizant of the outcome and significance of their acts, they are doomed to replay their lives forever. As everything has already happened, characters and spectators alike freely accept the roles as inevitable. But by the same token, the characters are so firmly rooted in their present condition that they are unable to break away and relive their pasts. Consequently, the slightest dramatic disclosure is inconceivable: Oreste cannot, in the heat of confrontation, suddenly discover that he will kill (or has just killed) Egisthe not out of revenge but out of desire for purity. The fragment is a dead end.

In *L'Alouette* the characters are again beyond their lives in some vague, stagy afterworld, represented by an equally vague and theatrical setting. As the curtain rises on a cast gathering up properties left behind from an earlier performance, the spectator immediately understands that he is witnessing a re-enactment; the tragedy is inescapable. Unlike the cast of *Oreste,* these people are effective actors: they have the capacity to escape their present condition and to lose themselves in scenes from their past. Thus they actually relive for the audience that dramatically charged moment of revelation. The dramatist's technical knowhow had evidently blossomed in the intervening years,

for the utter freedom of treatment here and the graceful interplay of time and mood are overpowering. Simple narration, lighting changes, strong situations, dreams—anything may suddenly lift the spectator from one world and plunge him into another, more fanciful or more real, more joyous or more rending. The very ambiguity of time is turned to advantage. Early in the play it is implied that *L'Alouette* is taking place just after Jeanne's abjuration, while she is still in prison in Rouen. The object is to present the heroine's rise and fall as inevitable, and to approach the climax—that is, her retraction and her martyrdom—as part of the immediate, dramatic present. But even this present is far from a naturalistic one. Numerous interpolations and contradictions have already set the play in some fairy-tale world beyond reality, where theatricalism and ambiguity compound to render the lark's fate inevitable.[3]

If the climax of *L'Alouette* has any weaknesses, they are less of form than of content: Anouilh did not find a very ennobling motif for Jeanne's retraction. He fitted the scene into standard mold of a protagonist suddenly discovering the meaning of his role, but he did so on a disappointingly homey level. After she has abjured, Jeanne is visited in her cell by Warwick, and the two begin musing about her future. Jeanne is depressed at the picture of herself growing old, fat, and complacent. She realizes now—but in retrospect, thus not very forcefully—that her true self is the maiden warrior. To recapture this true self and to hold it forever, she retracts her confession and invites death. Certainly, Anouilh's Jeanne d'Arc is a refreshing figure; but her revelation is less glorious than ingenious. The dramatist found no better motive for his lark's firmness of principle than a feminine fear of aging. . . .

[3] For example, Cauchon: "In the course of this trial"; Cauchon: "We're not at the trial"; Jeanne: "You're confusing everything. At the beginning when I hear my Voices or at the end of the trial . . . when I abjured and then took it back"; Warwick: "Evidently, in reality it didn't happen quite like

that"; etc. (*PC*, pp. 16–17, 20, 23 82). The air of fatality is furthered by an occasional direct remainder, for example: "There's nothing we can do . . . We can only play our parts, each of us his own, good or bad, the way they're written, and in our turn" (*ibid.*, p. 30).

◆◆◆ Part Five

IBSEN

CHEKHOV

WILLIAMS

BECKETT

I'll be through with the job ... the school house, and tonight ...hing the steamer back to town. *...utters*). *Bon voyage.*

...D. Thank you, my child. They're ...ting the new Orphanage here to-...w, and there'll be celebrations, with ...icating liquor. And no one shall say ...acob Engstrand that he can't turn his ...k on temptation. (REGINA *laughs scorn-...ly*.) Yes, well, there'll be a lot of tip-...p people coming here tomorrow. Pastor ...anders is expected from town.

...INA. He's arriving today.

...GSTRAND. Well, there you are. And I'm ...damned if I'm going to risk getting into ...his bad books.

...NA. Oh, so that's it.

...STRAND. What do you mean?

...EGINA (*looks knowingly at him*). What ...are you trying to fool the Pastor into this ...time?

...NGSTRAND. Hush! Are you mad? Me try to fool Pastor Manders? Oh no, Pastor Manders is much too good a friend to me for that. Now what I wanted to talk to you about is this. I'm going back home tonight.

REGINA. The sooner you go the better.

ENGSTRAND. Yes, but I want to take you with me, Regina.

REGINA (*her jaw drops*). You want to take me—? What are you talking about?

ENGSTRAND. I want to take you with me, I say.

REGINA (*scornfully*). Home with you? Not likely I won't!

ENGSTRAND. Oh, we'll see, we'll see.

REGINA. You bet your life we'll see. You expect me to go back and live with you? In that house? After Mrs. Alving's brought me up in her own home, treats me as though I was one of the family? Get out!

ENGSTRAND. What the hell's this? Are you setting yourself up against your father, my girl?

REGINA (*mutters without looking at him*). You've said often enough that I'm no concern of yours.

ENGSTRAND. Oh—you don't want to take any notice of that—

REGINA. What about all the times you've

sworn at me and called me a—oh, *mon dieu!*

ENGSTRAND. May God strike me dead if I ever used such a vile word!

REGINA. Oh, I know what word you used.

ENGSTRAND. Yes, but that was only when I wasn't myself. Hm. The temptations of this world are manifold, Regina.

REGINA. Ugh!

ENGSTRAND. And when your mother was being difficult. I had to think up some way to nark her. She was always acting the fine lady. (*Mimics.*) "Let me go, Engstrand! Stop it! I've been in service for three years with Chamberlain Alving at Rosenvold, and don't you forget it!" (*Laughs.*) She never could forget the Captain had been made a Chamberlain when she was working for him.

REGINA. Poor Mother! You killed her soon enough with your bullying.

ENGSTRAND (*uncomfortably*). That's right, blame me for everything.

REGINA (*turns away and mutters beneath her breath*). Ugh! And that leg!

ENGSTRAND. What's that you said, my child?

REGINA. *Pied de mouton!*

ENGSTRAND. What's that, English?

REGINA. Yes.

ENGSTRAND. Ah, well. They've made a scholar of you out here anyway, and that'll come in handy now, Regina.

REGINA (*after a short silence*). And—what was it you wanted me for in town?

ENGSTRAND. Fancy asking such a question! What should a father want from his only child? Aren't I a lonely, forsaken widower?

REGINA. Oh, don't try to fool me with that rubbish. What do you want me up there for?

ENGSTRAND. Well, it's like this. I'm thinking of starting out on something new.

REGINA (*sniffs*). You've tried that often enough. And you've always made a mess of it.

ENGSTRAND. Yes, but this time, you'll see, Regina! God rot me if I don't—!

REGINA (*stamps her foot*). Stop swearing!

ENGSTRAND. Ssh, ssh! How right you are, my child! Now what I wanted to say was this.

◆◆ Ghosts

By HENRIK IBSEN

Translated by Michael Meyer

Characters

MRS. HELEN ALVING, widow of Captain Alving, late Chamberlain to the King.
OSWALD ALVING, her son, a painter.
PASTOR MANDERS.
ENGSTRAND, a carpenter.
REGINA ENGSTRAND, Mrs. Alving's maid.

The action takes place on MRS. ALVING'S *country estate by a large fjord in Western Norway.*

ACT ONE

A spacious garden-room, with a door in the left-hand wall and two doors in the right-hand wall. In the centre of the room is a round table with chairs around it; on the table are books, magazines and newspapers. Downstage left is a window, in front of which is a small sofa with a sewing-table by it. Backstage the room opens out into a slightly narrower conservatory, with walls of large panes of glass. In the right-hand wall of the conservatory is a door leading down to the garden. Through the glass wall a gloomy fjord landscape is discernible, veiled by steady rain.

Henrik Ibsen, "Ghosts," in *Ghosts and Three Other Plays,* trans. by Michael Meyer (Garden City, N.Y.: Doubleday, 1966), pp. 124–198.

ENGSTRAND, *a carpe*
the garden door. His
crooked; under the sol
fixed a block of wood. RE
empty garden syringe in he
his entry.

REGINA (*keeping her voice low*). Wh
you want? Stay where you are! Yo
dripping wet!
ENGSTRAND. It is God's blessed rain, my chil
REGINA. The Devil's damned rain, more like.
ENGSTRAND. Why, Regina, the way you talk!
(*Limps a few steps into the room.*) What
I wanted to say is—
REGINA. Here, you! Don't make such a noise
with that foot. The young master's asleep
upstairs.
ENGSTRAND. In bed—at this hour? Why, the
day's half gone.
REGINA. That's none of your business.
ENGSTRAND. I was out drinking last night—
REGINA. I'm sure.
ENGSTRAND. We are but flesh and blood,
my child—
REGINA (*drily*). Quite.
ENGSTRAND. And the temptations of this world
are manifold. But God is my witness; I
was at my bench by half past five this
morning.
REGINA. Yes, yes. Come on now, clear off.
I don't want to be caught having a rendez-
vous with you.
ENGSTRAND. You don't what?
REGINA. I don't want anyone to see you here.
Come on, go away, get out.
ENGSTRAND (*comes a few steps nearer*). Not
before I've had a word with you. This

468

afternoon
down a
I'm cat
REGINA (
ENGSTRA
dedica
morr
into
of
bac
fu
to
N
RE
N
C

afternoon I'll be through with the job down at the school house, and tonight I'm catching the steamer back to town.

REGINA (*mutters*). *Bon voyage.*

ENGSTRAND. Thank you, my child. They're dedicating the new Orphanage here to-morrow, and there'll be celebrations, with intoxicating liquor. And no one shall say of Jacob Engstrand that he can't turn his back on temptation. (REGINA *laughs scorn-fully.*) Yes, well, there'll be a lot of tip-top people coming here tomorrow. Pastor Manders is expected from town.

REGINA. He's arriving today.

ENGSTRAND. Well, there you are. And I'm damned if I'm going to risk getting into his bad books.

REGINA. Oh, so that's it.

ENGSTRAND. What do you mean?

REGINA (*looks knowingly at him*). What are you trying to fool the Pastor into this time?

ENGSTRAND. Hush! Are you mad? Me try to fool Pastor Manders? Oh no, Pastor Man-ders is much too good a friend to me for that. Now what I wanted to talk to you about is this. I'm going back home tonight.

REGINA. The sooner you go the better.

ENGSTRAND. Yes, but I want to take you with me, Regina.

REGINA (*her jaw drops*). You want to take *me—*? What are you talking about?

ENGSTRAND. I want to take you with me, I say.

REGINA (*scornfully*). Home with you? Not likely I won't!

ENGSTRAND. Oh, we'll see, we'll see.

REGINA. You bet your life we'll see. You expect me to go back and live with you? In that house? After Mrs. Alving's brought me up in her own home, treats me as though I was one of the family? Get out!

ENGSTRAND. What the hell's this? Are you setting yourself up against your father, my girl?

REGINA (*mutters without looking at him*). You've said often enough that I'm no concern of yours.

ENGSTRAND. Oh—you don't want to take any notice of that—

REGINA. What about all the times you've

sworn at me and called me a—oh, *mon dieu!*

ENGSTRAND. May God strike me dead if I ever used such a vile word!

REGINA. Oh, I know what word you used.

ENGSTRAND. Yes, but that was only when I wasn't myself. Hm. The temptations of this world are manifold, Regina.

REGINA. Ugh!

ENGSTRAND. And when your mother was be-ing difficult. I had to think up some way to nark her. She was always acting the fine lady. (*Mimics.*) "Let me go, Eng-strand! Stop it! I've been in service for three years with Chamberlain Alving at Rosenvold, and don't you forget it!" (*Laughs.*) She never could forget the Cap-tain had been made a Chamberlain when she was working for him.

REGINA. Poor Mother! You killed her soon enough with your bullying.

ENGSTRAND (*uncomfortably*). That's right, blame me for everything.

REGINA (*turns away and mutters beneath her breath*). Ugh! And that leg!

ENGSTRAND. What's that you said, my child?

REGINA. *Pied de mouton!*

ENGSTRAND. What's that, English?

REGINA. Yes.

ENGSTRAND. Ah, well. They've made a scholar of you out here anyway, and that'll come in handy now, Regina.

REGINA (*after a short silence*). And—what was it you wanted me for in town?

ENGSTRAND. Fancy asking such a question! What should a father want from his only child? Aren't I a lonely, forsaken widower?

REGINA. Oh, don't try to fool me with that rubbish. What do you want me up there for?

ENGSTRAND. Well, it's like this. I'm thinking of starting out on something new.

REGINA (*sniffs*). You've tried that often enough. And you've always made a mess of it.

ENGSTRAND. Yes, but this time, you'll see, Regina! God rot me if I don't—!

REGINA (*stamps her foot*). Stop swearing!

ENGSTRAND. Ssh, ssh! How right you are, my child! Now what I wanted to say was this.

Ghosts

By HENRIK IBSEN

Translated by Michael Meyer

Characters

MRS. HELEN ALVING, widow of Captain Alving, late Chamberlain to the King.

OSWALD ALVING, her son, a painter.

PASTOR MANDERS.

ENGSTRAND, a carpenter.

REGINA ENGSTRAND, Mrs. Alving's maid.

The action takes place on MRS. ALVING'S *country estate by a large fjord in Western Norway.*

ACT ONE

A spacious garden-room, with a door in the left-hand wall and two doors in the right-hand wall. In the centre of the room is a round table with chairs around it; on the table are books, magazines and newspapers. Downstage left is a window, in front of which is a small sofa with a sewing-table by it. Backstage the room opens out into a slightly narrower conservatory, with walls of large panes of glass. In the right-hand wall of the conservatory is a door leading down to the garden. Through the glass wall a gloomy fjord landscape is discernible, veiled by steady rain.

Henrik Ibsen, "Ghosts," in *Ghosts and Three Other Plays*, trans. by Michael Meyer (Garden City, N.Y.: Doubleday, 1966), pp. 124–198.

ENGSTRAND, *a carpenter, is standing at the garden door. His left leg is slightly crooked; under the sole of his boot is fixed a block of wood.* REGINA, *with an empty garden syringe in her hand, bars his entry.*

REGINA (*keeping her voice low*). What do you want? Stay where you are! You're dripping wet!

ENGSTRAND. It is God's blessed rain, my child.

REGINA. The Devil's damned rain, more like.

ENGSTRAND. Why, Regina, the way you talk! (*Limps a few steps into the room.*) What I wanted to say is—

REGINA. Here, you! Don't make such a noise with that foot. The young master's asleep upstairs.

ENGSTRAND. In bed—at this hour? Why, the day's half gone.

REGINA. That's none of your business.

ENGSTRAND. I was out drinking last night—

REGINA. I'm sure.

ENGSTRAND. We are but flesh and blood, my child—

REGINA (*drily*). Quite.

ENGSTRAND. And the temptations of this world are manifold. But God is my witness; I was at my bench by half past five this morning.

REGINA. Yes, yes. Come on now, clear off. I don't want to be caught having a rendezvous with you.

ENGSTRAND. You don't what?

REGINA. I don't want anyone to see you here. Come on, go away, get out.

ENGSTRAND (*comes a few steps nearer*). Not before I've had a word with you. This

I've put quite a bit of money aside out of the work I've been doing at this new Orphanage.

REGINA. Have you? Good for you.

ENGSTRAND. Well, there ain't much for a man to spend his money on out here in the country, is there?

REGINA. Well? Go on.

ENGSTRAND. Yes, well, you see, so I thought I'd put the money into something that might bring me in a bit. A kind of home for sailors—

REGINA (*disgusted*). Oh, my God!

ENGSTRAND. A real smart place, you understand—not one of those low waterfront joints. No, damn it, this is going to be for captains and officers and—tip-top people, you understand.

REGINA. And I'm to—?

ENGSTRAND. You're going to help me. Just for appearance's sake, of course. You won't have to work hard, my child. You can fix your own hours.

REGINA. I see!

ENGSTRAND. Well, we've got to have a bit of skirt on show, I mean that's obvious. Got to give them a little fun in the evenings—dancing and singing and so forth. You must remember these men are wandering mariners lost on the ocean of life. (*Comes closer.*) Now don't be stupid and make things difficult for yourself, Regina. What can you make of yourself out here? What good is it going to do you, all this fine education Mrs. Alving's given you? I hear you're going to look after the orphans down the road. Is that what you want to do? Are you so anxious to ruin your health for those filthy brats?

REGINA. No, if things work out the way I— Ah well, they might. They might.

ENGSTRAND. What are you talking about?

REGINA. Never you mind. This money you've managed to save out here—is it a lot?

ENGSTRAND. All told I'd say it comes to between thirty-five and forty pounds.

REGINA. Not bad.

ENGSTRAND. Enough to make a start with, my child.

REGINA. Aren't you going to give me any of it?

ENGSTRAND. Not damn likely I'm not.

REGINA. Aren't you even going to send me a new dress?

ENGSTRAND. You just come back to town and set up with me, and you'll get dresses enough.

REGINA. (*laughs scornfully*). I could do *that* on my own, if I wanted to.

ENGSTRAND. No, Regina, you need a father's hand to guide you. There's a nice house I can get in Little Harbour Street. They don't want much cash on the nail; and we could turn it into a sort of—well—sailors' mission.

REGINA. But I don't want to live with *you!* I don't want anything to do with you. Come on, get out.

ENGSTRAND. You wouldn't need to stay with me for long, my child. More's the pity. If you play your cards properly. The way you've blossomed out these last few years, you—

REGINA. Yes?

ENGSTRAND. You wouldn't have to wait long before some nice officer—perhaps even a captain—

REGINA. I don't want to marry any of them. Sailors haven't any *savoir vivre.*

ENGSTRAND. Haven't any what?

REGINA. I know sailors. There's no future in marrying them.

ENGSTRAND. All right then, don't marry them. You can do just as well without. (*Lowers his voice.*) The Englishman—him with the yacht—fifty pounds he paid out—and she wasn't any prettier than you.

REGINA (*goes towards him*). Get out!

ENGSTRAND (*shrinks*). Now, now, you wouldn't hit your own father!

REGINA. Wouldn't I? You say another word about mother, and you'll see! Get out, I tell you! (*Pushes him towards the garden door.*) And don't slam the door. Young Mr. Alving's—

ENGSTRAND. Yes, I know. He's asleep. Why do you fuss so much about him? (*More quietly.*) Ah-ha! You wouldn't be thinking of *him*, would you?

REGINA. Out, and be quick about it! You're out of your mind. No, not that way. Here's

Pastor Manders. Go out through the kitchen.

ENGSTRAND (*goes right*). All right, I'll go. But you ask *him*—his Reverence. He'll tell you what a child's duty is to its father. I am your father, you know, whatever you say. I can prove it from the parish register.

He goes out through the second door, which REGINA *has opened and closed behind him. She looks quickly at herself in the mirror, dusts herself with her handkerchief, and straightens her collar; then she begins to water the flowers.* PASTOR MANDERS, *in an overcoat and carrying an umbrella, and with a small travelling bag on a strap from his shoulder, enters through the garden door into the conservatory.*

MANDERS. Good morning, Miss Engstrand.

REGINA (*turns in surprise and delight*). Why, Pastor Manders! Has the boat come already?

MANDERS. It arrived a few minutes ago. (*Enters the garden room.*) Very tiresome this rain we're having.

REGINA (*follows him*). A blessing for the farmers, though, sir.

MANDERS. Yes, you are right. We city people tend to forget that. (*Begins to take off his overcoat.*)

REGINA. Oh, please let me help you! There. Oh, it's soaking! I'll hang it up in the hall. Oh, and the umbrella! I'll open it out to let it dry.

She takes the coat and umbrella out through the other door, right. MANDERS *takes his bag from his shoulder and puts it and his hat on a chair. Meanwhile* REGINA *comes back.*

MANDERS. Ah, it's good to be under a dry roof again. Well, I trust all is well here?

REGINA. Yes, thank you, sir.

MANDERS. Everyone very busy, I suppose, getting ready for tomorrow?

REGINA. Oh, yes, there are one or two things to be done.

MANDERS. Mrs. Alving is at home, I hope?

REGINA. Oh, dear me, yes, she's just gone upstairs to make a cup of chocolate for the young master.

MANDERS. Ah, yes. I heard when I got off the boat that Oswald had returned.

REGINA. Yes, he arrived the day before yesterday. We hadn't expected him until today.

MANDERS. In good health and spirits, I trust?

REGINA. Oh yes, thank you, I think so. He felt dreadfully tired after his journey, though. He came all the way from Paris in one go—*par rapide*. I think he's having a little sleep just now, so we'd better talk just a tiny bit quietly.

MANDERS. Ssh! We'll be like mice!

REGINA (*moves an armchair near the table*). Now sit down and make yourself comfortable, sir. (*He sits. She puts a footstool under his feet.*) There now. Are you quite comfortable?

MANDERS. Thank you, thank you; yes, very comfortable. (*Looks at her.*) Do you know, Miss Engstrand, I really believe you've grown since I last saw you.

REGINA. Do you think so? Madam says I've rounded out a bit too.

MANDERS. Rounded out? Well, yes, a little perhaps. Not too much.

Short pause.

REGINA. Shall I tell madam you've come?

MANDERS. Thank you, there's no hurry, my dear child. Er—tell me now, Regina, how is your father getting on out here?

REGINA. Thank you, Pastor, he's doing very well.

MANDERS. He came to see me when he was last in town.

REGINA. No, did he really? He's always so happy when he gets a chance to speak to you, sir.

MANDERS. And you go down and see him quite often?

REGINA. I? Oh yes, of course—whenever I get the chance—

MANDERS. Your father hasn't a very strong character, Miss Engstrand. He badly needs a hand to guide him.

REGINA. Oh—yes, I dare say you're right there.

MANDERS. He needs to have someone near him whom he is fond of, and whose judgment he respects. He admitted it quite openly the last time he visited me.

REGINA. Yes, he said something of the sort to me too. But I don't know whether Mrs. Alving will want to lose me, especially now we've the new Orphanage to look after. Besides, I'd hate to leave Mrs. Alving. She's always been so kind to me.

MANDERS. But my dear girl, a daughter's duty! Naturally we would have to obtain your mistress's permission first.

REGINA. But I don't know that it'd be right and proper for me to keep house for an unmarried man at my age.

MANDERS. What! But my dear Miss Engstrand, this is your own father we're talking about!

REGINA. Yes—but all the same—Oh yes, if it was a nice house, with a real gentleman—

MANDERS. But my dear Regina—!

REGINA. Someone I could feel affection for and look up to as a father—

MANDERS. But my dear good child—!

REGINA. Oh, I'd so love to go and live in the city. Out here it's so dreadfully lonely—and you know, don't you, sir, what it means to be all alone in the world? And I'm quick and willing—I think I can say that. Oh, Pastor Manders, don't you know of a place I could go to?

MANDERS. I? No, I'm afraid I don't know of anyone at all.

REGINA. Oh, but do please think of me if ever you should, dear, dear Pastor Manders.

MANDERS (*gets up*). Yes, yes, Miss Engstrand, I certainly will.

REGINA. You see, if only I—

MANDERS. Will you be so good as to call Mrs. Alving for me?

REGINA. Yes, sir. I'll call her at once.

She goes out left. PASTOR MANDERS *walks up and down the room a couple of times, stands for a moment upstage with his hands behind his back and looks out into the garden. Then he comes back to the part of the room where the table is, picks up a book and glances at its title page, starts and looks at some of the others.*

MANDERS. Hm! I see!

MRS. ALVING *enters through the door left. She is followed by* REGINA, *who at once goes out through the door downstage right.*

MRS. ALVING (*holds out her hand*). Welcome to Rosenvold, Pastor.

MANDERS. Good morning, Mrs. Alving. Well, I've kept my promise.

MRS. ALVING. Punctual as always.

MANDERS. But you know it wasn't easy for me to get away. All these blessed boards and committees I sit on—

MRS. ALVING. All the kinder of you to arrive in such good time. Now we can get our business settled before lunch. But where's your luggage?

MANDERS (*quickly*). My portmanteau is down at the village store. I shall be sleeping there.

MRS. ALVING (*represses a smile*). I can't persuade you to spend a night in my house even now?

MANDERS. No, no, Mrs. Alving—it's very kind of you, but I'll sleep down there as usual. It's so convenient for when I go on board again.

MRS. ALVING. As you please. Though I really think two old people like you and me could—

MANDERS. Bless me, you're joking. But of course you must be very happy. The great day tomorrow—and you have Oswald home again.

MRS. ALVING. Yes, you can imagine how happy that makes me. It's over two years since he was home last. And now he's promised to stay with me the whole winter.

MANDERS. No, has he really? Well, that's nice of him. He knows his filial duty. I fancy life in Paris and Rome must offer altogether different attractions.

MRS. ALVING. Yes, but his home is here; and his mother. Ah, my dear boy; he loves his mother, God bless him.

MANDERS. It would be sad indeed if distance and dabbling in art and such things should blunt his natural affections.

MRS. ALVING. It certainly would. But luckily there's nothing wrong with him. I'll be amused to see whether you recognize him again. He'll be down later; he's upstairs now taking a little rest on the sofa. But please sit down, my dear Pastor.

MANDERS. Thank you. Er—you're sure this is a convenient moment—?

MRS. ALVING. Certainly.

She sits down at the table.

MANDERS. Good. Well, then— (*Goes over to the chair on which his bag is lying, takes out a sheaf of papers, sits down on the opposite side of the table and looks for a space to put down the papers.*) Well, to begin with, here are the— (*Breaks off.*) Tell me, Mrs. Alving, how do *these* books come to be here?

MRS. ALVING. Those books? I'm reading them.

MANDERS. You read writings of this kind?

MRS. ALVING. Certainly I do.

MANDERS. And does this kind of reading make you feel better or happier?

MRS. ALVING. I think they make me feel more secure.

MANDERS. How extraordinary! In what way?

MRS. ALVING. Well, they sort of explain and confirm many things that puzzle me. Yes, that's what's so strange, Pastor Manders— there isn't really anything new in these books—there's nothing in them that most people haven't already thought for themselves. It's only that most people either haven't fully realized it, or they won't admit it.

MANDERS. Well, dear God! Do you seriously believe that most people—?

MRS. ALVING. Yes, I do.

MANDERS. But surely not in this country? Not people like us?

MRS. ALVING. Oh, yes. People like us too.

MANDERS. Well, really! I must say—!

MRS. ALVING. But what do you object to in these books?

MANDERS. Object to? You surely don't imagine I spend my time studying such publications?

MRS. ALVING. In other words, you've no idea what you're condemning?

MANDERS. I've read quite enough about these writings to disapprove of them.

MRS. ALVING. Don't you think you ought to form your own opinion—?

MANDERS. My dear Mrs. Alving, there are many occasions in life when one must rely on the judgment of others. That is the way things are and it is good that it should be so. If it were not so, what would become of society?

MRS. ALVING. Yes, yes. You may be right.

MANDERS. Of course I don't deny there may be quite a lot that is attractive about these writings. And I cannot exactly blame you for wishing to keep informed of these intellectual movements in the great world outside about which one hears so much. After all, you have allowed your son to wander there for a number of years. But—

MRS. ALVING. But—?

MANDERS (*lowers his voice*). But one does not have to talk about it, Mrs. Alving. One really does not need to account to all and sundry for what one reads and thinks within one's own four walls.

MRS. ALVING. No, of course not. I quite agree with you.

MANDERS. Remember the duty you owe to this Orphanage which you decided to found at a time when your attitude towards spiritual matters was quite different from what it is now—as far as *I* can judge.

MRS. ALVING. Yes, yes, that's perfectly true. But it was the Orphanage we were going to—

MANDERS. It was the Orphanage we were going to discuss, yes. But—be discreet, dear Mrs. Alving! And now let us turn to our business. (*Opens the packet and takes out some of the papers.*) You see these?

MRS. ALVING. Are those the deeds?

MANDERS. All of them. Ready and completed. As you can imagine, it's been no easy task to get them all through in time. I really had to get out my whip. The authorities are almost painfully conscientious when you want a decision from them. But here we have them nevertheless. (*Leafs through them.*) Here is the executed conveyance of the farmstead named Solvik in the Manor of Rosenvold, with its newly constructed buildings, schoolrooms, staff accommodation and chapel. And here is the settlement of the endowment and the trust deed of the institution. Look. (*Reads.*) Deed of trust for the Captain Alving Memorial Home.

MRS. ALVING (*stares for a long while at the paper*). So there it is.

MANDERS. I thought I'd say Captain rather than Chamberlain. Captain looks less ostentatious.

MRS. ALVING. Yes, yes, as you think best.

MANDERS. And here is the bankbook for the capital which has been placed on deposit to cover the running expenses of the Orphanage.

MRS. ALVING. Thank you; but I think it would be more convenient if you kept that, if you don't mind.

MANDERS. Certainly, certainly. I think we may as well leave the money on deposit to begin with. Admittedly the interest isn't very attractive—four per cent with six months notice of withdrawal. If we could obain a good mortgage later—of course it would have to be a first mortgage and of unimpeachable security—we might reconsider the matter.

MRS. ALVING. Yes, well, dear Pastor Manders, you know best about all that.

MANDERS. Anyway, I'll keep my eyes open. But now there's another matter I've several times been meaning to ask you about.

MRS. ALVING. And what is that?

MANDERS. Should the buildings of the Orphanage be insured or not.

MRS. ALVING. Yes, of course they must be insured.

MANDERS. Ah, but wait a minute, Mrs. Alving. Let us consider this question a little more closely.

MRS. ALVING. Everything I have is insured—buildings, furniture, crops, livestock.

MANDERS. Naturally. On your own estate. I do the same, of course. But you see, this is quite a different matter. The Orphanage is, so to speak, to be consecrated to a higher purpose.

MRS. ALVING. Yes, but—

MANDERS. As far as I personally am concerned, I see nothing offensive in securing ourselves against all eventualities—

MRS. ALVING. Well, I certainly don't.

MANDERS. But what is the feeling among the local people out here? You can judge that better than I can.

MRS. ALVING. The feeling?

MANDERS. Are there many people with a right to an opinion—I mean, people who really have the right to hold an opinion—who might take offence?

MRS. ALVING. Well, what do you mean by people who have the right to hold an opinion?

MANDERS. Oh, I am thinking chiefly of people sufficiently independent and influential to make it impossible for one to ignore their opinions altogether.

MRS. ALVING. There are quite a few people like that who I suppose might take offence—

MANDERS. You see! In town, we have a great many such people. Followers of other denominations. People might very easily come to the conclusion that neither you nor I have sufficient trust in the ordinance of a Higher Power.

MRS. ALVING. But my dear Pastor, as long as you yourself—

MANDERS. I know, I know—my conscience is clear, that is true. But all the same, we couldn't prevent a false and unfavourable interpretation being placed on our action. And that might well adversely influence the purpose for which the Orphanage has been dedicated.

MRS. ALVING. If that were so I—

MANDERS. And I can't altogether close my eyes to the difficult—I might even say deeply embarrassing—position in which I might find myself. Among influential circles in town there is a great interest in the cause of the Orphanage. After all, it is to serve the town as well, and it is hoped that it may considerably ease the burden of the ratepayers in respect to the poor. But since

I have acted as your adviser and been in charge of the business side I must admit I fear certain over-zealous persons might in the first place direct their attacks against me—

MRS. ALVING. Well, you mustn't lay yourself open to that.

MANDERS. Not to speak of the attacks which would undoubtedly be launched against me in certain newspapers and periodicals, and which—

MRS. ALVING. Enough, dear Pastor Manders. That settles it.

MANDERS. Then you do not wish the Orphanage to be insured?

MRS. ALVING. No. We will forget about it.

MANDERS (*leans back in his chair*). But suppose an accident should occur—you never can tell—would you be able to make good the damage?

MRS. ALVING. No, quite frankly I couldn't.

MANDERS. Well, but you know, Mrs. Alving, this is really rather a serious responsibility we are taking on our shoulders.

MRS. ALVING. But do you think we have any alternative?

MANDERS. No, that's just it. I don't think there is any real alternative. We must not lay ourselves open to misinterpretation. And we have no right to antagonize public opinion.

MRS. ALVING. At any rate you, as a clergyman, must not.

MANDERS. And I really think we must believe that such an institution will have luck on its side—nay, that it stands under special protection.

MRS. ALVING. Let us hope so, Pastor Manders.

MANDERS. Shall we take the risk, then?

MRS. ALVING. Yes, let us.

MANDERS. Good. As you wish. (*Makes a note.*) No insurance, then.

MRS. ALVING. It's strange you happened to mention this today—

MANDERS. I've often thought of raising the matter with you—

MRS. ALVING. Because yesterday we almost had a fire down there.

MANDERS. What!

MRS. ALVING. Well, it was nothing much really. Some shavings caught fire in the carpentry shop.

MANDERS. Where Engstrand works?

MRS. ALVING. Yes. They say he's very careless with matches.

MANDERS. He's got so many things to think about, poor man—so many temptations. Thank heaven I hear he has now resolved to lead a virtuous life.

MRS. ALVING. Oh? Who says so?

MANDERS. He has assured me so himself. And he's a good worker.

MRS. ALVING. Oh, yes—as long as he keeps sober—

MANDERS. Yes, that is a grievous weakness! But he is often compelled to yield to it because of his bad leg, he says. The last time he was in town I was quite touched. He came to see me and thanked me so sincerely because I had got him this job here, so that he could be near Regina.

MRS. ALVING. I don't think he sees her very often.

MANDERS. Oh yes, he told me himself. He talks to her every day.

MRS. ALVING. Oh, well. Possibly.

MANDERS. He is so conscious of his need to have someone who can restrain him when temptation presents itself. That is what is so lovable about Jacob Engstrand, that he comes to one like a child and accuses himself and admits his weakness. The last time he came up and talked to me—Tell me, Mrs. Alving, if it were absolutely vital for the poor man to have Regina back to live with him again—

MRS. ALVING (*rises swiftly*). Regina!

MANDERS. You must not oppose it.

MRS. ALVING. I certainly shall. Anyway, Regina is going to work at the Orphanage.

MANDERS. But don't forget, he is her father—

MRS. ALVING. Oh, I know very well the kind of father he's been to her. No, I shall never consent to her going back to him.

MANDERS (*rises*). But my dear Mrs. Alving, you mustn't get so emotional about it. You seem quite frightened. It's very sad the way you misjudge this man Engstrand.

MRS. ALVING (*more quietly*). Never mind that. I have taken Regina into my house, and here she shall stay. (*Listens*) Hush now, dear Pastor Manders, let's not say anything more about it. (*Happily.*) Listen! There's Oswald coming downstairs. Now we will think of nothing but him.

OSWALD ALVING, *in a light overcoat, with his hat in his hand and smoking a big meerschaum pipe, enters through the door left.*

OSWALD (*stops in the doorway*). Oh, I'm sorry—I thought you were in the study. (*Comes closer.*) Good morning, Pastor.

MANDERS (*stares*). Why—! Most extraordinary!

MRS. ALVING. Well, Pastor Manders, what do you think of him?

MANDERS. I think—I think—! But is this really—?

OSWALD. Yes, this is the Prodigal Son, Pastor.

MANDERS. Oh, but my dear young friend—!

OSWALD. Well, the son, anyway.

MRS. ALVING. Oswald is thinking of the time when you used to be so strongly opposed to his becoming a painter.

MANDERS. Many a step which to human eyes seems dubious often turns out— (*Shakes his hand.*) Anyway, welcome, welcome! My dear Oswald—! I trust you will allow me to call you by your Christian name?

OSWALD. What else?

MANDERS. Excellent. Now, my dear Oswald, what I was going to say was this. You mustn't think I condemn the artistic profession out of hand. I presume there are many who succeed in keeping the inner man untarnished in that profession too.

OSWALD. Let us hope so.

MRS. ALVING (*happily*). I know one person who has remained pure both inwardly and outwardly. Just look at him, Pastor Manders.

OSWALD (*wanders across the room*). Yes, yes, Mother dear, please.

MANDERS. Unquestionably—there's no denying that. Besides, you have begun to acquire a name now. The newspapers often speak of you, and in most flattering terms. Well—that is to say, I don't seem to have read about you quite so much lately.

OSWALD (*by the flowers upstage*). I haven't done so much painting lately.

MRS. ALVING. Even painters have to rest now and then.

MANDERS. I suppose so. To prepare themselves and conserve their energies for some great work.

OSWALD. Yes. Mother, shall we be eating soon?

MRS. ALVING. In about half an hour. He still enjoys his food, thank heaven.

MANDERS. And his tobacco, I see.

OSWALD. I found Father's pipe upstairs in the bedroom, so I—

MANDERS. Of course!

MRS. ALVING. What do you mean?

MANDERS. When Oswald appeared in that doorway with that pipe in his mouth, it was just as though I saw his father alive again.

OSWALD. Oh? Really?

MRS. ALVING. Oh, how can you say that? Oswald takes after me.

MANDERS. Yes; but there's an expression at the corner of his mouth, something about his lips, that reminds me so vividly of Alving— at any rate now when he's smoking.

MRS. ALVING. How can you say that? Oswald has much more the mouth of a clergyman, I think.

MANDERS. True, true. Some of my colleagues have a similar expression.

MRS. ALVING. But put away that pipe, my dear boy. I don't want any smoke in here.

OSWALD (*obeys*). I'm sorry. I only wanted to try it. You see, I smoked it once when I was a child.

MRS. ALVING. What?

OSWALD. Yes. I was quite small at the time. I remember, I went upstairs to see Father in his room one evening. He was so happy and cheerful.

MRS. ALVING. Oh, you don't remember anything from that time.

OSWALD. Oh, yes, I remember very clearly, he picked me up and sat me on his knee and let me smoke his pipe. "Puff away, boy," he said, "puff hard." And I puffed as hard as

I could. I felt myself go pale and the sweat broke out on my forehead in great drops. And that made him roar with laughter—

MANDERS. How very strange.

MRS. ALVING. My dear, it's just something Oswald has dreamed.

OSWALD. No, Mother, I didn't dream it. Surely you must remember—you came in and carried me back into the nursery. Then I was sick and I saw you crying. Did Father often play jokes like that?

MANDERS. In his youth he was an extremely gay young man—

OSWALD. And yet he managed to achieve so much. So much that was good and useful; although he died so young.

MANDERS. Yes, you have inherited the name of an industrious and worthy man, my dear Oswald Alving. Well, I hope this will spur you on.

OSWALD. Yes, it ought to, oughtn't it?

MANDERS. In any case it was good of you to come home and join us in honouring him.

OSWALD. It was the least I could do for Father.

MRS. ALVING. And the best thing of all is that I'm going to have him here for so long.

MANDERS. Yes, I hear you're staying the winter.

OSWALD. I am here for an indefinite period, Pastor. Oh, but it's good to be home!

MRS. ALVING (*warmly*). Yes, Oswald. It is, isn't it?

MANDERS (*looks at him sympathetically*). Yes, you went out into the world early, my dear Oswald.

OSWALD. I did. Sometimes I wonder if it wasn't too early.

MRS. ALVING. Oh, nonsense. It's good for a healthy lad; especially if he's an only child. It's bad for them to stay at home with their mother and father and be pampered.

MANDERS. That is a very debatable point, Mrs. Alving. When all is said and done, the parental home is where a child belongs.

OSWALD. I agree with you there, Pastor.

MANDERS. Take your own son. Well, it will do no harm to talk about it in his presence. What has been the consequence for him? Here he is, twenty-six or twenty-seven years old, and he's never had the opportunity to know what a real home is like.

OSWALD. I beg your pardon, sir, but there you're quite mistaken.

MANDERS. Oh? I thought you had spent practically all your time in artistic circles.

OSWALD. I have.

MANDERS. Mostly among young artists.

OSWALD. Yes.

MANDERS. But I thought most of those people lacked the means to support a family and make a home for themselves.

OSWALD. Some of them can't afford to get married, sir.

MANDERS. Yes, that's what I'm saying.

OSWALD. But that doesn't mean they can't have a home. Several of them have; and very good and comfortable homes at that.

MRS. ALVING *listens intently and nods, but says nothing.*

MANDERS. But I'm not speaking about bachelor establishments. By a home I mean a family establishment, where a man lives with his wife and children.

OSWALD. Quite. Or with his children and their mother.

MANDERS (*starts and claps his hands together*). Merciful heavens! You don't—?

OSWALD. Yes?

MANDERS. Lives with—with the mother of his children?

OSWALD. Yes, would you rather he disowned the mother of his children?

MANDERS. So you are speaking of unlegalized relationships! These so-called free marriages!

OSWALD. I've never noticed anything particularly free about the way such people live.

MANDERS. But how is it possible that—that any reasonably well brought up man or young woman can bring themselves to live like that—openly, for everyone to see?

OSWALD. But what else can they do? A poor young artist—a poor young girl—It costs a lot of money to get married. What can they do?

MANDERS. What can they do? I'll tell you, Mr. Alving, what they can do. They should have kept away from each other in the first place—that's what they should have done.

OSWALD. That argument won't get you far with young people who are in love and have red blood in their veins.

MRS. ALVING. No, that won't get you very far.

MANDERS (*takes no notice*). And to think that the authorities tolerate such behaviour! That it is allowed to happen openly! (*Turns to* MRS. ALVING.) Wasn't I right to be so concerned about your son? In circles where immorality is practised openly and is, one might almost say, accepted—

OSWALD. Let me tell you something, sir, I have been a regular Sunday guest in one or two of these irregular households—

MANDERS. On Sundays!

OSWALD. Yes, that's the day when one's meant to enjoy oneself. But I have never heard an offensive word there, far less ever witnessed anything which could be called immoral. No; do you know when and where I have encountered immorality in artistic circles?

MANDERS. No, I don't, thank heaven.

OSWALD. Well, I shall tell you. I have encountered it when one or another of our model husbands and fathers came down there to look around a little on their own— and did the artists the honour of visiting them in their humble bistros. Then we learned a few things. Those gentlemen were able to tell us about places and things of which we had never dreamed.

MANDERS. What! Are you suggesting that honourable men from this country—!

OSWALD. Have you never, when these honourable men returned home, have you never heard them hold forth on the rampancy of immorality in foreign countries?

MANDERS. Yes, of course—

MRS. ALVING. I've heard that, too.

OSWALD. Well, you can take their word for it. Some of them are experts. (*Clasps his head.*) Oh, that beautiful life of freedom— that it should be so soiled!

MRS. ALVING. You mustn't get over-excited, Oswald. It isn't good for you.

OSWALD. No, you're right, Mother. It isn't good for my health. It's that damned tired-

ness, you know. Well, I'll take a little walk before dinner. I'm sorry, Pastor. I know you can't see it from my point of view. But I had to say what I felt.

He goes out through the second door on the right.

MRS. ALVING. My poor boy—!

MANDERS. Yes, you may well say that. So it's come to this.

MRS. ALVING *looks at him but remains silent.*

MANDERS (*walks up and down*). He called himself the prodigal son. Alas, alas!

MRS. ALVING *still looks at him.*

MANDERS. And what do you say to all this?

MRS. ALVING. I say that Oswald was right in every word he said.

MANDERS (*stops dead*). Right? Right! In expressing those principles!

MRS. ALVING. Here in my loneliness I have come to think like him, Pastor Manders. But I have never dared to bring up the subject. Now my son shall speak for me.

MANDERS. I feel deeply sorry for you, Mrs. Alving. But now I will have to speak to you in earnest. I am not addressing you now as your business manager and adviser, nor as your and your late husband's old friend. I stand before you now as your priest, as I did at the moment when you had strayed so far.

MRS. ALVING. And what has the priest to say to me?

MANDERS. First I wish to refresh your memory, Mrs. Alving. The occasion is appropriate. Tomorrow will be the tenth anniversary of your husband's death. Tomorrow the memorial to him who is no longer with us is to be unveiled. Tomorrow I shall address the whole assembled flock. But today I wish to speak to you alone.

MRS. ALVING. Very well, Pastor. Speak.

MANDERS. Have you forgotten that after barely a year of marriage you stood on the very brink of the abyss? That you abandoned your house and home—that you deserted your husband—yes, Mrs. Alving, deserted, deserted—and refused to return to him, although he begged and entreated you to do so?

MRS. ALVING. Have you forgotten how desperately unhappy I was during that first year?

MANDERS. Yes, that is the sign of the rebellious spirit, to demand happiness from this earthly life. What right have we to happiness? No, Mrs. Alving, we must do our duty! And your duty was to remain with the man you had chosen, and to whom you were bound by a sacred bond.

MRS. ALVING. You know quite well the kind of life Alving led at that time; the depravities he indulged in.

MANDERS. I am only too aware of the rumours that were circulating about him; and I least of anyone approve his conduct during his youthful years, if those rumours contained the truth. But a wife is not appointed to be her husband's judge. It was your duty humbly to bear that cross which a higher will had seen fit to assign to you. But instead you rebelliously fling down that cross, abandon the erring soul you should have supported, hazard your good name, and very nearly ruin the reputations of others.

MRS. ALVING. Others? Another's, you mean?

MANDERS. It was extremely inconsiderate of you to seek refuge with me.

MRS. ALVING. With our priest? With an old friend?

MANDERS. Exactly. Well, you may thank God that I possessed the necessary firmness—that I was able to dissuade you from your frenzied intentions and that it was granted to me to lead you back on to the path of duty and home to your lawful husband.

MRS. ALVING. Yes, Pastor Manders, that was certainly your doing.

MANDERS. I was merely a humble tool in the hand of a higher purpose. And that I persuaded you to bow to the call of duty and obedience, has not that proved a blessing which will surely enrich the remainder of your days? Did I not foretell all this? Did

not Alving turn from his aberrations, like a man? Did he not afterwards live a loving and blameless life with you for the remainder of his days? Did he not become a public benefactor, did he not inspire you so that in time you became his right hand in all his enterprises? And a very capable right hand—oh, yes, I know that, Mrs. Alving, I give you credit for that. But now I come to the next great error of your life.

MRS. ALVING. And what do you mean by that?

MANDERS. Once you disowned your duties as a wife. Since then, you have disowned your duties as a mother.

MRS. ALVING. Ah—!

MANDERS. All your days you have been ruled by a fatal spirit of wilfulness. You have always longed for a life unconstrained by duties and principles. You have never been willing to suffer the curb of discipline. Everything that has been troublesome in your life you have cast off ruthlessly and callously, as if it were a burden which you had the right to reject. It was no longer convenient to you to be a wife, so you left your husband. You found it tiresome to be a mother, so you put your child out to live among strangers.

MRS. ALVING. Yes, that is true. I did.

MANDERS. And in consequence you have become a stranger to him.

MRS. ALVING. No, no! That's not true!

MANDERS. It is. It must be. And how have you got him back? Think well, Mrs. Alving! You have sinned greatly against your husband. You admit that by raising the monument to him down there. Confess too, now, how you have sinned against your son. There may still be time to bring him back from the paths of wantonness. Turn; and save what may still be saved in him. (*With raised forefinger.*) For verily, Mrs. Alving, as a mother you carry a heavy burden of guilt. This I have regarded as my duty to say to you.

Silence.

MRS. ALVING (*slow and controlled*). You have had your say, Pastor; and tomorrow you will speak publicly at my husband's cere- mony. I shall not speak tomorrow. But now I shall say a few words to you, just as you have said a few words to me.

MANDERS. Of course. You wish to excuse your conduct—

MRS. ALVING. No. I simply want to tell you what happened.

MANDERS. Oh?

MRS. ALVING. Everything that you have just said about me and my husband and our life together after you, as you put it, had led me back on to the path of duty—all that is something of which you have no knowl- edge from your own observations. From that moment you, who used to visit us every day, never once set foot in our house.

MANDERS. You and your husband moved from town shortly afterwards.

MRS. ALVING. Yes. And you never came out here to see us while my husband was alive. It was only the business connected with the Orphanage that compelled you to visit me.

MANDERS (*quietly and uncertainly*). Helen— if this is intended as a reproach, I must beg you to consider the—

MRS. ALVING. The duty you owed to your position, yes. And then I was a wife who had run away from her husband. One can never be too careful with such unprincipled women.

MANDERS. My dear . . . Mrs. Alving, you exaggerate grotesquely.

MRS. ALVING. Yes, yes, well, let us forget it. What I wanted to say was that when you judge my conduct as a wife, you are con- tent to base your judgment on common opinion.

MANDERS. Yes, well; what of it?

MRS. ALVING. But now, Manders, now I shall tell the truth. I have sworn to myself that one day you should know it. Only you.

MANDERS. And what is the truth?

MRS. ALVING. The truth is that my husband died just as dissolute as he had always lived.

MANDERS (*gropes for a chair*). What did you say?

MRS. ALVING. Just as dissolute, at any rate in

his desires, after nineteen years of marriage, as he was before you wedded us.

MANDERS. You call these youthful escapades —these irregularities—excesses, if you like— evidence of a dissolute life!

MRS. ALVING. That is the expression our doc- tor used.

MANDERS. I don't understand you.

MRS. ALVING. It doesn't matter.

MANDERS. I cannot believe my ears. You mean your whole married life—all those years you shared with your husband—were nothing but a façade!

MRS. ALVING. Yes. Now you know.

MANDERS. But—but this I cannot accept! I don't understand—I cannot credit it! But how on earth is it possible—how could such a thing be kept secret?

MRS. ALVING. I had to fight, day after day, to keep it secret. After Oswald was born I thought things became a little better with Alving. But it didn't last long. And now I had to fight a double battle, fight with all my strength to prevent anyone knowing what kind of a man my child's father was. And you know what a winning personality Alving had. No one could believe anything but good of him. He was one of those people whose reputations remain untarn- ished by the way they live. But then, Manders—you must know this too—then came the most loathsome thing of all.

MANDERS. More loathsome than this!

MRS. ALVING. I had put up with him, al- though I knew well what went on secretly outside the house. But when he offended within our four walls—

MANDERS. What are you saying? Here!

MRS. ALVING. Yes, here in our own home. In there— (*Points to the first door on the right.*) —it was in the dining-room I first found out about it. I had something to do in there and the door was standing ajar. Then I heard our maid come up from the garden to water the flowers in there.

MANDERS. Oh, yes?

MRS. ALVING. A few moments later I heard Alving enter the room. He said something to her. And then I heard— (*Gives a short laugh.*) —I still don't know whether to laugh or cry—I heard my own servant whisper: "Stop it, Mr. Alving! Let me go!"

MANDERS. What an unseemly frivolity! But it was nothing more than a frivolity, Mrs. Alving. Believe me.

MRS. ALVING. I soon found out what to believe. My husband had his way with the girl. And that relationship had consequences, Pastor Manders.

MANDERS (*petrified*). And all this took place in this house! In this house!

MRS. ALVING. I had endured much in this house. To keep him at home in the evenings—and at night—I had to make myself his companion in his secret dissipations up in his room. There I had to sit alone with him, had to clink my glass with his and drink with him, listen to his obscene and senseless drivelling, had to fight him with my fists to haul him into bed—

MANDERS (*shocked*). I don't know how you managed to endure it.

MRS. ALVING. I had to, for my little son's sake. But when the final humiliation came—when my own servant—then I swore to myself: "This must stop!" And so I took over the reins of this house; both as regards him and everything else. For now, you see, I had a weapon against him; he dared not murmur. It was then that I sent Oswald away. He was nearly seven and was beginning to notice things and ask questions, the way children do. I couldn't bear that, Manders. I thought the child could not help but be poisoned merely by breathing in this tainted home. That was why I sent him away. And so now you know why he was never allowed to set foot in his home while his father was alive. No one knows what it cost me.

MANDERS. You have indeed been sorely tried.

MRS. ALVING. I could never have borne it if I had not had my work. Yes, for I think I can say that I have worked! All the additions to the estate, all the improvements, all the useful innovations for which Alving was praised—do you imagine he had the energy to initiate any of them? He, who spent the whole day lying on the sofa reading old court circulars? No; let me tell you

this too; I drove him forward when he was in his happier moods; and I had to bear the whole burden when he started again on his dissipations or collapsed in snivelling helplessness.

MANDERS. And it is to this man that you raise a memorial.

MRS. ALVING. There you see the power of a guilty conscience.

MANDERS. A guilty—? What do you mean?

MRS. ALVING. I always believed that some time, inevitably, the truth would have to come out, and that it would be believed. The Orphanage would destroy all rumours and banish all doubt.

MANDERS. You certainly made no mistake there, Mrs. Alving.

MRS. ALVING. And then I had another motive. I wanted to make sure that my own son, Oswald, should not inherit anything whatever from his father.

MANDERS. You mean it was Alving's money that—?

MRS. ALVING. Yes. The annual donations that I have made to this Orphanage add up to the sum—I have calculated it carefully—the sum which made Lieutenant Alving, in his day, "a good match."

MANDERS. I understand—

MRS. ALVING. It was the sum with which he bought me. I do not wish that money to come into Oswald's hands. My son shall inherit everything from me.

OSWALD ALVING *enters through the second door on the right; he has removed his hat and overcoat outside.*

MRS. ALVING (*goes towards him*). Are you back already? My dear, dear boy!

OSWALD. Yes; what's one to do outside in this eternal rain? But I hear we're about to have dinner. How splendid.

REGINA (*enters from the kitchen with a parcel*). A parcel has just come for you, madam. (*Hands it to her.*)

MRS. ALVING (*with a glance at* PASTOR MANDERS). Copies of the songs for tomorrow's ceremony, I suppose.

MANDERS. Hm—

REGINA. Dinner is served, madam.

MRS. ALVING. Good. We'll come presently. I just want to— (*Begins to open the parcel.*)

REGINA (*to* OSWALD). Shall it be white port or red port, Mr. Oswald?

OSWALD. Both, Miss Engstrand.

REGINA. *Bien*—very good, Mr. Oswald.

She goes into the dining-room.

OSWALD. I'd better help her open the bottles— (*Follows her into the dining-room. The door swings half open behind him.*)

MRS. ALVING. (*who has opened the parcel*). Yes, that's right. It's the copies of the songs, Pastor Manders.

MANDERS (*with folded hands*). How I am to make my address tomorrow with a clear conscience. I—!

MRS. ALVING. Oh, you'll find a way—

MANDERS (*quietly, so as not to be heard in the dining-room*). Yes, there mustn't be any scandal.

MRS. ALVING (*firmly, in a low voice*). No. But now this long, loathsome comedy is over. From the day after tomorrow, it will be as if the dead had never lived in this house. There will be no one here but my boy and his mother.

From the dining-room is heard the crash of a chair being knocked over. At the same time REGINA *says sharply, but keeping her voice low:*

REGINA. Oswald! Are you mad? Let me go!

MRS. ALVING (*starts in fear*). Ah!

She stares distraught at the half open door. OSWALD *coughs and begins to hum. A bottle is uncorked.*

MANDERS (*indignantly*). What is going on, Mrs. Alving? What was that?

MRS. ALVING (*hoarsely*). Ghosts. The couple in the conservatory—walk.

MANDERS. What are you saying! Regina—? Is she the child you—?

MRS. ALVING. Yes. Come. Not a word.

She grips PASTOR MANDERS' *arms and walks falteringly towards the door of the dining-room.*

ACT TWO

The same room. The mist still lies heavily over the landscape. PASTOR MANDERS *and* MRS. ALVING *enter from the dining-room.*

MRS. ALVING (*still in the doorway*). I'm glad you enjoyed it, Pastor Manders. (*Speaks into the dining-room.*) Aren't you joining us, Oswald?

OSWALD (*offstage*). No, thank you. I think I'll go out and take a walk.

MRS. ALVING. Yes, do. It's stopped raining now. (*Closes the door of the dining-room, goes over to the hall door and calls.*) Regina!

REGINA (*offstage*). Yes, madam.

MRS. ALVING. Go down to the wash-house and give them a hand with the garlands.

REGINA. Very good, madam.

MRS. ALVING *makes sure that* REGINA *has gone, then closes the door.*

MANDERS. He can't hear anything from in there, can he?

MRS. ALVING. Not when the door is shut. Anyway, he's going out.

MANDERS. I am still stunned. I don't understand how I managed to swallow a mouthful of that excellent meal.

MRS. ALVING (*restless but controlled, walks up and down*). Neither do I. But what is to be done?

MANDERS. Yes, what is to be done? Upon my word, I don't know. I'm so sadly inexperienced in matters of this kind.

MRS. ALVING. I am convinced that no harm has been done yet.

MANDERS. No, heaven forbid! Nevertheless, it's a most improper situation.

MRS. ALVING. It's only a casual whim of Oswald's. You can be certain of that.

MANDERS. Well, as I said, I don't know about these things; but I'm sure—

MRS. ALVING. She must leave the house. And at once. That's obvious—

MANDERS. Yes, naturally.

MRS. ALVING. But where to? We can't just—

MANDERS. Where to? Home to her father, of course.

MRS. ALVING. To whom, did you say?

MANDERS. To her—oh, no, Engstrand isn't her—! But, dear God, Mrs. Alving, how can this be possible? Surely you must be mistaken.

MRS. ALVING. Unfortunately I know I'm not mistaken. In the end Johanna had to confess to me; and Alving couldn't deny it. So there was nothing to be done but hush the matter up.

MANDERS. Yes, I suppose that was the only thing to do.

MRS. ALVING. The girl left my service at once, and was given a considerable sum of money to keep her mouth shut. The remaining difficulties she solved for herself when she got to town. She renewed an old acquaintance with Engstrand, let it be known, I dare say, how much money she had, and spun him a story about some foreigner or other who'd been here with a yacht that summer. Then she and Engstrand got themselves married in a hurry. Well, you married them yourself.

MANDERS. But how can that be true? I remember clearly how Engstrand came to me to arrange the wedding. He was completely abject, and accused himself most bitterly of having indulged with his betrothed in a moment of weakness.

MRS. ALVING. Well, he had to take the blame on himself.

MANDERS. But to be so dishonest! And to me! I certainly would never have believed that of Jacob Engstrand. I'll speak to him seriously about this. He can be sure of that. And the immorality of it! For money! How much was it you gave the girl?

MRS. ALVING. Fifty pounds.

MANDERS. Just imagine! To go and marry a fallen woman for a paltry fifty pounds!

MRS. ALVING. What about me? I went and married a fallen man.

MANDERS. Good God Almighty, what are you saying? A fallen man!

MRS. ALVING. Do you think Alving was any purer when I accompanied him to the altar than Johanna was when Engstrand married her?

MANDERS. But the two things are utterly different—

MRS. ALVING. Not so different. Oh, yes, there was a big difference in the price. A paltry fifty pounds against an entire fortune.

MANDERS. But how can you compare two such different situations? After all, you were obeying the counsels of your heart, and of your family.

MRS. ALVING (does not look at him). I thought you understood the direction in which what you call my heart had strayed at that time.

MANDERS (distantly). If I had understood anything of the kind, I should not have been a daily guest in your husband's house.

MRS. ALVING. Anyway, I didn't follow my own counsel. That is certain.

MANDERS. Well then, you obeyed your nearest relatives. Your mother and your two aunts. As was your duty.

MRS. ALVING. Yes, that is true. The three of them worked out a balance-sheet for me. Oh, it's incredible how patly they proved that it would be utter madness for me to turn down such an offer. If my mother could look down now and see what all that promise of splendour has led to.

MANDERS. No one can be held responsible for the outcome. And this much at least is sure, that your marriage was celebrated in an orderly fashion and in full accordance with the law.

MRS. ALVING (by the window). All this talk about law and order. I often think that is what causes all the unhappiness in the world.

MANDERS. Mrs. Alving, now you are being sinful.

MRS. ALVING. Yes, perhaps I am. But I can't

stand being bound by all these obligations and petty considerations. I can't! I must find my own way to freedom.

MANDERS. What do you mean by that?

MRS. ALVING (*taps on the window frame*). I should never have concealed the truth about Alving's life. But I dared not do otherwise—and it wasn't only for Oswald's sake. I was such a coward.

MANDERS. Coward?

MRS. ALVING. If people had known, they would have said: "Poor man, it isn't surprising he strays now and then. After all, his wife ran away from him."

MANDERS. Perhaps they would not have been altogether unjustified.

MRS. ALVING (*looks hard at him*). If I were a real mother, I would take Oswald and say to him: "Listen, my boy. Your father was a degenerate—"

MANDERS. But great heavens above—!

MRS. ALVING. And I would tell him everything I have told you. The whole story.

MANDERS. You scandalize me, Mrs. Alving.

MRS. ALVING. Yes, I know. I know! I scandalize myself. (*Comes away from the window.*) That's how cowardly I am.

MANDERS. You call it cowardice to do your simple duty! Have you forgotten that a child shall love and honour its father and mother?

MRS. ALVING. Let us not generalize so. Let us ask: "Shall Oswald love and honour Captain Alving?"

MANDERS. Is there not a voice in your mother's heart which forbids you to destroy your son's ideals?

MRS. ALVING. Yes, but what about the truth?

MANDERS. Yes, but what about the ideals?

MRS. ALVING. Oh, ideals, ideals! If only I weren't such a coward!

MANDERS. Don't despise our ideals, Mrs. Alving. Retribution will surely follow. Take Oswald in particular. He hasn't many ideals, I'm afraid. But this much I have discovered, that his father is to him an ideal.

MRS. ALVING. You are right there.

MANDERS. And you yourself have awakened and fostered these ideas of his, by your letters.

MRS. ALVING. Yes. I was bound by these obligations and considerations, so I lied to my son, year out and year in. Oh, what a coward, what a coward I have been!

MANDERS. You have established a happy illusion in your son, Mrs. Alving—and you should certainly not regard that as being of little value.

MRS. ALVING. Hm. I wonder. But I shan't allow him to use Regina as a plaything. He is not going to make that poor girl unhappy.

MANDERS. Good heavens, no! That would be dreadful.

MRS. ALVING. If I knew that he meant it seriously, and that it would make him happy—

MANDERS. Yes? What then?

MRS. ALVING. But that's impossible. Unfortunately Regina isn't that type.

MANDERS. How do you mean?

MRS. ALVING. If only I weren't such an abject coward, I'd say to him: "Marry her, or make what arrangements you please. As long as you're honest and open about it—"

MANDERS. Merciful God! You mean a legal marriage! What a terrible idea! It's absolutely unheard of—!

MRS. ALVING. Unheard of, did you say? Put your hand on your heart, Pastor Manders, and tell me—do you really believe there aren't married couples like that to be found in this country—as closely related as these two?

MANDERS. I simply don't understand you.

MRS. ALVING. Oh, yes you do.

MANDERS. You're thinking that by chance possibly—? Yes, alas, family life is indeed not always as pure as it should be. But in that kind of case, one can never be sure—at any rate, not absolutely—But in this case—! That you, a mother, could want to allow your own—

MRS. ALVING. But I don't *want* to. I wouldn't allow it for any price in the world. That's just what I'm saying.

MANDERS. No, because you are a coward, as you put it. But if you weren't a coward—! Great God in heaven, what a shocking relationship!

MRS. ALVING. Well, we all stem from a relationship of that kind, so we are told. And who was it who arranged things like that in the world, Pastor Manders?

MANDERS. I shall not discuss such questions with you, Mrs. Alving. You are not in the right spiritual frame of mind for that. But that you dare to say that it is cowardly of you—!

MRS. ALVING. I shall tell you what I mean. I am frightened, because there is in me something ghostlike from which I can never free myself.

MANDERS. What did you call it?

MRS. ALVING. Ghostlike. When I heard Regina and Oswald in there, it was as if I saw ghosts. I almost think we are all ghosts —all of us, Pastor Manders. It isn't just what we have inherited from our father and mother that walks in us. It is all kinds of dead ideas and all sorts of old and obsolete beliefs. They are not alive in us; but they remain in us none the less, and we can never rid ourselves of them. I only have to take a newspaper and read it, and I see ghosts between the lines. There must be ghosts all over the country. They lie as thick as grains of sand. And we're all so horribly afraid of the light.

MANDERS. Aha—so there we have the fruits of your reading. Fine fruits indeed! Oh, these loathsome, rebellious, freethinking books!

MRS. ALVING. You are wrong, my dear Pastor. It was you yourself who first spurred me to think; and I thank and bless you for it.

MANDERS. I?

MRS. ALVING. Yes, when you forced me into what you called duty; when you praised as right and proper what my whole spirit rebelled against as something abominable. It was then that I began to examine the seams of your learning. I only wanted to pick at a single knot; but when I had worked it loose, the whole fabric fell apart. And then I saw that it was machine-sewn.

MANDERS (*quiet, shaken*). Is this the reward of my life's hardest struggle?

MRS. ALVING. Call it rather your life's most pitiful defeat.

MANDERS. It was my life's greatest victory, Helen. The victory over myself.

MRS. ALVING. It was a crime against us both.

MANDERS. That I besought you, saying: "Woman, go home to your lawful husband," when you came to me distraught and cried: "I am here! Take me!" Was that a crime?

MRS. ALVING. Yes, I think so.

MANDERS. We two do not understand each other.

MRS. ALVING. No; not any longer.

MANDERS. Never—never even in my most secret moments have I thought of you except as another man's wedded wife.

MRS. ALVING. Oh? I wonder.

MANDERS. Helen—

MRS. ALVING. One forgets so easily what one was like.

MANDERS. I do not. I am the same as I always was.

MRS. ALVING (*changes the subject*). Well, well, well—let's not talk any more about the past. Now you're up to your ears in commissions and committees; and I sit here fighting with ghosts, both in me and around me.

MANDERS. I will help you to bring to heel the ghosts around you. After all the dreadful things you have told me today, my conscience will not permit me to allow a young and unprotected girl to remain in your house.

MRS. ALVING. Don't you think it would be best if we could get her taken care of? I mean—well, decently married.

MANDERS. Indubitably. I think it would be desirable for her in every respect. Regina is just now at the age when—well, I don't really understand these things, but—

MRS. ALVING. Regina matured early.

MANDERS. Yes, didn't she? I seem to remember that she was noticeably well developed from a physical point of view when I prepared her for confirmation. But for the present at any rate she must go home. To her father's care—no, but of course,

Engstrand isn't—! That he—that *he* could conceal the truth from me like that!

There is a knock on the door leading to the hall.

MRS. ALVING. Who can that be? Come in.

ENGSTRAND (*appears in the doorway in his Sunday suit*). Begging your pardon, madam, but—

MANDERS. Aha! Hm!

MRS. ALVING. Oh, is it you, Engstrand?

ENGSTRAND. There weren't any of the servants about, so I took the liberty of giving a little knock.

MRS. ALVING. Yes, yes. Well, come in. Do you want to speak to me about something?

ENGSTRAND (*enters*). No, thank you, ma'am. It's the Pastor I really wanted to have a word with.

MANDERS (*walks up and down*). Hm; really? You want to speak to me? Do you indeed?

ENGSTRAND. Yes, I'd be so terribly grateful if—

MANDERS (*stops in front of him*). Well! May I ask what is the nature of your question?

ENGSTRAND. Well, it's like this, Pastor. We've been paid off down there now—a thousand thanks, Mrs. Alving—and now we're ready with everything—and so I thought it'd only be right and proper if we who have worked so well together all this time—I thought we might conclude with a few prayers this evening.

MANDERS. Prayers? Down at the Orphanage?

ENGSTRAND. Well, of course, sir, if you don't think it's the right thing to do—

MANDERS. Oh yes, yes, indeed I do, but—hm—

ENGSTRAND. I've been in the habit of holding a little service myself down there of an evening—

MANDERS. Have you?

ENGSTRAND. Yes, now and then. Just a little edification, as you might say. But I'm only a poor humble man and haven't the proper gifts, God forgive me—and so I thought, seeing as Pastor Manders happens to be out here—

MANDERS. Now look here, Engstrand, first I must ask you a question. Are you in the correct frame of mind for such a meeting? Do you feel your conscience is clear and free?

ENGSTRAND. Oh, God forgive us, let's not talk about conscience, Pastor.

MANDERS. Yes, that's just what we are going to talk about. Well? What is your answer?

ENGSTRAND. Well—a man's conscience can be a bit of a beggar now and then—

MANDERS. Well, at least you admit it. But now, will you tell me the truth! What's all this about Regina?

MRS. ALVING (*quickly*). Pastor Manders!

MANDERS (*soothingly*). Leave this to me—

ENGSTRAND. Regina? Good heavens, how you frighten me! (*Looks at* MRS. ALVING.) Surely nothing's happened to Regina?

MANDERS. Let us hope not. But what I meant was, what's all this about you and Regina? You call yourself her father, don't you? Hm?

ENGSTRAND (*uncertainly*). Well—hm—you know all about me and poor Johanna.

MANDERS. Now I want no more prevarication. Your late wife told the whole truth to Mrs. Alving before she left her service.

ENGSTRAND. Well, may the—! No, did she really?

MANDERS. So now you are unmasked, Engstrand.

ENGSTRAND. And she promised and swore on the Bible that she—

MANDERS. Swore on the Bible—!

ENGSTRAND. No, she only promised, but so sincerely.

MANDERS. And all these years you have concealed the truth from me. Concealed it from *me*, who trusted you so implicitly.

ENGSTRAND. Yes, I'm afraid I have, I suppose.

MANDERS. Have I deserved this from you, Engstrand? Haven't I always been ready to assist you with help, both spiritual and material, as far as lay within my power? Answer! Haven't I?

ENGSTRAND. Things would often have looked black for me if it hadn't been for your Reverence.

MANDERS. And this is how you reward me! You cause me to enter false statements in the parish register, and withhold from me over a period of years the information which you owed both to me and to the cause of truth! Your conduct has been completely indefensible, Engstrand. From now on, I wash my hands of you.

ENGSTRAND (*with a sigh*). Yes, of course, sir. I appreciate that.

MANDERS. I mean, how could you possibly justify yourself?

ENGSTRAND. But wouldn't it have made things even worse for poor Johanna if the truth had been allowed to come out? Now just imagine if your Reverence had been in the same situation as her—

MANDERS. I!

ENGSTRAND. Oh, for heaven's sake, I don't mean exactly the same. But I mean, suppose your Reverence had something to be ashamed of in the eyes of the world, as the saying goes. We men mustn't judge a poor woman too harshly, your Reverence.

MANDERS. But I'm not. It's you I'm reproaching.

ENGSTRAND. May I ask your Reverence a tiny question?

MANDERS. Yes, yes, what is it?

ENGSTRAND. Isn't it right and proper for a man to raise up the fallen?

MANDERS. Of course it is.

ENGSTRAND. And isn't it a man's duty to stand by his word?

MANDERS. Certainly it is: but—

ENGSTRAND. That time when Johanna fell into misfortune through that Englishman—or maybe he was an American, or a Russian, as they call them—well, she came up to town. Poor creature, she'd turned up her nose at me once or twice; for she only looked at what was handsome and fine, poor thing; and of course I had this thing wrong with my leg. Well, your Reverence will remember how I'd ventured into a dancing-hall where foreign sailors were indulging in drunkenness and excess, as the saying goes. And when I tried to exhort them to start leading a better life—

MRS. ALVING (*by the window*). Hm—

MANDERS. I know, Engstrand. The ruffians threw you down the stairs. You've told me about it before. Your injury is something to be proud of.

ENGSTRAND. Oh, I take no pride in it, your Reverence. But what I was going to say was, so she came along and poured out all her troubles to me amid weeping and gnashing of teeth. I'll be frank, your Reverence; it nearly broke my heart to listen to her.

MANDERS. Did it really, Engstrand? Well, go on.

ENGSTRAND. Yes, well, so I said to her: "This American is a vagrant on the sea of life," I said. "And you, Johanna, you've committed a sin and are a fallen creature. But Jacob Engstrand," I said, "he's got both feet firmly on the ground"—speaking figuratively, you understand—

MANDERS. I understand you perfectly. Go on.

ENGSTRAND. Well, that's how I raised her up and made an honest woman of her so that people shouldn't get to know the wanton way she'd behaved with foreigners.

MANDERS. You acted very handsomely. The only thing I can't understand is how you could bring yourself to accept money—

ENGSTRAND. Money? I? Not a penny!

MANDERS (*glances questioningly at* MRS. ALVING). But—!

ENGSTRAND. Oh yes, wait a moment—now I remember. Johanna did have a few shillings with her. But I wouldn't have any of it. "Fie!" I said, "that's Mammon, that's the wages of sin. We'll throw that wretched gold—or notes, or whatever it was—back in the American's face," I said. But he'd taken his hook and disappeared across the wild sea, your Reverence.

MANDERS. Had he, my dear Engstrand?

ENGSTRAND. Oh yes. And so Johanna and I agreed that the money was to be used to bring up the child, and that's what happened; and I can account for every shilling of it.

MANDERS. But this puts quite a different face on things.

ENGSTRAND. That's the way it was, your Reverence. And I think I can say I've been a real father to Regina—as far as stood within my power—for unfortunately I'm an ailing man.

MANDERS. Now, now, my dear Engstrand—

ENGSTRAND. But this I can say, that I've brought up the child tenderly and been a loving husband to poor Johanna and ordered my household the way the good book says. But it would never have entered my head to go along to your Reverence in sinful pride and boast that for once I too had done a good deed. No, when anything of that kind happens to Jacob Engstrand, he keeps quiet about it. I don't suppose that's always the way, more's the pity. And when I do go to see Pastor Manders I've always more than enough of wickedness and weakness to talk to him about. For I said it just now and I say it again—a man's conscience can be a real beggar now and then.

MANDERS. Give me your hand, Jacob Engstrand.

ENGSTRAND. Why, good heavens, Pastor—!

MANDERS. No argument, now. (*Presses his hand.*) There!

ENGSTRAND. And if I was to go down on my bended knees and humbly to beg your Reverence's forgiveness—?

MANDERS. You? No, on the contrary. It is I who must ask your pardon—

ENGSTRAND. Oh no, really—

MANDERS. Indeed, yes. And I do so with all my heart. Forgive me that I could ever have misjudged you so. And if there is any way in which I can show the sincerity of my regrets and of my good-will towards you—

ENGSTRAND. Would your Reverence really do that?

MANDERS. Most gladly.

ENGSTRAND. Well, in that case there's a real opportunity just now. With the money I've managed to put aside through the blessed work here, I'm thinking of starting a kind of home for sailors in the city.

MANDERS. *You* are?

ENGSTRAND. Yes, a kind of refuge like the one here, in a manner of speaking. The temptations for a sailor wandering on shore are so manifold. But in this house, with me there, it'd be like them having a father to take care of them, I thought.

MANDERS. What have you to say to that, Mrs. Alving!

ENGSTRAND. My means are rather limited, God knows. But if only someone would stretch out a helping hand—

MANDERS. Yes, well, let us consider the matter more closely. Your project interests me very deeply. But go along now and get everything in order and light candles so as to make the place cheerful, and we'll have a little edification together, my dear Engstrand. For now I think you're in the right frame of mind.

ENGSTRAND. Yes, I think I am. Well, goodbye, Mrs. Alving, and thank you for everything. And take good care of Regina for me. (*Wipes a tear from his eye.*) Poor Johanna's child! Hm—it's strange, but—it's just as though she'd grown to be a part of me. It is really, yes. (*Touches his forehead and goes out through the door.*)

MANDERS. Well, what have you to say about that man now, Mrs. Alving? That was quite a different explanation we were given there.

MRS. ALVING. It was indeed.

MANDERS. You see how terribly careful one must be about condemning one's fellows. But then, again, it is a deep joy to discover that one has been mistaken. Or what do you say?

MRS. ALVING. I say: you are a great baby, Manders. And you always will be.

MANDERS. I?

MRS. ALVING (*places both her hands on his shoulders*). And I say: I'd like to throw both my arms round your neck.

MANDERS (*frees himself quickly*). No, no, bless you! Such impulses—!

MRS. ALVING (*with a smile*). Oh, you needn't be frightened of me.

MANDERS (*by the table*). You have such an extravagant way of expressing yourself sometimes. Now let me just gather these documents together and put them in my case. (*Does so.*) There! And now, *au revoir*. Keep your eyes open when Oswald comes back. I'll be with you again presently. (*Takes his hat and goes out through the hall.*)

MRS. ALVING (*sighs, looks out of the window for a moment, tidies the room a little and is about to go into the dining-room, but stops in the doorway and calls softly*). Oswald, are you still at table?

OSWALD (*offstage*). I'm just finishing my cigar.

MRS. ALVING. I thought you'd gone for a little walk.

OSWALD. In this weather?

There is the clink of a glass. MRS. ALVING *leaves the door open and sits down with her sewing on the sofa by the window.*

OSWALD (*still offstage*). Wasn't that Pastor Manders who left just now?

MRS. ALVING. Yes, he's gone down to the Orphanage.

OSWALD. Hm. (*Clink of decanter and glass again.*)

MRS. ALVING (*with a worried glance*). Oswald dear, you ought to be careful with that liqueur. It's strong.

OSWALD. It keeps out the damp.

MRS. ALVING. Won't you come in and talk to me?

OSWALD. I can't smoke in there.

MRS. ALVING. You know I don't mind cigars.

OSWALD. All right, I'll come, then. Just one tiny drop more. There. (*He enters with his cigar and closes the door behind him. Short silence.*)

OSWALD. Where's the Pastor gone?

MRS. ALVING. I told you, he went down to the Orphanage.

OSWALD. Oh yes, so you did.

MRS. ALVING. You oughtn't to sit at table so long, Oswald.

OSWALD (*holding his cigar behind his back*). But I think it's so nice, Mother. (*Strokes and pats her.*) To come home, and sit at my mother's own table, in my mother's dining-room, and eat my mother's beautiful food.

MRS. ALVING. My dear, dear boy.

OSWALD (*walks and smokes a trifle impatiently*). And what else is there for me to do here? I can't work—

MRS. ALVING. Can't you?

OSWALD. In this weather? Not a glimmer of sunlight all day. (*Walks across the room.*) That's the worst thing about it—not to be able to work—

MRS. ALVING. Perhaps you shouldn't have come home.

OSWALD. Yes, Mother, I had to.

MRS. ALVING. I'd ten times rather sacrifice the happiness of having you with me than that you should—

OSWALD (*stops by the table*). Tell me, Mother. Does it really make you so happy to have me home?

MRS. ALVING. Does it make me happy?

OSWALD (*crumples a newspaper*). I think it must be almost the same for you whether I'm alive or not.

MRS. ALVING. How can you have the heart to say that to your mother, Oswald?

OSWALD. But you managed so well to live without me before.

MRS. ALVING. Yes. I have lived without you. That is true.

Silence. Dusk begins to gather slowly. OSWALD *paces up and down the room. He has put down his cigar.*

OSWALD (*stops beside* MRS. ALVING). Mother, may I sit down on the sofa with you?

MRS. ALVING (*makes room for him*). Yes, of course, my dear boy.

OSWALD (*sits*). There's something I have to tell you, Mother.

MRS. ALVING (*tensely*). Yes?

OSWALD (*stares vacantly ahead of him*). I can't keep it to myself any longer.

MRS. ALVING. What? What do you mean?

OSWALD (*as before*). I couldn't bring myself to write to you about it; and since I came home I—

MRS. ALVING (*grips his arm*). Oswald, what is this?

OSWALD. Yesterday and today I've been trying to forget. To escape. But it's no good.

MRS. ALVING (*rises*). Tell me the truth, Oswald.

OSWALD (*pulls her down on to the sofa again*). Sit still and I'll try to tell you about it. I've complained so much about how tired I felt after the journey—

MRS. ALVING. Yes. Well?

OSWALD. But it isn't that that's wrong with me. It isn't any ordinary tiredness—

MRS. ALVING (*tries to rise*). You're not ill, Oswald!

OSWALD (*pulls her down again*). Sit still, Mother. Just keep calm. No, I'm not really ill; not what people usually call ill. (*Clasps his hands to his head.*) Mother, I'm spiritually broken—my will's gone—I shall never be able to work any more!

He throws himself into her lap, with his hands over his face, and sobs.

MRS. ALVING (*pale and trembling*). Oswald! Look at me! No, no, it isn't true!

OSWALD (*looks up at her despairingly*). Never to be able to work again! Never. Never. To be dead while I'm still alive. Mother, can you imagine anything so dreadful?

MRS. ALVING. My poor boy. How did this frightful thing happen to you?

OSWALD (*sits upright again*). Yes, that's just what I can't understand. I've never lived intemperately. Not in any way. You mustn't believe that of me, Mother. I've never done that.

MRS. ALVING. Of course I don't believe it, Oswald.

OSWALD. And yet it's happened to me. This dreadful thing.

MRS. ALVING. Oh, but my dear, dear boy, it'll be all right. You've just overworked. You take my word for it.

OSWALD (*heavily*). That's what I thought at first. But it isn't that.

MRS. ALVING. Tell me the whole story.

OSWALD. I shall, yes.

MRS. ALVING. When did you first notice it?

OSWALD. It was soon after the last time I'd been home, and had gone back again to Paris. I began to feel the most violent pains in my head—mostly at the back of my head, it seemed. It was as though a tight iron ring had been screwed round my neck and just above it.

MRS. ALVING. Yes?

OSWALD. At first I thought it was just the usual headaches I used to have so often while I was a child.

MRS. ALVING. Yes, yes—

OSWALD. But it wasn't. I soon realized that. I couldn't work any more. I wanted to begin on a new painting, but it was as though my powers had failed me. It was as though I was paralysed—I couldn't see anything clearly—everything went misty and began to swim in front of my eyes. Oh, it was dreadful! In the end I sent for the doctor. And he told me the truth.

MRS. ALVING. How do you mean?

OSWALD. He was one of the leading doctors down there. I had to tell him how I felt. And he began to ask me a lot of questions, which seemed to me to have absolutely nothing to do with it. I didn't understand what the man was driving at—

MRS. ALVING. Yes!

OSWALD. In the end he said: "You've been worm-eaten from birth." That was the word he used: *vermoulu*.

MRS. ALVING (*tensely*). What did he mean by that?

OSWALD. I didn't understand either, and asked him to explain more clearly. And then the old cynic said— (*Clenches his fist.*) Oh—!

MRS. ALVING. What did he say?

OSWALD. He said: "The sins of the fathers shall be visited on the children."

MRS. ALVING (*rises slowly*). The sins of the fathers—!

OSWALD. I nearly hit him in the face—

MRS. ALVING (*walks across the room*). The sins of the fathers—

OSWALD (*smiles sadly*). Yes, what do you think of that? Of course I assured him it was quite out of the question. But do you think he gave in? No, he stuck to his opinion; and it was only when I brought out your letters and translated to him all the passages that dealt with Father—

MRS. ALVING. But then he—?

OSWALD. Yes, then of course he had to admit he was on the wrong track. And then I learned the truth. The incredible truth! This wonderfully happy life with my comrades, I should have abstained from. It had

been too much for my strength. In other
words, I have only myself to blame.

MRS. ALVING. Oswald! Oh, no, you mustn't
think that!

OSWALD. There was no other explanation possible, he said. That's the dreadful thing. Beyond cure—ruined for life—because of my
own folly. Everything I wanted to accomplish in the world—not even to dare to
think of it—not to be *able* to think of it.
Oh, if only I could start my life over again,
and undo it all!

Throws himself face down on the sofa.
MRS. ALVING *wrings her hands and
walks to and fro, fighting silently with
herself.*

OSWALD (*after a while, looks up and remains
half-leaning on his elbow*). If it had been
something I'd inherited. Something I wasn't
myself to blame for. But this! To have
thrown away in this shameful, thoughtless,
light-hearted way one's whole happiness
and health, everything in the world—one's
future, one's life—

MRS. ALVING. No, no, my dear, blessed boy—
this is impossible! (*Leans over him.*)
Things are not as desperate as you think.

OSWALD. Oh, you don't know—! (*Jumps up.*)
And then, Mother, that I should cause you
all this grief! I've often almost wished and
hoped that you didn't care very much
about me.

MRS. ALVING. I, Oswald! My only son! The
only possession I have in the world—the
only thing I care about!

OSWALD (*seizes both her hands and kisses
them*). Yes, yes, I know. When I am at
home, of course I know it. And that's one
of the hardest things to bear. But now you
know. And now we won't talk about it
any more today. I can't bear to think about
it for long. (*Walks across the room.*) Get
me something to drink, Mother.

MRS. ALVING. Drink? What do you want to
drink now?

OSWALD. Oh, anything. You have some cold
punch in the house, haven't you?

MRS. ALVING. Yes, but, my dear Oswald—

OSWALD. Oh, Mother, don't be difficult. Be
nice now! I *must* have something to help
me forget these worries. (*Goes into the
conservatory.*) Oh, how—how dark it is in
here! (MRS. ALVING *pulls a bell-rope, right.*)
And this incessant rain. It goes on week
after week; sometimes for months. Never
to see the sun! In all the years I've been
at home I don't remember ever having seen
the sun shine.

MRS. ALVING. Oswald! You are thinking of
leaving me!

OSWALD. Hm— (*Sighs deeply.*) I'm not thinking about anything. I *can't* think about
anything. (*Softly.*) I take good care not to.

REGINA (*enters from the dining-room*). Did
you ring, madam?

MRS. ALVING. Yes, bring in the lamp.

REGINA. Yes, madam, at once. I've already lit
it. (*Goes.*)

MRS. ALVING (*goes over to* OSWALD). Oswald,
don't hide anything from me.

OSWALD. I'm not, Mother. (*Goes over to the
table.*) Haven't I told you enough?

*REGINA enters with the lamp and puts
it on the table.*

MRS. ALVING. Oh, Regina, you might bring
us half a bottle of champagne.

REGINA. Very good, madam. (*Goes.*)

OSWALD (*takes* MRS. ALVING'S *head in his
hands*). That's the way. I knew my Mother
wouldn't let her boy go thirsty.

MRS. ALVING. My poor, dear Oswald! How
could I deny you anything now?

OSWALD (*eagerly*). Is that true, Mother? Do
you mean it?

MRS. ALVING. Mean what?

OSWALD. That you wouldn't deny me anything?

MRS. ALVING. But, my dear Oswald—

OSWALD. Ssh!

REGINA (*brings a tray with a half-bottle of
champagne and two glasses, and puts it
down on the table*). Shall I open—?

OSWALD. No, thank you, I'll do it myself.

REGINA goes.

MRS. ALVING (*sits down at the table*). What did you mean just now, when you said I mustn't deny you anything?

OSWALD (*busy trying to open the bottle*). Let's taste this first.

> *The cork jumps out. He fills one glass and is about to do likewise with the other.*

MRS. ALVING (*puts her hand over it*). Thank you, not for me.

OSWALD. Well, for me, then. (*Empties the glass, refills it and empties it again. Then he sits down at the table.*)

MRS. ALVING (*tensely*). Well?

OSWALD (*not looking at her*). Tell me, Mother—I thought you and Pastor Manders looked so strange—hm—quiet—at dinner.

MRS. ALVING. Did you notice?

OSWALD. Yes—hm. (*Short silence.*) Tell me— what do you think of Regina?

MRS. ALVING. What do I think?

OSWALD. Yes, isn't she splendid?

MRS. ALVING. Oswald dear, you don't know her as well as I do—

OSWALD. Oh?

MRS. ALVING. Regina spent too much time at home, I'm afraid. I ought to have brought her here to live with me sooner.

OSWALD. Yes, but isn't she splendid to look at, Mother? (*Fills his glass.*)

MRS. ALVING. Regina has many great faults—

OSWALD. Oh, what does that matter? (*Drinks again.*)

MRS. ALVING. But I'm fond of her all the same. And I am responsible for her. I'd rather anything in the world happened than that she should come to any harm.

OSWALD (*jumps up*). Mother, Regina's my only hope!

MRS. ALVING (*rises*). What do you mean by that?

OSWALD. I can't bear all this misery alone.

MRS. ALVING. But you have your mother to bear it with you.

OSWALD. Yes, that's what I thought. And that's why I came home to you. But it won't work. I can see it; it won't work. I can't bear this life here.

MRS. ALVING. Oswald!

OSWALD. Oh, I must live differently, Mother. That's why I have to leave you. I don't want you to see.

MRS. ALVING. My poor, sick boy! Oh, but Oswald, as long as you're not well—

OSWALD. If it was just the illness, I'd stay with you, Mother. You're the best friend I have in the world.

MRS. ALVING. Yes, I am, Oswald, aren't I?

OSWALD (*walks around restlessly*). But it's all the remorse, the gnawing, the self-reproach. And then the fear! Oh—this dreadful fear!

MRS. ALVING (*follows him*). Fear? What fear? What do you mean?

OSWALD. Oh, don't ask me any more about it. I don't know. I can't describe it.

> MRS. ALVING *crosses and pulls the bell-rope.*

OSWALD. What do you want?

MRS. ALVING. I want my boy to be happy. He shan't sit here and brood. (*To* REGINA *who appears in the doorway.*) More champagne. A whole bottle.

> REGINA *goes.*

OSWALD. Mother!

MRS. ALVING. Do you think we don't know how to live here, too?

OSWALD. Isn't she splendid to look at? The way she's made! And so healthy and strong!

MRS. ALVING (*sits at the table*). Sit down, Oswald, and let's talk calmly together.

OSWALD (*sits*). You don't know this, Mother, but I have done Regina a wrong. And I've got to put it right.

MRS. ALVING. A wrong?

OSWALD. Well, a little thoughtlessness—whatever you care to call it. Quite innocently, really. When I was home last—

MRS. ALVING. Yes?

OSWALD. She asked me so often about Paris, and I told her this and that about the life down there. And I remember, one day I happened to say: "Wouldn't you like to come there yourself?"

MRS. ALVING. Oh?

OSWALD. Well, she blushed violently, and then she said: "Yes, I'd like to very much." "Well, well," I replied, "that might be arranged"—or something of the sort.

MRS. ALVING. Yes?

OSWALD. Well, of course I forgot the whole thing. But the day before yesterday, when I asked her if she was glad that I was going to stay at home so long—

MRS. ALVING. Yes?

OSWALD. She gave me such a strange look and then she asked: "But then, what's going to become of my trip to Paris?"

MRS. ALVING. Her trip!

OSWALD. And then I got it out of her that she'd taken the whole thing seriously, that she'd been going around here thinking about me the whole time, and that she'd begun to learn French—

MRS. ALVING. I see—

OSWALD. Mother—when I saw that splendid, handsome, healthy girl standing there in front of me—well, I'd never really noticed her before—but now, when she stood there, so to speak, with open arms ready to receive me—

MRS. ALVING. Oswald!

OSWALD. Then I realized that in her I could find salvation; for I saw that she was full of the joy of life.

MRS. ALVING (starts). The joy of life! But how could that help?

REGINA (enters from the dining-room with a bottle of champagne). I'm sorry I was so long. I had to go down to the cellar— (Puts the bottle on the table.)

OSWALD. And fetch another glass.

REGINA (looks at him, surprised). There is Mrs. Alving's glass.

OSWALD. But fetch one for yourself, Regina.

REGINA starts and throws a quick glance at MRS. ALVING.

OSWALD. Well?

REGINA (quietly, hesitantly). Do you wish me to, madam?

MRS. ALVING. Fetch the glass, Regina.

REGINA goes into the dining-room.

OSWALD (watches her go). Do you see how she walks? With such purpose and gaiety!

MRS. ALVING. This must not happen, Oswald.

OSWALD. It's already decided. Surely you can see. It's no use trying to stop it.

REGINA enters with an empty glass, which she keeps in her hand.

OSWALD. Sit down, Regina. (She glances questioningly at MRS. ALVING.)

MRS. ALVING. Sit down.

REGINA sits on a chair by the dining-room door, with the empty glass still in her hand.

MRS. ALVING. Oswald, what was it you were saying about the joy of life?

OSWALD. Oh, yes—the joy of life, Mother—you don't know much about that here. I never feel it here.

MRS. ALVING. Not when you are with me?

OSWALD. Not when I'm at home. But you don't understand that.

MRS. ALVING. Oh, yes—I think I do now—almost.

OSWALD. The joy of life and the love of one's work. They're practically the same thing. But that you don't know anything about, either.

MRS. ALVING. No, I don't suppose we do. Oswald, tell me more about this.

OSWALD. Well, all I mean is that here people are taught to believe that work is a curse and a punishment, and that life is a misery which we do best to get out of as quickly as possible.

MRS. ALVING. A vale of tears, yes. And we do our best to make it one.

OSWALD. But out there, people don't feel like that. No one there believes in that kind of teaching any longer. They feel it's wonderful and glorious just to be alive. Mother, have you noticed how everything I've painted is concerned with the joy of life? Always, always, the joy of life. Light and sunshine and holiday—and shining, contented faces. That's what makes me afraid to be here at home with you.

MRS. ALVING. Afraid? What are you afraid of here with me?

OSWALD. I'm afraid that everything in me will degenerate into ugliness here.

MRS. ALVING (*looks hard at him*). You think that would happen?

OSWALD. I know it. Live the same life here as down there, and it wouldn't be the same life.

MRS. ALVING (*who has listened intently, rises, her eyes large and thoughtful*). Now I see.

OSWALD. What do you see?

MRS. ALVING. Now I understand for the first time. And now I can speak.

OSWALD (*rises*). Mother, I don't follow you.

REGINA (*who has also risen*). Shall I go?

MRS. ALVING. No, stay. Now I can speak. Now, my boy, you shall know everything. And then you can choose. Oswald! Regina!

OSWALD. Ssh! The Pastor—!

MANDERS (*enters from the hall*). Well, we've had a most splendid and profitable hour down there.

OSWALD. So have we.

MANDERS. We must assist Engstrand with this sailors' home. Regina must go and help him—

REGINA. No thank you, Pastor.

MANDERS (*notices her for the first time*). What! You here! And with a glass in your hand!

REGINA (*puts the glass down quickly*). Oh, pardon—

OSWALD. Regina is leaving with me, sir.

MANDERS. Leaving! With you!

OSWALD. Yes. As my wife. If she so wishes.

MANDERS. But, good heavens—!

REGINA. It isn't my doing, sir.

OSWALD. Or she will stay here, if I stay.

REGINA (*involuntarily*). Here?

MANDERS. I am petrified at you, Mrs. Alving.

MRS. ALVING. She will neither leave with you nor stay with you. Now I can speak the truth.

MANDERS. But you mustn't! No, no, no!

MRS. ALVING. I can and I will. And I shan't destroy any ideals, either.

OSWALD. Mother, what have you been hiding from me?

REGINA (*listens*). Madam! Listen! People are shouting outside!

She goes into the conservatory and looks out.

OSWALD (*at the window, left*). What's going on? Where's that light coming from?

REGINA (*cries*). The Orphanage is on fire!

MRS. ALVING (*at the window*). On fire!

MANDERS. On fire? Impossible! I've only just left it.

OSWALD. Where's my hat? Oh, never mind! Father's Orphanage—! (*Runs out through the garden door.*)

MRS. ALVING. My shawl, Regina! The whole building's alight!

MANDERS. Terrible! Mrs. Alving, there blazes the judgment of God upon this sinful house!

MRS. ALVING. Perhaps you are right. Come, Regina. (*She and* REGINA *hurry out through the hall.*)

MANDERS (*clasps his hands*). And not insured either! (*He follows them.*)

ACT THREE

The same. All the doors are standing open. The lamp is still burning on the table. Outside it is dark, with only a faint glow from the fire in the background, left. MRS. ALVING, *with a big shawl over her head, is standing in the conservatory, looking out.* REGINA, *also with a shawl round her, stands a little behind her.*

MRS. ALVING. All burnt. Burnt to the ground.

REGINA. It's still burning in the basement.

MRS. ALVING. Why doesn't Oswald come back? There's nothing to save.

REGINA. Would you like me to go down and take him his hat?

MRS. ALVING. Hasn't he even got his hat?

REGINA (*points to the hall*). No, it's hanging there.

MRS. ALVING. Let it hang. He must come up now. I'll go and look for him myself. (*Goes out through the garden door.*)

MANDERS (*enters from hall*). Isn't Mrs. Alving here?

REGINA. She's just this minute gone into the garden.

MANDERS. This is the most terrible night I have ever experienced.

REGINA. Yes, sir, isn't it a dreadful tragedy?

MANDERS. Oh, don't talk about it! I hardly dare even to think about it.

REGINA. But how can it have happened—?

MANDERS. Don't ask me, Miss Engstrand. How can I know? Are you, too, going to—? Isn't it enough that your father—?

REGINA. What's he done?

MANDERS. Oh, he's completely confused me.

ENGSTRAND (*enters from the hall*). Your Reverence—

MANDERS (*turns, alarmed*). Are you still pursuing me?

ENGSTRAND. Yes, well, God rot me if—oh, good heavens! But this is a terrible business, your Reverence.

MANDERS (*walks up and down*). It is indeed, it is indeed.

REGINA. What is?

ENGSTRAND. Well, you see, it all began with this prayer service. (*Aside.*) Now we've got him, my girl! (*Aloud.*) Fancy me being to blame for Pastor Manders being to blame for something like this.

MANDERS. But I assure you, Engstrand—

ENGSTRAND. But there was no one except your Reverence mucking around with the candles down there.

MANDERS (*stops*). Yes, so you keep on saying. But I'm sure I don't remember ever having had a candle in my hand.

ENGSTRAND. And I saw as plain as plain could be your Reverence take the candle and snuff it with your fingers and throw the wick right down among the shavings.

MANDERS. And you saw this?

ENGSTRAND. Yes, with these eyes.

MANDERS. That I cannot understand. It's not usually my habit to snuff out candles with my fingers.

ENGSTRAND. Yes, it looked a bit careless, I thought. But it can't really be as bad as you say, can it, your Reverence?

MANDERS (*paces uneasily up and down*). Oh, don't ask me.

ENGSTRAND (*walks with him*). And of course you haven't insured it, either?

MANDERS (*still walking*). No, no, no. I've told you.

ENGSTRAND (*still with him*). Not insured. And then to go straight over and set fire to it all. Oh, good heavens, what a tragedy.

MANDERS (*wipes the sweat from his forehead*). Yes, Engstrand, you may well say that.

ENGSTRAND. And that such a thing should happen to a charitable institution which was to have served the city as well as the countryside. The newspapers won't be too gentle with your Reverence, I'm afraid.

MANDERS. No, that's just what I'm thinking. That's almost the worst part of it. All these hateful attacks and accusations—! Oh, it's frightful to think about.

MRS. ALVING (*enters from the garden*). I can't persuade him to come away from the fire.

MANDERS. Ah, it's you, Mrs. Alving.

MRS. ALVING. Well, now you won't have to make that speech after all, Pastor Manders.

MANDERS. Oh, I'd have been only too happy to—

MRS. ALVING (*in a subdued voice*). It was all for the best. Nothing good would have come of this Orphanage.

MANDERS. You think not?

MRS. ALVING. What do you think?

MANDERS. Nevertheless, it was a terrible tragedy.

MRS. ALVING. We'll discuss it simply as a business matter. Are you waiting for the Pastor, Engstrand?

ENGSTRAND (*in the doorway to the hall*). That's right, madam.

MRS. ALVING. Well, sit down, then.

ENGSTRAND. Thank you, I'm happy standing.

MRS. ALVING (*to* MANDERS). I suppose you'll be leaving with the steamer?

MANDERS. Yes. In an hour.

MRS. ALVING. Would you be kind enough to take all the papers along with you? I don't want to hear another word about this. Now I have other things to think about—

MANDERS. Mrs. Alving—

MRS. ALVING. I'll send you a power of attorney so that you can take any measures you think fit.

MANDERS. I shall be only too happy to shoulder that responsibility. I fear the original purpose of the endowment will now have to be completely changed.

MRS. ALVING. I appreciate that.

MANDERS. Yes, I'm provisionally thinking of arranging for the Solvik property to be handed over to the parish. The freehold cannot by any means be said to be without value. It can always be put to some purpose or other. And the interest from the capital in the savings bank I could perhaps most suitably employ in supporting some enterprise or other which could be said to be of benefit to the town.

MRS. ALVING. As you please. It's a matter of complete indifference to me.

ENGSTRAND. Remember my home for sailors, your Reverence.

MANDERS. Yes, indeed, you have a point there. We shall have to consider that possibility carefully.

ENGSTRAND. Consider? To hell with—oh, good heavens!

MANDERS (*with a sigh*). And I'm afraid I don't know how long these matters will remain in my hands. Public opinion may force me to withdraw. It all depends on the outcome of the enquiry into the cause of the fire.

MRS. ALVING. What are you saying?

MANDERS. And one cannot possibly predict the outcome.

ENGSTRAND (*comes closer*). Oh, yes one can. Don't I stand here, and isn't my name Jacob Engstrand?

MANDERS. Yes, yes, but—

ENGSTRAND (*more quietly*). And Jacob Engstrand isn't the man to fail his blessed benefactor in his time of need, as the saying goes.

MANDERS. But, my dear man, how—?

ENGSTRAND. Jacob Engstrand can be likened to an angel of deliverance, as you might say, your Reverence.

MANDERS. No, no, I really cannot accept this.

ENGSTRAND. Oh, that's the way it's going to be. I know someone who's taken the blame for another man's wickedness once before.

MANDERS. Jacob! (*Presses his hand.*) You are indeed a rare person. Well, you too shall receive a helping hand. For your seamen's home. That you can rely upon.

ENGSTRAND *wants to thank him, but is too moved to speak.*

MANDERS (*hangs his travelling bag on his shoulder*). Well, let's be off. We two shall go together.

ENGSTRAND (*at the dining-room door, says quietly to* REGINA). You come with me, my girl. You'll live as tight as the yolk in an egg.

REGINA (*tosses her head*). Merci! (*Goes into the hall and fetches* MANDERS' *overcoat.*)

MANDERS. Farewell, Mrs. Alving. And may the spirit of law and order soon enter into this house.

MRS. ALVING. Goodbye, Manders.

She goes towards the conservatory, as she sees OSWALD *come in through the garden door.*

ENGSTRAND (*while he and* REGINA *help* MANDERS *on with his overcoat*). Goodbye, my child. And if ever you find yourself in any trouble, you know where Jacob Engstrand is to be found. (*Quietly.*) Little Harbour Street—hm—! (*To* MRS. ALVING *and* OSWALD.) And the house for wandering sailors is going to be called Captain Alving's Home. And if I am allowed to run it according to my ideas, I think I can promise you it'll be a worthy memorial to him, God rest his soul.

MANDERS (*in the doorway*). Hm—hm! Come along, my dear Engstrand. Goodbye, goodbye. (*He and* ENGSTRAND *go out through the hall.*)

OSWALD (*goes over towards the table*). What was that he was talking about?

MRS. ALVING. Some kind of home that he and Pastor Manders are going to found.

OSWALD. It'll burn down just like this one.

MRS. ALVING. Why do you say that?

OSWALD. Everything will burn. There will be nothing left to remind people of Father. I, too, am burning.

REGINA *starts and stares at him.*

MRS. ALVING. Oswald! You ought not to have stayed down there so long, my poor boy.

OSWALD (*sits down at the table*). I think you're right.

MRS. ALVING. Let me wipe your face, Oswald. It's soaking wet. (*She dries him with her handkerchief.*)

OSWALD (*stares indifferently ahead of him*). Thank you, Mother.

MRS. ALVING. Aren't you tired, Oswald? Wouldn't you like to go upstairs and sleep?

OSWALD (*frightened*). No, no, I won't sleep. I never sleep. I only pretend to. (*Heavily.*) It'll come soon enough.

MRS. ALVING (*looks worried at him*). My dear boy, you really are ill.

REGINA (*tensely*). Is Mr. Alving ill?

OSWALD (*impatiently*). And shut all the doors! Oh, this fear that haunts me—!

MRS. ALVING. Close them, Regina.

REGINA *closes the doors and remains standing by the hall door.* MRS. ALVING *takes off her shawl.* REGINA *does likewise.*

MRS. ALVING (*brings a chair over to* OSWALD'S *and sits down beside him*). There now. I'll sit beside you—

OSWALD. Yes, do. And Regina must stay here too. Regina must always be near me. You'll save me, Regina. Won't you?

REGINA. I don't understand—

MRS. ALVING. Save you—?

OSWALD. Yes. When the time comes.

MRS. ALVING. But Oswald, you have your mother.

OSWALD. You? (*Smiles.*) No, Mother, you wouldn't do this for me. (*Laughs heavily.*) You? Ha, ha! (*Looks earnestly at her.*)

Though really you're the one who ought to. (*Violently.*) Why don't you speak to me as though I was your friend, Regina? Why don't you call me Oswald?

REGINA (*quietly*). I don't think Mrs. Alving would like it.

MRS. ALVING. You may do so presently. Come over and sit down here with us. (REGINA *sits quietly and diffidently on the other side of the table.*) And now, my poor, tormented boy, now I shall remove the burden from your mind—

OSWALD. You, Mother?

MRS. ALVING (*continues*). All this remorse and self-reproach you speak of—

OSWALD. You think you can do that?

MRS. ALVING. Yes, Oswald, now I can. You spoke of the joy of life; and that seemed to throw a new light over everything that has happened to me in my life.

OSWALD (*shakes his head*). I don't understand.

MRS. ALVING. You should have known your father when he was a young lieutenant. He was full of the joy of life, Oswald.

OSWALD. Yes, I know.

MRS. ALVING. It was like a sunny morning just to see him. And the untamed power and the vitality he had!

OSWALD. Yes?

MRS. ALVING. And this happy, carefree child—for he was like a child, then—had to live here in a little town that had no joy to offer him, only diversions. He had to live here with no purpose in life; simply a position to keep up. He could find no work into which he could throw himself heart and soul—just keeping the wheels of business turning. He hadn't a single friend capable of knowing what the joy of life means; only idlers and drinking-companions—

OSWALD. Mother—!

MRS. ALVING. And in the end the inevitable happened.

OSWALD. The inevitable?

MRS. ALVING. You said yourself this evening what would happen to you if you stayed at home.

OSWALD. You mean that Father—?

MRS. ALVING. Your poor father never found

any outlet for the excess of vitality in him. And I didn't bring any sunshine into his home.

OSWALD. You didn't?

MRS. ALVING. They had taught me about duty and things like that, and I sat here for too long believing in them. In the end everything became a matter of duty—*my* duty, and *his* duty, and—I'm afraid I made his home intolerable for your poor father, Oswald.

OSWALD. Why did you never write and tell me about this?

MRS. ALVING. Until now I never saw it as something that I could tell you, because you were his son.

OSWALD. And how did you see it?

MRS. ALVING (*slowly*). I only saw that your father was a depraved man before you were born.

OSWALD (*quietly*). Ah—! (*Gets up and goes over to the window.*)

MRS. ALVING. And day in and day out I thought of only one thing, that Regina really belonged here in this house—just as much as my own son.

OSWALD (*turns swiftly*). Regina—!

REGINA (*jumps up and asks softly*). I?

MRS. ALVING. Yes, now you both know.

OSWALD. Regina!

REGINA (*to herself*). So Mother was one of them.

MRS. ALVING. Your mother was in many ways a good woman, Regina.

REGINA. Yes, but still, she was one of them. Yes, I've sometimes wondered; but—! Well, madam, if you'll allow me I think I'd better leave. At once.

MRS. ALVING. Do you really want to, Regina?

REGINA. Yes, I certainly do.

MRS. ALVING. Of course you must do as you please, but—

OSWALD (*goes over to* REGINA). Go now? But you belong here.

REGINA. *Merci*, Mr. Alving—yes, I suppose I'm allowed to say Oswald now. But it certainly isn't the way I'd hoped.

MRS. ALVING. Regina, I haven't been open with you—

REGINA. I should say not. If I'd known that Oswald was ill like this, I—Now that there can never be anything serious between us—No, I'm not going to stay out here in the country and wear myself out looking after invalids.

OSWALD. Not even for someone who is so close to you?

REGINA. I should say not. A poor girl has got to make the best of her life while she's young. Otherwise she'll be left high and dry before she knows where she is. And I've got the joy of life in me too, Mrs. Alving.

MRS. ALVING. Yes, I'm afraid you have. But don't throw yourself away, Regina.

REGINA. Oh, what will be will be. If Oswald takes after his father, I shouldn't be surprised but what I'll take after my mother. May I ask, madam, does Pastor Manders know this about me?

MRS. ALVING. Pastor Manders knows everything.

REGINA (*begins to put on her shawl*). Well then, I'd better get down to the steamer as quick as I can. The Pastor's such a nice man to get along with. And I'm sure I've as much a right to a little of that money as he has—that awful carpenter.

MRS. ALVING. I'm sure you're very welcome to it, Regina.

REGINA (*looks spitefully at her*). You might have brought me up like the daughter of a gentleman. It'd have been more appropriate considering. (*Tosses her head.*) Oh, what the hell does it matter? (*With a bitter glance at the bottle, still unopened.*) I can still drink champagne with gentlemen.

MRS. ALVING. And if ever you need a home, Regina, come to me.

REGINA. No thank you, madam. Pastor Manders will take care of me. And if things go really wrong, I know a house where I belong.

MRS. ALVING. Where is that?

REGINA. In Captain Alving's home for sailors.

MRS. ALVING. Regina—I can see it. You will destroy yourself.

REGINA. Oh, rubbish. *Adieu!* (*Curtseys and goes out through the hall.*)

OSWALD (*stands by the window, looking out*). Has she gone?

MRS. ALVING. Yes.

OSWALD (*mumbles to himself*). I think it was wrong, all this.

MRS. ALVING (*goes over behind him and places her hands on his shoulders*). Oswald, my dear boy, has this news upset you very much?

OSWALD (*turns his face towards her*). All this about Father, you mean?

MRS. ALVING. Yes, about your poor father. I'm so afraid it may have been too much for you.

OSWALD. What on earth makes you think that? Of course it came as a great surprise to me. But I can't really feel it makes any difference.

MRS. ALVING (*takes her hands away*). No difference! That your father was so miserably unhappy!

OSWALD. I feel sorry for him of course, as I would for anyone, but—

MRS. ALVING. Nothing else? For your own father!

OSWALD (*impatiently*). Oh, Father, Father! I never knew anything about Father. I don't remember anything about him, except that once he made me sick.

MRS. ALVING. This is terrible! Surely a child ought to love its father whatever may happen?

OSWALD. Even when a child has nothing to thank its father for? Has never known him? Do you really cling to that old superstition —you, who are otherwise so enlightened?

MRS. ALVING. Do you really think it's only a superstition—?

OSWALD. Yes, Mother, surely you realize that. It's one of those truisms people hand down to their children—

MRS. ALVING (*shudders*). Ghosts!

OSWALD (*walks across the room*). Yes, that's not a bad word for them. Ghosts.

MRS. ALVING (*emotionally*). Oswald! Then you don't love me either!

OSWALD. At least I know you—

MRS. ALVING. Know me, yes. But is that all?

OSWALD. And of course I know how fond you are of me; and for that I must be grateful to you. And you can do so much for me now that I'm ill.

MRS. ALVING. Yes, Oswald, I can, can't I? Oh, I could almost bless your sickness for bringing you home to me. I realize it now. You aren't mine. I must win you.

OSWALD (*impatiently*). Yes, yes, yes. These are just empty phrases. You must remember I'm sick, Mother. I can't be expected to bother about others. I've enough worry thinking about myself.

MRS. ALVING (*quietly*). I shall be patient and undemanding.

OSWALD. And cheerful, Mother!

MRS. ALVING. Yes, my dear boy—I know. (*Goes over to him.*) Have I freed you from all your anxiety and self-reproach now?

OSWALD. Yes, you have. But who will take away the fear?

MRS. ALVING. The fear?

OSWALD (*walks across the room*). Regina would have done it for the asking.

MRS. ALVING. I don't understand you. What's all this about fear—and Regina?

OSWALD. Is it very late, Mother?

MRS. ALVING. It's early morning. (*Looks out into the conservatory.*) The dawn's beginning to show upon the mountains. It's going to be a fine day, Oswald. In a little while you'll be able to see the sun.

OSWALD. I'll look forward to that. Oh, there's still so much for me to look forward to and live for—

MRS. ALVING. Of course there is!

OSWALD. Even if I can't work, there's—

MRS. ALVING. Oh, you'll soon be able to work again, my dear boy. You haven't all these gnawing and oppressing thoughts to brood over any longer now.

OSWALD. No, it was a good thing you managed to rid me of all those ideas. Once I've got over this one thing—! (*Sits on the sofa.*) Let's sit down and talk, Mother.

MRS. ALVING. Yes, let's. (*Moves an armchair over to the sofa, and sits close to him.*)

OSWALD. And while we talk the sun will rise. And then you'll know. And then I won't have this fear any longer.

MRS. ALVING. What will I know?

OSWALD (*not listening to her*). Mother, didn't

you say earlier tonight that there wasn't anything in the world you wouldn't do for me if I asked you?

MRS. ALVING. Certainly I did.

OSWALD. And you'll keep your promise, Mother?

MRS. ALVING. Of course I will, my dearest, my only boy. I've nothing else to live for. Only you.

OSWALD. Yes, well, listen then. Mother, you're brave and strong, I know that. Now you must sit quite still while I tell you.

MRS. ALVING. But what is this dreadful thing you—?

OSWALD. You mustn't scream. You hear? Promise me that. We'll sit and talk about it quite calmly. Do you promise me that, Mother?

MRS. ALVING. Yes, yes, I promise. Only tell me.

OSWALD. Well then, all that business about being tired—and not being able to think about work—that isn't the real illness—

MRS. ALVING. What is the real illness?

OSWALD. The illness which is my inheritance —(*Points to his forehead and says quite quietly.*) That's in here.

MRS. ALVING (*almost speechless*). Oswald! No! No!

OSWALD. Don't scream. I can't bear it. Yes, Mother, it sits in here, watching and waiting. And it may break out any time; any hour.

MRS. ALVING. Oh, how horrible—!

OSWALD. Now keep calm. That's the way it is—

MRS. ALVING (*jumps up*). It isn't true, Oswald! It's impossible! It can't be true!

OSWALD. I had one attack down there. It soon passed. But when I found out what I had been like, this raging fear began to hunt me; and that's why I came back home to you as quickly as I could.

MRS. ALVING. So that's the fear—

OSWALD. Yes—it's so unspeakably repulsive, you see. Oh, if only it had been an ordinary illness that would have killed me—! Because I'm not so frightened of dying; though I'd like to live as long as I can.

MRS. ALVING. Yes, yes, Oswald, you must!

OSWALD. But this is so revolting. To be turned back into a slobbering baby; to have to be fed, to have to be—! Oh—! I can't think about it—!

MRS. ALVING. The child has its mother to nurse it.

OSWALD (*jumps up*). No, never! That's just what I won't allow! I can't bear to think that I might stay like that for years, growing old and grey. And perhaps you might die and leave me. (*Sits in* MRS. ALVING'S *chair.*) It might not mean that I'd die at once, the doctor said. He called it a softening of the brain or something. (*Smiles sadly.*) I think that sounds so beautiful. I shall always think of cherry-coloured velvet curtains—something delicious to stroke.

MRS. ALVING (*screams*). Oswald!

OSWALD (*jumps up again and walks across the room*). And now you've taken Regina from me. If only I had her! She would have saved me. I know.

MRS. ALVING (*goes over to him*). What do you mean by that, my beloved boy? Is there anything I wouldn't do to save you?

OSWALD. When I had recovered from the attack down there, the doctor told me that when it comes again—and it will come again—then there's no more hope.

MRS. ALVING. How could he be so heartless as to—?

OSWALD. I made him tell me. I told him I had arrangements to make. (*Smiles cunningly.*) And so I had. (*Takes a small box from his inside breast pocket.*) Mother, do you see this?

MRS. ALVING. What's that?

OSWALD. Morphine powders.

MRS. ALVING (*looks at him in horror*). Oswald—my boy—!

OSWALD. I've managed to collect twelve capsules—

MRS. ALVING (*tries to take it*). Give that box to me, Oswald.

OSWALD. Not yet, Mother. (*Puts it back in his pocket.*)

MRS. ALVING. I can't bear this!

OSWALD. You must bear it. If Regina had been here now, I'd have told her how things were with me—and asked her to do me this last service. I'm sure she would have helped me.

MRS. ALVING. Never!

OSWALD. When the horror was on me and she saw me lying there like a new-born baby, helpless, lost—beyond all hope—

MRS. ALVING. Regina would never have done it.

OSWALD. She would have. Regina was so splendidly carefree. And she would soon have got bored with looking after an invalid like me.

MRS. ALVING. Then thank God that Regina is not here!

OSWALD. Yes, well, so now you will have to do this last service for me, Mother.

MRS. ALVING (screams aloud). I?

OSWALD. Who else?

MRS. ALVING. I! Your mother!

OSWALD. Exactly.

MRS. ALVING. I, who gave you life!

OSWALD. I didn't ask you for life. And what kind of a life have you given me? I don't want it. Take it back.

MRS. ALVING. Help! Help! (Runs out into the hall.)

OSWALD (goes after her). Don't leave me! Where are you going?

MRS. ALVING (in the hall). To fetch the doctor, Oswald. Let me go!

OSWALD (also offstage). You're not going anywhere. And no one's coming here. (A key is turned.)

MRS. ALVING (comes back). Oswald! Oswald—my child!

OSWALD (follows her). If you have a mother's love for me, how can you see me suffer like this?

MRS. ALVING (after a moment's silence, says in a controlled voice). Very well. (Takes his hand.) I give you my word.

OSWALD. You promise?

MRS. ALVING. If it becomes necessary. But it won't be. No, no, it's impossible.

OSWALD. Yes, let us hope so. And let us live together as long as we can. Thank you, Mother.

He sits in the armchair, which MRS. ALVING *has moved over to the sofa. The*

day breaks. The lamp continues to burn on the table.

MRS. ALVING (approaches him cautiously). Do you feel calm now?

OSWALD. Yes.

MRS. ALVING (leans over him). You've just imagined these dreadful things, Oswald. You've imagined it all. All this suffering has been too much for you. But now you shall rest. At home with your own mother, my own dear, blessed boy. Point at anything you want and you shall have it, just like when you were a little child. There, there. Now the attack is over. You see how easily it passed! Oh, I know it! And, Oswald, do you see what a beautiful day we're going to have? Bright sunshine. Now you can really see your home.

She goes over to the table and puts out the lamp. The sun rises. The glacier and the snow-capped peaks in the background glitter in the morning light.

OSWALD (sits in the armchair facing downstage, motionless. Suddenly he says). Mother, give me the sun.

MRS. ALVING (by the table, starts and looks at him). What did you say?

OSWALD (repeats dully and tonelessly). The sun. The sun.

MRS. ALVING (goes over to him). Oswald, how are you feeling?

OSWALD *seems to shrink small in his chair. All his muscles go slack. His face is expressionless. His eyes stare emptily.*

MRS. ALVING (trembles with fear). What's this? (Screams loudly.) Oswald! What is it? (Throws herself on her knees beside him and shakes him.) Oswald! Oswald! Look at me! Don't you know me?

OSWALD (tonelessly as before). The sun. The sun.

MRS. ALVING (jumps to her feet in despair, tears her hair with both hands and screams). I can't bear this! (Whispers as though numbed.) I can't bear it! No!

(*Suddenly.*) Where did he put them? (*Fumbles quickly across his breast.*) Here! (*Shrinks a few steps backwards and screams.*) No; no; no! Yes! No; no! (*She stands a few steps away from him with her* hands twisted in her hair, speechless, and stares at him in horror.*)

OSWALD (*still motionless*). The sun. The sun.

◆◆ The Cherry Orchard

By ANTON CHEKHOV

Translated by Robert W. Corrigan

Characters

LYUBOV ANDREYEVNA RANEVSKY, owner of the
cherry orchard

ANYA, her daughter, age 17

VARYA, her adopted daughter, age 24

LEONID ANDREYEVICH GAEV, Lyubov's brother

YERMOLAY ALEXEYEVICH LOPAHIN, a business
man

PYOTR SERGEYEVICH TROFIMOV, a student

BORIS BORISOVICH SEMYONOV-PISHCHIK, a land-
owner

CHARLOTTA IVANOVNA, a governess

SEMYON PANTALEYEVICH EPIHODOV, a clerk on
the Ranevsky estate

DUNYASHA, a maid

FEERS, an old servant, age 87

YASHA, a young servant

A TRAMP

THE STATION MASTER

A POST-OFFICE CLERK

GUESTS and SERVANTS

*The action takes place on the estate of
Madame Ranevsky.*

ACT I

*A room which used to be the children's
room and is still called the nursery. Several doors, one leading into* ANYA's *room.
It is early in the morning and the sun is
rising. It is early in May, but there is a
morning frost. The windows are closed
but through them can be seen the
blossoming cherry trees. Enter* DUN-
YASHA, *carrying a candle, and* LOPAHIN
with a book in his hand.

LOPAHIN. The train's arrived, thank God.
What time is it?

DUNYASHA. It's nearly two. (*Blows out the
candle.*) It's daylight already.

LOPAHIN. The train must have been at least
two hours late. (*Yawns and stretches.*) And
what a fool I am! I make a special trip out
here to meet them at the station, and then
I fall asleep. . . . Just sat down in the chair
and dropped off. What a nuisance. Why
didn't you wake me up?

DUNYASHA. I thought you'd gone. (*Listens.*)
I think they're coming.

LOPAHIN (*also listens*). No . . . I should've
been there to help them with their luggage
and other things . . . (*Pause.*) Lyubov
Andreyevna has been abroad for five years.
I wonder what she's like now. She used to
be such a kind and good person. So easy
to get along with and always considerate.
Why, I remember when I was fifteen, my
father—he had a store in town then—hit me
in the face and it made my nose bleed. . . .
We'd come out here for something or other,
and he was drunk. Oh, I remember it as
if it happened yesterday. . . . She was so
young and beautiful . . . Lyubov Andreyevna brought me into this very room—the
nursery, and she fixed my nose and she

Anton Chekhov, "The Cherry Orchard," in *Six
Plays of Chekhov*, trans. by Robert W. Corrigan

(New York: Holt, Rinehart and Winston, 1962),
pp. 289–340.

said to me, "Don't cry, little peasant, it'll be better by the time you get married" . . . (*Pause.*) "Little peasant" . . . She was right, my father was a peasant. And look at me now—going about in a white waist-coat and brown shoes, like a crown in pea-cock's feathers. Oh, I am rich all right, I've got lots of money, but when you think about it, I'm still just a peasant. (*Turning over pages of the book.*) Here, I've been reading this book, and couldn't understand a word of it. Fell asleep reading it. (*Pause.*)

DUNYASHA. The dogs have been awake all night: they know their mistress is coming.

LOPAHIN. Why, what's the matter with you, Dunyasha?

DUNYASHA. My hands are shaking. I think I'm going to faint.

LOPAHIN. You've become too delicate and re-fined, Dunyasha. You get yourself all dressed up like a lady, and you fix your hair like one, too. You shouldn't do that, you know. You must remember your place.

Enter EPIHODOV *with a bouquet of flow-ers; he wears a jacket and brightly pol-ished high boots which squeak loudly. As he enters he drops the flowers.*

EPIHODOV (*picks up the flowers*). The gar-dener sent these. He says they're to go in the dining room. (*Hands the flowers to* DUNYASHA.)

LOPAHIN. And bring me some kvass.

DUNYASHA. All right.

EPIHODOV. It's chilly outside this morning, three degrees of frost, and here the cherry trees are all in bloom. I can't say much for this climate of ours, you know. (*Sighs.*) No, I really can't. It doesn't contribute to—well, you know, things . . . And what do you think, Yermolay Alexeyevich, the day before yesterday I bought myself a pair of boots and they squeak so much . . . well, I mean to say, they're impossible. . . . What can I use to fix them?

LOPAHIN. Oh, be quiet! And don't bother me!

EPIHODOV. Every day something unpleasant happens to me. But I don't complain; I'm used to it, why I even laugh. (*Enter* DUN-YASHA: *she serves* LOPAHIN *with kvass.*) Well, I have to be going. (*Bumps into a chair which falls over.*) There, you see! (*Triumphantly.*) You can see for yourself what I mean, you see . . . so to speak . . . It's absolutely amazing! (*Goes out.*)

DUNYASHA. I must tell you a secret, Yermolay Alexeyevich. Epihodov proposed to me.

LOPAHIN. Really!

DUNYASHA. I don't know what to do. . . . He's a quiet man, but then sometimes he starts talking, and then you can't understand a word he says. It sounds nice, and he says it with so much feeling, but it doesn't make any sense. I think I like him a little, and he's madly in love with me. But the poor man, he's sort of unlucky! Do you know, something unpleasant seems to happen to him every day. That's why they tease him and call him "two-and-twenty misfortunes."

LOPAHIN (*listens*). I think I hear them com-ing. . . .

DUNYASHA. Coming! . . . Oh, what's the matter with me. . . . I feel cold all over.

LOPAHIN. Yes, they're really coming! Let's go and meet them at the door. I wonder if she'll recognize me? We haven't seen each other for five years.

DUNYASHA (*agitated*). I'm going to faint . . . Oh, I'm going to faint! . . .

The sound of two carriages driving up to the house can be heard. LOPAHIN *and* DUNYASHA *hurry out. The stage is empty. Then there are sounds of people arriving in the next room.* FEERS, *who has gone to meet the train, enters the room leaning on a cane. He crosses the stage as rapidly as he can. He is dressed in an old-fashioned livery coat and a top hat and is muttering to himself, though it is impossible to make out what he is saying. The noises off-stage become louder.*

VOICE (*off-stage*). Let's go through here.

Enter LYUBOV ANDREYEVNA, ANYA, *and* CHARLOTTA IVANOVNA, *leading a small dog, all in traveling clothes,* VARYA, *wear-*

ing an overcoat and a kerchief over her head, GAEV, SEMYONOV-PISHCHIK, LO-PAHIN, DUNYASHA, *carrying a bundle and parasol and other servants with luggage.*

ANYA. Let's go through here. Do you remember what room this is, Mamma?

LYUBOV (*joyfully, through her tears*). The nursery!

VARYA. How cold it is! My hands are numb. (*To* LYUBOV.) Your rooms are the same as always, Mamma dear, the white one, and the lavender one.

LYUBOV. The nursery, my dear, beautiful room! . . . I used to sleep here when I was little. (*Cries.*) And here I am again, like a little child . . . (*She kisses her brother, then* VARYA, *then her brother again.*) And Varya hasn't changed a bit, looking like a nun. And I recognized Dunyasha, *too.* (*Kisses* DUNYASHA.)

GAEV. The train was two hours late. Just think of it! Such efficiency!

CHARLOTTA (*to* PISHCHIK). And my dog eats nuts, too.

PISHCHIK (*astonished*). Think of that!

They all go out except ANYA *and* DUNYASHA.

DUNYASHA. We've waited and waited for you . . . (*Helps* ANYA *to take off her hat and coat.*)

ANYA. I haven't slept for four nights . . . I'm freezing.

DUNYASHA. It was Lent when you left, and it was snowing and freezing; but it's spring now. Darling! (*She laughs and kisses her.*) Oh, how I've missed you! I could hardly stand it. My pet, my precious . . . But I must tell you . . . I can't wait another minute . . .

ANYA (*without enthusiasm*). What time is it? . . .

DUNYASHA. Epihodov, the clerk, proposed to me right after Easter.

ANYA. You never talk about anything else . . . (*Tidies her hair.*) I've lost all my hairpins. . . . (*She's so tired she can hardly keep on her feet.*)

DUNYASHA. I really don't know what to think. He loves me . . . he loves me very much!

ANYA (*looking through the door into her room, tenderly*). My own room, my own windows, just as if I'd never left them! I'm home again! Tomorrow I'm going to get up and run right to the garden! Oh, if only I could fall asleep! I couldn't sleep all the way back, I've been so worried.

DUNYASHA. Pyotr Sergeyevich came the day before yesterday.

ANYA (*joyfully*). Pyeta!

DUNYASHA. We put him in the bathhouse, he's probably asleep now. He said he didn't want to inconvenience you. (*Looks at her watch.*) I should have gotten him up, but Varya told me not to. "Don't you dare get him up," she said.

Enter VARYA *with a bunch of keys at her waist.*

VARYA. Dunyasha, get some coffee, and hurry! Mamma wants some.

DUNYASHA. I'll get it right away. (*Goes out.*)

VARYA. Thank God, you're back! You're home again. (*Embracing her.*) My little darling's come home! How are you, my precious?

ANYA. If you only knew what I've had to put up with!

VARYA. I can just imagine . . .

ANYA. You remember, I left just before Easter and it was cold then. And Charlotta never stopped talking the whole time, talking and those silly tricks of hers. Why did you make me take Charlotta?

VARYA. But you couldn't go all alone, darling. At seventeen!

ANYA. When we got to Paris it was cold and snowing. My French was terrible. Mamma was living on the fifth floor, and the place was filled with people—some French ladies, and an old priest with a little book, and the room was full of cigarette smoke. It was so unpleasant. All of a sudden I felt so sorry for Mamma that I put my arms around her neck and hugged her and wouldn't let go I was so upset. Later Mamma cried and was very kind.

VARYA (*tearfully*). I can't stand to hear it! . . .

ANYA. She had already sold her villa at Mentone, and she had nothing left, not a thing. And I didn't have any money left either, not a penny. In fact, I barely had enough to get to Paris. And Mamma didn't understand it at all. On the way, we'd eat at the best restaurants and she'd order the most expensive dishes and tip the waiters a rouble each. Charlotta's the same way. And Yasha expected a full-course dinner for himself; it was horrible. You know, Yasha is Mamma's valet, now, we brought him with us.

VARYA. Yes, I've seen the scoundrel.

ANYA. Well, how's everything here? Have you paid the interest on the mortgage?

VARYA. With what?

ANYA. Oh dear! Oh dear!

VARYA. The time runs out in August, and then it will be up for sale.

ANYA. Oh dear!

LOPAHIN (*puts his head through the door and moos like a cow*). Moo-o. . . . (*Disappears.*)

VARYA (*tearfully*). I'd like to hit him . . . (*Clenches her fist.*)

ANYA (*her arms round* VARYA, *dropping her voice*). Varya, has he proposed to you? (VARYA *shakes her head.*) But he loves you. . . . Why don't you talk to him, what are you waiting for?

VARYA. Nothing will come of it. He's too busy to have time to think of me . . . He doesn't notice me at all. It's easier when he isn't around, it makes me miserable just to see him. Everybody talks of our wedding and congratulates me, but in fact there's nothing to it, it's all a dream. (*In a different tone.*) You've got a new pin, it looks like a bee.

ANYA (*sadly*). Mamma bought it for me. (*She goes into her room and then with childlike gaiety.*) Did you know that in Paris I went up in a balloon?

VARYA. My darling's home again! My precious one's home. (DUNYASHA *returns with a coffeepot and prepares coffee. Standing by* ANYA's *door.*) You know, all day long, as I go about the house doing my work, I'm always dreaming. If only we could marry you to some rich man, I'd be more at peace.

Then they could go away; first I'd go to the cloisters, and then I'd go on a pilgrimage to Kiev, and then Moscow . . . I'd spend my life just walking from one holy place to another. On and on. Oh, what a wonderful life that would be!

ANYA. The birds are singing in the garden. What time is it?

VARYA. It must be nearly three. Time you went to bed, darling. (*Goes into* ANYA's *room.*) Oh, what a wonderful life!

Enter YASHA, *with a blanket and a small bag.*

YASHA (*crossing the stage, in an affectedly genteel voice*). May I go through here?

DUNYASHA. My, how you've changed since you've been abroad, Yasha. I hardly recognized you.

YASHA. Hm! And who are you?

DUNYASHA. When you went away, I was no bigger than this . . . (*Shows her height from the floor.*) I'm Dunyasha, Fyodor's daughter. You don't remember me!

YASHA. Hm! You're quite a little peach! (*Looks around and embraces her; she screams and drops a saucer.* YASHA *goes out quickly.*)

VARYA (*in the doorway, crossly*). What's happening in here?

DUNYASHA (*tearfully*). I've broken a saucer.

VARYA. That's good luck.

ANYA (*coming out of her room*). We ought to warn Mamma that Petya's here.

VARYA. I gave strict orders not to wake him up.

ANYA (*pensively*). Six years ago father died, and then a month later Grisha was drowned in the river. He was such a beautiful little boy—and only seven! Mamma couldn't stand it so she went away . . . and never looked back. (*Shivers.*) How well I understand her! If she only knew! (*Pause.*) And, Petya was Grisha's tutor, he might remind her . . .

Enter FEERS, *wearing a jacket and a white waistcoat.*

FEERS (*goes over and is busy with the samovar*). The mistress will have her coffee in here. (*Puts on white gloves.*) Is it ready? (*To* DUNYASHA, *severely.*) Where's the cream?

DUNYASHA. Oh, I forgot! (*Goes out quickly.*)

FEERS (*fussing around the coffeepot*). That girl's hopeless. . . . (*Mutters.*) They've come from Paris . . . Years ago the master used to go to Paris . . . Used to go by carriage . . . (*Laughs.*)

VARYA. Feers, what are you laughing at?

FEERS. What would you like? (*Happily.*) The mistress has come home! Home at last! I don't mind if I die now . . . (*Weeps with joy.*)

Enter LYUBOV, LOPAHIN, GAEV *and* SEMYONOV-PISHCHIK, *the latter in a long peasant coat of fine cloth and full trousers tucked inside high boots.* GAEV, *as he comes in, moves his arms and body as if he were playing billiards.*

LYUBOV. How does it go now? Let me think . . . The red off the side and into the middle pocket!

GAEV. That's right! Then I put the white into the corner pocket! . . . Years ago we used to sleep in this room, and now I'm fifty-one, strange as it may seem.

LOPAHIN. Yes, time flies.

GAEV. What?

LOPAHIN. Time flies, I say.

GAEV. This place smells of patchouli . . .

ANYA. I'm going to bed. Goodnight, Mamma. (*Kisses her.*)

LYUBOV. My precious child! (*Kisses her hands.*) Are you glad you're home? I still can't get used to it.

ANYA. Goodnight, Uncle.

GAEV (*kisses her face and hands*). God bless you. You're so much like your mother! (*To his sister.*) You looked exactly like her at her age, Lyuba.

ANYA *shakes hands with* LOPAHIN *and* PISHCHIK, *goes out and shuts the door after her.*

LYUBOV. She's very tired.

PISHCHIK. It's been a long trip for her.

VARYA (*to* LOPAHIN *and* PISHCHIK). Well, gentlemen? It's nearly three o'clock, time to say good-bye.

LYUBOV (*laughs*). You haven't changed a bit, Varya. (*Draws* VARYA *to her and kisses her.*) Let me have some coffee, then we'll all turn in. (FEERS *places a cushion under her feet.*) Thank you, my dear. I've got into the habit of drinking coffee. I drink it day and night. Thank you, my dear old friend. (*Kisses* FEERS.)

VARYA. I'd better see if they brought all the luggage in. (*Goes out.*)

LYUBOV. Is it really me sitting here? (*Laughing.*) I'd like to dance and wave my arms about. (*Covering her face with her hands.*) But am I just dreaming? God, how I love it here—my own country! Oh, I love it so much, I could hardly see anything from the train, I was crying so hard. (*Through tears.*) Here, but I must drink my coffee. Thank you, Feers, thank you, my dear old friend. I'm so glad you're still alive.

FEERS. The day before yesterday.

GAEV. He doesn't hear very well.

LOPAHIN. I've got to leave for Kharkov a little after four. What a nuisance! It's so good just to see you, and I want to talk with you . . . You look as lovely as ever.

PISHCHIK (*breathing heavily*). Prettier. In her fancy Parisian clothes . . . She's simply ravishing!

LOPAHIN. Your brother here—Leonid Andreyevich—says that I'm nothing but a hick from the country, a tight-fisted peasant, but it doesn't bother me. Let him say what he likes. All I want is that you trust me as you always have. Merciful God! My father was your father's serf, and your grandfather's, too, but you've done so much for me that I've forgotten all that. I love you as if you were my own sister . . . more than that even.

LYUBOV. I just can't sit still, I can't for the life of me! (*She jumps up and walks about in great excitement.*) I'm so happy, it's too much for me. It's all right, you can laugh at me. I know I'm being silly . . . My wonderful old bookcase! (*Kisses bookcase.*) And my little table!

GAEV. You know, the old Nurse died while you were away.

LYUBOV (*sits down and drinks coffee*). Yes, you wrote to me about it. May she rest in peace.

GAEV. Anastasy died, too. And Petrushka quit and is working in town for the chief of police. (*Takes a box of gumdrops out of his pocket and puts one in his mouth.*)

PISHCHIK. My daughter, Dashenka, sends you her greetings.

LOPAHIN. I feel like telling you some good news, something to cheer you up. (*Looks at his watch.*) I'll have to leave in a minute, so there's not much time to talk. But briefly it's this. As you know, the cherry orchard is going to be sold to pay your debts. They've set August 22nd as the date for the auction, but you can sleep in peace and not worry about it; there's a way out. Here's my plan, so please pay close attention. Your estate is only twenty miles from town, and the railroad is close by. Now, if the cherry orchard and the land along the river were subdivided and leased for the building of summer cottages, you'd have a yearly income of at least twenty-five thousand roubles.

GAEV. Such nonsense!

LYUBOV. I'm afraid I don't quite understand, Yermolay Alexeyevich.

LOPAHIN. You'd divide the land into one acre lots and rent them for at least twenty-five roubles a year. I'll bet you, that if you advertise it now there won't be a lot left by the fall; they'll be snapped up almost at once. You see, you're saved! And really, I must congratulate you; it's a perfect setup. The location is marvelous and the river's deep enough for swimming. Of course, the land will have to be cleared and cleaned up a bit. For instance, all those old buildings will have to be torn down . . . And this house, too . . . but then it's not really good for anything any more. . . . And then, the old cherry orchard will have to be cut down . . .

LYUBOV. Cut down? My good man, forgive me, but you don't seem to understand. If there's one thing that's interesting and really valuable in this whole part of the country, it's our cherry orchard.

LOPAHIN. The only valuable thing about it is that it's very large. It only produces a crop every other year and then who wants to buy it?

GAEV. Why, this orchard is even mentioned in the Encyclopedia.

LOPAHIN (*looking at his watch*). If you don't decide now, and do something about it before August, the cherry orchard as well as the estate will be auctioned off. So make up your minds! There's no other way out, I promise you. There's no other way.

FEERS. In the old days, forty or fifty years ago, the cherries were dried, preserved, pickled, made into jam, and sometimes. . . .

GAEV. Be quiet, Feers.

FEERS. And sometimes, whole wagon-loads of dried cherries were shipped to Moscow and Kharkov. We used to make a lot of money on them then! And the dried cherries used to be soft, juicy, sweet, and very good . . . They knew how to do it then . . . they had a way of cooking them . . .

LYUBOV. And where is that recipe now?

FEERS. They've forgotten it. Nobody can remember it.

PISHCHIK (*to* LYUBOV). What's it like in Paris? Did you eat frogs?

LYUBOV. I ate crocodiles.

PISHCHIK. Well, will you imagine that!

LOPAHIN. Until recently only rich people and peasants lived in the country, but now lots of people come out for the summer. Almost every town, even the small ones, is surrounded with summer places. And probably within the next twenty years there'll be more and more of these people. Right now, all they do is sit on the porch and drink tea, but later on they might begin to grow a few things, and then your cherry orchard would be full of life again . . . rich and prosperous.

GAEV (*indignantly*). Such a lot of nonsense!

Enter VARYA *and* YASHA.

VARYA. There were two telegrams for you, Mamma dear. (*Takes out the keys and opens the old bookcase, making a great deal of noise.*) Here they are.

LYUBOV. They're from Paris. (*Tears them up without reading them.*) I'm through with Paris.

GAEV. Do you know, Lyuba, how old this bookcase is? Last week I pulled out the bottom drawer, and I found the date it was made burned in the wood. Just think, it's exactly a hundred years old. What do you think of that, eh? We ought to celebrate its anniversary. I know it's an inanimate object, but still—it's a bookcase!

PISHCHIK (*astonished*). A hundred years! Can you imagine that!

GAEV. Yes . . . That's quite something. (*Feeling round the bookcase with his hands.*) Dear, most honored bookcase! I salute you! For one hundred years you have served the highest ideals of goodness and justice. For one hundred years you have made us aware of the need for creative work; several generations of our family have had their courage sustained and their faith in a brighter future fortified by your silent call; you have fostered in us the ideals of public service and social consciousness. (*Pause.*)

LOPAHIN. Yes . . .

LYUBOV. You haven't changed a bit, Leonia.

GAEV (*slightly embarrassed*). I shoot it off the corner into the middle pocket! . . .

LOPAHIN (*looks at his watch*). Well, I've got to go.

YASHA (*brings medicine to LYUBOV*). Would you like to take your pills now; it's time.

PISHCHIK. You shouldn't take medicine, my dear . . . they don't do you any good . . . or harm either. Let me have them. (*Takes the box from her, pours the pills into the palm of his hand, blows on them, puts them all into his mouth and drinks them down with kvass.*) There!

LYUBOV (*alarmed*). You're out of your mind!

PISHCHIK. I took all the pills.

LOPAHIN. What a stomach! (*All laugh.*)

FEERS. His honor was here during Holy Week, and he ate half a bucket of pickles. (*Mutters.*)

LYUBOV. What's he saying?

VARYA. He's been muttering like that for three years now. We're used to it.

YASHA. It's his age. . . .

CHARLOTTA IVANOVNA, *very thin, and tightly laced in a white dress, with a lorgnette at her waist, passes across the stage.*

LOPAHIN. Excuse me, Charlotta Ivanovna, for not greeting you. I didn't have a chance. (*Tries to kiss her hand.*)

CHARLOTTA (*withdrawing her hand*). If I let you kiss my hand, then you'd want to kiss my elbow next, and then my shoulder.

LOPAHIN. This just isn't my lucky day. (*All laugh.*) Charlotta Ivanovna, do a trick for us.

CHARLOTTA. Not now. I want to go to bed. (*Goes out.*)

LOPAHIN. I'll be back in three weeks. (*Kisses LYUBOV's hand.*) It's time I'm going so I'll say good-bye. (*To GAEV.*) Au revoir. (*Embraces PISHCHIK.*) Au revoir. (*Shakes hands with VARYA, then with FEERS and YASHA.*) I don't want to go, really. (*To LYUBOV.*) Think over the idea of the summer cottages and if you decide anything, let me know, and I'll get you a loan of at least fifty thousand. So think it over seriously.

VARYA (*crossly.*) Won't you ever go?

LOPAHIN. I'm going, I'm going. (*Goes out.*)

GAEV. What a boor! I beg your pardon . . . Varya's going to marry him, he's Varya's fiancé.

VARYA. Please don't talk like that, Uncle.

LYUBOV. Well, Varya, I'd be delighted. He's a good man.

PISHCHIK. He's a man . . . you have to say that . . . a most worthy fellow . . . My Dashenka says so too . . . she says all sorts of things. . . . (*He drops asleep and snores, but wakes up again at once.*) By the way, my dear, will you lend me two hundred and forty roubles? I've got to pay the interest on the mortgage tomorrow . . .

VARYA (*in alarm*). We haven't got it, really we haven't!

LYUBOV. It's true, I haven't got a thing.

PISHCHIK. It'll turn up. (*Laughs.*) I never lose hope. There are times when I think everything's lost, I'm ruined, and then—suddenly!—a railroad is built across my land, and they pay me for it! Something's bound to happen, if not today, then tomorrow, or the next day. Perhaps Dashenka will win two hundred thousand—she's got a lottery ticket.

LYUBOV. Well, we've finished our coffee; now we can go to bed.

FEERS (*brushing* GAEV, *admonishing him*). You've got on those trousers again! What am I going to do with you?

VARYA (*in a low voice*). Anya's asleep. (*Quietly opens a window.*) The sun's rising and see how wonderful the trees are! And the air smells so fragrant! The birds are beginning to sing.

GAEV (*coming to the window*). The orchard is all white. You haven't forgotten, Lyuba? How straight that lane is . . . just like a ribbon. And how it shines on moonlight nights. Do you remember? You haven't forgotten, have you?

LYUBOV (*looks through the window at the orchard*). Oh, my childhood, my innocent childhood! I used to sleep here, and I'd look out at the orchard and every morning when I woke up I was so happy. The orchard was exactly the same, nothing's changed. (*Laughs happily.*) All, all white! Oh, my orchard! After the dark, gloomy autumn and the cold winter, you are young again and full of joy; the angels have not deserted you! If only this burden could be taken from me, if only I could forget my past!

GAEV. Yes, and now the orchard's going to be sold to pay our debts, how strange it all is.

LYUBOV. Look, there's Mother walking through the orchard . . . dressed all in white! (*Laughs happily.*) It is Mother!

GAEV. Where?

VARYA. Oh, please, Mamma dear!

LYUBOV. You're right, it's no one, I only imagined it. Over there, you see, on the right, by the path that goes to the arbor; there's a small white tree that's bending so it looks just like a woman.

Enter TROFIMOV. *He is dressed in a shabby student's uniform, and wears glasses.*

What a wonderful orchard! Masses of white blossoms, the blue sky . . .

TROFIMOV. Lyubov Andreyevna! (*She turns to him.*) I'll just say hello and leave at once. (*Kisses her hand warmly.*) They told me to wait until morning, but I couldn't wait any longer. (LYUBOV *looks at him, puzzled.*)

VARYA (*through tears*). This is Petya Trofimov.

TROFIMOV. Petya Trofimov, I was Grisha's tutor. Have I changed that much?

LYUBOV *puts her arms round him and weeps quietly.*

GAEV (*embarrassed*). Now, now, Lyuba . . .

VARYA (*weeps*). Didn't I tell you to wait until tomorrow, Petya?

LYUBOV. My Grisha . . . my little boy . . . Oh, Grisha . . . my son . . .

VARYA. Don't cry, Mamma darling. There's nothing we can do, it was God's will.

TROFIMOV (*gently, with emotion*). Don't, don't . . . please.

LYUBOV (*weeping quietly*). My little boy was lost . . . drowned . . . Why? Why, my friend? (*More quietly.*) Anya's asleep in there, and here I'm crying and making a scene. But tell me, Petya, what's happened to your good looks? You've aged so.

TROFIMOV. A peasant woman on the train called me "that moth-eaten man."

LYUBOV. You used to be such an attractive boy, a typical young student. But now your hair is thin and you wear glasses. Are you still a student? (*She walks to the door.*)

TROFIMOV. I expect I'll be a student as long as I live.

LYUBOV (*kisses her brother, then* VARYA). Well, go to bed now. You have aged, too, Leonid.

PISHCHIK (*following her*). Yes, I suppose it's

time to get to bed. Oh, my gout! I'd better spend the night here, and in the morning, Lyubov Andreyevna, my dear, I'd like to borrow the two hundred and forty roubles.

GAEV. Don't you ever stop?

PISHCHIK. Just two hundred and forty roubles . . . To pay the interest on my mortgage.

LYUBOV. I haven't any money, my friend.

PISHCHIK. Oh, I'll pay you back, my dear. It's not much, after all.

LYUBOV. Oh, all right. Leonid will give it to you. You give him the money, Leonid.

GAEV. Why, of course; glad to. As much as he wants!

LYUBOV. What else can we do? He needs it. He'll pay it back.

LYUBOV, TROFIMOV, PISHCHIK and FEERS *go out.* GAEV, VARYA and YASHA *remain.*

GAEV. My sister hasn't lost her habit of throwing money away. (*To* YASHA.) Get out of the way, you smell like a barnyard.

YASHA (*with a sneer*). And you haven't changed either, have you Leonid Andreyevich?

GAEV. What's that? (*To* VARYA.) What did he say?

VARYA (*to* YASHA). Your mother came out from town yesterday to see you, and she's been waiting out in the servants' quarters ever since.

YASHA. I wish she wouldn't bother me.

VARYA. Oh, you ought to be ashamed of yourself.

YASHA. What's she in such a hurry for? She could have come tomorrow. (YASHA *goes out.*)

VARYA. Mamma hasn't changed a bit. She'd give away everything we had, if she could.

GAEV. Yes . . . You know, when many things are prescribed to cure a disease, that means it's incurable. I've been wracking my brains to find an answer, and I've come up with several solutions, plenty of them—which means there aren't any. It would be wonderful if we could inherit some money, or if our Anya were to marry some very rich man, or if one of us went to Yaroslavl and

tried our luck with our old aunt, the Countess. You know she's very rich.

VARYA (*weeping*). If only God would help us.

GAEV. Oh, stop blubbering! The Countess is very rich, but she doesn't like us . . . To begin with, my sister married a lawyer, and not a nobleman . . . (ANYA *appears in the doorway.*) She married a commoner . . . and since then no one can say she's behaved in the most virtuous way possible. She's good, kind, and lovable, and I love her very much, but no matter how much you may allow for extenuating circumstances, you've got to admit that her morals have not been beyond reproach. You can sense it in everything she does . . .

VARYA (*in a whisper*). Anya's standing in the doorway.

GAEV. What? (*A pause.*) Isn't that strange, something's gotten into my right eye . . . I'm having a terrible time seeing. And last Thursday, when I was in the District Court . . . (ANYA *comes in.*)

VARYA. Anya, why aren't you asleep?

ANYA. I don't feel like sleeping. I just can't.

GAEV. My dear little girl! (*Kisses* ANYA's *face and hands.*) My child! (*Tearfully.*) You're not just my niece, you're an angel, my whole world. Please believe me, believe . . .

ANYA. I believe you, Uncle. Everyone loves you, respects you . . . but, dear Uncle, you shouldn't talk so much, just try to keep quiet. What were you saying just now about mother, about your own sister? What made you say that?

GAEV. Yes, yes! (*He takes her hand and puts it over his face.*) You're quite right, it was a horrible thing to say! My God! My God! And that speech I made to the bookcase . . . so stupid! As soon as I finished it, I realized how stupid it was.

VARYA. It's true, Uncle dear, you oughtn't to talk so much. Just keep quiet, that's all.

ANYA. If you keep quiet, you'll find life is more peaceful.

GAEV. I'll be quiet. (*Kisses* ANYA's *and* VARYA's *hands.*) I'll be quiet. But I must tell you something about all this business, it's important. Last Thursday I went to the District Court, and I got talking with some friends, and from what they said it looks as if it might be possible to get a second mortgage so we can pay the interest to the bank.

VARYA. If only God would help us!

GAEV. I'm going again on Tuesday to talk with them some more. (*To* VARYA.) Oh, stop crying. (*To* ANYA.) Your mother's going to talk with Lopahin, and he certainly won't refuse her. And after you've had a little rest, you can go to Yaroslavl to see your grandmother, the Countess. You see, we'll attack the problem from three sides, and—it's as good as solved! We'll pay the interest, I'm sure of it. (*He eats a gumdrop.*) On my honor, on anything you like, I swear the estate'll not be sold! (*Excited.*) I'll bet my happiness on it! Here's my hand, you can call me a worthless liar if I allow the auction to take place. I swear it with all my soul!

ANYA (*calmer, with an air of happiness*). How good you are, Uncle, and how sensible! (*Embracing him.*) I'm not afraid anymore. I feel so happy and at peace.

Enter FEERS.

FEERS (*reproachfully*). Leonid Andreyevich, aren't you ashamed of yourself? When are you going to bed?

GAEV. In a minute. Now you go away, Feers. I can get ready for bed myself. Come along, children, time for bed. We'll talk about it some more tomorrow, you must go to bed now. (*Kisses* ANYA *and* VARYA.) You know, I'm a man of the 'eighties. People don't think much of that period these days, but still I can say that I've suffered a great deal in my lifetime because of my convictions. There's a reason why the peasants love me. You have to know the peasants! You have to know . . .

ANYA. You're beginning again, Uncle!

VARYA. Yes, you'd better keep quiet, Uncle dear.

FEERS (*sternly*). Leonid Andreyevich!

GAEV. I'm coming, I'm coming! Go to bed now! Bank the white into the side pocket. There's a shot for you . . . (*Goes out;* FEERS *hobbles after him.*)

ANYA. I feel better now, although I don't want to go to Yaroslavl, I don't like the Countess at all, but then, thanks to Uncle, we really don't have to worry at all. (*She sits down.*)

VARYA. I've got to get some sleep. I'm going. Oh, by the way, we had a terrible scene while you were gone. You know, there are only a few old servants left out in the servants' quarters: just Yefmushka, Polya, Yevstignay, and Karp. Well, they let some tramp sleep out there, and at first I didn't say anything about it. But then later, I heard people saying that I had given orders to feed them nothing but beans. Because I was stingy, you see . . . Yevstignay was the cause of it all. "Well," I think to myself, "if that's how things are, just you wait!" So I called Yevstignay in. (*Yawns.*) So he came. "What's all this, Yevstignay," I said to him, "you're such a fool." (*She walks up to* ANYA.) Anichka! (*A pause.*) She's asleep! . . . (*Takes her arm.*) Let's go to bed! Come! (*Leads her away.*) My darling's fallen asleep! Come . . . (*They go towards the door. The sound of a shepherd's pipe is heard from far away, beyond the orchard.* TROFIMOV *crosses the stage, but, seeing* VARYA *and* ANYA, *stops.*) Sh-sh! She's asleep . . . asleep . . . Come along, come along.

ANYA (*softly, half-asleep*). I'm so tired. . . . I can hear the bells ringing all the time . . . Uncle . . . dear . . . Mamma and Uncle. . . .

VARYA. Come, darling, come. . . . (*They go into* ANYA's *room.*)

TROFIMOV (*deeply moved*). Oh, Anya . . . my sunshine! My spring!

Curtain

ACT II

An old abandoned chapel in a field. Beside it are a well, an old bench, and some tombstones. A road leads to the Ranevsky estate. On one side a row of poplars casts a shadow; at that point the cherry orchard begins. In the distance, a line of telegraph poles can be seen, and beyond them, on the horizon is the outline of a large town, visible only in very clear weather. It's nearly sunset. CHARLOTTA, YASHA *and* DUNYASHA *are sitting on the bench;* EPIHODOV *is standing near by, playing a guitar; everyone is lost in thought.* CHARLOTTA *is wearing an old hunting cap; she has taken a shotgun off her shoulder and is adjusting the buckle on the strap.*

CHARLOTTA (*thoughtfully*). I don't know how old I am. For you see, I haven't got a passport . . . but I keep pretending that I'm still very young. When I was a little girl, my father and mother traveled from fair to fair giving performances—oh, very good ones. And I used to do the *"salto-mortale"* and all sorts of other tricks, too. When Papa and Mamma died, a German lady took me to live with her and sent me to school. So when I grew up I became a governess. But where I come from and who I am, I don't know. Who my parents were —perhaps they weren't even married—I don't know. (*Taking a cucumber from her pocket and beginning to eat it.*) I don't know anything. (*Pause.*) I'm longing to talk to someone, but there isn't anybody. I haven't anybody . . .

EPIHODOV (*plays the guitar and sings*). "What care I for the noisy world? . . . What care I for friends and foes?" How pleasant it is to play the mandolin!

DUNYASHA. That's a guitar, not a mandolin. (*She looks at herself in a little mirror and powders her face.*)

EPIHODOV. To a man who's madly in love this is a mandolin. (*Sings quietly.*) "If only my heart were warmed by the fire of love requited.". . . (YASHA *joins in.*)

CHARLOTTA. How dreadfully these people sing! . . . Ach! Like a bunch of jackals.

DUNYASHA (*to* YASHA). You're so lucky to have been abroad!

YASHA. Of course I am. Naturally. (*Yawns, then lights a cigar.*)

EPIHODOV. Stands to reason. Abroad everything's reached its maturity . . . I mean to say, everything's been going on for such a long time.

YASHA. Obviously.

EPIHODOV. Now, I'm a cultured man, I read all kinds of extraordinary books, you know, but somehow I can't seem to figure out where I'm going, what it is I really want, I mean to say—whether to live or to shoot myself. Nevertheless, I always carry a revolver on me. Here it is. (*Shows the revolver.*)

CHARLOTTA. That's finished, so now I'm going. (*Slips the strap of the gun over her shoulder.*) Yes, Epihodov, you are a very clever man, and frightening, too; the women must be wild about you! Brrr! (*Walks off.*) All these clever people are so stupid, I haven't anyone to talk to. I'm so lonely, always alone, I have nobody and . . . and who I am and what I'm here for, nobody knows . . . (*Wanders out.*)

EPIHODOV. Frankly, and I want to keep to the point, I have to admit that Fate, so to speak, treats me absolutely without mercy, like a small ship is buffeted by the storm, as it were. I mean to say, suppose I'm mistaken, then why for instance should I wake up this morning and suddenly see a gigantic spider sitting on my chest? Like this . . . (*Showing the size with both hands.*) Or if I pick up a jug to have a drink of kvass, there's sure to be something horrible, like a cockroach, inside it. (*Pause.*) Have you read Buckle? (*Pause.*) May I trouble you for a moment, Dunyasha? I'd like to speak with you.

DUNYASHA. Well, go ahead.

EPIHODOV. I'd very much like to speak with you alone. (*Sighs.*)

DUNYASHA (*embarrassed*). Oh, all right . . . But first bring me my little cape . . . It's hanging by the cupboard. It's getting terribly chilly . . .

EPIHODOV. Very well, I'll get it. . . . Now I know what to do with my revolver. (*Takes his guitar and goes off playing it.*)

YASHA. Two-and-twenty misfortunes! Just between you and me, he's a stupid fool. (*Yawns.*)

DUNYASHA. I hope to God he doesn't shoot himself. (*Pause.*) He makes me so nervous and I'm always worrying about him. I came to live here when I was still a little girl. Now I no longer know how to live a simple life, and my hands are as white . . . as white as a lady's. I've become such a delicate and sensitive creature. I'm afraid of everything . . . so frightened. If you deceive me, Yasha, I don't know what will happen to my nerves.

YASHA (*kisses her*). You sweet little peach! Just remember, a girl must always control herself. Personally I think nothing is worse than a girl who doesn't behave herself.

DUNYASHA. I love you so much, so passionately! You're so intelligent, you can talk about anything. (*Pause.*)

YASHA (*yawns*). Yes, I suppose so . . . In my opinion, it's like this; if a girl loves someone it means she's immoral. (*Pause.*) I enjoy smoking a cigar in the fresh air . . . (*Listens.*) Someone's coming. It's the ladies and gentlemen. . . . (DUNYASHA *impulsively embraces him.*) Go to the house now, as though you'd been swimming down at the river. No, this way or they'll see you. I wouldn't want them to think I was interested in you.

DUNYASHA (*coughing softly*). That cigar has given me such a headache . . . (*Goes out.*)

YASHA *remains sitting by the shrine. Enter* LYUBOV, GAEV *and* LOPAHIN.

LOPAHIN. You've got to make up your minds once and for all; there's no time to lose. After all, it's a simple matter. Will you lease your land for the cottages, or won't you? You can answer in one word: yes or no? Just one word!

LYUBOV. Who's been smoking such wretched cigars? (*Sits down.*)

GAEV. How very convenient everything is with the railroad nearby. (*Sits down.*) Well, here we are—we've been to town, had lunch and we're home already. I put the red into the middle pocket! I'd like to go in . . . just for one game. . . .

LYUBOV. You've got lots of time.

LOPAHIN. Just one word! (*Beseechingly.*) Please give me an answer!

GAEV (*yawns*). What did you say?

LYUBOV (*looking into her purse*). Yesterday I had lots of money, but today there's practically none left. My poor Varya feeds us all milk soups to economize; the old servants in the kitchen have nothing but dried peas, and here I am wasting money senselessly, I just don't understand it. . . . (*She drops her purse, scattering gold coins.*) Now I've dropped it again. . . . (*Annoyed.*)

YASHA. Allow me, madam, I'll pick them right up. (*Picks up the money.*)

LYUBOV. Thank you, Yasha . . . And why did we go out for lunch today? And that restaurant of yours . . . the food was vile, the music ghastly, and the tablecloths smelled of soap. And Leonia, why do you drink so much? And eat so much? And talk so much? Today at the restaurant you were at it again, and it was all so pointless. About the seventies, and the decadents. And to whom? Really, talking to the waiters about the decadents!

LOPAHIN. Yes, that's too much.

GAEV (*waving his hand*). I know I'm hopeless. (*To* YASHA, *irritably.*) Why are you always bustling about in front of me?

YASHA (*laughs*). The minute you open your mouth I start laughing.

GAEV (*to his sister*). Either he goes, or I do. . . .

LYUBOV. Get along, Yasha, you'd better leave us now.

YASHA (*hands the purse to* LYUBOV). I'm going. (*He can hardly restrain his laughter.*) Right this minute. . . . (*Goes out.*)

LOPAHIN. You know, that rich merchant Deriganov is thinking of buying your estate. They say he's coming to the auction himself.

LYUBOV. Where did you hear that?

LOPAHIN. That's what they say in town.

GAEV. Our Aunt in Yaroslavl has promised to send us some money, but when and how much we don't know.

LOPAHIN. How much wil she send? A hundred thousand? Two hundred?

LYUBOV. Well, hardly . . . Ten or fifteen thousand, perhaps. And we should be thankful for that.

LOPAHIN. Forgive me for saying it, but really, in my whole life I've never met such unrealistic, unbusinesslike, queer people as you. You're told in plain language that your estate's going to be sold, and you don't seem to understand it at all.

LYUBOV. But what are we to do? Please, tell us.

LOPAHIN. I keep on telling you. Every day I tell you the same thing. You must lease the cherry orchard and the rest of the land for summer cottages, and you must do it now, as quickly as possible. It's almost time for the auction. Please, try to understand! Once you definitely decide to lease it for the cottages, you'll be able to borrow as much money as you like, and you'll be saved.

LYUBOV. Summer cottages and vacationers! Forgive me, but it's so vulgar.

GAEV. I agree with you entirely.

LOPAHIN. Honestly, I'm going to burst into tears, or scream, or faint. I can't stand it any more! It's more than I can take! (*To* GAEV.) And you're an old woman!

GAEV. What did you say?

LOPAHIN. I said, you're an old woman!

LYUBOV (*alarmed*). No, don't go, please stay. I beg you! Perhaps we can think of something.

LOPAHIN. What's there to think of?

LYUBOV. Please don't go! I feel so much more cheerful when you're here. (*Pause.*) I keep expecting something horrible to happen . . . as though the house were going to collapse on top of us.

GAEV (*in deep thought*). I bank it off the cushions, and then into the middle pocket. . . .

LYUBOV. We've sinned too much. . . .

LOPAHIN. Sinned! What sins have you . . .

GAEV (*putting a gumdrop into his mouth*). They say I've eaten up my fortune in gumdrops. (*Laughs.*)

LYUBOV. Oh, my sins! Look at the way I've always wasted money. It's madness. And then I married a man who had nothing but debts. And he was a terrible drinker . . . Champagne killed him! And then, as if I hadn't enough misery, I fell in love with someone else. We went off together, and just at that time—it was my first punishment, a blow that broke my heart—my little boy was drowned right here in this river . . . so I went abroad. I went away for good, never to return, never to see this river again . . . I just shut my eyes and ran away in a frenzy of grief, but *he* . . . he followed me. It was so cruel and brutal of him! I bought a villa near Mentone because he fell ill there, and for three years, day and night, I never had any rest. He was very sick, and he completely exhausted me; my soul dried up completely. Then, last year when the villa had to be sold to pay the debts, I went to Paris, and there he robbed me of everything I had and left me for another woman. . . . I tried to poison myself. . . . It was all so stupid, so shameful! And then suddenly I felt an urge to come back to Russia, to my own country, to my little girl . . . (*Dries her tears.*) Oh, Lord, Lord, be merciful, forgive my sins! Don't punish me any more! (*Takes a telegram out of her pocket.*) This came from Paris today. He's asking my forgiveness, he's begging me to return. (*Tears up the telegram.*) Sounds like music somewhere. (*Listens.*)

GAEV. That's our famous Jewish orchestra. Don't you remember, four violins, a flute, and a bass?

LYUBOV. Are they still playing? Sometime we should have a dance and they could play for us.

LOPAHIN (*listens*). I can't hear anything . . . (*Sings quietly.*) "And the Germans, if you pay, will turn Russians into Frenchmen, so they say" . . . (*Laughs.*) I saw a wonderful play last night. It was so funny.

LYUBOV. It probably wasn't funny at all. Instead of going to plays, you should take a good look at yourself. Just think how dull your life is, and how much nonsense you talk!

LOPAHIN. That's true, I admit it! Our lives are stupid . . . (*Pause.*) My father was a peasant, an idiot. He knew nothing and he taught me nothing. He only beat me when he was drunk, and always with a stick. And as a matter of fact, I'm just as much an idiot myself. I don't know anything and my handwriting's awful. I'm ashamed for people to see it—it's like a pig's.

LYUBOV. You ought to get married, my friend.

LOPAHIN. Yes . . . That's true.

LYUBOV. You ought to marry our Varya. She's a fine girl.

LOPAHIN. Yes.

LYUBOV. She comes from simple people, and she works hard all day long without stopping. But the main thing is she loves you, and you've liked her for a long time yourself.

LOPAHIN. Well. . . . I think it's a fine idea . . . She's a nice girl. (*Pause.*)

GAEV. I've been offered a job at the bank. Six thousand a year. Did I tell you?

LYUBOV. Yes, you did. You'd better stay where you are.

FEERS enters, bringing an overcoat.

FEERS (*to* GAEV). Please put it on, sir, you might catch cold.

GAEV (*puts on the overcoat*). Oh, you *are* a nuisance.

FEERS. You must stop this! You went off this morning without letting me know. (*Looks him over.*)

LYUBOV. How you've aged, Feers!

FEERS. What can I do for you, Madam?

LOPAHIN. She says you've aged a lot.

FEERS. I've lived for a long time. They were planning to marry me before your father was born. (*Laughs.*) Why, I was already head butler at the time of the emancipation, but I wouldn't take my freedom, I stayed on with the master and mistress. . . . (*Pause.*) I remember everyone was happy at the time, but what they were happy about, they didn't know themselves.

LOPAHIN. That was the good life all right! All the peasants were flogged!

FEERS (*not having heard him*). That's right! The peasants belonged to their masters, and the masters belonged to the peasants; but now everything's all confused, and people don't know what to make of it.

GAEV. Be quiet, Feers. Tomorrow I've got to go to town. I've been promised an introduction to some general or other who might lend us some money for the mortgage.

LOPAHIN. Nothing will come of it. And how would you pay the interest, anyway?

LYUBOV. He's talking nonsense again. There aren't any generals.

Enter TROFIMOV, ANYA and VARYA.

GAEV. Here come the children.

ANYA. There's Mamma.

LYUBOV. Come here, my dears. Oh, my darling children. . . . (*Embraces ANYA and VARYA.*) If you only knew how much I love you! Here now, sit down beside me. (*All sit down.*)

LOPAHIN. Our perennial student is always with the girls.

TROFIMOV. It's none of your business.

LOPAHIN. He'll soon be fifty, and he's still a student.

TROFIMOV. Oh, stop your stupid jokes.

LOPAHIN. What's bothering you? My, you *are* a strange fellow!

TROFIMOV. Why do you keep pestering me?

LOPAHIN (*laughs*). Just let me ask you one question: what's your opinion of me?

TROFIMOV. My opinion of you, Yermolay Alexeyevich, is this: you're a rich man, and soon you'll be a millionaire. For the same reason that wild beasts are necessary to maintain nature's economic laws, you are necessary, too—each of you devours everything that gets in his way. (*Everybody laughs.*)

VARYA. You'd better talk about the planets, Petya.

LYUBOV. No, let's go on with the conversation we had yesterday.

TROFIMOV. What was that?

GAEV. About pride.

TROFIMOV. We talked for a long time yesterday, but we didn't agree on anything. The proud man, the way you use the word, has some mysterious quality about him. Perhaps you're right in a way, but if we look at it simply, without trying to be too subtle, you have to ask yourself why should we be proud at all? Why be proud when you realize that Man, as a species, is poorly constructed physiologically, and is usually coarse, stupid, and profoundly unhappy, too? We ought to put an end to such vanity and just go to work. That's right, we ought to work.

GAEV. You'll die just the same, no matter what you do.

TROFIMOV. Who knows? And anyway, what does it mean—to die? It could be that man has a hundred senses, and when he dies only the five that are known perish, while the other ninety-five go on living.

LYUBOV. How clever you are, Petya!

LOPAHIN (*ironically*). Oh, very clever!

TROFIMOV. Humanity is continually advancing, is continually seeking to perfect its powers. Someday all the things which we can't understand now, will be made clear. But if this is to happen, we've got to work, work with all our might to help those who are searching for truth. Up until now, here in Russia only a few have begun to work. Nearly all of the intelligentsia that I know have no commitment, they don't do anything, and are as yet incapable of work. They call themselves "the intelligentsia," but they still run roughshod over their servants, and they treat the peasants like animals, they study without achieving anything, they read only childish drivel, and they don't do a thing. As for their knowledge of science, it's only jargon, and they have no appreciation of art either. They are all so serious, and they go about with solemn looks on their faces; they philosophize and talk about important matters; and yet before our very eyes our workers are poorly fed, they live in the worst kind of squalor, sleeping not on beds, but on the floor thirty to forty in a room—with roaches, odors, dampness, and depravity everywhere. It's perfectly clear that all our moralizing is intended to deceive not only ourselves, but others as well. Tell me, where are the nursery schools we're always talking about, where are the libraries? We only write about them in novels, but in actuality there aren't any. There's nothing but dirt, vulgarity, and decadent Orientalism. . . . I'm afraid of those serious faces, I don't like them; I'm afraid of serious talk. It would be better if we'd just keep quiet.

LOPAHIN. Well, let me tell you that *I'm* up before five every morning, and I work from morning till night. I always have money, my own and other people's, and I have lots of opportunities to see what the people around me are like. You only have to start doing something to realize how few honest, decent people there are. Sometimes, when I can't sleep, I start thinking about it. God's given us immense forests, and wide-open fields, and unlimited horizons—living in such a world we ought to be giants!

LYUBOV. But why do you want giants? They're all right in fairy tales, anywhere else they're terrifying.

EPIHODOV *crosses the stage in the background, playing his guitar.*

LYUBOV (*pensively*). There goes Epihodov. . . .

ANYA (*pensively*). There goes Epihodov. . . .

GAEV. The sun's gone down, my friends.

TROFIMOV. Yes.

GAEV (*in a subdued voice, as if reciting a poem*). Oh, glorious Nature, shining with eternal light, so beautiful, yet so indifferent to our fate . . . you, whom we call Mother, the wellspring of Life and Death, you live and you destroy. . . .

VARYA (*imploringly*). Uncle, please!

ANYA. You're doing it again, Uncle!

TROFIMOV. You'd better bank the red into middle pocket.

GAEV. All right, I'll keep quiet.

They all sit deep in thought; the only thing that can be heard is the muttering of FEERS. *Suddenly there is a sound in the distance, as if out of the sky, like the sound of a harp string breaking, gradually and sadly dying away.*

LYUBOV. What was that?

LOPAHIN. I don't know. Sounded like a cable broke in one of the mines. But it must've been a long way off.

GAEV. Perhaps it was a bird . . . a heron, maybe.

TROFIMOV. Or an owl. . . .

LYUBOV (*shudders*). Whatever it was, it sounded unpleasant . . . (*A pause.*)

FEERS. It was the same way before the disaster: the owl hooted and the samovar was humming.

GAEV. What disaster?

FEERS. Before they freed us. (*A pause.*)

LYUBOV. We'd better get started, my friends. It's getting dark and we should get home. (*To* ANYA.) You're crying, my darling! What's wrong? (*She embraces her.*)

ANYA. Nothing, Mamma. It's nothing.

TROFIMOV. Someone's coming.

Enter A TRAMP *in a battered white hunting cap and an overcoat; he's slightly drunk.*

TRAMP. Excuse me, but can I get to the station through here?

GAEV. Yes, just follow the road.

TRAMP. Much obliged to you, sir. (*Coughs.*) It's a beautiful day today. (*Declaiming.*) "Oh, my brother, my suffering brother! . . . Come to the Volga, whose groans . . ." (*To* VARYA.) Mademoiselle, could a poor starving Russian trouble you for just enough to . . . (VARYA *cries out, frightened.*)

LOPAHIN (*angrily*). Really, this is too much!

LYUBOV (*at a loss what to do*). Here, take this . . . here you are. (*Looks in her purse.*) I haven't any silver . . . but that's all right, here's a gold one. . . .

TRAMP. Thank you very much! (*Goes off. Laughter.*)

VARYA (*frightened*). I'm going. . . . I'm going . . . Oh, Mamma, you know there's not even enough to eat in the house, and you gave him all that!

LYUBOV. Well, what can you do with a silly woman like me? I'll give you everything I've got as soon as we get home. Yermolay Alexeyevich, you'll lend me some more, won't you?

LOPAHIN. Why of course I will.

LYUBOV. Come, it's time to go now. By the way, Varya, we've just about arranged your marriage. Congratulations!

VARYA (*through her tears*). Don't joke about things like that, Mother!

LOPAHIN. Go to a nunnery, Okhmelia! . . .

GAEV. Look at how my hands are trembling: I haven't had a game for so long.

LOPAHIN. Okhmelia, nymph, remember me in your prayers!

LYUBOV. Come along, everybody. It's almost supper time.

VARYA. That man frightened me so. My heart's still pounding.

LOPAHIN. My friends, just one thing, please just a word: the cherry orchard's to be sold on the 22nd of August. Remember that! Think of what. . . .

All go out except TROFIMOV *and* ANYA.

ANYA (*laughs*). We can thank the tramp for a chance to be alone! He frightened Varya so.

TROFIMOV. Varya's afraid—she's afraid we might fall in love—so she follows us about all day long. She's so narrow-minded, she can't understand that we're above falling in love. To free ourselves of all that's petty and ephemeral, all that prevents us from being free and happy, that's the whole aim and meaning of our life. Forward! We march forward irresistibly towards that bright star shining there in the distance! Forward! Don't fall behind, friends!

ANYA (*raising her hands*). How beautifully you talk! (*A pause.*) It's wonderful here today.

TROFIMOV. Yes, the weather's marvelous.

ANYA. What have you done to me, Petya? Why don't I love the cherry orchard like I used to? I used to love it so very much, I used to think that there wasn't a better place in all the world than our orchard.

TROFIMOV. The whole of Russia is our orchard. The earth is great and beautiful and there are many wonderful places in it. (*A

pause.) Just think, Anya: Your grandfather, and your great grandfather, and all
your ancestors were serf owners—they
owned living souls. Don't you see human
beings staring at you from every tree in
the orchard, from every leaf and every
trunk? Don't you hear their voices? . . .
They owned living souls—and it has made
you all different persons, those who came
before you, and you who are living now,
so that your mother, your uncle and you
yourself don't even notice that you're living
on credit, at the expense of other people,
people you don't admit any further than
your kitchen. We're at least two hundred
years behind the times; we have no real
values, no sense of our past, we just philosophize and complain of how depressed we
feel, and drink vodka. Yet it's obvious that
if we're ever to live in the present, we
must first atone for our past and make a
clean break with it, and we can only atone
for it by suffering, by extraordinary, un-
ceasing work. You've got to understand
that, Anya.

ANYA. The house we live in hasn't really
been ours for a long time. I'll leave it, I
promise you.

TROFIMOV. Yes, leave it, and throw away
the keys. Be free as the wind.

ANYA (*in rapture*). How beautifully you say
things.

TROFIMOV. You must believe me, Anya, you
must. I'm not thirty yet, I'm young, and
I'm still a student, but I've suffered so
much already. As soon as winter comes, I'll
be hungry and sick and nervous, poor as a
beggar. Fate has driven me everywhere!
And yet, my soul is always—every moment
of every day and every night—it's always
full of such marvelous hopes and visions. I
have a premonition of happiness, Anya, I
can sense its coming. . . .

ANYA (*pensively*). The moon's coming up.

EPIHODOV *is heard playing the same
melancholy tune on his guitar. The
moon comes up. Somewhere near the
poplars* VARYA *is looking for* ANYA *and
calling.*

VARYA (*off-stage*). Anya! Where are you?

TROFIMOV. Yes, the moon is rising. (*A pause.*)
There it is—happiness—it's coming nearer
and nearer. Already, I can hear its footsteps. And if we never see it, if we never
know it, what does it matter? Others will
see it!

VARYA'S VOICE. Anya! Where are you?

TROFIMOV. It's Varya again! (*Angrily.*) It's
disgusting!

ANYA. Well? Let's go to the river. It's lovely
there.

TROFIMOV. Yes, let's. (TROFIMOV *and* ANYA
go out.)

VARYA'S VOICE. Anya! Anya!

Curtain.

ACT III

*The drawing room separated by an arch
from the ballroom. The same Jewish
orchestra that was mentioned in Act II,
is playing off-stage. The chandelier is
lighted. It is evening. In the ballroom
they are dancing the Grand-rond.* SEM-
YONOV-PISHCHIK *is heard calling: "Prom-
enade à une paire!" Then they all enter
the drawing room.* PISHCHIK *and* CHAR-
LOTTA IVANOVNA *are the first couple,
followed by* TROFIMOV *and* LYUBOV,
ANYA *and a* POST-OFFICE CLERK, VARYA
and THE STATION MASTER, *etc.* VARYA *is
crying softly and wipes away her tears
as she dances.* DUNYASHA *is in the last
couple.* PISHCHIK *shouts: "Grand-rond
balancez!" and "Les cavaliers à genoux
et remerciez vos dames!"* FEERS, *wearing
a dress coat, crosses the room with soda
water on a tray.* PISHCHIK *and* TROFIMOV
come back into the drawing room.

PISHCHIK. I've got this high blood-pressure—
I've had two strokes already, you know—
and it makes dancing hard work for me;
but, as they say, if you're one of a pack,

you wag your tail, whether you bark or not. Actually I'm as strong as a horse. My dear father—may he rest in peace—had a little joke. He used to say that the ancient line of Semyonov-Pishchik was descended from the very same horse that Caligula made a member of the Senate. (*Sitting down.*) But my trouble is, I haven't any money. A starving dog can think of nothing but food . . . (*Starts to snore, but wakes up almost at once.*) That's just like me—I can't think of anything but money . . .

TROFIMOV. You know, you're right, there *is* something horsy about you.

PISHCHIK. Well, a horse is a fine animal, you can sell a horse. . . .

The sound of someone playing billiards is heard in the next room. VARYA *appears under the arch to the ballroom.*

TROFIMOV (*teasing her*). Madam Lopahin! Madame Lopahin!

VARYA (*angrily*). The "moth-eaten man"!

TROFIMOV. Yes, I am a moth-eaten man, and I'm proud of it.

VARYA (*thinking bitterly*). Now we've hired an orchestra—but how are we going to pay for it? (*Goes out.*)

TROFIMOV (*to* PISHCHIK). If all the energy you've spent during your life looking for money to pay the interest on your debts had been used for something useful, you'd have probably turned the world upside down by now.

PISHCHIK. The philosopher Nietzsche, the greatest, the most famous—a man of the greatest intelligence, in fact—says it's quite all right to counterfeit.

TROFIMOV. Oh, you've read Nietzsche?

PISHCHIK. Of course not, Dashenka told me. But right now I'm in such an impossible position that I could forge a few notes. The day after tomorrow I've got to pay 310 roubles. I've borrowed 130 already. . . . (*Feels in his pockets, in alarm.*) The money's gone! I've lost the money. (*Tearfully.*) Where's the money? (*Joyfully.*) Oh, here it is, inside the lining! I'm so upset, I'm sweating all over! . . .

Enter LYUBOV *and* CHARLOTTA.

LYUBOV (*humming the "Lezginka"*). What's taking Leonid so long? What's he doing in town? (*To* DUNYASHA.) Dunyasha, offer the musicians some tea.

TROFIMOV. The auction was probably postponed.

LYUBOV. The orchestra came at the wrong time, and the party started at the wrong time . . . Oh, well . . . never mind . . . (*She sits down and hums quietly.*)

CHARLOTTA (*hands a deck of cards to* PISHCHIK). Here's a deck of cards—think of any card.

PISHCHIK. I've thought of one.

CHARLOTTA. Now shuffle the deck. That's right. Now give it to me, my dear Monsieur Pishchik. "*Ein, zwei, drei!*" Why look! There it is, in your coat pocket.

PISHCHIK (*takes the card out of his coat pocket*). The eight of spades, that's right! (*In astonishment.*) Isn't that amazing!

CHARLOTTA (*holding the deck of cards on the palm of her hand, to* TROFIMOV). Quickly, which card's on the top?

TROFIMOV. Well . . . ahh . . . the queen of spades.

CHARLOTTA. You're right, here it is! Now, which card?

PISHCHIK. The ace of hearts.

CHARLOTTA. Right again! (*She claps her hand over the pack of cards, which disappears.*) What beautiful weather we're having today! (*A woman's voice, as if coming from underneath the floor, answers her.*)

VOICE. Oh yes, indeed, the weather's perfectly marvelous!

CHARLOTTA (*addressing the voice*). How charming you are! I'm fond of you!

VOICE. And I like you very much, too.

STATION MASTER (*applauding*). Bravo, Madame ventriloquist! Bravo!

PISHCHIK (*astonished*). Isn't that amazing! Charlotta Ivanovna, you're absolutely wonderful! I'm completely in love with you!

CHARLOTTA (*shrugging her shoulders*). In love? What do you know about love? "*Guter Mensch, aber schlechter Musikant.*"

TROFIMOV (*slaps* PISHCHIK *on the shoulder*).

He's just an old horse, he is!

CHARLOTTA. Your attention please! Here's one more trick. (*She takes a shawl from a chair.*) Now there's this very nice shawl . . . (*Shakes it out.*) Who'd like to buy it?

PISHCHIK (*amazed*). Imagine that!

CHARLOTTA. "Ein, zwei, drei!"

She lifts up the shawl and ANYA *is standing behind it;* ANYA *curtsies, runs to her mother, gives her a hug, and runs back to the ballroom. Everybody's delighted.*

LYUBOV (*clapping*). Bravo, bravo!

CHARLOTTA. Once more. "Ein, zwei, drei!"

Lifts the shawl again; behind it is VARYA, *who bows.*

PISHCHIK (*amazed*). Isn't that amazing!

CHARLOTTA. It's all over! (*She throws the shawl over* PISHCHIK, *curtsies, and runs into the ballroom.*)

PISHCHIK (*going after her*). You little rascal! . . . Have you ever seen anything like her? What a girl . . . (*Goes out.*)

LYUBOV. Leonid's still not here. I can't understand what's keeping him all this time in town. Anyway, by now everything's been settled; either the estate's been sold or the auction didn't take place. Why does he wait so long to let us know?

VARYA (*trying to comfort her*). Uncle's bought it, I'm sure he did.

TROFIMOV (*sarcastically*). Why of course he did!

VARYA. Our great-aunt sent him power of attorney to buy it in her name, and transfer the mortgage to her. She's done it for Anya's sake . . . God will look after us, I'm sure of it—Uncle will buy the estate.

LYUBOV. Your great-aunt sent us fifteen thousand to buy the estate in her name—she doesn't trust us—but that's not enough to even pay the interest. (*She covers her face with her hands.*) My fate is being decided today, my fate. . . .

TROFIMOV (*to* VARYA, *teasingly*). Madame Lopahin!

VARYA (*crossly*). The pepetual student! Why, you've been thrown out of the University twice already!

LYUBOV. But why get so cross, Varya? He's only teasing you about Lopahin, there's no harm in that, is there? If you want to, why don't you marry him; he's a fine man, and he's interesting, too. Of course, if you don't want to, don't. No one's trying to force you, darling.

VARYA. I'm very serious about this, Mother . . . and I want to be frank with you . . . he's a good man and I like him.

LYUBOV. Then marry him. What are you waiting for? I don't understand you at all.

VARYA. But, Mother, I can't propose to him myself, can I? It's been two years now since everybody began talking to me about him, and everybody's talking, but he doesn't say a word, or when he does, he just jokes with me. I understand, of course. He's getting rich and his mind's busy with other things, and he hasn't any time for me. If only I had some money, even a little, just a hundred roubles, I'd leave everything and go away, the farther the better. I'd go into a convent.

TROFIMOV. How beautiful!

VARYA (*to* TROFIMOV). Of course, a student like you has to be so intelligent! (*Quietly and tearfully.*) How ugly you've become, Petya, how much older you look! (*To* LYUBOV, *her tearfulness gone.*) The only thing I can't stand, Mother, is not having any work to do. I've got to stay busy.

Enter YASHA.

YASHA (*with difficulty restraining his laughter*). Epihodov's broken a cue! . . . (*Goes out.*)

VARYA. But what's Epihodov doing here? Who let him play billiards? I don't understand these people. . . . (*Goes out.*)

LYUBOV. Please don't tease her, Petya. Don't you see she's upset already?

TROFIMOV. Oh, she's such a busy-body—always sticking her nose into other people's business. She hasn't left Anya and me alone all summer. She's afraid we might fall in love. What difference should it make to her? Besides, I didn't give her any reason to think so. I don't believe in such trivialities. We're above love!

LYUBOV. And I suppose I'm below love. (*Uneasily.*) Why isn't Leonid back? If only I knew whether the estate's been sold or not. It's such an incredible calamity that for some reason I don't know what to think, I feel so helpless. I think I'm going to scream this very minute . . . I'll do something silly. Help me, Petya. Talk to me, say something!

TROFIMOV. What difference does it make whether the estate's sold today or not? It was gone a long time ago. You can't turn back, the path's lost. You mustn't worry, and above all you mustn't deceive yourself. For once in your life you must look the truth straight in the face.

LYUBOV. What truth? *You* know what truth is and what it isn't, but I've lost such visionary powers. I don't see anything. You're able to solve all your problems so decisively—but, tell me, my dear boy, isn't that because you're young, because life is still hidden from your young eyes, because you can't believe anything horrible will ever happen to you and you don't expect it to? Oh, yes, you're more courageous and honest and serious than we are, but put yourself in our position, try to be generous —if only a little bit—and have pity on me. I was born here, you know, and my father and mother lived here, and my grandfather, too, and I love this house—I can't conceive of life without the cherry orchard, and if it really has to be sold, then sell me with it . . . (*Embraces* TROFIMOV, *kisses him on the forehead.*) You know, my little boy was drowned here. . . . (*Weeps.*) Have pity on me, my dear, kind friend.

TROFIMOV. You know that I sympathize with you from the bottom of my heart.

LYUBOV. But you should say it differently . . . differently. (*Takes out her handkerchief and a telegram falls on to the floor.*) There's so much on my mind today, you can't imagine. It's so noisy around here that my soul trembles with every sound, and

I'm shaking all over—yet I can't go to my room because the silence of being alone frightens me. . . . Don't blame me, Petya. . . . I love you as if you were my own son. I'd gladly let Anya marry you, honestly I would, but, my dear boy, you must study, you've got to graduate. You don't do anything, Fate tosses you from one place to another—it's so strange—Well, it is, isn't it? Isn't it? And you should do something about your beard, make it grow somehow. . . . (*Laughs.*) You look so funny!

TROFIMOV (*picks up the telegram*). I don't care how I look. That's so superficial.

LYUBOV. This telegram's from Paris. I get one every day . . . Yesterday, today. That beast is sick again, and everything's going wrong for him. . . . He wants me to forgive him, he begs me to return, and really, I suppose I should go to Paris and stay with him for a while. You're looking very stern, Petya, but what am I to do, my dear boy, what am I to do? He's sick, and lonely, and unhappy, and who'll take care of him, who'll stop him from making a fool of himself, and give him his medicine at the right time? And anyway, why should I hide it, or keep quiet about it? I love him; yes, I love him. I do, I do. . . . He's a stone around my neck, and I'm sinking to the bottom with him—but I love him and I can't live without him. (*She presses* TROFIMOV's *hand.*) Don't think I'm evil, Petya, don't say anything, please don't. . . .

TROFIMOV (*with strong emotion*). Please—forgive my frankness, but that man's swindling you!

LYUBOV. No, no, no, you mustn't talk like that. . . . (*Puts her hands over her ears.*)

TROFIMOV. But he's a scoundrel, and you're the only one who doesn't know it! He's a despicable, worthless scoundrel. . . .

LYUBOV (*angry, but in control of herself*). You're twenty-six or twenty-seven years old, but you're talking like a schoolboy!

TROFIMOV. Say whatever you want!

LYUBOV. You should be a man at your age, you ought to understand what it means to be in love. And you should be in love. . . . Tell me, why haven't you fallen in love!

(*Angrily.*) Yes, yes! Oh, you're not so "pure," your purity is a perversion, you're nothing but a ridiculous prude, a freak. . . .

TROFIMOV (*horrified*). What is she saying?

LYUBOV. "I'm above love!" You're not above love, you're useless, as Feers would say. Imagine not having a mistress at your age! . . .

TROFIMOV (*horrified*). This is terrible! What's she saying? (*Goes quickly toward the ballroom, clutching his head between his hands.*) This is dreadful. . . . I can't stand it, I'm going. . . . (*Goes out, but returns at once.*) Everything's over between us! (*Goes out through the door into the hall.*)

LYUBOV (*calls after him*). Petya, wait! You funny boy, I was only joking! Petya!

Someone can be heard running quickly downstairs and suddenly falling down with a crash. ANYA *and* VARYA *scream, and then begin laughing.*

What's happened?

ANYA *runs in.*

ANYA (*laughing*). Petya fell down the stairs. (*Runs out.*)

LYUBOV. What a strange boy he is!

The STATION MASTER *stands in the middle of the ballroom and begins to recite "The Sinner" by Alexey Tolstoy. The others listen to him, but he's hardly had time to recite more than a little bit when a waltz is played, and he stops. Everyone dances.* TROFIMOV, ANYA, VARYA *come in from the hall.*

Poor Petya . . . there, my dear boy . . . Please forgive me . . . Come, let's dance . . . *She dances with* PETYA. ANYA *and* VARYA *dance. Enter* FEERS, *then* YASHA. FEERS *leans on his cane by the side door.* YASHA *looks at the dancers from the drawing room.*

YASHA. How are you, old boy?

FEERS. Not too well . . . We used to have generals, barons, and admirals at our parties . . . long ago, but now we send for the post-office clerk and the station master, and even they don't want to come it seems. I seem to be getting weaker somehow . . . My old master, the mistress' grandfather, used to make everyone take sealing wax no matter what was wrong with them. I've been taking it every day for the last twenty years, maybe even longer. Perhaps that's why I'm still alive.

YASHA. How you bore me, old man! (*Yawns.*) Why don't you just go away and die . . . It's about time.

FEERS. Eh, you! . . . You're useless . . . (*Mutters.*)

TROFIMOV *and* LYUBOV *dancing, come into the drawing room.*

LYUBOV. Thank you. I think I'll sit down for a bit. (*Sits down.*) I'm tired.

Enter ANYA.

ANYA (*agitated*). There's a man in the kitchen who's been saying that the cherry orchard was sold today.

LYUBOV. Sold? To whom?

ANYA. He didn't say. He's gone.

She and TROFIMOV *dance into the ballroom.*

YASHA. There was some old man gossiping there. A stranger.

FEERS. Leonid Andreyevich isn't back yet, he hasn't come yet. And he's only got his light overcoat on; he'll probably catch a cold. Oh, these youngsters!

LYUBOV. I've got to know, or I think I'll die. Yasha, go and find out who bought it.

YASHA. But the old guy went away a long time ago. (*Laughs.*)

LYUBOV (*with a touch of annoyance*). What are you laughing at? What's so humorous?

YASHA. Epihodov's so funny—he's so stupid. Two-and-twenty misfortunes!

LYUBOV. Feers, if the estate's sold, where will you go?

FEERS. I'll go wherever you tell me to go.

LYUBOV. Why are you looking like that? Aren't you well? You ought to be in bed.

FEERS. Yes . . . (*With a faint smile.*) But if I went to bed, who'd take care of the guests and keep things going? There's no one in the house but me.

YASHA (*to* LYUBOV). Lyubov Andreyevna! I want to ask you something! If you go back to Paris, will you please take me with you? I couldn't stand staying here. (*Looking round and speaking in a low voice.*) I don't have to say it, you can see for yourself how uncivilized everything is here. The people are immoral, it's frightfully dull, and the food is terrible. And then there's that Feers walking about the place and muttering all sorts of stupid things. Take me with you please!

Enter PISHCHIK.

PISHCHIK. May I have this dance, beautiful lady . . . (LYUBOV *gets up to dance.*) I'll have that 180 roubles from you yet, you enchantress . . . Yes, I will . . . (*Dances.*) Just 180 roubles, that's all . . . (*They go into the ballroom.*)

YASHA (*sings quietly*). "Don't you understand the passion in my soul? . . ."

In the ballroom a woman in a grey top hat and check trousers starts jumping and throwing her arms about; shouts of: "Bravo, Charlotta Ivanovna!"

DUNYASHA (*stops to powder her face*). Anya told me to dance: there are so many men and not enough ladies; but I get so dizzy from dancing and it makes my heart beat so fast. Feers Nikolayevich, the post-office clerk said something to me just now that completely took my breath away. (*The music stops.*)

FEERS. What did he say?

DUNYASHA. You're like a flower, he said.

YASHA (*yawns*). What ignorance! . . . (*Goes out.*)

DUNYASHA. Like a flower . . . I'm so sensitive, I love it when people say beautiful things to me.

FEERS. You'll be having your head turned if you're not careful.

Enter EPIHODOV.

EPIHODOV. Avdotya Fyodorovna, you act as if you don't want to see me . . . as if I were some kind of insect. (*Sighs.*) Such is life!

DUNYASHA. What do you want?

EPIHODOV. But then, you may be right. (*Sighs.*) Of course, if one looks at it from a certain point of view—if I may so express myself, and please excuse my frankness, you've driven me into such a state . . . Oh, I know what my fate is; every day some misfortune's sure to happen to me, but I've long since been accustomed to that, so I look at life with a smile. You gave me your word, and though I . . .

DUNYASHA. Please, let's talk later, just let me alone now. I'm lost in a dream. (*Plays with her fan.*)

EPIHODOV. Some misfortune happens to me every day, but I—how should I put it—I just smile, I even laugh.

VARYA *enters from the ballroom.*

VARYA. Are you still here, Semyon? Your manners are abominable, really! (*To* DUNYASHA.) You'd better go now, Dunyasha. (*To* EPIHODOV.) First you play billiards and break a cue, and now you're going about the drawing room, like one of the guests.

EPIHODOV. Permit me to inform you, but you have no right to attack me like this.

VARYA. I'm not attacking, I'm telling you. You just wander from one place to another, instead of doing your work. We've hired a clerk, but why no one knows.

EPIHODOV (*offended*). Whether I work, wander, eat, or play billiards, the only people who are entitled to judge my actions are those who are older than me and have some idea of what they're talking about.

VARYA. How dare you say that to me? (*Beside herself in anger.*) You dare to say that? Are you suggesting that I don't know what

I'm talking about? Get out of here! Right now!

EPIHODOV (*cowed*). I wish you'd express yourself more delicately.

VARYA (*beside herself*). Get out this minute! Get out! (*He goes to the door, she follows him.*) Two-and-twenty misfortunes! Get out of here! I don't want ever to see you again!

EPIHODOV (*goes out; his voice is heard from outside the door*). I'm going to complain.

VARYA. Oh, you're coming back, are you? (*She seizes the stick which* FEERS *left by the door.*) Well, come along, come in . . . I'll show you! So, you're coming back . . . are you? There, take that . . . (*Swings the stick, and at that moment* LOPAHIN *comes in.*)

LOPAHIN (*whom the stick did not, in fact, touch*). Thank you very much!

VARYA (*angry and ironically*). I'm sorry!

LOPAHIN. Don't mention it. I'm much obliged to you for the kind reception.

VARYA. That's quite all right. (*Walks away and then looks around and asks gently.*) I haven't hurt you, have I?

LOPAHIN. No, not at all. . . . But there's going to be a huge bump, though.

VOICES (*in the ballroom*). Lopahin's here! Yermolay Alexeyevich!

PISHCHIK. There he is! You can see him, do you hear him? . . . (*Embraces* LOPAHIN.) You smell of cognac, my good fellow! . . . Well we're having a party here, too.

Enter LYUBOV.

LYUBOV. It's you, Yermolay Alexeyevich? What's taken you so long? Where's Leonid?

LOPAHIN. Leonid Andreyevich's here, he'll be along in a minute.

LYUBOV (*agitated*). Well, what happened? Was there an auction? Tell me!

LOPAHIN (*embarrassed, afraid of betraying his joy*). The auction was over by four o'clock . . . We missed our train and had to wait until nine-thirty. (*Sighs heavily.*) Ugh! I feel a little dizzy . . .

Enter GAEV; *he carries packages in his right hand and wipes away his tears with his left.*

LYUBOV. Leonia, what happened? Leonia? (*Impatiently, with tears.*) Tell me quickly, for God's sake! . . .

GAEV (*doesn't answer, but waves his hand*). (*To* FEERS, *crying.*) Here, take these . . . it's some anchovies and Kerch herrings . . . I haven't eaten all day . . . What I've been through!

Through the open door leading to the ballroom a game of billiards can be heard and YASHA's *voice is heard.*

YASHA. Seven and eighteen.

GAEV (*his expression changes and he stops crying*). I'm very tired. Come, Feers, I want to change my things. (*Goes out through the ballroom, followed by* FEERS.)

PISHCHIK. Well, what happened at the auction? Come on, tell us!

LYUBOV. Has the cherry orchard been sold?

LOPAHIN. It has.

LYUBOV. Who bought it?

LOPAHIN. I did.

A pause. LYUBOV *is overcome; only the fact that she is standing beside a table and a chair keeps her from falling.* VARYA *takes the keys from her belt, throws them on the floor in the middle of the room and goes out.*

I bought it. Wait a moment, ladies and gentlemen, please. I'm so mixed up, I don't quite know what to say . . . (*Laughs.*) When we got to the auction, Deriganov was already there. Leonid had only fifteen thousand roubles, and immediately Deriganov bid thirty thousand over and above the mortgage. I saw how things were so I stepped in and raised it to forty. He bid forty-five, I went to fifty-five; he kept on raising five thousand and I raised it ten thousand. Well, finally it ended—I bid ninety thousand over and above the mortgage, and it went to me. The cherry orchard's mine now! All right, tell me I'm drunk, tell me I'm crazy and that I'm just imagining all this. . . . (*Stamps his feet.*) Don't laugh at me! If only my father and grandfather could rise from their graves and see all that's happened . . . how their Yermolay, their ignorant, beaten Yermolay, the little boy that ran around in his bare feet in the winter . . . if only they could see that he's bought this estate, the most beautiful place in the world! Yes, he's bought the very estate where his father and grandfather were slaves and where they weren't even admitted to the kitchen! I must be asleep, I'm dreaming, it only seems to be true . . . it's all just my imagination, my imagination must be confused . . . (*Picks up the keys, smiling gently.*) She threw these down because she wanted to show that she's not the mistress here anymore. (*Jingles the keys.*) Well, never mind. (*The orchestra is heard tuning up.*) Hey there! you musicians, play something for us! I want some music! My friends, come along and soon you'll see Yermolay Lopahin take an axe to the cherry orchard, you'll see the trees come crashing to the ground! We're going to build hundreds of summer cottages, and our children and our grandchildren will see a whole new world growing up here . . . So play, let's have some music!

The band plays. LYUBOV *has sunk into a chair and is crying bitterly. Reproachfully.*

Why, why didn't you listen to me? My poor, dear lady, you'll never get it back now. (*With tears.*) Oh, if only all this could be over soon, if only we could change this unhappy and disjointed life of ours somehow!

PISHCHIK (*taking his arm, in a low voice*). She's crying. Come into the ballroom, let her be by herself . . . Come on . . . (*Takes his arm and leads him away to the ballroom.*)

LOPAHIN. What's the matter! Where's the music? Come on, play! Play! Everything will be as I want it now. (*Ironically.*) Here comes the new owner, here comes the owner of the cherry orchard! (*He tips over a little table accidentally and nearly upsets the candelabra.*) Don't worry about it, I can pay for everything! (*Goes out with* PISHCHIK.)

There is no one left in the ballroom or drawing room, but LYUBOV, *who sits huddled up in a chair, crying bitterly. The orchestra continues to play quietly.* ANYA *and* TROFIMOV *enter quickly;* ANYA *goes up to her mother and kneels beside her,* TROFIMOV *remains at the entrance to the ballroom.*

ANYA. Mamma! . . . Mamma, you're crying. Dear, kind, good Mamma, my percious one, I love you! God bless you, Mamma! The cherry orchard's sold, that's true, it's gone, but don't cry, Mamma, you still have your life ahead of you, you still have your good, innocent heart. You must come with me, Mamma, away from here! We'll plant a new orchard, even more wonderful than this one—and when you see it, you'll understand everything, and your heart will be filled with joy, like the sun in the evening; and then you'll smile again, Mamma! Come, dearest one, come with me! . . .

Curtain.

ACT IV

The same setting as for Act I. There are no pictures on the walls or curtains at the windows; most of the furniture is gone and the few remaining pieces are stacked in a corner, as if for sale. There is a sense of desolation. Beside the door, suitcases and other luggage have been piled together. The voices of VARYA *and* ANYA *can be heard through the door on the left, which is open.* LOPAHIN *stands waiting;* YASHA *is holding a tray with glasses of champagne. In the hall* EPIHODOV *is tying up a large box. Off-stage there is a low hum of voices; the peasants have called to say good-bye.* GAEV's *voice from off-stage.*

GAEV. Thank you, friends, thank you.

YASHA. The peasants have come to say good-bye. In my opinion, Yermolay Alexeyevich, they're good people, but they don't know much.

The hum subsides. LYUBOV *and* GAEV *enter from the hall;* LYUBOV *is not crying but her face is pale and it quivers. She is unable to speak.*

GAEV. You gave them everything you had, Lyuba. You shouldn't have done that. You really shouldn't.

LYUBOV. I couldn't help it! I couldn't help it! (*Both go out.*)

LOPAHIN (*calls after them through the door*). Please, have some champagne, please do! Just a little glass before you go. I didn't think to bring some from town, and at the station I could find only this one bottle. Please have some. (*A pause.*) You don't want any, my friends? (*Walks away from the door.*) If I'd known that, I wouldn't have brought it. . . . Well, then I won't have any either. (YASHA *carefully puts the tray on a chair.*) Have a drink, Yasha, nobody else wants any.

YASHA. To the travelers! And to those staying behind. (*Drinks.*) This champagne isn't the real thing, believe me.

LOPAHIN. What do you mean, eight roubles a bottle. (*A pause.*) God, it's cold in here.

YASHA. The stoves weren't lit today. What difference does it make since we're leaving? (*Laughs.*)

LOPAHIN. Why are you laughing?

YASHA. Because I feel good.

LOPAHIN. It's October already, but it's still sunny and clear, just like summer. Good building weather. (*Looks at his watch, then at the door.*) Ladies and gentlemen, the train leaves in forty-seven minutes. We've got to start in twenty minutes. So hurry up.

TROFIMOV, *wearing an overcoat, comes in from outdoors.*

TROFIMOV. It's time we get started. The horses are ready. God knows where my goloshes are, they've disappeared. (*Calls through the door.*) Anya, my goloshes aren't here; I can't find them.

LOPAHIN. I've got to go to Kharkov. I'm taking the same train. I'll be spending the winter in Kharkov: I've stayed around here too long, and it drives me crazy having nothing to do. I can't be without work: I just don't know what to do with my hands; they hang there, as if they didn't belong to me.

TROFIMOV. We'll be gone soon, then you can start making money again.

LOPAHIN. Have a drink.

TROFIMOV. No, thanks.

LOPAHIN. So, you're going to Moscow?

TROFIMOV. Yes, I'll go with them to town, and then, tomorrow I'll leave for Moscow.

LOPAHIN. I suppose the professors are waiting for you to come before they begin classes.

TROFIMOV. That's none of your business.

LOPAHIN. How many years have you been studying at the university?

TROFIMOV. Can't you say something new for a change, that's getting pretty old. (*Looks for his goloshes.*) By the way, since we probably won't see each other again, let me give you a bit of advice, as we say good-bye: stop waving your arms! Try to get rid of that habit of making wide, sweeping gestures. And another thing, all this talk about building estates, these calculations about summer tourists that are going to buy property, all these predictions—they're all sweeping gestures, too. . . . You know, in spite of everything, I like you. You've got beautiful delicate fingers, like an artist's, you've a fine, sensitive soul. . . .

LOPAHIN (*embraces him*). Good-bye, my friend. Thanks for everything. I can give you some money for your trip, if you need it.

TROFIMOV. What for? I don't need it.

LOPAHIN. But you haven't got any!

TROFIMOV. Yes, I have, thank you. I got some money for a translation. Here it is, in my pocket. (*Anxiously.*) But I can't find my goloshes.

VARYA (*from the other room*). Here, take the nasty things! (*She throws a pair of rubber goloshes into the room.*)

TROFIMOV. What are you so angry about, Varya? Hm . . . but these aren't my goloshes!

LOPAHIN. I sowed three thousand acres of poppies last spring, and I've made forty thousand on it. And when they were in bloom, what a picture it was! What I mean to say is that I've made the forty thousand, so now I can lend you some money. Why be so stuck up? So I'm a peasant . . . I speak right out.

TROFIMOV. Your father was a peasant, mine was a druggist. What's that got to do with it? (LOPAHIN *takes out his wallet.*) Forget it, put it away . . . Even if you offered me two hundred thousand, I wouldn't take it. I'm a free man. And all that you rich men— and poor men too—all that you value so highly doesn't have the slightest power over me—it's all just so much fluff floating about in the air. I'm strong and I'm proud! I can get along without you, I can pass you by. Humanity is advancing towards the highest truth, the greatest happiness that it's possible to achieve on earth, and I'm one of the avant-garde!

LOPAHIN. Will you get there?

TROFIMOV. Yes. (*A pause.*) I'll get there myself, or show others the way to get there.

The sound of an axe hitting a tree is heard in the distance.

LOPAHIN. Well, my friend, it's time to go. Good-bye. We show off in front of one another, and all the time life is slipping by. When I work all day long, without resting, I'm happier and sometimes I even think I know why I exist. But how many people there are in Russia, my friend, who exist for no reason at all. But, never mind, it doesn't matter. They say Leonid Andreyevich has a job at the bank, at six thousand a year. That won't last long; he's too lazy. . . .

ANYA (*in the doorway*). Mamma begs you not to let them cut down the orchard until we've left.

TROFIMOV. Really, haven't you got any tact? (*Goes out through the hall.*)

LOPAHIN. All right, I'll take care of it. . . . These people! (*Follows* TROFIMOV.)

ANYA. Has Feers been taken to the hospital?

YASHA. I told them to take him this morning. He's gone, I think.

ANYA (*to* EPIHODOV, *who passes through the ballroom*). Semyon Pantaleyevich, will you please find out whether Feers has been taken to the hospital?

YASHA (*offended*). I told Yegor this morning. Why ask a dozen times?

EPIHODOV. That old Feers—frankly speaking, I mean—he's beyond repair, it's time he joined his ancestors. As for me, I can only envy him. (*He places a suitcase on top of a cardboard hatbox and squashes it.*) There you are, you see! . . . I might have known it! (*Goes out.*)

YASHA (*sardonically*). Two-and-twenty misfortunes!

VARYA (*from behind the door*). Has Feers been taken to the hospital?

ANYA. Yes.

VARYA. Why wasn't the letter to the doctor taken then?

ANYA. I'll send someone after them with it . . . (*Goes out.*)

VARYA (*from the adjoining room*). Where's Yasha? Tell him his mother is here and wants to say good-bye to him.

YASHA (*waves his hand*). This is too much! I'll lose my patience.

While the foregoing action has been taking place, DUNYASHA *has been busy with the luggage; now that* YASHA *is alone, she comes up to him.*

DUNYASHA. If only you'd look at me just once, Yasha! You're going . . . you're leaving me! . . . (*She cries and throws her arms around his neck.*)

YASHA. What are you crying for? (*Drinks champagne.*) In a week I'll be in Paris again. Tomorrow we'll get on the train—

and off we'll go—gone! I can't believe it. *"Vive la France!"* I can't stand it here and could never live here—nothing ever happens. I've seen enough of all this ignorance. I've had enough of it. (*Drinks.*) What are you crying for? Behave yourself properly, then you won't cry.

DUNYASHA (*looking into a handmirror and powdering her nose*). Please, write to me from Paris. You know how much I've loved you, Yasha. Oh, I've loved you so much! I'm very sensitive, Yasha!

YASHA. Sshh, someone's coming. (*Pretends to be busy with a suitcase, humming quietly.*)

Enter LYUBOV ANDREYEVNA, GAEV, ANYA *and* CHARLOTTA IVANOVNA.

GAEV. We've got to leave soon. There isn't much time left. (*Looks at* YASHA.) What a smell! Who's been eating herring?

LYUBOV. We'll have to leave in the carriage in ten minutes. (*Looks about the room.*) Good-bye, dear house, the home of our fathers. Winter will pass and spring will come again, and then you won't be here any more, you'll be torn down. How much these walls have seen! (*Kisses her daughter passionately.*) My little treasure, how radiant you look, your eyes are shining like diamonds. Are you glad? Very glad?

ANYA. Oh, yes, very glad, Mamma! Our new life is just beginning!

GAEV (*gaily*). Really, everything's all right now. Before the cherry orchard was sold we were all worried and upset, but as soon as things were settled once and for all, we all calmed down and even felt quite cheerful. I'm working in a bank now, a real financier. . . . The red into the side pocket . . . And say what you like, Lyuba, you're looking much better. No doubt about it.

LYUBOV. Yes, that's true, my nerves are better. (*Someone helps her on with her hat and coat.*) I'm sleeping better, too. Take out my things, Yasha, it's time. (*To* ANYA.) My little darling, we'll be seeing each other again soon. I'm going to Paris—I'll live on the money which your Grandmother sent us to buy the estate—God bless Grandmamma!—but that money won't last very long either.

ANYA. You'll come back soon, Mamma . . . won't you? I'll study and pass my exams and then I'll work and help you. We'll read together, Mamma . . . all sorts of things . . . won't we? (*She kisses her mother's hands.*) We'll read during the long autumn evenings. We'll read lots of books, and a new wonderful world will open up before us . . . (*Dreamily.*) Mamma, come back soon . . .

LYUBOV. I'll come back, my precious. (*Embraces her.*)

Enter LOPAHIN. CHARLOTTA *quietly sings to herself.*

GAEV. Happy Charlotta! She's singing.

CHARLOTTA (*picks up a bundle that looks like a baby in a blanket*). Bye-bye, little baby. (*A sound like a baby crying is heard.*) Hush, be quiet, my darling, be a good little boy. (*The "crying" continues.*) Oh, my baby, you poor thing! (*Throws the bundle down.*) Are you going to find me another job? If you don't mind, I've got to have one.

LOPAHIN. We'll find you one, Charlotta Ivanovna, don't worry.

GAEV. Everybody's leaving us, Varya's going away . . . all of a sudden nobody wants us.

CHARLOTTA. There's no place for me to live in town. I'll have to go. (*Hums.*) Oh, well, what do I care. (*Enter* PISHCHIK.)

LOPAHIN. Look what's here!

PISHCHIK (*gasping for breath*). Oohhh, let me get my breath . . . I'm worn out . . . My good friends. . . . Give me some water . . .

GAEV. I suppose you want to borrow some money? I'm going . . . Excuse me . . . (*Goes out.*)

PISHCHIK. I haven't seen you for a long time . . . my beautiful lady . . . (*To* LOPAHIN.) You're here, too . . . glad to see you . . . you're a man of great intelligence . . . here . . . take this . . . (*Gives money to* LOPAHIN.) Four hundred roubles . . . I still owe you eight hundred and forty. . . .

LOPAHIN (*shrugging his shoulders in amazement*). It's like a dream . . . Where did you get it?

PISHCHIK. Wait a minute . . . I'm so hot . . . A most extraordinary thing happened. Some Englishmen came along and discovered some kind of white clay on my land. . . . (*To* LYUBOV.) Here's four hundred for you also, my dear . . . enchantress . . . (*Gives her the money.*) You'll get the rest later. (*Takes a drink of water.*) A young man on the train was just telling me that some great philosopher advises people to jump off roofs. You just jump off, he says, and that settles the whole problem. (*Amazed at what he has just said.*) Imagine that! More water, please.

LOPAHIN. What Englishmen?

PISHCHIK. I leased the land to them for twenty-four years. . . . And now you must excuse me, I'm in a hurry and have to get on. I'm going to Znoikov's, then to Kardamonov's . . . I owe then all money. (*Drinks.*) Your health. I'll come again on Thursday . . .

LYUBOV. We're just leaving for town, and tomorrow I'm going abroad.

PISHCHIK. What's that? (*In agitation.*) Why to town? Oh, I see . . . this furniture and the suitcases. . . . Well, never mind . . . (*Tearfully.*) What difference does it make. . . . These Englishmen, you know, they're very intelligent . . . Never mind. . . . I wish you all the best, God bless you. Never mind, everything comes to an end eventually. (*Kisses* LYUBOV's *hand.*) And when you hear that my end has come, just think of a horse, and say: "There used to be a man like that once . . . his name was Semyonov-Pishchik—God bless him!" Wonderful weather we're having. Yes . . . (*Goes out embarrassed, but returns at once and stands in the doorway.*) Dashenka sends her greetings. (*Goes out.*)

LYUBOV. Well, we can get started now. I'm leaving with two worries on my mind. One is Feers—he's sick. (*Glances at her watch.*) We've still got five minutes. . . .

ANYA. Mamma, Feers has been taken to the hospital. Yasha sent him this morning.

LYUBOV. The other is Varya. She's used to getting up early and working, and now, with nothing to do, she's like a fish out of water. She's gotten so thin and pale, and she cries a lot, the poor dear. (*A pause.*) You know very well, Yermolay Alexeyevich, that I've been hoping you two would get married . . . and everything pointed to it. (*Whispers to* ANYA *and motions to* CHARLOTTA, *and they both go out.*) She loves you, and you're fond of her, too . . . I just don't know, I don't know why you seem to avoid each other. I don't understand it.

LOPAHIN. Neither do I, I admit it. The whole thing's so strange. . . . If there's still time, I'm ready to. . . . Let's settle it at once— and get it over with! Without you here, I don't feel I'll ever propose to her.

LYUBOV. That's an excellent idea! You won't need more than a minute. I'll call her at once.

LOPAHIN. And there's champagne here, too, we'll celebrate. (*Looks at the glasses.*) They're empty, someone's drunk it all. (YASHA *coughs.*) They must have poured it down.

LYUBOV (*with animation*). Oh, I'm so glad. I'll call her, and we'll leave you alone. Yasha, "*allez!*" (*Through the door.*) Varya, come here for a minute, leave what you're doing and come here! Varya! (*Goes out with* YASHA.)

LOPAHIN (*looking at his watch*). Yes. . . .

A pause. Whispering and suppressed laughter are heard behind the door, then VARYA *comes in and starts fussing with the luggage. At last she says:*

VARYA. That's strange, I can't find it. . . .

LOPAHIN. What are you looking for?

VARYA. I packed it myself, and I can't remember . . . (*A pause.*)

LOPAHIN. Where are you going to now, Varvara Mihailovna?

VARYA. I? To the Rogulins. I've taken a job as their housekeeper.

LOPAHIN. That's in Yashnevo, isn't it? Almost seventy miles from here. (*A pause.*) So this is the end of life in this house. . . .

VARYA (*still fussing with the luggage*). Where could it be? Perhaps I put it in the trunk? Yes, life in this house has come to an end . . . there won't be any more. . . .

LOPAHIN. And I'm going to Kharkov. . . . On the next train. I've got a lot of work to do there. I'm leaving Epihodov here. . . . I've hired him.

VARYA. Really! . . .

LOPAHIN. Remember, last year at this time it was snowing already, but now it's still so bright and sunny. Though it's cold . . . Three degrees of frost.

VARYA. I haven't looked. (*A pause.*) Besides, our thermometer's broken. . . .

A pause. A voice is heard from outside the door.

VOICE. Yermolay Alexeyevich!

LOPAHIN (*as if he had been waiting for it*). I'm coming! Right away! (*Goes out quickly.*)

VARYA *sits on the floor, with her head on a bundle of clothes, crying quietly. The door opens,* LYUBOV *enters hesitantly.*

LYUBOV. Well? (*A pause.*) We must be going.

VARYA (*stops crying and wipes her eyes*). Yes, Mamma, it's time we got started. I'll just have time to get to the Rogulins today, if we don't miss the train.

LYUBOV (*calls through the door*). Anya, put your things on.

Enter ANYA, *followed by* GAEV *and* CHARLOTTA. GAEV *wears a heavy overcoat with a hood. Servants and coachmen come into the room.* EPIHODOV *is picking up the luggage.*

Now we can begin our journey!

ANYA (*joyfully*). Our journey!

GAEV. My friends, my dear, beloved friends! As I leave this house forever, how can I be silent, how can I refrain from expressing to you, as I say good-bye for the last time, the feelings which now overwhelm me. . . .

ANYA (*begging*). Uncle!

VARYA. Uncle, please don't!

GAEV (*downcast*). I put the red into the corner and then . . . I'll keep quiet.

Enter TROFIMOV *and* LOPAHIN.

TROFIMOV. Well, ladies and gentlemen, it's time we get started.

LOPAHIN. Epihodov, my coat!

LYUBOV. I'll just stay for one more minute. It seems as if I'd never seen the walls and ceilings of this house before, and now I look at them with such longing, such love. . . .

GAEV. I remember when I was six—it was Trinity Sunday . . . I was sitting here at this window watching father on his way to church. . . .

LYUBOV. Have they taken everything out?

LOPAHIN. It looks like it. (*To* EPIHODOV, *as he puts on his coat.*) Be sure to take care of everything, Epihodov.

EPIHODOV (*in a husky voice*). Don't worry, Yermolay Alexeyevich!

LOPAHIN. What is wrong with your voice?

EPIHODOV. I just had some water, and it went down the wrong throat.

YASHA (*with contempt*). What a fool!

LYUBOV. After we leave, there won't be a soul here. . . .

LOPAHIN. Not until spring.

VARYA (*pulls an umbrella from a bundle of clothes;* LOPAHIN *pretends to be afraid*). What are you doing that for? . . . I didn't mean to. . . .

TROFIMOV. Ladies and gentlemen, hurry up, it's time. The train will be here soon.

VARYA. Petya, here are your goloshes beside the suitcase. (*Tearfully.*) How dirty and old they are! . . .

TROFIMOV (*puts them on*). Hurry up, ladies and gentlemen!

GAEV (*greatly embarrassed, afraid of breaking into tears*). The train, the station . . . The red off the white into the middle pocket. . . .

LYUBOV. Let us go!

LOPAHIN. Are we all here? No one left? (*Locks the door on the left.*) There are some things stored in there, best to keep it locked up. Come along!

ANYA. Good-bye, old house! Good-bye, old life!

TROFIMOV. Welcome to the new life! . . . (*Goes out with* ANYA.)

> VARYA *looks around the room and goes out slowly.* YASHA *and* CHARLOTTA, *with her little dog, follow.*

LOPAHIN. And so, until the spring. Come, my friends. . . . Au revoir! (*Goes out.*)

> LYUBOV *and* GAEV *alone. They seem to have been waiting for this moment, and now they embrace each other and cry quietly, with restraint, so as not to be heard.*

GAEV (*in despair*). Sister, my sister. . . .

LYUBOV. Oh, my orchard, my beloved, my beautiful orchard! My life, my youth, my happiness . . . good-bye! . . . Good-bye!

ANYA (*off-stage, calling gaily*). Mama! . . .

TROFIMOV (*off-stage, gaily and excitedly*). Yoo-hoo! . . .

LYUBOV. Just one last time—to look at these walls, these windows. . . . Mother loved to walk in this room. . . .

GAEV. Sister, my sister . . .

ANYA (*off-stage*). Mamma!

TROFIMOV (*off-stage*). Yoo-hoo!

LYUBOV. We're coming . . . (*They go out.*)

The stage is empty. The sound of doors being locked and then of carriages driving off. Silence. In the stillness the dull sounds of an axe striking on a tree can be heard. They sound mournful and sad. Footsteps are heard and from the door on the right FEERS *enters. He is dressed, as usual, in a coat and white waistcoat, and is wearing slippers. He is ill.*

FEERS (*walks up to the middle door and tries the handle*). Locked. They've gone . . . (*Sits down on a sofa.*) They've forgotten me. Never mind. . . . I'll sit here for a bit. I don't suppose Leonid Andreyevich put on his fur coat, he probably wore his light one. (*Sighs, preoccupied.*) I didn't take care of it . . . These young people! . . . (*Mutters something unintelligible.*) My life's slipped by as if I'd never lived. . . . (*Lies down.*) I'll lie down a bit. You haven't got any strength left, nothing's left, nothing. . . . Oh, you . . . you old good-for-nothing! . . . (*Lies motionless.*)

A distant sound that seems to come out of the sky, like a breaking harp, slowly and sadly dying away. Then all is silent, except for the sound of an axe striking a tree in the orchard far away.

Curtain.

◆◆ A Streetcar Named Desire

By TENNESSEE WILLIAMS

Characters

BLANCHE
STELLA
STANLEY
MITCH
EUNICE
STEVE
PABLO
A NEGRO WOMAN
A DOCTOR
A NURSE
A YOUNG COLLECTOR
A MEXICAN WOMAN

The action of the play takes place in the spring, summer, and early fall in New Orleans.

SCENE ONE

The exterior of a two-story corner building on a street in New Orleans which is named Elysian Fields and runs between the L & N tracks and the river. The section is poor but, unlike corresponding sections in other American cities, it has a raffish charm. The houses are mostly white frame, weathered grey, with rickety outside stairs and galleries and quaintly ornamented gables. This building contains two flats, upstairs and

down. Faded white stairs ascend to the entrances of both.

It is first dark of an evening early in May. The sky that shows around the dim white building is a peculiarly tender blue, almost a turquoise, which invests the scene with a kind of lyricism and gracefully attenuates the atmosphere of decay. You can almost feel the warm breath of the brown river beyond the river warehouses with their faint redolences of bananas and coffee. A corresponding air is evoked by the music of Negro entertainers at a barroom around the corner. In this part of New Orleans you are practically always just around the corner, or a few doors down the street, from a tinny piano being played with the infatuated fluency of brown fingers. This "Blue Piano" expresses the spirit of the life which goes on here.

Two women, one white and one colored, are taking the air on the steps of the building. The white woman is Eunice, who occupies the upstairs flat; the colored woman a neighbor, for New Orleans is a cosmopolitan city where there is a relatively warm and easy intermingling of races in the old part of town.

Above the music of the "Blue Piano" the voices of people on the street can be heard overlapping.

[Two men come around the corner, Stanley Kowalski and Mitch. They are about twenty-eight or thirty years old,

Tennessee Williams, A Streetcar Named Desire (New York: New Directions, 1947), pp. 9–166.

roughly dressed in blue denim work clothes. Stanley carries his bowling jacket and a red-stained package from a butcher's. They stop at the foot of the steps.]

STANLEY [*bellowing*]. Hey, there! Stella, Baby!

[*Stella comes out on the first floor landing, a gentle young woman, about twenty-five, and of a background obviously quite different from her husband's.*]

STELLA [*mildly*]. Don't holler at me like that. Hi, Mitch.
STANLEY. Catch!
STELLA. What?
STANLEY. Meat!

[*He heaves the package at her. She cries out in protest but manages to catch it: then she laughs breathlessly. Her husband and his companion have already started back around the corner.*]

STELLA [*calling after him*]. Stanley! Where are you going?
STANLEY. Bowling!
STELLA. Can I come watch?
STANLEY. Come on. [*He goes out.*]
STELLA. Be over soon. [*To the white woman*] Hello, Eunice. How are you?
EUNICE. I'm all right. Tell Steve to get him a poor boy's sandwich 'cause nothing's left here.

[*They all laugh; the colored woman does not stop. Stella goes out.*]

COLORED WOMAN. What was that package he th'ew at 'er? [*She rises from steps, laughing louder.*]
EUNICE. You hush, now!
NEGRO WOMAN. Catch *what!*

[*She continues to laugh. Blanche comes around the corner, carrying a valise. She looks at a slip of paper, then at the*

building, then again at the slip and again at the building. Her expression is one of shocked disbelief. Her appearance is incongruous to this setting. She is daintily dressed in a white suit with a fluffy bodice, necklace and earrings of pearl, white gloves and hat, looking as if she were arriving at a summer tea or cocktail party in the garden district. She is about five years older than Stella. Her delicate beauty must avoid a strong light. There is something about her uncertain manner, as well as her white clothes, that suggests a moth.*]

EUNICE [*finally*]. What's the matter, honey? Are you lost?
BLANCHE [*with faintly hysterical humor*]. They told me to take a street-car named Desire, and then transfer to one called Cemeteries and ride six blocks and get off at—Elysian Fields!
EUNICE. That's where you are now.
BLANCHE. At Elysian Fields?
EUNICE. This here is Elysian Fields.
BLANCHE. They mustn't have—understood—what number I wanted . . .
EUNICE. What number you lookin' for?

[*Blanche wearily refers to the slip of paper.*]

BLANCHE. Six thirty-two.
EUNICE. You don't have to look no further.
BLANCHE [*uncomprehendingly*]. I'm looking for my sister, Stella DuBois. I mean—Mrs. Stanley Kowalski.
EUNICE. That's the party.—You just did miss her, though.
BLANCHE. This—can this be—her home?
EUNICE. She's got the downstairs here and I got the up.
BLANCHE. Oh. She's—out?
EUNICE. You noticed that bowling alley around the corner?
BLANCHE. I'm—not sure I did.
EUNICE. Well, that's where she's at, watchin' her husband bowl. [*There is a pause*] You want to leave your suitcase here an' go find her?

BLANCHE. No.

NEGRO WOMAN. I'll go tell her you come.

BLANCHE. Thanks.

NEGRO WOMAN. You welcome. [*She goes out.*]

EUNICE. She wasn't expecting you?

BLANCHE. No. No, not tonight.

EUNICE. Well, why don't you just go in and make yourself at home till they get back.

BLANCHE. How could I—do that?

EUNICE. We own this place so I can let you in.

[*She gets up and opens the downstairs door. A light goes on behind the blind, turning it light blue. Blanche slowly follows her into the downstairs flat. The surrounding areas dim out as the interior is lighted.*]

[*Two rooms can be seen, not too clearly defined. The one first entered is primarily a kitchen but contains a folding bed to be used by Blanche. The room beyond this is a bedroom. Off this room is a narrow door to a bathroom.*]

EUNICE [*defensively, noticing Blanche's look*]. It's sort of messed up right now but when it's clean it's real sweet.

BLANCHE. Is it?

EUNICE. Uh-huh, I think so. So you're Stella's sister?

BLANCHE. Yes. [*Wanting to get rid of her*] Thanks for letting me in.

EUNICE. *Por nada*, as the Mexicans say, *por nada!* Stella spoke of you.

BLANCHE. Yes?

EUNICE. I think she said you taught school.

BLANCHE. Yes.

EUNICE. And you're from Mississippi, huh?

BLANCHE. Yes.

EUNICE. She showed me a picture of your home-place, the plantation.

BLANCHE. Belle Reve?

EUNICE. A great big place with white columns.

BLANCHE. Yes . . .

EUNICE. A place like that must be awful hard to keep up.

BLANCHE. If you will excuse me, I'm just about to drop.

EUNICE. Sure, honey. Why don't you set down?

BLANCHE. What I meant was I'd like to be left alone.

EUNICE [*offended*]. Aw. I'll make myself scarce, in that case.

BLANCHE. I didn't mean to be rude, but—

EUNICE. I'll drop by the bowling alley an' hustle her up. [*She goes out the door.*]

[*Blanche sits in a chair very stiffly with her shoulders slightly hunched and her legs pressed close together and her hands tightly clutching her purse as if she were quite cold. After a while the blind look goes out of her eyes and she begins to look slowly around. A cat screeches. She catches her breath with a startled gesture. Suddenly she notices something in a half opened closet. She springs up and crosses to it, and removes a whiskey bottle. She pours a half tumbler of whiskey and tosses it down. She carefully replaces the bottle and washes out the tumbler at the sink. Then she resumes her seat in front of the table.*]

BLANCHE [*faintly to herself*]. I've got to keep hold of myself!

[*Stella comes quickly around the corner of the building and runs to the door of the downstairs flat.*]

STELLA [*calling out joyfully*]. Blanche!

[*For a moment they stare at each other. Then Blanche springs up and runs to her with a wild cry.*]

BLANCHE. Stella, oh, Stella, Stella! Stella for Star!

[*She begins to speak with feverish vivacity as if she feared for either of them to stop and think. They catch each other in a spasmodic embrace.*]

BLANCHE. Now, then, let me look at you. But don't you look at me, Stella, no, no, no, not till later, not till I've bathed and rested! And turn that over-light off! Turn that off! I won't be looked at in this merciless glare! [*Stella laughs and complies*] Come back here now! Oh, my baby! Stella! Stella for Star! [*She embraces her again*] I thought you would never come back to this horrible place! What am I saying? I didn't mean to say that. I meant to be nice about it and say—Oh, what a convenient location and such—Ha-a-ha! Precious lamb! You haven't said a *word* to me.

STELLA. You haven't given me a chance to, honey! [*She laughs, but her glance at Blanche is a little anxious.*]

BLANCHE. Well, now you talk. Open your pretty mouth and talk while I look around for some liquor! I know you must have some liquor on the place! Where could it be, I wonder? Oh, I spy, I spy!

[*She rushes to the closet and removes the bottle; she is shaking all over and panting for breath as she tries to laugh. The bottle nearly slips from her grasp.*]

STELLA [*noticing*]. Blanche, you sit down and let me pour the drinks. I don't know what we've got to mix with. Maybe a coke's in the icebox. Look'n see, honey, while I'm—

BLANCHE. No coke, honey, not with my nerves tonight! Where—where—where is—?

STELLA. Stanley? Bowling! He loves it. They're having a—found some soda!—tournament . . .

BLANCHE. Just water, baby, to chase it! Now don't get worried, your sister hasn't turned into a drunkard, she's just all shaken up and hot and tired and dirty! You sit down, now, and explain this place to me! What are you doing in a place like this?

STELLA. Now, Blanche—

BLANCHE. Oh, I'm not going to be hypocritical, I'm going to be honestly critical about it. Never, never, never in my worst dreams could I picture—Only Poe! Only Mr. Edgar Allan Poe!—could do it justice! Out there I suppose is the ghoul-haunted woodland of Weir! [*She laughs.*]

STELLA. No, honey, those are the L & N tracks.

BLANCHE. No, now seriously, putting joking aside. Why didn't you tell me, why didn't you write me, honey, why didn't you let me know?

STELLA [*carefully, pouring herself a drink*]. Tell you what, Blanche?

BLANCHE. Why, that you had to live in these conditions!

STELLA. Aren't you being a little intense about it? It's not that bad at all! New Orleans isn't like other cities.

BLANCHE. This has got nothing to do with New Orleans. You might as well say—forgive me, blessed baby! [*She suddenly stops short*] The subject is closed!

STELLA [*a little drily*]. Thanks.

[*During the pause, Blanche stares at her. She smiles at Blanche.*]

BLANCHE [*looking down at her glass, which shakes in her hand*]. You're all I've got in the world, and you're not glad to see me!

STELLA [*sincerely*]. Why, Blanche, you know that's not true.

BLANCHE. No?—I'd forgotten how quiet you were.

STELLA. You never did give me a chance to say much, Blanche. So I just got in the habit of being quiet around you.

BLANCHE [*vaguely*]. A good habit to get into . . . [*then, abruptly*] You haven't asked me how I happened to get away from the school before the spring term ended.

STELLA. Well, I thought you'd volunteer that information—if you wanted to tell me.

BLANCHE. You thought I'd been fired?

STELLA. No, I—thought you might have resigned . . .

BLANCHE. I was so exhausted by all I'd been through my—nerves broke. [*Nervously tamping cigarette*] I was on the verge of—lunacy, almost! So Mr. Graves—Mr. Graves is the high school superintendent—he suggested I take a leave of absence. I couldn't put all those details into the wire . . . [*She drinks quickly*] Oh, this buzzes right through me and feels so *good!*

STELLA. Won't you have another?

BLANCHE. No, one's my limit.

STELLA. Sure?

BLANCHE. You haven't said a word about my appearance.

STELLA. You look just fine.

BLANCHE. God love you for a liar! Daylight never exposed so total a ruin! But you—you've put on some weight, yes, you're just as plump as a little partridge! And it's so becoming to you!

STELLA. Now, Blanche—

BLANCHE. Yes, it is, it is or I wouldn't say it! You just have to watch around the hips a little. Stand up.

STELLA. Not now.

BLANCHE. You hear me? I said stand up! [*Stella complies reluctantly*] You messy child, you, you've spilt something on that pretty white lace collar! About your hair—you ought to have it cut in a feather bob with your dainty features. Stella, you have a maid, don't you?

STELLA. No. With only two rooms it's—

BLANCHE. What? *Two* rooms, did you say?

STELLA. This one and—[*She is embarrassed.*]

BLANCHE. The other one? [*She laughs sharply. There is an embarrassed silence.*]

BLANCHE. I am going to take just one little nip more, sort of to put the stopper on, so to speak. . . . Then put the bottle away so I won't be tempted. [*She rises*] I want you to look at *my* figure! [*She turns around*] You know I haven't put on one ounce in ten years, Stella? I weigh what I weighed the summer you left Belle Reve. The summer Dad died and you left us . . .

STELLA [*a little wearily*]. It's just incredible, Blanche, how well you're looking.

BLANCHE. [*They both laugh uncomfortably*] But, Stella, there's only two rooms, I don't see where you're going to put me!

STELLA. We're going to put you in here.

BLANCHE. What kind of bed's this—one of those collapsible things? [*She sits on it.*]

STELLA. Does it feel all right?

BLANCHE [*dubiously*]. Wonderful, honey. I don't like a bed that gives much. But there's no door between the two rooms, and Stanley—will it be decent?

STELLA. Stanley is Polish, you know.

BLANCHE. Oh, yes. They're something like Irish, aren't they?

STELLA. Well—

BLANCHE. Only not so—highbrow? [*They both laugh again in the same way*] I brought some nice clothes to meet all your lovely friends in.

STELLA. I'm afraid you won't think they are lovely.

BLANCHE. What are they like?

STELLA. They're Stanley's friends.

BLANCHE. Polacks?

STELLA. They're a mixed lot, Blanche.

BLANCHE. Heterogeneous—types?

STELLA. Oh, yes. Yes, types is right!

BLANCHE. Well—anyhow—I brought nice clothes and I'll wear them. I guess you're hoping I'll say I'll put up at a hotel, but I'm not going to put up at a hotel. I want to be *near* you, got to be *with* somebody, I *can't* be *alone*! Because—as you must have noticed—I'm—*not* very *well* . . . [*Her voice drops and her look is frightened.*]

STELLA. You seem a little bit nervous or over-wrought or something.

BLANCHE. Will Stanley like me, or will I be just a visiting in-law, Stella? I couldn't stand that.

STELLA. You'll get along fine together, if you'll just try not to—well—compare him with men that we went out with at home.

BLANCHE. Is he so—different?

STELLA. Yes. A different species.

BLANCHE. In what way; what's he like?

STELLA. Oh, you can't describe someone you're in love with! Here's a picture of him! [*She hands a photograph to Blanche.*]

BLANCHE. An officer?

STELLA. A Master Sergeant in the Engineers' Corps. Those are decorations!

BLANCHE. He had those on when you met him?

STELLA. I assure you I wasn't just blinded by all the brass.

BLANCHE. That's not what I—

STELLA. But of course there were things to adjust myself to later on.

BLANCHE. Such as his civilian background!

[*Stella laughs uncertainly*] How did he take it when you said I was coming?

STELLA. Oh, Stanley doesn't know yet.

BLANCHE [*frightened*]. You—haven't told him?

STELLA. He's on the road a good deal.

BLANCHE. Oh. Travels?

STELLA. Yes.

BLANCHE. Good. I mean—isn't it?

STELLA [*half to herself*]. I can hardly stand it when he is away for a night . . .

BLANCHE. Why, Stella!

STELLA. When he's away for a week I nearly go wild!

BLANCHE. Gracious!

STELLA. And when he comes back I cry on his lap like a baby . . . [*She smiles to herself.*]

BLANCHE. I guess that is what is meant by being in love . . . [*Stella looks up with a radiant smile.*] Stella—

STELLA. What?

BLANCHE [*in an uneasy rush*]. I haven't asked you the things you probably thought I was going to ask. And so I'll expect you to be understanding about what *I* have to tell *you.*

STELLA. What, Blanche? [*Her face turns anxious.*]

BLANCHE. Well, Stella—you're going to reproach me, I know that you're bound to reproach me—but before you do—take into consideration—you left! I stayed and struggled! You came to New Orleans and looked out for yourself! *I* stayed at *Belle Reve* and tried to hold it together! I'm not meaning this in any reproachful way, but *all* the burden descended on *my* shoulders.

STELLA. The best I could do was make my own living, Blanche.

[*Blanche begins to shake again with intensity.*]

BLANCHE. I know, I know. But you are the one that abandoned Belle Reve, not I! I stayed and fought for it, bled for it, almost died for it!

STELLA. Stop this hysterical outburst and tell me what's happened? What do you mean fought and bled? What kind of—

BLANCHE. I knew you would, Stella. I knew you would take this attitude about it!

STELLA. About—what?—please!

BLANCHE [*slowly*]. The loss—the loss . . .

STELLA. Belle Reve? Lost, is it? No!

BLANCHE. Yes, Stella.

[*They stare at each other across the yellow-checked linoleum of the table. Blanche slowly nods her head and Stella looks slowly down at her hands folded on the table. The music of the "blue piano" grows louder. Blanche touches her handkerchief to her forehead.*]

STELLA. But how did it go? What happened?

BLANCHE [*springing up*]. You're a fine one to ask me how it went!

STELLA. Blanche!

BLANCHE. You're a fine one to sit there *accusing me* of it!

STELLA. *Blanche!*

BLANCHE. I, I, *I* took the blows in my face and my body! All of those deaths! The long parade to the graveyard! Father, mother! Margaret, that dreadful way! So big with it, it couldn't be put in a coffin! But had to be burned like rubbish! You just came home in time for the funerals, Stella. And funerals are pretty compared to deaths. Funerals are quiet, but deaths—not always. Sometimes their breathing is hoarse, and sometimes it rattles, and sometimes they even cry out to you, "Don't let me go!" Even the old, sometimes, say, "Don't let me go." As if you were able to stop them! But funerals are quiet, with pretty flowers. And, oh, what gorgeous boxes they pack them away in! Unless you were there at the bed when they cried out, "Hold me!" you'd never suspect there was the struggle for breath and bleeding. You didn't dream, but I saw! *Saw! Saw!* And now you sit there telling me with your eyes that I let the place go! How in hell do you think all that sickness and dying was paid for? Death is expensive, Miss Stella! And old Cousin Jessie's right after

Margaret's, hers! Why, the Grim Reaper had put up his tent on our doorstep! . . . Stella. Belle Reve was his headquarters! Honey—that's how it slipped through my fingers! Which of them left us a fortune? Which of them left a cent of insurance even? Only poor Jessie—one hundred to pay for her coffin. That was all, Stella! And I with my pitiful salary at the school. Yes, accuse me! Sit there and stare at me, thinking I let the place go! *I* let the place go? Where were *you!* In bed with your— Polack!

STELLA [*springing*]. Blanche! You be still! That's enough! [*She starts out.*]

BLANCHE. Where are you going?

STELLA. I'm going into the bathroom to wash my face.

BLANCHE. Oh, Stella, Stella, you're crying!

STELLA. Does that surprise you?

BLANCHE. Forgive me—I didn't mean to—

[*The sound of men's voices is heard. Stella goes into the bathroom, closing the door behind her. When the men appear, and Blanche realizes it must be Stanley returning, she moves uncertainly from the bathroom door to the dressing table, looking apprehensively towards the front door. Stanley enters, followed by Steve and Mitch. Stanley pauses near his door, Steve by the foot of the spiral stair, and Mitch is slightly above and to the right of them, about to go out. As the men enter, we hear some of the following dialogue.*]

STANLEY. Is that how he got it?

STEVE. Sure that's how he got it. He hit the old weather-bird for 300 bucks on a six-number-ticket.

MITCH. Don't tell him those things; he'll believe it.

[*Mitch starts out.*]

STANLEY [*restraining Mitch*]. Hey, Mitch— come back here.

[*Blanche, at the sound of voices, retires in the bedroom. She picks up Stanley's photo from dressing table, looks at it, puts it down. When Stanley enters the apartment, she darts and hides behind the screen at the head of bed.*]

STEVE [*to Stanley and Mitch*]. Hey, are we playin' poker tomorrow?

STANLEY. Sure—at Mitch's.

MITCH [*hearing this, returns quickly to the stair rail*]. No—not at my place. My mother's still sick!

STANLEY. Okay, at my place . . . [*Mitch starts out again*] But you bring the beer!

[*Mitch pretends not to hear,—calls out "Goodnight all," and goes out, singing. Eunice's voice is heard, above.*]

Break it up down there! I made the spaghetti dish and ate it myself.

STEVE [*going upstairs*]. I told you and phoned you we was playing. [*To the men*] Jax beer!

EUNICE. You never phoned me once.

STEVE. I told you at breakfast—and phoned you at lunch . . .

EUNICE. Well, never mind about that. You just get yourself home here once in a while.

STEVE. You want it in the papers?

[*More laughter and shouts of parting come from the men. Stanley throws the screen door of the kitchen open and comes in. He is of medium height, about five feet eight or nine, and strongly, compactly built. Animal joy in his being is implicit in all his movements and attitudes. Since earliest manhood the center of his life has been pleasure with women, the giving and taking of it, not with weak indulgence, dependently, but with the power and pride of a richly feathered male bird among hens. Branching out from this complete and satisfying center are all the auxiliary channels of his life, such as his heartiness with men, his appreciation of rough humor, his love of good*] *drink and food and games, his car, his radio, everything that is his, that bears his emblem of the gaudy seed-bearer. He sizes women up at a glance, with sexual classifications, crude images flashing into his mind and determining the way he smiles at them.*]

BLANCHE [*drawing involuntarily back from his stare*]. You must be Stanley. I'm Blanche.

STANLEY. Stella's sister?

BLANCHE. Yes.

STANLEY. H'lo. Where's the little woman?

BLANCHE. In the bathroom.

STANLEY. Oh. Didn't know you were coming in town.

BLANCHE. I—uh—

STANLEY. Where you from, Blanche?

BLANCHE. Why, I—live in Laurel.

[*He has crossed to the closet and removed the whiskey bottle.*]

STANLEY. In Laurel, huh? Oh, yeah. Yeah, in Laurel, that's right. Not in my territory. Liquor goes fast in hot weather.

[*He holds the bottle to the light to observe its depletion.*]

Have a shot?

BLANCHE. No, I—rarely touch it.

STANLEY. Some people rarely touch it, but it touches them often.

BLANCHE [*faintly*]. Ha-ha.

STANLEY. My clothes're stickin' to me. Do you mind if I make myself comfortable? [*He starts to remove his shirt.*]

BLANCHE. Please, please do.

STANLEY. Be comfortable is my motto.

BLANCHE. It's mine, too. It's hard to stay looking fresh. I haven't washed or even powdered my face and—here you are!

STANLEY. You know you can catch cold sitting around in damp things, especially when you been exercising hard like bowling is. You're a teacher, aren't you?

BLANCHE. Yes.

STANLEY. What do you teach, Blanche?

BLANCHE. English.

STANLEY. I never was a very good English student. How long you here for, Blanche?

BLANCHE. I—don't know yet.

STANLEY. You going to shack up here?

BLANCHE. I thought I would if it's not inconvenient for you all.

STANLEY. Good.

BLANCHE. Traveling wears me out.

STANLEY. Well, take it easy.

[*A cat screeches near the window. Blanche springs up.*]

BLANCHE. What's that?

STANLEY. Cats . . . Hey, Stella!

STELLA [*faintly, from the bathroom*]. Yes, Stanley.

STANLEY. Haven't fallen in, have you? [*He grins at Blanche. She tries unsuccessfully to smile back. There is a silence*] I'm afraid I'll strike you as being the unrefined type. Stella's spoke of you a good deal. You were married once, weren't you?

[*The music of the polka rises up, faint in the distance.*]

BLANCHE. Yes. When I was quite young.

STANLEY. What happened?

BLANCHE. The boy—the boy died. [*She sinks back down*] I'm afraid I'm—going to be sick!

[*Her head falls on her arms.*]

SCENE TWO

It is six o'clock the following evening. Blanche is bathing. Stella is completing her toilette. Blanche's dress, a flowered print, is laid out on Stella's bed.

Stanley enters the kitchen from outside, leaving the door open on the perpetual "blue piano" around the corner.

STANLEY. What's all this monkey doings?

STELLA. Oh, Stan! [*She jumps up and kisses him which he accepts with lordly composure*] I'm taking Blanche to Galatoire's for supper and then to a show, because it's your poker night.

STANLEY. How about my supper, huh? I'm not going to no Galatoire's for supper!

STELLA. I put you a cold plate on ice.

STANLEY. Well, isn't that just dandy!

STELLA. I'm going to try to keep Blanche out till the party breaks up because I don't know how she would take it. So we'll go to one of the little places in the Quarter afterwards and you'd better give me some money.

STANLEY. Where is she?

STELLA. She's soaking in a hot tub to quiet her nerves. She's terribly upset.

STANLEY. Over what?

STELLA. She's been through such an ordeal.

STANLEY. Yeah?

STELLA. Stan, we've—lost Belle Reve!

STANLEY. The place in the country?

STELLA. Yes.

STANLEY. How?

STELLA [*vaguely*]. Oh, it had to be—sacrificed or something. [*There is a pause while Stanley considers. Stella is changing into her dress*] When she comes in be sure to say something nice about her appearance. And, oh! Don't mention the baby. I haven't said anything yet, I'm waiting until she gets in a quieter condition.

STANLEY [*ominously*]. So?

STELLA. And try to understand her and be nice to her, Stan.

BLANCHE [*singing in the bathroom*]. "From the land of the sky blue water, They brought a captive maid!"

STELLA. She wasn't expecting to find us in such a small place. You see I'd try to gloss things over a little in my letters.

STANLEY. So?

STELLA. And admire her dress and tell her she's looking wonderful. That's important with Blanche. Her little weakness!

STANLEY. Yeah. I get the idea. Now let's skip back a little to where you said the country place was disposed of.

STELLA. Oh!—yes . . .

STANLEY. How about that? Let's have a few more details on that subjeck.

STELLA. It's best not to talk much about it until she's calmed down.

STANLEY. So that's the deal, huh? Sister Blanche cannot be annoyed with business details right now!

STELLA. You saw how she was last night.

STANLEY. Uh-hum, I saw how she was. Now let's have a gander at the bill of sale.

STELLA. I haven't seen any.

STANLEY. She didn't show you no papers, no deed of sale or nothing like that, huh?

STELLA. It seems like it wasn't sold.

STANLEY. Well, what in hell was it then, give away? To charity?

STELLA. Shhh! She'll hear you.

STANLEY. I don't care if she hears me. Let's see the papers!

STELLA. There weren't any papers, she didn't show any papers, I don't care about papers.

STANLEY. Have you ever heard of the Napoleonic code?

STELLA. No, Stanley, I haven't heard of the Napoleonic code and if I have, I don't see what it—

STANLEY. Let me enlighten you on a point or two, baby.

STELLA. Yes?

STANLEY. In the state of Louisiana we have the Napoleonic code according to which what belongs to the wife belongs to the husband and vice versa. For instance if I had a piece of property, or you had a piece of property—

STELLA. My head is swimming!

STANLEY. All right. I'll wait till she gets through soaking in a hot tub and then I'll inquire if *she* is acquainted with the Napoleonic code. It looks to me like you have been swindled, baby, and when you're swindled under the Napoleonic code I'm swindled *too*. And I don't like to be *swindled*.

STELLA. There's plenty of time to ask her questions later but if you do now she'll go to pieces again. I don't understand what happened to Belle Reve but you don't know how ridiculous you are being when you suggest that my sister or I or anyone of our family could have perpetrated a swindle on anyone else.

STANLEY. Then where's the money if the place was sold?

STELLA. Not sold—*lost, lost!*

[*He stalks into bedroom, and she follows him.*]

Stanley!

[*He pulls open the wardrobe trunk standing in middle of room and jerks out an armful of dresses.*]

STANLEY. Open your eyes to this stuff! You think she got them out of a teacher's pay?

STELLA. Hush!

STANLEY. Look at these feathers and furs that she come here to preen herself in! What's this here? A solid-gold dress, I believe! And this one! What is these here? Fox-pieces [*He blows on them*] Genuine fox fur-pieces, a half a mile long! Where are your fox-pieces, Stella? Bushy snow-white ones, no less! Where are your white fox-pieces?

STELLA. Those are inexpensive summer furs that Blanche has had a long time.

STANLEY. I got an acquaintance who deals in this sort of merchandise. I'll have him in here to appraise it. I'm willing to bet you there's thousands of dollars invested in this stuff here!

STELLA. Don't be such an idiot, Stanley!

[*He hurls the furs to the daybed. Then he jerks open small drawer in the trunk and pulls up a fist-full of costume jewelry.*]

STANLEY. And what have we here? The treasure chest of a pirate!

STELLA. Oh, Stanley!

STANLEY. Pearls! Ropes of them! What is this sister of yours, a deep-sea diver? Bracelets of solid gold, too! Where are your pearls and gold bracelets?

STELLA. Shhh! Be still, Stanley!

STANLEY. And diamonds! A crown for an empress!

STELLA. A rhinestone tiara she wore to a costume ball.

STANLEY. What's rhinestone?

STELLA. Next door to glass.

STANLEY. Are you kidding? I have an acquaintance that works in a jewelry store. I'll have him in here to make an appraisal of this. Here's your plantation, or what was left of it, here!

STELLA. You have no idea how stupid and horrid you're being! Now close that trunk before she comes out of the bathroom!

[*He kicks the trunk partly closed and sits on the kitchen table.*]

STANLEY. The Kowalskis and the DuBois have different notions.

STELLA [*angrily*]. Indeed they have, thank heavens!—*I'm* going outside. [*She snatches up her white hat and gloves and crosses to the outside door*] You come out with me while Blanche is getting dressed.

STANLEY. Since when do you give me orders?

STELLA. Are you going to stay here and insult her?

STANLEY. You're damn tootin' I'm going to stay here.

[*Stella goes out to the porch. Blanche comes out of the bathroom in a red satin robe.*]

BLANCHE [*airily*]. Hello, Stanley! Here I am, all freshly bathed and scented, and feeling like a brand new human being!

[*He lights a cigarette.*]

STANLEY. That's good.

BLANCHE [*drawing the curtains at the windows*]. Excuse me while I slip on my pretty new dress!

STANLEY. Go right ahead, Blanche.

[*She closes the drapes between the rooms.*]

BLANCHE. I understand there's to be a little

card party to which we ladies are cordially *not* invited!

STANLEY [*ominously*]. Yeah?

[*Blanche throws off her robe and slips into a flowered print dress.*]

BLANCHE. Where's Stella?

STANLEY. Out on the porch.

BLANCHE. I'm going to ask a favor of you in a moment.

STANLEY. What could that be, I wonder?

BLANCHE. Some buttons in back! You may enter!

[*He crosses through drapes with a smoldering look.*]

How do I look?

STANLEY. You look all right.

BLANCHE. Many thanks! Now the buttons!

STANLEY. I can't do nothing with them.

BLANCHE. You men with your big clumsy fingers. May I have a drag on your cig?

STANLEY. Have one for yourself.

BLANCHE. Why, thanks! . . . It looks like my trunk has exploded.

STANLEY. Me an' Stella were helping you unpack.

BLANCHE. Well, you certainly did a fast and thorough job of it!

STANLEY. It looks like you raided some stylish shops in Paris.

BLANCHE. Ha-ha! Yes—clothes are my passion!

STANLEY. What does it cost for a string of fur-pieces like that?

BLANCHE. Why, those were a tribute from an admirer of mine!

STANLEY. He must have had a lot of—admiration!

BLANCHE. Oh, in my youth I excited some admiration. But look at me now! [*She smiles at him radiantly*] Would you think it possible that I was once considered to be —attractive?

STANLEY. Your looks are okay.

BLANCHE. I was fishing for a compliment, Stanley.

STANLEY. I don't go in for that stuff.

BLANCHE. What—stuff?

STANLEY. Compliments to women about their looks. I never met a woman that didn't know if she was good-looking or not without being told, and some of them give themselves credit for more than they've got. I once went out with a doll who said to me, "I am the glamorous type, I am the glamorous type!" I said, "So what?"

BLANCHE. And what did she say then?

STANLEY. She didn't say nothing. That shut her up like a clam.

BLANCHE. Did it end the romance?

STANLEY. It ended the conversation—that was all. Some men are took in by this Hollywood glamor stuff and some men are not.

BLANCHE. I'm sure you belong in the second category.

STANLEY. That's right.

BLANCHE. I cannot imagine any witch of a woman casting a spell over you.

STANLEY. That's—right.

BLANCHE. You're simple, straightforward and honest, a little bit on the primitive side I should think. To interest you a woman would have to—[*She pauses with an indefinite gesture.*]

STANLEY [*slowly*]. Lay . . . her cards on the table.

BLANCHE [*smiling*]. Well, I never cared for wishy-washy people. That was why, when you walked in here last night, I said to myself—"My sister has married a man!"— Of course that was all that I could tell about you.

STANLEY [*booming*]. Now let's cut the re-bop!

BLANCHE [*pressing hands to her ears*]. Ouuuuu!

STELLA [*calling from the steps*]. Stanley! You come out here and let Blanche finish dressing!

BLANCHE. I'm through dressing, honey.

STELLA. Well, you come out, then.

STANLEY. Your sister and I are having a little talk.

BLANCHE [*lightly*]. Honey, do me a favor. Run to the drug-store and get me a lemon-coke with plenty of chipped ice in it!— Will you do that for me, Sweetie?

STELLA [*uncertainly*]. Yes. [*She goes around the corner of the building.*]

BLANCHE. The poor little thing was out there listening to us, and I have an idea she doesn't understand you as well as I do. . . . All right; now, Mr. Kowalski, let us proceed without any more double-talk. I'm ready to answer all questions. I've nothing to hide. What is it?

STANLEY. There is such a thing in this State of Louisiana as the Napoleonic code, according to which whatever belongs to my wife is also mine—and vice versa.

BLANCHE. My, but you have an impressive judicial air!

[*She sprays herself with her atomizer; then playfully sprays him with it. He seizes the atomizer and slams it down on the dresser. She throws back her head and laughs.*]

STANLEY. If I didn't know that you was my wife's sister I'd get ideas about you!

BLANCHE. Such as what!

STANLEY. Don't play so dumb. You know what!

BLANCHE [*she puts the atomizer on the table*]. All right. Cards on the table. That suits me. [*She turns to Stanley.*] I know I fib a good deal. After all, a woman's charm is fifty per cent illusion, but when a thing is important I tell the truth, and this is the truth: I haven't cheated my sister or you or anyone else as long as I have lived.

STANLEY. Where's the papers? In the trunk?

BLANCHE. Everything that I own is in that trunk.

[*Stanley crosses to the trunk, shoves it roughly open and begins to open compartments.*]

BLANCHE. What in the name of heaven are you thinking of! What's in the back of that little boy's mind of yours? That I am absconding with something, attempting some kind of treachery on my sister?—Let me do that! It will be faster and simpler . . . [*She crosses to the trunk and takes out a box*] I keep my papers mostly in this tin box. [*She opens it.*]

STANLEY. What's them underneath? [*He indicates another sheaf of paper.*]

BLANCHE. These are love-letters, yellowing with antiquity, all from one boy. [*He snatches them up. She speaks fiercely*] Give those back to me!

STANLEY. I'll have a look at them first!

BLANCHE. The touch of your hands insults them!

STANLEY. Don't pull that stuff!

[*He rips off the ribbon and starts to examine them. Blanche snatches them from him, and they cascade to the floor.*]

BLANCHE. Now that you've touched them I'll burn them!

STANLEY [*staring, baffled*]. What in hell are they?

BLANCHE [*on the floor gathering them up*]. Poems a dead boy wrote. I hurt him the way that you would like to hurt me, but you can't! I'm not young and vulnerable any more. But my young husband was and I—never mind about that! Just give them back to me!

STANLEY. What do you mean by saying you'll have to burn them?

BLANCHE. I'm sorry, I must have lost my head for a moment. Everyone has something he won't let others touch because of their—intimate nature . . .

[*She now seems faint with exhaustion and she sits down with the strong box and puts on a pair of glasses and goes methodically through a large stack of papers.*]

Ambler & Ambler. Hmmmmm. . . . Crabtree. . . . More Ambler & Ambler.

STANLEY. What is Ambler & Ambler?

BLANCHE. A firm that made loans on the place.

STANLEY. Then it *was* lost on a mortgage?

BLANCHE [*touching her forehead*]. That must've been what happened.

STANLEY. I don't want no ifs, ands or buts! What's all the rest of them papers?

[*She hands him the entire box. He carries it to the table and starts to examine the papers.*]

BLANCHE [*picking up a large envelope containing more papers*]. There are thousands of papers, stretching back over hundreds of years, affecting Belle Reve as, piece by piece, our improvident grandfathers and father and uncles and brothers exchanged the land for their epic fornications—to put it plainly! [*She removes her glasses with an exhausted laugh*] The four-letter word deprived us of our plantation, till finally all that was left—and Stella can verify that!— was the house itself and about twenty acres of ground, including a graveyard, to which now all but Stella and I have retreated. [*She pours the contents of the envelope on the table*] Here all of them are, all papers! I hereby endow you with them! Take them, peruse them—commit them to memory, even! I think it's wonderfully fitting that Belle Reve should finally be this bunch of old papers in your big, capable hands! . . . I wonder if Stella's come back with my lemon-coke . . .

[*She leans back and closes her eyes.*]

STANLEY. I have a lawyer acquaintance who will study these out.

BLANCHE. Present them to him with a box of aspirin tablets.

STANLEY [*becoming somewhat sheepish*]. You see, under the Napoleonic code—a man has to take an interest in his wife's affairs— especially now that she's going to have a baby.

[*Blanche opens her eyes. The "blue piano" sounds louder.*]

BLANCHE. Stella? Stella going to have a baby? [*dreamily*] I didn't know she was going to have a baby!

[*She gets up and crosses to the outside door. Stella appears around the corner with a carton from the drugstore.*]

[*Stanley goes into the bedroom with the envelope and the box.*]

[*The inner rooms fade to darkness and the outside wall of the house is visible. Blanche meets Stella at the foot of the steps to the sidewalk.*]

BLANCHE. Stella, Stella for star! How lovely to have a baby! It's all right. Everything's all right.

STELLA. I'm sorry he did that to you.

BLANCHE. Oh, I guess he's just not the type that goes for jasmine perfume, but maybe he's what we need to mix with our blood now that we've lost Belle Reve. We thrashed it out. I feel a bit shaky, but I think I handled it nicely, I laughed and treated it all as a joke. [*Steve and Pablo appear, carrying a case of beer.*] I called him a little boy and laughed and flirted. Yes, I was flirting with your husband! [*as the men approach*] The guests are gathering for the poker party. [*The two men pass between them, and enter the house.*] Which way do we go now, Stella—this way?

STELLA. No, this way. [*She leads Blanche away.*]

BLANCHE [*laughing*]. The blind are leading the blind!

[*A tamale Vendor is heard calling.*]

VENDOR'S VOICE. Red-hot!

SCENE THREE

The Poker Night

There is a picture of Van Gogh's of a billiard-parlor at night. The kitchen now suggests that sort of lurid nocturnal brilliance, the raw colors of childhood's spectrum. Over the yellow linoleum of the kitchen table hangs an electric bulb with a vivid green glass shade. The poker players—Stanley, Steve, Mitch and Pablo—wear colored shirts, solid blues, a purple, a red-and-white check, a light green, and they are men at the peak of their physical manhood, as coarse and direct and powerful as the primary colors. There are vivid slices of watermelon on the table, whiskey bottles and glasses. The bedroom is relatively dim with only the light that spills between the portieres and through the wide window on the street.

For a moment, there is absorbed silence as a hand is dealt.

STEVE. Anything wild this deal?

PABLO. One-eyed jacks are wild.

STEVE. Give me two cards.

PABLO. You, Mitch?

MITCH. I'm out.

PABLO. One.

MITCH. Anyone want a shot?

STANLEY. Yeah. Me.

PABLO. Why don't somebody go to the Chinaman's and bring back a load of chop suey?

STANLEY. When I'm losing you want to eat! Ante up! Openers? Openers! Get y'r ass off the table, Mitch. Nothing belongs on a poker table but cards, chips and whiskey.

[He lurches up and tosses some watermelon rinds to the floor.]

MITCH. Kind of on your high horse, ain't you?

STANLEY. How many?

STEVE. Give me three.

STANLEY. One.

MITCH. I'm out again. I oughta go home pretty soon.

STANLEY. Shut up.

MITCH. I gotta sick mother. She don't go to sleep until I come in at night.

STANLEY. Then why don't you stay home with her?

MITCH. She says to go out, so I go, but I don't enjoy it. All the while I keep wondering how she is.

STANLEY. Aw, for the sake of Jesus, go home, then!

PABLO. What've you got?

STEVE. Spade flush.

MITCH. You all are married. But I'll be alone when she goes.—I'm going to the bathroom.

STANLEY. Hurry back and we'll fix you a sugar-tit.

MITCH. Aw, go rut. *[He crosses through the bedroom into the bathroom.]*

STEVE *[dealing a hand]*. Seven card stud. *[Telling his joke as he deals]* This ole farmer is out in back of his house sittin' down th'owing corn to the chickens when all at once he hears a loud cackle and this young hen comes lickety split around the side of the house with the rooster right behind her and gaining on her fast.

STANLEY *[impatient with the story]*. Deal!

STEVE. But when the rooster catches sight of the farmer th'owing the corn he puts on the brakes and lets the hen get away and starts pecking corn. And the old farmer says, "Lord God, I hopes I never gits *that* hongry!"

[Steve and Pablo laugh. The sisters appear around the corner of the building.]

STELLA. The game is still going on.

BLANCHE. How do I look?

STELLA. Lovely, Blanche.

BLANCHE. I feel so hot and frazzled. Wait till I powder before you open the door. Do I look done in?

STELLA. Why no. You are as fresh as a daisy.

BLANCHE. One that's been picked a few days.

[Stella opens the door and they enter.]

STELLA. Well, well, well. I see you boys are still at it!

STANLEY. Where you been?

STELLA. Blanche and I took in a show. Blanche, this is Mr. Gonzales and Mr. Hubbell.

BLANCHE. Please don't get up.

STANLEY. Nobody's going to get up, so don't be worried.

STELLA. How much longer is this game going to continue?

STANLEY. Till we get ready to quit.

BLANCHE. Poker is so fascinating. Could I kibitz?

STANLEY. You could not. Why don't you women go up and sit with Eunice?

STELLA. Because it is nearly two-thirty. [*Blanche crosses into the bedroom and partially closes the portieres*] Couldn't you call it quits after one more hand?

[*A chair scrapes. Stanley gives a loud whack of his hand on her thigh.*]

STELLA [*sharply*]. That's not fun, Stanley.

[*The men laugh. Stella goes into the bedroom.*]

STELLA. It makes me so mad when he does that in front of people.

BLANCHE. I think I will bathe.

STELLA. Again?

BLANCHE. My nerves are in knots. Is the bathroom occupied?

STELLA. I don't know.

[*Blanche knocks. Mitch opens the door and comes out, still wiping his hands on a towel.*]

BLANCHE. Oh!—good evening.

MITCH. Hello. [*He stares at her.*]

STELLA. Blanche, this is Harold Mitchell. My sister, Blanche DuBois.

MITCH [*with awkward courtesy*]. How do you do, Miss DuBois.

STELLA. How is your mother now, Mitch?

MITCH. About the same, thanks. She appreciated your sending over that custard.—Excuse me, please.

[*He crosses slowly back into the kitchen, glancing back at Blanche and coughing a little shyly. He realizes he still has the towel in his hands and with an embarrassed laugh hands it to Stella. Blanche looks after him with a certain interest.*]

BLANCHE. That one seems—superior to the others.

STELLA. Yes, he is.

BLANCHE. I thought he had a sort of sensitive look.

STELLA. His mother is sick.

BLANCHE. Is he married?

STELLA. No.

BLANCHE. Is he a wolf?

STELLA. Why, Blanche! [*Blanche laughs.*] I don't think he would be.

BLANCHE. What does—what does he do?

[*She is unbuttoning her blouse.*]

STELLA. He's on the precision bench in the spare parts department. At the plant Stanley travels for.

BLANCHE. Is that something much?

STELLA. No. Stanley's the only one of his crowd that's likely to get anywhere.

BLANCHE. What makes you think Stanley will?

STELLA. Look at him.

BLANCHE. I've looked at him.

STELLA. Then you should know.

BLANCHE. I'm sorry, but I haven't noticed the stamp of genius even on Stanley's forehead.

[*She takes off the blouse and stands in her pink silk brassiere and white skirt in the light through the portieres. The game has continued in undertones.*]

STELLA. It isn't on his forehead and it isn't genius.

BLANCHE. Oh. Well, what is it, and where? I would like to know.

STELLA. It's a drive that he has. You're standing in the light, Blanche!

BLANCHE. Oh, am I!

[*She moves out of the yellow streak of light. Stella has removed her dress and puts on a light blue satin kimono.*]

STELLA [*with girlish laughter*]. You ought to see their wives.

BLANCHE [*laughingly*]. I can imagine. Big, beefy things, I suppose.

STELLA. You know that one upstairs? [*More*

laughter] One time [*laughing*] the plaster —[*laughing*] cracked—

STANLEY. You hens cut out that conversation in there!

STELLA. You can't hear us.

STANLEY. Well, you can hear me and I said to hush up!

STELLA. This is my house and I'll talk as much as I want to!

BLANCHE. Stella, don't start a row.

STELLA. He's half drunk!—I'll be out in a minute.

[*She goes into the bathroom. Blanche rises and crosses leisurely to a small white radio and turns it on.*]

STANLEY. Awright, Mitch, you in?

MITCH. What? Oh!—No, I'm out!

[*Blanche moves back into the streak of light. She raises her arms and stretches, as she moves indolently back to the chair.*

[*Rhumba music comes over the radio. Mitch rises at the table.*]

STANLEY. Who turned that on in there?

BLANCHE. I did. Do you mind?

STANLEY. Turn it off!

STEVE. Aw, let the girls have their music.

PABLO. Sure, that's good, leave it on!

STEVE. Sounds like Xavier Cugat!

[*Stanley jumps up and, crossing to the radio, turns it off. He stops short at the sight of Blanche in the chair. She returns his look without flinching. Then he sits again at the poker table.*

[*Two of the men have started arguing hotly.*]

STEVE. I didn't hear you name it.

PABLO. Didn't I name it, Mitch?

MITCH. I wasn't listenin'.

PABLO. What were you doing, then?

STANLEY. He was looking through them drapes. [*He jumps up and jerks roughly at curtains to close them*] Now deal the hand over again and let's play cards or quit. Some people get ants when they win.

[*Mitch rises as Stanley returns to his seat.*]

STANLEY [*yelling*]. Sit down!

MITCH. I'm going to the "head." Deal me out.

PABLO. Sure he's got ants now. Seven five-dollar bills in his pants pocket folded up tight as spitballs.

STEVE. Tomorrow you'll see him at the cashier's window getting them changed into quarters.

STANLEY. And when he goes home he'll deposit them one by one in a piggy bank his mother give him for Christmas. [*Dealing*] This game is Spit in the Ocean.

[*Mitch laughs uncomfortably and continues through the portieres. He stops just inside.*]

BLANCHE [*softly*]. Hello! The Little Boys' Room is busy right now.

MITCH. We've—been drinking beer.

BLANCHE. I hate beer.

MITCH. It's—a hot weather drink.

BLANCH. Oh, I don't think so; it always makes me warmer. Have you got any cigs? [*She has slipped on the dark red satin wrapper.*]

MITCH. Sure.

BLANCHE. What kind are they?

MITCH. Luckies.

BLANCHE. Oh, good. What a pretty case. Silver?

MITCH. Yes. Yes; read the inscription.

BLANCHE. Oh, is there an inscription? I can't make it out. [*He strikes a match and moves closer*] Oh! [*reading with feigned difficulty*]:
   "And if God choose,
   I shall but love thee better—after—death!"
Why, that's from my favorite sonnet by Mrs. Browning!

MITCH. You know it?

BLANCHE. Certainly I do!

MITCH. There's a story connected with that inscription.

BLANCHE. It sounds like a romance.

MITCH. A pretty sad one.

BLANCHE. Oh?

MITCH. The girl's dead now.

BLANCHE [*in a tone of deep sympathy*]. Oh!

MITCH. She knew she was dying when she give me this. A very strange girl, very sweet —very!

BLANCHE. She must have been fond of you. Sick people have such deep, sincere attachments.

MITCH. That's right, they certainly do.

BLANCHE. Sorrow makes for sincerity, I think.

MITCH. It sure brings it out in people.

BLANCHE. The little there is belongs to people who have experienced some sorrow.

MITCH. I believe you are right about that.

BLANCHE. I'm positive that I am. Show me a person who hasn't known any sorrow and I'll show you a shuperficial—Listen to me! My tongue is a little—thick! You boys are responsible for it. The show let out at eleven and we couldn't come home on account of the poker game so we had to go somewhere and drink. I'm not accustomed to having more than one drink. Two is the limit—and *three!* [*She laughs*] Tonight I had three.

STANLEY. Mitch!

MITCH. Deal me out. I'm talking to Miss—

BLANCHE. DuBois.

MITCH. Miss DuBois?

BLANCHE. It's a French name. It means woods and Blanche means white, so the two together mean white woods. Like an orchard in spring! You can remember it by that.

MITCH. You're French?

BLANCHE. We are French by extraction. Our first American ancestors were French Huguenots.

MITCH. You are Stella's sister, are you not?

BLANCHE. Yes, Stella is my precious little sister. I call her little in spite of the fact she's somewhat older than I. Just slightly. Less than a year. Will you do something for me?

MITCH. Sure. What?

BLANCHE. I bought this adorable little colored paper lantern at a Chinese shop on Bourbon. Put it over the light bulb! Will you, please?

MITCH. Be glad to.

BLANCHE. I can't stand a naked light bulb, any more than I can a rude remark or a vulgar action.

MITCH [*adjusting the lantern*]. I guess we strike you as being a pretty rough bunch.

BLANCHE. I'm very adaptable—to circumstances.

MITCH. Well, that's a good thing to be. You are visiting Stanley and Stella?

BLANCHE. Stella hasn't been so well lately, and I came down to help her for a while. She's very run down.

MITCH. You're not—?

BLANCHE. Married? No, no. I'm an old maid schoolteacher!

MITCH. You may teach school but you're certainly not an old maid.

BLANCHE. Thank you, sir! I appreciate your gallantry!

MITCH. So you are in the teaching profession?

BLANCHE. Yes. Ah, yes . . .

MITCH. Grade school or high school or—

STANLEY [*bellowing*]. *Mitch!*

MITCH. *Coming!*

BLANCHE. Gracious, what lung-power! . . . I teach high school. In Laurel.

MITCH. What do you teach? What subject?

BLANCHE. Guess!

MITCH. I bet you teach art or music? [*Blanche laughs delicately*] Of course I could be wrong. You might teach arithmetic.

BLANCHE. Never arithmetic, sir; never arithmetic! [*with a laugh*] I don't even know my multiplication tables! No, I have the misfortune of being an English instructor. I attempt to instill a bunch of bobby-soxers and drug-store Romeos with reverence for Hawthorne and Whitman and Poe!

MITCH. I guess that some of them are more interested in other things.

BLANCHE. How very right you are! Their literary heritage is not what most of them treasure above all else! But they're sweet things! And in the spring, it's touching to notice them making their first discovery of love! As if nobody had ever known it before!

[*The bathroom door opens and Stella*

comes out. Blanche continues talking to Mitch.]

Oh! Have you finished? Wait—I'll turn on the radio.

[*She turns the knobs on the radio and it begins to play "Wien, Wien, nur du allein." Blanche waltzes to the music with romantic gestures. Mitch is delighted and moves in awkward imitation like a dancing bear.*]

[*Stanley stalks fiercely through the portieres into the bedroom. He crosses to the small white radio and snatches it off the table. With a shouted oath, he tosses the instrument out the window.*]

STELLA. *Drunk—drunk—animal thing, you!* [*She rushes through to the poker table*] All of you—please go home! If any of you have one spark of decency in you—
BLANCHE [*wildly*]. Stella, watch out, he's—

[*Stanley charges after Stella.*]

MEN [*feebly*]. Take it easy, Stanley. Easy, fellow.—Let's all—
STELLA. You lay your hands on me and I'll—

[*She backs out of sight. He advances and disappears. There is the sound of a blow. Stella cries out. Blanche screams and runs into the kitchen. The men rush forward and there is grappling and cursing. Something is overturned with a crash.*]

BLANCHE [*shrilly*]. My sister is going to have a baby!
MITCH. This is terrible.
BLANCHE. Lunacy, absolute lunacy!
MITCH. Get him in here, men.

[*Stanley is forced, pinioned by the two men, into the bedroom. He nearly throws them off. Then all at once he subsides and is limp in their grasp.*

[*They speak quietly and lovingly to him and he leans his face on one of their shoulders.*]

STELLA [*in a high, unnatural voice, out of sight*]. I want to go away, I want to go away!
MITCH. Poker shouldn't be played in a house with women.

[*Blanche rushes into the bedroom*]

BLANCHE. I want my sister's clothes! We'll go to that woman's upstairs!
MITCH. Where is the clothes?
BLANCHE [*opening the closet*]. I've got them! [*She rushes through to Stella*] Stella, Stella, precious! Dear, dear little sister, don't be afraid!

[*With her arms around Stella, Blanche guides her to the outside door and upstairs.*]

STANLEY [*dully*]. What's the matter; what's happened?
MITCH. You just blew your top, Stan.
PABLO. He's okay, now.
STEVE. Sure, my boy's okay!
MITCH. Put him on the bed and get a wet towel.
PABLO. I think coffee would do him a world of good, now.
STANLEY [*thickly*]. I want water.
MITCH. Put him under the shower!

[*The men talk quietly as they lead him to the bathroom.*]

STANLEY. Let the rut go of me, you sons of bitches!

[*Sounds of blows are heard. The water goes on full tilt.*]

STEVE. Let's get quick out of here!

[*They rush to the poker table and sweep up their winnings on their way out.*]

MITCH [*sadly but firmly*]. Poker should not be played in a house with women.

[*The door closes on them and the place is still. The Negro entertainers in the bar around the corner play "Paper Doll" slow and blue. After a moment Stanley comes out of the bathroom dripping water and still in his clinging wet polka dot drawers.*]

STANLEY. Stella! [*There is a pause*] My baby doll's left me!

[*He breaks into sobs. Then he goes to the phone and dials, still shuddering with sobs.*]

Eunice? I want my baby! [*He waits a moment; then he hangs up and dials again*] Eunice! I'll keep on ringin' until I talk with my baby!

[*An indistinguishable shrill voice is heard. He hurls phone to floor. Dissonant brass and piano sounds as the rooms dim out to darkness and the outer walls appear in the night light. The "blue piano" plays for a brief interval.*]

[*Finally, Stanley stumbles half-dressed out to the porch and down the wooden steps to the pavement before the building. There he throws back his head like a baying hound and bellows his wife's name: "Stella! Stella, sweetheart! Stella!"*]

STANLEY. Stell-lahhhhh!
EUNICE [*calling down from the door of her upper apartment*]. Quit that howling out there an' go back to bed!
STANLEY. I want my baby down here. Stella, Stella!
EUNICE. She ain't comin' down so you quit! Or you'll git th' law on you!
STANLEY. Stella!
EUNICE. You can't beat on a woman an' then call 'er back! She won't come! And her goin' t' have a baby! . . . You stinker! You whelp of a Polack, you! I hope they do

haul you in and turn the fire hose on you, same as the last time!
STANLEY [*humbly*]. Eunice, I want my girl to come down with me!
EUNICE. Hah! [*She slams her door.*]
STANLEY [*with heaven-splitting violence*]. STELL-LAHHHHH!

[*The low-tone clarinet moans. The door upstairs opens again. Stella slips down the rickety stairs in her robe. Her eyes are glistening with tears and her hair loose about her throat and shoulders. They stare at each other. Then they come together with low, animal moans. He falls to his knees on the steps and presses his face to her belly, curving a little with maternity. Her eyes go blind with tenderness as she catches his head and raises him level with her. He snatches the screen door open and lifts her off her feet and bears her into the dark flat.*]

[*Blanche comes out on the upper landing in her robe and slips fearfully down the steps.*]

BLANCHE. Where is my little sister? Stella? Stella?

[*She stops before the dark entrance of her sister's flat. Then catches her breath as if struck. She rushes down to the walk before the house. She looks right and left as if for a sanctuary.*]

[*The music fades away. Mitch appears from around the corner.*]

MITCH. Miss DuBois?
BLANCHE. Oh!
MITCH. All quiet on the Potomac now?
BLANCHE. She ran downstairs and went back in there with him.
MITCH. Sure she did.
BLANCHE. I'm terrified!
MITCH. Ho-ho! There's nothing to be scared of. They're crazy about each other.
BLANCHE. I'm not used to such—
MITCH. Naw, it's a shame this had to happen

when you just got here. But don't take it serious.

BLANCHE. Violence! Is so—

MITCH. Set down on the steps and have a cigarette with me.

BLANCHE. I'm not properly dressed.

MITCH. That don't make no difference in the Quarter.

BLANCHE. Such a pretty silver case.

MITCH. I showed you the inscription, didn't I?

BLANCHE. Yes. [During the pause, she looks up at the sky] There's so much—so much confusion in the world . . . [He coughs diffidently] Thank you for being so kind! I need kindness now.

SCENE FOUR

It is early the following morning. There is a confusion of street cries like a choral chant.

Stella is lying down in the bedroom. Her face is serene in the early morning sunlight. One hand rests on her belly, rounding slightly with new maternity. From the other dangles a book of colored comics. Her eyes and lips have that almost narcotized tranquility that is in the faces of Eastern idols.

The table is sloppy with remains of breakfast and the debris of the preceding night, and Stanley's gaudy pyjamas lie across the threshold of the bathroom. The outside door is slightly ajar on a sky of summer brilliance.

Blanche appears at this door. She has spent a sleepless night and her appearance entirely contrasts with Stella's. She presses her knuckles nervously to her lips as she looks through the door, before entering.

BLANCHE. Stella?

STELLA [stirring lazily]. Hmmh?

[Blanche utters a moaning cry and runs into the bedroom, throwing herself down beside Stella in a rush of hysterical tenderness.]

BLANCHE. Baby, my baby sister!

STELLA [drawing away from her]. Blanche, what is the matter with you?

[Blanche straightens up slowly and stands beside the bed looking down at her sister with knuckles pressed to her lips.]

BLANCHE. He's left?

STELLA. Stan? Yes.

BLANCHE. Will he be back?

STELLA. He's gone to get the car greased. Why?

BLANCHE. Why! I've been half crazy, Stella! When I found out you'd been insane enough to come back in here after what happened—I started to rush in after you!

STELLA. I'm glad you didn't.

BLANCHE. What were you thinking of? [Stella makes an indefinite gesture] Answer me! What? What?

STELLA. Please, Blanche! Sit down and stop yelling.

BLANCHE. All right, Stella. I will repeat the question quietly now. How could you come back in this place last night? Why you must have slept with him!

[Stella gets up in a calm and leisurely way.]

STELLA. Blanche, I'd forgotten how excitable you are. You're making much too much fuss about this.

BLANCHE. Am I?

STELLA. Yes, you are, Blanche. I know how it must have seemed to you and I'm awful sorry it had to happen, but it wasn't anything as serious as you seem to take it. In the first place, when men are drinking and playing poker anything can happen. It's always a powder-keg. He didn't know what he was doing. . . . He was as good as a lamb when I came back and he's really very, very ashamed of himself.

BLANCHE. And that—that makes it all right?

STELLA. No, it isn't all right for anybody to make such a terrible row, but—people do sometimes. Stanley's always smashed things. Why, on our wedding night—soon as we came in here—he snatched off one of my slippers and rushed about the place smashing the light-bulbs with it.

BLANCHE. He did—*what?*

STELLA. He smashed all the light-bulbs with the heel of my slipper! [*She laughs.*]

BLANCHE. And you—you *let* him? Didn't *run*, didn't *scream?*

STELLA. I was—sort of—thrilled by it. [*She waits for a moment*] Eunice and you had breakfast?

BLANCHE. Do you suppose I wanted any breakfast?

STELLA. There's some coffee left on the stove.

BLANCHE. You're so—matter of fact about it, Stella.

STELLA. What other can I be? He's taken the radio to get it fixed. It didn't land on the pavement so only one tube was smashed.

BLANCHE. And you are standing there smiling!

STELLA. What do you want me to do?

BLANCHE. Pull yourself together and face the facts.

STELLA. What are they, in your opinion?

BLANCHE. In my opinion? You're married to a madman!

STELLA. No!

BLANCHE. Yes, you are, your fix is worse than mine is! Only you're not being sensible about it. I'm going to *do* something. Get hold of myself and make myself a new life!

STELLA. Yes?

BLANCHE. But you've given in. And that isn't right, you're not old! You can get out.

STELLA [*slowly and emphatically*]. I'm not in anything I want to get out of.

BLANCHE [*incredulously*]. What—Stella?

STELLA. I said I am not in anything that I have a desire to get out of. Look at the mess in this room! And those empty bottles! They went through two cases last night! He promised this morning that he was going to quit having these poker parties, but you know how long such a promise is going to keep. Oh, well, it's his pleasure, like mine is movies and bridge. People have got to tolerate each other's habits, I guess.

BLANCHE. I don't understand you. [*Stella turns toward her*] I don't understand your indifference. Is this a Chinese philosophy you've—cultivated?

STELLA. Is what—what?

BLANCHE. This—shuffling about and mumbling—'One tube smashed—beer-bottles—mess in the kitchen!'—as if nothing out of the ordinary has happened! [*Stella laughs uncertainly and picking up the broom, twirls it in her hands.*]

BLANCHE. Are you deliberately shaking that thing in my face?

STELLA. No.

BLANCHE. Stop it. Let go of that broom. I won't have you cleaning up for him!

STELLA. Then who's going to do it? Are you?

BLANCHE. I? I!

STELLA. No, I didn't think so.

BLANCHE. Oh, let me think, if only my mind would function! We've got to get hold of some money, that's the way out!

STELLA. I guess that money is always nice to get hold of.

BLANCHE. Listen to me. I have an idea of some kind. [*Shakily she twists a cigarette into her holder*] Do you remember Shep Huntleigh? [*Stella shakes her head*] Of course you remember Shep Huntleigh. I went out with him at college and wore his pin for a while. Well—

STELLA. Well?

BLANCHE. I ran into him last winter. You know I went to Miami during the Christmas holidays?

STELLA. No.

BLANCHE. Well, I did. I took the trip as an investment, thinking I'd meet someone with a million dollars.

STELLA. Did you?

BLANCHE. Yes. I ran into Shep Huntleigh—I ran into him on Biscayne Boulevard, on Christmas Eve, about dusk . . . getting into his car—Cadillac convertible; must have been a block long!

STELLA. I should think it would have been—inconvenient in traffic!

BLANCHE. You've heard of oil-wells?

STELLA. Yes—remotely.

BLANCHE. He has them, all over Texas. Texas is literally spouting gold in his pockets.

STELLA. My, my.

BLANCHE. Y'know how indifferent I am to money. I think of money in terms of what it does for you. But he could do it, he could certainly do it!

STELLA. Do what, Blanche?

BLANCHE. Why—set us up in a—shop!

STELLA. What kind of a shop?

BLANCHE. Oh, a—shop of some kind! He could do it with half what his wife throws away at the races.

STELLA. He's married?

BLANCHE. Honey, would I be here if the man weren't married? [*Stella laughs a little. Blanche suddenly springs up and crosses to phone. She speaks shrilly*] How do I get Western Union?—Operator! Western Union!

STELLA. That's a dial phone, honey.

BLANCHE. I can't dial, I'm too—

STELLA. Just dial O.

BLANCHE. O?

STELLA. Yes, "O" for Operator! [*Blanche considers a moment; then she puts the phone down.*]

BLANCHE. Give me a pencil. Where is a slip of paper? I've got to write it down first—the message, I mean . . .

[*She goes to the dressing table, and grabs up a sheet of Kleenex and an eyebrow pencil for writing equipment.*]

Let me see now . . . [*She bites the pencil*] 'Darling Shep. Sister and I in desperate situation.'

STELLA. I beg your pardon!

BLANCHE. 'Sister and I in desperate situation. Will explain details later. Would you be interested in—?' [*She bites the pencil again*] 'Would you be—interested—in . . .' [*She smashes the pencil on the table and springs up*] You never get anywhere with direct appeals!

STELLA [*with a laugh*]. Don't be so ridiculous, darling!

BLANCHE. But I'll think of something, I've *got* to think of—*some*-thing! Don't, don't laugh at me, Stella! Please, please don't—I—I want you to look at the contents of my purse! Here's what's in it! [*She snatches her purse open*] Sixty-five measly cents in coin of the realm!

STELLA [*crossing to bureau*]. Stanley doesn't give me a regular allowance, he likes to pay bills himself, but—this morning he gave me ten dollars to smooth things over. You take five of it, Blanche, and I'll keep the rest.

BLANCHE. Oh, no. No, Stella.

STELLA [*insisting*]. I know how it helps your morale just having a little pocket-money on you.

BLANCHE. No, thank you—I'll take to the streets!

STELLA. Talk sense! How did you happen to get so low on funds?

BLANCHE. Money just goes—it goes places. [*She rubs her forehead*] Sometime today I've got to get hold of a bromo!

STELLA. I'll fix you one now.

BLANCHE. Not yet—I've got to keep thinking!

STELLA. I wish you'd just let things go, at least for a—while . . .

BLANCHE. Stella, I can't live with him! You can, he's your husband. But how could I stay here with him, after last night, with just those curtains between us?

STELLA. Blanche, you saw him at his worst last night.

BLANCHE. On the contrary, I saw him at his best! What such a man has to offer is animal force and he gave a wonderful exhibition of that! But the only way to live with such a man is to—go to bed with him! And that's your job—not mine!

STELLA. After you've rested a little, you'll see it's going to work out. You don't have to worry about anything while you're here. I mean—expenses . . .

BLANCHE. I have to plan for us both, to get us both—out!

STELLA. You take it for granted that I am in something that I want to get out of.

BLANCHE. I take it for granted that you still have sufficient memory of Belle Reve to find this place and these poker players impossible to live with.

STELLA. Well, you're taking entirely too much for granted.

BLANCHE. I can't believe you're in earnest.

STELLA. No?

BLANCHE. I understand how it happened—a little. You saw him in uniform, an officer, not here but—

STELLA. I'm not sure it would have made any difference where I saw him.

BLANCHE. Now don't say it was one of those mysterious electric things between people! If you do I'll laugh in your face.

STELLA. I am not going to say anything more at all about it!

BLANCHE. All right, then, don't!

STELLA. But there are things that happen between a man and a woman in the dark—that sort of make everything else seem—unimportant. [*Pause.*]

BLANCHE. What you are talking about is brutal desire—just—Desire!—the name of that rattle-trap street-car that bangs through the Quarter, up one old narrow street and down another . . .

STELLA. Haven't you ever ridden on that street-car?

BLANCHE. It brought me here.—Where I'm not wanted and where I'm ashamed to be . . .

STELLA. Then don't you think your superior attitude is a bit out of place?

BLANCHE. I am not being or feeling at all superior, Stella. Believe me I'm not! It's just this. This is how I look at it. A man like that is someone to go out with—once—twice—three times when the devil is in you. But live with? Have a child by?

STELLA. I have told you I love him.

BLANCHE. Then I *tremble* for you! I just—*tremble* for you. . . .

STELLA. I can't help your trembling if you insist on trembling!

[*There is a pause.*]

BLANCHE. May I—speak—*plainly?*

STELLA. Yes, do. Go ahead. As plainly as you want to.

[*Outside, a train approaches. They are silent till the noise subsides. They are both in the bedroom.*]

[*Under cover of the train's noise Stanley enters from outside. He stands unseen by the women, holding some packages in his arms, and overhears their following conversation. He wears an undershirt and grease-stained seersucker pants.*]

BLANCHE. Well—if you'll forgive me—he's *common!*

STELLA. Why, yes, I suppose he is.

BLANCHE. Suppose! You can't have forgotten that much of our bringing up, Stella, that you just *suppose* that any part of a gentleman's in his nature! *Not one particle, no!* Oh, if he was just—*ordinary!* Just *plain*—but good and wholesome, but—*no.* There's something downright—*bestial*—about him! You're hating me saying this, aren't you?

STELLA [*coldly*]. Go on and say it all, Blanche.

BLANCHE. He acts like an animal, has an animal's habits! Eats like one, moves like one, talks like one! There's even something—sub-human—something not quite to the stage of humanity yet! Yes, something—ape-like about him, like one of those pictures I've seen in—anthropological studies! Thousands and thousands of years have passed him right by, and there he is—Stanley Kowalski—survivor of the stone age! Bearing the raw meat home from the kill in the jungle! And you—*you* here—*waiting* for him! Maybe he'll strike you or maybe grunt and kiss you! That is, if kisses have been discovered yet! Night falls and the other apes gather! There in the front of the cave, all grunting like him, and swilling and gnawing and hulking! His poker night!—you call it—this party of apes! Somebody growls—some creature snatches at something—the fight is on! *God!* Maybe we are a long way from being made in God's image, but Stella—my sister—there has been *some* progress since then! Such things as art—as poetry and music—such kinds of new light have come into the world since then!

In some kinds of people some tenderer feelings have had some little beginning! That we have got to make *grow!* And *cling* to, and hold as our flag! In this dark march toward whatever it is we're approaching.... *Don't—don't hang back with the brutes!*

[*Another train passes outside. Stanley hesitates, licking his lips. Then suddenly he turns stealthily about and withdraws through front door. The women are still unaware of his presence. When the train has passed he calls through the closed front door.*]

STANLEY. Hey! Hey, Stella!
STELLA [*who has listened gravely to Blanche*]. Stanley!
BLANCHE. Stell, I—

[*But Stella has gone to the front door. Stanley enters casually with his packages.*]

STANLEY. Hiyuh, Stella. Blanche back?
STELLA. Yes, she's back.
STANLEY. Hiyuh, Blanche. [*He grins at her.*]
STELLA. You must've got under the car.
STANLEY. Them darn mechanics at Fritz's don't know their ass fr'm—*Hey!*

[*Stella has embraced him with both arms, fiercely, and full in the view of Blanche. He laughs and clasps her head to him. Over her head he grins through the curtains at Blanche.*]

[*As the lights fade away, with a lingering brightness on their embrace, the music of the "blue piano" and trumpet and drums is heard.*]

SCENE FIVE

Blanche is seated in the bedroom fanning herself with a palm leaf as she reads over a just completed letter. Suddenly she bursts into a peal of laughter. Stella is dressing in the bedroom.

STELLA. What are you laughing at, honey?
BLANCHE. Myself, myself, for being such a liar! I'm writing a letter to Shep [*She picks up the letter*] "Darling Shep. I am spending the summer on the wing, making flying visits here and there. And who knows, perhaps I shall take a sudden notion to *swoop* down on *Dallas!* How would you feel about that? Ha-ha! [*She laughs nervously and brightly, touching her throat as if actually talking to Shep*] Forewarned is forearmed, as they say!"—How does that sound?
STELLA. Uh-huh . . .
BLANCHE [*going on nervously*]. "Most of my sister's friends go north in the summer but some have homes on the Gulf and there has been a continued round of entertainments, teas, cocktails, and luncheons—"

[*A disturbance is heard upstairs at the Hubbell's apartment.*]

STELLA. Eunice seems to be having some trouble with Steve.

[*Eunice's voice shouts in terrible wrath.*]

EUNICE. I heard about you and that blonde!
STEVE. That's a damn lie!
EUNICE. You ain't pulling the wool over my eyes! I wouldn't mind if you'd stay down at the Four Deuces, but you always going up.
STEVE. Who ever seen me up?
EUNICE. I seen you chasing her 'round the balcony—I'm gonna call the vice squad!
STEVE. Don't you throw that at me!
EUNICE [*shrieking*]. You hit me! I'm gonna call the police!

[*A clatter of aluminum striking a wall is heard, followed by a man's angry roar, shouts and overturned furniture. There is a crash; then a relative hush.*]

BLANCHE [*brightly*]. Did he *kill* her?

[*Eunice appears on the steps in daemonic disorder.*]

STELLA. No! She's coming downstairs.

EUNICE. Call the police, I'm going to call the police! [*She rushes around the corner.*]

[*They laugh lightly. Stanley comes around the corner in his green and scarlet bowling shirt. He trots up the steps and bangs into the kitchen. Blanche registers his entrance with nervous gestures.*]

STANLEY. What's a matter with Eun-uss?

STELLA. She and Steve had a row. Has she got the police?

STANLEY. Naw. She's gettin' a drink.

STELLA. That's much more practical!

[*Steve comes down nursing a bruise on his forehead and looks in the door.*]

STEVE. *She here?*

STANLEY. Naw, naw. At the Four Deuces.

STEVE. That rutting hunk! [*He looks around the corner a bit timidly, then turns with affected boldness and runs after her.*]

BLANCHE. I must jot that down in my notebook. Ha-ha! I'm compiling a notebook of quaint little words and phrases I've picked up here.

STANLEY. You won't pick up nothing here you ain't heard before.

BLANCHE. Can I count on that?

STANLEY. You can count on it up to five hundred.

BLANCHE. That's a mighty high number. [*He jerks open the bureau drawer, slams it shut and throws shoes in a corner. At each noise Blanche winces slightly. Finally she speaks*] What sign were you born under?

STANLEY [*while he is dressing*]. Sign?

BLANCHE. Astrological sign. I bet you were born under Aries. Aries people are forceful and dynamic. They dote on noise! They love to bang things around! You must have had lots of banging around in the army and now that you're out, you make up

for it by treating inanimate objects with such a fury!

[*Stella has been going in and out of closet during this scene. Now she pops her head out of the closet.*]

STELLA. Stanley was born just five minutes after Christmas.

BLANCHE. Capricorn—the Goat!

STANLEY. What sign were *you* born under?

BLANCHE. Oh, my birthway's next month, the fifteenth of September; that's under Virgo.

STANLEY. What's Virgo?

BLANCHE. Virgo is the Virgin.

STANLEY [*contemptuously*]. Hah! [*He advances a little as he knots his tie*] Say, do you happen to know somebody named Shaw?

[*Her face expresses a faint shock. She reaches for the cologne bottle and dampens her handkerchief as she answers carefully.*]

BLANCHE. Why, everybody knows somebody named Shaw!

STANLEY. Well, this somebody named Shaw is under the impression he met you in Laurel, but I figure he must have got you mixed up with some other party because this other party is someone he met at a hotel called the Flamingo.

[*Blanche laughs breathlessly as she touches the cologne-dampened handkerchief to her temples.*]

BLANCHE. I'm afraid he does have me mixed up with this "other party." The Hotel Flamingo is not the sort of establishment I would dare to be seen in!

STANLEY. You know of it?

BLANCHE. Yes, I've seen it and smelled it.

STANLEY. You must've got pretty close if you could smell it.

BLANCHE. The odor of cheap perfume is penetrating.

STANLEY. That stuff you use is expensive?

BLANCHE. Twenty-five dollars an ounce! I'm

nearly out. That's just a hint if you want to remember my birthday! [*She speaks lightly but her voice has a note of fear.*]

STANLEY. Shaw must've got you mixed up. He goes in and out of Laurel all the time so he can check on it and clear up any mistake.

[*He turns away and crosses to the portieres. Blanche closes her eyes as if faint. Her hand trembles as she lifts the handkerchief again to her forehead.*]

[*Steve and Eunice come around corner. Steve's arm is around Eunice's shoulder and she is sobbing luxuriously and he is cooing love-words. There is a murmur of thunder as they go slowly upstairs in a tight embrace.*]

STANLEY [*to Stella*]. I'll wait for you at the Four Deuces!

STELLA. Hey! Don't I rate one kiss?

STANLEY. Not in front of your sister.

[*He goes out. Blanche rises from her chair. She seems faint; looks about her with an expression of almost panic.*]

BLANCHE. Stella! What have you heard about me?

STELLA. Huh?

BLANCHE. What have people been telling you about me?

STELLA. Telling?

BLANCHE. You haven't heard any—unkind—gossip about me?

STELLA. Why, no, Blanche, of course not!

BLANCHE. Honey, there was—a good deal of talk in Laurel.

STELLA. About *you*, Blanche?

BLANCHE. I wasn't so good the last two years or so, after Belle Reve had started to slip through my fingers.

STELLA. All of us do things we—

BLANCHE. I never was hard or self-sufficient enough. When people are soft—soft people have got to shimmer and glow—they've got to put on soft colors, the colors of butterfly wings, and put a—paper lantern over the light. . . . It isn't enough to be soft. You've got to be soft *and attractive*. And I—I'm fading now! I don't know how much longer I can turn the trick.

[*The afternoon has faded to dusk. Stella goes into the bedroom and turns on the light under the paper lantern. She holds a bottled soft drink in her hand.*]

BLANCHE. Have you been listening to me?

STELLA. I don't listen to you when you are being morbid! [*She advances with the bottled coke.*]

BLANCHE [*with abrupt change to gaiety*]. Is that coke for me?

STELLA. Not for anyone else!

BLANCHE. Why, you precious thing, you! Is it just coke?

STELLA [*turning*]. You mean you want a shot in it!

BLANCHE. Well, honey, a shot never does a coke any harm! Let me! You mustn't wait on me!

STELLA. I like to wait on you, Blanche. It makes it seem more like home. [*She goes into the kitchen, finds a glass and pours a shot of whiskey into it.*]

BLANCHE. I have to admit I love to be waited on . . .

[*She rushes into the bedroom. Stella goes to her with the glass. Blanche suddenly clutches Stella's free hand with a moaning sound and presses the hand to her lips. Stella is embarrassed by her show of emotion. Blanche speaks in a choked voice.*]

You're—you're—so *good* to me! And I—

STELLA. Blanche.

BLANCHE. I know, I won't! You hate me to talk sentimental! But honey, *believe* I feel things more than I *tell* you! I *won't* stay long! I won't, I *promise* I—

STELLA. Blanche!

BLANCHE [*hysterically*]. I won't, I promise, *I'll* go! Go *soon*! I will *really*! I *won't* hang around until he—throws me out . . .

STELLA. Now will you stop talking foolish?

BLANCHE. Yes, honey. Watch how you pour —that fizzy stuff foams over!

[*Blanche laughs shrilly and grabs the glass, but her hand shakes so it almost slips from her grasp. Stella pours the coke into the glass. It foams over and spills. Blanche gives a piercing cry.*]

STELLA [*shocked by the cry*]. Heavens!

BLANCHE. Right on my pretty white skirt!

STELLA. Oh . . . Use my hanky. Blot gently.

BLANCHE [*slowly recovering*]. I know—gently —gently . . .

STELLA. Did it stain?

BLANCHE. Not a bit. Ha-ha! Isn't that lucky? [*She sits down shakily, taking a grateful drink. She holds the glass in both hands and continues to laugh a little.*]

STELLA. Why did you scream like that?

BLANCHE. I don't know why I screamed! [*continuing nervously*] Mitch—Mitch is coming at seven. I guess I am just feeling nervous about our relations. [*She begins to talk rapidly and breathlessly*] He hasn't gotten a thing but a goodnight kiss, that's all I have given him, Stella. I want his respect. And men don't want anything they get too easy. But on the other hand men lose interest quickly. Especially when the girl is over— thirty. They think a girl over thirty ought to—the vulgar term is—"put out." . . . And I—I'm not "putting out." Of course he—he doesn't know—I mean I haven't informed him—of my real age!

STELLA. Why are you sensitive about your age?

BLANCHE. Because of hard knocks my vanity's been given. What I mean is—he thinks I'm sort of—prim and proper, you know! [*She laughs out sharply*] I want to *deceive* him enough to make him—want me . . .

STELLA. Blanche, do you want *him*?

BLANCHE. I want to *rest*! I want to breathe quietly again! Yes—I *want* Mitch . . . *very badly*! Just think! If it happens! I can leave here and not be anyone's problem . . .

[*Stanley comes around the corner with a drink under his belt.*]

STANLEY [*bawling*]. Hey, Steve! Hey, Eunice! Hey, Stella!

[*There are joyous calls from above. Trumpet and drums are heard from around the corner.*]

STELLA [*kissing Blanche impulsively*]. It *will* happen!

BLANCHE [*doubtfully*]. It will?

STELLA. It *will*! [*She goes across into the kitchen, looking back at Blanche.*] It will honey, it will. . . . But don't take another drink! [*Her voice catches as she goes out the door to meet her husband.*]

[*Blanche sinks faintly back in her chair with her drink. Eunice shrieks with laughter and runs down the steps. Steve bounds after her with goat-like screeches and chases her around corner. Stanley and Stella twine arms as they follow, laughing.*]

[*Dusk settles deeper. The music from the Four Deuces is slow and blue.*]

BLANCHE. Ah, me, ah, me, ah, me . . .

[*Her eyes fall shut and the palm leaf fan drops from her fingers. She slaps her hand on the chair arm a couple of times. There is a little glimmer of lightning about the building.*]

[*A Young Man comes along the street and rings the bell.*]

BLANCHE. Come in.

[*The Young Man appears through the portieres. She regards him with interest.*]

BLANCHE. Well, well! What can I do for *you*?

YOUNG MAN. I'm collecting for *The Evening Star*.

BLANCHE. I didn't know that stars took up collections.

YOUNG MAN. It's the paper.

BLANCHE. I know, I was joking—feebly! Will you—have a drink?

YOUNG MAN. No, ma'am. No, thank you. I can't drink on the job.

BLANCHE. Oh, well, now, let's see. . . . No, I don't have a dime! I'm not the lady of the house. I'm her sister from Mississippi. I'm one of those poor relations you've heard about.

YOUNG MAN. That's all right. I'll drop by later. [*He starts to go out. She approaches a little.*]

BLANCHE. Hey! [*He turns back shyly. She puts a cigarette in a long holder*] Could you give me a light? [*She crosses toward him. They meet at the door between the two rooms.*]

YOUNG MAN. Sure. [*He takes out a lighter*] This doesn't always work.

BLANCHE. It's temperamental? [*It flares*] Ah!—thank you. [*He starts away again*] Hey! [*He turns again, still more uncertainly. She goes close to him*] Uh—what time is it?

YOUNG MAN. Fifteen of seven, ma'am.

BLANCHE. So late? Don't you just love these long rainy afternoons in New Orleans when an hour isn't just an hour—but a little piece of eternity dropped into your hands—and who knows what to do with it? [*She touches his shoulders.*] You—uh—didn't get wet in the rain?

YOUNG MAN. No, ma'am. I stepped inside.

BLANCHE. In a drug store? And had a soda?

YOUNG MAN. Uh-huh.

BLANCHE. Chocolate?

YOUNG MAN. No, ma'am. Cherry.

BLANCHE [*laughing*]. Cherry!

YOUNG MAN. A cherry soda.

BLANCHE. You make my mouth water. [*She touches his cheek lightly, and smiles. Then she goes to the trunk.*]

YOUNG MAN. Well, I'd better be going—

BLANCHE [*stopping him*]. Young man!

[*He turns. She takes a large, gossamer scarf from the trunk and drapes it about her shoulders.*

[*In the ensuing pause, the "blue piano" is heard. It continues through the rest of this scene and the opening of the*

next. *The young man clears his throat and looks yearningly at the door.*]

Young man! Young, young, young man! Has anyone ever told you that you look like a young Prince out of the Arabian Nights?

[*The Young Man laughs uncomfortably and stands like a bashful kid. Blanche speaks softly to him.*]

Well, you do, honey lamb! Come here. I want to kiss you, just once, softly and sweetly on your mouth!

[*Without waiting for him to accept, she crosses quickly to him and presses her lips to his.*]

Now run along, now, quickly! It would be nice to keep you, but I've got to be good—and keep my hands off children.

[*He stares at her a moment. She opens the door for him and blows a kiss at him as he goes down the steps with a dazed look. She stands there a little dreamily after he has disappeared. Then Mitch appears around the corner with a bunch of roses.*]

BLANCHE [*gaily*]. Look who's coming! My Rosenkavalier! Bow to me first . . . now present them! *Ahhhh—Merciiii!*

[*She looks at him over them, coquettishly pressing them to her lips. He beams at her self-consciously.*]

SCENE SIX

It is about two A.M. on the same evening. The outer wall of the building is visible. Blanche and Mitch come in. The utter exhaustion which only a neur-

asthenic personality can know is evident in Blanche's voice and manner. Mitch is stolid but depressed. They have probably been out to the amusement park on Lake Pontchartrain, for Mitch is bearing, upside down, a plaster statuette of Mae West, the sort of prize won at shooting-galleries and carnival games of chance.

BLANCHE [*stopping lifelessly at the steps*]. Well—

[*Mitch laughs uneasily.*]

Well . . .

MITCH. I guess it must be pretty late— and you're tired.

BLANCHE. Even the hot tamale man has deserted the street, and he hangs on till the end. [*Mitch laughs uneasily again*] How will you get home?

MITCH. I'll walk over to Bourbon and catch an owl-car.

BLANCHE [*laughing grimly*]. Is that street-car named Desire still grinding along the tracks at this hour?

MITCH [*heavily*]. I'm afraid you haven't gotten much fun out of this evening, Blanche.

BLANCHE. I spoiled it for *you*.

MITCH. No, you didn't, but I felt all the time that I wasn't giving you much—entertainment.

BLANCHE. I simply couldn't rise to the occasion. That was all. I don't think I've ever tried so hard to be gay and made such a dismal mess of it. I get ten points for trying!—I *did* try.

MITCH. Why did you try if you didn't feel like it, Blanche?

BLANCHE. I was just obeying the law of nature.

MITCH. Which law is that?

BLANCHE. The one that says the lady must entertain the gentleman—or no dice! See if you can locate my door-key in this purse. When I'm so tired my fingers are all thumbs!

MITCH [*rooting in her purse*]. This it?

BLANCHE. No, honey, that's the key to my trunk which I must soon be packing.

MITCH. You mean you are leaving here soon?

BLANCHE. I've outstayed my welcome.

MITCH. This it?

[*The music fades away.*]

BLANCHE. Eureka! Honey, you open the door while I take a last look at the sky. [*She leans on the porch rail. He opens the door and stands awkwardly behind her.*] I'm looking for the Pleiades, the Seven Sisters, but these girls are not out tonight. Oh, yes they are, there they are! God bless them! All in a bunch going home from their little bridge party. . . . Y' get the door open? Good boy! I guess you—want to go now . . .

[*He shuffles and coughs a little.*]

MITCH. Can I—uh—kiss you—goodnight?

BLANCHE. Why do you always ask me if you may?

MITCH. I don't know whether you want me to or not.

BLANCHE. Why should you be so doubtful?

MITCH. That night when we parked by the lake and I kissed you, you—

BLANCHE. Honey, it wasn't the kiss I objected to. I liked the kiss very much. It was the other little—familiarity—that I—felt obliged to—discourage. . . . I didn't resent it! Not a bit in the world! In fact, I was somewhat flattered that you—desired me! But, honey, you know as well as I do that a single girl, a girl alone in the world, has got to keep a firm hold on her emotions or she'll be lost!

MITCH [*solemnly*]. Lost?

BLANCHE. I guess you are used to girls that like to be lost. The kind that get lost immediately, on the first date!

MITCH. I like you to be exactly the way that you are, because in all my—experience—I have never known anyone like you.

[*Blanche looks at him gravely; then she bursts into laughter and then claps a hand to her mouth.*]

MITCH. Are you laughing at me?

BLANCHE. No, honey. The lord and lady of the house have not yet returned, so come in. We'll have a night-cap. Let's leave the lights off. Shall we?

MITCH. You just—do what you want to.

[*Blanche precedes him into the kitchen. The outer wall of the building disappears and the interiors of the two rooms can be dimly seen.*]

BLANCHE [*remaining in the first room*]. The other room's more comfortable—go on in. This crashing around in the dark is my search for some liquor.

MITCH. You want a drink?

BLANCHE. I want *you* to have a drink! You have been so anxious and solemn all evening, and so have I; we have both been anxious and solemn and now for these few last remaining moments of our lives together—I want to create—*joie de vivre!* I'm lighting a candle.

MITCH. That's good.

BLANCHE. We are going to be very Bohemian. We are going to pretend that we are sitting in a little artists' cafe on the Left Bank in Paris! [*She lights a candle stub and puts it in a bottle.*] *Je suis la Dame aux Camellias! Vous êtes—Armand!* Understand French?

MITCH [*heavily*]. Naw. Naw, I—

BLANCHE. *Voulez-vous couchez avec moi ce soir? Vous ne comprenez pas? Ah, quelle dommage!*—I mean it's a damned good thing. . . . I've found some liquor! Just enough for two shots without any dividends, honey . . .

MITCH [*heavily*]. That's—good.

[*She enters the bedroom with the drinks and the candle.*]

BLANCHE. Sit down! Why don't you take off your coat and loosen your collar?

MITCH. I better leave it on.

BLANCHE. No. I want you to be comfortable.

MITCH. I am ashamed of the way I perspire. My shirt is sticking to me.

BLANCHE. Perspiration is healthy. If people didn't perspire they would die in five minutes. [*She takes his coat from him*] This is a nice coat. What kind of material is it?

MITCH. They call that stuff alpaca.

BLANCHE. Oh. Alpaca.

MITCH. It's very light weight alpaca.

BLANCHE. Oh. Light weight alpaca.

MITCH. I don't like to wear a wash-coat even in summer because I sweat through it.

BLANCHE. Oh.

MITCH. And it don't look neat on me. A man with a heavy build has got to be careful of what he puts on him so he don't look too clumsy.

BLANCHE. You are not too heavy.

MITCH. You don't think I am?

BLANCHE. You are not the delicate type. You have a massive bone-structure and a very imposing physique.

MITCH. Thank you. Last Christmas I was given a membership to the New Orleans Athletic Club.

BLANCHE. Oh, good.

MITCH. It was the finest present I ever was given. I work out there with the weights and I swim and I keep myself fit. When I started there, I was getting soft in the belly but now my belly is hard. It is so hard now that a man can punch me in the belly and it don't hurt me. Punch me! Go on! See? [*She pokes lightly at him.*]

BLANCHE. Gracious. [*Her hand touches her chest.*]

MITCH. Guess how much I weigh, Blanche?

BLANCHE. Oh, I'd say in the vicinity of—one hundred and eighty?

MITCH. Guess again.

BLANCHE. Not that much?

MITCH. No. More.

BLANCHE. Well, you're a tall man and you can carry a good deal of weight without looking awkward.

MITCH. I weigh two hundred and seven pounds and I'm six feet one and one half inches tall in my bare feet—without shoes on. And that is what I weigh stripped.

BLANCHE. Oh, my goodness, me! It's awe-inspiring.

MITCH [*embarrassed*]. My weight is not a very interesting subject to talk about. [*He hesitates for a moment*] What's yours?

BLANCHE. My weight?

MITCH. Yes.

BLANCHE. Guess!

MITCH. Let me lift you.

BLANCHE. Samson! Go on; lift me. [*He comes behind her and puts his hands on her waist and raises her lightly off the ground*] Well?

MITCH. You are light as a feather.

BLANCHE. Ha-ha! [*He lowers her but keeps his hands on her waist. Blanche speaks with an affection of demureness*] You may release me now.

MITCH. Huh?

BLANCHE [*gaily*]. I said unhand me, sir. [*He fumblingly embraces her. Her voice sounds gently reproving*] Now, Mitch. Just because Stanley and Stella aren't at home is no reason why you shouldn't behave like a gentleman.

MITCH. Just give me a slap whenever I step out of bounds.

BLANCHE. That won't be necessary. You're a natural gentleman, one of the very few that are left in the world. I don't want you to think that I am severe and old maid school-teacherish or anything like that. It's just—well—

MITCH. Huh?

BLANCHE. I guess it is just that I have—old-fashioned ideals! [*She rolls her eyes, knowing he cannot see her face. Mitch goes to the front door. There is a considerable silence between them. Blanche sighs and Mitch coughs self-consciously.*]

MITCH [*finally*]. Where's Stanley and Stella tonight?

BLANCHE. They have gone out. With Mr. and Mrs. Hubbell upstairs.

MITCH. Where did they go?

BLANCHE. I think they were planning to go to a midnight prevue at Loew's State.

MITCH. We should all go out together some night.

BLANCHE. No. That wouldn't be a good plan.

MITCH. Why not?

BLANCHE. You are an old friend of Stanley's?

MITCH. We was together in the Two-forty-first.

BLANCHE. I guess he talks to you frankly?

MITCH. Sure.

BLANCHE. Has he talked to you about me?

MITCH. Oh—not very much.

BLANCHE. The way you say that, I suspect that he has.

MITCH. No, he hasn't said much.

BLANCHE. But what he *has* said. What would you say his attitude toward me was?

MITCH. Why do you want to ask that?

BLANCHE. Well—

MITCH. Don't you get along with him?

BLANCHE. What do you think?

MITCH. I don't think he understands you.

BLANCHE. That is putting it mildly. If it weren't for Stella about to have a baby, I wouldn't be able to endure things here.

MITCH. He isn't—nice to you?

BLANCHE. He is insufferably rude. Goes out of his way to offend me.

MITCH. In what way, Blanche?

BLANCHE. Why, in every conceivable way.

MITCH. I'm surprised to hear that.

BLANCHE. Are you?

MITCH. Well, I—don't see how anybody could be rude to you.

BLANCHE. It's really a pretty frightful situation. You see, there's no privacy here. There's just these portieres between the two rooms at night. He stalks through the rooms in his underwear at night. And I have to ask him to close the bathroom door. That sort of commonness isn't necessary. You probably wonder why I don't move out. Well, I'll tell you frankly. A teacher's salary is barely sufficient for her living-expenses. I didn't save a penny last year and so I had to come here for the summer. That's why I have to put up with my sister's husband. And he has to put up with me, apparently so much against his wishes. . . . Surely he must have told you how much he hates me!

MITCH. I don't think he hates you.

BLANCHE. He hates me. Or why would he insult me? The first time I laid eyes on him I thought to myself, that man is my executioner! That man will destroy me, unless ——

MITCH. Blanche—

BLANCHE. Yes, honey?

MITCH. Can I ask you a question?

BLANCHE. Yes. What?

MITCH. How old are you?

[*She makes a nervous gesture.*]

BLANCHE. Why do you want to know?

MITCH. I talked to my mother about you and she said, "How old is Blanche?" And I wasn't able to tell her. [*There is another pause.*]

BLANCHE. You talked to your mother about me?

MITCH. Yes.

BLANCHE. Why?

MITCH. I told my mother how nice you were, and I liked you.

BLANCHE. Were you sincere about that?

MITCH. You know I was.

BLANCHE. Why did your mother want to know my age?

MITCH. Mother is sick.

BLANCHE. I'm sorry to hear it. Badly?

MITCH. She won't live long. Maybe just a few months.

BLANCHE. Oh.

MITCH. She worries because I'm not settled.

BLANCHE. Oh.

MITCH. She wants me to be settled down before she—[*His voice is hoarse and he clears his throat twice, shuffling nervously around with his hands in and out of his pockets.*]

BLANCHE. You love her very much, don't you?

MITCH. Yes.

BLANCHE. I think you have a great capacity for devotion. You will be lonely when she passes on, won't you? [*Mitch clears his throat and nods.*] I understand what that is.

MITCH. To be lonely?

BLANCHE. I loved someone, too, and the person I loved I lost.

MITCH. Dead? [*She crosses to the window and sits on the sill, looking out. She pours herself another drink.*] A man?

BLANCHE. He was a boy, just a boy, when I was a very young girl. When I was sixteen, I made the discovery—love. All at once and much, much too completely. It was like you suddenly turned a blinding light on something that had always been half in shadow, that's how it struck the world for me. But I was unlucky. Deluded. There was something different about the boy, a nervousness, a softness and tenderness which wasn't like a man's, although he wasn't the least bit effeminate looking— still—that thing was there. . . . He came to me for help. I didn't know that. I didn't find out anything till after our marriage when we'd run away and come back and all I knew was I'd failed him in some mysterious way and wasn't able to give the help he needed but couldn't speak of! He was in the quicksands and clutching at me —but I wasn't holding him out, I was slipping in with him! I didn't know that. I didn't know anything except I loved him unendurably but without being able to help him or help myself. Then I found out. In the worst of all possible ways. By coming suddenly into a room that I thought was empty—which wasn't empty, but had two people in it . . . the boy I had married and an older man who had been his friend for years . . .

[*A locomotive is heard approaching outside. She claps her hands to her ears and crouches over. The headlight of the locomotive glares into the room as it thunders past. As the noise recedes she straightens slowly and continues speaking.*]

Afterwards we pretended that nothing had been discovered. Yes, the three of us drove out to Moon Lake Casino, very drunk and laughing all the way.

[*Polka music sounds, in a minor key faint with distance.*]

We danced the Varsouviana! Suddenly in the middle of the dance the boy I had married broke away from me and ran out of the casino. A few moments later—a shot!

[*The Polka stops abruptly.*

[*Blanche rises stiffly. Then, the Polka resumes in a major key.*]

I ran out—all did!—all ran and gathered about the terrible thing at the edge of the lake! I couldn't get near for the crowding. Then somebody caught my arm. "Don't go any closer! Come back! You don't want to see!" See? See what! Then I heard voices say—Allan! Allan! The Grey boy! He'd stuck the revolver into his mouth, and fired—so that the back of his head had been —blown away!

[*She sways and covers her face.*]

It was because—on the dance-floor—unable to stop myself—I'd suddenly said—"I saw! I know! You disgust me . . ." And then the searchlight which had been turned on the world was turned off again and never for one moment since has there been any light that's stronger than this—kitchen— candle . . .

[*Mitch gets up awkwardly and moves toward her a little. The Polka music increases. Mitch stands beside her.*]

MITCH [*drawing her slowly into his arms*]. You need somebody. And I need somebody, too. Could it be—you and me, Blanche?

[*She stares at him vacantly for a moment. Then with a soft cry huddles in his embrace. She makes a sobbing effort to speak but the words won't come. He kisses her forehead and her eyes and finally her lips. The Polka tune fades out. Her breath is drawn and released in long, grateful sobs.*]

BLANCHE.   Sometimes — there's   God — so quickly!

SCENE SEVEN

It is late afternoon in mid-September.

The portieres are open and a table is set for a birthday supper, with cake and flowers.

Stella is completing the decorations as Stanley comes in.

STANLEY. What's all this stuff for?
STELLA. Honey, it's Blanche's birthday.
STANLEY. She here?
STELLA. In the bathroom.
STANLEY [*mimicking*]. "Washing out some things"?
STELLA. I reckon so.
STANLEY. How long she been in there?
STELLA. All afternoon.
STANLEY [*mimicking*]. "Soaking in a hot tub"?
STELLA. Yes.
STANLEY. Temperature 100 on the nose, and she soaks herself in a hot tub.
STELLA. She says it cools her off for the evening.
STANLEY. And you run out an' get her cokes, I suppose? And serve 'em to Her Majesty in the tub? [*Stella shrugs*] Set down here a minute.
STELLA. Stanley, I've got things to do.
STANLEY. Set down! I've got th' dope on your big sister, Stella.
STELLA. Stanley, stop picking on Blanche.
STANLEY. That girl calls *me* common!
STELLA. Lately you been doing all you can think of to rub her the wrong way, Stanley, and Blanche is sensitive and you've got to realize that Blanche and I grew up under very different circumstances than you did.
STANLEY. So I been told. And told and told and told! You know she's been feeding us a pack of lies here?
STELLA. No, I don't, and—
STANLEY. Well, she has, however. But now the cat's out of the bag! I found out some things!

STELLA. What—things?

STANLEY. Things I already suspected. But now I got proof from the most reliable sources—which I have checked on!

[*Blanche is singing in the bathroom a saccharine popular ballad which is used contrapuntally with Stanley's speech.*]

STELLA [*to Stanley*]. Lower your voice!

STANLEY. Some canary-bird, huh!

STELLA. Now please tell me quietly what you think you've found out about my sister.

STANLEY. Lie Number One: All this squeamishness she puts on! You should just know the line she's been feeding to Mitch. He thought she had never been more than kissed by a fellow! But Sister Blanche is no lily! Ha-ha! Some lily she is!

STELLA. What have you heard and who from?

STANLEY. Our supply-man down at the plant has been going through Laurel for years and he knows all about her and everybody else in the town of Laurel knows all about her. She is as famous in Laurel as if she was the President of the United States, only she is not respected by any party! This supply-man stops at a hotel called the Flamingo.

BLANCHE [*singing blithely*]. "Say, it's only a paper moon, Sailing over a cardboard sea —But it wouldn't be make-believe If you believed in me!"*

STELLA. What about the—Flamingo?

STANLEY. She stayed there, too.

STELLA. My sister lived at Belle Reve.

STANLEY. This is after the home-place had slipped through her lily-white fingers! She moved to the Flamingo! A second-class hotel which has the advantage of not interfering in the private social life of the personalities there! The Flamingo is used to all kinds of goings-on. But even the management of the Flamingo was impressed by Dame Blanche! In fact they was so impressed by Dame Blanche that they requested her to turn in her room-key—for

permanently! This happened a couple of weeks before she showed here.

BLANCHE [*singing*]. "It's a Barnum and Bailey world, Just as phony as it can be— But it wouldn't be make-believe If you believed in me!"

STELLA. What—contemptible—lies!

STANLEY. Sure, I can see how you would be upset by this. She pulled the wool over your eyes as much as Mitch's!

STELLA. It's pure invention! There's not a word of truth in it and if I were a man and this creature had dared to invent such things in my presence—

BLANCHE [*singing*]. "Without your love, It's a honky-tonk parade! Without your love, It's a melody played In a penny arcade . . ."

STANLEY. Honey, I told you I thoroughly checked on these stories! Now wait till I finished. The trouble with Dame Blanche was that she couldn't put on her act any more in Laurel! They got wised up after two or three dates with her and then they quit, and she goes on to another, the same old line, same old act, same old hooey! But the town was too small for this to go on forever! And as time went by she became a town character. Regarded as not just different but downright loco—nuts.

[*Stella draws back.*]

And for the last year or two she has been washed up like poison. That's why she's here this summer, visiting royalty, putting on all this act—because she's practically told by the mayor to get out of town! Yes, did you know there was an army camp near Laurel and your sister's was one of the places called "Out-of-Bounds"?

BLANCHE. "It's only a paper moon, Just as phony as it can be— But it wouldn't be make-believe If you believed in me!"

STANLEY. Well, so much for her being such a refined and particular type of girl. Which brings us to Lie Number Two.

STELLA. I don't want to hear any more!

STANLEY. She's not going back to teach school!

* Copyright 1933 by Harms, Inc. Used by permission. Permission for performance must be obtained from Harms, Inc.

In fact I am willing to bet you that she never had no idea of returning to Laurel! She didn't resign temporarily from the high school because of her nerves! No, siree, Bob! She didn't. They kicked her out of that high school before the spring term ended—and I hate to tell you the reason that step was taken! A seventeen-year-old boy—she'd gotten mixed up with!

BLANCHE. "It's a Barnum and Bailey world, Just as phony as it can be—"

[*In the bathroom the water goes on loud; little breathless cries and peals of laughter are heard as if a child were frolicking in the tub.*]

STELLA. This is making me—sick!

STANLEY. The boy's dad learned about it and got in touch with the high school superintendent. Boy, oh, boy, I'd like to have been in that office when Dame Blanche was called on the carpet! I'd like to have seen her trying to squirm out of that one! But they had her on the hook good and proper that time and she knew that the jig was all up! They told her she better move on to some fresh territory. Yep, it was practickly a town ordinance passed against her!

[*The bathroom door is opened and Blanche thrusts her head out, holding a towel about her hair.*]

BLANCHE. Stella!

STELLA [*faintly*]. Yes, Blanche?

BLANCHE. Give me another bath-towel to dry my hair with. I've just washed it.

STELLA. Yes, Blanche. [*She crosses in a dazed way from the kitchen to the bathroom door with a towel.*]

BLANCHE. What's the matter, honey?

STELLA. Matter? Why?

BLANCHE. You have such a strange expression on your face!

STELLA. Oh—[*She tries to laugh*] I guess I'm a little tired!

BLANCHE. Why don't you bathe, too, soon as I get out?

STANLEY [*calling from the kitchen*]. How soon is that going to be?

BLANCHE. Not so terribly long! Possess your soul in patience!

STANLEY. It's not my soul, it's my kidneys I'm worried about!

[*Blanche slams the door. Stanley laughs harshly. Stella comes slowly back into the kitchen.*]

STANLEY. Well, what do you think of it?

STELLA. I don't believe all of those stories and I think your supply-man was mean and rotten to tell them. It's possible that some of the things he said are partly true. There are things about my sister I don't approve of—things that caused sorrow at home. She was always—flighty!

STANLEY. Flighty!

STELLA. But when she was young, very young, she married a boy who wrote poetry. . . . He was extremely good-looking. I think Blanche didn't just love him but she worshipped the ground he walked on! Adored him and thought him almost too fine to be human! But then she found out—

STANLEY. What?

STELLA. This beautiful and talented young man was a degenerate. Didn't your supply-man give you that information?

STANLEY. All we discussed was recent history. That must have been a pretty long time ago.

STELLA. Yes, it was—a pretty long time ago . . .

[*Stanley comes up and takes her by the shoulders rather gently. She gently withdraws from him. Automatically she starts sticking little pink candles in the birthday cake.*]

STANLEY. How many candles you putting in that cake?

STELLA. I'll stop at twenty-five.

STANLEY. Is company expected?

STELLA. We asked Mitch to come over for cake and ice-cream.

[*Stanley looks a little uncomfortable. He lights a cigarette from the one he has just finished.*]

STANLEY. I wouldn't be expecting Mitch over tonight.

[*Stella pauses in her occupation with candles and looks slowly around at Stanley.*]

STELLA. *Why?*

STANLEY. Mitch is a buddy of mine. We were in the same outfit together—Two-forty-first Engineers. We work in the same plant and now on the same bowling team. You think I could face him if—

STELLA. Stanley Kowalski, did you—did you repeat what that—?

STANLEY. You're goddam right I told him! I'd have that on my conscience the rest of my life if I knew all that stuff and let my best friend get caught!

STELLA. Is Mitch through with her?

STANLEY. Wouldn't you be if—?

STELLA. I said, *Is Mitch through with her?*

[*Blanche's voice is lifted again, serenely as a bell. She sings "But it wouldn't be make-believe if you believed in me."*]

STANLEY. No, I don't think he's necessarily through with her—just wised up!

STELLA. Stanley, she thought Mitch was—going to—going to marry her. I was hoping so, too.

STANLEY. Well, he's not going to marry her. Maybe he *was,* but he's not going to jump in a tank with a school of sharks—now! [*He rises*] Blanche! Oh, Blanche! Can I please get in my bathroom? [*There is a pause.*]

BLANCHE. Yes, indeed, sir! Can you wait one second while I dry?

STANLEY. Having waited one hour I guess one second ought to pass in a hurry.

STELLA. And she hasn't got her job? Well, what will she do!

STANLEY. She's not stayin' here after Tuesday. You know that, don't you? Just to make sure I bought her ticket myself. A bus-ticket!

STELLA. In the first place, Blanche wouldn't go on a bus.

STANLEY. She'll go on a bus and like it.

STELLA. No, she won't, no, she won't, Stanley!

STANLEY. *She'll go!* Period. P.S. She'll go Tuesday!

STELLA [*slowly*]. What'll—she—do? What on earth will she—*do!*

STANLEY. Her future is mapped out for her.

STELLA. What do you mean?

[*Blanche sings.*]

STANLEY. Hey, canary bird! Toots! Get OUT of the *BATHROOM!*

[*The bathroom door flies open and Blanche emerges with a gay peal of laughter, but as Stanley crosses past her, a frightened look appears in her face, almost a look of panic. He doesn't look at her but slams the bathroom door shut as he goes in.*]

BLANCHE [*snatching up a hair-brush*]. Oh, I feel so good after my long, hot bath, I feel so good and cool and—rested!

STELLA [*sadly and doubtfully from the kitchen*]. Do you, Blanche?

BLANCHE [*brushing her hair vigorously*]. Yes, I do, so refreshed! [*She tinkles her high-ball glass.*] A hot bath and a long, cold drink always give me a brand new outlook on life! [*She looks through the portieres at Stella, standing between them, and slowly stops brushing*] Something has happened! —What is it?

STELLA [*turning away quickly*]. Why, nothing has happened, Blanche.

BLANCHE. You're lying! Something has!

[*She stares fearfully at Stella, who pretends to be busy at the table. The distant piano goes into a hectic breakdown.*]

SCENE EIGHT

Three-quarters of an hour later.

The view through the big windows is fading gradually into a still-golden dusk. A torch of sunlight blazes on the side of a big water-tank or oil-drum across the empty lot toward the business district which is now pierced by pinpoints of lighted windows or windows reflecting the sunset.

The three people are completing a dismal birthday supper. Stanley looks sullen. Stella is embarrassed and sad.

Blanche has a tight, artificial smile on her drawn face. There is a fourth place at the table which is left vacant.

BLANCHE [*suddenly*]. Stanley, tell us a joke, tell us a funny story to make us all laugh. I don't know what's the matter, we're all so solemn. Is it because I've been stood up by my beau?

[*Stella laughs feebly.*]

It's the first time in my entire experience with men, and I've had a good deal of all sorts, that I've actually been stood up by anybody! Ha-ha! I don't know how to take it. . . . Tell us a funny little story, Stanley! Something to help us out.

STANLEY. I didn't think you liked my stories, Blanche.

BLANCHE. I like them when they're amusing but not indecent.

STANLEY. I don't know any refined enough for your taste.

BLANCHE. Then let me tell one.

STELLA. Yes, you tell one, Blanche. You used to know lots of good stories.

[*The music fades.*]

BLANCHE. Let me see, now. . . . I must run through my repertoire! Oh, yes—I love parrot stories! Do you all like parrot stories? Well, this one's about the old maid and the parrot. This old maid, she had a parrot that cursed a blue streak and knew more vulgar expressions than Mr. Kowalski!

STANLEY. Huh.

BLANCHE. And the only way to hush the parrot up was to put the cover back on its cage so it would think it was night and go back to sleep. Well, one morning the old maid had just uncovered the parrot for the day —when who should she see coming up the front walk but the preacher! Well, she rushed back to the parrot and slipped the cover back on the cage and then she let in the preacher. And the parrot was perfectly still, just as quiet as a mouse, but just as she was asking the preacher how much sugar he wanted in his coffee—the parrot broke the silence with a loud—[*She whistles*]—and said—"God *damn*, but that was a short day!"

[*She throws back her head and laughs. Stella also makes an ineffectual effort to seem amused. Stanley pays no attention to the story but reaches way over the table to spear his fork into the remaining chop which he eats with his fingers.*]

BLANCHE. Apparently Mr. Kowalski was not amused.

STELLA. Mr. Kowalski is too busy making a pig of himself to think of anything else!

STANLEY. That's right, baby.

STELLA. Your face and your fingers are disgustingly greasy. Go and wash up and then help me clear the table.

[*He hurls a plate to the floor.*]

STANLEY. That's how I'll clear the table! [*He seizes her arm*] Don't ever talk that way to me! "Pig — Polack — disgusting — vulgar — greasy!"—them kind of words have been on your tongue and your sister's too much around here! What do you two think you are? A pair of queens? Remember what Huey Long said—"Every Man is a King!" And I am the king around here, so don't forget it! [*He hurls a cup and saucer to the floor*] My place is cleared! You want me to clear your places?

[*Stella begins to cry weakly. Stanley stalks out on the porch and lights a cigarette.*

[*The Negro entertainers around the corner are heard.*]

BLANCHE. What happened while I was bathing? What did he tell you, Stella?
STELLA. Nothing, nothing, nothing!
BLANCHE. I think he told you something about Mitch and me! You know why Mitch didn't come but you won't tell me! [*Stella shakes her head helplessly*] I'm going to call him!
STELLA. I wouldn't call him, Blanche.
BLANCHE. I am, I'm going to call him on the phone.
STELLA [*miserably*]. I wish you wouldn't.
BLANCHE. I intend to be given some explanation from someone!

[*She rushes to the phone in the bedroom. Stella goes out on the porch and stares reproachfully at her husband. He grunts and turns away from her.*]

STELLA. I hope you're pleased with your doings. I never had so much trouble swallowing food in my life, looking at that girl's face and the empty chair! [*She cries quietly.*]
BLANCHE [*at the phone*]. Hello. Mr. Mitchell, please. . . . Oh. . . . I would like to leave a number if I may. Magnolia 9047. And say it's important to call. . . . Yes, very important. . . . Thank you. [*She remains by the phone with a lost, frightened look.*]

[*Stanley turns slowly back toward his wife and takes her clumsily in his arms.*]

STANLEY. Stell, it's gonna be all right after she

goes and after you've had the baby. It's gonna be all right again between you and me the way that it was. You remember that way that it was? Them nights we had together? God, honey, it's gonna be sweet when we can make noise in the night the way that we used to and get the colored lights going with nobody's sister behind the curtains to hear us!

[*Their upstairs neighbors are heard in bellowing laughter at something. Stanley chuckles.*]

Steve an' Eunice. . .
STELLA. Come on back in. [*She returns to the kitchen and starts lighting the candles on the white cake.*] Blanche?
BLANCHE. Yes. [*She returns from the bedroom to the table in the kitchen.*] Oh, those pretty, pretty little candles! Oh, don't burn them, Stella.
STELLA. I certainly will.

[*Stanley comes back in.*]

BLANCHE. You ought to save them for baby's birthdays. Oh, I hope candles are going to glow in his life and I hope that his eyes are going to be like candles, like two blue candles lighted in a white cake!
STANLEY [*sitting down*]. What poetry!
BLANCHE [*she pauses reflectively for a moment*]. I shouldn't have called him.
STELLA. There's lots of things could have happened.
BLANCHE. There's no excuse for it, Stella. I don't have to put up with insults. I won't be taken for granted.
STANLEY. Goddamn, it's hot in here with the steam from the bathroom.
BLANCHE. I've said I was sorry three times. [*The piano fades out.*] I take hot baths for my nerves. Hydro-therapy, they call it. You healthy Polack, without a nerve in your body, of course you don't know what anxiety feels like!
STANLEY. I am not a Polack. People from Poland are Poles, not Polacks. But what I am is a one hundred percent American,

born and raised in the greatest country on earth and proud as hell of it, so don't ever call me a Polack.

[*The phone rings. Blanche rises expectantly.*]

BLANCHE. Oh, that's for me, I'm sure.

STANLEY. *I'm* not sure. Keep your seat. [*He crosses leisurely to phone.*] H'lo. Aw, yeh, hello, Mac.

[*He leans against wall, staring insultingly in at Blanche. She sinks back in her chair with a frightened look. Stella leans over and touches her shoulder.*]

BLANCHE. Oh, keep your hands off me, Stella. What is the matter with you? Why do you look at me with that pitying look?

STANLEY [*bawling*]. QUIET IN THERE!— We've got a noisy woman on the place.— Go on, Mac. At Riley's? No, I don't wanta bowl at Riley's. I had a little trouble with Riley last week. I'm the team-captain, ain't I? All right, then, we're not gonna bowl at Riley's, we're gonna bowl at the West Side or the Gala! All right, Mac. See you!

[*He hangs up and returns to the table. Blanche fiercely controls herself, drinking quickly from her tumbler of water. He doesn't look at her but reaches in a pocket. Then he speaks slowly and with false amiability.*]

Sister Blanche, I've got a little birthday remembrance for you.

BLANCHE. Oh, have you, Stanley? I wasn't expecting any, I—I don't know why Stella wants to observe my birthday! I'd much rather forget it—when you—reach twenty-seven! Well—age is a subject that you'd prefer to—ignore!

STANLEY. Twenty-seven?

BLANCHE [*quickly*]. What is it? Is it for *me*?

[*He is holding a little envelope toward her.*]

STANLEY. Yes, I hope you like it!

BLANCHE. Why, why—Why, it's a—

STANLEY. Ticket! Back to Laurel! On the Greyhound! Tuesday!

[*The Varsouviana music steals in softly and continues playing. Stella rises abruptly and turns her back. Blanche tries to smile. Then she tries to laugh. Then she gives both up and springs from the table and runs into the next room. She clutches her throat and then runs into the bathroom. Coughing, gagging sounds are heard.*]

Well!

STELLA. You didn't need to do that.

STANLEY. Don't forget all that I took off her.

STELLA. You needn't have been so cruel to someone alone as she is.

STANLEY. Delicate piece she is.

STELLA. She is. She was. You didn't know Blanche as a girl. Nobody, nobody, was tender and trusting as she was. But people like you abused her, and forced her to change.

[*He crosses into the bedroom, ripping off his shirt, and changes into a brilliant silk bowling shirt. She follows him.*]

Do you think you're going bowling now?

STANLEY. Sure.

STELLA. You're not going bowling. [*She catches hold of his shirt*] Why did you do this to her?

STANLEY. I done nothing to no one. Let go of my shirt. You've torn it.

STELLA. I want to know why. Tell me why.

STANLEY. When we first met, me and you, you thought I was common. How right you was, baby. I was common as dirt. You showed me the snapshot of the place with the columns. I pulled you down off them columns and how you loved it, having them colored lights going! And wasn't we happy together, wasn't it all okay till she showed here?

[*Stella makes a slight movement. Her look goes suddenly inward as if some interior voice had called her name. She begins a slow, shuffling progress from the bedroom to the kitchen, leaning and resting on the back of the chair and then on the edge of a table with a blind look and listening expression. Stanley, finishing with his shirt, is unaware of her reaction.*]

And wasn't we happy together? Wasn't it all okay? Till she showed here. Hoity-toity, describing me as an ape. [*He suddenly notices the change in Stella*] Hey, what is it, Stel? [*He crosses to her.*]

STELLA [*quietly*]. Take me to the hospital.

[*He is with her now, supporting her with his arm, murmuring indistinguishably as they go outside.*]

SCENE NINE

A while later that evening. Blanche is seated in a tense hunched position in a bedroom chair that she has recovered with diagonal green and white stripes. She has on her scarlet satin robe. On the table beside chair is a bottle of liquor and a glass. The rapid, feverish polka tune, the "Varsouviana," is heard. The music is in her mind; she is drinking to escape it and the sense of disaster closing in on her, and she seems to whisper the words of the song. An electric fan is turning back and forth across her.

Mitch comes around the corner in work clothes: blue denim shirt and pants. He is unshaven. He climbs the steps to the door and rings. Blanche is startled.

BLANCHE. Who is it, please?

MITCH [*hoarsely*]. Me. Mitch.

[*The polka tune stops.*]

BLANCHE. Mitch!—Just a minute.

[*She rushes about frantically, hiding the bottle in a closet, crouching at the mirror and dabbing her face with cologne and powder. She is so excited that her breath is audible as she dashes about. At last she rushes to the door in the kitchen and lets him in.*]

Mitch!—Y'know, I really shouldn't let you in after the treatment I have received from you this evening! So utterly uncavalier! But hello, beautiful!

[*She offers him her lips. He ignores it and pushes past her into the flat. She looks fearfully after him as he stalks into the bedroom.*]

My, my, what a cold shoulder! And such uncouth apparel! Why, you haven't even shaved! The unforgivable insult to a lady! But I forgive you. I forgive you because it's such a relief to see you. You've stopped that polka tune that I had caught in my head. Have you ever had anything caught in your head? No, of course you haven't, you dumb angel-puss, you'd never get anything awful caught in your head!

[*He stares at her while she follows him while she talks. It is obvious that he has had a few drinks on the way over.*]

MITCH. Do we have to have that fan on?

BLANCHE. No!

MITCH. I don't like fans.

BLANCHE. Then let's turn it off, honey. I'm not partial to them!

[*She presses the switch and the fan nods slowly off. She clears her throat uneasily as Mitch plumps himself down on the bed in the bedroom and lights a cigarette.*]

I don't know what there is to drink. I—haven't investigated.

MITCH. I don't want Stan's liquor.

BLANCHE. It isn't Stan's. Everything here isn't Stan's. Some things on the premises are actually mine! How is your mother? Isn't your mother well?

MITCH. Why?

BLANCHE. Something's the matter tonight, but never mind. I won't cross-examine the witness. I'll just— [*She touches her forehead vaguely. The polka tune starts up again.*] —pretend I don't notice anything different about you! That—music again . . .

MITCH. What music?

BLANCHE. The "Varsouviana"! The polka tune they were playing when Allan— Wait!

[*A distant revolver shot is heard. Blanche seems relieved.*]

There now, the shot! It always stops after that.

[*The polka music dies out again.*]

Yes, now it's stopped.

MITCH. Are you boxed out of your mind?

BLANCHE. I'll go and see what I can find in the way of— [*She crosses into the closet, pretending to search for the bottle.*] Oh, by the way, excuse me for not being dressed. But I'd practically given you up! Had you forgotten your invitation to supper?

MITCH. I wasn't going to see you any more.

BLANCHE. Wait a minute. I can't hear what you're saying and you talk so little that when you do say something, I don't want to miss a single syllable of it. . . . What am I looking around here for? Oh, yes— liquor! We've had so much excitement around here this evening that I *am* boxed out of my mind! [*She pretends suddenly to find the bottle. He draws his foot up on the bed and stares at her contemptuously.*] Here's something. Southern Comfort! What is that, I wonder?

MITCH. If you don't know, it must belong to Stan.

BLANCHE. Take your foot off the bed. It has a light cover on it. Of course you boys don't notice things like that. I've done so much with this place since I've been here.

MITCH. I bet you have.

BLANCHE. You saw it before I came. Well, look at it now! This room is almost—dainty! I want to keep it that way. I wonder if this stuff ought to be mixed with something? Ummm, it's sweet, so sweet! It's terribly, terribly sweet! Why, it's a *liqueur,* I believe! Yes, that's what it *is,* a liqueur! [*Mitch grunts.*] I'm afraid you won't like it, but try it, and maybe you will.

MITCH. I told you already I don't want none of his liquor and I mean it. You ought to lay off his liquor. He says you been lapping it up all summer like a wild-cat!

BLANCHE. What a fantastic statement! Fantastic of him to say it, fantastic of you to repeat it! I won't descend to the level of such cheap accusations to answer them, even!

MITCH. Huh.

BLANCHE. What's in your mind? I see something in your eyes!

MITCH [*getting up*]. It's dark in here.

BLANCHE. I like it dark. The dark is comforting to me.

MITCH. I don't think I ever seen you in the light. [*Blanche laughs breathlessly*] That's a fact!

BLANCHE. Is it?

MITCH. I've never seen you in the afternoon.

BLANCHE. Whose fault is that?

MITCH. You never want to go out in the afternoon.

BLANCHE. Why, Mitch, you're at the plant in the afternoon!

MITCH. Not Sunday afternoon. I've asked you to go out with me sometimes on Sundays but you always make an excuse. You never want to go out till after six and then it's always some place that's not lighted much.

BLANCHE. There is some obscure meaning in this but I fail to catch it.

MITCH. What it means is I've never had a real good look at you, Blanche. Let's turn the light on here.

BLANCHE [*fearfully*]. Light? Which light? What for?

MITCH. This one with the paper thing on it. [*He tears the paper lantern off the light bulb. She utters a frightened gasp.*]

BLANCHE. What did you do that for?

MITCH. So I can take a look at you good and plain!

BLANCHE. Of course you don't really mean to be insulting!

MITCH. No, just realistic.

BLANCHE. I don't want realism. I want magic! [*Mitch laughs*] Yes, yes, magic! I try to give that to people. I misrepresent things to them. I don't tell truth, I tell what *ought* to be truth. And if that is sinful, then let me be damned for it!—*Don't turn the light on!*

[*Mitch crosses to the switch. He turns the light on and stares at her. She cries out and covers her face. He turns the light off again.*]

MITCH [*slowly and bitterly*]. I don't mind you being older than what I thought. But all the rest of it—Christ! That pitch about your ideals being so old-fashioned and all that malarkey that you've dished out all summer. Oh, I knew you weren't sixteen any more. But I was a fool enough to believe you was straight.

BLANCHE. Who told you I wasn't—'straight'? My loving brother-in-law. And you believed him.

MITCH. I called him a liar at first. And then I checked on the story. First I asked our supply-man who travels through Laurel. And then I talked directly over long-distance to this merchant.

BLANCHE. Who is this merchant?

MITCH. Kiefaber.

BLANCHE. The merchant Kiefaber of Laurel! I know the man. He whistled at me. I put him in his place. So now for revenge he makes up stories about me.

MITCH. Three people, Kiefaber, Stanley and Shaw, swore to them!

BLANCHE. Rub-a-dub-dub, three men in a tub! And such a filthy tub!

MITCH. Didn't you stay at a hotel called The Flamingo?

BLANCHE. Flamingo? No! Tarantula was the name of it! I stayed at a hotel called The Tarantula Arms!

MITCH [*stupidly*]. Tarantula?

BLANCHE. Yes, a big spider! That's where I brought my victims. [*She pours herself another drink*] Yes, I had many intimacies with strangers. After the death of Allan— intimacies with strangers was all I seemed able to fill my empty heart with. . . . I think it was panic, just panic, that drove me from one to another, hunting for some protection—here and there, in the most— unlikely places—even, at last, in a seventeen-year-old boy but—somebody wrote the superintendent about it—"This woman is morally unfit for her position!"

[*She throws back her head with convulsive, sobbing laughter. Then she repeats the statement, gasps, and drinks.*]

True? Yes, I suppose—unfit somehow—anyway. . . . So I came here. There was nowhere else I could go. I was played out. You know what played out is? My youth was suddenly gone up the water-spout, and —I met you. You said you needed somebody. Well, I needed somebody, too. I thanked God for you, because you seemed to be gentle—a cleft in the rock of the world that I could hide in! But I guess I was asking, hoping—too much! Kiefaber, Stanley and Shaw have tied an old tin can to the tail of the kite.

[*There is a pause. Mitch stares at her dumbly.*]

MITCH. You lied to me, Blanche.

BLANCHE. Don't say I lied to you.

MITCH. Lies, lies, inside and out, all lies.

BLANCHE. Never inside, I didn't lie in my heart . . .

[*A Vendor comes around the corner. She is a blind Mexican woman in a dark shawl, carrying bunches of those gaudy tin flowers that lower class Mexicans display at funerals and other festive occasions. She is calling barely audibly. Her figure is only faintly visible outside the building.*]

MEXICAN WOMAN. Flores. Flores. Flores para los muertos. Flores. Flores.

BLANCHE. What? Oh! Somebody outside . . . [_She goes to the door, opens it and stares at the Mexican Woman._]

MEXICAN WOMAN [_she is at the door and offers Blanche some of her flowers_]. Flores? Flores para los muertos?

BLANCHE [_frightened_]. No, no! Not now! Not now!

[_She darts back into the apartment, slamming the door._]

MEXICAN WOMAN [_she turns away and starts to move down the street_]. Flores para los muertos.

[_The polka tune fades in._]

BLANCHE [_as if to herself_]. Crumble and fade and—regrets—recriminations . . . 'If you'd done this, it wouldn't've cost me that!'

MEXICAN WOMAN. Corones para los muertos. Corones . . .

BLANCHE. Legacies! Huh. . . . And other things such as bloodstained pillow-slips— 'Her linen needs changing'—'Yes Mother. But couldn't we get a colored girl to do it?' No, we couldn't of course. Everything gone but the—

MEXICAN WOMAN. Flores.

BLANCHE. Death—I used to sit here and she used to sit over there and death was as close as you are. . . . We didn't dare even admit we had ever heard of it!

MEXICAN WOMAN. Flores para los muertos, flores—flores . . .

BLANCHE. The opposite is desire. So do you wonder? How could you possibly wonder! Not far from Belle Reve, before we had lost Belle Reve, was a camp where they trained young soldiers. On Saturday nights they would go in town to get drunk—

MEXICAN WOMAN [_softly_]. Corones . . .

BLANCHE.—and on the way back they would stagger onto my lawn and call—'Blanche! Blanche!'—The deaf old lady remaining suspected nothing. But sometimes I slipped outside to answer their calls. . . . Later the paddy-wagon would gather them up like daisies . . . the long way home . . .

[_The Mexican Woman turns slowly and drifts back off with her soft mournful cries. Blanche goes to the dresser and leans forward on it. After a moment, Mitch rises and follows her purposefully. The polka music fades away. He places his hands on her waist and tries to turn her about._]

BLANCHE. What do you want?

MITCH [_fumbling to embrace her_]. What I been missing all summer.

BLANCHE. Then marry me, Mitch!

MITCH. I don't think I want to marry you any more.

BLANCHE. No?

MITCH [_dropping his hands from her waist_]. You're not clean enough to bring in the house with my mother.

BLANCHE. Go away, then. [_He stares at her_] Get out of here quick before I start screaming fire! [_Her throat is tightening with hysteria_] Get out of here quick before I start screaming fire.

[_He still remains staring. She suddenly rushes to the big window with its pale blue square of the soft summer light and cries wildly._]

Fire! Fire! Fire!

[_With a startled gasp, Mitch turns and goes out the outer door, clatters awkwardly down the steps and around the corner of the building. Blanche staggers back from the window and falls to her knees. The distant piano is slow and blue._]

SCENE TEN

It is a few hours later that night.
Blanche has been drinking fairly stead-

ily since Mitch left. *She has dragged her wardrobe trunk into the center of the bedroom. It hangs open with flowery dresses thrown across it. As the drinking and packing went on, a mood of hysterical exhilaration came into her and she has decked herself out in a somewhat soiled and crumpled white satin evening gown and a pair of scuffed silver slippers with brilliants set in their heels.*

Now she is placing the rhinestone tiara on her head before the mirror of the dressing-table and murmuring excitedly as if to a group of spectral admirers.

BLANCHE. How about taking a swim, a moonlight swim at the old rock-quarry? If anyone's sober enough to drive a car! Ha-ha! Best way in the world to stop your head buzzing! Only you've got to be careful to dive where the deep pool is—if you hit a rock you don't come up till tomorrow . . .

[*Tremblingly she lifts the hand mirror for a closer inspection. She catches her breath and slams the mirror face down with such violence that the glass cracks. She moans a little and attempts to rise.*]

[*Stanley appears around the corner of the building. He still has on the vivid green silk bowling shirt. As he rounds the corner the honky-tonk music is heard. It continues softly throughout the scene.*]

[*He enters the kitchen, slamming the door. As he peers in at Blanche, he gives a low whistle. He has had a few drinks on the way and has brought some quart beer bottles home with him.*]

BLANCHE. How is my sister?

STANLEY. She is doing okay.

BLANCHE. And how is the baby?

STANLEY [*grinning amiably*]. The baby won't come before morning so they told me to go home and get a little shut-eye.

BLANCHE. Does that mean we are to be alone in here?

STANLEY. Yep. Just me and you, Blanche. Unless you got somebody hid under the bed. What've you got on those fine feathers for?

BLANCHE. Oh, that's right. You left before my wire came.

STANLEY. You got a wire?

BLANCHE. I received a telegram from an old admirer of mine.

STANLEY. Anything good?

BLANCHE. I think so. An invitation.

STANLEY. What to? A fireman's ball?

BLANCHE [*throwing back her head*]. A cruise of the Caribbean on a yacht!

STANLEY. Well, well. What do you know?

BLANCHE. I have never been so surprised in my life.

STANLEY. I guess not.

BLANCHE. It came like a bolt from the blue!

STANLEY. Who did you say it was from?

BLANCHE. An old beau of mine.

STANLEY. The one that give you the white fox-pieces?

BLANCHE. Mr. Shep Huntleigh. I wore his ATO pin my last year at college. I hadn't seen him again until last Christmas. I ran into him on Biscayne Boulevard. Then— just now—this wire—inviting me on a cruise of the Caribbean! The problem is clothes. I tore into my trunk to see what I have that's suitable for the tropics!

STANLEY. And come up with that—gorgeous— diamond—tiara?

BLANCHE. This old relic? Ha-ha! It's only rhinestones.

STANLEY. Gosh. I thought it was Tiffany diamonds. [*He unbuttons his shirt.*]

BLANCHE. Well, anyhow, I shall be entertained in style.

STANLEY. Uh-huh. It goes to show, you never know what is coming.

BLANCHE. Just when I thought my luck had begun to fail me—

STANLEY. Into the picture pops this Miami millionaire.

BLANCHE. This man is not from Miami. This man is from Dallas.

STANLEY. This man is from Dallas?

BLANCHE. Yes, this man is from Dallas where gold spouts out of the ground!

STANLEY. Well, just so he's from somewhere! [*He starts removing his shirt.*]

BLANCHE. Close the curtains before you undress any further.

STANLEY [*amiably*]. This is all I'm going to undress right now. [*He rips the sack off a quart beer-bottle*] Seen a bottle-opener?

[*She moves slowly toward the dresser, where she stands with her hands knotted together.*]

I used to have a cousin who could open a beer-bottle with his teeth. [*Pounding the bottle cap on the corner of table*] That was his only accomplishment, all he could do— he was just a human bottle-opener. And then one time, at a wedding party, he broke his front teeth off! After that he was so ashamed of himself he used t' sneak out of the house when company came . . .

[*The bottle cap pops off and a geyser of foam shoots up. Stanley laughs happily, holding up the bottle over his head.*]

Ha-ha! Rain from heaven! [*He extends the bottle toward her*] Shall we bury the hatchet and make it a loving-cup? Huh?

BLANCHE. No, thank you.

STANLEY. Well, it's a red letter night for us both. You having an oil-millionaire and me having a baby.

[*He goes to the bureau in the bedroom and crouches to remove something from the bottom drawer.*]

BLANCHE [*drawing back*]. What are you doing in here?

STANLEY. Here's something I always break out on special occasions like this. The silk pyjamas I wore on my wedding night!

BLANCHE. Oh.

STANLEY. When the telephone rings and they say, "You've got a son!" I'll tear this off and wave it like a flag! [*He shakes out a brilliant pyjama coat*] I guess we are both entitled to put on the dog. [*He goes back to the kitchen with the coat over his arm.*]

BLANCHE. When I think of how divine it is going to be to have such a thing as privacy once more—I could weep with joy!

STANLEY. This millionaire from Dallas is not going to interfere with your privacy any?

BLANCHE. It won't be the sort of thing you have in mind. This man is a gentleman and he respects me. [*Improvising feverishly*] What he wants is my companionship. Having great wealth sometimes makes people lonely! A cultivated woman, a woman of intelligence and breeding, can enrich a man's life—immeasurably! I have those things to offer, and this doesn't take them away. Physical beauty is passing. A transitory possession. But beauty of the mind and richness of the spirit and tenderness of the heart—and I have all of those things—aren't taken away, but grow! Increase with the years! How strange that I should be called a destitute woman! When I have all of those treasures locked in my heart. [*A choked sob comes from her*] I think of myself as a very, very rich woman! But I have been foolish—casting my pearls before swine!

STANLEY. Swine, huh?

BLANCHE. Yes, swine! Swine! And I'm thinking not only of you but of your friend, Mr. Mitchell. He came to see me tonight. He dared to come here in his work-clothes! And to repeat slander to me, vicious stories that he had gotten from you! I gave him his walking papers . . .

STANLEY. You did, huh?

BLANCHE. But then he came back. He returned with a box of roses to beg my forgiveness! He implored my forgiveness. But some things are not forgivable. Deliberate cruelty is not forgivable. It is the one unforgivable thing in my opinion and it is the one thing of which I have never, never been guilty. And so I told him, I said to him, "Thank you," but it was foolish of me to think that we could ever adapt ourselves to each other. Our ways of life are too different. Our attitudes and our backgrounds are incompatible. We have to be realistic about such things. So farewell, my friend! And let there be no hard feelings . . .

STANLEY. Was this before or after the telegram came from the Texas oil millionaire?

BLANCHE. What telegram? No! No, after! As a matter of fact, the wire came just as—

STANLEY. As a matter of fact there wasn't no wire at all!

BLANCHE. Oh, oh!

STANLEY. There isn't no millionaire! And Mitch didn't come back with roses 'cause I know where he is—

BLANCHE. Oh!

STANLEY. There isn't a goddam thing but imagination!

BLANCHE. Oh!

STANLEY. And lies and conceit and tricks!

BLANCHE. Oh!

STANLEY. And look at yourself! Take a look at yourself in that worn-out Mardi Gras outfit, rented for fifty cents from some rag-picker! And with the crazy crown on! What queen do you think you are?

BLANCHE. Oh—God . . .

STANLEY. I've been on to you from the start! Not once did you pull any wool over this boy's eyes! You come in here and sprinkle the place with powder and spray perfume and cover the light-bulb with a paper lantern, and lo and behold the place has turned into Egypt and you are the Queen of the Nile! Sitting on your throne and swilling down my liquor! I say—Ha!—Ha! Do you hear me? Ha—ha—ha! [*He walks into the bedroom.*]

BLANCHE. Don't come in here!

[*Lurid reflections appear on the walls around Blanche. The shadows are of a grotesque and menacing form. She catches her breath, crosses to the phone and jiggles the hook. Stanley goes into the bathroom and closes the door.*]

Operator, operator! Give me long-distance, please. . . . I want to get in touch with Mr. Shep Huntleigh of Dallas. He's so well-known he doesn't require any address. Just ask anybody who—Wait!!—No, I couldn't find it right now. . . . Please understand,

I—No! No, wait! . . . One moment! Someone is—Nothing! Hold on, please!

[*She sets the phone down and crosses warily into the kitchen. The night is filled with inhuman voices like cries in a jungle.*

[*The shadows and lurid reflections move sinuously as flames along the wall spaces.*

[*Through the back wall of the rooms, which have become transparent, can be seen the sidewalk. A prostitute has rolled a drunkard. He pursues her along the walk, overtakes her and there is a struggle. A policeman's whistle breaks it up. The figures disappear.*

[*Some moments later the Negro Woman appears around the corner with a sequined bag which the prostitute had dropped on the walk. She is rooting excitedly through it.*

[*Blanche presses her knuckles to her lips and returns slowly to the phone. She speaks in a hoarse whisper.*]

BLANCHE. Operator! Operator! Never mind long-distance. Get Western Union. There isn't time to be—Western—Western Union!

[*She waits anxiously.*]

Western Union? Yes! I want to—Take down this message! "In desperate, desperate circumstances! Help me! Caught in a trap. Caught in—" Oh!

[*The bathroom door is thrown open and Stanley comes out in the brilliant silk pyjamas. He grins at her as he knots the tasseled sash about his waist. She gasps and backs away from the phone. He stares at her for a count of ten. Then a clicking becomes audible from the telephone, steady and rasping.*]

STANLEY. You left th' phone off th' hook.

[*He crosses to it deliberately and sets it back on the hook. After he has replaced it, he stares at her again, his mouth slowly curving into a grin, as he weaves between Blanche and the outer door.*]

[*The barely audible "blue piano" begins to drum up louder. The sound of it turns into the roar of an approaching locomotive. Blanche crouches, pressing her fists to her ears until it has gone by.*]

BLANCHE [*finally straightening*]. Let me—let me get by you!

STANLEY. Get by me? Sure. Go ahead. [*He moves back a pace in the doorway.*]

BLANCHE. You—you stand over there! [*She indicates a further position.*]

STANLEY [*grinning*]. You got plenty of room to walk by me now.

BLANCHE. Not with you there! But I've got to get out somehow!

STANLEY. You think I'll interfere with you? Ha-ha!

[*The "blue piano" goes softly. She turns confusedly and makes a faint gesture. The inhuman jungle voices rise up. He takes a step toward her, biting his tongue which protrudes between his lips.*]

STANLEY [*softly*]. Come to think of it—maybe you wouldn't be bad to—interfere with . . .

[*Blanche moves backward through the door into the bedroom.*]

BLANCHE. Stay back! Don't you come toward me another step or I'll—

STANLEY. What?

BLANCHE. Some awful thing will happen! It will!

STANLEY. What are you putting on now?

[*They are now both inside the bedroom.*]

BLANCHE. I warn you, don't, I'm in danger!

[*He takes another step. She smashes a bottle on the table and faces him, clutching the broken top.*]

STANLEY. What did you do that for?

BLANCHE. So I could twist the broken end in your face!

STANLEY. I bet you would do that!

BLANCHE. I would! I will if you—

STANLEY. Oh! So you want some rough-house! All right, let's have some rough-house!

[*He springs toward her, overturning the table. She cries out and strikes at him with the bottle top but he catches her wrist.*]

Tiger—tiger. Drop the bottle-top! Drop it! We've had this date with each other from the beginning!

[*She moans. The bottle-top falls. She sinks to her knees. He picks up her inert figure and carries her to the bed. The hot trumpet and drums from the Four Deuces sound loudly.*]

SCENE ELEVEN

It is some weeks later. Stella is packing Blanche's things. Sound of water can be heard running in the bathroom.

The portieres are partly open on the poker players—Stanley, Steve, Mitch and Pablo—who sit around the table in the kitchen. The atmosphere of the kitchen is now the same raw, lurid one of the disastrous poker night.

The building is framed by the sky of turquoise. Stella has been crying as she arranges the flowery dresses in the open trunk.

Eunice comes down the steps from her flat above and enters the kitchen. There is an outburst from the poker table.

STANLEY. Drew to an inside straight and made it, by God.

PABLO. *Maldita sea tu suerte!*

STANLEY. Put it in English, greaseball.

PABLO. I am cursing your rutting luck.

STANLEY [*prodigiously elated*]. You know what luck is? Luck is believing you're lucky. Take at Salerno. I believed I was lucky. I figured that 4 out of 5 would not come through but I would . . . and I did. I put that down as a rule. To hold front position in this rat-race you've got to believe you are lucky.

MITCH. You . . . you . . . you. . . . Brag . . . brag . . . bull . . . bull.

[*Stella goes into the bedroom and starts folding a dress.*]

STANLEY. What's the matter with him?

EUNICE [*walking past the table*]. I always did say that men are callous things with no feelings, but this does beat anything. Making pigs of yourselves. [*She comes through the portieres into the bedroom.*]

STANLEY. What's the matter with her?

STELLA. How is my baby?

EUNICE. Sleeping like a little angel. Brought you some grapes. [*She puts them on a stool and lowers her voice.*] Blanche?

STELLA. Bathing.

EUNICE. How is she?

STELLA. She wouldn't eat anything but asked for a drink.

EUNICE. What did you tell her?

STELLA. I—just told her that—we'd made arrangements for her to rest in the country. She's got it mixed in her mind with Shep Huntleigh.

[*Blanche opens the bathroom door slightly.*]

BLANCHE. Stella.

STELLA. Yes, Blanche?

BLANCHE. If anyone calls while I'm bathing take the number and tell them I'll call right back.

STELLA. Yes.

BLANCHE. That cool yellow silk—the bouclé.

See if it's crushed. If it's not too crushed I'll wear it and on the lapel that silver and turquoise pin in the shape of a seahorse. You will find them in the heart-shaped box I keep my accessories in. And Stella . . . Try and locate a bunch of artificial violets in that box, too, to pin with the seahorse on the lapel of the jacket.

[*She closes the door. Stella turns to Eunice.*]

STELLA. I don't know if I did the right thing.

EUNICE. What else could you do?

STELLA. I couldn't believe her story and go on living with Stanley.

EUNICE. Don't ever believe it. Life has got to go on. No matter what happens, you've got to keep on going.

[*The bathroom door opens a little.*]

BLANCHE [*looking out*]. Is the coast clear?

STELLA. Yes, Blanche. [*To Eunice*] Tell her how well she's looking.

BLANCHE. Please close the curtains before I come out.

STELLA. They're closed.

STANLEY. —How many for you?

PABLO. —Two.

STEVE. —Three.

[*Blanche appears in the amber light of the door. She has a tragic radiance in her red satin robe following the sculptural lines of her body. The "Varsouviana" rises audibly as Blanche enters the bedroom.*]

BLANCHE [*with faintly hysterical vivacity*]. I have just washed my hair.

STELLA. Did you?

BLANCHE. I'm not sure I got the soap out.

EUNICE. Such fine hair!

BLANCHE [*accepting the compliment*]. It's a problem. Didn't I get a call?

STELLA. Who from, Blanche?

BLANCHE. Shep Huntleigh . . .

STELLA. Why, not yet, honey!

BLANCHE. How strange! I—

[*At the sound of Blanche's voice Mitch's arm supporting his cards has sagged and his gaze is dissolved into space. Stanley slaps him on the shoulder.*]

STANLEY. Hey, Mitch, come to!

[*The sound of this new voice shocks Blanche. She makes a shocked gesture, forming his name with her lips. Stella nods and looks quickly away. Blanche stands quite still for some moments—the silverbacked mirror in her hand and a look of sorrowful perplexity as though all human experience shows on her face. Blanche finally speaks but with sudden hysteria.*]

BLANCHE. What's going on here?

[*She turns from Stella to Eunice and back to Stella. Her rising voice penetrates the concentration of the game. Mitch ducks his head lower but Stanley shoves back his chair as if about to rise. Steve places a restraining hand on his arm.*]

BLANCHE [*continuing*]. What's happened here? I want an explanation of what's happened here.

STELLA [*agonizingly*]. Hush! Hush!

EUNICE. Hush! Hush! Honey.

STELLA. Please, Blanche.

BLANCHE. Why are you looking at me like that? Is something wrong with me?

EUNICE. You look wonderful, Blanche. Don't she look wonderful?

STELLA. Yes.

EUNICE. I understand you are going on a trip.

STELLA. Yes, Blanche *is*. She's going on a vacation.

EUNICE. I'm green with envy.

BLANCHE. Help me, help me get dressed!

STELLA [*handing her dress*]. Is this what you—

BLANCHE. Yes, it will do! I'm anxious to get out of here—this place is a trap!

EUNICE. What a pretty blue jacket.

STELLA. It's lilac colored.

BLANCHE. You're both mistaken. It's Della Robbia blue. The blue of the robe in the old Madonna pictures. Are these grapes washed?

[*She fingers the bunch of grapes which Eunice had brought in.*]

EUNICE. Huh?

BLANCHE. Washed, I said. Are they washed?

EUNICE. They're from the French Market.

BLANCHE. That doesn't mean they've been washed. [*The cathedral bells chime*] Those cathedral bells—they're the only clean thing in the Quarter. Well, I'm going now. I'm ready to go.

EUNICE [*whispering*]. She's going to walk out before they get here.

STELLA. Wait, Blanche.

BLANCHE. I don't want to pass in front of those men.

EUNICE. Then wait'll the game breaks up.

STELLA. Sit down and . . .

[*Blanche turns weakly, hesitantly about. She lets them push her into a chair.*]

BLANCHE. I can smell the sea air. The rest of my time I'm going to spend on the sea. And when I die, I'm going to die on the sea. You know what I shall die of? [*She plucks a grape*] I shall die of eating an unwashed grape one day out on the ocean. I will die—with my hand in the hand of some nice-looking ship's doctor, a very young one with a small blond mustache and a big silver watch. "Poor lady," they'll say, "the quinine did her no good. That unwashed grape has transported her soul to heaven." [*The cathedral chimes are heard*] And I'll be buried at sea sewn up in a clean white sack and dropped overboard—at noon —in the blaze of summer—and into an ocean as blue as [*Chimes again*] my first lover's eyes!

[*A Doctor and a Matron have appeared around the corner of the building and climbed the steps to the porch. The gravity of their profession is exaggerated —the unmistakable aura of the state in-*

stitution with its cynical detachment. The Doctor rings the doorbell. The murmur of the game is interrupted.]

EUNICE [*whispering to Stella*]. That must be them.

[*Stella presses her fists to her lips.*]

BLANCHE [*rising slowly*]. What is it?
EUNICE [*affectedly casual*]. Excuse me while I see who's at the door.
STELLA. Yes.

[*Eunice goes into the kitchen.*]

BLANCHE [*tensely*]. I wonder if it's for me.

[*A whispered colloquy takes place at the door.*]

EUNICE [*returning, brightly*]. Someone is calling for Blanche.
BLANCHE. It *is* for me, then! [*She looks fearfully from one to the other and then to the portieres. The "Varsouviana" faintly plays*] Is it the gentleman I was expecting from Dallas?
EUNICE. I think it is, Blanche.
BLANCHE. I'm not quite ready.
STELLA. Ask him to wait outside.
BLANCHE. I . . .

[*Eunice goes back to the portieres. Drums sound very softly.*]

STELLA. Everything packed?
BLANCHE. My silver toilet articles are still out.
STELLA. Ah!
EUNICE [*returning*]. They're waiting in front of the house.
BLANCHE. They! Who's "they"?
EUNICE. There's a lady with him.
BLANCHE. I cannot imagine who this "lady" could be! How is she dressed?
EUNICE. Just—just a sort of a—plain-tailored outfit.
BLANCHE. Possibly she's—[*Her voice dies out nervously.*]
STELLA. Shall we go, Blanche?

BLANCHE. Must we go through that room?
STELLA. I will go with you.
BLANCHE. How do I look?
STELLA. Lovely.
EUNICE [*echoing*]. Lovely.

[*Blanche moves fearfully to the portieres. Eunice draws them open for her. Blanche goes into the kitchen.*]

BLANCHE [*to the men*]. Please don't get up. I'm only passing through.

[*She crosses quickly to outside door. Stella and Eunice follow. The poker players stand awkwardly at the table—all except Mitch, who remains seated, looking down at the table. Blanche steps out on a small porch at the side of the door. She stops short and catches her breath.*]

DOCTOR. How do you do?
BLANCHE. You are not the gentleman I was expecting. [*She suddenly gasps and starts back up the steps. She stops by Stella, who stands just outside the door, and speaks in a frightening whisper*] That man isn't Shep Huntleigh.

[*The "Varsouviana" is playing distantly.*

[*Stella stares back at Blanche. Eunice is holding Stella's arm. There is a moment of silence—no sound but that of Stanley steadily shuffling the cards.*

[*Blanche catches her breath again and slips back into the flat. She enters the flat with a peculiar smile, her eyes wide and brilliant. As soon as her sister goes past her, Stella closes her eyes and clenches her hands. Eunice throws her arms comfortingly about her. Then she starts up to her flat. Blanche stops just inside the door. Mitch keeps staring down at his hands on the table, but the other men look at her curiously. At last she starts around the table toward the bedroom. As she does, Stanley suddenly pushes back his chair and rises as if to* block her way. The Matron follows her into the flat.]

STANLEY. Did you forget something?

BLANCHE [*shrilly*]. Yes! Yes, I forgot something!

[*She rushes past him into the bedroom. Lurid reflections appear on the walls in odd, sinuous shapes. The "Varsouviana" is filtered into a weird distortion, accompanied by the cries and noises of the jungle. Blanche seizes the back of a chair as if to defend herself.*]

STANLEY [*sotto voce*]. Doc, you better go in.

DOCTOR [*sotto voce, motioning to the Matron*]. Nurse, bring her out.

[*The Matron advances on one side, Stanley on the other. Divested of all the softer properties of womanhood, the Matron is a peculiarly sinister figure in her severe dress. Her voice is bold and toneless as a firebell.*]

MATRON. Hello, Blanche.

[*The greeting is echoed and re-echoed by other mysterious voices behind the walls, as if reverberated through a canyon of rock.*]

STANLEY. She says that she forgot something.

[*The echo sounds in threatening whispers.*]

MATRON. That's all right.

STANLEY. What did you forget, Blanche?

BLANCHE. I— I—

MATRON. It don't matter. We can pick it up later.

STANLEY. Sure. We can send it along with the trunk.

BLANCHE [*retreating in panic*]. I don't know you—I don't know you. I want to be—left alone—please!

MATRON. Now, Blanche!

ECHOES [*rising and falling*]. Now, Blanche—now, Blanche—now, Blanche!

STANLEY. You left nothing here but spilt talcum and old empty perfume bottles—unless it's the paper lantern you want to take with you. You want the lantern?

[*He crosses to dressing table and seizes the paper lantern, tearing it off the light bulb, and extends it toward her. She cries out as if the lantern was herself. The Matron steps boldly toward her. She screams and tries to break past the Matron. All the men spring to their feet. Stella runs out to the porch, with Eunice following to comfort her, simultaneously with the confused voices of the men in the kitchen. Stella rushes into Eunice's embrace on the porch.*]

STELLA. Oh, my God, Eunice help me! Don't let them do that to her, don't let them hurt her! Oh, God, oh, please God, don't hurt her! What are they doing to her? What are they doing? [*She tries to break from Eunice's arms.*]

EUNICE. No, honey, no, no, honey. Stay here. Don't go back in there. Stay with me and don't look.

STELLA. What have I done to my sister? Oh, God, what have I done to my sister?

EUNICE. You done the right thing, the only thing you could do. She couldn't stay here; there wasn't no other place for her to go.

[*While Stella and Eunice are speaking on the porch the voices of the men in the kitchen overlap them. Mitch has started toward the bedroom. Stanley crosses to block him. Stanley pushes him aside. Mitch lunges and strikes at Stanley. Stanley pushes Mitch back. Mitch collapses at the table, sobbing.*]

[*During the preceding scenes, the Matron catches hold of Blanche's arm and prevents her flight. Blanche turns wildly and scratches at the Matron. The heavy woman pinions her arms. Blanche cries out hoarsely and slips to her knees.*]

MATRON. These fingernails have to be trimmed. [*The Doctor comes into the room and she looks at him.*] Jacket, Doctor?

DOCTOR. Not unless necessary.

[*He takes off his hat and now he becomes personalized. The unhuman quality goes. His voice is gentle and reassuring as he crosses to Blanche and crouches in front of her. As he speaks her name, her terror subsides a little. The lurid reflections fade from the walls, the inhuman cries and noises die out and her own hoarse crying is calmed.*]

DOCTOR. Miss DuBois.

[*She turns her face to him and stares at him with desperate pleading. He smiles; then he speaks to the Matron.*]

It won't be necessary.

BLANCHE [*faintly*]. Ask her to let go of me.

DOCTOR [*to the Matron*]. Let go.

[*The Matron releases her. Blanche extends her hands toward the Doctor. He draws her up gently and supports her with his arm and leads her through the portieres.*]

BLANCHE [*holding tight to his arm*]. Whoever you are—I have always depended on the kindness of strangers.

[*The poker players stand back as Blanche and the Doctor cross the kitchen to the front door. She allows him to lead her as if she were blind. As they go out on the porch, Stella cries out her sister's name from where she is crouched a few steps up on the stairs.*]

STELLA. Blanche! Blanche, Blanche!

[*Blanche walks on without turning, followed by the Doctor and the Matron. They go around the corner of the building.*

[*Eunice descends to Stella and places the child in her arms. It is wrapped in a pale blue blanket. Stella accepts the child, sobbingly. Eunice continues downstairs and enters the kitchen where the men, except for Stanley, are returning silently to their places about the table. Stanley has gone out on the porch and stands at the foot of the steps looking at Stella.*]

STANLEY [*a bit uncertainly*]. Stella?

[*She sobs with inhuman abandon. There is something luxurious in her complete surrender to crying now that her sister is gone.*]

STANLEY [*voluptuously, soothingly*]. Now, honey. Now, love. Now, now, love. [*He kneels beside her and his fingers find the opening of her blouse*] Now, now, love. Now, love. . . .

[*The luxurious sobbing, the sensual murmur fade away under the swelling music of the "blue piano" and the muted trumpet.*]

STEVE. This game is seven-card stud.

Curtain

◆◆ All That Fall

By SAMUEL BECKETT

Characters

MRS. ROONEY (MADDY), a lady in her seventies
CHRISTY, a carter
MR. TYLER, a retired bill-broker
MR. SLOCUM, Clerk of the Racecourse
TOMMY, a porter
MR. BARRELL, a station-master
MISS FITT, a lady in her thirties
A FEMALE VOICE
DOLLY, a small girl
MR. ROONEY (DAN), husband of Mrs. Rooney, blind
JERRY, a small boy

Rural sounds. Sheep, bird, cow, cock, severally, then together.

Silence.

Mrs. Rooney advances along country road towards railway-station. Sound of her dragging feet.

Music faint from house by way. "Death and the Maiden." The steps slow down, stop.

MRS. ROONEY. Poor woman. All alone in that ruinous old house.

Music louder. Silence but for music playing.

The steps resume. Music dies. Mrs. Rooney murmurs melody. Her murmur dies.

Samuel Beckett, "All That Fall," in *Krapp's Last Tape and Other Dramatic Pieces* (New York: Grove Press, 1960), pp. 29–91.

Sound of approaching cartwheels. The cart stops. The steps slow down, stop.

MRS. ROONEY. Is that you, Christy?
CHRISTY. It is, Ma'am.
MRS. ROONEY. I thought the hinny was familiar. How is your poor wife?
CHRISTY. No better, Ma'am.
MRS. ROONEY. Your daughter then?
CHRISTY. No worse, Ma'am.

Silence.

MRS. ROONEY. Why do you halt? (*Pause.*) But why do I halt?

Silence.

CHRISTY. Nice day for the races, Ma'am.
MRS. ROONEY. No doubt it is. (*Pause.*) But will it hold up? (*Pause. With emotion.*) Will it hold up?

Silence.

CHRISTY. I suppose you wouldn't—
MRS. ROONEY. Hist! (*Pause.*) Surely to goodness that cannot be the up mail I hear already?

Silence. The hinny neighs. Silence.

CHRISTY. Damn the mail.
MRS. ROONEY. Oh thank God for that! I could have sworn I heard it, thundering up the track in the far distance. (*Pause.*) So hinnies whinny. Well, it is not surprising.
CHRISTY. I suppose you wouldn't be in need of a small load of dung?
MRS. ROONEY. Dung? What class of dung?

CHRISTY. Stydung.

MRS. ROONEY. Stydung . . . I like your frankness, Christy. (*Pause.*) I'll ask the master. (*Pause.*) Christy.

CHRISTY. Yes, Ma'am.

MRS. ROONEY. Do you find anything . . . bizarre about my way of speaking? (*Pause.*) I do not mean the voice. (*Pause.*) No, I mean the words. (*Pause. More to herself.*) I use none but the simplest words, I hope, and yet I sometimes find my way of speaking very . . . bizarre. (*Pause.*) Mercy! What was that?

CHRISTY. Never mind her, Ma'am, she's very fresh in herself to-day.

Silence.

MRS. ROONEY. Dung? What would we want with dung, at our time of life? (*Pause.*) Why are you on your feet down on the road? Why do you not climb up on the crest of your manure and let yourself be carried along? Is it that you have no head for heights?

Silence.

CHRISTY (*to the hinny*). Yep! (*Pause. Louder.*) Yep wiyya to hell owwa that!

Silence.

MRS. ROONEY. She does not move a muscle. (*Pause.*) I too should be getting along, if I do not wish to arrive late at the station. (*Pause.*) But a moment ago she neighed and pawed the ground. And now she refuses to advance. Give her a good welt on the rump. (*Sound of welt. Pause.*) Harder! (*Sound of welt. Pause.*) Well! If someone were to do that for me I should not dally. (*Pause.*) How she gazes at me to be sure, with her great moist cleg-tormented eyes! Perhaps if I were to move on, down the road, out of her field of vision . . . (*Sound of welt.*) No, no, enough! Take her by the snaffle and pull her eyes away from me. Oh this is awful! (*She moves on. Sound of her dragging feet.*) What

have I done to deserve all this, what, what? (*Dragging feet.*) So long ago . . . No! No! (*Dragging feet. Quotes.*) "Sigh out a something something tale of things, Done long ago and ill done." (*She halts.*) How can I go on, I cannot. Oh let me just flop down flat on the road like a big fat jelly out of a bowl and never move again! A great big slop thick with grit and dust and flies, they would have to scoop me up with a shovel. (*Pause.*) Heavens, there is that up mail again, what will become of me! (*The dragging steps resume.*) Oh I am just a hysterical old hag I know, destroyed with sorrow and pining and gentility and church-going and fat and rheumatism and childlessness. (*Pause. Brokenly.*) Minnie! Little Minnie! (*Pause.*) Love, that is all I asked, a little love, daily, twice daily, fifty years of twice daily love like a Paris horse-butcher's regular, what normal woman wants affection? A peck on the jaw at morning, near the ear, and another at evening, peck, peck, till you grow whiskers on you. There is that lovely laburnum again.

Dragging feet. Sound of bicycle-bell. It is old Mr. Tyler coming up behind her on his bicycle, on his way to the station. Squeak of brakes. He slows down and rides abreast of her.

MR. TYLER. Mrs. Rooney! Pardon me if I do not doff my cap, I'd fall off. Divine day for the meeting.

MRS. ROONEY. Oh, Mr. Tyler, you startled the life out of me stealing up behind me like that like a deer-stalker! Oh!

MR. TYLER (*playfully*). I rang my bell, Mrs. Rooney, the moment I sighted you I started tinkling my bell, now don't you deny it.

MRS. ROONEY. Your bell is one thing, Mr. Tyler, and you are another. What news of your daughter?

MR. TYLER. Fair, fair. They removed everything, you know, the whole . . . er . . . bag of tricks. Now I am grandchildless.

Dragging feet.

MRS. ROONEY. Gracious how you wobble! Dismount, for mercy's sake, or ride on.

MR. TYLER. Perhaps if I were to lay my hand lightly on your shoulder, Mrs. Rooney, how would that be? (*Pause.*) Would you permit that?

MRS. ROONEY. No, Mr. Rooney, Mr. Tyler I mean, I am tired of light old hands on my shoulders and other senseless places, sick and tired of them. Heavens, here comes Connolly's van! (*She halts. Sound of motor-van. It approaches, passes with thunderous rattle, recedes.*) Are you all right, Mr. Tyler? (*Pause.*) Where is he? (*Pause.*) Ah there you are! (*The dragging steps resume.*) That was a narrow squeak.

MR. TYLER. I alit in the nick of time.

MRS. ROONEY. It is suicide to be abroad. But what is it to be at home, Mr. Tyler, what is it to be at home? A lingering dissolution. Now we are white with dust from head to foot. I beg your pardon?

MR. TYLER. Nothing, Mrs. Rooney, nothing, I was merely cursing, under my breath, God and man, under my breath, and the wet Saturday afternoon of my conception. My back tire has gone down again. I pumped it hard as iron before I set out. And now I am on the rim.

MRS. ROONEY. Oh what a shame!

MR. TYLER. Now if it were the front I should not so much mind. But the back. The back! The chain! The oil! The grease! The hub! The brakes! The gear! No! It is too much!

Dragging feet.

MRS. ROONEY. Are we very late, Mr. Tyler, I have not the courage to look at my watch.

MR. TYLER (*bitterly*). Late! I on my bicycle as I bowled along was already late. Now therefore we are doubly late, trebly, quadrupedly late. Would I had shot by you, without a word.

Dragging feet.

MRS. ROONEY. Whom are you meeting, Mr. Tyler?

MR. TYLER. Hardy. (*Pause.*) We used to climb together. (*Pause.*) I saved his life once. (*Pause.*) I have not forgotten it.

Dragging feet. They stop.

MRS. ROONEY. Let us a halt a moment and this vile dust fall back upon the viler worms.

Silence. Rural sounds.

MR. TYLER. What sky! What light! Ah in spite of all it is a blessed thing to be alive in such weather, and out of hospital.

MRS. ROONEY. Alive?

MR. TYLER. Well half alive shall we say?

MRS. ROONEY. Speak for yourself, Mr. Tyler. I am not half alive nor anything approaching it. (*Pause.*) What are we standing here for? This dust will not settle in our time. And when it does some great roaring machine will come and whirl it all skyhigh again.

MR. TYLER. Well, shall we be getting along in that case?

MRS. ROONEY. No.

MR. TYLER. Come, Mrs. Rooney—

MRS. ROONEY. Go, Mr. Tyler, go on and leave me, listening to the cooing of the ringdoves. (*Cooing.*) If you see my poor blind Dan tell him I was on my way to meet him when it all came over me again, like a flood. Say to him, Your poor wife, she told me to tell you it all came flooding over her again and . . . (*the voice breaks*) . . . she simply went back home . . . straight back home . . .

MR. TYLER. Come, Mrs. Rooney, come, the mail has not yet gone up, just take my free arm and we'll be there with time and to spare.

MRS. ROONEY (*sobbing*). What? What's all this now? (*Calmer.*) Can't you see I'm in trouble? (*With anger.*) Have you no respect for misery? (*Sobbing.*) Minnie! Little Minnie!

MR. TYLER. Come, Mrs. Rooney, come, the mail has not yet gone up, just take my free arm and we'll be there with time and to spare.

MRS. ROONEY (*brokenly*). In her forties now she'd be, I don't know, fifty, girding up her lovely little loins, getting ready for the change . . .

MR. TYLER. Come, Mrs. Rooney, come, the mail—

MRS. ROONEY (*exploding*). Will you get along with you, Mr. Rooney, Mr. Tyler I mean, will you get along with you now and cease molesting me? What kind of a country is this where a woman can't weep her heart out on the highways and byways without being tormented by retired bill-brokers! (*Mr. Tyler prepares to mount his bicycle.*) Heavens, you're not going to ride her flat! (*Mr. Tyler mounts.*) You'll tear your tube to ribbons! (*Mr. Tyler rides off. Receding sound of bumping bicycle. Silence. Cooing.*) Venus birds! Billing in the woods all the long summer long. (*Pause.*) Oh cursed corset! If I could let it out, without indecent exposure. Mr. Tyler! Mr. Tyler! Come back and unlace me behind the hedge! (*She laughs wildly, ceases.*) What's wrong with me, what's wrong with me, never tranquil, seething out of my dirty old pelt, out of my skull, oh to be in atoms, in atoms! (*Frenziedly.*) ATOMS! (*Silence. Cooing. Faintly.*) Jesus! (*Pause.*) Jesus!

Sound of car coming up behind her. It slows down and draws up beside her, engine running. It is Mr. Slocum, the Clerk of the Racecourse.

MR. SLOCUM. Is anything wrong, Mrs. Rooney? You are bent all double. Have you a pain in the stomach?

Silence. Mrs. Rooney laughs wildly.

Finally.

MRS. ROONEY. Well, if it isn't my old admirer, the Clerk of the Course, in his limousine.

MR. SLOCUM. May I offer you a lift, Mrs. Rooney? Are you going in my direction?

MRS. ROONEY. I am, Mr. Slocum, we all are. (*Pause.*) How is your poor mother?

MR. SLOCUM. Thank you, she is fairly comfortable. We manage to keep her out of pain. That is the great thing, Mrs. Rooney, is it not?

MRS. ROONEY. Yes, indeed, Mr. Slocum, that is the great thing, I don't know how you do it. (*Pause. She slaps her cheek violently.*) Ah these wasps!

MR. SLOCUM (*coolly*). May I then offer you a seat, Madam?

MRS. ROONEY (*with exaggerated enthusiasm*). Oh that would be heavenly, Mr. Slocum, just simply heavenly. (*Dubiously.*) But would I ever get in, you look very high off the ground to-day, these new balloon tires, I presume. (*Sound of door opening and Mrs. Rooney trying to get in.*) Does this roof never come off? No? (*Efforts of Mrs. Rooney.*) No . . . I'll never do it . . . you'll have to get down, Mr. Slocum, and help me from the rear. (*Pause.*) What was that? (*Pause. Aggrieved.*) This is all your suggestion, Mr. Slocum, not mine. Drive on, Sir, drive on.

MR. SLOCUM (*switching off the engine*). I'm coming, Mrs. Rooney, I'm coming, give me time, I'm as stiff as yourself.

Sound of Mr. Slocum extracting himself from driver's seat.

MRS. ROONEY. Stiff! Well I like that! And me heaving all over back and front. (*To herself.*) The dry old reprobate!

MR. SLOCUM (*in position behind her*). Now, Mrs. Rooney, how shall we do this?

MRS. ROONEY. As if I were a bale, Mr. Slocum, don't be afraid. (*Pause. Sounds of effort.*) That's the way! (*Effort.*) Lower! (*Effort.*) Wait! (*Pause.*) No, don't let go! (*Pause.*) Suppose I do get up, will I ever get down?

MR. SLOCUM (*breathing hard*). You'll get down, Mrs. Rooney, you'll get down. We may not get you up, but I warrant you we'll get you down.

He resumes his efforts. Sound of these.

MRS. ROONEY. Oh! . . Lower! . . Don't be

afraid! . . We're past the age when . . . There! . . Now! . . Get your shoulder under it . . . Oh! . . (*Giggles.*) Oh glory! . . Up! Up! . . Ah! . . I'm in! (*Panting of Mr. Slocum. He slams the door. In a scream.*) My frock! You've nipped my frock! (*Mr. Slocum opens the door. Mrs. Rooney frees her frock. Mr. Slocum slams the door. His violent unintelligible muttering as he walks round to the other door. Tearfully.*) My nice frock! Look what you've done to my nice frock! (*Mr. Slocum gets into his seat, slams driver's door, presses starter. The engine does not start. He releases starter.*) What will Dan say when he sees me?

MR. SLOCUM. Has he then recovered his sight?

MRS. ROONEY. No, I mean when he knows, what will he say when he feels the hole? (*Mr. Slocum presses starter. As before. Silence.*) What are you doing, Mr. Slocum?

MR. SLOCUM. Gazing straight before me, Mrs. Rooney, through the windscreen, into the void.

MRS. ROONEY. Start her up, I beseech you, and let us be off. This is awful!

MR. SLOCUM (*dreamily*). All morning she went like a dream and now she is dead. That is what you get for a good deed. (*Pause. Hopefully.*) Perhaps if I were to choke her. (*He does so, presses the starter. The engine roars. Roaring to make himself heard.*) She was getting too much air!

He throttles down, grinds in his first gear, moves off, changes up in a grinding of gears.

MRS. ROONEY (*in anguish*). Mind the hen! (*Scream of brakes. Squawk of hen.*) Oh mother, you have squashed her, drive on, drive on! (*The car accelerates. Pause.*) What a death! One minute picking happy at the dung, on the road, in the sun, with now and then a dust bath, and then— bang!—all her troubles over. (*Pause.*) All the laying and the hatching. (*Pause.*) Just one great squawk and then . . . peace.

(*Pause.*) They would have slit her weasand in any case. (*Pause.*) Here we are, let me down. (*The car slows down, stops, engine running. Mr. Slocum blows his horn. Pause. Louder. Pause.*) What are you up to now, Mr. Slocum? We are at a standstill, all danger is past and you blow your horn. Now if instead of blowing it now you had blown it at that unfortunate—

Horn violently. Tommy the porter appears at top of station steps.

MR. SLOCUM (*calling*). Will you come down, Tommy, and help this lady out, she's stuck. (*Tommy descends the steps.*) Open the door, Tommy, and ease her out.

Tommy opens the door.

TOMMY. Certainly, Sir. Nice day for the races, Sir. What would you fancy for—

MRS. ROONEY. Don't mind me. Don't take any notice of me. I do not exist. The fact is well known.

MR. SLOCUM. Do as you're asked, Tommy, for the love of God.

TOMMY. Yessir. Now, Mrs. Rooney.

He starts pulling her out.

MRS. ROONEY. Wait, Tommy, wait now, don't bustle me, just let me wheel round and get my feet to the ground. (*Her efforts to achieve this.*) Now.

TOMMY (*pulling her out*). Mind your feather, Ma'am. (*Sounds of effort.*) Easy now, easy.

MRS. ROONEY. Wait, for God's sake, you'll have me beheaded.

TOMMY. Crouch down, Mrs. Rooney, crouch down, and get your head in the open.

MRS. ROONEY. Crouch down! At my time of life! This is lunacy!

TOMMY. Press her down, Sir.

Sounds of combined efforts.

MRS. ROONEY. Merde!

TOMMY. Now! She's coming! Straighten up, Ma'am! There!

Mr. Slocum slams the door.

MRS. ROONEY. Am I out?

The voice of Mr. Barrell, the station-master, raised in anger.

MR. BARRELL. Tommy! Tommy! Where the hell is he?

Mr. Slocum grinds in his gear.

TOMMY. (*hurriedly*). You wouldn't have something for the Ladies Plate, Sir, I was given Flash Harry.

MR. SLOCUM (*scornfully*). Flash Harry! That carthorse!

MR. BARRELL (*at top of steps, roaring*). Tommy! Blast your bleeding bloody—(*He sees Mrs. Rooney.*) Oh, Mrs. Rooney . . . (*Mr. Slocum drives away in a grinding of gears.*) Who's that crucifying his gearbox, Tommy?

TOMMY. Old Cissy Slocum.

MRS. ROONEY. Cissy Slocum! That's a nice way to refer to your betters. Cissy Slocum! And you an orphan!

MR. BARRELL (*angrily to Tommy*). What are you doing stravaging down here on the public road? This is no place for you at all! Nip up there on the platform now and whip out the truck! Won't the twelve thirty be on top of us before we can turn round?

TOMMY (*bitterly*). And that's the thanks you get for a Christian act.

MR. BARRELL (*violently*). Get on with you now before I report you! (*Slow feet of Tommy climbing steps.*) Do you want me to come down to you with the shovel? (*The feet quicken, recede, cease.*) Ah, God forgive me, it's a hard life. (*Pause.*) Well, Mrs. Rooney, it's nice to see you up and about again. You were laid up there a long time.

MRS. ROONEY. Not long enough, Mr. Barrell. (*Pause.*) Would I were still in bed, Mr. Barrell. (*Pause.*) Would I were lying stretched out in my comfortable bed, Mr. Barrell, just wasting slowly painlessly away, keeping up my strength with arrowroot and calves-foot jelly, till in the end you wouldn't see me under the blankets any more than a board. (*Pause.*) Oh no coughing or spitting or bleeding or vomiting, just drifting gently down into the higher life, and remembering, remembering . . . (*the voice breaks*) . . . all the silly unhappiness . . . as though . . . it had never happened . . . what did I do with that handkerchief? (*Sound of handkerchief loudly applied.*) How long have you been master of this station now, Mr. Barrell?

MR. BARRELL. Don't ask me, Mrs. Rooney, don't ask me.

MRS. ROONEY. You stepped into your father's shoes, I believe, when he took them off.

MR. BARRELL. Poor Pappy! (*Reverent pause.*) He didn't live long to enjoy his ease.

MRS. ROONEY. I remember him clearly. A small ferrety purple-faced widower, deaf as a doornail, very testy and snappy. (*Pause.*) I suppose you'll be retiring soon yourself, Mr. Barrell, and growing your roses. (*Pause.*) Did I understand you to say the twelve thirty would soon be upon us?

MR. BARRELL. Those were my words.

MRS. ROONEY. But according to my watch, which is more or less right—or was—by the eight o'clock news, the time is now coming up to twelve . . . (*pause as she consults her watch*) . . . thirty-six. (*Pause.*) And yet upon the other hand the up mail has not yet gone through. (*Pause.*) Or has it sped by unbeknown to me? (*Pause.*) For there was a moment there, I remember now, I was so plunged in sorrow I wouldn't have heard a steam roller go over me. (*Pause. Mr. Barrell turns to go.*) Don't go, Mr. Barrell! (*Mr. Barrell goes. Loud.*) Mr. Barrell! (*Pause. Louder.*) Mr. Barrell!

Mr. Barrell comes back.

MR. BARRELL (*testily*). What is it, Mrs. Rooney, I have my work to do.

Silence. Sound of wind.

MRS. ROONEY. The wind is getting up. (*Pause. Wind.*) The best of the day is over. (*Pause. Wind. Dreamily.*) Soon the rain will begin to fall and go on falling, all afternoon. (*Mr. Barrell goes.*) Then at evening the clouds will part, the setting sun will shine an instant, then sink, behind the hills. (*She realizes Mr. Barrell has gone.*) Mr. Barrell! Mr. Barrell! (*Silence.*) I estrange them all. They come towards me, uninvited, bygones bygones, full of kindness, anxious to help . . . (*the voice breaks*) . . . genuinely pleased . . . to see me again . . . looking so well . . . (*Handkerchief.*) A few simple words . . . from my heart . . . and I am all alone . . . once more . . . (*Handkerchief. Vehemently.*) I should not be out at all! I should never leave the grounds! (*Pause.*) Oh there is that Fitt woman, I wonder will she bow to me. (*Sound of Miss Fitt approaching, humming a hymn. She starts climbing the steps.*) Miss Fitt! (*Miss Fitt halts, stops humming.*) Am I then invisible, Miss Fitt? Is this cretonne so becoming to me that I merge into the masonry? (*Miss Fitt descends a step.*) That is right, Miss Fitt, look closely and you will finally distinguish a once female shape.

MISS FITT. Mrs. Rooney! I saw you, but I did not know you.

MRS. ROONEY. Last Sunday we worshipped together. We knelt side by side at the same altar. We drank from the same chalice. Have I so changed since then?

MISS FITT (*shocked*). Oh but in church, Mrs. Rooney, in church I am alone with my Maker. Are not you? (*Pause.*) Why, even the sexton himself, you know, when he takes up the collection, knows it is useless to pause before me. I simply do not see the plate, or bag, whatever it is they use, how could I? (*Pause.*) Why even when all is over and I go out into the sweet fresh air, why even then for the first furlong or so I stumble in a kind of daze as you might say, oblivious to my co-religionists. And they are very kind, I must admit—the vast majority—very kind and understanding. They know me now and

take no umbrage. There she goes, they say, there goes the dark Miss Fitt, alone with her Maker, take no notice of her. And they step down off the path to avoid my running into them. (*Pause.*) Ah yes, I am distray, very distray, even on week-days. Ask Mother, if you do not believe me. Hetty, she says, when I start eating my doily instead of the thin bread and butter, Hetty, how can you be so distray? (*Sighs.*) I suppose the truth is I am not there, Mrs. Rooney, just not really there at all. I see, hear, smell, and so on, I go through the usual motions, but my heart is not in it, Mrs. Rooney, but heart is in none of it. Left to myself, with no one to check me, I would soon be flown . . . home. (*Pause.*) So if you think I cut you just now, Mrs. Rooney, you do me an injustice. All I saw was a big pale blur, just another big pale blur. (*Pause.*) Is anything amiss, Mrs. Rooney, you do not look normal somehow. So bowed and bent.

MRS. ROONEY (*ruefully*). Maddy Rooney, née Dunne, the big pale blur. (*Pause.*) You have piercing sight, Miss Fitt, if you only knew it, literally piercing.

Pause.

MISS FITT. Well . . . is there anything I can do, now that I am here?

MRS. ROONEY. If you would help me up the face of this cliff, Miss Fitt, I have little doubt your Maker would requite you, if no one else.

MISS FITT. Now now, Mrs. Rooney, don't put your teeth in me. Requite! I make these sacrifices for nothing—or not at all. (*Pause. Sound of her descending steps.*) I take it you want to lean on me, Mrs. Rooney.

MRS. ROONEY. I asked Mr. Barrell to give me his arm, just give me his arm. (*Pause.*) He turned on his heel and strode away.

MISS FITT. Is it my arm you want then? (*Pause. Impatiently.*) Is it my arm you want, Mrs. Rooney, or what is it?

MRS. ROONEY (*exploding*). Your arm! Any

arm! A helping hand! For five seconds! Christ, what a planet!

MISS FITT. Really . . . Do you know what it is, Mrs. Rooney, I do not think it is wise of you to be going about at all.

MRS. ROONEY (*violently*). Come down here, Miss Fitt, and give me your arm, before I scream down the parish!

Pause. Wind. Sound of Miss Fitt descending last steps.

MISS FITT (*resignedly*). Well, I suppose it is the Protestant thing to do.

MRS. ROONEY. Pismires do it for one another. (*Pause.*) I have seen slugs do it. (*Miss Fitt proffers her arm.*) No, the other side, my dear, if it's all the same to you, I'm left-handed on top of everything else. (*She takes Miss Fitt's right arm.*) Heavens, child, you're just a bag of bones, you need building up. (*Sound of her toiling up steps on Miss Fitt's arm.*) This is worse than the Matterhorn, were you ever up the Matterhorn, Miss Fitt, great honeymoon resort. (*Sound of toiling.*) Why don't they have a handrail? (*Panting.*) Wait till I get some air. (*Pause.*) Don't let me go! (*Miss Fitt hums her hymn. After a moment Mrs. Rooney joins in with the words.*) . . . the encircling gloo-oom (*Miss Fitt stops humming*) . . . tum tum me on. (*Forte.*) The night is dark and I am far from ho-ome, tum tum—

MISS FITT (*hysterically*). Stop it, Mrs. Rooney, stop it, or I'll drop you!

MRS. ROONEY. Wasn't it that they sung on the Lusitania? Or Rock of Ages? Most touching it must have been. Or was it the Titanic?

Attracted by the noise a group, including Mr. Tyler, Mr. Barrell and Tommy, gathers at top of steps.

MR. BARRELL. What the—

Silence.

MR. TYLER. Lovely day for the fixture.

Loud titter from Tommy cut short by Mr. Barrell with backhanded blow in the stomach. Appropriate noise from Tommy.

FEMALE VOICE (*shrill*). Oh look, Dolly, look!

DOLLY. What, Mamma?

FEMALE VOICE. They are stuck! (*Cackling laugh.*) They are stuck!

MRS. ROONEY. Now we are the laughing-stock of the twenty-six counties. Or is it thirty-six?

MR. TYLER. That is a nice way to treat your defenceless subordinates, Mr. Barrell, hitting them without warning in the pit of the stomach.

MISS FITT. Has anybody seen my mother?

MR. BARRELL. Who is that?

TOMMY. The dark Miss Fitt.

MR. BARRELL. Where is her face?

MRS. ROONEY. Now, deary, I am ready if you are. (*They toil up remaining steps.*) Stand back, you cads!

Shuffle of feet.

FEMALE VOICE. Mind yourself, Dolly!

MRS. ROONEY. Thank you, Miss Fitt, thank you, that will do, just prop me up against the wall like a roll of tarpaulin and that will be all, for the moment. (*Pause.*) I am sorry for all this ramdam, Miss Fitt, had I known you were looking for your mother I should not have importuned you, I know what it is.

MR. TYLER (*in marvelling aside*). Ramdam!

FEMALE VOICE. Come, Dolly darling, let us take up our stand before the first-class smokers. Give me your hand and hold me tight, one can be sucked under.

MR. TYLER. You have lost your mother, Miss Fitt?

MISS FITT. Good-morning, Mr. Tyler.

MR. TYLER. Good-morning, Miss Fitt.

MR. BARRELL. Good-morning, Miss Fitt.

MISS FITT. Good-morning, Mr. Barrell.

MR. TYLER. You have lost your mother, Miss Fitt?

MISS FITT. She said she would be on the last train.

MRS. ROONEY. Do not imagine, because I am silent, that I am not present, and alive, to all that is going on.

MR. TYLER (*to Miss Fitt*). When you say the last train—

MRS. ROONEY. Do not flatter yourselves for one moment, because I hold aloof, that my sufferings have ceased. No. The entire scene, the hills, the plain, the racecourse with its miles and miles of white rails and three red stands, the pretty little wayside station, even you yourselves, yes, I mean it, and over all the clouding blue, I see it all, I stand here and see it all with eyes . . . (*the voice breaks*) . . . through eyes . . . oh, if you had my eyes . . . you would understand . . . the things they have seen . . . and not looked away . . . this is nothing . . . nothing . . . what did I do with that handkerchief?

Pause.

MR. TYLER (*to Miss Fitt*). When you say the last train—(*Mrs. Rooney blows her nose violently and long*)—when you say the last train, Miss Fitt, I take it you mean the twelve thirty.

MISS FITT. What else could I mean, Mr. Tyler, what else could I *conceivably* mean?

MR. TYLER. Then you have no cause for anxiety, Miss Fitt, for the twelve thirty has not yet arrived. Look. (*Miss Fitt looks.*) No, up the line. (*Miss Fitt looks. Patiently.*) No, Miss Fitt, follow the direction of my index. (*Miss Fitt looks.*) There. You see now. The signal. At the bawdy hour of nine. (*In rueful afterthought.*) Or three alas! (*Mr. Barrell stifles a guffaw.*) Thank you, Mr. Barrell.

MISS FITT. But the time is now getting on for—

MR. TYLER (*patiently*). We all know, Miss Fitt, we all know only too well what the time is now getting on for, and yet the cruel fact remains that the twelve thirty has not yet arrived.

MISS FITT. Not an accident, I trust! (*Pause.*) Do not tell me she has left the track!

(*Pause.*) Oh darling mother! With the fresh sole for lunch!

Loud titter from Tommy, checked as before by Mr. Barrell.

MR. BARRELL. That's enough old guff out of you. Nip up to the box now and see has Mr. Case anything for me.

Tommy goes.

MRS. ROONEY (*sadly*). Poor Dan!

MISS FITT (*in anguish*). What terrible thing has happened?

MR. TYLER. Now now, Miss Fitt, do not—

MRS. ROONEY (*with vehement sadness*). Poor Dan!

MR. TYLER. Now now, Miss Fitt, do not give way . . . to despair, all will come right . . . in the end. (*Aside to Mr. Barrell.*) What is the situation, Mr. Barrell? Not a collision surely?

MRS. ROONEY (*enthusiastically*). A collision! Oh that would be wonderful!

MISS FITT (*horrified*). A collision! I knew it!

MR. TYLER. Come, Miss Fitt, let us move a little up the platform.

MRS. ROONEY. Yes, let us all do that. (*Pause.*) No? (*Pause.*) You have changed your mind? (*Pause.*) I quite agree, we are better here, in the shadow of the waiting-room.

MR. BARRELL. Excuse me a moment.

MRS. ROONEY. Before you slink away, Mr. Barrell, please, a statement of some kind, I insist. Even the slowest train on this brief line is not ten minutes and more behind its scheduled time without good cause, one imagines. (*Pause.*) We all know your station is the best kept of the entire network, but there are times when that is not enough, just not enough. (*Pause.*) Now, Mr. Barrell, leave off chewing your whiskers, we are waiting to hear from you —we the unfortunate ticket-holders' nearest if not dearest.

Pause.

MR. TYLER (*reasonably*). I do think we are

owed some kind of explanation, Mr. Barrell, if only to set our minds at rest.

MR. BARRELL. I know nothing. All I know is there has been a hitch. All traffic is retarded.

MRS. ROONEY (*derisively*). Retarded! A hitch! Ah these celibates! Here we are eating our hearts out with anxiety for our loved ones and he calls that a hitch! Those of us like myself with heart and kidney trouble may collapse at any moment and he calls that a hitch! In our ovens the Saturday roast is burning to a shrivel and he calls that—

MR. TYLER. Here comes Tommy, running! I am glad I have been spared to see this.

TOMMY (*excitedly, in the distance*). She's coming. (*Pause. Nearer.*) She's at the level-crossing!

Immediately exaggerated station sounds. Falling signals. Bells. Whistles. Crescendo of train whistle approaching. Sound of train rushing through station.

MRS. ROONEY (*above rush of train*). The up mail! The up mail! (*The up mail recedes, the down train approaches, enters the station, pulls up with great hissing of steam and clashing of couplings. Noise of passengers descending, doors banging, Mr. Barrell shouting "Boghill! Boghill!," etc. Piercingly.*) Dan! . . Are you all right? . . Where is he? . . Dan! . . Did you see my husband? . . Dan! . . (*Noise of station emptying. Guard's whistle. Train departing, receding. Silence.*) He isn't on it! The misery I have endured, to get here, and he isn't on it! . . Mr. Barrell! . . Was he not on it? (*Pause.*) Is anything the matter, you look as if you had seen a ghost. (*Pause.*) Tommy! . . Did you see the master?

TOMMY. He'll be along, Ma'am, Jerry is minding him.

Mr. Rooney suddenly appears on platform, advancing on small boy Jerry's arm. He is blind, thumps the ground with his stick and pants incessantly.

MRS. ROONEY. Oh, Dan! There you are! (*Her dragging feet as she hastens towards him. She reaches him. They halt.*) Where in the world were you?

MR. ROONEY (*coolly*). Maddy.

MRS. ROONEY. Where were you all this time?

MR. ROONEY. In the men's.

MRS. ROONEY. Kiss me!

MR. ROONEY. Kiss you? In public? On the platform? Before the boy? Have you taken leave of your senses?

MRS. ROONEY. Jerry wouldn't mind. Would you, Jerry?

JERRY. No, Ma'am.

MRS. ROONEY. How is your poor father?

JERRY. They took him away, Ma'am.

MRS. ROONEY. Then you are all alone?

JERRY. Yes, Ma'am.

MR. ROONEY. Why are you here? You did not notify me.

MRS. ROONEY. I wanted to give you a surprise. For your birthday.

MR. ROONEY. My birthday?

MRS. ROONEY. Don't you remember? I wished you your happy returns in the bathroom.

MR. ROONEY. I did not hear you.

MRS. ROONEY. But I gave you a tie! You have it on!

Pause.

MR. ROONEY. How old am I now?

MRS. ROONEY. Now never mind about that. Come.

MR. ROONEY. Why did you not cancel the boy? Now we shall have to give him a penny.

MRS. ROONEY (*miserably*). I forgot! I had such a time getting here! Such horrid nasty people! (*Pause. Pleading.*) Be nice to me, Dan, be nice to me today!

MR. ROONEY. Give the boy a penny.

MRS. ROONEY. Here are two halfpennies, Jerry. Run along now and buy yourself a nice gobstopper.

JERRY. Yes, Ma'am.

MR. ROONEY. Come for me on Monday, if I am still alive.

JERRY. Yessir.

He runs off.

MR. ROONEY. We could have saved sixpence. We have saved fivepence. (*Pause.*) But at what cost?

They move off along platform arm in arm. Dragging feet, panting, thudding stick.

MRS. ROONEY. Are you not well?

They halt, on Mr. Rooney's initiative.

MR. ROONEY. Once and for all, do not ask me to speak and move at the same time. I shall not say this in this life again.

They move off. Dragging feet, etc. They halt at top of steps.

MRS. ROONEY. Are you not—
MR. ROONEY. Let us get this precipice over.
MRS. ROONEY. Put your arm round me.
MR. ROONEY. Have you been drinking again? (*Pause.*) You are quivering like a blancmange. (*Pause.*) Are you in a condition to lead me? (*Pause.*) We shall fall into the ditch.
MRS. ROONEY. Oh, Dan! It will be like old times!
MR. ROONEY. Pull yourself together or I shall send Tommy for the cab. Then, instead of having saved sixpence, no, fivepence, we shall have lost . . . (*calculating mumble*) . . . two and three less six one and no plus one one and no plus three one and nine and one ten and three two and one . . . (*normal voice*) two and one, we shall be the poorer to the tune of two and one. (*Pause.*) Curse that sun, it has gone in. What is the day doing?

Wind.

MRS. ROONEY. Shrouding, shrouding, the best of it is past. (*Pause.*) Soon the first great drops will fall splashing in the dust.
MR. ROONEY. And yet the glass was firm. (*Pause.*) Let us hasten home and sit before the fire. We shall draw the blinds.

You will read to me. I think Effie is going to commit adultery with the Major. (*Brief drag of feet.*) Wait! (*Feet cease. Stick tapping at steps.*) I have been up and down these steps five thousand times and still I do not know how many there are. When I think there are six there are four or five or seven or eight and when I remember there are five there are three or four or six or seven and when finally I realize there are seven there are five or six or eight or nine. Sometimes I wonder if they do not change them in the night. (*Pause. Irritably.*) Well? How many do you make them to-day?
MRS. ROONEY. Do not ask me to count, Dan, not now.
MR. ROONEY. Not count! One of the few satisfactions in life?
MRS. ROONEY. Not steps, Dan, please, I always get them wrong. Then you might fall on your wound and I would have that on my manure-heap on top of everything else. No, just cling to me and all will be well.

Confused noise of their descent. Panting, stumbling, ejaculations, curses. Silence.

MR. ROONEY. Well! That is what you call well!
MRS. ROONEY. We are down. And little the worse (*Silence. A donkey brays. Silence.*) That was a true donkey. Its father and mother were donkeys.

Silence.

MR. ROONEY. Do you know what it is, I think I shall retire.
MRS. ROONEY (*appalled*). Retire! And live at home? On your grant!
MR. ROONEY. Never tread these cursed steps again. Trudge this hellish road for the last time. Sit at home on the remnants of my bottom counting the hours—till the next meal. (*Pause.*) The very thought puts life in me! Forward, before it dies!

They move on. Dragging feet, panting, thudding stick.

MRS. ROONEY. Now mind, here is the path . . . Up! . . Well done! Now we are in safety and a straight run home.

MR. ROONEY (*without halting, between gasps*). A straight . . . run! . . She calls that . . . a straight . . . run! . .

MRS. ROONEY. Hush! do not speak as you go along, you know it is not good for your coronary. (*Dragging steps, etc.*) Just concentrate on putting one foot before the next or whatever the expression is. (*Dragging feet, etc.*) That is the way, now we are doing nicely. (*Dragging feet, etc. They suddenly halt, on Mrs. Rooney's initiative.*) Heavens! I knew there was something! With all the excitement! I forgot!

MR. ROONEY (*quietly*). Good God.

MRS. ROONEY. But you must know, Dan, of course, you were on it. What ever happened? Tell me!

MR. ROONEY. I have never known anything to happen.

MRS. ROONEY. But you must—

MR. ROONEY (*violently*). All this stopping and starting again is devilish, devilish! I get a little way on me and begin to be carried along when suddenly you stop dead! Two hundred pounds of unhealthy fat! What possessed you to come out at all? Let go of me!

MRS. ROONEY (*in great agitation*). No, I must know, we won't stir from here till you tell me. Fifteen minutes late! On a thirty minute run! It's unheard of!

MR. ROONEY. I know nothing. Let go of me before I shake you off.

MRS. ROONEY. But you must know! You were on it! Was it at the terminus? Did you leave on time? Or was it on the line? (*Pause.*) Did something happen on the line? (*Pause.*) Dan! (*Brokenly.*) Why won't you tell me!

Silence. They move off. Dragging feet, etc.

They halt. Pause.

MR. ROONEY. Poor Maddy! (*Pause. Children's cries.*) What was that?

Pause for Mrs. Rooney to ascertain.

MRS. ROONEY. The Lynch twins jeering at us.

Cries.

MR. ROONEY. Will they pelt us with mud to-day, do you suppose?

Cries.

MRS. ROONEY. Let us turn and face them. (*Cries. They turn. Silence.*) Threaten them with your stick. (*Silence.*) They have run away.

Pause.

MR. ROONEY. Did you ever wish to kill a child? (*Pause.*) Nip some young doom in the bud. (*Pause.*) Many a time at night, in winter, on the black road home, I nearly attacked the boy. (*Pause.*) Poor Jerry! (*Pause.*) What restrained me then? (*Pause.*) Not fear of man. (*Pause.*) Shall we go on backwards now a little?

MRS. ROONEY. Backwards?

MR. ROONEY. Yes. Or you forwards and I backwards. The perfect pair. Like Dante's damned, with their faces arsy-versy. Our tears will water our bottoms.

MRS. ROONEY. What is the matter, Dan? Are you not well?

MR. ROONEY. Well! Did you ever know me to be well? The day you met me I should have been in bed. The day you proposed to me the doctors gave me up. You knew that, did you not? The night you married me they came for me with an ambulance. You have not forgotten that, I suppose? (*Pause.*) No, I cannot be said to be well. But I am no worse. Indeed I am better than I was. The loss of my sight was a great fillip. If I could go deaf and dumb I think I might pant on to be a hundred. Or have I done so? (*Pause.*) Was I a hundred to-day? (*Pause.*) Am I a hundred, Maddy?

Silence.

MRS. ROONEY. All is still. No living soul in sight. There is no one to ask. The world is feeding. The wind—(*brief wind*)—scarcely stirs the leaves and the birds—(*brief chirp*)—are tired singing. The cows —(*brief moo*)—and sheep—(*brief baa*)—ruminate in silence. The dogs—(*brief bark*)—are hushed and the hens—(*brief cackle*)—sprawl torpid in the dust. We are alone. There is no one to ask.

Silence.

MR. ROONEY (*clearing his throat, narrative tone*). We drew out on the tick of time, I can vouch for that. I was—

MRS. ROONEY. How can you vouch for it?

MR. ROONEY (*normal tone, angrily*). I can vouch for it, I tell you! Do you want my relation or don't you? (*Pause. Narrative tone.*) On the tick of time. I had the compartment to myself, as usual. At least I hope so, for I made no attempt to restrain myself. My mind—(*Normal tone.*) But why do we not sit down somewhere? Are we afraid we should never rise again?

MRS. ROONEY. Sit down on what?

MR. ROONEY. On a bench, for example.

MRS. ROONEY. There is no bench.

MR. ROONEY. Then on a bank, let us sink down upon a bank.

MRS. ROONEY. There is no bank.

MR. ROONEY. Then we cannot. (*Pause.*) I dream of other roads, in other lands. Of another home, another—(*he hesitates*)—another home. (*Pause.*) What was I trying to say?

MRS. ROONEY. Something about your mind.

MR. ROONEY (*startled*). My mind? Are you sure? (*Pause. Incredulous.*) My mind? . . (*Pause.*) Ah yes. (*Narrative tone.*) Alone in the compartment my mind began to work, as so often after office hours, on the way home, in the train, to the lilt of the bogeys. Your season-ticket, I said, costs you

twelve pounds a year and you earn, on an average, seven and six a day, that is to say barely enough to keep you alive and twitching with the help of food, drink, tobacco and periodicals until you finally reach home and fall into bed. Add to this—or subtract from it—rent, stationery, various subscriptions, tramfares to and fro, light and heat, permits and licences, hairtrims and shaves, tips to escorts, upkeep of premises and appearances, and a thousand unspecifiable sundries, and it is clear that by lying at home in bed, day and night, winter and summer, with a change of pyjamas once a fortnight, you would add very considerably to your income. Business, I said—(*A cry. Pause. Again. Normal tone.*) Did I hear a cry?

MRS. ROONEY. Mrs. Tully, I fancy. Her poor husband is in constant pain and beats her unmercifully.

Silence.

MR. ROONEY. That was a short knock. (*Pause.*) What was I trying to get at?

MRS. ROONEY. Business.

MR. ROONEY. Ah yes, business. (*Narrative tone.*) Business, old man, I said, retire from business, it has retired from you. (*Normal tone.*) One has these moments of lucidity.

MRS. ROONEY. I feel very cold and weak.

MR. ROONEY (*narrative tone*). On the other hand, I said, there are the horrors of home life, the dusting, sweeping, airing, scrubbing, waxing, waning, washing, mangling, drying, mowing, clipping, raking, rolling, scuffling, shovelling, grinding, tearing, pounding, banging and slamming. And the brats, the happy little hearty little howling neighbours' brats. Of all this and much more the week-end, the Saturday intermission and then the day of rest, have given you some idea. But what must it be like on a working-day? A Wednesday? A Friday! What must it be like on a Friday! And I fell to thinking of my silent, back-street, basement office, with its obliterated plate, rest-couch and velvet hangings, and what it means to be buried there alive, if only from ten to five, with convenient to the one hand a bottle of light pale ale and to the other a long ice-cold fillet of hake. Nothing, I said, not even fully certified death, can ever take the place of that. It was then I noticed we were at a standstill. (*Pause. Normal tone. Irritably.*) Why are you hanging out of me like that? Have you swooned away?

MRS. ROONEY. I feel very cold and faint. The wind — (*whistling wind*) — is whistling through my summer frock as if I had nothing on over my bloomers. I have had no solid food since my elevenses.

MR. ROONEY. You have ceased to care. I speak —and you listen to the wind.

MRS. ROONEY. No no, I am agog, tell me all, then we shall press on and never pause, never pause, till we come safe to haven.

Pause.

MR. ROONEY. Never pause . . . safe to haven . . . Do you know, Maddy, sometimes one would think you were struggling with a dead language.

MRS. ROONEY. Yes indeed, Dan, I know full well what you mean, I often have that feeling, it is unspeakably excruciating.

MR. ROONEY. I confess I have it sometimes myself, when I happen to overhear what I am saying.

MRS. ROONEY. Well, you know, it will be dead in time, just like our own poor dear Gaelic, there is that to be said.

Urgent baa.

MR. ROONEY (*startled*). Good God!

MRS. ROONEY. Oh, the pretty little woolly lamb, crying to suck its mother! Theirs has not changed, since Arcady.

Pause.

MR. ROONEY. Where was I in my composition?

MRS. ROONEY. At a standstill.

MR. ROONEY. Ah yes. (*Clears his throat. Narrative tone.*) I concluded naturally that we had entered a station and would soon be on our way again, and I sat on, without misgiving. Not a sound. Things are very dull to-day, I said, nobody getting down, nobody getting on. Then as time flew by and nothing happened I realized my error. We had not entered a station.

MRS. ROONEY. Did you not spring up and poke your head out of the window?

MR. ROONEY. What good would that have done me?

MRS. ROONEY. Why to call out to be told what was amiss.

MR. ROONEY. I did not care what was amiss. No, I just sat on, saying, If this train were never to move again I should not greatly mind. Then gradually a—how shall I say—a growing desire to—er—you know—welled up within me. Nervous probably. In fact now I am sure. You know, the feeling of being confined.

MRS. ROONEY. Yes yes, I have been through that.

MR. ROONEY. If we sit here much longer, I said, I really do not know what I shall do. I got up and paced to and fro between the seats, like a caged beast.

MRS. ROONEY. That is a help sometimes.

MR. ROONEY. After what seemed an eternity we simply moved off. And the next thing was Barrell bawling the abhorred name. I got down and Jerry led me to the men's, or Fir as they call it now, from Vir Viris I suppose, the *V* becoming *F,* in accordance with Grimm's Law. (*Pause.*) The rest you know. (*Pause.*) You say nothing? (*Pause.*) Say something, Maddy. Say you believe me.

MRS. ROONEY. I remember once attending a lecture by one of these new mind doctors, I forget what you call them. He spoke—

MR. ROONEY. A lunatic specialist?

MRS. ROONEY. No no, just the troubled mind, I was hoping he might shed a little light on my lifelong preoccupation with horses' buttocks.

MR. ROONEY. A neurologist.

MRS. ROONEY. No no, just mental distress, the

name will come back to me in the night. I remember his telling us the story of a little girl, very strange and unhappy in her ways, and how he treated her unsuccessfully over a period of years and was finally obliged to give up the case. He could find nothing wrong with her, he said. The only thing wrong with her as far as he could see was that she was dying. And she did in fact die, shortly after he washed his hands of her.

MR. ROONEY. Well? What is there so wonderful about that?

MRS. ROONEY. No, it was just something he said, and the way he said it, that have haunted me ever since.

MR. ROONEY. You lie awake at night, tossing to and fro and brooding on it.

MRS. ROONEY. On it and other . . . wretchedness. (*Pause.*) When he had done with the little girl he stood there motionless for some time, quite two minutes I should say, looking down at his table. Then he suddenly raised his head and exclaimed, as if he had had a revelation, The trouble with her was she had never been really born! (*Pause.*) He spoke throughout without notes. (*Pause.*) I left before the end.

MR. ROONEY. Nothing about your buttocks? (*Mrs. Rooney weeps. In affectionate remonstrance.*) Maddy!

MRS. ROONEY. There is nothing to be done for those people!

MR. ROONEY. For which is there? (*Pause.*) That does not sound right somehow. (*Pause.*) What way am I facing?

MRS. ROONEY. What?

MR. ROONEY. I have forgotten what way I am facing.

MRS. ROONEY. You have turned aside and are bowed down over the ditch.

MR. ROONEY. There is a dead dog down there.

MRS. ROONEY. No no, just the rotting leaves.

MR. ROONEY. In June? Rotting leaves in June?

MRS. ROONEY. Yes dear, from last year, and from the year before last, and from the year before that again. (*Silence. Rainy wind. They move on. Dragging steps, etc.*) There is that lovely laburnum again. Poor thing, it is losing all its tassels. (*Drag-

ging steps, etc.*) There are the first drops. (*Rain. Dragging feet, etc.*) Golden drizzle. (*Dragging steps, etc.*) Do not mind me, dear, I am just talking to myself. (*Rain heavier. Dragging steps, etc.*) Can hinnies procreate, I wonder.

They halt, on Mr. Rooney's initiative.

MR. ROONEY. Say that again.

MRS. ROONEY. Come on, dear, don't mind me, we are getting drenched.

MR. ROONEY (*forcibly*). Can what what?

MRS. ROONEY. Hinnies procreate. (*Silence.*) You know, hinnies, or is it jinnies, aren't they barren, or sterile, or whatever it is? (*Pause.*) It wasn't an ass's colt at all, you know, I asked the Regius Professor.

Pause.

MR. ROONEY. He should know.

MRS. ROONEY. Yes, it was a hinny, he rode into Jerusalem or wherever it was on a hinny. (*Pause.*) That must mean something. (*Pause.*) It's like the sparrows, than many of which we are of more value, they weren't sparrows at all.

MR. ROONEY. Than many of which . . . You exaggerate, Maddy.

MRS. ROONEY (*with emotion*). They weren't sparrows at all!

MR. ROONEY. Does that put our price up?

Silence. They move on. Wind and rain. Dragging feet, etc. They halt.

MRS. ROONEY. Do you want some dung? (*Silence. They move on. Wind and rain, etc. They halt.*) Why do you stop? Do you want to say something?

MR. ROONEY. No.

MRS. ROONEY. Then why do you stop?

MR. ROONEY. It is easier.

MRS. ROONEY. Are you very wet?

MR. ROONEY. To the buff.

MRS. ROONEY. The buff?

MR. ROONEY. The buff. From buffalo.

MRS. ROONEY. We shall hang up all our things in the hot-cupboard and get into our dressing-gowns. (*Pause.*) Put your arm round me. (*Pause.*) Be nice to me! (*Pause. Gratefully.*) Ah Dan! (*They move on. Wind and rain. Dragging feet, etc. Faintly same music as before. They halt. Music clearer. Silence but for music playing. Music dies.*) All day the same old record. All alone in that great empty house. She must be a very old woman now.

MR. ROONEY (*indistinctly*). Death and the Maiden.

Silence.

MRS. ROONEY. You are crying. (*Pause.*) Are you crying?

MR. ROONEY (*violently*). Yes! (*They move on. Wind and rain. Dragging feet, etc. They halt. They move on. Wind and rain. Dragging feet, etc. They halt.*) Who is the preacher to-morrow? The incumbent?

MRS. ROONEY. No.

MR. ROONEY. Thank God for that. Who?

MRS. ROONEY. Hardy.

MR. ROONEY. "How to be Happy though Married"?

MRS. ROONEY. No no, he died, you remember. No connexion.

MR. ROONEY. Has he announced the text?

MRS. ROONEY. "The Lord upholdeth all that fall and raiseth up all those that be bowed down." (*Silence. They join in wild laughter. They move on. Wind and rain. Dragging feet, etc.*) Hold me tighter, Dan! (*Pause.*) Oh yes!

They halt.

MR. ROONEY. I hear something behind us.

Pause.

MRS. ROONEY. It looks like Jerry. (*Pause.*) It is Jerry.

Sound of Jerry's running steps approaching. He halts beside them, panting.

JERRY (*panting*). You dropped—

MRS. ROONEY. Take your time, my little man, you will burst a bloodvessel.

JERRY (*panting*). You dropped something, Sir, Mr. Barrell told me to run after you.

MRS. ROONEY. Show. (*She takes the object.*) What is it? (*She examines it.*) What is this thing, Dan?

MR. ROONEY. Perhaps it is not mine at all.

JERRY. Mr. Barrell said it was, Sir.

MRS. ROONEY. It looks like a kind of ball. And yet it is not a ball.

MR. ROONEY. Give it to me.

MRS. ROONEY (*giving it*). What *is* it, Dan?

MR. ROONEY. It is a thing I carry about with me.

MRS. ROONEY. Yes, but what—

MR. ROONEY (*violently*). It is a thing I carry about with me!

Silence. Mrs. Rooney looks for a penny.

MRS. ROONEY. I have no small money. Have you?

MR. ROONEY. I have none of any kind.

MRS. ROONEY. We are out of change, Jerry. Remind Mr. Rooney on Monday and he will give you a penny for your pains.

JERRY. Yes, Ma'am.

MR. ROONEY. If I am alive.

JERRY. Yessir.

Jerry starts running back towards the station.

MRS. ROONEY. Jerry! (*Jerry halts.*) Did you hear what the hitch was? (*Pause.*) Did you hear what kept the train so late?

MR. ROONEY. How would he have heard? Come on.

MRS. ROONEY. What was it, Jerry?

JERRY. It was a—

MR. ROONEY. Leave the boy alone, he knows nothing! Come on!

MRS. ROONEY. What was it, Jerry?

JERRY. It was a little child, Ma'am.

Mr. Rooney groans.

MRS. ROONEY. What do you mean, it was a little child?

JERRY. It was a little child fell out of the carriage. On to the line, Ma'am. (*Pause.*) Under the wheels, Ma'am.

    Silence. Jerry runs off. His steps die away. *Tempest of wind and rain. It abates. They move on. Dragging steps, etc. They halt. Tempest of wind and rain.*

◆ Ibsen's Notes to *Ghosts*

By MICHAEL MEYER

. . . Ibsen's original draft for *Ghosts* has not been preserved, and the differences between his second draft and the final version as we know it are few and insignificant. After Ibsen's death, however, six brief sets of notes presumably relating to *Ghosts* were discovered among his papers, some (nos. 1–4) on two sheets of quarto, some (no. 5) on the back of an envelope, and some (no. 6) on a torn newspaper wrapper. They are undated, but probably belong to the winter and spring of 1881:

1. The play to be a realistic picture of life. Faith undetermined—but people daren't admit it. The "Orphanage"—for the sake of others. They want to be happy—but this, too, is only an illusion—Everything is ghosts—

An important point: She has been a believer and a romantic—and this can't completely be eradicated by the attitude she has subsequently adopted—"Everything is ghosts."

To marry for the wrong reasons, even though they be religious or moral, brings a Nemesis on the children.

She, the illegitimate child, can be saved by being married to—the son—but then—?

2. He in his youth was depraved, a debauchee; then she appeared, a woman who had "seen the light"; she saved him; she was rich. He had wanted to marry a girl who was thought unworthy. His wife bore him a son; then he turned back to the girl; a daughter—

3. These modern women, misused as daughters, as sisters, as wives, not educated according to their talents, barred from their vocation, robbed of their inheritance, their minds embittered—these are the women who are to provide the mothers for the new generation. What will be the consequence?

4. She became passionately religious in her youth; partly because of this, but partly also from affection, she married him, the "bright genius," the "prodigal." They move away from town; he "gets on," eventually becomes a judge, a model public servant, a model man in every way, religious too. They had a son, then another who died young. Very early in his life the eldest was put to lodge with a clergyman, then sent to a boarding school, was seldom allowed to visit his home. The judge performed his duties for many years, much honoured and respected; she too was honoured as his "good genius," who had been worthily rewarded for her magnanimity. Then he died; a large part of the fortune into which he unexpectedly came after his marriage has been formed into a trust, and now this memorial is about to be dedicated.

Here the play begins.

5. The main theme must be: the fine flowering of our spiritual life *via* literature, art, etc.— and, in contrast, all mankind wandering blindly on the wrong track.

6. The perfect man is no longer a natural product, he is something cultivated like corn and fruit-trees and the Creole race and thoroughbred horses and breeds of dogs, vines, etc.—

The trouble is that mankind as a whole is a failure. If a human being demands to live and develop according to his nature as a human being, it's regarded as megalomania. All humanity, especially Christians, suffers from megalomania.

We raise monuments to the *dead*; because we feel a duty towards them; we allow lepers to marry; but their offspring—? The unborn—?

Michael Meyer, "Ibsen's Notes to *Ghosts*," in *Ghosts and Three Other Plays*, trans. by Michael Meyer (Garden City, N.Y.: Doubleday, 1966), pp. 119–120.

◆ Three Letters

By ANTON CHEKHOV

TO A. S. SOUVORIN, MOSCOW:
OCTOBER 27, 1888

In conversation with my literary colleagues I always insist that it is not the artist's business to solve problems that require a specialist's knowledge. It is a bad thing if a writer tackles a subject he does not understand. We have specialists for dealing with special questions: it is their business to judge of the commune, of the future, of capitalism, of the evils of drunkenness, of boots, of the diseases of women. An artist must judge only of what he understands, his field is just as limited as that of any other specialist—I repeat this and insist on it always. That in his sphere there are no questions, but only answers, can be maintained only by those who have never written and have had no experience of thinking in images. An artist observes, selects, guesses, combines—and this in itself presupposes a problem: unless he had set himself a problem from the very first there would be nothing to conjecture and nothing to select. To put it briefly, I will end by using the language of psychiatry: if one denies that creative work involves problems and purposes, one must admit that an artist creates without premeditation or intention, in a state of aberration; therefore, if an author boasted to me of having written a novel without a preconceived design, under a sudden inspiration, I should call him mad.

You are right in demanding that an artist should take an intelligent attitude to his work, but you confuse two things: *solving a problem and stating a problem correctly*. It is only the second that is obligatory for the artist. In *Anna Karenina* and *Evgeni Onegin* not a single problem is solved, but they satisfy you completely because all the problems in these works are correctly stated. It is the business of the judge to put the right questions, but the answers must be given by the jury according to their own lights.

Anton Chekhov, "Three Letters," in *Letters of Anton Tchehov to his Family and Friends*, trans.

TO KONSTANTIN STANISLAVSKI, YALTA:
OCTOBER 30, 1903

Thank you very much for the letter and for the telegram. Letters are always very precious to me because, one, I am here all alone, and two, I sent the play off three weeks ago and your letter came only yesterday; if it were not for my wife, I would have been entirely in the dark and would have imagined any old thing that might have crept into my head. When I worked on the part of Lopahin, I thought it might be for you. If for some reason it doesn't appeal to you, take Gayev. Lopahin, of course, is only a merchant, but he is a decent person in every sense, should conduct himself with complete decorum, like a cultivated man, without pettiness or trickery, and it did seem to me that you will be brilliant in this part, which is central for the play. (If you do decide to play Gayev, let Vishnevski play Lopahin. He won't make an artistic Lopahin but still he won't be a petty one. Lujski would be a cold-blooded foreigner in this part and Leonidov would play it like a little kulak. You mustn't lose sight of the fact that Varya, an earnest, devout young girl is in love with Lopahin; she wouldn't love a little kulak.)

I want so much to go to Moscow but I don't know how I can get away from here. It is turning cold and I hardly ever leave the house; I am not used to fresh air and am coughing. I do not fear Moscow, or the trip itself, but I am afraid of having to stay in Sevastopol from two to eight, and in the most tedious company.

Write me what role you are taking for yourself. My wife wrote that Moskvin wants to play Epihodov. Why not, it would be a very good idea, and the play would gain from it.

My deepest compliments and regards to Maria Petrovna, and may I wish her and you all the best. Keep well and gay.

You know, I haven't yet seen *The Lower*

by Constance Garnett (New York: Macmillan, 1920), pp. 99–100, 407–408.

Depths or *Julius Caesar.* I would so much like to see them.

TO VLADIMIR NEMIROVICH-DANCHENKO,
YALTA: NOVEMBER 2, 1903

Two letters from you in one day, thanks a lot! I don't drink beer, the last time I drank any was in July; and I cannot eat honey, as it gives me a stomach ache. Now as to the play.

1. Anya can be played by any actress you'd like, even an utter unknown, if only she is young and looks like a young girl, and talks in a young, resonant voice. This role is not one of the important ones.

2. Varya's part is more on the serious side, if only Maria Petrovna would take it. If she doesn't the part will turn out rather flat and coarse, and I would have to do it over and soften it. M.P. won't repeat herself because, firstly, she is a gifted actress, and secondly, because Varya does not resemble Sonya or Natasha; she is a figure in a black dress, a little nun-like creature, somewhat simple-minded, plaintive and so forth and so on.

3. Gayev and Lopahin—have Stanislavski try these parts and make his choice. If he takes Lopahin and feels at home in the part, the play is bound to be a success. Certainly if Lopahin is a pallid figure, played by a pallid actor, both the part and the play will fail.

4. Pishchik—the part for Gribunin. God have mercy on you if you assign the part to Vishnevski.

5. Charlotta—a big part. It would of course be impossible to give the part to Pomyalova; Muratova might be good, perhaps, but not funny. This is the part for Mme. Knipper.

6. Epihodov—if Moskvin wants the part let him have it. He'll be a superb Epihodov. . . .

7. Firs—the role for Artem.

8. Dunyasha—for Khalutina.

9. Yasha. If it is the Alexandrov you wrote about, the one that is assistant to your producer, let him have it. Moskvin would make a splendid Yasha. And I haven't anything against Leonidov for the part.

10. The passer-by—Gromov.

11. The stationmaster who reads "The Sinner" in Act III should have a bass voice.

Charlotta speaks with a good accent, not broken Russian, except that once in a while she gives a soft sound to a consonant at the end of a word rather than the hard sound that is proper, and she mixes masculine and feminine adjectives. Pishchik is an old Russian fellow broken down with gout, old age and satiety, plump, dressed in a long Russian coat (à la Simov) and boots without heels. Lopahin wears a white vest and tan shoes, flails his arms when he is in motion, takes long strides, is lost in thought when he moves about and walks in a straight line. He doesn't cut his hair short and so he frequently tosses his head back; in reflection he strokes his beard back and forth, i.e., from his neck to his lips. I think Trofimov is clearly sketched. Varya wears a black dress and wide belt.

I have been intending to write *The Cherry Orchard* these past three years and for three years have been telling you to hire an actress who could play a part like Lyubov Andreyevna. This long waiting game never pays.

I have got into the stupidest position: I am here alone and don't know why. But you are unjust in saying that despite your work it is "Stanislavski's theatre." You are the one that people speak about and write about while they do nothing but criticize Stanislavski for his performance of Brutus. If you leave the theatre, so will I. Gorki is younger than we and has his own life to lead. As to the Nizhni-Novgorod theatre, this is only an episode in his life; Gorki will try it, sniff at it and cast it aside. I may say in this connection that people's theatres and people's literature are plain foolishness, something to sweeten up the people. Gogol shouldn't be pulled down to the people, but the people raised to Gogol's level.

I would like so much to visit the Hermitage Restaurant, eat some sturgeon and drink a bottle of wine. Once I drank a bottle of champagne solo and didn't get drunk, then I had some cognac and didn't get drunk either.

I'll write you again and in the meantime send my humble greetings and thanks. Was it Lujski's father that died? I read about it in the paper today.

Why does Maria Petrovna insist on playing Anya? And why does Maria Fyodorovna think she is too aristocratic to play Varya? Isn't she playing in *The Lower Depths,* after all? Well, the devil take them. I embrace you, keep well.

Translated by Constance Garnett

◆ Beckett by the Madeleine

By TOM F. DRIVER

Nothing like Godot, he arrived before the hour. His letter had suggested we meet at my hotel at noon on Sunday, and I came into the lobby as the clock struck twelve. He was waiting.

My wish to meet Samuel Beckett had been prompted by simple curiosity and interest in his work. American newspaper reviewers like to call his plays nihilistic. They find deep pessimism in them. Even so astute a commentator as Harold Clurman of *The Nation* has said that "Waiting for Godot" is "the concentrate . . . of the contemporary European . . . mood of despair." But to me Beckett's writing had seemed permeated with love for human beings and with a kind of humor that I could reconcile neither with despair nor with nihilism. Could it be that my own eyes and ears had deceived me? Is his a literature of defeat, irrelevant to the social crises we face? Or is it relevant because it teaches us something useful to know about ourselves?

I knew that a conversation with the author would not settle such questions, because a man is not the same as his writing: in the last analysis, the questions had to be settled by the work itself. Nevertheless I was curious.

My curiosity was sharpened a day or two before the interview by a conversation I had with a well-informed teacher of literature, a Jesuit father, at a conference on religious drama near Paris. When Beckett's name came into the discussion, the priest grew loud and told me that Beckett "hates life." That, I thought, is at least one thing I can find out when we meet.

Beckett's appearance is rough-hewn Irish. The features of his face are distinct, but not fine. They look as if they had been sculptured with an unsharpened chisel. Unruly hair goes straight up from his forehead, standing so high that the top falls gently over, as if to

Tom F. Driver, "Beckett by the Madeleine," *Columbia University Forum,* IV (Summer, 1961, pp. 21–25.

show that it really is hair and not bristle. One might say it combines the man's own pride and humility. For he has the pride that comes of self-acceptance and the humility, perhaps of the same genesis, not to impose himself upon another. His light blue eyes, set deep within the face, are actively and continually looking. He seems, by some unconscious division of labor, to have given them that one function and no other, leaving communication to the rest of the face. The mouth frequently breaks into a disarming smile. The voice is light in timbre, with a rough edge that corresponds to his visage. The Irish accent is, as one would expect, combined with slight inflections from the French. His tweed suit was a baggy gray and green. He wore a brown knit sports shirt with no tie.

We walked down the Rue de L'Arcade, thence along beside the Madeleine and across to a sidewalk cafe opposite that church. The conversation that ensued may have been engrossing but it could hardly be called world-shattering. For one thing, the world that Beckett sees is already shattered. His talk turns to what he calls "the mess," or sometimes "this buzzing confusion." I reconstruct his sentences from notes made immediately after our conversation. What appears here is shorter than what he actually said but very close to his own words.

"The confusion is not my invention. We cannot listen to a conversation for five minutes without being acutely aware of the confusion. It is all around us and our only chance now is to let it in. The only chance of renovation is to open our eyes and see the mess. It is not a mess you can make sense of."

I suggested that one must let it in because it is the truth, but Beckett did not take to the word truth.

"What is more true than anything else? To swim is true, and to sink is true. One is not more true than the other. One cannot speak anymore of being, one must speak only of the mess. When Heidegger and Sartre speak of a contrast between being and existence, they may be right, I don't know, but their language is too philosophical for me. I am not a philosopher. One can only speak of what is in front of him, and that now is simply the mess."

Then he began to speak about the tension in art between the mess and form. Until recently, art has withstood the pressure of chaotic things. It has held them at bay. It realized that to admit them was to jeopardize form. "How could the mess be admitted, because it appears to be the very opposite of form and therefore destructive of the very thing that art holds itself to be?" But now we can keep it out no longer, because we have come into a time when "it invades our experience at every moment. It is there and it must be allowed in."

I granted this might be so, but found the result to be even more attention to form than was the case previously. And why not? How, I asked, could chaos be admitted to chaos? Would not that be the end of thinking and the end of art? If we look at recent art we find it preoccupied with form. Beckett's own work is an example. Plays more highly formalized than "Waiting for Godot," "Endgame," and "Krapp's Last Tape" would be hard to find.

"What I am saying does not mean that there will henceforth be no form in art. It only means that there will be new form, and that this form will be of such a type that it admits the chaos and does not try to say that the chaos is really something else. The form and the chaos remain separate. The latter is not reduced to the former. That is why the form itself becomes a preoccupation, because it exists as a problem separate from the material it accommodates. To find a form that accommodates the mess, that is the task of the artist now."

Yet, I responded, could not similar things be said about the art of the past? Is it not characteristic of the greatest art that it confronts us with something we cannot clarify, demanding that the viewer respond to it in his own never-predictable way? What is the history of criticism but the history of men attempting to make sense of the manifold elements in art that will not allow themselves to be reduced to a single philosophy or a single aesthetic theory? Isn't all art ambiguous?

"Not this," he said, and gestured toward the Madeleine. The classical lines of the church, which Napoleon thought of as a Temple of Glory, dominated all the scene where we sat. The Boulevard de la Madeleine, the Boulevard Malesherbes, and the Rue Royale ran to it with graceful flattery, bearing tidings of the Age of Reason. "Not this. This is clear. This does not allow the mystery to invade us. With classical art, all is settled. But it is different at Chartres. There is the unexplainable, and there art raises questions that it does not attempt to answer."

I asked about the battle between life and death in his plays. Didi and Gogo hover on the edge of suicide; Hamm's world is death and Clov may or may not get out of it to join the living child outside. Is this life-death question a part of the chaos?

"Yes. If life and death did not both present themselves to us, there would be no inscrutability. If there were only darkness, all would be clear. It is because there is not only darkness but also light that our situation becomes inexplicable. Take Augustine's doctrine of grace given and grace withheld: have you pondered the dramatic qualities in this theology? Two thieves are crucified with Christ, one saved and the other damned. How can we make sense of this division? In classical drama, such problems do not arise. The destiny of Racine's Phèdre is sealed from the beginning: she will proceed into the dark. As she goes, she herself will be illuminated. At the beginning of the play she has partial illumination and at the end she has complete illumination, but there has been no question but that she moves toward the dark. That is the play. Within this notion clarity is possible, but for us who are neither Greek nor Jansenist there is not such clarity. The question would also be removed if we believed in the contrary—total salvation. But where we have both dark and light we have also the inexplicable. The key word in my plays is 'perhaps.'"

Given a theological lead, I asked what he thinks about those who find a religious significance to his plays.

"Well, really there is none at all. I have no religious feeling. Once I had a religious emotion. It was at my first Communion. No more. My mother was deeply religious. So was my brother. He knelt down at his bed as long as he could kneel. My father had none. The family was Protestant, but for me it was only irksome and I let it go. My brother and mother got no value from their religion when they died. At the moment of crisis it had no more depth than an old-school tie. Irish Catholicism is not attractive, but it is deeper. When you pass a church on an Irish bus, all the hands flurry in the sign of the cross. One day the dogs of Ireland will do that too and perhaps also the pigs."

But do the plays deal with the same facets of experience religion must also deal with?

"Yes, for they deal with distress. Some people object to this in my writing. At a party an English intellectual—so-called—asked me why I write always about distress. As if it were perverse to do so! He wanted to know if my father had beaten me or my mother had run away from home to give me an unhappy childhood. I told him no, that I had had a very happy childhood. Then he thought me more perverse than ever. I left the party as soon as possible and got into a taxi. On the glass partition between me and the driver were three signs: one asked for help for the blind, another, help for orphans, and the third for relief for the war refugees. One does not have to look for distress. It is screaming at you even in the taxis of London."

Lunch was over, and we walked back to the hotel with the light and dark of Paris screaming at us.

The personal quality of Samuel Beckett is similar to qualities I had found in the plays. He says nothing that compresses experience within a closed pattern. "Perhaps" stands in place of commitment. At the same time, he is plainly sympathetic, clearly friendly. If there were only the mess, all would be clear; but there is also compassion.

As a Christian, I know I do not stand where Beckett stands, but I do see much of what he sees. As a writer on the theater, I have paid close attention to the plays. Harold Clurman is right to say that "Waiting for Godot" is a reflection (he calls it a distorted reflection) "of the impasse and disarray of Europe's present politics, ethic, and common way of life." Yet it is not only Europe the play refers to. "Waiting for Godot" sells even better in America than in France. The consciousness it mirrors may have come earlier to Europe than to America, but it is the consciousness

that most "mature" societies arrive at when their successes in technological and economic systematization propel them into a time of examining the not-strictly-practical ends of culture. America is now joining Europe in this "mature" phase of development. Whether any of us remain in it long will depend on what happens as a result of the technological and economic revolutions now going on in the countries of Asia and Africa, and also of course on how long the cold war remains cold. At present no political party in Western Europe or America seems possessed of a philosophy of social change adequate to the pressures of current history.

In the Beckett plays, time does not go forward. We are always at the end, where events repeat themselves ("Waiting for Godot"), or hover at the edge of nothingness ("Endgame"), or turn back to the long-ago moment of genuine life ("Krapp's Last Tape"). This retreat from action may disappoint those of us who believe that the events of the objective world must still be dealt with. Yet it would be wrong to conclude that Beckett's work is "pessimistic." To say "perhaps," as the plays do, is not to say "no." The plays do not say that there is no future but that we do not see it, have no confidence about it, and approach it hopelessly. Apart from messianic Marxism, where is there today a faith asserting the contrary that succeeds in shaping a culture?

The walls that surround the characters of Beckett's plays are not walls that nature and history have built irrespective of the decisions of men. They are the walls of one's own attitude toward his situation. The plays are themselves evidence of a human capacity to see one's situation and by that very fact to transcend it. That is why Beckett can say that letting in "the mess" may bring with it a "chance of renovation." It is also why he is wrong, from philosophy's point of view, to say that there is *only* "the mess." If that were all there is, he could not recognize it as such. But the plays and the novels contain more, and that more is transcendence of the self and the situation.

In "Waiting for Godot" Beckett has a very simple and moving description of human self-transcendence. Vladimir and Estragon (Didi and Gogo) are discussing man, who bears his "little cross" until he dies and is forgotten. In a beautiful passage that is really a duet composed of short lines from first one pair of lips and then the other, the two tramps speak of their inability to keep silent. As Gogo says, "It's so we won't hear . . . all the dead voices." The voices of the dead make a noise like wings, sand, or leaves, all speaking at once, each one to itself, whispering, rustling, and murmuring.

VLADIMIR. What do they say?
ESTRAGON. They talk about their lives.
VLADIMIR. To have lived is not enough for them.
ESTRAGON. They have to talk about it.
VLADIMIR. To be dead is not enough for them.
ESTRAGON. It is not sufficient.

    (*Silence*)

VLADIMIR. They make a noise like feathers.
ESTRAGON. Like leaves.
VLADIMIR. Like ashes.
ESTRAGON. Like leaves.

In this passage, Didi and Gogo are like the dead, and the dead are like the living, because all are incapable of keeping silent. The description of the dead voices is also a description of living voices. In either case, neither to live nor to die is "enough." One must talk about it. The human condition is self-reflection, self-transcendence. Beckett's plays are the whispering, rustling, and murmuring of man refusing merely to exist.

Is it not true that self-transcendence implies freedom, and that freedom is either the most glorious or the most terrifying of facts, depending on the vigor of the spirit that contemplates it? It is important to notice that the rebukes to Beckett's "despair" have mostly come from the dogmatists of humanist liberalism, who here reveal, as so often they do, that they desire the reassurance of certainty more than they love freedom. Having recognized that to live is not enough, they wish to fasten down in dogma the way that life ought to be lived. Beckett suggests something more free— that life is to be seen, to be talked about, and that the way it is to be lived cannot be stated unambiguously but must come as a response to that which one encounters in "the mess." He has devised his works in such a way that those who comment upon them actually comment upon themselves. One cannot say, "Beckett has said so and so," for Beckett has said, "Perhaps." If the critics and the public see only images of despair, one can only deduce that they are themselves despairing.

Beckett himself, or so I take it, has repented of the desire for certainty. There are therefore released in him qualities of affirmation that his interpreters often miss. That is why the laughter in his plays is warm, his concern for his characters affectionate. His warm humor and affection are not the attributes of defeatism but the consequences of what Paul Tillich has called "the courage to be."

◆◆◆ Part Six

GENERAL DISCUSSION

◆ *from* The Poetics

By ARISTOTLE
Translated and edited by G. M. A. Grube

. . . Tragedy, then, is the imitation of a good action, which is complete and of a certain length, by means of language made pleasing for each part separately; it relies in its various elements not on narrative but on acting; through pity and fear it achieves the purgation (catharsis) of such emotions.

By "language made pleasing" I mean language which has rhythm, melody, and music. By "separately for the parts" I mean that some parts use only meter while others also have music. And as it is through acting that the poets present their imitation, one first and necessary element of a tragedy is the arranging of the spectacle. Then come music and diction, for these are the means used in the imitation. By diction I mean the actual composition of the verses, while the effect of music is clear to all.

THE SIX ELEMENTS OR ASPECTS OF TRAGEDY

Since it is an action which is imitated, it is performed by persons who must have qualities of character and mind, and from them we transfer these predicates to the actions also. Character and thought are the two natural causes of action; through actions men succeed or fail. The imitation of the action is the plot, for this is what I mean by plot, namely, the arrangement of the incidents. Character, on the other hand, is that which leads us to attribute certain qualities to the persons who act. Thought is present in all they say to prove a point or to express an opinion. Every tragedy, therefore, has these six necessary elements which make it what it is: plot, character, diction, thought, spectacle, and music. Two of these elements are the means of imitation, one is the manner, three belong to the objects imitated, and besides these there are no others. We may say that most poets use these elements; every tragedy, in much the

Aristotle, "The Poetics," in *Poetry and Style,* trans. and ed. by G. M. A. Grube (Indianapolis: Bobbs-Merrill, 1958), pp. 12–26, 29–33.

same manner, has spectacle, character, plot, diction, music, and thought.

PLOT AND CHARACTER

The most important of these is the arrangement of incidents, for tragedy is an imitation, not of men but of action and life, of happiness and misfortune. These are to be found in action, and the goal of life is a certain kind of activity, not a quality. Men are what they are because of their characters, but it is in action that they find happiness or the reverse. The purpose of action on the stage is not to imitate character, but character is a by-product of the action. It follows that the incidents and the plot are the end which tragedy has in view, and the end is in all things the most important. Without action there could be no tragedy, whereas a tragedy without characterization is possible.

The tragedies of most of our recent poets have no characterization and, generally speaking, there are many such poets. This is the difference, among painters, between Zeuxis and Polygnotus, for Polygnotus expresses character very well, while Zeuxis does not express it at all. Moreover, a series of speeches expressing character, well written and well thought-out though they might be, would not fulfill the essential function of a tragedy; this would be better achieved by a play which had a plot and structure of incidents, even though deficient in respect to character. Besides, the most important means by which a tragedy stirs the emotions reside in the plot, namely, Reversals and Recognitions. Another argument is that those who begin to write poetry attain mastery in diction and characterization before they attain it in plot structure. Nearly all our early poets are examples of this.

The plot is the first essential and the soul of a tragedy; character comes second. Pretty much the same is true of painting: the most beautiful colors, laid on at random, give less pleasure than a black-and-white drawing. It is the action which is the object of the imitation; the individual characters are subsidiary to it.

THOUGHT AND CHARACTER

Thought is the third element in tragedy. It is the capacity to express what is involved in, or suitable to, a situation. In prose this is the function of statesmanship and rhetoric. Earlier writers made their characters speak like statesmen; our contemporaries make them speak like rhetoricians. A person's character makes clear what course of action he will choose or reject where this is not clear. Speeches, therefore, which do not make this choice clear, or in which the speaker does not choose or reject any course of action at all, do not express character. Thought comes in where something is proved or disproved, or where some general opinion is expressed.

DICTION, MUSIC, SPECTACLE

Diction is the fourth of the elements we mentioned. By diction I mean, as I said before, the use of words to express one's meaning. Its function is the same in verse and prose. Of the remaining elements, music is most important among the features of tragedy which give pleasure. As for the spectacle, it stirs the emotions, but it is less a matter of art than the others, and has least to do with poetry, for a tragedy can achieve its effect even apart from the performance and the actors. Indeed, spectacular effects belong to the craft of the property man rather than to that of the poet.

VII

PLOT: BEGINNING, MIDDLE, AND END

Having now defined these elements, our next point is what the plot structure should be, as this is the first and most important part of a tragedy. We have established that a tragedy is the imitation of an action which is whole and complete, and also of a certain length, for a thing can be whole without being of any particular size. "Whole" means having a beginning, a middle, and an end.

The beginning, while not necessarily following something else, is, by definition, followed by something else. The end, on the contrary, follows something else by definition, either always or in most cases, but nothing else comes after it. The middle both itself follows something else and is followed by something else. To construct a good plot, one must neither begin nor end haphazardly but make a proper use of these three parts.

SIZE OR LENGTH

However, an animal, or indeed anything which has parts, must, to be beautiful, not only have these parts in the right order but must also be of a definite size. Beauty is a matter of size and order. An extraordinarily small animal would not be beautiful, nor an extraordinarily large one. Our view of the first is confused because it occupies only an all but imperceptible time, while we cannot view the second all at once, so that the unity of the whole would escape us if, for example, it were a thousand miles long. It follows that, as bodies and animals must have a size that can easily be perceived as a whole, so plots must have a length which can easily be remembered. However, the limit set to length by the circumstances of the dramatic presentation or by the perceptive capacity of the audience is not a matter of dramatic art. If a hundred tragedies were competing at once, the poets would compete with their eye on the water clock, and this they say happened at one time. What is a matter of art is the limit set by the very nature of the action, namely, that the longer is always the more beautiful, provided that the unity of the whole is clearly perceived. A simple and sufficient definition is: such length as will allow a sequence of events to result in a change from bad to good fortune or from good fortune to bad in accordance with what is probable or inevitable.

VIII

UNITY OF PLOT

A story does not achieve unity, as some people think, merely by being about one person. Many things, indeed an infinite number of things, happen to the same individual, some of which have no unity at all. In the same way one individual performs many actions which do not combine into one action. It seems, then, that all those poets who wrote a *Heracleid*, a *Theseid*, and the like, were in error, for they believed that, because Heracles is one person, a story about him cannot avoid having unity. Now Homer, outstanding as he is in other respects also, seems to have perceived this clearly, whether as a conscious artist or by instinct. He did not include in the *Odyssey* all that happened to Odysseus—for example, his being wounded on Parnassus or his feigning madness when the troops were being levied—because no thread of probability or necessity linked those events. He built his plot around the one action which we call the *Odyssey*; and the same is true of the *Iliad*. As in other kinds of imitative art each imitation must have one object, so with the plot: since it is the imitation of an action, this must be one action and the whole of it; the various incidents must be so constructed that, if any part is displaced or deleted, the whole plot is disturbed and dislocated. For if any part can be inserted or omitted without manifest alteration, it is no true part of the whole.

IX

TRAGEDY AND HISTORY

It also follows from what has been said that it is not the poet's business to relate actual events, but such things as might or could happen in accordance with probability or necessity. A poet differs from a historian, not because one writes verse and the other prose (the work of Herodotus could be put into verse, but it would still remain a history, whether in verse or prose), but because the historian relates what happened, the poet what might happen. That is why poetry is more akin to philosophy and is a better thing than history; poetry deals with general truths, history with specific events. The latter are, for example, what Alcibiades did or suffered, while general truths are the kind of thing which a certain type of person would probably or inevitably do or say. Poetry aims to do this by its choice of names; this is clearly seen in comedy, for when the writers of comedy have constructed their plots in accordance with probability, they give their characters typical names, nor are they, like the writers of iambic lampoons, concerned with a particular individual.

NAMES OF CHARACTERS: TRADITIONAL LEGENDS

The tragedians cling to the names of historical persons. The reason is that what is possible is convincing, and we are apt to distrust what has not yet happened as not possible, whereas what has happened is obviously possible, else it could not have happened. However, there are tragedies which use only one or two of the well-known names, the others being fictitious; indeed a few tragedies have no well-known names at all, the *Antheus* of Agathon for example. Both the names and the events of that play are fictitious, yet it is enjoyable nonetheless. It is not, therefore, absolutely necessary to cling to the traditional stories which are the usual subjects of tragedy. In fact, it is absurd to strive to do so, for even the familiar stories are familiar only to a few, yet are enjoyed by all. All this shows that it is the plot, rather than the verse, which makes a (tragic) poet, for he is a poet in virtue of his imitation, and he imitates actions. He is no less a poet if he happens to tell a true story, for nothing prevents some actual events from being probable or possible, and it is this probability or possibility that makes the (tragic) poet.

TYPES OF PLOTS

The episodic are the worst of all plots and actions; and by an episodic plot I mean one in which the episodes have no probable or inevitable connection. Poor poets compose such plots through lack of talent, good poets do it to please the actors. As they write in competition and stretch the plot too far, they are thereby compelled to distort the sequence of events.

The object of the imitation is not only a complete action but such things as stir up pity and fear, and this is best achieved when the events are unexpectedly interconnected.

This, more than what happens accidentally and by chance, will arouse wonder. Even chance events arouse most wonder when they have the appearance of purpose, as in the story of the man who was responsible for the death of Mitys and was watching a festival at Argos when the statue of his victim fell upon him and killed him. Things like that do not seem to happen without purpose, and plots of this kind are necessarily better.

X

SIMPLE AND COMPLEX PLOTS

Some plots are simple, others are complex, just as the actions which they imitate are clearly one or the other. I call simple an action which is one and continuous, as defined above, and in the course of which the change of fortune occurs without recognition or reversal. A complex action is one wherein the change of fortune is accompanied either by recognition or reversal, or by both. These must emerge from the plot structure itself so that they are connected with what has gone before as the inevitable or probable outcome. It makes all the difference whether one incident is caused by another or merely follows it.

XI

REVERSALS AND RECOGNITIONS

Reversal (*peripeteia*) is a change of the situation into its opposite, and this too must accord with the probable or the inevitable.[1] So in the *Oedipus* the man comes to cheer Oedipus and to rid him of his fear concerning his mother; then, by showing him who he is, he does the opposite; also in the *Lynceus* the hero is brought in to die and Danaus follows, intending to kill him, but in the event it is Danaus who dies and the other who is saved.

Recognition (*anagnorisis*), as the name implies, is a change from ignorance to knowledge of a bond of love or hate between persons who are destined for good fortune or the reverse. The finest kind of recognition is accompanied by simultaneous reversals, as in the *Oedipus*. There are, to be sure, other forms of recognition: the knowledge acquired may be of inanimate objects, indeed of anything; one may recognize that someone has, or has not, done something. But the recognition which is most fully part of the plot and of the action is the kind we noted first. This kind of recognition and reversal will evoke pity or fear. Tragedy is the imitation of such actions, and good or ill fortune results from them.

This recognition is between persons. Sometimes the identity of one person is known, and then only one person is recognized by the other; at other times both have to be recognized, as when Iphigenia is recognized by Orestes as soon as she sends the letter, but another recognition scene is necessary for her to recognize Orestes.

These things, reversal and recognition, are two parts of the plot. A third is suffering. We have discussed two of the three, namely reversal and recognition. Suffering (*pathos*) is a fatal or painful action like death on the stage, violent physical pain, wounds, and everything of that kind.

XII

THE SECTIONS OF A TRAGEDY

We have previously mentioned the parts of tragedy in the sense of its qualitative parts. The quantitative sections, on the other hand, into which a tragedy is divided are the following: *prologos, epeisodion, exodos,* and the

---

[1] Peripety or reversal should not be confused with the change of fortune which Aristotle calls μετάβασις. The metabasis refers to this change only, from bad fortune to good or, and this Aristotle considered better, from good fortune to bad (see ch. 14), and it involves no more than this change. Reversal, on the other hand, means that a situation that seems to or is intended to develop in one direction suddenly develops in the reverse direction. In *Oedipus King*, a messenger brings news that the king of Corinth is dead. Hearing that Oedipus had left Corinth because an oracle which foretold he would kill his father and marry his mother, the messenger seeks to rid him of this fear by showing that he is not the son of the Corinthian king. But instead of relief, this disclosure leads to the revelation that Laius (whom he killed) was his father and, ultimately, that Iocasta is his mother and that the oracle is fulfilled. The *Lynceus* is attributed to Theodectes, but is unknown to us.

choral part, itself subdivided into *parodos* and *stasima*. These occur in all tragedies; there may also be actors' songs and *kommoi*.

The *prologos* is that whole section which precedes the entrance of the chorus; the *epeisodion* is a whole section between complete choral odes; the *exodos* is that whole section of a tragedy which is not followed by a choral ode. In the choral part, the entrance song (*parodos*) is the first complete statement of the chorus, a *stasimon* is a song of the chorus without anapaests or trochees; a *kommos* is a dirge in which actors and chorus join.

We spoke previously of the parts which must be considered as qualitative elements of tragedy; these are the quantitative parts.

XIII

POSSIBLE CHANGES OF FORTUNE

We must discuss next what a writer should aim at and what he should avoid in constructing his plot, how tragedy will come to fulfill its proper function. As already stated, the plot of the finest tragedies must not be simple but complex, it must also represent what is fearful or pitiful, as this is characteristic of tragic imitation. It clearly follows that, in the first place, good men must not be seen suffering a change from prosperity to misfortune; this is not fearful or pitiful but shocking. Nor must the wicked pass from misfortune to prosperity; this, of all things, is the least tragic; nothing happens as it should, it is neither humane nor fearful nor pitiful. A thoroughly wicked man must not pass from prosperity to misfortune either; such a plot may satisfy or feeling of humanity, but it does not arouse pity or fear. We feel pity for a man who does not deserve his misfortune; we fear for someone like ourselves; neither feeling is here involved.

THE TRAGIC CHARACTER

We are left with a character in between the other two; a man who is neither outstanding in virtue and righteousness, nor is it through wickedness and vice that he falls into misfortune, but through some flaw. He should also be famous or prosperous, like Oedipus, Thyestes, and the noted men of such noble families.

THE BEST PLOTS

A good plot must consist of a single and not, as some people say, of a double story; the change of fortune should not be from misfortune to prosperity but, on the contrary, from prosperity to misfortune. This change should not be caused by outright wickedness but by a serious flaw in a character such as we have just described, or one better rather than worse. This is proved by what has happened: at first tragic poets related any kind of story, but now the best tragedies are constructed around the fortunes of a few families, and are concerned with Alcmaeon, Oedipus, Orestes, Meleager, Thyestes, Telephus, and any other such men who have endured or done terrible things. The best products of the tragic art have this kind of plot structure.

People are therefore mistaken when they criticize Euripides on this very point, because his tragedies are of this kind and many of them end unhappily, for this, as I said, is right. There is convincing proof of this: in the theater and in dramatic contests such dramas are seen to be the most tragic if they are well performed, and even though Euripides manages his plays badly in other respects, he obviously is the most tragic of the poets.

THE DOUBLE PLOT OF COMEDY

The double plot, such as we find in the *Odyssey*, where, at the end, the good are rewarded and the bad punished, is thought by some to be the best, but in fact it holds only second place. It is the weakness of our audiences that places it first, and the poets seek to please the spectators. The pleasure provided in this way, however, belongs to comedy rather than to tragedy; it is in comedy that those who, in the story, are the greatest enemies, like Orestes and Aegisthus, are reconciled in the end, walk off the stage as friends, and no one kills anybody.

XV

FOUR AIMS IN CHARACTERIZATION

In expressing character there are four things to aim at. Of these the first and foremost is that the characters should be good. Words and action express character, as we stated, if they bring out a moral choice, and the character is good if the choice is right. This applies to every type: even a woman or a slave can be good, though the former of these is a weaker being and the slave is altogether inferior. In the second place, characters must be appropriate or true to type: there is a manly character, but it is not appropriate for a woman to be manly or a clever speaker. The third aim is to be true to life, and this is different from being good or true to type. The fourth is consistency. Even if the character represented displays inconsistency as a character trait, he must be consistent in his inconsistency.

Menelaus in the *Orestes* provides an example of a character which is unnecessarily evil; the lament of Odysseus in the *Scylla* and the speech of Melanippe are unsuitable and inappropriate; Iphigenia in *Iphigenia at Aulis* shows inconsistency: her supplication is quite unlike the character she displays later.

In characterization as in plot structure, one must always aim at either what is probable or what is inevitable, so that a certain character will say or do certain things in a way that is probable or inevitable, and one incident will follow the other in the same way.

THE SUPERNATURAL

The solution of the plot should also emerge from the story itself; it should not require the use of the supernatural, as it does in the *Medea* and in the threatened departure of the Greeks in the *Iliad*. The supernatural should be used only in connection with events that lie outside the play itself, things that have happened long ago beyond the knowledge of men, or future events which need to be foretold and revealed, for we attribute to the gods the power of seeing all things. In the incidents of the play there should be nothing inexplicable or, if there is, it should be outside the actual play, as in the *Oedipus* of Sophocles.

CHARACTERIZATION

Since tragedy is the imitation of characters better than those we know in life, we should imitate good portrait painters. They too render the characteristic appearance of their subject in a good likeness which is yet more beautiful than the original. So when the poet is imitating men who are given to anger, indolence, and other faults of character, he should represent them as they are, and yet make them worthy. As such an example of violent temper we have the Achilles of Agathon and Homer.

CARE FOR DETAILS OF PRESENTATION

These things the poet must keep in mind. Besides these, he must also pay attention to the visual and other impressions which, apart from its essential effects, a poetic presentation inevitably makes upon the audience, for frequent errors are possible here also. These are adequately dealt with in my published works.

XVI

KINDS OF RECOGNITION

What recognition is has already been stated. As to its different kinds, the first, least artistic but most frequently used through lack of talent, is recognition by tokens or signs. Some of these signs are congenital, like the spear-shaped birthmark of the Sons of Earth, or the stars which Carcinus used in his *Thyestes;* others are acquired, whether marks on the body like wounds, external possessions like necklaces, or the skiff which was the means of recognition in the *Tyro.* There is a better and a worse way of using these signs; both his old nurse and the swineherds recognize Odysseus by his scar, but the manner of their recognition is quite different. Recognitions deliberately brought about to prove one's identity are less artistic, as are all recognitions of this kind; but those that emerge from the circumstances of the reversal are better, as in the bath scene with Odysseus' old nurse.

The second kind of recognition is that contrived by the poet; it is inartistic for this very reason, as Orestes in the *Iphigenia* brings about the recognition that he is Orestes. The recognition of Iphigenia follows from the letter, but Orestes says himself what the poet, not the plot, requires him to say. This is why it comes very close to the fault mentioned above in the case of Odysseus and the swineherds, for Orestes too could have had some tokens with him. The cry of the shuttle in the *Tyreus* of Sophocles also belongs here.

The third kind of recognition is through memory: we see one thing and recall another, as a character in the *Cyprians* of Dicaeogenes saw the picture and wept, or the recognition scene in the lay of Antinous, where Odysseus listens to the bard and weeps at his memories, and this leads to the recognition.

Recognition of the fourth kind is by inference, as in the *Choephori*: someone like me has come, there is no one like me except Orestes, therefore Orestes has come. The same

applies to Iphigenia in the work of the sophist Polyidus, for it was likely for Orestes to reflect that his sister was sacrificed and that the same thing was now happening to him, or for Tydeus in the play of Theodectes to say that he had come to find his son and was being killed himself. Similarly, in the *Phineidae,* the women, on seeing the place, reflected on their fate: that they were fated to die in this place from which they had been cast out.

There is a further kind of composite recognition based upon a wrong inference by one of the two parties involved, as in *Odysseus the False Messenger,* where one said he would know the bow he had never seen, and the other understood him to say he would recognize it, and thus made a false inference.

Of all these, the best recognition is that which emerges from the events themselves, where the amazement and the surprise are caused by probable means, as in the *Oedipus* of Sophocles and the *Iphigenia*, for it was probable that Iphigenia should wish to send a letter. This is the only kind of recognition which dispenses with contrived tokens and necklaces. The second best is recognition based on a correct inference.

◆ Theatre for Pleasure or Theatre for Instruction

By BERTOLT BRECHT

A few years back, anybody talking about the modern theatre meant the theatre in Moscow, New York and Berlin. He might have thrown in a mention of one of Jouvet's productions in Paris or Cochran's in London, or *The Dybbuk* as given by the Habima (which is to all intents and purposes part of the Russian theatre, since Vakhtangov was its director). But broadly speaking there were only three capitals so far as modern theatre was concerned.

Russian, American and German theatres differed widely from one another, but were alike in being modern, that is to say in introducing technical and artistic innovations. In a sense they even achieved a certain stylistic resemblance, probably because technology is international (not just that part which is directly applied to the stage but also that which influences it, the film for instance), and because large progressive cities in large industrial countries are involved. Among the older capitalist countries it is the Berlin theatre that seemed of late to be in the lead. For a period all that is common to the modern theatre received its strongest and (so far) maturest expression there.

The Berlin theatre's last phase was the so-

Bertolt Brecht, "Theatre for Pleasure or Theatre for Instruction," in *Brecht on Theatre*, trans. by John Willett (New York: Hill and Wang, 1964), pp. 69–76.

called epic theatre, and it showed the modern theatre's trend of development in its purest form. Whatever was labelled 'Zeitstück' or 'Piscatorbühne' or 'Lehrstück' belongs to the epic theatre.

THE EPIC THEATRE

Many people imagine that the term 'epic theatre' is self-contradictory, as the epic and dramatic ways of narrating a story are held, following Aristotle, to be basically distinct. The difference between the two forms was never thought simply to lie in the fact that the one is performed by living beings while the other operates via the written word; epic works such as those of Homer and the medieval singers were at the same time theatrical performances, while dramas like Goethe's *Faust* and Byron's *Manfred* are agreed to have been more effective as books. Thus even by Aristotle's definition the difference between the dramatic and epic forms was attributed to their different methods of construction, whose laws were dealt with by two different branches of aesthetics. The method of construction depended on the different way of presenting the work to the public, sometimes via the stage, sometimes through a book; and independently of that there was the 'dramatic element' in epic works and the 'epic element' in dramatic. The bourgeois novel in the last century developed much that was 'dramatic,' by which was meant the strong centralization of the story, a momentum that drew the separate parts into a common relationship. A particular passion of utterance, a certain emphasis on the clash of forces are hallmarks of the 'dramatic.' The epic writer Döblin provided an excellent criterion when he said that with an epic work, as opposed to a dramatic, one can as it were take a pair of scissors and cut it into individual pieces, which remain fully capable of life.

This is no place to explain how the opposition of epic and dramatic lost its rigidity after having long been held to be irreconcilable. Let us just point out that the technical advances alone were enough to permit the stage to incorporate an element of narrative in its dramatic productions. The possibility of projections, the greater adaptability of the stage due to mechanization, the film, all completed the theatre's equipment, and did so at a point where the most important transactions between people could no longer be shown simply by personifying the motive forces or subjecting the characters to invisible metaphysical powers.

To make these transactions intelligible the environment in which the people lived had to be brought to bear in a big and 'significant' way.

This environment had of course been shown in the existing drama, but only as seen from the central figure's point of view, and not as an independent element. It was defined by the hero's reactions to it. It was seen as a storm can be seen when one sees the ships on a sheet of water unfolding their sails, and the sails filling out. In the epic theatre it was to appear standing on its own.

The stage began to tell a story. The narrator was no longer missing, along with the fourth wall. Not only did the background adopt an attitude to the events on the stage—by big screens recalling other simultaneous events elsewhere, by projecting documents which confirmed or contradicted what the characters said, by concrete and intelligible figures to accompany abstract conversations, by figures and sentences to support mimed transactions whose sense was unclear—but the actors too refrained from going over wholly into their role, remaining detached from the character they were playing and clearly inviting criticism of him.

The spectator was no longer in any way allowed to submit to an experience uncritically (and without practical consequences) by means of simple empathy with the characters in a play. The production took the subject-matter and the incidents shown and put them through a process of alienation: the alienation that is necessary to all understanding. When something seems 'the most obvious thing in the world' it means that any attempt to understand the world has been given up.

What is 'natural' must have the force of what is startling. This is the only way to expose the laws of cause and effect. People's activity must simultaneously be so and be capable of being different.

It was all a great change.

The dramatic theatre's spectator says: Yes, I have felt like that too—Just like me—It's only natural—It'll never change—The sufferings of this man appal me, because they are inescapable—That's great art; it all seems the most obvious thing in the world—I weep when they weep, I laugh when they laugh.

The epic theatre's spectator says: I'd never have thought it—That's not the way—That's extraordinary, hardly believable—It's got to stop—The sufferings of this man appal me, because they are unnecessary—That's great art: nothing obvious in it—I laugh when they weep, I weep when they laugh.

THE INSTRUCTIVE THEATRE

The stage began to be instructive.

Oil, inflation, war, social struggles, the family, religion, wheat, the meat market, all became subjects for theatrical representation. Choruses enlightened the spectator about facts unknown to him. Films showed a montage of events from all over the world. Projections added statistical material. And as the 'background' came to the front of the stage so people's activity was subjected to criticism. Right and wrong courses of action were shown. People were shown who knew what they were doing, and others who did not. The theatre became an affair for philosophers, but only for such philosophers as wished not just to explain the world but also to change it. So we had philosophy, and we had instruction. And where was the amusement in all that? Were they sending us back to school, teaching us to read and write? Were we supposed to pass exams, work for diplomas?

Generally there is felt to be a very sharp distinction between learning and amusing oneself. The first may be useful, but only the second is pleasant. So we have to defend the epic theatre against the suspicion that it is a highly disagreeable, humourless, indeed strenuous affair.

Well: all that can be said is that the contrast between learning and amusing oneself is not laid down by divine rule; it is not one that has always been and must continue to be.

Undoubtedly there is much that is tedious about the kind of learning familiar to us from school, from our professional training, etc. But it must be remembered under what conditions and to what end that takes place.

It is really a commercial transaction. Knowledge is just a commodity. It is acquired in order to be resold. All those who have grown out of going to school have to do their learning virtually in secret, for anyone who admits that he still has something to learn devalues himself as a man whose knowledge is inadequate. Moreover the usefulness of learning is very much limited by factors outside the learner's control. There is unemployment, for instance, against which no knowledge can protect one. There is the division of labour, which makes generalized knowledge unnecessary and impossible. Learning is often among the concerns of those whom no amount of concern will get any forwarder. There is not much knowledge that leads to power, but plenty of knowledge to which only power can lead.

Learning has a very different function for different social strata. There are strata who cannot imagine any improvement in conditions: they find the conditions good enough for them. Whatever happens to oil they will benefit from it. And: they feel the years beginning to tell. There can't be all that many years more. What is the point of learning a lot now? They have said their final word: a grunt. But there are also strata 'waiting their turn' who are discontented with conditions, have a vast interest in the practical side of learning, want at all costs to find out where they stand, and know that they are lost without learning; these are the best and keenest learners. Similar differences apply to countries and peoples. Thus the pleasure of learning depends on all sorts of things; but none the less there is such a thing as pleasurable learning, cheerful and militant learning.

If there were not such amusement to be had from learning the theatre's whole structure would unfit it for teaching.

Theatre remains theatre even when it is instructive theatre, and in so far as it is good theatre it will amuse.

THEATRE AND KNOWLEDGE

But what has knowledge got to do with art? We know that knowledge can be amusing, but not everything that is amusing belongs in the theatre.

I have often been told, when pointing out

the invaluable services that modern knowledge and science, if properly applied, can perform for art and specially for the theatre, that art and knowledge are two estimable but wholly distinct fields of human activity. This is a fearful truism, of course, and it is as well to agree quickly that, like most truisms, it is perfectly true. Art and science work in quite different ways: agreed. But, bad as it may sound, I have to admit that I cannot get along as an artist without the use of one or two sciences. This may well arouse serious doubts as to my artistic capacities. People are used to seeing poets as unique and slightly unnatural beings who reveal with a truly godlike assurance things that other people can only recognize after much sweat and toil. It is naturally distasteful to have to admit that one does not belong to this select band. All the same, it must be admitted. It must at the same time be made clear that the scientific occupations just confessed to are not pardonable side interests, pursued on days off after a good week's work. We all know how Goethe was interested in natural history, Schiller in history: as a kind of hobby, it is charitable to assume. I have no wish promptly to accuse these two of having needed these sciences for their poetic activity; I am not trying to shelter behind them; but I must say that I do need the sciences. I have to admit, however, that I look askance at all sorts of people who I know do not operate on the level of scientific understanding: that is to say, who sing as the birds sing, or as people imagine the birds to sing. I don't mean by that that I would reject a charming poem about the taste of fried fish or the delights of a boating party just because the writer had not studied gastronomy or navigation. But in my view the great and complicated things that go on in the world cannot be adequately recognized by people who do not use every possible aid to understanding.

Let us suppose that great passions or great events have to be shown which influence the fate of nations. The lust for power is nowadays held to be such a passion. Given that a poet 'feels' this lust and wants to have someone strive for power, how is he to show the exceedingly complicated machinery within which the struggle for power nowadays takes place? If his hero is a politician, how do politics work? If he is a business man, how does business work? And yet there are writers who find business and politics nothing like so passionately interesting as the individual's lust for power. How are they to acquire the necessary knowledge? They are scarcely likely to learn enough by going round and keeping their eyes open, though even then it is more than they would get by just rolling their eyes in an exalted frenzy. The foundation of a paper like the *Völkischer Beobachter* or a business like Standard Oil is a pretty complicated affair, and such things cannot be conveyed just like that. One important field for the playwright is psychology. It is taken for granted that a poet, if not an ordinary man, must be able without further instruction to discover the motives that lead a man to commit murder; he must be able to give a picture of a murderer's mental state 'from within himself.' It is taken for granted that one only has to look inside oneself in such a case; and then there's always one's imagination. . . . There are various reasons why I can no longer surrender to this agreeable hope of getting a result quite so simply. I can no longer find in myself all those motives which the press or scientific reports show to have been observed in people. Like the average judge when pronouncing sentence, I cannot without further ado conjure up an adequate picture of a murderer's mental state. Modern psychology, from psychoanalysis to behaviourism, acquaints me with facts that lead me to judge the case quite differently, especially if I bear in mind the findings of sociology and do not overlook economics and history. You will say: but that's getting complicated. I have to answer that it *is* complicated. Even if you let yourself be convinced, and agree with me that a large slice of literature is exceedingly primitive, you may still ask with profound concern: won't an evening in such a theatre be a most alarming affair? The answer to that is: no.

Whatever knowledge is embodied in a piece of poetic writing has to be wholly transmuted into poetry. Its utilization fulfils the very pleasure that the poetic element provokes. If it does not at the same time fulfil that which is fulfilled by the scientific element, none the less in an age of great discoveries and inventions one must have a certain inclination to penetrate deeper into things—a desire to make the world controllable—if one is to be sure of enjoying its poetry.

IS THE EPIC THEATRE SOME KIND OF 'MORAL INSTITUTION'?

According to Friedrich Schiller the theatre is supposed to be a moral institution. In making this demand it hardly occurred to Schiller that by moralizing from the stage he might drive the audience out of the theatre. Audiences had no objection to moralizing in his day. It was only later that Friedrich Nietzsche attacked him for blowing a moral trumpet. To Nietzsche any concern with morality was a depressing affair; to Schiller it seemed thoroughly enjoyable. He knew of nothing that could give greater amusement and satisfaction than the propagation of ideas. The bourgeoisie was setting about forming the ideas of the nation.

Putting one's house in order, patting oneself on the back, submitting one's account, is something highly agreeable. But describing the collapse of one's house, having pains in the back, paying one's account, is indeed a depressing affair, and that was how Friedrich Nietzsche saw things a century later. He was poorly disposed towards morality, and thus towards the previous Friedrich too.

The epic theatre was likewise often objected to as moralizing too much. Yet in the epic theatre moral arguments only took second place. Its aim was less to moralize than to observe. That is to say it observed, and then the thick end of the wedge followed: the story's moral. Of course we cannot pretend that we started our observations out of a pure passion for observing and without any more practical motive, only to be completely staggered by their results. Undoubtedly there were some painful discrepancies in our environment, circumstances that were barely tolerable, and this not merely on account of moral considerations. It is not only moral considerations that make hunger, cold and oppression hard to bear. Similarly the object of our inquiries was not just to arouse moral objections to such circumstances (even though they could easily be felt—though not by all the audience alike; such objections were seldom for instance felt by those who profited by the circumstances in question) but to discover means for their elimination. We were not in fact speaking in the name of morality but in that of the victims. These truly are two distinct matters, for the victims are often told that they ought to be contented with their lot, for moral reasons. Moralists of this sort see man as existing for morality, not morality for man. At least it should be possible to gather from the above to what degree and in what sense the epic theatre is a moral institution.

CAN EPIC THEATRE BE PLAYED ANYWHERE?

Stylistically speaking, there is nothing all that new about the epic theatre. Its expository character and its emphasis on virtuosity bring it close to the old Asiatic theatre. Didactic tendencies are to be found in the medieval mystery plays and the classical Spanish theatre, and also in the theatre of the Jesuits.

These theatrical forms corresponded to particular trends of their time, and vanished with them. Similarly the modern epic theatre is linked with certain trends. It cannot by any means be practised universally. Most of the great nations today are not disposed to use the theatre for ventilating their problems. London, Paris, Tokyo and Rome maintain their theatres for quite different purposes. Up to now favourable circumstances for an epic and didactic theatre have only been found in a few places and for a short period of time. In Berlin Fascism put a very definite stop to the development of such a theatre.

It demands not only a certain technological level but a powerful movement in society which is interested to see vital questions freely aired with a view to their solution, and can defend this interest against every contrary trend.

The epic theatre is the broadest and most far-reaching attempt at large-scale modern theatre, and it has all those immense difficulties to overcome that always confront the vital forces in the sphere of politics, philosophy, science and art.

['Vergnügungstheater oder Lehrtheater?,' from *Schriften zum Theater*, 1957]

◆ Catharsis and the Modern Theater

By JOHN GASSNER

It is difficult to think of a more academic concept than that of catharsis. It is encrusted with antiquity and bears the rust of much speculation justly suspect to the practical worker. The concept is, nevertheless, one of those insights that philosophers sometimes achieve in spite of themselves. Aristotle touched bottom when he declared the effect of tragedy to be purgation of the soul by pity and fear.

The Aristotelian formula, supremely empirical, has a dual importance: the spectator is given a definition of his experience, and the playwright is provided with a goal for which certain means are requisite, the goal set for him being no other than the effect he must achieve if he is to hold an audience with high and serious matter of a painful nature. Unfortunately, however, Aristotle's analysis was altogether too fragmentary, and his *Poetics* has come down to us as little more than a collection of notes. We do not even know precisely what catharsis meant for him and how he thought "pity and fear" produced the purgation.

The subject has exercised commentators since the Renaissance when they seized upon the short passage: "Tragedy through pity and fear effects a purgation of such emotions." Each age has added its own interpretation, naturally reflecting its own interests and its own kind of drama. According to the Sixteenth Century pundits, including the famous Castelvetro, tragedy hardened the spectator to suffering by subjecting him to pity- and fear-inducing scenes of misery and violence. Corneille, who gave much thought to his craft, held that tragedy forced the spectator to fear for himself when he observed a character's passions causing disaster and that the resolve to rule one's own passions effected the purgation. Others, including John Milton, took the homeopathic view

that pity and terror on the stage counteracted the disturbing elements of pity and terror in the spectator. For the liberals or humanitarians of the Enlightenment, including the author of *Nathan the Wise,* tragedy purified the observer by enabling him to exercise his sympathies. For Hegel tragedy reconciled conflicting views, thereby effecting catharsis. And so it went until Jacob Bernays, Wilhelm Stekel, and other psychologists arrived at the view that accords most easily with both the findings of psychopathology and common sense—namely, that catharsis is simply the expulsion of disturbing drives and conflicts.

Without adhering to any specific school of psychopathology, it is safe to say that if Aristotelian catharsis is a valid definition of tragic effect (and I believe it is), it means one thing above all: In the tragic experience we temporarily expel troublesome inner complications. We expel "pity" and "fear," to use Aristotle's terms, and the terms are broad enough to cover the most pathological or near-pathological elements—namely, anxieties, fears, morbid grief or self-pity, sadistic or masochistic desires, and the sense of guilt that these engender and are engendered by. In a successful tragedy we see these drives enacted on the stage directly or through their results by characters with whom we can identify ourselves. They are our proxies, so to speak.

We must observe, however, that the expulsion would certainly prove ephemeral and perhaps even incomplete or ineffective if the expelled matter were merely brought to the surface (to our "pre-conscious," if you will) instead of being fully recognized by our consciousness. Evoked "pity and fear" on the tragic stage may effect expulsion, but at least one other force is needed if real recognition is to be effectuated.

John Gassner, "Catharsis and the Modern Theater," in Barrett H. Clark, ed., *European Theories* *of the Drama* (New York: Crown Publishers, 1964), pp. 549–552.

That something more is needed is evidenced by the whole history of the theater. The distinction between tragedy and melodrama is grounded in the opinion that excitement is not enough, that it does not produce the most satisfactory effects. Where the excitement emanates plausibly and serves an end beyond itself there is, we say, tragedy. Where the excitement exists solely for itself and is accomplished without the operation of reason or credibility we have melodrama. If purgation in tragedy were confined solely to the effects of pity and fear there could be little dramatic distinction between *Hamlet* and *The Bat*.

Has it not always been recognized that the superiority of the great tragedies, if we exclude purely stylistic differences, has resided in their powerful blending of passion with enlightenment? This is what we mean when we attribute their superiority to the significance of their content, the depth and scope of their conflict, or the relevance of their action to the major aspects and problems of humanity. In tragedy there is always a precipitate of final enlightenment—some inherent, cumulatively realized, understanding. We have seen an experience enacted on the stage, and have externalized its inner counterpart in ourselves by the process of vibrating to the acted passions; or possibly by some other means, since unconscious processes are open to infinite debate. Then, ensuring the externalization of the inner drives, we have given them form and meaning—that is, understood their causes and effects, which brings us to the furthest point from the unconscious, or from nebulous emotion, ever reached by the individual. Enlightenment is, therefore, the third component of the process of purgation.

It exists in perfect harmony with the components of "pity and fear," and it is even supported by them. "Pity and fear," (using these terms to cover the emotional experience) are the *fixatives* of tragic enlightenment, for without their agency the meaning of a play would be superficial and fleeting; enlightenment unrooted in the emotions or unsupported and unevoked by them would be something imposed from without, unprecipitated from the struggle of the drama, and devoid of persuasive growth or cumulative effect. Moreover, pity and terror have mnemonic values which the drama cannot dispense

with, because of its rapid course of action. Who would remember the significances of *Hamlet* without its anguish?

Finally, but keeping the above qualifications strictly in mind, we can maintain that enlightenment is not only the third element in catharsis, but the decisive one. The ultimate relief comes when the dramatist brings the tragic struggle to a state of rest. This cannot occur so long as we are left in a state of tension. No matter how well the action or the main character's destiny is resolved and concluded, the anarchic forces, "the pity and fear," evoked by the tragedy cannot establish a suitable inner equilibrium. Only enlightenment, a clear comprehension of what was involved in the struggle, an understanding of cause and effect, a judgment on what we have witnessed, and an induced state of mind that places it above the riot of passion—can effect this necessary equilibrium. And it is a necessary one if there is to be purgation, and if for the moment we are to be healed of the wounds self-inflicted in the unconscious, inflicted on us from without by external circumstance before they settle our inmost self, then inflicted once more by the tragic story enacted before our eyes on the stage. Only enlightenment can therefore round out the esthetic experience in tragedy, can actually ensure complete esthetic gratification. True tragic exaltation, which we require of a tragedy, also lies in this. For the exaltation comes only if we have prevailed over the anarchy of our inner life and the ever present and ever pressing life around us; and how can we master this anarchy without understanding it, without putting order into this house of disorder?

Had Aristotle pursued his investigation of classic drama further, he would have surely arrived at this view himself. The author of the *Nichomachean Ethics* and the *Politics* could not have failed to discover the conclusive element of enlightenment in the purgation afforded by the tragedies of Aeschylus, Sophocles, and Euripides. To adopt Nietzschean (*The Birth of Tragedy*) terminology, Greek tragedy imposed the Apollonian world of light and reason upon the dynamic Dionysian world of passion. The Apollonian element in the warp and woof of the plays, including the great choral passages, ordered and so mastered the Dionysiac excitement or disequilibrium. I believe the same thing can be demonstrated in Elizabethan tragedy, in the work of Corneille and Racine, and in modern tragedy.

To conclude this argument, I should, I suppose, try to disabuse anyone who would look askance at this insistence on enlightenment because it suggests a moral in the outmoded Victorian sense. The "moral" is imposed from without by a convention; that was the prime limitation of William Winter's criticism. Enlightenment is not actually imposed, but wells up from the stream of the play itself, from the enacted events, actions, and reactions. The moral, in other words, is a predigested judgement, whereas enlightenment is empirical. The moral is a summation or tag; enlightenment is a process. The moral of a play can be put into a sententious sentence. The element of enlightenment can also be summarized, but the summary is only a portion of the whole. It is a state of grace, so to speak, a civilized attitude achieved in the course of experiencing the play: an Apollonian attitude, Santayana's "life of reason," a clarity of mind and spirit, a resilience and cheerfulness even. The moral is a law. The enlightenment is a state of mind, and includes specific conclusions only as a necessary concomitant of every state of mind that is now vacuous. It is even a kind of poetry of the mind, no matter how earnest, somber or sultry.

Acceptance of the function of enlightenment in tragic catharsis is particularly essential if we are to cope with the modern drama, if we are to understand, write, and produce it. In the case of modern drama, many problems arise and many distinctions must be made. For instance, we must realize that many serious modern plays are not tragedies at all but a new form of tragicomedy for which no term has yet been found. In this essay let us, however, continue to hew close to the matter of enlightenment.

The fact is that many who would grant my premise, out of conviction or from sheer exhaustion, will stickle at one other point as much as they would at the possibility that "enlightenment" is just an undercover term for a moral. They will insist on confining the matter of enlightenment to "universals"

and proceed to flail post-Ibsen drama because it so often treats immediate issues and problems.

I have nothing against "universals," but it seems to me that the only universals these critics favor are *dead* ones; or let us say that, for reasons that could bear some scrutiny, they prefer them to be conveniently remote from contemporary social conflicts. Otherwise a universal is not universal for them. A fallacy, I believe, since how can something be universal if it no longer functions, what life is there in it if it lacks direct applicability to what pinches us, and what is left in it but a platitude that fobs us off with a cold compress while the diseased body teems with microbes.

A hard and fast distinction between the topical and the universal is impossible in practice. We live amid the immediacies of our time and place. Are these distinguishable, can these be separated from, fundamental realities and human drives? The immediate realities contain and project the universal ones. Even our most unvarnished economic and political struggles relate to the universals of anxiety, fear of deprivation, pain and extinction; they involve love and hate, loyalty and treason, selfishness and self-sacrifice, honor and dishonor, falsehood and truth, good and evil. And all this is also only another way of saying that anything we call universal is only a generalization of immediate and specific interests or concerns. If we could put ourselves in the place of an Athenian spectator at the first performance of *The Trojan Women,* the Oresteian trilogy, or any other tragedy that stirred that spectator either as an individual or as a member of a group, we would not speak so glibly of universals. It is safe to conjecture that everything we consider universal in these plays was once very immediate—socially, politically, psychologically.

No, the failure of any contemporary topical or even downright propaganda play as tragic art has other causes than the substitution of the "topical" for the "universal." These cannot be examined in this essay; they are many, and they also require particularization in individual cases. Still hewing to my theme, I should like to add only that perhaps the overall cause will be found in the social dramatist's and the propagandist's failure to achieve a catharsis. He fails chiefly because in striving so conscientiously for enlightenment, he so often substitutes statement for dramatic process and neglects to effectuate the "pity and fear"—that is, the tensions and emotional rapport or identification implicit in the Aristotelian terms. Although it is the combination of "pity," "fear," and "enlightenment" that produces tragic catharsis, his assault strategy makes the frontal attack with "enlightenment" but forgets about the flanks. The general assault fails, and the unsupported frontal attack soon crumbles, since there is no effective enlightenment when the play fails. There is even a school of social drama that in one way or other denies the value of catharsis. According to Berthold Brecht, the champion of the epic or "learning-play" (*Lehrstück*), sympathy and emotional identification (*Einfühlung*) represent enticements or evasions of social understanding and action. He objects to "all the illusion which whips up the spectator for two hours and leaves him exhausted and full of vague recollection and vaguer hope." Brecht's view is only a forthright version of an attitude that underlies much social drama which, regardless of its merits, must remain fundamentally untragic. Perhaps proponents of anti-emotional drama should go one step further and arraign tragedy itself as a wrong for their purposes.

◆ The Tragic Form

By RICHARD B. SEWALL

A discussion of tragedy is confronted at the outset with the strenuous objections of Croce, who would have no truck with genres. "Art is one," he wrote in his famous *Britannica* article,[1] "and cannot be divided." For convenience, he would allow the division of Shakespeare's plays into tragedies, comedies, and histories, but he warned of the dogmatism that lay in any further refining of distinctions. He made a special point of tragedy, which as usual was the fighting issue. No artist, he said, will submit to the servitude of the traditional definition: that a tragedy must have a subject of a certain kind, characters of a certain kind, and a plot of a certain kind and length. Each work of art is a world in itself, "a creation, not a reflection, a monument, not a document." The concepts of aesthetics do not exist "in a transcendent region" but only in innumerable specific works. To ask of a given work "is it a tragedy?" or "does it obey the laws of tragedy?" is irrelevant and impertinent.

Although this may be substituting one dogmatism for another, there is sense in it.

Nothing is more dreary than the textbook categories; and their tendency, if carried too far, would rationalize art out of existence. The dilemma is one of critical means, not ends: Croce would preserve tragedy by insuring the autonomy of the artist; the schoolmen would preserve it by insuring the autonomy of the form.

But the dilemma is not insurmountable, as Eliot and a number of others have pointed out. There is a life-giving relationship between tradition and the individual talent, a "wooing both ways" (in R. P. Blackmur's phrase) between the form which the artist inherits and the new content he brings to it. This wooing both ways has been especially true of the development of tragedy, where values have been incremental, where (for instance) each new tragic protagonist is in some degree a lesser Job and each new tragic work owes an indispensable element to the Greek idea of the chorus. So I should say that, provided we can get beyond the stereotypes Croce seems to have had in mind, we should continue to talk about tragedy, to make it grow in meaning, impel more artists, and attract a greater and more discerning audience.

But we must first get a suitable idea of

Richard B. Sewall, "The Tragic Form," *Essays in Criticism*, IV (October, 1954), pp. 345–358.

[1] Eleventh edition, article "Aesthetics."

form. Blackmur's article[2] from which I have just quoted provides, I think, a useful suggestion. It is the concept of "theoretic form," which he distinguishes from technical or "executive" form. "Technical form," he writes, "is our means of getting at . . . and then making something of, what we feel the form of life itself is: the tensions, the stresses, the deep relations and the terrible disrelations that inhabit them. . . . This is the form that underlies the forms we merely practice. . . ." This (and here Croce's full concept of form is more adequately represented) is "what Croce means by theoretic form for feeling, intuition, insight, what I mean by the theoretic form of life itself." Discussion of the "form" of tragedy in this sense need be neither prescriptive nor inhibiting, but it may define a little more precisely a vital area of thought and feeling.

Here is the kind of situation in which such a discussion might be helpful: Two years ago, in *Essays in Criticism* (October 1952), Miss K. M. Burton defended what she called the "political tragedies" of Ben Jonson and George Chapman as legitimate tragedies, although non-Aristotelian. *Sejanus* was perhaps the clearest case in point. Herford and Simpson, in their commentary, had set the play down as at best "the tragedy of a satirist," a "proximate" tragedy, with no tragic hero and with no cathartic effect. "Whatever effect (Jonson) aimed at," they wrote, "it was not the purifying pity excited by the fatal errors of a noble nature." Miss Burton's reply lay in her concept of political tragedy. She saw Jonson's tragic theme as "the manner in which evil penetrates the political structure." The "flaw" that concerned him lay "within the social order," and whatever purifying pity we feel would come from contemplating the ordeal of society, not the fatal errors of a noble nature. The play for her had "tragic intensity"; it was both "dramatic, and a tragedy."

Whether one agrees with her or not, the question, despite Croce, is out: "Is the play a tragedy?" And many others follow. Can

there be a tragedy without a tragic hero? Can "the social order" play his traditional role? Is catharsis the first, or only, or even a reliable test? In a recent article, Professor Pottle wrote, "I shall be told Aristotle settled all that." And added, "I wish he had." The disagreement on *Sejanus* is symptomatic. F. L. Lucas once pointed out that (on much the same issues) Hegel thought only the Greeks wrote true tragedy; and I. A. Richards, only Shakespeare. Joseph Wood Krutch ruled out the moderns, like Hardy, Ibsen and O'Neill; and Mark Harris ruled them in.[3] The question arises about every new "serious" play or novel; we seem to care a great deal about whether it is, or is not, a tragedy.

I have little hope of settling all this, but I am persuaded that progress lies in the direction of theoretic form, as Blackmur uses the term. It is not possible to bring the dominant feelings, intuitions, insights that we meet in so-called tragic writings into some coherent relationship to which the word "form" could be applied without too great violence? This is not to tell artists what to do, nor to set up strict *a priori* formulae, nor to legislate among the major genres. The problem of evaluating the total excellence of a given work involves much more than determining its status as a tragedy, or as a "proximate" tragedy, or as a non-tragedy. It involves, among other things, the verbal management within the work and the ordering of the parts. Furthermore, our discussion need not imply the superiority of tragedy over comedy (certainly not as Dante conceived of comedy) or over epic, although, if we look upon these major forms as presenting total interpretations of life, the less inclusive forms (lyric, satire) would seem to occupy inferior categories. But as we enter the world of any play or novel to which the term tragedy is at all applicable, we may well judge it by what we know about the possibilities of the form, without insisting that our judgment is absolute. If, set against the full dimensions of the tragic form, Jonson's *Sejanus* or Hemingway's *A Farewell to Arms* (for instance)

---

2 "The Loose and Baggy Monsters of Henry James: Notes on the Underlying Classic Form in the Novel," *Accent*, Summer, 1951; see also Eliseo Vivas, "Literature and Knowledge," *Sewanee Review*, Autumn, 1952.

3 F. A. Pottle, "Catharsis," *Yale Review*, Summer, 1951; F. L. Lucas, *Tragedy in Relation to Aristotle's Poetics*, N.Y., 1928; Joseph Wood Krutch, *The Modern Temper*, N.Y., 1929; Mark Harris, *The Case for Tragedy*, N.Y., 1932.

reveal undeveloped possibilities or contrary elements, we can still respect their particular modes of expression.

In indicating these dimensions of tragedy, I shall be mindful of Unamuno's warning[4] that tragedy is not a matter, ultimately, to be systematized. He speaks truly, I think, about "the tragic sense of life." He describes it as a sub-philosophy, "more or less formulated, more or less conscious," reaching deep down into temperament, not so much "flowing from ideas as determining them." It is the sense of ancient evil, of the mystery of human suffering, of the gulf between aspiration and achievement. It colors the tragic artist's vision of life (his theoretic form) and gives his works their peculiar shade and tone. It speaks, not the language of systematic thought, but through symbolic action, symbol and figure, diction and image, sound and rhythm. Such a recognition should precede any attempt to talk "systematically" about tragedy, while not denying the value of the attempt itself.

Two more comments remain to be made about method. The first is the problem of circular evidence,[5] the use of tragedies to define tragedy. I am assuming that we can talk meaningfully about a body of literature which reveals certain generic qualities and which can be distinguished from the body of literature called comedy, epic, satire, or the literature of pathos. My purpose is to isolate these qualities and to refer to the works themselves as illustrations rather than proof.

The second comment involves the problem of affectivism, which is the problem of catharsis: "This play is a tragedy because it makes me feel thus and so." As Max Scheler puts it, this method would bring us ultimately to the contemplation of our own ego. Thus, I would reverse the order of F. L. Lucas' discussion, which assumes that we must know what tragedy does before we can tell what it is: "We cannot fully discuss the means," Lucas wrote, "until we are clear about the ends." It is true that the usual or "scientific" way is to define natures by effects, which are observable. But rather than found a defi-

nition of tragedy on the infinite variables of an audience's reactions, I would consider first the works themselves as the "effects" and look in them for evidences of an efficient cause: a world-view, a form that "underlies the forms we merely practice." What are the generic qualities of these effects? Do they comprise a "form"? I think they do; and for convenience I shall use the term from the start as if I had already proved its legitimacy.

Basic to the tragic form is its recognition of the inevitability of paradox, of unresolved tensions and ambiguities, of opposites in precarious balance. Like the arch, tragedy never rests—or never comes to rest, with all losses restored and sorrows ended. Problems are put and pressed, but not solved. An occasional "happy ending," as in *The Oresteia* or *Crime and Punishment,* does not mean a full resolution. Though there may be intermittences, there is no ultimate discharge in the war. Although this suggests formlessness, as it must in contrast with certain types of religious orthodoxy or philosophical system, it would seem the essence of the tragic form. Surely it is more form than chaos. For out of all these tensions and paradoxes, these feelings, intuitions, insights, there emerges a fairly coherent attitude towards the universe and man. Tragedy makes certain distinguishable and characteristic affirmations, as well as denials, about (I) the cosmos and man's relation to it; (II) the nature of the individual and his relation to himself; (III) the individual in society.

(I) *The tragic cosmos.* In using the term cosmos to signify a theory of the universe and man's relation to it, I have, of course, made a statement about tragedy: that tragedy affirms a cosmos of which man is a meaningful part. To be sure, the characteristic locale of tragedy is not the empyrean. Tragedy is primarily humanistic. Its focus is an event in this world; it is uncommitted as to questions of ultimate destiny, and it is non-religious in its attitude toward revelation. But it speaks, however vaguely or variously, of an order that transcends time, space and matter.[6]

[4] *The Tragic Sense of Life,* tr. J. E. C. Flitch, London, 1921, pp. 17–18.

[5] Cf. Max Scheler, "On the Tragic," *Cross Currents,* Winter, 1954. This is a selection from Scheler's

Vom Umsturtz der Werte, vol. I (1923), tr. Bernard Stambler.

[6] Cf. Susan Taubes, "The Nature of Tragedy," *Review of Metaphysics,* December 1953.

It assumes man's connection with some super-sensory or supernatural, or metaphysical being or principle, whether it be the Olympians, Job's Jehovah or the Christian God; Fate, Fortune's Wheel, the "elements" that Lear invoked, or Koestler's "oceanic sense," which comes in so tentatively (and pathetically) at the end of *Darkness at Noon*. The first thing that tragedy says about the cosmos is that, for good or ill, it is; and in this respect tragedy's theoretic opposite is naturalism or mechanism. Tragedy is witness (secondly) to the cosmic mystery, to the "wonderful" surrounding our lives; and in literature the opposite of tragedy is not only writing based upon naturalistic theory but also upon the four-square, "probable"[7] world of satire and rationalistic comedy. Finally, what distinguishes tragedy from other forms which bespeak this cosmic sense—for tragedy of course is not unique in this—is its peculiar and intense preoccupation with the evil in the universe, whatever it is in the stars that compels, harasses, and bears man down. Tragedy wrestles with the evil of the mystery—and the mystery of the evil. And the contest never ends.

But, paradoxically, its view of the cosmos is what sustains tragedy. Tragedy discerns a principle of goodness that coexists with the evil. This principle need be nothing so pat as The Moral Order, the "armies of unalterable law," and it is nothing so sure as the orthodox Christian God. It is nearer the folk sense that justice exists somewhere in the universe, or what Nietzsche describes as the orgiastic, mystical sense of oneness, of life as "indestructibly powerful and pleasurable." It may be a vision of some transcendent beauty and dignity against which the present evil

may be seen as evil and the welter as welter. This is what keeps tragedy from giving up the whole human experiment, and in this respect its opposite is not comedy or satire but cynicism and nihilism, as in Schopenhauer's theory of resignation. The "problem of the good" plays as vital a part in tragedy as the "problem of evil." It provides the living tension without which tragedy ceases to exist.

Thus tragedy contemplates a universe in which man is not the measure of all things. It confronts a mystery. W. Macneile Dixon[8] pointed out that tragedy started as "an affair with the gods"; and the extent to which literature has become "secularized and humanized," he wrote, is a sign of its departure from (to use our present term) the tragic form. While agreeing with him as to the tendency, one may question the wholesale verdict which he implies. The affair with the gods has not, in the minds of all our artists, been reduced to an affair with the social order, or the environment, or the glands. But certainly where it becomes so, the muse of tragedy walks out; the universe loses its mystery and (to invoke catharsis for a moment) its terror.

The terms "pessimism" and "optimism," in view of the universe as conceived in the tragic form, do not suggest adequate categories, as Nietzsche first pointed out.[9] Tragedy contains them both, goes beyond both, illuminates both, but comes to no conclusion. Tragedy could, it is true, be called pessimistic in its view of the evil in the universe as unremitting and irremediable, the blight man was born for, the necessary condition of existence. It is pessimistic, also, in its view of the overwhelming proportion of evil to good and in its awareness of the mystery of

---

[7] The "wonderful" and the "probable" are the basic categories in Albert Cook's distinction between tragedy and comedy. (*The Dark Voyage and the Golden Mean*, Cambridge, Mass., 1949, chap. I.)
[8] *Tragedy*, London, 1924. The extent of my indebtedness to this book, and to the other discussions of tragedy mentioned in this paper, is poorly indicated by such passing references as this. Since observations on tragedy and the theory of tragedy appear in innumerable discussions of particular authors, eras, and related critical problems, a complete list would be far too cumbersome. Among them would be, surely, the standard work of A. C. Bradley and Willard Farnham on Shakespearean tragedy; C. M. Bowra and Cedric Whitman on Sophocles; W. L.

Courtney (*The Idea of Tragedy*, London, 1900); Maxwell Anderson, *The Essence of Tragedy*, Washington, 1939; Northrop Frye, "The Archetypes of Literature," *Kenyon Review*, Winter, 1951; Moody Prior, *The Language of Tragedy*, N.Y., 1947; and Herbert Weisinger, *Tragedy and the Paradox of the Fortunate Fall*, Michigan State College Press, 1953, which makes rich use of the archaeological and mythographic studies of the origin of tragedy (Cornford, Harrison, Murray). I am indebted, also, to my colleague Laurence Michel, for frequent conversations and helpful criticism.
[9] See also Reinhold Niebuhr, *Beyond Tragedy*, London, 1938.

why this should be—the "unfathomable element" in which Ahab foundered. But it is optimistic in what might be called its vitalism, which is in some sense mystical, not earthbound; in its faith in a cosmic good; in its vision, however fleeting, of a world in which all questions could be answered.

(II) *Tragic man.* If the tragic form asserts a cosmos, some order behind the immediate disorder, what does it assert about the nature of man, other than that he is a being capable of cosmic affinities? What is tragic man as he lives and moves on this earth? Can he be distinguished meaningfully from the man of comedy, satire, epic, or lyric? How does he differ from "pathetic man" or "religious man"? or from man as conceived by the materialistic psychologies? Tragic man shares some qualities, of course, with each of these. I shall stress differences in the appropriate contexts.

Like the cosmos which he views, tragic man is a paradox and a mystery. He is no child of God; yet he feels himself more than a child of earth. He is not the plaything of Fate, but he is not entirely free. He is "both creature and creator" (in Niebuhr's phrase) —"fatefully free and freely fated" (in George Schrader's). He recognizes "the fact of guilt" while cherishing the "dream of innocence" (Fiedler), and he never fully abandons either position. He is plagued by the ambiguity of his own nature and of the world he lives in. He is torn between the sense in commonsense (which is the norm of satire and rationalistic, or corrective, comedy) and his own uncommon sense. Aware of the just but irreconcilable claims within and without, he is conscious of the immorality of his own morality and suffers in the knowledge of his own recalcitrance.

The dynamic of this recalcitrance is pride. It sustains his belief, however humbled he may become by later experience, in his own freedom, in his innocence, and in his uncommon sense. Tragic man is man at his most prideful and independent, man glorying in his humanity. Tragic pride, like everything else about tragedy, is ambiguous; it can be tainted with arrogance and have its petty side; but it is not to be equated with sin or weakness. The Greeks feared it when it threatened the gods or slipped into arrogance, but they honored it and even worshiped it

in their heroes. It was the common folk, the chorus, who had no pride, or were "flawless." [10] The chorus invariably argues against pride, urging caution and moderation, because they know it leads to suffering; but tragedy as such does not prejudge it.

While many of these things, again, might be said of other than tragic man, it is in the peculiar nature of his suffering, and in his capacity for suffering, that his distinguishing quality lies. For instance (to ring changes on the Cartesian formula), tragic man would not define himself, like the man of corrective comedy or satire, "I think, therefore I am"; nor like the man of achievement (epic): "I act, or conquer, therefore I am": nor like the man of sensibility (lyric): "I feel, therefore I am": nor like the religious man: "I believe, therefore I am." Although he has all these qualities (of thought, achievement, sensibility, and belief) in various forms and degrees, the essence of his nature is brought out by suffering: "I suffer, I will to suffer, I learn by suffering; therefore I am." The classic statement, of course, is Aeschylus': "Wisdom comes alone through suffering" (Lattimore's translation); perhaps the most radical is Dostoevski's: "Suffering is the sole origin of consciousness."[11]

This is not to say that only tragic man suffers or that he who suffers is tragic. Saints and martyrs suffer and learn by suffering; Odysseus suffered and learned; Dante suffered and learned on his journey with Virgil. But tragic man, I think, is distinguishable from these others in the nature of his suffering as conditioned by its source and locus, in its characteristic course and consequences (that is, the ultimate disaster and the "knowledge" it leads to), and in his intense preoccupation with his own suffering.

But to consider these matters in turn and to illustrate them briefly:

I have already suggested the main sources and locus of tragic man's suffering. He suffers because he is more than usually sensitive to the "terrible disrelations" he sees about him and experiences in himself. He is more than

---

10 Cf. Arthur Miller, "Tragedy and the Common Man," *New York Times,* February 27th, 1949.
11 *Notes from Underground,* tr. B. G. Guerney.

usually aware of the mighty opposites in the universe and in man, of the gulf between desire and fulfilment, between what is and what should be. This kind of suffering is suffering on a high level, beyond the reach of the immature or brutish, and for ever closed to the extreme optimist, the extreme pessimist,[12] or the merely indifferent. It was Job on the ash-heap, the proto-type of tragic man, who was first struck by the incongruity between Jehovah's nature and His actions, between desert and reward in this life; and it was he who first asked, not so much for a release from physical suffering as a reasonable explanation of it. But above all, the source of tragic suffering is the sense, in the consciousness of tragic man, of simultaneous guilt and guiltlessness. Tillich called tragedy "a mixture of guilt and necessity." If tragic man could say, "I sinned, therefore I suffer" or "He (or They or God) sinned, therefore I suffer," his problem would be resolved, and the peculiar poignancy of his suffering would be removed. If he felt himself entirely free or entirely determined, he would cease to be tragic. But he is neither—he is, in short, a paradox and mystery, the "riddle of the world."

To draw further distinctions: The element of guilt in tragic suffering distinguishes it from the pathetic suffering of the guiltless and from the suffering of the sentimentalist's bleeding heart. On the other hand, tragic man's sense of fate, and of the mystery of fate, distinguishes his suffering from the suffering (which is little more than embarrassment) of the man of corrective comedy and satire. The suffering of the epic hero has little of the element of bafflement or enigma; it is not, characteristically, spiritual suffering. The Christian in his suffering can confess total guilt and look to the promise of redemption through grace.[13] The martyr seeks suffering, accepts it gladly, "glories in tribulation." Tragic man knows nothing of grace and never glories in his suffering. Although he may come to acquiesce in it partly and "learn" from it (a stage I shall discuss below), his characteristic mood is resentment and dogged endurance. He has not the stoic's patience, although this may be

part of what he learns. Characteristically, he is restless, intense, probing and questioning the universe and his own soul (Job, Lear, Ahab). It is true that, from Greek tragedy to tragedy written in the Christian era (Shakespeare and beyond) emphasis shifts from the universe to the soul, from the cosmic to the psychological. But Prometheus had an inner life; Antigone, for all her composure, suffered an ultimate doubt; Oedipus suffered spiritually as he grew to understand the dark ambiguities in his own nature. And we should be mistaken if we tried to interpret the divine powers in the plays of Shakespeare simply as "allegorical symbols for psychological realities."[14]

Tragic man, then, placed in a universe of irreconcilables, acting in a situation in which he is both innocent and guilty, and peculiarly sensitive to the "cursed spite" of his condition, suffers. What in the tragic view is the characteristic course of this suffering and what further aspects of tragic man are revealed by it? The tragic form develops, not only the partial outlines of a cosmology and psychology, but of an ethic.

(III) *Tragic man and society.* The tragic sufferer may now be viewed in his social and moral relationships. In the tragic world there are several alternatives. A man can default from the human condition—"Curse God and die"—and bring his suffering to an end: he can endure and be silent; he can turn cynic. Tragic man understands these alternatives, feels their attractions, but chooses a different way. Rising in his pride, he protests: he pits himself in some way against whatever, in the heavens above and in the earth beneath, seems to him to be wrong, oppressive, or personally thwarting. This is the hero's commitment, made early or late, but involving him necessarily in society and in action— with Prometheus and Antigone early, with Hamlet late. What to the orthodox mind would appear to be the wisdom or folly, the goodness or badness, of the commitment is not, in the beginning, the essence of the matter. In the first phase of his course of suffering, the hero's position may be anarchic, individual, romantic. Herein tragedy tests all norms—as, by contrast, satire,[15] comedy, or

[12] Cf. William Van O'Connor, *Climates of Tragedy,* Baton Rouge, La., 1943.
[13] Cf. Karl Jaspers, *Tragedy Is Not Enough,* tr. Reiche, Moore, Deutsch; Boston, 1952.

[14] Susan Taubes, *op. cit.,* p. 196.
[15] Cf. Maynard Mack, "The Muse of Satire," *Yale Review,* Spring, 1952.

epic tend to confirm them. The commitment may even be expressed in what society knows as a crime, but, as with tragic pride (of which the commitment is in part the expression) tragedy does not prejudge it. Thus it is said that tragedy studies "the great offenders," and Dostoevski sought among criminals and outcasts for his greatest spiritual discoveries. But the commitment must grow in meaning to include the more-than-personal. Ultimately, and ideally, the tragic hero stands as universal man, speaking for all men. The tragic sufferer, emerging from his early stage of lament or rebellion (Job's opening speech; the first scenes of Prometheus; Lear's early bursts of temper), moves beyond the "intermittences" of his own heart and makes a "pact with the world that is unremitting and sealed."[16]

Since the commitment cannot lead in the direction of escape or compromise, it must involve head-on collision with the forces that would oppress or frustrate. Conscious of the ambiguities without and within, which are the source of his peculiar suffering, tragic man accepts the conflict. It is horrible to do it, he says, but it is more horrible to leave it undone. He is now in the main phase of his suffering—the "passion."[17]

In his passion he differs from the rebel, who would merely smash; or the romantic hero, who is not conscious of guilt; or the epic hero, who deals with emergencies rather than dilemmas. Odysseus and Aeneas, to be sure, face moral problems, but they proceed in a clear ethical light. Their social norms are secure. But the tragic hero sees a sudden, unexpected evil at the heart of things that infects all things. His secure and settled world has gone wrong, and he must oppose his own ambiguous nature against what he loves. Doing so involves total risk, as the chorus and his friends remind him. He may brood and pause, like Hamlet, or he may proceed with Ahab's fury; but proceed he must.

He proceeds, suffers, and in his suffering "learns." This is the phase of "perception." Although it often culminates in a single apocalyptic scene, a moment of "recognition," as in *Oedipus* and *Othello,* it need not be separate in time from the passion phase. Rather, perception is all that can be summed up in the spiritual and moral change that the hero undergoes from first to last and in the similar change wrought by his actions or by his example in those about him.

For the hero, perception may involve an all-but-complete transformation in character, as with Lear and Oedipus; or a gradual development in poise and self-mastery (Prometheus, Hamlet); or the softening and humanizing of the hard outlines of a character like Antigone's. It may appear in the hero's change from moody isolation and self-pity to a sense of his sharing in the general human condition, of his responsibility for it and to it. This was one stage in Lear's pilgrimage ("I have ta'en too little care of this") and as far as Dostoevski's Dmitri Karamazov ever got. In all the manifestations of this perception there is an element of Hamlet's "readiness," of an acceptance of destiny that is not merely resignation. At its most luminous it is Lear's and Oedipus' hard-won humility and new understanding of love. It may transform or merely inform, but a change there must be.

And it is more, of course, than merely a moral change, just as the hero's problem is always more than a moral one. His affair is still with the gods. In taking up arms against the ancient cosmic evil, he transcends the human situation, mediating between the human and the divine. It was Orestes' suffering that, in the end, made the heavens more just. In the defeat or death which is the usual lot of the tragic hero, he becomes a citizen of a larger city, still defiant but in a new mood, a "calm of mind," a partial acquiescence. Having at first resented his destiny, he has lived it out, found unexpected meanings in it, carried his case to a more-than-human tribunal. He sees his own destiny, and man's destiny, in its ultimate perspective.

But the perception which completes the tragic form is not dramatized solely through the hero's change, although his pilgrimage

[16] Wallace Fowlie, "Swann and Hamlet: A Note on the Contemporary Hero," *Partisan Review,* 1942.
[17] Cf. Francis Fergusson, *The Idea of a Theater,* Princeton, N.J., 1949, chap. I, "The Tragic Rhythm of Action." Fergusson translates Kenneth Burke's formulation "Poiema, Pathema, Mathema" into "Purpose, Passion, Perception." (See *A Grammar of Motives,* pp. 38ff.) Cf. also Susan Taubes, *op. cit.,* p. 199.

provides the traditional tragic structure.[18] The full nature and extent of the new vision is measured also by what happens to the other figures in the total symbolic situation—to the hero's antagonists (King Creon, Claudius, Iago); to his opposites (the trimmers and hangers-on, the Osrics); to his approximates (Ismene, Horatio, Kent, the Chorus). Some he moves, some do not change at all. But his suffering must make a difference somewhere outside himself. After Antigone's death the community (even Creon) re-forms around her; the "new acquist" at the end of *Samson*

Agonistes is the common note, also at the end of the Shakespearean tragedies. For the lookers-on there is no sudden rending of the veil of clay, no triumphant assertion of The Moral Order. There has been suffering and disaster, ultimate and irredeemable loss, and there is promise of more to come. But all who are involved have been witness to new revelations about human existence, the evil of evil and the goodness of good. They are more "ready." The same old paradoxes and ambiguities remain, but for the moment they are transcended in the higher vision.

[18] Indeed, it has been pointed out that, in an age when the symbol of the hero as the dominating center of the play seems to have lost its validity with artist and audience, the role is taken over by the artist himself, who is his own tragic hero. That is, "perception" is conveyed more generally, in the total movement of the piece and through all the parts. The "pact with the world" and the suffering are not objectified in a hero's ordeal but seem peculiarly the author's. This quality has been noted in Joyce's *Ulysses*; Berdiaev saw it in Dostoevski; Hardy, Conrad, Faulkner are examples that come to mind. At any rate, the distinction may be useful in determining matters of tone, although it is not clear cut, as distinctions in tone seldom are. But it is one way of pointing to the difference between the tragic tone and the Olympian distance of Meredithian comedy, or the ironic detachment of satire. . . .

◆ The Elements of Drama: Plot

By ELDER OLSON

Poetry and fiction of one sort or another seem to have existed in almost every kind of society, from the most primitive to the most cultivated, and in almost every period. You would, I think, find it somewhat difficult offhand to indicate any very extensive period of which you could say positively that neither existed anywhere. I prefer to ignore Horace's "Many unwept and unknown are swept into eternal night, because they lack the sacred bard," together with Alexander Pope's paraphrase of it, "They had no poet, and are dead." This proves nothing: the sacred bard, with all his huge literary luggage, may also have been swept into oblivion, for all we know. Like poetry and fiction, music, dancing, painting, and sculpture seem to have flourished practically at all times and among all peoples. The case of drama is different. Drama generally develops late, as compared with other arts. A complex art requires the fulfillment of many conditions before it can exist, and of many more before it can develop significantly. Some of these conditions cannot possibly be fulfilled in certain societies, and in consequence drama does not exist in them or reach any significant development. Great dramatic periods themselves seem to be brief.

Despite all this, there is an enormous mass of what we call dramatic literature—so enormous and so varied that you may well wonder how to deal with it. Suppose I ask you: How many forms of drama are there? You are likely to answer in one or two opposed ways, according as you are a Lumper or Splitter. These are not my terms, but terms which a biologist friend of mine tells me are in use, nowadays, among biologists quarrelling over problems of classification. A Lumper lumps everything into the same classes, to get as few classes as possible. As the Splitters put it, a Lumper sees a flying fish, a flying squirrel, a pterodactyl, a bee, and a duck, and lumps them all under *Bird*. A Splitter splits until there are as many classes almost as individuals: as the Lumpers put it, if a Splitter sees a sparrow with one feather missing, he wants to call it a new species. Polonius seems to have been a Splitter: you remember his famous "tragedy, comedy, history, pastoral, pastoral-comical, historical-pastoral, tragical-historical, tragical-comical-historical-pastoral, scene individable or poem unlimited," which continues to bring such glee and comfort to the hearts of Lumpers.

The difficulty with the position of the Lumpers is obvious. If you take the view of a late distinguished playwright and critic (who was a Lumper) that comedy is comedy, whether written by Aristophanes or Shakespeare or Molière or Goldoni or Shaw, you not merely ignore the development of different species out of primitive ones, but also ignore any development within a given species. What is worse, you force yourself to talk in such general terms that you can discuss nothing specifically. But it would be wise, also, to consider before you embrace the position of the Splitters. A Splitter cannot really deal with developments either, for he cannot find enough continuity to do so; he can only find a succession of mere differences. What is worse, lost as he is in a wilderness of apparently infinite forms, he finds it impossible to say anything about drama in general.

The Lumper can see nothing but resemblance; the Splitter, nothing but difference. Fortunately for the discussion of drama, these are both incomplete discussions, therefore; for the fact is that dramas both resemble one another and differ from one another. When we discuss anything completely, we discuss *all* of its characteristics; a play has individual

Elder Olson, "The Elements of Drama: Plot," *Tragedy and the Theory of Drama* (Detroit, Wayne State University Press, 1961), pp. 29–54.

characteristics, specific characteristics, characteristics which it shares with other forms of drama, and so on; even characteristics which it shares with every other kind of existence.

Even if the forms of drama were infinite or indefinitely numerous, however, it would still be possible to reduce them to their elements and to discuss these. No matter how great the complexity of structures, in their full proliferation and development, they cannot have generated out of infinite elements. If the *elements* of a structure were infinite in number, no such structure could ever have existed; for nothing can result from an infinite process such as would be required to assemble infinitely numerous elements. On the other hand, where elements are finite in number, it is always possible to discuss through them —that is, their number, nature, different possibilities of assembly and correlation and so on—the structures even of great complexity into which they combine. In fact, in this fashion physics and chemistry find it possible to discuss the fabric of the whole universe and everything within it.

Very well, then: What are the elements of drama?

I do not want to do what it is customary to do at the posing of this question: flourish my Aristotle and intone, Why, of course, Plot, Character, Thought, Diction, Music, and Spectacle. In the first place, these are not the elements of drama as such, but the specific parts of tragedy, derived in fact from the definition of tragedy. In the second place, not one of these terms means in Aristotle what it is likely to mean to a modern reader, and they are likely to be entirely misleading. I pass over the fact that their interpretation is a matter of some considerable controversy, has been so indeed for centuries, and that the debate is still far from being settled.

For the sake of simplicity and clarity I prefer to put the whole thing another way. If we think about the things a dramatist must do, as a *minimum*, to make a play, it becomes clear that he must (1) devise some sort of action, together with characters who can appropriately carry it out, (2) contrive a scenario which shows what actions are to be enacted on the stage in what order, and (3) compose the dialog, or at least indicate roughly what sort of thing shall be said by the actors. It appears that no play is possible without these three things; and that, on the other hand, the moment these three are completed, a play—good, bad, or indifferent, but a *play*—results. It is true that stage directions might be furnished, music composed, scenery designed, and so on; but these seem mere superadditions, ornaments and enhancements which are inessential to drama since drama can exist without them. Not a given *form* of drama, perhaps, such as Greek tragedy, Nō, or opera; but certainly drama.

These three things, then—action, scenario, and dialog—seem to be closely related to the elements of drama; and whatever ultimate constituents or parts these may divide into are in all probability the elements themselves, the ultimate particles out of which everything in the universe of drama is created.

We generally speak of the action of drama as *plot*: unfortunately, however, we tend to use that term in a variety of senses, some of them less accurate, or at any rate less useful, than others. Perhaps it would be wise to look into these before we do anything further.

The most general meaning of *plot* is that of the argument, synopsis, or summary of a narrative or drama. In this sense you tell someone the "plot" of a movie. The fact that you are frequently surprised and disappointed by your listener's reaction shows that your synopsis is not really the "plot" devised by the dramatist. Had your listener seen the movie himself, his reaction would have been similar to yours, in all probability. A synopsis or summary never precludes the possibility of opposite emotional effects; a plot is always aimed at some definite effect. A synopsis of the Pyramus and Thisbe play in *A Midsummer Night's Dream* is closely similar to a synopsis of *Romeo and Juliet*. In both plays we have "two star-crossed lovers," parents averse to their union, clandestine meetings, the lover killing himself on the mistaken supposition that his beloved is dead, but it would be absurd to say that these plays have the same *plot*; one is comic, the other tragic.

For the same reason, plot is not a system of bare events or incidents in complete abstraction from character. Birth, marriage, parenthood, poverty, riches, death—any event, as *mere* event—can produce any number of different effects upon us, and thus no determinate effect. The death of a tyrant can bring joy, the marriage of an innocent girl to a villain can bring sorrow, though we commonly think of death as a sorrowful and marriage as a joyful event.

We also apply the term *plot* to a myth, legend, or series of historical happenings. This, too, seems inaccurate usage. Sophocles, Seneca, Corneille, Dryden, Voltaire, Hofmannsthal, Gide, and Cocteau all composed plays about Oedipus; can we say with any accuracy that all of these plays have the same *plot*?

Again, plot hardly appears to be mere intrigue or "conflict," although post-Elizabethan theorists often made it synonymous with the former, and nineteenth-century theorists often equated it with the latter. There are many plots—that of Sophocles' *Oedipus Tyrannus*, for example—which involve no intrigue whatsoever; similarly, there are plots in which no conflict is involved. What basic conflict can we find in *Our Town*?

Finally—and this is a subtler matter—plot is not the dramatic representation, or what we have just called the *scenario*. Parts of the plot, indeed crucial and central ones, may be omitted from the representation, that is, may occur off-stage; the murder of Duncan, the death of Lady Macbeth and of Macbeth himself are obviously important parts of the plot, but they are not shown on the stage. Conversely, events may be shown on the stage which form no part of the plot. For example, Act I Scene i of *Julius Caesar* is not a part of the plot. It has no effect whatsoever upon the train of consequences which make up the action; it is merely an expository scene, intended to exhibit the fickleness of the Roman rabble, and so establish the probability of important events which happen later.

Other considerations go to show the difference between plot and representation. The plot may begin before the representation, or after it, or simultaneously with it; similarly, the plot may end before or after or simultaneously with the ending of the representation. It would be wearisome, perhaps pedantic, to illustrate all of this: I may simply remark that the representation in *Hamlet* begins long before the plot, which has its initiating incident in the information which the Ghost gives to Hamlet; that of *King Lear* begins almost immediately before the initiating incident of the plot, which is Lear's questioning of his daughters; while the representation of *Oedipus Tyrannus* begins after the beginning of the plot.

Further, the incidents of the plot are *time-bound*, that is, must occur in a given chronological order, and are consequently not convertible. The incidents of the representation are not time-bound, and conversions of chronological order are common. The commonest instance is the flash-back; only a little less common is the successive representation of simultaneous events—the well-known "In the meantime" of the silent movies. There is even what we might call the "flash-ahead," such as the Prolog to *Marco Millions*, which depicts events twenty-three years *after* the events of Act I Scene i.

If the matter is still not clear, one further reflection should set it beyond all doubt: when the dramatist has completed his plot, he must still determine what he will show upon the stage, in what order, on what scale. The scenario or representation cannot possibly be devised until the corresponding parts of the plot have been invented, for the representation is *what represents*, whereas the plot is *what is represented*. They are thus, obviously, distinct.

Both representation and plot are actions, and dramatic actions. But the representation is a "dramatic action" primarily, in the sense precisely which we discovered in Chapter I, whereas a plot is "dramatic" secondarily, in the sense that it admits of being set before us by the representation. In other words, *any* plot is a dramatic one—regardless of the "actability" or "stageability" of the incidents which comprise it—so long as a dramatic scenario can be contrived to imply it. It is, thus, secondarily dramatic, as contingent upon the possibility of devising a dramatic scenario or representation. Henry James failed as a dramatist, not because he could not contrive dramatic plots, but because he could not contrive dramatic scenarios. The great success of some of his plays, as reworked by competent dramatists, establishes this beyond question.

If plot is evidently neither the representation nor any of the other things we have been considering, what is it? For simplicity's sake

I shall define it first and argue the definition afterward. *Plot is a system of actions of a determinate moral quality.* I use the word "actions" in a very general sense, to include the inner workings of the soul as well as external actions. In this sense, any actualization of a capacity for thought, emotion, or action is to be considered as "action."

I say "system of actions" because it seems unlikely that anyone would ever consider a single action or incident as a plot. A single, absolutely simple and indivisible activity, such as we find in the simplest forms of imagistic poetry, has never been called "plot" by anyone, so far as I know. Indeed, I suppose a good many people will balk at the notion of a plot as containing two, perhaps even three or four, incidents only. I shall come back to that later; for the moment, I say "system" as implying an activity (1) divisible into at least two activities, and (2) made into a system by some unifying principle. In saying "*some* unifying principle," I mean of course to imply that there are different possible ones.

The matter of "actions of a determinate moral quality" threatens to give us a little trouble. I shall simply give you the reasoning which leads me to insist upon this. I assume, as I said before, that plot is always aimed at some specific effect; that it is absurd to say that a tragic and a comic version of one and the same story have identical plots. If we then respond differently—as in fact we do—to events which in general synopsis are identical, that difference of response must be due to the different particular presentations of the events. Now, if we feel different emotions at the sight of the fortunes or misfortunes of characters in a play, we are of course feeling pleasures or pains, for the emotions are forms of mental pleasures or pains. Why do we feel these pleasures or pains? Because what we are seeing is in accordance with or in opposition to our wishes for the characters. What leads us to wish good or bad fortune for characters whom we have never known, and whose fortunes or misfortunes could never conceivably affect our own? Because we favor some, and hold others in disfavor. Why should we hold in favor or disfavor absolutely fictitious persons who exist in absolute detachment from our own self-interest? I can find only one answer to this last question: We feel toward

them, this way or that, upon precisely the same grounds on which we feel one way or another toward persons who have existed in remote periods of history, or who are otherwise absolutely detached from our advantage or disadvantage; that is, upon *grounds of moral approval or disapproval*. But an action which incurs moral approval or disapproval must itself be possessed of a certain moral quality; thus the foundation of emotional effectiveness in plot must clearly be moral, and plot itself is morally determinate action.

Certain objections offer themselves at once to this view. As I see them, they appear only for immediate dismissal. First: Why should not we simply say that all our emotional reactions in drama are based upon general human sympathy? This can mean one of two things: that we feel, emotion for emotion, precisely what the character is feeling, or that our reactions are based upon the general love of man for man. The latter is patently false, for drama is filled with characters toward whom we feel the extremest antipathy. The former is false, too. Time and again we feel emotions which are the very opposites of those felt by the character. For example, we do not share the wicked glee of the villain at the apparent success of his plan, nor do we share the calm confidence of the heroine as she moves among unsuspected dangers.

Well, then, cannot we simply say that we identify ourselves with the characters? This is another very widely held view, and it can also mean one of two things. It can mean that we absolutely "put ourselves into the shoes" of the characters, that is, imagine ourselves as them, or that we identify our own interests with theirs. Both again are false and contrary to fact. These may possibly be principles of certain schools of *acting;* they are positively not principles underlying the reactions of the *audience.* Do we, in fact, in watching a play, fancy ourselves now as Claudius, now as Gertrude, now as Hamlet, now Horatio, and now Polonius? Or identify our own interests with theirs? In that case we should view the outcome with very mixed emotions indeed. If we identify ourselves with some but not with others, on what grounds do we do so? For identification cannot itself then be the *principle* underlying our reactions: it requires something further to explain it. Do we, in fact, identify ourselves with *anybody*? Is it not rather manifestly the case that as we watch, absorbed in what we see, nothing is further from our thoughts than ourselves and our self-interest?

The fundamental fault in both of these views is that each assumes that we cannot be moved emotionally without reflection upon our self-interest, and that our attitudes towards others must consequently be based upon self-interest. Man does not happen to be so insensitive nor so self-concerned. I will leave the matter there; David Hume has beautifully argued the rest of the case for me; I will merely say that our feelings at a play are such feelings as we have, not for ourselves, but for others.

There is one other objection, which a very able British critic, Mr. John Holloway, has brought against my definition of plot as morally determinate action. This would apply, Mr. Holloway observes, to the crude plots of Saturday matinee movie-melodramas, and the naive "good-guy and bad-guy" reactions of the children who go to see them; if so, how can it also be the basis of the subtlest reactions to the greatest drama?

I must answer that, in the first place, the question is not one of good plots and bad plots, but of what is and is not plot. In the second place, a definition of plot must offer universal attributes of plot, ones common to the highest and to the lowest kinds. Mr. Holloway's objection, far from being a real one, seems to me rather to make for my case; I should be disturbed indeed if my definition did *not* cover the movie-melodramas. Besides, the possibility of a crude moral attitude in no way precludes the possibility of a more subtle and refined one. On the contrary, the subtle is possible only if the crude—or basic—attitude has been established.

Very well, then, we have our definition of plot, and we must ask another question: In how many ways may plots differ from each other?

First of all, they can differ in magnitude, in the extension of the action. The magnitude of the action is a function of the number of situations and of the number of characters which it contains. We can thus distinguish four kinds of magnitudes:

(1) the activity of a single character in a single closed situation
(2) the activity of two or more characters in a single closed situation
(3) the activity of two or more characters in a series of situations centering about a single principal event
(4) the activity of two or more characters in a series of situations involving more than one principal event.

The action involving a single character in a single closed situation is not common in drama as the whole action of a play. It can form a scene in a play, certainly; but as a whole action it is commonly found in lyrics, of which it is perhaps the commonest form of all. By a "closed situation" I mean one in which there is no external intervention of any kind; the character is as it were hermetically sealed off from the rest of the world, so that his action, thought, or emotion runs its uninterrupted course from beginning to end. This is the kind of action you will find in Keats's "Ode to a Nightingale," Milton's "Lycidas," Yeats's "Sailing to Byzantium," and similar lyrics.

The action involving two or more persons in a single closed situation is one that permits of many more possible developments, and so it is frequently found in short plays, and sometimes even in rather extended ones, such as Sartre's *No Exit* (*Huis Clos*). Even here, however, complication of the action can arise only out of the characters themselves, and not from external interruption or intervention. As a consequence, it is difficult to develop an extended action of this sort.

When external causes or agencies are combined with internal, however, the case is very different. If you have two characters in a given situation and can bring in a third who can change that situation, you can proceed indefinitely. The third may appear in person or may be represented only as the writer of a letter or someone invisible on the other end of the telephone; it does not matter. Whether or not he figures in the *Dramatis Personae,* he is still an agent in the drama; and it is obvious that as we multiply agents or agencies we multiply the possibilities of development and hence of extension.

The last two kinds of action, thus, as permitting external intervention, offer far greater possibilities of developing an action of some length. Suppose we call the action of situations centering about a principal event by the name of *episode,* and the one which centers about more than one principal event by the name of *grand plot.* They are clearly distinct: the action of the *Agamemnon* is an episode, with everything centering about the murder of Agamemnon; whereas the action of *Macbeth* is a grand plot, for it is impossible to designate in it any one event about which everything else centers.

So far as magnitude or mere extension of plot is concerned, I can think of nothing which goes beyond grand plot. But there is a matter of thickness or thinness, so to speak, as well as length. This is the matter of the number of lines or threads of action involved in a plot. A line of action is a chain of cause and effect, separable at least in part from other such lines. Plots are either linear or polylinear. The plot of the *Agamemnon* is linear, as consisting of a single line of action. The plot of *Oedipus Tyrannus,* on the other hand, is polylinear, and you can easily distinguish such different threads as Oedipus' investigations, the events happening at Corinth, and so on. When lines of action as such as to have an independent interest and constitute a story in their own right, they are called sub-plots, by-plots, or under-plots. The actions of Fortinbras and of Laertes in *Hamlet* I should consider lines of action simply; similarly, the successive actions of Albany in *King Lear* are merely a line of action, although a very important one. On the other hand, the Gloucester story is an under- or sub-plot.

Lines of action, whether or not they are sub-plots, either converge or diverge or run parallel. If you diagram a plot and find two or more lines of action stemming from a single cause or incident, this is divergence. If you find chains of causation concurring in a single effect or situation, this is convergence. If they are wholly independent of each other, they are parallel. Divergence is commonest at the beginning of an action, as permitting complication; convergence is commonest at the end, to achieve resolution. Threatened convergence is one way of obtaining suspense, when the convergence is such as to affect the outcome materially; sudden convergence is one way of obtaining surprise. In *King Lear,* for instance, Albany almost understands the true state of affairs at certain points, and since he has the power to put an end to the villainy, may help Lear's situation: his line threatens to converge with Lear's. The unexpected return of Lovewit in *The Alchemist* is an instance of sudden convergence.

When lines of action are not merely causally related, as producing complication or resolution, they serve to enhance the effect of the main line of action, either through resemblance to it or contrast with it. Thus a comic sub-plot in a serious play contrasts with the main plot, and conversely. There are other more subtle possibilities: the Fortinbras and Laertes lines in *Hamlet* both reflect the main lines as similars and contrast with it, for Fortinbras is like Hamlet a dispossessed prince, and Laertes is like Hamlet the son of a murdered father, and yet both act in sharp contrast to Hamlet. In the same manner the Gloucester line in *King Lear* is both similar and dissimilar to the main line.

You can see at once that this offers all sorts of possibilities. Plots can begin with a single incident which produces a divergence of lines which never meet again. In John Buchan's *A Gap in the Curtain,* five men, after participating in an experiment in prevision, work out their separate destinies. Plots can end in the convergence, in a single incident, of lines previously more or less independent, as in *The Bridge of San Luis Rey.* They can involve lines which converge and diverge repeatedly, like the lines of Henry and the Master in *The Master of Ballantrae.* They can have lines that start independently and converge halfway through, to diverge and become independent again, as in Barrie's *Dear Brutus;* they can diverge from a single incident, run parallel for awhile, and then converge in the denouement; and they can do many another thing besides, which you may work out on your own by drawing lines on paper in the form of hourglasses, diamonds, strings of diamonds, zigzags, and whatnots. You will only need to bear in mind that divergence is the stemming of separate lines from a single cause, while convergence is the coming together of lines in a single effect.

I want to move on to another aspect of plot: its unifying principle, the thing which makes it a system and a single system. This is one of the aspects of plot construction about which critics have been most dogmatic, and it is one of the things about which it is most dangerous to be dogmatic. To prevent dogmatism as much as we can, let us consider four plays and ask ourselves what makes the plot of each *one* plot. I choose *Macbeth, Our Town*, Schnitzler's *Reigen* (*La Ronde*), and *Ghosts*.

The plot of *Macbeth* has the unity of a train of consequences. The train has a beginning, an initiating incident (the meeting with the Witches), and it has a terminating incident (the killing of Macbeth and the passage of the crown to Malcolm). Everything in between is in some way an effect of the beginning and a cause of the end; the whole has the unity of a causal sequence. The plot of *Our Town* is quite different. There is a certain amount of causal relation, to be sure, but it is not terribly important, and it is not the unifying principle of the plot. The plot is intended to catch an image of life in a small American town, and it is complete when it has caught that image completely, at least in its more nostalgic aspects. In this respect it resembles the plot of Dylan Thomas' *Under Milk Wood*; only it attempts to capture the image of town life through the three phases of youth, marriage, and death, whereas Thomas' plot attempts to reflect its image in the activities of a townful of people on a single day. This difference of organization is unimportant, however; the significant thing about this sort of plot is that it is complete in the sense in which a description is complete when it has adequately described its object. The incidents are present in it, not because they have any necessary causal relation, but because they show different aspects of the object in view. The plots of documentaries, chronicle plays, and many historical, biographical, and pageant pieces are of this order.

Schnitzler's *Reigen* has a different sort of plot again. The events are in no way causes or effects of each other, and they do not deal with any one object. They all deal with the theme of sexual love, but they are not intended to offer any very adequate description even of that. There are ten scenes: The Whore has sexual relations with the Soldier,

the Soldier with the Parlormaid, the Parlormaid with the Young Gentleman, the Young Gentleman with the Young Wife, the Young Wife with the Husband, the Husband with the Little Miss, the Little Miss with the Poet, the Poet with the Actress, the Actress with the Count, and finally, the Count with the Whore. There you are: A and B, B and C, and so on, till we come full circle back to A. What sort of unity has this? Why, none, I say—unless you are willing to admit that a circle has unity or, more generally, that a pattern has unity. We can call this the *pattern plot*. Of course there are many possible patterns.

The plot of *Ghosts* is of still another kind. There is a causal sequence, but Ibsen is apparently so little concerned with it that he allows things to happen by convenient coincidence—for example, the outbreak of fire at a particular time—rather than go to the trouble of making them probable occurrences. It is hard to say what the initiating incident is. Is it the marriage of the Alvings? Or Mrs. Alving's flight from her husband? Or her return? Or his catching syphilis? Or the birth of Oswald? Or what? And what is the end? Does she poison Oswald or not? There are elements of the descriptive, too; but the unity of the plot is hardly that of a description. There is even a pattern of sorts; but that isn't primary either. The play is a *pièce à thèse*; the action and the characters are designed to prove, by example, that in a society in which duty is invariably opposed to pleasure, the good must suffer or become corrupt, while the wicked flourish in hypocrisy.

We have, thus, at least four different kinds of unifying principle in plots: the consequential, the descriptive, the pattern, and the didactic. I say, at *least* four; there may be many more.

We are likely to think that a plot cannot be complete unless it deals with a complete, and therefore finite, action. But in fact this applies only to the consequential plot. It is perfectly possible for a finite plot to convey the idea of an indefinitely continuing, perhaps eternal, process. There are a good many examples of this: *The Long Christmas Dinner, The Skin of Our Teeth*, and *Huis Clos* come to mind immediately. Some plots are complete when they afford an adequate basis for a certain emotion, some when they have made possible a certain inference. Some plots are stories; others, considered as stories, have no story at all, or are chronicles of very small beer indeed. What they do have in common is some end or other in view, and it is important to consider what that end may possibly be, for it is in terms of that and nothing else that the plot is complete.

To return to the question of other differences among plots: they can differ in terms of their laws of probability. This is a very difficult and complex question, and I can only deal lightly with it here. What I have in mind is that events which are probable or even inevitable in fantasy may very well be impossible in realistic drama, and that events which are probable or inevitable in farce may be impossible in ordinary comedy. The various forms of drama are in a sense different universes regulated by different laws, and the beings and objects within them operate according to those laws. We can distinguish several different systems of such laws or probabilities. We think an event probable if it happens daily or usually or frequently, to most people, or to most people at some time or other, or at any rate to people of a certain kind; and we think an action probable if everyone or most people or people of a certain kind have the power and the inclination to do it. This is common natural probability, and it is the kind of probability on which realistic and naturalistic plots are based.

We also think that rare and unusual occurrences are probable too, in certain circumstances, providing we believe that adequate causes exist, or that there are adequate indications that the occurrences happened. This is conditional natural probability, the probability of the unusual. Tragedy depends on it, and so does melodrama of the better sort.

We also accept as probable certain things of a highly exaggerated nature, because we recognize that the exaggeration, patently preposterous as it is, is only figurative and contains an element of truth. This is hyperbolical probability, and it underlies farce.

We even accept as probable the actions of beings we know do not exist, or actions which existent beings could not possibly perform, provided these follow upon a certain hypothesis. If witches, ghosts, and fairies existed, they *would* do such and such; *if* a dog could

talk, he *would* talk like that. This is hypothetical probability, and it underlies all fantasy and stories of the supernatural.

We will accept anything as probable which corresponds to something already accepted. Thus a plot which follows a familiar legend or a familiar version of historical events will be accepted as probable, even though these latter contain improbabilities or impossibilities. No one will question the feats of Paul Bunyan, or George Washington's cherry tree. This holds, too, of certain forms; for instance, we expect certain things to happen in a Western, improbable as they may be. This is the probability of custom, or conventional probability.

There is emotional probability, too. This may be completely irrational and in no way connected with logical probability. A given emotion predisposes us to believe certain things, even though they may be impossible. A man in a gloomy frame of mind finds it doubtful that anything good can happen; an audience in a certain emotional state will similarly accept things that in another it would question.

When I spoke earlier of "different universes regulated by different laws of probability," I did not mean to imply that these universes could not coincide, or at least impinge upon each other to some degree. They can, and often do. A plot of natural probability can turn to hypothetical probability (fantasy) and subsequently return to the natural: instances are *A Midsummer Night's Dream,* Dunsany's *If,* Barrie's *Dear Brutus,* and Shaw's *Man and Superman.* The natural probability can turn to the hyperbolical, as in Androcles' waltz with the lion in *Androcles and the Lion.* There are many other possibilities, one of the most fruitful of which seems to be the reversal of conventional probabilities; that is, the establishment of a different system of probabilities—within the framework of a legend or literary form—from those associated with that form or legend. This is one of Shaw's characteristic devices; he uses it in *Arms and the Man, Caesar and Cleopatra, Man and Superman, St. Joan,* and other plays. It has been used repeatedly also by Gide, Cocteau, Giraudoux, Sartre, and Anouilh to provide startlingly different versions of classical legend.

These shiftings of probabilities, or mixtures of them, seem to depend for their success upon a single principle; they must be required by the form, and themselves made probable within it. In *A Midsummer Night's Dream* separate lines are established at the outset, the human and the faery, each with its own probabilities. When the lines of action converge in the Wood, the natural and the hypothetical probabilities operate together; subsequently they draw apart again. The whole is probable because the convergence and the divergence have been made probable. In *St. Joan* an action which has been principally one of natural probability shifts, in the Epilog, into hypothetical. There has been much objection to the Epilog as "unnecessary," "improbable," and "destructive of the tragic effect"; I think these charges are very ill-founded. *St. Joan* is not tragedy, but a certain kind of comedy. As Shaw says, "The angels may weep at the murder, but the gods laugh at the murderers"; and he arranges matters so that Joan herself may have the last laugh—albeit a melancholy one. Her last laugh came with her canonization in the twentieth century, and so, if she is to enjoy the joke on her murderers, fantasy is required. The Epilog is essential to the play, for it contains the comic reversal; to delete it would be to alter the very form and significance of the play. This is a matter of the probability of form, and it underlies many of the great tragic denouements of Shakespeare.

If we consider probability in a different light, everything that is probable is so either intrinsically or through its connection with other things. In *St. Joan,* since we have been speaking of that, Shaw subverts the idea of the "miracles" as miraculous by supplanting them with events of intrinsic natural probability. The natural probability is always more probable intrinsically than any other. Normally we are more willing to believe that something is coincidence, or has been foolishly interpreted or knavishly misreported, than that it is actually miraculous. It would seem that this is the position of the Roman Catholic Church itself, since it submits all supposed miracles, I understand, to extremely rigorous tests.

On the other hand, extrinsic probability can very powerfully overcall intrinsic probability in some instances. Witch and fairy must do what witch and fairy would do, although both are impossible. Again, the spell of a particular emotion may be so powerful that under it we may doubt what we should normally believe, and believe what we should normally doubt.

There is probability even within the realm of accident and coincidence. That is, although we think of these as improbabilities, not all accidents are equally improbable. It is more probable that a car will collide with another than that it will be struck by a meteorite; that such-and-such will happen in the jungle than that it will happen in a city, and so on.

Plots of consecutive action are either simple or complex. A simple plot is one that moves in a single direction, as when the fortunes of the protagonist steadily decline or improve. A complex plot is one that involves a change of direction, as when the protagonist moves toward greater and greater good fortune, and then suffers reverses. A straight line and a bent line will give you the idea; the former is simple, the latter, complex. The complex is always divisible into distinct parts, while the simple is not: you can see that the bent line is made up of two discrete parts, but the straight line is continuous, and any point of division is arbitrary. The point at which the fortunes alter is the peripety or reversal. Discovery of some sort is usually associated with reversal, either as producing it or resulting from it. Someone learns that he has committed a dreadful mistake, or finds out in time to prevent it, and so on.

All complex plots involve at least two factors which we may call *force* and *counterforce.* The force is what carries the action initially in one direction; the counter-force is what produces the change of direction. Both must be probable, of course, as causes; but if the reversal is to be unexpected, the counter-force must be concealed, or made to seem improbable, while the force must be obvious and apparently irresistible. On the other hand, if the reversal is to be probable, the counter-force must be, in retrospect, far more probable than the force. The superiority of the complex plot lies in that it permits of the unexpected and hence of greater emotional power, since emotions that come upon us unexpectedly are always more violent and powerful.

Complex plots always involve complication, as their name suggests. There are two kinds of complication, the continuous and the incidental. The continuous operates from the first and throughout; the incidental operates only in a given part, is resolved and done with in that part, and another incidental complication must be introduced if further development is to result. The great Shakespearian tragedies involve continuous complication; Shaw chiefly uses the incidental. Thus in

Pygmalion Doolittle appears, threatens to break up Lisa's arrangement with Higgins, and withdraws. All momentary obstacles are of this order. Continuous complication depends primarily upon extrinsic probability, and incidental complication depends primarily upon intrinsic.

◆ The Tragic Fallacy

By JOSEPH WOOD KRUTCH

Through the legacy of their art the great ages have transmitted to us a dim image of their glorious vitality. When we turn the pages of a Sophoclean or a Shakespearean tragedy we participate faintly in the experience which created it and we sometimes presumptuously say that we "understand" the spirit of these works. But the truth is that we see them, even at best and in the moments when our souls expand most nearly to their dimensions, through a glass darkly.

It is so much easier to appreciate than to create that an age too feeble to reach the heights achieved by the members of a preceding one can still see those heights towering above its impotence, and so it is that, when we perceive a Sophocles or a Shakespeare soaring in an air which we can never hope to breathe, we say that we can "appreciate" them. But what we mean is that we are just able to wonder, and we can never hope to participate in the glorious vision of human life out of which they were created—not even to the extent of those humbler persons for whom they were written; for while to us the triumphant voices come from far away and tell of a heroic world which no longer exists, to them they spoke of immediate realities and revealed the inner meaning of events amidst which they still lived.

When the life has entirely gone out of a work of art come down to us from the past, when we read it without any emotional comprehension whatsoever and can no longer even imagine why the people for whom it was intended found it absorbing and satisfying, then, of course, it has ceased to be a work of art at all and has dwindled into one of those deceptive "documents" from which we get a false sense of comprehending through the intellect things which cannot be compre-

Joseph Wood Krutch, "The Tragic Fallacy," *The Modern Temper* (New York: Harcourt, Brace & World, 1956), pp. 79–97.

hended at all except by means of a kinship of feeling. And though all works from a past age have begun in this way to fade there are some, like the great Greek or Elizabethan tragedies, which are still halfway between the work of art and the document. They no longer can have for us the immediacy which they had for those to whom they originally belonged, but they have not yet eluded us entirely. We no longer live in the world which they represent, but we can half imagine it and we can measure the distance which we have moved away. We write no tragedies today, but we can still talk about the tragic spirit of which we would, perhaps, have no conception were it not for the works in question.

An age which could really "appreciate" Shakespeare or Sophocles would have something comparable to put beside them—something like them, not necessarily in form, or spirit, but at least in magnitude—some vision of life which would be, however different, equally ample and passionate. But when we move to put a modern masterpiece beside them, when we seek to compare them with, let us say, a *Ghosts* or a *Weavers*, we shrink as from the impulse to commit some folly and we feel as though we were about to superimpose Bowling Green upon the Great Prairies in order to ascertain which is the larger. The question, we see, is not primarily one of art but of the two worlds which two minds inhabited. No increased powers of expression, no greater gift for words, could have transformed Ibsen into Shakespeare. The materials out of which the latter created his works—his conception of human dignity, his sense of the importance of human passions, his vision of the amplitude of human life—simply did not and could not exist for Ibsen, as they did not and could not exist for his contemporaries. God and Man and Nature had all somehow dwindled in the course of the intervening centuries, not because the realistic creed of modern art led us to seek out mean people, but because this meanness of human life was somehow thrust upon us by the operation of that same process which led to the development of realistic theories of art by which our vision could be justified.

Hence, though we still apply, sometimes, the adjective "tragic" to one or another of those modern works of literature which describe human misery and which end more sadly even than they begin, the term is a misnomer since it is obvious that the works in question have nothing in common with the classical examples of the genre and produce in the reader a sense of depression which is the exact opposite of that elation generated when the spirit of a Shakespeare rises joyously superior to the outward calamities which he recounts and celebrates the greatness of the human spirit whose travail he describes. Tragedies, in that only sense of the word which has any distinctive meaning, are no longer written in either the dramatic or any other form, and the fact is not to be accounted for in any merely literary terms. It is not the result of any fashion in literature or of any deliberation to write about human nature or character under different aspects, any more than it is of either any greater sensitiveness of feeling which would make us shrink from the contemplation of the suffering of Medea or Othello or of any greater optimism which would make us more likely to see life in more cheerful terms. It is, on the contrary, the result of one of those enfeeblements of the human spirit not unlike that described in the previous chapter of this essay, and a further illustration of that gradual weakening of man's confidence in his ability to impose upon the phenomenon of life an interpretation acceptable to his desires which is the subject of the whole of the present discussion.

To explain that fact and to make clear how the creation of classical tragedy did consist in the successful effort to impose such a satisfactory interpretation will require, perhaps, the special section which follows, although the truth of the fact that it does impose such an interpretation must be evident to any one who has ever risen from the reading of *Oedipus* or *Lear* with that feeling of exultation which comes when we have been able,

by rare good fortune, to enter into its spirit as completely as it is possible for us of a remoter and emotionally enfeebled age to enter it. Meanwhile one anticipatory remark may be ventured. If the plays and the novels of today deal with littler people and less mighty emotions it is not because we have become interested in commonplace souls and their unglamorous adventures but because we have come, willy-nilly, to see the soul of man as commonplace and its emotions as mean.

II

Tragedy, said Aristotle, is the "imitation of noble actions," and though it is some twenty-five hundred years since the dictum was uttered there is only one respect in which we are inclined to modify it. To us "imitation" seems a rather naïve word to apply to that process by which observation is turned into art, and we seek one which would define or at least imply the nature of that interposition of the personality of the artist between the object and the beholder which constitutes his function and by means of which he transmits a modified version, rather than a mere imitation, of the thing which he has contemplated.

In the search for this word the aestheticians of romanticism invented the term "expression" to describe the artistic purpose to which apparent imitation was subservient. Psychologists, on the other hand, feeling that the artistic process was primarily one by which reality is modified in such a way as to render it more acceptable to the desires of the artist, employed various terms in the effort to describe that distortion which the wish may produce in vision. And though many of the newer critics reject both romanticism and psychology, even they insist upon the fundamental fact that in art we are concerned, not with mere imitation but with the imposition of some form upon the material which it would not have if it were merely copied as a camera copies.

Tragedy is not, then, as Aristotle said, the *imitation* of noble actions, for, indeed, no one knows what a *noble* action is or whether or not such a thing as nobility exists in nature apart from the mind of man. Certainly the action of Achilles in dragging the dead body of Hector around the walls of Troy and under the eyes of Andromache, who had begged to be allowed to give it decent burial, is not to us a noble action, though it was such to Homer, who made it the subject of a noble passage in a noble poem. Certainly, too, the same action might conceivably be made the subject of a tragedy and the subject of a farce, depending upon the way in which it was treated; so that to say that tragedy is the *imitation* of a *noble* action is to be guilty of assuming, first, that art and photography are the same and, second, that there may be something inherently noble in an act as distinguished from the motives which prompted it or from the point of view from which it is regarded.

And yet, nevertheless, the idea of nobility is inseparable from the idea of tragedy, which cannot exist without it. If tragedy is not the imitation or even the modified representation of noble actions it is certainly a representation of actions *considered* as noble, and herein lies its essential nature, since no man can conceive it unless he is capable of believing in the greatness and importance of man. Its action is usually, if not always, calamitous, because it is only in calamity that the human spirit has the opportunity to reveal itself triumphant over the outward universe which fails to conquer it; but this calamity in tragedy is only a means to an end and the essential thing which distinguishes real tragedy from those distressing modern works sometimes called by its name is the fact that it is in the former alone that the artist has found himself capable of considering and of making us consider that his people and his actions have that amplitude and importance which make them noble. Tragedy arises then when, as in Periclean Greece or Elizabethan England, a people fully aware of the calamities of life is nevertheless serenely confident of the greatness of man, whose mighty passions and supreme fortitude are revealed when one of these calamities overtakes him.

To those who mistakenly think of it as something gloomy or depressing, who are incapable of recognizing the elation which its celebration of human greatness inspires, and who, therefore, confuse it with things merely miserable or pathetic, it must be a paradox that the happiest, most vigorous, and most confident ages which the world has ever known—the Periclean and the Elizabethan— should be exactly those which created and which most relished the mightiest tragedies; but the paradox is, of course, resolved by the fact that tragedy is essentially an expression, not of despair, but of the triumph over despair and of confidence in the value of human life. If Shakespeare himself ever had that "dark period" which his critics and biographers have imagined for him, it was at least no darkness like that bleak and arid despair which sometimes settles over modern spirits. In the midst of it he created both the elemental grandeur of Othello and the pensive majesty of Hamlet and, holding them up to his contemporaries, he said in the words of his own Miranda, "Oh, rare new world that hath *such* creatures in it."

All works of art which deserve their name have a happy end. This is indeed the thing which constitutes them art and through which they perform their function. Whatever the character of the events, fortunate or unfortunate, which they recount, they so mold or arrange or interpret them that we accept gladly the conclusion which they reach and would not have it otherwise. They may conduct us into the realm of pure fancy where wish and fact are identical and the world is remade exactly after the fashion of the heart's desire or they may yield some greater or less allegiance to fact; but they must always reconcile us in one way or another to the representation which they make and the distinctions between the genres are simply the distinctions between the means by which this reconciliation is effected.

Comedy laughs the minor mishaps of its characters away; drama solves all the difficulties which it allows to arise; and melodrama, separating good from evil by simple lines, distributes its rewards and punishments in accordance with the principles of a naïve justice which satisfies the simple souls of its audience, which are neither philosophical enough to question its primitive ethics nor critical enough to object to the way in which its neat events violate the laws of probability. Tragedy, the greatest and the most difficult of the arts, can adopt none of these methods; and yet it must reach its own happy end in its own way. Though its conclusion must be, by its premise, outwardly calamitous, though it must speak to those who know that the good man is cut off and that the fairest things are the first to perish, yet it must leave them, as *Othello* does, content that this is so. We must be and we are glad that Juliet dies and glad that Lear is turned out into the storm.

Milton set out, he said, to justify the ways of God to man, and his phrase, if it be interpreted broadly enough, may be taken as describing the function of all art, which must, in some way or other, make the life which it seems to represent satisfactory to those who see its reflection in the magic mirror, and it must gratify or at least reconcile the desires of the beholder, not necessarily, as the naïver exponents of Freudian psychology maintain, by gratifying individual and often eccentric wishes, but at least by satisfying the universally human desire to find in the world some justice, some meaning, or, at the very least, some recognizable order. Hence it is that every real tragedy, however tremendous it may be, is an affirmation of faith in life, a declaration that even if God is not in his Heaven, then at least Man is in his world.

We accept gladly the outward defeats which it describes for the sake of the inward victories which it reveals. Juliet died, but not before she had shown how great and resplendent a thing love could be; Othello plunged the dagger into his own breast, but not before he had revealed that greatness of soul which makes his death seem unimportant. Had he died in the instant when he struck the blow, had he perished still believing that the world was as completely black as he saw it before the innocence of Desdemona was revealed to him, then, for him at least, the world would have been merely damnable, but Shakespeare kept him alive long enough to allow him to learn his error and hence to die, not in despair, but in the full acceptance of the tragic reconciliation to life. Perhaps it would be pleasanter if men could believe what the child is taught—that the good are happy and that things turn out as they should—but it is far more important to be able to believe, as Shakespeare did, that however much things in the outward world may go awry, man has, nevertheless, splendors of his own and that, in a word, Love and Honor and Glory are not words but realities.

Thus for the great ages tragedy is not an expression of despair but the means by which they saved themselves from it. It is a profession of faith, and a sort of religion; a way of looking at life by virtue of which it is robbed of its pain. The sturdy soul of the tragic author seizes upon suffering and uses it only as a means by which joy may be wrung out of existence, but it is not to be forgotten that he is enabled to do so only because of his belief in the greatness of human nature and because, though he has lost the child's faith in life, he has not lost his far more important faith in human nature. A tragic writer does not have to believe in God, but he must believe in man.

And if, then, the Tragic Spirit is in reality the product of a religious faith in which, sometimes at least, faith in the greatness of God is replaced by faith in the greatness of man, it serves, of course, to perform the function of religion, to make life tolerable for those who participate in its beneficent illusion. It purges the souls of those who might otherwise despair and it makes endurable the realization that the events of the outward world do not correspond with the desires of the heart, and thus, in its own particular way, it does what all religions do, for it gives a rationality, a meaning, and a justification to the universe. But if it has the strength it has also the weakness of all faiths, since it may—nay, it must—be ultimately lost as reality, encroaching further and further into the realm of imagination, leaving less and less room in which that imagination can build its refuge.

III

It is, indeed, only at a certain stage in the development of the realistic intelligence of a people that the tragic faith can exist. A naïve people may have, as the ancient men of the north had, a body of legends which are essentially tragic, or it may have only (and need only) its happy and childlike mythology which arrives inevitably at its happy end, where the only ones who suffer "deserve" to do so and in which, therefore, life is represented as directly and easily acceptable. A too sophisticated society on the other hand— one which, like ours, has outgrown not merely the simple optimism of the child but also that vigorous, one might almost say adolescent, faith in the nobility of man which marks a Sophocles or a Shakespeare—has neither fairy tales to assure it that all is always right in the end nor tragedies to make it believe that it rises superior in soul to the outward calamities which befall it.

Distrusting its thought, despising its passions, realizing its impotent unimportance in the universe, it can tell itself no stories except those which make it still more acutely aware of its trivial miseries. When its heroes (sad misnomer for the pitiful creatures who people contemporary fiction) are struck down it is not, like Oedipus, by the gods that they are struck but only, like Oswald Alving, by syphilis, for they know that the gods, even if they existed, would not trouble with them, and they cannot attribute to themselves in art an importance in which they do not believe. Their so-called tragedies do not and cannot end with one of those splendid calamities which in Shakespeare seem to reverberate through the universe, because they cannot believe that the universe trembles when their love is, like Romeo's, cut off or when the place where they (small as they are) have gathered up their trivial treasure is, like Othello's sanctuary, defiled. Instead, mean misery piles on mean misery, petty misfortune follows petty misfortune, and despair becomes intolerable because it is no longer even significant or important.

Ibsen once made one of his characters say that he did not read much because he found reading "irrelevant," and the adjective was brilliantly chosen because it held implications even beyond those of which Ibsen was consciously aware. What is it that made the classics irrelevant to him and to us? Is it not just exactly those to him impossible premises which make tragedy what it is, those assumptions that the soul of man is great, that the universe (together with whatever gods may be) concerns itself with him and that he is, in a word, noble? Ibsen turned to village politics for exactly the same reason that his contemporaries and his successors have, each in his own way, sought out some aspect of the common man and his common life—because, that is to say, here was at least something small enough for him to be able to believe.

Bearing this fact in mind, let us compare a modern "tragedy" with one of the great works of a happy age, not in order to judge of their relative technical merits but in order to determine to what extent the former deserves its name by achieving a tragic solution capable of purging the soul or of reconciling the emotions to the life which it pictures. And in order to make the comparison as fruitful as possible let us choose *Hamlet* on the one hand and on the other a play like *Ghosts* which was not only written by perhaps the most powerful as well as the most typical of modern writers but which is, in addition, the one of his works which seems most nearly to escape that triviality which cannot be entirely escaped by anyone who feels, as all contemporary minds do, that man is relatively trivial.

In *Hamlet* a prince ("in understanding, how like a god!") has thrust upon him from the unseen world a duty to redress a wrong which concerns not merely him, his mother, and his uncle, but the moral order of the universe. Erasing all trivial fond records from his mind, abandoning at once both his studies and his romance because it has been his good fortune to be called upon to take part in an action of cosmic importance, he plunges (at first) not into action but into thought, weighing the claims which are made upon him and contemplating the grandiose complexities of the universe. And when the time comes at last for him to die he dies, not as a failure, but as a success. Not only has the universe regained the balance which had been upset by what *seemed* the monstrous crime of the guilty pair ("there is nothing either good nor ill but thinking makes it so"), but in the process by which that readjustment is made a mighty mind has been given the opportunity, first to contemplate the magnificent scheme of which it is a part and then to demonstrate the greatness of its spirit by playing a rôle in the grand style which it called for. We do not need to despair in *such* a world if it has *such* creatures in it.

Turn now to *Ghosts*—look upon this picture and upon that. A young man has inherited syphilis from his father. Struck by a to him mysterious malady he returns to his northern village, learns the hopeless truth about himself, and persuades his mother to poison him. The incidents prove, perhaps, that pastors should not endeavor to keep a husband and wife together unless they know what they are doing. But what a world is this in which a great writer can deduce nothing more than that from his greatest work and how are we to be purged or reconciled when we see it acted? Not only is the failure utter, but it is trivial and meaningless as well.

Yet the journey from Elsinore to Skien is precisely the journey which the human spirit has made, exchanging in the process princes for invalids and gods for disease. We say, as Ibsen would say, that the problems of Oswald Alving are more "relevant" to our life than the problems of Hamlet, that the play in which he appears is more "real" than the other more glamorous one, but it is exactly because we find it so that we are condemned. We can believe in Oswald but we cannot believe in Hamlet, and a light has gone out in the universe. Shakespeare justifies the ways of God to man, but in Ibsen there is no such happy end and with him tragedy, so called, has become merely an expression of our despair at finding that such justification is no longer possible.

Modern critics have sometimes been puzzled to account for the fact that the concern of ancient tragedy is almost exclusively with kings and courts. They have been tempted to accuse even Aristotle of a certain naïveté in assuming (as he seems to assume) that the "nobility" of which he speaks as necessary to a tragedy implies a nobility of rank as well as of soul, and they have sometimes regretted that Shakespeare did not devote himself more than he did to the serious consideration of those common woes of the common man which subsequent writers have exploited with increasing pertinacity. Yet the tendency to lay the scene of a tragedy at the court of a king is not the result of any arbitrary convention but of the fact that the tragic writers believed easily in greatness just as we believe easily in meanness. To Shakespeare, robes and crowns and jewels are the garments most appropriate to man because they are the fitting outward manifestation of his inward majesty, but to us they seem absurd because the man who bears them has, in our estimation, so pitifully shrunk. We do not write about kings because we do not believe that any man is worthy to be one and we do not write about courts because hovels seem to us to be dwellings more appropriate to the creatures who inhabit them. Any modern attempt to dress characters in robes ends only by making us aware of a comic incongruity and any modern attempt to furnish them with a language resplendent like Shakespeare's ends only in bombast.

True tragedy capable of performing its function and of purging the soul by reconciling man to his woes can exist only by virtue of a certain pathetic fallacy far more inclusive than that to which the name is commonly given. The romantics, feeble descendants of the tragic writers to whom they are linked by their effort to see life and nature in grandiose terms, loved to imagine that the sea or the sky had a way of according itself with their moods, of storming when they stormed and smiling when they smiled. But the tragic spirit sustains itself by an assumption much more far-reaching and no more justified. Man as it sees him lives in a world which he may not dominate but which is always aware of him. Occupying the exact center of a universe which would have no meaning except for him and being so little below the angels that, if he believes in God, he has no hesitation in imagining Him formed as he is formed and crowned with a crown like that which he or one of his fellows wears, he assumes that each of his acts reverberates through the universe. His passions are important to him because he believes them important throughout all time and all space; the very fact that he can sin (no modern can) means that this universe is watching his acts; and though he may perish, a God leans out from infinity to strike him down. And it is exactly because an Ibsen cannot think of man in any such terms as these that his persons have so shrunk and that his "tragedy" has lost that power which real tragedy always has of making that infinitely ambitious creature called man content to accept his misery if only he can be made to feel great enough and important enough. An Oswald is not a Hamlet chiefly because he has lost that tie with the natural and supernatural world which the latter had. No ghost will leave the other world to warn or encourage him, there is no virtue and no vice which he can possibly have which can be really important, and when he dies neither his death nor the manner of it will be, outside the circle of two or three people as unnecessary as himself, any more important than that of a rat behind the arras.

Perhaps we may dub the illusion upon which the tragic spirit is nourished the Tragic, as opposed to the Pathetic, Fallacy, but fallacy though it is, upon its existence depends not merely the writing of tragedy but the existence of that religious feeling of which tragedy is an expression and by means of which a people aware of the dissonances of life manages nevertheless to hear them as harmony. Without it neither man nor his passions can seem great enough or important enough to justify the sufferings which they entail, and literature, expressing the mood of a people, begins to despair where once it had exulted. Like the belief in love and like most of the other mighty illusions by means of which human life has been given a value, the Tragic Fallacy depends ultimately upon the assumption which man so readily makes that something outside his own being, some "spirit not himself"—be it God, Nature, or that still vaguer thing called a Moral Order—joins him in the emphasis which he places upon this or that and confirms him in his feeling that his passions and his opinions are important. When his instinctive faith in that correspondence between the outer and the inner world fades, his grasp upon the faith that sustained him fades also, and Love or Tragedy or what not ceases to be the reality which it was because he is never strong enough in his own insignificant self to stand alone in a universe which snubs him with its indifference.

In both the modern and the ancient worlds tragedy was dead long before writers were aware of the fact. Seneca wrote his frigid melodramas under the impression that he was following in the footsteps of Sophocles, and Dryden probably thought that his *All for Love* was an improvement upon Shakespeare, but in time we awoke to the fact that no amount of rhetorical bombast could conceal the fact that grandeur was not to be counterfeited when the belief in its possibility was dead, and turning from the hero to the common man we inaugurated the era of realism. For us no choice remains except that between

mere rhetoric and the frank consideration of our fellow men, who may be the highest of the anthropoids but who are certainly too far below the angels to imagine either that these angels can concern themselves with them or that they can catch any glimpse of even the soles of angelic feet. We can no longer tell tales of the fall of noble men because we do not believe that noble men exist. The best that we can achieve is pathos and the most that we can do is to feel sorry for ourselves. Man has put off his royal robes and it is only in sceptered pomp that tragedy can come sweeping by.

IV

Nietzsche was the last of the great philosophers to attempt a tragic justification of life. His central and famous dogma—"Life is good *because* it is painful"—sums up in a few words the desperate and almost meaningless paradox to which he was driven in his effort to reduce to rational terms the far more imaginative conception which is everywhere present but everywhere unanalyzed in a Sophocles or a Shakespeare and by means of which they rise triumphant over the manifold miseries of life. But the very fact that Nietzsche could not even attempt to state in any except intellectual terms an attitude which is primarily unintellectual and to which, indeed, intellectual analysis is inevitably fatal is proof of the distance which he had been carried (by the rationalizing tendencies of the human mind) from the possibility of the tragic solution which he sought; and the confused, half-insane violence of his work will reveal, by the contrast which it affords with the serenity of the tragic writers whom he admired, how great was his failure.

Fundamentally this failure was, moreover, conditioned by exactly the same thing which has conditioned the failure of all modern attempts to achieve what he attempted—by the fact, that is to say, that tragedy must have a hero if it is not to be merely an accusation against, instead of a justification of, the world in which it occurs. Tragedy is, as Aristotle said, an imitation of noble actions, and Nietzsche, for all his enthusiasm for the Greek tragic writers, was palsied by the universally modern incapacity to conceive man as noble. Out of this dilemma, out of his need to find a hero who could give to life as he saw it the only possible justification, was born the idea of the Superman, but the Superman is, after all, only a hypothetical being, destined to become what man actually was in the eyes of the great tragic writers—a creature (as Hamlet said) "how infinite in capacities, in understanding how like a god." Thus Nietzsche lived half in the past through his literary enthusiasms and half in the future through his grandiose dreams, but for all his professed determination to justify existence he was no more able than the rest of us to find the present acceptable. Life, he said in effect, is not a Tragedy now but perhaps it will be when the Ape-man has been transformed into a hero (the *Übermensch*), and trying to find that sufficient, he went mad.

He failed, as all moderns must fail when they attempt, like him, to embrace the tragic spirit as a religious faith, because the resurgence of that faith is not an intellectual but a vital phenomenon, something not achieved by taking thought but born, on the contrary, out of an instinctive confidence in life which is nearer to the animal's unquestioning allegiance to the scheme of nature than it is to that critical intelligence characteristic of a fully developed humanism. And like other faiths it is not to be recaptured merely by reaching an intellectual conviction that it would be desirable to do so.

Modern psychology has discovered (or at least strongly emphasized) the fact that under certain conditions desire produces belief, and having discovered also that the more primitive a given mentality the more completely are its opinions determined by its wishes, modern psychology has concluded that the best mind is that which most resists the tendency to believe a thing simply because it would be pleasant or advantageous to do so. But justified as this conclusion may be from the intellectual point of view, it fails to take into account the fact that in a universe as badly adapted as this one to human as distinguished from animal needs, this ability to will a belief may bestow an enormous vital advantage as it did, for instance, in the case at present under discussion where it made possible for Shakespeare the compensations of a tragic faith completely inaccessible to Nietzsche. Pure intelligence, incapable of being influenced by

desire and therefore also incapable of choosing one opinion rather than another simply because the one chosen is the more fruitful or beneficent, is doubtless a relatively perfect instrument for the pursuit of truth, but the question (likely, it would seem, to be answered in the negative) is simply whether or not the spirit of man can endure the literal and inhuman truth.

Certain ages and simple people have conceived of the action which passes upon the stage of the universe as of something in the nature of a Divine Comedy, as something, that is to say, which will reach its end with the words "and they lived happily ever after." Others, less naïve and therefore more aware of those maladjustments whose reality, at least so far as outward events are concerned, they could not escape, have imposed upon it another artistic form and called it a Divine Tragedy, accepting its catastrophe as we accept the catastrophe of an *Othello,* because of its grandeur. But a Tragedy, Divine or otherwise, must, it may again be repeated, have a hero, and from the universe as we see it both the Glory of God and the Glory of Man have departed. Our cosmos may be farcical or it may be pathetic but it has not the dignity of tragedy and we cannot accept it as such.

Yet our need for the consolations of tragedy has not passed with the passing of our ability to conceive it. Indeed, the dissonances which it was tragedy's function to resolve grow more insistent instead of diminishing. Our passions, our disappointments, and our sufferings remain important to us though important to nothing else and they thrust themselves upon us with an urgency which makes it impossible for us to dismiss them as the mere trivialities which, so our intellects tell us, they are. And yet, in the absence of tragic faith or the possibility of achieving it, we have no way in which we may succeed in giving them the dignity which would not only render them tolerable but transform them as they were transformed by the great ages into joys. The death of tragedy is, like the death of love, one of those emotional fatalities as the result of which the human as distinguished from the natural world grows more and more a desert.

Poetry, said Santayana in his famous phrase, is "religion which is no longer believed," but it depends, nevertheless, upon its power to revive in us a sort of temporary or provisional credence and the nearer it can come to producing an illusion of belief the greater is its power as poetry. Once the Tragic Spirit was a living faith and out of it tragedies were written. Today these great expressions of a great faith have declined, not merely into poetry, but into a kind of poetry whose premises are so far from any we can really accept that we can only partially and dimly grasp its meaning.

We read but we do not write tragedies. The tragic solution of the problem of existence, the reconciliation to life by means of the tragic spirit is, that is to say, now only a fiction surviving in art. When that art itself has become, as it probably will, completely meaningless, when we have ceased not only to write but to *read* tragic works, then it will be lost and in all real senses forgotten, since the devolution from Religion to Art to Document will be complete.